THE OXFORD HAN]

SOCIAL
MOVEMENTS

THE OXFORD HANDBOOK OF

SOCIAL

MOVEMENTS

Edited by

DONATELLA DELLA PORTA

and

MARIO DIANI

OXFORD

UNIVERSITY PRESS

OXFORD
UNIVERSITY PRESS

Contents

PART III MICRO-DYNAMICS OF CONTENTION

PART IV HOW MOVEMENTS ORGANIZE

PART V REPERTOIRES OF COLLECTIVE ACTION

PART VI CULTURES OF CONTENTION

PART VII POLITICAL AND NON-POLITICAL OPPORTUNITIES AND CONSTRAINTS

PART VIII MOVEMENTS' CONTRIBUTIONS TO SOCIAL AND POLITICAL CHANGE

About the Contributors

Eitan Y. Alimi is Senior Lecturer in Political Sociology at the Hebrew University, Jerusalem

Massimiliano Andretta is Assistant Professor in the Department of Political Science at the University of Pisa

Helmut K. Anheier is Professor of Sociology and President and Dean at the Hertie School of Governance and holds a chair of Sociology at Heidelberg University

Philip Balsiger is Assistant Professor of Sociology at the University of Neuchâtel

Colin Barker retired from the Sociology Department at Manchester Metropolitan University in 2002

Mark R. Beissinger is the Henry W. Putnam Professor of Politics at Princeton and Director of the Princeton Institute for International and Regional Studies (PIIRS)

W. Lance Bennett is Professor of Political Science and Ruddick C. Lawrence Professor of Communication at University of Washington, Seattle, USA, where he is also Director of the Center for Communication & Civic Engagement

Mary Bernstein is Professor of Sociology at the University of Connecticut and past-president of Sociologists for Women in Society

Lorenzo Bosi is Assistant Professor of Sociology at the Scuola Normale Superiore and Research Fellow at the Center on Social Movement Studies-Cosmos, Florence

Ondřej Císař is Associate Professor in the Department of Sociology at the Faculty of Social Sciences, Charles University in Prague, and an affiliate to the Institute of Sociology of the Czech Academy of Sciences

Aysenur Dal is a graduate student in Communication at the Ohio State University

Frank G. A. de Bakker is Associate Professor of Strategic Management in the Department of Organization Sciences at Free University, Amsterdam

Donatella della Porta is Professor of Sociology at the European University Institute, Professor of Political Science at the Scuola Normale Superiore, and the Director of the Center on Social Movement Studies-Cosmos, Florence

Frank den Hond is the Ehrnrooth Professor of Management and Organization at Hanken School of Economics and Associate Professor at Free University Amsterdam

Mario Diani is Professor of Sociology at the University of Trento and ICREA Research Professor at UPF Barcelona

Nicole Doerr is Assistant Professor in International Relations at Mount Holyoke College

Jennifer Earl is Professor of Sociology at the University of Arizona

Julia Eckert is Professor of Social Anthropology at the University of Bern

Klaus Eder is retired Professor of Comparative Sociology at Humboldt-Universität zu Berlin and Professor at the Scuola Normale Superiore in Florence

Nina Eggert is SNSF Postdoctoral Research Fellow in the Department of Political Science at the University of Antwerp

Ron Eyerman is Professor of Sociology at Yale University

Olivier Fillieule is Professor of Political Sociology at the University of Lausanne (IEPHI—CRAPUL) and Senior Researcher at CNRS, Sorbonne-Paris 1, CEESP

Helena Flam is Professor of Sociology at the University of Leipzig

Beth Gharrity Gardner is a PhD candidate at the University of California, Irvine

R. Kelly Garrett is Associate Professor of Communication at the Ohio State University

Marco Giugni is Professor in the Department of Political Science and International Relations and Director of the Institute of Citizenship Studies (InCite) at the University of Geneva

Jack A. Goldstone is Hazel Professor of Public Policy at George Mason University and Director of the International Research Laboratory on Political Demography and Social Macrodynamics at the Russian Academy of National Economy and Public Administration

Jeff Goodwin is Professor of Sociology at New York University

Hatem M. Hassan is a PhD student at the University of Pittsburgh

Jayson Hunt is a PhD candidate in Sociology at the University of California, Irvine

Hank Johnston is Professor of Sociology at San Diego State University and founding editor/publisher of *Mobilization: An International Quarterly*

James M. Jasper teaches Sociology at the Graduate Center of the City University of New York

Jeffrey S. Juris is Associate Professor of Anthropology in the Department of Sociology and Anthropology at Northeastern University

Şahan Savaş Karataşli is Post-Doctoral Fellow at the Arrighi Center for Global Studies at the Johns Hopkins University (USA) and Post-Doctoral Research Associate at Princeton University Institute for International and Regional Studies (USA)

Alex Khasnabish is Associate Professor of Anthropology in the Department of Sociology and Anthropology at Mount Saint Vincent University

Brayden G. King is Professor of Management at the Northwestern University's Kellogg School of Management

Bert Klandermans is Research Professor of Applied Social Psychology in the Department of Sociology of the Free University, Amsterdam

Hanspeter Kriesi holds the Stein Rokkan Chair in Comparative Politics at the European University Institute in Florence

Lene Kühle is Associate Professor in Sociology of Religion at Aarhus University

Michael Lavalette is Professor of Social Work at Liverpool Hope University

Lasse Lindekilde is Associate Professor at the Department of Political Science, Aarhus University

Stefan Malthaner is Assistant Professor of Political Science at Aarhus University

Raffaele Marchetti is Assistant Professor in International Relations at LUISS Rome

John Markoff is Distinguished University Professor of Sociology, History, and Political Science at the University of Pittsburgh

Alice Mattoni is Research Fellow at the Centre on Social Movement Studies, European University Institute

Holly J. McCammon is Professor of Sociology and Affiliated Faculty in American Studies and Women and Gender Studies, Vanderbilt University

Michele Micheletti holds the Lars Hierta chair of Political Science at Stockholm University

Ann Mische is Associate Professor of Sociology and Peace Studies at the University of Notre Dame

Minyoung Moon is a PhD candidate in the Department of Sociology at Vanderbilt University

Kevin Moran is a graduate student in Sociology at City University New York

Diego Muro is Assistant Professor in Comparative Politics at the Institut Barcelona d'Estudis Internacionals (IBEI)

Kate Nash is Professor of Sociology and Director of the Centre for the study of Global Media and Democracy at Goldsmiths College, University of London

Eugene Nulman is Lecturer in Sociology at Birmingham City University, and Associate of the Centre for the Study of Social & Political Movements, at the University of Kent, Canterbury, England

Pamela E. Oliver is the Conway-Bascom Professor of Sociology at the University of Wisconsin—Madison

Abby Peterson is Professor of Sociology at the Department of Sociology and Work Science, University of Gothenburg, Sweden

Gianni Piazza is Associate Professor of Political Sociology at the University of Catania

Francesca Polletta is Professor of Sociology at the University of California, Irvine

Daniel P. Ritter is Assistant Professor of Politics and International Relations at the University of Nottingham

Kenneth M. Roberts is Professor of Government at Cornell University

Rene Rojas is a PhD candidate in Sociology at New York University

Christopher Rootes is Professor of Environmental Politics and Political Sociology and Director, Centre for the Study of Social & Political Movements, at the University of Kent, Canterbury, England

Paul Routledge is Professor of Contentious Politics and Social Change at the University of Leeds

Nikolas Scherer is a PhD Candidate at the Hertie School of Governance

Alexandra Segerberg is Research Fellow in the Department of Political Science at Stockholm University

Beverly J. Silver is Professor of Sociology and Director of the Arrighi Center for Global Studies at Johns Hopkins University, Baltimore

Jackie Smith is Professor of Sociology at the University of Pittsburgh

Nikolai Smith is a PhD candidate at the University of California, San Diego

David A. Snow is Distinguished Professor of Sociology at the University of California, Irvine

Sarah A. Soule is the Morgridge Professor of Organizational Behavior at Stanford University, Graduate School of Business

Suzanne Staggenborg is Professor of Sociology at the University of Pittsburgh

Dietlind Stolle is Professor of Political Science at McGill University and Director of the Inter-University Quebec Centre for the Study of Democratic Citizenship

Anna Subirats is a PhD researcher at the European University Institute and researcher at the Center on Social Movement Studies-Cosmos, Florence

Anna E. Tan is a PhD candidate at the University of California, Irvine

Julien Talpin is Research Fellow in Political Science at the CNRS, University of Lille

Sidney Tarrow is Emeritus Professor of Government and Visiting Professor of Law at Cornell University

Verta Taylor is Professor of Sociology at the University of California, Santa Barbara

Simon Teune is Research Fellow at the Berlin Social Science Center and TU Berlin

David B. Tindall is Associate Professor in the Department of Sociology at the University of British Columbia

Marisa Tramontano is a graduate student in Sociology at City University New York

David Waddington is Professor of Communications and Head of the Communication and Computing Research Centre, Sheffield Hallam University

Mattias Wahlström is Senior Researcher at the Department of Sociology and Work Science, University of Gothenburg, Sweden

Elisabeth Jean Wood is Professor of Political Science, International and Area Studies at Yale University and a member of the External Faculty of the Santa Fe Institute

Stephen Wulff is a graduate student in the Department of Sociology at the University of Minnesota

CHAPTER 1

....

INTRODUCTION

The Field of Social Movement Studies

....

DONATELLA DELLA PORTA AND MARIO DIANI

MAPPING THE FIELD

....

THE publication of an Oxford Handbook represents in the last instance a statement about a scientific field: not only about the principles and ideas guiding research activities and shaping discussions within it, but also about its very existence. Had the Oxford Handbooks been around in the 1960s, few would have probably thought of a volume focussing on "social movements." And this not because issues of social conflict or citizens' participation in political life were ignored by social scientists (they were not), but because a set of core ideas was missing, capable of connecting different lines of research and thinking around the concept of social movement. Analysts of large-scale societal changes took an obvious interest in collective action processes (e.g., Wallerstein 1974) while students of individual political and social participation were similarly intent on exploring involvement in protest activities alongside conventional ones (e.g., Barnes and Kaase 1979), yet there was a shortage of analytic tools, focussing on social movements, enabling broader conversations between promoters of different lines of investigation. Of course, even today, many analysts of macro social change, or of individual protest behavior, happily go on with their business without defining themselves as "social movement scholars," sometimes even without engaging with the concept. At the same time, however, social movements have consolidated as a distinct field of investigation and theorizing, with specialized journals such as *Mobilization, Social Movement Studies*, or most recently *Interface*, and annuals such as *Research in Social Movements, Conflict and Change*.

Here we are not interested in viewing the social movement field, à la Bourdieu (1988), as a structure of power relations between actors competing for influence and status. Rather, borrowing on DiMaggio and Powell's (1983) classic definition of organizational fields, we conceive of a scientific field as a "set of actors that, in the aggregate, constitute a recognized area of institutional life." In this chapter, we do not intend to trace the evolution of this particular field from the point of view of the interactions between social movement researchers (for this, see, if restricted to Europe, Diani and Cisar 2014). We intend, instead, to explore the criteria on the basis of which certain lines of research and their advocates may be recognized as social movement scholarship. While scientific boundaries are inevitably—and luckily—porous, still they may define professional identities, encourage attention to specific issues to the detriment of others, nurture specific theoretical or methodological approaches, and hamper the growth of others. What then are the factors that enable us to identify social movements as a distinct field of research? Far from being a purely academic exercise, exploring at least some of them provides an opportunity to map the range of empirical phenomena and the kind of intellectual questions shared among a significant number of social movement scholars and analysts.

First of all, the social movement field may be defined, in a purely empiricist way, by the set of actors on which social movement researchers primarily focus. A substantive amount of research has treated movements as sets of actors with specific characteristics. These have often been individuals. Building on the long-established tradition of survey research, the growing interest in protest politics has first resulted in specific questions included in surveys of the general population such as the World Values Survey or the European Social Survey (e.g., Dalton 2008), and later (since the late 1990s) in the promotion of specific surveys of demonstrators (e.g., Norris, Walgrave, and Van Aelst 2005; Walgrave and Rucht 2010) or of members of movement organizations (e.g., Tindall 2004). Deeper, more qualitative analyses have also been devoted to explore subjective feelings, motivations, and life stories of movement activists (e.g., della Porta 1995; Blee 2003) or, more rarely, of movement leaders (e.g., Barker, Johnson, and Lavalette 2001; Nepstad Erickson and Bob 2006). Other times, the focus has been on organizations, with studies of "social movement organizations" ranging again from the qualitative, in-depth observation of specific cases to larger population surveys (Zald and McCarthy 1980; Minkoff 1995; Kriesi 1996; Andrews and Edwards 2005; Diani 2015). All in all, it is fair to say that investigations of individual protestors and their motives, or of "social movement organizations," were largely promoted by people with a specific identification with social movements as a distinct area of research. At the same time, the boundaries have been far from impenetrable: the study of protest behavior has significantly overlapped with the study of political participation at large (van Deth and Kreuter 1998; Dalton 2008), while the difference between studies of "social movement organizations" and "public interest groups" has sometimes depended more on the individual orientation of specific researchers than on substantive differences in the object of study (see, e.g., Burstein 1998).

Social movement studies also stand apart as a field because of their attention to the practices through which actors express their stances in a broad range of social and political conflicts. Since the 1980s, the analysis of public challenges to existing authorities in the form of protest events has attracted considerable attention (Tarrow 1989; Kriesi et al. 1995; Rootes 2003; Soule and Earl 2005; McCarthy, Rafail, and Gromis 2013). While the study of public demonstrations as displays of worthiness, unity, numbers, and commitment ("wunc": Tilly 2004: 54) has been focal to the social movement field, attention has always been paid to the broader and more diverse forms taken by contention across time and space (Tilly, Tilly, and Tilly 1975; Tilly 2005; Tilly and Tarrow 2007). As the institutionalization of the protest movements of the 1960s and 1970s proceeded, analysts also became increasingly wary of too rigidly identifying public protest as their main distinctive feature. The role played within conventional political processes, through the use of conventional repertoires, by organizations as well as individuals, emerged from, or still engaged in, protest activities, has been repeatedly recognized (Burstein 1998; Giugni, McAdam, and Tilly 1999; Goldstone 2003). The spread of Internet-based and related forms of communication has also been hailed as an important transformation in practices of collective action, as public challenges may lose their centrality and be replaced by various forms of online campaigning, giving more autonomy to individual choices and rendering forms of action promoted by organizations, and in particular public protest, less relevant (e.g., Bennett and Segerberg 2013, this volume).

Analysts have become similarly aware of the fact that collective action does not always imply the formulation of political demands (through confrontational as well as conventional repertoires). It may also take the form of the direct production of collective goods, through a broad range of actions that stretch from the communitarian enactment of alternative lifestyles to various forms of mutual help and service delivery. In reference to the latter, while service delivery has been mostly the preserve of voluntary, charitable organizations, addressed by a different tradition of study, the boundaries between these two sectors of civil society have not always been rigid. Movement organizations have often been involved in service delivery to their members/sympathizers/beneficiaries (think for instance of environmental, women's or LGBT groups), while charitable organizations (including formal charities, if in an oblique way) have been on occasion involved in protest on issue linked, for example, to welfare dismantling, deprivation, or global inequalities. This has reflected in some analysts working as bridges between the corresponding scientific fields (Anheier 2004; Anheier and Kendall 2002; Anheier and Scherer this volume).

Even a superficial and partial glance at social movement research, such as the one we have just presented, suggests that its empirical focus is at the same time relatively distinctive and overlapping with several cognate fields. One can certainly argue that the social movement field has been disproportionately characterized by the interest in (a) individuals critical of the status quo and prepared to engage in protest; (b) organizational forms intent on encouraging rank and file participation and bottom-up forms of deliberation; (c) public challenges to powerholders, often linked in chains of protest events; (d) actions providing goods to movement constituencies, and facilitating experimentation with alternative lifestyles. There is a clear community of scholars who define themselves as social movement analysts and interact in a variety of ways around these and related topics. At the same time, they are by no means the monopolistic owners of those themes, to which understanding analysts from fields as diverse as political participation, interest groups, voluntary and non-profit organizations, cultural studies, organizational studies, communication studies, to name just a few, also contribute.

The most probing criterion to explore the profile and consistence of a field is through the main theoretical questions it addresses, and the responses it has provided. In our previous work (della Porta and Diani 2006:1) we have suggested that the bulk of social movement research in both North America and Europe developed since the 1960s around four main sets of questions, concerning (a) the relationship between structural change and transformations in patterns of social conflict; (b) the role of cultural representations in enabling collective action; (c) the mechanisms that render it rational to mobilize on collective goals; and (d) the effects of the political and institutional context on social movements' development and evolution. Since the 1970s, "new social movement" theorists (e.g., Touraine 1981; Melucci 1989) noted how movements like feminism or environmentalism reflected the shifting focus of contemporary societies from the production of material goods to the production of knowledge, broadly conceived. They also suggested that new forms of social conflict differed from those embodied in the experiences of class and nationalist movements because of a critical ideology in relation to modernism and progress; decentralized and participatory organizational structures; defense of interpersonal solidarity against the great bureaucracies; and the reclamation of autonomous spaces, rather than material advantages; and how new movements tried to oppose the intrusion of the state and the market into social life, reclaiming individuals' right to determine their own life projects and identities, against the omnipresent and manipulative systemic apparatuses. At the same time, new social movement theorists were not alone in keeping an interest in the relation between structural change and collective action. Notable lines of inquiry were pursued, among others, by Manuel Castells, whose focus shifted from changes in the urban sphere and in patterns of collective consumption (Castells 1984) to changing patterns of conflict in the network society, characterized by the pervasive presence of new technologies (Castells 1997, 2012); and by proponents of world system theory, exploring various forms of resistance to corporate and financial globalization in both the South and the North of the world (Arrighi, Hopkins, and Wallerstein 1989; Smith and Wiest 2012).

Other lines of research have taken the presence of structural grievances of various natures as a starting point for the analysis, focussing instead on the conditions under which certain structural tensions turned into collective action while others failed to do so. One approach to these issues has concentrated on cultural dynamics such as the production of proper frames, capable of providing motives and interpretations of situations enabling action, and the construction of collective identities. Building on the tradition of the collective behavior school and symbolic interactionism (e.g., Gusfield 1963) analysts have focussed on processes of symbolic production and identity construction as the essential mechanisms that enable actors to recognize aspects of their condition as worthy of collective action, and to define themselves as distinct carriers of collective goals and orientations (Snow et al. 1986; Benford and Snow 2000; Oliver and Johnston 2000). Since the 1990s, some researchers have expanded the cultural perspective by stressing that symbolic production is not only (or mainly) strategically oriented, but that movements produce condensing symbols and rhetoric oriented to provoke various types of emotional responses (e.g., Jasper 1997; Goodwin, Jasper, and Polletta 2001).

A different way to address the relation between structural conditions and action has originated from attempts to address the dilemma posed by Olson's (1963) seminal discussion of the "irrationality of collective action." Why should people participate in the production of collective goods that they will enjoy in any case if the attempt will be successful, while facing selective costs in case of failure? Theorists of resource mobilization (McCarthy and Zald 1977) identified in the presence of leaders acting as political entrepreneurs and in the availability of organizational and personal resources, some of the most important factors altering the terms of the rational calculation on the basis of which people decide whether to get involved or not in collective projects. Research has also highlighted the role of inter-personal, as well as inter-organizational networks in the circulation of resources and the creation of the solidarities that encourage action in pursuit of collective goals (Oberschall 1973; Marwell and Oliver 1993).

Finally, the perspective usually defined as "political process" (Tilly 1978; McAdam 1982; Tarrow 1994) has shared with resource mobilization theory a strategic view of action paying more systematic attention to the political and institutional environment in which social movements operate. Such environmental conditions have often been summarized under the heading of "political opportunity structure," combining the degree of openness or closure of formal political access, the degree of stability or instability of political alignments, the availability and strategic posture of potential allies, and political conflicts between and within elites (Tarrow 1994). Characteristics relating to the functional division of power and also to geographical decentralization have also been taken into account in order to explore which stable or "mobile" characteristics of the political system influence the growth of less institutionalized political action in the course of what are defined as protest cycles.

In this Handbook, we do not devote systematic attention to reconstructing the evolution of social movement research since the 1970s. This is so for two main reasons. First, those contributions have been repeatedly explored and summarized over the last few years, to different levels of detail (see, e.g., Crossley 2002; della Porta and Diani 2006; Opp 2009; Buechler 2011; Neveu 2011; Johnston 2014). Second, we do not want to contribute further to the reification of the different questions shaping the field as the basis of distinctive, objectified theoretical currents. While differentiating between "European" and "American" approaches (Klandermans and Tarrow 1988) or identifying the attention to frames, mobilizing structures and opportunities as the building blocks of a "classic agenda" of social movement research (McAdam, Tarrow, and Tilly 2001) has certainly helped to start conversations at crucial points in time, there are also costs attached to this approach. For example, scholars who are routinely associated, even by ourselves (della Porta and Diani 2006: ch. 1), with one or the other theoretical current, are actually far more complex and richer in their thinking. To name just two major cases, the late Alberto Melucci's analysis of identity-building mechanisms and small group network dynamics prevent us from associating him rigidly with the structural, deterministic version of new social movement theory; and David Snow's work on framing can also be read (see, e.g., Gamson 1992) as strongly conversant in resource mobilization theory.

Accordingly, we found it more useful to abandon any attempt to identify distinct "schools" of social movement research, and to focus instead on the responses that social movement researchers have attempted to provide to a few key themes and issues, mapping some of the different lines of investigation that have developed in recent years. Oftentimes, such questions have been identified, and answers to them have been elaborated, in close and explicit dialogue with dominant paradigms; other times, however, recent research has sprung out of dissatisfaction with such paradigms, and their basic assumptions. Both the strengths and the limitations of traditional approaches have been made more explicit following the growth of attention for social movement research in disparate intellectual and scientific fields (from anthropology to geography), as well as in areas other than the West (e.g., Routledge in this volume; Juris and Alex Khasnabish in this volume; della Porta 2014). With this purpose in mind, the structure of the Handbook reflects both the embeddedness of recent research in the basic questions that have emerged since the 1970s, and its sustained efforts to transcend its disciplinary and geographical limitations.

EXPANDING THE FIELD

The aim of this Handbook is to map, but also to expand the field of social movement studies, opening up to recent developments in cognate areas of studies, within and beyond sociology and political science. With this purpose in mind, we have looked for contributions which open conversations between classic social movement agendas and those developed on other issues and in diverse discipline. While we used quite traditional social movement concepts to structure the Handbook into parts, we tried in each Part to combine the purpose of mapping the state of the art with the one of broadening our knowledge of social movements finding inspiration outside of the classic agenda, as well as suggesting what contributions social movement studies can give to other fields of knowledge.

In structuring the different Parts of this Handbook, we have tried to use some main concepts around which research has converged within the fields of social movement studies, in each trying however to broaden the perspective by looking in cognate fields of research. After we cover some core theoretical perspectives, we go on to look at big social transformations that affect social movements, moving then to the analysis of microdynamics of collective action. We look then, at the meso-level, at movements' cultures, organizational models, and repertoires of action. Finally, we look at the political and non-political opportunities for social movements' development, as well as at the social movement effects on their environment.

The first Part of the Handbook, devoted to "Core Theoretical Perspectives," attempts to locate what we have just summarized as the "classic agenda" of social movement research in a broader intellectual context. In the opening chapter, Klaus Eder elaborates on the ways in which social theory has been used in social movement studies and, vice versa, how social movements were addressed in social theory, proposing a novel and promising relations between the two fields. Reviewing the classical contributions of social theories to social movement studies, he distinguishes between a macro-theoretical approach, including Alain Touraine's, Juergen Habermas', and Nikolas Luhmann's analysis of the role of social movements within structural transformations, and the "micro-theoretical" tradition, embedded especially in rational-choice explanations. In order to avoid a misleading opposition between structure and agency, he suggests looking then at the micro-foundation of collective action as well as at the emergency of complexity from within these social relations. Social movements are in fact theorized as structures of social relations that link social action events by circulating meaning through these relations. The narrative turn in social theory, the development of a network perspective, and the emergence of evolutionary theory are addressed in the search for new analytical tools to mobilize for this purpose.

In his chapter, Ondrej Cisar offers a parallel overview of the relations between social movement research and political science, looking at classical contributions in the field, with particular attention paid to the interactions between interest representation and social movement studies. As he observes, social movement studies did indeed develop in the United States within a paradigm of interest representation rooted in the pluralist approach that, from Madison to Truman, had then reached research on social movements. If this perspective has offered important contributions to our understanding of social movements, the chapter also points however to the importance of the (European) tradition that, with a Weberian sensitivity, pays attention to the state and its intervention in the regulation of interest representation. Rather than a neutral arena, in the corporatist vision of interest representation, the state is an actor itself, actively promoting some interests against which social movements struggle either, in a Marxist vision, to overcome capitalism or, in a Polanyi's approach, in order to balance the free market with (some) social protection. To what extent the Keynesian belief in macro-economic management as well as interest concentration based on state coordination will survive neoliberal capitalism remains an open question.

Historical research has also played an important role in social movement studies. In his chapter, John Markoff addresses the various ways in which history matters for the development of social movements. Covering a huge variety of literature in different fields of the social sciences, he discusses first of all big cross-historical comparisons that have located social movements within broad historical changes in the state and capitalism. The duration of some phenomena—from enduring to evanescent—is another way in which time matters for social movement studies that have been also interested in singling out trends and cycles in economic as well as electoral terms. Punctuated events such as big shocks or critical junctures are also ways in which history affects movements—as research on the interactions between social movements and wars or eventful protests have demonstrated. If this points at contingent (often, underdetermined) effects, path dependency as historical rootedness is however very important as well in social movement development and in the ways in which states deal with them.

The effort to connect social movements studies to other streams of political research, often from a strong historical angle, has shaped the contentious politics program, whose achievements and limits one of its promoters, Sidney Tarrow, discusses in the following chapter. At the very core of the project was indeed the bridging of different areas of studies: on social movements but also strike waves, revolutions, civil wars, and democratization processes. The main agenda was to innovate in the theory and empirics of social movement studies by singling out the recurrent causal mechanisms and more complex processes which are at the basis of the emergence and development of these various phenomena, which had been investigated through different lenses in fields that had remained strangely apart from each other. Some initial lacunae in the approach are discussed: a focus on episodes, which does not allow for an understanding of origins, developments or effects of contentious politics; the multiplication of mechanisms as well as an unclear definition of the concept of mechanism itself; the lack of reflection on structures and agencies. At the same time, the potential of contentious politics is stressed with examples coming from recent developments of the contentious politics approach in research on civil wars and revolutions, internal relations within movements, as well as their external relations with political parties.

Stephen Wulff, Mary Bernstein, and Verta Taylor focus then on gender theorizing and its impact on social movement theory. They analyze the ways in which the studies on gender and sexuality movements have influenced the broader field of social movement studies. In doing this, they look at the centrality of gender in shaping movements' emergence, trajectory, and outcomes. Challenging masculinist assumptions in the dominant approaches in the field, feminist, gay, and queer scholars have studied gender and sexuality movements, challenging political process and resource mobilization approaches by a reconceptualization of the role of power in its multiple sources and forms, collective identity (with particular attention to how collective identities are deployed as a social movement strategy), multi-institutional politics (as movements target also non-state institutions), as well as emotions.

Part II, on "Social Movements and Structural Processes," explores how some major recent changes in structural—in particular spatial—dynamics may have affected patterns of collective action. At their origins, especially in Europe, social movement studies used to pay attention to the ways in which social transformations affected social action. This attention had developed especially within the "new social movements" approach that had represented a critique of Marxism, which had however kept as a core question the relations between a post-industrial society and the specific characteristics of social movements within a new societal mode of production and reproduction. While still central in research in the global South, this question had however become more and more marginal in mainstream research on social movements that either considered them as middle-class phenomena or as non-class based ones. As it is often the case in a research field, this gap resulted in calls to bring classes, capitalism, and the like back into social movement studies (Hetland and Jeff Goodwin 2013; Barker, Cox, Krinski, and Gunvald Nilsen 2013; della Porta 2015). In the opening chapter, Beverly J. Silver and Sahan Savas Karatasli discuss the reemerging attention for class, especially labor, conflict in globalized societies. After a few decades in which issues of capital-ism and class had almost disappeared not only from social movement studies (Hetland and Goodwin 2013; della Porta 2015), but even from economic sociology (Arrighi 2001), the authors forcefully call for returning capitalism and labor/class-based move-ments to a prominent position in the social movement literature. In particular, look-ing at class-based conflict, with special attention at the timing, location, and changing character of labor movement upsurges, they suggest that the temporal–geographical framework of the analysis should be lengthened and widened, but also that elements of a theory of "historical capitalism" should be brought back in, allowing for an under-standing of the long-run dynamics of global capitalist development.

Jack Goldstone looks then at demography in order to address two main questions of how the demographic characteristics of the participants in social movements shape their collective expressions as well as how the demographic trends of socie-ties shape those of social movements. Following various suggestions in demographic studies, he points in particular at the important effects of the growth of specific popu-lation groups. Special attention is paid to the demographic effects of globalization in terms of the emergence of a large cohort of young people budge with high proportion of well-educated, as well as the potential development of a global middle class.

As one of the effects of globalization is indeed the movement of large groups of migrant people, with related social and cultural effects, the next two chapters look at the reciprocal contributions between social movement studies and two disciplinary fields that have grown to address the consequence of massive movements of people: migration studies and the sociology of religion.

Nina Eggert and Marco Giugni focus on the main structural changes in Western soci-eties that might affect social movements related with migration. The increasing size and, especially, diversity (among other aspects, of religion) of the migrant population are analyzed together with the changing social and political cleavages (with opposi-tion between "winners" and "losers" of globalization) as well as European integration as prompting both protest and counterprotest on migration issues. As migration is becom-ing an increasingly salient and politicized issue in politics and in academia, some new research trends are singled out with a more theoretical focus on resources and oppor-tunities for migrants as well as an empirical focus on Muslin groups as well as on global mobilization on migrant rights. In a cross-national comparison, the characteristics of claim-making on migration are linked to citizens' regimes.

Lasse Lindekilde and Lene Kühle look at structural transformations which affected religiosity and, then, religious revivalism as a foundation of social movement activities since the 1980s. Revisiting some classical studies in the sociology of religion, that had wrongly predicted a trend towards secularism, the authors locate religious revivalism within a greater visibility of religion, especially in its fundamentalist forms (Roy 2007) and a de-privatization of religion (Casanova 1994). The multiplication of religious com-munities on the same territory has not implied a loss of sacred canopy. The related effect is an intensified importance of religious-based social movements, both in the form of political expressions of religiosity (voice) as well as in a religious retreat (exit). As the authors suggest, the sociology of religion, looking at the cultural and ideological aspects of the phenomenon, could offer important tools in order to understand the prefigurative dimensions of collective action, moved by desire for salvation rather than mere interests.

In the following chapter, Diego Muro analyzes the relations between ethnicity, nationalism, and social movements. A main claim here too is that social movement studies would benefit from broadening the range of the analyzed forms of contentious politics by including nationalist and ethnic movements, that have been much studied in the social sciences, but within different approaches than the ones more commonly employed in social movement studies. From this perspective, the chapter addresses the wide variety of demands, activities, and goals displayed by ethnic and nationalist movements in their targeting of the state in their search for cultural recognition, territorial autonomy, and/or special rights or public goods provision. The research on repertoires of action, especially violent ones, on identity building, as well as on the structural conditions which make ethnic and national cleavages salient, are all central topics in research on ethnic and nationalist movements whose results could usefully be included in reflections on other types of social movements.

The transformations in the urban dimension of conflict are addressed by Massimiliano Andretta, Gianni Piazza, and Anna Subirats. As these authors note, even though the central role of cities for social mobilization emerges as more and more central, and with it the relationship between space and contentious politics, the contributions from literature on urban social movements and social movement studies have not been much integrated as yet. Their chapter attempts to build bridges between the two, looking at specific urban movements and locating them within a broader transformation in urban policies and in urban structures. Attention to broad transformations in the urban context allows us to open up social movement studies to contributions from fields such as urban planning or even architecture. While constrained by their environment, social movements are presented however as relevant players within cities, given their capacity to address the implementation of urban policies so, the authors note, "redefining the process of urban transformation through social and political practice, by producing new ways of experiencing and perceiving the city and opening new windows of opportunity " (in this volume).

The third Part, "Micro-Dynamics of Contention," focusses upon processes of individual involvement in collective action. One leading motive behind the development of social movement studies in the 1960s and 1970s was notoriously challenging views of political protest as irrational, anomic behavior (McAdam 2003). While this resulted in an emphasis on rational action and calculation, it also prompted critical responses that stressed the role of emotions in collective dynamics (e.g., Goodwin et al. 2001) or at least pointed at different rationalities operating for different social groups with uneven access to resources (e.g., Piven and Cloward 1977). Here we chart the different sides of this debate and some recent developments.

In the opening chapter, Bert Klandermans maps, from a social psychological perspective, the main steps of the process that brings individuals to enter into and remain involved in collective action. He differentiates between the demand-side of protest (individuals and their motives), the supply-side (organizations and their appeals), and the mobilizations that try to bring demand and supply together. He further differentiates between three types of motives (instrumentality, identification, and expressiveness) as well as between consensus mobilization (turning individuals into sympathizers) and action mobilization (turning sympathizers into participants).

While being far from the only important factor for individual choices, embeddedness in social networks involving people already active has been regarded as a major determinant of individual participation in protest activities. In his chapter, David Tindall discusses some of the theoretical processes that lie behind the empirical association between having network ties to other activists, and participating in a social movement. He looks at how the production of new network ties, or the strengthening of existing ones, may be regarded as an outcome of social movements. He also considers networks at different scales in terms of units of focus, and geography. Literature on the social psychology of initial mobilization, and the importance of networks for targeting others for recruitment, and participation is reviewed.

Pamela Oliver's assessment of the main contributions of rational action approaches to the study of collective action also has a strong network component. While she starts from an individualistic premise, she is quick to point out that the genuine contribution of this line of thinking has been at the group level, as "simplifying and even simplistic assumptions about individuals have permitted genuine insights into the differences between different kinds of actions and the differences between groups with different group-level properties" (Oliver, this volume). Group-level properties also need to be combined with a theory of strategic agency if they are to fulfill their potential.

While approaches focussing on the role of emotions have developed in stark opposition to rational-choice type of theories, one should not assume that the sudden exposure to highly emotional stimuli and the resulting moral outrage, as reflected in concepts such as "hot cognition" or "moral shock," are sufficient to account for collective action dynamics. Tracing the development of such important concepts, Helena Flam notes that even the perception of certain stimuli as sources of shock/outrage necessitates deeper and longer-term work focussed on the reframing of reality and changes in habitus. The relational contexts in which such work takes place may vary substantially depending on the characteristics of specific societies and political systems, and should certainly include movement organizations. Flam also identifies some basic mechanisms through which emotions may contribute to long-term activism and not merely to short-term outbursts of indignation, and impact both relations within movement groups and the latter's interaction with their environment.

This Part is rounded off by Olivier Fillieule's discussion of disengagement. While it may refer to processes that involve social movements or sustained campaigns as a whole, the concept also applies to individual activists and their life-careers. That is actually the main focus of the analysis, with special emphasis on the literature that has dealt with the biographical consequences of activism. Fillieule shows how many of the mechanisms that account for recruitment also apply to withdrawal from collective action.

However, if we are to achieve a genuinely process-oriented view of disengagement, we need to pay more attention to how the properties of a given social or political system may affect paths of disengagement, for example, through the creation of opportunities for people to take up different, more conventional lifestyles (a problem particularly acute in the case of withdrawal from terrorist organizations or cults).

The following Part on "How Movements Organize" explores the variety of forms through which collective action gets coordinated. While organizational approaches have been central to the development of the "classic agenda" of social movement research, some critics (e.g., Soule 2013) have lamented their relative marginalization since the 1990s. This is due not only to the simultaneous development of approaches focussing respectively on the political process or on culture and emotions, but also to the growing attention paid to networks and participatory, leaderless action (Soule 2013: 108). Attempts to bridge organizational and social movement analysis in a new synthesis did actually flourish in the late 2000s (e.g., Davis et al. 2005, 2008). However, even when they look at fields of organizations, the focus of those attempts is really on the organizations that make up their fields, on their properties, and on isomorphic mechanisms (or lack of them), rather than on the broader ways through which collective actors relate. While these studies provide a rich documentation of a long established fact—namely, the heterogeneity of the specific organizations that operate within social movements—they pay less attention to the relationship between different organizational forms, and to the conditions under which certain organizational forms may prevail over others.

In this Part we try to remedy this situation. Rather than pitching (more or less formal) organizations against networks, we bring them under a common framework, that is, to conceive of "organization" more broadly, as the set of principles through which resources are pooled and coordinated. Two chapters set the tone for this approach. In their contribution, Frank den Hond, Frank de Bakker, and Nikolai Smith provide "an alternative answer to the question of whether 'organization' is beneficial or detrimental to mobilization, as this depends on the contingent balance between various organizational elements." In particular, they suggest we focus on "several constitutive elements [of organizations]: membership, rules, hierarchy, monitoring and sanctioning" (in this volume), and on their changing weight and different combinations under different contingencies. Their distinction (borrowed from Ahrne and Brunsson 2011) between networks as "emergent" and organizations as "decided" orders in social life enables them to highlight the nature of social movements as a variable blend of both modes. The exploration of a specific case of mobilization in the Occupy movement shows how hierarchical and leadership mechanisms do not disappear even in the most "horizontal" forms of collective action.

The view of social movements as emerging forms of social organization is also central to Mario Diani's and Ann Mische's discussion of relational thinking in social movement analysis. They provide some analytic tools that may help the transition from treatments of collective phenomena as aggregates of the properties of their individual components, towards an interactive view of movements as embedded in collective action fields. After a preliminary discussion of the difference between two cognate yet different concepts such as "relations" and "interactions," the chapter takes up the fundamental question of what represents a tie in the context of collective action processes (see also Mische 2011). It then looks at how ties combine in distinct relational patterns, or "modes of coordination" (Diani 2015) and at the factors (agendas, ideological stances, political opportunities, contingent interactions) that may facilitate the emergence of some tie configurations over others. Finally, it takes up one of the most important open issues of network analytic research, namely, how to map network evolution.

Two chapters then follow, that look in greater depth at some organizational forms among those highlighted by the first two contributions, namely, social movement coalitions and social movement communities. While coalitions are not necessarily equivalent to social movements (Tarrow 2005: 164–165; Diani 2015), they represent one of their building blocks. It is indeed difficult not to think of social movements as "nested coalitions." In their chapter, Holly McCammon and Minyoung Moon discuss the principal mechanisms that may facilitate or discourage coalition building. They note that "shared beliefs and identities, prior social ties among activists, opportunities and threats in the broader context, and organizational resources all can play a role in coalition formation," yet sometimes with ambiguous effects. In particular the opening of opportunities may both encourage and discourage coalition building, depending on the broader configuration of local conditions. McCammon and Moon's contribution also tackles a less explored terrain, namely, the impact of coalitions over both social movement processes and actors in a mid-term perspective, and the political process in general.

At the same time, as important as coalitions may be, the interactions between movement actors are not limited to purposive collaborations in pursuit of specific goals between the best resourced organizations. To the contrary, they develop among a variety of actors, focussing not necessarily on campaigning but also on cultural activities and service delivery to movement actors or their constituents/beneficiaries. The concept of "social movement communities," explored by Hatem Hassam and Suzanne Staggenborg in their contribution, tries to capture this relational pattern. It would be a mistake to reduce the heuristic value of the concept to a representation of subcultural or countercultural settings, a dimension which is often emphasized by scholars looking at democratic societies. As Hassam and Staggenborg show in relation to cases from the Middle East, the concept also yields a high potential for the analysis of collective action in non-democratic regimes, as it enables forms of coordination that are less exposed than formal, purposive organizations to regime repression (see also Diani and Moffatt 2016).

One important question is, of course, to what extent new communication technologies have affected collective action, its forms, and its coordination. Jennifer Earl, Jayson Hunt, Kelly Garrett, and Aysenur Dal show how ICT facilitates "ephemeral" forms of individual engagement from petitioning to attacks on specific sites, that do not require sustained commitments from participants; how it enables individuals with similar views to coordinate, sharing information and resources, without having to join organizations; how it changes existing organizations' ways of operating; how it facilitates in particular forms of transnational organizing, and the spread of broader identities and solidarities, no longer confined within national boundaries. They conclude their chapter with a discussion of the ways in which the spread of ICT can stimulate the dialogue between social movement and political communication analysts, in particular on the mechanisms through which information circulates and is interpreted, both by the general public and by agenda setters and policy makers.

Earl et al.'s concerns are echoed in the next contribution, where Lance Bennett and Alexandra Segerberg explore how the advent of new digital technologies has transformed public communication, and the implications of those transformations for the ways in which mass contention is organized. Drawing upon their recent work (Bennett and Segerberg 2013), they point at "the use of digital and social media to supplement and even displace mass media in terms of reaching broad publics, often involving them in far more active roles than the spectator or bystander publics of the mass media era…. [T]he uses of media to create organizational networks among populations that lack more conventional institutional forms of political organization" (this volume). The overall result of such changes is the emergence of a new model of coordination of activism, "connective action," which differs from modern collective action because of the reduced role of organizations and collective identity mechanisms and the greater reliance on individual choices.

Discussions of the role of new technologies in collective action processes regularly point at their potential contribution in overcoming spatial limitations and increasing opportunities for the promotion and coordination of contention across space. At the same time, most episodes of collective action are still heavily embedded in specific territories. In his chapter, Paul Routledge outlines the different forms through which space influences action, as an object of contention and source of "spatial inequalities," as a source of specific resources and networks, and as an important symbolic reference in the construction of collective identities. Actors' variable relation to geographical space also highlights some of the distinctive traits of the most recent waves of contention, in which social movements may be better conceived as temporary assemblages of actors in different localities than as a quasi stable aggregation of locally bound actors. While it covers multiple aspects of the relationship between geography and collective action, Routledge's chapter nicely complements the overview of organizational mechanisms covered in this Part of the Handbook.

The next Part addresses "Repertoires of Collective Action." The exploration of the characteristics of action repertoires—that is, of the "know how" which movement activists draw upon in order to promote their causes—and of their changes over time has represented a cornerstone of social movement research in the last decades (McAdam, McCarthy, and Zald 1996; della Porta 2013). Many earlier works tended (a) to associate movements with quite distinctive repertoires of unconventional tactics, and (b) to associate specific configurations of political opportunities to specific movement traits and repertoires (contra, e.g., Kitschelt 1986; Flam 1994; Kriesi et al. 1995). Recently, there has been growing recognition of the fact that movements' courses of action are also—for some analysts, primarily—driven by strategic interactions within specific arenas.

In the opening chapter of the Part, James Jasper, Kevin Moran, and Marisa Tramontano offer some analytic criteria that may be useful in capturing the strategic dimension of social movements. They focus in particular on four elements: the players pursuing relevant goals, the arenas in which they interact, the types of interactions, and the means used by the different actors. Taking into account both cooperative and conflictive relations, among movement actors as well as between them and their allies and opponents, they document recent attempts to go beyond rigid opposition between structuralist and culturalist perspectives.

While he is more embedded in the political process tradition than Jasper et al., Eitan Alimi shares their attention to the interplay of structure and strategy in his chapter on the dynamics of repertoire selection and change. First he shows how repertoires are selected through a complex set of interactions including contingent and strategic choices that involve movement organizations and broader constituents as well as authorities and security forces. Then, he proceeds to illustrate how repertoire change and selection are particularly salient during cycles of contention, when a broader set of actors is involved, including the general public, countermovements, and other non-state external actors. In such a context in particular, events with high emotional content may play a highly significant roles alongside more tactical and contingent calculations.

The association of social movements with disruptive, radical forms of collective action has long been recognized to be far from perfect, as different phases and contexts display different balances of institutionalized and unconventional tactics (della Porta 1995; Norris et al. 2005; Soule and Earl 2005; Dalton 2008; McCarthy et al. 2013 see among many others Tarrow 1989). The relationship to violence, and even the definition of what represents violence, has been a crucial issue for movement activists and observers alike (see, e.g., Tilly 2003: 1). In particular, the largely unplanned, spontaneous forms of collective action often defined as "riots" have attracted widespread (mostly negative) attention from media and institutions. In his chapter, David Waddington attempts to identify the underlying political motives and rationality behind forms of behavior that are regularly stigmatized as "self-defeating, irrational, and wantonly criminal" (Waddington, this volume). Focussing mainly on the 2008 Greek and the 2011 UK riots, he explores the "relationship between the political contexts in which each episode of rioting occurred, the processes by which they were instigated and developed, and the political 'meanings' which can therefore be attached to their defining sentiments and forms of behaviour."

The following chapter by Bosi and Malthaner complements Waddington's, as its main empirical focus is on organized and higher levels forms of political violence. However, it shares with the previous chapter a view of different types of violent tactics (and indeed of social movement tactics without further qualification) as somehow connected parts of a broader repertoire, rather than as "discrete and mutually exclusive types." Their discussion of recent contributions in this field highlights the importance of both contextual and dynamic variables, as violent repertoires are not so much the result of strategic planning alone, but are part of broader processes of contention, and heavily dependent on the forms taken by the escalation of conflicts.

At times, challenges to powerholders exceed actions undertaken by small, clandestine groups and result in guerrilla or generalized civil war or insurrection. Traditionally at the margin of social movement research focussed on Western societies, this form of contention has repeatedly occurred in other areas of the globe. A consequence of differences in territorial focus has been the very limited overlap between analysts of movements and those of civil wars. In her chapter, Elisabeth Wood sets out to fill this gap through the identification of common themes to the two fields. These include, among others, escalation and de-escalation dynamics, the mobilization of affected publics, and the analysis of the outcomes of conflict. In drawing her parallels, Wood relies heavily on concepts from the classic agenda, such as political opportunities and framing.

It is worth stressing, however, that radical contentious challenges do not necessarily go along with violent repertoires. In his contribution, Daniel Ritter discusses nonviolent challenges to powerholders, including "un-armed insurrections." Drawing upon a range of examples from different historical phases, Ritter shows how nonviolent civil resistance is not just a set of specific protest tactics but also a way of conducting major forms of the modern protest repertoire such as strikes or mass demonstrations. In doing so he provides a bridge between social movement and nonviolent action research, that has so far been relatively (if surprisingly) disconnected. He also devotes specific attention to those cases in which nonviolent mass protest actually succeeds in overturning powerholders despite the latter's heavy reliance on repressive strategies.

Consumerism represents another, very different, form of challenge to corporate power, with strong cultural overtones. It has assumed growing relevance since the 1980s, in parallel although not overlapping with the rise of "new social movements." In their chapter, Michele Micheletti and Dietlind Stolle show how critical consumerism is actually located at the crossroads of more conventional political pressure and practices of personal transformation. They illustrate this point looking at a range of examples, coming from the African–American civil rights movement, Nestlé boycott, gay rights' movement, and the movement against the Israeli occupied territories. In particular they focus on four major practices (boycotts, buycotts, discursive actions, and lifestyle commitments), highlighting their strengths and weaknesses.

Finally, it is also important to notice the dual link between social movements and non-contentious forms like voluntary collective action. The relationship is dual because on the one hand, social movements often act to generate themselves the public goods in which they are interested, this way locating themselves close to a form of voluntary action oriented to service delivery; on the other hand, voluntary groups often connect in broad informal networks, sharing broad identities, that is, in a manner close to a social movement mode of coordination (Diani and Moffatt 2016; Diani and Mische, this volume).

In their chapter, Helmut Anheier and Nikolas Scherer discuss some aspects of the relations between volunteering and social movements. Even though addressing similar, sometimes overlapping, empirical cases, the two fields of studies have developed in parallel, remaining largely unconnected. This chapter aims at bridging insights from both, explaining how and why they could learn from each other. In doing so, they point to evidence that activities such as volunteering and political activism increasingly take place in voluntary organizations, that is organizations that are mainly based on the voluntary contributions of money, in-kind, and of time; pursue political goals; and uphold or promote certain social or political values. Moreover, social movements mobilize both civic activists and volunteers in their claim-making activities. Finally, in their recent development social movements have often adopted more formalized structures as well as voluntary forms of help and self-help. In fact, as the authors stress, "Non-governmental or voluntary organizations are thus often both vehicle and outcome of social movements" (p. 495, in this volume).

The role of cultural dynamics in social movement processes is explored in this Part 6, devoted to "Cultures of Contention." From being, if not totally absent, at least marginal, cultural issues and approaches have acquired centrality and relevance in social movement studies. This Part addresses different ways in which culture is conceptualized since when it was "brought back in" to social movement studies as well as to the potential bridges to be built on cultural issues with other fields of knowledge such as the sociology of art, literature studies, subaltern studies, visual analysis, and anthropology.

Anna Tan and David Snow provide a broad overview of such complex relations, drawing upon a notion of culture that comprises products, practices, and meanings. They show how culture is at the same time a major structural source of the conflicts in which social movements are engaged,[1] and an important tool for collective action and social change. They classify social movements' cultural claims and challenges as focussing on embracement, reform, or rejection of dominant cultural models. Then they shift their attention to the basic mechanisms through which cultural symbols are manipulated by social movement actors both to generate action and affect its outcomes.

In their chapter, Francesca Polletta and Beth Gharrity Gardner show how stories represent a powerful resource for social movement activists, but they add that, while the use of narratives has a strategic component, narratives are also part of the cultural fabric of a given society. Getting movements' stories accepted in public discourse also implies undermining those deeper narratives, and represents an important indicator of movement success. Stories are also essential to the establishment of connections between events, phases, actors, and contentious episodes. As such, they are essential to the formation of movements' identities (Mische 2003; White, Godart, and Corona 2007; White 2008).

While symbolic production is by no means reducible to the action of artistically gifted individuals or even professionals, the arts have historically provided an important source of inspiration and support for social movement activity, beyond representing arguably a distinctive form of social movements in their own right. In his chapter, Ron Eyerman builds on his view of movements as "cognitive praxis" (Eyerman and Jamison 1991) to illustrate how the arts enable the representation of movement causes and motives in a particularly effective form. Covering various forms of artistic expression, he also pays special attention to the role of "movements against the arts," showing how certain cultural forms may become a primary target for countermovements and an object of contention in their own right.

The concept of performative protest is also central to Nicole Doerr, Alice Mattoni, and Simon Teune, as part of their discussion of the role of visual analysis in social movements. They note that, despite the obvious relevance of images in order to convey the emotions associated with political activism, the worthiness of certain causes, or the brutality of movement opponents, their analysis has not (yet) made it fully into mainstream social movement research. They also pay special attention to the role of different types of media in making movement practices and cultural productions visible to broader publics. Their attention to new technologies renders their contribution complementary to essays by Earl et al. in Part III of this volume.

The strong attention to cultural processes among movement researchers represents an important reminder of the fact that social movements cannot be equated to political challenges, a criticism that has long been leveled against the "classic agenda" of social movement research (Melucci 1996; Oliver and Snow 1995; Snow, Soule, and Kriesi 2004). At the same time, as Tan and Snow's chapter also illustrates, critics have largely focussed on cultural movements that expressed an explicit criticism of dominant or emerging values and/or social structures. These took the form either of alternative life-worlds in which different cultural models might be put into practice, or of attempts to re-establish a moral order they considered to be undermined by the forces of modernization and social change. In her chapter, Julia Eckert adds an important element to the range of culture-based forms of collective action by looking at what she calls "practice movements." These are forms of unorganized collective action, often based in urban areas and carried on by the most deprived sectors of the population. They focus on the appropriation or redistribution of basic goods rather than on a critique of systemic dominant values. This is achieved neither through explicit political representation nor through the creation of alternative worlds but rather through the exploitation of the opportunities that the system presents at the border between conformity and transgression. Building on her familiarity with non-Western societies, Eckert builds on the intellectual tradition focussing on the "weapons of the weak" (Scott 1985) to highlight a pattern of action that the global crisis might well render more relevant even in the most affluent areas of the world.

A sustained conversation with anthropology may also be found in the chapter by Jeffrey Juris and Alex Khasnabish, yet with a stronger methodological focus. They address one of the key issues in the study of cultural processes within social movements, namely, how to approach cultural forms which are not reducible to texts. They suggest that ethnographic approaches may usefully contribute to the exploration of how social movement activists experience everyday life, how intra- and inter-group tensions and conflicts are managed, and how meanings are generated in collective action processes. They look in particular at four different modes of activist practice: everyday cultural production, local–global networking, new media activism, and performative protest. They also address promises and limitations of engaged ethnographic research.

The next Part addresses "Political and Non-political Opportunities and Constraints." Political opportunities are a core concept in social movement studies, which have mainly considered social movements as actors of normal politics. Even if criticized as stretched and too vague, the concept has nonetheless proved a very useful heuristic device to investigate conditions for the expression of contention in particular in democracies. The chapters in this Part revise some of these contributions, but also go well beyond them by bridging social movements with recent trends in comparative politics, as well as international relations, international political economy, history, and law.

In both the classic political process approach and in the contentious politics agenda, the state does indeed occupy a central function. States and state transformations are thus at the core of the next three chapters. The transformation of states is addressed by Marc Beissinger in terms of increasing complexity of state activities, and therefore effects of state actions on everyday life, but also in terms of claims on identity and culture. Looking at states as arenas of conflicts, but also social movement targets and actors within them, the chapter addresses the broad trend of increasing competences of the state but also the effects of globalization in term of a reduction of state capacity as well as the development of informal relations at the border of state and society, to which the spread of corruption testifies. Moreover, from the cultural point of view, while the idea of national self-determination is more and more rooted, the ubiquitous conflicts over national borders testifies that "There is no such thing as a culturally-neutral state; all states, to varying degrees, represent repositories of cultural interest—even more so in a world beset by massive movements of populations across state borders" (Beissinger, this volume).

The effects of globalization are addressed by Jackie Smith who locates a growing attention of international relations studies to non-state action within the increasing success of the constructivist approach. This approach can indeed contribute to social movement studies its focus on the role of ideas and norms, as well as on their diffusion within organizations and across them. From the international political economy comes instead attention to power, in particular to the position of specific states within world system capitalism. While international organizations attempt to deradicalize challengers by a selective inclusion of NGOs, global social movements have nonetheless mounted important challenges against global (as well as local) political institutions.

A similar plea is presented in the following chapter by Hank Johnston who focuses on authoritarian regimes. As social movement studies have developed on the assumption that social movements need some openness in political opportunities, their interaction with research on authoritarian regimes as well as democratization has been very limited. Looking at this literature, the chapter singles out the importance of considering the differences within typologies of authoritarian regimes that vary significantly in terms of degree of liberalization as well as of state capacity. It also maps the specific repertoires of actions that social movements tend to develop. It is suggested that from the literature on authoritarian regimes as well as on transition, important contributions could be made to social movement studies: among others, their attention to agency, to the role of critical junctures, and to the building of cross-class coalitions.

Authoritarian regimes are particularly oriented toward repression. However, repression is not a peculiarity of non-democracies. Rather, the governance of internal dissent is a main occupation for state actors all around the globe. Delving into sociology and political science, but also criminology, law, geography, and developmental studies, Abby Peterson and Matthias Wahlstrom map practices of repression by distinguishing its scale (from interpersonal relations to international police cooperation), its institution (public in the shape of the police and the army, but also private in the forms of corporation and countermovements), and its different forms.

Private politics is at the core of Philip Balsiger's contribution on the broad repertoire of political action that corporations develop in order to respond to and manage protest. Avoidance, acquiescence, compromise, sidestepping, confrontation, and prevention are selected as part of this repertoire. Bridging comparative political economy with social movement studies, the chapter reflects on some of the main transformations in the organization of corporate actors, such as the growth of firm internal units specializing in the management of protest, and the trends toward deregulation, the development of conceptions of corporate citizenship, as well as the potential effects of "varieties of capitalism" on corporate political strategies. As business interests tend to be more influential in "quiet times," contentious politics represent a challenge indeed to firms' power.

Within the political process approach as well as within the contentious politics approach, political parties have been considered as important potential allies and opponents for social movements. After revising this tradition (to whose development he has contributed greatly), Hanspeter Kriesi adds a new focus on how movements affect parties as well as party systems, by promoting the rise of new parties and the reshaping of existing ones. Bridging social movement and party studies, the chapter suggests a distinction between mainstream versus peripheral parties to be added at the more traditional one between party-in-government and party-in-opposition. At the same time, however, it also warns against too clear-cut a distinction between insiders and outsiders within a quickly changing and increasingly volatile party system.

The topic of political parties is also addressed in Kenneth Roberts' contribution on populism and social movements. Distinguishing between definitions of populism as mere rhetoric and those that look instead at populist regimes, he insists in fact on the differences between social movements as grass-roots, horizontal forms of political participation, and populism as instead socio-political mobilization controlled from above by authority figures. As he writes, "Whereas social movements emerge from autonomous forms of collective action undertaken by self-constituted civic groups or networks, populism typically involves an appropriation of popular subjectivity by dominant personalities who control the channels, rhythms, and organizational forms of social mobilization. Indeed, populism does not require that mass constituencies engage in collective action at all, beyond the individual act of casting a ballot in national elections or popular referendums. Although both forms of popular subjectivity contest established elites, social movements mobilize such contestation from the bottom-up, whereas populism typically mobilizes mass constituencies from the top-down behind the leadership of a counter-elite" (this volume). While both social movements and populist parties emerge from the crisis of representative politics, with the former sometimes contributing to the rise of the latter, the chapter refers to research on populist regimes in Latin America to stress the tensions between participatory visions within social movements and populist regimes as forms of incorporation within a specific socio-economic system. Indeed, the author argues for more interaction between studies on social movements and studies of populist politics, both increasingly important given the crisis of representative democracies.

Sarah A. Soule and Brayden G. King are also in many ways conversant with the political process approach when they address transformation in corporations, firms, and markets, and how they influence the social movement dynamics. The concept of *corporate opportunity structure* is developed in order to link markets and social movements. They show how the level of competition among firms, as well as the extent of public and private regulation and the degree of concentration of specific sectors, constitute opportunities and constraints for social movements. The same applies to firms' reputation and visibility as well as their corporatist culture. Attention is then focussed on some recent trends in the business world and their potential effects on contentious politics.

The final Part is devoted to "Movements' Contributions to Social and Political Change." For a long time, there has been a common lament about the lack of research on the effects of social movements. This gap was explained by the difficulties of singling out the specific impacts of civil society actors in complex processes as well as the long-term perspective from which outcomes had to be assessed. Addressing these challenges through process tracing and complex research designs, empirical analyses have however made progress on assessing the policy impacts of social movements at local, national, and international levels, and also on their cultural consequences (Giugni, McAdam, and Tilly 1999). In this Part of our Handbook, without aiming to paint a complete picture, we single out the scientific debates in some areas in which social movements had visible impacts.

First, two contributions look mainly at the policy effects in two important policy areas, namely, welfare and the environment. Colin Barker and Michael Lavalette analyze the intersection of welfare and social movements, both in terms of how changing welfare provisions affect social movements, but also how movements were able to transform, through long struggles, the provision of housing, monetary benefits, education and health, "and all manner of social and public policies and services." In doing this, the authors bridge the literature on the different forms of welfare (social–democratic, corporatist, and liberal) with social movement studies, looking at the effects of class stratification as well as the interactions between unions and parties in labor politics on the forms and extension of welfare. The degree of overlapping of work and community struggles is referred to in order to explain in particular the specificity of the weak (liberal) protection of the US welfare state. Social movements are moreover addressed as producers of welfare, which offer protection and alternative forms of de-commodification of goods and their constructions as rights.

If the welfare state has been a typical area of intervention of the "old" labor movements, the protection of the environment has been instead a main claim by so-called "new" social movements. By looking at transformations in environmental policies and politics, Christopher Rootes and Eugene Nulman analyze the impacts of environmental movements, both direct and indirect, positive and negative. The main puzzle addressed is the one of a movement which appears able to enjoy many successes, and is indeed often celebrated for its influence, while at the same time "the assault on the global environment proceeds at an unprecedented pace." The long lasting and complex processes of mobilization of sympathies in the public opinion, but also among policy makers at different levels, are therefore investigated and the differential effects in the global North versus global South pointed out.

The complex interaction of international politics and social movements is at the core of the next two chapters that both look at normative changes as co-produced by social movements.

In her chapter on human rights, Kate Nash mobilizes concepts from international relations and social movement studies to cover the emergence and content of a human right regime. International law and global constitutionalism contribute to the understanding of the formal introduction of human rights as international norms, but social movement studies are also referred to in order to point to the limits of a legal perspective. The universalistic approach of a North-based international NGO is in fact scrutinized in the definition of an "elitist" view of human rights which is contrasted with the grass-roots version of subaltern cosmopolitanism.

In a similar vein, Raffaele Marchetti looks at the development in international organizations of pro-civil society participatory norms, which tend to selectively integrate professionalized NGOs and to exclude grass-roots social movement organizations. With reference to normative theory, the development of this specific normative approach is linked to the spread at international level of the stakeholder principle, the reliance on expertize, and the liberalism of Western principles. The participatory governance of stakeholders is however contrasted with the conceptions and practices of democracy from below developed within the global justice movement.

The characteristics of these conceptions and practices, as well as their capacity to affect institutional policies, are addressed in the next chapter. Here, Donatella della Porta analyzes progressive social movements as important actors in the development of conceptions and practices of democracy that go beyond representative ones. Bridging social movement studies with normative theory, the chapter reviews the main contributions to participatory and deliberative democracy by past and contemporary social movements—from the labor movement to new social movements, the global justice movements, and recent anti-austerity protests. It is observed that, while far from achieving their ideals of democracy, progressive movements play an important prefigurative role for the development of inclusive and transparent forms of internal decision making, with increasing emphasis on grass-roots participation and consensus building. As stressed in the final part, both external and internal factors impact on internal practices of decision making in social movements, with innovation and adaptation which follows activists' critical self-reflections and attempts to overcome past failures.

Democratic innovations have indeed often travelled from social movements to public institutions. In his chapter, Julien Talpin notes the potential exchanges between research on social movements and research on democratic innovations and democratic theory. He suggests that social movements have played an important role in promoting, participating in or, sometimes, boycotting various institutions that have developed to compensate for the weakness of representative democracy. Participatory principles were embedded in several reforms in local politics in the 1960s as well as in most recent attempts to involve the public in decision making beyond the elections. Inspired by the participatory budgeting developed in Porto Alegre, Brasil, public institutions have experimented with ways of extending participation and, at the same time, improving deliberation through high-quality communication. The potential for expanding the public sphere as well as the limits in terms of atomization and depoliticization of some of these experiments are discussed.

Social movements might produce also most radical effects. As Jeff Goodwin and Rene Rojas observe, revolutionary situations are quite common situations in which substantial changes are claimed by revolutionary movements, defined as a special type of movement that tries to bring about broad changes, including minimally a change of political regime, and potentially encompassing transformation in class structures and the socio-economic institutions or mode of production. They observe however that revolutionary movements rarely succeed in overthrowing political regimes as, in order to win, they require previous weakening of the infrastructural power of the state due to economic circumstances, war, or élite divisions. Revolutionary situations then are situations of dual power as revolutionary movements clash with incumbent institutions. In these situations, regime repression, especially if indiscriminate and inconsistent, strengthens the resonance of revolutionary ideologies that depict the existing regime as fundamentally unjust, calling instead for drastic political and social changes.

In sum, we believe that these contributions facilitate not only the mapping of the current position in the field of social movements but also its reception to contributions and inspiration from other fields. This might be considered a satisfactory achievement in itself, yet it remains an inherently provisional one, as disciplinary borders seem to become more permeable with each new global wave of contentious politics. This means that the coverage of the "expanded field" could never be complete, and it is indeed our hope that the Handbook will pave the way for new conversations to be opened and new bridges to be built between different fields of knowledge. In particular, while we have tried to expand the focus of the research beyond the Western world, we must acknowledge that a sustained conversation with analysts located outside the West is still missing, and our focus on non-Western objects remains limited. We hope, however, that this Handbook can at least provide the starting point toward the expansion of these broader conversations.

Note

1. As theorized most forcefully by the late Alberto Melucci (1989, 1996).

References

Ahrne, Göran and Brunsson, Nils (2011). "Organization Outside Organizations: The Significance of Partial Organization," *Organization*. 18: 83–104.

Andrews, Kenneth T. and Edwards, Bob (2005). "The Organizational Structure of Local Environmentalism," *Mobilization*. 10: 213–234.

Anheier, Helmut and Kendall, Jeremy (2002). "Interpersonal Trust and Voluntary Associations: Examining Three Approaches," *British Journal of Sociology*. 53: 343–362.

Anheier, Helmut (2004). *Civil Society. Measurement, Evaluation, Policy*. London: Earthscan.

Arrighi, Giovanni, Hopkins, Terence K., and Wallerstein, Immanuel (1989). *Antisystemic Movements*. London: Verso.

Arrighi, Giovanni (2001). "Braudel, Capitalism and the New Economic Sociology," *Review* (Fernand Braduel Center). 24: 107–123.

Barker, Colin, Johnson, Alan, and Lavalette, Michael, eds. (2001). *Leadership in Social Movements*. Manchester: Manchester University Press.

Barker, Colin, Cox, Laurence, Krinski, John, and Gunvald Nilsen, Alf, eds. (2013). *Marxism and Social Movements*. Leiden: Brill, 83–102.

Barnes, Samuel H. and Kaase, Max, eds. (1979). *Political Action. Mass Participation in Five Western Democracies*. Beverly Hills/London: Sage.

Benford, Robert D. and Snow, David A. Snow (2000). "Framing Processes and Social Movements: An Overview and Assessment," *Annual Review of Sociology*. 26: 611–639.

Bennett, W. Lance and Segerberg, Alexandra (2013). *The Logic of Connective Action*. Cambridge/New York: Cambridge University Press.

Blee, Kathleen (2003). *Inside Organized Racism*. Los Angeles: University of California Press.

Bourdieu, Pierre (1988). *Homo Academicus*. Stanford, CA: Stanford University Press.

Buechler, Steven (2011). *Understanding Social Movements: Theories from the Classical Era to the Present*. New York: Paradigm.

Burstein, Paul (1998). "Interest Organizations, Political Parties, and the Study of Democratic Politics." In *Social Movements and American Political Institutions*, edited by Anne Costain and Andrew McFarland, 39–56. Lanham: Rowman & Littlefield.

Casanova, José (1994). *Public Religions in the Modern World*. Chicago: University of Chicago Press.

Castells, Manuel (1984). *The City and the Grassroots: A Cross-Cultural Theory of Urban Social Movements*. Berkeley and Los Angeles, CA: University of California Press.

Castells, Manuel (1997). *The Power of Identity*. Oxford: Blackwell.

Castells, Manuel (2012). *Networks of Outrage and Hope. Social Movements in the Internet Age*. Cambridge: Polity.

Crossley, Nick (2002). *Making Sense of Social Movements*. Buckingham: Open University Press.

Dalton, Russell (2008). *Citizen Politics*. Washington, DC: CQ Press.

Davis, Gerald F., Morrill, Calvin, Rao, Hayagreeva, and Soule, Sarah (2008). "Introduction: Social Movements in Organizations and Markets," *Administrative Science Quarterly*. 53: 389–394.

Davis, Gerald F., McAdam, Doug, Scott, Richard W., and Zald, Mayer N., eds. (2005). *Social Movements and Organization Theory*. Cambridge: Cambridge University Press.

della Porta, Donatella (1995). *Social Movements, Political Violence and the State*. Cambridge: Cambridge University Press.

della Porta, Donatella (2013). *Clandestine Political Violence*. Cambridge: Cambridge University Press.

della Porta, Donatella (2014). *Mobilizing for Democracy. Comparing 1989 and 2011*. Oxford: Oxford University Press.

della Porta, Donatella (2015). *Social Movements in Times of Austerity*. Cambridge: Polity.

della Porta, Donatella and Mario Diani (2006). *Social Movements*. Oxford: Blackwell.

Diani, Mario (2015). *The Cement of Civil Society: Studying Networks in Localities*. Cambridge/New York: Cambridge University Press.

Diani, Mario and Moffatt, Caelum (2016). "Modes of Coordination of Collective Action in the Middle-East: Has the Arab Spring Made a Difference?" In *Contention, Regimes, and Transition*, edited by Eitan Alimi, Avraham Sela, and Mario Sznajder, 27–45. Oxford/New York: Oxford University Press.

Diani, Mario and Cisar, Ondrej (2014). "The Emergence of a Social Movement Research Field." In *Routledge Handbook of European Sociology*, edited by Sokratis Kodornios and Alexander Kyrtsis, 173–195. London/New York: Routledge.

DiMaggio, Paul and Powell, Walter W. (1983). "The Iron Cage Revisited: Institutional Isomorphism and Collective Rationality in Organizational Fields," *American Sociological Review*. 48: 147–160.

Eyerman, Ron and Jamison, Andrew (1991). *Social Movements: A Cognitive Approach*. Cambridge: Polity Press.

Flam, Helena, ed. (1994). *States and Anti-Nuclear Movements*. Edinburgh: Edinburgh University Press.

Gamson, William (1992). "The Social Psychology of Collective Action." In *Frontiers of Social Movement Theory*, edited by Aldon Morris and Carol Mueller, 29–50. New Haven, CT: Yale University Press.

Giugni, Marco, McAdam, Doug, and Tilly, Charles, eds. (1999). *How Movements Matter*. Minneapolis, MN: Minnesota University Press.

Goldstone, Jack (2003). "Introduction: Bridging Institutionalized and Noninstitutionalized Politics." In *States, Parties and Social Movements*, edited by Jack Goldstone, 1–25. New York: Cambridge University Press.

Goodwin, Jeff, Jasper, James M., and Polletta, Francesca, eds. (2001). *Passionate Politics*. Chicago: Chicago University Press.

Hetland, Gabriel and Goodwin, Jeff (2013). "The Strange Disappearance of Capitalism from Social Movement Studies." In *Marxism and Social Movements*, edited by Colin Barker, Laurence Cox, John Krinski, and Alf Gunvald Nilsen, 83–102. Leiden: Brill.

Jasper, James (1997). *The Art of Moral Protest*. Chicago: University of Chicago Press.

Johnston, Hank (2014). *What Is a Social Movement?* Cambridge/Malden, MA: Polity Press.

Kitschelt, Herbert (1986). "Political Opportunity Structures and Political Protest. Antinuclear Movements in Four Democracies," *British Journal of Political Science*. 16: 57–85.

Klandermans, Bert and Tarrow, Sidney (1988). "Mobilization into Social Movements: Synthesizing European and American Approaches," *International Social Movement Research*. 1: 1–38.

Kriesi, Hanspeter (1996). "The Organizational Structure of New Social Movements in a Political Context." In *Comparative Perspective on Social Movements. Political Opportunities, Mobilizing Structures, and Cultural Framing*, edited by Doug McAdam, John McCarthy, and Mayer N. Zald, 152–184. Cambridge/New York: Cambridge University Press.

Kriesi, Hanspeter, Koopmans, Ruud, Duyvendak, Jan Willem, and Giugni, Marco (1995). *New Social Movements in Western Europe*. Minneapolis/London: University of Minnesota Press.

Marwell, Gerald and Oliver, Pamela E. (1993). *The Critical Mass in Collective Action. A Micro-Social Theory*. Cambridge/New York: Cambridge University Press.

McAdam, Doug (1982). *Political Process and the Development of Black Insurgency. 1930–1970*. Chicago: University of Chicago Press.

McAdam, Doug (2003). "Beyond Structural Analysis: Toward a More Dynamic Understanding of Social Movements." In *Social Movements and Networks*, edited by Mario Diani and Doug McAdam, 281–298. Oxford: Oxford University Press.

McAdam, Doug, McCarthy, John D., and Zald, Mayer N. (1996). *Comparative Perspective on Social Movements*. Cambridge: Cambridge University Press.

McAdam, Doug, Tarrow, Sidney, and Tilly, Charles (2001). *Dynamics of Contention*. Cambridge: Cambridge University Press.

McCarthy, John D., Rafail, Patrick, and Gromis, Ashley (2013). "Recent Trends in Public Protest in the U.S.A.: The Social Movement Society Thesis Revisited." In *The Future of Social Movement Research: Dynamics, Mechanisms, and Processes*, edited by Jacqueline van Stekelenburg, Conny Roggeband, and Bert Klandermans, 369–396. Minneapolis, MN: University of Minnesota Press.

McCarthy, John D. and Zald, Mayer N. (1977). "Resource Mobilization and Social Movements: A Partial Theory," *American Journal of Sociology*. 82: 1212–1241.

Melucci, Alberto (1989). *Nomads of the Present: Social Movements and Individual Needs in Contemporary Society*. London: Hutchinson.

Melucci, Alberto (1996). *Challenging Codes*. Cambridge/New York: Cambridge University Press.

Minkoff, Debra (1995). *Organizing for Equality*. New Brunswick: Rutgers University Press.

Mische, Ann (2003). "Cross-Talk in Movements: Reconceiving the Culture-Network Link." In *Social Movements and Networks*, edited by Mario Diani and Doug McAdam, 258–280. Oxford: Oxford University Press.

Mische, Ann (2011). "Relational Sociology, Culture, and Agency." In *The Sage Handbook of Social Network Analysis*, edited by Peter Carrington and John Scott, 80–97. London: Sage.

Nepstad Erickson, Sharon and Bob, Clifford (2006). "When Do Leaders Matter? Hypotheses on Leadership Dynamics in Social Movements," *Mobilization*. 11: 1–22.

Neveu, Erik (2011). *Sociologie Des Mouvements Sociaux*. Paris: La Decouverte.

Norris, Pippa, Walgrave, Stefaan, and Van Aelst, Peter (2005). "Who Demonstrates? Antistate Rebels, Conventional Participants, or Everyone?" *Comparative Politics*. 37: 189–205.

Oberschall, Anthony (1973). *Social Conflict and Social Movements*. Englewood Cliffs, NJ: Prentice Hall.

Oliver, Pamela and Johnston, Hank (2000). "What a Good Idea! Ideologies and Frames in Social Movement Research," *Mobilization*. 5(1): 37–54.

Oliver, Pamela and Snow, David A. (1995). "Social Movements and Collective Behavior." In *Sociological Perspectives on Social Psychology*, edited by Karen Cook, Gary A. Fine, and James House, 571–599. Boston, MA: Allyn and Bacon.

Olson, Mancur (1963). *The Logics of Collective Action*. Cambridge, MA: Harvard University Press.

Opp, Karl-Dieter (2009). *Theories of Political Protest and Social Movements: A Multidisciplinary Introduction, Critique, and Synthesis*. London: Taylor & Francis.

Piven, Frances Fox and Cloward, Richard (1977). *Poor People's Movements*. New York: Pantheon.

Rootes, Christopher, ed. (2003). *Environmental Protest in Western Europe*. Oxford: Oxford University Press.

Roy, Olivier (2007). *Secularism Confronts Islam*. New York: Columbia University Press.

Scott, James C. (1985). *Weapons of the Weak. Everyday Forms of Peasant Resistance*. New Haven: Yale University Press.

Smith, Jackie and Wiest, Dawn (2012). *Social Movements in the World-System*. New York: Russell Sage.

Snow, David A., Burke Rochford, E., Jr., Worden, Steven K., and Benford, Robert D. (1986). "Frame Alignment Processes, Micromobilization, and Movement Participation," *American Sociological Review.* 51(4): 464–481.

Snow, David A., Soule, Sarah, and Kriesi, Hanspeter (2004). *The Blackwell Companion to Social Movements*. Oxford: Blackwell.

Soule, Sarah (2013). "Bringing Organizational Studies Back into Social Movement Scholarship." In *The Future of Social Movement Research: Dynamics, Mechanisms, and Processes*, edited by Jacquelien van Stekelenburg, Conny Roggeband, and Bert Klandermans, 145–168. Minneapolis, MN: University of Minnesota Press.

Soule, Sarah and Earl, Jennifer (2005). "A Movement Society Evaluated: Collective Protest in the United States, 1960–1986," *Mobilization.* 10: 345–364.

Tarrow, Sidney (1989). *Democracy and Disorder*. Oxford: Clarendon Press.

Tarrow, Sidney (1994). *Power in Movement. Social Movements, Collective Action and Politics*. New York/Cambridge: Cambridge University Press.

Tarrow, Sidney (2005). *The New Transnational Activism*. Cambridge: Cambridge University Press.

Tilly, Charles (1978). *From Mobilization to Revolution*. Reading, MA: Addison-Wesley.

Tilly, Charles (2003). *The Politics of Collective Violence*. Cambridge: Cambridge University Press.

Tilly, Charles (2004). *Social Movements 1768-2004*. Boulder, CO: Paradigm.

Tilly, Charles (2005). *Popular Contention in Great Britain 1758-1834*. Boulder, CO: Paradigm.

Tilly, Charles and Tarrow, Sidney (2007). *Contentious Politics*. Boulder, CO: Paradigm.

Tilly, Charles, Tilly, Louise, and Tilly, Richard (1975). *The Rebellious Century 1830-1930*. Cambridge, MA: Harvard University Press.

Tindall, David (2004). "Social Movement Participation Over Time: An Ego-Network Approach to Micro-Mobilization," *Sociological Focus.* 37: 163–184.

Touraine, Alain (1981). *The Voice and the Eye*. Cambridge: Cambridge University Press.

Van Deth, Jan W. and Kreuter, Frauke (1998). "Membership of Voluntary Associations." In *Comparative Politics. The Problem of Equivalence*, edited by Jan W. van Deth, 135–155. London: Routledge.

Walgrave, Stefaan and Rucht, Dieter, eds. (2010). *The World Says No to War: Demonstrations Against the War in Iraq*. Minneapolis: University of Minnesota Press.

Wallerstein, Immanuel (1974). *The Modern World System: Capitalist Agriculture and the Origins of the European World Economy in the Sixteenth Century*. New York: Academic Press.

White, Harrison, Godart, Frederict, and Corona, Victor (2007). "Mobilizing Identities—Uncertainty and Control in Strategy," *Theory Culture & Society.* 24: 181–202.

White, Harrison (2008). *Identity and Control. How Social Formations Emerge*. Princeton: Princeton University Press.

Zald, Mayer N. and McCarthy, John D. (1980). "Social Movement Industries: Competition and Cooperation Among Movement Organizations," *Research In Social Movements, Conflict and Change.* 3: 1–20.

PART I

CORE THEORETICAL PERSPECTIVES

....

CHAPTER 2

SOCIAL MOVEMENTS IN SOCIAL THEORY

....

KLAUS EDER

SOCIAL MOVEMENTS HAVING A HARD TIME IN SOCIAL THEORY

....

SOCIAL movements have always been an irritating phenomenon in social theory (as they are in social reality). Their preoccupation with the problem of social order moved social movements to a residual category in social theorizing. The central issue has been to find out how to transform movement into order, how to contain and channel deviance toward orderly life. This has made them an object of theorizing that remained at the margin of social theory. Looking into the "giants upon which we stand" (Merton 1965) such as Weber, Durkheim, or Simmel, they do not tell us much about social movements. This even holds for Marx who engaged in social movements but who did not produce a compelling theory about social movements. All this has to do with the preoccupation with order—even Marx considered the working class movement as a step toward a new order—socialism and communism. We could take this as a hint that there is not much to gain from looking into social theory for making sense of social movements. The contrary is the case: by keeping social movements conceptually at the margin of social theorizing, they tell us a lot about the margins where the reproduction of order does not succeed. The more these social theorists were preoccupied with order, the more interesting social movements became as analytical keys to the problem of creating order in the permanent movement produced by social action.

This preoccupation with social order contrasts with the fact that modern social theory has emerged from a social movement: the movement against the old order in the eighteenth and nineteenth century. The Enlightenment saw itself as a social movement producing organizational forms such as clubs, associations that the old order looked at with suspicion, mobilizing everything to censure political communication and to destroy the networks formed to organize collective action (Habermas 1989 [1962]). Even the nineteenth century has been full of other types of protest (Tilly, Tilly, and Tilly 1975). Yet the theoretical analysis of social movements did not make it into the heart of social theory.

Nevertheless, Marx and the Left Hegelians provide a special case in this modern genealogy of social theory: they offered elements of a theory of social movements grounded upon a fundamental critique of the enlightenment movement. Contrary to the conservative critiques of the Enlightenment who saw the Enlightenment as an attempt to set fire (light) to the house, Marx radicalized the Enlightenment critique by extending it into a theory of class conflict which he linked to an analysis of the crisis-ridden evolution of capitalist forms of social relations of production. The central variables explaining collective action were the existence of an objective class ("Klasse an sich") which becomes conscious of itself ("Klasse für sich"). Yet this theoretical program fell short of its realization. Class conflict and class mobilization remained undertheorized in the decades to follow.

The Historical Baggage

The Marxian Heritage

The Marxian heritage found a theoretically consequential "sociological" translation in the seventies and eighties of the last century. An important step in the re-appropriation of the theoretical intentions of Marx is offered by the work of Jürgen Habermas (1979). In a similar vein, and using a genuinely sociological–historical perspective, Craig Calhoun (Calhoun 1982) focussed the link of the theory of capitalist development with the theory of class action. He made clear the issue of a necessary link between the structural contradictions of capitalism and the class contradictions that sometimes fostered class conflict and sometimes not. The theoretical question of why the mobilization of class conflict increases or decreases thus needed an answer that required further theoretical development. The general Marxian explanation provided a necessary but not a sufficient condition for social movements.

The theoretical construction of the mechanism producing class action, namely class consciousness, also marks the weak point of Marx's theoretical strategy. Ideological framings of reality block—as Marx argues—the awareness of the real world; yet a scientific account of the real forces generating the reality of capitalist development can overcome this blockage. Instead of developing a theory of social movements, a theory of an intellectual avant-garde came to the fore, which undermined the development of a genuine theory of social movements.

What is left is the theoretical proposition that social movements are practices that result from groups becoming aware of their position in social relations of production. Exactly how this works remains unclear. Marx however gives casual examples of why social movements do not arise, the most famous being contained in the metaphor of the "sack of potatoes" in the eighteenth Brumaire (Marx 1953). This metaphor describes the unconnected small land laborers who share nothing but the fact they all work on a little piece of land. There is no connection among the land laborers themselves; they are linked via the landowner who lives far away in Paris. This can be seen as a first network analytical account of why the mobilization of workers fails, an idea taken up a hundred years later in the social sciences.

Durkheim's Effervescence Collective

Another classic has touched upon social movements, providing the grounds for a debate in social movement theory that has become important in recent decades: the role of collective sentiments in the making of collective action. This theoretical idea emerged—paradoxically enough—when Emile Durkheim turned to social–anthropological studies and developed an explanation of collective practices in "primitive" societies that culminated in his book on the elementary forms of religious life (Durkheim 1968 [1912]). Observing the phenomenon he called "effervescence collective," Durkheim explained how people were able to act together. The elements necessary for making intensive collective action possible is get out of everyday life and to enter a ritual process which binds the group together and enables the group to defend itself against the bads that threaten it. Such rituals accompanied preparations for warfare, distributive quarrels, or collective responses to natural disasters.

What is important in Durkheim's account is the emphasis on the emotional energy invested in and reproduced by such collective actions. Acting together releases a collective excitement that transcends individual intentionality by orienting collective action toward a collectively shared goal. This is the reason why Durkheim described these practices as a case of "religious life": transcending the will of the individual and being oriented toward securing the group is something that requires binding forces enacted in religious life. Apart from the question of what "religious" means, the important theoretical insight is into the non-individual, that is, the social nature of collective action.

Durkheim's ideas gained momentum in different analytical directions. Some emphasized the interaction processes taking place in collective action providing the basis for theorizing different types of sequences of collective action, ranging from casual encounters to institutionalized collective action (such as voting). Recent modifications of symbolic interactionism have drawn on these premises (Collins 2004) as well as more recent theories on investing emotional energy in collective action such as social movements (Collins 2008) (see later).

Reformulating the Marxian Perspective: Touraine and Habermas

The Marxian heritage returned in the new wave of theorizing social movements that started in the sixties of the last century with the work of Alain Touraine in France (Touraine 1981). He was the most important social theorist of social movements at that time, preparing the ground for what was to become the theory of the "new social movements" (NSM). He attempted to shift social movements from the margins to the center of social theory.

Conceiving society as something permanently produced in collective action, Touraine discards the idea of order as the core issue for sociological analysis (Touraine 1977). Reacting against Parsonian functionalism, Touraine sought to replace the concept of society by the concept of "historical action systems" that act permanently against attempts to produce social order. Building on a post-Parsonian model of structures of historical action systems, the role of social movements thus becomes paramount as they are viewed as the carriers of historical action. Emphasizing process over order, the central problem of social theory is no longer the issue of institutional order (focussing mostly on the state as the main guarantor of social order). The focus is on the issue of who is able to intervene in social processes and how such interventions shape the direction of social processes. This capacity of directing social change is variable, depending upon the strength of social movements as the main carriers of systems of historical action. The explanation of social change is therefore located in the very structure of historical action, which Touraine conceptualizes as being constituted by three factors: (i) a collective actor with an (ii) identity who has an idea of the enemy while referring to a (iii) "totality," which means to the ensemble of historical processes in which historical action is embedded.

This theoretical construction of social movements is an implication of a radical interpretation of modernity as a situation in which societies engage in permanent self-production. Social reality appears as though in permanent flux, structured by the diversity of historical action events taking place in the here and now. In modernity, social movements multiply, and the working class movement is just one of the many movements competing for the direction of social change. The "old" movement (the working class movement) is only a first step in the constitution of a modernity generating itself in the medium of "old" and "new" social movements.

The long-term theoretical effect of this way of conceptualizing social movements has been a new concern with the methodological issue of the "objectivity" of the observer of social movements. Touraine articulated this problem as the link between the voice of social movements and the eye of the observer (Touraine 1981). Since the eye constitutes a permanent intrusion into the object of research which are the voices in society, the effect of the eye has to be controlled methodologically. The solution Touraine offers for this problem is the idea of seeing the sociological analysis of social movements as a sociological intervention into movement practices. The method of "sociological intervention" tries to figure out the extent to which social movements were able to see their collective action as the kind of historical action that sociological analysts assumed it might be. The theory of social movements provides hypotheses about the possibility of historical action in a concrete situation of protest. The empirical results produced by this coupling of theory and method in the analysis of social movements, however, have been more or less disappointing: the movement society remained a hypothesis that could not be proven empirically (Touraine et al. 1979; Touraine et al. 1980; Touraine 1981; Touraine, Wieviorka, and Dubet 1984). Yet the idea of reflexivity introduced into social movement studies adds a meta-theoretical perspective lacking so far in this field.

Habermas, a German contemporary of Touraine, provided an equally strong link between grand theory and social movements. The main argument in the theory of communicative action (Habermas 1987) is that social movements can be seen as mechanisms triggering collective learning processes in societies. Social movements on the one hand acted against the systemic decoupling of state and markets from the life-world while drawing upon the resources that only life-worlds can offer, that is, the reference to basic moral standards contained in the structure of communicative action among free and equal people. Social movements are phenomena, situated between systems and the life-world and fostered by the capacity to reclaim the normative standards betrayed by the systemic decoupling of politics and economic exchange as executed in the modern state and in capitalism. Such normative standards not only included universalist moral standards of justice, but also standards of equal recognition and standards of cognitive knowledge made available by modern science. This framework in fact well-suited social movements such as the anti-nuclear movement and anti-racist movements, yet turned out to be insufficient to grasp the rise of collective action and protest not only in the West, but also in the rest of the world, above all the rise of religious movements.

From Macro to Micro

The Paradox of Collective Action and the Challenge of RC Theory—The Rationalist Turn

Given the strong macro-theoretical approach dominating the post-'68 period in Western social science, the opportunities of a backlash against macro-structural theorizing favoring micro-structural approaches have grown. Under the label "from structure to action" (Klandermans, Kriesi, and Tarrow 1988) the turn to the actor's perspective not only promised new explanatory advantages, but also a normative claim: bringing the actor back in as something which is good in itself. Introduced by a series of refinements of analyzing collective action that ranged from resource mobilization theory (McCarthy and Zald 1977; Jenkins 1983) to Olson's paradox of collective action (Olson 1965), the notion of strategic action gained ground in social movement analysis.

This turn engendered a bifurcation of the theoretical debate. On the one hand, the implicit rationalist conception of resource mobilization theory joined the theoretical move toward a neo-utilitarian paradigm in the social sciences, that is, rational choice theories. On the other hand, the limits of rationalist assumptions of human action came to the fore, pointing out the identity-related aspects of social action, considered as irreducible to notions of strategic action (Cohen 1985).

The rationalist paradigm produced a series of insights into the dynamics of collective action (Opp 1989). Rationalist assumptions allowed for the resolution of some of the paradoxes in collective action. It added the idea of a "critical mass" of actors necessary for getting social movements off the ground (Marwell and Oliver 1993). Yet theory development stopped. The model offered by Opp, the "structural–cognitive model," combines structural and cognitive factors within an individualist theory perspective and offers, in the author's view, an alternative to failed theory programs (Opp 2009). Yet theory development in the social sciences had already gone beyond the confines of this model. Social relations (transcending the individual) and narrative semantics (transcending the cognitive model) point to the new elements that go beyond such a theorizing of social movements.

Adding Emotions and Identity Claims—The Emotional Turn

The critique of this rationalist individualist paradigm within social movement studies followed another path. It pointed to the neglect of non-rational factors in collective action, yet kept the individualistic (or non-relational) premises. Alberto Melucci (a student of Touraine) already in the eighties of the last century added the idea that identity offers a central motivation for taking part in social movements (Melucci 1980, 1988, 1995). In recent debates the idea that actors do not only act strategically, but also defend an identity, gained ground. This has a parallel development in empirical economic theory, which increasingly takes into account non-rational motivations in economic action (Gintis et al. 2006; Fehr and Gintis 2007). These empirical additions to a theory of the social actor however retained the basic assumptions of the individualistic model of explanation. The postulate to bring back agency against structure even gave it some moral support.

The emphasis on emotions brought back the "individual" in an even more radical way, namely as a body. The idea that social actors decipher the meaning of ongoing interaction from the presentation of the body and the theoretical idea that the body is a medium of creating social bonds among those acting together has its roots in the Durkheimian tradition. Yet the role of emotions taken up in the recent "turn" in social movement theory (Jasper 2011) remains within the individualistic paradigm of sociological explanation since it offers no more than an extension of the motivational basis on which collective action can draw. The theory of social movements therefore lived—as did much of the social sciences—in a fruitless debate over rationalist versus non-rationalist theories of action.

The increasing decline of rational choice theories and the emphasis on non-rational factors in the last decade opened up a new opportunity for theory development in social movement research, reacting and adding to general social theory construction in the social sciences. Introducing emotional factors allowed the theoretical eye to be turned on forms of social action in which the focus was less on language and on argumentative forms of addressing the other but rather on bodily movements and non-argumentative forms of communication. Keywords indicating the new pathways of theory construction are affective solidarity, emotional energy, emotional liberation, pride, and shame (Polletta 2006; Polletta and Chen 2012). This provided the ground for linking such research to the "narrative turn" in social theory (Eder 2009). *Homo narrans* became part of social movement theory and opened new paths explaining the dynamics of social movements.

A final effect of these theoretical innovations regards the double nature of the human actor. He or she is no longer as a mere voice making claims, but a body sending signals. Protest in particular is something that involves the body—exposure to police actions, organizing everyday life in social movements. The methodological implications closely join the conceptual–analytical advances. The focus on emotions and the body as the carrier of emotions invites a return to behavioral social science. This means to observe not only speech acts, but also practices; less what people say, rather what they do. Yet this is not a return to the behaviorism in the social sciences of the last century; it is rather behaviorism turned constructivist. As Clark McPhail put it: the idea is to "extend G. H. Mead's theory of the act as a closed-loop, negative-feedback model of purposive action" (McPhail 2006: 433). It is meaningful behavior emerging in and reproduced through "practices" (Reckwitz 2003).

RE-EMBEDDING THE ACTOR: FROM THE INDIVIDUAL TO MICRO-STRUCTURES

Theoretical Challenges in Empirical Social Movement Research

Social movement research provides a particularly appropriate empirical field for theoretical debates on the status of the individual in collective action. The fluidity of social movements pinpoints the issue of keeping people together by providing a network of social relations that continues even in times of non-action. This ephemeral nature of social movements requires particularly strong mechanisms overcoming the natural tendency to dissolve in time. The theoretical issue that results from extending the varying motivational sources of human agency is to provide a model of how social reality emerges from these motivational sources of agency.

Focussing on this emergent trans-individual level of analysis, theory building has to separate two issues: the issue of the interactional nature of agency events and the issue of the macro-level effects of the interactional nature of social action. Regarding the first issue, the question is how agency affects existing social relations and how these social relations affect agents. The second issue is how collective action events produce macro-effects and how the latter affect collective action events. We will deal with each issue in turn, beginning with the first and most critical central issue for social theory since it addresses the very question of what constitutes the social as opposed to the individual.[1]

Since social actors interact based on shared presuppositions about the world around them, a central hypothesis in sociological theory is that social reality is constructed and objectified in institutions. This implies a close, even reciprocally constitutive, link between interaction processes and shared framings of this world. This theoretical assumption has produced empirical research since the time when Ervin Goffman developed his version of symbolic interactionism and the idea of frames of reality construction (Goffman 1974, 1983). This idea has been taken up in social movement research in a series of publications by David Snow and Robert Benford (for an overview, see Benford and Snow 2000) introducing the notions of frames and framing as a way to explain the way collective action in social movements emerges and continues to exist. The semantic reality of shared frames, manifest in words, concepts, arguments, images, and stories that circulate between social actors, adds an important dimension of theoretically modeling social movements. Yet it runs the risk of a culturalist bias in theorizing social movements.

There is a theoretical position claiming to provide a link between the micro-reality of actors, shaped by power and material resources, and the objectivity of the situation in which they relate to each other. This position, so far less well established in social movement research, draws upon the work of Pierre Bourdieu. In his work, the late Bourdieu did not analyze social movements in a systematic way, yet he was sympathetic to them. This relates to the opposite research interest: how to explain that actors tend to reproduce the power structures to which they are exposed. It is easy to explain why this holds for those having power (it serves their interest), yet a paradox for explaining the social action of those who suffer from these power relations; the powerless paradoxically reproduce the "rules of the game" by playing the game, while creating an illusionary representation of this reality. Social movement then can be considered as a form of collective action that breaks this illusionary reality and its institutional supports, based on turning upside down the rules of the game played in a social situation.

Nick Crossley has applied this idea in a double argument (Crossley 2002). The first refers to the argument that social movements develop "working utopias" which generate a radical habitus, and create knowledge and justifications, all of which leads to a particular "movement illusion" (Crossley 1999, 2003). The second argument refers to the creation of networks providing a particular movement capital, to be invested in collective mobilization and constituting a particular movement field. This is an attempt to apply directly the implicit social theory of Bourdieu, an attempt that Crossley has rectified and pushed further in his later work (Crossley 2008, 2009). He no longer repeats the claim that the structural and cultural aspects of social reality should be better "integrated," as

Snow and Benford have done.[2] He goes a step further by drawing on the observation that protesters not only create shared symbolic worlds (which he finally conceptualizes as "conventions," but also while doing so, they interact, engage in practices, fight with each other, include some and exclude others in interaction networks, while drawing on the resources these actors can command. As he states: "Networks, resources and conventions are not discrete structures then but rather interlocking aspects of a single structure, centered upon social interaction" (Crossley 2009: 28).

This return of the world of social interaction conceptualized as emerging from network structures and creating network structures marks an important break in social theory, produced by the evolution triggered not only in social movement studies but also in other research fields such as migration studies. The theoretical challenge is how to conceptualize the social dimension without reducing it to its cultural components.

Network–analytic techniques offer solutions to the problem of describing social relations without reducing them to symbolic constructions. Theoretical concepts such as social capital fostered such rectification offering possibilities of the re-embedding frames and identity constructions in social relations. A side effect of these analytical moves is the discovery of the multi-functionality of social capital (as networks of social relation). Social capital fosters structures of power and social inequality. However, social relations practiced in associational settings can also foster democracy. This brought back an old social–theoretical (or normative) debate that started with Alexis de Tocqueville on the role of social associations for fostering democracy (Tocqueville 2008a, 2008b), which Robert Putnam continued (Putnam 1993, 2000), and which is now taken up in social movement research (Diani and McAdam 2003).

The current debates on associational social capital and its impact on the structure of collective action (Baldassarri and Diani 2007) involve two important theoretical points. The first is to offer an entrance point for arguments on the structures of social relations as constitutive elements for organizing social action. This argument provides an important challenge to and break with individualistic assumptions in social and political theory. It claims an analytic priority for the structure of social action, that is, the rules organizing social relations within which action events (normally produced by individuals)[3] gain a shared meaning. This ontological priority of the social over the individual provides the possibility to explain social action (individual and collective) in a non-psychological way. Instead of opposing agency and structure, the claim is that agency is the producer of events, which are linked to each other by structures of social relations and not by the psychological properties of the agents.

Focusing on the micro-structures of social relations has equally affected the theoretical status of normative claims in social theory. Given the old split between "normative theories" and "empirical theories" (pinpointed in the debate over value-free or value-loaded social-scientific research), the challenge is to argue that this distinction is useless and misleading. The empirical side of the emerging theoretical argument is the emphasis on the link between norms and agency. Norms are not only a special kind of motivation (as foreseen by Parsons) but they are rules which regulate the relations between action events; such rules foster, forbid, support, and command, thus situating action events in a sequence of action events. Unpacking the notion of norms is the empirical aspect of this theoretical endeavor. Providing an analytical model of the internal structure of norms (analogous to the structure of the genetic information in living organisms) is the other aspect of this theoretical endeavor. The particular difficulty that has accompanied empirical research addressing issues of norms has been that there is an internal link between normative rules and the structuring of social relations.

Linking normative theories with the micro-structures of social relations offers a new basis for linking democratic theory with civil society (della Porta 2013; della Porta and Rucht 2013). On a concrete level, this linkage is under scrutiny in ongoing research as the reciprocal effect of claiming democratic norms and organizing civic social relations in the course of collective action. Instead of using normative claims as yardsticks for good politics, theory development goes toward clarifying the constraints that occur when claiming democratic norms. In this way, we can explain the dynamics of hiding real social relations by producing illusions about them, equally in the political/economic institutional realm (through symbolic politics and ideological communication) as well as explaining the dynamics of civil society that has to defend itself against incivility. The complex semantics of democracy and its use by social actors in fighting for democracy or against distorted forms of democracy are part of an evolving theoretical model that does three things. First, the model makes explicit the implicit normativity of the micro-structures of social relations. Secondly, it makes visible the ideological distortions of the semantics representing these relations. Thirdly, it identifies those practices that realign the normative structures of social relations with their semantic representation.

Meaning Circulating through Movement Networks

Introducing the notion of micro-structures of social relations provides the analytical tool for describing and explaining the way collectively shared worlds emerge. The explanation of this emergence no longer takes place on the individual level or on the institutional level. It is taking place on the level of social relations. Roger Gould has made a strong argument in this direction (Gould 1993, 2003). Assuming that the (micro-)structure of network relations fosters or hinders collective action, he designed an explanatory strategy that, using historical and ethnographic case studies, showed the role of different forms of social relations (hierarchical versus egalitarian; boundary crossing and boundary defending) for success or failure of collective action.[4] A further step has been taken in a collection of papers (Diani and McAdam 2003) which introduce the methodological and analytic advances in the field of social movement research.

Yet there remains the task of linking networks with what circulates through these networks as "meaning." This is still an open issue. The most important strand of further theorizing continues the tradition of Harrison White (White, Godart, and Corona 2007; White and Godart 2007; White 2008). As they argue, the observation that narratives (stories) run through networks requires the assumption of their co-emergence and co-evolution. The micro-structures of social relations are channels for social interaction in which semantic forms (stories) circulate. Both channels and stories condition each other in the process of constructing social reality.[5]

The debate on the micro-structures of social relations shows that social movement research has become not only a borrower of social theory developments, it is also catalyzing theory development. This is due to the particular property of its object: being a network of ephemeral social relations that must survive against institutional power and in which stories circulate that run against established ideological delusion and illusions.

THE RETURN OF MACRO-THEORY IN THE MICRO-ANALYSIS OF SOCIAL MOVEMENTS

Movements as Devices that "Irritate" Social Systems

A final aspect of theory development in the field of social movement research is the issue of how to bring back the macro-perspective that was so dominant in the historical beginning of theorizing social movements (see earlier) into this theory development.

The "macro-perspective" has never been lost in social movement studies as the tradition of the "political opportunity structure approach" and its development testifies (McAdam, McCarthy, and Zald 1996; McAdam, Tarrow, and Tilly 2001). This approach describes how actors act under the constraints of institutional structures that provide them with "opportunities." This theoretical model of going from the individual to opportunity structures bypasses the reality of social relations and assumes a direct link between individual actors and institutional "macro-structures." Reducing the complexities of the relational nature of social movements (the micro-structures of social relations among actors) to an individualistic explanatory strategy simplified the explanatory task: the political opportunity structure model simply claimed that actors react rationally to the opportunities (and constraints) posed by the social/institutional/structural context. If there is more than one actor interacting with other actors (which normally is the case), then game-theoretic models have taken over the task of explaining the aggregate outcome as a rational response a group of game-playing actors. Such two-level theorizing has been attractive, providing a motivation and a particular (compatible with the rationalist action assumption) group process (games) for explaining the variety of situations and effects that can be observed in comparative social movement research. As has been noted in this chapter, there is a strong theoretical argument against the claim that game-theoretic modeling of social relations can grasp the micro-structures of social relations in which social actors are involved when acting together. Thus, the political opportunity structure model is theoretically deficient since it is based on a short cut between the individual actor and the macro-structures of social institutions (Meyer 2010), social systems (Luhmann 1995) or (recently) social fields (Fligstein and McAdam 2012).

Macro-realities (whether conceived as fields, systems, or institutions) matter, which also holds for social movements. Their effect is normally linked to the state (especially in social movement research), but this is just one of many macro-structural constraints collective action is facing. It can equally be the family (at times a favorite object of collective action), the market (which has been rediscovered as an object in recent collective action events), or religion (a topic of increasing importance in the analysis of collective action). Another implication is the possibility of updating the established notion of the (political and non-political) opportunity structure of collective action. All this requires that we distinguish carefully between (macro-)"structures" used for describing contexts of collective action (such as fields, institutions, or systems) and (micro-)"structures" that constitute collective action by relating action events.

Among the theoretical contributions that assess the role of macro-structures in the making of the social world in general and in the making of social movements in particular, functionalist theory still plays an important role. Apart from earlier functionalist accounts (Smelser 1962), the most consequential formulation of such a perspective is contained in the work of Niklas Luhmann who has opened up new theoretical insights into what social movements "do" in a world of social structures and systems. Luhmann's two books on that topic start with the initial irritation that social movements do not fit the property of social systems to be "autopoietic" systems (a central claim in Luhmann's sociological theory), thus challenging the theory of the autopoieis of social systems (Luhmann 1989, 1996). Luhmann's contribution finally has been to see social movements as irritations for social systems, forcing them to redraw their boundaries and to specify their functional position regarding other social systems. To conceptualize and model these effects Luhmann has that evolutionary theorizing be taken up again. This has been his proposal—yet he has left it to others to make sense of it.

The use of the Darwinian theory of evolution in fact provides a conceptual model of the mechanisms that work upon each other and promise to explain the otherwise chaotic effects of human collective action. It is with recent trends in evolutionary theory that this theoretical hunch has opened a new path of theory construction. The central issue in evolutionary theory (already discarded by many researchers in the life sciences including psychology and rational choice theory) is the recognition that evolution works not only on the level of the individual but also on the level of groups. Both levels, the individual and the group level, permanently interact yet follow different logics (Wilson 2002). This has to do with the century-old observation that not everything that is good for a group is good for the individual and vice versa in a given environment. Social processes therefore are the product of a three-level reality in which groups (and the micro-structures constituting them) play a mediating role between individuals and their given environments.

This shift in theoretical argument offers new possibilities for analyzing and explaining the emergence, the role, and the effects of social movements. It allows us to go beyond Luhmann's observation that social movements are like those elements in the human body that produce reactions and often overreactions against failures of systemic autopoiesis, that is, they are like the fever that warns the system and at the same time contributes—under specific conditions—to the repair of social systems. It rather turns Luhmann's hunch on its head: social movements constitute an important phenomenon the micro-structures of which irritate institutions. Moreover, it offers the possibility of bringing the actor back, but not as the idealized autonomous individual, but as a body and a person that is involved in social relations.

From the Individual to the Group and Back: The Promises of Evolutionary Theory

This return of macro-structures in fact corrects for the exclusivity of the individual as a causal factor in the construction of the social world. It argues for the causal effects of macro-structures (as Marx already did). Nevertheless, it still does not provide the causal mechanisms for explaining such effects. This brings back again the problem of the missing link between (macro)-structure and action (Koopmans 2005). Network theory has offered a solution in terms of describing micro-structures of social relations that mediate between macro-structures (institutions or "infrastructures") and action events. Evolutionary theory offers a possible solution in terms of mechanisms selecting for micro-structures of social relations. The missing link between actors and the macro-reality of state, economy, and society are the micro-structures of social relations.

The theoretical solution to the problem consists of a two-step model: individuals are selected into groups and groups are selected into existing social environments. Koopmans argues that the media (and no longer the direct confrontation on a site) provide the selection mechanism for protest groups (Koopmans 2004a). This is an empirical claim based on a theoretical hunch offered by evolutionary theory: movements compete with the groups opposing them in the medium of the mass media, thus producing effects equally on the groups based on the institutional stability of the state and on groups based on the institutional stability of civil society. Since this is an open process, we can expect cycles of protest characterizing the process in the long run (Koopmans 2004b).[6]

Explaining the macro-effects of social movements within a model that privileges the intentionalism introduced by the action theoretical turn (under the guise of providing micro-structural explanation) shows serious flaws. Such an explanation must capitulate in that face of the erratic picture of outcomes that do not correspond to intentions, neither in the short run nor in the long run. To enhance the explanatory capacity of social theory in social movement research, the return to macro-structures provided an outcome, but a return not to the static conceptions of social structures or opportunity structures whose variation over time was left to historical accounts and good story telling (Tilly 2002). The theoretical issue is to account for the micro-structural processes shaping the selection of individuals into (opposing) groups. Selection then often means that some are excluded, which sets into motion again the formation of new groups made out of those selected. Evolution here does not mean that we are heading forward in a process of ongoing all-inclusion as some normative theories try to justify as the only reasonable end of social action. Rather, it claims that by selecting some (as individuals or as groups) the possibilities of newly emerging groups exist which can call into question the power that groups have in controlling existing social relations. Without such selective processes, we would not have social movements and we would not need social movements. Therefore making such a selection process visible is a way to explain how counter-power emerges. Instead of claiming a mechanism of all-inclusion, the theory proposes exclusion as a mechanism for forming new groups capable of undermining the power of necessarily partially inclusive groups. Social movements then are a particular social form that organizes such counter-power, thus keeping the evolutionary process going.[7]

What is then left of macro-structures as an analytical tool for explaining the constitution, reproduction, or change of social movements? Macro-structures are emergent "organizational" properties of social relations backed up by semantic representations that justify these organizations.[8] They delimit the range of possible justifications ("conventions," forms of legitimation) available at a certain point in time. They delimit the rules of the game that can be played in a given situation. Whether we describe the emergent naturalness of such situations as objectivation (Berger and Luckmann 1966) or as social fields (Bourdieu and Wacquant 1992; Fligstein and McAdam 2012) or as social systems (Luhmann 1995) is open to further theoretical debate. Social movements certainly are not institutions or fields, or systems, but actors in institutional environment, playing field-specific games or marking systemic dysfunctionalities. What they do is to exert permanent pressure on these emergent forms of complexity thus pushing the evolutionary process also on the level of the "self-objectification" of social relations in ever more complex forms of social life.

Leaving Old Debates and Entering New Debates—Conclusion

Social theory is turning toward the micro-structural level of social reality, avoiding equally psychological reductionism and macro-sociological determinism. Social movement research has fostered this process and has been pushed by this process. It has revised the Marxian beginnings of social movement theories as well as the theories of social action offered by the classics of social theory. Debates on issues such as the structure–action link or the macro–micro link are waning; explanatory models turn up that defy the structure–action or micro–macro distinction. The analysis of rules making social interaction in general, collective action in particular possible, has brought forward the idea of micro-structures of social relations which constitute social action and which force macro-structures to adapt. Micro-structures of social relations start to overcome the actor centrism of theories of social action as well as the determinism of theories of macro-structures conceived as systems, institutions, or even fields. The discovery of micro-structures of social relations is generating new theoretical insights, pushing and being pushed to a not insignificant part by the dynamic field of theorizing collective action in social movements.

NOTES

1. The second issue will be dealt with later as the issue of the functional consequences of collective action events on the self-organizing capacities of societies.
2. In a critique of the framing approach Benford called for a better integration of the cultural and the structural approaches in social movement research (Benford 1997). This critique points at a general problem in social theory, which is the co-evolution of semantic structures and network structures. Given this co-evolution, the conceptual mapping by Benford is unclear since having "structural" properties applies equally to micro-social and to macro-social realities.
3. Some academics claim that action events can also be produced by things (Callon 1999; Latour 2005). This is a secondary yet interesting aspect of the debate. It adds support to the claim that action events produced by whoever makes sense only by their socially mediated relation to other events.
4. Even some researchers coming from the tradition of rational choice theory have moved in this direction as the work of Gerald Marwell and Pamela Oliver has shown (Marwell and Oliver 1993; Oliver and Myers 2003).
5. Promising attempts of linking networks structures with semantic forms in the field of explaining protest/collective action exist (Bearman and Everett 1993; Kim and Bearman 1997).
6. In a similar vein, selection theory accounts for organizational change (while considering organizations as a special type of groups) (Haveman, Rao, and Paruchuri 2007). This is related to the problem of the emergence of complexity for which recent organizational theory provides new analytical tools (Padgett and Powell 2012).
7. Another way of conceptualizing social–evolutionary processes is to describe the way social relations are structured as a mechanism of "collective learning." This is saying that aggregates of actors forming a group oppose existing ideas and provide new ideas to be tested in ongoing social relations (Podolny and Page 1998: 62ff).
8. This is the classic definition of an "institution": an organization coupled with a collectively accepted meaning (Meyer and Rowan 1977).

REFERENCES

Baldassarri, Delia and Diani, Mario (2007). "The Integrative Power of Civic Networks," *American Journal of Sociology*. 113(3): 735–780.

Bearman, Peter S. and Everett, K. D. (1993). "The Structure of Social Protest, 1961–1983," *Social Networks*. 15: 171–200.

Benford, Robert D. (1997). "An Insider's Critique of the Social Movements Framing Perspective," *Sociological Inquiry*. 67: 409–430.

Benford, Robert D. and Snow, David A. (2000). "Framing Processes and Social Movements: An Overview and Assessment," *Annual Review of Sociology*. 26: 611–639.

Berger, Peter L. and Luckmann, Thomas (1966). *Die gesellschaftliche Konstruktion der Wirklichkeit. Eine Theorie der Wissenssoziologie.* Frankfurt/Main: Fischer.

Bourdieu, Pierre and Wacqunat, Loic J. (1992). *An Invitation to Reflexive Sociology.* Cambridge: Polity Press.

Calhoun, Craig J. (1982). *The Question of Class Struggle. Social Foundations of Popular Radicalism during the Industrial Revolution.* Chicago, IL: University of Chicago Press.

Callon, Michel (1999). "Actor-Network Theory—The Market Test." In *Actor Network Theory and After,* edited by John Law and John Hassard, 181–195. Oxford: Blackwell.

Cohen, Jean L. (1985). "Strategy or Identity. New Theoretical Paradigms and Contemporary Social Movements," *Social Research.* 52(4): 663–716.

Collins, Randall (2004). *Interaction Ritual Chains.* Princeton, NJ: Princeton University Press.

Collins, Randall (2008). *Violence: A Micro-Sociological Theory.* Princeton, NJ: Princeton University Press.

Crossley, Nick (1999). "Working Utopias and Social Movements: An Investigation Using Case Study Materials from Radical Mental Health Movements in Britain," *Sociology.* 33(4): 809–830.

Crossley, Nick (2002). *Making Sense of Social Movements.* Buckingham: Open University Press.

Crossley, Nick (2003). "From Reproduction to Transformation: Social Movement Fields and the Radical Habitus," *Theory, Culture and Society.* 20(6): 43–68.

Crossley, Nick (2008). "Pretty Connected: The Social Network of the Early UK Punk Movement," *Theory, Culture & Society.* 25(6): 89–116.

Crossley, Nick (2009). "The Man whose Web Expanded: Network Dynamics in Manchester's Post/Punk Music Scene 1976–1980," *Poetics.* 37(1): 24–49.

della Porta, Donatella (2013). *Can Democracy Be Saved: Participation, Deliberation and Social Movements.* Hoboken: Wiley.

della Porta, Donatella and Rucht, Dieter, eds. (2013). *Meeting Democracy: Power and Deliberation in Global Justice Movements.* Cambridge: Cambridge University Press.

Diani, Mario and McAdam, Doug, eds. (2003). *Social Movements and Networks. Relational Approaches to Collective Action.* Oxford: Oxford University Press.

Durkheim, Emile (1968 [1912]). *Les formes élémentaires de la vie religieuse. Le système totemique en Australie.* Paris: Presses Universitaires de France.

Eder, Klaus (2009). "Communicative Action and the Narrative Structure of Social Life: The Social Embeddedness of Discourse and Market—A Theoretical Essay." In *Critical Turns in Critical Theory: New Directions in Social and Political Thought: New Directions in Social and Political Thought,* edited by Seamus O'Tuama, 63–79. London: Tauris & Co Ltd.

Fehr, Ernst and Gintis, Herbert (2007). "Human Motivation and Social Cooperation: Experimental and Analytical Foundations," *Annual Review of Sociology* 33(1): 43–64.

Fligstein, Neil and McAdam, Doug (2012). *A Theory of Fields.* New York, London: Oxford University Press.

Gintis, Herbert, Bowles, Samuel, Boyd, Robert, and Fehr, Ernst (2006). "Moral Sentiments and Material Interests: Origins, Evidence, and Consequences." In *Moral Sentiments and Material Interests: The Foundation of Cooperation in Economic Life,* edited by Herbert Gintis, Samuel Bowles, Robert Boyd, and Ernst Fehr, 3–39. Cambridge, MA: MIT Press.

Goffman, Ervin (1974). *Frame Analysis. An Essay on the Organization of Experience.* New York: Harper & Row.

Goffman, Ervin (1983). "The Interaction Order," *American Sociological Review.* 48: 1–17.

Gould, Roger V. (1993). "Collective Action and Network Structure," *American Sociological Review*. 58: 182–196.

Gould, Roger V. (2003). "Why do Networks Matter? Rationalist and Structuralist Interpretations." In *Social Movements and Networks. Relational Approaches to Collective Action*, edited by Mario Diani and Doug McAdam, 233–257. Oxford: Oxford University Press.

Habermas, Jürgen (1979). *Communication and the Evolution of Society*. London: Heinemann.

Habermas, Jürgen (1987). *The Theory of Communicative Action. Lifeworld and System. A Critique of Functionalist Reason. Volume II*. Boston, MA: Beacon Press.

Habermas, Jürgen (1989 [1962]). *The Structural Transformation of the Public Sphere. An Inquiry into a Category of Bourgeois Society*. Cambridge, MA: MIT Press.

Haveman, Heather A., Rao, Hayagreeva, and Paruchuri, Srikanth (2007). "The Winds of Change: The Progressive Movement and the Bureaucratization of Thrift," *American Sociological Review*. 72(1): 117–142.

Jasper, James M. (2011). "Emotions and Social Movements: Twenty Years of Theory and Research," *Annual Review of Sociology*. 37(1): 285–303.

Jenkins, J. C. (1983). "Resource Mobilization Theory and the Study of Social Movements," *Annual Review of Sociology*. 9: 527–553.

Kim, Hyojoung and Bearman, Peter S. (1997). "The Structure and Dynamics of Movement Participation," *American Sociological Review*. 62: 70–93.

Klandermans, Bernd, Kriesi, Hanspeteri, and Tarrow, Sidney G., eds. (1988). *From Structure to Action. Comparing Social Movement Research Across Cultures*. Greenwich, CT: JAI Press.

Koopmans, Ruud (2004a). "Movements and Media: Selection Processes and Evolutionary Dynamics in the Public Sphere," *Theory and Society*. 33: 367–391.

Koopmans, Ruud (2004b). "Protest in Time and Space: The Evolution of Waves of Contention." In *The Blackwell Companion to Social Movements*, edited by David A. Snow, S. A. Soule, and Hanspeter Kriesi, 19–46. Oxford: Blackwell.

Koopmans, Ruud (2005). "The Missing Link Between Structure and Agency: Outline of an Evolutionary Approach to Social Movements Mobilization," *Mobilization*. 10(1): 19–33.

Latour, Bruno (2005). *Reassembling the Social. An Introduction to Actor-Network-Theory*. Oxford: Oxford University Press.

Luhmann, Niklas (1989). *Ecological Communication*. Chicago, IL: University of Chicago Press.

Luhmann, Niklas (1995). *Social Systems*. Stanford, CA: Stanford University Press.

Luhmann, Niklas (1996). *Protest. Systemtheorie und soziale Bewegungen*. Frankfurt/Main: Suhrkamp.

Marwell, Gerald and Oliver, Pamela E. (1993). *The Critical Mass in Collective Action. A Micro-Social Theory*. Cambridge, MA: Cambridge University Press.

Marx, Karl (1953). "Der achtzehnte Brumaire des Louis Bonaparte." In *Marx Engels Werke*, edited by Institut für Marxismus-Leninismus beim ZK der SED, 111–207. Berlin (DDR): Dietz.

McAdam, Doug, McCarthy, John D., and Zald, Mayer N., eds. (1996). *Comparative Perspectives on Social Movements. Political Opportunities, Mobilizing Structures, and Cultural Framings*. Cambridge: Cambridge University Press.

McAdam, Doug, Tarrow, Sidney G., and Tilly, Charles (2001). *Dynamics of Contention*. New York: Cambridge University Press.

McCarthy, John D. and Zald, Mayer N. (1977). "Resource Mobilization and Social Movements. A Partial Theory," *American Journal of Sociology*. 82: 1212–1241.

McPhail, Clark (2006). "The Crowd and Collective Behavior: Bringing Symbolic Interaction Back In," *Symbolic Interaction*. 29(4): 433–464.

Merton, Robert K. (1965). *On the Shoulders of Giants: A Shandean Postscript*. New York, San Diego, CA: Free Press.

Melucci, Alberto (1980). "The New Social Movements. A Theoretical Approach," *Social Science Information*. 19: 199–226.

Melucci, Alberto (1988). "Getting Involved. Identity and Mobilization in Social Movements." In *From Structure to Action. Comparing Social Movement Research Across Cultures*, edited by Bernd Klandermans, Hanspeter Kriesi, and Sidney G. Tarrow, 329–348. Greenwich, CT: JAI Press.

Melucci, Alberto (1995). "The Process of Collective Identity." In *Social Movements and Culture*, edited by Hank Johnston and Bernd Klandermans, 41–64. Minneapolis, MN: University of Minnesota Press.

Meyer, John W. (2010). "World Society, Institutional Theories, and the Actor," *Annual Review of Sociology*. 36(1): 1–20.

Meyer, John W. and Rowan, Brian (1977). "Institutionalized Organizations. Formal Structure as Myth and Ceremony," *American Journal of Sociology*. 83: 340–363.

Oliver, Pamela E. and Myers, Daniel J. (2003). "Networks, Diffusion, and Cycles of Collective Action." In *Social Movements and Networks. Relational Approaches to Collective Action*, edited by Mario Diani and Doug McAdam, 173–203. Oxford: Oxford University Press.

Olson, Mancur (1965). *The Logic of Collective Action: Public Goods and the Theory of Groups*. Cambridge, MA: Harvard University Press.

Opp, Karl-Dieter (1989). *The Rationality of Political Protest. A Comparative Analysis of Rational Choice Theory*. Boulder, CO: Westview Press.

Opp, Karl-Dieter (2009). *Theories of Political Protest and Social Movements: A Multidisciplinary Introduction, Critique, and Synthesis*. London: Routledge.

Padgett, John F. and Powell, Walter W., eds. (2012). *The Emergence of Organizations and Markets*. Princeton: Princeton University Press.

Podolny, Joel M. and Page, Karen L. (1998). "Network Forms of Organization," *Annual Review of Sociology*. 24: 57–76.

Polletta, Francesca (2006). *It was Like a Fever: Storytelling in Protest and Politics*. Chicago, IL: University of Chicago Press.

Polletta, Francesca and Chen, Pang C. B. (2012). "Narrative and Social Movements." In *The Oxford Handbook of Cultural Sociology*, edited by Jeffrey C. Alexander, Ronald N. Jacobs, and Philip Smith, 487–506. New York: Oxford University Press.

Putnam, Robert D. (1993). *Making Democracy Work. Civic Traditions in Modern Italy*. Princeton, NJ: Princeton University Press.

Putnam, Robert D. (2000). *Bowling Alone. The Collapse and Revival of American Community*. New York: Simon & Schuster.

Reckwitz, Andreas (2003). "Grundelemente einer Theorie sozialer Praktiken. Eine sozialtheoretische Perspektive," *Zeitschrift für Soziologie*. 32: 282–301.

Smelser, Neil J. (1962). *Theory of Collective Behavior*. New York: Free Press.

Tilly, Charles (2002). *Stories, Identities, and Political Change*. Lanham, MD: Rowman & Littlefield.

Tilly, Charles, Tilly, Louise A., and Tilly, Richard (1975). *The Rebellious Century*. Cambridge, MA: Harvard University Press.

Tocqueville, Alexis de (2008a). *Democracy in America V1 (1862)*. Whitfish, MT: Kessinger Publishing.

Tocqueville, Alexis de (2008b). *Democracy in America V2 (1862)*. Whitfish, MT: Kessinger Publishing.

Touraine, Alain (1977). *The Self-Production of Society*. Chicago, IL: University of Chicago Press.

Touraine, Alain (1981). *The Voice and the Eye*. Cambridge: Cambridge University Press.

Touraine, Alain, Dubet, François, Hegedus, Zsuzsa, and Wieviorka, Michel (1979). *La lutte étudiante*. Paris: Le Seuil.

Touraine, Alain (1981). *Le pays contre l'Etat. Luttes occitanes*. Paris: Le Seuil.

Touraine, Alain, Hegedus, Zsuzsa, Dubet, François, and Wieviorka, Michel (1980). *La prophetie anti-nucléaire*. Paris: Le Seuil.

Touraine, Alain, Wieviorka, Michel, and Dubet, François (1984). *Le mouvement ouvrier*. Paris: Fayard.

White, Harrison C. (2008). *Identity and Control: How Social Formations Emerge*. 2nd edn. Princeton, NJ: Princeton University Press.

White, Harrison C., Godart, Frederic C., and Corona, Victor P. (2007). "Mobilizing Identities: Uncertainty and Control in Strategy," *Theory, Culture & Society*. 24(7–8): 181–202.

White, Harrison C. and Godart, Frédéric C. (2007). "Stories from Identity and Control," *Sociologica*. (3), doi: 10.2383/25960

Wilson, David S. (2002). *Darwin's Cathedral: Evolution, Religion, and the Nature of Society*. Chicago: University of Chicago Press.

CHAPTER 3

....

SOCIAL MOVEMENTS IN POLITICAL SCIENCE

....

ONDŘEJ CÍSAŘ

As stressed by this very volume, social movement research has been constituted as an interdisciplinary field of study. Still, this chapter aims at presenting social movements through the lenses of political science, summarizing political science's most important contributions to the study of social movements.[1] By taking this perspective, the chapter clearly goes beyond the field of social movement studies as narrowly defined. Moreover, unlike previous reflections on this subject, which either try to provide an exhaustive list of political science work (Meyer and Lupo 2007) or present a very short overview (Andretta 2013), this chapter focuses on broader research traditions that can be traced back to the founding fathers of the social sciences.

Since contemporary mainstream social movement studies as developed especially within US academia are rooted in liberal pluralism (Meyer and Lupo 2007: 113), we need to start with James Madison. Most criticisms of the pluralist paradigm pointed to its inability to capture the power asymmetries in the field of modern politics. Drawing on this insight, the political science view of social movements generally sees them as an expression of collective power interacting with other coordinated powers, be they capitalism, state, counter-movements, or the plurality of civil society groups. Based on this and other relevant dimensions, Table 3.1 gives an overview of the particular traditions to be discussed in this chapter.

In the Marxist view, social movements fight capitalism, envisioning an alternative social arrangement to be built "from below." According to the Weberians, movements are shaped by institutionalized power in the form of the modern state, they provide the tools of collective expression to those not included in the formal decision-making structure. Followers of K. Polanyi see movements as a regulatory reaction to capitalist expansion, they aim at its democratically based regulation; while participation researchers following in the footsteps of A. de Tocqueville see them as the collective expression of individual political action reflecting unequally distributed resources within the

Table 3.1 Four Views of Social Movements in Political Science

Tradition	Marxist	Weberian	Polanyian	Tocquevillean
Opportunities and threats (context)	Capitalist economy	Modern state	Corporatism	Civil society
The concept of the movement	Anti-capitalist movements	State challengers	Contra-movements	Associations and advocacy groups
Interaction with the system	Anti-systemic	Challenging	Regulatory and reformist	Representation of social pluralism
Represented groups	Socially excluded groups	Groups without access to decision-making	Occupational groups	A wide range of social interests

population. The associations and advocacy groups reflecting the pluralism of modern democratic society form various social movements.

MADISONIAN ROOTS: PLURALITY OF INTEREST GROUPS

In line with the general liberal understanding, Madison feared the tyranny that ensues whenever a certain group, especially the majority of society, monopolizes political power, which can thus be used in the oppression of the rest of its citizens. Like virtually every liberal, Madison did not believe in the possibility of finding a single enlightened ruler, but viewed the plurality of various competing groups in civil society, and the division of powers in the institutional arena, as the only safeguards against tyranny. This perspective on democracy as the rule of many minorities based on the principle of open competition, which ensures both their mutual control and the curbing of state power, was further developed by modern American pluralists.

Originating in Bentley, and fully expressed by David Truman's pluralism (1951), interest groups were conceived as a collective vehicle in a democratic society, more or less available to every segment of the population, through which citizens aggregate and articulate their preferences and interests. According to this view, the state is institutionally structured and at the same time a neutral arena in which various interest groups interact and try to influence public policies, counterbalancing one another. In this Madisonian view, a plurality of organized groups and open competition among them prevents narrow interests from gaining uncontrolled domination over the state (Dahl 1961). As recalled by S. Tarrow (2006: 7), Truman's view of interest groups as interacting *within* the state in the sense of being structured by its institutions and rules, was later behind ideas about the state structuring not only political insiders, but also its *outside challengers*, that is, social movements. The original pluralist approach has undergone an important transformation in this process of reformulation.

Besides conflating the state with American government, Truman was mostly criticized for his lack of a theory of the state going beyond the group-based interpretation. In fact, pluralism captures the particular American situation more than the general features of modern politics, which include many more configurations of state-interest group relations than the one described by pluralism. Reflecting both the general political science research on the effects of different patterns of democracy (e.g., Lijphart 1984, 1999) and the structural foundations of social power (e.g., Lukes 1974), contemporary social movement theory goes well beyond its original pluralist limitations by meticulously theorizing about the general structure of the state, and hypothesizing the effects of its variable configurations across nations, as well as their differing elite strategies towards institutional outsiders.

This is basically the main contribution of the political process model, with its central concept of political opportunity structure (see Kriesi et al. 1995; Kriesi 2004 and below). By investing the state with active powers and ideological characteristics, and focussing on their various configurations, social movement theory transformed original Truman's model into one with a more Weberian understanding, which views the state as an autonomous source of power in society, stemming from its monopoly of the legitimate use of violence (see Tilly 1978, 1985, 1995). Before coming to this approach, the chapter will focus on a supposedly excluded tradition within the social movement field, Marxism. Although often unrecognized, it has not only shaped the terrain of current mainstream approaches to social movements (see Tilly 1978, esp. ch. 2), but also forms a paradigm of its own (see Hetland and Goodwin 2013 on the disappearance from social movement studies of capitalism in general and the Marxist perspective in particular).

Marx's Followers: Movements and the (Capitalist) System

According to Karl Marx, the modern society's class structure was divided between two main social classes, the privileged capitalists and underprivileged proletarians. It was the latter who were expected to help bring about epochal social change in the direction of a truly free society. Regarding social movements, the most important insights derived from Marxism were the class-based interpretation of political conflicts ("class struggle"), a stress on the structural grievances produced by capitalism leading to their political articulation in the form of movements, and the concept of social movements as the agents of systemic social change voiced "from below" (see della Porta and Diani 2006; Tarrow 2011; Barker et al. 2013).

In general, Marxism frames social movements as the expression of an alternative world to established capitalist society. Like Marx, who believed in an emancipatory potential of the working class, his followers have regarded the progressive movements of the twentieth century as agents of human liberation and emancipation. This has been most forcefully manifested by the paradigm of the new social movements, which were seen as the expression of resistance by the new middle class against a supposedly depoliticized technocratic capitalism (cf. della Porta and Diani 2006: ch. 2). Although the Marxist perspective does not, explicitly at least, dominate the current research agenda on social movements, it has always been present among the most visible approaches to these studies; moreover, the ongoing economic crisis has given the critical Marxist perspective on capitalism an even more prominent place in the current debate (Barker et al. 2013).

From "Voices from Below" to "Another World Is Possible"

In a broadly Marxist perspective, Piven and Cloward (1977) famously argued that extra-institutional protest of the poor is the only tool left to the underprivileged and under-resourced classes in a capitalist society to achieve real change in policy, in opposition to the power and resources of the economic and political elite. In normal times this elite maintains control over the political output; only in times of crises and upheaval is there a chance for the unprivileged to disrupt business as usual. Such extraordinary times opening up opportunities for political change are very rare; most commonly the situation is under the control of the elite, who strive to coopt any potential disruption through organizational inclusion. Therefore the lesson for the poor is clear: stay unorganized and disruptive, since institutionalization takes away the only weapon you have at your disposal: protest (see Meyer and Lupo 2007: 116–117).

Looking at the potential for a genuine transformation of the social order, the neo-Marxist world-systems theory (Wallerstein 2004) also points out the danger of institutional cooptation. Although modern anti-systemic movements such as socialism and feminism originally challenged the capitalist hegemony, they ended up reinforcing it. According to Wallerstein, there are two main reasons for this: (1) these movements were unable to establish coalitions; on the contrary, they often spent as much time fighting one another as challenging capitalism; and (2) they relied on "a two-step agenda for action": first take over the state, then begin political reforms. In this respect, they prioritized attaining the positions of power and working for limited political change (change within the system) rather than a more radical program of transforming the cultural hegemony underpinning capitalism (changing the system). Still, according to Wallerstein, the potential for a systemic transformation remains open.

In times of systemic stability, the structure of capitalism keeps all political agents within its limits. Only recently has the systemic crisis of the capitalist system itself opened up a real opportunity for change. Since the hegemony of capitalism began to crumble after 1968, symbolized among other things by the mobilization of new social movements, a relatively open battlefield has replaced the previous structural stability. Therefore the current anti-systemic movements, associated by Wallerstein with the forces of alter-globalization and anti-capitalism (he groups them together as the "spirit of Porto Alegre"), are in a unique position to bring about a more just world than the capitalist system (Wallerstein 2003). The result of this battle is yet unclear—gone is the original historical optimism of Marx—since the current progressive forces are being actively resisted by the privileged class of the global economic and political elite ("spirit of Davos").

Probably the most influential (post-)Marxist take on social movements was the theory of new social movements related to the rise of the post-materialist movements in the late 1960s and 1970s (Cohen and Arato 1992). Like the working class in the nineteenth century, which was a manifestation of the systemic conflict within industrial modernity over the social product and its distribution, the new social movements are a manifestation of the new systemic conflicts within post-industrial (or late) modernity over autonomy, quality of life, and recognition of minority life styles (identity politics). In this view, post-industrial society is no longer defined by the struggle between two dominant classes, but oscillates around new varying conflicts over human rights, gender equality, individual autonomy, political participation, and environmental protection. At the same time, global capitalism "in the last instance"—to paraphrase famous Althusser's dictum—shapes the field on which these conflicts take place.

Marxism has not only been a theory of social movements, but for social movements (see Barker et al. 2013). Therefore these variable new movements should, on the basis of their mutual equivalences, articulate a single political project of "democratic hegemony" which would present a progressive alternative to the neoliberalism ideologically underpinning capitalist rule (Laclau and Mouffe 1985). This new Left counter-hegemony project created a never-realized political ethos, which would be taken up by later movements, most importantly some components of the alter-globalization and Occupy Wall Street movements (the so-called new new Left), proclaiming the values of individual autonomy and self-fulfillment.

WEBER'S FOLLOWERS: MOVEMENTS AND THE (STATE) INSTITUTIONS

Although Max Weber admired Marx's analysis of capitalism, he refused to see it as the only force shaping modern societies. According to Weber, the state played an even more important role in constituting the terrain of modern politics. Like the capitalists in the sphere of economy who monopolized the control of productive forces, the state monopolized control of physical coercion on a given territory. Charles Tilly famously depicted the state as a legitimized protection racket which, by crowding out other mafias, appropriated the control of violence on a given territory for itself (Tilly 1985), consequently creating a centralized arena for modern (movement-based) democratic politics (Tilly 1995). According to Tilly, the state originated from the processes of war making, state making, protection provision, and resource extraction. Similarly, Tarrow (2011: 81) recognizes three ways in which state making in the form of "making war, collecting taxes, and providing food" contributed to the formation of modern social movements in Britain, France, and the United States. In short, state making preceded and contributed to modern social movement making (Tilly 1992, 2004).

Unlike the Marxist literature, which largely views the state as a derivative of capitalism, the neo-Weberians understand it as an equally important causal force in the generation of modern social movements. The state is both an actor and the main arena—electoral and non-electoral—in which modern politics takes place. According to this political process model, variable institutional arrangements produce various patterns of collective action. This perspective can be applied both longitudinally (such as in Tilly 1995, for more see Tarrow 2011) and cross-sectionally (such as in Kriesi et al. 1995, for more see della Porta and Diani 2006). On a more general level, since the end of the 1970s this approach to social movements has developed with the general drift of political science analysis towards (neo)institutionalist approaches, which aim to explain political outcomes by looking at institutional variables and their configurations. Social movement studies have drawn on the rationalist version of institutionalism, as well as its historical and sociological versions (for this differentiation see Hall and Taylor 1996).

Models of Democracy, Political Opportunity Structure, and Political Culture

In political science this approach has been very visibly manifested in the comparative literature on political institutions that studies models of democratic governance for divided societies. In the form of consociational and consensus models (for the difference, see Lijphart 2008: 6–9) of democracy, A. Lijphart famously argued (e.g., 1984, 1999, 2008) for a power-sharing model of democracy as an alternative to its competitive majoritarian version based on power concentration. Although not primarily concerned about political mobilization and social movements, when compared to the majoritarian model Lijphart claimed that by incorporating interest groups into policy making the power-sharing consensual model has displayed a pacifying effect on mobilization and industrial conflict. The result is fewer strikes, generally less political violence (fewer riots and political deaths), and kinder and gentler public policies (Lijphart 1999: chs 15–16).

Importantly, research on social movements and collective action has come up with similar results when comparing institutional structures of states closed to external actors with their counterparts characterized by more open access. While closed institutions induce less but more radical collective action, open institutions produce more action but of a less radical nature (Kriesi et al. 1995; Kriesi 2004). In social movement research, the well-established concept of political opportunity structure captures this institutional context of social movement mobilization. The basic idea of this approach is that open political institutions facilitate mobilization (up to the point where protest gives way to institutionalized politics made possible by very open systems; see Tilly 1978), while closed institutions impede and radicalize it.

The comparative and state-centric version of the political process model (see Tarrow 2011 for other approaches) also overlaps with the comparative literature on political institutions in the way that openness/closeness are measured. Lijphart (1999: ch. 1) distinguishes between two dimensions—federal-unitary and executive-parties—that shape the two-dimensional space in which the world's democracies are positioned according to their particular placement in these dimensions (for more see Lijphart 1999). Likewise, in measuring the level of access to the political system, Kriesi and his colleagues focus on the level of a state's territorial decentralization and functional power-separation (largely Lijphart's first dimension) and the configuration of its elite actors (basically Lijphart's second dimension). Drawing on Lijphart, Kriesi (2004: 71) summarizes: "majoritarian democracy concentrates political power within and between institutions, which limits their accessibility ..., while consensus democracies divide political power and thus increase the institutional accessibility ... " Thus open opportunities can be operationalized as the existence of the formal and informal mechanisms and procedures for inclusion of social movements in the policy process. Closed opportunities display the opposite value. While more open access facilitates political mobilization and invites movement actors into the political process (such as in the federated United States), closed opportunities exclude them from the process, and increase the costs of collective action (such as unitary France, or semi- and non-democratic regimes; see also Tilly 2004; Tarrow 2011; della Porta 2013).

Being part of the more general "cultural turn" in political science and policy analysis, sometimes conceptualized as the fourth type of institutionalism (so-called "discursive institutionalism," see Schmidt 2010), social movement research has pointed out that political mobilization is not only determined by the level of institutional access, but that the structures within which social movements interact possess a symbolic/ cultural dimension. For example, Kriesi and colleagues distinguish between exclusive and inclusive strategies in the way political elites deal with institutional outsiders. Put into the mainstream political science language, we might say that there is a differentiation among various configurations of political culture, some more and some less facilitative of political mobilization (for a review see Vráblíková and Císař 2015; the political science classic here is Almond and Verba 1963). In social movement studies, Koopmans and his collaborators have successfully coined the term "discursive opportunity structure" in order to highlight the idea that the context of political mobilization is not only shaped by formal political institutions, but also by the prevailing interpretative schemata that make some ideas and claims generally acceptable, "sensible," "realistic," and " 'legitimate' within a certain polity at a specific time" (Koopmans and Statham 1999: 228).

International Political Opportunity Structure

The processes of globalization, internationalization, and Europeanization have played an important role in political science and international relations (IR) since the beginning of the 1990s. Reflecting these processes, the political process model has applied its originally state-level concept to the study of international organizations too (see Tarrow 2005; della Porta and Caiani 2009). Thus the available contributions have pointed out that political opportunities are provided not only by national institutions: an international opportunity structure is also developing which influences both state institutions and social movements operating within national boundaries (Keck and Sikkink 1998; Meyer 2003; Tarrow 2005; della Porta and Caiani 2009; Císař and Vráblíková 2013). In the same way as state institutions provided, and still provide, political opportunities for political actors at the nation-state level, supranational institutions such as the International Monetary Fund (IMF), the World Bank, and the European Union provide opportunity spaces for social movements to interact, cooperate, and clash.

Research has mostly focussed on the interaction between national politics and international relations/global politics. First, in a "partially globalized world," to borrow a phrase from leading IR scholar Robert Keohane, international institutions interfere with national political opportunities: "Changes in the international context can, by altering political and economic conditions, and/or perceptions of those conditions, change the opportunities for activists within a country" (Meyer 2003: 20). Second, international institutions provide social movements with additional opportunities to mobilize at the supranational level. Nowhere are these opportunities more developed than in the context of an integrating Europe (Imig and Tarrow 2001; della Porta and Caiani 2009; Císař and Vráblíková 2013). In terms of theory building, S. Tarrow (2005) has probably offered the most comprehensive catalogue of international-national interaction mechanisms, defining them in terms of six main processes of transnational contention.

POLANYI'S FOLLOWERS: MOVEMENTS COUNTERING (UNREGULATED) CAPITALISM

While the initially US-centric field of social movement studies originated in American pluralism, Europe-centered interest groups studies grew out of post-war European attempts to tame capitalism into the form of liberal corporatism. This tradition can be traced back to Karl Polanyi (for a classical and somewhat different view see Schmitter 1974). Like Marx, Polanyi sees capitalism as a transformative destructive force changing the structure of pre-modern society, thus bringing about a Great Transformation. Unlike Marx, whose revolutionary proletariat was supposed ultimately to dismantle capitalism, Polanyi's counter-movement aims at the political regulation and taming of capitalist market society without necessarily changing its basic logic. In Polanyi's view, we need political regulation to make modern capitalism socially acceptable. Since, unlike unregulated capitalism, political institutions can be democratically controlled, capitalism can only contribute to social well-being if it is under collective (democratic) control.

Here reside two interconnected ideas of post-1945 democratic capitalism, namely the Keynesian belief in macroeconomic management, and the neo-corporatist concept of interest concertation based on non-competitive coordination between the state, employers, and the representatives of working classes, trade unions. According to the corporatist approach, the incorporation of trade unions and employers together with the state in coordinated tripartite institutions made the economic management of modern societies more effective and the distribution of national product fairer (also see Lijphart's research on consensus democracies discussed above; corporatism is one of their characteristics).

Regimes of Interest Representation

Neo-corporatism, unlike pluralism but like both Marxist and Weberian social movement theory, acknowledges the privileged access to politics enjoyed by some interest groups; however, it parts company with both traditions of social movement studies by making these privileged groups—trade unions and employers' associations—the sole focus of scholarship (see Schmitter 1974). As a result, it has developed as a distinctive paradigm in interest group studies, in isolation from the broader social movement field, especially its US version. This is partly because while neo-corporatism was clearly Euro-centric in its focus, the empirical studies of social movements were originally developed in the American context. The very different trajectories of Europe and the United States after the Second World War account for the separate development of these two fields of study. By including employers and trade unions in policy making, European societies started to experiment with and build corporatist institutions to coordinate their post-War economic boom; in contrast, starting in the 1950s, the United States experienced consequential social movements, most notably the civil rights struggle and the various successors it inspired (see Císař 2013).

For some time a division of labor seemed to exist: interest group studies (pluralism, neo-corporatism) were primarily defined by their focus on institutional insiders, while social movement scholars concentrated on outsiders. While essentially capturing the same type of phenomenon, namely the interest organization, interest group studies focussed on those organizations integrated into the policy process, while social movement scholars looked at the extra-institutional challengers (see Beyers et al. 2008). In general, by focussing on a model of interest representation different from US pluralism, neo-corporatism generally contributed to our knowledge of the variability of interaction patterns between interest organizations and their environment, the state.

Drawing on a rare synthesis of interest group and social movement literature, Balme and Chabanet (2008) distinguish among three different regimes of interaction between interest groups/social movements and political institutions. So-called regimes of collective action are "combined institutional, political, sociological, and cognitive elements shaping the forms and intensity of collective action" (Balme and Chabanet 2008: 29, further description draws on 33–35). These are the clusters of variables, including political opportunities, organizational capacities, framing, and repertoire, that shape political mobilization and its characteristics.

In a *pluralist regime* such as the United States, opportunities are relatively open to a variety of policy-oriented groups that have developed the organizational capacity for a sustained exchange with the political system. They largely use political framing; in terms of their repertoire they rely on lobbying and legal action. In a *corporatist regime* such as that of the Scandinavian countries, opportunities for recognized, mostly occupational, groups are open and institutionalized. Compared to the pluralist regime, interest groups are more concentrated and incorporated into the institutional processes. As a result they use bureaucratic framing, and instead of lobbying engage in consultation and co-management of public policies. In a *protest regime* such as France's, the political opportunity structure is unfavorable to external groups, which compensate for this closeness by seizing opportunities provided by the media. Interest organizations are diffused; their capacity is limited to agenda-setting and vetoing. They use public opinion framing, and rely on extra-institutional mass mobilization and media-centered strategies. In this typology, the corporatist regime of state-interest group interaction embodies the logic of Polanyi.

The same type of reasoning for dealing with the challenges of yet another Great Transformation, namely economic globalization, has recently been inspired by Polanyi, this time on the global (or rather international) level. According to this view, like the modern state which had to catch up the capitalist expansion in order to subject it to political regulation during the era of industrial modernity, the globalization of our late modern era requires international political regulation to catch up with globalized capitalism in order to make it manageable and socially acceptable (Habermas 2001). As a result of international institutionalization, opportunities for social movements open up at the international level; here, too, the political process model explicitly draws on Polanyi's logic (see Tarrow 2005: especially ch. 2).

TOCQUEVILLE'S FOLLOWERS: POLITICAL PARTICIPATION AND POLICY ADVOCACY

According to Alexis de Tocqueville, modern society is driven by a progressive equalization of citizens that endangers their political freedom. This equalization, which actually created the conditions for democracy, at the same threatens democracy with its ultimate destruction. First, modern democratic society melted down the traditional intermediary institutions such as churches and guilds, creating an unstructured mass devoid of any collective capacity to counter the centralized power of the state. Second, democratic equality transformed individuals into isolated individuals fully focussed on their private life, with no interest in public affairs. As a result, atomized individuals are left unprotected from the potentially tyrannical state, and completely immersed in minding their own business. Under such conditions democracy is not likely to survive, and is open to displacement by a "new despotism" transforming a democratic citizenry into the passive receivers of state-driven programs. Democracy gives way to paternalistic care.

Alexis de Tocqueville not only diagnosed this danger, but also saw its potential cure in the form of a developed civil society; that is, a society of participating and associating individuals able to coordinate their individual forces in a collective venture. Two types of political science literature relevant to social movements originate here: individual-level political participation literature, and meso-level policy advocacy literature.

Individual Participation

Unlike research on social movements which mostly focusses on the meso-level of social movements, organizations and their protest events, political participation research primarily works with individual-level data. Substantively, while social movement research studies sustained activism, political participation research focusses on non/participation: *activism* refers to what activists and their organizations do, while *participation* captures what ordinary citizens do. Activists are individuals who devote a substantial part of their time or/and other resources to the political activities of particular organization(s). Others are non-activists, that is, ordinary citizens, who may or may not participate in politics: research on political participation calls it action by ordinary citizens aimed at direct or indirect influencing governmental officials (see Verba et al. 1995: 37–39).

Applying this distinction, there are three logically possible combinations of activism and participation: activism with participation (traditional participatory activism; see, e.g., Tilly 2004), activism with limited participation (professionalized advocacy groups without members, the specter haunting some analysts especially of contemporary American civil society; see below and Putnam 1995, 2000; Skocpol 1999), and participation without activism, characteristic of some self-organized and episodic protest events and/or personalized engagement (Bennett and Segerberg 2012).

Although originally focussing on elections, campaigning, and lobbying, in line with the research on social movements (Meyer and Tarrow 1998), participation researchers have recently observed a massive broadening of political participation, from demonstrations and other types of direct elite-challenging actions (e.g., Inglehart 1997) to community activism and consumer politics (Micheletti 2003; Dalton 2008). As a result of the recent digital media revolution, political participation now includes novel repertoires, including episodic flash mobs, personalized connective action, clictivism, and trolling (Dalton 2008; Bennett and Segerberg 2012). Moreover, Inglehart (1997) and Dalton (2008) in particular demonstrate that the rise of direct elite-challenging (protest) forms of political participation in the industrial democracies indicates the arrival of self-expressive (in Inglehart's original dictum, post-materialist) values, and thus engaged citizens who are critical of their political elites, but at the same time firmly allegiant to the principles of democracy. In this perspective, protest indicates a developed democracy.

When explaining political participation, the research originally focussed on the micro-level. Individual-level variables based on resources, such as indicators of socio-economic status, and variables based on motivations, especially political efficacy and attitudes towards politics, have traditionally been used to explain differences in political participation (the so-called "civic voluntarism" model, see Verba et al. 1995; Norris 2002). Although this approach observed the influence of socioeconomic inequalities on participation similar to that which social movement research showed in focussing on resource mobilization by movement organizations, it actually overlooked the structuring effect of organized movements at the individual level. Unlike social movement literature, these micro-level approaches treat individuals almost as isolated units (Vráblíková and Císař 2015).

Contrary to this understanding, the meso-level explanation focusses primarily on people's connections to their peers, social groups, and the organizations that recruit them for collective action. While individual-level explanations also focus on mobilization agents such as social movement organizations, they see their effect as mediated by individual predispositions. In line with Tocqueville's concept of "schools of democracy," this approach sees organizations as building the human capital, that is, civic skills, of active citizens. On the other hand, meso-level explanations conceptualize the effect of group membership differently, namely through the mechanism of relational social capital: group members are not only cultivated to be active citizens, but are also much more exposed to encouragement by other group members. In this respect, besides social recruitment by acquaintances within inter-personal networks, movement organizations provide individuals with a genuine basis for political mobilization, that is, recruitment by strangers (the paragraph mostly draws on Teorell 2003).

Organizations, Members, and Policy Advocacy

The relationship between individual participants and their organizations has assumed a prominent place in the recent political science literature on the transformation of American civil society. Theda Skocpol (1999) argues that American civic life has undergone a profound change since the mobilization of the anti-Vietnam War movement and related rights-based movements of the 1960s and 1970s. While all these movements at first brought an innovative repertoire of disruptive action, over the course of time they have become established as "public interest groups," combining occasional direct action with moderate lobbying strategies, within the formal structure of federal political institutions. In response to the changing opportunity structure of US politics, these groups increasingly focussed their attention on the federal level. This naturally evolved into a growing number of Washington offices devoted to routine lobbing, and the politics of influence rather than contentious politics.

Mirroring Putnam's (1995, 2000) famous diagnosis of the decline of social capital in America, Skocpol shows that the new advocacy groups display a different pattern from the traditional membership organizations, which relied on their membership bases not only in order to gain influence, but also to sustain themselves financially. Instead of collecting membership dues, these organizations seek funding from external sources, that is, foundations, corporations, and governmental agencies, and solicit individual contributions via direct mail techniques and media advertising. As a result, even an organization claiming to represent a large constituency "does not absolutely need members" (Skocpol 1999: 494). According to Skocpol, this threatens the very democratic system in the United States.

However, in contrast to Skocpol, a series of recent studies try to show that while there has been an increasing absolute number of professionalized advocacy organizations dependent on external funding, their proportion has not changed over time (Walker et al. 2011); and that they represent just one organizational model among many others (Minkoff et al. 2008). According to these studies, although democracy is undergoing a profound transformation, there is no decline as diagnosed by Skocpol. This debate forms part of a broader discussion on the decline (R. Putnam) versus transformation (R. Dalton, R. Inglehart, P. Norris) of the industrial democracies in general, and the American democracy in particular.

Marx, Weber, Polanyi, and Tocqueville in the Twenty-first Century

"Marx was right" or "Marx is back" are common titles among the books and articles reflecting on contemporary societies. The same trend seems to apply to developments in social movement research (see above and Barker et al. 2013). The political economy of late capitalism is finding its way back into social movement research, reflected in the increasing attention paid to structural grievances and socioeconomic issues highlighted by the economic crisis (see della Porta and Diani 2006: ch. 2). According to some, this crisis is threatening the very legitimacy of democracy, which might be reloaded only if the current wave of social movement mobilizations translates into tangible changes towards a more participatory and deliberative model (della Porta 2013). While clearly drawing on the political economy perspective, this renewed interest in critical scholarship is often framed more in Polanyian than Marxist terms. Either of them can help open up the long-awaited debate on the politico-economic conditions of collective action and its relation to contemporary democracy.

Further challenges include the interactions between various arenas of action, and novel ways of claims making, especially important to Weberian scholars. Although social movement studies traditionally prioritized the protest arena of action (for exceptions see Meyer and Lupo 2007: 120–122), recently there have been important contributions pointing out the need to focus on the electoral arena, political parties, and their interactions with movement politics (Goldstone 2003; della Porta and Diani 2006; Kriesi et al. 2012; McAdam and Tarrow 2013). This is especially important in studying those segments of the population that tend to express their grievances not through street protest, but through the protest vote, which compared to the movements of the Left is more common among those siding with the (radical) Right (Koopmans et al. 2005). While the relationship between the electoral and protest arenas is reinforcing in case of the Left, it seems to be substitutive for the political Right (Hutter and Kriesi 2013).

Moreover, the varieties of current popular resistance seem to cry out for novel conceptualization of their action repertoire (see, e.g., Tilly 1995, 2004). Especially in response to the economic recession and technological innovations, there has recently been an upsurge in new repertoires of resistance. These repertoires seem to transcend the usual dualism of anti-establishment mobilization in the form of either (left-wing) social movements or (right-wing) party populism. On one hand, one can find innovative protest repertoire traveling in unexpected directions (from the global periphery to the industrial core); on the other hand, different types of capital make unexpected inroads into democratic politics, for example in the form of wealthy businessmen and popular celebrities demanding the end of the political system as we know it. As previously mentioned, liberal democratic governance may be in question for some time to come (della Porta 2013).

Research on participation focusses in particular on novel methods of political expression, and aims at incorporating a wider political context into its perspective. Drawing significantly on social movement studies, most of the recent conceptual innovations concentrate on the study of macro-context. Three basic dimensions of context are analyzed: (1) formal political institutions, (2) socio-economic development, and (3) political culture (for a review, see Vráblíková and Císař 2015). Regarding political institutions, the insights of social movement theory, particularly the political process model, are combined with the contributions of comparative literature on institutions (majoritarian vs. consensual models), and electoral studies (types of electoral systems). Concerning economic development, modernization theories usually serve as the perspective for generating explanations of political participation. Last but not least, political culture studies focus on the effects of national patterns of political attitudes.

These developments offer a broader potential for incorporating the results of the last four decades of social movement research more firmly into political science, which has traditionally viewed them either as a marginal alternative to institutionalized politics, or a disruptive outburst of popular dissatisfaction. Since social movements have seemingly defied the readily available political science categories such as state institutions, parties, and interest groups, they previously stood outside the mainstream research. However, as demonstrated by recent research (e.g., Goldstone 2003 on the interrelationship of state, parties and movements, or della Porta 2013 on democracy and social movements), and hopefully also by this chapter, a dialogue between social movement research and the broader field of political science is able to bring important insights to the functioning of our late modern societies, which seem to be defined by a much higher degree of fluidity and change than might have seemed possible some decades ago. There are many important factors shaping our current political life, and the social movements are one of them.

NOTE

1. The author gratefully acknowledges funding from the Czech Science Foundation (grants "Collective Action and Protest in East-Central Europe," code GAP404/11/0462 and "Protestors in Context: An Integrated and Comparative Analysis of Democratic Citizenship in the Czech Republic," code GA13-29032S).

REFERENCES

Almond, Gabriel A. and Verba, Sidney (1963). *The Civic Culture: Political Attitudes and Democracy in Five Nations.* Princeton: Princeton University Press.

Andretta, Massimiliano (2013). "Political Science and the Study of Social Movements." In *Encyclopedia of Social and Political Movements, vol. 3,* edited by David Snow, Donatella della Porta, Bert Klandermans, and Doug McAdam, 965–968. London: Blackwell.

Balme, Richard and Chabanet, Didier (2008). *European Governance and Democracy.* Lanham: Roman and Littlefield.

Barker, Colin, Cox, Laurence, Krinsky, John and Nilsen, Alf Gunvald, eds. (2013). *Marxism and Social Movements.* Leiden: Brill.

Bennett, Lance and Segerberg, Alexandra (2012). "The Logic of Connective Action." *Information, Communication and Society.* 15(5): 739–768.

Beyers, Jan, Eising, Rainer, and Maloney, William (2008). "Researching Interest Group Politics in Europe and Elsewhere: Much We Study, Little We Know?" *West European Politics.* 31(6): 1103–1128.

Císař, Ondřej and Vráblíková, Kateřina (2013). "Transnational Activism of Social Movement Organizations: The Effect of European Union Funding on Local Groups in the Czech Republic." *European Union Politics.* 14(1): 140–160.

Císař, Ondřej (2013). "Interest Groups and Social Movements." In *Encyclopedia of Social and Political Movements, vol. 2,* edited by David Snow, Donatella della Porta, Bert Klandermans, and Doug McAdam, 616–620. London: Blackwell.

Cohen, Jean L. and Arato, Andrew (1992). *Political Theory and Civil Society.* Cambridge, M.A.: MIT Press.

Dahl, Robert (1961). *Who Governs? Democracy and Power in an American City.* New Haven: Yale University Press.

Dalton, Russel (2008). *The Good Citizen. How a Younger Generation Is Reshaping American Politics.* Washington, DC: CQ Press.

della Porta, Donatella and Caiani, Manuela (2009). *Social Movements and Europeanization.* Oxford: Oxford University Press.

della Porta, Donatella and Diani, Mario (2006). *Social Movements. An Introduction.* Blackwell: Oxford.

della Porta, Donatella (2013). *Can Democracy Be Saved? Participation, Deliberation and Social Movements*. Cambridge, Malden: Polity Press.

Goldstone, Jack, ed. (2003). *States, Parties, and Social Movements*. Cambridge: Cambridge University Press.

Hall, Peter A. and Taylor, Rosemary C. R. (1996). "Political Science and the Three New Institutionalisms." *Political Studies*. 44: 936–957.

Habermas, Jürgen (2001). *The Postnational Constellation*. Cambridge, MA: The MIT Press.

Hetland, Gabriel and Goodwin, Jeff (2013). "The Strange Disappearance of Capitalism from Social Movement Studies." In *Marxism and Social Movements*, edited by Colin Barker, Laurence Cox, John Krinsky and Alf Gunvald Nilsen, 83–102. Leiden: Brill.

Hutter, Swen and Kriesi, Hanspeter (2013). "Movements of the Left, Movements of the Right Reconsidered." In *The Future of Social Movement Research: Dynamics, Mechanisms, and Processes*, edited by Jacquelien Van Stekelenburg, Conny Rogeband, and Bert Klandermans, 281–298. Mineapolis, London: University of Minnesota Press.

Imig, Doug and Tarrow, Sidney, eds. (2001). *Contentious Europeans. Protest and Politics in an Emerging Polity*. Lanham, Boulder, New York, Oxford: Rowman and Littlefield.

Inglehart, Ronald (1997). *Modernization and Postmodernization*. Princeton: Princeton University Press.

Keck, Margaret and Sikkink, Kathryn (1998). *Activists Beyond Borders. Advocacy Networks in International Politics*. Ithaca, London: Cornell University Press.

Koopmans, Ruud and Statham, Paul (1999). "Ethnic and Civic Conceptions of Nationhood and the Differential Success of the Extreme Right in Germany and Italy." In *How Social Movements Matter*, edited by Marco Giugni, Doug McAdam, and Charles Tilly, 225–252. Minneapolis: University of Minnesota Press.

Koopmans, Ruud, Statham, Paul, Giugni, Marco, and Passy, Florence (2005). *Contested Citizenship: Immigration and Cultural Diversity in Europe*. Mineapolis, London: University of Minnesota Press.

Kriesi, Hanspeter, Koopmans, Ruud, Duyvendak, Jan Willem, and Giugni, Marco (1995). *New Social Movements in Western Europe. A Comparative Analysis*. London: UCL Press.

Kriesi, Hanspeter (2004). "Political Context and Opportunity." In *The Blackwell Companion to Social Movements*, edited by David Snow, Sarah Soule, and Hanspeter Kriesi, 67–90. Malden, Oxford, Carlton: Blackwell Publishing.

Kriesi, Hanspeter, Grande, Edgar, Dolezal, Martin, Helbling, Marc, Höglinger, Dominic, Hutter, Swen, and Wüest, Bruno (2012). *Political Conflict in Western Europe*. Cambridge: Cambridge University Press.

Laclau, Ernesto and Mouffe, Chantal (1985). *Hegemony and Socialist Strategy*. London and New York: Verso.

Lijphart, Arend (1984). *Democracies: Patterns of Majoritarian and Consensus Government in Twenty One Countries*. New Haven: Yale University Press.

Lijphart, Arend (1999). *Patterns of Democracy: Government Forms and Performance in Thirty-Six Countries*. New Haven and London: Yale University Press.

Lijphart, Arend (2008). *Thinking about Democracy: Power Sharing and Majority Rule in Theory and Practice*. London and New York: Routledge.

Lukes, Steven (1974). *Power: A Radical View*. London: Macmillan Press.

McAdam, Doug and Sidney Tarrow (2013). "Social Movements and Elections: Toward a Broader Understanding of the Political Context of Contention." In *The Future of Social Movement*

Research: Dynamics, Mechanisms, and Processes, edited by Jacquelien Van Stekelenburg, Conny Rogeband, and Bert Klandermans, 325–346. Mineapolis, London: University of Minnesota Press.

Meyer, David and Lupo, Lindsey (2007). "Assessing the Politics of Protest. Political Science and the Study of Social Movements." In *Handbook of Social Movements across* Disciplines, edited by Bert Klandermans and Conny Roggeband, 111–156. New York: Springer.

Meyer, David and Tarrow, Sidney, eds. (1998). *The Social Movement Society.* Lanham: Rowman and Littlefield.

Meyer, David (2003). "Political Opportunity and Nested Institutions." *Social Movement Studies.* 2(1): 17–35.

Micheletti, Michele (2003). *Political Virtue and Shopping: Individuals, Consumerism, and Collective Action.* New York: Palgrave Macmillan.

Minkoff, Debra, Aisenbrey, Silke, and Agnone, Jon (2008). "Organizational Diversity in the U.S. Advocacy Sector." *Social Problems.* 55(4): 525–548.

Norris, Pippa (2002). *Democratic Phoenix: Reinventing Political Activism.* New York: Cambridge University Press.

Piven, Frances Fox and Cloward, Richard A. (1977). *Poor People's Movements: Why They Succeed, How They Fail.* New York: Vintage Books/Random House.

Putnam, Robert D. (1995). "Bowling Alone: America's Declining Social Capital." *Journal of Democracy.* 6(1): 65–78.

Putnam, Robert D. (2000). *Bowling Alone: The Collapse and Revival of American Community.* New York: Simon & Schuster.

Schmidt, Vivien A. (2010). "Taking Ideas and Discourse Seriously: Explaining Change through Discursive Institutionalism as the Fourth 'New Institutionalism.'" *European Political Science Review.* 2(1): 1–25.

Schmitter, Philippe C. (1974). "Still the Century of Corporatism?" *The Review of Politics.* 36(1): 85–131.

Skocpol, Theda (1999). "Advocates without Members: The Recent Transformation of American Civic Life." In *Civic Engagement in American Democracy*, edited by Theda Skocpol and Morris P. Fiorina, 461–509. Washington D.C., New York: Brookings Institution Press and Russell Sage Foundation.

Tarrow, Sidney (2005). *The New Transnational Activism.* New York, Cambridge: Cambridge University Press.

Tarrow, Sidney (2006). "Confessions of a Recovering Structuralist." *European Political Science.* 5: 7–20.

Tarrow, Sidney (2011). *Power in Movement. Social Movements and Contentious Politics, 3rd edition.* Cambridge: Cambridge University Press.

Teorell, Jan (2003). "Linking Social Capital to Political Participation: Voluntary Associations and Network of Recruitment in Sweden." *Scandinavian Political Studies.* 26(1): 49–66.

Tilly, Charles (1978). *From Mobilization to Revolution.* Reading, MA: Addison-Wesley.

Tilly, Charles (1985). "War Making and State Making as Organized Crime." In *Bringing the State Back*, edited by Peter R. Evans, Dietrich Rueschemeyer and Theda Skocpol, 169–191. Cambridge: Cambridge University Press.

Tilly, Charles (1992). *Coercion, Capital, and European States, AD 990–1992.* Cambridge: Blackwell.

Tilly, Charles (1995). *Popular Contention in Great Britain 1758–1834.* Cambridge, London: Harvard University Press.

Tilly, Charles (2004). *Social Movements, 1768–2004.* Boulder, London: Paradigm Publishers.

Truman, David (1951). *The Governmental Process: Political Interests and Public Opinion*. Knopf, New York.

Verba, Sidney, Schlozman, Kay L., and Brady, Henry E. (1995). *Voice and Equality: Civic Voluntarism in American Politics*. Cambridge: Harvard University Press.

Vráblíková, Kateřina and Císař, Ondřej (2015). "Individual Political Participation and Macro Contextual Determinants." In *Political and Civic Engagement: Multidisciplinary Perspectives*, eds. Martyn Barrett and Bruna Zani, 33–53. London: Routledge.

Walker, Edward T., McCarthy, John D., and Baumgartner, Frank (2011). "Replacing Members with Managers? Mutualism among Membership and Nonmembership Advocacy Organizations in the United States." *American Journal of Sociology*. 116(4): 1284–1337.

Wallerstein, Immanuel (2003). *Decline of American Power: The U.S. in a Chaotic World*. New York: New Press.

Wallerstein, Immanuel (2004). *World-Systems Analysis. An Introduction*. Durham and London: Duke University Press.

CHAPTER 4

....

HISTORICAL ANALYSIS AND SOCIAL MOVEMENTS RESEARCH

....

JOHN MARKOFF

INTRODUCTION

....

SOCIAL movement scholars commonly find their way to history, sooner or later. Or both. Charles Tilly's first book, *The Vendée* (1964), was a pathbreaking study of a peasant counterrevolution in the 1790s. The book he was working on when he died, *Contentious Performances* (2008), traced changes in the forms of public conflict over decades of English history. They represent two very different ways that history matters for social movement studies. The first is the study of a dramatic episode in the past. The second treats the unfolding of a variety of processes over a significant span of time. Historical analysis is a capacious label that embraces both the study of past events, institutions, practices, and epochs as well as the search for meaningful connections between things that happened earlier and things that happened later on, that is to say, the search for causes and consequences across time.

Small wonder that students of social movements find themselves exploring histories. The ancestral nineteenth-century works that served as models or anti-models for subsequent theory and research about contentious collective action were anchored in awareness of rapid change in Europe's ongoing urbanizing, industrializing, and sometimes democratizing transformations, kickstarted by fears and hopes generated by the French Revolution. Observers were paying a lot of attention to collective actions from below (Barrows 1981; Harrison 1988). In following or repudiating theorists as different as Gustave LeBon and Karl Marx, later students were reading reflections on social conflict that drew on the past for examples illustrating one or another theoretical proposition, including propositions about how changing social processes altered forms of contention. One could also find in these nineteenth-century writers accounts of how later patterns of contention drew on or grew out of earlier ones. When Marx ([1852] (1955) is explaining how successive historical epochs generate characteristic forms of conflict or arguing that categories of understanding developed in earlier conflicts infuse identities and actions in later ones, attention to history is central. When LeBon ([1895] 1960) rummages through history for a grab bag of examples illustrating one or another variant of the irrational behavior of human collectivities, he, too, is drawing on history. The study of social movements has never strayed very far from such origins.

We may approximately classify the varying forms of historical analysis deployed by scholars of social movements according to the ways time figures in that analysis.

- Time may figure as a *dimension* along which we may locate particular events, institutions, or processes. Just as comparative research may explore events in a diversity of geographic locales to expand the range of variation of phenomena of interest, we may do the same in the temporal realm. We are not necessarily interested in the connections of events, institutions, or processes across space or time. Studying movements in the past is a way of enlarging the variety of movements taken into account in our theoretical understandings.
- We may be interested in *duration*, in why particular institutions or processes were as evanescent or as enduring as they proved to be. Why, for example, are there times and places characterized by heightened social activism that after a longer or shorter interval recedes? And, conversely, why are there times and places of more or less long-lasting quiescence?
- We may be interested in *trends* in significant processes that have consequences for movements, like the long-term growth in the capacities of European states over centuries, the rise of literacy, and changes in communications technologies. And we may be interested in trends in movement activism, such as long-term changes in the frequency of strikes and in how such movement trends may be causally connected to those changing contexts.
- We may be concerned with *cycles*, with repetitive processes that intermittently generate collective action of various kinds, like the seasonally driven rhythms of agricultural labor so important for understanding rural movements. We may be interested in shorter or longer cycles and sometimes in the superimposition of a variety of cycles and trends upon each other, including cyclical features of movements.
- We may be interested in *punctual* events that have significant consequences for movements as well as dramatic movement actions that have significant consequences. We are likely to be intrigued by powerful events that disrupt customary routines and alter the conditions of possibility of movements or the things about which people are in conflict. These are likely to be particularly attractive as research sites to the extent that the causally powerful episode is shorter and the impact is of long duration. A great deal of historical research has therefore been clustered around revolutions, when a lot of very consequential things happen over a short time span.

- We may be in interested the *causal dependence* of subsequent events on prior ones, and therefore be led to study sequences of events. We sometimes weave these sequences into causally plausible stories. An important sub-class of such studies is research into *critical junctures*, moments when important relations change so that there are actors' properties and connections among actors and properties that work differently before and after that juncture, including differences in the dynamics of collective action.
- In many ways adding geographic range and adding temporal range work in tandem. Taking account of temporal patterns and their specificities implies paying attention to the particular places where that distinctive history has happened. Historical analysis therefore is often the study of *the distinctiveness of place* and research on history is enmeshed with geography. There is a broad range of spatial scales. One study may be concerned with forms of conflict characteristic of particular urban neighborhoods, another with aggregate national differences, and others still with linkages among separate sites of conflict.

These various approaches to time will be elaborated below.

HISTORICAL ANALYSIS AS AN EXPANSION OF COMPARATIVE ANALYSIS

In some work, one turns to history for specific facts or for broad contextual understanding of specific facts. Time is but another dimension for identifying facts or contexts and plays little role in the analysis of social processes. A great deal of comparative research—perhaps most—pays no attention whatsoever to *place* or to the connections among places. US counties or national states may be compared for the co-occurrence of certain attributes, but the locational aspect of the counties or countries often plays no role in the analysis. Data points might be labelled New York and San Francisco but whether they are next to each other or a continent apart is irrelevant. In the same vein, much use of history simply adds another dimension to the search for data, but that dimension is not part of the theory or the data analysis.

In developing his *Theory of Collective Behavior*, for example, Neil Smelser (1962) scours historical works for a large number of disconnected examples that constitute instantiations of the theoretical processes he is depicting. In arguing, for example, that radical movements sometimes attract the "politically disinherited," he points to early Christianity's appeal to "the poor, simple, and low in Roman society" and also to protest movements among "[r]ecent migrants to American cities" (Smelser 1962: 325–326); that the two instances are separated by two millennia plays no role whatsoever in his theories. Since the considerable variety of human social arrangements at the moment any scholar is writing is very much less than the vastly greater variety of social arrangements humans have ever created, admitting historical instances vastly expands the power of comparison.

In thus expanding the array of human experience under study, one can frequently demonstrate that causal connections that seemed plausible when one's vision was restricted to the present were misstated. For example, reflecting on the social movement activism of the 1960s and beyond, many scholars thought they discerned "new social movements" focussed on a whole range of new issues—the environment, gender, lifestyle freedoms, emergent identities. Such movements had arisen, one plausible account went, because conflicts over distributional issues and over basic rights and freedoms were radically reduced in post-World War Two's prosperous democracies. With those sources of contention much less significant, people mobilized around other concerns. But Craig Calhoun (1993) showed that many of the attributes of these post-war movements can be found in social movements in the early nineteenth century, suggesting strongly that some other explanation than recently achieved democratic prosperity was needed for a full account. Perhaps the lesson was that certain emphases are cyclically recurrent themes of social movements across historical epochs. History is a fine source of instances that challenge theory and, with luck, trigger better theory.

Some important large-n statistical analyses would be simply impossible without making use of historical materials for the elementary reason that one couldn't get a large enough n otherwise. When Erica Chenoweth and Maria Stephan (2011) study the relative effectiveness of violent and nonviolent tactics in overthrowing regimes, they not only assemble a worldwide database on oppositional movements but span the more than a century from 1900 to 2006. This permits them, for example, to observe that of the twenty-five largest such campaigns, twenty were nonviolent and that these had a very much greater success rate than the violent ones (2011: 33). So here history not only deepens comparative analysis, it makes it possible. But when the same study tracks changes over time in the relative effectiveness of violent and nonviolent tactics (2011: 7–8), they are using history in a different way, one in which time matters.

TIME MATTERS

We can hone in on this distinction by taking a look at two different ways Tilly uses history in developing his important arguments on how democracy and social movements have shaped each other. There are many such connections. Democratization and social movements have developed together, Tilly argues, because of three broad kinds of causal connection: 1) democratization promotes movements; 2) movements promote democratization; and 3) important social processes promote both of them. To take a more concrete instance of each category: 1) Democratization fosters electoral campaigns, political parties, and a great variety of associations that also are vehicles for movement mobilization; 2) Social movements with some frequency advocate more democracy; 3) An increase in the numbers and connections of politically active people on the one hand fosters democratic politics and on the other fuels social movement recruitment (Tilly and Wood 2012).

Tilly then uses history in different ways to push this argument in different directions. In *Regimes and Repertoires* (2006), he attempts to show that distinctive forms of engaging in conflict are characteristic of different kinds of political systems, with "social movements" being particularly characteristic of democracy. For this analysis what matters are a democratic context, wherever and whenever it might happen to be found, and its common forms of contention. Looking at history is valuable because it gives you a lot more cases. But in *Contentious Performances* (2008) history matters in a deeply different way because here what is addressed is how relevant phenomena change over time. In this study, Tilly shows how new patterns of contentious action were built out of previous forms within changing circumstances, including democratization considered not as a state but as a process. Certain things happened after other things and the sequencing is part of the causal analysis.

So let us turn from history as a vast collection of dazzlingly varied forms of social life to history as the study of the operation of time in human affairs. Much of what we are looking at when we study social movements extends over time. Individual participants' relation to movements change as their lives unfold; movement organizations are shaped by the sequence with which they adopt identities, strategies, and structures; broad and changing historical contexts make some grievances, tactics, diagnoses, and identities more or less likely to become the stuff of social movement action; consequential trends, cyclical social processes, and sudden shocks cause all sorts of things to happen, including movements.

Movement Microhistory

Two studies suggest new ways of thinking about movement microhistory. The first addresses the ways in which the life cycles of participants intersect the movements in which they take part, while the second addresses the history of patterns of collective action and identity within individual organizations.

The basic insight that people are more or less likely to assume certain social roles at different points in their lives has been known for millennia and is embodied in names that exist in diverse cultures that designate stages in a life cycle. What are the implications for social movements? Catherine Corrigall-Brown (2012) has explored the diversity of ways in which movement activism fits into individual life histories. Youthful commitments endure for some, come to an end for others, and are the beginning of a lifetime of intermittent engagement for still others. How does having had certain kinds of movement experience earlier in life shape what sorts of engagement there might be later on? We are much in need of understanding how these individual life histories may be located in longer trajectories. In what ways, for example, are such commitments following in family or neighborhood traditions and in what ways in defiance of them?

Kathleen Blee (2012) opened up organizational microhistory by examining the initial phases in the development of new movements. Her evidence clearly shows that at quite an early stage in the history of newly formed movement organizations, decisions about membership, organizational structures, desirable tactics, how meetings will be run, and even who "we" are powerfully constrain everything that follows afterwards. Differently put, history matters inside movement organizations. As with participants' individual life histories, we need to understand how these histories of individual movement organizations mesh with broader patterns.

But Arthur Stinchcombe (1965) has made a strong case that organizational forms have a significant macrohistorical dimension: at particular historical moments certain forms are commonly assumed by newly founded organizations, in part driven by the use of available technologies, in part by what is culturally defined as respectable in that era, in part by mutually emulative processes, in part by new participants' experiences of other organizations from that historical moment. Many analysts have argued in that vein that the development of new communications technologies was encouraging new forms of social movement organization in the early twenty-first century, particularly highly decentralized structures of decision making (e.g., Castells 2012). Other analysts held that the new technologies permitted extensive mobilizations with very much less organization altogether (e.g., Earl and Kimport 2011). We need to understand better how organization microhistory and macrohistory work together.

Rhythms of Contention

On a larger timescale one can explore changes over decades in forms of contentious action, as in Danielle Tartakovsky's (2004, 2007) research on the history of demonstrations in twentieth-century France or Shorter and Tilly's (1974) account of very long-term changes in patterns of French strikes. Tartakovsky shows that French demonstrations have a long history of connection to broad revolutionary themes and struggles but that in the early twenty-first century they were shifting toward brief displays by large numbers mobilized on behalf of single, specific issues. Shorter and Tilly show that from the early nineteenth century to the mid-twentieth century, French strikes changed from being rare, small, and very long to frequent, large, and very brief. Such changes show a dynamic interaction of movement actors and others. Unions on the one hand and police, administrative authorities, and courts on the other, come to develop conventions of interaction. At the same time labor organizers learn from success and failures. Over the decades, it becomes easier to call strikes, to mobilize larger numbers for them, to resolve their issues faster, and to more quickly be able to call them off, too. The critical thing is to see these changes as the outcome of a variety of interactions within changing contexts.

Generally speaking, it is extremely rewarding to look for long-term changes in targets and tactics within some coherent field of contentious actions. Jean Nicolas

(2008), for example, has gathered data on collective contention in France from the mid-tseventeenth century down to the opening of the French Revolution, which allows tracing the ebb and flow of struggles around taxes, subsistence, religion, wages, and the seigneurial regime across time and space. Similarly, Edward Amenta et al. (2009) have traced the shifts in the US movements most covered year by year in the *New York Times* over the course of the twentieth century.

Contentious rhythms may be rooted in patterns of everyday life, in the dynamic quality of contentious action itself, and in powerful shocks. These may be observed in the ebb and flow of peasant mobilizations during the French Revolution (Markoff 1996). There was a weekly rhythm. Many actions were planned where and when rural communities came together, which typically meant on Sunday at Church after mass. Most actions, moreover, were small in scale and locally organized, and protest routines were well-known and needed little rehearsal. The result was that Sunday was by far the most common day for riot and rebellion. However, certain actions divided the rural community (conflicts over wages, e.g.). These could not be planned by the community collectively and so didn't fit the general Sunday pattern.

There was also a seasonal rhythm, with conflict avoiding times of sowing and harvest, which would bring ruin to all concerned. In addition, the specific threats and opportunities generated by big, revolutionary events did not necessarily adhere to standard temporal patterns. As the wars of the revolution, for example, led to labor shortages with military service drawing off many young men, scarce rural wage-workers pressed their advantage and strikes rose. But in regions where many were already turning against the revolution for other reasons, huge counterrevolutionary actions were sparked by military recruitment.

Superimposed on these already multiple rhythms were the ways in which rural communities learned which actions brought success by observing other communities. Over the tumultuous months of revolution, rural people tried out an increasing range of tactics, which shows up statistically as more actions per incident. But with the further passage of time, the number of actions per incident declined, as they zeroed in on those most effective, so that there is first a rise and then a fall in the sheer variety of tactics followed.

We see that some things of keen interest to social movement scholars exhibit trends, others cycles, and that both matter—and sometimes there are both trends and cycles, including multiple cycles, to be sorted out. Comparison of trends and cycles across movements or contexts is often especially rewarding.

Here are some more examples.

Some trends. Jackie Smith's work on transnationally organized social movement organizations shows a clear upward trend in their numbers from the 1950s to the early twenty-first century. There are, moreover, striking trends in the issues they address, with human rights and environmental issues on the rise. By contrast, labor unions were declining as transnational actors (Smith and Wiest 2012). Such trends may serve as important contexts for more finely focussed research. The declining clout of unions that these trends point up sheds some light on the development of new forms of labor organizing in the early twenty-first century (e.g., Walsh 2014).

Some cycles. While pre-revolutionary French rural conflict was muted in harvest season, this is precisely when agricultural strikes proliferated in southern Spain in the early twentieth century (Domènech 2015). This is because the organizations of rural workers would typically be negotiating labor contracts at moments of peak labor demand and strikes were an effective accompaniment to negotiation. This difference in the annual cycles of rural conflict is telling us something important about the institutionalized character of labor struggles in the twentieth-century Spanish case, one of the reasons a major goal of those who overthrew Spain's Second Republic in 1936 was the destruction of effective worker organizations.

Sometimes what is causally important is the intersection of different kinds of cycle. Consider the analysis of urban squatting as a social movement in Montevideo by María José Rivadulla Álvarez (2014), who provides a compelling analysis of the joint importance of economic and political cycles. Previously rare in comparison with other places in Latin America, illegal land occupation and housing construction became an important part of Montevideo's urban scene with the ending of military rule in the 1980s. It sometimes took the form of collectively organized actions of land seizure and sometimes consisted of individuals or separate families moving in one at a time. Both forms of squatting rise as economic circumstances deteriorate and both are affected by the timing of municipal elections.

But while the political cycle has an important impact on squatting, it has different impacts on different forms of action. When a group of squatters has been organized in advance to enable concerted action, the run-up to the election provides an opportunity for their spokespersons to bargain with contenders for office, including current incumbents, so squatting precedes the election itself. This means there is an important role for brokers between the would-be squatters and office-seeking politicians. Some brokers are activists on the political left, ideologically inclined to challenge capitalist property rights on behalf of the marginalized. Some are connected to mainstream parties and advancing their political careers. Some are poor people desperately seeking housing. But all are involved in a negotiated process that results in organized occupations taking place during the run-up to elections. On the other hand, individuals and families who are not part of such organized collectivities may also move onto unoccupied land and start to build, one individual or family at a time. Such cautious individuals await the victory of favorable candidates, so their squatting tends to happen after the election has been held and the left has won.

These distinctive paths to squatting leave enduring differences in their outcomes, too. Communities established by collective action are more secure because they have negotiated with authorities and are better organized for self-defense. They build with more durable materials and their neighborhoods often come to look indistinguishable from other poor but legal settlements. But communities formed by unorganized individuals look notably shabbier even after the passage of time.

The common thread of all these examples is that cyclical patterns of movement activity may be telling us important things about the rootedness of protest in the rhythms of daily life as well as the cyclical creation of opportunities, threats, and resources by both economic and political processes. What is important for historical analysis is studying the superimposition of these various cycles—and sometimes trends and sudden shocks as well.

Long-term comparison of cyclical patterns has much to tell us. In a broad look at the successes and failures of multi-country movement waves in the nineteenth and twentieth centuries, Kurt Weyland (2014) points to the spectacularly rapid diffusion of revolutionary actions in Europe in 1848 and the equally spectacular failure of those actions to bring about enduring change in desired directions. In striking contrast, the transnational diffusion of democratic waves in the late twentieth century was notably slower but had a stronger track record of enduring achievement. The key difference, Weyland argues, is that in 1848 disgruntled citizens, unorganized and undisciplined, almost instantly challenged and toppled governments as they heard the news of each other's successes, all triggered by the overthrow of the French monarchy. By contrast, in the twentieth century, more disciplined and organized collective actors reflected on the potentials and perils of particular actions, took longer to imitate each other, but were better prepared for the long haul. (It is interesting to explore the ways the Arab Spring of 2011 resembles 1848, and why.)

Consequential Trends and Cyclical Event Generators

Certain large historical processes quite regularly reshape interests, identities, opportunities, and threats and therefore figure in accounts of movements in a great variety of ways. Some of these are trends, others cyclical. Their close study is important for scholars of movements. Among the more consequential of these processes are the ways in which the rhythms of the seasons and longer-term features of the natural world shape human production; the ways in which technological change alters the rhythms of daily life; long-term growth or decline in the range and intrusiveness of states; long-term growth or decline in economic interconnection; and long-term changes in where people live and in their ways of livelihood. Some examples of the importance of their historical study for movement scholars follow.

As national arenas became more significant in European history, local actors found new fields to conquer and new rivals to ward off. Resisting the state or bidding for influence within it became increasingly significant foci of conflict. As state agents sought common cause with local actors to advance their own agendas and local actors sought the support of state agents, patterns of local conflict could alter drastically. Tocqueville ([1856] 1955), for example, argued that as the French state pushed aside the authority of local lords, the lord's considerable remaining privileges came to be experienced as theft, generating both an increasing sense of injustice among the peasantry and increasing resentment from envious well-off commoners. This shows up in a shift toward insurrectionary actions targeting the lords (as shown empirically by Nicolas [2008]). The key is to see that the growing reach of the state not only altered the ways in which movements addressed that state but altered the ways in which they acted in the local arena as well. Spanish historians, for example, are paying increasing attention to the role of local movements acting in local arenas in the nineteenth and twentieth centuries (Herrera and Markoff, 2013).

In the twenty-first century, it seems likely that we will have to pay increasing attention to transnational arenas as well and the ways that states are diminished or enhanced by actions beyond their borders, including the growing agencies of transnational decision making. Social movement scholars, therefore, have been examining, and debating, how movements are responding to these changes (della Porta 2007; Smith and Wiest 2012; Koopmans 2013). So two big trends, first the growth of effective states and then the growth of transnational structures of decision making, matter a lot for understanding movements.

From Structural Contexts to Cultures of Conflict

Big changes in the scale of economic interrelations are also major shapers of interests and identities, something central to the historical interpretations of Marx (e.g., [1852] 1955), and changes in state control and market connections are often closely connected. In European history, one major concern of states was provisioning their urban populations and their military forces, both as a general rule potentially far more dangerous to officials than hungry peasants. So states became engaged in promoting and protecting national markets in foodstuffs. Those whose access to food was thereby threatened in the seventeenth and eighteenth centuries responded by blocking exports of grain, terrorizing bakers into selling at acceptable prices, or demanding that officials release stored grain.

Both the development of national markets and the policies of growing states are major, intertwined contexts. Tilly did much to advance this general picture (1975), but he added a major cultural agenda as well for scholars of collective action. Tilly (1995) proposed that of all the imaginable ways human beings engage in conflict there are a relatively small number of well-established forms that are common at a specific time and place. There is thus a historically specific repertoire of contention that is learned and understood by participants. The new repertoire that developed in nineteenth-century Europe and North America included such actions as strikes and demonstrations just as earlier it had included food riots and insurrectionary tax resistance. There is therefore a cultural dimension to conflict, and one may speak of a performative aspect to the modern social movement and to other ways of engaging in conflict as well. People learn these performances.

This is an important part of what enabled insurrectionary movements to spread so rapidly in the French countryside from 1789 on without any organization on a larger terrain than the local rural community. Although the targets were not always traditional ones the insurrections involved very familiar routines, readily emulated when they seemed to work in a neighboring village (Markoff 1996: 261–269). Big changing structural contexts like the reach of states and markets matter for understanding repertoire change. But they are not automatic responses that people everywhere and at all times would opt for in the same circumstances. We need therefore to explore how repertoires are born and how they are transmitted.

Such repertoires have their geographic as well as temporal specificities. Federico Rossi (2015) has shown that in Argentina in the 1990s a diversity of political actors developed very similar forms of conflictive action for very different purposes, raising the questions of why blockading roads became part of an Argentine contentious repertoire and why Argentines adopted this rather than some other new form of struggle. Sidney Tarrow (2011) has developed the useful notion of "modularity": forms of collective action are modular to the extent that they are replicable in different times and places, for different purposes, by groups engaged in different struggles. But we need to understand better why some forms of action migrate far and others don't as well as why they migrate to some places but not others. Progress towards this theoretical objective will be greatly helped by more research into the histories of different forms of action in different places, and Rossi's work on late twentieth-century Argentina provides a strong example. Understanding big changes in contentious repertoires remains a major agenda for the historical understanding of contentious collective action.

Long-term comparative studies seem a good way to make headway on this big question. The trajectories of European states and markets that Tilly made so familiar to social movement scholars are not identical to those found elsewhere (as vividly demonstrated for Latin America by Miguel Angel Centeno (2002) or for China by R. Bin Wong (1997)). So how might different patterns have shaped contention differently? Ho-fung Hung (2011) addresses this in his exploration of Chinese protest history. Noting long-term cycles of state strengthening and decline in China, he suggests a consequent long-term alternation in protest forms. In eras when the state was strengthening, protesters engaged that increasingly effective state with nonviolent forms of mobilization. They might, for example, perform public displays of filial loyalty. During periods when the state was declining in effectiveness but was nonetheless intrusive, state actions were resisted violently. The data Hung meticulously assembled on thousands of eighteenth- and nineteenth-century protests strongly support his case. But Hung argues further that Chinese repertoires of contention are not simply invented and reinvented *ex nihilo* as a response to changes in state capacities. He suggests that they embody learned routines that are transmitted over generations, perhaps as folk legends about protest episodes. Late twentieth-century Chinese protests have some striking points of resemblance to those developed in earlier centuries, a point revealed by comparing protestor gestures captured in twentieth-century photographs with eighteenth-century woodcuts, so that we have, as his title has it, *Protest with Chinese Characteristics*. We need much more research on the transmission of protest cultures as part of our research into the genesis and decay of contentious repertoires.

The Overlay of Economic and Political Cycles

French economic historian Camille-Ernest Labrousse (1944) argued that in the pre-industrial past, harvest cycles were major engines of social protest. There was an annual rhythm, with grain prices lowest right after harvest, rising with increasing scarcity until next year's ripening grain could be turned into food. With bread so important for the great majority of Europeans in a world of generalized food insecurity, as prices rose spending on anything else plummeted. This meant, in bad years, major unemployment in manufacturing trades. So harvest failures were major events, reverberating through whole economies and societies, and a major source of protest and even revolution. Sewell (2005) argues that the development of industrial capitalism made the recurrent business cycle a similarly event-generating engine.

Since such recurrent causes of hardship interact in diverse ways with the political rhythms of possibility, much valuable analysis by historians and others is devoted to unravelling the intersection of different kinds of processes. Research on the development of the major wave of land occupations in early twenty-first century Brazil (Hidalgo et al. 2010), for example, has stressed the importance of a relatively sympathetic national political scene since the mid-1990s that is sometimes willing to grant ownership to rural people who have found the courage to seize some land. But land seizure remains a high-risk endeavor since large landholders often respond with violence and there is no guarantee that even the newly sympathetic state will grant title. In 2003, for example, fifty-five land invaders were killed (Hidalgo et al. 2010: 507). If there is a decent food supply, risk-averse poor people are a great deal less likely to organize those seizures. In often parched rural Brazil this is frequently a question of how much it rains so land occupations are highly correlated, negatively, with rainfall. The key is the superimposition of the rhythms of nature upon a period of political opportunity.

At a more general level, the rhythms of capitalism's expansion and contraction encapsulated by Schumpeter's (1950: 83) felicitous summary expression "creative destruction" are major generators of shifts in threats, resources, ideas, and opportunities. They deserve keen attention for historical analysts of social movements. Extremely consequential as well are changes in the form of the state. More democratic regimes differ from more authoritarian ones in the range of organizations, publicly avowable goals, and tactics that can be engaged in without crushing repression. So big swings between more authoritarian and more democratic regimes matter. But democracy itself has important cyclical processes. The regularity of elections encourages important relationships between movements and parties, sometimes mutually supportive or even mutually constitutive, sometimes antagonistic. And the histories of democracy and movements are deeply intertwined (Goldstone 2004; Markoff 2011; Tilly and Wood 2012).

It is not surprising that electoral cycles are often important for understanding movements and have cropped up at points in this chapter. Less often analyzed in long-term perspective have been cyclical alternations between more democratic and more authoritarian forms. Paul Almeida's (2008) delineation of eight decades of protest history in El Salvador shows how rewarding such a long-term approach can be because this is a place where shorter and longer moments of political opening alternated with murderously repressive regimes and civil wars. What Almeida finds is that liberalizing moments within authoritarian orders provide occasions for the development of diverse organizations and that these organizations, in the next democratic episode, are at the center of protest mobilization, much of it nonviolent. The shutting down of those opportunities in the next authoritarian turn of the wheel then leads some organizations to defend previous achievements with violence. Pointing ahead into the twenty-first century, Almeida's work indicates a new wrinkle: the combination of nationally democratic politics with enmeshment in the globalized economy is generating some new protest patterns directed at the transnationally fashionable policies of privatization and austerity. In summary, and instructively, we find both cyclicity and novelty in Almeida's account.

Taking an even longer run perspective, the development of a more effective state over centuries of European history or of broad decades-long swings in state capacities as in China seem major contexts for understanding forms of contentious action. Police, political parties, state administrators, and rival movements are actors to which movements respond and which in turn are often responding to those very same movements (della Porta et al. 1998). David Meyer and Suzanne Staggenborg (1996) have shown how dynamic the interplay of antagonistic movements can be. Tarrow (2011) has suggested a model of how movements and governing elites may respond to each other over time, generating considerable dynamism. John Markoff (1997) examines an instance of rebellious villagers and a national elite, each becoming more radical in interaction with the other over a few turbulent months of revolution. We need more fine-grained analyses of particular protest cycles in order to engage effectively in cross-cycle comparisons.

Big Shocks

We look to history for fairly stable features of social activism like contentious repertoires, for trends in both important contextual features like states and markets, and for powerful cyclical processes, including the weekly and seasonal rhythms of everyday life as well and the ebb and flow of economic and political circumstances. But we also look to history as well to learn something about dramatic shocks that alter social relations with a bang, including patterns of collective action, for things that drastically increase threats or opportunities, destroy familiar possibilities or open options unthinkable yesterday. Wars commonly do this. In changing borders they alter who's in charge locally. In the radically heightened demands of states for goods, services, and lives they create and destroy opportunities at high velocity. They upend peacetime social relations by radically changing the sorts of skills that are useful for coping with new environments, both on the battlefield and the home front.

So wars have multiple consequences for protest, suppressing some and enabling others. The effects of war, moreover, change over time. The First World War initially reduced movements as a result of heightened domestic repression, the shipment of young men to the front, the extension of work days, and patriotic conformism. But eventually, war-induced economic hardship, demand for labor, dismay at loss of life, and military mutinies opened the way for movements. In Beverly Silver's (2003) analysis of the large dataset she assembled on the world history of labor conflict from the late nineteenth to the late twentieth century, wartime and the immediate aftermath turn out to be extremely important contexts. Her data show the early years of the twentieth century's two world wars to be low on labor conflict. Massive conscription of young men, patriotic loyalty, politically cautious unions, and repression all probably played a part. But with war's end conflict exploded. The peak two years of the century were 1919–20 worldwide; the next largest peak was 1946–47 (2003: 125–126).

Some shocks are powerful enough to constitute "critical junctures," moments that send the future down a different path. Wars do so with some frequency. But what of other events? Demonstrating empirically that some events have had such a strong impact can be a difficult challenge. Students of history are apt to practice, informally or formally, counterfactual analysis as they speculate (with or without some well-crafted model) about possibilities that were unrealized. Comparative historical analysis sometimes convincingly reveals such moments. Fishman's comparative treatment of the consequences for each country of the different forms taken by Spanish and Portuguese democratization in the 1970s is exemplary (Fishman 2011). Two neighboring countries with many similarities in their histories, both long-term and recent, and many similarities in their social structures and cultures underwent deeply different democratizing movements at about the same time. The Spanish transition came to be known for its negotiation among political elites under the general leadership of regime insiders. The Portuguese transition was triggered by military mutiny and took on a revolutionary character. Fishman has demonstrated an array of subsequent differences in the political life, the policies, and even the youth cultures of the two countries that were not evident earlier. The Portuguese press, for example, became a forum for a wider variety of social movement voices than the Spanish because the Portuguese revolutionary process altered journalistic culture. In Fishman's judgment, while Spain is in comparative terms very prone to demonstrations, it is in Portugal that movements are paid more attention by those in power. So this is a case where a critical historical juncture in which movements played varying parts had consequences for movements downstream.

In addition to duration, trend, and cycle, therefore, we need to add punctual time. There are events that reshape movements. And some of these events are themselves movement actions. William Sewell (2005) has explored what it was that made an attack on a Paris prison and arms depot on July 14, 1789 so consequential, so emblematic of the ongoing revolutionary process. We need more studies of events, not just durations, trends, and cycles. Individual participants and movement organizations are often reacting to specific things decided by other actors, sometimes within significantly changing contexts. Movement scholars attending to such things commonly understand movement processes and outcomes as contingent (things would have happened differently if some other actor had done something else). Some contingencies are important enough to deeply constrain the future actions of many actors, and when we notice this we have evidence of critical junctures.

Revolutions are historical episodes in which contingency may be seen with relative clarity, because many people find that day after day they are facing situations in which their established routines are inadequate and they have to keep inventing new ones. Scholars of the Russian Revolution, for example, recognize that in the crisis following the abdication of the Tsar in early 1917, the Bolsheviks confronted a wholly unknown web of possibility and threat. Their famous organizational blueprint, as developed in Lenin's *What Is To Be Done?* of 1902, had no relationship to the organization that actually seized power in 1917 when decisions were improvised from one day to the next (Rabinowitch 1976). Methodologically, contingency means that movement scholars need to be paying attention to sequences of events connected by causal chains (Abbott 2001; Pierson 2004).

CONCLUSION

History matters for movements and for scholars of movements. It matters because the human past is replete with examples that expand our sense of what is possible and therefore what our theories need to account for. It matters because important processes unfold over time: in the lives of individual participants in movements, in the histories of individual organizations, in the rhythms of daily life that open some options and close others, in big contextual features that pose threats and opportunities. Some of these big features are broad trends, others are cyclical, and others still are powerful, unrepeatable shocks. All demand the study of history. And since these histories are different in different places, they demand the study of a broad variety of places, taking the analysis of human collective action well beyond the limited though important terrain of the contemporary wealthy democracies that have been the setting for the lion's share of empirical research.

But there is one other kind of time to consider, one other kind of moment, for which "momentous" is the adjectival form. There is the moment that is experienced as a rupture in history, not just following a trend or enmeshed in a cyclical routine, the moments when dreams and nightmares are part of waking life and the world feels transformed. We can recognize "critical junctures" by measurable indicators—the point where some trend changes direction, for example. But there is an experiential dimension, too, and it needs attention from movement scholars. These moments in between two different kinds of routine time (the Greeks had a term for this: the *kairos*) remain a challenge for scholarship.

REFERENCES

Abbott, Andrew (2001). *Time Matters. On Theory and Method*. Chicago and London: University of Chicago Press.

Almeida, Paul D. (2008). *Waves of Protest. Popular Struggles in El Salvador, 1925–2000*. Minneapolis: University of Minnesota Press.

Álvarez Rivadulla, María José (2014). "Squatters and Politics in Montevideo at the Turn of the Century." *Handbook of Social Movements across Latin America*, edited by Paul Almeida and Allan Cordero, 205–220. New York: Springer Press.

Amenta, Edwin, Caren, Neal, Olasky, Sheera Joy, and Stobaugh, James E. (2009). "All the Movements Fit to Print: Who, What, When, Where, and Why SMO Families Appeared in the New York Times in the Twentieth Century," *American Sociological Review*. 74 (August): 636–656.

Barrows, Susanna (1981). *Distorting Mirrors. Visions of the Crowd in Late Nineteenth-Century France*. New Haven: Yale University Press.

Blee, Kathleen M. (2012). *Democracy in the Making. How Activist Groups Form*. New York: Oxford University Press.

Calhoun, Craig (1993). "'New Social Movements' of the Early Nineteenth Century," *Social Science History*. 17(3): 385–427.

Castells, Manuel (2012). *Networks of Outrage and Hope. Social Movements in the Internet Age*. Cambridge: Polity Press.

Centeno, Miguel Angel (2002). *Blood and Debt. War and the State in Latin America*. University Park, PA: Pennsylvania State University Press.

Chenoweth, Erica and Stephan, Maria (2011). *Why Civil Resistance Works. The Strategic Logic of Nonviolent Conflict*. New York: Columbia University Press.

Corrigall-Brown, Catherine (2012). *Patterns of Protest. Trajectories of Participation in Social Movements*. Stanford: Stanford University Press.

della Porta, Donatella, ed. (2007). *The Global Justice Movement. Cross-National and Transnational Perspectives*. Boulder, CO: Paradigm.

della Porta, Donatella, Fillieule, Olivier, and Reiter, Herbert (1998). "Policing Protest in France and Italy: From Intimidation to Cooperation?" In *The Social Movement Society. Contentious Politics for a New Century*, edited by David S. Meyer and Sidney Tarrow, 111–130. Lanham, MD: Rowman & Littlefield.

Domènech, Jordi (2015). "Land Tenure Inequality, Harvests, and Rural Conflict. Evidence from Southern Spain during the Second Republic (1931–1934)," *Social Science History* 39: 253–286.

Earl, Jennifer and Kimport, Katrina (2011). *Digitally Enabled Social Change. Activism in the Internet Age*. Cambridge: MIT Press.

Fishman, Robert (2011). "Democratic Practice after the Revolution: The Case of Portugal and Beyond," *Politics and Society*. 39(2): 233–267.

Goldstone, Jack A. (2004). "More Social Movements or Fewer? Beyond Political Opportunity Structures to Relational Fields," *Theory and Society*. 33: 333–365.

Harrison, Mark (1988). *Crowds and History. Mass Phenomena in English Towns, 1790–1935*. New York: Cambridge University Press.

Herrera González de Molina, Antonio and Markoff, John, eds. (2013). "Democracia y mundo rural en España," special issue of *Ayer*, 89(1): 13–119.

Hidalgo, F. Daniel, Naidu, Suresh, Nichter, Simeon, and Richardson, Neal (2010). "Economic Determinants of Land Invasions," *Review of Economics and Statistics*. 92(3): 505–523.

Hung, Ho-fung (2011). *Protest with Chinese Characteristics. Demonstrations, Riots, and Petitions in the Mid-Qing Dynasty*. New York: Columbia University Press.

Koopmans, Ruud (2013). "The End of the Social Movement as We Know It? Adaptive Challenges in Changed Contexts." In *The Future of Social Movement Research*, edited by Jacquelien van Stekelenburg, Conny Roggeband and Bert Klandermans, 315–323. Minneapolis: University of Minnesota Press.

Labrousse, Camille-Ernest (1944). *La Crise de l'économie française à la fin de L'Ancien Régime et au début de la Révolution*. Paris: Presses Universitaires de France.

LeBon, Gustave ([1895] 1960). *The Crowd*. New York: Viking Press.

Markoff, John (1996). *The Abolition of Feudalism. Peasant, Lords, and Legislators in the French Revolution*. University Park, PA: Penn State Press.

Markoff, John (1997). "Peasants Help Destroy an Old Regime and Defy a New One: Lessons from (and for) the Study of Social Movements," *American Journal of Sociology*. 102: 1113–1142.

Markoff, John (2011). "A Moving Target: Democracy," *Archives Européennes de Sociologie/ European Journal of Sociology*. 52: 239–276.

Marx, Karl ([1852] 1955). "The Eighteenth Brumaire of Louis Bonaparte." In *Selected Works*, by Karl Marx and Frederick Engels, 1: 247–344. Moscow: Foreign Languages Publishing House.

Meyer, David and Staggenborg, Suzanne (1996). "Movements, Countermovements, and the Structure of Political Opportunity," *American Journal of Sociology*. 101: 1628–1660.

Nicolas, Jean (2008). *La rébellion française. Mouvements populaires et conscience sociale, 1661-1789*. Paris: Gallimard.

Pierson, Paul (2004). *Politics in Time. History, Institutions, and Social Analysis*. Princeton: Princeton University Press.

Rabinowitch, Alexander (1976). *The Bolsheviks Come to Power: The Revolution of 1917 in Petrograd*. New York: Norton.

Rossi, Federico M. (2015). "Conceptualizing Strategy Making in a Historical and Collective Perspective." In *Social Movement Dynamics: New Perspectives on Theory and Research from Latin America*, edited by Federico M. Rossi and Marisa von Bülow, 15–41. Farnham: Ashgate.

Schumpeter, Joseph A. (1950). *Capitalism, Socialism and Democracy*, third edition. New York: Harper.

Sewell, William H., Jr. (2005). *The Logics of History. Social Theory and Social Transformation*. Chicago: University of Chicago Press.

Shorter, Edward and Tilly, Charles (1974). *Strikes in France, 1830-1968*. London and New York: Cambridge University Press.

Silver, Beverly (2003). *Forces of Labor. Worker's Movements and Globalization since 1870*. Cambridge: Cambridge University Press.

Smelser, Neil J. (1962). *Theory of Collective Behavior*. New York: The Free Press.

Smith, Jackie and Wiest, Dawn (2012). *Social Movements in the World-System. The Politics of Crisis and Transformation*. New York: Russell Sage Foundation.

Stinchcombe, Arthur (1965). "Social Structure and Organizations." In *Handbook of Organizations*, edited by James March, 142–193. Chicago: Rand-McNaly.

Tarrow, Sidney (1989). *Democracy and Disorder. Protest and Politics in Italy, 1965-1975*. Oxford: Clarendon Press.

Tarrow, Sidney (2011). *Power in Movement. Social Movements and Contentious Politics*. Revised and updated third edition. Cambridge: Cambridge University Press.

Tartakovsky, Danielle (2004). *La Manif en éclats*. Paris: La Dispute.

Tartakovsky, Danielle (2007). *Les Manifestations de rue en France, 1918–1968*. Paris: Publications de la Sorbonne.

Tilly, Charles (1964). *The Vendée*. Cambridge: Harvard University Press.

Tilly, Charles, ed. (1975). *The Formation of National States in Western Europe*. Princeton: Princeton University Press.

Tilly, Charles (1995). "Contentious Repertoires in Great Britain, 1758–1834," *Social Science History*. 17(2): 253–280.

Tilly, Charles (2006). *Regimes and Repertoires*. Cambridge, MA: Cambridge University Press.

Tilly, Charles (2008). *Contentious Performances*. Cambridge: Cambridge University Press.

Tilly, Charles and Wood, Lesley (2012). *Social Movements, 1768–2012*. Third Edition. Boulder, CO: Paradigm Publishers.

Tocqueville, Alexis de ([1856] 1955). *The Old Regime and the French Revolution*. Garden City, NY.: Doubleday.

Walsh, Jane (2014). "'Our Struggles Are Not the Same But They Converge': Farmworkers, Allies, and the Fair Food Movement." Ph.D. dissertation, University of Pittsburgh.

Weyland, Kurt (2014). *Making Waves. Democratic Contention in Europe and Latin America since the Revolutions of 1848*. New York: Cambridge University Press.

Wong, R. Bin (1997). *China Transformed: Historical Change and the Limits of European Experience*. Ithaca, NY: Cornell University Press.

CHAPTER 5

....

CONTENTIOUS POLITICS

....

SIDNEY TARROW

OVER the past decade and more, students of social movements have begun to employ to a broader concept than movements—"contentious politics" (henceforth CP). Coined by the late Charles Tilly in a series of works he began in the 1970s[1] the term's use has grown dramatically since the early 1990s. Figure 5.1 presents an NGram analysis of the appearance of the combination "contentious politics" in Google Books between 1990 and 2008—the last year for which the NGram reader is currently available. As the graph shows, from a magnitude approaching zero in 1990, the term's use grew almost geometrically over a period of eighteen years.

Scholarly employment of the term, in particular, has grown. Examining Google Scholar for three-year periods from 1990 through 2013—the last year for which complete citations could be found—the total number of "hits" for the term "contentious politics" rose from 5,970 in 1990–92, to 24,200 in 2000–02, falling slightly to 19,400 for the two years 2012–13.

Why this rapid increase in the use of a term that was almost completely unknown two decades ago? One reason was surely its association with Tilly, his distinguished reputation, and its use by cohorts of his students and collaborators. But probably more important was the expanding range of contention in the post-9/11 world beyond classical social movements, to civil wars, guerilla insurgencies, clandestine armed conflict, suicide bombings, and the growing interest of scholars in these broader forms of contention. As these more lethal forms of conflict spread across the globe, scholars felt the need for a language of contention that went beyond the traditional term "social movements." Rather than sweep all forms of popular mobilization into the bin of social movements, scholars began to place movements in the context of a much wider variety of popular and violent struggles.

But a rapid inspection of how the term CP has been used produces a partially overlapping dichotomy. For some, it is an extension of the concept of "social movements" to other fields of conflict; while for others it refers to the *field of interaction* among collective actors or those who represent them, whether or not they are social movements. This tension was already obvious during the last decade of Tilly's work: In 2005, he published his well-known textbook, *Social Movements: 1768–2004* (Tilly and Wood, 2nd edn,

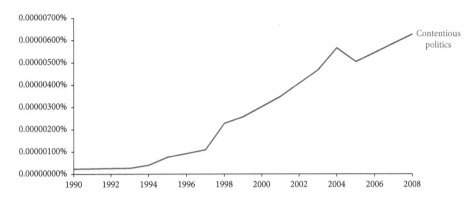

FIGURE 5.1. Appearance of "Contentious Politics" in an NGram Analysis of Google Books, 1990–2008.

2009). But two years later, with this author, Tilly devoted only one chapter to movements in a broader treatment of *Contentious Politics* (Tilly and Tarrow 2007). Soon after, Doug McAdam and Hillary Shaffer Boudet (2012) examined episodes of environmental conflict to "put social movements in their place."

For Tilly and many of his followers, the term "contentious politics" *includes* movements, but it focusses not on the objects of analysis but on the relational mechanisms in fields of contention. The instinct underlying this move was to allow scholars to study movements and institutional politics more interactively, facilitate analysis of the dynamics between movements and other actors, study the transitions from one form of contention to another, and examine broader and more systemic forms of collective action without stretching the meaning of the traditional term "social movements." As Tilly, with this author, wrote not long before his passing:

> Contentious episodes are all around us: they involve contentious interaction among claim-makers, their allies, their opponents, the government, the media, and the mass public. … their rise and fall describes a trajectory of mobilization and demobilization involving interactions among these actors
>
> (Tilly and Tarrow 2007: 92).

This chapter will refer to social movements but will leave aside the physiognomy, the ideology, and the organization of movements to focus on the broader and more relational version of CP. The underlying logic of the approach is both encompassing and differentiating. It can be summarized in five claims:[2]

- Revolutions, civil wars, ethnic conflicts, social movements, and other forms of contention result from similar causes in different combinations, sequences, and initial conditions.
- These causes can be broken down into recurrent mechanisms and processes. Explaining contention means identifying the mechanisms and processes that lie behind it.

- In all sorts of regimes, routine interactions between governments and political actors produce political opportunities that structure what forms of contention different potential makers of claims can actually initiate.
- Governmental action and popular contention interact to form repertoires of contention—limited arrays of known, feasible ways of making collective claims.
- All parties to contention are constantly innovating and negotiating, often attempting to persuade, block, defeat, punish, or collaborate with each other. That incessant give and take makes contentious politics a dynamic drama rather than a stale reenactment of old scenarios.

Section 1 of this chapter centers on the program first created by Tilly and reflected in the *Dynamics of Contention* project (henceforth *DOC*), as well as in other work he published in the last decade of his life. Section 2 summarizes some of the lacunae in that program, before turning, in Section 3, to examples of five avenues of research to which it has contributed: relational dynamics within movements; relations between movements and political parties; the process of radicalization; the mechanisms that drive civil wars; and the transition from mobilization to revolution. The chapter concludes with suggestions for further work.

THE CP PROGRAM

Tilly founded the school he came to call "contentious politics" in the 1970s, with his monumental text, *From Mobilization to Revolution* (1978), but in the next two decades, because he mainly focussed on historical analyses of Britain and France, the broader implications of the concept were somewhat obscured to students of social movements. But there were hints of what was coming: For example, already in the 1970s, writing with collaborators, Tilly began to develop event catalogs of both violence and strikes in France, using them to examine their relationship to cycles of political and institutional change (Snyder and Tilly 1972; Shorter and Tilly 1974). In the same decade, writing with Louise and Richard Tilly, he developed comparative analyses of historical episodes of contention (Tilly, Tilly, and Tilly 1975). In the 1980s he began to elaborate the concept of the "repertoire of contention"—which ranged from historical forms like the *charivari* to modern associational forms like the social movement, all the way to political violence—which began with *The Contentious French* and culminated with his masterwork, *Contentious Performances* (Tilly 1986, 2008a).

But it was only when he set out more deliberately to formalize his approach that Tilly was struck by what he saw as five major limitations in the way the field of contentious politics had developed. What he saw was:

- a limitation largely to the study of movements, and particularly reformist movements, mainly using case studies of individual movements;

- a largely separate specialty dedicated to the comparative study of revolutions, mainly using comparative/historical studies of small numbers of mainly social revolutions (Skocpol 1979; Goldstone 1991; Goodwin 2001);
- still another specialty, growing out of Ted R. Gurr's pathbreaking work in *Why Men Rebel* (1970), which used large-N comparisons of national level conflict events to study contention, but gave little attention to individual cases or to the distinctions among movements and other forms of conflict;
- a predominantly western bias; and
- a largely structuralist ontology, which paid more attention to the origins and outcomes of contentious episodes than to their internal processes.

These limitations have since been addressed by many other scholars, as the contributions to this volume demonstrate, and soon the field of social movement study began to broaden. Profiting from the cultural turn that was percolating out of anthropology, history, and literary studies in the 1980s (Johnston and Klandermans eds. 1995) and from the application of event history analysis from the organizational ecology tradition (Olzak 1992; Minkoff 1995; Soule 1997, 1999, 2004), the field also made increasingly more careful distinctions among movements, revolutions, civil wars, and guerilla movements. It drew increasingly on social network analysis, as theorists began to broaden the concept of movement organizations to broader and less formal networks (Gould 1995; Keck and Sikkink 1998; Diani and McAdam, eds. 2003). And it gave greater attention to contention in the Global East and South to address the predominantly western bias in the classical social movement tradition.[3]

But as research and writing on civil wars, guerilla insurgencies, terrorism, and revolutions began to explode, the segmentation of the field increased. A major problem was disciplinary: students working on these phenomena in political science seldom seemed aware of the rich lode of social movement and revolution studies in sociology, while few social movement scholars developed a knowledge of area studies and languages and the comparative frameworks used by political scientists.[4]

With the advent of global terrorism, an entirely new sector of contention was announced but this was largely developed by specialists in "national security" who had little knowledge of either social movements or of the broader field of contentious politics, as one of the editors of this volume has effectively shown (della Porta 2013). The problem was not that "terrorism" is no different than other forms of contention, but that its relations to these forms was obscured by scholarly concern with states' security dilemma. Soon "terrorism" became so widely employed as a term of political discourse that it became completely useless in the analysis of clandestine political violence (Tilly 2003; della Porta 2013).

A second problem was one of method: while social movement scholars like Tilly, Doug McAdam, Susan Olzak, and their students were perfecting the use of large-scale event catalogs, these methods were less familiar to political scientists, except for those who wandered into sociological circles.[5] Moreover, they were difficult to apply to contention in the Global South, where systematic newspaper records were either unavailable, unreliable, or both. As for the former Soviet bloc, only as it began to crumble did printed records of contention become widely available and reasonably reliable enough to form the basis of systematic event catalogs (Ekiert and Kubik 1999; Beissinger 2002).

Enter DOC

Tilly and his collaborators and students set out to address this segmentation. The most visible—if not universally welcomed—effort was *Dynamics of Contention*, published in 2001.[6] When it appeared, the book gave rise to spirited debates among social movement scholars and others. The program announced in that book had three overlapping features.

First, rather than focus on individual social movements or movement organizations, it sought to construct a largely interactive focus on *episodes of contention*. Episodes could be either short term—for example, among actors, the media, the police, and onlookers in a demonstration (Favre 1990); or longer term—for example, the cycle of contention in Italy after the First World War (Franzosi 1995, farm worker conflict in the United States (Jenkins 1986), or long revolutionary episodes, like the one in El Salvador in the 1980s (Wood 2000, 2003) or in Venezuela in the 1990s (Lopez-Maya, Smilde, and Stephany 2002). Episodes could be local, national, or transnational or cross those boundaries; they might be entirely peaceful, entirely violent, or more typically, made up of a mixture of conventional, disruptive, and violent interactions (Tarrow 1989; Kriesi et al. 1995).

Second, such many-sided episodes go well beyond social movements. We saw this in the 2013–14 confrontations among Ukrainian protesters, the government they challenged, the parties of the opposition, the countermovement of Russian-speaking opponents, and, ultimately, the Russian Federation and its local allies who took control of the Crimea in March 2014 (Tarrow 2015: ch. 1) and sponsored a separatist movement in Ukraine proper. We also see it in the now-defunct "Arab Spring," which created a movement but also engaged existing parties, unions, political opposition parties, and of course the military and the police. The latter—so often seen only in repressive duals with protesters—emerged in Egypt and Tunisia as key participants in the movements that overthrew long-standing presidents.

Third, rather than zeroing in on particular movements or movement organizations, students of CP emphasize the processes and mechanisms of contention in a dynamic political process. The "political process" approach became familiar for students of international relations and comparative politics in the last few decades (George 1979; George and Bennett 2005). But while George and his followers studied processes as sequences of events, Tilly and his collaborators specified the term through a number of intersecting "mechanisms."

Mechanisms, for these scholars, were defined as "delimited changes that alter relations among specified sets of elements in identical or closely similar ways over a variety of situations" (McAdam et al. 2001: 24–25). Mechanisms take three general forms: *dispositional mechanisms*—those that operate within individuals to determine or influence their behavior; *environmental mechanisms*—those that operate in the context of contentious actors; and *relational mechanisms*—those that shape or alter relations between actors or groups.

Although all three kinds of mechanisms operate in contentious politics, the CP program emphasizes relational ones: mechanisms like the *diffusion* of particular forms of action from one set of actors to another (Givan, Roberts, and Soule 2010); the *radicalization* of movement organizations (Alimi 2011; Alimi et al. 2012, 2015); the *goal displacement* of movement organizations (Zald and Ash 1966); the *suppression* of movement activists (Boykoff 2007; Boudreau 2015); or the *brokerage* of ties between two actors with no preceding connections by a third (McAdam et al. 2001: ch. 5).

Mechanisms build into processes either sequentially or in tandem. Consider the well-known process of *scale shift*.[7] Most episodes of contention begin locally; if there were no shift in scale, there would be few national or international waves of contention. Think of how the self-immolation of a street vendor in Tunisia gave rise to a national movement and then to "The Arab Spring." Scale shift not only diffuses contention across space or social sectors; it creates instances for new coordination at a higher or lower level than its initiation. Scale shift moves the locus of contention to new actors, touches on the interests and values of new targets, involves a shift in venue to sites that may be more dangerous or more institutionalized than its origin, and can threaten the survival of entire regimes.

There are at least two routes through which local contention scales upward to the national level: *direct diffusion*, which passes through individuals and groups whose previous contacts or similarities become the basis of their mobilization; and *mediated diffusion*, through brokers who connect people who would otherwise have no contact with each other. Scale shift, in addition to diffusion, involves the mechanisms of *emulation*, the *attribution of similarity*, and sometimes *coordination of action* between the originators of an action and those who follow their lead. The spread of the Arab spring was a classical case of transnational scale shift involving all these mechanisms and more, including—crucially—the *defection* of parts of the elite and the military.

DOC's Defects

In *Dynamics of Contention*, Tilly and his collaborators hoped to foment a conceptual and methodological reorientation of the study of non-routine collective action. Naturally, as with all ambitious projects, the greater the ambition, the larger the risk of falling short—perhaps well short—of one's goal. Critics, mainly coming from within the social movement field, complained that *Dynamics of Contention* had too little to say about too many episodes of contention, that it too casually adduced too many mechanisms, that it paid too little attention to empirically demonstrating them, and that it gave too little attention to the connections between contentious politics and different forms of regime.[8]

Four major lacunae in the original program are worth enumerating, before turning to the work that the CP program has given rise to, much of it from younger scholars outside the social movement canon:

First, by focussing on the mechanisms in episodes of contention, the program failed to provide thorough accounts of movement origins and outcomes. In this respect, it had more in common with the "analytic narratives" approach in the rationalist tradition than with the social movement field (Bates et al. 1998). Readers looking for well-rounded accounts of the origins, activism, and outcomes of social movements were bound to be disappointed with the sketches they found in *DOC*. The study also focussed almost exclusively on state-related contention, rather than on other forms of constituted authority.

Second, in empirically employing the CP perspective, Tilly and his collaborators painted with a broad brush. This was a virtue in one important respect: in contrast to the narrow temporal and geographic scope of most social movement scholarship, it encouraged scholars to study contention in many different times and places, enabling both comparison and analogy between them. Their book included seventeen episodes of contention, ranging from the French Revolution in the eighteenth century, to the American Civil War in the nineteenth, to American racial politics and the British suppression of the Mau Mau in the 1960s, to Italian contention in the 1960s and '70s, to the Nicaraguan revolution and Spanish democratization in the 1980s, and many others.

Third, the broad range of episodes led the authors to array mechanisms with abandon, making it difficult for readers to identify the key mechanisms that drive contentious politics in comparable situations. Nor was the ontological status of the concept of mechanisms entirely clear, leading to criticisms of the term's conceptual vagueness, the proliferation of mechanisms adduced, and the lack of methodological rigor in the production of mechanism-based analyses (Mahoney 2001). Most important, there was little attention to the methods by which mechanisms could be both identified and empirically verified, leaving the authors open to the charge that their key analytical concept could not be validated.[9]

Fourth, both classical structuralists working in the social movement tradition and the newer array of those who had taken the "cultural turn" found it hard to identify either structure or agency in the CP tradition. The authors of *DOC* argued, in response, that mechanisms bridge structure and agency: they were interested not in the strength of the correlations between variables but in how they are linked to one another—through mechanisms.[10]

Finally, *DOC* may have appeared too soon: 9/11 and the diffusion of post-9/11 violent movements and the repression that followed led many scholars to pay more attention to these other forms of contention; to interrogate the analogies between them and social movements; to examine the transitions from one form of contention to another; to study the escalation of conflict from relatively benign social movement campaigns to more violent forms of action; and to analyze the shift in scale from domestic conflicts to transnational movements and international conflicts (Alimi 2011; Alimi et al. 2015). These are the kinds of problems that recent scholars working in the broad contentious politics tradition are addressing, as we will see in the next section.

THE GROWTH IN CP-BASED RESEARCH

A growing literature either derives from or resonates with the aims of the program. Some of this work shows how a CP approach illuminates aspects of social movements that have remained obscure; other work examines the relations of movements to political parties and other institutions; still other work examines the dynamics of collective action and its shift in scale to more aggressive forms of contention—like civil wars and revolutions; other work focusses on these more aggressive forms themselves. This section provides examples of these strands in the CP literature, while the final section highlights some analytical problems that researchers face.

Relational Dynamics in Movements: Extending the Radical Flank Effect

A classical mechanism in the social movement field is the "radical flank effect." It has long been noted that social movements are frequently divided into moderate and radical factions. Despite a shared commitment to a common goal, they differ on what specific goals they should seek and the tactics that are best adapted to those goals. Scholars of social movements have long noted the radical flank effect (Haines 1984), but these conflicts have seldom been theorized effectively. One major problem is that sometimes the flank effect has positive results for the radicals and sometimes it helps their moderate opponents when the latter's tactics isolate them. Another problem is that third party strategies—and especially that of the state—have an outcome which is independent of these internal struggles. For example, while the radical flank effect had a positive effect for rent strikers in New York and Boston in the early civil rights movement—because liberal municipal authorities preferred to deal with them than with more radical activists (Lipsky 1968), by the end of the civil rights era, black radicals were suppressed by a state that was in the hands of the conservative Nixon administration (Bloom and Martin 2012).

The problem of bringing third parties into the contest between radicals and moderates within a movement is not insoluble. For example, using an applied game theory approach, Devashree Gupta has examined the consequences of this rivalry between moderate and militant groups in the nationalist movement in Northern Ireland. Her work shows how the British strategy affected the outcome of the struggle in which they were engaged.[11]

Repression by the British state and the dominant Protestant majority, plus the differences in ideology and strategy within the nationalist movement, had led to a split between the moderate Social Democratic and Labour Party (SDLP) and the Irish Republican Army (IRA) and its political arm, Sinn Féin. The IRA/Sinn Féin movement employed vicious violence against both Protestant opponents and those within the Catholic camp, while the SDLP chose a moderate, electoral strategy. As Gupta summarizes, the overarching goal of independence from Britain and unification with the Republic of Ireland did not prevent dissent among the nationalists themselves. As the moderate voice in the movement, the SDLP has always maintained that reunification can only occur with the explicit consent of all who live on the island, specifically Northern Ireland's Protestant population. By contrast the IRA and its political wing, Sinn Féin, have historically defended the right to engage in armed struggle, noting that the British army and Protestant paramilitaries themselves employed coercion and violence to dominant and colonize Northern Ireland (Gupta 2013: 21).

Gupta's work shows that the interactions among the two movement factions and the state provided a much more robust theoretical framework than the internal struggles in the movement alone. Internal power balances, she concluded, must be understood as the product of both intra-movement and external-to-the-movement interactions (Gupta 2013: 33). She concluded that "not all governments, corporations, or other conventional movement targets are equally endowed with the resources to resist demands being made on them. Some states have a higher capacity and appetite to meet movement demands with coercion, and others lack the wherewithal or desire to repress challengers" (Gupta 2013: 8–9).

Relating Movements to Parties and Courts

In his late work, Tilly became more and more interested in the relationship between contentious politics and difference forms of regime (2006), but he did not examine these relationships with respect to particular institutions. Two such institutions – party systems and courts – have long had a close interaction with movements, but only recently have movement scholars systematically focused on these relationships.

There has long been a disciplinary divide between the study of social movements and the study of political parties (McAdam and Tarrow 2010, 2013). But many parties begin life as movements.[12] Think of the labor movement that gave birth to social democratic parties in Western Europe; or the abolitionist movement that was at the core of the Republican Party during and after the American Civil War; or the indigenous peoples' movements that produced ethnically supported parties in Bolivia and Ecuador in recent decades. Movements frequently give rise to parties when movement activists *transfer their activism* to institutional politics.

But movements do not effortlessly transform into parties without intervening mechanisms of participation. They can engage in a variety of forms of electoral participation:

Proactive electoral mobilization. This occurs when movements become more active in the context of an electoral campaign. Typical of this is the mobilization of trade unions on behalf of allied parties in elections in both Europe and North America. More recent was the mobilization of grass-roots activists around the "Tea Party" label in the American 2010 congressional elections (Skocpol and Williamson 2012).

Reactive electoral mobilization. This involves escalating protest in the wake of a disputed election. We saw such an example in the Ukraine when opposition leader Viktor Yushchenko mobilized thousands of supporters against the corrupt election of Viktor Yanukovych in 2002. As Mark Beissinger (2007 and 2011) and Valerie Bunce and Sharon Wolchik have shown (2011), disputed elections have become one of the most common catalysts of protest movements in non-democratic states.

Movements induce shifts in electoral fortunes. If we consider the major turning points in electoral politics in the United States (i.e., the election of Abraham Lincoln in 1860 and of Franklin D. Roosevelt in the New Deal) they have mainly been linked to the intrusion of social movements into electoral politics. The latest intrusion of a movement into the party system—the delayed impact of the "Reagan revolution"—produced what McAdam and Karina Kloos call a "party-movement hybrid" (2014).[13]

Movement-induced polarization. Another link between movements and electoral politics comes via movement influence on the ideological character and unity of political parties. Typically, when movements enter the electoral arena, they do so in the name of broadly ideological missions, rather than following the practices of routine politics. Every major intrusion of movements into American electoral politics either coincided with, or produced, a major polarization of the party system (McAdam and Kloos 2014).

How do movement-based parties differ from parties with other kinds of origins? The question goes back to one of the classics in the parties literature, Maurice Duverger's *Political Parties* (1963). Although there are as many answers to this question as there are types of party systems, one variation stands out: movement-based parties are more likely to be driven by ideological militancy than by pragmatic political considerations. Consider two examples, one historical and the other contemporary: first, how the ideological passions of the Mountain led the Jacobin party to go to war against Prussia and Austria in 1792 (Tarrow 2015: ch. 2); second, how the advent of the Tea Party after the 2010 elections led the Republicans to resist any compromise with their Democratic opponents in Congress.

Movements also intersect with courts and the legal system more generally (Sarat and Scheingold 2001, 2006; Rosenberg 2008; Edelman et al. 2010; Ackerman 2014). One set of relationships is what Michael McCann calls "legal mobilization" – when movements go to court on behalf of movement claims (McCann 1994). Another is when "cause lawyers" organize themselves as a movement on behalf of common claims or interests (Goldsmith 2012). A third happens when court decisions animate a movement – either in support of the court's holdings, in opposition, or both. More generally, legal decisions frequently change cultural understandings of the law and may change the Constitution itself (McCann 2006; Ackerman 2014). This constructivist approach is close to social movement theories of the framing of the effects of collective action – but with institutions doing the framing (Snow 2004).

We see all three of these relationships between law and social movements in the effect of the *Brown* decision on civil rights in the United States after 1954. The Supreme Court's holding was the result of the legal efforts of the NAACP (McAdam 1999); it triggered a wave of movement and counter-movement activity (Andrews 2004); and it had a profound effect on the position of African-Americans and on other minorities in the United States, although this role of legal mobilization in this process has been vigorously contested (Rosenberg 2008). More recently, there were similar interactions among the law, politics, and movements in the campaign for marriage equality (Dorf and Tarrow 2013) and in the emergence of the legal conservative movement in the United States (Teles 2008). In both cases, lawyers were hired on behalf of social causes; they eventually mobilized as organized movements; and they contributed to major changes in legal and political culture.

The Radicalization Process: From Extremism to Terrorism

Ever since Robert Michels wrote his *Political Parties* (1962), students of social movements and left-wing parties have been taken with the mechanism that sociologists call "goal displacement" (Zald and Ash 1966), which political scientists are more inclined to call "institutionalization" (Lowi 1971). What often escapes notice is that movements are just as likely to radicalize as they are to moderate their tactics. Some students of collective action have referred to this process as "escalation" (Sambanis and Zinn 2003), but Eitan Alimi and his collaborators use a broader definition of the mechanism. They define radicalization as a process involving a shift from predominantly nonviolent forms of contention on the part of a movement organization to predominantly violent ones. Rather than seeing radicalization as a homogeneous phenomenon, they see it as a two-stage process beginning with nonviolent tactics in its early stages, but shifting inexorably to the use of political violence as either the sole or the predominant form of action (Alimi et al. 2015: ch. 1).

Alimi and his collaborators examined three radical movements that moved inexorably towards the use of political violence: the Salafi groups that grew out of the Afghan insurgency against the Soviet-dominated government in the 1980s and produced, among others, the al-Qaeda movement that was responsible for the bombings of September 11, 2001, and other outrages; the Italian Red Brigades, which grew out of the student and worker movements in Italy in the late 1960s and early 1970s; and the EOKA Movement against British occupation of Cyprus, which wanted the island (which had a Greek majority population and a Turkish minority population) to be transferred to the sovereignty of Greece, a claim that gave the movement its name—"*enosis*" (Greek for union). Although all three of these movements were "born radical" in general terms, each of them eventually adopted political violence as their predominant form of action.

Beyond Movements: Civil War Mechanisms

A wave of new scholarship on civil wars has focussed attention on the origins, the dynamics, and the outcomes of these phenomena.[14] Although there have been many such works—some of them using detailed quantitative comparisons and others based on historical case studies—Stathis Kalyvas' 2003 article and his 2006 book come closest to the relational perspective of the CP program in that they focus on the interaction of different sources and types of political violence.

Kalyvas structured his 2003 article around the vertical relationship between centers and peripheries within civil wars: that is, between the central ideological/political cleavage at the macro level of countries undergoing internal insurgencies and the congeries of local conflicts and violence that it either triggers or to which it adapts. He works with two parallel models of civil war organization: a *Hobbesian* model, which stresses an ontology of civil wars characterized by the breakdown of authority in which violence is privatized, and a *Schmittian* model, which entails violence that is based on abstract group loyalties and beliefs, and which stresses the fundamentally political nature of civil wars and its attendant processes (2003).

Kalyvas found both Hobbesian and Schmittian elements in the civil wars he studied, and— most importantly—that the peculiar dynamic and extreme brutality of civil war violence results from their interaction, rather than from properties of their participants, their histories, or their environments. In fact, one of the puzzles the book seeks to answer is that vicious violence often takes place in territories with no prior history of conflict. This is a complicated argument: Kalyvas discerns that the idea of a central cleavage, which dominates macro-level studies of civil wars, may not be at all central to the motives of the peripheral actors whose violence it triggers. Conversely, peripheral violence, which dominates much of the historical and anthropological literature on civil wars, cannot be understood apart from the political opportunities and threats posed by the central core conflict.

Rather than seeing violence as an outcome of civil wars, Kalyvas sees violence as a *process* linking core cleavages and peripheral actors. That leads him to the mechanisms that are central to this process. Uncertainty and preemption play a role, but rather than being linked by the same cleavage in core and periphery, which would depend on the existence of common preferences, core and peripheral actors in civil wars are connected despite the differences in their motives and alignments. The central mechanism linking center and periphery is not a single overarching cleavage but a set of *alliances* between people at the center and at the periphery who may have little in common.

Of course, as in many forms of contentious politics, alliance-building is only one mechanism. Its function in Kalyvas's book is that it allows him to go beyond a simple incentives model to a more *interactive* one that focusses on the relations between actors: central and peripheral, combatant and noncombatant. Though Kalyvas gives no attention to nonviolent forms of contention—in fact he denies their relevance to the story he tells—the role of alliances among disparate actors that he underscores parallels the recent renaissance of studies of coalition-building in social movements.

From Movements to Revolution: Mobilizing Mechanisms in the Maidan

The 2013–14 occupation of Independence Square (the Maidan) in the Ukrainian capital of Kiev closely paralleled what had happened there a decade earlier, when a coalition of parties, movements, and ordinary citizens carried out what Bunce and Wolchik call "an electoral revolution" (2012). As in other former Soviet systems from Serbia to Central Asia, it was the suspicion of electoral corruption that was the immediate cause of the protests in Kiev. But the astonishingly large mobilization of Ukrainian citizens of all kinds suggests deeper causes for the mobilization in 2002. In a surprisingly massive turnout of the population both in Kiev and around the country, protesters forced a corrupt national election to be overturned, followed by the election of the somewhat more liberal candidate, Viktor Yushchenko. In a European Social Survey a few months later, an astonishing 18–22 per cent of those Ukrainians surveyed claimed to have participated in a demonstration sometime over the precious twelve months (Beissinger 2011).

What explained this extraordinary national cycle of mobilization? In two richly documented articles (Beissinger 2007, 2011), Beissinger set out to answer this question, exploring a number of mechanisms in the process: critical mass, preference falsification, and bandwagoning processes—that is, endogenous processes that gained momentum in the wake of the initial mobilization by a sizeable group of core supporters. Multiple causal processes unfolding at several levels accounted for some portion of the oversized participation, each one of them dependent to some extent on processes occurring at other levels. He concludes:

> .... the Orange Revolution became a venue through which people with varied motivations—national, civil, and economic—linked up and interacted with one another in a single causal space, forging a diverse coalition united in opposition to the Kuchma regime. (Beissinger 2011: 40)

CONCLUSIONS

These examples come from different sectors of the academic community, focus on different forms of contention, and identify different kinds of relations among actors in episodes and processes of contention. By no means all of their authors would identify themselves with the tradition that Tilly founded, or with the CP program in general.

What they have in common is the effort they make to go beyond the traditional canon of social movement research to examine the relational dynamics of complex episodes of contention:

- in the Northern Irish case, relations among radical and moderate factions of a nationalist movement and the state they opposed;
- in western institutional politics, how social movements intersect with political parties and courts;
- in the radicalization of left-wing movements, the interaction between repressive governments and extremist movements;
- in civil wars, the relations between "peripheral" and "central" forms of violence;
- in the Orange Revolution, relations among social movements, parties and a weak authoritarian government.

In a field of study that is growing and changing as fast as contentious politics, it would be premature to examine these relationships in any depth. Instead, I have tried to show that both the core social movement canon and newer areas of research can profit from their interaction. Once exposed to examination through relational mechanisms like those employed by the authors whose work has been summarized in this chapter, new kinds of relationships can be unearthed and examined.

Here are four areas that promise further progress:

Movements and parties: While the forms of movement/party interaction summarized in this chapter focus on movements as the independent variables, in fact, these relationships are reciprocal: not only do movements structure parties but parties can also stimulate and shape movements. Examples from recent research illustrate this reciprocal causation: the Peronist Party shaped the movement that toppled the Argentine President in 2001 (Auyero 2007); between 2006 and the election of Barack Obama, the Democratic Party drained much of the energy from the anti-war movement of 2003 (Heaney and Rojas 2015).[15] In France, under Marine Le Pen, electoral competition brought about the evolution of the radical-right National Front into a party much closer to the conservative mainstream.[16]

Anti-capitalist protest: A second area of promising research has come from the recent waves of anti-austerity protest which have renewed scholarly interest in the relationships between capitalism and social movements. Earlier efforts to link movements to capitalism were hamstrung by an almost total reliance on structuralist models, which underestimated the relations between class cleavages and mobilization (Tilly 1998). Faced by a new wave of anti-capitalist protest during the great recession, a relational approach linking forms of inequality to forms of protest would be a logical next step, as one of the editors of this volume has suggested (della Porta 2015).

War and movements: Finally, what of the relationships between domestic contention and the most extreme form of contention—war?[17] Tilly taught that war was at the origin of modern states and of the citizenship rights that emerged from efforts of state-builders to gain the support of their subjects (1992). But once modern states were established, did war making also expand the right of citizens to contest government policy; reduce it; or produce cycles of movement repression followed by expansion of rights in war's wake? If the CP perspective can illuminate such forms of contention as insurgency in Northern Ireland, terrorism in Italy, Cyprus and the Middle East, civil war in Greece, and revolution in Ukraine, maybe it can help us to understand the relations among war, states, and movements in the wake of 9/11? Time will tell.

Author Note

I am grateful to Eitan Alimi, Vince Boudreau, Jack Goldstone, Juan Masullo, Doug McAdam, Ken Rogers, and the editors of this Handbook for comments on an earlier version of this chapter.

Notes

1. Tilly's classical contribution was *From Mobilization to Revolution* (1978), which went well beyond social movements. His most explicit statements of the process-based approach he began in that book are: *Popular Contention in Great Britain* (1995); "Mechanisms in Political Processes" (2000); "Social Boundary Mechanisms" (2004); "Mechanisms of the Middle Range" (2007); *Contentious Performances* (2008a); and "Explaining Social Processes" (2008b).
2. The summary is adapted from Charles Tilly and Sidney Tarrow, *Contentious Politics, Contentious Politics*, Paradigm Press, 2007, 196–197.
3. Among the many scholars who contributed to this broadening of the social movement field in Latin America, the most important were Arturo Escobar and Sonia Alvarez and their collaborators (1992). Extending and modifying the western social movement tradition in Asia was carried out by in a series of works by Vincent Boudreau (1996, 2004, and 2015); Mary Callahan (2003); and Dan Slater (2010). Quentin Wiktorowicz (2004) took on a similar task for the Middle East at the same time as Charles Kurzman was testing social movement and revolutionary theory for Iran (2004), followed by Carrie Rosofsky Wickham for the Muslim Brotherhood (2013). In the East, the most influential work was carried out by Valerie Bunce (1999), Mark Beissinger (2002), and Bunce and Sharon Wolchik (2011).
4. As with all sweeping generalizations, there are, of course, important exceptions. A conference organized by Bert Klandermans, Hanspeter Kriesi and this author presaged an increasing number of comparative and trans-Atlantic comparative studies (Klandermans, Kriesi and Tarrow 1988). Doug McAdam, John McCarthy and Mayer Zald's (1996) reader urged scholars of social movements to engage in comparative work; Kriesi and his collaborators' (1995) study of new social movements in four European countries was a

good example of what could be accomplished through systematic comparative methods. Lee Ann Banaszek's (1996) study of women's suffrage campaigns in the United States and Switzerland was a model of theoretically informed paired comparison. See della Porta (2013) for a richly theorized comparative analysis of four different kinds of clandestine political movements.

5. When this author, a card-carrying political scientist, employed a version of protest event analysis in Italy, the resulting book was almost exclusively read by sociologists and cordially ignored by his political science colleagues, except for those who specialized on Italy. See Tarrow 1989 for the report of this work.

6. For example, see the contributions to *Mobilization* (2003), and to *Qualitative Sociology* (2008). For further reflections on the program, see the special issue of *Mobilization* on *"Dynamics of Contention,* Ten Years On" (2011).

7. This section draws on Tarrow and McAdam (2005).

8. The early critics of *DOC*—most of them coming from the social movement field—were almost as numerous as those who took up its call for a broader approach to contentious politics. Some critics confused it with the earlier "political process" approach, conveniently ignoring the fact that it was constructed in direct polemic with that narrower framework.

9. To this we pled guilty, in our response to a symposium in *Qualitative Sociology* in 2008 by a group of constructive critics, including Jennifer Earl, Tullia Falleti and Julia Lynch, Mark Lichbach, and Suzanne Staggenborg.

10. An example illustrates the distinction: in the tradition of quantitative work on civil wars, a robust finding was that mountainous countries are more likely to produce internal insurgencies than flat ones (Fearon and Laitin 2003). But what remained unclear was the *mechanism* that produces this correlation: was it the difficulty of the terrain, the ability of insurgents to melt into the mountains, or the tight-knit nature of isolated communities that hid them from pursuers? These were the kind of dynamic gaps that the CP program set out to fill in.

11. Gupta's work is most accessible in her 2007b article and in a 2013 paper. For a fuller account, see her "Militant Flanks and Moderate Centers: The Struggle for Power and Influence in Nationalist Movements," Ph.D Dissertation, Cornell University Department of Government, 2007a.

12. This section draws on a series of works on the relations between movements and political parties, by Jack Goldstone and his collaborators (2003), and by McAdam and Tarrow (2010 and 2013), and McAdam and Karina Kloos (2014).

13. Whether this has permanently altered the character of the GOP it is too soon to tell (Parker and Barreto 2013). McAdam and Kloos' (2014) book implies a cyclical evolution in American politics that recent efforts by the Republican mainstream to throttle the power of the Tea Party seem to support.

14. Among scholars of civil war, Elisabeth Wood (2000 and 2003); James Fearon and David Laitin (2003); Stathis Kalyvas (2003 and 2006); Paul Collier and Nicholas Sambanis (2005); Jeremy Weinstein (2006); and Lars-Erik Cederman and his collaborators (2013) have made important contributions.

15. Michael Heaney and Fabio Rojas have shown how the election of a Democratic Congress in 2006 and the campaign of Barack Obama two years later not only led many anti-war activists to "spill over" into Democratic party politics; it also weakened and redirected the movement (Heany and Rojas 2015: ch. 5).

16. The tension between the "movement" origin of the party and its electoral commitments was illustrated publicly in the conflict over anti-semitism between Marine Le Pen and the founding-father of the party, Jean Le Pen, after the successful European election results of the party in 2014.
17. I take the liberty here of citing my own recent work on war and movements: Tarrow (2013 and 2015).

References

Ackerman, Bruce (2014). *We the People III. The Civil Rights Revolution.* Cambridge, MA, and London England: Harvard University Press.

Alimi, Eitan (2011). "Relational Dynamics in Factional Adoption of Terrorist Tactics," *Theory and Society.* 40: 95–118.

Alimi, Eitan, Bosi, Lorenzo, and Demetriou, Chares (2012). "Relational Dynamics and Processes of Radicalization: A Comparative Framework," *Mobilization.* 17: 7–26.

Alimi, Eitan, Demetriou Chares, and Bosi, Lorenzo (2015). *The Dynamics of Radicalization—A Relational Comparative Perspective.* New York and Oxford: Oxford University Press.

Andrews, Kenneth. 2004. *Freedom Is a Constant Struggle: The Mississippi Civil Rights Movement and Its Legacy.* Chicago and London: University of Chicago Press.

Auyero, Javier (2007). *Routine Politics and Collective Violence in Argentina: The Grey Zone of State Power.* Cambridge: Cambridge University Press.

Banaszak, Lee Ann (1996). *Why Movements Succeed or Fail: Opportunity, Culture, and the Struggle for Woman Suffrage.* Princeton: Princeton University Press.

Bates, Robert, Grief, Avner, Levi, Margaret, Rosenthal, Jean-Laurent, and Weingast, Barry (1998). *Analytic Narratives.* Princeton: Princeton University Press.

Beissinger, Mark R. (2002). *Nationalist Mobilization and the Collapse of the Soviet Union.* Cambridge: Cambridge University Press.

Beissinger, Mark R. (2007). "Structure and Example in Modular Political Phenomena: The Diffusion of Bulldozer/Rose/Orange/Tulip Revolutions," *Perspectives on Politics.* 5: 259–276.

Beissinger, Mark R. (2011). "Mechanisms of Maidan: The Structure of Contingency in the Making of Colored Revolution," *Mobilization.* 16.

Bloom, Joshua and Martin, Walter A. (2012). *Black Against Empire: The History and Politics of the Black Panther Party.* Berkeley CA: University of California Press.

Boudreau, Vincent (1996). "Northern Theory, Southern Protest: Opportunity Structure Analysis in a Cross-National Perspective," *Mobilization.* 1: 175–189.

Boudreau, Vincent (2004). *Resisting Dictatorship: Repression and Protest in Southeast Asia.* Cambridge and New York: Cambridge University Press.

Boudreau, Vincent (2015). "Liberal Violence: Strategies of Repression in Transitional Regimes." In *Breaking Down the State,* edited by J. Jasper and J. W. Duyvendak. Chicago and Amsterdam: University of Chicago Press/Amsterdam University Press, 179–202.

Boykoff, Jules (2007). *Beyond Bullets: The Suppression of Dissent in the United States.* Oakland: AK Press.

Bunce, Valerie (1999). *SubversiveInstitutions: The Design and Destruction of Socialism and the State.* Cambridge: Cambridge University Press.

Bunce, Valerie and Wolchik, Sharon (2011). *Defeating Authoritarian Leaders in Mixed Regimes: Electoral Struggles, U.S. Democracy Assistance, and International Diffusion in Post-Communist Europe and Eurasia*. New York and Cambridge: Cambridge University Press.

Callahan, Mary. (2003). *Making Enemies: War and State Building in Burma*. Ithaca and London: Cornell University Press.

Cederman, Lars-Erik, Skrede Gleditsch, Kristian, and Buhaug, Halvard (2013). *Inequality, Grievances, and Civil War*. New York and Cambridge: Cambridge University Press.

Collier, Paul and Sambanis, Nicholas, eds. (2005). *Understanding Civil War: Evidence and Analysis*. Washington D.C.: World Bank.

della Porta, Donatella (2013). *Clandestine Political Violence*. New York and Cambridge: Cambridge University Press.

della Porta, Donatella (2015). *Social Movements in Times of Austerity. Bringing Capitalism Back into Protest Analysis*. Cambridge: Polity.

Diani, Mario and McAdam, Doug, eds. (2003) *Social Movements and Networks: Relational Approaches to Collective Action*. Oxford and New York: Oxford University Press.

Dorf, Michael C. and Sidney Tarrow. 2013. "Strange Bedfellows: How an Anticipatory Countermovement Brought Same-Sex Marriage into the Public Arena" *Law and Social Inquiry*. 39: 449–473.

Duverger, Maurice (1963). *Political Parties: Their Organization and Activities in the Modern State*. New York: John Wiley.

Edelman, Lauren B, Gwendolyn Leachman, and Doug McAdam. 2010. "On Law, Organizations, and Social Movements" *Annual Review of Law and Society*. 6: 653–685.

Ekiert, Grzegorz and Kubik, Jan (1999). *Rebellious Civil Society: Popular Protest and Democratic Consolidation in Poland, 1989–1993*. Ann Arbor MI: University of Michigan Press.

Escobar, Arturo and Alvarez, Sonia, eds. (1992). *The Making of Social Movements in Latin America: Identity, Strategy, and Democracy*. Boulder CO: Westview.

Favre, Pierre (1990). *La Manifestation*. Paris: Presses de la Fondation Nationale des Sciences Politiques.

Fearon, James D. and Laitin, David (2003). "Ethnicity, Insurgency, and Civil War," *American Political Science Review*. 97: 75–90.

Franzosi, Roberto (1995). *The Puzzle of Strikes: Class and State Strategies in Postwar Italy*. Cambridge: Cambridge University Press.

George, Alexander L. (1979). "Case Studies and Theory Development: The Method of Structured, Focused Comparison." In *Diplomacy: New Approaches in History, Theory and Policy*, edited by P. G. Lauren, 43–68. New York: The Free Press.

George, Alexander L. and Bennett, Andrew, eds. (2005). *Case Studies and Theory Development in the Social Sciences*. Cambridge and London: MIT Press.

Givan, Rebecca K, Roberts, Kenneth, and Soule, Sarah A. (2010). *The Diffusion of Social Movements: Actors, Mechanism, and Political Effects*. New York and Cambridge: Cambridge University Press.

Goldsmith, Jack. (2012). *Power and Constraint: The Accountably Presidency After 9/11*. New York: Norton.

Goldstone, Jack A. (1991). *Revolution and Rebellion in the Early Modern World*. Berkeley and Los Angeles: University of California Press.

Goldstone, Jack A., ed. (2003). *State, Parties, and Social Movements*. New York and Cambridge: Cambridge University Press.

Goodwin, Jeff (2001). *No Other Way Out: States and Revolutionary Movements, 1945–1991.* Cambridge, U.K.; New York: Cambridge University Press.

Gould, Roger (1995). *Insurgent Identities: Class, Community, and Protest in Paris from 1848 to the Commune.* Chicago: University of Chicago Press.

Gupta, Devashree (2007a). "Militant Flanks and Moderate Centers: The Struggle for Power and Influence in Nationalist Movements." Ph.D dissertation, Department of Government, Cornell University.

Gupta, Devashree (2007b). "Selective Engagement and its Consequences for Social Movement Organizations: Lessons from British Policy in Northern Ireland," *Comparative Politics.* 39: 331–351.

Gupta, Devashree (2013). "The Strategic Logic of the Radical Flank Effect: Theorizing Power in Divided Social Movements." Presented to the annual meeting of the Midwest Political Science Association. Chicago, IL.

Gurr, Ted Robert (1970). *Why Men Rebel.* Princeton, NJ: Center for International Studies, Princeton University.

Haines, Herbert H. (1984). "Black Radicalization and the Study of Civil Rights: 1957–1970," *Social Problems.* 32: 21–43.

Heaney, Michael T. and Rojas, Fabio (2015). *Party in the Street: The Antiwar Movement and the Democratic Party After 9/11.* Cambridge and New York: Cambridge University Press.

Jenkins, J. Craig (1986). *The Politics of Insurgency: The Farm Worker Movement in the 1960s.* New York: Columbia University Press.

Johnston, Hank and Klandermans, Bert, eds. (1995). *Social Movements and Culture.* Minneapolis and St. Paul: University of Minnesota Press.

Kalyvas, Stathis N. (2003). "The Ontology of 'Political Violence': Action and Identity in Civil Wars," *Perspectives on Politics.* 1: 275–294.

Kalyvas, Stathis N. (2006). *The Logic of Violence in Civil War.* New York and Cambridge: Cambridge University Press.

Keck, Margaret and Sikkink, Kathryn (1998). *Activists beyond Borders: Transnational Activist Networks in International Politics.* Ithaca, NY and London: Cornell University Press.

Klandermans, Bert, Kriesi, Hanspeter, and Tarrow, Sidney, eds. (1988). *From Structure to Action: Comparing Social Movement Research Across Cultures.* Greenwich CT: JAI.

Kriesi, Hanspeter, et al. (1995). *The Politics of New Social Movements in Western Europe.* Minneapolis and St. Paul: University of Minnesota Press.

Kurzman, Charles (2004). *The Unthinkable Revolution in Iran.* Cambridge MA: Harvard University Press.

Lipsky, Michael (1968). "Protest as a Resource," *American Political Science Review.* 62: 1144–1158.

López Maya, Margarita, Smilde, David and Stephany, Keta (2002). *Protesta y Cultura en Venezuela. Los Marcos de Acción Colectiva en 1999.* Caracas: FACES-UCV, CENDES, FONACIT.

Lowi, Theodore (1971). *The Politics of Disorder.* New York: Basic Books.

Mahoney, James (2001). "Beyond Correlational Analysis: Recent Innovations in Theory and Method," *Sociological Forum.* 16: 575–593.

McAdam, Doug. (1999). *Political Process and the Rise of Black Insurgency.* Chicago and London: University of Chicago Press.

McAdam, Doug and Schaffer Boudet, Hillary (2012). *Putting Social Movements in their Place.* New York and Cambridge: Cambridge University Press.

McAdam, Doug and Kloos, Karina (2014). *Deeply Divided: Racial Politics and Social Movements in Post-War America*. New York and Oxford: Oxford University Press.

McAdam, Doug, McCarthy, John, and Zald, Mayer N., eds. (1996). *Comparative Perspectives on Social Movements: Political Opportunities, Mobilizing Structures and Cultural Framings*. Cambridge: Cambridge University Press.

Mcadam, Doug, Tarrow, Sidney, and Tilly, Charles (2001). *Dynamics of Contention*. New York and Cambridge: Cambridge University Press.

McAdam, Doug and Tarrow, Sidney (2010). "Ballots and Barricades: On the Reciprocal Relationship between Elections and Social Movements," *Perspectives on Politics*. 8: 529–542.

McAdam, Doug and Tarrow, Sidney (2013). "Social Movements and Elections: Towards a Better Understanding of the Political Context of Contention." In *The Changing Dynamics of Contention*, edited by Conny Roggeband, Bert Klandermans, and Jacquelien Van Stekelenburg, 325–346. Minneapolis and St. Paul: University of Minnesota Press.

McCann, Michael W. 1994. *Rights at Work: Pay Equity Reform and the Politics of Legal Mobilization*. Chicago and London: University of Chicago Press.

McCann, Michael W. 2006. "Law and Social Movements: Contemporary Perspectives" *Annual Review of Law and Society*. 6: 17–38.

Michels, Robert (1962). *Political Parties: A Sociological Study of the Oligarchical Tendencies of Modern Democracy*. New York: Collier Books.

Minkoff, Debra C. (1995). *Organizing for Equality: The Evolution of Women's and Racial-ethnic Organizations in America, 1955–1985*. New Brunswick: Rutgers University Press.

Mobilization (2003). "Book Symposium: Focus on Dynamics of Contention," *Mobilization*. 8: 107–141.

Mobilization (2011). "Dynamics of Contention, Ten Years On," *Mobilization*. 16: 1–116.

Olzak, Susan (1992). *Dynamics of Ethnic Competition and Conflict*. Stanford: Stanford University Press.

Parker, Christopher S. and Barreto, Matt A. (2013). *Change They Can't Believe In: The Tea Party and Reactionary Politics in America*. Princeton NJ: Princeton University Press.

Qualitative Sociology (2008). "Measuring Mechanisms of Contention: Symposium on McAdam, Tarrow, and Tilly, *Dynamics of Contention*," *Qualitative Sociology*. 31: 307–367.

Rosenberg, Gerald. 2008. *The Hollow Hope: Can Courts Bring About Social Change?* Chicago: University of Chicago Press.

Sambanis, Nicholas and Zinn, Annalisa (2003). "The Escalation of Self-Determination Movements: From Protest to Violence." Unpublished paper, Department of Political Science. New Haven.

Sarat, Austin and Stuart Scheingold, eds. 2001. *Cause Lawyering and the State in the Global Era*. Oxford and New York: Oxford University Press.

Sarat, Austin and Stuart Scheingold, eds. 2006. *Cause Lawyering and Social Movements*. Stanford, CA: Stanford University Press.

Shorter, Edward and Tilly, Charles (1974). *Strikes in France, 1830–1968*. Cambridge: Cambridge University Press.

Skocpol, Theda (1979). *States and Social Revolutions: A Comparative Analysis of France, Russia and China*. New York and Cambridge: Cambridge University Press.

Skocpol, Theda and Williamson, Vanessa (2012). *The Tea Party and the Remaking of Republican Conservatism*. New York: Oxford University Press.

Slater, Dan. (2010). *Ordering Power: Contentious Politics and Authoritarian Leviathans in Southeast Asia*. New York and Cambridge: Cambridge University Press.

Snow, David A. (2004). "Framing Processes, Ideology, and Discursive Fields" in Sarah A. Soule, and Hanspeter Kriesi, eds. 2004. *The Blackwell Companion to Social Movements*, 386-412. Malden MA and Oxford: Blackwell.

Snyder, David and Tilly, Charles (1972). "Hardship and Collective Violence in France, 1830–1960," *American Journal of Sociology*. 37: 520–532.

Soule, Sarah A. (1997). "The Student Divestment Movement in the United States and Tactical Diffusion: The Shantytown Protest," *Social Forces*. 75: 855–882.

Soule, Sarah A. (1999). "The Diffusion of an Unsuccessful Innovation: The Case of the Shantytown Protest Tactic," *The Annals of the American Academy of the Political and Social Sciences*. 566: 120–134.

Soule, Sarah A. (2004). "Diffusion Processes within and across Movements." In *The Blackwell Companion to Social Movements*, edited by D. A. Snow, S. A. Soule, and H. Kriesi, ch. 13. Malden MA and Oxford: Blackwell.

Tarrow, Sidney (1989). *Democracy and Disorder: Protest and Politics in Italy, 1965–1974*. Oxford: Oxford University Press.

Tarrow, Sidney (2013). "War, Rights, and Contention: Lasswell v. Tilly." In *Sovereignty, Citizenship, and Cosmopolitan Alternatives*, edited by S. Ben-Porath and R. Smith, 35–67. Philadelphia: University of Pennsylvania Press.

Tarrow, Sidney (2015). *War, States, and Contention*. Ithaca and London: Cornell University Press.

Tarrow, Sidney and McAdam, Doug (2005). "Scale Shift in Transnational Contention." In *Transnational Protest and Global Activism*, edited by Donatella della Porta and Sidney Tarrow, 121–150. Lanham MD: Rowman and Littlefield.

Teles, Steven M. (2008). *The Rise of the Conservative Legal Movement: The Battle for Control of the Law*. Princeton NJ: Princeton University Press.

Tilly, Charles (1978). *From Mobilization to Revolution*. Reading: Addison-Wesley.

Tilly, Charles (1992). *Coercion, Capital, and European States, AD 990–1992*. Cambridge, MA: Blackwell.

Tilly, Charles (1986). *The Contentious French*. Cambridge MA: Harvard University Press.

Tilly, Charles (1995). *Popular Contention in Great Britain, 1758–1834*. Cambridge, MA: Harvard University Press.

Tilly, Charles (1998). *Durable Inequality*. Berkeley: University of California Press.

Tilly, Charles (2000). "Mechanisms in Political Processes," *Annual Review of Political Science*. 4: 21–41.

Tilly, Charles (2003). *The Politics of Collective Violence*. New York and Cambridge: Cambridge University Press.

Tilly, Charles (2004). "Social Boundary Mechanisms," *Philosophy of the Social Sciences*. 34: 211–236.

Tilly, Charles (2006). *Regimes and Repertoires*. Cambridge: Cambridge University Press.

Tilly, Charles (2007). "Mechanisms of the Middle Range." Presented to the Conference on the Work of Robert K. Merton, and its implications for sociology and related fields today. Columbia University, 9–10 August.

Tilly, Charles (2008a). *Contentious Performances*. New York and Cambridge: Cambridge University Press.

Tilly, Charles (2008b). *Explaining Social Processes*. Boulder: Paradigm Publishers.

Tilly, Charles and Tarrow, Sidney (2007). *Contentious Politics*. Boulder, CO: Paradigm Publishers.

Tilly, Charles, Tilly, Louise A. Tilly, and Tilly, Richard (1975). *The Rebellious Century, 1830–1930*. Cambridge, MA: Harvard University Press.

Tilly, Charles and Wood, Lesley (2009). *Social Movements, 1768–2008*. Boulder CO: Paradigm Press.

Weinstein, Jeremy (2006). *Inside Rebellion. The Politics of Insurgent Violence*. New York and Cambridge: Cambridge University Press.

Wickham, Carrie Rosofsky (2013). *The Muslim Brotherhood: Evolution of an Islamist Movement*. Princeton NJ: Princeton University Press.

Wiktorowicz, Quentin, ed. (2004). *Islamic Radicalism: A Social Movement Approach*. Bloomington IN: University of Indiana Press.

Wood, Elisabeth Jean (2000). *Forging Democracy From Below: Insurgent Transitions in South Africa and El Salvador*. New York and Cambridge: Cambridge University Press.

Wood, Elisabeth Jean (2003). *Insurgent Collective Action and Civil War in El Salvador*. New York and Cambridge: Cambridge University Press.

Zald, Mayer N. and Ash, Roberta (1966). "Social Movement Organizations: Growth, Decay and Change," *Social Forces*. 44: 327–341.

CHAPTER 6

NEW THEORETICAL DIRECTIONS FROM THE STUDY OF GENDER AND SEXUALITY MOVEMENTS

Collective Identity, Multi-Institutional Politics, and Emotions

STEPHEN WULFF, MARY BERNSTEIN, AND VERTA TAYLOR

INTRODUCTION

SINCE the mid-1980s, a number of scholars have turned to social movement theory to study gender and sexuality movements. However, the dominant theoretical approaches in the field remain rooted in masculinist assumptions that narrowly define social movements and what counts as legitimate forms of protest (Taylor 2010). For example, for a long time social movement scholars overlooked the study of health movements, yet recent studies reveal that the radical branch of the women's movement became mobilized, in part, through women's alternative health institutions, like the Boston Women's Health Book Collective (Morgen 2002; Davis 2007). Resource mobilization and political process approaches have tended to treat institutions such as the state and economy as the only credible targets for studying the emergence, nature, and outcomes of social movements (Taylor 1996; Armstrong and Bernstein 2008). The gender bias that inheres in social movement theories is not altogether surprising though considering that these very institutions are fundamentally gendered, as some feminist sociologists have revealed (Connell 1987; Acker 1990).

A growing body of work by feminist scholars demonstrates that gender is indeed a pervasive feature of social movements (G. West and Blumberg 1990; Naples 1992, 1998; Ferree and Martin 1995; Schneider and Stoller 1995; Blee 1996, 1998; Ray 1999; Staggenborg and Taylor 2005). Such research has pushed scholars to rethink some fundamental concepts in the field, including the state (Klawiter 2008), collective identity (Taylor and Whittier 1992), organizations (Clemens 1993), framing processes (White 1999), and emotions (Einwohner 1999). Gender is a key explanatory factor in the emergence and trajectory of social protest (Ferree and Roth 1998; Abdulhadi 1998; J. Taylor 1998) and common features such as leadership patterns, mobilization, movement participation, strategies, ideology, discourse, consequences of activism, and social movement outcomes are also gendered (McAdam 1988, 1992; Blee 1991; Taylor and Whittier 1992; McNair Barnett 1993; Ferree 1994; Whittier 1995; Beckwith 1996; Robnett 1996, 1997; Taylor 1996; Irons 1998; Fonow 1998; Staggenborg 1998).

Some gender and social movement scholars have attempted to bridge both literatures by developing new theoretical frameworks. In her case study of the postpartum depression self-help movement, Verta Taylor (1999) offers an analytical approach linking gender and social movement theories by drawing on key sets of factors that have been postulated to explain the emergence and development of social movements: political opportunities, mobilizing structures, and framing processes. The movement activities that these three sets of concepts structure influence movements to adopt and elaborate strategic repertoires, which Ferree and Mueller (2004) have termed "gendered repertoires of contention." Building on Taylor (1996, 1999), Einwohner et al. (2000) develop a typology that takes into account gender composition, goals, tactics, identities, and attributions to more systematically analyze the different ways in which social movements are gendered.

Meanwhile, the study of gender and lesbian, gay, bisexual, and transgender (LGBT) movements have forced scholars to think about power in more complex ways. Political process theory assumes that domination is organized by and around one primary source of power (i.e., the state and the economy) and treats culture separate from domination and of secondary importance. In contrast, several studies on gender and LGBT movements reveal that domination is organized around not only the state but myriad institutions (e.g., non-profit organizations, workplaces, commercial establishments, religion, science, medicine, law) and that culture is, in fact, constitutive of domination (Gamson 1989; Melucci 1985, 1989; Taylor 1996; Epstein 1996; Katzenstein 1998; Naples 1998; Cohen 1999; Turner 1999; Armstrong 2002a; Bernstein 2003, 2005; Van Dyke, Soule, and Taylor 2004; Raeburn 2004; Bruce 2013). Although political process theories dismiss gender and sexuality movements that seek material and symbolic change in institutions or culture as merely "expressive" politics compared to "legitimate" forms of state-centric activism (Bernstein 2005), studies on the women's movement (e.g., Gilmore and Kaminski 2007) and LGBT movement (Creed and Scully 2000; Rupp and Taylor 2003; Hennen 2004; Engel 2007; Dugan 2008) reveal how the strategic use of identity, or "identity deployment" (Bernstein 1997), influences movement goals, outcomes, and the selection of state and non-state targets (Bernstein and Olsen 2009). The reconceptualization of power and the strategic use of identity in women's and LGBT movements have paved the way for a multi-institutional politics approach to studying all social movements (Armstrong and Bernstein 2008).

As this brief overview illustrates, the study of gender and sexuality movements has transformed the field in profound ways. In this chapter, we will discuss three fundamental ways in which this body of scholarship has influenced theoretical directions for the study of social movements by focusing, specifically, on the concepts of collective identity, multi-institutional politics, and emotions. Throughout our discussion we highlight how key concepts and theories from the fields of gender and sexuality have influenced the study of social movements more generally. After reviewing these fundamental contributions, we suggest promising avenues for future research.

Collective Identity

The notion of identity and how activist groups perceive themselves and others shapes and is shaped by their worldview and daily interactions with opponents and fellow activists, influencing the type of tactics and strategies they employ and the goals they seek to attain. Identity permeates various aspects of movements, including conversations, discourse, practices, and collective displays (Stryker, Owens, and White 2000; Reger, Myers, and Einwohner 2008). A major insight of new social movement theory is that collective identity, which translates structural inequality and injustice into individual dissatisfaction, is a primary social psychological dynamic of mobilization (Pizzorno 1978; Touraine 1985; Melucci 1989; Castells 1997). Research on gender and sexuality movements has contributed to our understanding of collective identity by illuminating the processes by which it is constructed, the strategic dilemmas that arise over the course of its construction, and its role in both sustaining and demobilizing movements. Debates over sameness and difference are central to our understanding of gender and sexuality movements, which, consequently, has led scholars to recognize the need for paying attention to the construction and deployment of collective identity in all social movements (Taylor 1989; Bernstein 1997).

In their study of lesbian feminist communities, Taylor and Whittier (1992) define collective identity as "the shared definition of a group that derives from members' common interests, experiences, and solidarity" (105) and present a formal model that specifies three dimensions of collective identity: boundary maintenance between group members and dominant groups; political consciousness, which manifests in the process of framing as groups seek to define and advance their interests; and negotiation whereby group members work to transform symbols and engage in strategic actions that challenge the status quo (see Hunt and Benford 2004 for a recent review of this research). While collective identity is a key concept in the European new social movement tradition (Touraine 1985; Melucci 1989), Taylor and Whittier's (1992) framework makes a unique contribution by providing conceptual tools that can be applied to examining how a wide range of movements construct contentious identities.

Some scholars have examined broader historical processes and/or the emergence of new models in cognitive science to reveal how challenging groups develop politicized identities (Polletta and Jasper 2001). For instance, D'Emilio (1983) examines how macrohistorical processes such as industrialization and urbanization, along with the rise of a new psychiatric paradigm of homosexuality, facilitated the social construction of a homosexual group identity that the dominant society considered deviant. While individuals engaged in isolated homosexual acts before the nineteenth century, it was these broader historical processes that enabled a collective identity to emerge in the twentieth century despite government repression, which was eventually met with collective resistance (D'Emilio 1983; Seidman 1993; Rupp 2011). This work unsettles prior understandings of homosexual identity as a "natural" category by revealing its historical and cultural variability (Polletta and Jasper 2001).

By examining institutional settings, movement scholars have introduced useful concepts for understanding the construction of contentious identities, including "sequestered social sites" (Scott 1990), "halfway houses" (Morris 1984), "free spaces" (Evans and Boyte 1986), "havens" (Hirsch 1990) and "submerged networks" (Melucci 1989; Mueller 1994). Meanwhile, Rupp and Taylor's (1987) analysis of the women's movement in *Survival in the Doldrums* introduced the new concept of "abeyance structures," which is useful for understanding how collective identity can sustain movements through periods of retrenchment and decline. Empirically, their work challenged the dominant view that the US women's movement died after the suffrage victory in the 1920s and was later reborn in the 1960s by showing how the movement sustained itself during the interim through its shared collective identity. Their findings also challenged prevailing mobilization theories that misinterpreted movement breakthroughs for "births" and movement decline for "deaths" by arguing instead for a more continuous understanding of movements as having turning points and thresholds (Taylor 1989).

Taylor and Whittier (1992) further specify—in their work on lesbian feminist communities—how boundary strategies, which involve a two-tiered process of building counterinstitutions and nurturing a unique culture separate from dominant society, are crucial to collective identity formation. Yet, establishing group membership may, at times, be contentious and engender bitter divisions, as several studies on feminist and gay/lesbian movements reveal (Echols 1989; Phelan 1989; Ryan 1992; Taylor and Rupp 1993; Bernstein 1997), although infighting can also produce positive dividends (Ghaziani 2008). In extreme cases, disputes might lead to exclusion of certain group members (Gamson 1997). Analyzing the Black community's inactive response to the AIDS crisis, Cohen (1999) asserts that struggles over inclusion have real material consequences, impacting the ways in which resources, services, and power are distributed within communities.

Gamson's (1995) analysis of "queer" politics in the gay and lesbian movement calls attention to a fundamental paradox facing stigmatized groups seeking to build a collective identity: essentialized identity categories form the basis of cultural oppression but are necessary for fighting institutional oppression (see also Epstein 1987 and Seidman 1993). A seemingly inescapable predicament, Gamson (1995) recognizes the utility of deconstructionist politics that aim to challenge cultural sources of oppression, on the one hand, and the need for an essentialized collective identity that challenges institutionalized sources of power, on the other hand. Turner (1999) reveals, in her study of the intersex movement, the challenges of collectively mobilizing behind a social identity, while simultaneously acknowledging a medicalized discourse that colonizes bodies. Intersexed activists describe themselves as "hermaphrodites with attitude" to ironically invoke quaint medical labels, yet, in doing so, run the risk of reinforcing the hetero/homo binary and perpetuating a pathologized identity. This "queer dilemma," as Gamson (1995) refers to it, is relevant beyond gender and sexuality movements. For example, with more and more people identifying as multiracial, racially based movements face similar predicaments (Lorber 1999).

Creating and sustaining a collective identity is no easy task though, thus requiring "identity work." Constructing a movement identity is shaped by the "activist environment" and involves both internal and external struggles and challenges at the macro, meso, and micro levels. Such work primarily rests on notions of "sameness" and "difference," which refer to the similarities and differences group members simultaneously share with dominant groups, their targets, and each other as well as the competing demands and challenges involved in negotiating between the two (Einwohner et al. 2008). Drawing on four campaigns for lesbian and gay rights statutes, Bernstein (1997) seeks to explain why groups shift their focus over time between strategies that celebrate and suppress differences from the majority, as they interact with social movement organizations, state actors, and opponents, and under what political conditions such identities are deployed strategically. Bernstein presents a general model of identity and argues that there are three analytic dimensions of "identity" that must remain distinct when studying the role of identity in social movements (1997, 2002, 2005, 2008, 2009). The first dimension, identity for empowerment, maintains that activists need to construct a collective identity in order to mobilize movement participants to take political action. Second, identity may be a movement goal as activists work to challenge stigmatized identities, receive recognition for new identities, and/or deconstruct oppressive social categories. The third dimension, identity as strategy or "identity deployment," refers to expressing identity such that the terrain of conflict becomes the individual person so that the values, categories, and practices of individuals become subject to debate. Identity deployment can be analyzed at the individual and collective level along a continuum from education to critique. A mixed model drawing on both strategies may also be employed (Bernstein 1997). And both state and non-state structures may be the targets of identity deployment strategies (Armstrong and Bernstein 2008). Identity for critique confronts the values, categories, and practices of the dominant culture, while identity for education challenges the dominant culture's perception of the minority or is used strategically to gain legitimacy by playing on uncontroversial themes, but both can be aimed toward cultural and political goals (1997). The interrelationships or "feedback loops" that connect these analytic levels remain understudied and should also be examined (Bernstein 2008). Ultimately, Bernstein (1997) finds that when faced with opposition and a closed polity, gay and lesbian activists sought to advance their civil rights by deploying critical identities that emphasized their differences from the majority. On the other hand, movement organizations faced with an open polity deployed identity for education. Rather than celebrating their differences they suppressed them, underscoring their similarities to the majority instead. At the same time, other activists found it necessary to adopt a mixed model as their strategy. Movements may also seek to avoid identity strategies altogether by invoking abstract concepts such as justice and fairness (Bernstein 2002). For movements that do strategically deploy identities, they invite what Bernstein (2008) refers to as an "identity contest," which takes places between various challengers and bystanders making competing claims over an issue.

Bernstein's (1997) concept "identity deployment" has been further developed in other studies on the lesbian and gay movement (Rupp and Taylor 2003; Hennen 2004; Engel 2007; Dugan 2008), the women's movement (Gilmore and Kaminski 2007), and a host of other movements beyond so-called "identity movements," like the gay and lesbian movement, and may be deployed performatively, rhetorically, and/or discursively by movements with or without face-to-face interaction (see Bernstein and Olsen 2009 for a recent review). For example, within the workplace, lesbian and gay employees deploy identities to achieve cultural goals, like fighting stigma, through casual encounters and educating co-workers, and by transforming corporate policies and practices (Taylor and Raeburn 1995; Creed and Scully 2000; Button 2004). Research on the gay and lesbian movement also reveals how identity can be strategically deployed in non-performative ways through rhetorical and discursive strategies such as printed materials (e.g., mass mailings of postcards and letters to the editor) (Dugan 2008). For example, Loeske and Cavendish (2001) demonstrate how the rhetoric of newsletters published by the gay Catholic organization Dignity created a narrative character that is, at the same time, both proudly gay and devoutly Catholic, seemingly contradictory identities. Finally, identity deployment can be used as an organizational strategy. In their analysis of the National Organization for Women, Gilmore and Kaminski (2007) demonstrate how rank-and-file members helped collectively shift the organization's identity by compelling it to be more inclusive of lesbian feminists. Over the past decade, research on gender and sexuality movements has also investigated the wide range of tactical and cultural repertoires that movements use to deploy collective identities, including music, street performance, ritual, art, theater, and practices of everyday life (Gamson 1989; Bernstein 1997; Staggenborg and Lang 2007; Kaminski and Taylor 2008; Rupp, Taylor, and Shapiro 2010; Reger 2012). Jasper (1997) finds that movements develop a "taste" for specific tactics, while Polletta and Jasper (2001) argue that activists often select strategies and adopt tactical styles that reflect their movement identities (Polletta 2002; Ferber 2004; Taylor and Van Dyke 2004). For instance, the ritualization of music in drag performances, which has a long history in the LGBT community, helps performers deploy identity strategically as a way to critique and educate audiences (Kaminski and Taylor 2008). Strategic preferences may be solidified by collective identities before a movement emerges and develop external to the movement (Ennis 1987) or internally, as Whittier's (1995) work on "micro-cohorts" in the women's movement illustrates (Polletta and Jasper 2001).

MULTI-INSTITUTIONAL POLITICS

Although some political process and contentious politics scholars continue to question whether collective challenges that do not target the state constitute social movements (McAdam, Tarrow, and Tilly 2001), in the past decade a number of scholars have conceptualized the study of social movements from a less state-centric perspective (Cress and Myers 2004; Snow 2004; Van Dyke, Soule, and Taylor 2004; Staggenborg and Taylor 2005; Jasper 2006; Snow and Soule 2010; Taylor and Zald 2010). Research on gender and sexuality movements, in particular, has pushed the field to recognize that movements target an array of state and non-state institutions (Taylor and Raeburn 1995; Taylor and Van Dyke 2004; Raeburn 2004; Taylor et al. 2009; Klawiter 2008; Taylor and Zald 2010). Drawing from the body of scholarship that situates movements within multiple institutional arenas, Armstrong and Bernstein (2008) developed a "multi-institutional politics" (MIP) approach that offers theoretical tools for studying a range of collective actions in modern society.

The political process model is rooted in a Marxist or neo-Marxist conception of power that narrowly defines power and politics as centralized in the state and the economy. By contrast, contemporary theories of power and politics, including approaches advanced by European new social movement theory (Giddens 1991; Touraine 1992; Melucci 1996), feminist theory (Collins 1990; Smith 1990; Naples 1998), contemporary cultural theory (Bourdieu 1977; Foucault 1977; Crossley 2002), and institutional theory (Fligstein 1991; Friedland and Alford 1991; Powell and DiMaggio 1991; Sewell 1992), conceptualize power in late modern societies as multidimensional and as both symbolic and material. Such a view of power calls for a more inclusive definition of social movements.

The MIP approach argues that domination in modern society can be best understood as resulting from multiple sources of power that are dispersed throughout numerous institutions. The state remains relevant, but its importance is historically and culturally variable, contrary to political process theories that view its significance as a constant. Society is seen as being comprised of a variety of institutions that operate on diverse and, at times, contradictory institutional logics, which shape movement goals and strategies. Institutional power is both symbolic and material and movements may challenge a variety of state and non-state targets (e.g., institutions, practices, cultural norms, and knowledge systems) when waging interconnected struggles over classification and distribution (Fraser 1997; Armstrong and Bernstein 2008; Bernstein 2013). The study of social movements in multi-institutional context has forced theorists to rethink how they understand who counts as an activist, what counts as activism, mobilization, strategies, goals, and outcomes.

In her comparative study on feminists in the American Catholic Church and US military, Katzenstein (1998) argues that the proximity of institutions to the state and law shape protest strategies and outcomes. Lacking access to the law, feminists in the

Catholic Church engaged in "discursive politics" to rethink the role of women in society and church, while feminists in the military—with access to the law—maintained the status quo by embracing liberal, interest-group strategies, as they fought for pay equity, access to jobs, and against sexual harassment.

To examine health-related movements, Taylor and Zald (2010) synthesize institutional and social movement theories. They argue that health movements form in myriad ways, including around alternative specializations and various systems of treatment and diagnosis. Such movements may also form around diseases, illnesses, and health-related issues (Taylor 1996; Brown 2007). For example, Klawiter (2004, 2008) argues that a paradigm shift in "disease regimes" transformed women's relationship to breast cancer from an either/or condition to a disease continuum. This changing relationship to the disease led to the creation of support groups that provided emotional comfort for women and fostered social networks and group solidarities that, in turn, fueled the breast cancer movement.

In some cases, different movements use different strategies when mobilizing around similar targets. The contemporary intersex movement challenges the ways in which the medical establishment assigns people to gender categories and doctors' authority to perform genital surgery. They wage these linked challenges over classification and corporeal body practices by drawing on lay understandings of their own bodies to question expert knowledge (Preves 2003). On the contrary, Epstein (1995, 1996) reveals how AIDS activists intentionally sought to blur the lay/expert dichotomy by acquiring scientific language and culture, which enabled them to establish scientific credibility and transform the way knowledge is constructed and research carried out by the biomedical community.

Meanwhile, some LGBT movements have targeted organizations as well as corporations. Corporations have become an increasingly important site for collective challenges (Soule 2009), especially in light of recent scholarly efforts to link theories from the fields of social movements and organizational sociology (Davis and Zald 2005). Raeburn (2004) demonstrates how lesbian and gay employees fighting for domestic partner benefits in Fortune 1000 companies formed networks and eventually inter-organizational ties through "virtual opportunities," which enabled them to win health benefits for domestic partners in hundreds of companies nationwide. Theoretically, she develops an "institutional opportunity framework" that elucidates key processes and structures, while advancing an understanding of how social movements form inside of organizations. Armstrong (2002a, 2002b, 2005) examines LGBT organizations and identities in San Francisco from 1950 to the 1990s. Dominant social movement theories were unable to explain the proliferation and diversity of organizations in the LGBT community, such as the institutionalization of gay pride parades, so she draws on institutional theory instead. Applying a MIP approach allows Armstrong and Bernstein (2008) to extend her analysis. They argue that the proliferation of organizations is a response to the multi-sited nature of heteronormativity. Situating the movement within a multi-institutional system provides greater clarity and a wider context for understanding the proliferation of organizations and the emergence of new identities and institutional challenges.

Joshua Gamson poses the question of "who is the enemy?" in his study on ACT UP (AIDS Coalition to Unleash Power), while seeking to explain the various strategies the movement employed as it challenged state and non-state targets. Like Armstrong, Gamson was unable to explain the movement's choice of targets from a political process approach. Instead, he draws on European New Social Movement theory and Foucault to argue that, apart from concrete state and non-state targets, ACT UP was targeting an "abstract, disembodied, invisible" enemy (1989). Applying a MIP approach extends Gamson's analysis by revealing how ACT UP was, in fact, fighting a concrete, embodied, and visible "enemy" in its efforts to challenge a multi-institutional system of domination that enacts and perpetuates heteronormativity (Armstrong and Bernstein 2008).

Bernstein (2003, 2005) compares the strategies of lesbian and gay activists seeking to decriminalize sodomy in the United States over different time periods. In the wake of the 1986 *Bowers v. Hardwick* decision, which denied the constitutional right to consensual "homosexual" sodomy, Bernstein found that activists responded to shifts in the political opportunity structure in ways that political process theories could not account for. While political opportunities can lead to successful policy outcomes, repealing repressive laws lacks meaningful change if hegemonic discourse remains unchallenged. That said, she found that activists at times prioritized changing the cultural consensus against homosexuality at the expense of legal and political goals. Understood through a MIP approach, state legal institutions are producers of cultural meaning as well as laws that have material and symbolic consequences, which pose strategic dilemmas for activists (Armstrong and Bernstein 2008).

Emotions

A wide range of emotions, including shame, fear, love, pride, depression, and anger, arise from an individual's and a group's social locations within hierarchies of status and power (Kemper 1978). As Jim Jasper observes: "[e]motions are present in every phase and every aspect of protest ... They can help or hinder mobilization efforts, ongoing strategies, and the success of social movements" (2011: 286). The study of women's movements, particularly women's self-help movements, and LGBT movements has pushed the field to examine the role of emotions within social movements and to rethink excessively structural and rational models. Early on, feminist scholars took the lead in challenging the rationalist assumptions of dominant frameworks, such as resource mobilization and political process theories, that for so long denied the place of emotions in movement mobilization and participation (Fraser 1997; Armstrong and Bernstein 2008; Bernstein 2013), a reality that emotion and social movement scholars also recognize (Goodwin and Jasper 1999). While, increasingly, researchers are conducting work on emotions in non-feminist movements (see Ferree and Merrill 2000; Goodwin et al. 2001; Aminzade and McAdam 2002; Einwohner 2002; Shrivasta 2006), the role of emotions in collective action was first seriously taken up in studies on gender and sexuality movements (Rupp and Taylor 1987; Taylor 1989, 1995, 1996, 2000, 2010; Taylor and Whittier 1992, 1995; Matthews 1994; Gamson 1995; Morgen 1995; Gould 2001, 2003, 2009).

All social movements engage, on some level, in what Hochschild (1983) calls "emotion labor" to help participants transform negative emotions that can be channeled constructively in ways that advance the goals and strategies of a movement (Taylor 2010). For example, the high rate of depression among women, which is tied to gender subordination (Mirowsky and Ross 1989; Jack 1991), spurred the development of a variety of women's health and self-help movements (Taylor 1996; Whittier 2009). Not altogether surprising, the emotional division of labor in movements has been found to be gendered. For example, in the civil rights movement, Robnett (1997) highlights how formal leaders, such as Martin Luther King, Jr., made emotional appeals to audiences in public forums, while women engaged in behind the scenes grass-roots organizing efforts by fostering emotional ties with local residents. Forging such ties was crucial to recruiting residents to engage in high-risk activism. Likewise, the rewards of emotion labor are also gendered. Kleinman (1996) argues in her study of a holistic health center that women and men were not rewarded equally for displaying the same emotions: men enhanced their status by expressing an ethic of care, while women were discouraged from acting overly emotional, thus ensuring the maintenance of structural inequalities along gender lines. In a similar vein, Groves (1995, 1997, 2001) finds, in her study of the animal rights movement, that women sought to constrain the expression of "irrational" emotions, which they feared would discredit the cause. Accommodating only the expression of "acceptable anger," they favored a "rational" approach that privileged scientific reasoning and a professional outlook. Although, historically, women comprised the majority of the movement, because women perceived men as more rational and therefore more credible, men occupied a disproportionate number of prominent positions within the movement.

Scholars have shown how movements develop distinctive *emotion cultures*, which are integral to mobilizing efforts. Social movement actors use emotion-laden rituals to engender solidarity and self-transformation among participants in ways that inspire and sustain activism. Social movements create distinctive emotion cultures that define the appropriate ways in which movement participants should express and manage emotions in the presence of fellow activists and when engaging with elites, opponents, and targets (Taylor and Whittier 1995; Taylor and Leitz 2010). For example, Taylor (1995) notes how the planning committee for the 1991 National Lesbian Conference designated several women as "vibes watchers" who were responsible for "staying alert to the collective emotional climate and advising us when to stop for a deep breath, a moment of silence or a group scream."

Yet emotional rules and conventions are not set in stone: they can change over the course of a movement's history. In her study on the radical AIDS activist group ACT UP, Gould defines her theoretical framework of *emotional habitus* as the "socially constituted, prevailing ways of feeling and emoting, as well as the embodied, axiomatic understandings and norms about feelings and their expression" (2009: 10). She argues that the emotional habitus of the LGBT community shifted over time and profoundly shaped movement participants' attitudes and actions (2009). For instance, at the height of gay liberation, pride and militant activism were linked. Early on in the AIDS crisis though, activists used pride to submerge anger, encourage volunteerism, remember the dead, and engage in quiet lobbying instead of "rocking the boat." As the crisis wore on and in the face of an ever-constraining political opportunity structure, the anger of the LGBT community ignited and pride once again became linked to oppositional politics (Gould 2001).

The emotion cultures of social movements may also form across cultures. In their study of the transnational women's movement that organized from the late nineteenth century through World War II, Taylor and Rupp (2002) find that the emotion culture was central to building solidarity and identity among activist groups from different countries. The movement fostered an emotional culture that allowed activists to forge a feminist collective identity that transcended national borders, ensuring the movement's survival and growth despite years of war, economic depression, revolution, and the emergence of fascism.

Whittier (2001) argues that emotional displays of participants in the movement against child sexual abuse were shaped, in part, by what she terms "emotional opportunities." Emotional opportunities become available depending on whether extra-movement contexts are favorable to activists. The concept of emotional opportunities is helpful for understanding how movement participants perceive the political and discursive opportunities in external environments and why some emotional strategies aid mobilizing efforts, while other feeling displays fail to resonate.

As movements continue to challenge state and non-state targets across a variety of institutional settings, it has become necessary to consider how activists learn and express emotions favorable to protest in diverse contexts (Taylor 2010). In their work on drag queen performances, Rupp and Taylor (2003) contend that drag shows are cultural repertoires through which performers render visible gay identities, transgress norms around gender and sexuality, while constructing a collective identity on stage. Kaminski and Taylor (2008) find that drag queens strategically use music and song to parody conventional understandings about femininity and masculinity, which elicits a range of emotions among audience members and fosters an oppositional community. While emotions are crucial for building collective identity, they can also be used strategically to achieve policy goals. Taylor and Leitz (2010) examined a pen-pal network of women sent to prison for committing infanticide while suffering postpartum depression and psychosis and found that active involvement in the network was emotionally transformative, compelling participants to seek policy change for other women who commit infanticide while suffering from the same illness.

While the relationship between emotions and perceptions of injustice are complicated (Goodwin et al. 2001; Jasper 1998), a substantial body of work on women's and sexuality movements (Hercus 2005; Reger 2004; Lyman 2004; Guenther 2009; Summers-Effler

2002; Gould 2001), and other movements more generally (e.g., Shrivasta 2006; Klandermans et al. 2008), have demonstrated the mobilizing potential of anger. In her case study of the New York City chapter of the National Organization for Women, Reger (2004) elucidates how feminist consciousness-raising groups empower women to transform personal emotions of hopelessness, frustration, alienation, and anger into a sense of injustice that promotes collective action. Taylor et al. (2009) examine the 2004 same-sex marriage protest in San Francisco and find that anger over the Supreme Court's invalidation of the marriages of more than 4,000 people who participated in the 2004 marriage protests played a significant role in mobilizing participants to join LGBT organizations promoting marriage equality. Most of the couples who engaged in the protest had been involved in previous social movements. Thus, anger was a mobilizing *affect* in what Gould (2009) terms the emotional habitus of the campaign for same-sex marriage. Meanwhile, Hercus (1999) finds that anger among feminists was a common reaction to frames that reflected feminist concerns and experiences. When feminists interacted with the broader community though, they felt the need to restrain their anger and other deviant emotions through emotion work. Her study advances an understanding of the role of emotions in bringing about collective action and the emotional costs and benefits involved in such an endeavor.

CONCLUSION

In this chapter, we have examined the ways in which studying gender and sexuality movements has influenced the study of social movements more generally. Feminist scholars have demonstrated how gender plays a central role in shaping the emergence, trajectory, and outcomes of movements. Studies on gender and sexuality movements have challenged dominant theories in the field by reconceptualizing power, the types of protest, tactics, and targets that count as legitimate and, in turn, the very definition of social movements. Our discussion has demonstrated contributions significant to the body of research on collective identity, multi-institutional politics, and emotions. We have highlighted key concepts and theories from the fields of gender and sexuality that have entered the field of social movements.

For instance, in our section on collective identity, we noted the influence of the concept "abeyance structures" that Taylor (1989) first introduced in a study of the women's movement (Taylor and Rupp 1987). The concept is useful for understanding how collective identity can sustain movements through periods of retrenchment and decline and has had real analytic staying power (Whittier 1995; Reger 2005; Grey and Sawer 2008). Scholars have also employed the concept to study various other movements, including submerged socialist movements in Australia, France, and Italy (Fillieule 2004), movements in democratic transition in Latin America, South Africa, and Asia (Klandermans 2008), and "digital abeyance structures" of online activism (Earl and Schussman 2003).

Research on gender and sexuality movements has also pushed scholars to examine not only how collective identities are constructed and help sustain movements but also how collective identities are deployed as a social movement strategy. Bernstein's (1997) political identity model, which specifies three analytic levels of identity (i.e., identity for empowerment, as goal, and as strategy), together with her notion of identity deployment, has been applied to study a wide range of movements (Bernstein and Olsen 2009). But there is ripe research still to be done in this area, especially with respect to examining identity as a goal of social movements—whether to deconstruct existing identities and/or secure recognition for new identities as well as examining the interrelationships or "feedback loops" that connect these three analytic levels of identity. Undertaking such research could help to answer central questions within social movement theory, including the types of relationships among the analytic levels of identity that impact mobilization, strategic decisions, and outcomes (Bernstein 2008).

At the same time, gender and sexuality movement scholars have reconceptualized power as emanating from multiple sources and myriad institutions, as opposed to dominant theories that view power as centralized in the state and the economy. This reconceptualization combined with analyses of social movements targeted at other non-state institutions such as science (e.g., Moore 1999), health (Taylor and Zald 2010), and religion (Kane 2013; Katzenstein 1998) has led to the development of a "multi-institutional politics" (MIP) approach to understanding social movements (Armstrong and Bernstein 2008; Taylor and Zald 2010). Beyond gender and sexuality-based movements, the MIP framework is currently being employed to analyze a wide range of social movements, including Islamic movements in Turkey (Gurbuz and Bernstein 2012), racial truth regimes in the multi-racial Hapa movement (Bernstein and De La Cruz 2009), protests targeting private businesses such as Wal-Mart (Ingram et al. 2010), and knowledge production practices (Waidzunas 2013). This approach provides theoretical tools for analyzing how different forms of power in a variety of institutional and cultural contexts create conditions favorable to the mobilization of protest. Future research should continue to investigate the impact that diverse institutional logics and their corresponding forms of power have on shaping movement participants, tactics and strategies, and goals, especially as movements seek to capitalize on institutional vulnerabilities. Attention should also be devoted to examining how movement participants interpret, negotiate, and understand the different forms of power that prevail in different institutional contexts. Furthermore, this approach may be particularly useful for understanding the rise of new transnational social movements (Armstrong and Bernstein 2008).

The study of gender and sexuality movements has challenged scholars to recognize the role of emotions within social movements and to move beyond excessively structural and rational models. Gould's (2009) emotional habitus framework could be applied to studies beyond LGBT movements to further theorize under which political conditions the emotional habitus of a movement shifts over time and the ways in which certain emotions both facilitate and hinder mobilization and collective action. The examination of cultural dimensions of protest and contentious politics answers a different set of questions from the structural and state-centered resource mobilization and political process theories. Practitioners of cultural approaches bring culture to the fore by paying attention to the everyday practices and meanings of movement participants, and employing a broader view of targets and tactics, while still paying close attention to institutional and political structures. Those who have focused on the salience of collective identity, multi-institutional politics, and emotions to social movements and their participants have not only expanded the scope of the field but have also been central to the cultural turn in social movement scholarship.

While the research on LGBT movements discussed in this chapter focuses primarily on LGBT movements in democratic regimes, this research can provide guidance for the study of LGBT and sexuality movements in authoritarian or hybrid regimes as well. For example, as the MIP approach suggests, the importance of the state is variable both cross-nationally and over time. This insight requires that scholars simultaneously take the state and forms of state power into account while also taking seriously the idea that in different national and local contexts other institutions may also be important and that the relationships between various institutions and the state is something that cannot be taken for granted as static but must be theorized in different contexts and different time periods. For example, the formal power of religious authorities over both gender and sexuality is variable and may affect our understanding of these movements in different types of regimes. Furthermore, concepts such as "discursive opportunity structure" (Ferree et al. 2002) remind us that not only do institutional structures matter to understanding gender and sexuality movements (and social movements more generally), but the cultural and discursive context matter as well, shaping what types of claims may be perceived as radical in one context or time period, but not another. Understanding the institutional context, including the state, as well as the discursive and cultural context can help to explain the emergence, development, strategies, goals, and targets of social movements and why they change over time in a variety of types of political regimes (e.g., Smith 2008; Currier 2009, 2012; Bernstein and Naples 2010; Ferree 2012).

AUTHOR NOTE

We would like to thank Alison Crossley for her assistance on this chapter.

REFERENCES

Abdulhadi, Rabab I. (1998). "The Palestinian Women's Autonomous Movement: Emergence, Dynamics, and Challenges," *Gender & Society*. 12(6): 649–673.

Acker, Joan (1990). "Hierarchies, Jobs, Bodies: A Theory of Gendered Organizations," *Gender & Society*. 4: 139–158.

Aminzade, Ronald and McAdam, Doug (2002). "Emotions and Contentious Politics." In *Silence and Voice in the Study of Contentious Politics*, edited by Ronald Aminzade et al., 14–50. New York: Cambridge University Press.

Armstrong, Elizabeth (2002a). *Forging Gay Identities: Organizing Sexuality in San Francisco, 1950–1994*. Chicago: University of Chicago Press.

Armstrong, Elizabeth (2002b). "Crisis, Collective Creativity, and the Generation of New Organizational Forms: The Transformation of Lesbian/Gay Organizations in San Francisco." In *Research in the Sociology of Organizations*, edited by Michael Lounsbury and Marc Ventresca, 361–95. Oxford: JAI Press.

Armstrong, Elizabeth (2005). "From Struggle to Settlement: The Crystallization of a Field of Lesbian/Gay Organizations in San Francisco, 1969–1973." In *Social Movements and Organization Theory*, edited by Gerald F. Davis, Doug McAdam, W. Richard Scott, and Mayer N. Zald, 161–87. Cambridge: Cambridge University Press.

Armstrong, E. A. and Bernstein, M. (2008). "Culture, Power, and Institutions: A Multi-Institutional Politics Approach to Social Movements," *Sociological Theory*. 26: 74–99.

Beckwith, Karen (1996). "Lancashire Women Against Pit Closures: Women's Standing in a Men's Movement," *Signs: Journal of Women in Culture and Society*. 21: 1034–1068.

Bernstein, Mary (1997). "Celebration and Suppression: The Strategic Uses of Identity by the Lesbian and Gay Movement," *American Journal of Sociology*. 103: 531–565.

Bernstein, Mary (2002). "Identities and Politics: Toward a Historical Understanding of the Lesbian and Gay Movement," *Social Science History*. 26(3): 531–581.

Bernstein, Mary (2003). "Nothing Ventured, Nothing Gained? Conceptualizing Social Movement 'Success' in the Lesbian and Gay Movement," *Sociological Perspectives*. 46: 353–379.

Bernstein, Mary (2005). "Identity Politics," *Annual Review of Sociology*. 31: 47–74.

Bernstein, Mary (2008). "The Analytic Dimensions of Identity: A Political Identity Framework." In *Identity Work in Social Movements*, edited by J. Reger, D. J. Meyers and R. L. Einwohner, 277–301. Minneapolis: University of Minnesota Press.

Bernstein, Mary (2013). "Power, Politics and Social Movements: A Multi-institutional Politics Approach," *Politics, Groups, and Identities*. 1(1): 87–93.

Bernstein, Mary and De la Cruz, Marcie (2009). "What Are You? Explaining Identity as a Goal of the Multiracial Hapa Movement," *Social Problems*. 56(4): 722–745.

Bernstein, Mary and Naples, Nancy A. (2010). "Sexual Citizenship and the Pursuit of Relationship Recognition Policies in Australia and the U.S," *Women's Studies Quarterly*. 38(1&2): 132–156.

Bernstein, Mary and Olsen, Kristine A. (2009). "Identity Deployment and Social Change: Understanding Identity as a Social Movement and Organizational Strategy," *Sociology Compass*. 3: 871–883.

Blee, Kathleen M. (1991). *Women of the Klan: Racism and Gender in the 1920s*. Berkeley: University of California Press.

Blee, Kathleen M. (1996). "Becoming a Racist: Women in Contemporary Ku Klux Klan and Neo-Nazi Groups," *Gender & Society*. 10: 680–702.

Blee, Kathleen M. (1998). *No Middle Ground: Women and Radical Protest*. New York: New York University Press.

Bourdieu, Pierre (1977). *Outline of a Theory of Practice*. New York: Cambridge University Press.

Brown, Phil (2007). *Toxic Exposures: Contested Illnesses and the Environmental Health Movement*. New York: Columbia University Press.

Bruce, Katherine M. (2013). "LGBT Pride as a Cultural Protest Tactic in a Southern City," *Journal of Contemporary Ethnography*. 42(5): 608–635.

Button, S. B. (2004). "Identity Management Strategies Utilized by Lesbian and Gay Employees," *Group & Organization Management*. 29(4): 470–494.

Castells, Manuel (1997). *The Power of Identity*. Malden, MA: Blackwell.

Clemens, Elisabeth S. (1993). "Organizational Repertoires and Institutional Change: Women's Groups and the Transformation of American Politics, 1890–1920," *American Journal of Sociology*. 98(4): 755–798.

Cohen, Cathy J. (1999). *The Boundaries of Blackness: AIDS and the Breakdown of Black Politics*. Chicago, IL: University of Chicago Press.

Collins, Patricia Hill (1990). *Black Feminist Thought: Knowledge, Consciousness and the Politics of Empowerment*. New York: Routledge.

Connell, R. W. (1987). *Gender and Power: Society, the Person, and Sexual Politics*. Sidney: Allen and Unwin.

Creed, W. E. D. and Scully, M. A. (2000). "Songs of Ourselves: Employees Deployment of Social Identity in Workplace Encounters," *Journal of Management Inquiry*. 9(4): 391–412.

Cress, Daniel, and Myers, Daniel (2004). "Authorities in Contention." In *Authorities in Contention, Research in Social Movements, Conflicts and Change*, vol. 25, edited by Daniel Myers and Daniel Cress, 279–93. San Diego: Elsevier.

Crossley, Nick (2002). *Making Sense of Social Movements*. Philadelphia: Open University Press.

Currier, Ashley (2009). "Deferral of Legal Tactics: A Global LGBT Social Movement Organization's Perspective." In *Queer Mobilizations: LGBT Activists Confront the Law*, edited by Scott Barclay, Mary Bernstein, and Anna-Maria Marshall, 21–37. New York: NYU Press.

Currier, Ashley (2012). *Out in Africa: LGBT Organizing in Namibia and South Africa*. Minneapolis: University of Minnesota Press.

D'Emilio, John (1983). *Sexual Politics, Sexual Communities*. Chicago, IL: University Chicago Press.

Davis, Kathy (2007). *The Making of Our Bodies, Ourselves: How Feminism Travels Across Borders*. Duke University Press.

Davis, G. F. and Zald, M. N. (2005). "Social Change, Social Theory, and the Convergence of Movements and Organizations." In *Social Movements and Organization Theory*, edited by G. F. Davis, D. McAdam, W. Richard Scott, and M. N. Zald, 335–350. Cambridge: Cambridge University Press.

Dugan, K. B. (2008). "Just Like You: The Dimensions of Identity Presentations in an Antigay Contested Context." In *Identity Work in Social Movements*, edited by J. Reger, D. J. Meyers and R. L. Einwohner, 21–46. Minneapolis: University of Minnesota Press.

Earl, Jennifer and Schussman, Alan (2003). "The New Site of Activism: On-line Organizations, Movement Entrepreneurs, and the Changing Location of Social Movement Decision-Making," *Research in Social Movements, Conflicts and Change*. 24: 155–187.

Echols, Alice (1989). *Daring to Be Bad: Radical Feminism in America, 1967–1975*. Minneapolis: University of Minnesota Press.

Einwohner, Rachel L. (1999). "Gender, Class, and Social Movement Outcomes: Identity and Effectiveness in Two Animal Rights Campaigns," *Gender & Society*. 13: 56–76.

Einwohner, Rachel L. (2002). "Bringing the Outsiders In: Opponents' Claims and the Construction of Animal Rights Activists' Identity," *Mobilization*. 7: 253–268.

Einwohner, Rachel L., Hollander, Jocelyn A., and Toska Olson (2000). "Engendering Social Movements: Cultural Images and Movement Dynamics," *Gender & Society*. 14(5): 679–699.

Einwohner, R., Reger, J., and Myers, D. J. (2008). "Identity Work, Sameness, and Difference in Social Movements." In *Identity Work in Social Movements*, edited by J. Reger, D. J. Meyers and R. L. Einwohner, 1–17. Minneapolis: University of Minnesota Press.

Engel, S. M. (2007). "Organizational Identity as a Constraint on Collective Action: A Comparative Analysis of Gay and Lesbian Interest Groups," *Studies in American Political Development*. 21(1): 66–91.

Ennis J. (1987). "Fields of Action: Structure in Movements' Tactical Repertoires," *Sociological Forum*. 2: 520–33.

Epstein S. (1987). "Gay Politics, Ethnic Identity: The Limits of Social Constructionism," *Socialist Review*. 93/94: 9–56.

Epstein S. (1996). *Impure Science: AIDS, Activism, and the Politics of Knowledge*. Berkeley: University of California Press.

Epstein S. (1995). "The Construction of Lay Expertise: AIDS Activism and the Forging of Credibility in the Reform of Clinical Trials," *Science, Technology, & Human Values*. 20(4): 408–37.

Evans, S., Boyte, H. (1986). *Free Spaces: The Sources of Democratic Change in America*. New York: Harper & Row.

Ferber, A. L., ed. (2004). *Home-Grown Hate: Gender and Organized Racism*. New York: Routledge.

Ferree, Myra Marx (1994). "'The Time of Chaos Was the Best': Feminist Mobilization and Demobilization in East Germany," *Gender & Society*. 8: 597–623.

Ferree, Myra Marx (1992). "The Political Context of Rationality: Rational Choice Theory and Resource Mobilization." In *Frontiers of Social Movement Theory*, edited by Aldon Morris and Carol Mueller, 29–52. New Haven CT: Yale University Press.

Ferree, Myra Marx (2012). *Varieties of Feminism: German Gender Politics in Global Perspective*. Stanford: Stanford University Press.

Ferree, Myra Marx, and Mueller, Carol McClurg (2004. "Feminism and the Women's Movement: A Global Perspective." In *The Blackwell Companion to Social Movements*, edited by David A. Snow, Sarah A. Soule, and Hanspeter Kriesi, 576–607. Oxford: Blackwell.

Ferree, Myra Marx and Merrill, David A. (2000). "Hot Movements, Cold Cognition: Thinking about Social Movements in Gendered Frames," *Contemporary Sociology*. 29(3): 454–62.

Ferree, Myra Marx, and Martin, Patricia Yancey, eds. (1995). *Feminist Organizations: Harvest of the New Women's Movement*. Philadelphia: Temple University Press.

Ferree, Myra Marx, and Roth, Silke (1998). "Gender, Class, and the Interaction Between Social Movements: A Strike of West Berlin Day Care Workers," *Gender & Society*. 12: 626–648.

Ferree, Myra Marx, Gamson, William A., Gerhards, Jürgen, and Rucht, Dieter (2002). *Shaping Abortion Discourse: Democracy and the Public Sphere in Germany and the United States*. Cambridge: Cambridge University Press.

Fillieule, Olivier (2004). *Devenirs Militants: Approches Sociologiques Du Desengagment*. Paris, France: Belin.

Fligstein, Neil (1991). "The Structural Transformation of American Industry: An Institutional Account of the Causes of Diversification in the Largest Firms, 1919–1979." In *The New Institutionalism in Organizational Analysis*, edited by Walter W. Powell and Paul J. DiMaggio, 311–36. Chicago: University of Chicago Press.

Fonow, Mary Margaret (1998). "Protest Engendered: The Participation of Women Steelworkers in the Wheeling-Pittsburgh Steel Strike of 1985," *Gender & Society*. 12: 710–728.

Foucault, Michel (1977). *Discipline and Punishment: The Birth of the Prison*. London: Penguin Books.

Fraser, N. (1997). *Justice Interruptus: Critical Reflections on the "Postsocialist" Condition*. New York: Routledge.

Friedland, Roger and Alford, Robert (1991). "Bringing Society Back in: Symbols, Practices, and Institutional Contradictions." In *The New Institutionalism in Organizational Analysis*, edited by Walter W. Powell and Paul J. DiMaggio, 232–66. Chicago: University of Chicago Press.

Gamson, Joshua (1989). "Silence, Death, and the Invisible Enemy: AIDS Activism and Social Movement 'Newness,'" *Social Problems*. 36: 351–367.

Gamson, Joshua (1995). "Must Identity Movements Self-Destruct? A Queer Dilemma," *Social Problems*. 42: 390–407.

Gamson, Joshua (1997). "Messages of Exclusion: Gender, Movement, and Symbolic Boundaries," *Gender & Society*. 11(2): 178–199.

Ghaziani, Amin (2008). *The Dividends of Dissent: How Conflict and Culture Work in Lesbian and Gay Marches on Washington*. Chicago: University of Chicago Press.

Giddens, Anthony (1991). *Modernity and Self-Identity: Self and Society in the Late Modern Age*. Stanford, CA: Stanford University Press.

Gilmore, S. and Kaminski, E. (2007). "A Part and Apart: Lesbian and Straight Feminist Activists Negotiate Identity in a Second-Wave Organization," *Journal of the History of Sexuality*. 16(1): 95–113.

Goodwin, Jeff and Jasper, James M. (1999). "Caught in a Winding, Snarling Vine: The Structural Bias of Political Process Theory," *Sociological Forum*. 14: 27–54.

Goodwin, Jeffrey, Jasper, James, and Polletta, Francesca (2001). *Passionate Politics: Emotions and Social Movements*. Chicago: University of Chicago Press.

Gould, Deborah (2001). "Rock the Boat, Don't Rock the Boat, Baby: Ambivalence and the Emergence of Militant AIDS Activism." In *Passionate Politics: Emotions and Social Movements*, edited by Jeff Goodwin, James Jasper, and Francesca Polletta, 135–57. Chicago: University of Chicago Press.

Gould, Deborah (2003). "Passionate Political Processes: Bringing Emotions Back into the Study of Social Movements." In *Rethinking Social Movements*, edited by J. Goodwin and J. M. Jasper, 282–302. Lanham, MD: Rowman & Littlefield.

Gould, Deborah (2009). *Moving Politics: Emotion and ACT UP's Fight against AIDS* Chicago. University of Chicago Press.

Grey, Sandra and Sawyer, Marian, eds. (2008). *Women's Movements: Flourishing or in Abeyance?* New York: Routledge.

Groves Julian M. (1995). "Learning to Feel: The Neglected Sociology of Social Movements," *Sociological Review*. 43: 435–461.

Groves Julian M. (1997). *Hearts and Minds: The Controversy over Laboratory Animals*. Philadelphia, PA: Temple University Press.

Groves Julian M. (2001). "Animal Rights and the Politics of Emotion: Folk Constructs of Emotions in the Animal Rights Movement." In *Passionate Politics: Emotions and Social Movements*, edited by Jeff Goodwin, James Jasper, and Francesca Polletta, 212–229. Chicago: University of Chicago Press.

Guenther, Katja M. (2009). "The Impact of Emotional Opportunity Structures on the Emotion Cultures of Feminist Organizations," *Gender & Society*. 23(3): 337–362.

Gurbuz, Mustafa and Bernstein, Mary (2012). " 'Thou Shall Not Protest!': Multi-Institutional Politics, Strategic Non-Confrontation and Islamic Mobilizations in Turkey," *Research in Social Movements, Conflict and Change*. 34: 63–91.

Hennen, P. (2004). "Fae Spirits and Gender Trouble: Resistance and Compliance Among the Radical Faeries," *Journal of Contemporary Ethnography* 33(5): 499–533.

Hercus, Cheryl (1999). "Identity, Emotion, and Feminist Collective Action," *Gender & Society*. 13: 34–55.

Hercus, Cheryl (2005). *Stepping Out of Line: Becoming and Being a Feminist*. New York and London: Routledge.

Hirsch, E. L. (1990). *Urban Revolt: Ethnic Politics in the Nineteenth-Century Chicago Labor Movement*. Berkeley: University of California Press.

Hochschild, A. (1983). *The Managed Heart: Commercialization of Human Feeling*. Berkeley: University of California Press.

Hunt Scott A. and Benford, Robert D. (2004). "Collective Identity, Solidarity, and Commitment." In *The Blackwell Companion to Social Movements*, edited by D. A. Snow, S. A. Soule, and H. Kriesi, 433–57. Oxford: Blackwell Publishing Ltd.

Ingram, Paul, Qingyuan Yue, Lori, and Rao, Hayagreeva (2010). "Trouble in Store: Probes, Protests, and Store Openings by Wal-Mart, 1998–2007," *American Journal of Sociology*. 116(1) (July): 53–92.

Irons, Jenny (1998). "The Shaping of Activist Recruitment and Participation: A Study of Women in the Mississippi Civil Rights Movement," *Gender & Society*. 12: 692–709.

Jack, Dana Crowley (1991). *Silencing the Self: Women and Depression*. Cambridge, MA: Harvard University Press.

Jasper, J. M. (1997). *The Art of Moral Protest*. Chicago: University Chicago Press.

Jasper, J. M. (1998). "The Emotions of Protest: Affective and Reactive Emotions in and around Social Movements," *Sociological Forum*. 13: 397–424.

Jasper, J. M. (2006). *Getting Your Way: Strategic Dilemmas in Social Life*. Chicago: University of Chicago Press.

Jasper, J. M. (2011). "Emotions and Social Movements: Twenty Years of Theory and Research," *Annual Review of Sociology*. 37: 285–303.

Kane, Melinda D. (2013). "LGBT Religious Activism: Predicting State Variations in the Number of Metropolitan Community Churches, 1974–2000," *Sociological Forum* 28(1): 135–158.

Katzenstein, M. F. (1998). *Faithful and Fearless: Moving Feminist Protest Instead the Church and Military*. Princeton: Princeton University Press.

Kaminski, Elizabeth and Taylor, Verta (2008). "'We're Not Just Lip-Synching Up Here': Music and Collective Identity in Drag Performances." In *Identity Work: Negotiating Sameness and Difference in Activist Environments*, edited by Rachel Einwohner, Dan Myers, and Jo Reger, 47–75. Minneapolis: University of Minnesota Press.

Kemper, Theodore (1978). *A Social Interactional Theory of Emotions*. New York: Wiley.

Klandermans, Bert (2008). "Movements in Times of Democratic Transition." Paper presented at a workshop in Belo Horizonte, Brazil. November, 19–21.

Klandermans, Bert, van der Toorn, Jojanneke, van Stekelenburg, Jackquelien (2008). "Embeddedness and Identity: How Immigrants Turn Grievances into Action," *American Sociological Review*. 73: 992–1012.

Klawiter, Maren (2008). *The Bio-Politics of Breast Cancer: Changing Cultures of Disease and Activism*. Minneapolis: University of Minnesota Press.

Klawiter, Maren (2004). "Breast Cancer in Two Regimes: The Impact of Social Movements on Illness Experience," *Sociology of Health & Illness*. 26: 845–874.

Kleinman, Sheryl (1996). *Opposing Ambitions*. Chicago: University of Chicago Press.

Loeske, D. R. and Cavendish, J. C. (2001). "Producing Institutional Selves: Rhetorically Constructing the Dignity of Sexually Marginalized Catholics," *Social Psychology Quarterly* 64(4): 347–362.

Lorber, Judith (1999). "Crossing Borders and Erasing Boundaries: Paradoxes of Identity Politics," *Sociological Focus*. 32(4): 355–370.

Lyman, Peter (2004). "The Domestication of Anger: The Use and Abuse of Anger in Politics," *European Journal of Social Theory*. 7(2): 133–147.

Matthews, Nancy A. (1994). *Confronting Rape: The Feminist Anti-Rape Movement and the State*. London: Routledge.

McAdam, Doug (1988). *Freedom Summer*. New York: Oxford University Press.

McAdam, Doug (1992). "Gender as a Mediator of the Activist Experience: The Case of Freedom Summer," *American Journal of Sociology*. 97: 1211–1240.

McAdam, Doug, Tarrow, Sidney, and Tilly, Charles (2001). *Dynamics of Contention*. Cambridge: Cambridge University Press.

McNair Barnett, Bernice (1993). "Invisible Southern Black Women Leaders in the Civil Rights Movement," *Gender & Society*. 7: 162–182.

Melucci, Alberto (1985). "The Symbolic Challenge of Contemporary Movements," *Social Research*. 52: 789–816.

Melucci, Alberto (1989). *Nomads of the Present: Social Movements and Individual Needs in Contemporary Society*. Philadelphia: Temple University Press.

Melucci, Alberto (1996). *Challenging Codes: Collection Action in the Information Age*. Cambridge: Cambridge University Press.

Mirowsky, John, and Ross, Catherine E. (1989). *Social Causes of Distress*. New York: Aldine de Gruyter.

Moore, Kelly (1999). "Political Protest and Institutional Change: The Anti-Vietnam War movement and American Science." In *How Social Movements Matter*, edited by Marco Giugni, Doug McAdam, and Charles Tilly, 97–115. Minneapolis: University of Minnesota Press.

Morgen, Sandra (1995). "'It Was the Best of Times, It Was the Worst of Times': Emotional Discourse in the Work Cultures of Feminist Health Clinics." In *Feminist Organizations: Harvest of the New Women's Movement*, edited by Myra Marx Ferree and Patricia Yancey Martin, 234–247. Philadelphia: Temple University Press.

Morgen, Sandra (2002). *Into Our Own Hands: The Women's Health Movement in the United States, 1969–1990*. New Brunswick: Rutgers University Press.

Morris Aldon D. (1984). *The Origins of the Civil Rights Movement*. New York: Free Press.

Mueller Carol (1994). "Conflict Networks and the Origins of Women's Liberation." In *New Social Movements: From Ideology to Identity*, edited by Enrique Laraña, Hank Johnston, and Joseph R. Gusfield, 234–263. Philadelphia: Temple University Press.

Naples, Nancy (1992). "Activist Mothering: Cross-Generational Continuity in the Community Work of Women from Low-Income Urban Neighborhoods," *Gender & Society*. 5: 478–494.

Naples, Nancy (1998). *Community Activism and Feminist Politics: Organizing Across Race, Class, and Gender*. New York: Routledge.

Phelan, Shane (1989). *Identity Politics: Lesbian Feminism and the Limits of Community*. Philadelphia: Temple University Press.

Pizzorno, Alessandro (1978). "Political Exchange and Collective Identity in Industrial Conflict." In *The Resurgence of Class Conflict in Western Europe Since 1968*, edited by Colin Crouch and Alessandro Pizzorno, 277–298. London: Macmillan.

Polletta Francesca (2002). *Freedom Is an Endless Meeting: Democracy in American Social Movements*. Chicago: University of Chicago Press.

Polletta, Francesca and Jasper, James (2001). "Collective Identity and Social Movements," *Annual Review of Sociology*. 27(1): 283–305.

Powell, Walter W. and DiMaggio, Paul J. (1991). *The New Institutionalism in Organizational Analysis*. Chicago: University of Chicago Press.

Preves, Sharon (2003). *Intersex and Identity: The Contested Self*. New Jersey: Rutgers University Press.

Raeburn, Nicole C. (2004). *Changing Corporate America from Inside Out: Lesbian and Gay Workplace Rights*. Minneapolis: University of Minnesota Press.

Ray, Raka (1999). *Fields of Protest: Women's Movements in India*. Minneapolis: University of Minnesota Press.

Reger, Jo (2004). "Organizational 'Emotion Work' Through Consciousness-Raising: An Analysis of a Feminist Organization," *Qualitative Sociology*. 27(2): 205–222.

Reger, Jo, ed. (2005). *Different Wavelengths: Studies of the Contemporary Women's Movement*. New York: Routledge.

Reger, Jo (2012). *Everywhere and Nowhere: Contemporary Feminism in the United States*. New York: Oxford University Press.

Reger, Jo, Myers, Daniel J., and Einwohner, Rachel, eds. (2008) *Identity Work in Social Movements*. Minneapolis: University of Minnesota Press.

Robnett, Belinda (1996). "African-American Women in the Civil Rights Movement, 1954–1965: Gender, Leadership, and Micromobilization," *American Journal of Sociology*. 101: 1661–1693.

Robnett, Belinda (1997). *How Long, How Long? African-American Women in the Struggle for Civil Rights*. New York: Oxford University Press.

Rupp, Leila J. (2011). "The Persistence of Transnational Organizing: The Case of the Homophile Movement," *American Historical Review*. 116(4) (October 2011): 1014–1039.

Rupp, Leila J. and Taylor, Verta (1987). *Survival in the Doldrums: The American Women's Rights Movement 1945 to the 1960s*. New York: Oxford University Press.

Rupp, Leila J. and Taylor, Verta (2003). *Drag Queens at the 801 Cabaret*. Chicago: University of Chicago Press.

Rupp, Leila, Taylor, Verta, and Shapiro, Eve Illana (2010). "Drag Queens and Drag Kings: The Difference Gender Makes," *Sexualities*. 13: 1–10.

Ryan, Barbara (1992). *Feminism and the Women's Movement: Dynamics of Change in Social Movement Ideology and Activism*. New York: Routledge.

Schneider, Beth E. and Stoller, Nancy E. (1995). *Women Resisting AIDS: Feminist Strategies of Empowerment*. Philadelphia: Temple University Press.

Scott, James C. (1990). *Domination and the Arts of Resistance: Hidden Transcripts*. New Haven: Yale University Press.

Seidman, Steven (1993). "Identity and Politics in a 'Postmodern' Gay Culture: Some Historical and Conceptual Notes." In *Fear of a Queer Planet: Queer Politics and Social Theory*, edited by M. Warner, 105–42. Minneapolis: University of Minnesota Press.

Sewell, William (1992). "A Theory of Structure: Duality, Agency and Transformation," *American Journal of Sociology*. 98(1): 1–30.

Shrivasta, Sarita (2006). "Tears, Fears, and Careers: Anti-racism and Emotion in Social Movement Organizations," *Canadian Journal of Sociology*. 31: 55–90.

Smith, Dorothy (1990). *The Conceptual Practices of Power: A Feminist Sociology of Knowledge*. Toronto: University of Toronto Press.

Smith, Miriam (2008). *Political Institutions and Lesbian and Gay Rights in the United States and Canada*. New York: Routledge.

Snow, David A. (2004). "Social Movements as Challenges to Authority: Resistance to an Emerging Conceptual Hegemony." In *Authority in Contention, Volume 25 of Research in Social Movements, Conflict and Change*, edited by Daniel J. Meyers and Daniel M. Cress, 3–26. Oxford: JAI Press.

Snow, David and Soule, Sarah A. (2010). *A Primer on Social Movements*. New York: W.W. Norton and Company.

Soule, Sarah A. (2009). *Contention and Corporate Social Responsibility*. New York: Cambridge University Press.

Summers-Effler, Erika (2002). "The Micro Potential for Social Change: Emotion, Consciousness, and Social Movement Formation," *Sociological Theory*. 20(1): 41–60.

Staggenborg, Suzanne (1998). *Gender, Family, and Social Movements*. Thousand Oaks, CA: Pine Forge.

Staggenborg, Suzanne and Lang, Amy (2007). "Culture and Ritual in the Montreal Women's Movement," *Social Movement Studies*. 6: 177–194.

Staggenborg, Suzanne and Taylor, Verta (2005). "Whatever Happened to the Women's Movement?" *Mobilization*. 10: 37–52.

Stryker, Sheldon, Owens, Timothy Joseph, and White, Robert W., eds. (2000). *Self, Identity, and Social Movements*. Minneapolis, MN: University of Minnesota Press.

Taylor, Judith (1998). "Feminist Tactics and Friendly Fire in the Irish Women's Movement," *Gender & Society*. 12: 674–691.

Taylor, Verta (1989). "Social Movement Continuity: The Women's Movement in Abeyance," *American Sociological Review*. 54(5): 761–75.

Taylor, Verta (1995). "Watching for Vibes: Bringing Emotions into the Study of Feminist Organizations." In *Feminist Organizations: Harvest of the New Women's Movement*, edited by Myra Marx Ferree and Patricia Yancey Martin, 223–233. Philadelphia: Temple University Press.

Taylor, Verta (1996). *Rock-a-by Baby: Feminism, Self-help and Postpartum Depression*. New York: Routledge.

Taylor, Verta (1999). "Gender and Social Movements: Gender Processes in Women's Self-Help Movements," *Gender & Society*. 13(1): 8–33.

Taylor, Verta (2000). "Emotions and Identity in Women's Self-help Movements." In *Self, Identity, and Social Movements*, edited by Sheldon Stryker, Timothy J. Owens, and Robert W. White, 271–99. Minneapolis: University of Minnesota Press.

Taylor, Verta (2010). "Culture, Identity, and Emotions: Studying Social Movements as if People Really Matter," *Mobilization*. 15(2): 113–134.

Taylor, Verta, Kimport, Katrina, Van Dyke, Nella, and Anderson, Ellen Ann (2009). "Culture and Mobilization: Tactical Repertoires, Same-Sex Weddings, and the Impact on Gay Activism," *American Sociological Review*. 74: 865–90.

Taylor, Verta and Leitz, Lisa (2010). "From Infanticide to Activism: Emotions and Identity in Self-Help Movements." In *Social Movements and the Transformation of American Health Care*, edited by Jane Banaszak-Holl, Sandra Levitsky, and Mayer N. Zald, 266–83. New York: Oxford University Press.

Taylor, Verta and Raeburn, Nicole C. (1995). "Identity Politics as High-Risk Activism: Career Consequences for Lesbian, Gay, and Bisexual Sociologists," *Social Problems*. 42: 252–73.

Taylor, Verta and Rupp, Leila J. (1993). "Women's Culture and Lesbian Feminist Activism: A Reconsideration of Cultural Feminism," *Signs: Journal of Women in Culture and Society*. 19(1): 32–61.

Taylor, Verta and Rupp, Leila J. (2002). "Loving Internationalism: The Emotion Culture of Transnational Women's Organizations, 1888–1945," *Mobilization*. 7(2): 125–144.

Taylor Verta and Van Dyke, Nella. (2004). "'Get Up, Stand Up': Tactical Repertoires of Social Movements." See Snow et al. 2004, 262–293.

Taylor, Verta and Whittier, Nancy (1992). "Collective Identity and Lesbian Feminist Mobilization." In *Frontiers in Social Movement Theory*, edited by Aldon D. Morris and Carol McClurg Mueller. New Haven, CT: Yale University Press.

Taylor, Verta and Whittier, Nancy (1995). "Analytical Approaches to Social Movement Culture: The Culture of the Women's Movement." In *Social Movements and Culture*, edited by Hank Johnston and Bert Klandermans, 163–87. Minneapolis: University of Minnesota Press.

Taylor, Verta and Zald, Mayer N. (2010). "Conclusion: The Shape of Collective Action in the U.S. Health Sector." In *Social Movements and the Transformation of American Health Care*. Edited by Jane Banaszak-Holl, Sandra Levitsky, and Mayer N. Zald, 300–317. New York: Oxford University Press.

Touraine, Alain (1985). "An Introduction to the Study of Social Movements," *Social Research*. 52: 749–87.

Touraine, Alain (1992). "Beyond Social Movements," *Theory, Culture and Society*. 9: 125–45.

Turner, Stephanie S. (1999). "Intersex Identities: Locating New Intersections of Sex and Gender," *Gender & Society*. 13(4): 457–479.

Van Dyke, Nella, Soule, Sarah A., and Taylor, Verta (2004). "The Targets of Social Movements: Beyond a Focus on the State," *Research in Social Movements, Conflict, and Change*. 25: 27–51.

Waidzunas, Tom J. (2013). "Intellectual Opportunity Structures and Science-Targeted Activism: Influence of the Ex-Gay Movement on the Science of Sexual Orientation," *Mobilization*. 18(1): 1–19.

West, Guida and Blumberg, Rhoda Lois (1990). *Women and Social Protest*. New York: Oxford University Press.

White, Aaronette M. (1999). "Talking Black: Micromobilization Processes in Collective Protest Against Rape," *Gender & Society*. 13: 77–100.

Whittier, Nancy E. (1995). *Feminist Generations: The Persistence of the Radical Women's Movement*. Philadelphia: Temple University Press.

Whittier, Nancy E. (2001). "Emotional Strategies: The Collective Reconstruction and Display of Oppositional Emotions in the Movement Against Child Sexual Abuse." In *Passionate Politics: Emotions and Social Movements*, edited by J. Goodwin, J. M. Jasper, and F. Polletta, 233–50. Chicago: University of Chicago Press.

Whittier, Nancy E. (2009). *The Politics of Child Sexual Abuse: Feminism, Social Movements, and the Therapeutic State*. New York: Oxford University Press.

PART II

SOCIAL MOVEMENTS AND STRUCTURAL PROCESSES

CHAPTER 7

....

HISTORICAL DYNAMICS OF CAPITALISM AND LABOR MOVEMENTS

....

BEVERLY J. SILVER AND ŞAHAN SAVAŞ KARATAŞLI

LABOR, CAPITALISM, AND THE SOCIAL MOVEMENT LITERATURE

....

THE mainstream of the social movement literature since the 1990s has in large measure dismissed the concept of "capitalism" from its toolkit for understanding social movements, while at the same time placing "labor movements" outside its field of inquiry. This state of affairs—particularly the "disappearance" of capitalism—has been the object of lamentations by a subset of social movement scholars who have grown in size and insistence since the 2008 financial crisis (see, e.g., Hetland and Goodwin 2013; Tejerina et al. 2013; Rosenhek and Shalev 2013; della Porta 2015). Moreover, the recent worldwide upsurge in protest movements from the Arab Spring to the Occupy Movements stimulated a significant resurgence of interest among social movement scholars in the dormant sub-field of rebellions and revolutions. Yet, while some noted the significant class-based component of these struggles (e.g., Rosenhek and Shalev 2013; Karataşlı et al. 2015), overall, the role of workers and workers' movements in these struggles has been underestimated or ignored.

This chapter will argue in favor of returning *both* capitalism *and* labor/class-based movements to a prominent position in the social movement literature. The virtual disappearance of "capitalism" from the social movement literature since the 1990s is, as Gabriel Hetland and Jeff Goodwin (2013: 83, 90) write, "a perplexing development... During an era in which global capitalism became ever more powerful... it also became increasingly invisible to scholars of popular movements." This perplexing disappearance (and recent partial resurgence) of capitalism is not unique to the social movement literature, but is rather a more general phenomenon across the social sciences. Giovanni Arrighi, for one, pointed to (and lamented) a parallel (and perhaps even more perplexing) disappearance of capitalism from the "new economic sociology" literature in the 1990s (Arrighi 2001; see also Arrighi 2010). Meanwhile, in the wake of the 2008 financial crisis, we can observe a resurgence of interest in "bringing capitalism back in" to economic sociology (see, e.g., Krippner 2011). Indeed, the "disappearance" and recent "resurgence" of interest in capitalism can be seen across the social sciences and humanities.

The virtual disappearance of labor movements from the purview of the social movement literature has multiple roots dating back to the 1960s and 1970s. The "new left" movements that arose in the 1960s were harsh critics of the organizations that had emerged out of the wave of struggles by the "old left" in the first half of the twentieth century, *especially* trade unions and labor/socialist parties. These organizations were viewed as having "sold out" (as being corrupt, weak, economistic and/or in collusion with dominant forces at the domestic and international[1] level), as "neglecting the truly dispossessed," or worse still, as actively excluding women, racial/ethnic minorities, and immigrants in order to protect the interests of a privileged labor aristocracy (for the critiques, see Clawson 2003: 51, 59; also Arrighi, Hopkins, and Wallerstein 1989: 221–222).

By the 1980s and 1990s, the dismissal of labor movements from the social movement and broader social science literature came not so much from a critique of their political stance as from an assessment of their diminishing structural power. As Aristide Zolberg (1995: 28) put it, the late twentieth-century transformations that have gone under the rubric of globalization have brought about the virtual disappearance of "the distinctive social formation we term 'working class'" (1995: 28). In a similar vein, Manuel Castells (1997: 354, 360) argued that the dawn of the "Information Age" had transformed the experience of work in ways that not only undermine the labor movement's ability to act as "a major source of social cohesion and workers' representation," but also in ways that undermine any possibility of workers becoming emancipatory "subjects" in the future—the source of a new "project identity" aimed at rebuilding the social institutions of civil society. Looking out from the 1990s, Castells argued that non-class-based identity movements were the only "potential subjects of the Information Age."[2]

THE PERSISTENCE AND RESURGENCE
OF LABOR AT THE MARGINS

Outside the geographical and thematic mainstream of the (US and western European) social movement literature, there were some important exceptions to this tendency to dismiss workers and workers' movements as irrelevant. The first was in so-called newly industrializing countries (NICs) such as Brazil (e.g., Keck 1989), South Africa (e.g., Seidman 1994), and South Korea (Koo 2001).[3] For while the decline of Fordist mass production industries in wealthy core countries was leading to a disempowerment of established working classes and their trade unions in the 1970s and 1980s, the rapid economic expansion of the NICs in the same years was leading to the creation of large industrial working classes and the emergence of powerful independent labor movements (Silver 2003).

These labor movements were not only successful in improving wages and working conditions, they were also key subjects behind the success of the broader struggles for democracy and social and economic justice. But as Ruth Collier (1999: 110) noted, "the comparative and theoretical literature [on democratization] largely missed the importance of the working class and the labor movement in the democratization process of the 1970s and 1980s… In the overwhelming majority of cases, the roles of unions and labor-affiliated parties were important to a degree that is at most hinted at in the literature." In country after country labor movements were intertwined with struggles of working and poor people more broadly and with cross-class struggles for democracy and national liberation (Chun and Williams 2013).

For example, in South Africa, the independent black trade unions that emerged in the late 1970s in mining and manufacturing were, by the mid-1980s, playing the leading role in the anti-apartheid movement, bringing "a distinctively working class perspective" to the question of national liberation (Obrery 1989: 34–35). The movement came to be dubbed "social movement unionism" as it was characterized by a "combination of productive and reproductive struggles" as well as a combination of resistance on the factory floor and resistance in the communities where workers lived (Webster 1988; Seidman 1994; von Holdt 2002; Chun and Williams 2013; Ashman and Pon-Vignon 2014).

Manufacturing capital had been attracted to the NICs in the 1960s and 1970s, partly for their relatively cheap labor and docile, but within less than a generation, this large inflow of capital created new working classes and new militant labor movements. In the late 1990s and first decade of the twenty-first century, manufacturing capital was attracted to China, partly in a further search for cheap and docile labor. At the turn of the century, most observers thought that the incorporation of China's vast labor supplies into global manufacturing production was destined to lead to a "race to the bottom" in global wages and working conditions. But as in the case of the NICs, within less than a generation, an industrial working class emerged in China that became the protagonists of a large and growing wave of strikes and labor unrest. It could easily be argued that by the second decade of the twenty-first century, China had become the new "epicenter of world labor unrest" (Silver and Zhang 2009). At the same time, China has become an epicenter of social scientific interest in labor and labor movements (see, e.g., Pun 2005; Lee 2007; Friedman 2014; Zhang 2015).

Another exception outside the mainstream of the social movement literature emerged in the late 1990s, and was inspired by the sudden upsurge of militancy among low-wage (often undocumented) immigrant workers in the United States, and in particular the impressive 1990 success of the Justice for Janitors campaign in gaining union recognition for workers cleaning the skyscrapers in the downtown commercial district in Los Angeles—a victory that sparked a wave of union organizing among immigrant workers (many undocumented) across the United States (Waldinger et al. 1998; Milkman 2006).[4] The upsurge in labor militancy led to a wave of scholarly interest in labor movements beginning in the late 1990s and 2000s among social scientists in the United States—the site where the obituary of workers' movements had been written most insistently in the prior decades. This wave of labor militancy shattered many of the assumptions on which the "irrelevance of workers as social actors" thesis had been based—that is, that labor had been fragmented and fatally weakened by the structural transformations associated with "globalization" and "post-Fordism" such that class-based mobilizations were a thing of the past. This new wave of organizing combined workplace and community struggles, thereby challenging the tendency to see workers' movements as particularistic, and outside the purview of the social movement field (Bronfenbrenner et al. 1998; Fine 2006; Chun 2011). The term "social movement unionism" was borrowed from the South African and Brazilian literature as a way of capturing this phenomenon (Clawson 2003).

METHODOLOGICAL IMPLICATIONS

The above examples point us toward some methodological insights for how to think about labor and social movements. First, they point to the importance of moving beyond a common approach in the social science literature (including the social movement literature) of generalizing from the experience of one or a handful of core countries to the world. What looks like a general crisis of labor movements in the 1980s when viewed from the core, looks very different when *the geographical frame of our analysis is widened.*

Second, they point to the importance of moving beyond the common approach in the social science literature (including the social movement literature) of taking a relatively short (and undynamic) time horizon as the framework for analysis. Based in part on extrapolations from short-term trends, the thesis that class-based movements had become irrelevant as social actors flourished in the United States, just as a new and proactive (largely immigrant) working class had begun to emerge.

A similar misapprehension of the longer-run dynamics for labor movements occurred almost 100 years ago as most early twentieth-century observers were convinced that the transformations associated with the rise of mass production spelled the death of labor movements—making the skills of most unionized (craft) workers obsolete and allowing employers to tap vast new sources of migrant labor. It was only *post facto*—with the successful wave of sitdown strikes beginning in 1936–37 by mass production workers in the United States—that Fordism came to be seen as inherently labor strengthening rather than inherently labor weakening. Thus, once we *lengthen the time horizon of our analysis* what looks like a terminal crisis of labor movements—the end of history—may turn out to be another lull between recurrent major labor movement upsurges (Silver 2003; Clawson 2003; cf. Piven and Cloward 1977).

To be sure, the protagonists of these recurrent major upsurges of labor unrest are fundamentally different working classes. As Clawson (2003: 13) notes "each period of labor upsurge redefines what we mean by 'the labor movement,' changing cultural expectations, the form that unions take, laws, structures, and accepted forms of behavior."

Labor Movements and Historical Capitalism

In order to understand the timing, location, and changing character of these labor movement upsurges, it is important not only to lengthen and widen the temporal–geographical framework for analysis; it is also important to embed the analysis of labor movements in elements of a theory of "historical capitalism"—this is, an understanding of the long-run dynamics of global capitalist development. In this section, we will sketch seven elements toward building such a theory. These seven elements are not meant to be comprehensive but rather to provide a set of initial building blocks toward a full theorization.[5]

The first is the notion that *labor unrest is endemic to capitalism*. Both Karl Marx and Karl Polanyi contended that one of the historical specificities of capitalism as a social system is the commodification of labor. Moreover, both Marx and Polanyi argued that labor is a "fictitious commodity" and that treating human beings as commodities like any other would necessarily lead to deeply felt grievances and resistance. For Marx (1959 [1867]) "labor power"—unlike other commodities purchased and deployed in the "hidden abode of production"—is embodied in human beings who complain and resist if they are made to work too long, too hard or too fast. Likewise, for Polanyi (1957 [1944]: 71, 130, 176–177), the commodity labor is "no other than the human beings themselves of which every society exists" and moves to incorporate labor as commodities in "free markets" necessarily calls forth a movement toward "the self protection of society," which takes a variety of forms such as agitation for state welfare provisions and trade union mobilization. Thus, from both Marxian and Polanyian perspectives, labor unrest should be expected anytime and anywhere we find the commodification of labor: sometimes at the point of production, sometimes in political struggles over regulation of the labor market, sometimes in the form of open resistance, but at other times taking "hidden forms" with deployment of the "weapons of the weak" (cf. Scott 1985).

The second theoretical element is the notion that capitalism is characterized by a tendency toward recurrent major transformations in the organization of production and consumption, which in turn, leads to the recurrent *making, unmaking, and remaking of working classes* on a world scale (Silver 2003). The idea that capitalism is characterized by bouts of massive change is captured by Joseph Schumpeter's (1954) concept of "creative-destruction" and by Marx's and Engel's famous phrase in *The Manifesto*: "all that is solid melts into air." Those who in recent decades have insisted on the death of the working class have tended to focus solely on the *unmaking* side of this process—most notably the unmaking of the industrial mass production working classes in much of the global North. However, the same mechanisms that bring about the "unmaking" of established working classes (e.g., capital mobility, labor migration, the rise/decline of industries), also lead to new working class formation. If we work from the premise that the world's working classes and workers' movements are recurrently made, unmade, and *remade*, then we are primed to be on the lookout for the outbreak of fresh struggles—both by new working classes in formation and by old working classes being unmade; that is, struggles by those experiencing the "creative" and "destructive" sides of the process of capital accumulation, respectively.

Beverly Silver (2003) labeled these two types of workers' struggles (1) Marx-type labor unrest—that is, struggles by newly emerging working classes; and (2) Polanyi-type labor unrest—that is, struggles by established working classes defending ways of life and livelihood that are in the process of being "unmade." In a similar vein, Ching Kwan Lee (2007) has labeled these two types "sunbelt" and "rustbelt" struggles with reference to the unmaking of the Chinese working-class that had formed in the Mao era (and were by the mid- and late 1990s being systematically laid-off from state-owned enterprises as part of the dismantling of the "iron rice bowl" social compact), on the one hand, and the simultaneous making of a new migrant working class in the coastal export manufacturing centers in China, on the other hand. Finally, David Harvey (2003) has proposed a conceptual distinction between "struggles against accumulation in production" and "struggles against accumulation by dispossession"—the latter concept having some parallels with the concept of Polanyi-type labor unrest since Harvey understands struggles by established working classes defending their existing ways of life and livelihood as a form of "struggles against accumulation by dispossession."

Third (and following from the first two theoretical elements), *labor unrest takes a broad range of forms* as the terrain on which workers struggle—including the sources of their bargaining power, the intensity and nature of their grievances, and the "face" of the working class—is recurrently transformed. Moreover, *labor unrest unfolds at a variety of levels—in the workplace, on the labor market, in the community and in national and international politics.* The twentieth-century social science literature tended to privilege struggles at the workplace. And while the "hidden abode of [factory] production" was indeed Marx's focus in the middle section of volume 1 of *Capital* [Parts 3–5]—where he catalogues an endemic labor–capital conflict over the duration, intensity, and pace of work—it is clear by the end of volume 1 of *Capital* that the logic of capitalist development, as Marx envisions it, not only leads to endemic struggles in the workplace but also to broader societal-level conflict as the accumulation of capital goes hand-in-hand with the "accumulation of misery," most notably in the form of an *expanding reserve army of unemployed, underemployed and precariously employed workers.*[6] This in turn brings to the fore questions of struggles over the conditions for the reproduction of labor power on which there is an important relevant feminist literature (see, e.g., Federici 2006) as well as what Nancy Fraser (2014) has recently called struggles over the wide range of "background conditions" that capitalist production presupposes.

A fourth theoretical consideration follows from the postulate that capitalist development is producing an enlarged reserve army of labor on a world scale. Earlier, we emphasized two divergent types of working-class protest: that is, protest by new working classes being "made" in areas where capital is expanding (the post-2010 wave of factory worker strikes and protests in China is a paradigmatic example) and protest by established working classes being "unmade" in areas where capital is disinvesting (the post-2009 wave of anti-austerity protests in Europe is a paradigmatic example). But, if historical capitalism is characterized, not only by a cyclical process of "creative-destruction," but also by a long-term tendency for the "destruction" of established livelihoods to proceed more quickly than the establishment of new livelihoods—and hence, an enlarging mass of unemployed, underemployed, and precariously employed workers—then we would expect *a third type of working-class protest to grow in importance over time*; that is, protest neither by working classes who are being "made" or "unmade" but those *segments of the working class who are deprived of the means of livelihood but who have not been absorbed into stable wage employment—those whom capital has essentially "bypassed"* (Karataşlı et al. 2015).

All three of these types of labor unrest are playing a key role in the post-2008 upsurge of global social protest, with protests by the vast numbers of unemployed youth around the world as a prominent paradigmatic example of our "third type" (Karataşlı et al. 2015). Yet while instances of this "third-type" of labor unrest are often described in the recent social movement literature—for example, the 2005 riots that erupted in French *banlieues*; the 2011 London riots; the role of the unemployed in the 2011 Tunisian and Egyptian revolutions—they are rarely categorized as labor unrest by the authors. The same is the case for much of what could be categorized as "Polanyi-type labor unrest." The failure to think of these protests as labor unrest is in part due to a tendency to deploy an excessively narrow and rigid definition of "the working class."[7] For example, Guy Standing (2011: 6) sees what he calls the *precariat* as a key force behind the recent upsurge of social protest, but he distinguishes the precariat from the proletariat, and restricts the use of the latter term to "workers in long-term, stable fixed-hour jobs with established routes of advancement, subject to unionization and collective agreements, with job titles their fathers and mothers would have understood, facing local employers whose names and features they were familiar with." Not only is the "reserve army of labor" excluded from this definition but also the vast majority of the world's wage workers throughout the history of capitalism are excluded by definition from the working class and/or the proletariat.

On the flip side, Slovj Žižek (2012: 11) sees the mid-twentieth century unionized wage worker in factories, shops, and offices (that is, Standing's proletariat), as a major force behind the recent wave of global social unrest; however, Žižek does not classify them as workers, but rather as a "salaried bourgeoisie" who are "resisting being reduced to proletarians." As we have implicitly argued above, a more useful and theoretically coherent definition of the working class (or proletariat) would include both Standing's *precariat* and the lower ranks of Žižek's *salaried bourgeoisie*. They represent two moments in the *making and unmaking* of working classes on a global scale. More specifically, a significant chunk of Žižek's *salaried bourgeoisie* are the working classes who made major advances as a result of the mid-twentieth century labor movement upsurges, and are now feeling the brunt of the "destructive" side of the process of creative destruction as their previous gains (and middle-class pretensions) come under attack. Meanwhile, a significant chunk of Standing's *precariat* are "new working classes in formation," the outcome of the "creative" side of capitalist development, some of whom may be on the route to (at least temporarily) making significant gains in wages and working conditions; that is, becoming a "stable working class" if not a "salaried bourgeoisie." At the same time, another chunk of Standing's *precariat* belong to our "third type"—members of a mushrooming global reserve army of labor, they are proletarianized but with little chance of ever finding stable employment as wage workers. All three of these "strata" of the working class are the outcome of different sides of the same processes of capitalist development; moreover, the fate of their struggles is deeply intertwined with one another.

This brings us to our fifth element for a theorization of the relationship between historical capitalism and labor movements. As Immanuel Wallerstein (1995: 25) has pointed out, historical capitalism is characterized by a "system-level problem": that is, profits can be made—even with the partial decommodification of labor and the establishment of expensive social contracts—as long as those concessions are made to only a small percentage of the world's workers (as was the case with the mass production social compacts that emerged after the Second World War in the core). Put differently, there is a fundamental tension in capitalism between profitability and legitimacy. Efforts to overcome the tendency toward a crisis of legitimacy through improving the condition of the working class as a whole (rising wages, improved working conditions, social welfare provisions) can only work for short amounts of time or small segments of the working class without provoking a crisis of profitability. If the crisis of global capitalism of the 1970s was largely precipitated by a squeeze on profitability, the current global crisis of capitalism is increasingly characterized by a deep crisis of legitimacy as inequality mushrooms and growing numbers have lost access to the means to produce their own livelihood without being provided with any opportunity to make a living within the circuits of capital (Silver 2003; Silver 2014; Karataşlı et al. 2015). Moreover, in addition to the limits imposed by the requirements of profitability on the generalization of mass consumption, the ecological and resource constraints on the extension of US-style consumption standards will be critical in determining what kind of social contracts are both generalizable and sustainable in the twenty-first century (cf. Arrighi 2007).

The sixth element for constructing a theory of the dynamics of historical capitalism and labor movements is *the intimate relationship between labor movements and status-based movements,* which, in turn, is rooted in the above-mentioned "system-level problem." Fundamental to historical capitalism has been the ways in which status-based distinctions are recurrently mobilized (by capitalists, by states, and/or by workers themselves) to carve out special protections from the worst ravages of an unregulated labor market for a *segment* of the world's working class marked for special treatment along lines of gender, race, ethnicity, and/or citizenship. Special protections seek to mitigate the deep tension between profitability and legitimacy—to square the circle, so to speak—by creating legitimating social compacts for some segments of the world working class while maintaining profitability by excluding the majority from those social compacts. However, the successful extension of benefits such as higher wages, job security, and welfare provisions to a privileged group becomes an important incentive for *working-class mobilizations along status lines* by both privileged and by excluded workers—mobilizations aimed, respectively, at *defending* or *overturning* racial, ethnic, national, and gender hierarchies. As a result, the history of workers' mobilizations has been deeply interconnected with mobilizations along racial, gender, ethnic, and citizenship lines. In a nutshell, mobilization based on class and mobilization based on status have been and will continue to be deeply intertwined.[8]

Throughout the twentieth century, the results of such mobilizations have sometimes been to draw status-based distinctions among workers *within* a country; but at other times these mobilizations have taken the form of worker-citizens demanding protection from their own states vis-à-vis workers of other states, contributing to the growing salience of status-based distinctions among workers *across* countries.

Social scientists witnessing the escalation of inter-imperialist rivalries and war in the late nineteenth and early twentieth centuries pointed to multiple links between mounting interstate and domestic conflict, including mass labor unrest. On the one hand, rulers facing intense social conflict at home were tempted into what they hoped would be short, popular wars—for example, the Spanish–American War for the US and the South African War for the UK—that would create a diversionary "rally-around-the-flag" effect as well as have a more direct material effect on boosting employment by opening up protected markets, cheap sources of raw materials and/or new colonial areas to which surplus labor at home could be exported.[9] According to E.H. Carr (1945: 204) the collapse of labor internationalism on the eve of the First World War was at least in part due to the success of states in convincing the mass of workers that "their bread was buttered" on the side of their own state's power. Yet observers from Lenin (1916) to Skocpol (1979) noted another empirical regularity—that is, that lost or otherwise unpopular wars opened up the space for major rebellions and revolutions. The result was a "vicious circle" of war, mass labor unrest, and revolution in the first half of the twentieth century—that is, during the crisis of British world hegemony and transition to US world hegemony (Arrighi and Silver 1999: ch. 3; Silver 2003: ch. 4).[10]

This brings us to our seventh and final theoretical element: *workers and workers' movements have been and will continue to be shaped by (and shape) the dynamics of geopolitics and interstate war.* To be sure, in order to understand the nature of this linkage today we have to take into account the major changes over the past half-century in the nature of warfare and the incorporation of the mass of workers and citizens into the war-making strategies of states—in the "global North" most notably the increasing automation of war (e.g., pilotless drones and cruise missiles), the elimination of mass compulsory conscription, the expanding reliance on private military contractors and mercenaries rather than citizen-soldiers (Silver 2015). But particularly as we move into a period of deepening crisis of US world hegemony (Silver and Arrighi 2011), the salience of the links between labor, war, and world politics will become increasingly apparent.

In this chapter we have argued for the importance of returning both capitalism and labor movements to a prominent position in the social movement literature. Moreover, since *profit-making and warmaking have been intimately intertwined in the history of capitalism*—a point emphasized in key works on the historical sociology of capitalism including Charles Tilly's (1990) *Coercion, Capital and European States* and Giovanni Arrighi's (2010) *The Long Twentieth Century: Money, Power and the Origins of Our Times* (see also Wallerstein 1983)—in advocating bringing labor and capitalism back into the social movement literature we are also advocating making geopolitical dynamics—including interstate conflict, war, and the rise/decline of world hegemonies—a central concern of the social movement literature.

NOTES

1. On the alliance between the main trade union federation in the United States and the US government in the sphere of foreign policy, see Kim Scipes (2011); on the link between labor rights, welfare states, war, and geopolitics more broadly, see Silver (2015).
2. The focus of this chapter is on labor/class-based movements; however, it is important to point out that the call for bringing capitalism back in to the social movement literature has broader relevance. Transformations over time in the structure, institutions and ideologies of capitalism have been crucial in shaping the trajectories of *non-class-based* social movements. Indeed, as Hetland and Goodwin (2013: 91) point out, if we look to the enduring classics of the social movement literature from the 1970s and early 1980s, the dynamics of capitalism formed a central (and highly productive) part of their theoretical frameworks, including for those studies focused on understanding what were largely *non-class-based* movements such as the US civil rights movement (e.g., Piven and Cloward 1977; McAdam 1982); second wave feminism (Klein 1984; see also Fraser 2013), and the LGBT movement (D'Emilio 1983; see also Valocchi 1999).
3. In many ways, the strong labor movements in the 1970s and 1980s in Poland (Singer 1982) and Iran (Abrahamian 1982) also fall in this category (see Silver 2003: ch. 4).
4. An indication of the strength of this resurgent scholarly interest—as well as the fact that it was largely taking place outside the existing centers of social movement research—was the formation in 2000 of a new section on Labor and Labor Movements of the American Sociological Association (ASA)—distinct from the already existing ASA section on Collective Behavior and Social Movements.
5. Among the useful resources for constructing a relevant theory of world capitalist development see: Wallerstein 1983; Arrighi and Silver 1999; Arrighi 2010; Harvey 2011; Silver and Arrighi 2011; Fraser 2014.
6. See, e.g., chapter 25 of volume 1 on the "general law of capital accumulation" and the reserve army of labor.
7. See Marcel Van der Linden (2014) for a particularly broad definition of the working class; see also Silver (2003: Appendix A) for an expanded definition of both the "labor" and "unrest" components of the concept of "labor unrest."
8. For theoretical elaborations along these lines, see Saxton 1971; Bonacich 1972; Arrighi 1990; Silver 2003.
9. In the words of Cecil Rhodes (quoted in Lenin 1916: ch. 6): "… in order to save the 40,000,000 inhabitants of the United Kingdom from a bloody civil war, we colonial

statesmen must acquire new lands to settle the surplus population, to provide new markets for the goods produced in the factories and mines. The Empire, as I have always said, is a bread and butter question. If you want to avoid civil war, you must become imperialists."

10. See Stohl (1980) for a review of the literature on the international–domestic conflict link.

References

Abrahamian, Ervand (1982). *Iran: Between Two Revolutions*. Princeton: Princeton University Press.

Arrighi, Giovanni (1990). "Marxist-Century, American-Century: The Making and Remaking of the World Labor Movement." *New Left Review*. 179, Jan–Feb: 29–63.

Arrighi, Giovanni (2001). "Braudel, Capitalism and the New Economic Sociology." *Review* (Fernand Braduel Center). 24(1): 107–123.

Arrighi, Giovanni (2007). *Adam Smith in Beijing: Lineages of the Twenty-First Century*. New York: Verso.

Arrighi, Giovanni (2010). *The Long Twentieth Century: Money, Power and the Origins of Our Times*. London: Verso.

Arrighi, Giovanni and Silver, Beverly J (1999). *Chaos and Governance in the Modern World System*. Minn: University of Minnesota Press.

Arrighi, Giovanni, Hopkins, Terence, and Wallerstein, Immanuel (1989). *Antisystemic Movements*. London: Verso.

Ashman, Sam and Pon-Vignon, Nicolas (2014). "NUMSA, the Working Class and Socialist Politics in South Africa," *Socialist Register*. 51: 93–113.

Bonacich, Edna (1972). "A Theory of Ethnic Antagonism: The Split Labor Market," *American Sociological Review*. 37(5): 547–559.

Bronfenbrenner, Kate et al., eds (1998). *Organizing to Win: New Research on Union Strategies*. Ithaca, NY: Cornell University Press.

Carr, Edward H. (1945). *Nationalism and After*. London: Macmillan.

Castells, Manuel (1997). *The Information Age, vol. 2: The Power of Identity*. Oxford: Blackwell.

Chun, Jennifer (2011). *Organizing at the Margins: The Symbolic Politics of Labor in South Korea and the United States*. Ithaca, NY: ILR Press.

Chun, Jennifer and Williams, Michelle (2013). "Labour as a Democratizing Force?: Lessons from South Africa and Beyond," *Rethinking Development and Inequality*. 2: 2–9.

Clawson, Dan (2003). *The Next Upsurge: Labor and the New Social Movements*. Ithaca, NY: Cornell University Press.

Collier, Ruth Berins (1999). *Paths Toward Democracy: The Working Class and Elites in Western Europe and South America*. Cambridge: Cambridge University Press.

della Porta, Donatella (2015). *Social Movements in Times of Austerity: Bringing Capitalism Back into Protest Analysis*. Polity, Cambridge (UK).

D'Emilio, John ([1983]; 2013). "Capitalism and Gay Identity." In *Making Trouble: Essays on Gay Identity, Politics and the University*, 3–16. New York: Routledge.

Federici, Silvia (2006). "Precarious Labor: A Feminist Viewpoint" https://www.scribd.com/fullscreen/3108724?access_key=key-27agtedsy1ivn8j2ycc1 (accessed January 10, 2015).

Fine, Janice (2006). *Worker Centers: Organizing Communities at the Edge of the Dream*. Ithaca, NY: ILR Press.

Fraser, Nancy (2013). *Fortunes of Feminism: From State-Managed Capitalism to Neoliberal Crisis and Beyond*. New York: Verso.

Fraser, Nancy (2014). "Behind Marx's Hidden Abode: For an Expanded Conception of Capitalism," *New Left Review*. 86, March–April: 55–72.

Friedman, Eli (2014). *Insurgency Trap: Labor Politics in Postsocialist China*. Ithaca, NY: ILR Press.

Harvey, David (2003). *The New Imperialism*. New York: Oxford University Press.

Harvey, David (2011). *The Enigma of Capital: and the Crises of Capitalism*, 2nd edn. New York: Oxford University Press.

Hetland, Gabriel and Goodwin, Jeff (2013). "The Strange Disappearance of Capitalism from Social Movement Studies." In *Marxism and Social Movements*, edited by Colin Barker, Laurence Cox, John Krinsky, and Alf Gunvald Nilsen, 83–102. Brill: Leiden.

Karataşlı, S. Savaş, Kumral, Şefika, Scully, Ben, and Upadhyay, Smriti (2015). "Class, Crisis, and the 2011 Protest Wave: Cyclical and Secular Trends in Global Labor Unrest." In *Overcoming Global Inequalities*, edited by Christopher Chase-Dunn, Immanuel Wallerstein, and Christian Suter, 184–200. New York: Paradigm Press.

Keck, Margaret (1989). "The New Unionism in the Brazilian Transition." In *Democratizing Brazil: Problems of Transition and Consolidation*, edited by Alfred Stepan, chapter 8, 252–296. New York: Oxford University Press.

Klein, Ethel (1984). *Gender Politics*. Cambridge, MA: Harvard University Press.

Koo, Hagen (2001). *Korean Workers: The Culture and Politics of Class Formation*. Ithaca, NY: Cornell University Press.

Krippner, Greta (2011). *Capitalizing on Crisis: The Political Origins of the Rise of Finance*. Cambridge, MA: Harvard University Press.

Lee, Ching Kwan (2007). *Against the Law: Labor Protests in China's Rustbelt and Sunbelt*. Berkeley, CA: University of California Press.

Lenin, Vladimir (1971). "Imperialism, the Highest Stage of Capitalism." In *V.I. Lenin Selected Works*, 169–263. New York: International Publishers (orig. 1916).

Marx, Karl ([1867]; 1959). *Capital. Vol 1*. Moscow: Foreign Languages Publishing House.

McAdam, Doug (1982). *Political Process and the Development of Black Insurgency, 1930–1970*. Chicago: University of Chicago Press.

Milkman, Ruth (2006). *LA Story: Immigrant Workers and the Future of the US Labor Movement*. New York: Russell Sage.

Obrery, Ingrid (1989). "COSATU Congress: Unity in Diversity," *Work in Progress* (South Africa). 60, August/September: 34–39.

Piven, Frances Fox and Cloward, Richard A (1977). *Poor Peoples Movements*. New York Vantage Books.

Polanyi, Karl ([1944]; 1957). *The Great Transformation*. Boston: Beacon.

Pun, Ngai (2005). *Made in China: Women Factory Workers in a Global Marketplace*. Durham, NC: Duke University Press.

Rosenhek, Zeev and Shalev, Michael (2013). "The Political Economy of Israel's 'Social Justice' Protests: A Class and Generational Analysis," *Contemporary Social Science*, http://dx.doi.org /10.1080/21582041.2013.851405

Saxton, Alexander (1971). *The Indispensable Enemy: Labor and the Anti-Chinese Movement in California*. Berkeley: University of California Press.

Schumpeter, Joseph (1954). *Capitalism, Socialism and Democracy*. London: Allen & Unwin.

Scipes, Kim (2011). *AFL-CIO's Secret War against Developing Country Workers: Solidarity or Sabotage?* Lanham: Lexington Books.

Scott, James (1985). *Weapons of the Weak*. New Haven: Yale University Press.

Seidman, Gay (1994). *Manufacturing Militance: Workers' Movements in Brazil and South Africa, 1970–1985*. Berkeley, CA: University of California Press.

Silver, Beverly (2003). *Forces of Labor: Workers Movements and Globalization since 1870.* New York: Cambridge University Press.

Silver, Beverly (2014). "Theorizing the Working-Class in Twenty-First Century Global Capitalism." In *Workers and Labour in a Globalised Capitalism*, edited by M. Atzeni, 46–69. Basingstoke: Palgrave Macmillan.

Silver, Beverly (2015). "Labor, War and World Politics: Contemporary Dynamics in World–Historical Perspective." In *Handbook of the International Political Economy*, edited by Kees van der Pilj, 6–22. Cheltenham: Edward Elgar Books.

Silver, Beverly J. and Arrighi, Giovanni (2011). "The End of the Long Twentieth Century." In *Business as Usual: The Roots of the Global Financial Meltdown*, edited by C. Calhoun and G. Derluguian, 53–68. New York: NYU Press.

Silver, Beverly J. and Zhang, Lu (2009). "China: Emerging Epicenter of World Labor Unrest." In *China and Global Capitalism*, edited by H. Hung, 174–187. Baltimore: Johns Hopkins University Press.

Singer, Daniel (1982). *The Road to Gdansk.* New York: Monthly Review Press.

Skocpol, Theda (1979). *States and Social Revolutions.* Cambridge: Cambridge University Press.

Standing, Guy (2011). *The Precariat: The New Dangerous Class.* New York: Bloomsbury Academic.

Stohl, Michael (1980). "The Nexus of Civil and International Conflict." In *Handbook of Political Conflict: Theory and Research*, edited by Ted Robert Gurr, 297–330. New York: The Free Press.

Tejerina, Benjamín, Perugorría, Ignacia, Benski, Tova, and Langman, Lauren (2013). "From Indignation to Occupation: A New Wave of Global Mobilization," *Current Sociology.* 61(4): 377–392.

Tilly, Charles (1990). *Coercion, Capital, and European States, A.D. 990–1990.* Cambridge, MA: Basil Blackwell.

Valocchi, Steve (1999). "The Class-Inflected Nature of Gay Identity," *Social Problems.* 46(2) May: 207–224.

Van der Linden, Marcel (2014). "Who is the Working Class? Wage Earners and Other Labourers," In *Workers and Labour in a Globalised Capitalism*, edited by M. Atzeni, 70–84. Basingstoke: Palgrave Macmillan.

von Holdt, Karl (2002). "Social Movement Unionism: The Case of South Africa," *Work, Employment and Society.* 16(2): 283–304.

Waldinger, Roger, Erickson, Chris, Milkman, Ruth, Mitchell, Daniel J.B., Valenzuela, Abel, Wong, Kent and Zeitlin, Maurice (1998). "Helots No More: A Case Study of the Justice for Janitors Campaign in Los Angeles." Chapter 6 in *Organizing to Win*, edited by Bronfenbrenner, K., Friedman, S., Hurd, R.W., Oswald, R.A. and Seeber, R.L., 102–119.

Wallerstein, Immanuel (1983). *Historical Capitalism.* London: Verso.

Wallerstein, Immanuel (1995). "Response: Declining States, Declining Rights?" *International Labor and Working Class History.* 47: 24–27.

Webster, Edward (1988). "The Rise of Social Movement Unionism: The Two Faces of Black Trade Union Movements in South Africa." In *State, Resistance and Change in South Africa*, edited by P. Frankel, N. Pines, and M. Swilling, 174–196. London: Croon Helm.

Zhang, Lu (2015). *Inside China's Automobile Factories: The Politics of Labor and Worker Resistance.* New York: Cambridge University Press.

Žižek, Slavoj (2012). *The Year of Dreaming Dangerously.* London: Verso.

Zolberg, Aristide (1995). "Response: Working-Class Dissolution," *International Labor and Working Class History.* 47: 28–38.

CHAPTER 8

DEMOGRAPHY AND SOCIAL MOVEMENTS

JACK A. GOLDSTONE

SOCIAL movements are made up of people, and so it is obvious that to understand social movements we must understand who are the people that compose them. But that is not as simple as it sounds. Even basic elements of the demography of social movement participants—how many they are, what are their ages, their gender, their ethnicity, their education, their geographic and class backgrounds—can be hard to ascertain. Moreover, social movements emerge from and are embedded in societies, so the demography of the society is important as well: what is happening to the size of a society's population, to its particular cohorts (especially youth) in regard to their education and opportunities, what shifts in culture or experience are affecting particular groups, and what is the ethnic or regional or religious breakdown of society and is that changing? Thus the analysis of the demography of social movements has to proceed simultaneously at two levels: how do the demographic characteristics of *movement participants* shape the emergence, tactics, ideology (framing and goals), and outcome of those movements, and how do the demographic characteristics *of societies (or for global movements, of globalized networks)* shape the opportunities, motivations, tactics, ideology, reception, and outcome of those movements.

BASIC DEMOGRAPHIC CONCEPTS: GROWTH DIFFERENTIALS, COHORTS

In the 1960s and early 1970s, when social movements were often seen as movements of the marginalized and discontent, the anomic and poorly integrated, rapid population growth in developing countries, and the rapid growth of education in previously illiterate populations, were seen as creating a situation in which institutions failed to keep pace with the growth in the numbers and aspirations of the populace (Huntington 1968; Gurr 1970. The result was large numbers of people not socialized into meaningful roles in society, who were readily available to join radical or revolutionary movements.

While this element—a large number of educated and underemployed youth— remains an important consideration in social movements, it is far too narrow a view of demography and social movements. It is recognized today that social movements are drawn from all walks of life, the young and the old, the socially marginal but also the elites. Moreover, a broad understanding of social movement actions recognizes not only participation in demonstrations and protests, but also efforts by organized groups to pursue programs of change by working through institutional means—lawsuits, legal strikes, legislative and election campaigns, and forming political parties (see Goldstone 2003 and Sidney Tarrow's entry "Contentious Politics" in this *Encyclopedia*). Thus we need an approach that embraces a much wider range of demographic factors, and that shows how they contribute to diverse campaigns of mobilization and move- ment action.

The most basic data in demography is the number of people in a category. That can be the whole society (total population), an educational category (college educated, liter- ate), a racial or ethnic or religious grouping, or a gender type. It can also be the number of people living in cities versus the countryside; the number of rich, middle class, and poor; the number in particular occupations (public versus private employment, manual labor); the number who are immigrants or children of immigrants versus native origin; and the numbers voting for particular political parties. The groups that are most salient in any given society also need to be determined empirically; in some societies kinship groups are very important but in most modern countries they are not. In some countries linguistic groups are of vital importance (e.g., Russian speakers within the Ukraine); in other countries religious groups matter far more (e.g., Sunni Muslims in Iraq or Christians in Nigeria).

The interesting dynamics in populations stem from the fact that these groupings often change at very different rates. For example, the number of people with college education may grow much faster than the number of people in society as a whole; or the number of people in a previously marginalized group that are urban and educated may be growing much more quickly than the overall rates of urbanization and educa- tional gains. The civil rights movement in the United States benefitted greatly from two major demographic shifts, both a consequence of the mechanization of cotton-picking in the early twentieth century. One was the movement of southern Blacks to southern cities, where they created educational opportunities and there emerged a small but vital Black urban professional class: ministers, doctors, teachers, and white-collar workers. A second was the vast movement of Blacks out of the south and into northern cities, where they became a considerable voting bloc. The southern Black professional class was critical in leading and organizing the civil rights movements and its actions in the south; the northern Black working class was equally critical in providing support for congressmen who were willing to vote for national legislation to end racial discrimina- tion (McAdam 1982).

Growth in the size of one population group is often seen as an opportunity by members of that group to seek greater rewards, but also as a threat by other groups. Growth in the number of homeless can lead to more advocacy on their behalf; yet it can also alarm people and lead to other movements to oppose government spending that is blamed for creating larger numbers of the idle (Snow 1993). Growth in the number of immigrants can lead to anti-immigrant mobilization, as has happened in Europe (van der Brug et al. 2000). In sum, shifts in the numbers of people in various groups, and in the characteristics of people comprising those groups, are a powerful factor promoting the emergence of social movements.

So far, I have mentioned mostly groups that people are readily aware of, which tend to be fairly visible: immigrants, racial or regional or religious groups, and gender types. There is one additional type of group—the age cohort—that is mainly familiar to demographers, but which is very important in the study of social movements.

An age cohort is simply a group of people of roughly the same age, who were born in a particular period. In the United States, it has become common to refer to those born between 1945 and 1960 as the "baby boomers;" those born from 1960 to 1980 as "Generation X;" and those born from 1980 to 2000 as "Millennials." However, cohorts do not always vary or form systematic groups (Gen X in the United States is known mainly for being very diverse and hard to classify). Rather their significance has more to do with whether a cohort experienced a major shift in its size, education, or experience relative to other cohorts (Mannheim 1974).

A political generation, as defined by Mannheim, is a cohort that has passed through a critical shared event that shapes their political outlook, values, and actions for the rest of their lives (Cavalli 2004). The generations that went through World War I as young men and women, or that experienced the Great Depression of the 1930s, remained cautious, driven by a sense of loss, and drawn to political solutions that promised stability and security. The cohorts of young women who came of age in America and Europe in the 1940s and early 1950s, who were focussed on rebuilding families and their roles as wives and mothers, were very different in their outlook and politics from the women who entered adulthood in the 1960s and 1970s with greater interests in careers, self-expression, and gender equality. And these were again different from the women who came of age in the 1980s and 1990s, for whom aggressive feminism seemed outdated and who sought a different path to reconcile femininity and equality in a different, post-civil rights context. Activists of different generations thus formed their own persistent outlooks, identities, and modes of movement action (Whittier 1995, 1997). More recently, the advent of a global "war on terror" between Islamic Jihadists and the West, triggered by the attack on New York and Washington on September 11, 2001, created a critical generational experience for those entering young adulthood and forming their impressions of politics throughout the Islamic world (Cavalli 2004). Thus the baby-boomers, born into a period of exceptional peace and prosperity after the Great Depression and World War II, and being much larger than earlier cohorts, felt unusually free to define their goals in an idealistic fashion and to act defiantly of their elders. As the baby-boom generation matured, it thus spawned an unusual number of social movements. When the generation was in their 20s (the 1960s), they led the counter-culture, free love, anti-war, student, women's liberation, Chicano and American Indian, women's, environmental and anti-nuclear movements (Goldstone and McAdam 2001). Today, the same generation is in their 50s and 60s, and with a very different outlook, plays a leading role in the conservative Tea Party movement (see more on that later).

Another important cohort effect can be seen in the dissolution of the Soviet Union. The Soviet generation that suffered through World War II sought stability above all else, and even as adults tended to accept the corruption and stagnation of the Brezhnev era in the 1970s. However, the generation that was born after 1950 had a very different world view, and expected more in the way of progress. This "thaw" generation, as they were called by David Remnick (1994), was more urban and educated than any in Soviet history. By the 1980s, they were experimenting with rock music, environmentalism, and regional nationalism in the republics. As members of this generation entered the government, they were more willing to shake things up and entertain ideas of change. As Lane and Ross (1994: 437) note, by 1989 (after the first semi-free elections, engineered by Mikhail Gorbachev), "a new elite in terms of its generational, occupational, and institutional background had replaced the professional politicians of the Brezhnev era." The Brezhnev leadership was dominated by individuals born before the war (indeed 23 per cent were still of the Bolshevik generation born before 1920), who were mainly of rural origins and who had worked their way up the ladder of Komsomol (Communist Youth), the Communist Party, and the Supreme Soviet. However, those who campaigned and were elected in 1989 were mainly persons with a professional or managerial background who had been educated in Moscow and Leningrad, with a wholly different outlook and much weaker attachment to communism. They were soon to dismantle the USSR and replace it and communism with independent national republics and post-communist regimes (Lane and Ross 1998).

In short, significant shifts in the relative size, education, and especially the critical experiences of various groups can play a dramatic role in motivating people to seek changes in social policies and institutions, thus spawning new outlooks, aspirations, and social movements.

DEMOGRAPHY AND INSTITUTIONS

The previous section emphasized the impact of demographic differentials on people within particular groups. However, demographic shifts also have important consequences for society as a whole, which can create new opportunities and conditions for social movement emergence and success.

A society's institutions—schools, families, government, voluntary associations, courts and jails, the military, business organizations—have the important task of moving people into and out of positions, and distributing penalties and rewards, over the course of their life. In most societies, people enter schools and when they complete schooling leave their families, enter jobs in business or government, and join voluntary associations. If unsuccessful, they may end up in encounters with the police, courts and jail. If successful, they may end up in leading roles in business or government. At the same time, all these institutions also have the crucial task of *reproducing society over time*. That is, each new generation must be socialized to prepare to move smoothly through these institutions, and in doing so to learn to operate these institutions and replace the older generations as they pass (Goldstone 2011).

All of this tends to work smoothly when the numbers of people in society are stable or changing slowly enough for growth in the economy and institutions to accommodate the change. However, rapid change in the size of cohorts, or of particular social groups, can easily disrupt this process and place great strains on institutions. Sudden increases in the number of young people, or of migrants, can place a burden on schools (and on government to finance them). Rapid urbanization and educational expansion can rapidly change outlooks and loyalties as people move out of familiar and traditional settings into more fluid ones, where they have a greater variety of choices to create and join voluntary organizations, including new religious and social movements.

Research has shown that in societies with a succession of ever-larger cohorts producing a substantial "youth bulge" (technically, a ratio of the 15–24 age group that is 25 per cent or more the size of the entire adult population), the odds that there will be political violence are considerably higher (Urdal 2011). It is not just that young people are more available for activism, often lacking the responsibilities of families or established careers and the burden of mortgages. It is also the case that young people tend to be more extreme in their views, and more willing to engage in violence for a valued goal. The 1960s thus produced in Europe, Japan, and the West not only a large number of fairly radical social movements embracing such causes as civil rights, women's rights, students' rights, environmental protection, and peace, but also a smaller but still significant number of violent youth-led movements as well (the American Weather Underground, the Italian Red Brigades, the Japanese Red Army, the German Red Army Faction (Baader-Meinhof Gang)).

By contrast, countries with a more mature age profile (i.e., with a mean age of 25 or above), have less violence and also have been shown to be more likely to make a stable transition to democracy (Cincotta and Doces 2011; Weber 2013). Older countries still have a rich variety of social movements, but they tend to be more civil and peaceful, rather than radical and violent, and to seek institutional change rather than extreme ideological goals. The new wave of "color revolutions" seeking democracy, and the success of non-violent movements for social change in recent years (Chenoweth 2011; Nepsted 2011), reflects this change in the demographic profiles of many countries toward less youthful populations.

In addition, societies that have systematically marginalized particular groups (women, gays and lesbians, racial or immigrant groups), are likely to be affected by social movements for change as the members of that group grow more numerous, educated, and concentrated within society. Moreover, as new generations arise for whom the issues making these groups marginal are less salient and meaningful, these movements are more likely to enjoy success. As one example, in the United States opposition to gay marriage is very strongly linked to age. While older generations, raised in an era when homosexuality was considered sinful and shameful and was widely illegal, still resist the idea that same-sex marriage should be treated just the same as man-woman marriage, for younger people this is barely an issue (Lax and Phillips 2009). So as younger generations grow more numerous and influential and older generations pass, the success of the gay marriage movement has gone from doubtful to inevitable in just a few decades.

Demography of Movements

To demonstrate the ways in which demographic analysis can illuminate the emergence, goals, and outcomes of social movements, we can consider three examples: the American civil rights movement of the 1950s and 1960s, America's Tea Party movement of the 2000s, and the Arab Uprisings of 2011.

The Civil Rights Movement

The civil rights movement in the United States went through several phases over many decades, but we will highlight here two of those: the legal and non-violent struggle in the 1940s and 1950s, and the increasingly aggressive and sometimes violent struggles in the 1960s.

From the founding of the National Association for the Advancement of Colored People (NAACP) in 1909, Black Americans fought discrimination mainly through lawsuits and lobbying. They gained limited success, including most notably the 1954 Supreme Court Decision in *Brown v. Board of Education* that made school segregation illegal, and integration in the armed forces during World War II. However, even after *Brown,* little had changed in practice for Blacks in the south. New urban organizations led by Black professionals, such as the Montgomery Improvement Association and the Southern Christian Leadership Conference (SCLC), began to spring up in the mid-1950s.

Most of the leaders of the SCLC had been born prior to the 1920s. The Reverend Martin Luther King, born in 1929, was the youngest of the leadership group. This was thus a mature set of leaders, mainly in their 40s, and they pursued a strategy of deliberate civil disobedience marked by boycotts, sit-ins, and non-violent marches. They had considerable success in the 1950s in getting local business and jurisdictions to change their segregationist policies. However, many states and regions still stood firm for the older racist policies.

In the late 1950s and early 1960s, the civil rights movement then sought out and attracted much more youth participation to support broader activities. The NAACP set up a youth council which started staging sit-ins across the south. The SCLC gave rise to a youth-based Student Nonviolent Coordinating Committee which supported Freedom Rides (to desegregate interstate bus travel) and voter registration drives. In addition, the civil rights movement sought out the participation of white youth for voter registration drives during "Freedom Summer." Black leaders recognized that they were still a marginal, fiercely discriminated against group in the American South, and that without white support they might not be able to break through old patterns. So they invited white northern students to volunteer to assist in drives to register Black voters in the South.

Doug McAdam (1988: 14) points out that the demography of the baby-boom deeply shaped the outlook of these volunteers: "The sheer size and extraordinary national attention lavished on the post-war generation helped produce a middle- to upper-middle class youth subculture uniquely optimistic about the future; certain, one might even say cocky, about its own capabilities, and enamored of its 'history-making' presence in the world." Riding a tide of generational confidence unprecedented in this century, white middle-class youth moved into the civil rights movement along with all the other anti-establishment movements of the 1960s, bringing not only youthful energy and enthusiasm, but the conviction of their generation that they could and would change the world.

Yet at the same time, many Black youths began to move in a different direction. Although by the mid-1960s the civil rights movement had won major national victories with the passage of Civil Rights Acts by Congress, a number of Black leaders began to grow impatient with the continued economic hardship, discrimination in hiring and housing, and hostility still experienced by many Blacks. These younger leaders, such as Stokely Carmichael (born 1941), Huey Newton (born 1942), and H. Rap Brown (born 1943) began to advocate for Black Power and the right to violence in self-defense. In 1969, the Student Non-Violent Coordinating Committee dropped the "non" from its name, while Newton and Brown helped found the Black Panther movement. In the mid- to late 1960s, violent race riots tore through major American cities, including Detroit, Los Angeles, and Newark, ending what had been the purely non-violent protest movement against discrimination that prevailed from the 1950s through 1964.

In sum, the civil rights movement was shaped by demography in many respects. Changes in the education and migration of Blacks created the grounds for the organization of the movement and electoral support for its success. Changes in the generational leadership of Black organizations heralded the shift from a deliberate and peaceful approach in the movement to the more confrontational and even violent acts of a younger generation. Finally, the baby-boom helped shape the confidence and participation of young middle and upper-middle class whites in American to engage in the movement and contribute to its success.

THE TEA PARTY MOVEMENT

Move forward fifty years from the 1960s, and we find the same generation that sought to reshape the world now organized to preserve the world they knew. The emergence of the "Tea Party movement," a collection of conservative, anti-immigration, anti-globalization, and anti-big government groups, has had a major influence on the Republican Party and national politics in 2008–13. They have mobilized their supporters to defeat more liberal Republicans, provide funds to conservative candidates and causes, and even dictated strategy to congressional leaders, promoting refusals to compromise on Federal Budget reductions and bitter opposition to President Barack Obama's national health care reforms (Skocpol and Williamson 2013; Van Dyke and Meyer 1914).

In contrast to the civil rights movement, which was a movement of a marginalized, discriminated-against group seeking greater rights, the Tea Party movement is composed of people who are generally better established and *more* successful than average Americans. According to a national poll by CBS News (2012), among the 18 per cent who identified themselves as Tea Party supporters, 89 per cent are white; just one per cent is black. Three-quarters of them are 45 years old or older, and 29 per cent are 65 plus. They are fairly spread out nationally: just over one-third are from the South, a quarter are from the West, 18 per cent are from the northeast, and 22 per cent are from the Midwest. However, they are far better educated than most Americans, with 37 per cent being college graduates compared to 25 per cent of all Americans. They also have above-average household incomes with 56 per cent making over $50,000 per year. In short, they would seem to be a cross-section of America's most successful; yet they are angry, mobilized, and determined to shape policy.

What motivates them? This is a generation that has prospered through the stock market and property booms that lasted from 1980 to the early 2000s. They looked forward to a very comfortable retirement in which to continue their pleasant lifestyle. Yet that is precisely what they now see threatened by factors beyond their control. In the dot-com bust of 2001 and the much bigger crash and Great Depression of 2007–09, they lost value on their homes and savings. They then grew livid at the government response to these events, with the Bush and Obama administrations spending billions to bail out banks and corporations, paying many more billions to support the unemployed, and even more billions on a health care reform that pays subsidies for medical insurance for those currently uninsured. At the same time, they received nothing to help make up their losses, and even had to suffer higher taxes on their income and dividends into the bargain. Worried that the government's hugely increased debts and easy money policies will generate inflation that will further eat away at their asset values, they want a sharp reduction of deficits and government spending, and an end to policies that they see as providing handouts and subsidies for those who are not working or paying their own way. In sum, the emergence of the Tea Party is a product of a particular generational experience for the baby-boom cohort galvanized by the economic turmoil of the early 2000s, acting not to create change, but to preserve what they see as their well-earned position against government actions that put them at risk.

THE ARAB UPRISINGS

In late 2010 and early 2011, several Arab countries of North Africa and the Middle East were suddenly shaken by massive waves of social protest. In Tunisia, a campaign of marches and demonstrations in all major cities forced the ruler, Zine El Abidine Ben Ali to flee. In Egypt, mass occupations of public spaces in Cairo and Alexanderia combined with waves of political strikes to similarly drive President Hosni Mubarak from power. In Libya and Syria, peaceful protests provoked a military response from the regimes of Muammar Qaddafi and Bashar al-Assad, leading the opposition to arm itself and producing civil wars. In Yemen, protests seeking to change the regime led America to broker the departure of the President, Ali Abdullah Saleh, and left a still-divided country seeking stability in the face of multiple religious and regional movements (Lynch 2012).

What all of these movements had in common is that they were led by youth. Young men and women in their twenties and early thirties in Egypt were behind the April 6 movement, which organized the initial demonstration on January 25, and then used social media to spread news of events throughout the world. To be sure, youth alone could not carry these uprisings forward, and it was only when the older generations followed youth into the streets and then joined movement actions and undertook strikes demanding change that the movements succeeding in overcoming the old regimes. Yet it was the perspective of youth on their societies that prompted the initial mobilizations and their radical goals.

Following an earlier wave of revolutions across the Arab world in the 1950s, inspired by the Arab nationalism and socialism of Gamal Abdel Nasser, Arab states had grown stronger, more centralized, and provided more patronage and subsidies to their populations. The generations of the 1950s to the 1980s were glad to have expanded opportunities for work, education, and subsidies for food and fuel. The result—supported in part by the flow of oil money into the region, but also by military support and foreign investment—was a period of stable and populist authoritarianism.

However, in the era following the 1980s new generations grew up with different experiences. By the 2000s, as a new wave of young people emerged from schools and universities, their relationship to governments had changed. The cohorts of the 1980s, 1990s, and 2000s were huge, as fertility across the region remained high while economic growth produced falling child mortality. The number of those aged 15–24 grew dramatically: in Egypt from 8.7 million in 1980 to 15.4 million in 2010; in Syria from 1.8 million to 4.4 million over the same period (United Nations 2013).

These large youth cohorts, pouring out of schools and universities, strained the capacity of states to continue to provide the guaranteed free education, the guaranteed government jobs for graduates, and the food and fuel subsidies for poorer families, that had been the basis of the social contract. While the first decade of the twenty-first century was generally one of strong economic growth for the Arab countries, the benefits of this growth went increasingly to those closely connected with the ruling families, while the social guarantees for the rest of the population were reduced or curtailed. The youth were particularly ill-served; youth unemployment across the region was among the highest in the world c. 2010, and oddly, the very highest unemployment rates were found among those with the highest level of education! This was because the concentrated, capital intensive growth did not provide adequate numbers of white collar and professional jobs for the vast number of youth who, having received a free college education, felt entitled to such jobs; nor could governments, whose payrolls had already grown to extraordinary levels hiring prior generations of graduates, make up the gap (Korotayev and Zinkina 2011).

The generation coming of age in the early 2000s thus felt particularly betrayed. Unable to find work, despite the promise bestowed by their education, and therefore unable to marry when expected, many felt that their entire life was being driven off track. The regimes, meanwhile, appeared ever more closed, corrupt, and resistant to change. Unsurprisingly, the Arab youth cohort in their early 20s and 30s thus began to seek ways to organize for change, and by the end of the decade was ready to take to the streets and demand a new regime.

The overall demographic structure of the Arab societies also made them more vulnerable to change. These countries had a relatively low median age, mostly in the high teens or low twenties, and thus had large reserves of youth who could be mobilized. They had also grown more urbanized and industrialized, giving greater political clout to urban crowds and workers.

The one exception to this general trend was Tunisia, where family control and fertility decline were more advanced, creating a significantly older age structure than in other Arab countries. Thus we would expect the social movement in Tunisia to be less violent, less radical, and show greater chances of a peaceful transition than in other countries of the region (Cincotta 2012). While it is too early to say whether this forecast will prove true, so far Tunisia has fit this pattern.

DEMOGRAPHY AND THE FUTURE
OF SOCIAL MOVEMENTS

The demographic trends that we now see around the world seem sure to generate a future of even more active social movements and protest. In the developed world, from North America and Western Europe to South Korea, Japan, and Australia and New Zealand, we see sharply slowing and even negative population growth, along with fast ageing populations. These conditions are likely to produce sharp generational conflicts. As the large baby-boom cohorts move into retirement, they will fight (as we have seen with the Tea Party) to keep the benefits they expect, despite the slow-down in economic growth and the smaller size of the workforce to support them. Meanwhile, the younger generation is likely to protest against paying high taxes to support an older generation that already benefitted from a period of exceptional prosperity. Generational social movements are thus likely to continue to be a feature of developed country politics.

At the same time, in the developing world, still surging youth populations with growing educational achievement are likely to be frustrated where economic opportunities do not keep pace with their expectations and demands, and are likely to continue to fuel both democratic and radical political movements. In the past few years, we have not only seen the revolutions in the Arab world and Ukraine, but also major protest movements in Turkey, Brazil, Thailand, Bosnia, and Venezuela. Both low-income and middle-income countries are feeling this wave.

While youth and student movements played a leading part in all of these movements, a crucial role was also played by the emerging urban middle class, demanding an end to corruption and more accountable government, blaming rulers for misgovernment and squandering the resources needed to move their countries forward (Fukuyama 2013). As globalization of the economy promotes a growing global middle class, which is projected to increase by several billion in the next two decades (Kharas 2010), we can expect to see this middle class pursue their goals by movement organization as well as through elections and mainstream political parties. The trends in global demography thus foreshadow a future with far more active and widespread social and protest movements.

REFERENCES

Cavalli, Allessandro (2004). "Generations and Value Orientations," *Social Compass*. 51(2): 155–168.

CBS News (2012). "Tea Party Supporters: Who They Are and What they Believe." CBS News on line: www.cbsnews.com/news/tea-party-supporters-who-they-are-and-what-they-believe/

Chenoweth, Erica and Stephan Maria J. (2011). *Why Civil Resistance Works*. New York: Columbia University Press.

Cincotta, Richard (2012). "Life Begins after 25: Demography and the Societal Timing of the Arab Spring." Foreign Policy Research Institute E-notes online: www.fpri.org/enotes/2012/201201.cincotta.demography_arabspring.html

Cincotta, Richard and Doces, John (2011). "The Age-Structural Maturity Thesis: The Impact of the Youth Bulge on the Advent and Stability of Liberal Democracy." In *Political Demography: How Population Changes Are Reshaping International Security and National Politics*, edited by Jack A. Goldstone, Eric P. Kaufmann, and Monica Duffy Toft, 98–116. New York: Oxford University Press.

Fukuyama, Francis (2013). "The Middle-Class Revolution." *Wall Street Journal online*, June 28, 2013. www.online.wsj.com/news/articles/SB10001424127887323873904578571472700348086

Goldstone, Jack A., ed. (2003). *States, Parties, and Social Movements*. New York: Cambridge University Press.

Goldstone, Jack A. (2011). "A Theory of Political Demography: Human and Institutional Reproduction," In *Political Demography: How Population Changes Are Reshaping*

International Security and National Politics, edited by Jack A. Goldstone, Eric P. Kaufmann, and Monica Duffy Toft, 10–30. New York: Oxford University Press.

Goldstone, Jack A. and McAdam, Doug (2001). "Contention in Demographic and Life-Course Context." In *Silence and Voice in the Study of Contentious Politics*, edited by Ronald R. Aminzade, Jack A. Goldstone, Doug McAdam, Elizabeth J. Perry, William H. Sewell, Jr., Sidney Tarrow and Charles Tilly, 195–221. Cambridge: Cambridge University Press.

Gurr, Ted Robert (1970). *Why Men Rebel*. Princeton: Princeton University Press.

Huntington, Samuel P. (1968). *Political Order in Changing Societies*. New Haven: Yale University Press.

Kharas, Homi (2010). "The Emerging Middle Class in Developing Countries." Brookings Research Paper. www.brookings.edu/research/papers/2010/01/global-consumers-khraras

Korotayev, Andrey V. and Zinkina, Julia V. (2011). "Egyptian Revolution: A Demographic Structural Analysis," *Entelequia. Revista Interdisciplinar*. 13 (Spring): 139–169.

Lax, Jeffrey R. and Phillips, Justin H. (2009). "Gay Rights in the States: Public Opinion and Policy Responsiveness," *American Political Science Review*. 103(3): 367–386.

Lane, David and Ross, Cameron (1994). "The Social Background and the Political Allegiance of the Political Elite of the Supreme Soviet of the U.S.S.R.: The Terminal Stage, 1984–1991," *Europe-Asia Studies*. 46: 437–463.

Lane, David and Ross, Cameron (1998). "The Russian Political Elites 1991–1995: Recruitment and Renewal." In *Postcommunist Elites and Democracy in Eastern Europe*, edited by John Higley, Jan Pakulsi, and Wlodzimeirz Wesolowski, 34–66. London: Macmillan.

Lynch, Marc (2012). *The Arab Uprising: The Unfinished Revolutions of the New Middle East*. New York: Public Affairs.

Mannheim, Karl (1974). "What is a Social Generation?" In *The Youth Revolution: The Conflict of Generations in Modern History*, edited by Anthony Esler, 7–14. Lexington, MA: D.C. Heath.

McAdam, Doug (1982). *Political Process and the Development of Black Insurgency, 1930–1970*. Chicago: University of Chicago Press.

McAdam, Doug (1988). *Freedom Summer*. New York: Oxford University Press.

Nepstad, Sharon (2011). *Non-Violent Revolutions: Civil Resistance in the Late 20th Century*. New York: Oxford University Press.

Remnick, David (1994). *Lenin's Tomb: The Last Days of the Soviet Empire*. New York: Vintage.

Skocpol, Theda and Williamson, Vanessa (2013). *The Tea Party and the Remaking of Republican Conservatism*. New York: Oxford University Press.

Snow, David A. and Anderson, Leon (1993). *Down on Their Luck: A Study of Homeless Street People*. Berkeley and Los Angeles: University of California Press.

United Nations, Department of Economic and Social Affairs, Population Division, Population Estimates and Projections Section (2013). "World Population Prospects: the 2012 Revision" on-line data base: www.esa.un.org/unpd/wpp/unpp/panel_population.htm

Urdal, Henrick (2011). "Youth Bulges and Violence," In *Political Demography: How Population Changes Are Reshaping International Security and National Politics*, edited by Jack A. Goldstone, Eric P. Kaufmann, and Monica Duffy Toft, 117–132. New York: Oxford University Press.

Van der Brug, Wouter, Fennema, Meindert, and Tillie, Jean. (2000). "Anti-immigrant Parties in Europe: Ideological or Protest Vote?" *European Journal of Political Research*. 37: 77–102.

Van Dyke, Nella and Meyer, David, eds. (2014). *Understanding the Tea Party Movement*. Farnham, Surrey: Ashgate.

Weber, Hannes (2013). "Demography and Democracy: the Impact of Youth Cohort Size on Democratic Stability in the World," *Democratization*. 20(2): 335–357.

Whittier, Nancy (1995). *Feminist Generations: The Persistence of the Radical Women's Movement*. Philadelphia: Temple University Press.

Whittier, Nancy (1997). "Political Generations, Micro-Cohorts, and the Transformation of Social Movements," *American Sociological Review*. 62(5): 760–778.

CHAPTER 9

MIGRATION AND SOCIAL MOVEMENTS

NINA EGGERT AND MARCO GIUGNI

INTRODUCTION

MIGRATION today is a salient issue across Europe. Political and public debates often deal with the status and rights of immigrants in the so-called host societies, the regulation of inflows of economic migrants as well as asylum seekers, the supposedly negative consequences of the "Islamization" of Western society due to an increasing number of immigrants from Muslim countries, and so forth. Similarly—and perhaps as a consequence of that—public opinion is often quite skeptical about giving more space and rights to new immigrants, if not overtly opposed to it.

Such a saliency and politicization of migration issues is both a cause and a result of the mobilization of certain political forces on such issues, most notably radical right parties which have gained increasing electoral success in recent years. But other political actors have contributed to placing immigration and immigrants high on the political and public agendas: mainstream parties, but also social movements, both from the Left and from the Right. These other actors, of course, include migrants' movements themselves. However, the latter are often absent from political and public debates, and more institutional actors tend to dominate the scene, although we have many important instances of such mobilizations such as, for example, the *sans papiers* or the unrest of 2005 and 2007 in France or the mobilization in the United States of migrant background workers supporting legalization policies.

In spite of such a relevant and close link between migration issues and popular mobilizations around such issues, scholarly work has traditionally developed along two separate paths. On the one hand, research has focussed on the sociology of migration as well as on policy making on immigration and ethnic relations (Brubaker 1992; Joppke 1998; Freeman 2011). On the other hand, students of social movements have sometimes—though not very often—examined the patterns and determinants of collective action by, on behalf, and against migrants (Ireland 1994; Koopmans et al. 2005).

In this chapter we examine the relation between migration and social movements by focussing on how the structural changes that have affected Western societies, in particular Western Europe, have led to the rise of collective mobilizations in this field (see Kastoryano and Schader 2014 for a review focussing on ethnic mobilizations). The latter take place in a space of contention in which various collective actors intervene publicly on issues pertaining to immigration and ethnic relations politics. Such interventions may take different forms, not only protest actions, but also "softer" ways of addressing migration issues, including speech acts. This is what in recent literature has been called "claims-making" (Koopmans and Statham 1999; Koopmans et al. 2005) and which is inspired by the fundamental work of McAdam, Tarrow, and Tilly (1996, 2001).[1] Here we follow this broader view of contentious politics to show how certain structural changes might impact on the claims-making in the field of immigration and ethnic relations politics.

STRUCTURAL CHANGES

It is a truism that the world has undergone a fundamental transformation in recent years. Often we refer to such a transformation as "globalization," that is, "the compression of the world and the intensification of the consciousness of the world as a whole" (Robertson 1992: 8) or the "'lifting out' of social relations from local contexts of interaction and their restructuring across indefinite spans of time–space" (Giddens 1990: 21). This has brought about some important structural changes in contemporary societies. Three such changes, all related to the process of globalization, are of particular relevance when it comes to social movements and collective action on migration issues. Let us describe them in some detail.

The first structural change that had—and is having—important consequences for collective action in this field refers to the movements of populations from one country to the other and, more broadly, from one region of the world to the other, in particular from the less wealthy region to the richest one (Bade 2003). Western Europe has come under particularly strong pressure since the end of the Second World War. Since then immigrants moved to a number of European countries mainly for three reasons: the search for better economic conditions (the so-called "guest workers"), family reunion with other family members, and political motives by asylum-seekers and refugees. This inflow of migrants has taken place in spite of attempts by receiving countries to put up some barriers to it, also due to the inherently liberal character—both in economic and political terms—of Western countries (Hollifield 1992). At the same time, however, the so-called "fortress Europe"—that is, the double-track process of increasing control at the borders of the union and facilitating internal movements, institutionally embodied by the creation of the Schengen space—has made access more difficult for migrants coming from extra-European countries.[2]

Yet, the most important changes in this respect lie not so much in the sheer number or share of residents of migrant origin as in the variety and diversity of this population. If, up until the 1990s, the migrant population of most immigration countries was made of a few nationalities coming from traditional emigration countries such as Italy,[3] Portugal, and Spain, or from former colonies (this applies in particular to Britain and France), in the past two or three decades this population has become more diversified. Immigration flows have started increasingly to come from extra-European countries, from Asia and Sub-Saharan Africa, most notably. Perhaps most importantly in relation to recent and current political debates, is the diversity in religious terms brought about by the inflow of Muslim immigrants.[4]

These structural changes in the size and diversity of the immigrant population may have two consequences. On the one hand, they might increase the likelihood to observe the rise of migrants' mobilizations, all other things being equal. On the other hand, they might also increase the likelihood that other actors—especially anti-migrant ones—might mobilize, either verbally or physically. Social movement theory, however, has shown that at least three intervening factors need to be taken into account for explaining if and how grievances translate into actual mobilization: the degree of endogenous organization of the movement, the framing of migration issues by social and political actors, and favorable political opportunities to mount collective challenges (McAdam et al. 1996; Tarrow 2011). In other words, structural change does not translate directly in social movements around migration issues, but depends on how organized movements are, how such issues are articulated in the public domain, and how the political–institutional context offers opportunities for the movements to mobilize.

Globalization has brought about a second important structural change for the claims-making on immigration and ethnic relations politics. This refers to the transformation of the structure of social and political cleavages in Europe. As Kriesi and his collaborators have argued (Kriesi et al. 2008, 2012), Europe has witnessed a transformation of the political space in recent years which has brought about a new cleavage opposing "winners" and "losers" of globalization and cutting across traditional lines of demarcation. This transformation of the cleavage structures, which has primarily affected the cultural dimension of the political space, has favored the rise and success of radical right parties in the 1990s and 2000s, which have made their opposition to immigration their main electoral selling point, but also to a transformation of the political agenda of established parties into right-wing populist parties supported by the losers of the globalization process: unskilled workers and the less well educated (Grande 2008; Oesch and Rennwald 2010). The success of these parties has been attributed to their use of a "magic formula" combining liberalism in the economic realm and authoritarianism in the cultural realm (Kitschelt 1995). The latter rests precisely on a strong anti-immigrant stance, especially when it comes to asylum-seekers and, more recently, Muslim immigrants. As a result, political debates on immigration become more polarized.

Finally, if the transformation of the political space just described is felt above all at the national level, though in most if not all European countries, a third structural change brought about by globalization—or perhaps better, characterizing globalization—and having important consequences for collective action on migration issues concerns the increasing importance of the supranational level. We refer to the process of European integration. In spite of recent and less recent instances of resistance to this process and increasing skepticism vis-à-vis the European project, the past few decades have witnessed a relative shift of power and sovereignty from the national to the supranational (European) level. In terms of social movement and collective action theory, this means that political opportunities for mobilization—including on migration issues—have emerged at the EU level (Marks and McAdam 1996). However, as some have shown (Balme and Chabanet 2008; Imig and Tarrow 2001; Rucht 2002), the structure and logic of European institutions favors interest groups as well as highly professionalized and formalized organizations rather than social movements and grass-roots associations, with little space for a Europeanization of protest, including in the field of immigration and ethnic relations (Giugni and Passy 2002).

CHANGING PATTERNS OF POLITICAL MOBILIZATION ON MIGRATION

How have these structural changes affected political mobilization in the field of immigration and ethnic relations? Two large-scale comparative studies provide empirical evidence to answer this question.[5] First and foremost, as already noted, this has led to an increasing salience of migration. The degree of intervention in the public domain, as measured by the number of claims, gives a rough indicator of salience. Although their study is more geared towards explaining differences across countries rather than changes over time, Koopmans et al. (2005) have stressed the increasing salience of migration issue in public discourse during the 1990s.

A more recent study—the Support and Opposition to Migration (SOM) project—allows us to take a closer look at the period up to the late 2000s. This study has looked, among other things at the changing patterns of claims-making in the politics of migration in Western Europe (Berkhout 2012). As we can see, in spite of day-to-day variation, there is a rising trend in terms of the number of claims since 1995 (Figure 9.1). The pattern, however, is curvilinear rather that linear: the number of claims peaked in 2004–05 and has fallen since then. Yet the level at the end of the period in 2009 remains higher than its initial level in 1995.

Migration policy has traditionally been divided into two main subfields: the regulation of immigration flows (including asylum-seekers and refugees) and the situation of resident migrants in the receiving society (in social, cultural, and political terms). These two policy fields have been captured by the distinction between immigration and

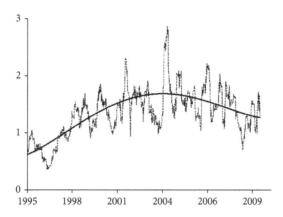

FIGURE 9.1 Salience of migration (number of claims per day and long-term trend line)

Source: Berkhout, Joost (2012). *Changing Claims and Changing Frames in the Politics of Migration in Western Europe, 1995–2009*. SOM Working Papers. Paper Number 2012-09.

immigrant policy (Hammar 1985). Political mobilization over migration accordingly addresses these two main issue fields. Koopmans et al. (2005) show that the thematic focus of claims varies very much across country as a result of different institutional and discursive opportunity structures. In some countries, such as Germany and Switzerland but to some extent also France, claims on immigration, asylum, and aliens politics largely surpass claims on minority integration politics, while in others, like Netherlands and Great Britain, it is the other way around. If, however, one includes in immigrant policy also claims pertaining to anti-racism, xenophobia, and inter-ethnic conflicts, then in all five countries but Switzerland the former represent the core of political debates and collective action in this field. So, in spite of a substantial share of claims being focussed on the regulation of immigration flows and in spite of the question of refugees taking central stage—in addition to being a real problem—in specific periods and in some contexts, most notably in the wake of the dramatic events occurred in the Middle East and Northern Africa after the Libyan and Syrian crises, in most countries the real stuff of political mobilization in this field seems to have to do with minority integration politics.

Again, the SOM project provides us with longitudinal data in order to see whether and how the thematic focus of claims has changed over time (Berkhout et al. 2013). The distinction between immigration and civic integration issues roughly reflects that between immigration and immigrant policy. The trends over time unveil something a cross-sectional analysis cannot show, namely that priorities have changed considerably. Once again, important annual variations can be observed, but the linear trend lines are quite explicit (Figure 9.2). Clearly, political mobilization in this field has shifted from a focus on immigration in the mid-1990s to a focus on civic integration in the late 2000s. The issue of accommodation of Islam in Europe is certainly not alien to this major shift (van Parys et al. 2013). In fact, if one looks at claims-making on Muslims only—hence excluding other types of migrants—minority integration politics became

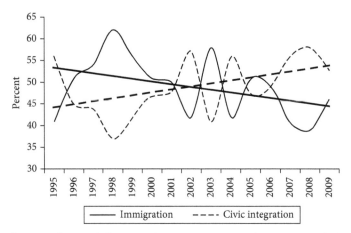

FIGURE 9.2 Thematic focus of claims-making on migration (proportion of claims per year and linear trend lines)

Source: Berkhout, Joost (2012). *Changing Claims and Changing Frames in the Politics of Migration in Western Europe, 1995–2009*. SOM Working Papers. Paper Number 2012-09.

overwhelmingly the most important priority in all countries, with only a small share of claims dealing with immigration, asylum, and aliens politics when it comes to this population.

Obviously, claims are made by actors. So, who lies behind interventions in claims-making? Has the relative weight of certain actors changed over time? We can get an idea of this by looking again at the SOM data (Figure 9.3). These show the distribution of claims on migration issues across types of actors. Perhaps the most immediately visible aspect is that both state and non-state actors have increased their interventions in the public domain on issues pertaining to immigration and ethnic relations politics during the period under scrutiny.[6] This applies in particular to governments as well as parliaments and political parties, on the one hand, and other civil society actors, on the other.[7] In contrast, the contribution of three key actors in this field seems to be more limited. These are extreme right (anti-immigrant) actors, anti-racist and pro-migrant actors, and of course migrants themselves.

The low presence (read: political mobilization) of the radical right may seem odd. It can however be explained in two ways. First, public attention has often been captured by some *éclatant* events, such as xenophobic violent attacks to centers of asylum-seekers—especially in Germany—in the 1990s or certain speeches by extreme right party leaders. This might convey the image of a very active radical right, while a more systematic view tells us that it is less so (see Caiani et al. 2012 for a recent comparative analysis of the mobilization of the extreme right).[8] Secondly, unlike leftist positions in favor of immigrants, the radical right most often takes the form of parties and uses the electoral channels rather than of social movements (Kriesi 1999; Hutter and Kriesi 2013). Protests on immigration only represent a small share of all protest events (Kriesi et al. 2012). In addition, it remains largely in the hand of

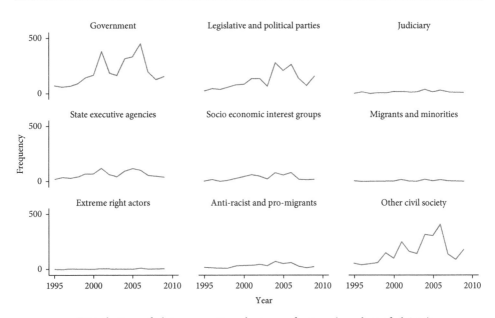

FIGURE 9.3 Distribution of claims over time by type of actors (number of claims)

Source: SOM project.

left-wing pro-migrant groups than of anti-migrants actors. The latter tend to pre-fer using the institutional venues, most notably interventions in the electoral arena. We should therefore not be too surprised to observe a low presence of radical rights actors in political claims-making on migration issues, a presence which has moreover remained quite stable over time. In addition Koopmans (1996) has shown that there is an inverse relationship between the electoral strength of the radical right and the level of extra-parliamentary mobilization by extreme right actors: the stronger the former, the weaker the latter and vice versa.

If mobilization by "anti-immigrant" actors is less important than one might expect, that of their counterpart is not much higher. As we can see, claims by anti-racist and pro-migrant actors are also at a relatively low level. In contrast to the radical right, how-ever, they have increased their presence during the peak of mobilization in the field, around 2004–05. Yet, research on anti-racist and pro-migrant movements is extremely limited. Apart from certain works on the *sans papiers* in France (Siméant 1998) and in the French-speaking literature more generally (Passy 1998), little has been done so far on this front (Koopmans 2001; Statham 2001).

In our earlier discussion of the structural changes, we referred to globalization as a major transformation which has had—and is still having—important consequences for migration. To what extent does it influence collective action and social movements on immigration and ethnic relations politics? During the 1990s, a number of important works argued that, under the thrust of globalization, the locus of conflicts around migra-tion issues has shifted from the national to the supranational arena and that the national level has become much less important in recent decades (Soysal 1994; Jacobson 1996).

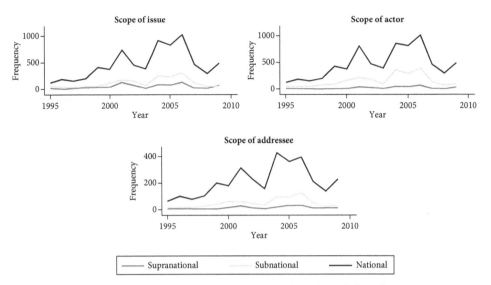

FIGURE 9.4 Distribution of claims over time by scope (number of claims)

Source: SOM project.

Koopmans et al. (2005), among others (Joppke 1999) have challenged this view, showing evidence that this is not the case and that the core of political debates and mobilizations has remained well anchored in the national level. The data from the SOM project lead to a similar conclusion. We can see the extent to which claims-making in this field went "beyond borders"—or perhaps has localized—by looking at the scope of claims-making (Figure 9.4). Regardless of whether we consider the scope of the issue, actor, or addressees—three indicators of the "supranationalization" of claims-making—the share of national-based claims remains overwhelmingly larger than that of both supranational and sub-national ones. In addition, while all levels have contributed to the rise in the first half of the 2000s, national claims take the lion's share in it.

Migrants' Movements

In our earlier discussion on claims-making by specific actors, migrants and minorities were deliberately not included, as their political mobilization is discussed in more detail here. The increasing salience of migration as an issue in the public domain and in contentious politics goes along with an increasing organization of migrants as collective political actors. Long considered as politically quiescent, in particular in European scholarship on contentious politics in the field of immigration, recent works show that migrants are politically active (Jacobs and Tillie 2004; Ramakrishnan and Bloemraad 2008; Morales and Giugni 2011). As can be seen in the data shown in Figure 9.3, migrants form only a small share of actors mobilizing on issues related to immigration and ethnic relations politics. In addition, migrant organizations use protest very sparingly (Eggert and Pilati 2014). However, they are increasingly organizing themselves, both nationally and supra-nationally, advancing claims on issues as diverse as the extension of their rights, the recognition of their cultural particularities, and the conditions of entry and stay in the receiving countries (Soysal 1997). In some countries, the presence of migrants in claims-making is actually quite large and can constitute as much as one fifth of all claims, as for example in Britain in the 1990s (Koopmans et al. 2005).

The structural changes discussed earlier have not only affected the patterns of claims-making and political mobilization on issues pertaining to immigration and ethnic relations, but also the ways in which scholars have addressed these issues. In Western Europe and most notably in long-standing immigration countries such as Britain, France, and Germany, research has long focussed on immigrant groups coming from Southern Europe in order to work or—especially in the case of Britain and France—on people from former colonies such as India, Pakistan, or the Maghreb region. In the last few years, however, the focus of scholars has shifted towards an analysis of new immigrant groups, including from Sub-Saharan Africa and, more recently, Muslims migrants have taken center stage.

Various approaches have accounted for the mobilization of migrants and their collective action. Reflecting the ways in which immigration has been dealt with more generally, in the 1970s and 1980s the study of collective action of migrants was dominated by the debate opposing class-based and ethnic-based approaches (Castles and Kosack 1974; Miles and Phizaclea 1977; Miller 1982; Rex 1991). In the 1990s and 2000s, however, there has been a paradigmatic shift towards theories stressing the role of resources and opportunities for the political mobilization of migrants (Ireland 1994; Soysal 1994, 1997; Koopmans and Statham 2000; Okamoto 2003; Koopmans et al. 2005; Steil and Vasi 2014). This theoretical turn has come in part under the lead of students of social movements who became interested in collective action in the field of immigration and ethnic relations politics. Studies undertaken in this theoretical tradition were able to show how collective action by migrants follow logics similar to any other social movement as well as its wide cross-national variation as a result of different sets of institutional and discursive opportunities. Thus, recent studies show that the use of protest activities by migrant organizations varies across countries: in countries where migrants have limited rights, migrants and their organizations tend to rely on native associations and actors to advance their claims (Pilati 2012; Eggert and Pilati 2014).

In sum, research on migrants' movements is still relatively limited. This is not because of a lack of "raw material," as different types of migrants do mobilize in spite of the fact that they are often to be found at the margins of society. Students of social movements have traditionally tended to focus on a limited number of "important" movements, such as peace and environmental movements in Europe or the civil rights movement in the United States. This has adversely affected not only the study of migrants' movements, but also of that of mobilizations against (i.e., radical rights movements) or on behalf (i.e., pro-migrant movements) of such movements. In addition, this relative shortage of studies on migrants' movements is to some extent hidden by the fact that there is a growing and quite important literature on the political participation of immigrants at the individual level (see Morales an Giugni 2011 for a recent study). While these works often look at different forms of participation or at participation in general, they provide important insights into the conditions and mechanisms of engagement in protest activities.

Conclusion

Migration and social movements have seldom been associated in the social science literature. Scholarly work has either looked at migration mainly in terms of policies or in its sociological dimension, leaving little room for discussion of collective action by, for, or against migrants. When scholars have addressed political mobilization on migration issues, they have mostly focussed on party politics, mainly in order to explain the rise and electoral breakthrough of radical right parties. And in the rare instances in which they have looked at social movements in this field, they have predominantly focussed on migrants as objects rather than protagonists of political mobilization.

Yet, the field is not completely empty. Scholarly interest in the topic has increased in recent years, partly as a consequence of certain structural changes that have had important consequences for collective action in this field, such as the increasing size and diversity of the immigrant population in Western Europe. As a result, migration has become a more salient issue, both in political debates and among scholars.

Research has been characterized by two major shifts in recent years. First, class and ethnicity theories, which dominated the field in the 1970s and 1980s, have been increasingly challenged by new approaches stressing the role of resources and opportunities. This is because students of social movements have become interested in the political mobilizing of migrants as well as more generally on immigration and ethnic relations politics. The resulting cross-fertilization between the field of migration studies and that of social movement studies cannot but be beneficial to both.

Secondly, in addition to this theoretical shift, scholars have shifted their attention away from traditional immigrant groups to other migrant populations, most notably Muslims. In addition, partly as a result of the structural changes described earlier, research has paid increasing attention to mobilizations occurring at the global and not only national or local levels.

While the gap between the research on migration and research on social movements, at least in part, has started to be closed, much more work is required in order to better understand under which conditions social movements by, for, and against migrants mobilize and through which processes and mechanisms. Work on migrants' movements is particularly necessary, as this represents one of the main blind spots in the extant literature. In addition, research on the consequences of social movements in the field of immigration has been lagging behind and therefore scholars should pay much more attention to this aspect in the future.

Notes

1. In this context, an instance of claims-making can be defined as any act involving "demands, criticisms, or proposals related to the regulation or evaluation of immigration, minority integration, or xenophobia" (Koopmans and Statham 1999: 207).

2. This does not apply, or only to a limited extent, to countries such as Switzerland that have made specific bilateral agreements with the European Union.

3. Britain is perhaps an exception, given the more varied migrant population coming from Commonwealth countries.

4. Of course, countries with former colonies in Muslim societies, like Britain and France, had already a large share of residents originating from those societies.

5. These are the MERCI (Mobilization on Ethnic Relations, Citizenship, and Immigration) project (covering France, Germany, Great Britain, Netherlands, and Switzerland) and the SOM (Support and Opposition to Migration) project (covering Austria, Belgium, Britain, Ireland, Netherlands, Spain, and Switzerland).

6. Since these data (and those presented by Koopmans et al. 2005) come from a content analysis of media sources, here we refer to the presence of actors in the public domain in this field. However, this is the most relevant aspect when it comes to examining patterns of political mobilization, both across countries and over time. The same applies to the other data presented in this chapter.

7. Other civil society actors include religious organizations, media and journalists, academics and experts, charity and social organizations.

8. It is important to note that we are speaking here of claims by radical rights actors, not xenophobic or racist claims made by other actors, such as mainstream parties for example. If we include the latter, obviously we find a much higher number of extreme right claims (Koopmans et al. 2005).

References

Bade, Klaus J. (2003). *Migration in European History*. Oxford: Basil Blackwell.

Balme, Richard and Chabanet, Didier (2008). *European Governance and Democracy: Power and Protest in the EU*. Lanham, MD: Rowman and Littlefield.

Berkhout, Joost (2012). *Changing Claims and Changing Frames in the Politics of Migration in Western Europe, 1995-2009*. SOM Working Papers No. 2012-09. Available at SSRN: http://ssrn.com/abstract=2168713 or http://dx.doi.org/10.2139/ssrn.2168713Berkhout 2012, working paper

Berkhout, Joost, Sudulich, Laura, Ruedin, Didier, Peintinger, Teresa, Meyer, Sarah, Vangoidsenhoven, Guido, Cunningham, Kevin, Ros, Virgina, Wunderlich, Daniel (2013) "Political Claims Analysis: Support and Opposition to Migration." http://hdl.handle.net/1902.1/17967

Brubaker, Roger (1992). *Citizenship and Nationhood in France and Germany*. Cambridge: Harvard University Press.

Castles, Stephen and Kosack, Godula (1974). "How Trade Unions Try to Control and Integrate Immigrant Workers in the German Federal Republic," *Race & Class*. 15: 497–514.

Caiani, Manuela, della Porta, Dontella, and Wageman, Claudius (2012). *Mobilizing on the Extreme Right. Germany. Italy, and the United States*. Oxford: Oxford University Press.

Eggert, Nina and Pilati, Katia (2014). "Networks and Political Engagement of Migrant Organizations in 5 European Cities," *European Journal of Political Research*. 53: 858–875.

Freeman, Gary P. (2011). "Comparative Analysis of Immigration Politics: A Retrospective," *American Behavioral Scientist*. 55: 1541–1560.

Giddens, Anthony (1990). *The Consequences of Modernity*. Cambridge: Polity Press.

Giugni, Marco and Passy, Florence (2002). "Le champ politique de l'immigration en Europe: Opportunités, mobilisations et héritage de l'Etat national." In *L'action collective en Europe*, edited by Richard Balme, Didier Chabanet, and Vincent Wright, 433–460. Paris: Presses de la Fondation Nationale des Sciences Politiques.

Grande, Edgar (2008). "Globalizing West European Politics: The Change of Cleavage Structures, Parties and Party Systems in Comparative Perspective." In *West European Politics in the Age of Globalization*, edited by Hanspeter Kriesi, Edgar Grande, Romain Lachat, Martin Dolezal, Simon Bornshier, and Timotheos Frey, 320–344. Cambridge: Cambridge University Press.

Hammar, Tomas (1985). *European Immigration Policy*. Cambridge: Cambridge University Press.

Hutter, Swen and Kriesi, Hanspeter (2013). "Movements of the Left, Movements of the Right Reconsidered." In *The Future of Social Movement Research: Dynamics, Mechanisms, and Processes*, edited by Jacquelien van Stekelenburg, Conny Roggeband, and Bert Klandermans, 281–298. Miineapolis: Minnesota University Press.

Hollifield, James (1992). *Immigrants, Markets, and States: The Political Economy of Postwar Europe*. Cambridge, MA: Harvard University Press.

Imig, Doug and Tarrow, Sidney (2001). *Contentious Europeans: Protest and Politics in an Emerging Polity*. Lanham, MD: Rowman and Littlefield.

Jacobs, Dirk and Tillie, Jean (2004). "Introduction: Social Capital and Political Integration of Migrants," *Journal of Ethnic and Migration Studies*. 30: 419–427.

Jacobson, David (1996). *Rights Across Borders: Immigration and the Decline of Citizenship*. Baltimore: Johns Hopkins University Press.

Joppke, Christian, ed. (1998). *Challenge to the Nation-State. Immigration in Western Europe and the United States*. Oxford: Oxford University Press.

Joppke, Christian (1999). *Immigration and the Nation-State: The United States, Germany and Great Britain*. Oxford: Oxford University Press.

Kriesi, Hanspeter (1999). "Movements of the Left, Movements of the Right: Putting the Mobilization of Two New Types of Social Movement into Political Context." In *Continuity and Change in Contemporary Capitalism*, edited by Herbert Kitschelt, Peter Lange, Gary Marks, and John D. Stephens, 398–423. Cambridge: Cambridge University Press.

Ireland, Patrick (1994). *The Policy Challenge of Ethnic Diversity: Immigrant Politics in France and Switzerland*. Cambridge: Harvard University Press.

Kastoryano, Riva and Schader, Miriam (2014). "A Comparative View of Ethnicity and Political Engagement," *Annual Review of Sociology*. 40: 241–260.

Kitschelt, Herbert (1995). *The Radical Right in Western Europe: A Comparative Analysis*. Ann Arbor, MI: The University of Michigan Press.

Koopmans, Ruud (1996). "Explaining the Rise of Racist and Extreme Right Violence in Western Europe: Grievances or Opportunities?" *European Journal of Political Research*. 30: 185–216.

Koopmans, Ruud (2001). "Better Off by Doing Good? Why Anti-Racism Must Mean Different Things to Different Groups." In *Political Altruism? Solidarity Movements in International Perspective*, edited by Marco Giugni and Florence Passy, 111–131. Lanham, MD: Rowman and Littlefield.

Koopmans, Ruud, Statham, Paul, Giugni, Marco, and Passy, Florence (2005). *Contested Citizenship: Immigration and Cultural Diversity in Europe*. Minneapolis: University of Minnesota Press.

Koopmans Ruud and Statham, Paul (1999). "Political Claims Analysis: Integrating Protest Event and Political Discourse Approaches," *Mobilization*. 4: 203–221.

Koopmans, Ruud, and Paulk Statham (2000). "Migration and Ethnic Relations as a Field of Political Contention: An Opportunity Structure Approach." In *Challenging Immigration and Ethnic Relations Politics: Comparative European Perspectives*, edited by Ruud Koopmans and Paul Statham, 13–56. Oxford: Oxford University Press.

Kriesi, Hanspeter, Grande, Edgar, Lachat, Romain, Dolezal, Martin, Bornschier, Simon, and Frey, Timotheos (2008). *West European Politics in the Age of Globalization*. Cambridge: Cambridge University Press.

Kriesi Hanspeter, Grande, Edgar, Dolezal, Martin, Helbling, Marc, Höglinger, Dominic, Hutter, Swen, and Wüest, Bruno (2012). *Political Conflict in Western Europe*. Cambridge: Cambridge University Press.

Marks, Gary and McAdam, Doug (1996). "Social Movements and the Changing Structure of Political Opportunity in the European Union," *West European Politics*. 19: 249–278.

McAdam, Doug, McCarthy, John D., and Zald, Mayer N., eds. (1996). *Comparative Perspectives on Social Movements: Political Opportunities, Mobilizing Structures, and Cultural Framings*. Cambridge: Cambridge University Press.

McAdam, Doug, Tarrow, Sidney, and Tilly, Charles (1996). "To Map Contentious Politics," *Mobilization*. 1: 17–34.

McAdam, Doug, Tarrow, Sidney, and Tilly, Charles (2001). *Dynamics of Contention*. Cambridge: Cambridge University Press.

Morales, Laura and Giugni, Marco, eds. (2011). *Social Capital, Political Participation and Migration in Europe. Making Multicultural Democracy Work?* Houndsmill: Palgrave Mcmillan.

Miles, R. and Phizaclea, V. (1977). "Class, Race, Ethnicity and Political Action," *Political Studies*. 25: 491–507.

Miller, Mark J. (1982). "The Political Impact of Foreign Labor: A Re-evaluation of the Western European Experience," *International Migration Review*. 16: 27–60.

Oesch, Daniel and Rennwald, Line (2010). "The Class Basis of Switzerland's Cleavage between the New Left and the Populist Right," *Swiss Political Science Review*. 16: 343–371.

Okamoto, Dina G. (2003). "Towards a Theory of Panethnicity: Explaining Asian-American Collective Action," *American Sociological Review*. 68: 811–842.

Passy, Florence (1998). *L'action altruiste*. Genève: Droz.

Pilati, Katia (2012). "Networks and Political Engagement of Migrant Organisations in Milan," *Journal of Ethnic and Migration Studies*. 38(4): 671–688.

Ramakrishnan, S. Karthic and Bloemraad, Irene, eds. (2008). *Civic Hopes and Political Realities: Immigrants, Community Organizations, and Political Engagement*. New York: Russell Sage Foundation.

Rex, John (1991). *Ethnic Identity and Ethnic Mobilisation in Britain*. Warwick: University of Warwick.

Robertson, Roland (1992). *Globalization. Social Theory and Global Culture*. London: Sage.

Rucht, Dieter (2002). "The EU as a Target of Political Mobilization: Is There a Europeanization of Conflict?" In *L'action collective en Europe*, edited by Richard Balme, Didier Chabanet, and Vincent Wright, 163–194. Paris: Presses de la Fondation Nationale des Sciences Politiques.

Siméant, Johanna (1998). *La cause des sans-papiers*. Paris: Presses de Science Politique.

Soysal, Yasemin Nuhoglu (1994). *Limits of Citizenship: Migrants and Postnational Membership in Europe*. Chicago: Chicago University Press.

Soysal, Yasemin Nuhoglu (1997). "Changing Parameters of Citizenship and Claims-Making: Organized Islam in European Public Sphere," *Theory and Society*. 26: 509–527.

Steil, Justin Peter and Vasi, Ion Bogdan (2014). "The New Immigration Contestation: Social Movements and Local Immigration Policy Making in the United States, 2000–2011," *American Journal of Sociology*. 119(4): 1104–1155.

Statham, Paul (2001). "The Role of State Policies in Influencing British Anti-racist and Pro-migrant Movements," In *Political Altruism? Solidarity Movements in International Perspective*, edited by Marco Giugni and Florence Passy, 133–158. Lanham, MD: Rowman and Littlefield.

Tarrow, Sidney (2011). *Power in Movement: Social Movements and Contentious Politics*. 3rd edn. Cambridge: Cambridge University Press.

Vanparys, Nathalie, Dirk Jacobs, and Corinne Torrekens (2013). "The Impact of Dramatic Events on Public Debate Concerning Accommodation of Islam in Europe." *Ethnicities*. 13: 209–228.

CHAPTER 10

....

RELIGIOUS REVIVALISM AND SOCIAL MOVEMENTS

....

LASSE LINDEKILDE AND LENE KÜHLE

INTRODUCTION

....

"REVITALIZATION of Religion" (Huntington 1996); "De-secularization" (Berger 1999); "De-privatization of Religion" (Casanova 1994, 2001); "The Revenge of God" (Kepel 1994). The reappearance of religion as a contentious issue in the public sphere and as a source of political protest and activism in many parts of the world in the last two decades of the twentieth century has many academic labels. Empirically this religious revivalism has been associated with diverse phenomena ranging from the Iranian revolution to terrorism associated with al-Qaeda, Pope John Paul II's support to the Solidarity movement in Poland, Catholic liberation theology in Latin America, Protestant fundamentalism in the United States, and outbursts of violence within new religious movements.

This chapter focusses on religious revivalism as the foundation of social movement activities since the 1980s. Generally speaking, this religious revivalism amounts to a greater visibility of religion in many parts of the world, especially in its fundamentalist forms (Roy 2007). The revivalism does not mean increased observance of religion or that religion prior to revivalism did not play a significant role as a source of cultural and ideological innovation. Historically there is no lack of examples of connections between religious practices and political mobilization. However, since the 1980s, religious revivalism has manifested itself as intensified importance of social movements advocating political change (Casanova 1994; Berger 1999).

Our purpose is not to give a comprehensive empirical account of the diverse empirical phenomena associated with the surge in visible religion over the last thirty years. Rather, we will, first, outline the structural transformations which contributed to changing conditions of religiosity in the period in order to, second, explore religious revivalism as the foundation of a variety of social movement activities. Finally, the chapter discusses potential future gains from further integrating insights from sociology of religion with social movement research, and points to a number of areas where theoretical integration would be productive.

Bridging sociology of religion and sociology of social movements to make sense of religious revivalism and the role of religion in modern political activism and cultural change is not a new idea. Already in 1987 Mayer Zald and John D. McCarthy stated that:

> It is clear that the study of social movements from a resource mobilisation perspective and the study of transformation of and within religion have much to offer each other ... Both the sociology of religion and the sociology of social movements can be invigorated by continuing this interchange. (Zald and McCarthy 1987: 12)

So far, however, the exchange of insights between sociology of religion and social movement research has been limited to a few research areas and questions. Three areas stand out. First, the study of new religious movements: The intensified interest in seemingly deviant forms of religiosity carried out in "cults" or "sects" incorporates insights from early social movement theory, stressing the importance of experienced, individual deprivation/strain, external circumstances, and charismatic leadership to explain recruitment and conversion (Robbins 1988). To some degree this theoretical integration helped advance the understanding of recruitment in new religious movements beyond simplistic readings highlighting "brainwashing" and manipulation (Furseth and Repsted 2006: 149). Second, research on the particularities of religious ideology and communities as a source of mobilization and recruitment stresses factors such as affective bonds, moral emotions, reference to divine authority, transcendental rewards, rituals, etc. as important resources for social movement activities (McAdam 1982; Smith 1996). Third, more recently a sub-field of research on a variety of state-church relations and related forms of religious mobilization and claims-making has emerged (Koopmans and Statham 1999; Fetzer and Soper 2005). These studies are theoretically inspired by the political process model and the concept of "political opportunity structures" in social movement research. The basic argument of much of this research is that the institutional incorporation and political claims-making of emerging religions (such as Islam in Europe) develop by adaptation to existing state-church relations.

STRUCTURAL TRANSFORMATIONS AND CHANGING CONDITIONS OF RELIGIOSITY

The concept of the secular is derived from Christian theology. The original theological meaning of the word secularization is a process of making worldly, that is, when a person leaves monastic life or when the church gave up property after the Protestant reformation (Casanova 2011: 56). While founding sociologists like Weber and Durkheim may be said to have promoted theories of secularization, detailed sociological theories of secularization were only formulated in the 1960s, emphasizing in particular processes of rationalization and differentiation as well as worldliness (internal religious organizational transformations) as the crucial ones (Tschannen 1991). Theories of secularization became the explicit foundational theory for the sociology of religion, at the same time as the fact that religion no longer played a major role in public life became an implicit assumption in the general social sciences. The consequences were isolation and insulation of the sociology of religion from broader sociological concerns (Beckford 1989): Religion rarely came up as a topic in mainstream social science, and sociologists of religion engaged less with general theories in the social sciences.

A thesis of the "return of the sacred" was introduced by Daniel Bell in 1977. According to Bell it simply cannot be the case that religion is losing its influence over societies: "[I]t is a constitutive aspect of human experience because it is a response to the existential predicaments which are the *ricorsi* of human culture" (Bell 1977: 442). It was, however, only through recurrent reformulations by other scholars from the late 1980s throughout the 1990s that the thesis of a return of religion gradually pushed the formerly dominant explicit as well as implicit theories of secularization aside. An important turning point is seen in the publications of sociologist Peter Berger, in the 1960s a leading figure in the formulation of sociological theories of secularization. In works like *The Sacred Canopy* he outlined how the plausibility of religious world views is seriously challenged by modern developments, in particular the pluralism caused by the rationalization and differentiation of society. When the truth claim of one religion is confronted with truth claims from other religions or from secular world views, it loses its taken-for-grantedness. This means that religion can no longer function as a "sacred canopy" and takes the position as an optional rather than a foundational feature of society. The shift from a primary to a secondary societal institution means that religion gradually but inevitably will lose societal as well as individual salience.

In his publications from the 1980s onwards, Berger however increasingly questions his own position. Could it be that the loss of a position as taken for granted does not necessarily undermine the plausibility of religion? The breakthrough of Berger's new views on religion and secularization is cemented in the often-cited introduction to the edited volume, *The Desecularization of the World* from 1999. Here Berger describes how he and the majority of his colleagues were wrong in trusting the secularization thesis, which may reflect the secular lifestyles of Western university elites, but in no way represents the state of affairs in a world which is "as furiously religious as it ever was, and in some places more so than ever" (Berger 1999: 2). The fact that religion becomes a choice may in fact enhance its vitality and in a world where secular ideologies have been imposed to uphold the power of elites, nothing mobilizes the masses better than religion (Berger 1999: 11). Berger's change of heart was followed by the warning that "those who neglect religion in their analysis of contemporary affairs do so at their great peril" (1999: 18).

Similar arguments may be found in José Casanova's seminal work on public religions (Casanova 1994). Coining the word "de-privatization," Casanova claims that the failure of the secularization thesis is a failure of confusing three distinct dimensions.

Secularization is commonly used to refer to differentiation of a secular sphere from religious institutions and norms, as well as to privatization and to religious decline. According to Casanova, only the first dimension, differentiation, "is not a modern structural trend, but, rather, a historical option" (Casanova 1994: 215). Some religious organizations may choose to offer privatized religion, while others—most noticeably Muslim and Catholic organizations—may de-privatize in order to formulate Catholic and Muslim versions of modernity (Casanova 2001: 1063). Working from a Habermasian perspective, it becomes a challenge for Casanova that church-state relations are among the strongest in well-functioning and secular democracies like Britain and the Scandinavian countries. Casanova denotes these state churches as "rather residual anachronisms" (Casanova 1994: 219), but the tendency to disregard state-church relations in otherwise "well-functioning" democratic and liberal societies is increasingly challenged by scholars who point out that religion is not only relevant for understanding the historical development of, for instance, welfare regimes (Van Kersbergen and Manow 2009), but also understanding the conditions for integration policies (Minkenberg 2008) and accommodation of new religious claims (Fetzer and Soper 2005). With the pressure on welfare states and the challenges posed by ethnic and religious diversity, states are likely to be more rather than less eager to engage religious communities in providing welfare and countering alleged threats to social cohesion caused by "radicalization" (Beckford 2010; Turner 2011).

Central to most accounts of the resurgence of religion is the emphasis on processes of globalization. Migration is related to religious change as migration often involves revitalization of religious identities. Global transportation systems and media also have well-known effects on religion, facilitating the innate transnational dimensions of many religions. Global media may install as well as undermine authorities.

Globalization also concerns religion on a more systemic level. According to American sociologist Roland Robertson, the idea of the secular state spread across the world from the early nineteenth century. Under globalization, the secular state and separateness of religious and political spheres are challenged by "religionization" of government on one hand and by politicization of religion on the other. The "religionization" of government refers both to how the state increasingly becomes involved with moral and ethical issues and to how the state-organized society becomes an object of veneration in itself. Politicization and religionization are to some extent mutually reinforcing processes: The new political agendas caused by religionization invite religious actors to become involved, while the politicization of religion fosters religious interpretation of the "state of affairs" (1989: 14). The consequences of the global situation for religion do escape simple descriptions, however. Whereas the fate of religion under processes of modernization was secularization, it is something much more complicated under globalization: "Hence, what stands out with respect to religion in the globalizing as opposed to modernizing world is not secularization but pluralization, the inclusion of different glocalizations of religion" (Beyer 2007: 99). There is nothing new in religion being the imperative for the establishment of a social movement. However, contemporary circumstances may be more conducive to a movement's success.

RELIGIOUS REVIVALISM AND SOCIAL MOVEMENTS

As indicated above, structural transformations and changed conditions of religiosity have been associated with religious revivalism since the 1980s. Obviously this religious revivalism has varied in degree and taken on many forms, depending on context. Religious revivalism has taken the forms of exclusionism or inclusionism, particularism or universalism, fundamentalism or progressive, foundation of the rise of powerless and excluded groups. Most attention has been given to the new forms of fundamentalism, especially the perceived rise in Islamic fundamentalism. The new forms of fundamentalism are said to be characterized by accultural religion, an alleged return to the pre-culturalized sources of religion (Roy 2007: 73–7). Religious trends such as Salafism within Islam and Christian evangelicalism have worked to "purify" and to separate religion from any cultural sentiments. Thus, traditionalist interpretations of sacred texts are often bypassed as irrelevant or even infidel. In a context of globalization, migration, and experienced loss of cultural identity, this sort of accultural religion provides the foundation on which global identities can form. In Europe, for example, Salafism spreads especially among migrant youth because it offers a clear oppositional identity to mainstream liberal society and at the same time a generational uproar vis-à-vis their parents' "cultural" Islam (Kühle and Lindekilde 2009).

In the following sections, we will discuss religious revivalism as the foundation of social movement activities and political challenges since the 1980s. The discussion is structured on the basis of a simple, heuristic distinction between religious revivalism as the source of "voice" and "exit," drawing upon Hirschman's (1970) framework. The distinction regards differences in response and coping strategies in regard to perceived grievances by religious communities (see also Aminzade and Perry 2001). Religious revivalism in the shape of "voice" covers the instances where revitalized religious communities mobilize to raise demands of recognition and fulfilment of needs external to the religious community. This is the kind of religious revivalism most scholars have in mind when they use terms like "de-privatization of religion." It is certainly the kind of religious revivalism that has caught the most attention in social movement studies (Smith 1996), as applied action repertoires often render it comparable to non-religious movements and place it firmly within standard definitions of social movement actions (Snow and Soule 2010: 15). However, there is also a different and, we argue, empirically important kind of religious activism which has caught more attention within the sociology of religion, namely the less visible, more internally oriented revivalism. Religious revivalism as "exit" refers to strategies of internal need fulfilment and more indirect challenges of the established authorities through prefigurative organization and transformation. Our central argument concerning this basic distinction is that there is an important element of social critique and political protest inherent to the prefigurative revivalist movements, which social movement scholars could benefit from paying more attention to. The distinction between religious revivalism as the source of "voice" and "exit" should be conceived of as analytical ideal types. In practice, strategies of voice and exit will often mix or follow each other in time, for example so that exit functions as a precursor for voice.

Religious Revivalism as "Voice"

In Europe, the Middle East, Asia, North Africa, and the Americas, religious revivalism has helped fuel mobilization for external change to a significant degree since 1980. At times, such religiously based mobilization has aimed at a complete transformation of the state, as was the case with the Iranian revolution, Catholic liberation theology in Latin America, the Solidarity movement in Poland, and parts of the Arab Spring. Research in this area has shown how religious communities and institutions under authoritarian or semi-authoritarian political conditions may serve as "safe havens" or "free spaces" in which political challenge to the established system may form (Kubik 1994; Burns 1996). Under such conditions, religion may become a privileged arena of activism and the only possibility of voicing political protest. In other cases, revitalized religious communities have mobilized for more modest aims of public recognition and institutional adaptation within existing legal frameworks and state-church relations. An example is "re-Islamized youth" mobilizing in European countries, advancing demands of the right to veiling in public schools, halal food in public institutions, prayer rooms at work, Muslim burial grounds, and purpose build mosques (Amiraux 2005). Around the globe, in Nigeria, Indonesia, the Sudan, or the Philippines, the advent of a revivalist "Southern" form of Christianity, while generally not overtly political, are fuelling political conflicts by combatting rival religions, struggling for converts, and attempting to enforce moral codes (Jenkins 2002).

Needless to say, religiously driven mobilization of political claims for change and institutional adaptation has used various action repertoires. Whereas the Iranian revolution quickly turned violent, the Solidarity movement in Poland managed to achieve significant political influence with predominantly peaceful means. Likewise, Swedish Muslims have obtained important institutional adaptations by mobilizing through established channels of interaction between religious communities and the state (Sander and Larsson 2002), while French Muslims have been forced to use non-institutionalized and more confrontational repertoires for voicing their claims (Wieviorka 2003). The immediate global appeal of images of peacefully protesting Buddhist Monks in saffron robes placed the monks as the central vehicle of global focus on the Burmese 2007-saffron revolution (Rogers 2008).

A further point should be made which seems valid for all forms of religious revivalist voicing: Religious revivalism, even within the same religious community, is rarely uniform or mono-vocal (see also Salvatore 2004). Rather than implying a deterministic relationship between religious interpretations and prescribed behavior or political claims, religious revivalism is pluralistic and often sectarian. Among young Muslims in Europe who have (re-)found Islam in search of identity and a sense of belonging, and who voice this identity in public, we find at least three broad positions, which vary greatly in degree of orthodoxy and adaptation to secular principles. At one end of the spectrum, Islamic revivalism morphs into ultra-orthodoxy and revolutionary Islam as exemplified by Hizb ut-Tahrir and al-Qaeda-inspired "home-grown" Jihadist groups. The overall goal is Islamization of the state and rejection of secularism (Schiffauer 2007). At the other end of the spectrum, and partly in reaction to the first, we find mobilization of a liberal or cultural Islam, calling for privatization, individualization, and "aggiorna-mento" of Islam, that is, adaptation to and acceptance of secular principles. Somewhere in between the two we find neo-orthodox Muslim groupings, who fundamentally accept the conditions of secularism but attempt to twist the principles and create "pri-vatized public spaces" (Roy 2007: 79)—spaces which are shared with non-believers, but occupied in a different manner with rules regarding, for example, gender separa-tion, handshakes, veiling, etc. that only apply to the believers. Here Islamic revivalism negotiates with authorities and engages in the secular public without compromising religious dogma.

Religious Revivalism as "Exit"

Among the untouchables, the Dalits, of India oppression by the Hindu system of caste is escaped through mass conversion to Islam, Buddhism, and Christianity (Jenkins 2002: 228). Religious revivalism within a community may also lead to physical exit through formations of a sect (Furseth and Repstad 2006: 133). Innovative theology marks new lines of division, which become the basis of mobilization. Again the re-Islamization of migrant youth in Europe is illustrative. Among ultra-orthodox Salafists in Europe, many groups—in fact the vast majority—seek isolation from the surrounding society instead of public claims-making and confrontation with authorities. They aim at ful-filling the needs of a pious lifestyle within a secluded community of "true believers," establishing their own mosques, supply of "halal" foods, religious books, etc. In a sense, these milieus are characterized by a double exit-strategy. They isolate themselves from mainstream secular society, which is perceived as "immoral" and "ungodly," but also from large parts of the Muslim community, which is seen as "misguided" and "fallen," not living up to the Salafists' standards of piousness and religious practice. However, an important part of these groups' activities is missionary work (*dawa*) calling "fallen" Muslims back to Islam (Wiktorowicz 2005). As pointed out by Hirschman in his origi-nal work on voice, exit, and loyalty (1970), exit need not be physical, but can be mental or emotional. Continuing the example of the Salafi movement in Europe, a central focus is personal or inner transformation—the purification of thought and mind, sometimes referred to as "inner Jihad" (Johnson 2002).

One may object that religious revivalism as exit, especially the more mentally escap-ist type, has little to do with social movements understood as collective action and challenges of authority. However, revivalist exit inherits important, indirect political challenges of established authorities through prefigurative organization and transformation (for a similar argument, see Kepel 1994). For example, by "living" the alternative to secular Western society and Muslim urban street culture, pious Salafists in European cities are quietly challenging mainstream political authorities, principles of democracy, Muslim religious authorities, cultural customs, etc. Prefigurative movements can be powerful carriers of change and sites of mobilization, especially when they manage to fulfil central community needs internally, and provide followers with identity, meaning, affective bonds, and a sense of being among the "chosen ones" (Wiktorowicz 2005). The political success of the Salafist movement in parts of North Africa and the Middle East in recent years is built on the movement's strong prefigurative organization in local communities, which has been activated for political gains (Bayat 2007).

An often cited risk of religious revivalism as exit and self-seclusion is related to social-psychological group dynamics in bordered enclaves leading to forms of extremism (Schkade, Sunstein, and Hastie 2010). Much research on cults and sects within the field of sociology of religion points to such dynamics of social desirability effects and group pressure in explaining, for example, social control and the difficulty of exit from these groups (Robbins 1988). Likewise, research on radicalization among re-Islamized Muslim youth in Europe, drawing on social movement theory, has underscored group dynamics in secluded milieus (online as well as offline) as important factors in explaining moral disengagement and legitimation of violence (Wiktorowicz 2005; Lindekilde 2013). Put differently, we can say that a potential risk of the combination of intense religiosity and interaction in bordered, prefigurative enclaves is that the cross-over between "exit" and "voice" is made using extreme or even violent means.

Sociology of Religion and Social Movement Research

A basic theoretical claim of this chapter is that there is a lot to be gained from further integrating elements of the sociological study of religion with the sociological study of social movements. Making sense of religious revivalism as a source of societal change calls for such integration. We have already suggested how the study of prefigurative movements in general, which is an underdeveloped area of social movement research, may look to the rich literature within the sociology of religion paying attention to the internal life of self-secluded religious communities, stressing the importance of passive daily resistance embedded in style of interaction, organization, rituals, language, etc. (Bayat 2007). In addition to this, we shall mention three areas of research where insights from the sociology of religion can fruitfully spill over into social movement studies. This is not to suggest that the sociology of religion cannot learn from social movement studies, only that, due to the focus of the book at hand, we delimit ourselves to a one-sided discussion of the potential gains of integration.

The first, and quite obvious, area regards the study of what we termed earlier "religious revivalism as voice." Social movement scholars of religious movements and claims-making have struggled to get a handle on the internal diversity of, for example, Muslim activism—even in local contexts. The result has at times been a tendency to reify and essentialize, and thus overlook the heterogeneous nature of revitalized religion. Dutch sociologist of religion, Marcel Maussen, has argued that social movement scholars studying Muslim mobilization assume that they know in advance what Muslims want and their reasons for wanting it, instead of considering it an empirical question (Maussen 2006: 36). These scholars miss important empirical variation (within and across borders) in how much, and for what reasons, for example, veiling has been politicized by Muslim communities. The point is that religion as both culture and ideology is subject to context-dependent interpretation and change, which leads to variation in prescriptions and claims-making, and that we should design our studies of religious activism to allow for this. Thus, we need to study empirically how the same religious doctrines are used to mobilize and frame divergent claims (for a similar point see Snow and Byrd 2007).

The second area of research we will highlight is the study of mobilization into deviant or counter-cultural milieus. Social movement scholars have struggled to capture the transitory nature of many such milieus and explain their often eclectic and diversified ideological nature. Colin Campbell (1972) coined the notion "the cultic milieu" to describe a counter-cultural environment in a society where different religious and philosophical currents flourish and intermingle, and occasionally provide the background for formation of cults. Campbell understands the cult as an "organization" encompassing unorthodox deviant views, which have no firm organizational form or fixed dogma. However, the cultic milieu is a "constant feature of society," which forms an important "cultural underground of society" (Campbell 1972: 122). A few studies have used the concept of the "cultic milieu" to investigate radical movements, stressing how participants in line with Campbell's understanding can often be understood as "seekers" of the cultic milieu in society, which helps to explain the transitory nature of participation in such movements and the common, innovative mixing of, for example, religious and political ideology in radical movements (Kaplan and Lööw 2006). The framework seems promising also to the study of counter-cultural movements online, and as an alternative explanatory model to the rigid linear phase models which are often used to make sense of "radicalization" of political activism (for an elaboration of this argument see Kühle and Lindekilde 2009).

Finally, insights from the sociological study of religion stressing the component of transcendental motivation (i.e. desire for salvation) and emotions of hope and comfort in religious life can serve as an important reminder to social movement scholars engaging with religious mobilization not to treat religion as purely instrumental vis-à-vis movement goals (for a good starting point, see Smith 1996). In other words, the study of religious activism must take into account both the elements of "instrumental" and "value" rationality (Weber 2002). Paying attention to both forms of rationality simultaneously when studying religious revivalism, as "voice" or "exit," can serve as a shield against instrumentalist reductionism *and* affective exaggeration.

REFERENCES

Aminzade, Ron and Perry, Elizabeth (2001). "The Sacred, Religious, and Secular in Contentious Politics: Blurring Boundaries." In *Silence and Voice in the Study of Contentious Politics*, edited by Ron Aminzade et al., 155–178. Cambridge: Cambridge University Press.

Amiraux, Valérie (2005). "Discrimination and Claims for Equal Rights amongst Muslims in Europe." In *European Muslims and the Secular State*, edited by Jocelyn Cesari and Seán Mcloughlin, 25–38. Aldershot: Ashgate Publishing.

Bayat, Asef (2007). *Making Islam Democratic: Social Movements and the Post-Islamist Turn.* Stanford: Stanford University Press.

Beckford, James A. (1989). *Religion and Advanced Industrial Society.* London & New York: Routledge.

Beckford, James A. (2010). "A Critical Assessment of a Popular Claim," *Nordic Journal of Religion and Society.* 23(2): 121–136.

Bell, Daniel (1977). "The Return of the Sacred? The Argument on the Future of Religion," *The British Journal of Sociology.* 28(4): 419–449.

Berger, Peter L. (1999). *The Desecularization of the World: Resurgent Religion and World Politics.* Grand Rapids: B. Eerdmans Publishing.

Beyer, Peter (2007). "Globalization and Glocalization." In *The SAGE Handbook of the Sociology of Religion*, edited by James A. Beckford and N.J. Demerath, 98–117. London: Sage.

Burns, Gene (1996). "Ideology, Culture and Ambiguity: The Revolutionary Process in Iran," *Theory and Society.* 25: 349–388.

Campbell, Colin (1972). "The Cult, the Cultic Milieu and Secularization," *A Sociological Yearbook of Religion in Britain.* 5: 119–136.

Casanova, José (1994). *Public Religions in the Modern World.* Chicago: The University of Chicago Press.

Casanova, José (2001). "Civil Society and Religion: Retrospective Reflections on Catholicism and Prospective Reflections on Islam," *Social Research.* 68(4): 1041–1080.

Casanova, José (2011). "Secular, Secularizations, Secularisms." In *Rethinking Secularism*, edited by Craig Calhoun, Mark Juergensmeyer, and Jonathan Van Antwerpen, 54–74. Oxford: Oxford University Press.

Fetzer, Joel S. and Soper, Christopher J. (2005). *Muslims and the State in Britain, France and Germany.* Cambridge: Cambridge University Press.

Furseth, Inger and Repstad, Pål (2006). *An Introduction to the Sociology of Religion.* Aldershot: Ashgate.

Hirschman, Albert O. (1970). *Exit, Voice, and Loyalty: Responses to Decline in Firms, Organizations, and States.* Cambridge: Harvard University Press.

Huntington, Samuel P. (1996). *The Clash of Civilizations and the Remaking of World Order.* New York: Simon & Schuster.

Jenkins, Philip (2002). *The Next Christendom: The Coming of Global Christianity.* Oxford: Oxford University Press.

Johnson, James Turner (2002). *The Holy War Idea in Western and Islamic Traditions.* Philadelphia: Pennsylvania University Press.

Kaplan, Jeffrey and Lööw, Heléne (2002). *The Cultic Milieu: Oppositional Subcultures in an Age of Globalization*. Walnu Creek: Rowman/Altamira Press.

Kepel, Gilles (1994). *The Revenge of God: The Resurgence of Islam, Christianity, and Judaism in the Modern World*. University Park: Pennsylvania State University Press.

Koopmans, Ruud and Statham, Paul (1999). "Challenging the Liberal Nation-State? Postnationalism, Multiculturalism and the Collective Claims Making of Migrants and Ethnic Minorities in Britain and Germany," *American Journal of Sociology*. 105(3): 652–696.

Kubik, Jan (1994). *The Power as Symbols against the Symbols of Power: The Rise of Solidarity and the Fall of State Socialism in Poland*. University Park: Pennsylvania State University Press.

Kühle, Lene and Lindekilde, Lasse (2009). *Radicalization among Young Muslims in Aarhus*. Research report conducted for the Centre for the study of Islamism and Radicalization Processes, Aarhus University 2009. See http://cir.au.dk/fileadmin/site_files/filer_statskund-skab/subsites/cir/radicalization_aarhus_FINAL.pdf

Lindekilde, Lasse (2013). "A Typology of Backfire Mechanisms: How Soft and Hard Forms of State Repression can have Perverse Effects in the Field of Counterterrorism." In *Dynamics of Political Violence: A Process-Oriented Perspective on Radicalization and the Escalation of Political Conflict*, edited by L. Bosi, C. Demetriou, and S. Malthaner, 51–69. Aldershot: Ashgate.

Maussen, Marcel (2006). "Anti-Muslim Sentiments and Mobilizationin the Netherlands. Discourse, Policies and Violence." In *Islamophobia in Western Europe*, edited by J. Cesari, P. DeWan, and M. Somos, 100–142. Paris: Challenge.

McAdam, Doug (1982). *Political Process and the Development of Black Insurgency*. Chicago: University of Chicago Press.

Ranger, Terence O., ed. (2008). *Evangelical Christianity and Democracy in Africa*. New York: Oxford University Press.

Robbins, Thomas (1988). *Cults, Converts and Charisma. The Sociology of New Religious Movements*. Thousand Oaks: Sage.

Robertson, Roland (1989). "Globalization, Politics and Religion." In *The Changing Face of Religion*, edited by James A. Beckford and Thomas Luckmann, 10–23. Beverly Hills: Sage.

Rogers, Benedict (2008). "The Saffron Revolution: The Role of Religion in Burma's Movement for Peace and Democracy," *Totalitarian Movements and Political Religions*. 9(1): 115–118.

Roy, Olivier (2007). *Secularism Confronts Islam*. New York: Columbia University Press.

Salvatore, Armando (2004). "Making Public Space: Opportunities and Limits of Collective Action Among Muslims in Europe," *Journal of Ethnic and Migration Studies*. 30(5): 1013–1031.

Sander, Åke, and Göran Larsson (2002). "The Mobilisation of Islam in Sweden 1990–2000. From Green to Blue and Yellow Islam." In *Religious Freedom and the Neutrality of the State: The Position of Islam in the European Union*, edited by W.A.R Shadid and P.S. van Koningsveld, 62–88. Leuven: Peeters.

Schiffauer, Werner (2007). "From Exile to Diaspora: The Development of Transnational Islam in Europe." In *Islam in Europe. Diversity, Identity and Influence*, edited by Aziz Al-Azmed and Effie Fokas, 68–95. Cambridge: Cambridge University Press.

Schkade, David, Sunstein, Cass R., and Hastie, Reid (2010). "When Deliberation Produces Extremism," *Critical Review*. 22(2–3): 227–252.

Smith, Christian (1996). "Correcting a Curious Neglect, or bringing Religion Back." In *Disruptive Religion. The Forth of Faith in Social Movement Activism*, edited by Christian Smith, 1–29. New York: Routledge.

Snow, David A. and Soule, Sarah A. (2010). *A Primer on Social Movements*. New York: W. W. Norton & Company.

Snow, David A. and Byrd, Scott C. (2007). "Ideology, Framing Process, and Islamic Terrorist Movements," *Mobilization*. 12(1): 119–136.

Tschannen, Olivier (1991). "The Secularization Paradigm: A Systematization," *Journal for the Scientific Study of Religion*. 30(4): 395–415.

Turner, Bryan S. (2011). *Religion and Modern Society: Citizenship, Secularisation and the State*. Cambridge: Cambridge University Press.

Van Kersbergen, Kees and Manow, Philip, eds. (2009). *Religion, Class Coalitions, and Welfare States*. Cambridge: Cambridge University Press.

Weber, Max (2002). *The Protestant Ethic and the "Spirit" of Capitalism and Other Writings*. Translated by Peter R. Baehr and Gordon C. Wells. New York: Penguin.

Wieviorka, Michel, ed. (2003). *L'avenir de l'islam en France et en Europe*. Paris: Balland.

Wiktorowicz, Quintan (2005). *Radical Islam Rising: Muslim Extremism in the West*. Lanham, Boulder, Toronto and Oxford: Rowan and Littlefield Publishers.

Zald, Mayer N. and McCarthy, John D. (1987). "Religious Groups as Crucibles of Social Movements." In *Social Movements in an Organisational Society: Collected Essays* edited by Mayer N. Zald and John D. McCarthy, 67–96. New Brunswick: Transaction Publishers.

CHAPTER 11

ETHNICITY, NATIONALISM, AND SOCIAL MOVEMENTS

DIEGO MURO

INTRODUCTION

POLITICAL claims based on identity are ubiquitous. Examples of purposeful collective actions which aim to transform the values and institutions of a society on behalf of separate cultural groups can be found all over the globe. From pious religious fundamentalists and land-grabbing ethno-nationalists to racist movements or gender equality activists, a plethora of social movements have developed as people attempt to take control of their own lives and immediate environments according to their identity preferences (Castells 1997).

In spite of the ever-present and important cultural distinctiveness, the study of identity was a peripheral concern of social and political theory for much of the twentieth century. The sociologist Zygmunt Bauman (2004: 17) acknowledged that the topic of "identity" was nowhere near the center of scholarly thought a few decades ago. Similarly, one of the foremost scholars of ethnicity and nationalism, Anthony D. Smith, complained that "ethnicity as a term and a subject of study is very recent" (Hutchinson and Smith 1996: v) and that the study of nationalism had "until recently been relatively neglected" (Hutchinson and Smith 1995: 3). Similar complaints were voiced by social scientists well into the 1990s (Horowitz 1985: 13) but the end of the Cold War facilitated the scholarly study of both ethnicity and nationhood in parallel with the weakening of the left–right ideological conflict in world politics. The result of this belated interest was an avalanche of books and papers on nationalism, and the publication of a number of specialized journals as well as the establishment of research centers and degree programs across the world (Ozkirimli 2005).

Unfortunately, the literature on social movements has paid little attention to the study of identity politics (Melucci and Diani 1983). With a few notable exceptions, ethnic and nationalist movements were rarely studied together (Conversi 2004; Olzak 2013;

Okamoto 2013). Social scientists studied ethnicity and nationalism as one of the possible variables in mobilization but mainly focussed on forms of relational conflicts (Fearon and Laitin 2003: Brubaker and Laitin 2004; Collier and Hoeffler 2004). Research on identity and protest emphasized the violent or rebellious element (Muro 2008; Cebotari and Vink 2013) but paid much less attention to nonviolent ethnic and national movements, in particular to "the borderland between contentious and routine politics" (Tarrow 2012). Scholarly work has begun to fill this gap but it can be argued that research on ethno-nationalist conflict and social movements has remained regrettably separate (Beissinger 2002; Yashar 2005; Stroschein 2012).

This chapter brings together existing work on ethnicity and nationalism and evaluates the contribution the field of identity politics can make to the study of social movements. The text is structured as five sections. The first focusses on conceptual issues related to ethnicity and nationhood. A second reviews existing theories of identity and examines how ethnic and national cleavages become salient. The third examines the alleged spread of ethnic and national conflict and a fourth deals with the research field of indigenous movements. Finally, a set of concluding remarks summarizes the main findings.

Conceptual Clarification

Ethnicity and nationhood are terms that denote a sense of belonging to a distinct social group. They also relate to the belief of being ethnic or national. But what do the terms "ethnic group" and "nation" truly mean? And how different is one from the other? This section aims to provide some conceptual clarity by providing working definitions of ethnic group, nation, and nationalism.

To start with, an *ethnic group* contains people who believe they are of common descent. Max Weber first identified common ancestry and shared pasts as building blocks of ethnicity but warned that the belief in "common blood" could be either real or putative. In his own words, ethnic groups would be those "human groups that entertain a subjective belief in their common descent because of similarities of physical type or of customs or both, or because of memories of colonization and migration; this belief must be important for group formation; furthermore it does not matter whether an objective blood relationship exists" (Weber 1922: 389). Since belief in the existence of descent-based attributes (instead of hard evidence) is needed for ethnicity, the idea of common ancestry is likely to involve the creation, invocation, and manipulation of notions of cultural distinctiveness to establish self/other dichotomies among people in a shared political and economic system. In short, ethnicity would be used to indicate the self-perception of cultural difference and collective identity. A *nation*, by contrast, can be defined as a "named population sharing a historic territory, common myths and historical memories, a mass public culture, a common economy and common legal rights and duties for its members" (Smith 1995: 57).

But how different is a nation from an ethnic group? One key difference is their political character. Whereas ethnicity is often pre-political, it would be almost impossible to envisage a nation devoid of a partisan dimension and deprived of its own political pro-gram (Conversi 2004: 815). Likewise, ethnic groups can exist without states but most nations (or, rather, nationalists) want to erect a political roof (i.e., a state) over their nation. Another key difference between the ethnic group and the nation is that the latter is sometimes seen as an upgraded version of the former. From this point of view, a line of continuity is occasionally drawn between pre-modern ethnic ties and modern national communities. Even though not every ethnic group of the past became a nation, some dominant "ethnic cores" (Prussia, England, Castille) consolidated their power over sub-ordinate ethnic groups and became central pillars of nations. Thus, ethnic groups can be seen as precursors of nations because they articulate a pre-modern form of collective sentiment and provide the cultural foundations of national political identities (Smith 1986; Hastings 1997).

In contrast to the position that regards ethnicity and nationhood as continuous, many more authors have emphasized the importance of "modern institutions" such as capital-ism, industrialization or mass education in explaining the transformation of ethnic com-munities into nations. In fact, the question "when was the nation?" was the core of the debate on nationalism that took off in the 1960s and gained momentum during the 1980s onwards with the publication of seminal works by Benedict Anderson, Eric J. Hobsbawm, Anthony D. Smith, and Ernest Gellner. The conclusion of the modernist grand narrative was that both nations and nationalism were the consequence of various processes associ-ated with modernization, such as urbanization, print capitalism, administrative central-ization, the collection of statistics, taxation, and the creation of centralized educational systems and military apparatuses.

On the basis of the definitions presented above, there is no problem about arguing that nations do not always have a state of their own and that most states have more than one nation within their borders. Similarly, many states, particularly large ones, host more than one ethnicity—China, Afghanistan, Laos, and Vietnam being examples—whereas nations within territories are exemplified by India, Bolivia, Canada, Russia, South Africa, the United Kingdom, and Belgium. And that is where nationalism comes into play for *nationalism* can be defined as both an ideology and a movement that aims to have a perfect one-to-one correspondence between nation and state.

Moving on from concepts of ethnic group, nation, and nationalism the next section reviews prevailing theories of identity politics and tries to answer the question, when are "ethnic" or "national" identities "activated"? A snapshot of primordialism, instrumental-ism, and constructivism will be provided in order to explain change and variation within and across cases of ethnic and national politics.

THEORIES OF IDENTITY

When do social movements frame issues and grievances in ethnic or national terms? Can one predict when social groups will base their political mobilization on the cultural distinctiveness of the people they claim to represent? Unfortunately, there is no single explanation or coherent theory that can predict when certain categorical cleavages—nations, ethnic groups, race or tribes—will become politically salient and the focus of popular identification (Wimmer 2012: 11). The resonance of ethnic and national claims will depend on the structural configuration of power in each case but also on the theoretical assumptions of the observer.

Academic explanations for the basis of identity can be divided into three schools of thought or paradigms: (1) primordialism; (2) instrumentalism; and (3) constructivism. The three approaches fundamentally differ in their understanding of how stable or malleable ethnic and national identities are. Whereas primordialists believe that identities are singular and fixed, both instrumentalists and constructivists believe in the evolving and fluid nature of identity. The importance of these paradigms lies in the fact that they show up the constraints political entrepreneurs face when trying to activate and manipulate identity categories in institutionalized politics. For the purposes of this review, it is useful to have an awareness of these theoretical paradigms when trying to establish the power and resonance of ethnic and national identities in social movements.

Primordialism

Primordialism is one the oldest traditions of enquiry in the sub-field of ethnicity and nationalism (and possibly one of the most discredited). The primordialist camp is made up of scholars who believe that identity is needed for basic human functioning. Primordialism argues that individuals need to have a relatively clear conception of the self and that both ethnic groups and nations are useful in providing strong cultural bonds between individuals. For them, humans have a need for identity that is tightly connected to the human need for order more generally. The emergence of ethnic or national organizations can be understood as the natural expression of deeply rooted identities (Shils 1975; Geertz 1977; Smith 1998).

The primordialist assumption is that individuals have fixed, singular identities which are exogenous to human processes. Individuals belong to one and only one ethnic group or nation and that unique group membership remains fixed over a lifetime, perhaps even across generations. The interesting aspect of primordialists is that their assumptions are commonly assumed by expert and lay circles alike. For example, there are numerous cases of research in politics and economics that test theories of the relationship between ethnicity and democratic stability, economic growth, civil war, state formation, the provision of public goods, and just about everything else, and they assume, almost without exception, that the identity of individuals and populations is singular, timeless and fixed for all time, and not created by political and economic processes (Chandra 2012). Furthermore, ethnic diversity (as measured by the ethno-linguistic fractionalization index or ELF) is often seen as a "problem" and many policy responses rest on the assumption that multi-ethnic societies are conflict-prone and that ethnic mobility needs to be lessened or eliminated where possible (Horowitz 1985; Kaufmann 1996, 1998; Petersen 2002). Finally, the argument about the primordial appeal of "ancient hatreds" has also been used by commentators and pundits to explain violent ethno-nationalist conflicts—in Burundi, Rwanda, Israel/Palestine, Indonesia or Yugoslavia—and to point out the allegedly intractable nature of these conflicts.

Various scholars have highlighted the limitations of primordialism but we will restrict this overview to the main two criticisms (Yashar 2005; Wimmer 2008; Chandra 2012). First, primordialism has been accused of holding an essentialist position that is unable to explain variation. If identity is so deeply rooted, critics argue, why does mobilization rise and fall at different times? Why do some groups live peacefully in some places, but not in others? Why do antagonistic identities lead to state collapse and civil war in some countries but not others? Second, identity conflicts are not always caused by old hostilities. Often, there is the quick politicization of identities. It may be possible to resort to "primordial" or "ancient" roots to explain the conflict between Shia and Sunni in the Middle East but the animosity between Iraq and Iran is much more recent. Could this variation be related to "greed and grievance" or could it be that elites sometimes use ethnic or national attributes to mobilize their supporters, as instrumentalists have argued?

Instrumentalism

Instrumental or rational choice analyses challenge the primordialist assumption that ethnic and national identities are "givens" that motivate collective action. The core idea of instrumentalism is that identity is neither inherent in human nature nor intrinsically valuable. Instrumentalists assume that individuals are utility-maximizing actors with fixed preferences who seek the most cost-effective means to achieve their goals and who never stop to reflect on the worthiness of those goals. From a rationalist perspective, ethnicity or nationhood becomes one of many available instruments (or frames) used by political entrepreneurs interested in seeking political or economic power. Conflicts take place because leaders strategically manipulate identity for the sake of political power, or simply for extracting resources from the state (Bates 1974; Hechter 1986; Laitin 1998; Chandra 2012).

One of the shortcomings of rationalists is that they study the politicization of identity as largely instrumental but they fail to explain why the ethnic or nationalist message resonates. If it is true that political entrepreneurs mobilize the masses by deploying invented myths and traditions, why do the masses come along? Is it because instrumental rationality is a feature that can be found only at an elite level, but not at the level of the masses? If we come to share the assumption that individuals have fixed preferences, are goal-oriented, and act intentionally, would it not be logical to expect more free-riding individuals? It would appear that a rationalist approach can provide little insight into why conflicts take an ethnic or national dimension. Another limitation is that instrumentalists cannot explain why utility-maximizing individuals would join movements that are likely to be costly, particularly in the early stages of mobilization when the risks are high and the tipping point has not been reached. In other words, by focussing on the individual and leaving context unexamined, instrumentalists are unable to explain why people commit the ultimate sacrifice of dying for their ethnic groups and nations.

Constructivism

Constructivism's point of departure is that identity is not a cultural given but the product of a social process. In the case of national identities, nations are seen as contingent constructs of the modern epoch that are constantly evolving. This claim is relatively straightforward for nations: work across a whole range of disciplines has shown the "invented," "imagined" or "constructed" nature of national identities. This is not to say that nationhood is "false" or "artificial" but simply that it is the result of social and political institutions with power. However, constructivists go beyond making the instrumentalist point that elites and intellectuals deliberately select and rework pre-existing social and cultural traditions to engineer products that resonate with the masses. In fact, constructivists are not only interested in how much fabrication is possible but why individuals think that ethnic and national boundaries are meaningful, valuable or useful (Barth 1969).

One of the clear advantages of constructivism is that it is well equipped to explain variation across social contexts. The ways in which identities are formed (e.g., ethnogenesis) and the ways in which identity changes in local, statewide, and interstate contexts can be explained by their own guiding assumptions and principles (Cederman 2001; Hale 2008; Wimmer 2008). Constructivists are also able to explain the process by which products of social engineering are reproduced everyday by informal institutions (private or from below) and state and civil society organizations (public or from above) (Brubaker 2004). In other words, the point is not to argue whether the Mexicans, Han Chinese, Koreans or Basques exist but to identify the mechanisms whereby these identities present themselves as "natural" and "inevitable." Rhetoric and discourses about ethnic and national homogeneity or uniqueness are studied by constructivists but also the endogenous processes by which change is made possible by political and economic processes. Indeed, discursive practices may be effective (and reproduced) but there may also be ambiguity and arguments. By focussing on the malleable nature of the phenomena of identity, constructivism shifts the emphasis from structure to agency and expands the research agenda to both hegemonic actors but also to subaltern ones (Brubaker 2004). Thus, disputes are likely to develop when peripheral social movements do not want to be incorporated into particular frameworks of consciousness and understanding. Hence, we can identify movements that do state-building and nation-building processes but also those that subscribe to colonial policies, institutions, and practices (Weber 1976; Anderson 1983; Hobsbawm and Ranger 1983; Wimmer 2002).

To recap, this section has argued that there is no unified grand theory able to predict when ethnic or national issues will become salient. The three theories reviewed—primordialism, instrumentalism, and constructivism—differ in their positions on two distinct debates: the changing character of identities (fixedness vs. fluidity) and the relationship of these identities to economic and political processes (endogeneity vs. exogeneity). Whereas primordialism focusses on explaining the effect of "fixed" identities on political and economic outcomes, and instrumentalism emphasizes the strategic interests of elites in "activating" identity attributes, constructivism prefers to emphasize the role of institutions (formal and informal) in constructing, reproducing, and contesting ethnic and national identities. To conclude, although it is not possible to forecast when social movements will frame their agendas in terms of identity, the paradigms examined in this chapter suggest that the relationship between the elites and the masses is crucial. The resonance of the ethnic message depends on whether elites are able to broadcast their political message on a wavelength that sympathizers are tuning in to. Needless to say, followers are no passive receivers of messages for they also participate in the process of constructing ethnic and national communities, as the next section shows.

THE SPREAD OF ETHNIC AND NATIONAL CONFLICT

In the aftermath of the Cold War there was talk about nationalism and ethnic conflict as the primary sources of conflict in world politics. As the world came to be dominated by a single super-power, a proliferation of intrastate conflicts appeared to bring greater international instability and human suffering across the globe. The conflicts in Yugoslavia, Rwanda or Chechnya popularized the terms "ethnic cleansing," "genocide," and "crimes against humanity" during the 1990s. But to what extent were ethnic and national conflicts new? Was there a real spread of these types of conflict? Why were culturally distinct movements more able to inflame passions at the turn of the century than ever before?

The prominence of ethnicity and nationalism in war escalated during the second half of the twentieth century and peaked during the 1990s. According to the sociologist Andreas Wimmer, the share of nationalist wars of secession and ethnic civil wars rose from 25 to 75 per cent over the course of the twentieth century (Wimmer 2012: 27). By the year 2000, over three-quarters of violent conflicts were fought either by groups seeking to establish a separate nation-state or to change the ethnic balance of power within an existing state. The likelihood of war more than doubled after nationalism gained a foothold as the key foundation of political legitimacy and changed the motivations and aims for which humanity goes to war. Nowadays, ethno-national wars for independence are commonly considered to be the main threat to international peace and regional security in the post-Cold War period (Marshall and Gurr 2003). These conflicts increased in importance during the previous century to the point that most of today's more prominent and protracted full-scale wars—those armed conflicts costing more than 1,000 battle deaths—are wars of self-determination (Wimmer 2012: 2–27).

In spite of the increasing importance of ethno-nationalist wars, it is paramount to distinguish between "conflict" and "violence." Only then does it become possible to establish whether ethnic and national principles have become more pervasive since the collapse of the USSR. In spite of the fact that conflict and violence are usually used as synonyms, a situation of conflict is simply one where two actors have mutually incompatible goals, and not necessarily a violent confrontation. Given the scarcity of resources and irreconcilable preferences, the potential for conflict around the world is great, both in authoritarian and democratic states. However, if conflict is a situation where two or more different players hold incompatible goals, one cannot expect the decline of conflict in the future, for scarcity is intrinsic to social life (Arendt 1970).

If conflict is a situation where several actors have incompatible goals, it is reasonably straightforward to argue that many ethnic and national conflicts are resolved peacefully. As Laitin (2007) has noted, violence is not intrinsically related to nationalism—on the contrary, inter-ethnic cooperation is much more frequent than radicalized conflict. In pluralistic democracies, for example, non-violent conflict is often expressed openly because opportunities for participation remain accessible. Social groups channel their protest through parliaments, assemblies, and bureaucracies, and the peaceful resolution of conflict is also made possible by democratic means. National minorities or ethnic groups use political institutions to voice their concerns about the language of instruction in schools, who should be allowed into the country, religious laws, whether religious dress can be allowed in public spaces, whether places of worship can be built without special permission, whether the provision of public goods should be indiscriminate or, by contrast, whether there should be affirmative action, etc. The public expression of dissent brings a given conflict to the surface, which makes it easier to deal with it, but this does not inoculate society against political violence. Unconventional political action such as strikes and nonviolent demonstrations does not always lead to violence but nor does it prevent the emergence of riots, pogroms, asymmetric warfare or civil wars.

The following section will shift the focus of the chapter from violent struggles to cases of ethno-national social movements that have used peaceful strategies. More specifically, the structure of nonviolent conflicts from Latin America will be examined in order to pay special attention to their grievances or perceived ethno-political inequality (Wimmer 2012: 28). By focussing on less well-known cases of mobilization, it should become possible to extract novel lessons that can enrich the literature on social movements (Trejo 2000).

ETHNIC POLITICS: LESSONS FROM INDIGENOUS MOVEMENTS IN LATIN AMERICA

How can the study of ethnic conflicts and indigenous groups enrich our understanding of social movements? What can be learned from the study of ethnic politics in Latin

America? This section provides an analytical narrative that examines cases of movements that demand rights from their respective nation-states and the international community. The histories, agendas, and dynamics of the "first people" movements are both similar and different. Indigenous movements and organization have a long history in Latin America where the term "indigenous" has been adopted as a tool for the social and political mobilization of people who now number over 40 million—roughly 8 to 10 per cent of the region's overall population. The empirical analysis enables us to identify elements of importance to ethnic and nationalist movements since the 1990s, namely (1) political contexts; (2) goals; and (3) strategies.

First, political contexts can facilitate or hamper the effectiveness of social movements. Agents of change find it easier to organize and be recognized as legitimate actors in favorable institutional settings. For example, in Latin America, democratization processes facilitated the (re-)surfacing of indigenous social movements. Before becoming electoral democracies, authoritarian regimes effectively repressed internal dissent and civil society was de-mobilized. Contrary to those who argue that unjust regimes provoke solid mobilizations, the Latin American example effectively demonstrates that stable autocracies can be ruthless in promoting cultural homogeneity and assimilation on the basis of an exclusive national identity and the idea of progress. Indeed, ethnic mobilization was a relatively rare phenomenon until the 1980s but, as transition from authoritarian rule across the continent allowed for the (re)emergence of grass-roots organizations, it was possible to trace indigenous movements gaining increasing relevance as political actors (Sieder 2002; Yashar 2005; Vom Hau and Wilde 2010).

The Latin American case provides a unique setup to argue that "institutions matter" but also to study the role of political opportunity structures such as democratization, economic and legal globalization, citizenship regimes or constitutional reform to explain the creation of new spaces of contestation (Sieder 2002; Postero and Zamosc 2004; Yashar 2005; Silva 2009). Beyond domestic conditions, scholars have identified the important role of international jurisprudence (Sieder 2002), non-governmental and inter-governmental networks (Brysk 2000) or transnational advocacy groups (Keck and Sikkink 1999) in the protection of indigenous rights and the legitimation of local claims in Latin America. The argument developed by these authors sustains the idea that the diffusion of global norms and legal resources has significantly contributed to the advance of indigenous platforms (Risse and Sikkink 1999; Van Cott 2000; Stavenhagen 2002).

Nevertheless, the opportunities for social action are largely determined by the state, not by the international context. The state is the main target of claim making and it is the key adversary of social movements, but it is also through state institutions that much of the contention is organized and directed (Tarrow and Tilly 2009). In other words, social movements target the state from outside but they also work within it. Variation with regard to social mobilization depends on regime type and on the internal configuration, from decentralized federations to unitary states. Whether a given country is an autocracy or a democracy often has an impact on the recognition of group rights and ethnic self-determination (della Porta 2014). For example, the instruments used by Canada to channel the Quebecoise claim to independence stand in contrast to the

Chinese policy response to the Ugyur minority. Needless to say, regime type also has an impact on whether ethnic or national movements use peaceful or violent means. With regard to internal factors of the state, potential for conflict or mobilization is more likely when power is noticeably distributed along ethnic or national lines. If there is political inequality or there is a perception that the ethno-political configuration of power privileges some ethnic or national groups over others, a grievance is more likely to be defined along identity cleavages (Wimmer 2002).

Secondly, and with regard to campaign goals, ethnic and nationalist movements want to influence the agenda setting. Social movements organize outside the state and yet their activities compel them to interact with government institutions, for these are the actors that can provide them with the policy responses they require. Within democratic polities, social movements want either to change the status quo, reform the state or to press the authorities to provide certain public goods. Needless to say, the ability to determine success in the public arena is also contingent on goals, activities, and forms of organization (Gamson 1990).

It is difficult to establish the precise political impact of social movements: challengers may fail to achieve their main goals but still win substantial advantages for their constituents. For example, it is possible to distinguish between three different types of returns or political consequences of social mobilization (Amenta et al. 2010: 289): (1) indigenous movements may manage to extend their democratic rights and practices by incorporating disenfranchised groups and adopting multicultural constitutional frameworks (Van Cott 2000); (2) indigenous mobilization may provide benefits to the movement's constituency in the form of major legislative change, social reform or affirmative action (Silva 2009); and (3) groups may also gain acceptance or political leverage by establishing connections with parties or the state, sometimes to the point of being included in institutional political processes (Tarrow 1998). None of these three outcomes may realize the full political program of indigenous movements but they will have contributed to the renewal and survival of the movement by proving that institutionalized politics pays off.

Thirdly, with regard to strategies, it can be argued that ethnic and nationalist social movements are no different from other social movements. They use a variety of tactics and strategies, they engage in both conventional and unconventional methods, they pressure the state from the inside but also from the outside, they make use of domestic as well as international campaigns, and so on and so forth. In the case of Latin America, the key difference with other movements is that since the 1990s ethnicity has become the key to explaining political activism, state politics, and public discourse (Van Cott 2000; Stavenhagen 2002; Jackson and Warren 2005; Yashar 2005). This is not to say that Indians have not organized in the past, but simply that they have not organized along ethnic lines to promote an explicitly indigenous agenda (Yashar 2005: 5).

Latin American indigenous movements have devoted much time to the "politics of difference" and defining who is indigenous and who is not. The invocation of a separate identity has been considered essential to movements that fight for recognition of their status as national, ethnic or indigenous. Immense effort has been devoted to the political recognition of the agent of change, whether the ethnic group, the indigenous group or the nation. While many groups are recognized as "indigenous" or "national" on the international scale, many still struggle for similar recognition from their national governments, who are wary of the legal consequences of the politics of recognition (Hodgson 2002: 1041–1042). To name an example, historically marginalized groups are "becoming" indigenous in order to seek recognition and demand rights. In line with constructivist approaches, social movements have reframed their long-term collective identities based on criteria such as ethnicity or livelihood to embrace a new identity as "indigenous." This term is now used by tribal or semi-tribal people and also by a wide range of disenfranchised groups to define and promote their movements. The adoption of the "indigenous" label allows these groups to homogenize their public images and identities to accord with "Western" stereotypes in order to seek recognition and demand rights (Hodgson 2002: 1040). Being recognized as an "indigenous group" is seen as the first step towards being acknowledged as a legitimate actor, able to participate in electoral politics and demand rights and resources from the state.

To recapitulate, this section has examined the interaction of identity repertoires, organizations, and contexts in which indigenous movements operate. Many of the structural conditions are no different from the ones that affect other social movements, and success ultimately depends on whether there is mass participation, whether the movement adapts its tactics to changing circumstances, and whether the state is receptive to its demands. However, a few elements that are specific to indigenous movements in Latin America have been identified. For example, instead of being defined by "identity," ethnic and national movements construct and manipulate identity issues, hence confirming the constructivist view about the fluid nature of identity. Another novel element is that these movements' successes depend on their ability to link issues of representation, recognition, resources, and rights. Finally, these movements achieve political influence by protest but also by electoral politics, hence transcending the more traditional concept of social movement.

CONCLUSION

Ethnicity and nationalism are key providers of identity in the modern world. The theorizing of mobilization for identity-based groups does not have to be different from other social movements but must concentrate attention on the politicization of identity. Existing theories suggest that ethnic and national identity is historically contingent, institutionally bound, and open to change. Identity is neither fixed, as primordialists argue, not completely malleable, as some instrumentalists suggest. Instead, the constructivist agenda of identifying the mechanisms that allow identities to be translated into political action and social mobilization seems to be the more fruitful one.

Ethnic and nationalist movements are generated by groups that question a particular aspect of society and encourage the formation of a new social order. Most of the time, these movements target the state with the aim of setting policy agendas and triggering a set of responses. A perception of ethno-political inequality and lack of legitimacy often drives the mobilization and interaction of elites and masses. Ethnic and nationalist movements try to reform the state or influence its institutions to get policy responses such as new rights, laws or political acceptance that have gone largely unrecognized by the state. The way that movements target political institutions varies from the conventional to the innovative and depends mainly on national and transnational opportunity structures. What is clear is that ethnic mobilization does not equal political violence.

The case of indigenous groups in Latin America indicates that peaceful social movements thrive in open democratic settings. Mobilizing groups frame their demands in ethnic or national terms in order to take control of the state, transform their social reality, and democratize access to conventional politics. The Latin American case also suggests that the international dimension is an additional structural condition that strengthens the indigenous community's ability to scale up and confront the state. Several indigenous groups have made substantial progress in institutionalizing their demands and rights in the international arena but their domestic successes have been more limited (Martí 2010). Finally, the Latin American case suggests that the concept and practice of indigenous movements needs to be understood within national and international processes such as democratization, economic globalization or the rise of a human rights regime.

References

Amenta, Edwin, Caren, Neal, Chiarello, Elizabeth, and Su, Yang (2010). "The Political Consequences of Social Movements," *Annual Review of Sociology.* 36(1): 287–307.

Anderson, Benedit (1983). *Imagined Communities: Reflections on the Origin and Spread of Nationalism.* London: Verso.

Arendt, Hannah (1970). *On Violence.* London: Allen Lane, Penguin Press.

Barth, Frederik, ed. (1969). *Ethnic Groups and Boundaries: The Social Organization of Culture Difference.* London: Allen & Unwin.

Bates, Robert (1974). "Ethnic Competition and Modernization in Contemporary Africa," *Comparative Political Studies.* 6 (Jan): 457–484.

Bauman, Zygmunt (2004). *Identity.* Cambridge: Polity.

Beissinger, Mark R. (2002). *Nationalist Mobilization and the Collapse of the Soviet State.* Cambridge: Cambridge University Press.

Brubaker, Rogers. 2004. *Ethnicity without Groups.* Cambridge, MA: Harvard University Press.

Brubaker, Rogers and Laitin, David (2004). "Ethnic and Nationalist Violence." In *Ethnicity without Groups,* edited by R. Brubaker, 88–115. Cambridge, MA: Harvard University Press.

Brysk, Alison (2000). "Democratizing Civil Society in Latin America," *Journal of Democracy.* 11(3): 151–166.

Castells, Manuel (1997). *The Power of Identity, the Information Age: Economy, Society and Culture Vol. II.* Cambridge, MA, Oxford: Blackwell.

Cebotari, Victor and Vink, Maarten P. (2013). "A Configurational Analysis of Ethnic Protest in Europe," *International Journal of Comparative Sociology.* 54(4): 298–324.

Cederman, Lars-Erik (2001). *Constructing Europe's Identity*. Boulder, CO: Lynne Rienner.

Chandra, Kanchan (2012). *Constructivist Theories of Ethnic Politics*. Oxford: Oxford University Press.

Collier, Paul and Hoeffler, Anka (2004). "Greed and Grievance in Civil War," *Oxford Economic Papers*. 56: 563–595.

Conversi, Daniele (2004). "Can Nationalism Studies and Ethnic/Racial Studies be Brought Together?," *Journal of Ethnic and Migration Studies*. 30(3): 815–829.

della Porta, Donatella (2014). *Mobilizing for Democracy. Comparing 1989 and 2011*. Oxford: Oxford University Press.

Fearon, James D. and Laitin, David D. (2003). "Ethnicity, Insurgency, and Civil War," *American Political Science Review*. 97: 91–106.

Gamson, William (1990). *Strategy of Social Protest*. Belmont: Wadsworth Publishing Company.

Geertz, Clifford (1977). "Religion as a Cultural System." In *The Interpretation of Cultures*, by C. Geertz, 87–125. New York: Basic Books.

Hale, Henry (2008). *The Foundations of Ethnic Politics: Separatism of States and Nations in Eurasia and the World*. New York: Cambridge University Press.

Hastings, Adrian (1997). *The Construction of Nationhood: Ethnicity, Religion and Nationalism*. Cambridge: Cambridge University Press.

Hechter, Michael (1986). "Rational Choice Theory and the Study of Race and Ethnic Relation." In *Theories of Race and Ethnic Relations*, by John Rex and David Mason, 264–279. Cambridge: Cambridge University Press.

Hutchinson, John and Smith, Anthony D. (1995). *Nationalism*. Oxford: Oxford University Press.

Hutchinson, John and Smith, Anthony D. (1996). *Ethnicity*. Oxford: Oxford University Press.

Hobsbawm, Eric and Ranger, Terence (1983). *The Invention of Tradition*. Cambridge: Cambridge University Press.

Hodgson, Dorothy L. (2002). "Introduction: Comparative Perspectives on the Indigenous Rights Movements in Africa and the Americas," *American Anthropologist*. 104(4): 1037–1049.

Horowitz, Donald (1985). *Ethnic Groups in Conflict*. Berkeley and Los Angeles: University of California Press.

Jackson, Jean E. and Warren, Kay B. (2005). "Indigenous Movements in Latin America, 1992–2004: Controversies, Ironies, New Directions," *Annual Review of Anthropology*. 34: 549–573.

Kaufmann, Chaim D. (1996). "Possible and Impossible Solutions to Ethnic Civil Wars," *International Security*. 20(4): 136–175.

Kaufman, Chaim D. (1998). "When All Else Fails: Ethnic Population Transfers and Partitions in the Twentieth Century," *International Security*. 23(2): 120–156.

Keck, Margaret E. and Sikkink, Kathryn (1999). "Transnational Advocacy Networks in International and Regional Politics," *International Social Science Journal*. 51(159): 89–102.

Laitin, David D. (1998). *Identity in Formation. The Russian-Speaking Populations in the New Abroad*. Cornell: Cornell University Press.

Laitin, David D. (2007). *Nations, States and Violence*. Oxford: Oxford University Press.

Marshall, Monty G. and Gurr, Ted R. (2003). *Peace and Conflict 2003: A Global Survey for Armed Conflicts, Self-Determination Movements, and Democracy*. College Park, MD: Center for International Development and Conflict Management, University of Maryland.

Martí Puig, Salvador (2010). "The Emergence of Indigenous Movements in Latin America and Their Impact on the Latin American Political Scene," *Latin American Perspectives*. 175(27): 74–92.

Melucci, Alberto and Diani, Mario (1983). *Nazioni senza stato: i movimenti etnico-nazionali in Occidente*. Torino: Loescher.

Muro, Diego (2008). *Ethnicity and Violence: The Case of Radical Basque Nationalism*. London and New York: Routledge.

Okamoto, Dina G. (2013). "Ethnic Movements." In *Blackwell Encyclopedia of Social and Political Movements*, edited by David A. Snow, Donatella della Porta, Bert Klandermans, and Doug McAdam. Oxford: Wiley-Blackwell.

Olzak, Susan (2013). "Ethnic, Racial, and Nationalist Social Movements." In *International Encyclopedia of Social and Behavioural Sciences*, edited by James D. Wright, 666–693. Oxford: Elsevier Ltd.

Ozkirimli, Umut (2005). *Contemporary Debates on Nationalism. A Critical Engagement*. Basingstoke: Palgrave.

Petersen, Roger D. (2002). *Understanding Ethnic Violence: Fear, Hatred, and Resentment in Twentieth-Century Eastern Europe*. Cambridge: Cambridge University Press.

Postero, Nancy and Zamosc, Leòn (2004). "Indigenous Movements and the Indian Question in Latin America." In *The Struggle for Indigenous Rights in Latin America*, edited by Nancy Postero and Leòn Zamosc, 1–31. Sussex: Sussex Academic Press.

Risse, Thomas and Sikkink, Kathryn (1999). "The Socialization of International Human Rights Norms into Domestic Practices." In *The Power of Human Rights: International Norms and Domestic Change*, edited by Thomas Risse, Stephen C. Ropp, and Kathryn Sikkink, 1–38. Cambridge: Cambridge University Press.

Shils, Edward (1975). "Charisma, Order, and Status." In *Center and Periphery: Essays in Macrosociology*, edited by Edward Shils, 256–275. Chicago: University of Chicago Press.

Sieder, Rachel, ed. (2002). *Multiculturalism in Latin America: Indigenous Rights, Diversity and Democracy*. New York: Palgrave Macmillan.

Silva, Eduardo (2009). *Challenging Neoliberalism in Latin America*. Cambridge: Cambridge University Press.

Smith, Anthony D. (1986). *The Ethnic Origin of Nations*. Oxford: Wiley-Blackwell.

Smith, Anthony D. (1995). *Nations and Nationalism in a Global Era*. Cambridge: Polity.

Smith, Anthony D. (1998). *Nationalism and Modernism*. London and New York: Routledge.

Stavenhagen, Rodolfo (2002). "Indigenous Peoples and the State in Latin America: An Ongoing Debate." In *Multiculturalism in Latin America: Indigenous Rights, Diversity, and Democracy*, edited by Rachel Sieder, 24–44. New York: Palgrave Macmillan.

Stroschein, Sherrill (2012). *Ethnic Struggle, Coexistence, and Democratization in Eastern Europe*. Cambridge: Cambridge University Press.

Tarrow, Sidney (1998). *Power in Movement: Social Movements and Contentious Politics*. Cambridge: Cambridge University Press.

Tarrow, Sidney (2012). *Strangers at the Gate. Movements and States in Contentious Politics*. Cambridge: Cambridge University Press.

Tarrow, Sidney and Tilly, Charles (2009). "Contentious Politics and Social Movements." In *The Oxford Handbook of Comparative Politics*, edited by Carles Boix and Susan C. Stokes, 435–460. Oxford: Oxford University Press.

Trejo, Guilermo (2000). "Etnicidad y movilización social. Una revisión teórica con aplicaciones a la 'cuarta ola' de movilizaciones indígenas en América Latina," *Política y Gobierno*. 8(1): 205–250.

Van Cott, Donna L. (2000). *The Friendly Liquidation of the Past. The Politics of Diversity in Latin America*. Pittsburgh, PA: University of Pittsburgh Press.

Vom Hau, Matthias and Wilde, Guillermo (2010). "We Have Always Lived Here': Indigenous Movements, Citizenship, and Poverty in Argentina," *Journal of Development Studies*. 46(7): 1283–1303.

Weber, Max (1922). *Economy and Society*. Berkeley: University of California Press, vol. 2, 389.

Weber, Eugene (1976). *Peasants into Frenchmen: The Modernization of Rural France, 1870–1914*. Stanford: Stanford University Press.

Wimmer, Andreas (2002). *Nationalist Exclusion and Ethnic Conflict: Shadows of Modernity*. Cambridge: Cambridge University Press.

Wimmer, Andreas (2008). "The Making and Unmaking of Ethnic Boundaries: A Multilevel Process Theory," *American Journal of Sociology*. 113(4): 970–1022.

Wimmer, Andreas (2012). *Waves of War: Nationalism, State Formation, and Ethnic Exclusion in the Modern World*. Cambridge: Cambridge University Press.

Yashar, Deborah (2005). *Contesting Citizenship in Latin America: The Rise of Indigenous Movements and the Postliberal Challenge*. Cambridge: Cambridge University Press.

CHAPTER 12

....

URBAN DYNAMICS
AND SOCIAL MOVEMENTS

....

MASSIMILIANO ANDRETTA, GIANNI PIAZZA,
AND ANNA SUBIRATS

THE ROLE OF CITIES IN SOCIAL
MOBILIZATION: AN INTRODUCTION

RECENT waves of protest in Tahrir Square in Cairo, Puerta del Sol in Madrid, and Gezy Park in Istanbul have illustrated the central role cities play as arenas of political action (Miller and Nicholls 2013; Barnett 2014: 1625; see also Swyngedouw 2011; Harvey 2012). Despite these prominent contemporary examples, the importance of urban settings for social and political mobilization is not a new phenomenon; the civil rights movement in the United States in the 1960s, urban protests in Hong Kong in the 1980s, and the global justice movement in the 2000s, are other examples.

Why are cities important for social movements? And what kinds of social mobilizations emerge in cities? The relationship between space and contentious politics has been a fast growing sub-field in social science since the 1990s (Slater 1997; Routledge 2003; Leitner et al. 2008); however, relatively little research has focussed on studying the conditions that enable political mobilization in cities. As Chris Pickvance (2003) highlighted some years ago, the literature on urban social movements and social movements have tended to follow different paths. Scholars researching urban social movements (Lefebvre 1968, 1970; Castells 1977, 1983; Fainstein and Hirst 1995; Hamel et al. 2000; Mayer 2006, 2009, 2013; Harvey 2008, 2012; Brenner et al. 2012) have tended to focus on the definition of the urban conflict and the identification of the macro-trends that transform cities. Attempts to identify the mechanisms that connect local political processes with urban mobilization dynamics, by contrast, have been relatively scarce. The literature on social movements, meanwhile, has addressed the concept of space in analyzing how the politics of place creates common collective identities (della Porta and

Piazza 2008), how social movements strategically approach and produce space (Bosi 2013), and how transnational social movement networks affect local organizations (Diani 2003). However, this literature has tended to leave aside the study of the specificities of the urban as such.

In recent years, however, there has been an increasingly prominent effort made to bridge the gap between social movements theory and urban sociology. Walter Nicholls (2008), for example, has explored the role cities play in fostering general social movements, by highlighting the need to incorporate space as an analytical category into social movements studies. Pickvance (2003), meanwhile, has advocated the concept of "urban movements" as a field of study in itself. He emphasizes the need to study the concrete and specific outcomes of such urban movements and the ways in which they change people's lives; the relationship between the state, local authorities, and urban protest; and the political context in which such movements develop, noting that they do not arise from spontaneous answers to objective inequalities or deprivations but are more or less easily formed under certain social and political conditions (2003: 103–105).

In this chapter we explore existing scholarship on urban social movements and consider under which conditions such movements emerge and how they are affected by different social and political contexts. The chapter proceeds in three sections. First, we review the literature on urban studies and social movements in order to provide a definition of urban social movements. Although the terms "urban social movements" (Castells 1983), "urban movements" (Pickvance 2003), "urban protest" and "urban conflict" remain contested in the literature (see Miller and Nicholls 2013), for the purpose of this chapter, however, we will understand the category of "urban social movements" as a specific type of social movement. Second, we will explore the conditions that enable or constrain urban mobilization. Third, we will present two types of urban social movements. The first type is often described as a simple reaction to urban planning and infrastructural policies, in which citizens attempt to overcome the pejorative "Nimby" (Not In My BackYard Movements) label that powerful urban actors attach to them in order to delegitimize their protests. The second type is represented by squatted houses and social centers and is often described as more radical in terms of action repertoire and collective identity. Despite their differences, both types of urban mobilization have as their purpose the social re-appropriation of the process by which cities and the conditions of urban life are produced. The chapter concludes by arguing that in favorable political conditions "urban social movements" can generate processes of social transformation and connect to broader social movements.

What is an "Urban Social Movement"?

The concept of "urban social movement" has given rise to a long and ongoing debate since it was introduced in the social sciences following the movements of the 1960s. The works of Lefebvre (1968) and Castells (1983) represented the beginning of critical urban thinking. Castells first addressed *"The Urban Question"* with a Marxist approach (1977). He asserted that when citizens mobilize in cities to address problems in the urban environment, and connect with other organizations that are engaged in the class struggle in the sphere of production, such citizens give rise to urban movements that have the capacity to generate structural and social change. Later, in *"The City and the Grassroots"* Castells defined "urban social movements" as collective mobilizations around demands for collective consumption, cultural identity, and political self-determination "that influence structural social change and transform the urban meaning" (1983: 305). From this perspective, urban movements become "social" when their activists are part of broader social movements, express solidarity with other movement activists, and maintain contact with media, professionals, and political parties, without conceding their autonomy (Castells 1983: 322).

More recently, "urban movements" have been defined by Pruijt (2007: 5115) as "social movements through which citizens attempt to achieve some control over their urban environment. The urban environment comprises the built environment, the social fabric of the city, and the local political process." Pruijt pointed to three prominent sets of issues in urban literature which citizens address, by means of protests and collective action. First those related to "collective consumption." In the global North, such issues encompass housing shortages, increasing gaps between rent and wages, and inadequate healthcare and education. In the global South issues relating to collective consumption include the absence of water supply, sewerage systems, and electricity for shantytown inhabitants. A second set of issues concerns problems connected to urban planning such as the relocation of uses and demolition of beloved cityscape. The third set of issues identified by Pruijt relates to discrete, specific issues around which particular groups mobilize, such as "squatters against anti-squatter policies, property owners against proposed social housing and against property tax, [or] racist groups against migrants" (Pruijt 2007: 5115). According to Pruijt, for urban mobilization to be considered as a movement, actors "do not need overarching goals—nor do they need a high level of organizational unification," but they have to fight for new conception of identity and way of life, or instrumentally for a specific aim such as affordable housing (Pruijt 2007: 5116).

In such an approach, there is a risk that every urban mobilization or protest campaign could be considered as a social movement. Some protests, however, may simply be reactions to urban policies at a lower level—as street or district citizens committees sometimes are—or may be the outcome of coalitions exclusively aimed at achieving a common goal without forging shared beliefs and identities. Other movements which arise at the urban level may go beyond the local dimension, reaching a national and transnational level and intertwining with other social movements as did, for example, "Critical Mass," "Reclaim the Streets," and some social centers.

In our view, the extent to which urban mobilizations ought to be defined as *urban social movements* is an empirical question to be investigated on a case-by-case basis. The understanding of urban social movements should be limited to conflict-oriented networks of informal relationships between individuals and groups/organizations, based on collective identities, shared beliefs, and solidarity, which mobilize around urban issues, through the frequent use of various forms of protest (Diani 1992).

CHANGING POLITICAL OPPORTUNITIES IN THE URBAN CONTEXT

Urban conflicts do not emerge spontaneously and in isolation but rather exist in relation to a host of social and political processes, institutional settings, and specific socio-economic structures. As a result, such conflicts are more likely to occur in some places rather than others (Trudelle 2003). In this section, we will explore the links between processes of urban transformation and urban mobilization, highlighting the political opportunity structures for urban social movements represented by factors such as the nature of urban redevelopment processes, the decision-making models employed in transformations of the urban space, and the general socio-economic context within which the city is embedded.

The rise of mobilization in cities has historically been related to economic reorganization and urban redevelopment (Fainstein and Fainstein 1985; Harvey 1989). Since the 1980s, the shift from the modern industrial city to the post-industrial global city has led to the emergence of the urban space as the "new strategic institutional arena" (Salet 2007: 5), which has an increasingly central and strategic role for the functioning of the global economy (Sassen 2001). Since the 1990s scholars from the fields of urban studies and urban politics (see Kearns and Paddison 2000; Jessop 2002; Davies 2003; Peck, Theodore, and Brenner 2009) have identified a hegemonic model of urban development characterized by large-scale physical renovation projects and the development of what has been called the "new urban policy" (NUP) agenda (Swyngedouw et al. 2002). This "new urbanism" (Salet and Gualini 2007) has aimed at reshaping the city environment and the urban socio-economic landscape to make cities more attractive to potential investors, giving an influential role to economic development and private economic actors.

The emergence of this model of urban development has been an international process. The privatization and commodification of urban resources, the processes of residential gentrification, the dispossession and displacement of low-income people, and the growing impact of tourism in central urban areas are increasingly prominent in cities across the world. The movement against the process of gentrification in the central Flower square in Zagreb between 2006 and 2008 (Misetic and Ursic 2010), the campaign against Hamburg's urban renewal policies in 2009 (Novy and Colomb 2013), and the movement against tourism in Barcelona throughout the summer of 2014, are examples of mobilization against comparable phenomena: cities for people against cities for profit (Brenner et al. 2012).

The need to be competitive and to constantly attract public and private investment has not only prompted conflicts between cities, but also within them; between those who stress the need for economic development policies and those who make claims for social and environmental policies for the community (Le Galés 1995). The process of standardization in the design and the implementation of urban renewal projects has provided the conditions for social movements to mobilize against similar types of developments. This has channeled collective action around the world and facilitated citizen mobilization by emphasizing the distinction between people who use the city principally as a place to live and to work and those who aim to use it as a source of profit. Consequently, over the last twenty years the classical Marxist distinction between use-value and exchange-value has been highly visible in framing the urban conflict (Brenner et al. 2012).

However, despite the conditions for social mobilization are also present in non-Western cities, collective action in the huge urban conglomerates of the developing world has often taken different forms than in other areas of the world. Referring primarily if not exclusively to Arab cities, Asef Bayat (2012) has spoken of social "non-movements" of the "urban subalterns," mainly composed of the poor and the young who are compelled by necessity to operate, spend time, work, and move their livelihoods in the city out-door public spaces, as the streets and the sidewalks. These "non-movements" have elaborated practices of informal resistance that may not be explicitly acknowledged and theorized, yet enable people to reduce the costs of mobilization under repressive conditions in authoritarian regimes and unresponsive governments. Although resistance mostly takes disperse or passive forms, it maintains a permanent state of latent mobilization in urban communities, enabling them to promote collective protests, or connect to broader political and social mobilization, when opportunities arise. This was the case for instance in the Arab uprisings (Bayat 2012).

Different municipal institutional settings and conflict-resolution models (Trudelle 2003) have led to variation in patterns of urban mobilization. For example, the characteristics of the decision-making process in urban planning policy, the interplay of actors participating at the local production of the space, and the level of consensus among the local political elite in urban policy are aspects of local political structures that have ramifications for the nature of citizen responses to urban development policy. As Nicholls (2008: 841) has argued, whether or not mobilization takes place "depends on the nature of local power relations between political authorities and civic organizations." At the local level, institutional and non-institutional dynamics are closely intertwined and in constant interaction. According to della Porta (2013: 183) "at the local, but also transnational, levels, social movements' criticism of representative democracy has been accompanied by proposals for alternative institutions." Going beyond institutionalized participatory processes and introducing some element of democratic innovation in processes of urban transformation can provide opportunities for urban movements (Font et al. 2014).

Finally, the broader socio-economic context within which planning and policy making takes place also influences the contours of urban mobilization. In Europe, the current financial crisis has been a significant turning point in the ongoing process of evolution of urban conflict, emerging as a political opportunity for movements. In recent years, the urban reality has been at the heart of the functioning and the contradictions of contemporary capitalism and since the credit crunch of 2007–08, the urban context has emerged as both epicenter and victim of the global crisis. As Margit Mayer has observed (2009: 370–371), "the rapidly unfolding recession is intensifying the breaking points around which urban social movements have been rallying, suddenly validating their claims and arguments about the lack of sustainability and the destructiveness of the neoliberal growth model."

The types of frame, repertoires of action, and organizational structures that characterize "urban social movements" are connected to the model of urban planning and types of urban policies being applied, the structure of local governance, and the broader socio-economic context. To explore the change and ramifications of the conditions that different institutional, political, and economic contexts provide, we present two types of urban mobilization taking place in Western cities, which are often interpreted by media and political authorities in contrasting ways. By reviewing the literature on those cases we will underline that those movements include "transformative" aspects, especially when they emerge in favorable local political contexts.

Case 1. Struggling for a Better Quality of Life: Between Nimby and Urban Movements

Urban transformations often provoke citizens reactions usually labeled as Nimby or LULU (Locally Unwanted Land Use) mobilizations, even if the first acronym has a negative connotation while the second does not. Researchers on a variety of disciplines ranging from social sciences to urban planning have often understood these phenomena as obstacles for the common or civic good. In this perspective, the Nimby label defines "the figure of a challenger who is at the same time rational utilitarian and pathologically irrational, able to rationally calculate costs and benefits and, at the same time, unable to base this calculation on rational arguments" (Jobert 1998: 72). If some see LULU opponents as exhibiting a "risk-averse strategy" (Fischel 2001) and characterize them as "producers for whom the potential gains on the economic market from a favourable public decision will far outweigh the considerable cost of effective participation" (Brion 1991: 43); others characterize Nimby movements as actors showing: "(1) parochial and localized attitudes toward the problem [to be addressed by the facility], which exclude broader implications; (2) distrust of project sponsors; (3) limited information about project siting, risks, and benefits; (4) high concern about project risks; and (5) highly emotional responses to the conflict" (Smith and Marquez: 2000). According to these definitions, it would be hard to consider citizens mobilizing on urban transformation as part of "urban social movements" as conceptualized above.

From an empirical perspective, however, citizens reacting to urban transformations have not been found necessarily to be affected by any kind of syndrome. Research

conducted in six Italian cities in the 2000s, surveying local committees of citizens protesting against urban authorities on issues ranging from security to the environment,
show that most of them were found to be mobilizing on a variety of issues that have
been framed under the label of "quality of life." Moreover, though they were formed on
a street or district level, they often networked with other committees, associations, and
social movements organizations to coordinate their mobilizations at the urban level.
Out of the eighty-six local committees surveyed in Turin, Milan, Bologna, Florence,
Catania, and Palermo, only 19 per cent were classified as Nimby type, while 33 per cent
were classified as urban movement organizations and the rest either a district or a urban
committee in that research (della Porta 2004: 21).

Indeed, those committees rather appeared to represent forms of bottom-up mobilizations of "citizen-workers" who try to exercise their citizens' rights (as workers do in their
places of work), by defending their quality of life (Gould et al. 1996: 4), rather than forms
of egoist reaction against the common good. It was, then, not a surprise to find, a couple
of years later, that among the Global Justice Movement's activists meeting in 2002 at the
first European Social Forums of Florence, around 20 per cent of Italians, Germans, and
English, 30 per cent of Spaniards, and 40 per cent of French were (also) members of local
committees (della Porta et al. 2006: 47). After all, their mobilizations have been interpreted (della Porta 2004) as conflicts emerging from cities' competition in the global
market for attracting private investment, which seem to transform them into "urban
growth machines" (Logan and Molotch 1987), increasingly under the control of business
imperatives (Levine 1989). This kind of "urban regime" (Stone 1993) is often challenged
by urban movements proposing an alternative organization of cities (more oriented
toward social inclusiveness and environmental respect), sometimes with a relevant policy impact, as in Detroit in the 1990s (Orr and Stoker 1994: 62) and in many other cities
among the 1,000 cities in thirty-eight countries studied by Clark (1994).

Urban-based citizens' mobilization, even when they "react" to urban policy implementation, is not, then, necessarily Nimby-oriented. Many researchers have, in fact,
contested this conventional interpretation of such mobilizations (Jobert 1998; Andretta
2004; Gibson 2005; Schively 2007), and propose examining them for their democratic
potential (McAvoy 1998). Gordon and Jasper (1996) underline that the more such mobilizations are able to generalize their frames the more they gain public attention, and,
consequently, increase the probability that they will achieve their policy goals; the process through which such actors build and/or transform their identities does not seem to
be only a function of their agency.

Local citizens' mobilization "frames" and "identities," as well as their organizational
features, are also the result of a combination of external factors such as social integration, social capital, human capital, and political opportunities (della Porta 2004).

Some scholars suggest locating the Nimby syndrome in the contentious field of
identity formation where challengers and authorities compete through conflicting arguments (Toulemin 1993: 7). While authorities try to label citizens' mobilization as Nimby (Tapie-Grime 1997; Jobert 1998), challengers seek to overcome this
label developing a "Not On the Planet Earth" (NOPE) discourse, and struggle to gain

public acknowledgement and legitimacy (Gordon and Jasper 1996). This "argumentative field" seems to be (also) shaped by political opportunities: when political parties more oriented toward citizens inclusion and environmental concerns have a certain centrality in the urban political system, citizens mobilizing for a better quality of life have been found to frame their discontent in a more democratic and generalized way (Andretta 2005), even when their central issue was the security of their district, an issue often mobilized by right-wing movements and political parties (Andretta and della Porta 2005).

Case 2. Squatting Movements from Housing to Social Centers

Squatting in the cities is a practice and a form of action which has also given rise to urban movements with, in some cases, an extra local dimension. If squatting in general is a long-lasting urban phenomenon which refers to the illegal occupation of empty properties used without the consent of their owners, the political dimension of squatting as a way of living and/or carrying out public activities (political, social, cultural) has only recently been highlighted[1] (SQEK 2013; SQEK et al. 2014). Political squatting is indeed considered not only a way to meet the need for housing and spaces of sociability through direct action, the rejection of the rules and logic of the market and legal regulations, and criticizing the extent to which these needs are satisfied in a capitalist society; it is also conceived as an attempt made by radical and antagonist left-wing activists to practice non-hierarchical and participatory organization models, offering an alternative mode of envisioning social relationships, and political and countercultural practices (SQEK et al. 2014). According to Martìnez indeed, not only is the "appropriation of abandoned spaces... a partial attack on the unjust distribution of urban goods, but it is also a grassroots political intervention at the core of urban politics. Squatters defy the rules of the urban growth machine both for the sake of their own needs and to promote citizens' protests" (2013: 871); they can give rise to "a persistent *autonomous* and *radical* urban movement with a pragmatic orientation, although some institutional bonds and constraints can also play a significant role in its expansion" (Martìnez 2013: 870).

In fact Martinez, using the concept of "socio-spatial framework of opportunities and constraints," has identified a permissive legal status and non-repressive policies over squatters as some of the conditions that may allow squatting to emerge; but, these conditions also need to be combined with a sufficient number of abandoned properties, a slow rhythm of urban renewal and restructuring, a connection with other social movements, and an independent mass media coverage (Martìnez 2013: 872–882). The political opportunity structure (POS) approach is also applied by Pruijt and Roggeband (2014) who, studying squatting in the United States and in the Netherlands, suggest that a "dual-movement structure"—a combination of autonomous and institutionalized social movements—is most relevant when the political system is selectively open, because even when the relations between these different types of movements are tense, they can create opportunities for each other. The POS framework has also been critically used in combination with the approach of strategic dilemmas, showing that the squatters filter the constraints and opportunities of the local political system through their cognitive lenses facing some dilemmas; in their turn the resulting strategic choices of the activists extend or reduce these constraints and opportunities, thus influencing the opening and/or closure of the POS (Piazza and Genovese 2015).

The best known typology of squatting has been developed by Pruijt (2013), consisting of five basic configurations: a) deprivation-based squatting implies middle class activists who open up squats for poor people to move into; b) in squatting as an alternative housing strategy people organize occupation of buildings to meet their own housing needs; c) entrepreneurial squatting offers opportunities for setting up various kind of establishment, among which are occupied social centers, without the need for large resources nor bureaucracy fulfilments; d) conservational squatting involves occupation of buildings or sites as a tactic used in the preservation of a cityscape or landscape against efficiency driven planned transformation; e) political squatting refers to squatters particularly engaged in anti-systemic politics. This typology, however, has faced some criticism of the denominations employed, above all the use of "political" only for the anti-systemic squatting, while also the other configurations all have a political dimension. Then, if for Martìnez (2013) the squatters' movement includes squatted houses, squatted and non-squatted autonomous social centers, rural squatting and tactical squatting like the occupation of squares, two main broader types can be identified: the squatted houses (squats) and social centers (Piazza 2012), even if the distances between the two types are gradually reducing and more recently in some cases the housing occupations are beginning to turn into social centers too (SQEK et al. 2014), or vice versa.

Squats are typically apartment buildings, previously vacant, which are occupied mainly for residential purposes, whose common activities mainly concern the management of the edifice. Over time, these squats have become particularly widespread in the cities of Central and Northern Europe (e.g., Berlin, Hamburg, Amsterdam, Copenhagen, Paris, London, Zurich, etc.), but especially after the recent economic crisis, squatting in houses as a way to live is becoming more common in Southern European cities, like Madrid, Barcelona, Milan, Rome, etc., thus characterizing the social and urban conflicts. For example, in Rome occupations by the "movements for housing rights" in recent years have been rescaled socially, now involving workers whose job prospects are precarious, the unemployed, students, and different groups of migrants; they squatted houses also for alternative living conditions, reclaiming the right to the city and providing "an effective form of welfare from below" (Mudu 2014: 158).

Squatting movements for housing are closely interconnected with the occupied social centers that arose in the 1970s in Italy, then spread to Spain (Madrid, Barcelona) and in the rest of Europe, particularly in the UK (London, Bristol, Brighton, etc.) (SQEK 2013). They can be considered at the same time "liberated spaces" and urban protest actors whose reach of action often goes beyond the local dimension. The properties are empty and disused large buildings, not previously used for housing (such as former factories, schools, theatres, cinemas, etc.), which are occupied by groups of radical/antagonist left-wing activists. Their aim is to self-manage political, social, and countercultural activities, practicing participatory and non-hierarchical modes of political and social relationships (Piazza 2012: 9) opposed to the logic of market, capitalism, and to public authorities. From these "liberated spaces," the occupants/activists often launch radical/ antagonist political and social protest campaigns, addressed outside the squatted places towards the neighborhood where are located, the city, and the urban fabric, and the society at large. In fact, social centers cannot be considered only physical spaces, but also collective actors of the radical/antagonist left (Piazza 2012: 14). They are indeed urban players because they are spatially localized in the city centers or in the periph-eral/working class districts but their reach of action is often also regional, national, and global; the issues faced are both urban (social spaces and services, housing, urban renewal, etc.), although always set in general framework, and extra-local. Moreover, when the squatted social centers develop cooperative relations with other squatting and social movement groups, they play a key political role inside the wider squatters' movement: they serve as an essential socio-spatial infrastructure for the coordination and public expression of the squatting as an autonomous urban movement (Martìnez 2013: 882).

Finally, the strands of research on squatting have developed comparative approaches and empirical case studies focussing on long- and medium-term structural factors that make squatting possible, the analysis of conflicts and dynamics, the networks of social centers/squats, and their politics and culture (SQEK et al. 2014); nevertheless, squat-ting as a practice and urban movement has received considerable attention in Western European cities, while the phenomenon is much less visible in the international liter-ature in Asia, the Americas, and Australia, though in Eastern Europe the first studies emerged very recently (Piotrowski 2014).

Urban Social Movements and the Right to the City: Some Conclusions

The movements described in this chapter are both constrained by the structure of politi-cal opportunities in the urban context. However, by directly asking for more open ways to make political decisions or by prefiguring new city policies with their activities and practices, they have the agency to transform the relations between citizens and structur-ally powerful political actors. In our view, even if they are both very different in terms of identity, repertoires, and relations with political and social actors, they both represent two different ways to claim the "Right to the City." As Harvey (2008) points out, the "Right to the City" "is far more than the individual liberty to access urban resources: it is the right to change ourselves by changing the city. It is, moreover, a common rather than an individual right since this transformation inevitably depends upon the exercise of a collective power to reshape the process of urbanisation" (2008: 2).

As Margit Mayer (1987) argued over twenty years ago, in contexts of economic crisis and austerity politics, urban movements emerge as the promoters of social innovation dynamics. The current social and economic crisis in Europe is providing evidence for this claim, as new alliances among urban social movements, advocacy networks, and community-based organizations seem to be emerging. These new coalitions are generating alternative discourses, performing new practices, and rethinking new types of relationship with the local state (Walliser 2013), "in seeking to respond to social demands that neither the market not the state have managed to do" (Parés et al 2014). Beyond Europe, in a global context of neoliberal urbanism, non-Western cities are also experiencing new waves of local protest. For example, since 2004 South Africa has experienced a massive movement against privatization of local services, inadequate investment in public goods, and lack of accountability by local councillors, which Peter Alexander (2010) has called "the rebellion of the poor." In some Middle Eastern cities, such as Cairo, the very process of urban neoliberalism, under authoritarian rule, including gentrification, zoning, the state retreat from public services and welfare, and deregulation, seem to have created the opportunities for social and political mobilization aiming at the repossession of urban spaces (Bayat 2012). In Africa and Latin America, a social conflict is emerging in the socially and spatially marginalized slums in both violent and more moderate forms (Davis 2006).

Mayer (2013) has argued that today's urban mobilizations are mainly emerging around two lines: the continuous commodification of the city and the dismantling of the welfare state system. In Barcelona, the "Platform of Citizens Affected by Mortgages" (PAH), a housing right movement born in 2009, is continuously responding to an increasing housing problem by combatting evictions and transforming empty houses held by financial institutions into social housing (Parés et al. 2014). Another example in Barcelona is Can Batlló, an example of citizen self-management of a disused urban space in order to defend its social use of the place against processes of privatization and enclosure. In Italy, citizens in Turin are occupying "La Cavallerizza Reale" in order to avoid its sale by the local administration to private developers. Similar examples are the occupations by precarious workers in the art, culture, and entertainment sectors of former theatres and cinemas in Italy—the *Teatro Valle* in Rome and the *Macao* in Milan—as a means of preventing their abandonment or transforming them into commercial malls, instead seeking to create free spaces of cultural and artistic production (Giorgi 2014).

All those mobilizations in different urban spaces of the world demonstrate that the neoliberal pressures, not only deprive citizens of their rights to the city, but also offer opportunities for what Bayat (2012: 124–125) calls "a new logic of repossession." Or, alternatively, that urban movements create new opportunities to mobilize even under constraining conditions.

According to Andrés Walliser (2013), these new experiences at the local level represent a new paradigm of urban mobilization since they are not formed around organized structures but rather as a constellation of groups that have a virtual logic and among people that are highly educated and who use their professional expertise for collaborative interventions in a context of social innovation.

These types of movements can be interpreted as an outcome of two interrelated dynamics. On the one hand, they are intertwined with the context of crisis as they try to cover the paralysis and the privatization process of the public administration. On the other hand, they take advantage of a new collaborative culture, such is the pro-common culture, to focus on the production of the urban space (Fuster 2012; Harvey 2012). Through their mobilization, purposely or not, such movements produce alternative spaces with the common goal of reinforcing local democracy and producing a more just city.

"Urban social movements" are, in this sense, transformative actors of the urban space, and contribute to the production of the "resources" available to citizens for the claiming of their right to the city. Thus, political structures are not only constraints on urban social movements but can also be transformed into opportunities through these very processes of mobilization. If, as we have argued, the city is a space of social, cultural, political, and economic production, it ought to be investigated. Both social movements and urban scholars would benefit from a more intense dialogue which would help to produce a deeper knowledge of the nature of the city, and how it is transformed by different actors and actions in different circumstances.

NOTE

1. Established in 2009, the *SQuatting Europe Kollective* is an open transnational and interdisciplinary network of critically engaged activist-researchers focussing on the housing and social centers squatters' movement in its various contexts, with the explicit aim of publishing reliable information not only as an end in itself, but also as a public resource for society and especially for squatters and activists, trying to involve them in research practices.

REFERENCES

Alexander, Peter (2010). "Rebellion of the Poor: South Africa's Service Delivery Protests—A Preliminary Analysis," *Review of African Political Economy*. 37 (123): 25–40.

Andretta, Massimiliano (2004). "L'identità dei comitati: tra egoismo e bene pubblico." In *Comitati di cittadini e democrazia urbana*, edited by Donatella della Porta, 71–96. Soveria Mannelli: Rubbettino.

Andretta, Massimiliano, and della Porta, Donatella (2005). "Quale sicurezza? Mobilitazioni locali e comitati di cittadini," *Rivista Italiana di Scienza dell'Amministrazione*. 4: 77–104.

Bayat, Asef (2012). "Politics in the City-Inside-Out," *City & Society*. 2(24): 110–128.

Barnett, Clive (2014). "What Do Cities Have to Do with Democracy?" *International Journal of Urban and Regional Research*. 38(5): 1625–1643.

Bosi, Lorenzo (2013). "Safe Territories and Violent Political Organizations." *Nationalism and Ethnic Politics*. 19(1): 80–101.

Brenner, Neil, Marcuse, Peter, and Mayer, Margit, eds. (2012). *Cities for People, Not for Profit*. London: Routledge.

Brion, Denis J. (1991). *Essential Industry and the NIMBY Phenomenon*. New York: Quorum.

Castells, Manuel (1977). *The Urban Question: A Marxist Approach*. Cambridge, MA: The MIT Press.

Castells, Manuel (1983). *The City and the Grassroots: A Cross-cultural Theory of Urban Social Movements*. Berkley: University of California Press.

Clark, Terry Nichols (1994). "Turbulence and Innovation in Urban America." In *Urban Innovation. Creative Strategies for Turbulent Times*, edited by Terry Nichols Clark, 1–20. London: Sage.

Davies, Jonathan (2003). "Partnerships versus Regimes: Why Regime Theory Cannot Explain Urban Coalitions in the UK," *Journal of Urban Affairs*. 25(3): 253–269.

Davis, Mike (2006). *Planet of Slums*. London/New York: Verso.

della Porta, Donatella (2004). "Comitati di cittadini e democrazia urbana: una introduzione." In *Comitati di cittadini e democrazia urbana*, edited by Donatella della Porta, 7–41. Soveria Mannelli: Rubettino.

della Porta, Donatella (2013). *Can Democracy Be Saved? Participation, Deliberation and Social Movements*. Cambridge: Polity Press.

della Porta, Donatella and Piazza, Gianni (2008). *Voices of the Valley, Voices of the Straits: How Protest Creates Communities*. New York: Berghahn Books.

della Porta, Donatella, Andretta, Massimiliano, Mosca, Lorenzo, and Reiter, Herbert (2006). *Globalization from Below*. Minnesota: University of Minnesota Press.

Diani, Mario (1992). "The Concept of Social Movement," *Sociological Review*. 40(1): 1–25.

Diani, Mario (2003). "Introduction. Social Movements, Contentious Actions, and Social Networks: from Metaphor to Substance." In *Social Movements and Networks: Relational Approaches to Collective Action*, edited by Mario Diani and Douglas McAdam, 1–19. Oxford: Oxford University Press.

Fainstein, Susan and Fainstein, Nornman (1985). "Economic Restructuring and the Rise of Urban Social Movements," *Urban Affairs Review*. 21(2): 187–206.

Fainstein, Susan and Hirst, Clifford (1995). "Urban Social Movements." In *Theories of Urban Politics*, edited by David Judge, Gerry Stoker and Harold Wolman, 181–204. London: Sage.

Fischel, William A. (2001). "Why are there NIMBYs?" *Land Economics*. 77(1): 144–152.

Font, Joan, della Porta, Donatella, and Sintomer, Yves (2014). *Participatory Democracy in Southern Europe. Causes, Characteristics and Consequences*. London: Rowman & Littlefield International.

Fuster, Morell M. (2012). "The Free Culture and 15M Movements in Spain: Composition, Social Networks and Synergies," *Social Movement Studies: Journal of Social, Cultural and Political Protest*. 11(3–4): 383–392.

Gibson, Timothy A. (2005), "NIMBY and the Civic Good," *City & Community*. 4(4): 381–401.

Giorgi, Alberta (2014). "Le mobilitazioni dei lavoratori della cultura, dell'arte e dello spettacolo." In *La nuova politica. Mobilitazioni, movimenti e conflitti in Italia*, edited by Luca Alteri and Luca Raffini, 91–113. Naples: Ediesse.

Gordon, Cyntia, and Jasper, James M. (1996). "Overcoming the 'Nimby' Label: Rhetorical and Organizational Links for Local Protestors," *Research in Social Movements, Conflict and Change*. 19(2): 159–181.

Gould, Kenneth A., Schnaiberg, Allan, and Weinberg, Adam (1996). *Local Environmental Struggles. Citizen Activism in the Treadmill of Production*. Cambridge: Cambridge University Press.

Hamel, Pierre, Lustiger-Thaler, Henri, and Mayer, Margit, eds. (2000) *Urban Movements in a Globalising World*. London: Routledge.

Harvey, David (1989). "From Managerialism to Entrepreneurialism: The Transformation in Urban Governance in Late Capitalism," *Geografiska Annaler. Series B, Human Geography.* 71: 13–17.

Harvey, David (2008). "The Right to the City," *New Left Review.* 53(September–October): 23–40.

Harvey, David (2012). *Rebel Cities: from the Right to the City to the Urban Revolution.* London: Verso.

Jessop, Bob (2002). "Liberalism, Neo-Liberalism and Urban Governance: A State Theoretical Perspective," *Antipode.* 34(3): 452–472.

Jobert, Arthur (1998). "L'aménagement en politique- ou ce que la syndrome NIMBY nous dit de l'intérêt general," *Politix.* 42: 67–92.

Kearns, Ade and Paddison, Ronan (2000). "New Challenges for Urban Governance," *Urban Studies.* 37(5–6): 845–850.

Lefebvre, Henri (1968). *Le Droit à la ville.* Paris: Anthropos.

Lefebvre, Henri (1970). *Le Révolution urbaine.* Paris: Gallimard.

Le Galés, Patrick (1995). "Du gouvernement des villes à la gouvernance urbaine," *Revue Française de Science Politique.* 45(1): 57–95.

Leitner, Helga, Sheppard, Eric, and Sziarto Kristin M. (2008). "The Spatialities of Contentious Politics," *Transactions of the Institute of British Geographers.* 33: 157–172.

Levine, Marc L. (1989). "The Politics of Partnership. Urban Redevelopment since 1945." In *Unequal Partnership,* edited by Gregory Squires, 12–34. New Brunswick, NJ: Rutgers University Press.

Logan, John R. and Molotch, Harvey L (1987). *Urban Fortunes. The Political Economy of Place.* Berkeley: University of California.

Martìnez, Miguel (2013). "The Squatters' Movement in Europe: A Durable Struggle for Social Autonomy in Urban Politics," *Antipode.* 45(4): 866–887.

Mayer, Margit (1987). "Restructuring and Popular Opposition in West German Cities." In *The Capitalist City. Global Restructuring and Community Politics,* edited by Michael P. Smith and Joe R. Feagin, 343–363. Oxford: Basil Blackwell.

Mayer, Margit (2006). "Manuel Castells' The City and the Grassroots," *International Journal of Urban and Regional Research.* 30(1): 202–206.

Mayer, Margit (2009). "The 'Right to the City' in the Context of Shifting Mottos of Urban Social Movements," *City.* 13(2–3): 362–374.

Mayer, Margit (2013). "First World Urban Activism. Beyond Austerity Urbanism and Creative City Politics," *City.* 17: 5–19.

McAvoy, Gregory E. (1998). "Partisan Probing and Democratic Decision Making: Rethinking the NIMBY Syndrome," *Policy Studies Journal.* 26(2): 274–293.

Miller, Byron and Nicholls, Walter (2013). "Social Movements in Urban Society: The City as a Space of Politicization," *Urban Geography.* 34(4): 452–473.

Misetic, Anka and Ursic, Sara (2010) "'The Right to the City': An Example of a Struggle to Preserve Urban Identity in Zagreb," *Sociologija i proctor.* 185(1): 3–18.

Mudu, Pierpaolo (2014). "'Ogni Sfratto Sarà una Barricata': Squatting for Housing and Social Conflict in Rome." In *The Squatters' Movement in Europe. Commons and Autonomy as Alternative to Capitalism,* edited by SQEK, Claudio Cattaneo, and Miguel Martìnez, 136–163. London: PlutoPress.

Nicholls, Walter (2008). "The Urban Question Revisited: The Importance of Cities for Social Movements," *International Journal of Urban and Regional Research.* 32(4): 841–859.

Novy, Johannes and Colomb, Claire (2013). "Struggling for the Right to the (Creative) City in Berlin and Hamburg: New Urban Social Movements, New 'Spaces of Hope'?" *International Journal of Urban and Regional Research*. 37(5): 1816–1838.

Orr, Marion E. and Stoker, Gerry (1994). "Urban Regimes and Leadership in Detroit," *Urban Affairs Quarterly*. 30(1): 48–73.

Parés, Marc, Martínez, Ruben, and Blanco, Ismael (2014). "Collaborative Governance under Austerity in Barcelona: A Comparison between evictions and empty urban space management," City Futures International Conference, Special Session: Collaborative Governance Under Austerity, Paris.

Peck, Jamie, Theodore, Nik, and Brenner, Neil (2009). "Neoliberal Urbanism: Models, Moments, Mutations," *SAIS Review of International Affairs*. 29(1), 49–66.

Piazza, Gianni (2012). "Il movimento delle occupazioni di *squat* e centri sociali in Europa: Una Introduzione." In *Il movimento delle occupazioni di squat e centri sociali in Europa*, edited by Gianni Piazza, special issue of *Partecipazione e Conflitto* 4(1): 4–18.

Piazza, Gianni and Genovese, Valentina (2016). "Between Political Opportunities and Strategic Dilemmas: The Choice of 'Double Track' by the Activists of an Occupied Social Centre in Italy," *Social Movement Studies*.

Pickvance, Chris (2003). "Symposium on Urban Movements," *International Journal of Urban and Regional Research*. 27(1): 102–177.

Piotrowski, Grzegorz (2014). "Squatting in the East—Rozbrat in Poland." In *The City Is Ours Squatting and Autonomous Movements in Europe from the 1970s to the Present*, edited by Bart van der Steen, Ask Katzeff and Leendert van Hoogenhuijze, 233–253. Oakland, CA: PM Pres.

Pruijt, Hans (2007). "Urban Movements." In *Blackwell Encyclopaedia of Sociology*, edited by George Ritzer, 5115–5119. Malden: Blackwell.

Pruijt, Hans (2013). "The Logic of Urban Squatting," *International Journal of Urban and Regional Research*. 1(37): 19–45.

Pruijt, Hans and Roggeband, Conny (2014). "Autonomous and/or Institutionalized Social Movements? Conceptual Clarification and Illustrative Cases," *International Journal of Comparative Sociology*. 55(2): 144–165.

Routledge, Paul (2003). "Convergence Space: Processes of Geographies of Grassroots Globalisation Networks," *Transactions of the Institute of British Geographers*. 28: 333–349.

Salet, Willem (2007). "Framing Strategic Urban Projects." In *Framing Strategic Urban Projects. Learning from Current Experiences in European Urban Regions*, edited by Willem Salet and Enrico Gualini, 3–19. London: Routledge.

Sassen, Saskia (2001). *The Global City*. New York: Princeton University Press.

Schively, Carissa (2007). "Understanding the NIMBY and LULU Phenomena: Reassessing Our Knowledge Base and Informing Future Research," *Journal of Planning Literature*. 21: 255–266.

Slater, David (1997). "Spatial Politics/Social Movements: Questions of (B)orders and Resistance in Global Times." In *Geographies of Resistance*, edited by Steve Pile and Michael Keith, 258–276. London: Routledge.

Smith, Eric R. A. N. and Marisela Marquez (2000). "The Other Side of the NIMBY Syndrome," *Society and Natural Resources*. 13(3): 273–280.

SQEK, ed. (2013). *Squatting in Europe. Radical Spaces, Urban Struggles*. New York: Minorcompositions/Autonomedia.

SQEK, Cattaneo, Claudio, and Martìnez, Miguel, eds. (2014). *The Squatters' Movement in Europe. Commons and Autonomy as Alternative to Capitalism*. London: PlutoPress.

Stone, Clarence N. (1993). "Urban Regimes and the Capacity to Govern," *Journal of Urban Affairs*. 15: 1–28.

Swyngedouw, Erik (2011). "Every Revolution has its Square." http://citiesmcr.wordpress.com/2011/03/18/every-revolution-has-its-square/ (accessed 30 January 2015).

Swyngedouw, Erik, Moulaert, Frank, and Rodriguez, Arantxa (2002). "Neoliberal Urbanism in Europe: Large-Scale Urban Development Projects and the New Urban Policy," *Antipode*. 34(3): 542–577.

Tapie-Grime, Muriel (1997). "Le nimby, une resource de démocratisation," *Ecologie et Politique*. 21: 13–27.

Toulemin, Stephan E. (1993). *Les usages de l'argomentation*. Paris, Presses Universitaires de France.

Trudelle, Catherine (2003). "Au-delà des mouvements sociaux: une typologie relationnelle des conflits urbains," *Cahiers de géographie du Québec*. 47(131): 223–242.

Walliser, Andres (2013). "New Urban Activism in Spain: Reclaiming Public Space in the Face of Crisis," *Policy&Politics*. 43(3): 329–350.

PART III

MICRO-DYNAMICS OF CONTENTION

CHAPTER 13

....

MOTIVATIONS TO ACTION

....

BERT KLANDERMANS

PROTESTS in the "new" democracies in Central Europe about "stolen elections," street demonstrations in the "old" democracies against austerity measures, ongoing protests in the Arab world for more democracy, and occupied city squares throughout the world to charge against inequality and claim better governance—almost daily our news media report on how people try to influence politics in contentious manners. This is not to say that political protest is something people regularly do. Facing some aversive situation most people continue to do what they were doing, namely nothing. In fact, participants in political protest are most of the time a minority. Even mass mobilization rarely encompasses more than a few percentage points of the population. Wright, Taylor and Moghaddam (1990) proposed a simple sequence of crossroads people pass if they are confronted with aversive politics (in Figure 13.1).

The first crossroad separates those who do nothing and those who take some action. The next separates those who take individual action (e.g., contacting a politician or writing a letter to the editor) from those who take collective action (e.g., taking part in a street demonstration or a strike). Finally, those who take collective action might take part in non-contentious action (e.g., a peaceful demonstration or a petition) or contentious action (e.g., a site-occupation or violent confrontations with the police). This raises a question that has always occupied students of contentious collective action: *Why do some individuals participate in contentious collective action while others don't?* This chapter on motivations to action attempts to review the answers to that question.

GRIEVANCES

....

It all starts with grievances, that is, "outrage about the way authorities are treating a social problem" (Klandermans 1997: 38). In *The Social Psychology of Protest* while expanding on this definition, a distinction is made between illegitimate inequality, suddenly imposed grievances, and violated principles. Suddenly imposed grievances—such as

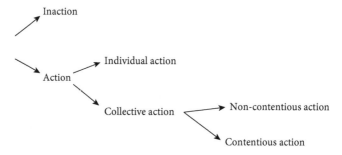

FIGURE 13.1 Action taxonomy

the establishment of a waste incinerator or a highway trajectory—are powerful mobilizers as are violated principles (Walsh and Warland 1983; Kriesi 1993). Illegitimate inequality is dealt with in the literatures on relative deprivation and social justice (Tyler and Smith 1998). Relative deprivation theory holds that feelings of relative deprivation result from a comparison of one's situation with a certain standard—one's past, someone else's situation, or an ideological standard such as equity or justice (Folger 1986). If a comparison results in the conclusion that one is not receiving what one deserves, a person experiences relative deprivation. The literature further distinguishes between relative deprivation based on personal comparisons (i.e., individual deprivation) and relative deprivation based on group comparisons (i.e., group deprivation: Kelly and Breinlinger 1996). Research demonstrates that group relative deprivation is particularly important for engagement in collective action (Major 1994), but work by Foster and Matheson (1999) suggests that so-called "double deprivation," that is, a combination of group and individual deprivation, is even more effective. On the basis of a meta-analysis, Van Zomeren et al. (2008) conclude that the cognitive component of relative deprivation (i.e., the observation that one receives less than the standard of comparison) has less influence on action participation than does the affective component (i.e., such feelings as dissatisfaction, indignation, and discontent about outcomes).

Social psychologists have applied social justice theory to the study of social movements (Tyler and Smith 1998). The social justice literature distinguishes between two classes of justice judgments: distributive and procedural justice. Distributive justice is related to relative deprivation in that it refers to the fairness of outcome distributions. Procedural justice, on the other hand, refers to the fairness of decision-making procedures and the relational aspects of the social process, that is, whether authorities treat people with respect and can be trusted to act in a beneficial and unbiased manner (Tyler and Lind 1992). Research has found that people care more about how they are treated than about outcomes. Based on these findings, Tyler and Smith (1998) propose that procedural justice might be a more powerful predictor of social movement participation than distributive justice; that is indeed what we found both in our research in South Africa (Klandermans, Roefs, and Olivier 2001) and among migrants in the Netherlands and New York (Klandermans, Van der Toorn, and Van Stekelenburg 2008).

DEMAND AND SUPPLY

Grievances are the raw material of the demand of protest. The demand-side of protest refers to the proportion of the population in a society that is sympathizing with the cause. The supply-side of protest refers to the opportunities of protest offered to people. If there is no supply of protest opportunities, the demand might be high but nothing will happen. If, on the other hand, there is no demand there is no point in offering opportunities to protest.

The demand-side of protest concerns the characteristics of an issue's mobilization potential. An issue's mobilization potential can be characterized in terms of its demographic composition (gender, age, social class, level of education, ethnicity, etc.) and its political composition (left–right, liberal–conservative); in terms of collective identities, shared grievances, and shared emotions; in terms of its internal organization; and in terms of its embeddedness in the society at large. The dynamics of demand refer to the formation of mobilization potential: grievances and identities must politicize and emotions must be aroused. Social movement organizations are more or less successful in satisfying demands for collective political participation and we may assume that movements that are successfully supplying what potential participants demand gain more support than movements that fail to do so. Movements and movement organizations can be compared in terms of their effectiveness in this regard.

The supply-side of protest concerns characteristics of the opposition in society (cf. Corrigall-Brown 2012). How contentious is the opposition and how dense? It regards such matters as the composition of the opposition's multi-organizational field; its allies and its opponents. Are traditional organizations such as churches, parties or unions involved, or any other societal organization? The supply-side also concerns action repertoires, the effectiveness of the opposition, the ideologies movements stand for, and the constituents of identification they offer. How well is the opposition in a society organized? What kinds of activities are they staging and are those activities effective one way or the other? What is the ideological position of these organizations? Do organizations have charismatic leaders people can identify with? Movement organizations are not isolated structures. On the contrary, they engage in coalition formation, negotiations with other movement organizations in order to stage collective action.

Studies of participation tend to concentrate on mobilization and to neglect the development of demand and supply factors. Yet, there is no reason to take either for granted. To be sure, grievances abound in a society, but that does not mean that we need not explain how grievances develop and how they are transformed into demands for protest. Nor does the presence of oppositional organizations in a society mean that there is no need to understand their formation and to investigate how they stage opportunities to protest and how these opportunities are seized by aggrieved people. Perhaps social movement scholars do not bother too much about how mobilization potential and the social movement sector is formed, as they tend to study contention when it takes place and mobilization potential and social movements are formed and mobilized already. Hence, little is known about the formation of mobilization potential and the movement sector in the ebb and flow of contentious politics. Basic questions remain unanswered, questions such as how consensus is formed, how individuals come to feel, think, and act in concert; why and how some grievances turn into claims, while other do not; why and how some identities politicize, while others do not. Similarly, we lack fundamental insight into how movement organizations come into being; how they are formed, how their leadership work; whether they are competing with other organizations, and so on.

INSTRUMENTAL VERSUS EXPRESSIVE

Instrumental action refers to action as an attempt to influence the social and political environment; *expressive action* refers to action as an expression of people's views. Instrumental action presumes that participants take part because they believe that they can change their social and political environment at affordable costs. Therefore, movement organizations try to make participation attractive by increasing the benefits and reducing the costs of participation. Authorities or opponents on their part may try to make participation less attractive by imposing costs upon participants. Instrumental action presupposes an effective movement that is able to enforce some wanted changes or at least to mobilize substantial support. Making an objective assessment of a movement's impact is not an easy task, but movement organizations will try to convey the image of an effective political force. They can do so by pointing to the impact they have had in the past, or to the powerful allies they have. They may lack all this, but then, they might be able to show other signs of movement strength. A movement may command a large constituency as witnessed by turnout on demonstrations, or by membership figures, or large donations. It may comprise strong organizations with strong charismatic leaders who have gained respect, and so on. From an instrumental perspective a solution must be found to the dilemma of collective action. Olson (1968) argued that a rational actor will choose to take a free ride, unless selective incentives (costs or benefits that are made contingent upon participation in the production of the collective good) prevent him from doing so. Therefore, instrumentality also implies the provision of selective incentives. Movements may vary considerably in the selective incentives for participation they provide. This is, obviously, also a matter of the resources a movement commands. Surprisingly little comparative information is available on the resources movements have at their disposal. In a similar vein, systematic documentation is lacking on the way in which the larger political system and the alliances and opponents of movement organizations influence movement participation. Indeed, repressive political environments may increase the costs of participation considerably (Tilly 1978): people may lose friends, they may risk their jobs or otherwise jeopardize their sources of income, they may be jailed, and they may even lose their lives.

Expressive action presumes that people take part in collective action because they want to express their views. In classic studies of social movements the distinction was made between instrumental and expressive movements or protest (Turner and Killian 1987). In those days, instrumental movements were seen as movements that aimed at some external goal, for example, the implementation of citizenship rights. Expressive movements, on the other hand, were movements that had no external goals. Participation was a goal in itself, for example, the expression of anger in response to experienced injustice. Movement scholars felt increasingly uncomfortable with the distinction, as it was thought that most movements have both instrumental and expressive aspects and that the emphasis on the two could change over time. Therefore, the distinction fell out of use. Recently, however, the idea that people might participate in movements to express their views has received renewed attention from movement scholars who were unhappy with the overly structural approach of resource mobilization and political process theory (Goodwin et al. 2001; Gould 2009). These scholars began to put an emphasis on the creative, cultural, and emotional aspects of social movements, such as music, symbols, rituals, narratives, and moral indignation. People are angry, they develop feelings of moral indignation about some state of affairs or some government decision, and wish to make that known. They participate in a social movement not necessarily to enforce political change, but to gain dignity in their lives through struggle and moral expression.

Acting on one's view is one of the fundamental motives of action participation and necessarily charged with emotion. Appraisal and action are socially constructed, that is to say, they are formed in interpersonal interaction, especially in the case of politically relevant emotions. Obviously, appraisals can be manipulated. Activists work hard to create moral outrage and anger and to provide a target against which these can be vented. They must weave together a moral, cognitive, and emotional package.

Social movements play a significant role in the diffusion of ideas and values. Rochon (1998) makes the important distinction between "critical communities" where new ideas and values are developed and "social movements" that are interested in winning social and political acceptance for those ideas and values. "In the hands of movement leaders, the ideas of critical communities become ideological frames," states Rochon (1998: 31), going on to argue that social movements are not simply extensions of critical communities. After all, not all ideas developed in critical communities are equally suited to motivate collective action. Social movement organizations, then, are carriers of meaning. Through processes such as consensus mobilization they seek to propagate their definition of the situation to the public at large. Social movements do not invent ideas from scratch, they borrow from the history of ideas. They build on an ideological heritage as they relate their claims to broader themes and values in society.

TYPES OF MOTIVES

The social psychology of protest distinguishes three fundamental reasons why people participate in collective action: people may want to change their circumstances, they may want to act in concert with the group they identify with, or they may want to express their views. Together these three motives account for most of the reasons why people take part in collective political action. Social movements may supply the opportunity to fulfil these motives and the better they do, the more movement participation turns into a satisfying experience. In brief the literature refers to these three motives as instrumentality, identity, and ideology. *Instrumentality* refers to movement participation as an attempt to influence the social and political environment; *identity* refers to movement participation as an expression of identification with a group; and *ideology* refers to movement participation as an expression of one's views. Different theories are associated with these three angles (Klandermans 1997; Tarrow 1998). Instrumentality is related to resource mobilization and political process theories of social movements and, at the psychological level, to rational choice theory and expectancy–value theories; identity is related to sociological approaches that emphasize the collective identity component of social movement participation and with the social psychological social identity theory; and ideology is related to approaches in social movement literature that focus on culture, meaning, narratives, moral reasoning, and emotion and, in psychology, to theories of social cognition and emotions.

These are not mutually exclusive motives, or competing views on collective action participation, although some parties in the debates in the literature seem to take that position. However, approaches that neglect any of these three motives are fundamentally flawed. This is not to say that each motive should necessarily be present, or should be equally strong. For some people a specific motive can be more important than the other and the same holds for some instances of collective action. One might imagine that in the case of the labor movement, instrumentality, that is, aiming for a better agreement, is more important. Identity motives, on the other hand, might be more important for the gay and lesbian movement, while ideological motives might have been more important for participants in the anti-Iraq War demonstrations.

Perceived Costs and Benefits

The instrumental motive to participate in collective action conceives of action participation as controlled by the perceived costs and benefits of participation. Klandermans presented his now classic expectancy–value model in the American Sociological Review in 1984. The model holds willingness to participate dependent on collective and selective incentives. The incentives are the expected outcomes of participation multiplied by the value of those outcomes. Between values and expectancies a multiplicative relationship exists which implies that each factor must be higher than zero. If an expected outcome is not valued it does not make a difference; if a valued outcome is not expected, it does not make any difference either. Some outcomes are called selective incentives because they are contingent upon participation. Other are characterized by jointness of supply, that is to say, that once they materialize everybody benefits, including those who did not take part in their realization. Therefore, they are called collective benefits. This makes collective action vulnerable to free rider behavior, that is, non-participation under the assumption that one will reap the collective benefits anyway. The key factor of this part of the model is the expectations: expectations about the behavior of others, expectations that the goal will be reached, and expectations about the contribution of one's own behavior.

Inner Social Obligation

The drive originating from identification with other participants is the felt inner social obligation to act on behalf of the collective. Stürmer and his collaborators demonstrate that the motivating force behind collective identity is such a felt inner obligation (Stürmer et al. 2003). In terms of motivation, a felt inner obligation to participate is important because it is impossible to take a free ride on such an obligation. An inner obligation to participate can only be met by acting upon it, that is to say, by participating.

Inner Moral Obligation

Ideology as a motivating force results in an inner obligation as well, but this time a felt moral obligation (Van Stekelenburg and Klandermans 2007). Where norms and values are violated, for instance, equality or protecting the weak and in order to maintain their moral integrity, people may choose to participate in collective action. And again, one cannot take a free ride on a felt inner obligation.

An Additive Model

Instrumental, identity, and ideological motives presumably combine in an additive manner. That is to say, each motive adds to the other two in explaining why people participate in collective action, although the relative contribution need not be equal on every occasion. This implies also that the three motives can compensate for one another. Indeed, someone can participate in a protest event although she is not convinced that it will have much impact on politics, but she identifies with the other participants and that is what makes her participate. Alternatively, someone can feel so upset about the violation of some core value, for example animal rights, that he wants to express his indignation irrespective of the expected political outcomes. Van Stekelenburg (2006) was the first to demonstrate that depending on the organizer or the issue the relative weight of the motives vary. She proposed and tested that movements might have different action orientations that appeal differentially to the three key motives. Borrowing Turner and Killian's distinction between power oriented, participation oriented, and value oriented movements, she argued that power oriented movements appeal more to instrumental motives, and value oriented movements more to ideological motives (Turner and Killian 1987).

Emotions

Recent work in sociology and social and political psychology has brought emotions to the study of collective action (Jasper 1998; Goodwin et al. 2001; Van Zomeren et al. 2004; Van Stekelenburg 2006). Emotions can be avoidance or approach oriented. Fear, which makes people refrain from taking action, is an example of an avoidance oriented emotion. Anger is an approach oriented emotion and is known to be an antecedent of protest participation (Van Zomeren et al. 2004). There appears to be a relation between emotions and efficacy. When people do not feel efficacious, they are more likely to experience fear; feeling efficacious, on the other hand, is associated with displaying anger (Mackie, Devos, and Smith 2000). Findings from our study among migrants confirm this, feelings of efficacy reinforced anger and reduced fear, while in their turn anger fostered collective action participation while fear undermined it (Klandermans et al. 2008). Anger and fear are not the only emotions relevant in the context of movement participation; indeed other emotions such as hope and despair are proposed as well (Gould 2009; Sturmer and Simon 2009; Taylor 2013). Anger moves people to adopt a more challenging relationship with authorities than subordinate emotions such as shame and despair (Taylor 2013) or fear (Klandermans et al. 2008).

An Integrating Framework

Strikingly, a comprehensive framework integrating identities, grievances, and emotions into a single model was lacking for a long time. Recently, however, Simon et al. (1998), Van Zomeren et al. (2008), and Van Stekelenburg and Klandermans (2007, 2009, 2011) have each attempted to build such models. The three models these authors have in common that they distinguish various pathways to collective action. While Simon et al. distinguish an instrumental and identity pathway, and Van Zomeren et al. distinguish between an emotion- and a problem focussed pathway, Van Stekelenburg and Klandermans distinguish instrumentality, identity, ideology, and anger as determinants of participation in collective action. Central to all three models are processes of identification; in order to develop the shared grievances and shared emotions that characterize demand, a shared identity is needed. Similarly, all three models include an instrumentality component with efficacy as a key aspect. In a comparison of the three models Van Zomeren and his colleagues concluded that injustice, identity, and efficacy each contributed to the explanation of collective action participation (2008).

Figure 13.2 summarizes the various models. As dependent variable, the strength of the preparedness to participate in collective action is taken. Such strength results from group-based anger, and instrumental and/or ideological motivation. Instrumental and ideological motivation each result from grievances and feelings of efficacy shared with a group with which the individual participants identify. Grievances may originate from interests and/or principles that are felt to be threatened. The more people feel that interests of the group and/or principles that the group values are threatened, the angrier they

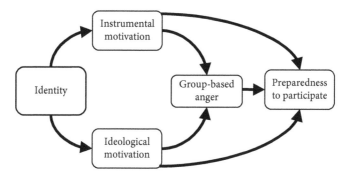

FIGURE 13.2 Motivational dynamics of Collective Action Participation

are and the more they are prepared to take part in collective action to protect their interests and/or to express their indignation. Whether a specific level of motivation turns into actual participation depends also on the supply of opportunities to act.

Consensus and Action Mobilization

To conclude, a brief discussion of mobilization is needed as motivation without mobilization would not get far. Mobilization can be distinguished into the processes of convincing and activating (Klandermans 1988). An actor's attempts to convince people is referred to as consensus mobilization. These attempts embrace grievance interpretation, causal attribution, possible measures to be taken, and so on. Consensus mobilization is a long-term enterprise. It takes time to convince people of the actor's points of view. However, possible success in activating people is limited by the degree of success of consensus mobilization. Action mobilization concerns the transformation of sympathizers into activists. Indeed, activating sympathizers is difficult enough let alone turning people into sympathizers. Therefore, action mobilization campaigns tend to concentrate on transforming sympathizers into participants.

Steps Toward Participation

Action mobilization is a process that evolves in four steps that each has its own explanation (see Figure 13.3). Motivation concerns one of the steps in the process.

As action mobilization concerns the transformation of sympathizers into participants, the process starts with that part of the population that sympathizes with the cause—in the literature often depicted as the mobilization potential of a social movement. The size of the mobilization potential reflects the success or failure of the consensus mobilization. The first problem to solve is targeting the sympathizers. This step seems obvious but its significance is often overlooked, both by organizers and researchers. Formal and

ACTION MOBILIZATION

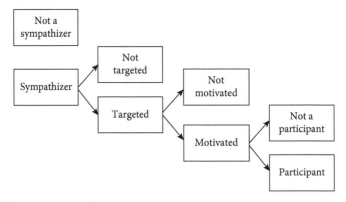

FIGURE 13.3 Four steps to action

informal networks, strong and weak ties to movement organizations, and all kinds of communication channels are important vehicles of mobilization at this stage.

The next step involves motivating people to participate. The fact that someone sympathizes with the cause of a movement does not guarantee that he or she is prepared to participate. Moreover, being motivated for one activity—let's say signing a petition—does not necessarily mean being motivated for another activity—for instance, joining a site-occupation. In the final step those who are motivated to participate must actually be persuaded to take part. This is still a significant step to take. For example, in a study of the mobilization campaign for a demonstration, 60 per cent of those who said that they were prepared to take part in the demonstration the next day eventually did not go (Klandermans and Oegema 1987). Indeed, this is a difficult step for organizers. What are they to do? People have been targeted; their motivation has been aroused, what more can an organizer do to make sure that people participate. At this final stage the strength of the motivation, the height of remaining barriers, *and* the influence of friends are what make the difference. This is understandable. If two friends decide to take part in an event, each of them will make sure that the other will go. It is your friends that make you live up to your promises.

REFERENCES

Corrigall-Brown, Catherine (2012). *Patterns of Protest. Trajectories of Participation in Social Movements*. Stanford: Stanford University Press.

Folger, R. (1986). "Rethinking Equity Theory: A Referent Cognitions Model." In *Justice in Social Relations*, edited by H. W. Bierhoff, R. L. Cohen, and J. Greenberg, 145–162. New York: Plenum.

Foster, M. D. and Matheson, K. (1999). "Perceiving and Responding to the Personal/Group Discrimination Discrepancy," *Personality and Social Psychology Bulletin*. 25: 1319–1329.

Goodwin, Jeff, Jasper, James, and Polletta, Francesca (2001). *Passionate Politics. Emotions and Social Movements*. Chicago: The University of Chicago Press.

Gould, D. (2009). *Moving Politics: Emotion and ACT UP's Fight Against AIDS*. Chicago: University of Chicago Press.

Jasper, James (1998). "The Emotions of Protest: Affective and reactive Emotions In and Around Social Movements," *Sociological Forum*. 13(3): 397–424.

Kelly, Caroline and Breinlinger, Sara (1996). *The Social Psychology of Collective Action: Identity, Injustice and Gender*. London: Taylor & Francis.

Klandermans, Bert (1984). "Mobilization and Participation: Social Psychological Expansions of Resource Mobilization Theory," *American Sociological Review*. 49: 583–600.

Klandermans, Bert (1988). "The Formation and Mobilization of Consensus." In *International Social Movement Research, vol.1, From Structure to Action: Comparing Movement Participation Across Cultures*, edited by Bert Klandermans, Hanspeter Kriesi, and Sidney Tarrow, 173–197. Greenwich, CN: JAI-Press.

Klandermans, Bert (1997). *The Social Psychology of Protest*. Oxford: Blackwell.

Klandermans, Bert and Oegema, Dirk (1987). "Potentials, Networks, Motivations and Barriers: Steps toward Participation in Social Movements," *American Sociological Review*. 5: 519–531.

Klandermans, Bert, Roefs, Marlene, and Olivier, Johan (2001). *The State of the People: Citizens, Civil Society and Governance in South Africa, 1994–2000*. Pretoria: Human Science Research Council.

Klandermans, Bert, Van der Toorn, Jojanneke, and Van Stekelenburg, Jacquelien (2008). "Embeddedness and Identity: How Immigrnats Turn Grievances into Action," *American Sociological Review*. 73: 992–1012.

Kriesi, Hanspeter (1993). *Political Mobilization and Social Change: The Dutch Case in Comparative Perspective*. Aldershot: Avebury.

Mackie, D. M., Devos, T., and Smith, E. R. (2000). "Intergroup Emotions: Explaining Offensive Action Tendencies in an Intergroup Context," *Journal of Personality and Social Psychology*. 79(4): 602–616.

Major, Brenda (1994). "From Social Inequality to Personal Entitlement: The Role of Social Comparisons, Legitimacy Appraisals, and Group Memberships," *Advances in Experimental Social Psychology*. 26: 293–355.

Olson, Mancur (1968). *The Logic of Collective Action. Public Goods and the Theory of Groups*. Cambridge, MA: Harvard University Press.

Rochon, Thomas R. (1998). *Culture Moves: Ideas, Activism, and Changing Values*. Princeton, NJ: Princeton University Press.

Simon, Bernd, Loewy, Michael, Stürmer, Stefan, Weber, Ulrike, Kampmeier, Claudia, Freytag, Peter, Habig, Corinna, and Spahlinger, Peter (1998). "Collective Identity and Social Movement Participation," *Journal of Personality and Social Psychology*. 74: 646–658.

Stürmer, Stefan and Simon, Bernd (2009. "Pathways to Collective Protest: Calculation, Identification, or Emotion? A Critical Analysis of the Role of Group-Based Anger in Social Movement Participation," *Journal of Social Issues*. 65: 681–705.

Stürmer, Stefan, Simon, Bernd, Loewy, Michael, and Jörger, Heike (2003). "The Dual-Pathway Model of Social Movement Participation: The Case of the Fat Acceptance Movement," *Social Psychology Quarterly*. 66(1): 71–82.

Tarrow, Sidney (1998). *Power in Movement. Social Movements, Collective Action and Mass Politics in the Modern State,* 2nd edn. Cambridge: Cambridge University Press.

Taylor, Verta (2013). Social Movement Participation in the Global Society: Identity, Networks and Emotions." In *The Future of Social Movement Research. Dynamics, Processes and Mechanisms,* edited by Jacquelien Van Stekelenburg, Conny M. Roggeband, and Bert Klandermans, 37–58. Minnesota: University of Minnesota Press.

Tilly, Charles (1978). *From Mobilization to Revolution.* Reading, MA: Addison-Wesley.

Turner, Ralph H. and Killian, Lewis M. (1987). *Collective Behavior,* 3rd edn. Englewood Cliffs, NJ: Prentice-Hall Inc.

Tyler, Tom R. and Lind, E. A. (1992). A Relational Model of Authority in Groups," *Advances in Experimental Social Psychology.* 25: 115–191.

Tyler, Tom. R. and Smith, Heather (1998). "Social Justice and Social Movements." In *Handbook of Social Psychology,* edited by D. Gilbert, S. T. Fiske, and G. Lindzey, 595–629. New York: McGraw-Hill.

Van Stekelenburg, Jacquelien (2006). "Promoting or Preventing Social Change: Instrumentality, Identity, Ideology and Group-based Anger as Motives of Protest Participation," Ph.D Thesis, VU-University, Amsterdam.

Van Stekelenburg, Jacquelien and Klandermans, Bert (2007). "Individuals in Movements: A Social Psychology of Contention." In *Social Movements Across Disciplines,* edited by Bert Klandermans and Conny Roggeband, 157–204. New York: Springer.

Van Stekelenburg, Jacquelien, Klandermans, Bert, and Van Dijk, Wilco W. (2009). "Context Matters. Explaining Why and How Mobilizing Context Influences Motivational Dynamics," *Journal of Social Issues.* 65: 815–838.

Van Stekelenburg, Jacquelien, Klandermans, Bert, and Van Dijk, Wilco W. (2011). "Combining Motivations and Emotion: The Motivational Dynamics of Collective Action Participation," *Revista de Psicología Social.* 26: 91–104.

Van Zomeren, Martijn, Postmes, Tom, and Spears, Russell (2008). "Toward an Integrative Social Identity Model of Collective Action: A Quantitative Research Synthesis of Three Socio-psychological Perspectives," *Psychological Bulletin.* 134: 504–535.

Van Zomeren, Martijn, Spears, Russell, Fischer, Agneta, and Leach, Collin W. (2004). "Put Your Money Where Your Mouth Is! Explaining Collective Action Tendencies Through Group-Based Anger and Group Efficacy," *Journal of Personality and Social Psychology.* 87: 649–664.

Walsh, Ed. J. and Warland, Rex (1983). "Social Movement Involvement in the Wake of a Nuclear Accident: Activists and Freeriders in the Three Mile Island Area," *American Sociological Review.* 48: 764–780.

Wright, Steven. C., Taylor, D. M., and Moghaddam, Fatali (1990). "Responding to Membership in a Disadvantaged Group: From Acceptance to Collective Protest," *Journal of Personality and Social Psychology.* 58: 994–1003.

CHAPTER 14

....

NETWORKS AS CONSTRAINTS AND OPPORTUNITIES

....

DAVID B. TINDALL

INTRODUCTION

....

SOCIAL networks are an integral part of social movement mobilization, and an important predictor of whether an individual joins a social movement organization (SMO), participates in a movement event, and/or engages in ongoing participation (Passy and Giugni 2001).[1] Networks can create opportunities. For example, they shape conditions for participation in collective action and social movements by acting as conduits for the flow of information, the development of pro-movement attitudes and values, and the development of collective identities. Importantly, networks also link individuals and groups to other movement actors and potential actors. Past social movement participants are often recruited for participation in new movements, and new episodes of mobilization. Networks can also provide non-movement related opportunities. For example, the ties developed through mobilization can act as a type of social capital that might be utilized in other contexts (Diani 1997; Tindall et al. 2012).

In addition to their role in facilitating mobilization, social network ties can also serve to constrain action in some circumstances. For example, a potential movement participant who has strong ties to individuals who oppose the values and goals of a movement may be constrained in their actions (McAdam and Paulsen 1993; Kitts 2000). In a related vein, Ho's (2010) study of environmental politics in Taiwan, provides an example where existing social ties were manipulated by industry to neutralize the local opposition to pollution.

While this chapter will focus primarily on the relevance of networks to individuals, network structures are important in a broader sense as articulated in social movement theorizing at the meso level. For instance, Mario Diani (2015) has conceptualized social network considerations as being central to a more theoretically informed definition of the concept of social movement (also see Diani and Mische, this volume).

Through empirical research, scholars have explored the relationship between networks and movements using a variety of different types of research methods and designs, including social surveys (Diani 1995; Tindall 2002), ethnographies (Stobbe 2011; Harris 2012; Barassi 2013), analysis of available documents (McAdam 1986; Osa 2001), and simulations (Marwell and Oliver 1993).[2]

Four types of network processes have been explored by social movement scholars: 1) personal networks that are implicated in the initial recruitment and ongoing mobilization of social movement members; 2) inter-organizational networks that link members of distinct social movement groups; 3) network structures that help transmit ideas and other aspects of culture; 4) networks that produce social capital for group members.

Less is known about the mechanisms that underlie these processes, and about the conditions under which network effects operate. Also, relatively less is known about the role that networks sometimes play in constraining social movement activity. Further, studies of networks and social movements have disproportionately been conducted on cases from the West. This essay will endeavor to address some of these lacunae.

In this chapter we will begin by considering the scale of social networks in terms of units of focus, and geography. Next we will briefly review some aspects of the social psychology of initial mobilization, the importance of networks for targeting others for recruitment, and the factors associated with different trajectories of participation. This will be followed by considering some of the main processes that are thought to underlie network explanations for individual participation in social movements. Most of this focus considers social ties as a type of "independent variable" that facilitates processes related to micromobilization. Thus, in the subsequent section, we will contrast this by considering some research on network ties as an outcome, or dependent variable—namely, network social capital. We will then provide a brief discussion of key network issues related to social media and social movement participation (Earl et al., this volume, provide a more detailed consideration of social media). Finally, in concluding we will examine some methodological considerations related to network dynamics and social movement participation.

SCALE OF NETWORKS

The focus of social network analysis can be "ego-networks" or, "whole networks." An ego-network is a focal actor, and the set of alters to which the focal actor is tied. A whole network is comprised of all of the nodes, and all of the ties amongst the nodes, in a bounded social grouping. Another distinction that is made by network analysts is between one-mode networks, and two-mode networks. In matrix terms, in one-mode networks the rows and the columns are the same actors. In two-mode networks, the rows and columns are different actors. For example, the rows might be individuals, while the columns might be organizations or events. With regard to the organization example, Breiger (1974) has introduced the concept of the duality of persons and groups where he notes that individuals are linked to one another through their joint membership in organizations, and organizations are linked together through the joint membership of individuals. This chapter will focus mostly on individuals (whether in terms of ego-networks, or as nodes in a whole or two-mode network).

The geographical scope of social networks is another dimension of analysis. Typically, network studies of social movement participants are local or regional. Recently, however, there has been an increasing interest in transnational movements, and networks (Keck and Sikkink 1998). Some scholars have investigated the intersection of local and transnational networks. For instance, Subramaniam et al.'s (2003) study of women's grass-roots organizing in India shows how a variety of intermediary networks are complexly intertwined within the nation-state, and internationally (see also Wiest 2007 on the role of the state, and its effects on activist networks related to transnational human rights mobilization in the Middle East and North Africa.)

Initial Mobilization, Targeting, Barriers, and Trajectories

Individual Mobilization

Klandermans (1997, 2004, this volume) has developed a model of individual mobilization. Becoming a participant in a social movement can be conceived as a process with four different steps (Klandermans and Oegema 1987). Two of these steps involve *"networks."* Motivation to participate in a collective action, such as a social movement activity, depends on the costs and benefits of participation, and these are often perceived, and evaluated in the context of social networks. However, as Klandermans and others point out, motivation is a necessary but insufficient condition of participation. Individuals have to be *motivated and also become the target of mobilization attempts.* Klandermans and Oegema (1987) state that people who have not been the targets of mobilization attempts are unlikely to participate in a collective action even if they are favorably disposed to its goals. Informal networks are crucial for the arousal of motivation to participate, as well as for the activation and coordination of motivated individuals.

Recruitment and Targeting

As noted above, affective support for a movement is usually not sufficient to ensure participation. Typically, those who are supportive of a movement also have to be targeted, and recruitment through pre-existing networks is an effective strategy. In studying the Wilderness Preservation Movement in Canada, Tindall (2002) found that the more weak ties, and strong ties, to SMO members an individual had, the more often they received requests to participate in movement activities. In turn, the more frequently they were targeted, the more active they were in low to medium cost activism. Often recruitment happens in blocs—where clusters of individuals (or groups) are simultaneously recruited.

Risk and Cost

Doug McAdam (1986: 70) has distinguished between low-risk/cost activism and high-risk/cost activism. Activities vary in terms of the risks that activists may face such as the likelihood of physical violence. Activities also vary in terms of money and time. While risks and costs are positively correlated, they are analytically distinct. This distinction is central to disentangling different network effects, such as the relative importance of weak versus strong ties to collective action within different governing conditions. For example, in countries where more authoritarian regimes exist, there are higher risks. Rizzo et al. (2012) studied networks and high-risk activism in Egypt. They found that in their study of an anti-sexual harassment campaign, the density of network ties at the local level played a significant role in facilitating a number of positive outcomes for the women activists involved, and for the movement more generally. As McAdam (1986) has noted, social networks can play an important role in high cost activism by providing access to social support. For example, Leenders (2012) describes the important supportive role that dense social networks played in collective action in Syria; they provided an important sense of solidarity and constituted the context in which recruitment for mobilization took place.

Continuity and Disengagement

In addition to developing a model of individual mobilization, Klandermans has also considered disengagement. In Klandermans's (2004) model, insufficient gratification and declining commitment contributes to a growing intention to leave the movement. Departure from the movement is then a function of a precipitating event. McAdam (1989) found that contrary to some stereotypes, many of the activists who were initially involved in the Freedom Summer project displayed remarkable continuity of commitment to political action over their life course. However, they often moved from one movement to another one. Similarly, Corrigall-Brown (2011) examines how the characteristics and life experiences of individual social movement participants affect the trajectory of their participation over time. She documents varying modes of engagement, and continuity.

Disengagement from social movement participation has received increasing attention in recent years (see Fillieule, this volume, for a review). The role of networks in disengagement, though, has received somewhat less attention. As Burt (2000) has noted, social relationships have a tendency to decline over time; in network terms, ties decay. In his analysis of network relations among bankers, Burt identifies several factors that work to speed up or slow down the rate at which relationships weaken and dissipate. The role of tie decay in social movement disengagement is a potential topic for social movement scholars.

NETWORK EXPLANATIONS: SOCIAL NETWORK PROCESSES

While there is strong evidence that network ties and social movement participation are empirically associated (e.g., see Passy and Giugni 2001), less is known about underlying mechanisms and processes. Kitts (2000) identifies three currents of microstructural explanation associated with networks: information, identity, and exchange. Passy (2001) includes identity within the larger explanatory category of socialization. She also points to the role that networks play in connecting individuals with others who share political interests, and in shaping individual preferences regarding decisions about whether or not to join a movement. Additionally, Kitts (2000) talks about the notion of multivalence, the tendency for social ties to inhibit as well as promote participation. This latter observation regarding constraint has been somewhat underemphasized. While many scholars have noted that pre-existing social ties (such as those to other movement participants) tend to facilitate entry into, and participation in a movement, it has also been noted (e.g., by Snow et al. 1980) that extra-movement ties can constrain movement participation. Some of the processes that are associated with the network-social movement linkage are described in the following text.

Communication, Information, and Social Comparison

Communication is a central function of social networks (Oliver and Marwell 2001; Tindall 2002, 2004; see Bennett and Segerberg, this volume, for a broader discussion of communication in social movements). Individuals learn about movement events and issues through their social ties with others. The structural characteristics of whole networks, and ego networks, can affect patterns of information transmission (Freeman 1979). For example, information can be disseminated more efficiently in more centralized networks. The relative centrality of a node (or actor) will affect the information that is received, and information about events and issues plays a role with who gets involved. Occupying a structural hole can be important to individuals in their ability to act as brokers (Burt 1993; Diani 2003). Being sociometrically close to others means that an individual will receive information more rapidly (Freeman 1979). Someone with higher degree centrality will be more likely to be an opinion leader.

A number of studies have demonstrated the linkage between networks and communication of information. For example, Holzner (2004), in a study of a Mexican squatter movement, argues that an individual's location in strong versus weak networks can restrict or expand their choice of action by making information about new political opportunities more or less available to them. Leenders (2012: 419), in a study of collective action in Syria, argues that dense social networks in the "peripheral" Dara region "contributed to the transfer, circulation, and interpretation of information whereby the shifting opportunities emanating from events in the region were recognized and the regime's threats were framed in ways that compelled people to act."

Of course communication can play other roles beyond dissemination of information about events and issues. For instance, information provided through social network plays an important role in "thresholds" or "critical mass" effects (Granovetter 1978; Macy 1991). Even when individuals have pro-movement interests, they may only be willing to participate if they believe there is a critical number of other actors committed to act. Such information is often assessed via informal social networks. More recently, social media has played a role in such processes—as potential movement participants are more visible through virtual networks. As Klandermans (2004) notes, expectations about the behavior of others is important. If too few people are expected to participate then one's own participation is useless. If very many people are expected to participate, then one's own participation is unnecessary.

Social comparison processes are another aspect of the linkage between social networks and the diffusion of information. Important here is the idea that network are not merely conduits for information. Rather, egos compare their contributions and outcomes with alters, and information about the alters is a key part of such processes. Individuals make comparisons when evaluating incentives to participate, and in monitoring the contributions of others (see Oliver 1984; Tindall and Gartrell 1990; Gould 1993). Social comparison is also implicated in other processes such as the formation of collective identities (Tindall 2002).

Social Influence

Another factor underlying social network effects on social movements is social influence (Snow et al. 1980; Kitts 2000; Tindall 2002; Gould 2003). Here a distinction between social influence and social selection is important (Friedkin 2006; Snijders et al. 2010). In the broader social network literature, social influence refers to phenomena like attitudes and behaviors that are shaped by an individual's social ties (Erickson 1988). Thus an individual with ties to members of environmental organizations will become more concerned about environmental issues. Social network analysts, however, argue that this relationship can also work in reverse. Thus an individual who has pro-environmental views, will be more motivated to form ties with people who belong to the environmental movement (Tindall 2007). While information exchange is one part of social influence, generally social influence effects are broader than information diffusion.

Social influence effects on social movement participation are often implicitly assumed by explanatory models, but these are rarely documented. There are at least three different ways in which social influence might happen. One is the information effect discussed earlier. Particular structures and/or ties are more likely to provide certain types of information that may facilitate (or constrain) participation. In this sense, by virtue of having such a tie and receipt of information via the tie, individuals will be more likely to act, and thus will be influenced. Another way in which this process works is through persuasion attempts by alters. The more ties an ego has to alters involved in a movement, and/or the more ties of a certain kind (e.g., strong ties), the more likely the ego is to be subject to such persuasion attempts by alters. A third argument, derived from balance theory, is that social ties are not merely information conduits, but they become part of the mechanism of social influence or social pressure. The assertion is that if person i has a positive social tie with person j, and person j has a positive tie to movement X, and if person j makes an attempt to recruit person i, then person i will feel pressure to either become affiliated with movement X (in order to please person j) or to adjust the nature of his or her relationship with person j. The activation of different processes is thought to be associated with tie strength. Those with whom an individual is strongly tied are thought to be able to exert greater social pressure and thus more social influence. Conversely, actors connected to others through weak ties are thought to be less able to exert social pressure—and thus their main avenue of social influence is through the provision of information. Gould (2003), however, argues that it is not credible that the average individual would cut a strong tie relationship just because an alter declined a social movement recruitment attempt.

Identity and Identification

Social psychologists and social movement researchers have observed that group identification can serve as a basis for collective action (McAdam 1986). In particular, Klandermans (1997, 2004, this volume) notes that identity can act as a motivation for participation, beyond the costs and benefits associated with instrumental considerations. This is partly a result of values and norms for behavior that are tied to identification. Further, as Friedman and McAdam (1992) suggest, acting is necessary in order to maintain a cherished identity "such as environmentalist" in the eyes of one's peers. McAdam and Paulsen (1993: 659) argue that network ties and identification interact to produce engagement in high-risk activism:

> The conclusion is unmistakable: neither organizational embeddedness nor strong ties to another volunteer are themselves predictive of high-risk activism. Instead it is a strong subjective identification with a particular identity, reinforced by organizational or individual ties, that is especially likely to encourage participation.

Diani (1992) has noted that a movement usually requires the involvement of more than one organization. From the vantage point of the individual, Tindall (2002) has theorized that it is range of ties to multiple SMOs, rather than number of ties to a single SMO, that is important for movement identification. In his studies of the wilderness preservation movement, Tindall (2002, 2004) found range of organization memberships, and range of interpersonal ties to people in different environmental organizations were positively correlated with their level of identification with the environmental movement. Further, results showed that level of identification was the strongest statistical predictor of level of activism in the movement.

Subjective Interests, Incentives, Sanctions, and Norms

Rational choice scholars see social movement activities as being instrumentally rational, and have examined the decisions that actors make in terms of perceived costs and benefits. Scholars working at the intersection of social networks and social movements have examined how networks shape decisions about instrumental action (Passy 2001), and have provided a critique of rational choice accounts (Kim and Bearman 1997; Gould 2003). Heckathorn (1988) has considered how various characteristics of groups affect the relationship between sanctioning systems and collective action. Thus, by considering the role of social networks, this body of work modifies and/or provides a counterpoint to rational choice approaches.

NETWORKS AS OUTCOMES: SOCIAL CAPITAL

Social ties are often thought of as an "independent variable" that facilitate intervening processes which in turn foster micromobilization (or constrain micromobilization). Relatively less emphasis has been placed on network ties as an outcome, or as a "dependent variable." There are several possible avenues for such investigation. At the individual level, actors can be thought of as leaders, followers, or brokers. Actors can take advantage of social structures to achieve goals. Conversely, social networks also shape actors. There are different views on how to bridge the agency–structure divide (Emirbayer and Mishe 1998). A primary focus of scholars examining the relationship between networks and movements has been on the role that network social structure plays in the mobilization process. Actors in leadership roles can take advantage of social structure to recruit others for collective action, and coordinate activities. There are a plethora of "indirect effects" linking network structures to activism.

    Participation in social movements and other types of collective action can also lead to the development of network social capital. Certain social structural properties can serve to foster the creation of social capital for individuals, and collective entities such as communities. In terms of collective benefits, network properties such as closure (related to density) facilitate the production of trust, and help groups to build norms and values (Erickson 1988). At the individual level, particular patterns of network embeddedness (such as higher extensity of ties) can be advantageous for individual goals such as social mobility. Burt (2009) has also talked about the advantages that accrue to individuals by their location in structural holes.

Diani (1997) has extended these ideas to consider the ties created through mobilization. He argues that social ties created between movement participants and non-movement participants through campaigns can serve as a form of social capital that might be drawn upon in the future. Following in this vein, Tindall et al. (2012) examined the relationship between individual participation in an environmental movement, and the range of ties that movement participants had to people in different occupations. They found that people who were more active developed greater network range. Using the logic of social capital, these enhanced networks might be drawn upon in the future for other purposes (such as future political activity, or individual instrumental goals such as job searches). Malinick et al. (2013) examined the network embeddedness of core environmental activists in Canada, and their propensity to get cited in news media coverage. The network structures developed by these activists served as a type of social capital in attracting reporters. Actors who were more central were cited significantly more often.

Virtual Social Networks

Earl et al. (this volume) discuss the implications of virtual social networks (social networks that are enabled through information communication technologies (ICTs)) and social movements. Here, we will briefly consider social networks in the context of social media and related technologies. In popular discourse, the term social network is often used as a synonym for social media such as Facebook. From a scholarly perspective, social media constitute one mode of social network interaction. However, (despite popular conceptions) non-digital interpersonal social networks have existed in human societies for many millennia. Of interest with regard to the phenomena covered in this chapter, social media (and other ICTs) can have subtle effects with regard to conventional interpersonal social networks. For instance, in terms of the concept of critical mass, social media can provide an indicator of the numbers of others who support or participate in a movement and which, from the individual perspective, may affect the tipping point or threshold for influencing one's participation. In terms of social comparison processes, social media can provide reference points for self–other comparisons that are utilized in the formation of collective identities. Indeed, social media can make people's social networks more visible (for instance, by showing the friends of your friends on Facebook). At the same time, they can also distort perceptions about the composition of a given actor's social network (e.g., when an individual "friends" strangers on Facebook or starts following unknown Twitter followers). Some of these potential network effects on the social psychology of micromobilization should be considered in investigations of whether social media is a "game changer" for individual participation in collective action and social movements (see Brym et al. 2014, for an analysis that compares the effects of social media with traditional interpersonal and organizational ties on participation in the Arab Spring).

Conclusions: Looking Ahead

As discussed in this chapter, social networks are a central part of social movement mobilization, and an important explanatory factor of whether an individual joins an SMO, participates in a movement event, and or engages in ongoing participation. Certain characteristics of networks can also serve to constrain social movement participation and/or neutralize micromobilization. Although there is a substantial literature on networks as an explanation for social movement participation, one challenge of research on networks and social movement participation is that it is not entirely clear whether networks are the "cause" or the "effect" of participation. Indeed, networks can be important for both providing opportunities for fostering and constraining activism. And new ties can be produced through social movement activities. While this latter insight has received somewhat less attention, a more general observation is that scholars need to consider "network dynamics" (Snijders 2011). As Passy notes, ideally, researchers should collect data on participants before and after their participation (see also Fillieule, this volume). And as McAdam and Paulsen (1993) have noted, comparative research on non-participants is also important, in order to avoid the problem of "sampling on the dependent variable." Most famously, McAdam has studied applicants to the Freedom Summer Project, and has data on participants and non-participants before and after their participation (McAdam 1986, 1989). See also, Klandermans and Oegema (1987); Passy (2001); Corrigall-Brown (2011). Next, we will consider several aspects of this issue.

Time and Network Dynamics

The link between behavior and social ties is shaped by two forces: persuasion (or social influence) and social selection (Knoke 1994). Social influence theory posits that when people interact, they influence each other's perceptions and actions (Friedkin 2006). Frequent interaction between individuals shapes political attitudes, and creates normative expectations that influence behavior, such as participation in social movement protests. Social selection theory highlights the tendency of people to make connections to similar others. People choose to form ties to individuals or groups (such as SMOs) who share their views, and in the process, embed themselves within a network which reinforces their attitudes. Thus, people's actions can be shaped by their networks, and their ideological preferences may also shape the formation of their networks. Relatedly, in a study of recruitment to Protestantism in China, Vala and O'Brien (2007) found that Protestant recruiters became adept at attracting non-networked individuals in relatively safe spaces, and they conclude that social bonds may be as much a result of recruitment as a precondition for it.

In order to tease out the difference between influence and selection, one needs to have longitudinal panel data on social movement actors, their relations, and accompanying "attribute" variables of interest. If one has two or more waves of data, then one approach is to utilize SIENA modeling (Snijders et al. 2010). This is a perspective that has received a great deal of attention in recent years (Snijders 2011), though it has not yet featured prominently in social movement scholarship. This is a potential avenue for future research. However, the difficulty of obtaining whole network data on social movement participants makes this challenging (see Diani and Mische, this volume, for a discussion of network evolution at the meso level).

Average Effects Versus Multiple Causal Pathways

The research literature on networks and social movements has evolved from focussing simply on the relation of social network ties to participation, to trying to understand the mechanisms that underlie this resilient correlation. For the most part this literature has focussed on network ties or structural properties as a key independent variable that explains participation. This is often considered an advance vis-à-vis earlier perspectives that focussed solely on social psychological factors. There has been some debate on exactly what are the key "intervening" variables or processes (Kitts 2000; Passy 2001; Tindall 2007). Some candidates include socialization and identity, but these are not all. A number of explanatory models have adopted multivariate regression-type approaches (e.g., McAdam 1986, 1989; McAdam and Paulsen 1993; Diani 1995; Tindall 2004). In these analyses various explanatory variables have been explored as potential intervening processes.

One shortcoming of this approach is that it models effects in terms of "average effects" for the entire sample, and does not allow the analyst to consider the possibilities that cases may differ, and that different configurations of variables may be important in different situations. Charles Ragin, in a number of works, has argued that a useful alternative to the variable centered approach of mainstream quantitative social science, is qualitative comparative analysis (QCA) focussing on cases instead of variables (Ragin 2009). A rare application of fuzzy set QCA to networks and social movement participation explored the combination of network and lifecycle effects to account for individual recruitment to, and sustained participation in activism (Hagan and Hansford-Bowles 2005; see also Ragin and Alexandrovna Sedziaka 2013 for an overview). QCA might also help us to disentangle the interplay of social ties and identification for explaining participation. While there is widespread agreement that both matter (e.g., McAdam and Paulsen 1993; Tindall 2002), their combination may vary for different individuals. In some instances people may jointly develop social ties and identification with a movement, and these factors may facilitate their participation. However, in alternative cases it may be that individuals participate because of an identification with a movement without having any "non-virtual" social ties to other participants. In yet other instances, ties may develop subsequent to participation rather than preceding participation.

Between movements, and within movements, it is likely to be the case that there are several different pathways that link networks and participation (Tindall 2007). These need to be explored more fully, especially outside the realm of liberal Western democracies. Further, it seems quite plausible that social media and other ICTs have increased the number of different configurations that produce individual participation (see Bennett and Segerberg's and Earl at al.'s chapters in this volume). It should also be added that this type of approach can also be used to explore the different configurations of variables that lead to non-participation—a topic that has been somewhat understudied.

Notes

1. I would like to thank Neil Guppy, Catherine Corrigall-Brown, Georgia Piggot, Rima Wilkes, Cohen Hocking, Neil Gross, and Noelani Dubeta for their useful feedback on an earlier draft.
2. See Diani (2002) for a review of key methodological issues.

References

Barassi, Veronica (2013). "Ethnographic Cartographies: Social Movements, Alternative Media and the Spaces of Networks," *Social Movement Studies*. 12: 48–62.

Breiger, Ronald L. (1974). "The Duality of Persons and Groups," *Social Forces*. 53: 181–190.

Brym, Robert, Godbout, Melissa, Hoffbauer, Andreas, Menard, Gabe, and Huiquan Zhang, Tony (2014). "Social Media in the 2011 Egyptian Uprising," *The British Journal of Sociology*. 65: 266–292.

Burt, Ronald S. (2000). "Decay Functions," *Social Networks*. 22: 1–28.

Burt, Ronald S. (2009). *Structural Holes: The Social Structure of Competition*. Cambridge, MA: Harvard University Press.

Corrigall-Brown, Catherine (2011). *Patterns of Protest: Trajectories of Participation in Social Movements*. Standford, CA: Stanford University Press.

Diani, Mario (1992). "The Concept of Social Movement," *The Sociological Review*. 40: 1–25.

Diani, Mario (1995). *Green Networks: A Structural Analysis of the Italian Environmental Movement*. Edinburgh: Edinburgh University Press.

Diani, Mario (1997). "Social Movements and Social Capital: A Network Perspective on Movement Outcomes," *Mobilization*. 2: 129–147.

Diani, Mario (2002). "Network Analysis." In *Methods of Social Movement Research*, edited by B. Klandermans and S. Staggenborg, 173–200. Minneapolis, MN: University of Minnesota Press.

Diani, Mario (2003). "'Leaders' or 'Brokers'? Positions and Influence in Social Movement Networks." In *Social Movements and Networks*, edited by M. Diani and D. McAdam, 105–122. Oxford: Oxford University Press.

Diani, Mario (2015). *The Cement of Society: Studying Collective Action Networks in Localities*. New York: Cambridge University Press.

Emirbayer, Mustafa and Mische, Ann (1998). "What Is Agency?," *American Journal of Sociology*. 103: 962–1023.

Erickson, Bonnie H. (1988). "The Relational Basis of Attitudes." In *Social Structures: A network Approach*, edited by B. Wellman and S. D. Berkowitz, 99–121. Cambridge: Cambridge University Press.

Freeman, Linton C. (1979). "Centrality in Social Networks Conceptual Clarification," *Social Networks*. 1: 215–239.

Friedkin, Noah E. (2006). *A Structural Theory of Social Influence*, vol. 13. Cambridge: Cambridge University Press.

Friedman, Debra and McAdam, Doug (1992). "Identity, Incentives, and Activism: Networks, Choices, and the Life of a Social Movement." In *Frontiers in Social Movement Theory*, edited by C. Mueller and A. Morris, 156–173. New Haven: Yale University Press.

Gould, Roger V. (1993). "Collective Action and Network Structure." *American Sociological Review* 58: 182–196.

Gould, Roger V. (2003). "Why do Networks Matter? Rationalist and Structuralist Interpretations." In *Social movements and Networks*, edited by M. Diani and D. McAdam, 233–257. Oxford: Oxford University Press.

Granovetter, Mark (1978). "Threshold Models of Collective Behavior," *American Journal of Sociology*. 83: 1420–1443.

Hagan, John and Hansford-Bowles, Suzanne (2005). "From Resistance to Activism: The Emergence and Persistence of Activism among American Vietnam War Resisters in Canada," *Social Movement Studies*. 4: 231–259.

Harris, Kevan (2012). "The Brokered Exuberance of the Middle Class: An Ethnographic Analysis of Iran's 2009 Green Movement," *Mobilization: An International Journal*. 17: 435–455.

Heckathorn, Douglas D. (1988). "Collective Sanctions and the Creation of Prisoner's Dilemma Norms." *American Journal of Sociology* 94: 535–562.

Ho, Ming-sho (2010). "Co-opting Social Ties: How The Taiwanese Petrochemical Industry Neutralized Environmental Opposition," *Mobilization: An International Journal*. 15: 447–463.

Holzner, Claudio A. (2004). "The End of Clientelism? Strong and Weak Networks in a Mexican Squatter Movement." *Mobilization: An International Journal*. 9: 223–240.

Keck, Margaret E. and Sikkink, Kathryn (1998). *Activists Beyond Borders: Advocacy Networks in International Politics*, vol. 35. Cambridge: Cambridge University Press.

Kim, Hyojoung and Bearman, Peter S. (1997). "The Structure and Dynamics of Movement Participation," *American Sociological Review*. 62: 70–93.

Kitts, James A. (2000). "Mobilizing in Black Boxes: Social Networks and Participation in Social Movement Organizations," *Mobilization*. 5: 241–257.

Klandermans, Bert (1997). *The Social Psychology of Protest*. Oxford: Blackwell Publishers.

Klandermans, Bert (2004). "The Demand and Supply of Participation: Social-psychological Correlates of Participation in Social Movements." In *The Blackwell Companion to Social Movements*, edited by D. A. Snow, S. A. Soule, and H. Kriesi, 360–379. Oxford: Wiley-Blackwell.

Klandermans, Bert and Oegema, Dirk (1987). "Potentials, Networks, Motivations, and Barriers: Steps towards Participation in Social Movements," *American Sociological Review*. 52: 519–531.

Knoke, David (1994). *Political Networks: The Structural Perspective*, vol. 4. Cambridge: Cambridge University Press.

Leenders, Reinoud (2012). "Collective Action and Mobilization in Dar'a: An Anatomy of the Onset of Syria's Popular Uprising," *Mobilization: An International Journal.* 17: 419–434.

Macy, Michael W. (1991). "Chains of Cooperation: Threshold Effects in Collective Action." *American Sociological Review.* 56: 730–747.

Malinick, Todd E., Tindall, D. B., and Diani, Mario (2013). "Network Centrality and Social Movement Media Coverage: A Two-mode Network Analytic Approach," *Social Networks.* 35: 148–158.

Marwell, Gerald and Oliver, Pamela (1993). *The Critical Mass in Collective Action.* Cambridge: Cambridge University Press.

McAdam, Doug (1986). "Recruitment to High-Risk Activism: The Case of Freedom Summer," *American Journal of Sociology.* 92: 64–90.

McAdam, Doug (1989). "The Biographical Consequences of Activism," *American Sociological Review.* 54: 744–760.

McAdam, Doug and Paulsen, Ronnelle (1993). "Specifying the Relationship between Social Ties and Activism," *American Journal of Sociology.* 99: 640–667.

Oliver, Pamela (1984). "'If You Don't Do It, Nobody Else Will': Active and Token Contributors to Local Collective Action," *American Sociological Review.* 49: 601–610.

Oliver, Pamela E. and Marwell, Gerald (2001). "Whatever Happened to Critical Mass Theory? A Retrospective and Assessment," *Sociological Theory.* 19: 292–311.

Osa, Maryjane (2001). "Mobilizing Structures and Cycles of Protest: Post-Stalinist Contention in Poland, 1954–1959," *Mobilization.* 6: 211–231.

Passy, Florence (2001). "Socialization, Connection, and the Structure/Agency Gap: A Specification of the Impact of Networks on Participation in Social Movements," *Mobilization.* 6: 173–192.

Passy, Florence and Giugni, Marco (2001). "Social Networks and Individual Perceptions: Explaining Differential Participation in Social Movements," *Sociological Forum.* 16: 123–153.

Ragin, Charles C. (2009). *Redesigning Social Inquiry: Fuzzy Sets and Beyond.* Chicago: University of Chicago Press.

Ragin, Charles C. and Sedziaka, Alesia Alexandrovna (2013). "QCA and Fuzzy Set Applications to Social Movement Research." In *The Wiley-Blackwell Encyclopedia of Social and Political Movements,* edited by David Snow, Donatella della Porta, Bert Klandermans, and Doug McAdam, 1031–1034. Oxford: Blackwell.

Rizzo, Helen, Price, Anne M., and Meyer, Katherine (2012). "Anti-Sexual Harrassment Campaign in Egypt," *Mobilization: An International Journal.* 17: 457–475.

Snijders, Tom A. B. (2011). "Statistical Models for Social Networks," *Annual Review of Sociology.* 37: 131–153.

Snijders, Tom A. B., van den Bunt, Gerhard G., and Steglich, Christian E. G. (2010). "Introduction to stochastic actor-based models for network dynamics," *Social Networks.* 32: 44–60.

Snow, David A., Zurcher, Louis A., Jr., and Ekland-Olson, Sheldon (1980). "Social Networks and Social Movements: A Microstructural Approach to Differential Recruitment," *American Sociological Review.* 45: 787–801.

Stobbe, Stephanie (2011). "The Soukhouan Ritual: The Legacy of Lao Women in Conflict Resolution," *Research in Social Movements, Conflicts and Change.* 32: 45–73.

Subramaniam, Mangala, Gupte, Manjusha, and Mitra, Debarashmi (2003). "Local to Global: Transnational Networks and Indian Women's Grassroots Organizing," *Mobilization: An International Journal.* 8: 335–352.

Tindall, David B. and Gartrell, C. David (1990). "Networks, Social Evaluation, and Collective Dilemmas," *Advances in Group Processes.* 7: 105–128.

Tindall, David B. (2002). "Social Networks, Identification and Participation in an Environmental Movement: Low-Medium Cost Activism within the British Columbia Wilderness Preservation Movement," *La Revue Canadienne de Sociologie et d'Anthropologie/ The Canadian Review of Sociology and Anthropology.* 39: 413–452.

Tindall, D. B. (2004). "Social Movement Participation over Time: An Ego-Network Approach to Micro-Mobilization," *Sociological Focus.* 37: 163–184.

Tindall, D. B. (2007). "From Metaphors to Mechanisms: Critical Issues in Networks and Social Movements Research," *Social Networks.* 29: 160–169.

Tindall, David B. and Gartrell, C. David (1990). "Networks, Social Evaluation, and Collective Dilemmas," *Advances in Group Processes.* 7: 105–128.

Tindall, D. B., Cormier, Jeffrey, and Diani, Mario (2012). "Network Social Capital as an Outcome of Social Movement Mobilization: Using the Position Generator as an Indicator of Social Network Diversity," *Social Networks.* 34: 387–395.

Vala, Carsten T. and O'Brien, Kevin J. (2007). "Attraction without Networks: Recruiting Strangers to Unregistered Protestantism in China," *Mobilization: An International Journal.* 12: 79–94.

Wiest, Dawn (2007). "A Story of Two Transnationalisms: Global Salafi Jihad and Transnational Human Rights Mobilization in the Middle East and North Africa," *Mobilization: An International Journal.* 12: 137–160.

CHAPTER 15

....

RATIONAL ACTION

....

PAMELA E. OLIVER

ATTEMPTS to assess the contributions and value of rational action approaches to studying social movements have to negotiate the thicket of matters of ideology and identity among scholars of social movements and the shifting significations they attach to the meaning of the words "rational" and "rational action." Some scholars have attached positive value to the word "rational" and have rejected claims that social movements were mindless or ill-conceived emotional responses to strain (e.g., Schwartz 1976). Others attach negative value to rationality and associate it with the disciplinary invasion of sociology by economics, unfettered capitalism, isolated individualized selfishness, a rejection of social structure, and patriarchy (e.g., Ferree 1992). Those who attach negative value to the term "rational action" typically use it to refer only to calculations by isolated selfish individuals and rational action theory as a single hegemonic project. By contrast, those who use the term positively tend to refer to the broader tradition of work that flowed from engagement with rational action ideas and rational action theory as a set of well-bounded tools for constructing explanations (Opp 1999, 2009, 2000; Lichbach 2003).

The assertion that all people pursue their individual self-interest is either empirically false or tautological, depending on how narrowly the concept of self-interest is defined. Similarly tautological and untestable are the symbolic interaction dicta that people act toward things based on the meaning things have for them, that meanings are derived from interaction, and that people engage in interpretive processes (Blumer 1969). Also tautological is Ferree's "feminist and social constructionist" alternative to rational action's core assumption: "all values, including those that appear to be 'natural' and 'objective' rest in social experience of some sort" (Ferree 1992). Ditto the core orienting premises of resource mobilization, political process, or any other general theory. Smelser (1992) argues that a theory that explains everything is a theory that explains nothing and may be considered degenerate. But tautological theoretical premises may be very useful if they lead to previously unrecognized insights into social processes, or even if they offer orderly accounting schemes for inventorying relevant factors.

This chapter ignores ideological debates about whether people are or are not rational, whether rationality is a stalking horse for patriarchy, and the political implications of assumptions of market rationality for social policies. It does not assume that everybody is rational, nor that individuals are isolated. It argues instead that the real contributions of rational action theory to understanding social movements have been made at the group level, where simplifying and even simplistic assumptions about individual motivations have permitted genuine insights into the differences between different kinds of actions and the differences between groups. These insights can be coupled with a theory of strategic agency to provide tools for understanding why collective action takes different forms in different contexts and how actors can make choices that change the strategic game they are playing. The real contributions of rational action theory cannot be reduced to slogans that fit on placards, and understanding these contributions requires a willingness to engage complexity and contingency.

OLSON AND COLLECTIVE ACTION

Any discussion of rational action theory in social movements must begin with the provocative claim by economist Mancur Olson's *The Logic of Collective Action* (1965) that "rational, self-interested individuals will *not* act to achieve their common or group interests" (2, emphasis added). Olson made social scientists realize that there was something essential to study in what happens in the gap between collective interests and collective action. His impact on social science was enormous, even though critics quickly showed that his sweeping verbal claims and nods to mathematics notwithstanding, whether it is rational or not for an individual to contribute to collective action depends very much on the properties of the situation (e.g., Frohlich et al. 1975; Frohlich and Oppenheimer 1970). Oliver (1993) provides a review of this early literature. Olson lumps together several dimensions of action situations that need to be disentangled. The central issue is *non-excludability*, which means that if a collective good is provided, there is no way to keep non-contributors from enjoying the good. Everybody experiences the same level of air pollution, regardless of how much greenhouse gas they personally exude; everybody experiences the same level of non-discrimination in housing, regardless of whether they personally participated in a civil rights march or not. Non-excludability throws a wrench in the usual microeconomic model of market pricing where people "buy" just the right amount of a good to maximize their satisfaction, subject to a resource constraint. The engine of Olson's mathematical argument is that each individual's share of a collective good—and thus her payoff—goes down with the number who share the good, while the cost of providing the good goes up with the number who share in it. Thus, he argues intuitively, people will not contribute to large-group goods because individual contributions have to be divided up among too many free-riding recipients. At first blush, this argument seems to hold a lot of water. The large group problem certainly seems to adhere to air pollution or voluntary contributions to national defense.

The problem with Olson's analysis is that most non-excludable goods also have high levels of *jointness of supply*, which means that the cost of provision is the same regardless of the number who enjoy the good. It costs a certain amount to build a bridge, for example, whether it will be used once or thousands of times. This is especially important because collective goods provided through political systems have high jointness of supply: the cost of lobbying or political pressure does not usually go up with the number of people who benefit from the law. Extensive levels of environmental cleanup were produced by activists lobbying for new laws to force businesses to reduce pollution (Mitchell 1979). Wealthy individuals or businesses often find it in their interest to lobby for a bill that benefits them and are typically indifferent as to whether the bill also benefits (or hurts) others.

What Olson referred to as one problem—the free rider problem—is really two quite different problems. One is the *noticeability* or *efficacy* problem: Can the individual actually do (or afford to do) anything that would make a noticeable difference in the collective good? This is the core of Olson's "large group" problem. No single individual can stop global warming through their own personal lifestyle choices. No single individual can create racial justice or world peace. The other problem is the real free rider dilemma: if there are more people willing to pay for a non-excludable jointly supplied good than are necessary for its provision, there may arise a "small group" strategic gaming problem where each hopes that someone else will pay the cost. This happens every day when roommates dodge housework and hope that someone else will wash the dishes. Similarly, the free rider dilemma is a real issue in social movement groups when it comes to dividing labor for unpleasant tasks like cleaning up after a meeting. But because of jointness of supply, there may be free riding with no dilemma. Wealthy patrons often pay for collective benefits like concert halls and are quite happy to let other people listen to the music. Some social movements have been underwritten by wealthy patrons who cared about the issue and were quite happy to let other people benefit, too. Free riding stymies collective action if people fail to act because they hope someone else will do the job. But free riding and efficacy are not the same problem and they have different solutions.

Olson is right that collective goods are rarely provided through the unorganized independent actions of isolated people whose individual contributions are too small to make a difference. But flipping his argument around (and consistent with his discussion of what he calls small groups), the implication is that collective goods can readily be provided when actors are coordinated or when the strategy for providing the good involves working through the political system. That is, a serious engagement with the logical consequences of Olson's arguments leads directly to recognizing the importance of organization and strategy.

IMPACT OF OLSON ON THE STUDY OF SOCIAL MOVEMENTS

By the early 1970s, it was already recognized that "Olson's problem" was not a single problem and that the dilemmas that existed under the assumption of independent isolated decision makers could be readily solved if people could talk to each other and coordinate their actions. Early social movement writers in the rational action tradition ignored these formal results and largely took Olson's claims at face value, using them as theoretical grounds for stressing the importance of groups and organization. That is, the most direct and substantial impact of rational action arguments on actual social movement theory was not an emphasis on models of isolated individuals but, to the contrary, an emphasis on the problem of mobilization and its dependence on organizations, social networks, and social structure.

One of the first works on social movements to deeply engage the implications of Olson's arguments was Oberschall's *Social Conflict and Social Movements* (1973). Oberschall built his theory by putting the character of a latent group's social organization at the center of the theory and developed hypotheses for how mobilization varies depending on the social organizational structure. Writing a few years later, Oberschall (1978) used the label "solidarity theory" for writers like Tilly who "stress that conditions that lead to violent protest are essentially the same as those that produce other forms of collective action; view all forms of collective action, including violent ones, as essentially purposeful, rational pursuits or defenses of collective interests…. "because, for him, rational action encompasses issues of networks and collective solidarity.

McCarthy and Zald's first resource mobilization paper (McCarthy and Zald 1973) stressed the importance of resources for movements but also of structure, saying, "This view does not necessarily deny the existence of grievances. It stresses the structural conditions that facilitate the expression of grievances" (1). This paper mentioned Olson only in a footnote (fn. 14 at 22) that argued that resources made it relatively easy to provide incentives for action. However, by the time they published their programmatic statement in the *American Journal of Sociology* (McCarthy and Zald 1977), McCarthy and Zald had moved Olson to the foreground, saying: "The resource mobilization perspective adopts as one of its underlying problems Olson's (1965) challenge: since social movements deliver collective goods, few individuals will 'on their own' bear the costs of working to obtain them. Explaining collective behavior requires detailed attention to the selection of incentives, cost-reducing mechanisms or structures, and career benefits that lead to collective behavior (see, especially, Oberschall 1973)." Tilly's theoretical statement *From Mobilization to Revolution* (Tilly 1978) similarly give central place to the problem of networks and social organization of challenging groups with his concepts of "catness" and "netness."

Thus, social movement theory emerged from its encounter with Olson as a theory of mobilization, as a theory of the social stuff that happens in the middle between grievances or interests or goals on the one hand and action in pursuit of those ends on the other. Virtually all of the impact of rational action theory in the actual study of social movements was to focus attention on the matter of networks and organization and social structure. The idea that social structure matters is argued by the most ardent partisans of rational action theory. For example, Hechter (1992) argues that game theory alone is insufficient without direct consideration of the actual social arrangements and mechanisms that structure the information available to participants while Hechter and Okamoto (2001) build their discussion of minority group formation around a rational action consideration of free riding, but also stress the importance of identity formation and institutional structures.

INCENTIVES

Olson argued for the importance of what he called selective incentives (also known as side payments), that is, benefits offered to individuals that are contingent on participation, or costs that are imposed on non-participants. "Only a separate and selective incentive will stimulate a rational individual in a latent group to act in a group-oriented way.... The incentive must be 'selective' so that those who do not... contribute to the attainment of the group's interest, can be treated differently from those who do" (Olson 1965: 51). Although Olson thought only about the impact of incentives on individuals, the incentive idea rapidly led to consideration of issues of social organization.

Drawing on ideas about incentives in organizations originally written before Olson's book was published (Clark and Wilson 1961), James Q. Wilson (Wilson 1974) directly engaged and repacked Olson's incentive arguments by attacking the idea that incentives could only be material. In addition to material incentives, there are two other broad types that were well-recognized to affect organizational participation: solidary (tied to other people) and purposive (tied to internal motivations of morality or ethics). Solidary incentives include things like simple sociability from being with others, other people's approval for one's actions, and respect or honor for leadership roles. When solidary incentives are important, it matters who one is with and how other people feel about the collective action. Some solidary incentives have jointness of supply where everyone can share in them without diminishing the value to anyone else, such as when people simply enjoy being with other people in the action, or when friends and family approve of the participation. Other solidary incentives are more like private goods, like the value of being recognized as a leader.

A purposive or moral incentive is the benefit of participating (or not) that arises from within a person such as when a person's sense of personal morality or ethnics depends on doing what is right. Purposive incentives are typically linked to religious, ethical, or political philosophies and identities. Carden (1978) points to purposive incentives as one of the central features of social movements and voluntary action more broadly: because people are motivated to do what seems important to them, movements often focus on actions that fit the participants' sense of rightness, whether or not they promote the collective good in some instrumental way. The idea of a purposive or moral incentive is akin to the idea of identity as a motivator, that a person participates because they are that kind of person.

The concepts of solidary and purposive selective incentives provide a way of talking within a rational action framework about the importance of social influence, ideology, identity, and solidarity. Treating these as types of incentives permits them to be treated alongside collective goals and material incentives as factors that, in combination, affect how people act. It permits a consideration of how different factors might reinforce each other sometimes but be balanced against each other or run at cross purposes in others.

Of course, other theories also address these issues, and rational action theory itself has little to offer as an explanation for why people want to be with a particular group or have a particular ideology or identity that motivates them, although some of the theories of social influence (discussed later) do offer some explanations. The point is not that the idea of incentives makes other theoretical approaches unnecessary or irrelevant, but rather that rational action theory has places where the insights from other types of theory can be plugged in and merged. For example, Melucci's (1985, 1988, 1995) arguments about the importance of symbolism and identity in movements are not rational action theories by any means, but Melucci's insights can be linked with rational action ideas to treat symbolic expression as a desirable outcome or goals, or the very process of constructing the collective actor as relevant to whether a solidary or purposive incentive exists for action.

ACTION IN CROWDS

In the wake of the Black urban riots, the social scientists collaborating on the report of the National Advisory Commission on Civil Disorders (Kerner et al. 1968) and at least half a dozen other studies by sociologists and political scientists published between 1968 and 1970 (cited by Marx 1970) argued that the riots should fundamentally be understood as protests against racial discrimination, police brutality, and adverse social conditions. Such studies cited evidence about differentiation of behaviors within an event, choices of targets, and observable processes within crowd events, and verbal claims of the rioters. Authors argued that crowd participants were no less rational than the social scientists studying them and that people's actions could be understood as rule-governed or ends-oriented behavior under conditions of interdependence (e.g., Berk 1974). This line of argument had become so strong by 1970 that Gary Marx was moved to write "Issueless Riots" (Marx 1970), arguing that not all riots were instrumental, and offering hypotheses about the differences between instrumental and non-instrumental riots.

Much of the theorizing that derives from this tradition gives little attention to motives for participation, but instead draws on research that found little evidence of heightened emotionality or new beliefs in self-reports of decisions to riot, but only information about when and where the riot was occurring (e.g., Singer 1968; Singer et al. 1970) and focuses on the problem of mobilization, in line with the resource mobilization emphasis on social movements. For example, McPhail and his colleagues stressed the importance of the mobilization process itself as central in crowd action (McPhail 1969, 1971, 1991; McPhail and Miller 1973; McPhail and Wohlstein 1983). In his comprehensive review and critique of theorizing about crowds, McPhail (1991) gives many examples of cases demonstrating clear evidence of planning, organization, and goal-oriented behavior in episodes of crowd violence in lynchings and riots, and argues for the importance of recognizing what he later calls "the dark side of purpose" (McPhail 1994).

Formal models of crowd behavior from the 1970s focus on how people's decisions are affected by others' actions. Building on arguments by Schelling (1973) and Berk (1974), Granovetter (1978) makes no assumption about motivations except that people's willingness to join a collective behavior depends on how many others are already acting and that each person has a threshold X such that they will not join if the number of others is below X and will join if the number of others is X or above. He shows that whether collective action cascades or stalls depends on the heterogeneity of the group and the presence or absence of gaps in the distribution of thresholds. Oliver (1993) shows that the engine in Granovetter's models is actually the proportion of a group's members who are self-starters (i.e., have thresholds of zero). Granovetter and Soong (1983) provide further elaborations. Macy (1991) reworks Granovetter's models in stochastic learning terms, finding similar results. The image in these models is that collective action happens not from coordination and planning, but spontaneously through local interactional influence. This is not entirely different from some of the older collective behavior models of contagion, except that this attention to others' behavior is treated as unproblematic and not in need of a psychological explanation.

The Usefulness and Ultimate Inadequacy of One- and Two-Person Models

Empirical research grounded in collective action accounting models has demonstrated that participants tend to have collective rationality in the sense that they value the goals of the movement and to believe that the collective action will promote those goals (Muller and Opp 1986; Opp 1990, 1988; Finkel and Muller 1998). However, free riding as a psychological dynamic does not seem to arise. Individual personal gain is less predictive of action than collective gain (Muller and Opp 1986). Costs or constraints matter (Klandermans and Oegema 1987) and incurring the costs of repression can hinder action (Opp 1994; Opp and Roehl 1990). Consistent with ideas of social or purposive incentives, participants are more likely than non-participants to identify with movement groups or to have network ties to participants or to say people approve of their participation (Klandermans and Oegema 1987; Finkel et al. 1989; Klandermans 2002; Klandermans et al. 2008).

Work grounded in the rational action tradition has also provided clear evidence for the social construction of costs and benefits, as well as group identities. Movement participants actively resist attempts to get them to divorce the impact of their individual actions from that of the group as a whole and are motivated by the perceived efficacy of the collective action, not the marginal difference their own showing up might make (Muller and Opp 1986; Klosko et al. 1987; Klandermans 1988); studies also find that participants perceive higher costs of acting than non-participants do (Muller and Opp 1986; Opp 1990). People's beliefs about the costs and benefits of collective action change after their participation (Finkel and Muller 1998) and the experience of being repressed leads to a greater since of grievance (Opp and Roehl 1990; Opp 1994, 2004).

Overall, empirical research inspired by the rational action tradition has shown the importance of the group identities and collective orientations as well as of instrumental considerations of the consequences of actions. However, formal rational action models grounded in predicting the behavior of one person at a time have not helped to generate new theoretical insights.

Although some early works in social movements included individual-level equations for rational choices, these equations did no analytic work except as simple accounting schemes or heuristics to support a verbal argument. An individual-level rational action model would take a form like $V(a) = \Delta B|a - C$, $C<R$ or maybe $V(a) = (\Delta p|a)B - C$, $C<R$, where $V(a)$ is the value of doing action a, $\Delta B|a$ is the change in the benefit or value given that action a is done, C is the cost of doing action a, and R is the resource constraint on C. In the second specification, B is a benefit and it is multiplied by $\Delta p|a$, the change in probability of getting B if action a is done. If B and C are in the same metric, a number $V(a)$ can be calculated and a prediction can be made that the likelihood of doing a will be a function of $V(a)$.

The trouble is that B and C never are in the same metric and in addition there are often multiple benefits and multiple costs that all have different metrics. If things don't have common metrics, they cannot be added. Benefits like civil rights and costs like marching or getting beaten just don't have the same metrics. Moreover, the conditional difference $\Delta B|a$ or $(\Delta p|a)B$ itself is generally not a static number but rather a complex function of the inputs from other people in the situation. In short, it is not actually possible to write an equation for individuals' decisions that would yield any kind of determinate or meaningful number that would predict their behavior. Instead, individual-level equations are used only heuristically to guide a verbal discussion of the kinds of factors that are expected to influence behavior, and as a guide to the kinds of things that should be considered. What do people think the benefits are? Do they think the action is an efficacious way to achieve the benefit? Does the person have the resources to incur the cost that is big enough to produce the desired benefit? Does the expected change in benefit outweigh the cost?

Similarly, 2×2 game theory payoff matrices treat "the individual" and "the group" as a unitary actor whose decision considerations can be summarized into one net payoff. The free rider problem has been equated to the prisoner's dilemma, in which an individual always gains more by defecting regardless of the other's action, but both actors will receive more if both cooperate than if both defect, and there have been many discussions of the factors that affect social movements that are organized around the solutions to this dilemma (see Lichbach 1995). As Lichbach's exhaustive discussion shows, the 2×2 matrices provide a vocabulary for talking about strategic dynamics and the wide variety of solutions to the game that are possible, but no formal tools for deciding which strategic situation a group actually is in. Further, collapsing "the group" and treating it as "the other" means that the 2×2 game is really a unitary actor model. As such, it provides no tools for attending to issues of group size or group social organization or network structure. In addition, many collective action situations are not prisoner's dilemmas but assurance games (individuals will gain more by cooperating as long as they are sure everyone else is cooperating too) or coordination games (individuals gain as long as their behavior matches others' behavior).

Even seemingly more-complex models resolve to unitary actors and provide only heuristic guidance. For example, Ahlquist and Levi (2013) develop a rational action model within the theory of clubs in which there is enough profit to be made from group action to pay a leader extra to provide the coordination, and use this model as a foil for discussing the differences between corrupt unions whose leaders extract material payments and political unions whose leaders extract participation in radical political activities, starting from the premise that there is a finite "rent" to be paid to leaders one way or another. But the formal model is not tied to the rich historical detail of their case studies, nor does their later discussion of the endogeneity of radical ideology and the importance of governance structures make its way back into any refined formal theoretical model.

CRITICAL MASS THEORY AND SOCIAL SOLUTIONS TO SOCIAL DILEMMAS

The metaphor of the critical mass has been used at least since the 1960s by social movement activists to refer to the number of people who could get some kind of protest movement going. The first newsletter of the Collective Behavior and Social Movements section of the American Sociological Association was called the *Critical Mass Bulletin*. Sullivan (1977) discusses how the critical mass in riots involves not only sheer numbers but the social relations among people. In a series of articles collected into their book, Marwell and Oliver (1993) picked up on the metaphor to use the phrase "critical mass" as a label for theories of the ways in which a few individuals can create the conditions for providing collective goods to a whole group. This built on discussions of what is often called the second order collective action problem (Oliver 1980), that is, why should someone pay to provide selective incentives to get others to contribute to a collective good? Because positive incentives are paid to cooperators but negative incentives to non-cooperators, they have different cost structures and are, thus, associated with different kinds of collective actions. Rewards are efficient for motivating a few to act to benefit the many, while the threat of punishment is efficient for maintaining unanimous action. Thinking about incentive structures made it obvious that the formal problem of incentivizing collective action in a group could not be correctly analyzed with individual-level models but required specific attention to the nature of the collective action and the nature of the group.

While its model of individual choice is oversimplified, the rational action frame-work has led to a careful recognition and specification of the great diversity of col-lective action problems. As highlighted by Elinor Ostrom (1998), the key insight of Oliver and Marwell's line of work called critical mass theory is their rejection of monocausal arguments when they say: "This is not to say that general theoretical pre-dictions are impossible using our perspective, only that they cannot be simple and global. Instead, the predictions that we can validly generate must be complex, interac-tive, and conditional" (Marwell and Oliver 1993: 25). To repeat, the most important lesson of critical mass theory specifically and rational action theory more broadly is that there is no one-size-fits-all simple theory of collective action. Useful theory is not placard-sized slogans about individualism, but rather entails complex, inter-active, and conditional arguments about the differences among groups, actions, and situations.

For example, instead of a slogan-sized debate about whether group size has a posi-tive or negative effect on collective action, Oliver and Marwell (1988, also Marwell and Oliver 1993: ch. 3) argue that the nature of the group size effect interacts with the level of heterogeneity and the level of jointness of supply. Paradoxically, when groups are heterogeneous, the size of the critical mass of people who have both the interest and resources to be willing to act together to provide a jointly supplied collective good may actually be smaller in a larger group. Intuitively, this can happen because a more het-erogeneous group has greater inequality and thus is more likely to have a few wealthy benefactors. This is a complex and contingent finding about interactions effects among the type of good (degree of jointness of supply), group size, group heterogeneity, and the correlation between interests and resources and not (contra too many sloganized citations to their work) a simplistic bivariate assertion that either group size or het-erogeneity promote collective action. Or, again, in place of Olson's under-theorized and undifferentiated "free rider problem," Oliver and her colleagues (Oliver et al. 1985) stress the importance of the exact form of the production function that relates inputs of units of collective action to outputs of units of collective good. When production functions are non-linear, people's choices are interdependent, in that each person's best choice depends upon what others are doing. They contrast the convex or diminishing returns case with the concave or increasing returns case, showing that the critical mass plays a different role in each: in the convex case, the most interested and resourceful actors provide the good while others free ride, while in the concave case the interested and resourceful actors solve the start-up problem and bring others into the collective action. Oliver and Marwell devoted most of the rest of their work on the critical mass to organizer-centered models in the concave case that assumed that a small group of self-starters were absorbing the second-order costs of recruiting or coordinating oth-ers for collective action (Prahl et al. 1991; Marwell et al. 1988; Marwell and Oliver 1993). These models attend to group heterogeneity, social network properties, and the costs of information and communication, and find complex interactions among these fac-tors leading to thresholds that partition the response space into areas with different dynamics.

This investigation of complexity and contingency is the main thrust of most formal sociological work on collective action. Heckathorn (1996) dug into the second order problem, showing that production functions for collective goods and production functions for incentive systems could interact in complex ways to generate many different dynamic patterns. Incentives can promote cooperation that benefits everyone, but they can also lead people to do things that are against their self-interest or to motivate or police a revolt against a collective effort. Heckathorn argued that parameters for production functions and incentives jointly define a space divided by thresholds into five regions with different strategic dilemmas that are equivalent to the five games in a standard two-person game matrix and that these five regions of the strategy space correspond to five distinct political ideologies for reconciling potential conflicts between individual and collective interests Heckathorn (1998). Kitts (2006, 2008) builds on Heckathorn's work to show how incentives can affect the development of norms that either promote or hinder collective action, again depending on complex and interactive conditions.

One line of work in the rational action tradition actually replaces the individual-level assumption of a forward-looking rational actor with a backward-looking adaptive learner who responds to the current level of reward or punishment in the environment (e.g., Macy 1990). Such models produce both the thresholds characteristics of critical mass situations and the division of labor consistent with free rider arguments.

In short, this line of work has demonstrated that there is not one dynamic of collective action, but many dynamics. Providing the collective good is unproblematic in some situations and impossible in others. In some contexts, incentive systems help promote collective action, while in other parts of the space, incentive systems can actually lead people to enforce outcomes that no one wants. For people interested in the concrete problems of social movements, the lesson of these theoretical exercises is that problems of collective action are not typically simple, and incentives can be perverse. But the situation is not theoretically anarchic: there are conceptual tools for distinguishing among different situations.

ACTION IN NETWORKS

A substantial body of work in the rational action tradition makes no assumption at all that people are selfish or individually rational, but instead examines the effects of influence or sideways processes wherein people's choices are affected by the behavior of the people around them, either through norms of fairness and balance or through influence. Social networks affect these influence processes. Consistent with critical mass ideas, most of these models exhibit threshold effects and complex interactions among different factors. The Gould (1993) model assumes fairness norms and finds that the location of an initial group of unconditional cooperators in the network interacts with network density and group size. In a similar vein, Kim and Bearman (1997) assume that people value both the collective good and equality of contributions, finding that collective action occurs where network power and interests are positively correlated.

A growing body of research investigates network effects, generally finding that influence and new or initially unpopular ideas spread most effectively when societies have segmented networks in which people are more likely to have social ties to people like themselves (Centola et al. 2005; Centola and Macy 2007; Siegel 2009; Janssen 2011; Centola 2013). What these formal results show, in essence, is that initially unpopular ideas can be nurtured in relatively homogeneous networks where people are protected from the influences of the larger society, and these networks can expand by influencing people at their edges. This is an important set of findings for understanding how social movement ideologies can spread.

This insight is an important one to take into empirical studies of social movements. And, again, all these models reveal that even this general theme is an interaction effect, and that the dynamics of influence vary greatly depending on both the initial distribution of opinions and the structure of networks.

Strategic Dynamics

Most theoretical and empirical attention in the study of social movements is given to mobilization processes broadly construed. But social movements are inherently relational: there is always some other collective actor in the system, either a target or an opponent, and there may also be allies or audiences. Rationalist theories of strategic action abound in the study of international relations and warfare. Despite this, relatively little formal theoretical attention in the study of social movements is given to the relationships between movements and their targets or opponents. Although formal game theory provides models of strategic interaction, most use of game theory in studies of social movements has focussed on equating the collective action dilemma to the two-person prisoner's dilemma game between an individual and "the group" in a 2×2 payoff matrix (e.g., Lichbach 1995, 1996), not to the relation between movements and their opponents or targets.

There are some two- and multi-actor models. Chong (1991) developed a supply and demand model for the interactions between movements and regimes where movements produce mobilization and regimes produce policies. Hoover and Kowalewski (1992) use simulation software to develop their own model in which dissidents and regimes have grievances and resources and third party support that respond positively, negatively, or not to the intensity and scope of the others' actions. There is a longstanding concern in both sociology and political science with the relation between protest and repression, with the core question being the balance between the "repression works" effect in which repression reduces further protest, and the backlash effect, in which repression increases protest by way of increasing grievance. Francisco (1995) tests two predator–prey models from mathematical biology to assess the relation between protest and repression in three cases (German Democratic Republic, Czechoslovakia, and the Palestinian Intifada) and concludes that protesters adapt to coercion by changing tactics. Pierskalla (2010) develops an extensive strategic game between the government and an opposition group with incomplete information and third-party threat, arguing that it permits identification of equilibria that result either in successful repression or escalating violence. Francisco (2010) brings a great deal of empirical evidence to bear on models of the strategic dynamics between dissenters and regimes, arguing that most forms of symbolic protest converge on equilibria as protesters and regimes adapt to each other, while interactions between terrorists and regimes depend upon network structures between terrorists and a larger population and the regime's ability to target terrorists without harming the surrounding population.

The idea that the relation between movements and regimes should be understood in co-evolutionary terms as a process of mutual adaptation is gaining adherents. Koopmans (2005) argues for reconceiving political opportunity in co-evolutionary terms, as movements and regimes interact with and respond to each other, shaping their actions over time. Oliver and Myers (2003) employ a co-evolutionary framework and focus on carefully examining patterns in observed data about protests over time and their relation to proposed relational mechanisms, including diffusion and external or mutual reinforcement by other groups. They argue that most theories cannot account for either the spikiness of real protest data or its cycles, in which protest declines as well as rises. They show that random external reinforcement can produce the spiky patterns characteristic of real protest data and that models that presume there are several movements competing for attention/response from a common audience or regime are most capable of exhibiting the large cycles of ups and downs that characterize protest data.

Conclusions: On the Relevance of Rational Action Theory for Understanding Social Movements

Simple-minded rational action models are useless for understanding social movements, but so are simple-minded theories of any stripe. Theorists in the rational action tradition have used formal tools to show how complex collective action situations can be. Theorists and empirical researchers in the rational action tradition have themselves probed and critiqued the limits of early claims and assumptions. They have shown empirically that collective rather than individual orientations predominate in social movements. Formal theorists have shown that there are complex interactions that create qualitatively different strategic dynamics depending on the combinations of different factors. Any simplistic bivariate statement that any single factor helps or hurts collective action or the likelihood of movement success is simply wrong. The only correct statements are complex, interactive, and conditional. Group structure—organizations and networks—always matter, and qualitative differences in group structure make huge differences in the dynamics of collective action.

If one is trying to make simplistic predictions, all this complexity is a nightmare. But the complexity also shows the importance of human agency. Jasper (2004) argues that analysis of strategy clearly points to the role of leadership and agency in negotiating strategic dilemmas, as well as to the importance of the cultural and institutional contexts that shape strategic choices. Rational action theory does not deny agency but rather provides tools for understanding the dynamics of different strategic situations.

Consider the classic large group problem, clean air or clean water. It is impossible that the air or water supply will become cleaner through the independent actions of isolated individuals, and genuinely difficult and probably impossible to persuade enough individuals to change their habits to clean the air or water. But it is not at all impossible for concerned activists to get cleaner air and cleaner water through mobilizing an environmental movement and lobbying legislatures to pass laws that create water treatment plants, impose clean-up standards on polluting industries backed up by fines for noncompliance, mandate efficiency standards for vehicles and electrical appliances, and impose taxes and offer tax credits to shape desired consumer actions (Mitchell 1979). And, as Elinor Ostrom and her colleagues have amply demonstrated (Ostrom 1998, 1999), it is not at all impossible for traditional communities to organize themselves to preserve environmental resources across generations. There are explicable modes of social organization that make this possible. Rational actors transcend the dilemmas of individualized action by creating structures for collective action. They can use the results of formal theory to think about their strategic choices within their structural constraints. They can choose actions that require the resources and personnel they have. They can also use agency to change some of their structural constraints, for example by working to increase network ties among group members.

Many of the terms in rational action models are potentially endogenous or changeable. People can choose actions with different production functions, but they can also be persuaded to change their subjective interests or their perceptions of the likelihood of success of an action. New network ties can be created. These influence processes themselves can be and have been studied with the tools of formal analysis in the rational action tradition. Motivations that are not part of the standard rational action cost–benefit framework such as symbolic or expressive protest, or emotional dynamics, may well show influence patterns that are similar to those that have been found in models of the spread of ideas.

If theorizing is seen as a war between competing armies, it is important to wear uniforms and be sure friends and enemies can be distinguished. If theorizing is seen as an ecological competition for turf, then it is important to kill off pioneer members of species invading new terrain before they take over and choke off local species. If theorizing is a war of position in a profession, it is important to prevent other theorists from gaining any advantage and it is important to make distinctions. But if theorizing is seen as a cooperative enterprise that is trying to understand how the world works, it may not matter where the boundary of one theory ends and another begins. The rigorous tools developed in the rational action tradition have illuminated important processes in social movements that go far beyond the isolated economistic market-driven automaton that is the bugbear of some theorists in other traditions.

References

Ahlquist, J. S. and Levi, M. (2013). *In the Interest of Others Organizations and Social Activism.* Princeton: Princeton University Press.

Berk, R. A. (1974). "A Gaming Approach to Crowd Behavior," *American Sociological Review.* 39: 355–373.

Blumer, Herbert. (1969). Symbolic Interactionism. Perspective and Method. Englewood Cliffs, NJ: Prentice-Hall.

Carden, M. L. (1978). "The Proliferation of a Social Movement: Ideology and Individual Incentives in the Feminist Movement," *Research in Social Movements, Conflicts and Change.* 1: 179–196.

Centola, D. M. (2013). "Homophily, Networks, and Critical Mass: Solving the Start-up Problem in Large Group Collective Action," *Rationality and Society.* 25: 3–40.

Centola, D. and Macy, M. (2007). "Complex Contagions and the Weakness of Long Ties," *American Journal of Sociology.* 113: 702–734.

Centola, D., Willer, R., and Macy, M. (2005). "The Emperor's Dilemma: A Computational Model of Self-Enforcing Norms." *American Journal of Sociology.* 110: 1009–1040.

Chong, D. (1991). *Collective Action and the Civil Rights Movement.* Chicago: University of Chicago Press.

Clark, P. B. and Wilson, J. Q. (1961). "Incentive Systems: A Theory of Organizations," *Administrative Science Quarterly.* 6: 129–166.

Ferree, M. M. (1992). "The Political Context of Rationality: Rational Choice Theory and Resource Mobilization." In *Frontiers in Social Movement Theory*, edited by A. D. Morris and C. M. Mueller, 221–240. New Haven, CN: Yale University Press.

Finkel, S. E. and Muller, E. N. (1998). "Rational Choice and the Dynamics of Collective Political Action: Evaluating Alternative Models with Panel Data," *American Political Science Review.* 92: 37–49.

Finkel, S. E., Muller, E. N., and Opp, K.-D. (1989). "Personal Influence, Collective Rationality, and Mass Political Action," *The American Political Science Review.* 83: 885–903.

Francisco, R. A. (1995). "The Relationship between Coercion and Protest," *Journal of Conflict Resolution.* 39: 263–283.

Francisco, R. A. (2010). *Collective Action Theory and Empirical Evidence.* Dordrecht: Springer.

Frohlich, N. and Oppenheimer, J. A. (1970). "I Get by with a Little Help from My Friends," *World Politics.* 23: 104–120.

Frohlich, N., Hunt, T., Oppenheimer, J., and Wagner, R. H. (1975). "Individual Contributions for Collective Goods: Alternative Models," *The Journal of Conflict Resolution.* 19: 310–329.

Gould, R. V. (1993). "Collective Action and Network Structure," *American Sociological Review.* 58: 182–196.

Granovetter, M. (1978). "Threshold Models of Collective Behavior," *American Journal of Sociology.* 83: 1420–1443.

Granovetter, M. and Soong, R. (1983). "Threshold Models of Diffusion and Collective Behaviour," *Journal of Mathematical Sociology*. 9: 165.

Hechter, M. (1992). "The Insufficiency of Game Theory for the Resolution of Real-World Collective Action Problems," *Rationality & Society*. 4: 33–40.

Hechter, M. and Okamoto, D. (2001). "Political Consequences of Minority Group Formation," *Annual Review of Political Science*. 4: 189–215.

Heckathorn, D. D. (1996). "The Dynamics and Dilemmas of Collective Action," *American Sociological Review*. 61: 250–277.

Heckathorn, D. D. (1998). "Collective Action, Social Dilemmas and Ideology," *Rationality and Society*. 10: 451–480.

Hoover, D. and Kowalewski, D. (1992). "Dynamic Models of Dissent and Repression," *Journal of Conflict Resolution*. 36: 150–182.

Janssen, M.. (2011). "Targeting individuals to catalyze collective action in social networks." Presented at the Computational Social Science Society of the Americas. http://computation-alsocialscience.org/conferences/17-2/csssa-2011-papers/

Jasper, J. M. (2004). "A Strategic Approach to Collective Action: Looking for Agency in Social-Movement Choices," *Mobilization*. 9: 1–16.

Kerner, O., Lindsay, J. V., and Harris, F. (1968). *Report of the National Advisory Commission on Civil Disorders*. Washington DC: US Government Printing Office.

Kim, H. and Bearman, P. S. (1997). "The Structure and Dynamics of Movement Participation," *American Sociological Review*. 62: 70–93.

Kitts, J. A. (2006). "Collective Action, Rival Incentives, and the Emergence of Antisocial Norms," *American Sociological Review*. 71: 235–259.

Kitts, J. A. (2008). "Dynamics and Stability of Collective Action Norms," *Journal of Mathematical Sociology*. 32: 142–163.

Klandermans, B. (1988). "Union Action and the Free-Rider Dilemma," *Research in Social Movements, Conflicts and Change*. 10: 77–91.

Klandermans, B. (2002). "How Group Identification Helps to Overcome the Dilemma of Collective Action," *American Behavioral Scientist*. 45: 887.

Klandermans, B. and Oegema, D. (1987). "Potentials, Networks, Motivations and Barriers: Steps Towards Participation in Social Movements," *American Sociological Review*. 52: 519–531.

Klandermans, B., Van Der Toorn, J., and Van Stekelenburg, J. (2008). "Embeddedness and Identity: How Immigrants Turn Grievances into Action," *American Sociological Review*. 73: 992–1012.

Klosko, G., Muller, E. N., and Opp, K. D. (1987). "Rebellious Collective Action Revisited," *The American Political Science Review*. 81: 557–564.

Koopmans, R. (2005). "The Missing Link between Structure and Agency: Outline of an Evolutionary Approach to Social Movements," *Mobilization: An International Journal*. 10: 19–35.

Lichbach, M. I. (1995). *The Rebel's Dilemma*. Ann Arbor, University of Michigan Press.

Lichbach, M. I. (1996). *The Cooperator's Dilemma*. Ann Arbor, University of Michigan Press.

Lichbach, M. I. (2003). *Is Rational Choice Theory All of Social Science?* Ann Arbor, University of Michigan Press.

Macy, M. W. (1990). "Learning Theory and the Logic of Critical Mass," *American Sociological Review*. 55: 809–826.

Macy, M. W. (1991). "Chains of Cooperation: Threshold Effects in Collective Action," *American Sociological Review*. 56: 730–747.

Marwell, G. and Oliver, P. (1993). *The Critical Mass in Collective Action: A Micro-social Theory*. Cambridge, New York: Cambridge University Press.

Marwell, G., Oliver, P. E., and Prahl, R. (1988). "Social Networks and Collective Action: A Theory of the Critical Mass. III," *American Journal of Sociology*. 94: 502–534.

Marx, G. T. (1970). "Issueless Riots," *The Annals of the American Academy of Political and Social Science*. 391: 21–33.

McCarthy, J. D. and Zald, M. N. (1973). *The Trend of Social Movements in America: Professionalization and Resource Mobilization*. Morristown, NJ, General Learning Press.

McCarthy, J. D. and Zald, M. N. (1977). "Resource Mobilization and Social Movements: A Partial Theory," *American Journal of Sociology*. 82: 1212–1241.

McPhail, C. (1969). "Student Walkout: A Fortuitous Examination of Elementary Collective Behavior," *Social Problems*. 16: 441–455.

McPhail, C. (1971). "Civil Disorder Participation: A Critical Examination of Recent Research," *American Sociological Review*. 36: 1058–1073.

McPhail, C. (1991). *The Myth of the Madding Crowd*, New York, Walter DeGruyter.

McPhail, C. (1994). "The Dark Side of Purpose: Individual and Collective Violence in Riots," *Sociological Quarterly*. 35: 1–32.

McPhail, C. and Miller, D. (1973). "The Assembling Process: A Theoretical and Empirical Examination," *American Sociological Review*. 38: 721–735.

McPhail, C. and Wohlstein, R. T. (1983). "Individual and Collective Behaviors Within Gatherings, Demonstrations, and Riots," *Annual Review of Sociology*. 9: 579.

Melucci, A. (1985). "The Symbolic Challenge of Contemporary Movements," *Social Research*. 52: 789–816.

Melucci, A. (1988). "Getting Involved: Identity and Mobilization in Social Movements," *International Social Movement Research*. 1: 329–348.

Melucci, A. (1995). "The Process of Collective Identity." In *Social Movements and Culture*, edited by H. Johnston and B. Klandermans, 41–63. Minneapolis, MN: U of Minnesota Press.

Mitchell, R. C. (1979). "National Environmental Lobbies and the Apparent Illogic of Collective Action." In *Collective Decision Making: Applications From Public Choice Theory*, edited by C. S. Russell. Baltimore: Johns Hopkins University Press.

Muller, E. N. and Opp, K.-D. (1986). "Rational Choice and Rebellious Collective Action," *The American Political Science Review*. 80: 471–488.

Oberschall, A. (1973). *Social Conflict and Social Movements*. Englewood Cliffs., NJ: Prentice-Hall.

Oberschall, A. (1978). "Theories of Social Conflict," *Annual Review of Sociology*. 4: 291–315.

Oliver, P. (1980). "Rewards and Punishments as Selective Incentives for Collective Action: Theoretical Investigations," *American Journal of Sociology*. 85: 1356–1375.

Oliver, P. E. (1993). "Formal Models of Collective Action," *Annual Review of Sociology*. 19: 271–300.

Oliver, P. E. and Marwell, G. (1988). "The Paradox of Group Size in Collective Action: A Theory of the Critical Mass. II," *American Sociological Review*. 53: 1–8.

Oliver, P. E. and Myers, D. J. (2003). "The Coevolution of Social Movements," *Mobilization*. 8: 1–24.

Oliver, P., Marwell, G., and Teixeira, R. (1985). "A Theory of the Critical Mass. I. Interdependence, Group Heterogeneity, and the Production of Collective Action," *American Journal of Sociology*. 91: 522–556.

Olson, M. (1965). *The Logic of Collective Action; Public Goods and the Theory of Groups.* Cambridge, MA: Harvard University Press.

Opp, K.-D. (1988). "Grievances and Participation in Social Movements," *American Sociological Review.* 53: 853–864.

Opp, K.-D. (1990). "Postmaterialism, Collective Action, and Political Protest," *American Journal of Political Science.* 34: 212.

Opp, K.-D. (1994). "Repression and Revolutionary Action: East Germany in 1989," *Rationality & Society.* 6: 101–138.

Opp, K.-D. (1999). "Contending Conceptions of the Theory of Rational Action," *Journal of Theoretical Politics.* 11: 171.

Opp, K.-D. (2000). "Adverse Living Conditions, Grievances, and Political Protest after Communism: The Example of East Germany," *Social Forces.* 79: 29–71.

Opp, K.-D. (2004). "How Does Postcommunist Transformation Affect Political Protest? The Example of East Germany," *Mobilization: An International Journal.* 9: 127–147.

Opp, K.-D. (2009). "Das individualistische Erklärungsprogramm in der Soziologie. Entwicklung, Stand und Probleme," (German). *The Individualistic Research Program in Sociology. Development, Present State, and Problems (English).* 38: 26–47.

Opp, K.-D. and Roehl, W. (1990). "Repression, Micromobilization, and Political Protest," *Social Forces.* 69: 521–547.

Ostrom, E. (1998). "A Behavioral Approach to the Rational Choice Theory of Collective Action Presidential Address," *American Political Science Review.* 92: 1–22.

Ostrom, E. (1999). "Coping With Tragedies of the Commons," *Annual Review of Political Science.* 2: 493–535.

Pierskalla, J. H. (2010). "Protest, Deterrence, and Escalation: The Strategic Calculus of Government Repression," *Journal of Conflict Resolution.* 54: 117–145.

Prahl, R., Marwell, G., and Oliver, P. E. (1991). "Reach and Selectivity as Strategies of Recruitment for Collective Action: A Theory of the Critical Mass, V," *The Journal of Mathematical Sociology.* 16: 137–164.

Schelling, T. C. (1973). "Hockey Helmets, Concealed Weapons, and Daylight Saving: A Study of Binary Choices with Externalities," *Journal of Conflict Resolution.* 17: 381–428.

Schwartz, M. (1976). *Radical Protest and Social Structure: The Southern Farmers' Alliance and Cotton Tenancy, 1880–1890.* New York, Academic Press.

Siegel, D. A. (2009). "Social Networks and Collective Action," *American Journal of Political Science.* 53: 122–138.

Singer, B. D. (1968). "Mass Media and Communication Process in the Detroit Riot of 1967," *Public Opinion Quarterly.* 34: 236–245.

Singer, B. D., Geschwender, J. A., and Osborn, R. W. (1970). *Black Rioters: A Study of Social Factors and Communication in the Detroit Riot.* Lexington, MA: Heath Lexington Books.

Smelser, Neil J. (1992). "The Rational Choice Perspective," *Rationality & Society.* 4(4): 381–410.

Sullivan, T. J. (1977). "The 'Critical Mass' in Crowd Behavior: Crowd Size, Contagion and the Evolution of Riots," *Humboldt Journal of Social Relations.* 4: 46–59.

Tilly, C. (1978). *From Mobilization to Revolution.* Reading, MA: Addison-Wesley.

Wilson, J. Q. (1974). *Political Organizations.* New York: Basic Books.

CHAPTER 16

MICROMOBILIZATION
AND EMOTIONS

HELENA FLAM

INTRODUCTION

In the post-Second World War era of the 1960s and 1970s, the burgeoning research on social movements fought for its own legitimacy in the United States and Europe by insisting on the rationality of movements and their participants. On the high tide of the "cultural" turn, in the early 1990s the "emotional turn" signaled its arrival. Today's research on social movements welcomes the exploration of emotions, offering differing approaches but little debate between their proponents.

The following text teases out opposing ideas about emotions as mobilization prerequisites in democratic and repressive contexts, also inspecting power asymmetries jeopardizing social movements. It looks at the mobilizing potential of the seemingly individualizing emotions, such as grief and sorrow, to then turn to cross-border emotions.

INSTANT VERSUS AGONIZINGLY SLOW MOBILIZATION

Two concepts—"hot cognition" and "moral shock"—are currently much in use to explain why individuals come together in protest and/or form social movements (Gamson 1992: 7.31–7.32; Jasper and Poulsen 1995: 493). Their attractiveness lies in their ability to convey instantly intensely felt moral outrage or shock allegedly catapulting one into immediate political action. The two concepts also seem to free one from the burden of explaining at length *why* moral outrage or shock was felt. A quick glance at their original formulations shows, however, that accounts of initial mobilization should not be short-cut by mere references to "hot cognition" or "moral shock."

Moral outrage as a key prerequisite of collective protest against "unjust" authorities has a long history. As a concept it was always associated with slow and problematic mobilization. Although some individuals react with immediate disbelief, anger, and disgust at the transgressions of authorities, collective moral outrage is an outcome of a longer, deeply contingent process because it takes time to sort out who is to lead, what frames fit all, and if mutual bonding and cooperation work (Fireman et al. 1979; Moore 1987). Similarly, a hydraulic model of anger posits relations of domination making the dominated feel anger, yet for long hiding it behind a mask of apathy for fear of sanctions which also prompt engaging in anonymous, hard to detect forms of low-cost resistance (Scott 1990). When top-down controls relax, the dominated create their own defiant cultures—varying from resignedembittered to subversive, and might convert anger into moral outrage. Unpredictably the accumulated moral outrage explodes in the face of the dominant.

This is to say that there is nothing easy, self-explanatory, or immediate about moral outrage or open protest. The same goes for moral shocks defined as strong responses to violations of taken-for-granted trust and moral standards. This concept was originally brought in to (re-)insert moral concerns and culture into the study of social movements. It stood for an individual response to an event, intensely questioning deeply held societal, religious, or professional values (Goodwin, Jasper, and Polletta 2004: 422) that could explain why a random person might become moved to protest action even in the absence of previous social ties or networks (Jasper and Poulsen 1995: 493; Jasper 1998).

True, some examples implied immediacy between the felt moral shock and protest, since these were cast as responses to "public events, unexpected and highly publicized...such as the [nuclear plant] accident at the Three Mile Island" (Jasper and Poulsen 1995: 498). But this immediacy becomes qualified, if not contradicted, in the same text: moral shocks are defined as an outcome of diagnostic framing and powerful condensed symbols used by social movement organizers trying to "generate" moral shocks through their rhetorical appeals—all of which implies time lost due to framing trial-and-error.

Indeed, a transgression of deeply held values is often not enough to produce an immediate moral shock and to mobilize to action. It may instead be followed by resignation, debilitating self-blame, or hatred towards scapegoats. These emotions are among the very many *cementing emotions* that underpin the extant relations of domination (Flam 2005, 2010). Among these we also find awe for the powerful, love and loyalty to our families, partners, religions, and countries, contempt and hatred for the "other." They all bind members of the society to the elements of the prevailing order. That is why it takes not only cognitive liberation (McAdam 1988) but also emotional liberation for the individual to adopt a dissenting stand (Flam 1993, 2005: 19, 31–32). This is where self-help groups or social movements, but also specific professions, thinkers, or artists, offering alternative feeling rules and visions of society (Flam 2005), come in. They try to undermine some emotions, such as fear, shame, or hatred of scapegoats, while re-appropriating, re-redirecting and intensifying other emotions, such as pride, anger, or solidarity, all along specifying collective actors or public goods to whom they should be attached. Social movements highlight the "outlaw" emotions of the "subordinated individuals who pay a disproportionately high price for maintaining the status quo," such as fear, irritability, revulsion, or anger, to promote critical thought (Jaggar 1989: 160, 161). If successful, they transform cementing, status quo-supporting emotions into *subversive, mobilizing emotions* that bring about social change (Flam 2005).

The Power of Strong Bonds in and across Self-help Groups and "Shielding" Institutions

Cementing and subversive emotions directly address emotions underpinning relations of domination. A well-known approach takes a detour via the nexus of culture, identity, and emotions to address these relations. It has made focal *stigmatized identities* of women, homosexuals, breast-cancer patients, transsexuals and crossdressers, victims of sexual abuse, and others who came together to form self-help groups (Taylor and Van Willingen 1996; Britt and Heise 2000; Whittier 2009).

Its key theoretical contribution is pinpointing that self-help groups and related broader movements are not merely expressive or sub-cultural groups. Instead they are political challengers to the status quo *when* they reframe reality, re-pool emotions, and pursue various reforms of the prevailing cultural, institutional, and legal–political order.

As this approach argues, those subject to discrimination and imprisoned by stigmatized identities suffer shame, guilt, self-doubt, low-esteem, and self-hate—an array of painful (social order-cementing) emotions, motivating some to join self-help groups. These offer support and solidarity, assisting their members in improving their self-images and moving them from the debilitating emotions to the mobilizing emotions, such as anger and pride. They also enable protest: either directly as when they encourage members to become involved in the public efforts to effect change or indirectly when they enable them to join other more militant social movements (Schrock et al. 2004; Whittier 2009).

Although welcome exceptions highlighting the difficulties and failures of self-help groups can be found (Schrock et al. 2004), overall this particular approach views self-help groups and the social movements they feed with great optimism. Self-selection processes and the difficulties faced by self-help groups or their movements are blended out. Comparative studies on the emotional make-up of those who join in contrast to those who do not or on individuals who drop out are missing—a research gap that needs to be closed since these groups might not resemble each other at all.

Social movements become portrayed as successful emotional strategists, superbly informed about which emotions are required in which arenas and acting accordingly: orchestrating a mixture of victimization-related and self-assertive oppositional emotions in self-help groups, displaying victimization-related emotions for the media and courts, while forsaking self-assertion in order not to alienate, and responding to counter-arguments with cool rationality in professional settings (Whittier 2009; Kenney 2009).

The opposite approach stresses how hard it is to move away from debilitating or at best ambivalent emotions. Members of the stigmatized minorities, even after coming together to form a broader movement, may for long remain self-divided or ambivalent in their emotions about themselves and society at large (Gould 2009: 32–42, 106, 119, 166–171, 427). Their very emotional habitus keeps them from becoming aware of their own anger or expressing it in public. This habitus sets a specific political horizon and a range of—moderate—protest activities. It takes long-term processes and extreme events to tip the balance of ambivalent emotions in the direction of anger. It takes again much mobilizing (framing) effort to convert it into moral outrage that helps generate new political horizons and more decisive, militant protest forms. Freed and legitimated anger can feel exhilarating and empowering, freeing one's energies and fantasy, setting them ready for a new action course.

In sum some scholars approach social movements as instantly successful strategists of emotions, while others see social movements as caught in a Houdini-like emotional habitus-trap. Both attribute little emotional–normative flexibility to the outer world. But while the first approach sees member emotions as a well-calibrated bullet, easy to employ, the second approach draws attention to the difficulties attending transforming debilitating into mobilizing emotions. It focusses on mobilizing and converting anger into moral outrage powerful enough to generate confrontational tactics. An explicit debate about these two contrasting conceptualizations of emotions in social movements is missing.

So far the focus has mostly been on the United States—a formally democratic system. It highlighted the significance of self-help groups and social movements as potential agents of cultural and political change. Next the focus shifts away from the United States to repressive political systems to continue the inquiry into the emotional prerequisites of micro-mobilization.

While research on the United States points to voluntary organizations as the crucibles of mobilization, in repressive systems or contexts, universities, coffee shops, church-related organizations as well as trade unions play an equivalent role. Just like the private gatherings, known in some countries as "kitchen seminars," they make the emergence of strong social ties and shared frames possible. Can research concerned with these throw an additional light on the question of whether collective mobilization is spontaneous or deliberated?

For many repressive societies, here exemplified by Franco's Catalonian Spain and pre-1987 South Korea, findings indicate that for collective expressions of moral outrage or moral shock to occur, it takes not only years of separate micro-level mobilization in separate social groups but also their opening to each other. A gradual development of friendship ties is just as important as the emergence of cross-institutional support networks and shared frames among earlier ideological strangers/enemies (della Porta 1991, 1995; Flam 1998; Fehr 2006). Initially, these flourish in separate institutional realms of the universities, factories, and religious centers. Under the protective umbrella of the militant clergymen and trade union leaders, they begin to blossom.

In the late 1960s and the 1970s in Catalonia gradual *rapprochement* between Marxists and National-Catholics, on the one hand, and these two groups and working class trade unionists arrived from other Spanish regions, on the other, was taking place. Radicalism inspired by Marxism and the Second Vatican Council just as the anti-Catalanism of Franco's regime and the pro-Catalanism of the trade unions thrived thanks to the enabling institutional infrastructure provided by the student associations, coffee-shops, church schools and associations, and religious, regionalist and trade union events. Intensifying personal attachments meant that arrests, beatings, and torture affected one not in the abstract but at a "visceral level" (Johnston 1991: 77). In turn personal bonds reinforced the efforts to work out new personal and collective frames. The search for shared frames was far from unproblematic, however, marked as it was by severe personal agonies. It was a cause of much cognitive dissonance, guilt feelings, intense personal anguish, and diverse social conflicts with own families and milieus (Johnston 1991: 96–99, 108–117, 190). That is why "although the concept of reframing is abstract, distant, and even sterile, more likely than not it represents anguished conflict among the social movement adherents who actually accomplish it. Without the tortured reconciliation.... of ideas and values, cross-class alliances would not have been possible." (Johnston 1991: 190; see also Flam 1993, 2005 on "emotional liberation").

Rapproachement between strangers and even ideological enemies first within and then across the institutions of higher education, trade unions, and the Church occurred also in South Korea. The burgeoning coalition movement for democracy coalesced around the Minjung-myth of national suffering and the Han-emotions of both resignation and tenacity in the face of this suffering replayed in rituals, performances of folk theater, mask dance and folk music groups as well as in religious–ecstatic ceremonies (Kern 2005: 202–216). Performances evoking these emotions were staged at every suitable opportunity—for instance, a strike of an extremely exploited workers group, a protest suicide, or an "obvious" case of violent repression. When student, Lee Han-yeol, was hit by a gas grenade, a widely circulated picture showed him wounded and unconsciousness, held up by his fellow student. It ignited moral outrage and nationwide protests. Lee Han-yeol became a symbol of the suffering Minjung's desperate struggle for freedom (Kern 2005: 215). Two months into the protests, he died from his wounds, and an umbrella organization coordinated nationwide expressions of grief. South Korea had never before witnessed such an outpouring of protest. As in the case of Spain, it took a long time for emotional investments in the shared ideas and ties as well as for the willingness to partake in each other's suffering to develop. One day these led to a massive protest and a sustained, open movement for democracy.

Long-term Activism

Deep Mutual Bonds in Jeopardy

Long-term activism is predicated on the development of a variety of deep bonds. To the members of the Italian movement of left-wing students, who lived, discussed, and engaged in protest as groups in the 1960s, the other members of their groups felt like "brothers" and "sisters"—a family. They offered warmth and a sense of belonging during a period of escalating and horrifying confrontations with police violence and the recalcitrant state (della Porta 1995). Combined with loyalty, these bonds compelled many Italian extreme left-wing students to go "underground." Later, when some of their comrades were captured and imprisoned, out of loyalty, they chose to stay rather than leaving the country.

Researchers often argue that solidarity, friendship, camaraderie, or family-like ties sustain social movements (Taylor 1989; Taylor and Rupp 2002). Yet little systematic attention is devoted to these concepts. Neither is their national or international meaning compared nor are they contextualized or their emotional correlates explored. If they indeed sustain movements, however, it seems crucial to specify their substance, pinpointing the conditions under which they emerge, thrive, and become threatened.

Internal conflicts prompting the dissolution of social movements point decisively to power differentials as a serious threat to friendship and solidarity bonds, even to loosely knit alliances. This finding confirms what Theodore Kemper, Thomas Sheff, and Randall Collins, the pioneers in the sociology of emotions, postulated: social bonds become threatened when power asymmetries assert themselves. Power asymmetries are felt by both interaction partners. When the blame for the sensed lack of autonomy and power is attributed to the other—in this case, an ally, comrade in arms, or friend—frustration can be overlaid with anger. When the blame for the sensed overuse of power is attributed to oneself, shame and guilt follow.

Scarce empirical research confirms that power asymmetries result in anger leading to a take-over or to self-shame leading to a withdrawal of the newcomers to a prestigious movement (Kleres 2001; Polletta 2002). Also longstanding activists who feel marginalized and unacknowledged may come to express their anger—this was the case when, for example, Maori and lesbian feminists challenged white heterosexual dominance in the New Zealand "second wave" women's movement (Holmes 2004) or when white, middle-class HIV-infected men felt betrayed and resentful as other ACT UP activists called for more attention to Latinas/os and African-Americans, and, when these men insisted that their HIV/AIDS should remain a priority, were accused of sexism and racism (Gould 2009: 373–378).

It is important to investigate under what conditions 'anger performed' can generate positive uptake and lead to power re-structuring. Scant research suggests that personalized, moralizing, and resentful–hostile anger either debilitates or leads to (defensive) expressions of contempt, superiority, and counter-moralizing, hindering constructive discussions. Power asymmetries can be reduced when anger is expressed in moderate and impersonal ways and when the larger moral–discursive field and the context in which it is embedded allow for positive uptake (Holmes 2004: 217–221; Gould 2009).

Anger and upset can be expressed by both the dominated and the dominant group. Painstaking analysis is necessary to decide whether they are expressed to defend or thwart relations of domination. Both white feminists and white middle-class male activists within ACT UP, when they are reproached about their racism and sexism, describe their sense of victimization and hurt feelings in response—they proclaim that such criticism makes the movement space less safe or comfortable (Holmes 2004: 220/221; Gould 2009: 373; Srivastava in Russo 2013: 45). The teary defense pattern fore-closes any further discussion, focussing all the attention on the suffering of those criti-cized. It is successful since it is compatible with the moral–discursive field in which it emerges. Those feeling victimized—"the strong reduced to tears" (in Holmes 2004: 220)—receive much support from their white peers who also feel anxious not to dis-cuss the shame of enjoying the privileges attached to being white (Holmes 2004; Gould 2009; Russo 2013: 40–46).

Painstaking analysis is necessary also to unveil the emotional difficulties attend-ing alliance-building or forging friendship bonds across the divisive lines of "race," class, gender, religion, sexual preference, etc. in various national contexts and across national borders (see Lloyd 2002; Patel 2002: 141–145; Mahrouse 2010: 172–177). In the present-day Olympics of Suffering, nearly each mobilized identity group clamors for exclusive attention. Although there is much need for space for all, "without fear of being straitjacketed into fixed identities" (Patel 2002: 142), not only the societal rela-tions of domination, but also the very identity politics frustrates the attempts to build intersectional movements striving for universal rather than particularistic goals (Lloyd 2002; Russo 2013: 42–46; Gould 2009). The therapeutic discourse that ennobles suffer-ing and its emotional expressions sustains status and power hierarchies both within and between identity-stressing movements. It also privileges "emotional expression over critical analysis" (Srivastava in Russo 2013: 45) and keeps constructive conflicts from emerging.

The Mobilizing Force of Grief and Sorrow

Although emotions such as love, grief, or sorrow are considered deeply private and asso-ciated with withdrawal from social life, they are in fact bi-modal in their action conse-quences and can mobilize to collective protest action.

Disquiet, worry, sorrow, and grief have moved hundreds of "grieving mothers" to break the silence about the murderous regimes responsible for the political disap-pearances, torture, and political killings of their children (Flam 2013a). Las Madres de Playa de Mayo were the first to walk around a fountain across from the government building in Buenos Aires in April 1977 and every week ever since. Their example has been followed in Chile, Cuba, El Salvador, Israel, Guatemala, Nicaragua, Russia, China, Kashmir, Iran, and many other countries. Even though they have been ridiculed, beaten up, arrested, and persecuted, hundreds of grieving mothers dare to form and sustain their protest across the globe.

Just like Las Madres, the Israeli Women in Black (WiB) have served as a model worthy of emulation. Starting in 1988 every Friday WiB defied the Israeli state and the ban on showing solidarity with the Palestinians. Their shared grief about war victims and their moral outrage about warmongers compelled them to protest (Benski 2005). Along with friendship ties they helped face public expressions of hatred and disdain. Sorrow and grief have also motivated lovers, friends, and families of AIDS victims to organize public quilt displays as recurring commemorative events, offering a chance to mourn, to protest, and to sympathize (Power 2011: 145–159).

RE-ENTER MOVEMENT ORGANIZATIONS (MOs)

If genuine grief and sorrow over the lost bonds can sustain long-term activism, Mothers Against Drunk Driving (MADD) show that a cultural construction and organization of a perpetual trauma is equally effective. Inge Schmidt (2013) casts MOs in the new role of cultural producers. MOs construct a narrative, and find the means and the settings to stage and to work on the emotions of those they try to mobilize.

MADD defines drunk driving as a tragedy compelling collective suffering and leaving a mark on group consciousness (Schmidt 2013: 2–5). It constructs drunk driving as an event which occurs in real time and the future. When staging public events, MADD relies on a variety of dramaturgical devices to evoke a very personal sense of danger attached to drunken driving (Schmidt 2013: 6–9, 13). The class/audience experiences first the horror, the fear, the pain, and the guilt associated with being the victim or perpetrator in a drunken-driving accident. When the emotional crescendo has been reached, MADD offers relief from the painful emotions: making the right choice. If you do not drive when you drink, all will be well.

This particular case highlights a distinction between social movements that work on emotions in a by-the-way fashion and those that explicitly work on the emotions of their members and/or audiences—a distinction that should be explored more systematically.

CROSS-BORDER EMOTIONS

Research on both transnational movements and emotions is still very modest, but a few examples that focus on the Arab Spring and transnational activism will be offered.

The Arab regimes had become known for encouraging discourses, institutions, and practices conducive to dispiriting emotions, such as fear, cynicism, and pessimism, among their citizens. Consequently a shared emotional state of apathy underwritten by fear and cynicism prevailed. Quite unexpectedly Tunisians responded with anger to the moral shock of self-immolation by Bouazizi and others. Making a powerful argument against rational-choice and value-stressing approaches, Pearlman (2013; see also Johnston 1991: 191–192) argues that this anger was transformative as it focussed blame on the powerholders, reinforced the value of freedom, and helped assess the benefits of action as greater than its costs, thus mobilizing to collective action. In what I would call an emotional domino-effect, Egyptians followed. Although dispiriting emotions were pervasive also in Egypt, the Tunisian revolution made Egyptians feel neighbor-envy and hurt self-pride that their great nation was not the first to rise. These new emotions deepened the feelings of anger, disdain, and impatience directed at the elites (see also Gribbon and Hawas 2012). Together they reduced fear, leading to public protest. Hope that things would improve soon, exhilaration of freedom as well as the camaraderie, kept that anger from turning violent. In both countries, citizens switched from the dispiriting emotions of fear, cynicism, and pessimism, to the emboldening emotions, such as moral outrage and hope.

Two studies examine what emotions transnational organizations of the "North" active in the "South" advocate in relation to the South (Boltanski 1999 [1993]; Leebaw 2007). The Humanitarian Movement, exemplified by the Red Cross, used to urge political neutrality for the sake of immediate compassion for human suffering. The Human Rights Movement, exemplified by Amnesty International, took time necessary to amass compelling evidence against repressive political regimes in order to pinpoint the perpetrators. During the past twenty years, these movements have come to resemble each other. Neither easily offers compassion, investigating facts first. Their new indignation is directed not only at states but also at non-state perpetrators causing human suffering.

My own study investigates feeling rules proposed for distant suffering by the prominent Western "armchair critics" of the West, these movements, and the advocates of transitional justice (TJ) who debate what the perpetrators and victims facing international criminal courts and truth commissions should feel (Flam 2013b). All three discourses advocate "mindful" compassion for the victims and "cooled" indignation for the perpetrators. The movement for TJ attempts to square the circle by equating the suffering of victims, perpetrators, and by-standers, calling for compassion for all three.

At the micro-level one investigation shows that many activists of humanitarian and human rights initiatives can identify when they feel vulnerable or endangered. Their strategies include embracing risk-taking morally and emotionally, routinizing alertness, and avoiding "unnecessary" risk. Some try to build up friendship and solidarity ties with the locals as a shield, and let their concern and guilt about the locals who cannot fall upon the privilege of being able to withdraw counteract their own fears (Roth 2011).

Another investigation focusses on the activists and helpers from the North who often act upon, although some become self-critical of, their racist, top-down, voyeuristic emotional take on their comrades or aid recipients in the South (Mahrouse 2008). The desire for intimacy with the Other is (mis)taken for solidarity, while white "feel-good" multicultural aspirations translate into counterproductive, life-endangering recruitment of non-whites as human shields meant to protect human rights (Mahrouse 2010: 172–177).

CONCLUSION

Much has been written about micro-mobilization. Yet gaps remain. Social movement research would greatly benefit from sustained debates across schools of thought and types of regimes about whether or not collective mobilization is instant or excruciatingly slow, involves unproblematic or deeply emotional, soul-wrenching identity shifts, and how internal emotional movement dynamics interacts with the emotionality of the institutional settings and actors to decide for or against different courses of action. Its corollary would be comparative research on those who join and make movement careers in contrast to those who do join but drop out and those who do not join in the first place although they belong to the identical social category. Only then would we obtain a realistic assessment of movement accomplishments for individuals—both stigmatized and exploited. Similarly, research on social movements asserts that friendship or family-like ties, solidarity, and camaraderie sustain social movements. But these concepts are often empty shells. Sorely needed is focus on their cultural and movement-attached meanings and emotional contents. It is also necessary to pay heed to internal power differentials causing much ill feeling and, if not constructively expressed and responded to, movement conflicts or even demise. Rather than just celebrating social movements and human solidarity, we should pay attention to problems they face and often fail to resolve, admitting that today many movements mobilize also around shared grief, sorrow, or humiliation and, as their predecessors, do not know how to cope with the frustration, anger, guilt, or hatred bred by internal power asymmetries. There is a huge gap in research on transnational movements and emotions. The little research that does exist signals that the activists of the North have possibly cooled their compassion for the victims and their indignation for the perpetrators, professionalizing for the sake of their own safety. They have to stay on alert about their own latent racist "feel-good" tendencies or guilt parading as solidarity.

REFERENCES

Benski, Tova (2005). "Breaching Events and the Emotional Reactions of the Public: Women in Black in Israel." In *Emotions and Social Movement*, edited by Helena Flam and Debra King, 57–78. London/New York: Routledge.

Boltanski, Luc (1999 [1993]). *Distant Suffering: Morality, Media and Politics.* Cambridge: Cambridge University Press.

Britt, Lory and Heise, David (2000). "From Shame to Pride in Identity Politics" In *Self, Identity, and Social Movements*, edited by Sheldon Stryker, Timothy J. Owens, and Robert W. White, 252–268. Minneapolis: University of Minnesota Press.

della Porta, Donatella. (1991). "Die Spirale der Gewalt und Gegengewalt: Lebensberichte von Links- und Rechtsradikalen in Italien," *Forschungsjournal Neue Soziale Bewegungen*. 4(2): 53–62.

della Porta, Donatella (1995). *Social Movements, Political Violence and the State: A Comparative Analysis of Italy and Germany*. Cambridge: Cambridge University Press.

Fehr, Helmut (2006). *Unabhängige Öffentlichkeit und soziale Bewegungen: Fallstudien über Bürgerbewegungen in Polen und der DDR*. Opladen: Leske+Budrich.

Fireman, Bruce, Gamson, William A., Rytina, Steven, and Taylor, B. (1979). "Encounters with Unjust Authority." In *Research in Social Movements, Conflicts and Change* Volume 2, edited by L. Kriesberg. Greenwich/Conn.: JAI Press.

Flam, Helena (1993). "Die Erschaffung und der Verfall oppositioneller Identität," *Forschungsjournal Neue Soziale Bewegungen*. 2: 83–97.

Flam, Helena (1998). *Mosaic of Fear: Poland and East Germany before 1989*. New York: East European Monographs distributed by Columbia University Press.

Flam, Helena (2005). "Emotion's Map: A Research Agenda." In *Emotions and Social Movement*, edited by Helena Flam and Debra King, 19–40. London/New York: Routledge.

Flam, Helena (2010). "Emotion, and the Silenced and Short-circuited Self." In *Conversations About Reflexivity*, edited by Margaret S. Archer, 187–205. London: Routledge.

Flam Helena (2013a). "The Politics of Grief and the "Grieving" Mothers." In *The Blackwell Encyclopedia of Social and Political Movements*, edited by David A. Snow, Donatella della Porta, Doug McAdam, and Bert Klandermanns, 978–983. Malden: Wiley-Blackwell.

Flam, Helena (2013b)."The Transnational Movement for Truth, Justice and Reconciliation as an Emotional (Rule) Regime?" *Special Issue on Power and Emotion*, guest edited by Jonathan G. Heaney and Helena Flam, *Journal of Political Power*. 6(3): 363–383.

Flam, Helena (2015). "Social Movements and Emotions." In *The Handbook of Political Citizenship and Social Movements*, edited by Hein-Anton v.d. Heijden, 308–333. Cheltenham/Camberley/Northampton: Edward Elgar Publishing.

Gamson, William (1992). *Talking Politics*. New York: Cambridge University Press.

Goodwin, Jeff, Jasper, James M., and Polletta, Francesca (2001). *Passionate Politics. Emotions and Social Movements*, Chicago/London: The University of Chicago Press.

Goodwin, Jeff, Jasper, James M., and Polletta, Francesca (2004). "Emotional Dimensions of Social Movements." In *The Blackwell Companion to Social Movements*, edited by David A. Snow, Sarah A. Soule, and Hanspeter Kriesi, 413–432. Oxford: Blackwell.

Gould, Deborah (2009). *Moving Politics: Emotion and ACT UP's Fight against AIDS*. Chicago: The University of Chicago Press.

Gribbon, Laura and Hawas, Sarah (2012)."Signs and Signifiers: Visual Translations of Revolt." In *Translating Egypt's Revolution. The Language of Tahrir*, edited by Samia Mehrez, 103–142. Cairo/New York. The American University in Cairo Press.

Holmes, Mary (2004). "Feeling Beyond Rules: Politicizing the Sociology of Emotions and Anger," *Special Issue on Anger in Political Life*, edited by Mary Holmes, *European Journal of Social Theory*. 7(2): 209–228.

Jaggar, Alison M. (1989). "Love and Knowledge: Emotions in Feminist Epistemology." In *Gender / Body / Knowledge: Feminist Reconstructions of Being and Knowing*, edited by Alison M. Jaggar and Susan R. Bordo, 145–171. New Brunswick, NJ: Rutgers University Press.

Jasper, James M. and Poulse, Jane D. (1995). "Recruiting Strangers and Friends: Moral Shocks and Social Network in Animal Rights and Anti-Nuclear Protests," *Social Problems*. 42(4): 493–512.

Jasper, James M. (1998). *The Art of Moral Protest: Culture, Biography and Creativity in Social Movements*. Chicago: The University of Chicago Press.

Johnston, Hank (1991). *Tales of Nationalism: Catalonia, 1939–1979*. New Brunswick, NJ: Rutgers University Press.

Kenney, Scott J. (2009). "Emotions and the Campaign for Victims' Rights in Canada," *Canadian Journal of Criminology and Criminal Justice*. 51(4): 473–510.

Kern, Thomas (2005). *Südkoreas Pfad zur Demokratie*. Frankfurt a.M.: Campus, 2005.

Kleres, Jochen (2001). "Cherries Blossoming in East(ern) Germany?" In *Pink, Purple, Green*, edited by Helena Flam, 135–149. New York: East European Monographs distributed by Columbia University Press.

Leebaw, Bronwyn (2007). "The Politics of Impartial Activism: Humanitarianism and Human Rights," *Perspectives on Politics*. 5(2): 223–239.

Lloyd, Cathie (2002). "Anti-racism, Social Movements and Civil Society." In *Re-thinking Anti-racisms*, edited by Floya Anthias and Cathie Lloyd, 60–77. London: Routledge.

Mahrouse, Gada (2008). "Race-conscious Transnational Activists with Cameras: Mediators of Compassion," *International Journal of Cultural Studies*. 11(1): 87–105.

Mahrouse, Gada (2010). "Questioning Efforts that Seek to 'Do Good': Insights from Transnational Solidarity Activism and Socially Responsible Tourism." In *States of Race. Critical Race Feminism for the 21th Century*, edited by Sherene Razack, Malinda Smith, and Sunera Thobani, 160–190. Toronto: Between the Lines.

McAdam Doug (1988). *Freedom Summer*. New York: Oxford University Press, 1988.

Moore, Barrington Jr. (1987). *Injustice. The Social Bases of Obedience and Revolt*. London: MacMillan Palgrave.

Patel, Pragna. (2002). "Back to the Future: Avoiding déjà vu in Resisting Racism." In *Re-thinking Anti-racisms*, edited by Floya Anthias and Cathie Lloyd, 128–148. London: Routledge.

Pearlman, Wendy (2013). "Emotions and the Microfoundations of the Arab Uprisings," *Perspectives on Politics*. 11(2): 387–409.

Polletta, Francesca (2002). *Freedom is an Endless Meeting: Democracy in American Social Movements*. Chicago: The University of Chicago.

Power, Jennifer (2011). *Movement, Knowledge, Emotion: Gay Activism and HIV/AIDS in Australia*. Canberra: Australian University Press.

Roth, Silke (2011). "Dealing with Danger—Risk and Security in the Everyday Lives of Aid Workers." In *Inside the Everyday Lives of Development Workers: the Challenges and Futures of Aidland*, edited by Anne-Meike Fechter and Heather Hindman, 151–168. Sterling, US: Kumarian Press.

Russo, Ann (2013). "Between Speech and Silence: Reflections on Accountability." In *Silence, Feminism, Power* edited by Sheena Malhotra and Aimee Carrillo Rowe, 34–49. London: Palgrave MacMillan.

Schmidt, Inge B. (2013). "Perpetual Trauma and its Organizations: Mothers Against Drunk Driving and Drunk Driving Revisited," *Memory Studies*. 7(2): 239–253.

Schrock Douglas, Holden, Daphne, and Reid, Lori (2004). "Creating Emotional Resonance: Interpersonal Emotion Work and Motivational Framing in a Transgender Community," *Social Problems*. 51(1): 61–81.

Scott, James (1990). *Domination and the Arts of Resistance: The Hidden Transcript of Subordinate Groups*. New Haven: Yale University Press, 1990.

Taylor, Verta (1989). "Social Movement Continuity: The Women's Movement in Abeyance," *American Sociological Review*. 54: 761–775.

Taylor, Verta and Rupp, Leila J. (2002). "Loving Internationalism: The Emotion Culture of Transnational Women's Organizations, 1888–1945," *Mobilization: International Journal of Theory and Research About Social Movements and Collective Behavior.* 7(2): 141–158.

Taylor, Verta and Van Willingen, Marieke (1996). "Women's Self-Help and the Reconstruction of Gender: The Postpartum Support and Breast Cancer Movements," *Mobilization. An International Journal.* 1(2): 123–142.

Whittier, Nancy (2009). *The Politics of Child Sexual Abuse.* Oxford/New York: Oxford University Press.

CHAPTER 17

DEMOBILIZATION AND DISENGAGEMENT IN A LIFE COURSE PERSPECTIVE

OLIVIER FILLIEULE

A NEGLECTED AREA OF RESEARCH

WE know little about the mechanisms governing the decline of social movements and the varied forms of individual or collective demobilization that prompt this decline or end it. Indeed, as Verta Taylor emphasizes, "scholars generally are more interested in movements undergoing cycles of mass mobilization and have done little research on movements in decline or equilibrium" (1989: 772). Yet, the logical counterpart of the initial recruitment and mobilization processes is clearly collective demobilization and individual disengagement. Thus, we might suggest that one of the permanent traits of political organizations, whether they are political parties, unions or non-governmental organizations (NGOs), is turnover and consequently defection (Fillieule 2010).

There are at least four explanations for the failure of the literature to address this. First, activism has been less studied for itself than through the analysis of organizations which frame it. This leads naturally to reasoning in terms of stock rather than flow. Secondly, microsociological approaches to behavior, except for their economicist version of *rational choice theory*, have long been discarded in the name of the struggle against the paradigm of collective behaviour. Thirdly, there is a scarcity of sources that can prove useful in understanding the activist flow. By definition, ex-activists are no longer present at the time of the investigation and, very often, organizations do not retain records of members which would allow researchers to track those no longer active or, if they do, they do not make them readily available to researchers. Fourthly, there is the difficulty of moving from static approaches to a true processual perspective which, in this particular case, is based on setting up longitudinal studies, whether prospective or retrospective (Fillieule 2001). However, in broadening the range of literature to review related questions or fields, the spectrum of potentially relevant research seems considerable. If we exclude the autobiographical works of priests, terrorists, and communist activists, literature that more or less directly broaches the question of disengagement emerges from life course sociology, especially concerning the question of the social effects of ageing; from social psychology, concerning the social functioning of small groups and sociability networks (e.g., Kanter 1972; McPherson et al. 1992); and the sociology of roles, in the Mertonian or interactionist tradition, especially in the literature on churches and cults, but also divorce and the professions (Vaughan 1986; Fuchs-Ebaugh 1988).

Definitions and Modalities

The notion of demobilization brings us back to a plurality of phenomena ranging from individual disengagement (Fillieule 2005) to the political demobilization of an entire society, the sum of individual behavior producing macrosocial cycles of involvement or, conversely, withdrawal to the private sphere (Hirschman 2002). More precisely, beyond cycles of political attention, analysis reveals four other distinct types of situations. First, there is the demobilization phenomenon in a multi-organizational field (Curtis and Zurcher 1973) that is, of an entire social movement industry, with its formal organizations, its support networks and those involved along the way. The brutal ending of the 1956 protest movement in Poland due to harsh repression (Osa 2003), the generalized decline of leftist movements in developed countries in the aftermath of the May 1968 crisis (e.g., Whalen and Flacks 1989), and the movement of de-unionization and disintegration of workers' struggles in Europe (Klandermans 1997) are several such examples. Second, demobilization may relate less to a specific sector than to the slow collapse of a mobilization campaign, as a result of its success or, conversely, its failure. The history of anti-nuclear struggles in the 1970s and 1980s provides an illustration of this. At the mesosociological level, demobilization may affect a specific social movement organization, whether due to its voluntarily disbanding, rare though it is, or a general decline in a cause, or even the effect of repression (e.g., the banning or removal of the leadership), as seen with numerous clandestine or semi-clandestine extreme leftist groups at the end of the 1970s in Japan and the United States (Zwerman and Steinhoff 2005), as well as in Europe (della Porta 1995 and Combes and Fillieule 2011 for a critical review).

The concept of demobilization brings us back to collective phenomena. At the microsociological level, we will refer instead to disengagement. This may fall within the rubric of demobilization but also brings us back to singular trajectories which may include a wide diversity of forms and determinants. Indeed, it is very likely that the process of disengagement changes in nature according to what causes it, the cost of defection, the manner in which it takes place and, therefore, what becomes of those who leave, which raises the question of the biographical consequences of activism.

Individual demobilization is not always voluntary. It may also result from a collective decision to dissolve an organization; from the decline of an ideology, as Taylor illustrates

(1989) with regards to American postwar feminism; from exclusion; from deprogramming; or from being sidelined due to forced exile or a prison sentence. The modalities of individual defection vary. It may be isolated or collective, on the occasion, for example, of an organizational split, or when groups with a certain affinity leave together. Introvigne distinguishes *defectors*, who leave in a negotiated manner, *apostates*, who become professional enemies of their organization, and *ordinary leavers*, who disappear without their withdrawal representing a significant cost, for either themselves or the organization (1999). This is a typology which needs to be completed by adding all forms of passive defection, but also all the cases in which withdrawal is followed, and sometimes provoked, by joining another organization. Nonetheless, in every case, the vast majority of the ordinary people who leave remain invisible.

Finally, the cost of the individual departure is related first to the way in which organizations impose various constraints on defections. The psychological or material cost of the defection and, therefore, its probability, are traceable to many factors. These include the extent of the sacrifices accepted to join the group (initiation rites, tests, hierarchization and the compartmentalization of groups); the degree of socialization within the group, which reinforces emotional attachment, related to the extent of renunciation of social relations outside of the group (networks of families and friends); and, finally, the rules governing defection, sometimes made impossible by material dependence or the threat of being hunted down as a traitor (Bennani-Chraibi and Fillieule 2003: 123). To these barriers, we must also add the existence of opportunities to reconvert acquired resources, the possibility of reconnecting with alternative sociability networks and, finally, the social legitimacy of defection. This is linked to the social acceptance of departure, as well as to society's readiness to grant those who leave an alternative social identity.

BIOGRAPHICAL CONSEQUENCES
OF ACTIVISM

We count some seventy publications intended to evaluate the biographical consequences of activist commitment, in various domains. A first direction of research deals with the study of black student activism in the civil rights and black power movements and of riot participants (Sears and McConahay 1973; Gurin and Epps 1975). It explores environmental influences as well as the impact of activism on political ideology and adult resocialization, suggesting, among other interesting results, that the riots themselves appeared to have generated a type of "riot ideology" that further resocialized not only the direct participants but those who only vicariously experienced them; a result that has recently been confirmed by studies on not-so-committed participants (Sherkat and Blocker 1997; Van Dyke et al. 2000). But the value of this research lies primarily in analyzing how movements accomplish their socializing role, teaching young blacks to question the overall white system of domination through specific mechanisms and set ups like mass meeting, workshops, and citizen and freedom schools.

A second direction stems from feminist research and deals with the development of a gender consciousness through the women's movement (Sapiro 1989; Whittier 1995; Klawiter 2008). The reason that this movement has served as an active agent of socialization is partly due to the fact that one of its central goals is to change women's self understanding: that is, to provide a social space in which women can consider and negotiate their social identity as women and its relationship to politics. Moreover, beyond the specific case of the women's movement, feminist research suggests that all protest movements may operate like gender workplaces. As a matter of fact, activism can play a liberating role for women in permitting them to leave the domestic universe and acquire social skills previously inaccessible to them. This is the reason why, even in movements where women are kept in positions of subjugation, mere participation can foster emancipation (Fillieule and Roux 2008).

A third and more prolific domain of research concerns what became of ex-activists between ten and twenty years after the decline of the movements of the 1960s, mainly in the United States, but also elsewhere, in Europe, in Latin America, and in the Arab world (Fillieule and Neveu 2014). They are very largely based on survey questionnaires, more rarely accompanied by a qualitative section. The research strategies deployed are distinguished by their sample selection methods, whether or not the study was replicated and the eventual composition of control groups. With a similar approach to that of Demerath (Demerath et al. 1971), in the early 1980s, D. McAdam studied the 1964 *Freedom Summer* project, which was designed to mobilize white students to participate in a southern voter registration campaign (McAdam 1988). The study was based on applications filed by the student candidates before the summer. Some amongst them did, in fact, participate while others withdrew. Based on the data contained in these files, the author managed to trace 73 per cent of the *no-shows* and 53 per cent of the volunteers. A mailed questionnaire was sent out, and this was combined with a campaign of interviews of around forty-eight individuals. For their part, J. Whalen and R. Flacks were interested in the anti-Vietnam War movement. More precisely, they started with the 1970 burning of a bank by members of the *Santa Barbara 19* group. Twenty-five people were subsequently arrested. It was from this core of ex-activists that R. Flacks started an investigation in 1979. He interviewed eleven people condemned in 1982 for burning the bank, and eight other activists. Moreover, a control group of those who were non-politicized students at the time was also questioned. In 1980, J. Whalen interviewed a second wave for his thesis. Seventeen activists and fifteen non-activists who had been questioned in 1979 were interviewed once again. This was followed by a third wave in 1983, and then a fourth in 1987–88, with almost the entire panel. A fine work published in 1989 presents a final overview of the research (Whalen and Flacks 1989).

This research does not exhaust all the strategies employed to answer the question of what happened to the activists from the 1960s. Yet, this is enough for us to appreciate the strengths and weaknesses of this literature. Indeed, a number of methodological questions arise. The first is that of timing. Most studies were conducted at the time when leftist radicalism was at its peak, so that it is difficult to distinguish the effect of the period from that of the generation. Secondly, the question arises of a comparison amongst samples over time and space. Only research based on comparisons of groups of ex-activists and non-activists can even venture beyond simple correlations. As well, consideration of the degrees of commitment and the nature of their experiences is a valuable addition. From this perspective, the research of Whalen, Flacks, and McAdam is exemplary. Yet all this work is based on participation in a movement which no longer existed at the time of the inquiry. Therefore, it is impossible to correlate the characteristics and trajectories of those who leave with those who remain committed, as was possible in more recent research (Fillieule and Blanchard 2013). Still along the same lines, we must stress that, doubtless, the work allowing us to link individual characteristics and opinions before and after activist involvement is the most promising and persuasive, since without having access to earlier information on activists, it is difficult to determine the extent and significance of changes brought about by participation.

Overall, despite the varied methodology employed, it is striking that research on the biographical consequences of activism is generally consistent on at least three elements. These are the long-term effects of activism, the determinants of the process of disengagement, and the typology of ways of leaving and forms of career change.

All the studies agree in emphasizing that life trajectories are considerably shaped by the activist experience, primarily in three areas: political participation, family life, and professional life. In terms of political participation and ideological orientation, there is a strong chance that ex-activists are permanently oriented towards the left and more interested and active in politics than those who have never participated. The family life of ex-activists is characterized by a late entry into adult life and the roles associated with it, and a greater instability of couples, with a higher divorce rate than the control groups. Finally, their academic careers were more likely to be interrupted or cut short. They were concentrated in the social welfare sphere and middle-ranking or upper intellectual professions, including the ministry or the priesthood for former members of the civil rights movement. Consequently, incomes are not very high. Their careers are also characterized by greater professional instability, notably due to their late entry into active adult life and their more frequent changes of employment. These elements allow Fendrich to analyze the ex-activists as a "generational unit," in the Mannheimian sense, which D. McAdam confirms when he demonstrates that the risks associated with the *Freedom Summer* undoubtedly greatly contributed to making this experience "unforgettable" for participants. In other words, the eventual direction of trajectories must be related to the nature of the activist experience, again, the moral career of individuals very likely having been affected to some degree by the duration and intensity of their activism.

Nonetheless, it is very difficult to determine whether activism has produced a reorientation of trajectories or whether, on the contrary, it is by virtue of the same initial dispositions that the individuals studied participated, had a more distant relation with their families and to marriage, and finally chose one profession over another. The only certainty is that the choice of career which does not enter into contradiction with an activist disposition is probably related to their continued involvement. This last point brings us to the question of the overlapping of factors possibly leading to disengagement. To respond to this, we must turn to the second generation of research to find some consideration of the process of defection.

For J. Whalen and R. Flacks, the primary cause of the ebb in activism of the 1960s was connected to a change in the political climate. The Vietnam War was ending while the repression of the movement was intensifying. Such a context led to a re-evaluation of the chances of success, as well as of the cost of activism. Specifically, it became increasingly difficult for young activists not to ask questions about their professional futures. Added to these external factors, the two sociologists add the idea that the movement didn't know how to maintain and tend the enthusiasm of activists or even of their organization. In their view, activists were caught in a certain form of community life that made it very difficult to protect themselves from excessive demands. Now, while at first, the strength of community bonds could have constituted the cement holding activists together, it finally gave rise to strong tensions and encouraged defection.

As for explanations for the later trajectories of the ex-activists, while statistical investigations indicate that their lives have followed a particular course, biographical analysis allows us to go further in characterizing them, in paying less attention to the point at which they arrive than to the paths that led them there. In the 1970s, in a context where the field of possible politics was narrowing, former activists took four types of routes. While a minority chose simply to withdraw from the ranks, most sought to reconcile their politics and their search for a future. From the outset, some were going to turn to the introspective aspects of the movement and develop a religious sentiment, those alternate lifestyles, which allowed them to preserve their personal aspirations and political beliefs. For others, as much as was feasible, the pursuit of professional projects occurred in conjunction with activist convictions, explaining the importance of professions linked to social work. Others still, who did not envision walking away from the struggle, devoted their efforts to creating small radical parties, or developing alternative institutions (*underground* newspapers, local radio, or associations), which allowed for professional career change without abandoning their activist convictions. As well, some sought to politicize the profession they embraced, for example through the creation of red unions, and the "invention" of the sociology of social movements.

The focus of research on the civil rights movements and opposition to the Vietnam War doubtless explains some of the astonishing consistency of the literature. Yet, more recent research on other contexts seems to corroborate those results (Fillieule and Bennani-Chraïbi 2003; and Fillieule 2005). The focus on the 1950s and 1960s has the further advantage of having given rise to reflection on questions of cycles of mobilization, on the transmission and evolution of action repertoires and activist know-how. From this perspective, the American left, as created and structured in the 1960s, functioned as an agency for "ethical development," in providing groups of individuals with political training which would later lead them to the causes of the 1970s and 1980s. It is this generation of former activists who opposed the Reagan administration and which, today, comprises much of the leadership of the anti-globalization movement.

A Processual Approach
to Disengagement

The literature to which we have just referred is characterized by a movement which went from the exclusive use of a retrospective questionnaire to using the life story (Linde 1993) as the only way to be able to approach the issue of how activism could have been experienced in the past and to take into consideration the order in which a withdrawal occurs. More recently, scholars started to combine life stories with life history calendars (LHC) and sequence analysis, which allow the systematic study of populations of biographies. The LHC amalgamates a number of different event histories in a unique, large chart (Freedman 1988: 40). This enables the respondent (as well as the researcher in the case of face-to-face interviews) to relate and cross-check the timing of events across different domains. One can recall the timing of past events more accurately and avoid chronological inconsistencies. The graphical presentation facilitates the recording of detailed and intricate sequences related to critical life periods. It also unloads the memory burden by providing an incremental and progressive record of memories, from the most readily available events to the most hidden and uncertain ones. Comparison with more traditional questionnaire designs has proven that the LHC provides a more accurate and more detailed record of the respondent's biography (Glasner and van der Vaart 2009). The second progress in life history methodology was chiefly made by Andrew Abbott's work on time and sequences in the social and historical sciences (Abbott 1983, 1995). The "narrative positivism" approach he proposed leaves aside the general linear model dominant in social statistics and sociological reasoning (Abbott 1988) and moves from abstract variables and causality to individuals, events, and processes. The method that resulted from this approach, sequence analysis, accounts at the same time for the three basic dimensions of biographies: the nature of the successive positions/statuses held by individuals, the order in which they occur, and their duration. The methodological package includes tools to code and format sequences, to compare them by pairs, to cluster them, to represent them in alphanumeric and graphical forms, to calculate specific statistics for sequences and groups of sequences, to mine sequences, and to extract prototypical sequences. All these tools will certainly prove to be dramatically fruitful for the study of activists' careers (see Fillieule and Blanchard 2013 for a first attempt).

This evolution of investigative techniques is related to the renewal of the sociology of activism inspired by interactionist approaches and, more broadly, life course sociology. In such an approach, the focus is on the processes leading to withdrawal (Björgo and Horgan 2009; Fillieule 2010) rather than on its determinants or what happens to those who withdraw. From this perspective, withdrawal is seen as resulting from the three interdependent levels: *exhaustion of the rewards* of involvement, *the loss of ideological meaning*, and the *transformation of relations of sociability*.

Attention to the variability of rewards involves examining the reasons for which, at a particular stage of the life course, involvement in protest activity becomes problematic, and determining under which conditions the benefits experienced from involvement are maintained or exhausted. This leads to identification, in different life spheres, of the "succession[s] of phases, of changes in individual behavior and perspectives" (Becker 1966). These critical moments prompt a fresh assessment of the rewards, knowing that their value in a given sphere is correlated to the value they are accorded in all other spheres. Examples abound of occasions when involvement in a cause, or withdrawal from it, corresponds almost exactly to the collapse or rise of new perspectives in the professional or affective sphere.

The impetus for individuals to re-evaluate the associated rewards must be examined. In addition to immediate reasons, such as the loss of a job or the end of a relationship, joining the workforce or entering a new serious relationship, we must also add a whole array of factors not directly related to the individual. Indeed, the price accorded to the rewards in a given universe is indexed to the value that other beneficiaries and the entire society accord it. In a context of political turmoil, for example in the 1960s, the rewards of involvement were very likely to be greater than those offered at a time of a loss of interest for politics.

Finally, we must attempt to understand how individuals seek to weigh the exhaustion experienced and the rewards, through turning back, distancing themselves from the role, and trying to transform the role or defect from it. It is at this point that the degree of dependence on the role and the existence of lateral possibilities, determined notably by the extent of compartmentalization of various spheres of life, constitute a universe of constraints making defection more or less difficult. It is as much the socializing power of the role that one is leaving as the manner in which one departs that explains the changing trajectory, once the individual has left and sometimes much later.

Withdrawal may also be observed in the erosion of acquired beliefs within groups, which may lessen the sacrifices one is willing to make for the cause. Here, we may discern two levels of possible determination. On one hand, the strength of beliefs may vary, depending on a change in political climate, whether from the perspective of a theory of social cycles (Hirschman 2002, the historical exhaustion of a commitment model (e.g. Fuchs Ebaugh 1988), or even a backlash and return to order. This is what Whalen and Flacks (1989), for example, show in their work on what became of American students opposed to the Vietnam War. According to them, the primary cause of the decline of the 1960s was related to a change in the *Zeitgeist*. The Vietnam War was coming to an end while the repression of leftist movements was intensifying. Such a context led to a re-evaluation of the revolution's chances for success, as well as of the cost of involvement. Specifically, it became more and more difficult for young activists to sacrifice their professional future to the increasingly remote possibility of reforming society. The question of the *personal versus the political* carried the day. In the same way, the success, rather than the decline, of a movement may erode convictions. Indeed, the satisfaction of demands, along with the eventual institutionalization of movements as they are integrated into the state's decision-making processes, may lead to a rethinking of priorities and demobilization. Examples are the demobilization of gay movements at the end of the 1970s and the emergence of state feminism.

On the other hand, the loss of ideological conviction may also stem from a *rupture of the consensus* within the movement, the appearance of factions or splinter groups. Social psychology, notably based on the study of small groups, shows under what conditions loyalty to the group can be maintained. For example, Kanter (1972) proposes a typology of elements likely to encourage attachment, constructed around the two mechanisms of *sacrifice* and *investment:* the more sacrifices required to enter a group and remain, the higher the cost of defection. Here, Kanter is inspired by the concept of cognitive dissonance to stress the psychological dimension of the cost: the more intense the efforts, the more difficult it is to acknowledge the futility of these efforts. The notion of disinvestment, for its part, is linked to the existence of alternatives. The more individuals are caught in a system which is the only one distributing rewards and costs, the more they remain involved.

Finally, disengagement may be interpreted in terms of the transformation of relations of sociability within groupings. Indeed, the manner in which groups support these relations both inside and outside the groups reveals an array of significant factors affecting withdrawal. For example, McPherson and his colleagues produced interesting results on networks of sociability, their role in maintaining commitment and the importance of intragroup relations in the decision to defect (McPherson et al. 1992; Cress et al. 1997). In particular, they show that when individuals are part of multiple networks, they are more likely to leave the organizations (*niche overlap hypothesis*). They also show that voluntary associations lose atypical members faster than more typical volunteers (*niche edge hypothesis*). This finding is consistent with Kanter's observations that, when groups are underrepresented in an organization, they experience tensions and are generally excluded from informal friendship networks created in the course of their activism. So, overall, individual withdrawal is often inseparable from tensions observable amongst generations of activists.

AVENUES FOR FUTURE RESEARCH

While research has certainly made progress in understanding the mechanisms of individual demobilization, a certain number of avenues remain insufficiently explored. Thus, for example, at the mesosociological level, we still lack a reliable typology of the diversity of routes chosen by social movement organizations that are undergoing a process of demobilization. Certain cases are clearly identifiable, starting with those of bureaucratization, institutionalization and assimilation by the state or, on the contrary, of radicalization, to which we add the periods of abeyance, highlighted by Taylor (1989) and perfectly illustrated by Osa (2003). Yet this is still insufficient.

In addition, research could more systematically study the way in which some macrosocial contexts discourage or encourage certain paths to demobilization. The existence or availability (most often via the state) of possibilities of reconversion is an example of this. From this point of view, the literature on so-called terrorist movements or on leaving armed conflicts, especially around the issue of rehabilitation programs, as well as that dealing with public policies to end crises and to encourage disarmament of armed groups, constitutes a valuable tool. This helps in understanding what impedes and what accelerates the phenomena of demobilization at both the meso- and micro-sociological level (Björgo and Horgan 2009). Finally, the consequences of phenomena of political demobilization over the short and long term also raise a series of fascinating questions which the literature has largely ignored, except with respect to the biographical consequences of involvement. Thus, for example, and to conclude, while there is considerable questioning on the spread of social movements from a positive perspective, it would also be interesting to explore the effects across time and space of the failure of a movement, a campaign, or an organization on other movements or campaigns, whether in an alliance network or a conflict network. Thus, to give only three examples, we would gain a more thorough understanding of the consequences of the crushing of the Paris Commune in 1871, the revolutions of 1848, or even the Chinese, Beijing student movement in 1989.

More broadly, research on disengagement suggests that activism can undoubtedly generate profound and widespread socialization effects on individuals by transforming their sense of identity and politicizing the resulting social identification. However, much work is needed in order to build a comprehensive and solid theoretical model for the study of the multiple socializing effects of social movements. And apart from a few exceptions, research has mainly dealt with committed activists, without exploring not-so-committed participants; little has been done in order to disentangle the respective effects of political organizations' molding and socialization due to the mere participation to protest events; and, in existing research, age seems not to be considered as playing a role in explaining individual outcomes. Indeed, age is considered as an important variable in explaining commitment propensity (see McAdam's notion of *biographical availability*). But when it comes to analysis of biographical consequences, age is no longer mobilized as a central variable; lastly, analysis of post-movement paths of individual development is less interested in the very process of subsequent life course than in understanding the socio-historical structuring of activists' careers.

References

Abbot, A. (1983). "Sequences of Social Events: Concepts and Methods for the Analysis of Order in Social Processes. *Historical Methods*. 16 (4): 129–147.

Abbot, A. (1988). "Transcending General Linear Reality." *Sociological Theory*. 6.

Abbot, A. (1995). "Sequence Analysis: New Methods for Old Ideas." *Annual Review of Sociology*. 21: 93–113.

Becker, H. (1966) *Outsiders*. Glencoe, IL: Free Press.

Bennani-Chraibi, M. and Fillieule, O., eds. (2003). *Résistances et protestations dans les sociétés musulmanes*. Paris: Presses de Sciences Po.

Björgo, T. and Horgan, J., eds. (2009). *Leaving Terrorism Behind. Individual and Collective Disengagement*. London and New York: Routledge.

Combes, H. and Fillieule, O. (2011). "Repression and Protest. Structural Models and Strategic Interactions." *Revue française de science Politique, English.* 6(61): 1–24.

Cress, D. J., McPherson, M., and Rotolo, Th. (1997). "Competition and Commitment in Voluntary Memberships: The Paradox of Persistence and Participation." *Sociological Perspectives.* 40: 61–80.

Curtis R. L. and Zurcher L. A. (1973). "Stable Resources of Protest Movements: The Multi-Organizational Field." *Social Forces.* 52 (1): 53–61.

della Porta, D. (1995). *Social Movements, Political Violence and the State. A Comparative Analysis of Italy and Germany.* New York: Cambridge University Press.

Demerath N. J. III, Marwell G., and Aiken M. T. (1971). *Dynamics of Idealism.* San Francisco: Jossey-Bass Inc Publishers.

Fillieule O. (2001). "Propositions pour une analyse processuelle de l'engagement individual." *Revue française de science politique.* 51(1–2): 199–215.

Fillieule, O., ed. (2005). *Le Désengagement militant.* Paris: Belin.

Fillieule O. (2010). "Some Elements of an Interactionist Approach to Political Disengagement." *Social Movement Studies.* 9(1): 1–15.

Fillieule, O. and Blanchard, P. (2013). "Fighting Together. Assessing Continuity and Change in Social Movement Organizations Through the Study of Constituencies' Heterogeneity." In *The New Political Sociology,* edited by Kauppi Niilo, 79–110. ECPR press.

Fillieule, O. and Neveu E., eds. (2014). *Activists Forever? The Long Term Impact of Political Activism in Various Contexts.* Minnesota: University of Minnesota Press.

Fillieule O. and Roux P. (dir.) (2008) *Le sexe du militantisme.* Paris: Presses de Sciences Po.

Freedman D. et al. (1988). "The Life-History Calendar: A Technique for Collecting Retrospective Data." *Sociological Methodology.* 37–68.

Fuchs-Ebaugh, H. R. (1988). *Becoming an Ex: The Process of Role Exit.* Chicago: University of Chicago Press.

Glasner, T. and van der Vaart, W. (2009). "Applications of Calendar Instruments in Social Surveys: A Review." *Quality and Quantity.* 43: 333–349.

Gurin, P. and Epps, E. (1975). *Black Consciousness, Identity and Achievement.* New York: Wiley.

Hirschman, A. O. (2002). *Shifting Involvements: Private Interest and Public Action* (Twentieth-Anniversary Edition). Princeton: Princeton University Press.

Introvigne, M. (1999). "Defectors, Ordinary Leavetakers and Apostates: A Quantitative Study of Former Members of New Acropolis in France." *Nova Religio, The Journal of Alternative and Emergent Religions.* 3(1): 83–99.

Kanter, R. M. (1972). *Commitment and Community: Communes and Utopias in Sociological Perspective.* Cambridge, MA: Harvard University Press.

Klandermans, B. (1997). *The Social Psychology of Protest.* Cambridge, MA: Blackwell.

Klawiter M. (2008). *The Biopolitics of Breast Cancer.* Minnesota: University of Minnesota Press.

Linde, C. (1993) *Life Stories. The Creation of Coherence,* Oxford: Oxford University Press.

McAdam, D. (1988). *Freedom Summer.* Oxford: Oxford University Press.

McPherson, J. M., Popielarz, P., and Drobnic, S. (1992). "Social Networks and Organizational Dynamics." *American Sociological Review.* 57(2): 153–170.

Osa, M. (2003). *Solidarity and Contention: Networks of Polish Opposition.* Minnesota: University of Minnesota Press.

Sapiro V. (1989). "The Women's Movement and the Creation of Gender Consciousness." In *Political Socialization for Democracy,* edited by O. Ichilov. Teachers College Press.

Sears, D. and McConahay, J. B. (1973). *The Politics of Violence: The New Urban Blacks and the Watts Riot*. Boston: Houghton-Mifflin.

Sherkat, D. E. and Blocker, T. J. (1997). "Explaining the Political and Personal Consequences of Protest." *Social Forces.* 75(3): 1049–1076.

Taylor. V. (1989). "Social Movement Continuity: The Women's Movement in Abeyance." *American Sociological Review.* 54(5): 761–775.

Van Dycke, N. et al. (2000). "Gendered Outcomes: Gender Differences in the Biographical Consequences of Activism." *Mobilization.* 5: 161–177.

Vaughan, D. (1986). *Uncoupling: Turning Points in Intimate Relationships*. Oxford: Oxford University Press.

Whalen, J. and Flacks, R. (1989). *Beyond the Barricades: The Sixties Generation Grows Up*. Philadelphia: TUP.

Whittier, N. (1995). *Feminist Generations: The Persistence of the Radical Women's Movement*. Philadelphia: TUP.

Zwerman, G. and Steinhoff, P. (2005). "When Activists Ask for Trouble: State-Dissident Interactions and the New Left Cycle of Resistance in the United-States and Japan." In *Repression and Mobilization*, edited by C. Davenport, H. Johnston, C. Mueller. Minnesota: University of Minnesota Press.

PART IV

....

HOW MOVEMENTS ORGANIZE

....

CHAPTER 18

SOCIAL MOVEMENTS AND ORGANIZATIONAL ANALYSIS

FRANK DEN HOND, FRANK G. A. DE BAKKER, AND NIKOLAI SMITH

I agree with the claim that there is no such thing as a structureless group that persists for any length of time. There is also no such thing as a protest movement that masters the basic tasks of communication and coordination, and that is nevertheless literally unorganized. So, finally, let us put those canards aside, and then maybe we can go on to consider the advantages and disadvantages to the movement of different kinds of structure or organization. (Piven 2013: 191)

INTRODUCTION

RESEARCH at the nexus of organizations and social movements has a long and rich history, in which both fields have learned a great deal from one another. Nevertheless, Soule (2013: 108) contends that the relationship has recently become "lopsided," as social movement scholarship has increasingly "turned a cold shoulder" to organizational scholarship. There might be various reasons for this development, beyond the traditional dispute as to whether "organization" is a benefit or a liability to movements. For example, Soule (2013: 108) suggests that "many movement scholars have become interested in loosely structured networks of social movement participants that deliberately eschew formal organizations." Or, they "have become interested in online activism, which may be possible without traditional social movement organizations" (Soule 2013: 108). Indeed, several contemporary social movements—opposing corporate globalization, advancing social justice—are increasingly inspired by participatory democracy, "horizontal, leaderless organization" (Sutherland, Land, and Böhm 2013) and other "post-bureaucratic" (Grey and Garsten 2001) or even anarchist principles (Graeber

2004; Benkler 2013). The apparent rejection of received principles of formal organiza-tion (March and Simon 1993) in and by these movements seems to advance an analysis on the basis of networks and collective identities. The relevance of organizational schol-arship for social movement studies can thus be perceived as being restricted to those parts of social movements that are formal organizations, that is, for social movement organizations (SMOs).

In this chapter, we seek to argue that organizational analysis has much more to offer to social movement scholarship than merely the study of formal organizations within movements.[1] More particularly, we want to convey the value of taking a less formal view on organizations to understand organization in social movements. To make this argu-ment, we need to break down the concept of "organization" in its several constitutive elements and to argue that the amount of "organization" may vary along each of them (Ahrne and Brunsson 2011). Of course, social movements are not organizations (Diani 2013), yet collective action in general and social movements in particular need organi-zation (cf. Freeman 1972), albeit not necessarily in the form of *formal* organization. We argue that both the presence and absence of organizational elements may be associated with issues, problems, tensions, and conflict within social movements, and that chang-ing the composition of the set of organizational elements is one way to address them. Benkler (2013: 216) illustrates this in his analysis of several "working anarchies" in move-ments around cooperative banking and open source software, confirming that—within these movements—"hierarchy and power reappear, to some extent and in some pro-jects, although they are quite different than the hierarchy of government or corporate organization." Similar reasoning may apply to other social movements. As the context for movements continuously changes, the presence of organizational elements will also vary over time, thus arguing against Michels' iron law of oligarchy (1962) that suggests an increasing bureaucratization over time. Moreover, this approach also provides an alter-native answer to the question of whether "organization" is beneficial or detrimental to mobilization, as this depends on the contingent balance between various organizational elements. In developing our analysis, we build on the conceptualization of "organiza-tion" by Ahrne and Brunsson (2011) to bridge ideas from social movement studies and organizational analysis.

Partial Organization of
Social Movements

Ahrne and Brunsson (2011) distinguish between networks[2] and institutions[3] that are "emergent" orders in social life, and organizations that are "decided" orders. Organizations are sometimes created *de novo*, but most often their creation builds in some way on pre-existing emergent orders. Organizations are created by decision mak-ing on various elements of organization—who is and who is not a member; which rules apply in which situations; who has what hierarchical position vis-à-vis others; what aspects of performance and behavior are monitored and how; and who is rewarded or punished, when, and how? For example, members can be recruited from pre-existing social networks and rules and hierarchy can be decided by formalizing pre-existing institutionalized patterns. When all these elements of membership, rules, hierarchy, monitoring, and sanctioning are substantially present, Ahrne and Brunsson (2011) speak of formal organizations that are "complete," as opposed to those instances of organization that are "partial" in the sense that one or more of these elements are absent. Partial organization may also be understood from the other side, when organizational elements are introduced into emergent orders. Seen in this light, organization is not a discrete entity, but a set of variables that can be present to varying degrees.

This perspective on organization is suited for the analysis of social movements and the way they organize. While many authors would agree on a conceptualization of social movements as a particular form of collective action—that is, some order in social life—that is in opposition to some political, cultural, economic, or other type of authority, there is less agreement on how to further characterize this particular form of collective action. This lack of agreement is undoubtedly related to the great variety that exists among what are or can be considered social movements. But it is also related to whether the analyst wishes to emphasize their "emergent" or their "decided" nature. In these terms, social movements have been variously conceptualized. For example, by emphasizing the beliefs and norms that are shared in a social movement, its institutional character is highlighted. Thus, social movements can be seen as "preference structures directed towards social change" (McCarthy and Zald 1977: 1218) that are the basis for a shared, collective identity, in political or cultural terms (Melucci 1995), and which can be tapped into through framing processes (Snow et al. 1986). By emphasizing the multiplexity of the inter-personal and inter-organizational relations between actors promoting collective action, their network character is highlighted (Diani 1992, 2013). Both emphases, on shared beliefs and norms and on networks, suggest that social movements are emergent orders. Meanwhile, by emphasizing the efforts that are required to make a social movement happen or even successful, its character as a decided order is emphasized (McCarthy and Zald 1977; Piven 2013).

In many cases social movements, at least parts thereof, are decided orders as decisions have been made along one or several of the five elements of organization that Ahrne and Brunsson (2011) distinguish. Although social movements can be studied as formal organizations (McCarthy and Zald 1977), or as populations of formal organizations (Zald and McCarthy 1980), they tend to escape the language and traditions of organization analysis as it is usually understood, because they are blends of emergent and decided orders. Social movements are emergent orders to the extent that people find and connect to one another, that is, build networks, on the basis of their interests, identity, and ideology (Klandermans 2004). They find each other in a common cause that needs to be articulated over time. Social movements are decided orders to the extent that (some of) the people associated with them intervene in the emergent order of social relations and shared beliefs by deliberately introducing elements of organization. Consequently, in a particular movement one finds individuals, informal groups, networks, SMOs, coalitions, and other organizations; taken together they might be conceptualized as social movement communities (Staggenborg 1998) or as organizational fields (Minkoff and McCarthy 2005; Diani 2013). Partial organization thus seems to offer an organizational approach to studying social movements.[4]

Organizational Elements in Social Movements

We consider social movements as partially organized orders, as blends of emergent and decided orders. Yet, how and why do such blended orders come into being? How and why do they change over time? After all, some of the more recent examples of protest seem to have occurred rather spontaneously. Think of the protests in the Arab world, the 2013 protests in Brazil and Turkey, the protest events around WTO meetings, and the mobilizations effectuated by Occupy. Often the role of social media and the availability of free spaces is considered to be critical in understanding whether and how such movements and their mobilizations can exist, when there is no apparent leadership or unitary organization (Bennett and Segerberg 2012; Castells 2012). This impression is reinforced through selective media coverage of the symbols of protest and the clashes with authorities. On this account Ishkanian and Glasius (2013: 9) assert that "mainstream media ignored the organisational aspects of the [Occupy] encampments," even though there was ample organization in each of these encampments, such as horizontal organizational structures, strictly enforced rules, and additional services such as classes or separate spaces for women.

In five subsections we discuss examples of seemingly "unorganized" social movement activities, drawing upon Ahrne and Brunsson's (2011) elements of organization, in order to suggest how this conceptualization of organizational analysis can speak to social movement fields and communities, and the protest events they organize. We supplement their elements with insights from the ideal-typical anarchist "organization" (Graeber 2004), which is characterized by a parallel set of principles—what may be termed "anti-organizational elements"—that closely relate to Ahrne and Brunsson's organizational elements: voluntary association versus membership, direct democracy versus hierarchy, autonomy versus rules, self-organization versus monitoring, and mutual aid versus sanction (Table 18.1). In combination, these typologies present the spectrum of the elements of organization.

Membership

Within social movement studies the notion of membership is contested. While social movements as such have participants rather than members, SMOs do have

Table 18.1 Organizational elements defined

Element	Definition*
Membership	Who is allowed to join
↕	↕
Voluntary association	Whoever joins takes part
Hierarchy	A right to oblige others to comply with central decisions
↕	↕
Direct democracy	A plight to develop consensus decisions, which are therefore binding
Rules	Explicit expectations about actions and classifications to follow
↕	↕
Autonomy	Libertarian freedom to act in the pursuit of the common cause
Monitoring	Observing performance and behavior of individuals
↕	↕
Social control	Confidence in the ability of people to oversee their own projects
Sanctions	Rewards and punishments upon individuals
↕	↕
Mutual aid	Solidarity and cooperation define relationships

* Based on Graeber (2004) and Ahrne and Brunsson (2011).

members—individuals (or organizations) that have some formalized relationship with the movement organization, such as paying a membership fee, that distinguishes them from participants, supporters, followers, bystanders, or sympathizers. Movement leaders may find it advantageous to organize the latter through membership. Members provide resources on a continuing basis. Because volunteers and constituents are scarce, SMOs compete for them and try to bind them to their respective organizations (McCarthy and Zald 1977). Membership can be a way to maintain a community of supporters during times when little or no protest goes on: "Organizations with more members have a greater pool of possible participants, and, like financial resources, larger numbers of members may signal broader legitimacy for a group and its claims" (Andrews et al. 2010: 1199–1200, commenting on the Sierra Club). Further, the number of individual members within an SMO can reduce the likelihood of its disbanding (Minkoff 1993). Membership is thus important, yet the meaning of membership in the context of social movements seems to have changed, posing new challenges to social movements.

On the one hand, various social movements are characterized by the presence of a limited number of very large SMOs who depend on membership contributions to keep their organizations "afloat" (Hensby, Sibthorpe, and Driver 2012: 812). Typically these SMOs lower the cost of participation in both financial terms and in terms of expectations of participation; they campaign "on behalf of" rather than "with" their constituents. It has been claimed that by stimulating such "checkbook activism" they pull away resources from smaller or local groups (Jordan and Maloney 2007). For them, gaining and maintaining such support can be seen as a branding strategy, intended at stabilizing their environment. Unlike the members of formal organizations, these members are not subject to other organizational elements; their bond is restricted to loyalty (cf. the members of the IKEA family). This approach to membership seems to be successful. For instance, younger members of such SMOs "feel a sense of loyalty and trust towards the SMO as an effective 'brand leader' in its field, though this is by no means unrelenting" (Hensby et al. 2012: 809). These SMOs make use of an organizational element—membership—to increase the organization of a movement.

On the other hand, some SMOs de-emphasize the use of membership as an organizational element. Early on, Melucci (1984: 829) argued that "the normal situation of today's 'movement' is to be a network of small groups submerged in everyday life." Part-time and short-time militants, whether individuals or small groups but typically with a strong need for personal involvement, could participate in various such networks; the organizational form then is "not just 'instrumental' for their goals. It is a goal in itself," intended to symbolically challenge dominant organizational patterns (Melucci 1984: 830). This trend has continued and is visible in, for example, "radical democratic networks" such as Indymedia (Pickard 2006), as well as in the many examples of post-bureaucratic "DIY" activism, in which membership of SMOs is increasingly unimportant, focussed as it is on specific protest events (Hensby et al. 2012). Regarding the latter, Bennett and Segerberg (2012: 742) point out how even established SMOs when participating in such protest events "step back from branding [them] in terms of particular organizations, memberships, or conventional collective action frames ... [but rather] cast a broader public engagement net using interactive digital media and easy-to-personalize action themes."[5] Making use of, and stimulating emergent order in movements is, indeed, an important feature of present day movements. Yet, these alternative forms of organizing give rise to specific issues that can be related to the presence or absence of organizational elements.

The Occupy London Stock Exchange (OLSX) protest camp provides a telling illustration.[6] Because the camp was open to all, it inevitably attracted homeless people looking for shelter and support. Its inclusiveness was heralded as the embodiment of Occupy's claim that current capitalism has become exclusive. It "defied capitalist ontology" by providing "food and shelter for the needy, homeless, and mentally ill ... [Thereby, it] reaffirmed humanity's potential for selfless, generous and caring ways of relating to other human beings" (Reinecke and Ansari 2013: 26). Any camper, including a homeless one, was automatically a campaigner by virtue of putting her body out there, a tactic needed to maintain the physical occupation. However, OLSX experienced that inclusiveness created, in the end, a seemingly irresolvable dilemma. There remained a clear distinction between activists and homeless people, and that was at the root of the dilemma: the ethical protest embodied in the presence of the camp depended on the camp's openness to anybody who wished to join, but the permanent presence of homeless people changed the very nature of the ethical protest as perceived from the outside, and severely drew on the encampment's resources (Reinecke and Costas 2013). For OLSX, the principle of inclusiveness invoked continuing debates on membership rules, objectives, and tactical preferences, but also on resource distribution, trust, and credibility of commitments. Attempts to resolve the issue included decision making on organizational elements, such as hierarchy, rules, monitoring, and sanctions, and resulted in a stratification of the camp's participants.

Hierarchy

Hierarchy refers to the "right that some have to oblige others to comply with central decisions" (Ahrne and Brunsson 2011: 86). Some movements choose to remain egalitarian. Hensby et al. (2012: 815) note that "Power in DIY groups [such as EarthFirst! or Rising Tide] is decentred and strictly anti-hierarchical." The protests in Brazil, Turkey, and Egypt have largely been without leaders—at least not leaders that were willing or able to represent protesters in discussions with authorities.[7] Yet, stratification of power within a movement is likely to occur. For example, Sutherland et al. (2013: 16) conclude from studying four radical, participative–democratic SMOs that "although individual leaders were not present, there was still evidence of leadership occurring." They reported on three tensions related to leadership: 1) the fact that "more outspoken members can take over and eclipse others" threatens the desire for participatory equality, 2) informality of inter-personal relationships could lead to cliques being formed where some "people had greater decision-making weight and gradually came to assume more permanent leadership positions," and 3) a gender inequality in which "the activist groups we studied unreflexively reproduced gender norms that permeated wider society" (Sutherland et al. 2013: 14–15). Such differences may be formalized, if only for limited periods of time, to create hierarchical relationships within a collective. For example, collectives may delegate tasks to particular individuals, such that these individuals become, temporary or even permanently, agents of the collective. An example might be someone taking minutes on a meeting, or another person keeping order in a meeting. The other way round, collectives may charge individuals with the discretion to represent them and to decide on their behalf in negotiations with other parties, such that these individuals become principals of the collective. Indeed, at times, three forms of hierarchy could be observed within Occupy: emergent stratification within the movement, the collective using agents for particular tasks, and the collective submitting to hierarchy entrusted upon specific individuals, for instance "based on their level of confidence, on recognition, or the length of their involvement" (Howard and Pratt-Boyden 2013: 739).

In many if not all Occupy camps, a non-hierarchical, leaderless perspective was embodied in the form of "General Assemblies," in which everybody present was allowed a voice. At various occasions it decided to create, overview, and coordinate various working groups within the camp, such as "OccupyFaith, Tent City University debates, and the High Court case" (Reinecke and Ansari 2013: 10–11). In a similar way Occupy Wall Street (OWS), set up various committees, for example, one that was responsible for media relations and a Direct Action Committee (Schneider 2011b). In the case of OLSX, this tool of decision making also led to the adoption of rules that allowed some campers to monitor and sanction other participants, specifically home-less occupants, thus challenging the perceived leaderless philosophy. A hierarchy of protest camp patrollers and enforcers were put in place to implement these new regula-tions (Reinecke and Costas 2013). In New York, Gamson and Sifry (2013: 161) observed, "There have been some attempts in the #Occupy movement to move from the pure 'general-assembly' hyper-democracy model. This includes … empowering the working groups to designate spokespeople (who rotate) but who are able to make some tactical decisions without them having to go to the whole General Assembly." Some such work-ing groups acted as agents to the General Assembly, others operated as principals of the General Assembly.

The introduction of hierarchy does not need to be permanent: working groups can be dissolved, and dedicated roles can be revoked. In the radical groups that Sutherland et al. (2013) studied such hierarchy and leadership issues tend to be temporal. The tem-porality of hierarchy, for instance through rotation, suggest that there is not always a clear build-up in organizational elements and that different organizational elements are called upon when needed. In many cases, though, hierarchy and rules of some sort go hand in hand. The presence of hierarchy seems to invoke another organizational ele-ment, rules, to confirm the hierarchy.

Rules

Rules are explicit, pronounced expectations about actions and classifications to fol-low. They come in a wide variety of sorts. Some relate to particular situations and others are more general in nature. Rules may be formulated and agreed upon when non-organizational equivalents, such as socialization or autonomy, are ambiguous or insufficiently effective. OWS for instance issued "March guidelines," formulated by its Direct Action Committee; they were posted on September 25, one day after the arrest of nearly 100 people during a protest march (Schneider 2011a) and addressed, among other things, how to respond to police and bystanders.[8] In this case, rule-setting was a direct response to previous events and were issued to reach beyond the behavioral expecta-tions communicated through socialization processes among participants.

In many Occupy camps rules were created to guide the debate, for instance to main-tain order in the General Assemblies or simply "to run the space." Collective action needs coordination and often comes with rules and procedures for how to develop to consent. Although everything can be brought up for debate, if this were done on a regu-lar basis, no collective action could ensue as hyper-democracy would paralyze all ini-tiative. Occupy's unwillingness to formulate specific demands, seen in this light, may be interpreted as an inability to develop demands, due to the complex functioning of the General Assemblies (Roberts 2012). The number of rules, and thus the frequent calling upon this element of organization, is an issue for debate. Although rules can be developed in their own right, their functioning will depend on the interplay with other organizational elements, especially their monitoring and the possible sanctioning involved.

Monitoring and Sanctions

Because monitoring and sanctions are difficult to separate in the context of social movements we here discuss them jointly. Adapted from Ahrne and Brunsson (2011), monitoring, as an organizational element for a social movement, means that compliance with its own rules or with those from extra-movement authorities—if endorsed by the movement—is attended to. Sanction refers to the use of incentives—material or immaterial rewards and punishments—that can be used when monitoring provides evidence of rule compliance or violation. Explicit monitoring and sanctioning typically occur within SMOs—such as in relation to task performance or financial control. But these elements are also found during protest events—think of crowd control in relation to previously agreed upon role performances. Although Sandy Nurse of Occupy Wall Street's Direct Action Committee (quoted in Schneider 2011b) says that "For us to go around and police everyone in the march is not respecting their way of expressing how they're participating in this movement or this action," protest events that build on a "logic of bearing witness" (della Porta and Diani 1999) depend for their success on a close mutual monitoring and adjustment by the participants during the action, in the dynamics between the event's script and the unfolding of the event. Often, this takes a form of self-monitoring that resembles "heedful interrelating" (Weick and Roberts 1993). Often, social movements attempt to maintain a certain culture, for example a commitment to nonviolence, especially during mobilizations and protest events. On the one hand, such a commitment—if shared by the participants—reduces the need for a "security culture" among the organizers of the event and fosters transparency about which behaviors participants in the event are expected to espouse, and which not (Schneider 2011b). On the other hand, techniques of nonviolent resistance need to be trained, as happened at various Occupy sites, and there might still be a need for monitoring. Schneider (2011b) reports that "The committee responsible for media relations for Occupy Wall Street has already begun preparing messaging—down to specific tweets—to use in case someone in the movement ends up using violence." At OLSX, monitoring took the form of protesters being monitored based on rules and statements decided on at the General Assembly. The "Homelessness Statement" created the role of the "Tranquility Team," also called the camp's "police force," set up to patrol the camp day and night (Reinecke and Costas 2013: 25). Tranquility Team "campaigners became enforcers of order and hygiene in the camp," thus not only patrolling, but "*managing*" homeless people, up to the point having the power "to temporarily or permanently exclude offenders from the camp" (Reinecke and Costas 2013: 26 (original emphasis)). Movements thus do decide about sanctions, both positive and negative. They can decide to give some participants more resources than others and to change a participant's status by using promotions, for example, and through negative sanctions, such as the "withholding of promotions,

or even through outright punishment, the sanction of exclusion can often be avoided"
(Ahrne and Brunsson 2011: 86).

DISCUSSION AND CONCLUSION

Because there is more organization in social movements that just SMOs, organizational analysis has more to offer than the study of formal organizations in movements. The strategies, tactics, daily activities, and outcomes of social movements are rife with organizational questions. Rather than seeing increased bureaucratization as a necessary and inevitable trend, or viewing post-bureaucratic and anarchistic principles as without any organization, we suggest that organization is a matter of variation along various dimensions. By breaking down the concept of organization in its constituting elements (Ahrne and Brunsson 2011), the notion of partial organization offers social movement scholars the language and conceptual tools to analyze and understand how "organization" matters to social movements.

Organization is not inherently good or bad to movements, nor is it necessarily and of itself beneficial or detrimental to mobilization; whether it is depends on the contingent balance between organizational elements. Likewise, from an organizational perspective, "collective action" and "connective action" (Bennett and Segerberg 2012) are not opposite categories but poles on a continuum; the discussion is not between "horizontal" organization versus "vertical" non-organization (Piven 2013), but on exactly which organizational choices are made in different situations. We may agree that in a functional way collective action critically depends on "communication and coordination" (Piven 2013: 192), but communication and coordination can be achieved in multiple ways: the question is how these prerequisites of collective action are variously organized in specific situations, and to what consequences. Partial organization is a helpful perspective to untangle this question.

Partial—instead of complete—organization can be a consequence of the inability to mobilize sufficient resources for complete organization, or it can be a choice based on ideological or strategic considerations. In either case, we expect that the partial organization of movements is not stable over time. We propose that the organization of movements changes over time, which can be conceptualized through a dialectical process model (e.g., Van de Ven and Poole 1995). At any moment in time, both the presence and the absence of organizational elements may be associated with issues, problems, tensions, or conflict within social movements, which can be addressed by changing the set of organizational elements present (that is, by the introduction or the removal of specific organizational elements). These elements, in turn, can also be present in varying degrees, as Graeber's (2004) characterization of the ideal-typical anarchist "organization" shows. After some time, new issues, problems, tensions, or conflict may emerge; these can also be addressed by changing the set of organizational elements. Hence, there is a continuing sequence of more, less, or changed organizational elements. The introduction or the removal of organizational elements is a choice that is contingent on the movement's recent past, as well as on the unfolding of events which in turn affects the movement's immediate future as well as enabling and constraining the further unfolding of events. In this sense, maintaining a purposeful order in a social movement requires considerable and continuing efforts (cf. March and Simon 1993). This observation calls for a longitudinal approach in studying the organization of social movements (Haug 2013).

Changing the set of organizational elements in a social movement may affect the character of a social movement: it may weaken or strengthen the movement. Social movements may see advantages in introducing or removing organizational elements. For example, a movement may rely for the efficacy of its mobilization on shared norms, on trust and friendship among its participants, on altruism, social capital, etc.; or it may decide to formalize these emergent orders by the introduction of one or more organizational elements, such as membership, hierarchy, rules, monitoring, or sanction. Similarly, social movement participants may resist attempts to introduce organizational elements into the movement, or they may demand their introduction. Further study is needed into such questions of how and why the partial organization of movements changes over time and how variation and change in the partial organization of social movements is associated with movement outcomes.

Partial organization is not only relevant for understanding how movements internally organize their communication and coordination; rule-setting, monitoring, and sanctioning can also be used as movement tactics toward external audiences. For example, parallel to viewing standards in the context of private regulation as "rule[s] for common and voluntary use, decided by one or several people or organizations" (Brunsson, Rasche, and Seidl 2012: 616), movements' claims can also be understood as a sort of rules oriented to the movement's targets. In this context, Occupy's unwillingness to formulate specific demands may be interpreted as a tactic in line with its ideology in the sense that making a demand would imply some recognition of the legitimacy of the institutions whose legitimacy it fundamentally contested. In a similar way monitoring and sanctioning can be used as tactics. Much of the work being done under the heading of "watch dog" groups[9] consists of collecting data about the entities they seek to "watch." To publicize these data, to espouse how targets do not comply to the rules that these groups seek their targets to adhere to, is intended to tarnish their reputations, that is, to sanction their non-compliance.

This is not to say that the framework we applied should be used without any critical assessment. Although Ahrne and Brunsson (2011) propose that organization as a decided order is distinct from networks and institutions, the exact boundaries between networks, institutions, and organization may be difficult to point out as all three sources of social order are simultaneously present in movements. For example, the interaction within networks may institutionalize such that norms appear as rules without having been formalized; however, at some point in time the possibility or need of contesting or confirming them may arise, which creates transparency and which explicates or transforms the norm as a rule. Furthermore, it might seem that organizational elements can be "switched on and off" at the organizers' will, suggesting a high level of voluntarism and agency in social movements. However, it is more likely that there are path dependencies and contingencies in a movement's social order; hierarchies may be connected with rules, and rules with monitoring and sanctioning. Yet, various organizational elements need not be permanently present at the same time for effective mobilization in the longer run.

The vocabulary of partial organization may thus advance the study of social movements—how they evolve over time and their consequences—adding another perspective on how organizational analysis remains relevant for social movement studies. Investigating the interplay between emergent and decided orders through the dynamics of organization along its various constituting elements is a challenging task that bridges organizational studies and social movement studies. Indeed, "Research is needed to investigate the situations and patterns or interactions between organizers and the organized that give rise to more or less organization" (Ahrne and Brunsson 2011: 96). Social movements provide an excellent domain to study this interplay. Therefore, our exploration also confirms the relevance of social movements as empirical grounds for advancing organization theory.

Acknowledgement

An earlier version of this chapter was presented at cbsCSR/Copenhagen Business School. Thanks to the seminar participants and to Andreas Rasche, Mario Diani, and Christoph Haug for their helpful comments.

Notes

1. Organizational analysis—the study of the structures, processes, workings, and outcomes of organizations—has focussed on formal organizations as well as on inter-organizational relations and networks, but typically on organizations and relation as discrete entities. It has a micro tradition—organizational behavior, and a macro tradition—organization theory. Each is characterized with multiple theories, often using widely diverging epistemological and ontological assumptions.
2. Ahrne and Brunsson (2011: 88) define networks as "informal structures of relationships linking social actors, which may be persons, teams or organizations."
3. Ahrne and Brunsson (2011: 89) define institutions as "stable, routine-reproduced pattern[s] of behaviour, combined with norms and conceptions that are taken for granted by larger or smaller groups of people … Institutions are built by common beliefs and norms."
4. In political economy, Ostrom (1990) provided a similar argument, noting that the management of common pool resources was facilitated by combining different organization elements.
5. Digital media have reinforced and strengthened this trend in an instrumental manner, but have not created it.
6. Similar illustrations can be told about other Occupy encampments.
7. "Gezocht: protestleiders (m/v) in Turkije, Brazilië en Egypte." *NRC Handelsblad*, June 24, 2013.

8. OccupyWallStreet. 2011. March guidelines. Available atwww.occupywallst.org/article/march-guidelines/, posted September 25, 2011, accessed November 25, 2013.
9. Examples include CorporateWatch, investigating social and environmental impact of corporations and corporate power (www.corporatewatch.org) or GM Watch, focussing on genetic modification (www.gmwatch.org).

REFERENCES

Ahrne, Göran and Brunsson, Nils (2011). "Organization outside Organizations: The Significance of Partial Organization," *Organization*. 18(1): 83–104.

Andrews, Kenneth T., Ganz, Marshall, Baggetta, Matthew, Han, Hahrie, and Lim, Chaeyoon (2010). "Leadership, Membership, and Voice: Civic Associations That Work," *American Journal of Sociology*. 115(4): 1191–1242.

Benkler, Yochai (2013). "Practical Anarchism: Peer Mutualism, Market Power, and the Fallible State," *Politics & Society*. 41(4): 213–251.

Bennett, W. Lance and Segerberg, Alexandra (2012). "The Logic of Connective Action," *Information, Communication & Society*. 15(5): 739–768.

Brunsson, Nils, Rasche, Andreas, and Seidl, David (2012). "The Dynamics of Standardization: Three Perspectives on Standards in Organization Studies," *Organization Studies*. 33(5/6): 613–632.

Castells, Manuel (2012). *Networks of Outrage and Hope: Social Movements in the Internet Age.* Oxford: Polity.

della Porta, Donatella and Diani, Mario (1999). *Social Movements: An Introduction.* Oxford: Blackwell.

Diani, Mario (1992). "The Concept of Social Movement," *Sociological Review*. 40: 1–25.

Diani, Mario (2013). "Organizational Fields and Social Movement Dynamics." In *The Future of Social Movement Research. Dynamics, Mechanisms, and Processes*, edited by Jacquelien van Stekelenburg, Conny Roggeband, and Bert Klandermans, 145–168. Minneapolis: University of Minnesota Press.

Freeman, Jo (1972). "The Tyranny of Structurelessness," *Berkeley Journal of Sociology*. 17: 151–165.

Gamson, William A. and Sifry, Micah L. (2013). "The #Occupy Movement: An Introduction," *Sociological Quarterly*. 54(2): 159–163.

Graeber, David R. (2004). *Fragments of an Anarchist Anthropology*. Chicago: Prickly Paradigm Press (available from www.prickly-paradigm.com/sites/default/files/Graeber_PPP_14_0.pdf).

Grey, Christopher and Garsten, Christina (2001). "Trust, Control and Post-Bureaucracy," *Organization Studies*. 22(2): 229–250.

Haug, Christoph (2013). "Organizing Spaces: Meeting Arenas as a Social Movement Infrastructure between Organization, Network, and Institution," *Organization Studies*. 34(5–6): 705–732.

Hensby, Alexander, Sibthorpe, Joanne, and Driver, Stephen (2012). "Resisting the 'Protest Business': Bureaucracy, Post-Bureaucracy and Active Membership in Social Movement Organizations," *Organization*. 19(6): 809–823.

Howard, Neil and Pratt-Boyden, Keira (2013). "Occupy London as Pre-Figurative Political Action," *Development in Practice*. 23(5/6): 729–741.

Ishkanian, Armine and Glasius, Marlies (with Irum S. Ali) (2013). *Reclaiming Democracy in the Square? Interpreting the Movements of 2011–12.* London: London School of Economics and Political Science, Department of Social Policy.

Jordan, Grant and Maloney, William A. (2007). *Democracy and Interest Groups: Enhancing Participation?* Basingstoke: Palgrave MacMillan.

Klandermans, Bert (2004). "The Demand and Supply of Participation: Social-Psychological Correlates of Participation in Social Movements." In *Blackwell Companion to Social Movements*, edited by David A. Snow, Sarah A. Soule, and Hanspeter Kriesi, 360–379. Oxford: Blackwell.

March, James G. and Simon, Herbert A. Simon (1993 [1958]). *Organizations*, 2nd edn. Cambridge: Blackwell.

McCarthy, John D. and Zald, Mayer N. (1977). "Resource Mobilization and Social Movements: A Partial Theory," *American Journal of Sociology.* 82(6): 1212–1241.

Melucci, Alberto (1984). "An End to Social Movements? Introductory Paper to the Sessions on 'New Movements and Change in Organizational Forms'," *Social Science Information.* 23(4–5): 819–835.

Melucci, Alberto (1995). "The Process of Collective Identity." In *Social Movements and Culture*, edited by Hank Johnston and Bert Klandermans, 41–63. Minneapolis: University of Minnesota Press.

Michels, Robert (1962 [1911]). *Political Parties: A Sociological Study of the Oligarchical Tendencies of Modern Democracy.* New York: Free Press.

Minkoff, Debra C. (1993). "The Organization of Survival: Women's and Racial-Ethnic Voluntarist and Activist Organizations, 1955–1985," *Social Forces.* 71(4): 887–908.

Minkoff, Debra C. and McCarthy, John D. (2005). "Reinvigorating the Study of Organizational Processes in Social Movements," *Mobilization.* 10(2): 289–308.

Ostrom, Elinor (1990). *Governing the Commons: The Evolution of Institutions for Collective Action.* Cambridge: Cambridge University Press.

Pickard, Victor W. (2006). "United Yet Autonomous: Indymedia and the Struggle to Sustain a Radical Democratic Network," *Media Culture Society.* 28(3): 315–336.

Piven, Frances F. (2013). "On the Organizational Question," *Sociological Quarterly.* 54(2): 191–193.

Reinecke, Juliane and Ansari, Shahzad M. (2013). "The Unintended Overflows of Social Movements: The Shifting Relationship between Occupy London and the Church of England." Paper presented at the annual colloquium of the European Group for Organizational Studies, Montreal, Québec, July 4–6.

Reinecke, Juliane and Costas, Jana (2013). "Homo Sacer and the Biopolitical Body: Struggles of Resistance in the Occupy London Protest Camp." Paper presented at the "Embodied Identities at Work" workshop, organized by the Stockholm University School of Business, Stockholm, Sweden, May 7–8.

Roberts, Alisdair (2012). "Why the Occupy Movement Failed," *Public Administration Review.* 72(5): 754–762.

Schneider, Nathan (2011a). "#OccupyWallStreet Bleeds and Leads." Available at www.waging-nonviolence.org/feature/occupywallstreet-bleeds-and-leads/ posted September 25, 2011, accessed November, 25 2013.

Schneider, Nathan (2011b). "What 'Diversity of Tactics' Really Means for Occupy Wall Street." Available at www.wagingnonviolence.org/feature/what-diversity-of-tactics-really-means-for-occupy-wall-street/ posted October 19, 2011, accessed November 25, 2013.

Snow, David A., Rochford, E. Burke, Worden, Steven K., and Benford, Robert D. (1986). "Frame Alignment Processes, Micromobilization, and Movement Participation," *American Sociological Review.* 51(4): 464–481.

Soule, Sarah A. (2013). "Bringing Organizational Studies back into Social Movement Scholarship." In *The Future of Social Movement Research. Dynamics, Mechanisms, and Processes*, edited by Jaquelien van Stekelenburg, Conny Roggeband, and Bert Klandermans, 107–123. Minneapolis: Minnesota University Press.

Staggenborg, Suzanne (1998). "Social Movement Communities and Cycles of Protest: The Emergence and Maintenance of a Local Women's Movement," *Social Problems.* 45(2): 180–204.

Sutherland, Neil, Land, Christopher, and Böhm, Steffen (2014). "Anti-Leaders(hip) in Social Movement Organizations: The Case of Autonomous Grassroots Groups," *Organization.* 21(6): 759–781. doi: 10.1177/1350508413480254

Van de Ven, Andrew H. and Poole, M. Scott (1995). "Explaining Development and Change in Organizations," *Academy of Management Review.* 20(3): 510–540.

Weick, Karl E. and Roberts, Karlene H. (1993). "Collective Mind in Organizations: Heedful Interrelating on Flight Decks," *Administrative Science Quarterly.* 38(3): 357–381.

Zald, Mayer N. and McCarthy, John D. (1980). "Social Movement Industries: Cooperation and Conflict amongst Social Movement Organizations," *Research in Social Movements, Conflicts and Change.* 3: 1–20.

....

CHAPTER 19

NETWORK APPROACHES
AND SOCIAL MOVEMENTS

....

MARIO DIANI AND ANN MISCHE

NETWORKS clearly affect social movements, but how are movement networks themselves configured and transformed? Some network theorists differentiate between
theories of networks, accounting for network properties, and network theories, identifying the impact of certain network configurations over different aspects of social life
(Borgatti and Lopez-Kidwell 2011). Among social movement scholars, the latter type of
theorizing has been overwhelmingly dominant, if focussed almost exclusively on personal networks as facilitators of individual activism (see, e.g., Passy 2003 and Tindall's
chapter in this volume; for exceptions: Diani 1995, 2015; Mische 2008). This view is
also reflected in the distinction between "social movements campaigns" (the classic
"sustained challenge to powerholders... ") and "social movement bases," consisting of
"movement organizations, networks, participants, and the accumulated cultural artifacts, memories and traditions that contribute to social movement campaigns" (Tilly
and Tarrow 2007: 114). When focus shifts to inter-organizational ties and interactions,
network concepts tend to be abandoned in favor of strategic ones, emphasizing the purposive exchanges in which movement actors become involved in the context of specific
events or campaigns (see, e.g., McCammon and Moon's chapter in this volume).

As the link between networks and individual activism is treated elsewhere (Tindall,
this volume), we do not address it here. Instead, we focus on "theories of networks," that
is, on the processes that lead to the emergence of networks. We view social movements
as a particular form of social organization that emerges out of repeated and patterned
interactions between multiple actors (Mische 2008; Diani 2015; see also Monge and
Contractor 2003: 14, and den Hond, de Bakker, and Smith in this volume). This enables us to avoid treating collective phenomena as aggregates of the properties of their
individual components, and move toward a relational and interactive view of collective
action processes (see, e.g., Crossley 2011). While few movement analysts would theorize
against such a view, most empirical research has been driven by aggregative conceptions of social structure. The "structure" of a movement has been mainly treated as the

distribution of the traits of the elements regarded as constitutive of a movement: individual sympathizers or activists (e.g., Walgrave and Rucht 2010), organizations (e.g., Andrews and Edwards 2005), or events (e.g., McCarthy, Rafail, and Gromis 2013). Change has been mapped as variations in the properties of actors or events rather than in relational patterns.[1]

However, if collectivities are best theorized as complex bundles of multiple social relations, it is also necessary to look at the properties of the relational patterns that connect individual and organizational actors, as well as non-agentic elements such as events or cultural forms, and to examine their evolution over time. This in turn requires that we replace a view of movements as sets of discrete cases with one focussing on collective action fields. The concept of field has long gained attention from analysts of collective action, from different angles (Melucci 1996; Crossley 2002; Armstrong 2002; Goldstone 2004; Davis et al. 2008). Expanding on earlier definitions, we define collective action fields as localized relational arenas characterized by mutual orientation, positioning, and (at times) joint action among multiple kinds of actors engaged in diverse forms of collective intervention and challenge. While the systematic exploration of direct relations between individuals and organizations is essential to capture the structure of a field (e.g., DiMaggio and Powell 1983: 64–65; Kenis and Knoke 2002), it is also important to look at the connecting role played by shared events or even practices (e.g., Breiger 1974; Crossley 2002; Mische 2008).

We should note that the concept of "field" is both structural and cultural; it refers to how actors are positioned in social space by their relations and affiliations, as well as how they endow those relations with meaning through mutual orientation and discursive positioning. The scope of a relevant field can move up or down: it can be intra-sectoral, such as the field of alliances or oppositions among student groups; or it can be multi-sectoral, such as the field of student, religious, professional, NGO, and business organizations that come together in a broader civic coalition (e.g., Mische 2008). If we focus on individuals, we can even think of fields at the intra-group level, referring to the power relations among leaders within a particular student group (or factions within a party). Fields are multiple and overlapping, and actors switch back and forth among them as different sets of relationships are perceived as mattering for the interaction at hand.

Our network approach to collective action fields, as developed in our own work over the past two decades (Diani 1995, 2015; Mische and Pattison 2000; Mische 2008), has many parallels to Fligstein and McAdam's (2012) recent exploration of the field concept. However, there are several important differences. First, we focus on complex networks of actors, promoting different forms of collective action, rather than on the challenger/incumbent distinction. In doing so we concur with those (e.g., Armstrong and Bernstein 2008; King 2014) who argue that this dichotomy is problematic, in that many actors engaged in collective intervention have inter-penetrating relationships with state and non-state elites. Second, we acknowledge symbolic and material power relations as constitutive of fields, but do not centrally thematize these here (although we recognize that power dynamics within and across movement networks are an important area of future study). Third, and most importantly, while Fligstein and McAdam downplay the importance of network analysis to field approaches, we argue that network analytic tools significantly contribute to our understanding of the constitution and dynamics of different kinds of collective action fields (see also Crossley 2002, 2011).

In this chapter, we offer some principles for a relational approach to collective action that dissects the idea of field in its basic components. Our argument develops as follows. First, we discuss the difference between two slippery concepts, "relations" and "interactions." This prompts us to undertake a more fundamental exploration of what a tie represents in the context of collective action processes. We then look at how ties combine in distinct relational patterns, and at the factors (agendas, organizational models, ideological stances, political opportunities, contingent interactions) that may facilitate the emergence of some tie configurations over others. Finally, we take up one of the most important open issues of network analytic research, namely, how to study network evolution, that is, the changing patterns of ties and tie formation over the life course of social movements and cycles of protest.

THE INTERPLAY OF INTERACTIONS AND RELATIONS

While there is relative consensus among movement analysts that "networks matter," there has been some debate about whether the proper focus of analytical attention should be on "relations" or "interactions." The term "relations" signals relative stability and durability over time, and thus is critical for understanding movements in terms of structured fields of collective action. In contrast, the term "interactions" highlights the dynamism and fluidity of social engagement within particular social sites. Network analysis has traditionally focussed on presenting static snapshots of relations, often with an implicit (usually black box) claim that these have durability over time. And yet social movements are, as the name implies, based on movement—that is, on *destabilizing* a given situation and contributing to a reorganization of positions and relations within a field. Given this core concern, one might reasonably argue that social interactions within fluid and dynamic *situations* are more important to social movement analysis than durable patterns of relations.

Structural analysts have handled the distinction between interactions and social relations in different ways. In an explicit critique of network analysis, Bourdieu associated networks with ephemeral and contingent interactions, while leaving the term "social relations" to designate deep differences between social positions in terms of power and access to material and symbolic resources (Bourdieu 1992: 113–114). In the social movements field, Tilly was the force behind attempts to bring relations more explicitly into the picture (Tilly 2005, 2008; Diani 2007; Krinsky and Mische 2013). While keeping a neat distinction between networks and interactions, he turned Bourdieu's approach on its head, using the term "networks" to designate the more stable social relations that facilitate collective action (see also Tilly and Tarrow 2007: 114).

Our position challenges the dichotomy while recognizing the distinction. We understand the interplay between durable relations and contingent interactions to be critical to the emergence and evolution of movements. We consider "social networks" to be the outcome of patterned, relatively stable interactions (see also Crossley 2011). That is, most social ties are not "one off" affairs or generated purely situationally, but entail shared histories, expectations, and (often) institutionally supported *logics* of interaction (take a family, workplace, or religious tie, for example). These shared pasts and futures—which are constituted culturally, through reporting, storytelling, and scenario-building—generate varying degrees of durability and reproducibility in social relations, which we can capture in static snapshots.

However, since networks are constructed through interactions—and interactions always entail a degree of contingency and fluidity—then of course, networks change. These changes can come gradually over long periods of time; Tilly emphasizes this slower pace in his work on changing repertoires of contention (e.g, Tilly 1994, 2008). Or they can come suddenly, either as the result of exogenous events in the world (e.g., regime shifts, economic crisis, wars or natural disasters, broad institutional restructurings), or in response to endogenous movement processes (e.g., tactical reassessments in response to changing opportunities and threats, internal dissension and fragmentation, reconfigurations of alliances). Movements go through more "settled" or "unsettled" times (Swidler 1986, 2001), which in network terms, means periods in which they are actively articulating (building or breaking) ties, or periods in which they can take these relations largely for granted.

Even during periods of relative network stability, certain types of ties can be more stable and indicate stronger links than others. We can note these differences by looking at the frequency of interactions, their emotional intensity, the amount of shared risks and resources, or the volume of information flows. For example, sharing resources in a series of jointly promoted campaigns may be seen as more demanding, and therefore as evidence of a stronger tie, than the exchange of information, or the sharing of some basic facilities (e.g., Diani 1995). Moreover, some kinds of ties may persist in a state of latency over a long period of time before they are *activated* in movement contexts as the basis for "participation identities" (Gould 1995; Mische 2008). For example, histories of joint movement or group participation, past friendships or workplace ties, as well as neighborhood, clan, religious or partisan affiliations might become the basis for social movement mobilization in certain situations, even if they are not particularly salient in day-to-day interactions. The challenge for social movement analysis becomes understanding how these latent or underlying (and often quite durable and long-lasting) ties are activated in particular movement settings during the mobilization process.

What are Ties?

The problem of understanding "types of ties" has long been considered as one of the most thorny and understudied questions in network analysis (White 1992). Often it is convenient to put this question into a black box—to rely vaguely on the enumeration and mappings of "connections" between actions without differentiating between different *types* of relations (and their associated histories, logics, and expectations). Harrison White's own inquiries into this question led him to narrative and temporality as constitutive of networks ties, as we will discuss below (White 1992; Mische and White 1998). Moreover, network ties have a *performative* dimension—discursive, embodied, and institutional work goes into the characterization of relations as "friendship" or "respect" or "alliance" or "enmity" (McLean 2007).

In the case of social movements, ties serve several functions: a) as recruitment contexts (see Tindall's chapter in this volume); b) as channels of informal communication and solidarity building among movements; and c) as resources for the articulation of alliances and coalitions across organizations, movements, and movement contexts. At the same time, movements are constituted through *multiple types of ties*, and in fact, it is often the interplay between multiple types of ties (and associated network formations) that is critical for movement dynamics (e.g., McAdam and Paulsen 1993; Gould 1995; Diani 1995, 2015; Mische 2003, 2008). Here, we single out four different ways in which movement ties can be understood and studied:

1) *Direct relationships:* One of the most straightforward ways in which to study movement networks is to examine direct relationships between actors, at either the individual or the organizational level. Here, a "tie" can represent a range of types of relationships, depending upon questions being examined. For example, researchers can ask participants about their friendship or collaboration ties with other activists, or to whom they go for information, support or advice. The study of individual ties within movements can be especially important for studies of movement recruitment, as well as for the maintenance of movement commitment over time (Passy 2003; Tindall, this volume). Researchers can also move from the individual to the organizational level by asking leaders about the types of connections their organization has to other movements or groups, such as joint projects, shared information, resource pooling, tactical affinity, or ideological proximity (von Bülow 2010; Diani 2015). Such ties can be assessed for their frequency, strength, salience, and durability over time, as well as for the extent to which these multiple types of ties are correlated or intertwined with each other (e.g., pragmatic resource exchanges may or may not overlap with ideological or tactical affinities). Moreover, they can also be assessed for the extent to which blocks of actors tend to maintain similar types of relationships with others sets of actors in the networks, thus constituting network *positions* (via structural equivalence) in addition to direct relationships.

2) *Co-memberships in organizations:* A second approach to the study of movement networks is to focus not on direct ties, but on overlapping affiliations. This approach builds on Breiger's (1974) classic formalization of the Simmelian notion of the "duality of persons and groups": individuals are linked by shared memberships, while groups are linked by the members they have in common. In this case, a "tie" represents a shared affiliation—perhaps in a social movement or civil

society organization, a neighborhood or workplace, an institution of worship or faith community, or some other formal or informal grouping. While there is no guarantee that people thus "tied" have met personally or are directly connected, the fact that they belong to two (or more) different groups can provide potential channels of communication within and between these groups. Such affiliations often represent membership in common discursive communities or circles of recognition (Pizzorno 1986), and (in some cases) can generate opportunities for interaction and communication. They can also generate potential bonds (real or imagined) among co-members of particular groups. Such shared memberships can contribute to solidaristic movement subcultures (Diani 1995, 2015) as well as to movement robustness in response to repression (Osa 2003) and to opportunities for mediation and brokerage across partially disconnected groups (Mische 2008).

3) *Co-presence at events:* A third approach to understanding how ties work is to study relations formed by joint participation in events. This is a variation on the duality principle described above, with ties here composed by co-presence rather than co-membership. This is an important kind of tie for understanding social movement mobilization, incorporating attention to the *social settings* in which the projects, strategies, and alliances of movements are articulated. What can be said, planned, or imagined depends upon who is present (or just as crucially, *not* present) at the meeting, activity or protest events. Likewise, the intermingling of previously disconnected groups in broad movement publics and protests can lead to the elaboration of new connections, the sharing of discourse and tactics, or the broader integration (or segmentation) of the field (e.g., Bearman and Everett 1993; Mische and Pattison 2000; Mische 2008; von Bülow 2010). The changing dynamics of individual and group participation in events can play an important role in the acceleration (or deceleration) of a cycle of protest, and thus are critical to movement careers, as we will explore more fully below.

4) *Shared projects and practices (ideological or tactical proximity):* Finally, movement participants are often connected not only by co-membership and co-presence, but by shared goals, projects, and repertoires of contention. These kinds of ideological, discursive, or tactical ties can be measured directly by asking an organization about the strength of their shared goals, practices, or worldviews with other actors (von Bülow 2010; Diani 2015). Alternatively, we can measure these ties more indirectly, by examining the overlap in projects or practices (or other kinds of cultural elements) as these appear in interviews, questionnaires, textual production, news reports, or public discourse (e.g., Mische and Pattison 2000). In this case, we can examine how particular combinations and distributions of discursive or tactical elements help to structure relations of proximity and distance in a field, based upon the actors who jointly affirm (or use) them. Conversely, we can see how actors are linked by shared narratives and practices. This approach is useful for understanding the interpenetration of organizational and cultural ties in a movement, as well as for understanding how positionality in a field is constituted by what people do and say.

How Do Ties Combine in Different Patterns?

Not all micro interactions combine in recognizable patterns, nor do they all display continuity over time.[2] In some cases, however, informal collaborations between different organizations, or interpersonal exchanges between activists and sympathizers of a given cause, take a certain regularity, and some informal, yet relatively stable network model of social organization emerges. While social movements have long been associated with network forms of organization (Diani 1992; Tilly 1994), a network perspective enables us to identify the broader variety of relational patterns through which collective action may be coordinated.

One way to study these relational patterns is by examining how they undergird processes of communication and coordination within collective action fields. For example, Diani (2012, 2015) describes how modes of coordination of collective action are defined by different combinations of network multiplexity. In particular, he shows how modes of coordination are formed by the different properties of the networks in which two essential mechanisms of collective action, *resource allocation* and *boundary definition*, are embedded. Sometimes, decisions about the allocation of personal and organizational resources are taken mostly within specific groups or organizations, with little negotiation with other actors in the same field. At other times, a considerable amount of energy may be devoted to the building of collaborative relations with other groups, and resources may flow through dense exchanges at the field level.

The definition of boundaries, that is, of criteria that assign social actors to different groups and categories, represents another essential dimension of collective action (Tilly 2005: 8), and indeed social action at large (Abbott 1995: 870; White 2008). Boundaries mirror processes of identity building, establishing connections across time and space, for example, within different phases of personal biographies, between generations, or between events occurring simultaneously in different locations (see, e.g., Pizzorno 1986; Somers 1994; Melucci 1996: ch. 4; Pizzorno 2008; Mische 2008). Analogously to what we noticed for resource allocation, boundary definition may largely equate with the work conducted by distinct groups or associations to strengthen their own separate identity. It may also, however, rest on diffuse network exchanges within fields. Through the joint forging and/or circulation of symbols, the expression of emotions, or the sharing of militancy and friendship with people across a field, actors may develop a sense of belonging to a broader collectivity that goes beyond the confines of any specific group or organization. Rather than implying the replacement of an organizational identity with a group identity, it is reasonable to expect a variable tension between the two levels of identification (Melucci 1996; Diani 2015).

The variable density of the network exchanges within a field, related to resource allocation and boundary definition, enables us to identify four basic modes of coordination: *the social movement, coalitional, subcultural/communitarian* and *organizational* modes (see Figure 19.1). These modes represent ideal types; any specific episode or any field of collective action is likely to be constituted by different combinations of these modes. Nevertheless, we think it is useful to distinguish between them analytically, given that that they represent quite distinct relational and cultural patterns (i.e., network structures and identity processes), which in turn enable and constrain different kinds of action.

First, the "social movement" mode of coordination is defined by the intersection of *dense networks of informal inter-organizational exchanges* and processes of *boundary definition* that operate at the level of broad collectivities rather than specific groups/ organizations. Coordination takes place through dense interpersonal networks, multiple affiliations, and symbolic production. The terms of inter-organizational collaboration are informal, and need to be renegotiated each time a new issue/opportunity/threat emerges. In other words, each collective action event can be regarded as the product of a specific negotiation on forms and content of resource allocation.

As for boundary definition processes, social movements have no formal boundaries and no formally defined criteria for inclusion or exclusion. Instead, the boundaries of a movement are defined by processes of mutual recognition whereby social actors recognize different elements as part of the same collective experience and identify some criteria that differentiate them from the rest (see also Mische and Pattison 2000; Mische 2008). Likewise, organizations do not belong in a movement because of their traits, but because they define themselves as part of that movement, and are perceived as such by significant others. Also, while inter-organizational exchanges are subject to constant negotiation, the establishing of new alliances is easier if there are routines and recurrent practices that also reflect in particular identities and definitions of boundaries. Accordingly, boundary definition is sustained by activists' multiple affiliations and

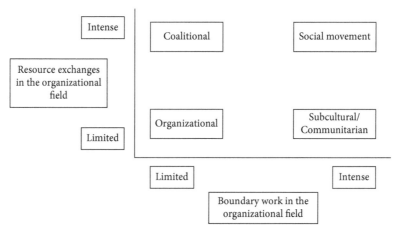

FIGURE 19.1 *Modes of coordination of collective action*

(source: adapted from Diani 2012, 110; reprinted by permission © 2012 by Cambridge University Press)

involvements in several experiences through membership, personal connections, and participation in activities (Carroll and Ratner 1996).

Multiplexity sets apart the social movement mode of coordination from another pattern that is often equated with it, namely, the "coalitional" mode. While it is very difficult to think of social movements without thinking of coalitions, the opposite does not necessarily apply (see, e.g., Tarrow 2005: 164–165). In principle, coalitions may be driven by purely instrumental motives, requiring no broader definitions of boundaries that outlive specific campaigns. Throughout the process of collective action, participants' loyalties and priorities may remain firmly within the boundaries of specific organizations. A lot of single-issue, local protest of the reactive type is best conceived as an instance of coalitional action rather than as a "social movement." Even much broader campaigns, however, may be more appropriately framed as coalitions, or at least treated as the product of multiple modes of coordination. For instance, the demonstrations that challenged the imminent war against Iraq in February 2003 seem to combine modes of coordination close on the one hand, to peace movements, on the other, to ad hoc anti-governmental coalitions, bringing together people and organizations with highly diverse agendas (Walgrave and Rucht 2010; see also Heaney and Rojas 2015).

A third mode of coordination—the "subcultural/communitarian" mode—occurs when inter-organizational linkages are sparse, yet feelings of identification with broad collectivity are widespread, and are embedded in shared practices and mutual affiliations by individual activists. In fields constituted primarily by this mode of coordination, several factors might account for the lack of dense inter-organizational networks. Sometimes, sectarianism may prevent extended alliances from developing, as in the case of radicalizing left-wing movements (della Porta 1995). In other cases, this may depend on repression, as alliance building may be discouraged by the high costs associated with public action in a repressive regime, as in post-Second World War Eastern European communist regimes (e.g., Osa 2003). In these cases, activists promote collective action primarily through the interpersonal connections developed in the context of their involvement in apparently neutral forms of social organization like cultural associations, churches, and neighborhood meeting points. At still other times, inter-organizational coalitions are missing because challenges do not take the form of public displays of organized action, but rather take place through the multiple involvement of people in cultural associations and events, in communitarian lifestyles, and in individualized alternative behaviors. Examples include significant sectors of new social movements or global justice activism (e.g., Melucci 1996; Juris 2008), as well as, more recently, in the online sphere (Earl and Kimport 2011). For all the substantive variation of content, these forms of action share the fact that the practices enacted by activists provide the main connection as well as the basis for boundary definition processes, in situations in which the role of groups and organizations is limited.

Finally, a substantive share of collective action, including of the radical type, is coordinated through "organizational" modes. Organizational forms may range from extremely hierarchical and formalized, such as twentieth-century mass parties, to extremely decentralized and informal, such as alternative communes or grass-roots groups. In all cases, however, action is promoted and coordinated by units that have an autonomous decisional capacity, whether this comes from formally appointed leaders or officers, or from the grass-roots, participatory deliberations of activists' meetings. The definition of boundaries and identity building is by no means less relevant in instances of collective action coordinated through an organizational model, than in other cases. Yet, the difference lies in the fact that loyalties and attachments are largely (in the case of sects, exclusively) focussed on specific groups and organizations rather than on broader collectivities.

If social movements and other modes of coordination may be regarded as emergent forms of social organization, it is also important not to associate the idea of organization with the idea of planned action. Although some networks may be deliberately created by organizations in order to pursue specific goals (e.g., Kahler 2009), network organizational forms, including those of civic fields, are rarely planned in their entirety (Monge and Contractor 2003: 11–16). Rather, they originate from repeated discrete decisions that a variety of groups and organizations take regarding their partners in projects and campaigns in specific local settings. It is therefore important to take a closer look at how ties are created.

WHAT FACILITATES TIE BUILDING?

If network ties can be constituted (and studied) in all of the different ways described above, this begs the question of how these ties are formed. We focus here on three conditions that facilitate tie formation: proximity in agenda, organizational model, and ideological affinity. The first of these is relatively straightforward: ties may be driven primarily by actors' proximity in agendas and goals. Organizations will be more likely to develop linkages if they have similar priorities; likewise, activists will be more likely to join organizations that are closer to their interests. However, while proximity in agendas indeed facilitates inter-organizational cooperation (e.g., McCammon and van Dyke 2010; Diani 2015: ch. 3), this is far from the only significant factor in tie formation.

In addition to shared goals, organizational models may also affect the chances and nature of ties in a variety of ways. Large organizations with a relatively well-articulated internal structure usually take different roles than grass-roots groups (Staggenborg 1986). This should in principle facilitate the development of symmetric relationships amongst actors with similar organizational properties, while asymmetric relationships should prevail between organizations which a different profile. These asymmetries in exchanges contribute both to functional differentiation (i.e., different organizations take responsibility for particular aspects of mobilization) and to power hierarchies in a field. For example, reciprocated cooperative ties between Milanese environmental organizations more frequently linked homogeneous pairs either of local branches of the most important national associations, or of neighborhood associations. In contrast, exchanges between large associations and grass-roots groups were largely asymmetrical: the former provided the latter mainly with cognitive resources, orientation or advice, while receiving mostly militancy resources in return (Diani 1995: ch. 5). More recent research on civic networks in Britain also points at the asymmetry of the relations between organizations with different network positions (Diani 2015: ch. 3).

However, relational patterns driven exclusively by interest agendas or functional division of labor are hard to find. Differences in organizational forms are often linked to ideological differences: for instance, loose organizational forms often reflect activists' commitment to principles of participatory politics and horizontal deliberation (see della Porta's chapter in this volume). More generally, differences in frames and identities—that is, in the ways in which movement actors represent themselves, their adversaries, and the object of their mobilization—can prevent ties between groups sharing interests in specific issues. Conversely, ideological proximity may bring together actors whose original agendas were not necessarily close. For examples, environmental activism in Italy in the 1970s was promoted by political ecology and conservation groups that stood on opposite sides in relation to the dominant left–right cleavage of the time. This did not facilitate the development of sustained ties, despite their shared concern for specific problems (Diani 1995). Most important, while cooperation among actors espousing different points of view is a permanent feature of movements, long-term ties cannot develop if actors differ on non-negotiable principles. Symbolic and value incentives often play a central role in promoting and subsequently maintaining the mobilization of movement activists. In contexts characterized by high sectarianism, connections with actors having even marginally different worldviews may be avoided; being seen as evidence of inclination to compromise, such connections might affect organizations' capacity to provide symbolic incentives to their own activists.

The impact of differences in organizational models, ideological stances, or other traits on tie construction may be expected to vary in different political contexts and phases of protest. However, the rare studies available to date do not provide consistent indications regarding the patterns of such relationships. On the one hand, limited or closing political opportunities may encourage network fragmentation. When a movement fails to achieve recognition and legitimacy, and/or concrete policy results, actors may rely increasingly on symbolic and solidaristic resources to counter trends to demobilization. The coupling of greater inter-organizational competition for scarce resources and heavier reliance on symbolic elements may create ever greater divisions within movement arenas. These divisions are proportional to the emphasis placed on the elements that divide as opposed to those that support convergence, sometimes up to the point of explicit factional conflict (see, e.g., della Porta 1995). However, the closing of opportunities may also strengthen activists' perception of growing threats, inducing them to engage in more coalition work than would normally be the case (see McCammon and Moon, this volume).

The picture is similarly ambiguous in contexts characterized by positive political opportunities. On the one hand, recourse to ideology as an instrument of mobilization may be reduced, as well as references to specific identities and solidarities. Accordingly, non-competitive forms of cooperation between diverse actors may increase, and criteria for alliance selection may become more inclusive. In the 1980s, for example, widespread attention to environmental problems in Italian public opinion, coupled with the reduced salience of the left–right cleavage, created favorable opportunities for the emerging environmental movement. This corresponded to a growth of the ties between groups holding different frames of environmental issues (Diani 1995). However, organizations operating in a more favorable environment might also be encouraged to act on their own without committing to broader alliances than might not be deemed so essential to achieve positive results.

One should also note that none of the factors described above can be conceived in purely static terms, as a rigid "antecedent" of tie creation. Tie building is a dynamic and situational process. Even if connections between movement organizations depended entirely on the proximity of their agendas, their interaction might still result in progressive adaptations and transformations of their original strategies and priorities. For this reason, we need to understand the processes by which relations are built, activated, nurtured, sustained, suppressed, and severed over the course of movement development. We can think about this as the "talking of the tie," or the *articulation* of linkage as a key component of the constitution of relationships (Mische 2008: ch. 5). As noted above, this is (at least in part) a cultural and discursive process; it involves the narration of a shared past, present, and future. These articulations—which evolve over the course of a movement—help to constitute the relationship as being, for example, one of friendship or enmity, of alliance or opposition, or of entailing varying degrees of shared goals, resources, tactics or ideas (Gould 2003; Mische 2003, 2008; McLean 2007).

As Sidney Tarrow (2013) has recently argued, language plays a critical role in the relational process that underlies movement networks. Language, storytelling, and symbolic displays of identity (Taylor and Whittier 1992; Tilly 2005) contribute to the activation and deactivation of identity boundaries, which, as we have shown above, are distinguishing components of modes of coordination in movement networks. Moreover, while network ties have varying degrees of durability over time, they are also situationally activated. Whether activists actively display (i.e., dramaturgically *perform*) their affiliations with political parties, religious associations, civil society organizations, racial–ethnic groups, or gender/sexuality categories may depend upon the contingencies of particular interaction settings. Such performances help to constitute "group styles," that is, joint *definitions of the situation* as to the purposes and practices that are appropriate in particular movement settings (Goffman 1959, 1974; Eliasoph and Lichterman 2003; Mische 2008). For example, Mische (2008) shows how Brazilian youth activists combined displays of partisanship with those of other forms of association (student, religious, labor, professional) in varying ways as they moved between movement settings, and engaged in different kinds of coalition building and political challenge. She also shows how these relations changed historically, mapping the coupling and decoupling of these different types of ties over the course of two decades of democratic reconstruction.

HOW TO EXPLORE NETWORK
CHANGE OVER TIME

In the sections above, we have discussed what ties are, how they combine to compose movement networks, and how they are generated. We turn now to a more field-level understanding of how networks develop and change over the life course of a movement. The social movements literature largely agrees that social networks contribute to movement dynamics, particularly via the mechanisms of recruitment, tactical diffusion, and coalition building, which are often seen as "building on" or "flowing through" pre-existing networks. However, this image of networks as "conduits" has been criticized in recent work as presenting a static and reified understanding of how networks are constituted (e.g., Mische 2011). Less attention has been paid to determining how movements generate change in networks, or how the careers of networks, movements, and broader collective action fields are intertwined. We consider this an area that is ripe for future study, with only a few recent initiatives in this direction.

The temporal dynamics of social movements have been considered in a number of ways, most importantly through the analysis of event sequences (Biggs 2002), cycles of protest (Tarrow 2011; McCarthy, Rafail, and Gromis 2013), and organizational growth and decay (Minkoff 1999). While this research has provided valuable insights, for the most part it has not directly incorporated attention to changing networks. We would like to suggest two ways in which we can study the interplay of network and movement dynamics, focussing on network changes across cycles of protest, and on the trajectories of activist cohorts across changing fields.

Network Change Across Cycles of Protest

One of the more obvious ways in which movements contribute to network change is through the dynamics of participation itself. In joining a movement—or heading to the streets with an existing organization or friendship group—people stand a high likelihood of coming into contact with previously unknown people, organizations, tactics, and ideas. Many of these new encounters will fall into the category of "weak ties" (Granovetter 1973), that is, potential points of connection with other actors (or practices or ideas) that can help to bridge structural or cultural holes (Burt 1992; Breiger and Pachucki 2010) and provide opportunities for brokerage, mediation, and coalition-building (e.g., McCammon and van Dyke 2010). Other relations may be stronger and more durable; relationships formed within the heat of joint struggle can be highly emotionally charged and can generate "strong ties" that persist across the life course, as McAdam (1988) documents in the case of participants in Freedom Summer. In either case, networks change as a result of movement participation.

One interesting line of research would be to track patterns of network change across different stages of a cycle of protest (Tilly and Tarrow 2007; Tarrow 2011). For example, during the early stages of an emerging protest cycle, as a protest begins to shift in scale and generates an exuberant intermingling of people, groups, and slogans, the potential for expansion of weak ties is probably at its height. Protesters are not likely to generate strong ties with most of the new people they encounter on the streets, but nevertheless, they may forge new connections and the beginnings of shared stories, which might become activated or expanded in future encounters. We might call this the *amplification* stage, as weak ties and loose chains of connections span structural holes and bring previously disconnected clusters of actors into movement activity (Mische 2008: ch. 5). In the language of modes of coordination highlighted earlier, we may be witnessing a growth of "coalitional" patterns, in which multiple collaborations develop, yet on what is still largely an ad hoc, issue-related basis.

As these bridges are formed (and structural holes thus eliminated or reduced in number), the shape of the network changes. Previous lines of segmentation (and associated cultural boundaries) break down, generating new lines of communication between people and groups. There is thus less need for brokers (in the classic sense). At the same time, there may be more need for cross-network negotiation and coordination as the field of actors engaged in joint movement activity becomes more heterogeneous and complex. We can call this the *consolidation* stage; this may be dominated by prominent and well-connected actors who take on the task of setting the discursive, tactical, and organizational parameters of the (still growing) collective action field. We expect the "social movement" modes of coordination to be prominent in this phase, with denser cooperation and more intensive boundary work required to hold heterogeneous actors together.

Later in a protest cycle, the relational dynamics change again. Over the course of a series of (repressive or accommodating) encounters with the state, sectors of the movement may begin to become more institutionalized, while others undergo radicalization and entrenchment. During this stage, the formation of strong ties may become more important, either through the joint construction of new organizational forms (which requires intense internal relational work), or through the formation of more intensely linked protest enclaves (underground cells, extremist factions), often in response to state repression. The formation of these more tightly bounded networks may require the cutting or weakening of some of the looser, bridging ties that helped to give dynamism and exuberance to the early stages of the movement. It may also require a dissociation from previous local networks (families, friendships, neighborhoods), as organizational participation becomes more demanding and exclusive. These changes in relational patterns may result in an increase in "organizational" modes of coordination, as bureaucratic organizations share with radical sects a focus on the organization itself to the detriment of the broader field in which it operates (Diani 2015).

If the movement goes through a process of internal competition and fragmentation, those tight-knit ties may themselves be severed and reconfigured through processes of factional segmentation and realignment. Thus in every stage in the protest cycle, networks may be in a process of change—whether through expansion and intermingling or through segmentation and boundary formation at the level of specific organizations.

Cohort Trajectories Across Changing Fields

Another way to study the temporal dynamics of movement networks is to approach them systemically—that is, by examining the changing patterns of large numbers of people moving through a system. As many scholars have demonstrated (e.g., see Walgrave and Rucht 2010), many movement activists not only have multiple affiliations at any particular point in time, but also move in and out of various types of involvements over the course of their activist careers. These may be within a particular movement sector (e.g., participating in multiple kinds of environmental or feminist organizations), or across them (e.g., moving from the civil rights to feminist to human rights to global justice movement). Activists can engage in multiple types of participation concurrently or over time; for example, they might belong to a political party or civil society organization before, during, or after participation in a broader protest movement. The movement participation itself might lead to decisions about whether to continue existing affiliations, or initiate new ones. These changes in individual trajectories in turn reconfigure the larger field of overlapping relationships through which they are moving.

We can think of this approach as "Simmel over time," providing a temporalized version of the "duality of persons and groups" concept described above (Mische 2008). Individuals can be considered as the intersection of the set of groups through which they pass over time, that is, their trajectory of overlapping affiliations. Conversely, the trajectories of groups—and their position in the broader field of relations—can be considered as the intersection of those individuals that pass through them over time. The members that they share across different time periods—and the ways that those members act upon their multiple identities in movement social encounters—help to constitute the changing structure of relations in broader fields of collective action. This approach can be very useful for mapping the changing structure of relationship between movement sectors, as composed by successive cohorts of activists moving through the field (e.g., Mische 2008).

Studying this systemic dimension requires a focus on the changing structure of intersecting relationships that may only be partly visible to actors, but that nevertheless constrain opportunities and choices. In other words, to understand what actors can see, say, and do, we have to understand where and with whom they are positioned in the larger system of overlapping relations. Activists' structural positions shape the kinds of careers that they develop, influencing which involvements they take on and which they drop or avoid. For example, becoming a student, labor or environmental activist may *entail* adopting a political party affiliation in some regions of a field, in order to gain recognition and legitimation; in other regions partisan engagement may be discouraged or proscribed. Such field-generated pressures and possibilities may change over time, in response to shifting political opportunities and threats as well as to internal reassessments of goals and tactics. The choices made by successive cohorts of activists in response to these pressures and possibilities influence the future structure of intersections in a multi-sectoral field.

CONCLUSIONS

The language of networks and fields has gained increasing popularity among social movement analysts, whether in an analytic or a metaphorical form. As such developments have been repeatedly charted (see, e.g., Armstrong and Bernstein 2008; Crossley 2002, 2011; Diani 2011; Mische 2011), here we have engaged in a more foundational exercise, looking at some of the mechanisms that generate network structures and shape their patterns. Starting from the vexed question of the distinctiveness of relations and interactions, we have then introduced various types of ties between movement actors, their combination into broader patterns or "modes of coordination" (Diani 2012, 2015), and some of their generative mechanisms.

Going through these different steps has enabled us to show how to re-establish the connection between networks, and in particular network analysis, and the study of social fields. Always disputed in some social science milieus (Bourdieu 1992), such a connection has recently been pointedly dismissed, in specific reference to social movement analysis (Fligstein and McAdam 2012). We are convinced that social network analysis may fruitfully contribute to what we regard as the main intellectual goal of field analysis in social movement research: namely, approaching collective action processes as the result of the patterned interactions between multiple, interdependent actors, rather than as the aggregation of individual actors' characteristics and orientations. While we happily accept that strategic choices by specific actors are important elements in the construction of a field, we also stress the importance of mapping how such choices combine in broader structural patterns. To this purpose, network analysis provides a range of useful conceptual and methodological tools. At the same time, network analysts certainly need to devote more energy to the exploration of network variation over time, an area correctly singled out by critics of current network analytic studies. There is an urgent need for proper datasets, enabling us to build on available contributions (Mische 2008; Wang and Soule 2012).

Finally, a network analytic approach may facilitate our understanding of the empirical complexity of collective action fields. Despite repeated theoretical claims to the contrary, when it comes to empirical research, there is still substantial confusion with the identification of the various forms of collective action. While social movements are inevitably diverse phenomena, we see little analytic gain from applying the same label to instances of collective action that range from single-issue, local campaigns to national (sometime, transnational) systemic challenges. Nor do we regard it as useful to treat as distinctive movements campaigns on issues that a field perspective shows to be actually just a fully integrated part of broader collective efforts (on this, Diani 2015: ch. 9).

Network analysis may help us to identify the different forms that collective action takes in the context of broader fields, without renouncing the aspiration to explore the links between them.

NOTES

1. Diani (2015: ch. 1) offers a broader discussion of this issue.
2. This section draws upon text from Diani 2015 (ch. 1). Reprinted by permission © 2015 by Cambridge University Press.

REFERENCES

Abbott, Andrew (1995). "Things of Boundaries." *Social Research.* 62: 857–882.

Andrews, Kenneth T. and Edwards, Bob (2005). "The Organizational Structure of Local Environmentalism," *Mobilization.* 10: 213–234.

Armstrong, Elizabeth A. (2002). *Forging Gay Identities: Organizing Sexuality in San Francisco, 1950–1994.* Chicago: University of Chicago Press.

Armstrong, Elizabeth A. and Bernstein, Mary (2008). "Culture, Power, and Institutions: A Mu lti-Institutional Politics Approach to Social Movements," *Sociological Theory.* 26: 74–99.

Bearman, Peter and Everett, Kevin D. (1993). "The Structure of Social Protest, 1961–1983," *Social Networks.* 15: 171–200.

Biggs, Michael (2002). "Strikes as Sequences of Interaction The American Strike Wave of 1886," *Social Science History.* 26: 583–617.

Borgatti, Stephen P. and Lopez-Kidwell, Virginie (2011). "Network Theory." In *The Sage Handbook of Social Network Analysis*, edited by Peter Carrington and John Scott, 40–54. London: Sage.

Bourdieu, Pierre (1992). *An Invitation to Reflexive Sociology.* Edited by Loic J.D. Wacquant. Cambridge: Polity Press.

Breiger, Ronald (1974). "The Duality of Persons and Groups," *Social Forces.* 53: 181–190.

Breiger, Ronald and Pachucki, Mark A. (2010). "Cultural Holes: Beyond Relationality in Social Networks and Culture," *Annual Review of Sociology.* 36: 205–224.

Burt, Ronald S. (1992). "The Social Structure of Competition." In *Networks and Organizations*, edited by Nitin Nohria and Robert Eccles, 57–91. Boston, MA: Harvard Business School Press.

Carroll, William K. and Ratner, Robert S. (1996). "Master Framing and Cross-Movement Networking in Contemporary Social Movements," *Sociological Quarterly.* 37: 601–625.

Crossley, Nick (2002). *Making Sense of Social Movements.* Buckingham: Open University Press.

Crossley, Nick (2011). *Towards Relational Sociology.* London: Routledge.

Davis, Gerald F., Morrill, Calvin, Rao, Hayagreeva, and Soule, Sarah (2008). "Introduction: Social Movements in Organizations and Markets," *Administrative Science Quarterly.* 53: 389–394.

della Porta, Donatella (1995). *Social Movements, Political Violence and the State.* Cambridge: Cambridge University Press.

Diani, Mario (1992). "The Concept of Social Movement," *Sociological Review.* 40: 1–25.

Diani, Mario (1995). *Green Networks. A Structural Analysis of the Italian Environmental Movement*. Edinburgh: Edinburgh University Press.

Diani, Mario (2007). "The Relational Element in Charles Tilly's Recent (and Not so Recent) Work," *Social Networks*. 29: 316–323.

Diani, Mario (2011). "Social Movements and Collective Action." In *The Sage Handbook of Social Network Analysis*, edited by Peter Carrington and John Scott, 223–235. London: Sage.

Diani, Mario (2012). "Modes of Coordination of Collective Action: What Actors in Policy Making?" In *Networks in Social Policy Problems*, edited by Marco Scotti and Balazs Vedres, 101–123. Cambridge/New York: Cambridge University Press.

Diani, Mario (2015). *The Cement of Civil Society: Studying Networks in Localities*. Cambridge/New York: Cambridge University Press.

DiMaggio, Paul and Powell, Walter W. (1983). "The Iron Cage Revisited: Institutional Isomorphism and Collective Rationality in Organizational Fields," *American Sociological Review*. 48: 147–160.

Earl, Jennifer and Kimport, Kathrin (2011). *Digitally Enabled Social Change Activism in the Internet Age*. Boston, MA: MIT Press.

Eliasoph, Nina and Lichterman, Paul (2003). "Culture in Interaction," *American Journal of Sociology*. 108: 735–794.

Fligstein, Neil and McAdam, Doug (2012). *A Theory of Fields*. Oxford: Oxford University Press.

Goffman, Erving (1959). *The Presentation of Self in Everyday Life*. New York: Anchor Books.

Goffman, Erving (1974). *Frame Analysis*. New York: Harper and Row.

Goldstone, Jack (2004). "More Social Movements or Fewer? Beyond Political Opportunity Structures to Relational Fields," *Theory and Society*. 33: 333–365.

Gould, Roger V. (1995). *Insurgent Identities*. Chicago: Chicago University Press.

Gould, Roger V. (2003). "Why Do Networks Matter?" In *Social Movements and Networks*, edited by Mario Diani and Doug McAdam, 233–257. Oxford: Oxford University Press.

Granovetter, Mark (1973). "The Strength of Weak Ties," *American Journal of Sociology*. 78: 1360–1380.

Heaney, Michael and Rojas, Fabio (2015). *Party in the Street: The Antiwar Movement and the Democratic Party after 9/11*. Cambridge/New York: Cambridge University Press.

Juris, Jeffrey S. (2008). *Networking Futures: The Movements against Corporate Globalization*. Durham, NC: Duke University Press.

Kahler, Miles (2009). "Collective Action and Clandestine Networks: The Case of Al-Qaeda." In *Networked Politics: Agency, Power, and Governance*, edited by Miles Kahler, 103–124. Ithaca, NY: Cornell University Press.

Kenis, Patrick and Knoke, David (2002). "How Organizational Field Networks Shape Interorganizational Tie-Formation Rates," *Academy of Management Review*. 27: 275–293.

King, Brayden (2014). Review of Neil Fligstein and Doug McAdam: A Theory of Fields. *Administrative Science Quarterly*. 60: NP4–NP6.

Krinsky, John and Mische, Ann (2013). "Formations and Formalisms: Charles Tilly and the Paradox of the Actor," *Annual Review of Sociology*. 39: 1–26.

McAdam, Doug (1988). *Freedom Summer*. New York: Oxford University Press.

McAdam, Doug and Paulsen, Ronnelle (1993). "Specifying the Relationship between Social Ties and Activism," *American Journal of Sociology*. 99: 640–667.

McCammon, Holly and van Dyke, Nella (2010). "Applying Qualitative Comparative Analysis To Empirical Studies of Social Movement Coalition Formation." In *Strategic Alliances: New*

Studies of Social Movement Coalitions, edited by Nella Van Dyke and Holly McCammon, 292–315. Minneapolis, MN: University of Minnesota Press.

McCarthy, John D., Rafail, Patrick, and Gromis, Ashley (2013). "Recent Trends in Public Protest in the U.S.A.: The Social Movement Society Thesis Revisited." In *The Future of Social Movement Research: Dynamics, Mechanisms, and Processes*, edited by Jacqueline van Stekelenburg, Conny Roggeband, and Bert Klandermans, 369–396. Minneapolis, MN: University of Minnesota Press.

McLean, Paul (2007). *The Art of the Network: Strategic Interaction and Patronage in Renaissance Florence*. Durham, NC: Duke University Press.

Melucci, Alberto (1996). *Challenging Codes*. Cambridge/New York: Cambridge University Press.

Minkoff, Debra (1999). "Bending with the Wind: Organizational Change in American Women's and Minority Organizations," *American Journal of Sociology*. 104: 1666–1703.

Mische, Ann (2003). "Cross-Talk in Movements: Reconceiving the Culture-Network Link." In *Social Movements and Networks*, edited by Mario Diani and Doug McAdam, 258–280. Oxford: Oxford University Press.

Mische, Ann (2008). *Partisan Publics*. Princeton, NJ: Princeton University Press.

Mische, Ann (2011). "Relational Sociology, Culture, and Agency." In *The Sage Handbook of Social Network Analysis*, edited by Peter Carrington and John Scott, 80–97. London: Sage.

Mische, Ann, and Pattison, Philippa (2000). "Composing a Civic Arena: Publics, Projects, and Social Settings," *Poetics*. 27: 163–194.

Mische, Ann, and White, Harrison C. (1998). "Between Conversation and Situation: Public Switching Dynamics across Network Domains." *Social Research*. 65: 695–724.

Monge, Peter R. and Contractor, Noshir S. (2003). *Theories of Communication Networks*. Oxford: Oxford University Press.

Osa, Maryjane (2003). *Solidarity and Contention. Networks of Polish Opposition*. Minneapolis, MN: University of Minnesota Press.

Passy, Florence (2003). "Social Networks Matter. But How?" In *Social Movements and Networks*, edited by Mario Diani and Doug McAdam, 21–48. Oxford: Oxford University Press.

Pizzorno, Alessandro (1986). "Some Other Kind of Otherness." In *Development, Democracy and the Art of Trespassing*, edited by Alejandro Foxley, Michael M. Pherson, and Guillermo O'Donnell, 353–373. Notre Dame, IN: University of Notre Dame Press.

Pizzorno, Alessandro (2008). "Rationality and Recognition." In *Approaches in the Social Sciences*, edited by Donatella della Porta and Michael Keating, 162–174. Cambridge: Cambridge University Press.

Somers, Margaret (1994). "The Narrative Constitution of Identity. A Relational and Network Approach," *Theory and Society*. 23: 605–649.

Staggenborg, Suzanne (1986). "Coalition Work in the Pro-Choice Movement," *Social Problems*. 33: 374–390.

Swidler, Ann (1986). "Culture in Action: Symbols and Strategies," *American Sociological Review*. 51: 273–286.

Swidler, Ann (2001). *Talk of Love: How Culture Matters*. Chicago: University of Chicago Press.

Tarrow, Sidney (2005). *The New Transnational Activism*. Cambridge: Cambridge University Press.

Tarrow, Sidney (2011). *Power in Movement*, 3rd edn. New York/Cambridge: Cambridge University Press.

Tarrow, Sidney (2013). *The Language of Contention: Revolutions in Words, 1688–2012.* Cambridge: Cambridge University Press.

Taylor, Verta and Nancy Whittier (1992). "Collective Identity in Social Movement Communities." In *Frontiers of Social Movement Theory*, edited by Aldon D. Morris and Carol Mueller, 104–129. New Haven, CT: Yale University Press.

Tilly, Charles (1994). "Social Movements as Historically Specific Clusters of Political Performances," *Berkeley Journal of Sociology.* 38: 1–30.

Tilly, Charles (2005). *Identities, Boundaries, and Social Ties.* Boulder, CO: Paradigm.

Tilly, Charles (2008). *Contentious Performances.* Cambridge: Cambridge University Press.

Tilly, Charles and Tarrow, Sidney (2007). *Contentious Politics.* Boulder, CO: Paradigm.

von Bülow, Marisa (2010). *Building Transnational Networks. Civil Society Networks and the Politics of Trade in the Americas.* New York/Cambridge: Cambridge University Press.

Walgrave, Stefaan, and Dieter Rucht, eds. (2010). *The World Says No to War: Demonstrations Against the War in Iraq.* Minneapolis: University of Minnesota Press.

Wang, Dan and Soule, Sarah (2012). "Social Movement Organizational Collaboration: Networks of Learning and the Diffusion of Protest Tactics, 1960–1995," *American Journal of Sociology.* 117: 1674–1722.

White, Harrison C. (1992). *Identity and Control: A Structural Theory of Social Action.* Princeton NJ: Princeton Universit Press.

White, Harrison C. (2008). *Identity and Control. How Social Formations Emerge.* Princeton: Princeton University Press.

CHAPTER 20

SOCIAL MOVEMENT COALITIONS

HOLLY J. MCCAMMON AND MINYOUNG MOON

In most cases, social movements are amalgamations of diverse groups, often with the same general goal, but with differences in specific agendas, identities, and strategic orientations. Increasingly social movement scholars note this complex nature of social movements and have begun to consider coalitions in social movements as an important means of orchestrating joint work. While a body of scholarship on movement coalitions is emerging, there remains additional work to be done. This chapter reviews this literature, examines its main themes, and identifies important avenues for future research.[1] After discussing definitions of movement coalitions, we discern two foci in the research: examinations of key facilitators of coalitions and studies of their consequences.

DEFINING SOCIAL MOVEMENT COALITIONS

Social movement coalitions occur when distinct activist groups mutually agree to cooperate and work together toward a common goal.[2] Zald and Ash (1966), in an early treatment of coordinated action among movement groups, distinguish coalitions from mergers, stating that a "coalition pools resources and coordinates plans, while keeping distinct organizational identities." Mergers, on the other hand, entail groups uniting into one organization with one organizational structure and a fused identity. More recently, Tarrow (2005: 163–164) differentiates networks and coalitions by defining networks as a set of loose ties among groups often with some information exchange but little or no actual purposive, collaborative action. Ellingson, Woodley, and Paik (2012) point out that information sharing in broader networks can bolster inter-organizational trust that, in turn, can lead to coalition activities, as groups build on weak ties and make decisions to pursue mutually-agreed-upon activism. Social movement coalitions, then, might be said to reside on a continuum between mergers and networks, as a mid-range relationship entailing cooperative joint action while distinct organizational identities and structures remain intact.

Social movement coalitions can form within social movements or can emerge across different social movements. Scholars note that a variety of movements reveal coalition work, including the LGBT (D'Emilio 1983), women's (Gilmore 2008); environmental (Lichterman 1995; Murphy 2005), civil rights (Mantler 2013), and labor movements (Williams 1999). Researchers also describe activist coalitions across social movements, between labor and other civil society organizations (Dixon and Martin 2012; Heery, Williams, and Abbott 2012), immigrant rights and queer movements (Luibheid and Khokha 2001), environmental and peace groups (Beamish and Luebbers 2009), and religious and environmental groups (Ellingson, Woodley, and Paik 2012).

Levi and Murphy (2006) add a temporal dimension, recognizing both short-lived and longer-term coalitions. They distinguish between "event" and "enduring" alliances, with event coalitions occurring when collaborators coordinate their actions only relatively briefly around a specific protest event. Enduring coalitions, on the other hand, take place when activist groups formalize a more durable cooperative relationship that often involves joint decision-making structures and agreed-upon rules for participation. These more permanent alliances may result in an umbrella organizational structure with its own staff and funding to coordinate coalition work.

In addition to the degree of formalization and permanency, social movement coalitions can vary along other dimensions. Di Gregorio's (2012) research considers the intensity of coalition structures, noting that some alliances are based on strong bonds with frequent interaction while others involve only a few concrete exchanges among groups. In addition, studies by both Van Dyke (2003) and Mix (2011) tell us that some coalitions form around single issues, while others are more expansive, encompassing multiple concerns.

Not surprisingly, scholarship on social movement coalitions reveals important diversity in membership composition as well, with considerations especially of race, ethnic, class, political, and religious diversity within alliances (Beamish and Luebbers 2009; Okamoto 2010; Roth 2010). Moreover, researchers (Banaszak 2010; Isaac 2010) observe that some movement organizations join in partnerships with state actors when they share social-change goals. Suh (2011) considers that such alliances may entail the institutionalization of social movement actors and in some cases even a moderation of their demands and tactics. Almeida (2010) investigates coordinated efforts between Latin American democratization movements and oppositional political parties, coining the term "social movement partyism." We note as well the rapidly growing literature on transnational social movement coalitions, which can include a variety of actors, for instance: local social movements, international non-governmental advocacy groups, the media, and regional and international inter-governmental organizations (Bandy and Smith 2005; Tarrow 2005; von Bülow 2011).

CIRCUMSTANCES FACILITATING AND HINDERING COALITION FORMATION

A sizeable portion of the scholarship on social movement coalitions explores circumstances facilitating alliances among movement groups (Van Dyke and McCammon 2010). Four sets of circumstances are prominent in this literature.

Shared Ideology, Identity, Interests, and Goals

A common finding is that groups sharing ideological orientations, similar identities, or common interests and goals are more likely to form alliances (Bandy and Smith 2005; Di Gregorio 2012; Park 2008). Research also confirms the reverse phenomenon: distinct ideologies can impede coalition formation (Barkan 1986; Gerhards and Rucht 1992; Diaz-Veizades and Chang 1996). Studies also reveal that partnerships become possible when an important ideological shift occurs for one group, bringing it more closely into ideological alignment with another group (McCammon and Campbell 2002; Cornfield and McCammon 2010).

But similar ideologies may not be a sufficient condition for coalition work. Scholarship affirms as well that sometimes challengers may share broad goals and have awareness of one another but still not engage in collective-action collaboration. A few studies help us understand why. Lichterman (1995) examines grass-roots environmental groups and finds agreement on broad environmental goals, but a "personalized" orientation with emphasis on traditions of individualism in the white, middle-class group he studies limits collaborations with other local environmental groups. Similarly, Roth (2010) investigates second-wave US feminist groups and finds that a politics of "organizing one's own" discouraged coalitions across racial and ethnic lines. Non-collaborative ideational orientations can override shared goals and impede collaborations. A similar avenue of scholarship considers the breadth or particularism of group beliefs and framing efforts to explain who coalesces. Van Dyke (2003), for instance, finds that among college-student groups, multi-issue groups with a broader expanse of interest areas were more likely to form alliances. Rohlinger and Quadagno (2009) similarly discover that as a politically conservative group framed its efforts using a more "particularized world view" with a narrower understanding of its political agenda, the group was less likely to engage in cooperative activism. Such scholarship alerts us to the need for more attention to the specific content of the belief systems and frames deployed by activists and how these can influence coalitions. For instance, when are ideological differences too extreme to overcome?

Social Ties

Just as prior social ties among individuals heighten chances of collective mobilization, pre-existing relationships between groups can determine who will become coalition partners (Van Dyke 2003). As noted, a growing body of research looks closely at how groups with diverging views can find a path to collaborative activism. This research fruitfully considers small group processes that occur as potential or actual coalition partners interact and negotiate differences in order to build and strengthen ties. Beamish and Luebbers (2009) examine cross-movement collaborations with race, class, gender, and place diversity and outline various steps that fuel successful exchanges, identifying both "cause affirmation" in which one group recognizes the grievances of another group, and "co-development of commitments" in which groups join the struggle of other groups, both as crucial ingredients heightening solidarity. In addition, movement coalition scholarship on social ties has begun to use advanced network analysis to examine links among groups (Park 2008; Di Gregorio 2012).

An intriguing area of research considers "bridge builders" or "brokers," that is, individuals with membership in more than one group who facilitate communication, trust, and coordinated efforts between organizations, both within and across movements (Grossman 2001; Obach 2004; Borland 2010; Reese, Petit, and Meyer 2010; von Bülow 2011). Such brokers, too, can help divergent groups negotiate differences. We view this as an exciting avenue of investigation that could dovetail with emerging social movement research on activist leadership (Morris and Staggenborg 2004). Further, coalition brokers can be critical to transnational movement coalitions, that draw on diverse groups and networks from around the globe (Bandy and Smith 2005; Tarrow 2005).

Opportunities and Threats in the Broader Context

Studies reveal that the broader political context can have an important influence on whether activist groups form coalitions. In her seminal study, Staggenborg (1986) finds that political opportunities, such as the repeal of anti-abortion laws, prompted pro-choice organizations to join together to take advantage of a more receptive political environment. But a variety of studies suggest that threats confronted by activists may be a more pivotal influence (McCammon and Van Dyke 2010). A number of researchers provide empirical evidence showing that threats to activist goals play an important role in sparking coalitions (Dolgon 2001; Grossman 2001; Van Dyke 2003; Meyer and Corrigall-Brown 2005; Dixon and Martin 2012). McCammon and Campbell (2002) study alliances between the US woman suffrage movement and temperance activists, revealing that when these groups face political defeats at the hands of legislators, they are more likely to engage in joint action. Similarly, Chang (2008), in a study of the democracy movement in South Korea, finds that government-sponsored repression heightens the likelihood of coalition formation among democracy proponents, even as state repression lowered the number of overall protest events.

McCammon and Campbell (2002) take the argument about threats even further, suggesting, based on their evidence, that while threats lead to alliance building, political opportunities do little to foster coalitions. This claim is echoed by Poloni-Staudinger's (2009) comparison of environmental movements in Britain, France, and Germany. She finds that open domestic political opportunity structures do not intensify environmental coalitions, while closed structures bolster coalition activism. Like McCammon and Campbell, Poloni-Staudinger concludes that when the political opportunity structure is open and thus more receptive to movement demands, there is little incentive for movement activists to seek coalition partners, and rather the costs of alliances can outweigh the benefits. Threats, on the other hand, can encourage activists to seek new strategies, coalition formation being one such option. della Porta's (1995) investigation of Italian activists, however, reveals that closed political opportunities can fragment movements. She finds that during such periods groups rely more heavily on ideological incentives to mobilize participants, and this can introduce ideological conflict that stands in the way of alliance formation.

The final chapter has not yet been written on the role of political opportunities and threats in fostering coalition work. An important direction for future research is to explore the conditions under which either or both may have their greatest influence. For instance, Obach (2010) reports that provisions in tax laws may encourage some groups to collaborate while discouraging other organizations from joint action. Additionally, as Staggenborg (1986) and Diani (1995) suggest, it may be that both political opportunities and threats can matter simultaneously. Moreover, the *degree* of political openness or closure may have ramifications for alliances, with highly open or extremely closed arenas derailing coalition work, albeit for different reasons. A recent study by Kadivar (2013) indicates an important avenue for additional research. Kadivar investigates alliances during the Iranian reform movement and examines activist perceptions of opportunities and threats as they make decisions about coalition formation. Using the concept of "perception profiles," Kadivar disaggregates distinct dimensions of the political landscape and the ways in which perceptions about these political dimensions can lead to or hinder activist alliances. At this juncture, we know little about the perceptions and incentives that encourage activist coalitions.

Resources

As resource mobilization theorists (McCarthy and Zald 1977) convey, activists are unlikely to mobilize without critical resources to support their efforts. Research suggests that a similar dynamic governs coalition work: group collaboration is more likely when resources are plentiful (Van Dyke 2003; Cornfield and Canak 2007) and when the sources of partner groups' funding are distinct and non-competitive (Hathaway and Meyer 1993). Barkan's (1986) study of the US civil rights movement supports these assertions. He finds that rivalries among civil rights organizations over scarce funding hindered the ability of these groups to coalesce. Diaz-Veizades and Chang (1996), in fact, find that when resources decline, coalitions are likely to dissolve.

But as Hathaway and Meyer (1993) point out, available resources are likely to be shaped by circumstances in the larger political environment. A crisis or threat may provide an influx of new resources to activists, such as occurred in the 1980s nuclear freeze movement. This, in turn, can heighten levels of coalition work. Broader circumstances driving resource levels and their impact on coalitions are not well understood. Moreover, we know little about which resources are crucial to coalition formation. Our review suggests that the role of resources is an understudied area generally in coalition studies and one warranting substantial further investigation.

Conjunctural Causation in Future Research

An important direction for future study of the circumstances producing social movement coalitions is consideration of conjunctural causality (Borland 2010; McCammon and Van Dyke 2010). While we have discussed the individual influence of a variety of factors, many of these circumstances combine to foster movement coalitions. For example, as Staggenborg (1986) suggests, when activist groups share members, overlapping constituents can help overcome ideological differences to smooth a path for activist partnerships. Additionally, McCammon and Van Dyke (2010) in a meta-analysis observe that the most fertile ground for coalition activity appears to be the combination of shared beliefs and plentiful resources. Additionally, the way in which threats interact with other conditions to foster coalitions calls for more attention; for instance, at what level of threat can ideological differences or lack of resources be ignored and coalitions occur? Understanding more fully such conjunctural causality is a necessary next step for future research.

CONSEQUENCES OF COALITIONS

While numerous studies consider the circumstances fostering coalition work, fewer examine the consequences coalitions produce. This remains an understudied area with a need for closer scrutiny (Staggenborg 2010). Among existing studies, we identify various types of outcomes that social movement coalitions have influenced: organizational change, movement mobilization, political outcomes, and survival of coalitions.

Organizational Change

Movement alliances can generate consequences for the member organizations within coalitions. As Lee (2011) and Mix (2011) show, one important organizational consequence is that coalitions can provide member organizations with resources and further network-building opportunities, which may, in turn, enhance their organizational stability. Collaborations also can affect organizations' deployment of tactics, ranging from tactical diffusion (Wang and Soule 2012) to tactical innovation (Meyer and Whittier 1994). Organizational framing can also be influenced. Croteau and Hicks (2003) and Luna (2010) document shifts in framing strategies as a result of alliance work, often when one group realigns its frames to better mesh with a coalition partner. These organizational influences are not surprising, given that coalition partners often closely interact, predisposing them to learn from one another. Meyer and Whittier (1994) show that coalition efforts between the US women's and peace movements in the 1980s resulted in a spillover of feminist frames and tactics into peace organizations.

A coalition not only affects the collaborating organizations; it can also influence the formation of new social movement groups, but the direction of the effect is not yet certain. In her study of the global environmental movement, Murphy (2005) finds that an increased number of coalitions limit access to resources generally, reducing founding rates of new, non-coalition organizations. On the other hand, in the Korean democracy movement, coalition activism helped found a new social movement organization, a large labor group during the democratization period (Lee 2011). Understanding the organizational consequences of movement coalitions is clearly an area in need of further examination.

Movement Mobilization

Coalitions can fuel social movement mobilization more generally, including the number of individual participants in a specific protest event and the overall scale of an ongoing campaign. Gerhards and Rucht (1992) examine two distinct protest campaigns in late-1980s West Germany and find that coalition structures bolstered the size of specific protests, turning them into large-scale events. Luna (2010) draws a similar conclusion, finding that *March for Women's Lives*, a 2004 march in support of reproductive justice, grew in size because of coalition participation. But while the mobilization goal of coalitions is often enhanced, not every attempt ends in success. Jones and his colleagues (2001) suggest some coalitions are more effective than others in recruiting large numbers of protest participants. They find that the most effective form is "network invocation." This occurs when a single movement organization leads the planning and decision making while drawing on other organizations to assist.

When it comes to transnational coalitions, their impact on domestic mobilization is not yet fully understood. Widener (2007) shows that cooperation with international organizations weakens domestic mobilization by discouraging network-building efforts at home. On the other hand, Juska and Edwards (2005) demonstrate that effective transnational collaboration between a US-based organization, the Animal Welfare

Institute, and a Polish farmers' organization, Samoobrona, brought new Polish allies into the mobilization, which ultimately was crucial to the success of the anti-corporate campaign. This may be another case where the causal influence varies depending on broader circumstances, conjunctural circumstances not yet being well understood by researchers.

Political Outcomes

Scholarly study provides evidence that coalitions can produce a third type of outcome: political results, such as legislative or policy changes. But the findings are not yet conclusive. Some scholars show the significance of coalition work for such political successes, while others argue that coalitions alone cannot achieve a political victory.

Studying social movement–political party coalitions in Latin America, Almeida (2010) shows that such coalitions achieve political success by preventing passage of unfavorable legislation. Banaszak's (2010) research on US feminist political insiders from the Kennedy to Clinton administration considers alliances between state and social movement actors and finds that state–movement partnerships contribute to policies promoting gender equality in employment and education. Moreover, transnational coalitions to eradicate child labor in Bangladesh also succeeded in establishing laws to protect children from under-aged labor exploitation (Brooks 2005). But Joyner (1982) proposes a different perspective, that coalitions alone may not be sufficient for political success. She analyzes allied women's groups' efforts to ratify the Equal Rights Amendment (ERA) in Illinois and concludes that even with a strong coalition the Illinois ERA Ratification Project was not able to win a political victory.

Various strains of research provide clues that may help us understand such divergent findings. Banaszak (1996) and Crawhall (2011) indicate that large coalitions encompassing a substantial number of groups increase the likelihood of a positive political outcome, although others suggest size may not matter (Joyner 1982; Knoke 1990). Dixon and colleagues (2013) as well ask what shapes coalition political success. They find that different political outcomes in two labor coalitions can be attributed in part to coalition "fit," where fit refers to collaborations between labor and non-labor organizations with mutual trust, a shared sense of commitment, and common objectives. Where such fit occurred, the coalition was more successful. A study by Arnold (2011) also indicates the importance of trust, shared knowledge, and the ability to jointly problem solve as key for politically successful coalitions. Haydu (2012) finds, however, that when coalition members' core objectives differ from one another, frame brokers were critical in that they played an important role in introducing new tactics to the coalition which eventually helped to win passage of important federal legislation. Researchers studying the political outcomes of coalitions are beginning to understand when such partnerships may succeed, but additional research will bring a more definitive understanding.

Survival of Coalitions

Finally, some scholars examine coalition longevity as a type of outcome. Long-lasting coalitions may not be the ultimate goal, but it can be critical to achieving other outcomes. Scholars have investigated why some coalitions survive while others dissolve quickly. They find that avoiding or managing conflict and threats, both internal and external, to the coalition is the key to an enduring coalition.

Coalitions are often composed of diverse organizations, and differences in ideologies, cultures, and strategies can create tensions. Williams (1999) argues that coalitions are more likely to endure when they acknowledge threats to cooperation and resolve internal conflicts. Kleidman (1993) finds that when internal tensions endure, coalition members eventually drift away. Avoiding competition for resources and constituents by differentiating one's group from other member organizations helps sustain functioning coalitions (Hathaway and Meyer 1993; Krinsky and Reese 2006). Moreover, Guenther (2010) finds that weak coalitions, in which organizations are loosely connected to one another with low demand for ideological unity, contributed to the durability of trans-regional feminist alliances in East Germany. In his study of coalitions between labor and environmental groups, Mayer (2008) demonstrates that developing a joint identity within blue–green coalitions was an important factor for their long-lasting collaboration.

Factors external to coalitions, such as a favorable context for mobilization generally, influence longevity as well. Krinsky and Reese (2006) show that some labor-community coalitions in US workfare-justice campaigns were able to persist because of relatively weak opposition from employers. On the other hand, unfavorable political contexts can make it hard to sustain coalitions. Meyer and Corrigall-Brown (2005) find that US coalitions against the war in Iraq weakened and member organizations turned their attention back to their core identities after experiencing political defeats when the US President rejected movement claims and instead framed the war as a success. Attempts to reconcile these findings, however, with the important role threats can play in coalition formation suggest that we do not yet fully understand how unfavorable political environments influence coalition efforts.

ADDITIONAL POSSIBILITIES FOR FUTURE RESEARCH ON SOCIAL MOVEMENT COALITIONS

A few scholars note other types of coalition outcomes, but as yet we know little about them. For instance, coalitions are likely to offer benefits for individuals who participate. Hathaway and Meyer (1993) and Lee (2011) discuss such individual-level outcomes, telling us that coalition actors gain training, mentoring, career benefits, and solidarity incentives. In addition, it may be that movement alliances produce negative effects for member groups, when such groups realize that the costs of coordinated action outweigh the benefits (Staggenborg 2010). Unexpected consequences can also occur. Murphy's (2005) study of the global environmental movement provides evidence that the growing number of transnational coalitions resulted in the unintended and negative outcome of curtailing movement expansion, by channeling available resources to coalition partners and making it difficult for new organizations to form outside the coalition. Few scholars as yet have examined the negative or unintended consequences of movement coalitions.

The study of social movement coalitions is a vibrant area of research, but one still in need of additional scholarship. For instance, researchers often do not consider that coalition types vary, for instance, in terms of duration, extent, size, and formalization. It may well be that different types have different antecedents and consequences. As this chapter shows, we have learned much thus far about alliances among movement groups, but study of movement coalitions is also an area ripe for additional scholarly attention.

NOTES

1. We thank Mario Diani and Donatella della Porta for helpful comments on an earlier draft of our chapter.
2. Here we focus on coalitions in social movements, acknowledging that coalitions occur in other domains as well, for instance, in party politics and military campaigns (see, e.g., Kreps 2011). See Diani and Bison (2004) for a discussion of types of coalitions.

REFERENCES

Almeida, Paul (2010). "Social Movement Partyism: Collective Action and Oppositional Political Parties." In *Strategic Alliances: Coalition Building and Social Movements*, edited by Nella Van Dyke and Holly J. McCammon, 170–196. Minneapolis: University of Minnesota Press.

Arnold, Gretchen (2011). "The Impact of Social Ties on Coalition Strength and Effectiveness: The Case of the Battered Women's Movement in St. Louis," *Social Movement Studies*. 10: 131–150.

Banaszak, Lee Ann (1996). *Why Movements Succeed or Fail: Opportunity, Culture, and the Struggle for Woman Suffrage*. Princeton: Princeton University Press.

Banaszak, Lee Ann (2010). *The Women's Movement Inside and Outside the State*. New York: Cambridge University Press.

Bandy, Joe and Smith, Jackie (2005). *Coalitions across Borders: Transnational Protest and the Neoliberal Order*. Lanham: Rowman & Littlefield Publishers.

Barkan, Steven E. (1986). "Interorganizational Conflict in the Southern Civil Rights Movement," *Sociological Inquiry*. 56: 190–209.

Beamish, Thomas D. and Luebbers, Amy J. (2009). "Alliance Building across Social Movements: Bridging Difference in a Peace and Justice Coalition," *Social Problems*. 56: 647–676.

Borland, Elizabeth (2010). "Crisis as a Catalyst for Cooperation? Women's Organizing in Buenos Aires." In *Strategic Alliances: Coalition Building and Social Movements*, edited by Nella Van Dyke and Holly J. McCammon, 241–265. Minneapolis: University of Minnesota Press.

Brooks, Ethel (2005). "Transnational Campaigns Against Child Labor: The Garment Industry In Bangladesh." In *Coalitions across Borders: Transnational Protest in the Neoliberal Order*, edited by Joe Bandy and Jackie Smith, 121–139. Lanham: Rowman & Littlefield Publishers.

Chang, Paul Y. (2008). "Unintended Consequences of Repression: Alliance Formation in South Korea's Democracy Movement (1970–1979)," *Social Forces*. 87: 651–677.

Cornfield, Daniel B. and Canak, William (2007). "Immigrants and Labor in a Globalizing City: Prospects for Coalition Building in Nashville." In *Labor in the New Urban Battlegrounds: Local Solidarity in a Global Economy*, edited by Lowell Turner and Daniel B. Cornfield, 163–177. Ithaca: ILR Press.

Cornfield, Daniel B. and McCammon, Holly J. (2010). "Approaching Merger: The Converging Public Policy Agendas of the AFL and CIO, 1938–1955." In *Strategic Alliances: Coalition Building and Social Movements*, edited by Nella Van Dyke and Holly J. McCammon, 79–98. Minneapolis: University of Minnesota Press.

Crawhall, Nigel (2011). "Africa and the UN Declaration on the Rights of Indigenous People," *The International Journal of Human Rights*. 15: 11–36.

Croteau, David and Hicks, Lyndsi (2003). "Coalition Framing and the Challenge of a Consonant Frame Pyramid: The Case of a Collaborative Response to Homelessness," *Social Problems*. 50: 251–272.

della Porta, Donatella. 1995. *Social Movements, Political Violence, and the State: A Comparative Analysis of Italy and Germany*. New York: Cambridge University Press.

D'Emilio, John (1983). *Sexual Politics, Sexual Communities*. Chicago: University of Chicago Press.

Di Gregorio, Monica (2012). "Networking in Environmental Movement Organisation Coalitions: Interest, Values or Discourse?" *Environmental Politics*. 21: 1–25.

Diani, Mario (1995). *Green Networks: A Structural Analysis of the Italian Environmental Movement*. Edinburgh: Edinburgh University Press.

Diani, Mario and Bison, Ivano (2004). "Organizations, Coalitions, and Movements," *Theory and Society*. 33: 281–309.

Diaz-Veizades, Jeannette and Chang, Edward T. (1996). "Building Cross-Cultural Coalitions: A Case-Study of the Black-Korean Alliance and the Latino-Black Roundtable," *Ethnic and Racial Studies*. 19: 680–700.

Dixon, Marc and Martin, Andrew W. (2012). "We Can't Win This on Our Own: Unions, Firms, and Mobilization of External Allies in Labor Disputes," *American Sociological Review*. 77: 946–969.

Dixon, Marc, Danaher, William F., and Kail, Ben Lennox (2013). "Allies, Targets, and the Effectiveness of Coalition Protest: A Comparative Analysis of Labor Unrest in the U.S. South," *Mobilization*. 18: 331–350.

Dolgon, Corey (2001). "Building Community amid the Ruins: Strategies for Struggle from the Coalition for Justice at Southampton College." In *Forging Radical Alliances across Difference*, edited by Jill Bystydzienski and Steven Schacht, 220–232. London: Rowman and Littlefield Publishers.

Ellingson, Stephen, Woodley, Vernon A., and Paik, Anthony (2012). "The Structure of Religious Environmentalism: Movement Organizations, Interorganizational Networks, and Collective Action," *Journal for the Scientific Study of Religion.* 51: 266–285.

Gerhards, Jürgen and Rucht, Dieter (1992). "Mesomobilization: Organizing and Framing in Two Protest Campaigns in West Germany," *American Journal of Sociology.* 98: 555–595.

Gilmore, Stephanie (2008). *Feminist Coalitions: Historical Perspectives on Second-Wave Feminism in the United States.* Champaign: University of Illinois Press.

Grossman, Zoltan (2001). "'Let's Not Create Evilness for This River': Interethnic Environmental Alliances of Native Americans and Rural Whites in Northern Wisconsin." In *Forging Radical Alliances across Difference,* edited by Jill Bystydzienski and Steven Schacht, 146–159. Lanham: Rowman & Littlefield Publishers.

Guenther, Katja M. (2010). "The Strength of Weak Coalitions: Transregional Feminist Coalitions in Eastern Germany." In *Strategic Alliances: Coalition Building and Social Movements,* edited by Nella Van Dyke and Holly J. McCammon, 119–142. Minneapolis: University of Minnesota Press.

Hathaway, Will and Meyer, David S. (1993). "Competition and Cooperation in Social Movement Coalitions: Lobbying for Peace in the 1980s," *Berkeley Journal of Sociology.* 38: 156–183.

Haydu, Jeffrey (2012). "Frame Brokerage in the Pure Food Movement, 1879–1906," *Social Movement Studies.* 11: 97–112.

Heery, Edmund, Williams, Steve, and Abbott, Brian (2012). "Civil Society Organizations and Trade Unions: Cooperation, Conflict, Indifference," *Work, Employment and Society.* 26: 145–160.

Isaac, Larry (2010). "Policing Capital: Armed Countermovement Coalitions against Labor in Late Nineteenth-Century Industrial Cities." In *Strategic Alliances: Coalition Building and Social Movements,* edited by Nella Van Dyke and Holly J. McCammon, 22–49. Minneapolis: University of Minnesota Press.

Jones, Andrew W., Hutchison, Richard N., Van Dyke, Nella, Gates, Leslie, and Companion, Michele (2001). "Coalition Form and Mobilization Effectiveness in Local Social Movements," *Sociological Spectrum.* 21: 207–231.

Joyner, Nancy Douglas (1982). "Coalition Politics: A Case Study of an Organization's Approach to a Single Issue," *Women & Politics.* 2: 57–70.

Juska, Arunas and Edwards, Bob (2005). "Refusing the Trojan Pig: The US-Poland Coalition Against Corporate Pork Production." In *Coalitions across Borders: Transnational Protest and the Neoliberal Order,* edited by Joe -Bandy and Jackie Smith, 187–207. Lanham: Rowman & Littlefield Publishers.

Kadivar, Mohammad Ali. 2013. "Alliances and Perception Profiles in the Iranian Reform Movement, 1997 to 2005," *American Sociological Review.* 78: 1063–1086.

Kleidman, Robert (1993). *Organizing for Peace: Neutrality, the Test Ban, and the Freeze.* Syracuse: Syracuse University Press.

Knoke, David (1990). *Organizing for Collective Action: The Political Economies of Associations.* Hawthorne, NY: Aldine de Gruyter.

Kreps, Sarah E. (2011). *Coalitions of Convenience: United States Military Interventions after the Cold War.* New York: Oxford University Press.

Krinsky, John and Reese, Ellen (2006). "Forging and Sustaining Labor-Community Coalitions: The Workfare Justice Movement in Three Cities," *Sociological Forum*. 21: 623–658.

Lee, Jung-eun (2011). "Insularity or Solidarity? The Impacts of Political Opportunity Structure and Social Movement Sector on Alliance Formation," *Mobilization*. 16: 303–324.

Levi, Margaret and Murphy, Gillian H. (2006). "Coalitions of Contention: The Case of the WTO Protests in Seattle," *Political Studies*. 54: 651–670.

Lichterman, Paul (1995). "Piecing Together Multicultural Community: Cultural Differences in Community Building Among Grass-Roots Environmentalists," *Social Problems*. 42(4): 513–534.

Luibheid, Eithne and Khokha, Sasha (2001). "Building Alliances between Immigrant Rights and Queer Movements." In *Forging Radical Alliances across Difference: Coalition Politics for the New Millennium*, edited by Jill M. Bystydzienski and Steven P. Schacht, 77–90. Lanham: Rowman & Littlefield Publishers.

Luna, Zakiya T. (2010). "Marching Toward Reproductive Justice: Coalitional (Re) Framing of the March for Women's Lives," *Sociological Inquiry*. 80: 554–578.

Mantler, Gordon K. (2013). *Power to the Poor: Black–Brown Coalition and the Fight for Economic Justice, 1960–1974*. Chapel Hill: University of North Carolina Press.

Mayer, Brian (2008). *Blue-Green Coalitions: Fighting for Safe Workplaces and Healthy Communities*. Ithaca: Cornell University Press.

McCammon, Holly J. and Campbell, Karen E. (2002). "Allies on the Road to Victory: Coalition Formation between the Suffragists and the Woman's Christian Temperance Union," *Mobilization*. 7: 231–251.

McCammon, Holly J. and Van Dyke, Nella (2010). "Applying Qualitative Comparative Analysis to Empirical Studies of Social Movement Coalition Formation." In *Strategic Alliances: Coalition Building and Social Movements*, edited by Nella Van Dyke and Holly J. McCammon, 292–315. Minneapolis: University of Minnesota Press.

McCarthy, John D. and Zald, Mayer N. (1977). "Resource Mobilization and Social Movements: A Partial Theory," *American Journal of Sociology*. 82(6): 1212–1241.

Meyer, David S. and Corrigall-Brown, Catherine (2005). "Coalitions and Political Context: US Movements Against the War in Iraq," *Mobilization*. 10: 327–344.

Meyer, David S. and Whittier, Nancy (1994). "Social Movement Spillover," *Social Problems*. 41: 277–298.

Mix, Tamara L. (2011). "Rally the People: Building Local–Environmental Justice Grassroots Coalitions and Enhancing Social Capital," *Sociological Inquiry*. 81: 174–194.

Morris, Aldon D. and Staggenborg, Suzanne (2004). "Leadership in Social Movements." In *The Blackwell Companion to Social Movements*, edited by David A. Snow, Sarah A. Soule, and Hanspeter Kriesi, 171–196. Malden: Blackwell Publishing.

Murphy, Gillian (2005). "Coalitions and the Development of the Global Environmental Movement: A Double-Edged Sword," *Mobilization*. 10: 235–250.

Obach, Brian K. (2004). *Labor and the Environmental Movement: A Quest for Common Ground*. Cambridge: MIT Press.

Obach, Brian (2010). "Political Opportunity and Social Movement Coalitions: The Role of Policy Segmentation and Nonprofit Tax Law." In *Strategic Alliances: Coalition Building and Social Movements*, edited by Nella Van Dyke and Holly J. McCammon, 197–218. Minneapolis: University of Minnesota Press.

Okamoto, Dina G. (2010). "Organizing across Ethnic Boundaries in the Post-Civil Rights Era: Asian American Panethnic Coalitions." In *Strategic Alliances: Coalition Building and Social Movements*, edited by Nella Van Dyke and Holly J. McCammon, 143–169. Minneapolis: University of Minnesota Press.

Park, Hyung Sam (2008). "Forming Coalitions: A Network-Theoretic Approach to the Contemporary South Korean Environmental Movement," *Mobilization*. 13: 99–114.

Poloni-Staudinger, Lori (2009). "Why Cooperate? Cooperation among Environmental Groups in the United Kingdom, France, and Germany," *Mobilization*. 14: 375–396.

Reese, Ellen, Petit, Christine, and Meyer, David S. (2010). "Sudden Mobilization: Movement Crossovers, Threats, and the Surprising Rise of the U.S. Antiwar Movement." In *Strategic Alliances: Coalition Building and Social Movements*, edited by Nella Van Dyke and Holly J. McCammon, 266–291. Minneapolis: University of Minnesota Press.

Rohlinger, Deanna A. and Quadagno, Jill (2009). "Framing Faith: Explaining Cooperation and Conflict in the U.S. Conservative Christian Political Movement," *Social Movement Studies*. 8: 341–358.

Roth, Benita (2010). "'Organizing One's Own' as Good Politics: Second Wave Feminists and the Meaning of Coalition." In *Strategic Alliances: Coalition Building and Social Movements*, edited by Nella Van Dyke and Holly J. McCammon, 99–118. Minneapolis: University of Minnesota Press.

Staggenborg, Suzanne (1986). "Coalition Work in the Pro-Choice Movement: Organizational and Environmental Opportunities and Obstacles," *Social Problems*. 33: 374–390.

Staggenborg, Suzanne (2010). "Conclusion: Research on Social Movement Coalitions." In *Strategic Alliances: Coalition Building and Social Movements*, edited by Nella Van Dyke and Holly J. McCammon, 316–329. Minneapolis: University of Minnesota Press.

Suh, Doowon (2011). "Institutionalizing Social Movements: The Dual Strategy of the Korean Women's Movement," *The Sociological Quarterly*. 52: 442–471.

Tarrow, Sidney (2005). *The New Transnational Activism*. New York: Cambridge University Press.

Van Dyke, Nella (2003). "Crossing Movement Boundaries: Factors That Facilitate Coalition Protest by American College Students, 1930–1990," *Social Problems*. 50: 226–250.

Van Dyke, Nella and McCammon, Holly J. (2010). *Strategic Alliances: Coalition Building and Social Movements*. Minneapolis: University of Minnesota Press.

von Bülow, Marisa (2011). "Brokers in Action: Transnational Coalitions and Trade Agreements in the Americas," *Mobilization*. 16: 165–180.

Wang, Dan J. and Soule, Sarah A. (2012). "Social Movement Organizational Collaboration: Networks of Learning and the Diffusion of Protest Tactics, 1960–1995," *American Journal of Sociology*. 117: 1674–1722.

Widener, Patricia (2007). "Benefits and Burdens of Transnational Campaigns: A Comparison of Four Oil Struggles in Ecuador," *Mobilization*. 12: 21–36.

Williams, Heather L. (1999). "Mobile Capital and Transborder Labor Rights Mobilization," *Politics and Society*. 27: 139–166.

Zald, Mayer N. and Ash, Robert (1966). "Social Movement Organizations: Growth, Decay and Change," *Social Forces*. 44: 327–341.

CHAPTER 21

....

MOVEMENTS AS COMMUNITIES

....

HATEM M. HASSAN AND SUZANNE STAGGENBORG

SOCIAL movements are diffuse phenomena with permeable boundaries consisting of a variety of actors, ideas, and events that change over time. Scholars have struggled to conceptualize movements in ways that capture their emergent qualities and ongoing interactions with supporters and targets. Tilly (1984: 305–306) sees social movements as shifting coalitions of actors in "sustained interaction" with authorities and other targets. In his view, movements are means of engaging in "public politics" that emerged in historically specific contexts in the Western world (Tilly 2004: 7). Tarrow (2011: 9) builds on Tilly's approach to offer a widely used definition of social movements as "collective challenges, based on common purposes and social solidarities, in sustained interaction with elites, opponents, and authorities." Other theorists propose more expansive definitions of social movements as operating in a variety of cultural and institutional as well as political arenas, targeting various types of authorities (Snow 2004) and including "ideologically structured action" as well as political movement organizations (Zald 2000). While scholars recognize the importance of the multiple social movement organizations (SMOs) that often mobilize and sustain social movements (McCarthy and Zald 1977; Gamson 1990), they also understand that movements are comprised of social networks, collective identities, and cultures as well as political campaigns and organizations (Melucci 1989, 1996; Diani 1992; Polletta 2008).

The notion of *social movement communities* aims to capture the interactions among diverse political and cultural elements that help to sustain social movements. The concept originated in studies of movements in Western countries, such as the women's movement, and has largely been employed to understand local or regional movements rather than national or international ones.

In this chapter, we begin by discussing the concept of social movement community and its usefulness in understanding the mobilization and maintenance of social movements, showing how it differs from related concepts. We then explore questions about its relevance and limitations when studying non-Western movements in authoritarian settings, using cases from the Middle East. In the recent revolutions, we have witnessed the emergence of "free spaces" (Polletta 1999) once denied by despots. Yet, many ruling governments in the region continue to deny movements and individuals of such spaces to freely express their demands. By asking whether movement communities can exist in the region, and studying them in different scenarios, we consider a range of possible avenues for participation and sources for social change in authoritarian contexts. Finally, we move beyond original conceptions to include alternative community structures while stressing the growing significance of information and communication technologies (ICTs) in allowing for the development of movement communities in authoritarian and non-Western contexts.

THE CONCEPT OF SOCIAL MOVEMENT COMMUNITY

A social movement community (SMC) consists of networks of individuals, cultural activities, institutional supporters, and alternative institutions as well as SMOs and other actors that support movement goals (Staggenborg 1998: 182). Movement communities vary on a range of characteristics that affect their cohesiveness and ability to maintain movement ideas and activities. Some local movement communities are linked to national and international ones, while others are strictly local. *Specific* movement communities, such as women's movement and environmental movement communities, may be more or less connected to one another via networks and organizations. During cycles of protest, a *general* movement community, such as a radical or progressive one, may connect activists with various interests and concerns (Staggenborg 1998). Within SMCs, networks between individuals and among groups may be more or less dense. Some SMCs contain movement centers or common meeting places that facilitate interaction while others are more decentralized. SMCs also vary in the number of SMOs they include and in their institutional support.

The concept is broader than some related concepts, including that of a "social movement industry" (SMI), which consists of all SMOs in a movement (McCarthy and Zald 1977), and that of a "multi-organizational field," which consists of various types of organizations within local communities, including both movement supporters and opponents (Curtis and Zurcher 1973; Klandermans 1992). Whereas the SMI and multi-organizational field concepts recognize a variety of organizations involved in movements, the SMC concept conceives of movements as including other actors besides organizations, such as individuals and cultural groups. The notion of an SMC is also broader than that of "civil society" in that the latter is typically used to identify non-governmental actors, whereas the former may include supporters from within the government, such as a government agency. The concept of a movement community is useful in that it allows us to emphasize informal and cultural elements of movements,

342 HATEM M. HASSAN AND SUZANNE STAGGENBORG

including amorphous social networks of individuals and the various rituals and events that support movement ideas, as well as explicitly political organizations and campaigns.

The SMC concept originated among American scholars who were trying to incorporate informal organizational structures and cultural elements into our understanding of how social movements emerge and maintain themselves. It was first used by Steven Buechler (1990), who argued that some aspects of social movements are better understood as communities than organizations. In his example, Buechler points out the absence of formal organizations in the American women's suffrage movement in its early years, describing how a network of women's rights activists, previously involved in the abolition and temperance movements, mobilized the movement through women's rights conventions held between 1848 and the Civil War (Buechler 1990: 45–46). Similarly, in the 1960s, the women's liberation movement in the United States created a "social movement community of like-minded, informally linked activists who are capable of rapid and intense mobilization around specific issue areas even in the absence of formal movement organization" (1990: 70). While various feminist groups came and went, a women's movement community maintained itself in places such as women's centers and women's studies programs at universities, feminist bookstores and cafes, women's health centers, rape crisis centers, women's music festivals, and issue-oriented projects (1990: 75–76). Taylor and Whittier (1992) argue that lesbian feminists are central to these networks and alternative institutions, and that "lesbian feminist communities sustain a collective identity that encourages women to engage in a wide range of social and political actions that challenge the dominant system" (1992: 105). Staggenborg (1998) also shows how cultural, institutional, and political elements of the women's movement community have maintained feminism in the United States.

Scholars examining other movements have also found the concept of social movement communities useful. Stoecker (1995) uses the concept to examine collective identity in a neighborhood movement, showing how individual and collective identities converge through interaction between participants and other community members. If such a convergence does occur, and when threatened or aroused by particular issues, local communities may turn into movement communities (Woliver 1993; Stoecker 1994). Also taking a local approach, Lichterman (1995) examines different types of movement communities in the environmental movement, showing how the cultural practices of groups affect efforts to build multicultural alliances. Lichterman (1996) also discovers that while some movement communities are based on pre-existing communal ties, such as those that are found within churches, others build on the personalized commitments of individuals.

Thus, the SMC concept allows theorists to explain movement-building dynamics within communities and how movements sustain themselves during periods when there is no visible protest. Much of the existing literature attempts to explain how movements are sustained after public protest disappears. This may occur in a variety of ways: as institutions, such as universities and state agencies, absorb movement goals and cultures of resistance (Staggenborg 1996, 1998); as one movement community spills over into another (Meyer and Whittier 1994); as cultural activities sustain movement networks and ideology (Taylor and Whittier 1992; Taylor and Rupp 1993; Staggenborg 2001); or as "elite sustained organizations" keep the movement community alive during a period of "abeyance" (Taylor 1989). Informal personal networks enable individuals with critical worldviews to experiment with new lifestyles and alternative cultural models even when movements are unable to mount public challenges to the existing powers. Melucci's (1989, 1996; see also Donati 1984) investigation of the youth, women's, ecological, and "new conscience" movement areas that emerged in Italy in the aftermath of the crisis of the opposition movements of the 1970s well illustrates these mechanisms.

A movement community may also precede political movement activity. Rochon (1998) argues that "critical communities" often help to create new values and ways of thinking about issues that are then be taken up by broader movements. Organizational structures in movement communities are also important to the growth of collective campaigns (Staggenborg 1998; Staggenborg and Lecomte 2009). For example, the Southern black church became an arm of the American civil rights movement, as leaders adapted and borrowed its rituals and frames (Morris 1984). Similarly, the American women's movement emerged not simply within political spaces, but also from cultural and commercial spaces, such as women's softball teams, coffeehouses, and bars (Enke 2007). In such instances, one important process to be explained is the transformation of a community into a *movement* community.

In relatively *undemocratic* contexts, sustained movement campaigns are unlikely, and it is reasonable to ask whether an SMC can exist at all in such settings. When protests do emerge, seemingly spontaneously, they are likely to build on community practices and structures. And in settings where repression makes public organizing implausible, alternative and often informal practices, traditions, and cultures might support future movements. In an attempt to explore the usefulness of the SMC concept in non-Western and non-democratic settings, we turn to cases in the Middle East.

MOVEMENT COMMUNITIES
IN THE MIDDLE EAST

The Middle East has not experienced the same kind of expansion, diffusion, and institutionalization of protest activity observed in Western settings. Moments of mass mobilization, such as the 2011 uprisings, emerged without the strong presence of organizations, influential leaders, or a unified ideology (Bamyeh 2011). Contentious episodes before the uprisings, however, were not uncommon (Beinin and Variel 2011). Class-based, grass-roots, student, and women's movements have been active throughout the twentieth and twenty-first centuries. In relatively democratic settings, such moments often lead to sustained protest campaigns or to the creation of free spaces where individuals can foster collective identity and aim towards a unified goal. Institutional access and competitive elections, even under dictators, can give individuals the space needed to form NGOs, cultural groups, and grass-roots organizations (Almeida 2003).

Here, we move beyond political opportunities structures by focussing on the relationship between political and cultural aspects of community and heightened periods of protest activity. Do the organizational, ideological, and cultural bases of pre-existing communities influence subsequent moments of mobilization? Do movement communities emerge from these episodes of protest and, if so, how does the state respond? We begin exploring these questions by looking at three spectacular moments in recent history: the 1987 Palestinian Intifada, the 2009 Iranian Green Movement, and the 2011 Egyptian revolution. The cases illustrate three different scenarios within the movement community process: a movement community that was quickly and violently suppressed, a developing (pre)movement community, and a virtual movement community in between two contentious episodes. In each case, the link between community and protest campaigns is contingent upon local and national cultures of resistance, pre-existing community infrastructures, the character of the contentious episode itself, and responses from the regime.

The Intifada: When Movement Community Meets the State

The 1987 Palestinian uprising gave birth to one of the most notable and recent examples of grass-roots organization within the region. It is difficult to explain the speed and scale of mobilization against Israeli forces without noting the rapid emergence of Palestinian neighborhood groups known as *popular committees* (PCs) (Hiltermann 1993). Responding to Israel's decisions to deploy troops to the occupied territories, the original neighborhood groups emerged during the first few days out of a necessity to provide food, protection, and basic healthcare services (Robinson 1997). Partly formed by local student, women's, and labor groups, committees gained popularity by connecting the everyday problems of ordinary Palestinians to Israel's occupation.

The authoritarian case forces us to consider how the *state's response* to protest activity might affect the likelihood of a future movement community. If PCs represented a potential building block for an emerging movement community—and indeed the pre-existing organizational infrastructure (e.g., women's movement, student movement, etc.) suggests that a movement community could have existed in the past—then Israeli authoritarianism coupled with the paternalism of nationalist political parties quickly eliminated such possibilities. Eventually, informal PC networks were unified and co-opted by the Unified National Leadership of the Uprising (UNLU), a coalition comprised of the PLO and its supporters. With national and international political elites competing over them, popular committees lost their intimate ties to local communities. It is no surprise, then, that these neighborhood groups were largely absent from the (2000–05) second Intifada (Hammami and Tamari 2001). One might argue that the UNLU had established a different *type* of movement community that privileged formal and national, rather than grass-roots, mobilization. What emerged was, in reality, an organizationally homogenous, NGO-dominated movement with little connection to the traditions and culture of community organizing witnessed during the first uprising.

Iran and the 2009 Green Movement: A (Pre)Movement Community

Whereas the Palestinian case provides an example of an emergent but quickly repressed SMC, the Iranian case allows us to see the gradual development of a movement community. In 2009, millions of Iranian citizens, many of whom were women from all sides of the political, religious, and class spectrum, took to the streets in response to the alleged rigging of the June election. In the weeks leading up to the final round, the public domain momentarily lost its repressive features and became a free space (Tahmasebi-Birgani 2010). The Convergence of Women, a newly formed coalition consisting of forty-two women's organizations, tapped into a dispersed network of activists, lawyers, public officials, students, and workers. Together, groups, coalitions, and informal networks converged, asserting the presence of women in the political realm, and doing so on a scale rivaled only by the 1979 revolution. But did the Green Movement emerge, at least partially, from a bourgeoning women's movement community, or was the presence of women symptomatic of a larger, heterogeneous campaign that needed no previous SMC to emerge?

The existence of a "true" Iranian women's movement is still hotly debated (Hoodfar and Sadeghi 2009). For nearly two decades, women had been establishing what Moghadam (2003) calls a "contemporary women's (pre)movement." Overlapping professional, grass-roots, and conscience communities (Aunio and Staggenborg 2011), have been responsible for palpable, though gradual, change in Iran despite the absence of sustained public demonstrations. In the mid-1990s, the vibrant feminist publications industry grew considerably by building solidarity, publicizing controversial issues, and promoting cultural events. One example was the 1995 Women's Week Festival, where famous female filmmakers, NGOs, women athletes, and academics came together for art exhibits, competitions, and seminars (Bayat 2007: 169). By the turn of the century, formal organizations, movement entrepreneurs, and women in parliament were consistently targeting the regime through single-issue campaigns, such as the international Campaign on the Elimination of All Forms of Discrimination Against Women (CEDAW) (Shekarloo 2005). In 2006, middle-class women formed the "One Million Signatures" and "Stop Stoning Forever" campaigns to reform traditional family laws. Meanwhile, ordinary Iranian women gradually made their presence felt in the public sphere, resisting patriarchy through their everyday practices, such as storming soccer stadiums to watch a tradition-ally male-only sport and pushing back the *hijab* (Islamic headscarf).

By identifying a (pre)movement community, with its overlapping but dispersed networks, formal organizations and campaigns, cultural organizations and alterna-tive institutions, and everyday resistance by ordinary people, we can better understand the collective character of social change in particularly repressive contexts. The free-dom that characterized the movement leading up to the 2009 election was ephemeral and was met with brutal repression by the Basij, the regime-backed paramilitary forces. But despite limited success, these movement-building activities provided the impetus for some to continue advocating for social change in less explicit ways. Many young Iranians, for example, continue to discuss the goals and ideas of the movement on their blogs, forums, and other ICTs. As the next section demonstrates, despite the strict polic-ing of physical spaces, young members of the community are often able to continue the discussions, expand the networks, and even sustain public protest in the years leading up to a moment of mass mobilization.

Egypt and the 2011 Revolution

If anything in Egypt resembled a movement community under Mubarak, it would look less like the Palestinian and Iranian models and more like the online virtual spaces that were established between the 2004 pro-democracy movement and the 2011 Revolution. In 2004, activists began a campaign to prevent Mubarak's re-election and to show sup-port for Palestinians under occupation (Oweidat et al. 2008). At the forefront of the movement was an ideologically diverse, but socially and economically homogenous, coalition. Though the Egyptian Movement for Change lost popular support by 2007 due to a combination of repression, arrests, and its elite orientation, it influenced future movements—most notably the April 6th movement in 2008—and paved the way for a virtual online community. Although decentralized like the Iranian example and grass-roots like the Palestinian PCs, Egyptian activists moved beyond physical spaces to sustain their movement goals and ideas years after formal groups had been crushed.

Eventually, we saw a re-emergence of some of these demands, albeit on a national scale. During the initial eighteen days of the Revolution, activists and ordinary Egyptians further developed already growing demands, beliefs, and ideas that had been introduced during the 2004 wave of protests. Like pieces in a puzzle, mobilization heav-ily relied on impromptu debate circles in Tahrir Square like those that occurred in the streets of Tehran in 2009; social media technologies; popular committees similar in the structure and function of those in Palestine; and a palpable, but ideologically nimble notion of "the people" (*al-sha'b*). Between the two waves of mobilization, free spaces were developed to sustain, at the very least, dialogue among activists. With central secu-rity forces monitoring both public and private spheres in Egypt, it is highly unlikely that physical communities and free spaces for dialogue could have emerged, let alone sus-tained, a movement campaign.

ALTERNATIVE CONCEPTUALIZATIONS
OF COMMUNITY

If we define a movement community as consisting of actors who advance the same concrete movement goals, consciously share a collective identity, meet in physical "free" spaces, and participate in sustained collective movement activities (Staggenborg 1998), then the three major episodes of contention just described do not always qualify. More often, they reflect what Scott (1990) refers to as the culture of everyday resistance. Although the SMC concept is not irrelevant to non-Western and non-democratic settings, the community is likely to take a different shape. To adapt the SMC concept to contexts such as the Middle East, we propose two models of community that might exist in authoritarian settings: (1) an informal community of individuals that participate in everyday resistance, and (2) an online community that evades repression of an authoritarian regime. In both models, we see the emergence of imagined communities (Anderson 1991).

Informality, Everyday Resistance, and Imagined Community

While recent scholarship has increasingly emphasized the decentralized networks and fluid organizational structures of Western movements, in authoritarian contexts the informal structure has been the very backbone of resistance and survival (Beinin and Variel 2011; Bayat 2013). Social and economic informality in Middle Eastern cities are responses to urbanization, increased economic inequality, closed political spaces, and failing states (Singerman 1995; Roy and AlSayyad 2004; Elyachar 2005). Most notably, the urban poor, through their everyday practices based on the principles of mutual aid and self-empowerment, have been able to "quietly encroach" onto public spaces (Bayat 2013). In Cairo, residents have created their own informal housing and economy, tapped into electricity grids, built their own ramps to major highways, and squatted in public parks for subsistence. In Tehran, women gradually pushed back the *hijab* after Khomeini's regime enforced conservative dress codes. Informal opposition, however, is not exclusive to one particular class or subaltern group. Egyptian intellectuals, active on university campuses between the 1960s and 1980s, continued their discussions into the twenty-first century through "more subtly activities in the literary field" when more formal leftist organizations were dismantled (Duboc 2011: 51). However, these individual practices alone cannot be seen as political.

Although everyday resistance and informality involves individual actions, a struggle for essential goods and services has kept community central to the equation. Local responses often allow both ordinary individuals and activists to evade the draconian tactics of authoritarian regimes (Duboc 2011). Egypt's Six-day and October wars; the Iraqi invasion of Kuwait; and Lebanon's civil war are examples of local neighborhood groups that emerged rapidly during moments of crisis. But at times, these community responses are as ephemeral as the events that provoked them. During revolutionary moments in Palestine and Egypt, for example, neighborhood committees emerged as a response to the security vacuums and disappeared shortly thereafter. And yet, the informality that characterizes the everyday lives of ordinary citizens across the Middle East can become a culture of resistance, especially in times of political and economic crisis.

But when do informal community responses to a particular event or crisis transform into a sustained movement community? Bayat (2013) suggests that, over time, seemingly atomized practices of everyday resistance accumulate and become a "nonmovement," leading to gradual but concrete social change. Using different language, Eckert suggests that "practice movements" endure over stretches of time, "stand[ing] out from other quotidian practices.... [by] explicitly transgress[ing] restrictions inherent in the nexus of the material organisation of space, property relations, status orders, and almost always normative regulations" (Eckert, this volume; Isin 2008). Yet, in order for us to be able to call this a movement, one can imagine the necessity of some sort of collective identity that unifies that action towards some goal. The accumulation of atomized practices becomes a movement towards social change only when, "identification of similarity, of comparability [exists].... what happened there could happen here; their situation is in some way comparable to ours; what they have done we could do" (Eckert, this volume; Eckert 2012). In this way, even citizens marginalized by oppressive systems of subordination can experience something akin to Anderson's (1991) imagined communities.

In Palestine, the establishment of an imagined community among neighborhood groups is inextricably linked to the traditions of nationalism and self-help. During the Intifada, a heightened patriotism coupled with a collective memory of occupation translated into solidarity, self-sufficiency, and mutual aid (Robinson 1997). Individuals and neighborhoods struggling to attain basic necessities, such as food and security, reached out to other PCs through their pre-existing networks of local, extended families (1997: 96). Fluid and amorphous, these "submerged networks" (Melucci 1989) provide a space where ordinary Palestinians can interact with one another in order to link their everyday actions and needs to the larger movements against Palestinian occupation.

This sense of "we"—one that emerges from below and through largely impersonal networks of ordinary individuals—is also what makes the actions of women in Iran a (pre) movement community. Overlapping feminist groups share a collective identity referred to as *hamdeli*, or "shared feeling.... about their inferior position in society and.... [their wish] to do something about it" (Bayat 2007: 169). The identity is, of course, not a concrete, neatly framed, or unified ideology constructed by movement professionals; its nimbleness is a reflection of dispersed collective action and grievances that Iranian women experience on a daily basis. But the consequences of this sense of "we" are anything but imagined, as can be seen by the communities of professional activists, academics and lawyers, artists and musicians, and, finally, ordinary Iranian women that have gradually coalesced to demand concrete change. Put simply, Iranian women with disparate political, social, and economic backgrounds can only come together through submerged networks that connect their everyday subordination to the larger structural inequality.

Collective identity is but one factor that can sustain an SMC; the larger point here is that an imagined community, which can transform a community into a movement community, may depend upon the informal cultures of resistance already present in a given environment. In many repressive settings in the Middle East, a tradition of everyday resistance and informality coupled with an *ethos* of mutual aid can take on a "transgressive character" (Eckert, this volume) when submerged networks are used by ordinary individuals pushing for gradual and less confrontational social change. In Egypt, groups comprised of well-known intellectuals and activists influenced the Kefaya movement through daily publications in leftist magazines and newspapers (Duboc 2011). The Egyptian case also provides another type of community, one that has grown through virtual organizing. Although relevant to social movements of all types (Earl and Kimport 2011; Bennett and Segerberg 2013), online communities are becoming particularly important in undemocratic states where physical free spaces are lacking or vanishing.

Virtual Communities

Everyday cultures of resistance may not be enough to provoke substantive social change. Indeed, the point here is not to romanticize informal and everyday resistance and equate it with more explicit forms of activism. "Hidden" practices can lead to demobilization, "enabling actors to keep their level of engagement minimal and thereby facilitating phasing down in their activism" (Duboc 2011: 53). However, movements in both repressive and relatively democratic settings have used ICTs to organize supporters and engage in targeted actions. If the SMC concept is to remain relevant to twenty-first-century movements, we need to incorporate such changes.

Using cases of online activism following the 2008 global financial crisis, Bennett and Segerberg (2013) argue that there is a "logic of *connective* action" distinct from more familiar, face-to-face *collective* action. While concepts like collective identity remain central to explaining the latter, the authors associate the former with an "individualized" form of citizenship in which participants seek "flexible association with causes, ideas, and political organizations" and wish to "personalize" collective action frames (2013: 5–6). One might argue that the increasing presence of online and individualized *connective* action renders SMCs obsolete. Yet, as we will see in the case of Egypt, a collective identity can emerge despite highly personalized ways of communicating grievances.

For example, Caren et al. (2012) reported the emergence of the social movement *online* community (SMOC) in their analysis of right-wing white nationalist forums. They argue that collective identity, network building, and claims-making remain central to both SMOCs and face-to-face SMCs. But because SMOCs are often comprised of geographically dispersed individuals rather than organizations, their networks are able to expand or contract more rapidly than other SMCs (2012: 171).

Returning to our Egyptian example, the role of ICTs in political movements remains contested (Diani 2011). We do not suggest that communication technologies were *the* central factor in mobilizing citizens during or even prior to the 2011 Revolution. Instead, we focus on how the use of ICTs sustained movement goals between the two episodes of contention. Virtual free spaces became increasingly important after 2005, when pro-democratic activists responded to brutal repression by creating a national and decentralized network of blogger activists. But as in more traditional SMCs, a blogger-activist identity emerged to sustain the beliefs, goals, and debates of the original *Kefaya*-led campaign, long after the formal group's repression.

In the wake of the second Palestinian Intifada and the American invasion of Iraq, an emerging "blogosphere" and pro-democratic movement *Kefaya* ("enough") came to reinforce one another in a campaign against the government's authoritarian practices. As both a platform for personal posts and an alternative to state-sponsored narratives, blogs and online forums immediately assumed a powerful role in the campaign against Mubarak (Al Malky 2007). But the community of bloggers was close-knit, consisting of no more than forty individuals at the time of their emergence, and only expanded in 2005 (Al-Sayyid 1993). In the face of continuing state repression and blatant authoritarianism, politics and online blogging became inseparable as the number of bloggers soared to 1,800 three years after its emergence. Although blogging was later used by the general public as an ordinary method of communication (1993: 8), "the blogger" became a concrete identity assumed by many young Egyptians tired of Mubarak's draconian policies.

The Egyptian blogger-activists created more than an identity; they established imagined communities that were participatory, inclusive, and geographically diffuse. The anonymous character of the blogger identity, coupled with an amorphous network of activists, rendered SMOCs the regime's biggest challenge. Even after the 2007 arrests of famous Egyptian blogger-activists and journalists, several communities of bloggers with explicitly political intentions remained active, now with a more fluid organizational structure:

> The core remained, yet a much larger group of activists developed and the country's blogosphere lost its center, becoming a network of identity communities linked in a virtual place by virtue of their Egyptianness. Having a blog became a necessity for staying up to date with activists and being an activist.
>
> (Al-Sayyid 1993: 9)

Blogs and other ICTs can be used as both one-directional and *interactive* tools. Between 2004 and 2011, blogs were used to update protestors and the general public and to document cases of police brutality and corruption. Yet, one of the blogosphere's most important contributions to creating free spaces was its ability to allow for open discourse and debate among activists with disparate ideologies—including even those who belong to formal opposition groups like the Muslim Brotherhood (Lim 2012). As a free space, the "blogosphere" in Egypt between 2004 and 2011 represented a novel approach to resisting undemocratic governments: a platform consisting of a sustainable network of diverse individuals and groups that shared broad goals and objectives while constructing a fluid, yet coherent, collective identity. Although Egyptian SMOCs were under fire by 2007, the network had become too agile, dispersed, and heterogeneous for a despot to dismantle. To be sure, physical free spaces and concrete collective identities continue to be central to social change in Egypt. Yet, during the period when pro-democratic movements were violently put on hold in Egypt, online communities became *movement* communities in order to maintain the movement's beliefs, debates, and networks.

CONCLUSION

Like movement communities in democratic environments, SMCs in authoritarian contexts often consist of an amalgam of organizations, coalitions, submerged networks, alternative institutions, and cultural groups. Yet, actors in repressive circumstances have also created and used hidden networks, everyday forms of resistance, and ICTs to advance their goals and demands. The *intentionality* of such actors, however, requires additional attention. Unlike movement actors in democratic settings, such as second wave feminists and American civil rights activists, it is often unclear whether individuals in repressive situations deliberately create and sustain these types of communities, or whether they are incidental to their overall accommodation strategies. Future research involving in-depth fieldwork in local settings can tap into these submerged networks and assess the intentionality of actors within these movement communities.

Thinking about movements as communities allows us to capture their diverse structures and participants, including informal and cultural as well as formal and political elements. The processes by which SMCs, as well as their characteristics and interactions, emerge vary in different settings. In relatively democratic contexts, SMCs are better able to establish diverse networks of movement organizers and supporters, create collective identity, sustain campaigns, and keep a movement in abeyance. In more authoritarian contexts such as the Middle East, movement communities are likely to emerge from alternative community infrastructures. Our three examples show different scenarios where movement communities can appear despite an authoritarian environment. At times, what can explain them best are informal, everyday structures of resistance and the construction of an imagined community—a sense of "we." At other times, online movement communities become particularly important, offering the free spaces that movements require in repressive contexts. The fluidity of the social movement community concept makes it a valuable tool in understanding how movements diffuse and maintain themselves in different environments.

REFERENCES

Al Malky, Rania (2007). "Blogging for Reform: the Case of Egypt," *Arab Media & Society.* 1: 1–31.
Al-Sayyid, Mustapha K. (1993). "A Civil Society in Egypt?" *Middle East Journal.* 47(2): 228–242.

Almeida, Paul D. (2003). "Opportunity Organizations and Threat-Induced Contention: Protest Waves in Authoritarian Settings," *American Journal of Sociology*. 109(2): 345–400.

Anderson, Benedict (1991). *Imagined Communities: Reflections on the Origin and Spread of Nationalism*, Revised edition. London: Verso.

Aunio, Anna-Liisa and Staggenborg, Suzanne (2011). "Transnational Linkages and Movement Communities," *Sociology Compass*. 5(5): 364–375.

Bamyeh, Mohammed (2011). "The Egyptian Revolution: First Impressions from the Field [Updated]." *Jadaliyya*. http://www.jadaliyya.com/pages/index/561/the-egyptian-revolution_first-mpressions-from-the

Bayat, Asef (2007). "A Women's 'Non-Movement': What it Means to be a Woman Activist in an Islamic State," *Comparative Studies of South Asia, Africa, and the Middle East*. 27(1): 161–175.

Bayat, Asef (2013). *Life as Politics: How Ordinary People Change the Middle East*. Stanford, CA: Stanford University Press.

Beinin, Joel and Vairel, Frédéric (2011). *Social Movements, Mobilization, and Contestation in the Middle East and North Africa*. Standford, CA: Stanford University Press.

Bennett, W. Lance and Segerberg, Alexandra (2013). *The Logic of Connective Action: Digital Media and the Personalization of Contentious Politics*. New York: Cambridge University Press.

Buechler, Steven M. (1990). *Women's Movements in the United States*. New Brunswick, NJ: Rutgers University Press.

Caren, Neal, Jowers, Kay, and Gaby, Sarah (2012). "A Social Movement Online Community: Stormfront and the White Nationalist Movement." *Research in Social Movements, Conflicts and Change*. 33: 163–193.

Curtis, Russell L. Jr. and Zurcher, Louis Jr. (1973). "Stable Resources of Protest Movements: The Multi-organizational Field," *Social Forces*. 52: 53–61.

Diani, Mario (1992). "The Concept of Social Movement," *The Sociological Review*. 40(1) Feb.: 1–25.

Diani, Mario (2011). "Networks and Internet into Perspective," *Swiss Political Science Review*. 17(4): 469–474.

Donati, P. R. (1984). "Organization between Movement and Institution," *Social Science Information*. 23(4–5): 837–859.

Duboc, Marie (2011). "Egyptian Leftist Intellectuals' Activism from the Margins: Overcoming the Mobilization/Demobilization Dichotomy." In *Social Movements, Mobilization, and Contestation in the Middle East and North Africa*, edited by Joel Beinin and Frédéric Vairel, 49–67. Stanford, CA: Stanford University Press.

Earl, Jennifer and Kimport, Katrina (2011). *Digitally Enabled Social Change: Activism in the Internet Age*. Cambridge, MA: MIT Press.

Eckert, Julia (2012). "Rumours of Rights." In *Law against the State: Ethnographic Foray's into Law's Transformations*, edited by J. Eckert, B. Donahoe, Ch. Struempell, and Z.Ö. Biner, 147–170. Cambridge: Cambridge University Press,.

Elyachar, Julia (2005). *Markets of Dispossession: NGOs, Economic Development, and the State in Cairo*. Durham, NC, Duke University Press Books.

Enke, Anne (2007). *Finding the Movement: Sexuality, Contested Space, and Feminist Activism*. Durham, NC: Duke University Press.

Gamson, William A. (1990). *The Strategy of Social Protest*, 2nd edn. Belmont, CA: Wadsworth.

Hammami, Rema and Tamari, Salim (2001). "The Second Uprising: End Or New Beginning?" *Journal of Palestine Studies*. 30(2): 5–25.

Hiltermann, Joost R. (1993). *Behind the Intifada: Labor and Women's Movements in the Occupied Territories*. Princeton University Press: Princeton, NJ.

Hoodfar, Homa and Sadeghi, Fatemeh (2009). "Against All Odds: The women's movement in the Islamic Republic of Iran," *Development*. 52(2): 215–223.

Isin, Engin (2008). "Theorizing Acts of Citizenship." In *Acts of Citizenship*, edited by Engin F. Isin and Greg Nielsen, 15–43. London: Macmillan.

Klandermans, Bert (1992). "The Social Construction of Protest and Multiorganizational Fields." In *Frontiers in Social Movement Theory*, edited by Aldon D. Morris and Carol McClurg Mueller, 77–103. New Haven: Yale University Press.

Lichterman, Paul (1995). "Piecing Together Multicultural Community: Cultural Differences in Community Building Among Grass-Roots Environmentalists," *Social Problems*. 42(4): 513–534.

Lichterman, Paul (1996). *The Search for Political Community: American Activists Reinventing Commitment*. Cambridge: Cambridge University Press.

Lim, Merlyna (2012). "Clicks, Cabs, and Coffee Houses: Social Media and Oppositional Movements in Egypt, 2004–2011," *Journal of Communication*. 62(2): 231–248.

McCarthy, John D. and Zald, Mayer N. (1977). "Resource Mobilization and Social Movements: A Partial Theory," *American Journal of Sociology*. 82(6): 1212–1241.

Melucci, Alberto (1989). *Nomads of the President: Social Movements and Individual Needs in Contemporary Society*. Philadelphia: Temple University Press.

Melucci, Alberto (1996). *Challenging Codes: Collective Action in the Information Age*. Cambridge: Cambridge University Press.

Meyer, David S. and Whittier, Nancy (1994). "Social Movement Spillover," *Social Problems*. 41(2): 277–298.

Moghadam, Valentine M. (2003). "Feminism in Iran and Algeria: Two Models of Collective Action for Women's Rights," *Journal of Iranian Research and Analysis*. 19(1): 18–31.

Morris, Aldon D. (1984). *The Origins of the Civil Rights Movement: Black Communities Organizing for Change*. New York: Free Press.

Oweidat, Nadia, Benard, Cheryl, Stahl, Dale, Kildani, Walid, O'Connell, Edward, and Grant, Audra K. Grant (2008). *The Kefaya Movement. A Case Study of a Grassroots Reform Initiative*. Santa Monica, CA: Rand Corporation.

Polletta, Francesca (1999). "'Free Spaces' in Collective Action," *Theory and Society*. 28: 1–38.

Polletta, Francesca (2008). "Culture and Movements," *Annals of the Academy of Political and Social Sciences*. 619(1): 78–96.

Robinson, Glenn E. (1997). *Building a Palestinian State: The Incomplete Revolution*. Bloomington, IN: Indiana University Press.

Rochon, Thomas R. (1998). *Culture Moves: Ideas, Activism, and Changing Values*. Princeton: Princeton University Press.

Roy, Ananya, and AlSayyad, Nezar, eds.(2004). *Urban Informality: Transnational Perspectives from the Middle East, Latin America, and South Asia*. Lanham, MD: Lexington Books.

Scott, James C. (1990). *Domination and the Arts of Resistance: Hidden Transcripts*. New Haven, CT: Yale University Press.

Shekarloo, Mahsa (2005). "Iranian Women Take On the Constitution," *Middle East Research and Information Project*. http://www.merip.org/mero/mero072105

Singerman, Diane (1995). *Avenues of Participation: Family, Politics, and Networks in Urban Quarters in Cario*. Princeton, NJ: Princeton University Press.

Snow, David A. (2004). "Social Movements as Challenges to Authority: Resistance to an Emerging Conceptual Hegemony," *Research in Social Movements, Conflict and Change*. 25: 3–25.

Staggenborg, Suzanne (1996). "The Survival of the Women's Movement: Turnover and Continuity in Bloomington, Indiana," *Mobilization*. 1(2): 143–158.

Staggenborg, Suzanne (1998). "Social Movement Communities and Cycles of Protest: The Emergence and Maintenance of a Local Women's Movement," *Social Problems*. 45(2): 180–204.

Staggenborg, Suzanne (2001). "Beyond Culture Versus Politics: A Case Study of a Local Women's Movement," *Gender & Society*. 15(4): 507–530.

Staggenborg, Suzanne and Lecomte, Josée (2009). "Social Movement Campaigns: Mobilization and Outcomes in the Montreal Women's Movement Community," *Mobilization*. 14(2): 405–422.

Stoecker, Randy (1994). *Defending Community: The Struggle for Alternative Redevelopment in Cedar-Riverside*. Philadelphia: Temple University Press.

Stoecker, Randy (1995). "Community, Movement, Organization: The Problem of Identity Convergence in Collective Action," *The Sociological Quarterly*. 36(1): 111–130.

Tahmasebi-Birgani, Victoria (2010). "Green Women of Iran: The Role of the Women's Movement During and After Iran's Presidential Election of 2009," *Constellations*. 17(1): 78–86.

Tarrow, Sidney (2011). *Power in Movement: Social Movements and Contentious Politics*, Revised and updated 3rd edn. New York: Cambridge University Press.

Taylor, Verta (1989). "Social Movement Continuity: The Women's Movement in Abeyance," *American Sociological Review*. 54: 761–775.

Taylor, Verta and Rupp, Leila J. (1993). "Women's Culture and Lesbian Feminist Activism: A Reconsideration of Cultural Feminism," *Signs*. 19(1): 32–61.

Taylor, Verta and Whittier, Nancy E. (1992). "Collective Identity in Social Movement Communities." In *Frontiers in Social Movement Theory*, edited by Aldon D. Morris and Carol M. Mueller, 104–130. New Haven, CT: Yale University Press.

Tilly, Charles (1984). "Social Movements and National Politics." In *Statemaking and Social Movements*, edited by Charles Bright, and Susan Harding, 297–317. Ann Arbor, Michigan: University of Michigan Press.

Tilly, Charles (2004). *Social Movements, 1768–2004*. Boulder, CO: Paradigm Publishers.

Woliver, Laura R. (1993). *From Outrage to Action: The Politics of Grass-Roots Dissent*. Urbana, IL: University of Illinois Press.

Zald, Mayer N. (2000). "Ideologically Structured Action: An Enlarged Agenda for Social Movement Research," *Mobilization*. 5(1): 1–16.

CHAPTER 22

....

NEW TECHNOLOGIES AND SOCIAL MOVEMENTS

....

JENNIFER EARL, JAYSON HUNT, R. KELLY GARRETT,
AND AYSENUR DAL

THE increasingly pervasive use of information and communication technologies (ICTs) in recent decades has yielded a wide variety of changes in social and political life. In this chapter, we examine how ICT use has affected protest and social movements (SMs), particularly in a global context. *First*, we focus on ICT-enabled infrastructural changes within movements, which: (1) introduce new formats of protest and a new model of power; (2) allow for greater movement activity outside of formal social movement organizations (SMOs) and/or within dramatically altered SMOs; and (3) facilitate transnational protest and SMs in non-Western countries in instrumental and less instrumental ways. *Second*, we argue that increasing ICT use changes the information environment in which activists and supporters operate, creating an information-saturated environment requiring SM scholars to import insights from political communication research. Although these topics highlight key infrastructural changes and scholarly opportunities brought by ICT use, we recognize that scholarship on ICTs and activism is far broader in scope and deeper in substance than we are able to review here (interested readers should see the following for more reviews: Earl, Hunt, and Garrett 2014; Garrett 2006).

ENABLING EPHEMERAL COLLECTIVE ACTION

....

One critical outgrowth of widescale ICT usage has been the rise of collective actions requiring only ephemeral engagements from participants, such as massive online petition drives, e-mail campaigns, distributed denial of service (DDoS) attacks (i.e., when a server is rendered inoperable by flooding it with requests), and viral campaigns (e.g, Kony 2012). In democratic nations, these new online actions are often fairly low cost (i.e., easy online petition signing) and don't require long-term or sustained commitments from participants. Online tactics such as these have become very widespread, making up the majority of protest opportunities online (Earl, Kimport, Prieto, Rush, and Reynoso 2010).

We argue that these ephemeral forms of engagement build on a new, alternative model of protest power, which research reveals can be effective in affecting agendas, policy decisions, corporate policies, etc. (see, for a review of related studies, Earl and Kimport 2011). Whereas power from social movements traditionally comes from sustained and persistent activism by a smaller but dedicated core of activists, this model uses a "flash flood" model of power in which short, massive bursts of activity by loosely (and even temporarily) engaged participants create pressure on targets (Bennett and Fielding 1999). Just as a flash flood can be devastating despite rapidly abating water levels, we expect that flash activism influences policy makers, public opinion, and subsequent media coverage by showcasing massive mobilizations and attracting widespread attention. In developing and authoritarian countries, where governments may be markedly less responsive to direct expressions of concern by their citizens, we expect that these tactics can still be influential by generating a deluge of international attention and concern. Although the now (in)famous Kony 2012 video was produced and released in the United States, it nonetheless illustrates this point. With over a hundred million views, the video did not "work" by persuading the Lord's Resistance Army to stop child abductions; instead, it generated significant international attention, which persuaded the Obama administration to prioritize and act on the issue (Kristof 2012) and led to a US Senate resolution.

However, many activists and scholars have been skeptical of these campaigns, often derisively referring to them as "slacktivism" and assuming their ineffectiveness. We believe that such cynical labeling is at least premature—and is more likely inaccurate—for several reasons. First, it discounts the flash flood model of power, presuming that only sustained activism can be successful. We join Earl (2011) in arguing that instead of assuming that either flash activism cannot be successful (which is not empirically supported in the literature) and/or assuming that street activism is always successful (which is also not empirically supported in the literature), scholars should move this discussion forward by investigating *the circumstances under which flash activism may be tactically useful* to movements.

Second, calling these actions slacktivism implies that ephemeral activism is consistently "easy," only undertaken by those too lazy to participate in more meaningful ways. This reveals a strong Western bias to such criticisms. In more authoritarian countries, engaging in such actions can entail considerable risk. Nevertheless, we suspect that these tactics will persist in authoritarian contexts (e.g., Lai 2005; Parker 2013): despite authorities' capacities for web-based surveillance and repression (Morozov 2011), flash activism is harder for authorities to control and less costly for protesters than street protests. Such tactics may be especially accessible when criticism of the state can be veiled through polysomic uses of words, phrases, or images. For instance, in China, two images and related phrases have become important digital markers for pro-free speech internet users: the grass mud horse and the river crab (Qiang 2011; Wines 2009). The grass mud horse is a Mandarin homophone for "f*ck your mother." Use of the phrase allows brazen displays of anger about online censorship and other government decisions but in a way that was initially difficult for Chinese officials to recognize and has subsequently proven hard to control. The river crab as a symbol is an even more barbed criticism of Chinese censorship, which is referred to by the government as "harmonizing." The river crab is a homonym for harmonize and symbolically can refer to a bully in Chinese culture. Thus, images of the river crab are used as a way of criticizing Chinese censorship. To describe posting and helping to popularize these critical tools as slacktivism is difficult to justify in the Chinese context.

Finally, the denigration of slacktivism is often paired with the empirically unsupportable assumption that *if not for* opportunities to engage in flash activism, participants would have chosen more costly forms of participation such as offline street protests. Decades of research on micro-mobilization reveals this assumption to be false for the vast majority of individuals. Even when people agree with the position of a movement only a very small fraction actually mobilize. The challenge for social movement scholarship has been explaining how to get someone to go from doing nothing to doing something. Instead of distracting would-be long-term movement participants from participating, flash activism likely allows millions of people who would otherwise never have been active to engage politically.

It is possible that engagement in new media and flash activism can also support later street mobilizations. For instance, early research shows that ICTs spread news of street protests quickly, driving offline protest and its diffusion (Castells 2012; Tufekci and Wilson 2012). Thus, we argue that SM studies would be well-served by moving past increasingly tired and empirically anemic debates about whether these new tactics and forms of power can be effective, and toward an understanding of the circumstances under which ephemeral mobilization might facilitate movement goals.

Organizing Outside of and through Different Organizations

ICT usage has also influenced the role and function of SMOs; we focus on two sets of impacts. First, ICT usage has increasingly allowed SM participation outside of organizations. Indeed, the literature contains numerous examples of organizing outside of organizations and the media has touted examples from multiple countries of relatively spontaneous protests erupting after individuals called for them on Facebook. More systematically, Earl (2013) shows that over half of protest-related websites across twenty different SM areas were not run by SMOs (i.e., being run instead by individuals, loose networks, etc.).

Rationales for why so much activity is happening online outside of organizations vary. For instance, Earl and Kimport (2011) argue that online tools can reduce the costs of organizing and participating so much that it is just as easy (and sometimes easier) to build and organize outside of organizations as within them. Bennett and Segerberg (2013) assert that digital communication networks have contributed to a new "logic of connective action," in which individuals are mobilized primarily by the exchange of personally relevant information across fluid social networks, not by the organizations to which they belong. Shirky (2008) claims that the desire to route around SMOs has resulted from diminishing returns for investing in SMOs and their maintenance, except for higher cost forms of activism like street protests (Earl 2013). Bimber, Flanagin, and Stohl (2005) suggest that the free rider dilemma is less relevant in the information age, implying that SMOs are less necessary for providing selective incentives to drive participation. Raine and Wellman (2012) claim that organizations of all types are being broadly displaced by ICT-facilitated extended social networks as a primary means of organizing. Still others argue the decline of standard media gatekeepers and the ability to garner public attention without forming long-term connections leads to a rise of online organizing (Chadwick 2011). In our view, these are all complementary accounts of an empirically well-established phenomenon—widespread organizing and mobilization outside of SMOs—and we suspect that future research will show many of these factors are in play at the same time.

Beyond establishing this change is occurring, it is important to understand its consequences. For instance, we suspect that organizing outside of organizations may facilitate illegal protest activity. SMOs have at times been held liable for the actions of members, effectively forcing SMOs to choose between going underground and disavowing members. Indeed, even nominally online "groups" that regularly engage in illegal conduct (e.g., Anonymous) are often actually networks of actors rather than organizations in a traditional sense, making repression of a central organization impossible (Beyer 2011).

Organizing outside of organizations may also assist protesters in more authoritarian contexts. In these contexts, official or state media are often highly censored and repression of specific SMOs is relatively easy. Social media, which often involves masses of user-generated content, further complicates the censorship of ideas, while still leaving SMOs vulnerable (Faris and Villeneuve 2008). Of course, authorities may begin to track individual protesters instead of groups, but this is a much more taxing form of repression for a regime, especially when a protest sentiment is widely held.

Organizational Adaptation

ICT usage has led to a second SMO-related shift: existing SMOs are being forced to adapt to new digital environments. Bimber, Flanagin, and Stohl (2012) argue that organizational members vary widely in their orientation to organizational authority and technology use, with some members happy to allow organizations to lead while other members push the boundaries of entrepreneurship within these organizations using technological tools. These differences are likely to force organizational accommodations over time. Similarly, Karpf (2012) forcefully argues SMOs are having to change, leading to "organizing through different organizations." He positions industry leading SMOs like MoveOn as spurring on these transitions throughout the SM sector. For instance, MoveOn's position as an issue generalist allows it to fundraise and act upon "hot" issues of the day, and in doing so, out-compete traditional advocacy organizations who must fundraise and organize about their specific issue, whether that issue has traction at a given moment or not. Over the long term, Karpf argues this will impact the viability of traditional, issue specialist organizations, requiring traditional SMOs to adapt to survive.

Many scholars see these two lines of work as in opposition to one another as if people were *either* organizing "outside of organizations" *or* "organizing in different organizations" (e.g., Karpf 2012). However, we argue that these two changes are not at odds as some have claimed: it is likely that both phenomena are happening simultaneously. Other scholars have also seen these phenomena as reconcilable (e.g., Bennett and Segerberg 2013). The empirical evidence shows that many people are routing around organizations but that others are changing SMOs. As Earl (2015) argues, the rise of organizing outside of SMOs is unlikely to spell the end of SMOs. SMOs will remain important in a variety of circumstances and they will increasingly adapt, but many people will also use ICTs to route around SMOs.

Transnational/Non-Western Online SM Activity

Transnational and non-Western SMs have achieved levels of continuity, visibility, size, and connectivity that would be impossible without ICTs (Diani 2000). According to della Porta and Mosca (2005), part of ICTs' contribution is instrumental: they allow for cheap, fast, and easy modes of communication and participation that facilitate activism, particularly for resource-poor actors, as they have for environmental organizations in China (Yang 2003) and NGOs in Africa (Wasserman 2003). ICT usage can also allow geographically dispersed actors to easily participate in online campaigns and usage may limit the need to travel across state-monitored political boundaries (Garrett and Edwards 2007; Reid and Chen 2007). ICT usage has allowed SMs to respond to transnational issues and actors with a rapidly evolving transnational repertoire of contention (Bennett 2003). These instrumental effects are fairly well-established and have received substantial research attention.

Less instrumental effects on movements have been studied less frequently, but this does not mean that such effects are nonexistent. For instance, research has found that ICT usage can help to build transnational movement cultures (e.g., Alest and Walgrave 2002) and collective movement identities across national borders (e.g., agrarian reform movements, see Mann 2008; the European Women's Lobby, see Pudrovska and Marx Ferree 2004). Likewise, social media (e.g., Facebook, Twitter, YouTube) further contribute to the creation of large, more inclusive SMs (Aouragh and Alexander 2011), promoting group identification and shared grievances, as when user-generated material shared on Facebook helped catalyze the "We are all Khaled Said" campaign in Egypt (Lim 2012).

In fact, scholars are only beginning to understand the significance of user-generated content for SMs. Early research shows that protesters' ability to document and share information can extend the reach of protests (Castells 2012), reduce the reliance on news organizations that ignore protest activity or parrot state discourse (Aday, Farrell, Freelon, Lynch, Sides, and Dewar 2013), and generate foreign pressure to resolve problems, as demonstrated in Burma (Chowdhury 2008) and Afghanistan (Kensinger 2003). User-generated content can also alter how people living under repressive regimes perceive the risks and efficacy of activism, which may alter individuals' willingness to participate. Illustratively, the real-time flow of online information (including SMS) about Arab Spring protests allowed would-be activists to track police responses to protests and gauge potential consequences of street protest (Aouragh and Alexander 2011; Tufekci and Wilson 2012). We suspect that additional research on the impacts of user-generated content will reveal other important movement implications.

Of course, we acknowledge that technology is not a panacea for problems facing transnational activists. ICTs do not eliminate all of the burdens facing SMs (e.g., Smith 2004), and they do not automatically enable all-inclusive and globally equitable means of participation and organization. Concerns about digital divides have lost some traction due to continuing ICT diffusion, but recent research on the Arab Spring demonstrates that differences in political, social, and economic contexts can significantly impact the manner and success with which ICTs are used for protest (Howard and Hussain 2013). Moreover, although research cited above suggests that ICT usage could limit repressive risks for protesters, others have countered that ICTs can increase repression by helping track activists or spread propaganda (Lynch 2011; Morozov 2011). Service providers are also vulnerable to pressure by states to act against their users' interests (Youmans and York 2012), and networks may be entirely shut down (as occurred in Egypt, although the strategy backfired, see Howard and Hussain 2011).

BRINGING SM STUDIES AND POLITICAL COMMUNICATION TOGETHER

In addition to the infrastructural changes discussed earlier (i.e., flash activism, altering the reliance on and role of SMOs in SMs, and supporting the growth of transnational activism), we argue that the widescale use of ICTs should change *how* we study SMs by forcing greater integration between research on political communication (PC) and SM studies, which have been hitherto oddly estranged.

Both fields share common theoretical concerns. For instance, SM scholars have long studied framing and how the media disseminates frames. Framing has also been widely studied within PC (Scheufele 1999). Likewise, both fields have been interested in agenda setting. As a central topic in media effects research (e.g., Scheufele and Tewksbury 2007), PC research on agenda setting finds that as a topic receives more news media coverage, the topic becomes increasingly important to the public (McCombs and Shaw 1993). SM scholars also study agenda setting, examining how media coverage and movement mobilization set policy agendas and influence public opinion.

Despite these common concerns, and other more general shared interests about messaging and influence, these two literatures have remained relatively independent. A primary exception has been in research on online activism, as evidenced by the large number of publications on online protest in interdisciplinary and communication journals and the departmental affiliations of key senior scholars in online activism (e.g., Castells, Bennett). This exchange has begun to bridge these fields; extending this initial bridging would be productive for SM studies (online *and* offline) for several reasons.

First, insights from PC could extend existing SM knowledge on shared concerns, a move that the information age makes ever more important. For instance, communication research has shown that agenda setting is influenced by increasing source choice (Stroud 2011), differences between online and offline cues about importance (Althaus and Tewksbury 2002), and increasing reliance on social media cues (Messing and Westwood 2012). These insights have not been accounted for in SM research on agenda setting, but should be.

Second, insights from PC could help identify unexamined effects on both offline and online movements. For example, the third leg of media effects theory, priming (Scheufele and Tewksbury 2007), asserts that information context influences how much weight people give to different factors (Roskos-Ewoldsen, Roskos-Ewoldsen, and Carpentier 2009). While well-known to sociologists doing survey designs, priming effects in information consumption or SM action have rarely been considered but may exist offline and online. What if all the money spent by LGBT (lesbian, gay, bisexual, and transgender) forces to defeat California's Proposition 8 to ban gay marriage could not overcome priming effects from voting in churches? SM scholars have not even considered this larger information and persuasion environment. Online, it is likely that the context in which web surfers find information about movements strongly affects its reception, and yet research on framing doesn't strongly attend to information context or the possibility of priming effects.

Third, SM scholars have not seriously theorized about information reception and interpretation, leaving the audience largely absent. PC scholars, however, have examined how people respond to messages about contentious issues. For instance, research suggests that people are cognitive misers, adopting satisficing strategies (Zaller 1992; Lupia and McCubbins 1998). Citizens also have numerous strategies to guard against persuasive messages and propaganda. Without this important skill, individuals' beliefs would be unstable and easily manipulated, but the ability to guard against manipulation can also lead individuals to reject legitimate critiques. Persuasive appeals can also boomerang, leading people to embrace their initial views more vigorously (Byrne and Hart 2009).

The Information Age and Political Communication

In addition to the benefits to SM research on both offline and online activism discussed earlier, we argue that incorporating PC research is critical in the information age. SM studies will become increasingly impoverished if research from PC is not seriously considered. Specifically, much of the SM literature tacitly assumes that if movements produce resonant frames and receive media attention, people will necessarily learn about movements and some proportion of attitudinally compatible people will be mobilized. This suggests that the core information problem facing movements is information scarcity: there is not enough information available to catalyze potential supporters.

But, widespread ICT usage has created both an avalanche of information and the ability to selectively search for information of interest and/or that fits with one's existing views. This makes information overload, not scarcity, a core SM problem. These changes elevate the importance of the audience-related questions raised earlier since movements must increasingly compete for attention against vast amounts of information and appeals. For instance, individuals may selectively expose or attend to information (Hart, Albarracín, Eagly, Brechan, Lindberg, and Merrill 2009), leading political attitudes to shape information consumption (though not necessarily at the expense of exposure to counter-attitudinal messages, see Garrett 2009). Political interest also shapes political information consumption, although there is some evidence that internet usage can independently increase political interest and do so more powerfully than other mass media (Boulianne 2011).

Despite the possibility of selective consumption, PC research shows that ICT usage exposes individuals to political information in non-political online spaces and that information in these contexts often conflicts with users' existing beliefs (Wojcieszak and Mutz 2009). This can lead to byproduct learning, which can help politically disinterested individuals become engaged (Jensen, Jorba, and Anduiza 2012). However, strong context-dependent priming effects may exist (e.g., learning about politics through a religious website).

Dozens more examples of meaningful overlaps between these fields are possible. Our goal in this section is not to fully map out how PC and SM research might be integrated, as we lack sufficient space to do so. Rather, we argue that future theorizing and research should place a premium on this integration because the questions, and potential answers, that PC holds for communication processes within SMs become ever more important as information environments become even more overloaded and increasing amounts of political information move online.

CONCLUSION

This chapter had two overarching goals: (1) to summarize research on some of the largest infrastructural changes in protest and SMs brought by the widescale use of ICTs; and (2) to argue for greater integration between SM and PC research. We reviewed research on three major infrastructural changes: (1) the rise in ephemeral forms of contention; (2) the changing necessity and roles of SMOs; and (3) the expansion of online transnational protest and online protest in authoritarian and/or developing states. We also argued that the integration of PC research and SM studies is long overdue. Even without consideration of ICTs, greater integration would be profitable. But, ICT-exacerbated information overload has made this integration critical. We suggest some lines for integration and hope that other scholars take up this cause.

AUTHOR NOTE

We would like to thank Heidi Reynolds-Stenson for her research assistance.

REFERENCES

Aday, Sean, Farrell, Henry, Freelon, Deen, Lynch, Marc, Sides, John, and Dewar, Michael. (2013). "Watching From Afar Media Consumption Patterns Around the Arab Spring." *American Behavioral Scientist*. 57: 899–919.

Alest, Peter Van and Walgrave, Stefaan. (2002). "New Media, New Movements? The Role of the Internet in Shaping the Anti-globalization Movement." *Information, Communication & Society*. 5: 465–493.

Althaus, Scott L. and Tewksbury, David. (2002). "Agenda Setting and the "New" News: Patterns of Issue Importance among Readers of the Paper and Online Versions of the New York Times." *Communication Research*. 29: 180–207.

Aouragh, Miryam and Alexander, Anne. (2011). "The Egyptian Experience: Sense and Nonsense of the Internet Revolution." *International Journal of Communication*. 5: 1344–1358.

Bennett, Daniel and Fielding, Pam. (1999). *The Net Effect: How Cyberadvocacy Is Changing the Political Landscape*. Merrifield, VA: e-advocates Press.

Bennett, W. Lance. (2003). "Communicating Global Activism: Strengths and Vulnerabilities of Networked Politics." *Information, Communication and Society*. 6: 143–168.

Bennett, W. Lance and Segerberg, Alexandra. (2013). *The Logic of Connective Action: Digital Media and the Personalization of Contentious Politics*. Cambridge: Cambridge University Press.

Beyer, Jessica Lucia. (2011). "Youth and the Generation of Political Consciousness Online." Unpublished Doctoral Dissertation Thesis, Department of Political Science, University of Washington, Washington.

Bimber, Bruce. (2012). *Collective Action in Organizations: Interaction and Engagement in an Era of Technological Change*. Cambridge: Cambridge University Press.

Bimber, Bruce, Flanagin, Andrew J., and Stohl, Cynthia. (2005). "Reconceptualizing Collective Action in the Contemporary Media Environment." *Communication Theory*. 15: 365–388.

Boulianne, Shelley. (2011). "Stimulating or Reinforcing Political Interest: Using Panel Data to Examine Reciprocal Effects Between News Media and Political Interest." *Political Communication*. 28: 147–162.

Byrne, Sahara and Hart, P. Sol. (2009). "The 'Boomerang' Effect: A Synthesis of Findings and a Preliminary Theoretical Framework." *Communication Yearbook*. 33: 3–37.

Castells, Manuel. (2012). *Networks of Outrage and Hope: Social Movements in the Internet Age*. Malden, MA: Polity Press.

Chadwick, Andrew. (2011). "Britain's First Live Televised Party Leader's Debate: From the News Cycle to the Political Information Cycle." *Parliamentary Affairs*. 64: 24–44.

Chowdhury, Mridul. (2008). *The Role of the Internet in Burma's Saffron Revolution*. The Berkman Center for Internet & Society, Cambridge, MA.

della Porta, Donatella and Mosca, Lorenzo. (2005). "Global-net for Global Movements? A Network of Networks for a Movement of Movements." *Journal of Public Policy*. 25: 165–190.

Diani, Mario. (2000). "Social Movement Networks Virtual and Real." *Information, Communication and Society*. 3: 386–401.

Earl, Jennifer (2011). "Protest Online: Theorizing the Consequences of Online Engagement." Paper presented at *Outcomes of Social Movements and Protest Conference*, Wissenschaftszentrum, Berlin, Germany, June 24, 2011.

Earl, Jennifer. (2013). "Spreading the Word or Shaping the Conversation: "Prosumption" in Protest Websites." *Research in Social Movements, Conflicts, and Change*. 36: 3–38.

Earl, Jennifer. (2015). "The Future of Social Movement Organizations: The Waning Dominance of SMOs Online." *American Behavioral Scientist*. 59: 35–52.

Earl, Jennifer and Kimport, Katrina. (2011). *Digitally Enabled Social Change: Activism in the Internet Age*. Cambridge, MA: MIT Press.

Earl, Jennifer, Kimport, Katrina, Prieto, Greg, Rush, Carly, and Reynoso, Kimberly. (2010). "Changing the World One Webpage at a Time: Conceptualizing and Explaining 'Internet Activism.'" *Mobilization*. 15: 425–446.

Earl, Jennifer, Hunt, Jayson, and Garrett, R. Kelly. (2014). "Social Movements and the ICT Revolution." In *Handbook of Political Citizenship and Social Movements*, edited by H.-A. van der Heijden, 359–383. Edward Elgar.

Faris, Robert and Villeneuve, Nart. (2008). "Measuring Global Internet Filtering." In *Access Denied: The Practice and Policy of Global Internet Filtering*, edited by R. Deibert, J. Palfrey, R. Rohozinski, and J. Zittrain, 6–27. Cambridge, MA: MIT Press.

Garrett, R. Kelly. (2006). "Protest in an Information Society: A Review of the Literature on Social Movement and New ICTs." *Information, Communication, and Society*. 9: 202–224.

Garrett, R. Kelly. (2009). "Politically Motivated Reinforcement Seeking: Reframing the Selective Exposure Debate." *Journal of Communication*. 59: 676–699.

Garrett, R. Kelly and Edwards, Paul N. (2007). "Revolutionary Secrets: Technology's Role in the South African Anti-Apartheid Movement." *Social Science Computer Review*. 25: 13–26.

Hart, William, Albarracín, Dolores, Eagly, Alice H., Brechan, Inge, Lindberg, Matthew J., and Merrill, Lisa. (2009). "Feeling Validated Versus Being Correct: A Meta-Analysis of Selective Exposure to Information." *Psychological Bulletin*. 135: 555–588.

Howard, Philip N. (2013). *Democracy's Fourth Wave: Digital Media and the Arab Spring*. New York: Oxford University Press.

Howard, Philip N. and Hussain, Muzammil M. (2011). "The Role of Digital Media." *Journal of Democracy*. 22: 35–48.

Jensen, Michael J., Jorba, Laia, and Anduiza, Eva. (2012). "Introduction." In *Digital Media and Political Engagement Worldwide: A Comparative Study*, edited by M. J. Jensen, L. Jorba, and E. Anduiza, 80–101. Cambridge: Cambridge University Press.

Karpf, Dave. (2012). *The MoveOn Effect*. Cambridge: Oxford University Press.

Kensinger, Loretta. (2003). "Plugged in Praxis: Critical Reflections on U.S. Feminism, Internet Activism, and Solidarity with Women in Afghanistan." *Journal of International Women's Studies*. 5: 1–28.

Kristof, Nicolas D. (2012). "Viral Video, Vicious Warlord." *New York Times*, 35.

Lai, On-Kwok. (2005). "Cultural Imperialism, State Power, and Civic Activism in and Beyond Cyberspace: Asia's Newly Industrializing Economies (NIEs) in Comparative Perspective." In *Cultural Imperialism: Essays on the Political Economy of Cultural Domination*, edited by B. Hamm and R. C. Smandych, 114–135. Toronto: University of Toronto Press.

Lim, Merlyna. (2012). "Clicks, Cabs, and Coffee Houses: Social Media And Oppositional Movements In Egypt, 2004–2011." *Journal of Communication*. 62: 231–248.

Lupia, Arthur and McCubbins, Matthew Daniel. (1998). *The Democratic Dilemma*. Cambridge: Cambridge University Press.

Lynch, Marc. (2011). "After Egypt: The Limits and Promise of Online Challenges to the Authoritarian Arab State." *Perspectives on Politics*. 9: 301–310.

Mann, Alana. (2008). "Spaces for Talk: Information and Communication Technologies (ICTs) and Genuine Dialogue in an International Advocacy Movement." *Asian Social Science* 4: 3–13.

McCombs, Maxwell E. and Shaw, Donald L. (1993). "The Evolution of Agenda-Setting Research: Twenty-Five Years in the Marketplace of Ideas." *Journal of Communication*. 43: 58–67.

Messing, Solomon and Westwood, Sean. (2012). "Selective Exposure in the Age of Social Media: Endorsements Trump Partisan Source Affiliation when Selecting News Online." *Communication Research*. X: 1–22.

Morozov, Evgeny. (2011). *The Net Delusion: The Dark Side of Internet Freedom*. New York: Public Affairs.

Parker, Emily. (2013). "The 20-Year-Old Crime That's Blowing Up on Chinese Social Media." *New Republic*, available online at: http://www.newrepublic.com/article/113116/zhu-l ing-attempted-murder-case-weibo, November 18, 2013.

Pudrovska, Tetyana and Ferree, Myra Marx. (2004). "Global Activism in "Virtual Space": The European Women's Lobby in the Network of Transnational Women's NGOs on the Web." *Social Politics*. 11: 117–143.

Qiang, Xiao. (2011). "The Battle for the Chinese Internet." *Journal of Democracy*. 22: 47–61.

Rainie, Lee and Barry Wellman. (2012). *Networked: The New Social Operating System*. Cambridge, MA: MIT Press.

Reid, Edna and Chen, Hsinchen. (2007). "Internet-savvy US and Middle Eastern Extremist Groups." *Mobilization* 12: 177–192.

Roskos-Ewoldsen, David R., Roskos-Ewoldsen, Beverly, and Dillman Carpentier, Francesca. (2009). "Media Priming: An Updated Synthesis." In *Media Effects: Advances in Theory and Research*, edited by J. Bryant and M. B. Oliver, 74–93. New York: Routledge.

Scheufele, Dietram A. (1999). "Framing as a theory of media effects." *Journal of Communication*. 49: 103–122.

Scheufele, Dietram A and Tewksbury, David. (2007). "Framing, Agenda Setting, and Priming: The Evolution of Three Media Effects Models." *Journal of Communication*. 57: 9–20.

Shirky, Clay. (2008). *Here Comes Everybody: The Power of Organizing Without Organizations*. New York: Penguin Press.

Smith, Jackie. (2004). *Transnational Processes and Movements*: Malden, MA: Blackwell Publishing.

Stroud, Natalie Jomini. (2011). *Niche News: The Politics of News Choice*. New York: Oxford University Press.

Tufekci, Zeynep and Wilson, Christopher. (2012). "Social Media and the Decision to Participate in Political Protest: Observations From Tahrir Square." *Journal of Communication*. 62: 363–379.

Wasserman, Herman (2003). "The Possibilities of ICTs for Social Activism in Africa: An Exploration." Paper presented at Intellectuals, Nationalism and the Pan-African Ideal Conference, Dakar, Senegal, December 8–11, 2003.

Wines, Michael. (2009). "A Dirty Pun Tweaks China's Online Censors." *New York Times*. 1.

Wojcieszak, Magdalena E. and Mutz, Diana C. (2009). "Online Groups and Political Discourse: Do Online Discussion Spaces Facilitate Exposure to Political Disagreement?" *Journal of Communication*. 59: 40–56.

Yang, Goubin. (2003). "Weaving a Green Web: The Internet and Environmental Activism in China." *China Environment Series*. 6: 89–93.

Youmans, William Lafi and York, Jillian C. (2012). "Social Media and the Activist Toolkit: User Agreements, Corporate Interests, and the Information Infrastructure of Modern Social Movements." *Journal of Communication*. 62: 315–329.

Zaller, John R. (1992). *The Nature and Origins of Mass Opinion*. New York: Cambridge University Press.

....

CHAPTER 23

COMMUNICATION IN
MOVEMENTS

....

W. LANCE BENNETT AND ALEXANDRA SEGERBERG

MODERN social movement scholarship came of age during a time of mature modern societies and mass media. Early and mid-twentieth century social protest formations were typically embedded in institutional platforms such as parties, unions, churches, social clubs, and other civil society organizations from which they drew membership, resources, collective identities, and network bridges to other groups and institutions. A next generation of "new" identity-oriented movements formed around social groups with common concerns about rights, equality, and various forms of discrimination against women, ethnic and racial groups, or sexual preference. Also developing through the last half of the twentieth century were numerous cause movements that focussed on issues such as environmental protection, human rights, freedom for various oppressed peoples, economic justice in the global South, and hundreds of other issues. Both identity and cause movements created a demand for new kinds of organizations and political relationships that helped spur the rapid growth of non-governmental organizations (NGOs) and an alphabet soup of other hybrids (INGOs, TSMOs, etc.) as the social platforms for public engagement and cause advocacy.

The symbolic worlds of recognition, power, and legitimacy in which these organization-based movements operated were largely constructed through the mass media that enabled distant citizens to include or exclude one another in "imagined communities" (Anderson 2006). The era of modern, mass mediated societies spanning roughly the last half of the twentieth century helped scholars define the role of communication in movements largely in terms of how collective identity was framed and how well those frames traveled across coalitions of organizations and into mass media representations of their activities. Media coverage, in turn, was thought to affect levels of popular support or opposition to movements.

Both movement and media landscapes have changed dramatically in the short period spanning the end of the twentieth century and the opening decades of the twenty-first. Joining the legacy movements noted above were a number of the largest protest mobilizations in human history, often spanning many nations, affecting large populations, and inviting participation at various levels, from direct physical action to voluminous shows of social support on digital media platforms. These protests include the anti war mobilizations in more than sixty nations before the US invasion of Iraq in 2003, the Icelandic "anthill" uprising following the banking crisis of 2008, the sustained protests in Tunisia and Egypt that have been referred to as the "Arab Spring," the M-15 "indignados" mobilization in Spain in 2011, and the Occupy Wall Street encampments and social media crowds that developed in the United States in 2011–12 and spread to many other locations around the globe (Bennett and Segerberg 2013). In addition, there have been waves of socially mediated protests about environmental and labor issues in authoritarian regimes such as China. These and other "socially mediated mobilizations" suggest the need for supplementing existing mass media perspectives to better understand the role of media in contentious politics.

Whether these more recent mobilizations count as true social movements seems to us not a particularly helpful question that is likely to invite definitional skirmishes and reification. Participants and observers in many such protests have referred to them as movements. However, they also differ in important ways from classic movements of the modern era. We can finesse the definitional issues by categorizing the entire range of collective action noted above under the broad category of contentious collective action developed by McAdam, Tarrow, and Tilly (2001). This move opens up more fruitful questions about how to compare different forms of mobilization in terms of organization, ideas, engagement mechanisms, participation patterns, goals, and outcomes. However, it would also be helpful to develop a broad organizational framework in which different kinds of movements can be located and compared. Toward this end, we are particularly interested in how the role of communication may be changing in contentious politics and how those changes reflect different logics of collective action rooted in different interactions among social structure, participant identities, and communication processes and technologies. In the course of our discussion, when we refer to "movements," we do so in the spirit of problematizing these analytical elements.

One interesting shift in thinking about the role of communication in contention involves the use of digital and social media to supplement and even displace mass media in terms of reaching broad publics, often involving them in far more active roles than the spectator or bystander publics of the mass media era. A second shift involves the uses of media to create organizational networks among populations that lack more conventional institutional forms of political organization. Mobilizations that rely importantly on social media for engagement, logistics, and planning suggest that communication and media involve more than the exchange of messages and ideas. Indeed, dense social media networks interact with often-dispersed physical populations to form networked organizations that may have few conventional bureaucratic organizations or clear leadership (Bennett, Segerberg, and Walker 2014). These changes in the role of communication in movements are often associated with important changes in modern social structure, from the decline of institutional memberships and loyalties in many postindustrial societies, to the challenges faced by many authoritarian regimes in policing online communication that has played key roles in uprisings in countries as different as China and Egypt. Understanding the relationships between social structure and communication processes offers a foundation for analyzing and comparing different kinds of contention. We begin with a look at the legacy movements and legacy media that defined contention in modern societies.

MOVEMENTS, MASS MEDIA, AND MODERN SOCIETY

As noted earlier, the study of modern era movements generally looked at communication in terms of spreading ideas. Communication involved creating messages that shaped collective identification among participants and potential coalition partners, and then getting those messages to bystander publics through mass media to publicize claims and demands (Koopmans 2004). The path-breaking work by Benford and Snow on "framing" processes highlighted movement actors' efforts to interpret relevant events and conditions, and in particular the ongoing framing work undertaken by movement organizations in order to mobilize participants, gain bystander support, and generally establish the legitimacy of their preferred frames in the broader public discourse (Snow and Benford 1988; Benford and Snow 2000). Extending Goffman's (1974) work on how individuals' "schemata of interpretation" help organize experience and guide action, mobilization was understood to depend on organizations' abilities to achieve resonance with the interpretative schemes of potential participants and coalition partners through a set of frame alignment processes (Snow et al. 1986).

In the view of many scholars, a movement's success hinged on getting positive messages based on framing into the mass media. Favorable mass media portrayal was deemed critical to achieve visibility, and to establish frames and legitimacy. Perhaps the starkest claim about the dependency of movements on media was by the German scholar, Joachim Rashke, who stated that "A movement that does not make the media is non-existent" (Rashke 1985: 343—quoted in Rucht 2004: 25). Mass media actors serve as communication gatekeepers who could play an important role for getting a movement's messages out, but more often than not, relations between contentious collectivities and the press are not harmonious.

Gaining favorable media attention is seldom a simple proposition. Movements often come from the excluded margins of society seeking to insert their values and demands into the mainstream. The mass media in many cases are the gatekeepers of the values of centrist society (Gans 1979). Moreover, the news tends to frame stories according to cues from elites in power (Bennett 1990). This leaves movements in the contradictory position of fighting to get their values and demands into a mainstream society and press that are not predisposed to accept them. The media thus often report on movements negatively, particularly when inability to achieve recognition and satisfy demands leads to civil disobedience and disruptive protest in order to get public attention. The result is typically a combination of negative coverage and media pressures to get movements to conform to accepted mainstream models of politics and political organization that in many cases the movements were seeking to change in the first place (Gitlin 1980; Gamson and Modigliani 1989; Gamson 2004).

This mass media paradox generated a good deal of interesting literature on the media strategies of movements aimed at understanding how the public communication imperatives of movements could be handled effectively. Gamson (1992) developed a symbolic logic for thinking about the fit between internal movement communication and the broader public values represented by media logics. Gamson and Wolfsfeld (1993) noted ways in which framing of actions could evoke broader public sympathy for causes, while satisfying media norms of drama and entertainment. Nonetheless, the sensation-value of street protests, clashes with police and civil disobedience, offered more compelling news fare, and thus the dominant media logic frequently resulted in negative coverage that failed to communicate movement messages effectively to broader publics (Altheide and Snow 1979).

Direct mass media strategies were often frustrated, leading to what Rucht (2004) observed as "Four As" of movement media strategy: abstention (frustration with negative coverage or no coverage resulting in giving up efforts to influence the mass media); attack (campaigning against mass media bias); adaptation (playing the media game and staging events to fit more favorable mass media logics); or creating alternative media (publishing magazines or producing radio more in keeping with movement values). Movements throughout the 1960s to the 1980s had some success in mixing variations on these strategies. Careful press relations also worked for some transnational movement organizations as noted by Kolb (2005) in his analysis of ATTAC (Action for a Tobin Tax to Assist the Citizen) in Germany.

Focussing on the mass media messages controlled by movement organizations makes sense when analyzing movements making claims on institutional targets in coherent modern societies dominated by mass media systems. However, this perspective also draws a sharp dichotomy between mainstream and alternative media, as well as between political strategies and deeper cultural processes in ways that divided the academic discussion and overshadowed other forms of communication and action (Downing 2000; Atton 2002). More recent thinking about movements and communication has expanded as both movement and media forms have changed with the transformation from modern to late modern social structures and as movements and their communication capacities have spilled beyond national borders and adopted social media, as discussed in the next section.

Movements and Media in Late Modern Societies

Many notable changes have occurred as the rise of neoliberal globalization in the late twentieth century has transformed social structures, everyday social life, political engagement, and communication systems. Many scholars have discussed these structural changes involving the separation of individuals from groups and institutions in variously termed late modern or post-industrial societies (Giddens 1991; Bauman 2000; Putnam 2000). Others have noted that as individuals disconnect from the modern social order, they do not necessarily drift in anomie, particularly when they have access to personal media devices and social networking technologies that give rise to new orders such as the network society (Castells 2000; Barney 2004; Benkler 2006). Different societies may undergo these changes at different rates and with different results depending on levels of economic and political development, culture, and geopolitical location. And, in most societies, these changes are generationally accented as older citizens often continue to participate in the legacy institutions of modern society (party, press, civil society organizations). The rise of nationalist and anti immigrant parties and movements in many nations is just one sign of a struggle to preserve a changing social order.

By contrast, younger generations coming of age in more fully globalized, neoliberal economies are less attracted to conventional politics, the press, and memberships in legacy movements even when they may share concerns about their causes. The demographic trend is toward loose affiliations in networked and often highly personalized forms of contention (Bennett and Segerberg 2013). The point here is not whether these forms of contention are necessarily more or less effective than classical movement forms, but that their social and communication underpinnings are importantly different, as indicated in the early work of Castells (2000) on networked protest, Bennett (2003a) on the permanent transnational campaigns against large corporations, and Olesen's (2004) analysis of the online and offline international solidarity networks that formed around the Zapatista uprising in Mexico. Among the most dramatic empirical contrasts is the side-by-side comparison of different kinds of movements in Spain by Anduiza, Cristancho, and Sabucedo (2013). Their field surveys contrasted participants in conventional movements such as labor, regional autonomy, and abortion, with participants in the *indignados* protests. When *indignados* named organizations with which they affiliated, those organizations had far fewer street addresses (38 per cent versus 86 per cent for general strike and 78–100 per cent for regional autonomy), and most of those mainly virtual organizations did not accept formal members (13 per cent versus 60–100 per cent in conventionally organized movement protests).

In general, as labor markets, political parties, and other institutions of modern democracy continue to erode in terms of popular support and participation in the global north, the relations between many movements and these institutions are also changing. A dilemma facing many activists involves figuring out just what to demand of political institutions that they regard as dysfunctional. Observers of some contemporary movements such as the M-15 in Spain and Occupy Wall Street were puzzled that they did not seek alliances with conventional organizations such as unions, parties, or other social movement organizations, nor did they seek entry into the political process by engaging with elections as many other movements have done. Such anomalies may be explained by what some prominent scholars are pointing to as a crisis of democratic legitimacy (Castells 2012; della Porta 2013). As fragmented societies become further burdened with legitimacy crises, individuated populations may share common grievances and causes, but are less inclined to join conventional organizations or embrace the collective identifications of classic movement frames.

As citizens disconnect from institutions, politics has become more personalized in a granular sense of being individualized, resulting in changing forms of movement organization, more flexible and inclusive framing of messages, and the growing importance of personal media. One implication of these changes for thinking about media in movements is that the old dichotomy between mass and alternative media is no longer helpful. Indeed, it gets in the way of grasping the importance of a new communication order supported by the internet, mobile networks, and a dizzying array of communication software that may now connect more people around the globe in ways they trust than mass media systems do. However, if we are going to remove the categorical distinction between mass and alternative media, how do we want to think about media? One approach is to recognize that media systems have become hybridized: media networks move more fluidly across devices and platforms and involve various kinds of actors, from professional journalists to politicians to activists (Chadwick 2013). Important political content now moves directly from social media platforms such as Facebook or YouTube to large audiences, and may reach those who continue to follow mass media by making the daily news.

Most of these hybrid media systems (and related movements) rise and fall fairly quickly, as when Wikileaks had its brief, high impact moment with the international publication of secret documents. Whether they are more or less enduring, social media networks are characterized by participation of audiences in both creating and distributing much of the information that travels through them, creating network connections with each other in the process. These content creation and networking preferences of younger digital media users add pressures on more established organizations to rethink their relationships with followers and their strategies for managing issues and campaigns. As we explain in the next section, many NGOs have relaxed their interests in controlling or branding issue campaigns, and offer many avenues for publics to engage directly with each other, and with other issues and organizations in cause networks. In many campaigns, sponsoring organizations move to the background while supporting online organizations that coordinate multiple paths for individual involvement with multiple political targets. This was the pattern in the Robin Hood Tax campaign in the United Kingdom, which failed to gain British government support for a tax on speculative financial transactions in Britain, yet successfully directed public pressure on the European Union, where eleven member states adopted versions of the tax (Bennett and Segerberg 2013: ch. 5).

In short, digital media networks not only display the capacity to reach broad publics, but unlike mass media, they often blur the distinction between information production and consumption by engaging members of those publics as participants at varying levels of involvement (Bennett 2003b, 2005; Bennett and Segerberg 2013; Bennett, Segerberg, and Walker 2014). In the process, activist choices about media strategies have become both more complex and numerous. Mass media may retain a distinctive role as a conduit to elites and political institutions, and as a link between elites and older civic generations who continue to consume journalism, but those information gates are not as easily kept as in past eras when other media forms were less evident.

In this context many established cause movements (e.g., feminist, minorities, peace, environment) have also become hybridized, moving fluidly across national borders, targets and issue boundaries, as the case of the Robin Hood Tax illustrates. NGOs and other movement organizations increasingly package interrelated issues in their agendas, making fewer distinctions among issue boundaries such as economic and environmental justice, or human and labor rights. Putting this back in social context, these trends correspond to the above mentioned social changes that disrupt individuals from forming more committed organizational memberships and free them to engage with multiple causes and adopt more "flexible political identities" (della Porta 2005). As a result, legacy movement organizations may have less control over memberships and strategies than in earlier eras (see Keck and Sikkink 1998), as they typically operate in protest spaces shared with less disciplined networks of direct activists who can use personal media to coordinate their own activities and even continue campaigns after NGOs have moved on (Bennett 2003a, 2005; Bennett and Segerberg 2013). These developments raise interesting theoretical questions about the implications of digital media for protest mobilization and organization.

COMMUNICATION, CONNECTIVE ACTION, AND LARGE-SCALE PROTEST

Shifts in social structure, political engagement patterns, and communication systems have implications both for forms of protest organization and the associated role of communication. This is particularly clear in the large-scale protests that marked the first decade of the twenty-first century. Although there had been large-scale protests against international organizations such as the G7, G8, G20, World Bank, and World Trade Organization (WTO) dating from the 1980s, the iconic "Battle of Seattle" that shut down the WTO meetings in 1999 marks something of a turning point in the hybrid forms of multi-issue, loosely organized, and personally mediated protests. Such events became more characteristic after the turn of the millennium, as protest waves followed international organizations around the world, and mediated crowds addressed diverse issues in different settings, from United Nations (UN) climate summits, to Tahrir Square and Occupy Wall Street.

Distinct logics of action yield diverse organizational dynamics in such protests (Bennett and Segerberg 2013). At one end of a spectrum of the principles of organization and participation in movements is the classic logic of collective action, as formulated by Mancur Olson (1965). Olson addressed mobilization and participation dilemmas in which obstacles and costs associated with participation become problematic for the formation of groups. Olson's classic "free rider problem" develops the paradox of why it is rational for an individual not to contribute to a collective endeavor even if everyone would be better off if everyone contributed. This logic has movement organizers working hard to overcome barriers to participation by offering inducements, providing consciousness-raising or education, developing framing, and facilitating peer mobilizing. While many movement scholars quickly moved away from strong assumptions about collective action contained in early resource mobilization theory (McCarthy and Zald 1977), many movement studies retain echoing roles for formal organizations, leadership, collective identity framing, social networks, and other aspects of movement organizing. Moving even farther across the scale are approaches favoring more cultural and epistemic models that generally echo the collective identification and framing assumptions (for reviews of variations among different legacy movement perspectives, see Tarrow 1998). These various types of movements that emphasize the centrality of organizations, coalitions, and collective action framing and frame alignment engage in what we term "organizationally brokered collective action" (Bennett and Segerberg 2013).

The role of communication in studies along this part of the movement spectrum generally involves organizations seeking message control by using framing to mobilize consensus and solidarity and to maximize what Tilly called WUNC (worthiness, unity, numbers, and commitment) in the demonstrations (Tilly 2004). Such collective action framing tends to be exclusive and demanding, requiring extensive brokerage between groups attempting to work together, with organizers using social technology primarily to manage participation, reduce the costs of reaching members, and circumvent often negative mass media coverage (Rucht 2004).

In the middle of our theoretical spectrum of action logics is a hybrid action type that we term "organizationally-enabled *connective* action," which is characterized by organizations relaxing their need to recruit and manage formal members and exclusively brand or frame their own campaigns. Instead, they join in loose, media rich networks with other organizations. Websites and other media sites (such as Facebook) in this part of the action spectrum offer personalized media affordances through which individuals may engage with issues and directly share ideas and action plans with each other. In many cases such as the Robin Hood Tax campaign, the networks become quite large (numbering in the hundreds and even thousands of organizations), enabled in part because the personalized framing of the action shifts the focus from organizations to networked publics. As organizations recede into the background of campaigns and events, the personalized face of the social network often appears in the form of web-based organizations such as the Robin Hood Tax and Put People First (Bennett and Segerberg 2013). Because social media enable considerable network organization among participants on their own terms, we shift the focus of communication logics here from collective action rooted in mass media to connective action rooted in social networking.

As we move farther along the connective action end of the organizational spectrum, the impact of changing social structures (i.e., individual separation from organizations and institutions) becomes more evident: neither the identity preferences of participants, nor the role of communication in movements are explained adequately by legacy organization-centered movement perspectives. The end of the movement spectrum that we term "crowd-enabled connective action," is characterized by large-scale mobilizations that have few central organizations, few formal leaders, little in the way of brokered coalitions, and action frames that are inclusive and individualized such as "We are the 99%" that captured the ethos of Occupy Wall Street, or "Real Democracy Now!" around which the M-15 Spanish *indignados* rallied (Anduiza et al. 2013). What enables organization in such mobilizations?

In contrast to the rational self-interest position of individuals being asked to share the costs and the identifications of creating common cause with others, the logic of connective action is rooted in self-motivated personal sharing across social networks. Action based on this logic is enhanced by easy access to digital communication technologies that facilitate personalized sharing and offer reinforcement for participation via recognition among individuals at a fine-grained level (Bennett and Segerberg 2013). Although they may face other challenges, organizers of connective action do not have to put the same kind of communication and organizational work or cost into overcoming the participation threshold.

Networks along the crowd-enabled range of the action spectrum are often densely mediated, with different media engaging different populations, and performing different kinds of work. These media networks may provide coordination among widely dispersed geographic populations, and engage supportive publics that in some cases may span the globe. The highly personalized action frames in these networks often arise from crowd production and transmission and typically enable individuals to attach their own stories, and share their own experiences via multi media artifacts such as photos, videos, and other easily shared objects (Bennett and Segerberg 2013). In important ways, the communication networks become the political organization.

These three ideal types of action organization contain different roles for communication, from *organizationally brokered* collective action networks in which communication may magnify and valorize (or limit and devalue) the public awareness of action, to *organizationally enabled* and *crowd-enabled* connective networks in which communication media take increasingly central organizing roles (Bennett and Segerberg 2013). Of course many protests encompass layers and pockets of all three types, not always harmoniously relating to each other. However, there are many events and movements that fall close enough to one of our three ideal types to illustrate the distinctive roles of communication in different types of contention. Recognizing the roles of communication in different types of movement organization can be facilitated by identifying different repertoires of communication, and seeing how these repertoires, along with the role of language and symbolism can change from one movement type to another.

REPERTOIRES OF COMMUNICATION AND
THE ROLE OF LANGUAGE AND SYMBOLISM

The above theoretical continuum of movement organization helps in recognizing both the variety of movements and the complexity of the media environments in which they are situated. Analyzing the patterns of communication and organization is easier if the researcher is sensitive to how convention, routine and beliefs play into strategic action (Polletta 2002, 2006). The media choices and communication practices of particular movement actors may reveal implicit models of the ideal movement. Different players may clearly regard one form of movement or protest organization as superior to another, and their communication preferences can reveal clues about those normative preferences. A useful step in this direction is Mattoni's idea of communication repertoires that encompass "the entire set of activist media practices that social movement actors might conceive as possible and then develop in both the latent and visible stages of mobilization, to reach social actors positioned both within and beyond the social movement milieu" (Mattoni 2013: 47; see also Kriesi et al. 2009; Teune 2011).

The attention to situated and dynamic activist "media practices" (Couldry 2004) brings focus squarely to movement actors (as opposed to conditioning media and technology) and emphasizes the embedded character of movement communication cultures in which practices reveal situated ideas about organization, identification, strategy, and media choices. As Mattoni (2013) demonstrates in her study of precarious workers' mobilizations in Italy, such an approach offers useful comparative potential for movements in the complex and layered—mass and social, public and restricted, online and offline—media environments that are typical of the digital age. Similarly, Kavada (2013) studied communication cultures in the European Social Forum movement factions, some of which favored a more transparently and hierarchically organized movement with clear frames and demands—"the verticals"—while others preferred to think of the forum as an open conversation space with no fixed agenda, leadership, or control—"the horizontals" (Juris 2005). While the verticals had clear communication strategies and repertoires reflecting their movement culture, the horizontals favored less structure, generating numerous e-mail lists, creating wikis to which almost anyone could add content, and perhaps most tellingly, blurring distinctions between communicators and audiences (a communication culture echoed in more recent movements such as Occupy). The horizontals favored a communication style which developed the inward-looking visions about the communication space of the movement, in contrast with the verticals who saw more clearly defined communication strategies as means of facilitating outward political goals aimed at social change.

However, as we move farther away from movements led by central organizations and leaders aiming particular claims at institutional targets using conventional in media strategies, it becomes more difficult to link communication repertoires to purposive organizational strategy. Costanza-Chock's (2013) notion of "transmedia mobilization" shows how participatory media networks often diffuse rather than focus the idea of communication: "Transmedia mobilization thus marks a transition in the role of movement communicators from content creation to aggregation, curation, remixing and circulation of rich media texts. Those social movement actors that embrace decentralization of the movement voice can reap great rewards, while those that attempt to maintain top-down control risk losing credibility" (Costanza-Chock 2013: 97). In such networked organizations, actors "shift from speaking *for* to speaking *with* social movements" (Costanza-Chock 2013: 97).

This raises the importance of the role of language and other content in different kinds of movement organization. For many scholars, movements involve inspiring leaders delivering great speeches that signify the worthiness of causes and their followers. While words and language—the stuff of framing—still matter they may matter less (or at least differently) in connective action than they do in more conventional protest organization, leaving some observers nostalgic for the grandiloquent rhetoric of past eras (Tarrow 2013). What matters more in crowd-enabled organization are the mundane personal stories and images shared over social networks, or the seemingly trivial logistics and rallying messages streaming over SMS and Twitter. At the same time, other kinds of symbols such as art, masks, costumes, and digital artifacts may matter more as they become *memes* that travel easily across network boundaries of culture, language, time, space, and group membership. Indeed, the study of visual elements is now becoming central to understanding the organization of protests both online and offline (Doerr, Mattoni, and Teune 2013). The idea of visual elements in protest surely dates to the beginning of human association, but the ways in which digital media can now capture, share, curate, and network these images may make them more than just expressive aspects of movements, but important organizational elements as well.

Setting various repertoires of communication alongside the different repertoires of contention invites closer analysis of when and how communication and organization repertoires cross and combine (Tilly 2006; Tilly and Tarrow 2007). In the process it may become easier to see when communication serves more as an expression of existing organization and when organization is the creation of communication.

COMMUNICATION AS ORGANIZATION

Perhaps the most significant indicator that a paradigm shift may be underway in thinking about movements and how they work is the idea that communication is not just a category that can give insight into movements, but rather one that is increasingly at the core of how movements work: determining how large and fast they grow, how they achieve some semblance of coherence, how long they last, and what kinds of impacts they may have. As more instances of what we term connective action become evident, it is important to consider how communication is implicated in the organizing process. As explained earlier, beyond carrying content, discourses, images, and technological mechanisms are also potential networking agents. Embedded in networks, these elements acquire relationship properties (closeness, distance, valence, avoidance, repetition of contact, etc.) that enable and constrain action, channel resources, establish relationships, and absorb events. These organizational capacities may be due in part to how technologies are designed, but also to what users do with them.

An important question for the study of communication in contemporary movements, then, is what kinds of organization can result from different kinds of communication technologies, and how they are used to accomplish different varieties of organizational work under different conditions. For example, our analysis of the Occupy movement identified dozens of dense technology layers doing different kinds of organizational work, with Twitter serving as an overarching network stitching mechanism connecting the plethora of layers in the large-scale movement. As a result, the crowd developed a capacity to allocate resources, respond to short-term external events such as police actions, and display adaptive long-term communication efforts using millions of fine-grained peer-to-peer mechanisms of production, curation, and dynamic integration (Bennett, Segerberg, and Walker 2014).

While networked media may explain the fortunes of crowd-enabled connective action, the same media (e.g., Facebook or Twitter) may not make much of a difference for the organizationally brokered collective action discussed earlier. Instead, the same media enable central actors to do more of what they were already doing, albeit possibly more efficiently, cheaply and on a larger scale (the "supersizing" effect described by Earl and Kimport 2011). More work remains to be done on how different communication processes operate in different contexts at macro- and micro-levels.

BRINGING THEORY FORWARD

Despite the notable reliance on digital media in the organization of movements that are more distributed and less reliant on mass media, there are still calls to return to the framework adapted to an earlier age of modern social structure and simpler communication options. Rucht (2013) lists fully a dozen reasons why a focus on the internet is misguided when attempting to understand communication in movements, and warns that the role of mass media and face-to-face communication is underestimated by those who focus on digital media. Perhaps this is true, for the very reasons we point out, when looking at traditional, organizationally brokered, movements. It is of course important to avoid letting a new set of enthusiasms overshadow everything else. However, the role of communication as framing and sending messages, expanding audiences and negotiating coalitions and legitimacy is just one package of communication that fits into particular types of movement organization. These roles for communication begin to fade and be supplemented by networked organizational capacities as we move across our theoretical spectrum to organizationally enabled and crowd-enabled forms of organization.

There are now many distinct forms of movement organization, and they entail other roles and repertoires of communication. From early activist experiments with digital media—such as Indymedia—to continuously innovative web platforms and the appropriation of commercial social media such as Facebook and Twitter (and counterparts such as Weibo in China), communication occupies myriad roles in different organizational schemas. The forms and dynamics of contention are expanding to include: direct digital action and hacktivism (Jordan 2002; Atton 2004; Lievrouw 2011; Milan 2013) and other purely digital repertoires of contention (Earl and Kimport 2011); and invasive methods of policing, surveillance, and authoritarian rule (Fuchs 2008; Braman 2009).

The pressing contemporary challenge is to understand the rich range of roles of communication in movements and to more fully theorize how different media fit into different kinds of movements. In doing this, we cannot assume that all movements are the same, or that some movement approaches to communication are more genuine than others. Rather, the key questions are how various movement forms are organized along different kinds of participatory and organizational logics with different kinds of goals, and how distinct kinds of communication reflect and constitute those varieties of contention.

REFERENCES

Altheide, David L. and Snow, Robert P. (1979). *Media Logic*. Beverly Hills: Sage.

Anderson, Benedict (2006). *Imagined Communities: Reflections on the Origin and Spread of Nationalism*. Rev. Ed. London: Verso.

Anduiza, Eva, Cristancho, Camilo, and Sabucedo, Jose M. (2013). "Mobilization Through Online Social Networks: The Political Protest of the Indignados in Spain," *Information, Communication & Society*. 17(6): 750–764.

Atton, Chris (2002). *Alternative Media*. London: Sage.

Atton, Chris (2004). *An Alternative Internet: Radical Media, Politics and Creativity*. Edinburgh: Edinburgh University Press.

Barney, Darin (2004). *The Network Society*. Cambridge: Polity.

Bauman, Zygmunt (2000). *Liquid Modernity*. Cambridge: Polity.

Benford, Robert D. and Snow, David A. (2000). "Framing Processes and Social Movements: An Overview and Assessment," *Annual Review of Sociology*. 26: 611–639.

Benkler, Yochai (2006). *The Wealth of Networks: How Social Production Transforms Markets and Freedom*. New Haven: Yale University Press.

Bennett, W. Lance (1990). "Towards a Theory of Press—State Relations," *Journal of Communication*. 40: 103–125.

Bennett, W. Lance (2003a). "Communicating Global Activism: Strengths and Vulnerabilities of Networked Politics," *Information, Communication & Society*. 6(2): 143–168.

Bennett, W. Lance (2003b). "New Media Power: The Internet and Global Activism." In *Contesting Media Power*, edited by Nick Couldry and James Curran, 17–37. Lanham, MD: Rowman & Littlefield.

Bennett, W. Lance (2005). "Social Movements beyond Borders: Organization, Communication and Political Capacity in Two Eras of Transnational Activism." In *Transnational Protest and*

Global Activism, edited by Donatella della Porta and Sidney Tarrow, 203–226. Boulder, CO: Rowman and Littlefield.

Bennett, W. Lance and Segerberg, Alexandra (2013). *Logic of Connective Action: Digital Media and the Personalization of Contentious Politics*. Cambridge & New York: Cambridge University Press.

Bennett, W. Lance, Segerberg, Alexandra, and Walker, Shawn (2014). "Organization in the Crowd: Peer Production in Large-scale Networked Protests," *Information, Communication & Society*. 17(2): 232–260.

Braman, Sandra (2009). *Change of State: Information, Policy, and Power*. Cambridge, MA: MIT Press.

Castells, Manuel (2000). *The Rise of the Network Society*. New York: Wiley.

Castells, Manuel (2012). *Networks of Outrage and Hope: Social Movements in the Internet Age*. Cambridge: Polity.

Chadwick, Andrew (2013). *The Hybrid Media System: Politics and Power*. New York: Oxford University Press.

Costanza-Chock, Sasha (2013). "Transmedia Mobilization in the Popular Association of the Oaxacan Peoples, Los Angeles." In *Mediation and Protest Movements*, edited by Bart Cammaerts, Alice Mattoni, and Patrick McCurdy, 95–114. Bristol: Intellect Press.

Couldry, Nick (2004). "Theorising Media as Practice," *Social Semiotics*. 14(2): 115–132.

della Porta, Donatella (2005). "Multiple Belongings, Flexible Identities and the Construction of 'Another Politics': Between the European Social Forum and the Local Social Fora." In *Transnational Protest and Global Activism*, edited by Donatella della Porta and Sidney Tarrow, 175–202. Boulder, CO: Rowman & Littlefield.

della Porta, Donatella (2013). "Bridging Research on Democracy, Social Movements and Communication." In *Mediation and Protest Movements*, edited by Bart Cammaerts, Alice Mattoni, and Patrick McCurdy, 21–38. Bristol: Intellect Press.

Doerr, Nicole, Mattoni, Alice, and Teune, Simon, eds. (2013). *Advances in the Visual Analysis of Social Movements*. Vol. 35 of the Series Research in Social Movements, Conflict and Change, Bingley UK: Emerald.

Downing, John (2000). *Radical Media: Rebellious Communication and Social Movements*. London: Sage.

Earl, Jennifer, and Kimport, Katrina (2011). *Digitally Enabled Social Change: Activism in the Internet age*. Cambridge, MA: MIT Press.

Fuchs, Christian (2008). *Internet and Society: Social Theory in the Information Age*. New York: Routledge.

Juris, Jeffrey (2005). "Social Forums and their Margins: Networking Logics and the Cultural Politics of Autonomous Space," *Ephemera: Theory and Politics in Organization*. 5(2): 253–272.

Kavada, Anastasia (2013). "Internet Cultures and Protest Movements: The Cultural Links Between Stratgey, Organizing and Online Communication." In *Mediation and Protest Movements*, edited by Bart Cammaerts, Alice Mattoni, and Patrick McCurdy, 75–94. Bristol: Intellect Press.

Keck, Margaret and Sikkink, Kathryn (1998). *Activists Beyond Borders: Advocacy Networks in International Politics*. Ithaca, NY: Cornell University Press.

Gamson, William A. (1992). *Talking Politics*. New York: Cambridge University Press.

Gamson, William A. (2004). "Bystanders, Public Opinion, and the Media." In *The Blackwell Companion to Social Movements*, edited by David A. Snow, Sarah A. Soule, and Hanspeter Kriesi, 242–261. Malden MA: Blackwell.

Gamson, William A. and Modigliani, Andre (1989). "Media Discourse and Public Opinion on Nuclear Power: A Constructionist Approach," *American Journal of Sociology*. 95: 1–37.

Gamson, William A. and Wolfsfeld, Gadi (1993). "Movements and Media as Interacting Systems," *Annals of the American Academy of Political and Social Science*. 528: 114–125.

Gans, Herbert J. (1979). *Deciding What's News: A Study of CBS Evening News, NBC Nightly News, Newsweek, and Time*. New York: Pantheon Books.

Giddens, Anthony (1991). *Modernity and Self Identity: Self and Society in the Late Modern Age*. Stanford: Stanford University Press.

Gitlin Todd (1980). *The Whole World is Watching: Mass Media in the Making and Unmaking of the Left*. Berkeley: University of California Press.

Goffman, Erving (1974). *Frame Analysis: An Essay on the Organization of Experience*. Cambridge MA: Harvard University Press.

Jordan, Tim (2002). *Activism! Direct Action, Hacktivism and the Future of Society*. London: Reaktion Books.

Kolb, Felix (2005). "The Impact of Transnational Protest on Social Movement Organizations: Mass Media and the Making of ATTAC Germany." In *Transnational Protest and Global Activism*, edited by Donatella della Porta and Sidney Tarrow, 95–120. Boulder, CO: Rowman & Littlefield.

Koopmans, Ruud (2004). "Movements and Media: Selection Processes and Evolutionary Dynamics in the Public Sphere," *Theory and Society*. 33(3–4): 367–391.

Kriesi, Hanspeter, Laurent, Bernhard, and Regula, Hänggli (2009). "The Politics of Campaigning—Dimensions of Strategic Action." In *Politik in der Mediendemokratie*, edited by Frank Marcinkowski and Barbara Pfetsch, 345–365. Wiesbaden: VS Verlag für Sozialwissenschaften.

Lievrouw, Leah A. (2011). *Alternative and Activist New Media*. Cambridge: Polity.

Mattoni, Alice (2013). "Repertoires of Communication in Social Movement Processes." In *Mediation and Protest Movements*, edited by Bart Cammaerts, Alice Mattoni, and Patrick McCurdy, 39–56. Bristol: Intellect Press.

McAdam, Doug, Tarrow, Sidney, and Tilly, Charles (2001). *Dynamics of Contention*. New York: Cambridge University Press.

McCarthy, John D. and Zald, Mayer N. (1977). "Resource Mobilization and Social Movements: A Partial Theory," *American Journal of Sociology*. 82: 1212–1241.

Milan, Stefania (2013). *Social Movements and their Technologies: Wiring Social Change*. Basingstoke, Hampshire: Palgrave.

Olesen, Thomas (2004). "The Transnational Zapatista Solidarity Network: An Infrastructure Analysis," *Global Networks*. 4: 89–107.

Olson, Mancur (1965). *The Logic of Collective Action: Collective Goods and the Theory of Groups*. Cambridge MA: Harvard University Press.

Polletta, Francesca (2002). *Freedom Is An Endless Meeting: Democracy in American Social Movements*. Chicago: University of Chicago Press.

Polletta, Francesca (2006). It Was Like A Fever: Storytelling in Protest and Politics. Chicago: University of Chicago Press.

Putnam, Robert D. (2000). *Bowling Alone: The Collapse and Revival of American Community*. New York: Simon and Schuster.

Rucht, Dieter (2004). "The Quadruple 'A': Media Strategies of Protest Movements Since the 1960s." In *Cyberprotest: New Media, Citizens and Social Movements*, edited by Wim Van De Donk, Brian D. Loader, Paul G. Nixon, and Dieter Rucht, 29–56. London: Routledge.

Rucht, Dieter (2013). "Protest Movements and their Media Usages." In *Mediation and Protest Movements*, edited by Bart Cammaerts, Alice Mattoni, and Patrick McCurdy, 249–268. Bristol: Intellect Press.

Snow, David A. and Benford, Robert D. (1988). "Ideology, Frame Resonance, and Participant Mobilization." In *From Structure to Action: Social Movement Participation across Cultures*, edited by Bert Klandermans, Hanspeter Kriesi, and Sidney Tarrow, 197–217. Greenwich, CN: JAI Press.

Snow, David A., Rochford, R. Burke, Jr., Worden, Steven K., and Benford, Robert D. (1986). "Frame Alignment Processes, Micromobilization, and Movement Participation," *American Sociological Review*. 51: 464–481.

Teune, Simon (2011). "Communicating Dissent: Diversity of Expression in the Protest Against the G8 Summit in Heiligendamm." In *Protest Beyond Borders: Contentious Politics in Europe Since* 1945, edited by Hara Kouki and Eduardo Romanos, 86–102. Oxford: Berghahn Books.

Tarrow, Sidney (1998). *Power in Movement: Social Movements and Contentious Politics*. New York: Cambridge University Press.

Tarrow, Sidney (2013). *The Language of Contention: Revolutions in Words* 1688–2012. New York: Cambridge University Press.

Tilly, Charles (2004). *Social Movements, 1768–2004*. Boulder, CO: Paradigm Publishers.

Tilly, Charles (2006). *Regimes and Repertoires*. Chicago: University of Chicago Press.

Tilly, Charles and Tarrow, Sidney G. (2007). *Contentious Politics*. Boulder, CO: Paradigm.

CHAPTER 24

GEOGRAPHY AND SOCIAL MOVEMENTS

PAUL ROUTLEDGE

DURING the 1970s, and drawing from Marxism and feminism, the discipline of Geography inquired into socio-spatially constituted inequalities and injustices. However, it was not until the early 1990s that a direct and sustained engagement with the geographies of social movements began (e.g., Routledge 1993; Miller 2000; Nicholls 2007). Although engaging with the theoretical traditions of resource mobilization and political process (e.g., Miller 2000; Nicholls 2007) and new social movements (e.g., Routledge 2000), geographers have been concerned with the *lack* of engagement with Geography in social movement studies, arguing that geographical (spatial) understandings of social movement practice are crucial to the interpretation of contentious action. Movements act from space, politically mobilizing from the material conditions of their (local) spaces; movements act on space appropriating it with a group identity; movements act in space, such as taking to the streets for protests, or occupying land; and movements make space: creating conditions to expand public political involvement, for example through the creation of solidaristic alliances (Dikeç 2001).

Geographers' encounters with social movements have tended either to ground collective action within territorially bounded (often local) contexts or interpret such activity as relational and networked. More recently, geographical approaches to contentious politics have sought to incorporate both perspectives and their interrelations, stressing the multiple spatialities of social movement practices.

SOCIO-SPATIAL POSITIONALITY AND THE POLITICS OF PLACE

Differently positioned subjects have distinct identities, experiences, and perspectives that shape their understanding of, and engagement with, the world. These emerge relationally through connections and interactions with differently positioned subjects, and are shot through with unequal power relations. It is within particular places where everyday politics is practiced and made real. This is because the processes undertaken by macro-scale institutions such as governments are both translated into being in such places and where they are contested and reworked by social movement actors (Agnew 1987; Harvey 1995). Through people's geographically situated practices, relations, and imaginaries, oppressive power relations are contested, frequently through social movements (Leitner et al. 2008).

This is because different social groups endow space with an amalgam of different meanings and values. Hence, particular places frequently become sites of conflict where the social structures and relations of power, domination, and resistance intersect. This is most evident in instances where different ethnic or nationalist groups contest the same political space (e.g., Israel/Palestine). Collective action is often focussed upon cultural codes which are themselves spatially specific, since culture and ethnicity influence a community's sense of place, that is, the subjective orientation that can be engendered by living in a place. This plays a distinct role in shaping both the political claims of actors and the perception of political opportunities (Martin 2003). The ideology that emanates from this articulates a process of positive assertion (of local values, beliefs, and lifestyles) and resistance to intervening values of domination.

Sensitivity to such processes when considering particular practices of contentious action acknowledges the subjective nature of people's perceptions, imaginations, and experiences when they are involved in political action. It locates such action in dynamic spatial contexts, as it sheds light upon how geographic spaces are transformed into places redolent with cultural meaning, memory, and identity under conditions of conflict. For example, the Zapatista insurgency was informed by the place-specific political and cultural economy of indigenous people in the Mexican state of Chiapas, Mexico. Place has a central role in shaping the claims, identities, and capacities of mobilized political agents, helping to explain why social movements occur where they do, how the particularities of specific places influence the character and emergence of various forms of contentious action, and the context within which movement agency interpolates the social structure. Such a context-based analysis of social movements seeks to understand how the geographically uneven modes of exercising state and economic power intersect with people's everyday lives, combining to generate particular "terrains of resistance" (Routledge 1993).

Spatial proximity enables strong social and cultural ties to be established (e.g., through trust and kinship networks, ethnic and religions affiliations, common history, shared language and traditions, etc.) which can then be drawn on to enable collective action (Miller 2000; Tarrow and McAdam 2005; Nicholls 2007). For example, trade unions in Canada and the United Kingdom have recognized the importance of developing ties with other social movements (concerned with immigration, religion, and women's rights) in the places where they operate, generating "community unionism" that addresses low levels of unionism and workplace protection for home workers (Tufts 1998; Wills 2001, 2005).

Moreover, social movements frequently draw upon local knowledge, cultural practices, and vernacular languages to articulate their resistances. Songs, poems, stories, myths, metaphors, and symbols are used to inform and inspire collective action evoking a sense of place, history, and community. Such cultural expressions of contentious action frequently form a place-specific discourse of dissent which motivates and informs social movement agency, and articulates a movement's resistance identity. The poetics that emerges from such place-based resistance—that is, the *geopolitics*—are deployed in order to mobilize, to educate, to propagandize, to teach tactics and explain strategies (Routledge 2000).

Spatial imaginaries—that is, individual and collective cognitive frameworks constituted through the lived experiences, perceptions and conceptions of space—mediate how actors evaluate the potential risks and opportunities of joining social movements (Oslender 2004). For example, in the context of agricultural restructuring, political openings, and religious mobilization in southern Brazil, landless framers used and reformulated their spatial imaginaries to embrace land occupation through *Movimento dos Trabalhadores Rurais Sem Terra* (MST), or the Landless Workers' Movement; while in the northeast, unemployed rural workers overcame the spatial imaginaries put in place by the local sugarcane economy to join the movement (Wolford 2004).

Finally, places are internally multiple with pluralistic exchanges between actors within these areas, and the possibility for relational interactions across different sites: places are connected to extensive economic, political, and cultural networks with varying geographical reach (Massey 2004; Nicholls 2007). Therefore, movement interests and identities are formed through relational exchanges between multiple actors within and between different sites (Featherstone 2008). As a result, movements must negotiate constructing alliances between folk with diverse socio-spatial identities, interests, and imaginaries—both in their own particular struggles, and when participating with other movements in broader networks (Leitner et al. 2008).

However, while social movements may be increasingly made up of extensive and pluralistic relational flows, a number of factors continue to require their territorialization. Research on transnational social movements has shown how they must negotiate political power primarily institutionalized through discrete territorial boundaries despite increased interdependencies and relational exchanges across state spaces. Hence territorially intensive and geographically extensive relations contribute distinct yet complementary resources to social movements (Beaumont and Nicholls 2007).

Spatial Inequalities

Economic and political processes are articulated in geographically uneven ways that produce variations in the grievances and development trajectories of social movements (Miller 2000). The uneven nature of capitalism both differentiates grievance structures across space, and concentrates and disperses the resources needed to make social movements possible (Nicholls 2007). For example, the urbanization process within the southern states of the United States resulted in the concentration of organizational resources of Black Americans (e.g., churches, people, money, social networks) in a handful of urban centers (McAdam 1982). Conversely, the increased mobility of people and resources can diffuse the resource base available to movements, weaken important social networks between potential collaborators (hence limiting the usefulness of networks for procuring key resources), and place movements into territorial competition with one another (Nicholls 2007).

The uneven character of economic cycles creates differential conditions of social movement mobilization (Miller 2000). Rapid economic growth in one location may create conditions of environmental degradation, gentrification, or urban redevelopment, while economic decline in another location may generate conditions of unemployment, factory closures, or inner city decline. Hence, the uneven articulation of economic and state power—at the macro level—geographically differentiates the grievance structures of social movements and presents different sets of political opportunities for actors in different locations (Nicholls 2007).

Between states and within them, geographical variations in the relationship between states and civil society actors are important in understanding the context from which social movements emerge. For example, trade unions are still accepted as legitimate "social partners" in much of Western Europe, though they have been under attack in North America, the United Kingdom, and Australia and are heavily censored or often state-dominated in parts of Asia, Eastern Europe, and the former Soviet Union. Social movements are confronted by a range of more or less democratic political systems, and hence must operate within political spaces that are more, or less, coercive which may increase the barriers to cooperation. In addition, the degree of political opportunities available to movements differs profoundly across political regimes (Nicholls 2007). The coercive powers of the state are deployed differentially across space, which creates an uneven pattern of regulatory and repressive controls to contain those places where social and political contention is articulated (Nelson 2006). At the sub-national level, variations are also evident in the relations between local state actors and civil society. For example, in the United States, the American Federation of Labour (AFL-CIO) has faced a more favorable organizing environment in northern states, than unions in the southern states (Herod 1998, 2001).

THE POLITICS OF SCALE

Social movements mostly operate at the intersection of a series of overlapping scales—from more local municipalities, through regions, to the nation-state and, increasingly international forums. These different politics of scale provide movements with a range of opportunities and constraints (Nicholls 2007). For example, subsuming national labor regulations to international conventions reduces the opportunities for social movements to use electoral threats to pressure national political leaders. Also, devolving welfare policies to local government diffuses resistance because social movements must make claims in countless local bodies rather than a single national one (Nicholls 2007).

Movements that are local or national in character derive their principal strength from acting at these scales rather than at the global level. For example, transnational corporations such as Nestlé, McDonalds, and Nike have usually been disrupted primarily due to the efficacy of local campaigns (Klein 2000). Where international campaigns are organized, local and national scales of action can be as important as international ones. For example, the Liverpool Dockers' international campaign was grass-roots-instigated and coordinated (by the Liverpool Dockers) and operationalized by dockers beyond the United Kingdom working within established union frameworks (Castree 2000). However, Kathryn Sikkink (2005) has argued that political opportunities for transnational social movements differ markedly between national and international scales depending on the political character of countries, international institutions, and the nature of the political issues at stake. Movements often utilize political opportunities at one scale to create opportunities at other scales. For example, trade unions have employed a range of multi-scalar spatial strategies to transcend national level organizational logics in order to challenge Multinational Corporations through lobbying key global institutions such as the World Bank and International Monetary Fund (IMF) (Cumbers et al. 2008).

The persecution of multi-scalar strategies is also an interactive and relational process that requires the development and reorganization of social networks across geographical and social boundaries (Nicholls 2007). In their work on the American civil rights movement, Tarrow and McAdam (2005) term this process "scale shift" achieved through "relational diffusion" that is, the spatial extension of a movement through pre-existing relational ties containing trust and shared identities; and "brokerage" that is, the spread of social movement mobilization (through various brokers) resulting from linking two or more social movement actors who were previously unconnected.

NETWORKS AND RELATIONAL SPACES
OF STRUGGLE

As noted earlier, geographers understand places as internally multiple with pluralistic exchanges between actors within these areas, and the possibility for relational interactions across different sites (Massey 2004). Moreover, places are not only internally plural, they are also connected to extensive economic, political, and cultural networks with varying geographical reach (Nicholls 2007). Therefore, it is important to avoid simple counter-posing notions of local and global, space and place since movement interests and identities are formed through relational exchanges between multiple actors within and between different sites (Featherstone 2003). Particular locations are crossed by a variety of power networks, with actors in different sites engaging with one another through multiple relational exchanges (Featherstone 2005).

However, while social movements may be increasingly made up of extensive and pluralistic relational flows, a number of factors continue to require their territorialization (Martin 2003; D'Arcus 2005; Bosco 2006; Nicholls 2007). For example, the strength of community embeddedness of social movement networks can facilitate collaborative attitudes towards dialogue and engagement with movement opponents (Ansell 2003).

Certainly, political power continues to be primarily institutionalized through discrete territorial boundaries despite increased interdependencies and relational exchanges across state spaces (Mann 1997; Tarrow 2005). Hence, when place-based struggles develop, or become part of, geographically flexible networks, they become embedded in different places at a variety of spatial scales. These different geographic scales (local, national, regional, global) are mutually constitutive parts, becoming links of various lengths in the network. Networks of agents act across various distances and through diverse intermediaries (Dicken et al. 2001; for networked trade unionism, see Waterman 1998).

Networks can create cultural and spatial configurations that connect places with each other (Escobar 2001). Moreover, particular places can also be important within the workings of those networks. For example, the *Madres de Plaza de Mayo* in Argentina protested in different places across space (e.g., the public meetings of *Madres* in plazas across Argentina) that enabled the sustainability of different movement communities and movement identities. By reinforcing moral commitments and group solidarity, activist identities were maintained both within particular groups and between movements and activists in wider solidarity networks (Bosco 2001).

The identification with particular places can be of strategic importance for the mobilization strategies of movements. Activists may deploy symbolic images of places to match the interests and collective identities of other groups and thereby mobilize others along common cause or grounds. Hence the ties to particular places can be mobile, appealing to, and mobilizing, different groups in different localities (Bosco 2001). However, international alliances have to negotiate between action that is deeply embedded in place, that is, local experiences, social relations, and power conditions, and action that facilitates more transnational coalitions. For example, People's Global Action Asia, a network of Asian peasant movements, had to negotiate the different power relationships (e.g., caste, class, and gender) within Indian, Nepali, and Bangladeshi movements while attempting to forge an effective alliance against the processes of neoliberal globalization (Routledge 2003; see also Featherstone 2003).

Geographically, social movement networks have been conceived of as "convergence spaces" (Routledge 2003; Cumbers et al. 2008; Routledge and Cumbers 2009) defined by the following characteristics. First, they comprise place-based, but not place-restricted movements. Second, they articulate certain "collective visions" (e.g., unifying values and organizational principles) that generate common ground between participants. Third, they involve a practical relational politics of solidarity, bound up in five forms of interaction and facilitation: communication, information sharing, solidarity actions, network coordination, and resource mobilization. Fourth, they facilitate spatially extensive political action by participant movements. Fifth, they require "networking vectors," that is, activists that intervene in the work of translation by which networks are formed and developed, conducting ideational work and acting across space to further the process of communication, information sharing and interaction within and between a network's participant movements and the communities in which they operate. However, recent work by Diani (2013, 2015) in Glasgow and Bristol, in the United Kingdom, challenges the importance given to the actions of such key individual actors, arguing that of equal or greater importance is the configuration of network structures and the relational dynamics in particular localities. Sixth, they are characterized by range of different operational logics, spanning from more horizontal (decentered, non-hierarchical) to more vertical (centralized, hierarchical) operational logics. Finally, they are sites of contested social and power relations, because the diversity of groups that comprise them articulate a variety of potentially conflicting goals (concerning the forms of social change), ideologies (e.g., concerning gender, class, and ethnicity), and strategies (e.g., institutional (legal) and extra-institutional (illegal) forms of protest).

Such relational approaches to collective action are seen as increasingly important in understanding the communicative organizational logics of transnational social movement practices. Such networked approaches has been informed, at times, by actor-network theory (ANT) in order to highlight how transnational activists are able to connect and share information, enrol people and other resources into social movement networks, and translate networked imaginaries to grass-roots communities. For example, Routledge (2008) has shown how such processes have operated in Bangladesh, as attempts were made to enrol village communities mobilized by the Bangladesh Krishok (farmer) Federation into the international anti-capitalist network of People's Global Action (PGA). They relied on the durability of interpersonal relations, mobility through space and the associated materials and processes of distance-spanning communication. This was also affected by the extent to which PGA strategies and ideas were able to be reproduced (or not) in a range of network instances and locations.

ASSEMBLAGES AND SOCIAL MOVEMENTS

Recent theorizations of the spatiality of social movement practices have attempted to draw together key insights from both territorial and relational approaches to fashion a synthesis of the multiple spatialities of contentious politics (Beaumont and Nicholls 2007; Featherstone 2008; Jessop et al. 2008; Leitner et al. 2008; Nicholls 2009; Nicholls et al. 2013). For example, Nicholls (2009) argues that territorial understandings of contentious politics highlight how place-based relations generate actionable political values and interests, strengthen group cohesion, and enhance solidarity. Relational, networked accounts meanwhile, highlight how places act as nodes that are enrolled within what he terms "social movement space," creating opportunities for convergence between collective actors that generate different relational dynamics from those that exist in particular places.

Developing from these insights some geographers have begun to use concepts of assemblage to understand social movement behaviors (e.g., Featherstone, 2011). Social formations are understood as temporary aggregates of objects and people that temporarily cohere at certain times and places before dispersing again. What then becomes of importance is how sets of relations produce specific spatialities that emerge at particular times of political action (Davies 2012). Utilizing such assemblage thinking, Colin McFarlane (2009) has shown how the geographies of social movements operate *trans-locally*. Such an approach attempts to understand how place-based movements aggregate into wider alliances while also focusing upon the vibrant yet contingent character of connections between sites of contentious action. For McFarlane, space is open to be shaped by social movement actors whose relations with other actors are produced yet alter over time, creating assemblages where spatially extensive relations between activists maintain and territorialize social movement organizations. Drawing from this work Andrew Davies (2012) has shown how particular processes and practices of connection and disconnection are produced in and between Tibet Support Groups (TSG) in order to explore how relations between the groups have been produced and held together over time. He has shown how often quite mundane practices within particular TSG office spaces help to reinforce connections between both people within a particular TSG and simultaneously between that group and others.

GEOGRAPHERS AND SOCIAL MOVEMENTS

Although Geography's concern with issues of social justice dates back to the 1970s, it is only since the mid-1990s that geographers have become increasingly concerned with active collaboration with social movements opening up "third spaces" within and between academia and activism (Routledge 1996). Heavily influenced by feminist geographers amongst others (e.g., England 1994; Gibson-Graham 1994; Nast 1994; Staeheli and Lawson 1995; Rose 1997; Katz 2001; Panelli 2007) and eschewing necessarily "macho" forms of activism in favor of more open and relational understandings (Maxey 1999), activist geographers have stressed that connection and negotiation between diverse (activist, academic, lay) communities is required to enable what Paul Chatterton terms "learning, acting and talking together on uncommon ground" (2006: 277). In considering how political intervention might develop against global neoliberalism at the local scale, Doreen Massey (2004) uses the phrase "Geographies of Responsibility" to make the point that, because places are relational, and social relations flow through them, connecting us increasingly to "distant others" in complex ways, we should think more about how our own actions and interventions locally could be politically important. Hence, activist geographers recognize that they have social responsibilities, given their training, access to information, and freedom of expression, to make a difference "on the ground." This involves a commitment to exposing the socio-spatial processes that (re)produce inequalities between people and places; challenging and changing those inequalities; and then bridging the divide between theorization and praxis (Fuller and Kitchen 2004).

Thus a variety of activist geographies have been practiced by various geographers operating from different institutional bases and with varying levels of involvement in different worldly situations of social injustice (in both the Global North and the Global South). Such initiatives include, but are not limited to: *people's geography*, as embodied in the People's Geography Project organized out of the University of Syracuse, with its effort at making research and geographical concepts relevant to social struggles "for" (and to an extent "by") the people, for example, through the Syracuse hunger project (see www.peoplesgeography.org); *participatory geographies*, which involve geographers participating in the life-worlds of research subjects, and/or the participation of those research subjects in the production of geographical research (Kindon et al. 2008); and *autonomous geographies*, as outlined by Jenny Pickerill and Paul Chatterton in 2006, studying but also actively seeking to contribute to the building of "spaces where there is a desire to constitute non-capitalist, collective forms of politics, identity and citizenship" (Pickerill and Chatterton 2006: 730; see also Autonomous Geographies Collective 2010).

Such activist geographies stress the inseparability of knowledge and action, impelling them to be self-consciously interventionist in approach. This generates activist methodologies conceptualized with an eye to both communication and emancipation, confronting, and seeking solutions to, issues of social, economic, and environmental injustice. They are conceptualized and carried out in collaboration with social movements, the precise contours of such collaboration being worked through in cooperation with those others (Routledge 2002).

Geographers' engagement with social movements has been concerned with (i) developing practices aimed at *social transformation* rather than merely the "production of knowledge" and/or the "solving" of "local" problems. These move beyond the acquisition, cataloguing, ordering, and the publishing of information towards jointly producing knowledge with social movements to produce critical interpretations and readings of the world which are accessible, understandable to all those involved, and actionable (Chatterton et al. 2008); (ii) engagement in a *politics of affinity* with social movements, the connections and solidarities forged being a key part of activist research, implying a common identification of problems and desires amongst groups or individuals committed to social change, as well as a desire to work together to confront and reverse a set of issues which have a common effect on all the people concerned (e.g., see Koopman 2008); (iii) being attentive to, and *negotiating problematic power relations*, that exist between (research) collaborators. Collaborations between activist geographers and others are neither relationships of difference articulated through an objectifying distance, nor relationships of sameness based upon entirely commensurate backgrounds, interests, and ambitions. Hence activist geographers ask how difference—for instance regarding power relations—is constituted, tracing its destabilizing emergence during the research process itself. Negotiating power relations means working with groups to uncover structures of power to empower people to take control of their own lives; (iv) engaging with emotions not least because transformative encounters based on solidarity often come from our deep emotional responses to the world (Pulido 2003; Routledge 2012); (v) attempting to *engage in prefigurative action*, that is, to embody visions of transformation as if they are already achieved, thereby calling them into being. Moreover, collaborations are not just about action in the research process, but how the research process can contribute to wider activism like protests, demonstrations, events, etc. (Chatterton et al. 2008); (vi) attempting to *create spaces for action*, that is, physical spaces that can be created and occupied in building commonality and connection between different groups unmediated by consumer relations or profit, those autonomous geographies discussed by Jenny Pickerill and Paul Chatterton. These common places seek opportunities for transformative dialogue, mutual learning, and (creative) conflict. They form participatory spaces for building modes of understanding, encounter, and action that are inclusive, which nurture creative interaction with others independent of electoral politics, and which can lead to critical reflection and interventions; (vii) *relational ethics*. Ethical considerations raise crucial questions concerning the role played by concepts of social (in)justice in geographical research, and the extent to which ethical conduct is desirable, definable and/or enforceable in the practice of geography (Routledge 2002).

In short, geographers have been concerned with the ethics of political responsibility to social movements that extend beyond teaching within the academy (to relatively privileged students), in order for academic research to "make its deliberations more consequential for the poorer eighty per cent of the population of the world" (Appadurai 2000: 3). Such geographical engagements with social movements prioritize grounded, embodied political action, the role of theory being to contribute to, be informed by, and be grounded in such action, in order to create and nurture mutual solidarity and collective action, and an emancipatory politics of affinity.

References

Agnew, J. (1987). *Place and Politics: The Geographical Mediation of State and Society.* London: Allen and Unwin.

Ansell, C. (2003). "Community Embeddedness and Collaborative Governance in the San Francisco Bay Area Environmental Movement." In *Social Movements and Networks: Relational Approaches to Collective Action*, edited by M. Diani, and D. McAdam, 123–144. Oxford: Oxford University Press.

Appadurai, A. (2000). "Grassroots Globalization and the Research Imagination," *Public Culture.* 12(1): 1–19.

Autonomous Geographies Collective. (2010). "Beyond Scholar Activism: Making Strategic Interventions Inside and Outside the Neoliberal University," *ACME: An International E-Journal for Critical Geographies.* 9(2): 245–275.

Beaumont, J. and Nicholls, W. (2007). "Between Relationality and Territoriality: Investigating the Geographies of Justice Movements in The Netherlands and the United States," *Environment and Planning A*. 39(11): 2554–2574.

Bosco, F. (2001). "Place, Space, Networks, and the Sustainability of Collective Action: The *Madres de Plaza de Mayo*," *Global Networks*. 1(4): 307–329.

Bosco, F. (2006). "The *Madres de Plaza de Mayo* and Three Decades of Human Rights' Activism: Embeddedness, Emotions, and Social Movements," *Annals of the Association of American Geographers*. 96(2): 342–357.

Castree, N. (2000). "Geographic Scale and Grassroots Internationalism The Liverpool Dock Dispute 1995–1998," *Economic Geography*. 76(3): 272–292.

Chatterton, P. (2006). "'Give up Activism' and Change the World in Unknown Ways: Or, Learning to Walk with Others on Uncommon Ground," *Antipode*. 38(2): 259–281.

Chatterton, P., Fuller, D., and Routledge, P. (2008). "Relating Action to Activism: Theoretical and Methodological Reflections." In *Participatory Action Research Approaches and Methods: Connecting People, Participation and Place*, edited by S. Kindon, R. Pain, and M. Kesby, 216–222. London: Routledge.

Cumbers, A., Routledge, P., and Nativel, C. (2008). "The Entangled Geographies of Global Justice Networks," *Progress in Human Geography*. 32(2): 179–197.

D'Arcus, B. (2005). *Boundaries Of Dissent: Protest And State Power In The Media Age*. London: Routledge.

Davies, A. (2012). "Assemblage and Social Movements: Tibet Support Groups and the Spatialities of Political Organization," *Transactions of the Institute of British Geographers*. 37: 273–286.

Diani, M. (2013). "Organizational Fields and Social Movement Dynamics." In *The Future of Social Movement Research: Dynamics, Mechanisms, and Processes*, edited by J. van Stekelenburg, C. Roggeband, and B. Klandermans, 145–168. Minneapolis, MN: University of Minnesota Press.

Diani, M. (2015). *The Cement of Civil Society: Studying Networks in Localities*. Cambridge: Cambridge University Press.

Dicken, P., Kelly, P. F., Olds, K., and Wai-Chung Yeung, H. (2001). "Chains and Networks, Territories and Scales: Towards a Relational Framework for Analysing the Global Economy," *Global Networks*. 1(2): 89–112.

Dikeç, M. (2001). "Justice and the Spatial Imagination," *Environment and Planning A*. 33: 1785–1805.

England, K. (1994). "Getting Personal: Reflexivity, Positionality, and Feminist Research," *The Professional Geographer*. 46: 80–89.

Escobar, A. (2001). "Culture Sits in Places: Reflections on Globalism and Subaltern Strategies of Localization," *Political Geography*. 20(2): 139–174.

Featherstone, D. (2003). "Spatialities of Transnational Resistance to Globalisation: The Maps of Grievance of the Inter-Continental Caravan," *Transaction of the Institute of British Geographers*. 28(4): 404–421.

Featherstone, D. (2005). "Towards the Relational Construction of Militant Particularisms: Or Why the Geographies of Past Struggles Matter for Resistance to Neoliberal Globalisation," *Antipode*. 37(2): 250–271.

Featherstone, D. (2008). *Resistance, Space and Political Identities: The Making of Counter-global Networks*. Oxford: Wiley-Blackwell.

Featherstone, D. (2011). "On Assemblage and Articulation," *Area*. 43(2): 139–142.

Fuller, D. and Kitchen, R., eds. (2004). *Critical Theory/Radical Praxis: Making a Difference Beyond the Academy?*. Vernon and Victoria, BC, Canada: Praxis (e)Press.

Gibson-Graham, J-K. (1994). "'Stuffed if I know!' Reflections on Post-modern Feminist social Research' *Gender, Place and Culture*. 1, (1994): 205–224.

Harvey, D. (1995). "Militant Particularism and Global Ambition: The Conceptual Politics of Place, Space and Environment in the Work of Raymond Williams," *Social Text*. 42: 69–98.

Herod, A., ed. (1998). *Organizing the Landscape: Geographical Perspectives of Labor Unionism*. Minnesota: University of Minnesota Press.

Herod, A. (2001). *Labor Geographies*. New York: Guildford Press.

Jessop, B., Brenner, N., and Jones, M. (2008). "Theorizing Sociospatial Relations," *Environment and Planning D: Society and Space*. 26: 389–401.

Katz, C. (2001). "On the Grounds of Globalization: A Topography for Feminist Political Engagement," *Signs*. 26(4): 1213–1229.

Kindon, S., Pain, R., and Kesby, M., eds. (2008). *Participatory Action Research Approaches and Methods: Connecting People, Participation and Place*. London: Routledge.

Klein, N. (2000). *No Logo*. London: Flamingo.

Koopman, S. (2008). "Cutting Through Topologies: Crossing Lines at the School of the Americas," *Antipode*. 40(5): 825–847.

Leitner, H., Sheppard, E., and Sziarto, K. M., "The Spatialities of Contentious Politics," *Transactions of the Institute of British Geographers*. 33(2): 157–172.

McAdam, D. (1982). *Political Process and the Development of Black Insurgency, 1930–1970*. Chicago: University of Chicago Press.

McFarlane, C. (2009). "Translocal Assemblage: Space, Power and Social Movements," *Geoforum*. 40: 561–567.

Martin, D. (2003). "'Place-framing' as Place-making: Constituting a Neighborhood for Organizing and Activism," *Annals of the Association of American Geographers*. 93(3): 730–750.

Mann, M. (1997). "Has Globalisation Ended the Rise and Rise of the Nation-State," *International Review of Political Economy*. 4(3): 472–496.

Massey, D. (2004). "Geographies of Responsibility," *Geografiska Annaler*. 86B(1): 5–18.

Maxey, I. (1999). "Beyond Boundaries? Activism, Academia, Reflexivity and Research," *Area*. 31: 199–208.

Miller, B. (2000). *Geography and Social Movements: Comparing Antinuclear Activism in the Boston Area*. Minneapolis: University of Minnesota Press.

Nast, H. (1994). "Opening Remarks on 'Women in the Field'," *The Professional Geographer*. 46: 54–66.

Nelson, L. "Geographies of State Power, Protest, and Women's Political Identity Formation in Michoacán, Mexico," *Annals of the Association of American Geographers*. 96(2): 366–389.

Nicholls, W. J. (2007). "The Geographies of Social Movements," *Geography Compass*. 1(3): 607–622.

Nicholls, W. J. (2009). "Place, Relations, Networks: The Geographical Foundations of Social Movements," *Transactions of the Institute of British Geographers*. 34(1): 78–93.

Nicholls, W. J., Miller, B., and Beaumont, J., eds. (2013). *Spaces of Contention: Spatialities and Social Movements*. Farnham, Surrey: Ashgate.

Oslender, U. (2004). "Fleshing out the Geographies of Social Movements: Black Communities on the Colombian Pacific Coast and the Aquatic Space," *Political Geography*, 23(8): 957–985.

Panelli, R. (2007). "Time-space Geometries of Activism and the Case of Mis/placing Gender in Australian Agriculture," *Transactions of the Institute of British Geographers.* 31: 46–65.

Pickerill, J. and Chatterton, P. (2006). "Notes Towards Autonomous Geographies: Creation, Resistance and Self-management as Survival Tactics," *Progress in Human Geography.* 30: 730–746.

Pulido, L. (2003). "The Interior Life of Politics," *Ethics, Place and Environment.* 6: 46–52.

Rose, G. (1997). "Situating Knowledges: Positionality, Reflexivities and Other Tactics," *Progress in Human Geography.* 21(3): 305–320.

Routledge, P. (1993). *Terrains of Resistance: Nonviolent Social Movements and the Contestation of Place in India.* Westport: Praeger.

Routledge, P. (1996). "The Third Space as Critical Engagement," *Antipode.* 28(4): 397–419.

Routledge, P. (2000). "Geopoetics of Resistance: India's Baliapal Movement," *Alternatives.* 25: 375–389.

Routledge, P. (2002). "Travelling East as Walter Kurtz: Identity, Performance and Collaboration in Goa, India," *Environment and Planning D: Society and Space.* 20: 477–498.

Routledge, P. (2003). "Convergence Space: Process Geographies of Grassroots Globalisation Networks," *Transactions of the Institute of British Geographers.* 28(3): 333–349.

Routledge, P. (2008). "Acting in the Network: ANT and the Politics of Generating Associations," *Environment and Planning D: Society and Space.* 25: 199–217.

Routledge, P. (2012). "Sensuous Solidarities: Emotion, Politics and Performance in the Clandestine Insurgent Rebel Clown Army," *Antipode.* 44(2): 428–452.

Routledge, P. and Cumbers, A. (2009). *Global Justice Networks: Geographies of Transnational Solidarity.* Manchester: Manchester University Press.

Sikkink, K. (2005). "Patterns of Dynamic Multilevel Governance and the Insider-Outsider Coalition." In *Transnational Protest & Global Activism*, edited by D. della Porta and S. Tarrow, 151–174. Lanham, MD: Rowman and Littlefield Publishers.

Staeheli, L. A. and Lawson, V. A. (1995). "Feminism, Praxis and Human Geography," *Geographical Analysis.* 27: 321–338.

Tarrow, S. (2005). *The New Transnational Activism.* Cambridge: Cambridge University Press.

Tarrow, S. and McAdam, D. (2005). "Scale Shift in Transnational Contention." In *Transnational Protest and Global Activism*, edited by D. della Porta, and S. Tarrow, 121–150. Boulder CO: Rowman & Littlefield.

Tufts, T. (1998). "Community Unionism in Canada and Labour's (Re)organization of Space," *Antipode.* 30(3): 227–250.

Waterman, P. (1998). *Globalization, Social Movements, and the New Internationalisms.* Washington, DC: Mansell.

Wills, J. (2001). "Community Unionism and Trade Union Renewal in the UK: Moving Beyond the Fragments at Last?" *Transactions of the Institute of British Geographers.* 26: 465–483.

Wills, J. (2005). "The Geography of Union Organising in Low-paid Service Industries in the UK: Lessons from the T&G's Campaign to Unionise the Dorchester Hotel," *Antipode.* 37: 139–159.

Wolford, W. (2004). "This Land Is Ours Now: Spatial Imaginaries and the Struggle for Land in Brazil," *Annals of the Association of American Geographers.* 94(2): 409–424.

PART V

REPERTOIRES OF COLLECTIVE ACTION

....

CHAPTER 25

STRATEGY

....

JAMES M. JASPER, KEVIN MORAN, AND MARISA TRAMONTANO

THIS chapter examines the major conceptual building blocks needed to understand the strategic dimensions of social movements: the players who pursue goals, the arenas in which they engage one another, the interactions that occur, and the means deployed. It also examines states as the most influential set of arenas in today's world. Finally it suggests paths for future research.

Strategic engagements occur when players with goals try to influence each other's thoughts, feelings, and actions, whether cooperatively or conflictually. The most obvious strategic engagements are between social movements and their opponents, but there is also strategic interaction between movements and their potential allies or recruits, the media, and various government players. Cooperation is a more common form of strategic interaction than conflict. In either case, players are trying to get something from others. Players' ends and means, as well as the arenas in which they interact, are the core of strategic action.

In recent years a strategic perspective has emerged which focusses equally on players and the arenas in which they interact (Duyvendak and Jasper 2014a, 2014b), moving beyond unhelpful debates between structuralists who focus on arenas and culturalists who focus on players (Goodwin and Jasper 2004, 2012). From a strategic viewpoint, the main constraints on what protestors can accomplish are not imposed directly by economic and political structures so much as they are imposed by other players with different goals and interests operating in the same arenas.

Game theory for a long time has focussed on the expectations and interactions of strategic engagement (e.g. Karklins and Petersen 1993), but its image of human motivation has been very narrow. Only recently have fuller social-psychological visions of motivations appeared (Pinard 2011). Other traditions in political science have highlighted strategic interaction, including that between protestors and the state (O'Brien and Li 2006). This view has filtered into the sociology of social movements (Jasper 2004), especially in recent work on the interactions between pairs of opposed movements (Fetner 2008; Bob 2012). Too often, a strategic analysis remains implicit in research and theory.

PLAYERS

Players are those who engage in strategic action with goals in mind. Simple players consist of individuals, compound players are teams of individuals. Compound players range from loose, informal groups to formal organizations all the way up to nations tentatively or seemingly united behind some purpose. Simple and compound players face many of the same challenges and dilemmas, but they differ in an important way: the individuals who comprise teams may depart, defect, partly defect, or pursue their own goals at the same time that they pursue the group goals. Compound players, even when they have names and bylaws, are never completely unified. They are "necessary fictions" that attract and inspire supporters through their promise of unity (Gamson 1995; McGarry and Jasper 2014).

Players vary in how tight or porous their boundaries are. Some compound players are composed of paid staff positions; some have security guards at the door to keep outsiders away. Many organizations have rules about who can speak at meetings. At the other extreme, a group may be open to anyone who shows up at a meeting or a rally—raising problems of infiltrators whose intent is to discredit or disrupt the player's projects, but also of well-intentioned participants with widely different goals or tastes in tactics.

Every player has multiple goals, which range from its official mission to other stated objectives to secret aspirations to murky motivations that are obscure even to the players themselves. It is difficult for a player to compare or rank-order its goals, in part because their salience shifts according to external circumstances and in part because there is always contention within a player over its priorities. The goals of compound players are especially unstable, because factions and individuals are forever competing to make their own goals into the official goals of the team. Leaders sometimes use movements to attain their own goals, rather than the other way around. They can use the fame they derive from leading a movement to advance their own careers, for example, as happened in the New Left (Gitlin 1980). In addition, goals change: new ones surface, old ones disappear, new twists and interpretations emerge.

For this reason groups and organizations that operate as players in external arenas can, from a different point of view, be seen as arenas themselves when we look at their internal procedures. Because subplayers never agree entirely on either goals or means, considerable time is devoted to arriving at decisions through formal and informal processes (Maeckelbergh 2009). The individuals who comprise a compound player typically devote more of their strategic attention to interacting with other members than with external players. Even players that have strict hierarchies, which are designed to reduce internal conflicts, have many ways that individuals and factions maneuver within them. Every player can be further subdivided, all the way down to individuals.

Goals impose a number of strategic tradeoffs on players. For instance the Survival or Success Dilemma: once a group is formed, its members (and especially its paid employees) have an interest in its survival, which may sometimes interfere with the goals it was formed to pursue in the first place (Piven and Cloward 1977). This is connected to the Today or Tomorrow Dilemma: short-run goals may interfere with long-run goals. For instance, a movement victory may inspire countermobilization by its opponents, who may turn out to be more effective in the long run (Jasper and Poulsen 1993).

Another pair of strategic dilemmas suggests how movements change over time through interaction with other players. There is a Dilemma of Shifting Goals (Jasper 2006: 75). Activists may wish to abandon some goals as unrealistic, or they may add goals that they come to feel are important and attainable. In other words, it is strategically realistic to adapt goals to available means. But some supporters may feel betrayed; opponents can accuse you of being duplicitous. This links to the Articulation Dilemma: the more you specify what your goals are, the more you attract those who share them, but the more accountable you will be for failing to reach them. Articulation makes it more costly to shift goals (Jasper 2006: 78).

Players have a variety of capacities at their disposal in pursuing their goals. Money, reputation, legal rights, technologies, even emotions of confidence are all helpful. Some capacities adhere to an organization, others are held primarily by individuals.

Compound players themselves are always shifting: appearing, merging, splitting, going through dormant periods, disappearing altogether, growing, shrinking, changing names and purposes. Tilly linked the emergence of new players to the opening of political arenas: create or empower a parliament, and political factions and parties will appear to pursue the stakes available within it. This structural insight was very fruitful, but such an emphasis on access to arenas meant that players were often taken for granted (Jasper 2012; Krinsky and Mische 2013). From Tilly's structural perspective, it is sometimes difficult to see how players move among arenas, trying to enter those where their capabilities will yield the greatest advantages, or to see how new goals emerge and inspire players to form around them.

From a strategic perspective, research begins with catalogues of the players involved on all sides. These lists often need to be quite extensive, and include the multiple goals and many capabilities a player has at its disposal, as well as the potential subplayers that could emerge.

ARENAS

An arena is a bundle of rules and resources that allow or encourage certain kinds of interactions to proceed, with something at stake. Players within an arena monitor each others' actions, although that capacity is not always equally distributed. Like players, arenas vary in the degree to which they are institutionalized with bureaucratic rules and legal recognition as opposed to informal traditions and expectations. They also vary in the extent to which they are literal physical settings, like a courtroom or Tahrir Square, or they are more metaphorical aggregates such as public opinion or world capitalism.

Some strategic moves are made clearly within the rules of the game, others are meant to change, ignore, or twist those rules. Some rules are formally written down, providing ammunition for any player who has a stake in seeing that they are enforced. Other rules are moral norms, and the cost of breaking these is usually a tarnished reputation among those who hold to the norms, but here again opponents must work to tarnish that repute. There are many combinations in between.

Arenas have a variety of formal and informal relationships with each other. In more formal cases there may be hierarchies of arenas, as with appeals courts. Most arenas can be further broken down into subarenas. Thus policy making can be seen as one arena, or as a number of distinct arenas, ranging from informal persuasion to registered lobbying to legislative chambers and votes. An outcome in one arena can be the opening move in another, like a new law that is challenged in court. Players can force each other into some arenas, but must entice them in other cases. (They face the Bystander Dilemma: you may wish to get outsiders involved in your strategic engagement, but you cannot always control what they do once they are involved: Jasper 2006: 123.) One arena may affect another merely by changing players' morale, as they carry a good or bad mood with them from one setting to another.

Because of these variations in both players and arenas, players can have an infinite variety of relationships to arenas, and they usually have several kinds at the same time. They can play in an arena through formal standing, or through the standing of individual sympathizers. They can try to influence other players in an arena through personal networks, by persuading third parties such as the media, or by creating their own versions of other players (establishing their own media or fielding their own candidates for office, say). Some arenas are defined by the players in them, as in games or in legislatures (which could not exist without legislators). Some prove to be "false arenas": as soon as a new player is admitted, the arena loses its influence (whether to enter such arenas, which are often intentional traps, is another dilemma: Jasper 2006: 169).

One kind of strategic project is to change arenas themselves. Some players may try to stabilize an arena to their advantage, or to change an existing one so that it favors them. Some arenas are changing constantly, without much stabilization; others are stable for long periods, punctuated by sudden changes that can be dramatic and which are often unexpected. But all arenas can be changed or abandoned. When they are stable for long periods, it is not mere inertia, but the result of active support from interested players.

New arenas provide new opportunities for action. You can't bring a lawsuit in a nation without courts. As Tilly (1997: 250) noted the increasing centrality of parliament in Great Britain in the early nineteenth century weakened the autonomy and power of the aristocracy and local dignitaries and reduced direct involvement of troops and other repressive forces in claims-making. The institutional changes did not entirely close off old arenas or entirely push action into new ones: it shifted the potential benefits and costs of various strategic programs. It promoted persuasion at the expense of payments and especially of coercion in domestic politics.

The positions they hold in arenas can help or hinder players, just as their resources and skills can. Like positions on a field of battle, positions in an arena such as a bureaucracy allow players to do certain things by providing them with a distinct bundle of rules and resources. They may still have to fight to enforce or bend those rules and to deploy those resources, despite the formalities of their positions. Some positions, like the high ground on a battlefield, are more advantageous than others, and a great deal of contestation centers around getting into position. In some cases attaining standing in an arena is a key position, but then in addition there are different positions within that arena. Attending a meeting is one advantage, facilitating it is another.

INTERACTIONS

By distinguishing players and arenas, we can observe the interactions among players. Why do players choose the arenas they do, often switching from one to another? How do they adapt their capabilities to arenas, and choose arenas that best suit their capabilities? What positions do they hold in an arena, and what do these positions allow them to do? We can also observe when there are good matches and when there are mismatches between a player's capacities and an arena. Players sometimes fail badly, or unexpectedly. By distinguishing arenas from players, we can also observe more dimensions of the arenas: formal rules versus informal traditions, status within the arena versus status outside it, soft and hard boundaries that define which players can participate. Players and arenas constantly adjust to each other, but they do not entirely define each other. Conflicts among players often spill across arenas.

Protest groups that manage to match their strategies to their institutional arenas are more likely to obtain their goals. For movements oriented toward public policy, as Amenta (2006) found in his study of the Townsend Movement, more assertive strategies work when elected politicians are uninterested or opposed and when bureaucrats are weak or opposed to the movement; otherwise, electoral or legislative arenas are more promising. Working within the system, however, always runs the risk of cooptation, in which the survival of the protest group or benefits for its leaders begin to crowd out its original goals.

By observing the strategic back-and-forth of engagement we can achieve a dynamic picture of politics, in the plans, initiatives, reactions, countermeasures, mobilizations, rhetorical efforts, arena switches, and other moves that players make. Recently scholars have begun to look at interactions between pairs of players who maneuver and counter maneuver across multiple arenas. For example, the US Christian right and the LGBT movement (Fetner 2008) and US Conservatives challenging progressive legislation in international arenas (Bob 2012).

A strategic approach highlights the tradeoffs, choice points, and dilemmas that players face as they negotiate arenas. Jasper (2006) catalogues dozens of these. Some choices are tough ones, in which each option carries risks. For this reason, players often try hard to back their opponents into a position in which their options are limited and treacherous. Sørensen and Martin (2014) dub this "the dilemma action." In many cases these actions force state agents to repress nonviolent protestors, leading to moral indignation in response. More generally, the point of these moves is to push an opponent to do something that conflicts with widely held or stated beliefs and values. Protest itself is an effort to force authorities (or other players) into actions they would prefer to avoid, whether concessions or repression or uncomfortable silence.

People have fewer choices than they think, as social structures, networks, institutional norms or logics all impose constraints. Various kinds of habits and routines also explain the stability of interactions. Blee (2012) shows how protest groups establish decision-making routines in their first few months which they do not need to revisit. But all routines were originally choices, implicit or explicit. All changes to routines are also choices. And within certain routines, there are still choices to be made, especially in reaction to the actions of other players. The purpose of routines is to allow a group to focus its attention on new decisions.

STATES

In the modern world, states are the dominant players and the main arenas in which protest unfolds, and so for several decades, the study of social movements has centered on the relationship between movements and the state. In older structural views "the state" is both opponent and judge for protestors, who are generally demanding admission to the polity—many scholars even *defined* social movements as efforts by the oppressed to become full citizens (McAdam 1982: 25).

A strategic perspective, by highlighting who actively does what, forces us to ask if both "movements" and "states" are not a bit of a fiction, implying a unity for each that does not really exist (McAdam et al. 2001; Slaughter 2004; Duyvendak and Jasper 2014a, 2014b). A state is more usefully seen as a web of subplayers (agencies, assemblies, executives, police forces, and so on) tied together by a set of rules (laws and traditions) that purport to govern their relationships, but do so incompletely. Each subplayer of the state brings a variety of capabilities to strategic engagements, which include many informal interactions as well as the formal ones covered by laws. Even laws are regularly reinterpreted, ignored, bent, broken, and changed as a result of strategic campaigns and accidents. Because strategic action is only partly covered by formal rules, the boundaries of state agents are porous, with a range of other players included in some ways at some times, excluded at others. In almost no cases does "the state" act as a unified player.

Whether we view a segment of the state as a player or as an arena depends on our analytic interests: all players are also at the same time arenas in which decisions are made. But as an initial approximation, if a group of people share goals, coordinate their action, and have some collective identity, they are a player. If they organize a place where interactions occur, with some rules and some outcome at stake, they are an arena. It is apparent why many groupings can be both player and arena at the same time.

Scholars of protest have occasionally called for more attention to the "internal workings of government" (Zald 1992: 339) to overcome the field's "movement-centered" bias (McAdam et al. 2001), but few researchers have heeded the call. O'Brien and Li (2006) focus on horizontal divisions of the Chinese state, following "rightful" resisters as they jump to higher levels to pursue their grievances, often expressing faith that the true intentions of the central government are being corrupted by local officials. This "principal-agent" challenge may be especially severe in a nation as large as China, but all states face some version of it in the implementation of official decisions. What is more, states are also divided into vertical segments, as industry ministries, for instance, battle budget offices or elected officials (Jasper 1990). "Political opportunities" are always there, in some form, rather than being special results of infrequent crises (Jasper 2012).

Fewer scholars of social movements today think of protestors as "challengers" or "outsiders" seeking entry to the polity, a view that was once at the heart of political-process theory. Rather Goldstone (2003: 9) offers "a continuum of alignment and influence, with some groups having very little access and influence through conventional politics, others having somewhat more, and still others quite a lot; but groups may move up and down this continuum fairly quickly, depending on shifts in state and party alignments." This view has a healthy dynamism, although it assumes that the main influence is through political parties, and it still seems to assume a relatively unified state.

Means

Strategic players have three basic families of means at their disposal: they can use physical coercion or threat, they can persuade others, or they can pay others to do what they want them to (Jasper 2014). Although they may use all three, social movements rely heavily on persuasion to accomplish their goals. To the extent they rely more on coercion, they become a rebel army or a band of criminals. To the extent they rely more on paid staff, they shade into the status of interest groups.

The threat of coercion is a way to disrupt economic and political systems, a strategy that Piven and Cloward (1977) believe is the only path open to those without monetary and other capacities. In a parallel inquiry, Gamson (1975) found that groups using violence were more likely to attain their goals. These works were an important breakthrough in our understanding of the effects of different strategies, shattering a complacent pluralist intuition that disruptive protest was somehow bad. Instead we see the Naughty or Nice Dilemma (Jasper 2006: 106): aggressive tactics can attain some ends, safe choices obtain others. Aggression runs the risk of arousing repression by authorities and the erosion of public support, but if it can seize gains that are hard to reverse later, it is often worth it.

Foremost in the study of persuasion have been the processes by which mobilizers must find the right frames to appeal to participants and potential participants (Snow et al. 1986), diagnosing a problem and motivating work toward a solution. Moral shocks

(Jasper 1997), dizzying experiences that challenge a person's assumptions about the world, are other processes by which recruits are first attracted to a movement. It seems framing and moral shocks are most effective in the context of social networks, motivating those already involved and sometimes pushing them toward more radical tactics (Ryan and Gamson 2006). For instance Gould (2009) demonstrates that lesbian and gay activists moved toward more disruptive tactics in the late 1980s because of the moral shock of the US Supreme Court decision, *Bowers v. Hardwick*, upholding anti-sodomy statutes.

In the affluent nations since the late twentieth century, protest groups have often paid staff to conduct many basic activities instead of relying on volunteers, a process famously analyzed by McCarthy and Zald (1973, 1977). Groups that choose this route come to depend on their financial backers, and frequently turn into interest groups. In addition, professional activists emerge who can move from one cause to another, bringing their specialized skills with them—for a price. With paid staff comes bureaucracy, which often undermines some of the basic moral goals of the protest groups.

Means and ends conflict in this and other ways. In the Dirty Hands Dilemma, there are certain goals that can only be obtained through means that are morally suspect (Jasper 2006: 70). For some participants, money and bureaucracy fall in this category, making it hard for them to sustain organizations. A few movements, notably nonviolent movements, define themselves by the tactics they reject on moral grounds, although often recognizing that more aggressive tactics might help them get what they want sooner. A good example is the American animal rights movement, which in its early years obtained powerful propaganda about the abuse of animals through spies and burglars.

Tactics originate from either invention or borrowing from other movements. Tactical innovation seems to occur through interaction with opponents, in a kind of strategic game (Ganz 2009). Diffusion of tactics is better studied (Soule 2004). The transmission mechanisms include direct influence through social networks (Morris 1981) and indirect inspiration through reportage by the media (Myers 2000). Diffusion involves varying degrees of active consideration on the part of either those transmitting or those adopting (and adapting) innovations (Snow and Benford 1999). Because strategic innovation always carries risks, protestors try to solve the Innovation Dilemma by observing what the costs, benefits, and risks have been for others before they do something new themselves (Jasper 2014).

FUTURE RESEARCH

A strategic approach to protest opens up several lines of research that have received little attention in other paradigms. For example, we know little about how activists make decisions about what to do, leaving the impression that they simply follow the scripts and routines they have learned in or from other movements, or what Tilly (e.g. 2006) called a repertoire of contention. But it is the ability to choose among options and to invent new actions and arguments that sometimes allows "David" to defeat "Goliath" (Ganz 2009). Good choices are more likely, according to Ganz, in groups with regular, open, and authoritative deliberation; diverse networks of supporters; knowledge about diverse tactics to choose between, amongst others factors. What is crucial is feedback about what is working, and flexible reactions to that feedback: in a word, the ability to learn (Krinsky and Barker 2009).

Some decisions are made by a single individual, who either persuades others, disposes of financial or coercive resources, or has some positional authority provided by a set of rules. We can only understand these decisions if we come to grips with the biography and psychology of that single person; such factors must find a place in social-science models (Jasper 1997: ch. 9). Even the most macro-level phenomena often reflect the influence of one or a few individuals.

Once we recognize the human beings who make decisions, we can see a range of additional mechanisms at work. For instance, people attach moral value to their means as well as their goals. They also know how to do some things and not others. Together these give people a "taste in tactics" (Jasper 1997: ch. 10) that is partly independent of the perceived efficacy of the tactics; tactics are rarely neutral means about which protestors do not care. Thus protestors face dilemmas having to do with clashes between means and ends.

Interactions among individuals and factions within groups is another new topic that a strategic perspective should highlight. Players overlap with each other. A protest group is part of a movement coalition. An MP is also a member of her party, occasionally pursuing its goals alongside legislative ones, and she may also be a member of a protest group seeking social change or justice. Individuals are especially clear cases of one player moving among and being a part of various other players, often pursuing activist careers (Fillieule 2010). Thanks to the individuals who compose them, protest movements can permeate a number of other players, even on occasion their targets and opponents.

As a subset of individuals, leaders are also a topic, long neglected in social movement research, that a strategic approach could help us understand. In even the most democratic of groups, some individuals have more influence than others. In most there is some formal division of labor. As part of their role, formal leaders set agendas, guide discussions, and make a number of smaller decisions on their own. Alliances of protest groups negotiate their stated goals and their means through formal mechanisms, although here too the decisions often come down to a small group of individuals. Factions, too, struggle to set agendas and formulate public statements.

Attention to strategic interactions promises to pull together various strands of research, including structural and cultural accounts and micro- and macro-level research. How players engage each other in various arenas can tell us about innovation and decision making, about individuals, leaders, and factions. Strategy permeates politics and protest, but we need to pay explicit attention to it in order to recognize its full impact.

REFERENCES

Amenta, Edwin (2006). *When Movements Matter.* Princeton: Princeton University Press.

Blee, Kathleen M. (2012). *Democracy in the Making: How Activist Groups Form.* New York: Oxford University Press.

Bob, Clifford (2012). *The Global Right Wing and the Clash of World Politics.* Cambridge: Cambridge University Press.

Duyvendak, Jan Willem and Jasper, James M., eds. (2014a.) *Breaking down the State: Protestors Engaged.* Amsterdam: Amsterdam University Press.

Duyvendak, Jan Willem and Jasper, James M., eds. (2014b). *Players and Arenas: The Interactive Dynamics of Protest.* Amsterdam: Amsterdam University Press.

Fetner, Tina (2008). *How the Religious Right Shaped Lesbian and Gay Activism.* Minneapolis: University of Minnesota Press.

Fillieule, Olivier (2010). "Some Elements of an Interactionist Approach to Political Disengagement," *Social Movement Studies.* 9: 1–15.

Gamson, Joshua (1995). "Must Identity Movements Self-Destruct? A Queer Dilemma," *Social Problems.* 42: 390–407.

Gamson, William A. (1975). *The Strategy of Social Protest.* Homewood, IL: Dorsey Press.

Ganz, Marshall (2009). *Why David Sometimes Wins.* New York: Oxford University Press.

Gitlin, Todd (1980). *The Whole World Is Watching.* Berkeley: University of California Press.

Goldstone, Jack, ed. (2003). *States, Parties and Social Movements.* Cambridge: Cambridge University Press.

Goodwin, Jeff and Jasper, James M., eds. (2004). *Rethinking Social Movements.* Lanham: Rowman and Littlefield.

Goodwin, Jeff and Jasper, James M., eds. (2012). *Contention in Context.* Stanford: Stanford University Press.

Gould, Deborah B. (2009). *Moving Politics: Emotion and ACT UP's Fight against AIDS.* Chicago: University of Chicago Press.

Jasper, James M. (1990). *Nuclear Politics: Energy and the State in the United States, Sweden, and France.* Princeton, NJ: Princeton University Press.

Jasper, James M. (1997). *The Art of Moral Protest.* Chicago: University of Chicago Press.

Jasper, James M. (2004). "A Strategic Approach to Collective Action: Looking for Agency in Social Movement Choices," *Mobilization.* 9: 1–16.

Jasper, James M. (2006). *Getting Your Way: Strategic Dilemmas in the Real World.* Chicago: University of Chicago Press.

Jasper, James M. (2012). "Introduction." In *Contention in Context*, edited by Jeff Goodwin and James M. Jasper. Stanford: Stanford University Press.

Jasper, James M. (2014). *Protest: A Cultural Introduction to Social Movements.* Cambridge: Polity Press.

Jasper, James M. and Poulsen, Jane (1993). "Fighting Back: Vulnerabilities, Blunders, and Countermobilization by the Targets in Three Animal Rights Campaigns," *Sociological Forum.* 8: 639–657.

Karklins, Rasma and Petersen, Roger (1993). "Decision Calculus of Protestors and Regimes: Eastern Europe 1989," *The Journal of Politics.* 55: 588–614.

Krinsky, John, and Barker, Colin (2009). "Movement Strategizing as Developmental Learning." In *Culture, Social Movements, and Protest*, edited by Hank Johnston. Farnham: Ashgate.

Krinsky, John, and Mische, Ann (2013). "Formations and Formalisms: Charles Tilly and the Paradox of the Actor," *Annual Review of Sociology*. 39: 1–26.

Maeckelbergh, Marianne (2009). *The Will of the Many: How the Alterglobalisation Movement is Changing the Face of Democracy*. London/ New York: Pluto Press.

McAdam, Doug, Tarrow, Sidney G., and Tilly, Charles (2001). *Dynamics of Contention*. Cambridge: Cambridge University Press.

McCarthy, John D. and Zald, Mayer N. (1973). *The Trend of Social Movements in America*. Morristown, NJ: General Learning Press.

McCarthy, John D. and Zald, Mayer N. (1977). "Resource Mobilization and Social Movements: A Partial Theory," *American Journal of Sociology*. 82: 1212–1241.

McGarry, Aidan, and Jasper, James (2014). *The Identity Dilemma. Publisher?*

Morris, Aldon (1981). "The Black Southern Sit-In Movement: An Analysis of Internal Organization," *American Sociological Review*. 46: 744–767.

Myers, Daniel J. (2000). "The Diffusion of Collective Violence: Infectiousness, Susceptibility, and Mass Media Networks," *American Journal of Sociology*. 106: 173–208.

O'Brien, Kevin J. and Li, Lianjiang (2006). *Rightful Resistance in Rural China*. Cambridge: Cambridge University Press.

Pinard, Maurice (2011). *Motivational Dimensions in Social Movements and Contentious Collective Action*. Montreal: McGill-Queen's University Press.

Piven, Frances Fox and Cloward, Richard A. (1977). *Poor People's Movements*. New York: Pantheon.

Ryan, Charlotte, and Gamson, William A. (2006). "The Art of Reframing Political Debates," *Contexts*. 5: 13–18.

Slaughter, Anne-Marie (2004). *A New World Order*. Princeton: Princeton University Press.

Snow, David A. and Benford, Robert D. (1999). "Alternative Types of Cross-National Diffusion in the Social Movement Arena." In *Social Movements in a Globalizing World*, edited by Donatella della Porta, Hanspeter Kriesi, and Dieter Rucht. London: Macmillan.

Sørensen, Majken Jul and Martin, Brian (2014). "The Dilemma Action: Analysis of an Activist Technique," *Peace & Change*. 39: 73–100.

Soule, Sarah A. (2004). "Diffusion Processes within and across Movements." In *The Blackwell Companion to Social Movements*, edited by David A. Snow, Sarah A. Soule, and Hanspeter Kriesi. Malden, MA: Blackwell.

Tilly, Charles (1997). "Parliamentarization of Popular Contention in Britain 1758–1834," *Theory and Society*. 26: 245–273.

Tilly, Charles (2006). *Regimes and Repertoires*. Chicago: University of Chicago Press.

Zald, Mayer N. (1992). "Looking Backward to Look Forward: Reflections on the Past and Future of the Resource Mobilization Program." In *Frontiers of Social Movement Theory*, edited by Aldon D. Morris and Carol McClurg Mueller. New Haven: Yale University Press.

CHAPTER 26

REPERTOIRES OF CONTENTION

EITAN Y. ALIMI

INTRODUCTION

WHY use a non-English word to capture the ways people act together in pursuit of shared interests? According to Tilly, who coined and developed the concept (1978, 1995, 2008), we should prefer the term repertoire over "stock," "inventory" or "means" for several important reasons. First, the term repertoire conjures up the notion of a stock of special skills, plays, and activities with which members of a group are already familiar and from which they select specific ones. Second, the term brings up the notion of performance, which is congruent with the idea that collective action involves not only what people *know* how to do, but also what those on the receiving end would expect and understand. Third, repertoire also implies innovation, which echoes Tilly's use of the analogy of *commedia dell'arte*, since performance essentially involves experimenting and improvising whether through imitation of other observed performances, through innovation at the margins of the known and handed-down templates and, perhaps most centrally, through interactions with other actors and parties involved. Indeed, as Tilly himself noted, the theatrical metaphor that captures the essence of the concept repertoire falls short in an important aspect: "Unlike the imagined situation of actors on a stage before a darkened house, all participants in contention learn continuously as they interact" (2008: 15).

In what follows, we will say little about how a particular repertoire of one or more contending actors or groups has come into being, a topic that necessitates a detailed journey into the historical development of a given population, which is beyond the scope of this essay.[1] What matters to our discussion concerns the analysis of how particular repertoires are selected and change during contentious interaction. To this end, we will examine how contention unfolding in three central, most recurring and distinguishable arenas or fields of interaction (Jasper 2004; Fligstein and McAdam 2012) helps to explain these selections and changes. These arenas (i.e., intra-movement, movement and authorities, and movement and security forces) are by no means empirically distinct in their influence; rather they influence and are influenced by each other. Nor are they the only arenas of interaction that are part of contention and shape movement repertoires. However, the influence of those additional "external" arenas (i.e., movement and general public forces, movement and countermovement, and movement and actors across state borders) on movement repertoires becomes most noticeable and meaningful during times of heightened conflict across the social system, what Tarrow has called "cycles of contention" (2011: 199).

Following this logic, we begin by examining repertoire choice and shift in each central arena during more delimited, short-term episodes of contention as well as cycles. We then examine how the broadening scope and arenas of interaction, and the higher levels of uncertainty and contingency that ensue, influence repertoire choice and shift, but also give rise to non-purposive, emergent ones.

REPERTOIRES, ARENAS OF INTERACTION, AND CONTENTION

Any episode of contention features three central contending parties that are most directly involved: movement actors, authorities, and security forces (i.e., police forces, military forces, etc.). As such, the most recurring and robust arenas are intra-movement interaction, movement—authorities interaction, and movement—security forces interaction.

Intra-Movement Interaction

Instances of single actor or unified movements are rare; social movements are best seen as a voluntary field or network of actors, which vary in their degree of organization, resources, ideologies, and preferable action strategies and repertoires. The ability to form *and* to sustain a common purpose, solidarity, and commitment to both the movement as a whole and its goals is a central challenge social movement leaders face.

Certain repertoires employed by movement leaders are meant to address this challenge. Vertically, between leaders and activists, inducement, benefaction, and teach-ins facilitate recruitment and commitment to the movement and its activities. They can be carried out face-to-face in consciousness-raising and efficacy-promotion meetings (Hirsch 1990), via "old" media channels (e.g., newsletters and leaflets), and, increasingly so, via "new" media channels (internet, blogs, podcasts, etc.), as is most notably the case with transnational movements (Smith 2008).

Sole reliance on incentives and benefits, however, may not be enough for sustaining commitment. Considerable efforts on the part of leaders and organizers are devoted to forging and maintaining commitment and loyalty through meshing of individual identity, solidarity, and consciousness with collective social and cultural levels and systems (Mansbridge 2001). Much of these efforts rest on frame alignment tasks within and between social movement organizations (SMOs), but also on contentious words that are meant to shape and maintain activists' consciousness and participation in contention (Snow et al. 2014; Ryan et al. 2012; Tarrow 2013). Noteworthy repertoires include designation of special events and days of commemoration (Armstrong and Crage 2006), transformation of common rituals into acts of mobilization (e.g., public weddings), and storytelling (Polletta 2006; Taylor et al. 2009). These repertoires often invoke moral rage, pride, honor, courage, and other emotions, and are linked to past memories and histories that serve as a pool to draw from in order to further consolidate collective identity, justify specific actions, and define adversaries (Gould 2009; Jasper 2011; Viterna 2013; Johnston 2014).

Additional repertoires are utilized for the purpose of minimizing competition between two or more groups or organizations over resources, legitimacy, goals, and action strategy. Through occasional meetings or conventions movement organizations deliberate and discuss goals and strategy, try to form and consolidate alliances, foster coordination, and divide labor (Diani 2003; Cornfield and McCammon 2010). These repertoires reflect the rationalist logic of the various SMOs' leadership concerning the expected benefit from presenting a united front and pooled resources. Concomitantly, they are indicative of movement leaders' understanding of the importance of trying to contain radical groups (or "spoilers" (Chenoweth and Stephan 2011)), through cooperation, as demonstrated in Diani's (2012) comparative study on the propensity to engage in riots among movement radical factions in Bristol and Glasgow during the early 2000s.

Not surprisingly, the more prolonged contention is, the more difficult it becomes to meet these two related challenges. In the face of harsh repression, difficulties to promote the movement goals or depletion of resources, leaders and organizers often oscillate between more and less assertive repertoires. For example, in cases of depletion of resources and decreased willingness on the part of activists to bear the cost of participation, we would observe not only infighting between organizations, but also the formation of disciplinary bodies meant to enforce directives made by certain movement organizations. But it is also possible that mutual recognition of the negative consequences of such infighting as well as demoralization on the part of activists and supporters would encourage leaders from various organizations and groups to initiate conciliatory gestures and forms of action. Certain organizations may lower their demands and initiate less violent forms of action, in the hope that this would reenergize participation. Other organizations, or a movement within a coalition of movements, in cases when an event that serves as a hinge for their mobilization is over, may go as far as hybridizing their issues and concerns with those of others for the purpose of continuing to promote their goals, as was the case in the US peace movement after 9/11 (Heaney and Rojas 2014).

Movement and Authorities Interaction

For the simple fact that state authorities control the principal concentrated means of coercion and have legislative, executive, and judiciary powers vis-à-vis specific population, authorities occupy the role of the ultimate target of claim making. Even if authorities act as the object of contention only indirectly (i.e., a firm or a corporate body acting as the direct target) and movement goals are not "political" in the narrow sense of the term (i.e., revolving around identity and/or economic issues), the structure and the nature of interaction in this arena suggest a great deal about repertoire selection and change. Since there is hardly any political establishment completely "closed" or completely "opened" to movement claims, and political arrangements as well as the balance of political power relations vary over time, it is more analytically useful to speak about the structure of political opportunities and constraints or threats movement actors face and seek to change (McAdam 1999).

Movement repertoires in this arena may be institutional and contained. In cases where movements face a fairly responsive political environment to their claims, repertoires may include lobbying, press conferences, litigation, but also demonstrations, street rallies, vigils, and human chain marches. These latter repertoires are meant not only to display to authorities determination, solidarity, size and scope of supporters the movement has, but also to strengthen the leverage of political allies. During election campaigns, most notably, movement repertoires may include setting up political action committees to support candidates, presenting their own candidates, engaging in bloc voting, or employing bolder repertoires like harassing politicians (McAdam and Tarrow 2013).

But there are other repertoires that aim to influence authorities in a more indirect manner, expressing claims embedded in conflicts that transcend the political (in the narrow, institutional sense of the term) and revolve around cultural, societal, moral, and personal conflict domains and issues. Symbolic issues that are often linked with issues of identity (individual and collective linked), consciousness, and solidarity characterize much of the work of movements like LGBT, religious, women, environmental, consumerism, and lifestyle. Identity deployment and presentation (Bernstein 2008) through unconventional, unique clothing and hairstyle, consumption and consumerism—all are repertoires that challenge institutional, cultural codes and practices. Tattooing, in particular, and the Straight Edge movement, in general, is a case in point of non-verbal self-expressions that challenge oppressive discourse and norms of class, status, and gender (Haenfler 2004). These repertoires are part of individual activists' daily practices of resistance, but they can also accompany more collective representations, as when demonstrations are peppered with theatrical tactics, such as wearing costumes and putting on street shows (Wood 2007).

While reliance on contained and institutional repertoires may prove effective when authorities are responsive, in many instances this is not the case. In these situations movement leaders may decide to engage in more disruptive, direct action repertoires as a means to force policy makers to attend to their claims. Strikes, traffic blocking, sit ins, squatting, boycotts, tax revolts, and conscientious objection, are meant to induce threat among authority members of greater, more outright violence by obstructing routine activities.

In political contexts where movement leaders and activists enjoy basic freedoms and rights, the threat of violence that is embodied in disruption may well remain latent. In authoritarian regimes, but also in democracies under specific circumstances or with regard to certain populations and issues, unruly and violent repertoires may be the *only* choice available to movement activists. This goes a long way in explaining engagement in violent repertoires not only against public property (i.e., rioting), but also against state actors (e.g., kidnapping and assassination, but also armed rebellion (Einwohner and Maher 2011)). Rioting is often the only recourse as well as resource aggrieved and disadvantaged populations have for expressing their discontent. That riots may begin spontaneously by no means implies they are bounded to remain disorganized and aimless, or that they are essentially violent. As research by della Porta and Gbikpi (2012) on riots in France 2005 and Greece 2008 demonstrates, disruptive and violent activities, such as vandalism, squatting, robberies, and assaults on governmental and law-and-order agents, often become purposive. Moreover, claims are being articulated, a certain level of constraining and restriction is exercised, and new and social media are used for coordinating, discussing, and catalyzing activities (for a useful review and examples from the Arab Spring, see the chapter by Earl, Hunt, Garrett, and Dal in this volume).

As the foregoing analysis has demonstrated, the structure and the nature of interaction in the arena between movement and authorities shape both selection of, and change in repertoires. The more excluded, disadvantaged, and decertified movement organizations are the more likely it is for them to employ more violent tactics, and vice-versa.

Movement and Security Forces Interaction

While disagreement persists over whether the state's capacity and propensity for repression of domestic challengers constitute a distinguishable dimension of political opportunities structure or a derivative of other dimensions (e.g., divided elites), a growing consensus has been developing regarding the distinct influence of *actual* interaction between movement activists and security forces on repertoires. The style of protest policing or the social control of protest may be brutal or soft, repressive or tolerant, diffused or selective, illegal and legal, reactive or preventive, formal or informal, and professional or artisanal (della Porta and Reiter 1998; Earl 2006). Regardless of regime type, security forces (i.e., the police, the military, etc.) separately or jointly can either tone-up a fairly tolerant governmental policy to the detriment of protesters or tone-down a fairly intolerant governmental policy to the benefit of protesters. It is not only because interacting with protesters on-the-ground has its own situational dynamics, but also because security forces have a considerable level of discretion in implementing policy guidelines which, admittedly, are not always clear. Moreover, factors that shape the nature of inter-action between both sides may include: (1) political culture regarding civil rights and institutional accountability; (2) whether membership in the force is professional or based on national duty and service; and (3) the extent to which the social composition of the force reflects societal cleavages (e.g., class, race, ethnicity) and how it reflects on the attitudes, perceptions, and prejudice regarding protesters' claims.

In those cases where security forces are known to be or perceived as tolerant, move-ment leaders are likely to try and negotiate and establish understandings regarding acceptable and legitimate levels, forms, and locations of protesting. When the lines are crossed on the part of individual activists or groups, movement leaders may engage in symbolic *bona fide* gestures, such as handing in weapons, condemning and marginaliz-ing transgressors, or even forming and training field organizers and marshals (Gillham and Noakes 2007).

All this does not imply that disruptive actions are not part of the repertoires of move-ments when interacting with one or more security force. In the face of failure to pro-mote their goals, movement leaders may employ disruptive repertoires that although illegal, are nonetheless legitimate and nonviolent. When leaders of the Jewish settler movement engaged in their first major contentious campaign to settle the Samaria region of the West Bank in 1974–75, it was also the time when they gradually developed their *fait accompli* tactic of illicitly setting up a settlement and engaging in passive resist-ance to eviction attempts. Despite governmental threats of forceful eviction leaders of the movement had good reasons to think otherwise. It was not only that the "creating facts on the ground" resonated with the illegalistic framework developed by the Zionist pioneers during the pre-State period, but also the rapidly growing presence of move-ment activists and supporters within the ranks of the military that explained the Chief of General Staff's objection to the governmental decision on forceful eviction and Prime Minister Rabin's willingness to accept a compromise.

A more frequent situation, admittedly, is that of security forces exercising a tougher hand than politically laid down which, at the extreme, may push movement leaders and activists to engage in violent repertoires and to devise new ones for the purpose of pro-tecting themselves as well as their constituents. When some legal, political, or public recourse is available movement leaders may engage in media work as a means to pub-licize acts of brutal repression. Either independently or with human rights advocacy groups, movement leaders typically seek legal defense and appeal to the court. When these recourse channels appear futile locally, movement leaders look outside their bor-ders and seek to mobilize supra-national institutions and other sympathetic govern-ments, NGOs, and other social movements to act on their behalf, based on networking and old/new media-based information campaign (Keck and Sikkink 1998; Tarrow 2005). As sourly realized by activists in Syria, the Ukraine, Chechnya, or Northern Ireland, but also in federated and confederated states (e.g., the Civil Rights movement in the United States), for example, outside sympathizers may prove to be a poor guarantor against brutality of security forces. In these cases, as in other local instances of contention where meaningful and effective recourse channels are absent, movement leaders may engage in violence against security forces targets, property and bodily alike, which can include sabotaging equipment, bombing of facilities, kidnappings, and assassinations.

As violence is usually met with greater violence, movement leaders place greater and harsher demands on themselves, activists, and constituents; the need for secrecy and resources becomes higher and often leads to the setting up of paramilitary forces for self-protection together with the forming or reassigning of existing disciplinary forces as vigilante-like "shock forces" meant to deter and punish collaborators. As counter-demands on movement activists and supporters are placed by security forces and contention stretches over time, radicalization and escalation often operate in tandem, heightening and broadening the cycle of the conflict.

CYCLE OF CONTENTION, INTERLOCKING ARENAS OF INTERACTIONS, AND EMERGENT REPERTOIRES

Repertoire selection and change may well be shaped by interaction with the general public, opposing movements, and outside, state, non-state, and supra-national actors. In addition to those repertoires we have mentioned in passing when discussing movement interaction with transnational actors (e.g., advocacy networking and information campaigns), other repertoires include fundraising and other forms of online activism, contained and disruptive, such as online petitions and hackerism (Earl and Kimport 2011; Bennett and Segerberg 2013). Regarding interaction with countermovements, movement leaders may seek to neutralize, discredit, and confront them by, for example, gathering and publicizing unlawful and illegitimate information on rivals' activists and activities, petitioning and appealing to court, or even disrupting rivals' protest activities (Zald and Useem 1987; Meyer and Staggenborg 2008; Luders 2010). Finally, regarding interaction with the general public, movement leaders typically try to influence public opinion indirectly via mass communication channels, such as advertising, but also more directly through face-to-face and in-house activities, special programs and services. In cases of targeting public or private firms or corporations, in addition to trying to change the costs and benefits of pursuing certain policies and practices through boycotts or lawsuits, leaders and activists also seek to penetrate organizations in order to change these policies and practices from the inside (Zald, Morrill, and Rao 2005).

Nonetheless, as much as these external arenas of interaction are at play in contention and exert their influence on movement repertoires, this influence becomes exponentially higher during cycles of contention. The intensification and continuation of the struggle and the high costs and stakes that come with it, push actors and forces in those external arenas to become more proactively involved in contention, externalities which, in turn, are seen as critical and consequential to the outcome of the cycle in the eyes of movements, authorities, and security forces. In this context of higher level of complexity of interactions and increased levels of uncertainty and contingency, new repertoires are introduced. Some of these repertoires, to be sure, are purposive, yet others are more expressive and emergent in response to transformative events—what della Porta has labeled "eventful protests" (2012). Let us relate to these two sets of repertoires as they pertain to interaction unfolding in each external arena.

Movement leaders devise particular repertoires that are meant to win the hearts and mind of the populace. Since members of the general public often pay a price during cycles of contention, at times as an indirect outcome of the movement's own actions, movement leaders seek to balance the situation by devising specific repertoires that are meant to cater for the population. They may engage in provision-like tactics, such as supply of food, water, medical treatment, and other basic necessities, such as public transportation, as was the case during the prolonged Montgomery bus boycott, often with the help of local businesses that are called upon to pull their weight.

As is usually the case, broad public support puts authorities on the defensive, pushing them to overreact and to engage in sweeping and indiscriminating oppressive and repressive measures meant to undermine the infrastructural bases of movement support. Shocked and outraged by authorities' excessive moves and fearing depletion of resources, material and non-material alike, movement leaders look for ways to preserve their bases of social support. Specific repertoires may express solidarity with the inflicted population in the hope that they would link with emotions of fear and anger and galvanize a sense of collective injustice, identity, and sympathy for the collective cause. Such repertoires can range from financial aid, condolences visits, aftercare committees to help with reconstruction efforts in cases of property damage, and transformation of mourning rituals, such as public funerals, into sites of mobilization. If these tactics are not enough and instances of diminishing public support and withdrawal accrue, movement leaders might radicalize their claims and raise demands of moral conduct on the population, a development that unfolded in Egypt during the first half of the 1990s between the Egyptian Islamic Jihad and its public constituency (Malthaner 2011). Instances of selective violence against specific civilians and their property because their actual or perceived behaviors or roles (e.g., collaborators, intellectuals, and businessmen) are deemed enemy are likely to ensue.

Emotional response can also translate into greater ideological rigidity as well as relational patterns of mergers and splits in the context of movement—countermovement contentious interaction. The ability of movements to sustain contention and the mere prospects of goal attainment often lead to the intensification of countermovements' mobilization and increased pressure on authorities to exert a tougher hand. When authorities are unwilling or unable to do so due to legal or political constraints (domestic as well as international), countermovement leaders and activists may engage in violent attacks against movement leaders, activists, and supporters. Leaders of the movement may try to take advantage of their opponents' illegal actions and engage in provocation in the hope that the violent response on the part of countermovement activists would prompt the authorities and security forces to react. When such hopes and tactical logic fail to materialize it is often the case that the movement as a whole or some movement organizations would form paramilitary groups for the purpose of protection from and in retaliation to their opponents' actions.

The balance of such tactical adaptation, which may well remain low in intensity, can be tipped when security forces, independently or with the backing of authorities, take a clear stance in support of the countermovement claims and goals. In addition to measures such as restriction of resources to the movement or refusal to open complaint files, police or military forces may go as far as turning a blind eye to countermovement attacks on movement activists and, in extreme cases, participate in such operations and even initiate their own. Under these circumstances, certain events can augment the salience of emotions in dictating tactics and push certain movement organizations to radicalize their worldviews and ideologies. In Italy, the neofascist bombing on December 12, 1969, at Piazza Fontana, Milan, and the proof that the Italian security forces not only helped protect the assassins, but also put the blame on a leftwing anarchist activist who mysteriously died while being interrogated, had a radicalizing effect on the extra-parliamentary new-left movement. In the immediate aftermath it generated an atmosphere of rage and revenge among movement leaders and activists in which the state was seen as "the state of the massacre" and interaction with neofascist activists was dictated by a logic of hatred and death. In the longer term, the Piazza Fontana was also pivotal in convincing activists to form militant and semi-clandestine organizations, fully devoted to the armed struggle ideology and tactics, and seeking to outflank the more moderate movement organizations by violent repertoires (Bosi and della Porta 2012; della Porta 2013). Where the lines dividing movements and countermovements are based on ethnonational, religious, or racial categories, such as the Protestant/Unionist and the Catholic/Republican movement in Northern Ireland, a policy of systematic favoritism of the majority population may develop into categorical terrorism (Goodwin 2006; Maney et al. 2012).

Finally, in addition to shifts in repertoires that stem from emotional salience and relational trends of mergers and splits within movements in the context of contentious interactions with the general public actors and countermovements, interaction with outside, state, non-state, and supra-national actors is likely to produce another source of innovations. Although cognitive work of identity formation and re-formation (e.g., definition and redefinition of the collective subject—"who we are") can be at play in the other arenas of interaction, interaction with those "outside" actors seems particularly relevant and salient. Much of the ability of movement leaders to attract or receive outside support rests on a bare minimum of pre-existing or the creation of shared values vis-à-vis both supra-national institutions and movement leaders and activists in bordering and non-bordering countries, the diffusion of which can be relational as well as nonrelational (Kolins Givan et al. 2010; Chabot 2012). During cycles of contention, both local and outside actors are likely to proactively capitalize on their ideational affinity and act upon it. Certain states, supra-national institutions (e.g., the EU, the UN or the Muslim World League), but, most central to our discussion, movements often lay claims on local authorities, launch boycott campaigns (e.g., the anti-Israel Boycott, Divestment and Sanctions movement) and may go as far as volunteering to participate in un/armed insurrections. The pro-Palestinian Gaza flotilla (de Jong 2012), the US-based Central America Solidarity movement (Nepstad 2006), and the Arab mujahedin's role in the anti-Soviet Afghan jihad (Sela and Fitchette 2014) are just three of many examples.

However, certain events may become eventful in the sense of gearing forward a process of re-definition of the movement's collective identity, by invoking deep cultural elements that solidified the affinity with outside movements and become compelling in shaping contentious repertoires. Returning to the abovementioned case of the Arab Mujahedin's struggle against the Soviet invader, such a cognitive process unfolded in the subsequent struggle against Russia's invasion into Chechnya. As Johnston and this author have shown (2012), despite deep-rooted Islamic elements in Chechen's culture, the first stages of the Chechen struggle against the Soviet rule were predominantly shaped by secular, nationalist cultural elements. A shift in Chechen insurgents' collective identity, deeply infused with salafi worldviews of bordering Arab Mujahedin organizations and, in the process, adoption of offensive jihad began, first, following Yeltsin-Russia's forceful attempt to regain its grip on Chechnya in late 1991. The process however reached critical height, with salafi jihadist warlords and militias fighting together with the Chechen National Guard and previously secular, nationalist leaders embracing jihadist worldviews, following Russian brutal invasion in the winter of 1994–95 and the eighteen-month ferocious war that ensued.

A FINAL NOTE

It would be fair to say that even when Tilly paid greater attention to the cultural and emotional dimensions of contention during the late years of his academic work, the expressive logic of repertoire selection and change remained fairly underdeveloped. Yet, it would be equally fair to say that Tilly's notion of repertoire has not only captured something fundamental to contention, but has also pointed out the key source of choice and change, namely, contentious interaction. It is contentious interaction that takes place in various arenas and the interplay among them that shapes repertoires and provides the context for learning process by the parties involved. Moreover, it is contentious interaction that acts as the basic situational framework in which contingencies gain meaning and, possibly, generate strong cognitive and emotional responses that could break away from the purposive logic, and yet become part of the routine forms of claim making in the next round of contention.

NOTE

1. We will say little about framing as a repertoire of contention, which is discussed in a separate chapter in this volume.

REFERENCES

Armstrong, Elizabeth A., and Crage, Suzanna M. (2006). "Movements and Memory: The Making of the Stonewall Myth," *American Sociological Review*. 71(5): 724–751.

Bennett, W. Lance, and Segerberg, Alexandra (2013). *The Logic of Connective Action: Digital Media and the Personalization of Contentious Politics*. New York: Cambridge University Press.

Bernstein, Marry (2008). "Afterward: The Analytic Dimensions of Identity: A Political Identity Framework." In *Identity Work in Social Movements*, edited by Jo Reger, Daniel J. Myers, and Rachel L. Einwohner, 277–302. Minneapolis: University of Minnesota Press.

Chenoweth, Erica and Stephan, Maria J. (2011). *Why Civil Resistance Works: The Strategic Logic of Nonviolent Conflict*. New York: Columbia University Press.

Cornfield, Daniel B., and McCammon Holly J. (2010). "Approaching Merger: The Converging Public Policy Agendas of the AFL and CIO, 1938–1955." In *Strategic Alliances: Coalition Building and Social Movements*, edited by Nella Van Dyke and Holly J. McCammon, 79–98. Minneapolis: University of Minnesota Press.

De Jong, Anne (2012). "The Gaza Freedom Flotilla: Human Rights, Activism and Academic Neutrality," *Social Movement Studies*. 11(2): 193–209.

della Porta, Donatella (2012). "Eventful Protest, Global Conflicts: Social Movements in the Reproduction of Protest." In *Contention in Context: Political Opportunities and the Emergence of Protest*, edited by Jeff Goodwin and James M. Jasper, 256–275. Stanford, CA: Stanford University Press.

della Porta, Donatella (2013). *Clandestine Political Violence*. Cambridge: Cambridge University press.

della Porta, Donatella, and Gbikpi, Bernard (2012). "The Riots: A Dynamic View." In *Violent Protest, Contentious Politics, and the Neoliberal State*, edited by Seraphim Seferiades and Hank Johnston, 87–100. Farnham and Burlington: Ashgate.

della Porta, Donatella, and Reiter, Herbert (1998). *Policing Protest. The Control of Mass Demonstration in Western Democracies*. Minneapolis: The University of Minnesota Press.

Diani, Mario (2003). "'Leaders' or Brokers? Positions and Influence in Social Movement Networks." In *Social Movements and Networks: Relational Approaches to Collective Action*, edited by Mario Diani and Doug McAdam, 105–122. New York: Oxford University Press.

Diani, Mario (2012). "The 'Unusual Suspects': Radical Repertoires in Consensual Settings." In *Violent Protest, Contentious Politics, and the Neoliberal State*, edited by Seraphim Seferiades and Hank Johnston, 71–85. Farnham and Burlington: Ashgate.

Earl, Jennifer (2006). "Introduction: Repression and the Social Control of Protest," *Mobilization*. 11(2): 129–143.

Earl, Jennifer, and Kimport, Katrina (2011). *Digitally Enabled Social Change: Activism in the Internet Age*. Cambridge, MA: The MIT Press.

Einwohner, Rachel L., and Maher, Thomas V. (2011). "Threat Assessment and Collective-Action Emergence: Death-Camp and Ghetto Resistance during the Holocaust," *Mobilization*. 16(2): 127–146.

Fligstein, Neil, and McAdam, Doug (2012). *A Theory of Fields*. New York: Oxford University Press.

Gillham, Patrick F., and Noakes, John A. (2007). "'More than a March in A Circle': Transgressive Protests and the Limits of Negotiated Management," *Mobilization*. 12(4): 341–357.

Givan Kolins, Rebecca, Roberts, Kenneth M., and Soule, Sarah A. (2010). *The Diffusion of Social Movements—Actors, Mechanisms, and Political Effects*. Cambridge: Cambridge University Press.

Goodwin, Jeff (2006). "A Theory of Categorical Terrorism," *Social Forces*. 84(4): 2027–2046.

Gould, Deborah (2009). *Moving Politics: Emotions and ACT UP's Fight Against AIDS*. Chicago: University of Chicago Press.

Haenfler, Ross (2004). "Collective Identity in the Straight Edge Movement: How Diffused Movements Foster Commitment, Encourage Individualized Participation, and Promote Cultural Change," *The Sociological Quarterly*. 45(4): 785–805.

Heaney, Michael T., and Rojas, Fabio (2014). "Hybrid Activism: Social Movement Mobilization in a Multimovement Environment." *American Journal of Sociology*. 119(4): 1–57.

Hirsch, Eric L. (1990). "Sacrifice for the Cause: Group Processes, Recruitment, and Commitment in a Student Social Movement," *American Sociological Review*. 55(2): 243–254.

Jasper, James M. (2004). "A Strategic Approach to Collective Action: Looking for Agency in Social-Movement Choices." *Mobilization*. 9(1): 1–16.

Jasper, James M. (2011). "Emotions and Social Movements: Twenty Years of Theory and Research," *Annual Review of Sociology*. 37: 1–19.

Johnston, Hank (2014). "The Mechanisms of Emotion in Violent Protest." In *Dynamics of Political Violence: A Process-Oriented Perspective on Radicalization and the Escalation of Political Conflict*, edited by Lorenzo Bosi, Chares Demetriou, and Stefan Malthaner, 27–49. Farnham and London: Ashgate.

Johnston, Hank, and Alimi, Eitan Y. (2012). "Primary Frameworks, Keying and the Dynamics of Contention in the Chechen and Palestinian National Movements," *Political Studies*. 60(3): 603–620.

Luders, Joseph E. (2010). *The Civil Rights Movement and the Logic of Social Change*. New York: Cambridge University Press.

Malthaner, Stefan (2011). *Mobilizing the Faithful: The Relationship between Militant Islamist Groups and their Constituencies*. Frankfurt and New York: Campus.

Maney, Gregory M., McCarthy, Michael A., and Yukich, Grace B. (2012). "Explaining Political Violence Against Civilians in Northern Ireland: A Contention-Oriented Approach," *Mobilization*. 17(1): 27–48.

Mansbridge, Jane (2001). "The Making of Oppositional Consciousness." In *Oppositional Consciousness: The Subjective Roots of Social Protest*, edited by Jane Mansbridge and Aldon Morris, 1–19. Chicago and London: University of Chicago Press.

McAdam, Doug (1999). *Political Process and the Development of Black Insurgency, 1930–1970*. Chicago: The University of Chicago Press.

McAdam, Doug, and Tarrow, Sydney (2013). "Social Movements and Elections: Toward a Broader Understanding of the Political Context of Contention." In *The Future of Social Movement Research: Dynamics, Mechanisms, and Processes*, edited by Jacquelien van Stekelnburg, Conny Roggeband, and Bert Klandermans, 325–346. Minneapolis: University of Minnesota Press.

Meyer, David S., and Staggenborg, Suzanne (2008). "Opposing Movement Strategies in US Abortion Politics." In *Research in Social Movements, Conflict, and Change*, edited by Patrick G. Coy, 207–238. Bingley: Emerald JAI.

Nepstad, Sharon E. (2006). *Convictions of the Soul: Religion, Culture, and Agency in the Central America Solidarity Movement*. Oxford and New York: Oxford University Press.

Polletta, Francesca (2006). *It Was Like a Fever*. Chicago: University of Chicago Press.

Ryan, Charlotte, Jeffreys, Karen, and Blozie, Linda (2012). "Raising Public Awareness of Domestic Violence: Strategic Communication and Movement Building." In *Strategies for Social Change*, edited by Gregory M. Maney, Rachel V. Kutz-Flamenbaum, Deana A. Rohlinger, and Jeff Goodwin, 61–92. Minneapolis: University of Minnesota Press.

Sela, Avraham, and Fitchette, Robert A. (2014). "State, Society, and Transnational Networks: The Arab Volunteers in the Afghan War (1984–1990)." In *Nonstate Actors in Intrastate Conflicts*, edited by Dan Miodownik and Oren Barak, 56–83. Philadelphia, PA: University of Pennsylvania Press.

Smith, Jackie (2008). *Social Movements for Global Democracy*. Baltimore, Maryland: John Hopkins University Press.

Snow, David A., Benford, Robert, McCammon, Holly, Hewitt, Lyndi, Fitzgerald, Scott (2014). "The Emergence and Development of Framing Perspective: Twenty-Five Years since the Publication of Frame Alignment and What Lies Ahead," *Mobilization*. 19(1): 23–45.

Tarrow, Sidney (2005). *The New Transnational Activism*. Cambridge: Cambridge University Press.

Tarrow, Sidney (2011). *Power in Movement: Social Movements and Contentious Politics*. Cambridge: Cambridge University Press.

Tarrow, Sidney (2013). *The Language of Contention: Revolutions in Words 1688–2012*. New York: Cambridge University Press.

Taylor, Verta, Kimport, Katrina, Van Dyke, Nella, and Andersen, Ellen A. (2009). "Culture and Mobilization: Tactical Repertoires, Same-sex Weddings, and the Impact on Gay Activism," *American Sociological Review*. 74(6): 865–890.

Tilly, Charles (1978). *From Mobilization to Revolution*. Reading, MA: Addison Wesley.

Tilly, Charles (1995). *Popular Contention in Great Britain 1758–1834*. Cambridge, MA: Harvard University Press.

Tilly, Charles (2008). *Contentious Performances*. Cambridge: Cambridge University Press.

Viterna, Jocelyn (2013). *Women in War: The Micro-Process of Mobilization in El Salvador*. New York: Oxford University Press.

Wood, Lesley J. (2007). "Breaking the Wave: Repression, Identity, and Seattle Tactics," *Mobilization*. 12(4): 377–388.

Zald, Mayer N., and Useem, Bert (1987). "Movement and Countermovement Interaction: Mobilization, Tactics, and State Involvement." In *Social Movements in an Organizational Society*, edited by Mayer N. Zald and John D. McCarthy, 247–272. New Brunswick: Transaction.

Zald, Mayer N., Morrill, Calvin, and Rao, Hayagreeva (2005). "The Impact of Social Movements on Organizations: Environment and Responses." In *Social Movements and Organization Theory*, edited by Gerald F. Davis, Doug McAdam, and W. Richard Scott, 253–279. Cambridge: Cambridge University Press.

CHAPTER 27

....

RIOTS

....

DAVID WADDINGTON

INTRODUCTION

....

RIOTS constitute a highly distinctive category of oppositional collective behavior. They differ fundamentally from social movements in the sense that, while the latter are characterized by their explicitly stated objectives and relatively stable protest repertoires, riots tend to be underpinned by more obscure (and often confusing) political agendas (Simiti 2012). According to Kotronaki and Seferiades (2012: 158), "One common, emblematic property of all riots—apparently at odds with the long history incubating them—is the unexpected, convulsive nature of their outburst." Adding to this characteristic "explosiveness" is the inescapable fact that rioting typically involves intensely distasteful and violent courses of behavior, including violence towards the police (and occasionally members of the public), and the often gleeful and celebratory destruction or theft of property (Waddington 2008). Such activities are inevitably condemned by politicians and the mass media as self-defeating, irrational, and wantonly criminal (Waddington 2008). The daunting task confronting academics is therefore to try and pinpoint the underlying political motives and rationality of the riots without ignoring their spontaneity, emotionality, and destructiveness (Waddington 2008).

The present chapter accepts this difficult challenge by closely focussing on two recent European examples—the nationwide riots that took place in Greece (in 2008), and in England three years later—each of which was politically condemned in each society for allegedly showcasing the "nihilistic" and "avaricious" propensities of the participants, rather than reflecting any justificatory "political" rationales. The chapter will begin with a section that sets out a brief conceptual basis on which to understand the rational (and political) dimensions of riots. Two further sections will then loosely adhere to this foundation in highlighting the crucial explanatory relationship between the political contexts in which each episode of rioting occurred, the processes by which they were instigated and developed, and the political "meanings" which can therefore be attached to their characteristic sentiments and behaviors.

CONCEPTUALIZING RIOTS

These outright political denunciations of the Greek and English riots reflect age-old tendencies in Western societies to: (i) pathologize such behavior as "criminal" or "irrational"; (ii) underemphasize the importance of the socio-political contexts in which rioting occurs; and (iii) play down any possible contribution of the conduct of the police to the instigation and escalation of violence (Waddington and King 2005). Ideological positions of this nature have their parallels in equally longstanding and archaic "theories of the crowd," which have their roots in the work of nineteenth-century French scholars, like Tarde and Le Bon:

> The central, unifying tenet of such theories is that the mere immersion of individuals in a crowd is sufficient to obliterate their moral faculties and customary powers of reason. Processes of anonymity, suggestibility, and contagion inevitably ensure that civilized and pro-social standards of behavior are supplanted by a more sinister, unfeeling and potentially barbaric "collective mind."
>
> (Waddington 2008: 676)

These notions of the crowd as homogeneous, unthinking, amoral, and prone to manipulation remain popular among police public order officers of all ranks (Waddington 2008).

In the late twentieth century, European and American social scientists started to expound more "rational" explanations of crowd behavior, which placed greater emphasis on its underlying meanings and motives. Such approaches were exemplified by Berk's (1974) "game theory," which posited that each riot participant would stop to calculate the possible "costs" and "benefits" involved in (say) directly abusing a police officer, throwing a brick at a vehicle, or looting from a store, before committing him- or herself to such action. Academic objections have since been voiced, alleging that "superrationalistic" explanations of this nature have swung too far in the opposite direction from the primitive ideas of Tarde and Le Bon, by denying the essentially spontaneous and "emotional" nature of rioting (Borch 2006).

One way of reconciling the apparent disjuncture between the definitively emotional, spontaneous, and rational features of riotous behavior is by pausing to consider Marx's (1972) distinction between two primary forms of rioting. According to Marx, there are some forms of riots in which "elements of protest, ideology, grievance, strain, lack of access to channels for redressing complaints, social change and social movements, are relatively insignificant factors, if not absent altogether" (Marx 1972: 49–50). Examples of these "issueless riots" are the "expressive outbursts which occasionally accompany victory celebrations or ritualized festivals" (Marx: 56). One such illustration relates to the "euphoric disorders" engaged in by supporters of the eighteenth-century British politician, John Wilkes, following his election to parliament.

In contrast there is a second category of disorders for which Smith (1983) has since coined the term "issue-oriented riots." Examples of these include the eighteenth-century "food riots" involving the seizure of consignments of grain from those merchants who stood accused of driving up prices by postponing the distribution of shipments of cereal into retail markets. Here, violence was employed as a highly selective and calculated form of resolving a collective sense of injustice. Marx also places into this category the American "ghetto riots" of the 1960s, in which scores of predominantly African-American communities responded to the injustice of police harassment, joblessness, political powerlessness, and social deprivation by electively attacking the police and vandalizing and/or looting businesses and stores held responsible for exploiting them.

In a highly relevant academic essay which asks "were the [English] riots political?," Angel (2012: 25) notes that the distinction "between the dramatic 'trigger' event and the underlying social, economic or political conditions that make the subsequent chain of events more likely is an important one in understanding the UK riots of 2011." There is an obvious resonance between this comment, the "spark and tinder box" (or "spark and powder keg") explanations of the American disorders of the 1960s (e.g., Hundley 1975; Spiegel 1969) and the Flashpoints Model of Public Disorder, developed by the present author in relation to countless examples of rioting in Europe and the United States (Waddington 1992, 2010; Waddington et al. 1989).

These "multivariate approaches" are comprehensively described in Waddington (2007: ch. 2). Each emphasizes the importance of pre-existing feelings of grievance related to a shared experience of some form(s) of inequality, discrimination or deprivation, and of the perception by community members that the authorities are not sufficiently sensitive to their plight. Particular significance is placed on the ongoing deterioration of police–community relations, highlighted by a growing frequency (and subsequent discussion) of negative encounters between the police and local residents.

The Flashpoints Model develops this theme by noting the importance of a prevailing political/ideological climate (generated by the mass media, politicians, and police spokespersons) which serves not only to vilify, "demonize" or, even, criminalize sections of a local population, but also to justify uncompromising policing "solutions" to the "problem." The model also uniquely emphasizes the importance of such cultural variables as the protest rituals or repertoires customarily enacted by local residents, or the "symbolic significance" of particular locations, for example, the site of a locally notorious police station, or section of "turf" to be taken by the police or defended by local youths.

Authors like Hundley, Spiegel, and Waddington all agree that the potency of the "proximate," "precipitating" or "flashpoint" incident (invariably an aggressive encounter between police and local civilians) lies in its inherent symbolic significance. Hundley (1975: 232–233) remarks, for example, how "The significance of this event is that it immediately focuses the attention on an overt act of suppression that is met with open hostility not because of the act itself, but because it is representative of a long history of such acts."

Spiegel (1969: 120) likewise contends that pivotal incidents of this nature serve as "concrete illustrations" of those factors most central to heightened grievance levels, while Waddington (1992) maintains that the strength of social reaction to such incidents is dependent on the presence or absence of what he calls "intensifiers"—that is, characteristics of the individuals involved (e.g., a high-ranking police officer or "vulnerable" person, such as a woman, elderly person or child), or of the activity itself (e.g., an especially rough or degrading arrest).

Conceptual linkages between the background conditions and "flashpoint" (or trigger) incidents that are most conducive to rioting to the resulting release of emotions and acts of aggression, looting, and destruction have recently been provided in commentaries on the Greek and English riots by Kotronaki and Seferiades (2012) and Akram (2014), respectively. Kotronaki and Seferiades also emphasize how riots tend to be "sparked off" by "the incidence of an extraordinary, non-normalized event of coercive violence... which upsets both standard conceptions of injustice as well as entrenched notions of how to cope with a 'bleak future'" (Kotronaki and Seferiades 2012: 158). Events of this nature serve not only to "detonate rage," but also to unleash an amplificatory process of "cognitive liberation" in which dormant but highly significant grievances rise up and fuel extreme forms of oppositional activity.

There is an obvious relationship between this approach and that of Akram, who uses Bordieu's notion of "habitus"—"the deeply held and practiced, but perhaps not discussed, taken-for-granted which is made up of the so many givens in any particular society" (Akram 2014: 10)—as a major key to understanding riots. For Akram, the constituent behaviors emerge because the triggering event represents a "rupture" in the rioter's habitus, inducing a "moment of critical reflection" in which the chronically troublesome issues which have become almost subconsciously submerged as "natural" parts of the everyday lives of particular sections of society suddenly become salient and contentious (Akram 2014: 13).

It is this capability of the triggering incident to enhance the salience of grievances related to the prevailing socio-political context which helps to explain the characteristic behaviors and emotions of any given riot. Instances of aggression, looting, and vandalism invariably exhibit patterns of selectivity and restraint that are directly related to important contextual factors, while the frequently reported sensations of "liberation," "joy," and "potency" commonly experienced by rioters stem from the collective feeling of having "turned the tables" on a repressive police force, having forced themselves to be heard by an otherwise unsympathetic and unyielding political system, and having temporarily reassumed some degree of control over their lives (Waddington 2008).

The suddenness with which rioting invariably occurs can blind us to the fact that such disorders depend for their escalation and development beyond the flashpoint incident on the activation of the participants' existing social ties and informal networks of communication (Simiti 2012). Messages (and images) transmitted, not only by word of mouth, but also via social media and other forms of mass communication, are liable to accelerate the formation of shared oppositional identities against the police (Reicher 1984). These emerging feelings of unity and solidarity will not only enhance the perceived legitimacy of the rioters' behavior, but will also embolden and encourage their acts of defiance and aggression—particularly in situations where the police are outnumbered or perceived to be lacking in resolve (Drury and Reicher 2000).

The importance of these links between the prevailing socio-political context, the triggering incident, and the meanings and motives underlying participants' emotions and behavior will become even more apparent as we move on to analyze our two featured riots, starting with the Greek disorders of December 2008.

THE GREEK RIOTS

The three weeks of rioting which took place in Greece in December 2008 were precipitated by an incident occurring in the Exarcheia area of central Athens, a bohemian locality which is home to sizable populations of students (mostly enrolled at the local Athens Polytechnic) and counter-cultural activists, well-known for their general adherence to anti-establishment values. It was here on Saturday, December 6 that a group of local youths allegedly threatened to attack a patrolling police car. The officers in question immediately parked up, left their vehicle, and shortly after came across a second group of local youths. In the brief confrontation that followed, a 15-year-old schoolboy, Alexis Grigoropoulos, was shot dead by one of the policemen.

News of the incident spread rapidly and rioting of an "unprecedented magnitude" then followed (Bratsis 2010). In the ensuing several days, "schoolchildren, students, migrants and members of extra-parliamentary radical left groups" were at the forefront of the riots, not only erecting barricades and throwing petrol bombs at police, but also attacking dozens of police stations, other state buildings (such as the main courthouse in Athens), and banks and retail outlets (Bratsis 2010) as the conflict proliferated nationwide. By the end of December, 800 such buildings had been torched or otherwise destroyed (Bratsis 2010). In a bizarre piece of irony, looters also entered and stole from the shop belonging to the parents of Alexis Grigoropoulos (Kovras and Andronikidou 2012).

Political Context

The Greek riots were engaged in by a broad coalition of working- and middle-class youth, said to be disproportionately affected by the advent of global crisis and accompanying neoliberal policies of recent governments which had set about producing a more flexible, compliant, and lower paid workforce (Sotoris 2010). In the build-up to the riots, the national rate of unemployment for people aged 15–24 approached 25 per cent, within a society in which even a highly expensive university degree offered no guarantee of a secure job. Figures revealed that, six years after completing their first degrees, one-third of Greek students had not found stable employment. Thus, the "common denominator and the unifying element" in the riots was this paucity of employment prospects (Sotoris 2010: 204).

Government ministers had shown themselves impervious to popular demands for reform, while faith in their capacity to respond with due fairness and compassion had been undermined by a "wide range of economic improprieties and scandals," involving nepotism, bribery and corruption, and illegal trading of state-owned land (Karamichas 2009: 290). Meanwhile, the trade unions and parties on the political Left were either being denied the opportunity to fulfil their representative role or were also urging acceptance of the government's austerity measures:

> Consensual bargaining arrangements between labour and capital were brought to an abrupt end, pulling the carpet under the feet of the unions and left parties accustomed to "social dialogue" and piecemeal reform. On most occasions, the latter attempted to address the problem by de-politicizing struggles and by abandoning all prospects of undertaking (or condoning) militant action in favour of a cooperative model.
>
> (Johnston and Seferiades 2012: 155)

Large sections of the Greek population were therefore feeling "silenced, non-recognized and alienated" by the political system generally and representative organizations in particular (Johnston and Seferiades 2012). Of these, the second-generation immigrants living in "utter destitution" in central Athens (Kotronaki and Seferiades 2012) were especially resentful: "Although many were born in Greece and may feel themselves to be Greek, they are often without official papers, endure much more extreme versions of humiliation at the hands of state bureaucracies, and have little hope or chance of social mobility" (Bratsis 2010: 194).

Sotoris (2010: 206) makes the point that instances of police violence had risen in parallel with the corresponding growth of youth protest, thus "providing the disciplinary and repressive aspect of the neoliberal agenda." The heavy-handed treatment of dissenting students had been witnessed on a weekly basis by television viewers (Karamichas 2009), reinforcing anti-police sentiments connected to the mounting number of deaths in police custody, and evidence of police brutality towards prisoners (Karamichas 2009; Andronikidou and Kovras 2012).

It was against this backdrop of political marginalization and police repression that the killing of Alexis Grigoropoulos took place. The emotional significance of this incident was greatly enhanced by the symbolic importance of the location in which the fatal shot was fired: the Exarcheia district of Athens constitutes an enclave of politically radical groupings pursuing "unconventional" artistic endeavors and lifestyles, and exhibiting a "sociopolitical elan" (Kotronaki and Seferiades 2012). Central to this culture is the Athens Polytechnic, a highly symbolic symbol of resistance since November 1973 when it was raided by soldiers acting on behalf of the military Junta of the day and forty student protesters were "assassinated" in the process (Vradis 2009: 147). It remains customary for groups of student demonstrators to retreat from physical confrontations with the police and take advantage of the protection afforded by the "Academic Asylum Law" (a statute forbidding the police and military from entering university grounds) by barricading themselves inside the Polytechnic (Vradis 2009: 147).

Recent media preoccupation with and vilification of the resident "koukouloforoi"—an anarchist group notorious for covering their heads and faces with hoods in an apparent attempt to avoid identification and incrimination—had provided an ideological rationale for growing police repression (Astrinaki 2009). Thus, as Kotronaki and Seferiades (2012: 162) explain:

> In this context, it is not surprising that wars of signification regarding the nature of the "Exarcheia identity" have been going on for quite some time. Though safe as few other areas in Athens, Exarcheia is casually referred to by the official media as an "independent state" and an "anarcho-bandits' grotto," and has been the target of proactive police surveillance of an intensity often resembling conditions in occupied areas (especially after the 2004 Olympic Games and the 2006 student outburst). The assassination of the teenager became the straw breaking the camel's back in the background of this accumulated experience of coercion. Or, as Sotoris (2010: 206) points out, this extreme example of police brutality served as a "metonymy" for the various forms of "social pressure," violence, and repression currently being endured by young people in Greek society.

The rioting was unceremoniously denounced by senior politicians, who regarded the violence and looting as having been driven by criminal, rather than political motivation. Thus, the Greek disorders were variously attributed to growing cultures of social irresponsibility, nihilism, and tolerance of civil disobedience; to the sinister influence of local anarchist groups; or to the equally "criminally-minded" or "poorly socialized" immigrant groups supposedly at the forefront of these events (Astrinakis 2009; Bratsis 2010; Sotris 2010).

Motives and Meanings

Aspects of local political culture played a key role in the diffusion of the conflict beyond its initial flashpoint. Within the Exarcheia district there already existed a highly receptive "emotional code" for interpreting the police action leading to the death of Alexis Grigoropoulos (Kotronaki and Seferiades 2012). The adjacent presence of such a greatly disaffected immigrant community further ensured that the message leaving Exarcheia "found ideal conditions to diffuse throughout the immediate central area—which in a different urban environment would have been absent" (Kotronaki and Seferiades 2012: 163). The dense and highly sophisticated solidarity bonds and formal or informal structures linking the residents of Exarcheia to nationwide social and political networks meant that accounts of the police misconduct were rapidly transmitted by all variety of blogs, websites, SMS, texts, emails, and word of mouth (Kotronaki and Seferiades 2012: 163–164; Andronikidou and Kovras 2012).

Kotronaki and Seferiades (2012: 165) emphasize that the emotionally shocking nature of the precipitating incident and the specific identities of the main protagonists were key contributors to the process of "identity amplification" that further encouraged the spread of rioting:

> The unexpected, non-normalized character of the shooting was immediately perceived as a supreme offence. The dramatis personae of the incident are here critical. To start with, a Greek school student, shot dead without rhyme or reason by a riot policeman, was someone with whom members of the same socio-demographic category (students and parents) as well as sections of the population systematically suffering the consequences of generalized injustice in the form of state coercion (especially immigrants and the "usual contentious subjects") could readily identify. Equally important was that the emergent injustice frame did not concern some abstract category (e.g. neoliberalism), but a specific moral and physical perpetrator (i.e, riot policeman Korkoneas), which served as a lever for the mobilization of rage, at least in the early stages of the eruption.

Of additional significance, here, was the hesitant and indecisive way in which the Greek riot police responded—that is, in such a way as to betray "strategic bewilderment on the part of the coercive apparatus" (Kotronaki and Seferiades 2012: 168). This emboldening effect on the rioters' mentality was consolidated by the chain reaction by which one city after another engaged in the riots: "The feedback of the sense that the insurrection was being generalized constituted, at the time, a key diffusing factor" (Kotronaki and Seferiades 2012: 168).

The action repertoires engaged in by participants became patently more organized and pre-calculated as the days of rioting unfolded. Initially, it was the immense anti-police "wrath" aroused by the Grigopoulous killing that was most clearly evident in the rioters' behavior (Astrinaki 2009). Within an hour of the incident, over 1,000 youths, many of them *koukouloforoi*, had gathered outside Athens Polytechnic, to hurl stones and petrol bombs at police and erect impromptu barricades out of burning cars and garbage cans (Astrinaki 2009). Subsequent attacks were waged on dozens of police cars and personnel, and several police stations firebombed; and as the rioters' actions took on a more pre-meditated character, student rallies occurred outside fifty police stations nationwide (Kalyvas 2010).

On the two days following the Grigopoulous incident, dozens of shops and boutiques were set ablaze in central Athens as "[s]ymbols of the consumer society promised by neoliberal ideology came under widespread attack by predominantly youthful crowds," and the slogans were chanted away from the theme of police violence onto more general anti-government and anti-establishment issues (Johnston and Seferiades 2012: 153). Indeed,

> One could sense this not only in tracts by leftist or anarchist groups but also in the way students expressed their rage against what they called the "policies that kill our dreams" and the popularity of slogans such as "down with the government of

murderers." Even the mass destruction of banks and retail stores in the centre of Athens on December 8th, was directed mainly against symbols of economic power, and even youths that opted for more "peaceful" ways to demonstrate experienced rioting as a necessary aspect of a collective effort to "make themselves heard."

(Sotoris 2010: 207)

The remaining three weeks of rioting were marked by a general reversion to more traditional Greek protest repertoires, such as street demonstrations, involving skirmishes between police and more transgressive groups. As the political issues became more focussed and more effectively articulated, organized groups of protesters adopted such communicative strategies as occupying television and radio stations, and interrupting programs in order to convey their points of view. Theater productions were similarly interrupted, while town halls and other municipal buildings were commandeered as venues for sit-ins and assemblies (Sotoris 2010).

THE ENGLISH RIOTS

The English riots of August 2011 were similar in origin to their Greek counterparts. Here, too, a police-related killing, in which a 29-year-old African-Caribbean man, Mark Duggan, was shot dead while being pursued by officers in the Tottenham area of north London, was pivotal. Initial newspaper reports maintained that Duggan (whom the press characterized as a well-known "gangster") was killed in the course of a shoot-out, in which a bullet from his gun lodged into one of the policemen's radios, thereby saving the latter's life (Riots Communities and Victims Panel 2012). However, large sections of the Broadwater Farm community fervently maintained that this was a bogus version of events, deliberately concocted to conceal something profoundly more sinister (Reicher and Stott 2011).

It was against this background of events that, on Saturday, August 6, a crowd of 200 protesters, consisting mainly of women and children, marched through the Broadwater Farm estate and gathered outside the Tottenham Court Road police station to demand further details of the nature and circumstances of Duggan's death. The protest remained peaceful for all of its two- to three-hour duration (Riots Communities and Victims Panel 2011). However, following its peaceful dispersal, rioting broke out which soon spread to other nearby areas. A day later, twelve neighboring London areas were also affected by disorder; and by Monday, August 8, rioting (and widespread arson and looting) had spread to sixty-six other areas nationwide, including such major cities as Birmingham and Manchester (Riots Communities and Victims Panel 2011).

In Britain, as in Greece, political reaction was exemplified by Prime Minister, David Cameron's, condemnation of the rioters as "simply selfish and avaricious barbarians basking in the fleeting pleasures of mob rule" (quoted by Winslow and Hall 2012: 153).

Such reaction deflected public attention away from possible societal causes of the rioting: "Put bluntly, no politics, just looting" (Valluvan et al. 2013: 166).

Political Context

The same crisis of European and global capitalism that contributed to the Greek disorders is central to explaining the rioting in England, where the ruling Conservative government was equally committed to an "austerity" program of economic survival, and also tarred by accusations of corruption. Adding to the worldwide "banking crisis" which had propelled major Western stock markets into a "downward spiralling freefall," the Cameron government was reeling from the arrest of its recently appointed communications director (and former editor of the English Sunday newspaper, the *News of the World*), Andy Coulson, in connection with the so-called Murdochgate scandal (Kellner 2012). It was alleged that it was during Coulson's tenure as editor of the paper that *News of the World* reporters had systematically "hacked" into the phone conversations of celebrities, and even members of the British royal family, in search of sensationalist news stories. Thus, by the time of the English riots,

> The British government was now in full-scale legitimation crisis mode as the Cameron government was oiled by its tawdry association with the Murdoch criminal media empire and had indeed carried out a right-wing agenda that cut social programs, education, and programs for youth and a deficit spending-cuts agenda that benefitted the rich while harming the working and middle classes—all the while spending lavishly on expensive wars in Afghanistan and Libya.
>
> (Kellner 2012: 21)

In contrast to the Greek riots, in which the immigrant population in the inner-city area of Athens was drawn into the disturbance once it had ignited, the London riots were notable for the immediate and pivotal involvement of the north London African Caribbean community of Broadwater Farm. Hallsworth and Brotherton (2011) observe how this initial location of the rioting, and the other London venues subsequently affected, all constituted areas of chronic economic and social disadvantage, each characterized by unacceptably high levels of youth unemployment, failing schools, and poor levels of educational attainment.

The "volatile and alienated young men" occupying these areas had thus resorted to "coping mechanisms," specifically designed to "compensate for the failure to provide jobs and work by attempting to find respect through alternative means, often through illegal means" (Hallsworth and Brotherton 2011: 10). In extreme cases, such coping strategies were manifested in *intra*-communal violence. The police were correspondingly subjected to intensified enhanced political pressures—in the form of a "moral panic" around gang-related activity, and stern directives to stem a rising tide of burglaries and street robberies (Hallsworth and Brotherton 2011: 10).

This increased onus on the police impacted detrimentally on their relations with local communities. Strategic responses to enhanced political pressure included a far more prominent role for Operation Trident, and increasingly pervasive "stop and search" procedures—invariably carried out by officers from outside the locality. Widespread complaints that the latter approach was dangerously indiscriminate were substantiated by statistical evidence that, of the 6,894 stops carried out by police officers in Tottenham and the surrounding area of Haringey between April and June 2011, only eighty-seven resulted in convictions. Local youths in particular objected to the brusque and disrespectful manner with which these searches were conducted (Reicher and Stott 2011: 73).

Of equal significance here was spiralling community resentment and distrust towards the police relating to several recent instances of deaths resulting from police raids or detention in police custody, of which the shooting of Mark Duggan was merely the latest example (Riots Communities and Victims Panel 2012). As we shall now see, it is possible that, had the Metropolitan Police paid greater heed to warnings by community leaders of rising local tension, and devoted more energy to assuaging the indignation and antagonism culminating in the death of Mark Duggan, the riots might well have been averted.

Motives and Meanings

This latter point is profoundly relevant to our understanding both of the precipitation and development of the riots. Especially germane here is the protest that focussed on the killing of Mark Duggan—which, according to the local Member of Parliament, assumed the character of a long-established ritual:

> Tottenham is no stranger to marches on the police station. These are quasi-scripted exchanges between the community and those that police them. The protesters will stand outside demanding answers, and a high-ranking police official will invite the most immediately aggrieved inside, defusing the anger in the crowd. Except that on this occasion, that didn't occur. The march arrived outside and the family demanded to speak to an officer who could tell them what had happened to their son. The officer put forward, a chief inspector, did not meet the family's expectations of seniority and they were asked to wait. And they waited. According to some accounts, they spent as long as five hours for the promised superintendent to make an appearance.
>
> (Lammy 2011: 10)

It was not long after the protesters had voluntarily dispersed—to be replaced by a growing crowd of local youths—that the first signs of disorder appeared. According to Reicher and Stott (2011: 80), it was the police who escalated the violence by deploying cordons of officers with the intention of breaking up the crowd and creating a "sterile zone" around the station. In the process, they allegedly bundled a 16-year-old black girl to the ground before striking her repeatedly: "All those who describe the incident agree that this was what actually 'sparked off all the riots' " (Reicher and Stott 2011: 81–82).

Rumors of the police assault on the girl spread quickly and were pivotal to further violence. Baker (2012) is dismissive of political claims, emerging in the immediate aftermath of the riots, that social media was used both to "orchestrate" naked criminal activity and encourage the spree of violence. For her, such "technological determinism" overlooks the fact that Britain has long tradition of rioting, predating the advent of mobile technologies, and distracts attention from what she calls the "emotional and cultural dimension of the unrest" (Baker 2012: 169). Baker notes that interviews with riot participants point to the significance of existing social networks and "word of mouth" in explaining how the rioting developed. Nevertheless, she maintains that it was in its capacity to convey such emotive visual imagery as burning cars in Tottenham and of protesters calling on people to avenge Mark Duggan's death that such technology greatly induced a sense of social solidarity (à la the Greek disorders) and hastened the growth and spreading of the conflict:

> A notable effect of new social media was that these mediums engendered a sense of social cohesion by connecting actors from disparate geographies into a common symbolic space. While new social media did not initiate the unrest, by representing one man's death as a vivid symbol of widespread social injustice, what I refer to as a "social tragedy"... these emergent mediums played a key role in facilitating the events.
>
> (Baker 2012: 175–176)

Being too few in number to effectively quell this escalation, the police concentrated on redirecting traffic away from the riot's epicenter, and clearing the way for fire engines rushing to emergencies. Resulting perceptions of police impotence and ineffectuality influenced further attacks on police lines and encouraged looting behavior, which, by Monday, August 8, had proliferated throughout the country (Reicher and Stott 2011).

In the wake of the riots, participants explained their actions largely in terms of a determination to exact revenge on the police ("the biggest gang on the block") for "all the grief they have caused to communities" (*Guardian*/LSE 2011). Anger extended "well beyond the black company" and was offered as a primary motive for rioting by 85 per cent of those interviewed (*Guardian*/LSE 2011). Forty-three per cent of female interviewees claimed to have been personally stopped and searched by police, but they were virtually unanimous in feeling angry about the police's treatment of their male peers occupying their social networks (Kelly and Gill 2012).

Explanations of the looting that took place have emphasized the significance of contemporary consumerist values. This is exemplified by Moxon's (2011) characterization of the looting and "general mayhem" associated with the English riots as primarily "acquisitive" or "nihilistic." Moxon attaches great importance to the fact that, during the "acquisitive moments" of the riots, looters helped themselves primarily to "positional goods," such as trainers, clothing, and flat-screen televisions, which confer distinction on their owners; and that, as the riots entered their "nihilistic moments," those involved in the destructive mayhem "were creating an exciting, edgy experience (as demanded by consumer culture)" (Moxon 2011: 5). Though some of this might well have looked like "protest, resistance or rebellion," it actually represented "conformity to the brutal underlying values of a free market consumerist society" (Moxon 2011: 6).

The problem with such a perspective is that it undoubtedly underplays the relationship between the looting and destruction and the underlying police–community tension. This feature of the rioting is explored in a more nuanced analysis by Reicher and Stott (2011), who saw how, not long after its instigation, the Tottenham riot began to involve numerous attacks on police vehicles and personnel. Shortly after this, participants began turning their wrath on other legal institutions, such as the Haringey and Enfield Magistrates Court and local probation offices, although a local fire engine was spared from similar destruction. The fact that subsequent patterns of looting, arson, and destruction were not as clear cut as this is not regarded by these authors as evidence of purely random and apolitical behavior:

> There is some evidence that rioters were willing to attack any target, whoever owned it, simply to show that the police could do absolutely nothing to stop them. This only underlines the argument that, in this riot, everything else was secondary to the desire to "teach the police a lesson" and to show them who is really in control. This raises a further theme: this riot was fundamentally about the assertion of power. It wasn't about using that power in any programmatic way. It was about displaying power as an end in itself—displaying power to the police. The pleasure that people got in doing so was palpable.
>
> (Reicher and Stott 2011: 91)

The subsequent nationwide rioting that spread to cities like Manchester, Salford, Liverpool, and Nottingham is interpreted by the same authors as an "assertion of power" over the police by roving gangs intent on looting shopping malls or retail parks, smashing shops, and destroying cars. Reicher and Stott speculate that those involved may also have been out to advance their reputation by proving themselves jut as capable of taking on the police as their peers elsewhere in the country (Reicher and Stott 2011: 109).

This is not to pretend that all instances of conflict and looting were directed exclusively at the police. Reicher and Stott maintain, for example, that unprovoked attacks on people and property in the affluent London boroughs of Croydon and Ealing constituted "class riots" in which "[p]eople describe(d) how 'brilliant' it was for them 'showing the rich people' and 'the police' that 'we can do what we want'" (Reicher and Stott 2011: 107). It is therefore evident that, as in the Greek riots, participants' emotions and behaviors reflected both longstanding resentment of the police and the perceived injustice of austerity measures that impacted primarily on the younger and poorer sections of society.

CONCLUSIONS

What our close analyses of the Greek and English riots have demonstrated with much clarity is that, whilst it is undeniable that riots are seldom associated with an explicit and thoroughly coherent statement of relevant grievances and objectives, such underlying meanings and motives may be comfortably discerned by linking the participants' emotions and behaviors to the prevailing socio-political context in which the disorder has occurred, and to the symbolic nature of the flashpoint incident which "ignited" the disorder.

The collective "rage" engendered in both cases by intensely arousing instances of insensitivity and brutality was, in large part, a reaction to what these incidents so shockingly symbolized in terms of the nature of everyday relations with the police. Anti-police sentiments were patently manifest in the countless attacks witnessed in each country on police personnel, vehicles, and property, as well as the various ways that rioters deliberately transgressed the law (e.g., by looting stores under the direct gaze of officers) in defiance of police authority.

We have also seen, however, that flashpoints of such vivid symbolic significance are apt to "rupture the habitus" and induce a profoundly critical awareness of negative, unsatisfactory (and often downright unjust) elements of the wider socio-political context that rarely assume such salience. Vengeful attacks on banks, corporate buildings, and even the residents of affluent localities were surely inseparable from the unjust austerity measures and "crises of legitimation" apparent in both societies. The arson, the looting, the attacks on police and civilian vehicles and personnel are all meaningful when viewed in their appropriate contexts. It may well be, as Astranaki (2009: 106) suggests, that "spectacular acts" of this nature "deride the regime of power but do not challenge it," but that does not make them any less "political."

REFERENCES

Akram, S. (2014). "Recognizing the 2011 United Kingdom Riots as Political Protest: A Theoretical Framework Based on Agency, Habitus and Preconscious," *British Journal of Criminology.* 54(3): 375–392.

Angel, A. (2012). "Viewpoint: Were the Riots Political?," *Safer Communities.* 11(1): 24–32.

Astrinaki, R. (2009). "(Un)hooding' a Rebellion: The December 2008 Events in Athens," *Social Text.* 27(4): 97–107.

Baker, S.A. (2012). "Policing the Riots: New Social Media as Recruitment, Resistance and Surveillance." In *The English Riots of 2011: A Summer of Discontent*, edited by D. Briggs, pp. 169–190, Hampshire: Waterside Press.

Berk, R.A. (1974). "A Gaming Approach to Crowd Behavior," *American Sociological Review.* 39: 355–373.

Borch, C. (2006). "The Exclusion of the Crowd: The Destiny of a Sociological Figure of the Irrational," *European Journal of Social Theory.* 9: 83–102.

Bratsis, P. (2010). "Legitimation Crisis and the Greek Explosion," *International Journal of Urban and Regional Research.* 34(1): 190–196.

Drury, J. and Reicher, S.D. (2000). "Collective Action and Psychological Change: The Emergence of New Social Identities," *British Journal of Social Psychology.* 39: 579–604.

Guardian, The/London School of Economics (LSE) (2011). *Reading the Riots: Investigating England's Summer of Disorder.* London: Guardian Books (Kindle edition).

Hallsworth, S. and Brotherton, D. (2011). *Urban Disorder and Gangs: A Critique and a Warning.* London: Runnymede.

Hundley, J.R. Jnr. (1975). "The Dynamics of Recent Ghetto Riots." In *Readings in Collective Behavior,* edited by R.R. Evans, pp. 480–492, Chicago, IL: Rand McNally.

Johnston, H. and Seferiades, S. (2012). "The Greek December, 2008." In *Violent Protest, Contentious Politics and the Neoliberal State,* edited by S. Seferiades and H. Johnston, pp. 149–156, Farnham, Surrey: Ashgate.

Kalyvas, A. (2010). "Some Reflections on the Greek December, 2008," *Constellations.* 17(2): 351–365.

Karamichas, J. (2009). "The December 2008 Riots in Greece," *Social Movement Studies.* 8(3): 289–293.

Kelly, L. and Gill, A.K. (2012). "Reading the Riots Through Gender: A Feminist's Reflection on England's 2011 Riots." In *The English Riots of 2011: A Summer of Discontent,* edited by D. Briggs, 215–234. Hampshire: Waterside Press.

Kellner, D. (2012). "The Dark Side of the Spectacle: Terror in Norway and the UK Riots," *Cultural Politics.* 8(1): 1–43.

Kotronaki, L. and Seferiades, S. (2012). "Along the Pathways of Rage: The Space-Time of an Uprising." In *Violent Protest, Contentious Politics and the Neoliberal State,* edited by S. Seferiades and H. Johnston, 157–170, Farnham, Surrey: Ashgate.

Kovras, I. and Andronikidou, A. (2012). "Cultures of Rioting and Anti-systemic Politics in Southern Europe," *West European Politics.* 35(4): 707–725.

Lammy, D. (2011). *Out of the Ashes: Britain after the Riots.* London: Guardian Books.

Marx, G. T. (1972). "Issueless Riots." in *Collective Violence,* edited by J.F. Short and M.E. Wolfgang, 46–59, Chicago, IL: Aldine, Atherton.

Moxon, D. (2011). "Consumer Culture and the 2011 'Riots'," *Sociological Research Online.* 16(4): 19.

Reicher, S. D. (1984). "The St Paul's Riot: An Exploration of the Limits of Crowd Action in Terms of a Social Identity Model," *European Journal of Social Psychology.* 14: 1–24.

Reicher, S. and Stott, C. (2011). *Mad Mobs and Englishmen: Myths and Realities of the 2011 Riots.* London: Robinson.

Riots Communities and Victims Panel. (2012). *After the Riots: The Final Report of the Riots Communities and Victims Panel.* London: Riots Communities and Victims Panel.

Simiti, M. (2012). "The Volatility of Urban Riots." In *Violent Protest, Contentious Politics and the Neoliberal State,* edited by S. Seferiades and H. Johnston, 133–145, Farnham, Surrey: Ashgate.

Smith, M.D. (1983). *Violence and Sport.* Toronto, ON: Butterworths.

Sotoris, P. (2010). "Rebels With a Cause: The December 2008 Greek Youth Movement as the Condensation of Deeper Social and Political Contradictions," *International Journal of Urban and Regional Research.* 34(1): 203–209.

Spiegel, J.P. (1969). "Hostility, Aggression and Violence." In *Racial Violence in the United States,* edited by A.D. Grimshaw, 331–339, Chicago, IL: Aldine Publishing Co.

Valluvan, S., Kapor, N., and Kalra, S. (2013). "Critical Consumers Run Riot in Manchester," *Journal for Cultural Research*. 17(2): 164–182.

Vradis, A. (2009). "Greece's Winter of Discontent," *City*. 13(1): 146–149.

Waddington, D. (1992). *Contemporary Issues in Public Disorder: A Comparative and Historical Approach*. London: Routledge.

Waddington, D. (2007). *Policing Public Disorder: Theory and Practice*. Cullompten: Willan Publishing.

Waddington, D. (2008). "The Madness of the Mob: Explaining the "Irrationality" and Destructiveness of Crowd Violence', *Sociology Compass*. 2(2): 675–687.

Waddington, D. (2010). "Applying the Flashpoints Model of Public Disorder to the 2001 Bradford Riot," *British Journal of Criminology*. 50(2): 342–359.

Waddington, D. and King, M. (2005). "The Disorderly Crowd: From Classical Psychological Reductionism to Socio-contextual Theory—The Impact on Public Order Policing Strategies," *Howard Journal*. 44: 490–503.

Waddington, D., Jones, K., and Critcher, C. (1989). *Flashpoints: Studies in Public Disorder*. London and New York: Routledge.

Winslow, S. and Hall, S. (2012). "Gone Shopping: Inarticulate Politics in the English Riots of 2011." In *The English Riots of 2011: A Summer of Discontent*, edited by D. Briggs, 149–165, Hook: Waterside Press.

CHAPTER 28

....

POLITICAL VIOLENCE

....

LORENZO BOSI AND STEFAN MALTHANER

POLITICAL violence involves a heterogeneous repertoire of actions oriented at inflicting physical, psychological, and symbolic damage to individuals and/or property with the intention of influencing various audiences for affecting or resisting political, social, and/or cultural change. It is used by actors across the political spectrum and includes actions such as attacks on property, bodily assaults, the planting of explosive devices, shooting attacks, kidnappings, hostage taking and the seizure of aircraft or ships, high profile assassinations, public self-immolation, to mention only a few. However, we should be aware that political violence is "culture-dependent" (Rucht 2003: 369) and that these radical forms of contentious politics may be called either terrorism or resistance "depending on the circumstances and who is doing the naming" (Steinhoff and Zwerman 2008: 213). In this chapter "political violence" is preferred to terms such as "terrorism," which, because of its strong normative and political connotations, is much more contested, has doubtful heuristic value, and has often been used to stigmatize rather than to explain the social phenomenon under examination (Tilly 2004).

Despite acknowledging the importance of state or state-sponsored political violence, ranging from police control of street protest to state-approved torture, to mass killings by militaries, this chapter, for reasons of space, focusses mainly on non-state actors as perpetuators of political violence. In particular, we focus on organized and higher-level forms of political violence, rather than on smaller-scale and less organized forms of violence that occur during street demonstrations or in the form of riots, as these have been addressed in the chapters by Alimi (on repertoires of action) and Waddington (riots) in this volume (on smaller-scale and less organized forms of collective violence, see also Myers 1997; Peterson 2001; Brockett 2005; Auyero 2007; Seferiades and Johnston 2012; Schneider 2014). Yet we explicitly emphasize that different forms of political violence are interlinked and are part of a continuum of violent tactics—rather than representing discrete and mutually exclusive types—and often occur successively or simultaneously during processes of escalation (see later).

In the first section of this chapter we introduce how social movement scholars have, in past decades, approached and analyzed political violence.[1] We also trace the development of the field in cognate areas of research dealing with political violence. In the subsequent section we suggest how terrorism studies, and research on militant Islamism and civil wars can contribute (and have contributed) to broadening and further developing the social movements field and in particular its perspective on processes of political violence. In the concluding section we will suggest a possible direction for future research on political violence recognizing the achievements of the social movements field so far.

"Protest by Other Means," the Social Movements Field and the Study of Political Violence

A new generation of scholars from the late 1960s on—in challenging the early "classical" model of collective behavior—has interpreted social movements as "politics by other means" (Tilly 1978). Following that breakthrough, an emerging line of research has understood political violence not as a *sui generis* phenomenon or as a social pathology, but as a collective effort to pursue goals with intelligible strategies. What characterizes the social movement perspective is, above all, an emphasis on locating political violence within broader processes of political contention and within the context of social, political, and cultural conflicts, and to examine its emergence as shifts from nonviolent towards more violent repertoires as a result of interactive dynamics involving various political actors.[2] Whatever forms it takes, political violence never emerges "from nothing," neither is it the mere result of "root causes" (the international system; material deprivation and economic grievances; processes of modernization or interrupted ones; political culture, such as cultural acceptance of violence) at the macro-level (Franks 2006) or radical ideologies, psycho-pathologies (dependency, circular reaction or identity-seeking personalities) at the micro-level (Victoroff 2005). Also, in contrast to many scholars within the field of "mainstream terrorism studies," for example, who "have been directly or indirectly involved in the business of counterterrorism" (Goodwin 2004: 259) and have often produced more or less "policy-oriented" knowledge (Goodwin 2004), social movement scholars have promoted, often from a sociological perspective, a critical approach that rejects examining protest movements and violent groups in isolation. Instead, they have fostered a perspective which entails the contextualization of the phenomenon in three respects.

First, violence is considered as one component of broader repertoires of action. Actors not only shift back and forth between violent and nonviolent forms of action, but also use them in various combinations. In other words, violence is not an entirely exceptional form of political action, but has to be examined in the context of other nonviolent and "routine" forms of political action. Thereby, the decision to use violent means or not is not only the result of available repertoires of action, but is shaped by the groups' goals and identity orientation and, particularly, responds to changing environments and actions of their opponents and/or allies. Thus, the second aspect of contextualizing political violence is that the decision to adopt violent means is considered to be not one taken in isolation but as being influenced by the fact that groups are embedded in complex webs of contingent relationships and strategic interactions among a variety of actors—including state agents, rival groups, or countermovements—all of whom shape the evolution of the conflict as they are linked by asymmetrical power balances. Approaches inspired by social movement theory, in other words, do not focus on the violent actor alone, be this an individual or an armed group, but take into account the wider social movements and constituencies, to which they are connected, as well as political opponents and government authorities and the patterns of interaction between them. Violence emerges as a result of relational dynamics that evolve as sequences of interaction in which mutual responses and adaptations contribute to the gradual escalation of violence. Such interactions are considered to be the result—and part—of temporal sequences of events and causal dynamics bounded together through their connection to the state—that is, through claims that implicate the state and through reactions by the state. Thus, a third aspect of contextualizing political violence is locating it within larger political and social conflicts. The social movement perspective recognizes that violent interactions are embedded in the wider processes of political contention that shape relations between actors and the trajectory of violent conflicts.

If all this is true, however, we should remember that the social movement literature, as diverse as it has been, was for quite some time characterized by a certain bias towards studying nonviolent movements as well as towards studying movements in Western countries rather than in other parts of the world. Accordingly, the first social movement scholars who started to focus on political violence also did so based on research on relatively small clandestine violent groups that emerged from protest movements in Western countries during the 1960s and 1970s (White 1993; Wieviorka 1993; della Porta 1995; Zwerman, Steinhoff, and della Porta 2000). This bias meant that research—as well as theoretical frameworks—tended to emphasize certain forms of institutional and cultural contexts (liberal democracies) as well as certain waves of mobilization (1960s–70s) and violent groups (small underground groups). Yet, in recent years, increasing contact and collaboration with other fields of research has led to a considerable broadening of perspectives. Among the most notable developments were that, in the aftermath of September 11, a growing number of scholars studying Islamist groups and Islamist violence (Hafez 2004; Wiktorowicz 2004; Gunning 2007; Hegghammer 2010; Malthaner 2011) as well as those interested in civil wars and violent insurgencies (Wood 2003; Wiktorowicz 2004; Kalyvas 2006; Weinstein 2007; Hazen 2009; Hegghammer 2010; Malthaner 2011; McCauley and Moskalenko 2011; Pearlman 2012; Viterna 2013; Grisham 2014) have increasingly adopted concepts and theoretical approaches from social movement studies, including the "classic" paradigms of resource mobilization, political opportunity structures, and framing, as well as elements of the "contentious politics" agenda as pioneered by Doug McAdam, Sidney Tarrow, and Charles Tilly (2001). This expansion into other fields of research has introduced social movement studies to a quite different type of actors and socio-cultural contexts: movements that draw on various forms of religio-political frames of action and notions of collective identity, involve different forms of actors and safe spaces, and face authoritarian regimes. Recent comparative works building on the "most-different" design draw on sets of cases that include leftist, right-wing, ethno–nationalist, as well as Islamist movements in order to illustrate the benefits this process had for further developing theoretical approaches and identifying a set of crucial relational dynamics that contribute to processes of escalation and radicalization (Alimi, Bosi, and Demetriou 2012; della Porta 2013; Bosi, Demetriou, and Malthaner 2014; Alimi, Demetriou, and Bosi 2015). Among the cardinal dynamics mentioned in these frameworks, which offer a mid-level approach to analysis, located between description and universal social laws, are, first, interactions between oppositional movements and government authorities, that is, the interrelation between protest and state reactions, most importantly different forms of policing, and their impact on the escalation of violence; and, secondly, competitive relations between different groups or organizations within a movement, that is, rivalries that entail forms of political outbidding leading to the radicalization of forms of action. In addition, interactions between movements and countermovements have been noted to contribute to processes of escalation, as well as dynamics of transnational diffusion and mechanisms of gradual organizational transformation, such as organizational compartmentalization and encapsulation.

In sum, the social movement perspective in research on political violence has introduced a processual understanding of the emergence of violence and has shifted attention from individual predispositions, collective behavior, or root causes towards the broader political conflicts and social environments in which violent forms of action emerge and towards the relational dynamics that shape them. Its value is strengthened by the synthesis of a variety of social theories, including rational choice, structural, cultural, and relational theory. This offers an integrated multi-level (micro–meso–macro) conceptual framework, which provides stronger explanatory value than single-level analysis of political violence (della Porta 1995, 2013; Bosi and della Porta 2012). So if on the one side it incorporates the subjective, constructed reality of those involved with violent politics, on the other hand it takes in serious consideration the organization factors and capacities (in material and cultural terms) as well as the dynamic environment in which inviduals and organizations operate. The social movement perspective's interaction with other fields has contributed—and may further contribute as we will suggest in the following section—to broadening comparative perspectives and further developing theoretical frameworks in several respects.

TERRORISM STUDIES, RESEARCH ON MILITANT ISLAMISM AND THE CIVIL WARS FIELD CONTRIBUTION TO SOCIAL MOVEMENT RESEARCH

Terrorism Studies

The interaction with what has been called "mainstream" terrorism studies shaped and enriched research on political violence, even if most works from within the social movement tradition were notable for their criticism and their self-distancing from this tradition. Yet, to some extent, it is thanks to this discussion and self-reflection with "mainstream terrorism studies" as a point of critical reference, that a new line of research has formed. After all, the "critical terrorism studies" school of research (Gunning 2009) was one of the first that emphasized the benefits of a social movement theory–perspective on political violence. And it is due to reflections about essentialist notions of "terrorist" violence that the debate was able to develop a more nuanced understanding and use of analytical concepts (Tilly 2004). Moreover, the two fields also influenced each other. A number of works within the terrorism studies literature have adopted elements from social movement studies, such as the concept of framing in studies of radicalization or network-based approaches to explain participation in violent groups (Sageman 2004, 2008; Wiktorowicz 2004, 2005; Hegghammer 2010), and issues such as, for example, radicalization and de-radicalization have instigated collaborative research involving scholars from both fields (della Porta and LaFree 2012; Bosi, Demetriou, and Malthaner 2014; Bosi, O'Dochartaigh and Pisoiu 2015). In fact, the field of terrorism studies offers a number of important insights which are relevant for social movement scholarship. The field of terrorism studies has undertaken significant efforts to understand why people choose to participate in political violence while others—the large majority—do not. In recent years there has been a shift away from relative deprivation, frustration–aggression, humiliation/revenge, identity-seeking personalities, and grievances hypotheses in favor of a search for pathways toward mobilization (Horgan 2008; McCauley and Moskalenko 2008/2011). Such reading challenges the erroneous assumption that individuals who mobilize, whether in violent or nonviolent forms of action, do this for the same motivations and in the same way (the one-dimensional perspective). Individual mobilization should be treated, instead, as a multifaceted, conjunctural, and complex phenomenon "across incrementally experienced stages" (Horgan 2008: 93), through the reconstruction of individual pathways.

In the aftermath of 9/11 a considerable number of scholars have focussed on what is commonly called "homegrown terrorism," that is, jihadist groups in European and other Western countries (see, e.g., Bakker 2006; Sageman 2008; Neumann 2009). This research is interesting for social movement studies insofar as it offers insights into new and quite complex forms of movements and relational dynamics, which not only combine local and transnational spaces and networks, but also include close personal as well as very abstract relationships (identification with the worldwide community of Muslims). The phenomenon of small, seemingly isolated jihadist groups which actually emerge from local milieus, involved in intensive internet communication, and embedded in transnational radical networks, are an important case in point. As a number of studies which connect the social movement and "terrorism studies" fields have shown, these cases can help to test the limits of contextualized process analysis as well as identify new forms of relational fields and interactions which shape the pathways of individuals and small jihadist groups (Kühle and Linedkilde 2010; Malthaner and Hummel 2012).

Moreover, social movement studies approaches, to a large extent, have focussed on *open* political organizations and networks of mobilization (Morrill, Zald, and Rao 2003). With respect to organizational forms and dynamics of a more clandestine nature (militant or not), even if we claim that they should be analyzed in the same terms as other organizations, research can benefit from insights from "terrorism studies" on structures of clandestine groups (cell structures and forms of compartmentalization) and transnational networks (Crenshaw 1990; Asal and Rethemeyer 2008), as well as organizational dynamics and forms of recruitment, leadership, or mechanisms of command and control (Crenshaw 1990; on terrorist organizations see also Mayntz 2004).

Furthermore, terrorism studies have devoted considerable attention to the particular meaning and strategic and communicative logic of terrorist violence ("propaganda by the deed") as a form of violent action that is designed and intended to exert an effect on certain audiences beyond the immediate target of an attack (to frighten enemies or paralyze hostile populations, but also to gain sympathies among constituencies) (Crenshaw 1995a; Waldmann 1998). Interpreting political violence as a form of communication has induced a number of works on the socio-psychological effects of this type of violence as well as on the role of news media (Schmid 1994), which is of particular importance in many processes of political conflict and militant protest. For example, we believe that the literature on target populations of violent attacks can be instrumental to developing research on the life-course patterns of movements' targets. Or, we can look at how terrorism studies have underlined the role that courts and public trials have for political violent groups for achieving their communication goals (De Graaf 2010).

Political Islam and Militant Islamist Movements

The study of political Islam and militant Islamist movements emerged in the 1980s, developed into a distinct line of research over the course of the 1990s, and gained particular prominence after the events of September 2001. It is rooted in and related to several research traditions. In addition to works related to classical Middle East and Islamic studies, which focussed on Muslim history, culture, and societies, as well as the emergence of new religious currents (such as "globalized Islam") (Kepel 1985, 2000; Roy

2004), militant Islam was a subject of "fundamentalism studies" that compared "radical" religions of different provenience (Marty and Appleby 1993), as well as of a specific line of works within "terrorism studies" that focussed on religious (or "sacred") violence (Juergensmeyer 1997). Initially, the focus of many works within this tradition was on the historical genesis of the phenomenon, on theological justifications and belief systems of violent Islamist groups, as well as on their organizational structure and specific violent strategies, in particular the phenomenon of suicide bombers. It tended towards culturalist explanations (Islamism as a particularly violence-prone ideology; failure of secular legitimacy in the Middle East), political and economic structuralism (failed modernization and ineffective authoritarian regimes in the Middle East), and individualistic approaches (psychology of young male suicide bombers). However, a number of more recent empirical works on Islamist movements (Wickham 2002; Wiktorowicz 2004, 2005; Hafez 2004; Haenni 2005; Hegghammer 2010) adopted sociological approaches—including elements of social movement theory—and contributed not only valuable case studies but also comparative and theoretical insights.

Social movement studies, for their part, can learn from this line of research particularly as Islamist movements, while in some respects similar to movements in Western countries, nevertheless display a number of particular patterns and elements of mobilization, with respect to frames, justifications, and symbols, as well as with respect to safe spaces, key leaders, and repertoires of action. Not only are notions of purity, martyrdom, sacrifice, or "sacred" obligations central to many militant Islamist movements; they also often revolve around religious leaders and mosques (Appleby 1997, 2000; Wickham 2002). Moreover, they entail particular patterns of mobilization and organization, emphasizing charitable work as well as education to a much greater degree than Western movements, and teacher–student (or –disciple) relations are of crucial importance in individual pathways towards participation as well as for maintaining activists' networks (Wickham 2002).

Of particular relevance for the study of political violence, finally, are some forms of violence displayed (inter alia) by Islamist movements as well as particular movement–society relations. While many characterizations of violence committed by Islamist groups as ritualistic or especially excessive are certainly overstated and neglect similarities to other militant movements, elements of Islamic symbolism nevertheless may shape violent campaigns to some extent (see Hoffman 1995; Juergensmeyer 1997). Of even greater relevance, however, are authoritarian elements in the way some militant Islamist groups engage with local populations, which may involve notions of imposing an Islamist socio-cultural order and moral codes (an attempt to "Islamicize" society) by force and punishing sinful behavior (Hafez 2004; Meijer 2009; Malthaner 2011). Whereas social movement studies often focus on progressive and emancipatory movements, emphasizing confrontations with elites and authorities, the study of Islamist movements makes clear—even if not all Islamist movements share these traits, of course—that social movements, too, can be authoritarian and oppressive towards the civilian population, or can turn that way during processes of escalation.

The Study of Civil War and Violent Insurgencies

Civil war studies have seen a number of theoretical approaches and paradigms. During the 1990s and early 2000s, the field was dominated, for example, by studies that emphasized "ethnic" cleavages and economic approaches (war economies and the greed versus grievance debate) (Fearon and Laitin 2003), the recent decade has seen two particularly influential developments. First, a line of research that explained patterns of insurgent violence and civilian responses in civil wars based on elements of rational choice theory—the Stathis Kalyvas' "control–compliance model"—has gained prominence (see Kalyvas 2006, 2012). Another parallel, influential trend was the adoption of social movement approaches in research on civil wars and violent insurgencies (see, e.g., Wood 2003; Viterna 2013). From the point of view of social movements studies, these latter works have produced inspiring research not only because they adapted elements of social movement theory to the study of new contexts (wars) and different kinds of movements (guerrilla armies), but also because they added new concepts and paradigms, such as Elizabeth Wood's notion of the "joy of agency" in explaining mobilization in repressive contexts (Wood 2003), and contributed to theoretical frameworks to explain participation in oppositional movements (Weinstein 2007; Viterna 2013). Beyond these obvious confluences, civil war studies represent an important source of inspiration and comparative insights for social movement scholars, because they have drawn attention, first, to the particularities of contentious politics in situations of extreme violence. Civil wars as militarized political conflicts create dependencies and constraints for armed actors as well as civilians that entail relational mechanisms in which basic survival considerations and coercive forms of control may supersede political preferences and notions of political legitimacy (Kalyvas 2006, 2012). Secondly, whereas social movement studies have to some extent focussed on movements as challengers of incumbent governments and established elites, civil wars make clear that power relations between states and non-state armed actors may be much more fluent, and armed groups and militant movements can shift into a position of "governing" certain areas and populations (see, e.g., Kalyvas 2006; Arjona 2010; Staniland 2012). Instances of "rebel government," thereby, entail particular relationships between armed groups and local populations, which follow a logic of compliance, control, and legitimacy created by providing some degree of order/security and basic social welfare, rather than a logic of mobilization, and which thus create an entirely new set of challenges for insurgents who have become local "rulers" (see also Schlichte 2009; Malthaner 2011). So, similar to research on militant Islamism, civil war studies have examined oppositional (insurgent) movements in different "roles" towards parts of the population, which they seek to mobilize but also to rule and control. There is certainly a confluence with parts of the literature on social movements and revolutions (Goldstone 2003). Taken together, these works have made clear that there is a continuum, rather than a clear distinction, between "official" government authorities and non-state armed groups with respect to forms of government and de facto statehood.

Moreover, earlier debates in the civil war literature research can help to re-consider the role of kinship networks and ethnic identities as well as the role of economic factors and dynamics in processes of violent contention, which have been downplayed in the majority of social movement studies in favor of political opportunity structures and resources.[3] Instead of reducing the role of economy in the study of political violence to a simplistic argument about whether poverty, grievances, and socio-economic deprivation motivates insurgents, as has been done in some studies, the work of scholars such as David Keen and Georg Elwert has pointed to self-reinforcing economic mechanisms in processes of political violence and to particular opportunities and constraints in war economies, which can contribute greatly to existing analytical frameworks focusing on relational mechanisms (Elwert 1999; Keen 2003).

DIRECTION FOR FUTURE RESEARCH

The social movement field seems to have contributed to the gradual formation of an integrated analytical perspective which analyzes political violence as a contextualized process shaped by relational dynamics, and as part of repertoires of action which include nonviolent mobilization as well as different patterns of violence, ranging from militant protest to clandestine attacks to large-scale violence during violent insurgencies and civil wars. Yet, such a perspective also implies theoretical challenges that we have so far only begun to address. One of these challenges is the connection and relation between forms of political violence. Recognizing variety, thereby, also requires identifying the interrelation between these different forms. In a review article in 2007, Sidney Tarrow noticed that what was missing in many studies on violent insurgencies was an examination of the relationship between civil wars and other ("lesser") forms of political violence: "Escalation to civil war from nonviolent contention or from less lethal forms of violence; transitions from civil wars to post-civil war conflict; co-occurrence between core conflicts in civil wars and the peripheral violence they trigger—none of these was exhaustively examined in these studies" (Tarrow 2007: 589). This holds true also for many studies on clandestine political violence and "terrorism," for example, which rarely address the process in which these develop into larger-scale patterns of violence. This challenge is complicated further by the fact that categories such as civil war, violent insurgency, "terrorism," clandestine political violence, etc, are terminological containers which each include a broad spectrum of different patterns of violent interactions, which the respective fields have only begun to address in a systematic or comparative manner (on patterns of violence in civil wars, e.g., see Kalyvas 2006; Wood 2012).

In other words, connecting different fields of research not only requires the recognition of variety in forms and contexts, but also the development of a more integrated analytical perspective on the emergence and trajectories of political violence: How do militant street protests, armed strikes, or clandestine violence develop (or not) into civil wars? How do patterns of violent interactions transform? This means that we not only need to delimit certain types, but also to identify the relation and boundaries between them, and to capture shifts and transformations. The challenge ahead might be, then, to produce conceptual differentiation between different types of political violence that is analytically integrating and allows for classification as well as for tracing trajectories that cross and connect different phenomena.

Notes

1. For recent reviews on the subject, see: Beck (2008) and Gunning (2009).
2. We should be clear that there had also been a body of literature outside social movements studies which, nevertheless, developed contextual and process-oriented perspectives (Crenshaw 1995b; Waldmann 1998; Horgan 2005; English 2009).
3. It should be emphasized that the social movement field is currently experiencing an "economic turn," also in reaction to the recent economic crisis (Hetland and Goodwin 2013; della Porta 2015).

References

Alimi, Eitan, Bosi, Lorenzo, and Demetriou, Chares (2012). "Relational Dynamics and Processes of Radicalization: A Comparative Framework," *Mobilization*. 17(1): 7–26.

Alimi, Eitan, Demetriou, Chares, and Bosi, Lorenzo (2015). *The Dynamics of Radicalization: A Relational Perspective*. Oxford: Oxford University Press.

Arjona, Ana (2010). *Social Order in Civil War*. Dissertation. Yale University.

Asal, Victor, and Rethemeyer, R. Karl. (2008). "The Nature of the Beast: Terrorist Organizational Characteristics and Organizational Lethality," *Journal of Politics*. 70(2): 437–449.

Auyero, Javier (2007). *Routine Politics and Violence in Argentina. The Gray Zone of State Power*. Cambridge: Cambridge University Press.

Bakker, Edwin (2006). "Jihadi terrorists in Europe: their characteristics and the circumstances in which they joined the jihad: an exploratory study." The Hague, Netherlands Institute of International Relations Clingendael. www.clingendael.info/publications/2006/20061200_cscp_csp_bakker.pdf; last accessed 24 July 2014.

Beck, Colin J. (2008). "The Contribution of Social Movement Theory to Understanding Terrorism," *Sociology Compass*. 2(5): 1565–1581.

Bosi, Lorenzo, Demetriou, Chares, and Malthaner, Stefan, eds. (2014). *Dynamics of Political Violence: A Process-Oriented Perspective on Radicalization and the Escalation of Political Conflict*. Farnham/London: Ashgate.

Bosi, Lorenzo and della Porta, Donatella (2012). "Micro-mobilization into Armed Groups: The Ideological, Instrumental and Solidaristic Paths," *Qualitative Sociology*. 35: 361–383.

Bosi, Lorenzo, Niall O'Dochartaigh and Daniela Pisoiu. (2015). *Political Violence in Context: Time, Space and Milieu*. Colchester: ECPR Press.

Brockett, Charles (2005). *Political Movements and Violence in Central America*. Cambridge: Cambridge University Press.

Crenshaw, Martha (1990). "Theories of Terrorism: Instrumental and Organizational Approaches. In *Inside Terrorist Organizations*, edited by David C. Rapoport, 13–31. New York: Columbia University Press.

Crenshaw, Martha (1995a). "An Organizational Approach to the Analysis of Political Terrorism," *Orbis*. 29(3): 465–489.

Crenshaw, Martha (1995b). *Terrorism in Context*. Pennsylvania: The Pennsylvania State University Press.

De Graaf, Beatrice (2010). *Theater van de angst. De strijd tegen terrorisme in Nederland, Duitsland, Italië en Amerika*. Amsterdam: Uitgeverij Boom.

della Porta, Donatella (1995). *Social Movements, Political Violence and the State*. New York: Cambridge University Press.

della Porta, Donatella (2013). *Clandestine Political Violence*. Cambridge: Cambridge University Press.

della Porta, Donatella (2015). *Bringing Capitalism Back In: Democracy and Social Movements in Times of Austerity*.

della Porta, Donatellá and LaFree, Gary, eds. (2012). "(De-)Radicalization," *Special-focus of the International Journal of Conflict and Violence*. 6(1): 4–10.

English, Richard (2009). *Terrorism. How to Respond*. Oxford: Oxford University Press.

Fearon, James and Laitin, David (2003). "Ethnicity, Insurgency, and Civil War," *American Political Science Review*. 97(1): 75–90.

Franks, Jason (2006). *Rethinking the Roots of Terrorism*. Basingstoke: Palgrave Macmillan.

Grisham, Kevin E. (2014). *Transforming Violent Political Movements. Rebels Today, What Tomorrow?* London: Routledge.

Goodwin, Jeff (2004). "Review Essays: What Must We Explain to Explain Terrorism?" *Social Movement Studies*. 3: 259–265.

Gunning, Jeroen (2007). *Hamas in Politics*. London: Hurst & Company.

Gunning, Jeroen (2009). "Social Movement Theory and the Study of Terrorism." In *Critical Terrorissm Study: A New Research Agenda*, edited by Richard Jackson, Marie Breen Smyth, and Jeroen Gunning, 156–177. London: Routledge.

Haenni, Patrick (2005). *L'ordre des caïds: conjurer la dissidence urbaine au Caire*. Paris: Karthala.

Hafez, Mark (2004). *Why Muslims Rebel: Repression and Resistance in the Islamic World*. Boulder and London: Lynne Rienner Publishers.

Hazen, Jennifer M. (2009). "From Social Movement to Armed Group: A Case Study from Nigeria," *Contemporary Security Policy*. 30(2): 281–300.

Hegghammer, Thomas (2010). *Jihadism in Saudi Arabia*. Cambridge: Cambridge University Press.

Hetland Gabriel and Goodwin, Jeff (2013). "The Strange Disappearance of Capitalism from Social Movement Studies." In *Marxism and Social Movements*, edited by Colin Barker, Laurence Cox, John Krinsky, and Alf Gunvald Nilsen, 83–102. Boston: Brill.

Horgan, John (2005). *The Psychology of Terrorism*. London: Routledge.

Horgan, John (2008). "From Profiles to Pathways and Roots to Routes: Perspectives from Psychology on Radicalization into Terrorism," *Annals of the American Academy of Political and Social Science*. 618(1): 80–94.

Juergensmeyer, Mark (1997). "Terror Mandated by God," *Terrorism and Political Violence*. 9(2): 16–23.

Kalyvas, Stathis N. (2006). *The Logic of Violence in Civil War*. Cambridge: Cambridge University Press.

Kalyvas, Stathis N. (2012). "Micro-level Studies of Violence in Civil War: Refining and Extending the Control–Collaboration Model," *Terrorism and Political Violence*. 24(4): 658–668.

Kepel, Giles (1985). *The Prophet and the Pharaoh*. Berkeley: University of California Press.

Kühle, Lene and Linedkilde, Lasse. (2010). Radicalization among Young Muslims in Aarhus. Research report prepared for the Centre for Studies in Islamism and Radicalisation (CIR), Aarhus University, Denmark, January 2010.

Mayntz, Renate (2004). "Organizational Forms of Terrorism: Hierarchy, Network, or a Type sui generis?" Max-Planck-Institut für Gesellschaftsforschung, MPIf6 Discussion Paper 04/4.

Malthaner, Stefan (2011). *Mobilizing the Faithful: The Relationship between Militant Islamist Groups and their Constituencies*. Frankfurt/New York: Campus.

Malthaner, Stefan and Hummel, Klaus (2012). "Islamistischer Terrorismus und salafistische Milieus: Die Sauerland Gruppe und ihr soziales Umfeld." In *Radikale Milieus: Das soziale Umfeld terroristischer Gruppen*, edited by Stefan Malthaner and Peter Waldmann, 245–278. Frankfurt/New York: Campus.

Marty, Martin E. and Appleby, R. Scott, eds. (1993). *Fundamentalism and the State: Remaking Polities, Economies, and Militance*. Chicago: The University of Chicago Press.

McAdam, Doug, Tarrow, Sidney, and Tilly, Charles (2001). *Dynamics of Contention*. Cambridge and NY: Cambridge University Press.

McCauley, Clark and Moskalenko, Sophia (2008). "Mechanisms of Political Radicalization: Pathways towards Terrorism," *Terrorism and Political Violence*. 20(3): 415–433.

McCauley, Clark and Moskalensko, Sophia (2011). *Friction: How Radicalization Happens to Them and Us*. New York: Oxford University Press.

Meijer, Roel (2009). "Commanding Right and Forbidding Wrong as a Principle of Social Action: The Case of al-Jamaa al-Islamiyya." In *Global Salafism: Islam's New Religious Movement*, edited by R. Meijer, 189–220. London: Hurst & Company.

Myers, Daniel J. (1997). "Racial Rioting in the 1960s: An Event History Analysis of Local Conditions," *American Sociological Review*. 62: 94–112.

Morrill, Calvin, Zald, Mayer, and Rao, Hayagreeva (2003). "Covert Political Conflict in Organizations: Challenges from Below," *Annual Review of Sociology*. 29: 391–415.

Neumann, Peter (2009). *Joining Al-Qaeda: Jihadist Recruitment in Europe*. London: Routledge.

Pearlman. Wendy (2012). "Precluding Nonviolence, Propelling Violence: The Effect of Internal Fragmentation on Movement Protest," *Studies in Comparative International Development*. 47: 23–46.

Peterson, Abby (2001). *Contemporary Political Protest. Essays on Political Militancy*. Aldershot: Ashgate.

Roy, Olivier (2004). *Globalized Islam: The Search for a New Ummah*. New York: Columbia University Press.

Rucht, D. (2003). "Violence and New Social Movements," in *International Handbook of Violence Research*, edited by W. Heitmeyer and J. Hagan, 369–383. Dordrecht: Kluwer Academic Publishers.

Sageman, Mark (2004). *Understanding Terror Networks*. Philadelphia: University of Pennsylvania Press.

Sageman, Mark (2008). *Leaderless Jihad: Terror Networks in Twenty-First Century*. Philadelphia: University of Pennsylvania Press.

Schneider, Cathy L. (2014). *Police Power and Race Riots. Urban Unrest in Paris and New York*. Philadelphia: University of Pennsylvania Press.

Seferiades, Seraphim and Johnston, Hank, eds. (2012). *Violent Protest, Contentious Politics, and the Neoliberal State*. Farnham: Ashgate Publishing Limited.

Staniland, Paul (2012). "States, Insurgents, and Wartime Political Orders," *Perspectives on Politics*. 10(2): 243–264.

Steinhoff, Patricia and Zwerman, Gilda (2008). "Introduction to the Special Issue on Political Violence," *Qualitative Sociology*. 31(3): 213–220.

Tarrow, Sidney (2007). "Inside Insurgencies: Politics and Violence in an Age of Civil War," Book Review Essay, *Perspectives on Politics*. 5(3): 587–600.

Tilly, Charles (1978). *From Mobilization to Revolution*. Reading: Addison-Wesley.

Tilly, Charles (2003). *The Politics of Collective Violence*. Cambridge: Cambridge University Press.

Tilly, Charles (2004). "Terror, Terrorism, Terrorists," *Sociological Theory*. 22(1): 5–13.

Victoroff, Jeff (2005). "The Mind of Terrorist: A Review and Critique of Psychological Approaches," *Journal of Conflict Resolution*. 49: 3–42.

Viterna, Jocelyn (2013). *Women in War: The Micro-processes of Mobilization in El Salvador*. New York: Oxford University Press.

Weinstein, Jeremy M. (2007). *Inside Rebellion: The Politics of Insurgent Violence*. New York: Cambridge University Press.

White, Robert W. (1993). *Provisional Irish Republicans: An Oral and Interpretive History*. Westport, CT: Greenwood Press.

Wickham, Carrie Rosefsky (2002). *Mobilizing Islam: Religion, Activism, and Political Change in Egypt*. New York: Columbia University Press.

Wieviorka, Michel (1993). *The Making of Terrorism*. Chicago: University of Chicago Press.

Wiktorowicz, Quintan (2004). *Islamic Activism: A Social Movement Theory Approach*. Bloomington, Indianapolis: Indiana University Press.

Wiktorowicz, Quintan (2005). *Radical Islam Rising: Muslim Extremism in the West*. Lanham: Rowman and Littlefield.

Wood, Elisabeth J. (2003). *Insurgent Collective Action and Civil War in El Salvador*. Cambridge: Cambridge University Press.

Wood, Elisabeth J. (2012). "Sexual Violence during War: Variation and Accountability." In *Collective Crimes and International Criminal Justice: an Interdisciplinary Approach*, edited by Alette Smeulers and Elies van Sliedregt, 297–324. Antwerp: Intersentia.

Zwerman, Gilda, Steinhoff, Patricia G., and della Porta, Donatella (2000). "Disappearing Social Movements: Clandestinity in the Cycle of New Left Protest in the U.S., Japan, Germany, and Italy," *Mobilization*. 5(1): 85–104.

CHAPTER 29

....

SOCIAL MOBILIZATION AND VIOLENCE IN CIVIL WAR AND THEIR SOCIAL LEGACIES

....

ELISABETH JEAN WOOD

SINCE 1945 the dominant form of large-scale violence has been civil wars. Although the annual count of extant civil wars (far larger than the number of interstate wars) peaked before the turn of the century, civil wars continue to inflict vast suffering—including displacement, sexual violence, and death—on millions of civilians each year.

Scholars in various disciplines, particularly political science, have increasingly turned their attention to analysis of civil war, especially after the turn of the century. An early theme was the identification of the structural determinants of civil war onset, largely addressed through cross-national quantitative studies (Collier and Hoeffler 2001, 2004; Fearon and Laitin 2003; Hegre and Sambanis 2006). In-depth analysis of sub-national patterns of violence and political participation in particular civil wars, often based on extensive field or archival research, increasingly provided a complementary focus and method. Recent works deploy more sophisticated research designs and methodologies to develop and test theoretical insights at either the cross-national or sub-national level (or both). Examples include the analysis of ethnic dyads across borders to study transnational dynamics (Cederman et al. 2013), patterns of order within civil war (Arjona 2010; Staniland 2012), trajectories of different insurgent organizations within a field of rebellion (Parkinson 2013; Staniland 2014), variation in wartime sexual violence across states as well as insurgents (Wood 2006; Leiby 2009; Cohen 2013; Wood 2015), negotiated settlements (Walter 2002, 2009; Hoddie and Hartzell 2007; Toft 2009), and the legacies of wartime violence and mobilization (Wood 2008; Bateson 2013).

Rather than attempt a synthesis of this burgeoning field of scholarship, I emphasize three themes that are particularly relevant for this volume. The first, patterns of violence against civilians during civil war, is particularly rich in its theoretical and policy implications. Specifically, scholars increasingly focus on documenting the repertoires of violence on the part of both states and non-state groups and on assessing the extent to which group institutions and ideology account for the wide variation in those repertoires. These emergent themes evoke key concepts of the social movements literature, including repertoires of contention, political opportunity, framing processes, and mobilizing structures. The second theme, political mobilization during civil war, more directly evokes those concepts, but the connections between their role in peacetime and in wartime are as yet not well established. The third, the social legacies of war, also echoes ongoing themes in the literature on social movements, particularly the legacies of political mobilization and the origins of pro-social norms.

I first discuss violence, emphasizing the recent turn to analysis of group institutions and ideologies to explain the sharp variation in patterns of violence observed across armed groups. I then assess the sparser literature on social mobilization and civil war, focussing on escalation from unarmed protest to armed insurgency; mobilization of both recruits and civilians by insurgents, the state, and its allies; and the consequences of both indiscriminate state violence and hearts-and-minds approaches to counterinsurgency. In the penultimate section, I discuss the social legacies of civil war, emphasizing its positive as well as negative legacies. In the conclusion, I identify particular topics for which scholarly understanding would benefit from increased exchange between scholars of civil wars and social movements as distinct forms of contentious politics.

PATTERNS OF VIOLENCE AGAINST CIVILIANS IN CIVIL WAR

In his magisterial *The Logic of Violence in Civil War* (2006), Stathis Kalyvas argues that an armed actor (either a state or non-state group) should exert selective violence based on civilian denunciations in the areas that it partially controls, and indiscriminate violence in areas that it does not control. The argument is based on a two-fold logic: because indiscriminate violence may be counterproductive, armed actors prefer to exert selective violence against civilian supporters of their rival. However, they need information from civilians to do so. Such information is not available in contested areas as civilians are too fearful to denounce their neighbors; and in areas of total control, no civilian would dare defect. Thus selective violence is exercised in the group's areas of partial control. In contrast, an armed group engages in indiscriminate violence in areas where its rival exerts total or partial control (if accessible) because it has no information with which to select victims. Data from the Greek civil war (Kalyvas 2006) and the Vietnam War (Kalyvas and Kocher 2009; Kocher, Pepinsky, and Kalyvas 2011) confirm several observable implications of the theory: selective and indiscriminate violence roughly occurred where the theory predicted. However the theory, in its focus on where violence occurs, does not account for other variation in violence across actors, particularly in its frequency and repertoire. Moreover, the theory treats collective targeting (when a group targets a particular ethnic, political or social group) as part of indiscriminate violence, which obscures other logics of violence (Balcells 2010; Steele 2009). (But see Kalyvas 2012 on extensions of his argument to account for non-lethal violence and motives for violence that do not stem from territorial control.)

In contrast to the territorial control model's emphasis on strategic logic, its presumption that all actors respond similarly to its imperatives, and its neglect of the principal agent challenges that armed groups confront, Jeremy Weinstein (2007) traces variation in violence against civilians across non-state actors to differences in their initial endowments. Those with access to economic endowments attract opportunistic recruits who are difficult to discipline, with the result that such groups engage in a broad repertoire of frequent violence against civilians. Those who rely on social endowments attract activist recruits amenable to the group's training and discipline, with the result that they engage in violence much more selectively. Thus non-state actors engage in either a broad repertoire of frequent violence against civilians, or only lethal and highly selective violence. However, his parsimonious emphasis on distinct pools of recruits neglects the powerful potential of socialization, which he rejects as unable to account for variation in group norms (2007: 125), a point to which I return later in discussing ideology. Moreover, the claimed correlation between reliance on lootable resources and abuse of civilians may not be true: Stanton (2009, 2013) shows that rebel reliance on contraband is not correlated with relevant patterns of violence against civilians in civil wars since 1989.

Scholars continue to document the wide variation in violence against civilians during civil war, exploring the extent to which it is explained by variation in territorial control, economic endowments, and other characteristics of the conflict or the armed organization. In particular, restraint in the use of violence toward civilians during civil war is a theme important for both its policy and theoretical significance. Stanton (2009, 2013) shows that more than 40 per cent of states and of rebels during civil conflicts since 1989 exercise restraint—the absence of massacres, scorched earth campaigns, forced displacement, bombing and strafing of civilian areas. Moreover, despite the emphasis in policy and media publications on wartime sexual violence, not all armed groups engage in high levels of rape: during civil wars in Africa from 2000–09, 59 per cent of the 177 armed groups (states, rebels, and militias) were not reported to have engaged in moderate or high levels of rape (Nordås 2011). (Importantly, by 2000, media and NGO organizations were actively documenting rape of civilians.) Restraint is particularly puzzling when exercised against an enemy that engages in violence against the group's civilian base. In a study of wartime rape by armed groups in all major civil wars between 1980 and 2009, Cohen (2013) found that in 38 per cent of wars where there were (at least) some reports of rape, only one side perpetrated the violence. (State forces are more likely than rebels to do so, she shows.) Countrywide social structures and cultural norms cannot explain such sustained asymmetry in rape, suggesting that characteristics of the armed group are important for explaining variation in wartime violence (Wood 2012, 2015; Cohen, Hoover Green, and Wood 2013).

Before assessing this "organizational turn" in the literature on civil war violence, it is important to note that scholars increasingly emphasize the importance of documenting and analyzing non-lethal elements of the armed group's repertoire of violence, including sexual violence (Wood 2006, 2009, 2015; Leiby 2009, 2011; Hoover Green 2011; Cohen 2013). Gutiérrez Sanín and Wood (2014b), for example, in defining what scholars should mean by "pattern of violence," analyze three distinct dimensions: the group's repertoire, and for each element of the repertoire, its targeting (selective, collective against groups defined by a specific ethnic, social or political identity, and indiscriminate) and for each element and target, its frequency. In contrast to Weinstein, they argue that variation in patterns of violence cannot be reduced to the binary all-forms-of-terror vs. restraint.

Much recent scholarly analysis has focussed on armed group institutions to explain the observed variation in violence against civilians, building on Weinstein's work but without his focus on initial endowments. A theoretically consequential question is the extent to which that variation is explained by unordered violence. To account for variation in unordered as well as ordered violence, many authors draw on principal agent approaches to organizations as their theoretical starting point (Gates 2002; Mitchell 2004; Weinstein 2007; Wood 2009, 2015; Hoover Green 2011). Such approaches build on a two-fold insight: commanders and combatants may have different preferences for violence, and combatants but not commanders have information about the violence they are in fact carrying out. Wood (2009) argues that group institutions mediate this tension: groups with strong institutions (as indicated by the ability to distribute financial resources across the organization without significant corruption, for example) implement commander preferences, while those with weak ones implement those of combatants (which evolve during war). In contrast to Weinstein, scholars increasingly emphasize the importance of socialization rather than endowments. For example, Stanton (2009, 2013) shows that rebels that have a political wing to their military organization are more likely to exhibit restraint; her other findings similarly emphasize the group's institutions and also those of its rival. In light of the social psychological dynamics of combat—dehumanization of victims, brutalization of combatants, etc.—Hoover Green (2011, 2014) argues that reiterated political training is necessary if armed groups are to engage in a narrow repertoire. Cohen (2013) shows that wartime rape is significantly more frequent by armed groups (rebel or state forces) that forcibly (particularly when also randomly) recruit their combatants: gang rape serves as a source of social cohesion for such groups, she argues. In their careful analyses of variation in patterns of violence, Hoover Green (2011) and Manekin (2012) show that internal group institutions explain differences in violence patterns between state and rebel forces in El Salvador (and among different constituent groups of each) and between different state forces in Israel, respectively.

These recent works of course beg the question: what is the origin of armed group institutions? Diffusion across non-state actors and also across state militaries clearly plays a role (Kalyvas and Balcells 2010), but the precise mechanisms of diffusion—learning (adaptation due to belief in an innovation's effectiveness), imitation, agent migration, coercion, or competition—are not well understood (Wood 2013).

One source is group ideology, another emergent theme in the literature. Gutiérrez Sanín and Wood (2014a: 215; see also Freeden 2004: 6) argue that ideology is best understood as "a more or less systematic set of ideas that includes the identification of a referent group (a class, ethnic, or other social group), an enunciation of the grievances or challenges that the group confronts, the identification of objectives on behalf of that group (political change—or defense against its threat), and a (perhaps vaguely defined) program of action." Thus in carrying out the political violence of civil war, armed groups (including ethnic nationalist groups) necessarily embrace ideologies, which vary from highly systematic doctrines on the part of some groups to loosely related ideas vaguely advanced by leaders of others. In short, if violence is political, it is ideological, to sharply varying degree. Moreover, ideologies prescribe—to widely varying extent, from no explicit blueprint to very specific instructions—particular institutions and strategies as the means to attain group goals. Latin American insurgent groups built different institutions, for example, depending on whether they followed Maoist, Guevarist, or Leninist ideology.

Ideologies also partly determine the perceived set of alternative strategies and tactics from which commanders develop not only institutions, but also group norms, rhetoric, and alliances. They do not calculate the costs and benefits of distinct possibilities through some abstract calculus but consider historically available options, possibly restricted by the strategic and normative constraints their ideology prescribes (Gutiérrez Sanín and Wood 2014a). Scott Straus (2012) argues that state ideology in some settings may serve as a source of de-escalation (rather than escalation) of violence, as in the case of Cote d'Ivoire, which contrasts sharply with Rwanda in terms of state ideology as well as mass killing. (Other scholars attribute differences in the type of warfare and in the duration of the conflict during and after the Cold War to ideological differences: Kalyvas and Balcells 2010; Balcells and Kalyvas 2014.)

However, the recent emphasis on group institutions and ideology—the "organizational turn"—runs the risk of neglecting other determinants of civil war violence. Three issues are particularly important. First, a narrow focus on the armed group may ignore the effects of its interaction with enemy organizations and with "on-side" rivals. Violence against civilians may escalate because of conflict dynamics, particularly looming defeat (Hultman 2007) or competition for resources with rivals (Metelits 2010). Patterns of violence may diffuse directly (without the mediation of institutions stressed earlier), as combatants imitate or learn enemy or rival repertoires. The emergence of revolutionary movements may reflect characteristics of the state, not just the armed organization (Goodwin 2001). Second, whether or not a fledgling rebel organization develops the coherence necessary to pose a sustained challenge to the state depends on its social embeddedness—the type and extent of its social networks—before (Staniland 2014) and during the conflict (Stearns 2015). Third, the emphasis on the principal agent approach to understanding civil war violence may obscure a distinct approach that focusses on collective action as the result of non-material, in-process benefits and the dynamic co-evolution of organizational culture and group institutions (Wood 2003).

SOCIAL MOBILIZATION AND CIVIL WAR

Despite the work of eminent scholars Doug McAdam, Sidney Tarrow, and Charles Tilly (McAdam et al. 2001; Tilly 2003, 2008; Tilly and Tarrow 2006) to build a unified field of "contentious politics," scholars who work primarily on social movements and on civil wars largely work in isolation from one another, with too few analyzing the relationship between the two forms of political opposition as instances of the broader field of contentious politics, as several scholars have argued (Tarrow 2007; Bosi and Giugni 2012; Goodwin 2012; Tarrow 2014, this volume). Yet scholars of social movements and civil wars share an emphasis on the dynamics of escalation of violence and social mobilization.

Escalation in violence takes many forms: it may mean an increase in the frequency and scale of attacks or a widening of the repertoire or the targeting of violence (Gutiérrez Sanín and Wood 2014b). Just as some social movements in peacetime develop explicit long-term strategies of escalation (particularly civil resistance campaigns, Sharp 2005), so too do some insurgent groups in wartime. For example, the Guevarist *foco* theory of revolution claims that small networks of insurgents can foment armed insurrections in cities (Guevara [1961] 1998). However, despite various attempts, armed insurrection to overthrow the regime has generally failed, with some exceptions (e.g., Nicaragua in 1979).

A particular form of escalation that spans the two fields of study is the decision by a hitherto nonviolent social movement to deploy violence. The recently released Nonviolent and Violent Campaigns and Outcomes (NAVCO) 2.0 dataset makes possible quantitative analysis of the distinct types of campaigns and the correlates of engaging in violence (Chenoweth and Lewis 2013). An important initial insight is the documentation that a significant fraction of nonviolent campaigns have a "radical flank" (for an analysis of radicalization of ethno-nationalist movements, see Alimi et al. 2012).

One reason often cited for the switch from nonviolence to violence is that indiscriminate state violence provokes moral outrage that legitimizes the turn to violence as in El Salvador in the late 1970s (Wood 2003), shifts the balance of power within the opposition to those that favor violence (Wood 2003), or leads civilians to perceive that they will be more secure by joining the insurgency than by not doing so (Kalyvas and Kocher 2007). However, the determinants of the onset of primarily violent and primarily nonviolent campaigns appear to be distinct: instead of poverty, mountainous terrain, oil, and a history of instability, nonviolent campaigns occur more frequently where there is a durable authoritarian regime (as well as the shared determinant, population size) (Chenoweth and Lewis 2013; see also Cunningham 2013). This suggests that scholars should not presume that violent campaigns generally originate as an escalation of previous nonviolent campaigns. Nonetheless, the same dataset shows that about 12 per cent of campaigns switch between primarily violent and nonviolent categories; with about 60 per cent of campaigns that switch beginning as primarily nonviolent (Wasser 2014). Moreover, in some settings, there are significant (often covert) ties between nonviolent and revolutionary activists and organizations, as in Central America (Wood 2003; Brockett 2005). These issues clearly merit more scholarly attention.

Less frequently analyzed is social mobilization *during* civil war. Such mobilization occurs not only in the obvious form of recruitment of combatants but also in the ongoing mobilization of civilian supporters of both insurgencies and the state (Wood 2008). For insurgents, survival as well as success in wars fought through irregular warfare—about half of civil wars (Kalyvas and Balcells 2010)—relies on the ongoing support of at least some civilians. Insurgent supports provide "cover" for non-state combatants as well as intelligence, supplies, transportation, and fresh recruits. While the last three can be coerced relatively effectively, as evident in the pattern of forced recruitment in many wars, the coercing of high-quality intelligence is much more problematic (Wood 2003). Despite a massive influx of aid and training to state forces and major counterinsurgent reforms, the insurgency in El Salvador was not defeated due to the provision of such intelligence by networks of deeply committed civilians, support that reflected moral outrage at state violence and the pleasure of agency on the part of hitherto subordinate actors (Wood 2003). Insurgencies vary sharply in the degree of coercion they exercise over civilians, from groups that require only a "coerced minimum" of not providing support to the state as in El Salvador, to those that recruit forcibly and brutally, to those that deploy a reign of terror to "cleanse" territory of civilians unlikely to support their project. Scholars increasingly document and analyze "rebel governance" as forms of order in the midst of civil war, tracing variation in its type and degree to the extent of state authority before the war, insurgent internal organization and ideology, and the cohesion of the local community, which facilitates its posing constraints on both insurgent and state forces (Arjona 2010; Mampilly 2011).

States (to varying extent) and actors allied to the state also attempt to mobilize not only recruits but also civilian support during civil war. State militaries often attempt to draw or conscript recruits from a wide range of sub-cultures in order to build national unity (Weber 1976). In particular, the state may promote the process of "ethnic defection" (Kalyvas 2008), recruiting disaffected members of an ethnic community on whose behalf an insurgent organization is seeking autonomy or secession. State actors may also bolster their forces by drawing on clientelist networks of local allies or organizations of retired soldiers to found civilian militias or defense forces, as in El Salvador.

In many settings, local elites also mobilize existing social networks, particularly kin and clientelist ties, to counter actors encroaching on their interests through the arming of these networks (Romero 2003; Wood 2008). They may target not only insurgent organizations and their presumed civilian supporters but also rival elites seeking advantage in the disorganized context of war. Rwanda represents an extreme case of such mobilization: local elites drew on kin and social networks to recruit participants in the genocidal killing of neighbors (Fujii 2011). In contrast, in other settings it is community leaders who found local militias to protect the community from insurgent violence. This form of collective action—community-initiated militias—spreads to other communities that have local cultures that resonate with its particular ideology and practices (Jentzsch 2014).

Returning to the state, the conditions under which counterinsurgency strategy based on cultivating hearts-and-minds through service provision and nation building will succeed are sharply contested, not only in recent policy debates over US policy in Iraq and Afghanistan but also among scholars. For example, major political science journals such as *Perspectives on Politics* (Review Symposium 2008) and *Politics and Society* (Branch 2010; Branch and Wood 2010; Hunt 2010; Peceny and Stanley 2010) have published special sections assessing the strategy and its unintended as well as intended effects. On the one hand, some scholars and military strategists emphasize the responsiveness of local residents to provision of services (US Army and Marine Corps 2007; Berman et al. 2011). On the other, the attempt to cultivate local support through such assistance may not succeed as it may not in the eyes of local residents compensate for former violence. Indiscriminate state violence against nonviolent protestors as well as the long history of marginalization, exclusion, and mis-rule led to significantly greater active support for the insurgents than for state forces in El Salvador even during periods when the state moved from indiscriminate violence to a hearts-and-minds approach (Wood 2003). The conditions for successful external intervention may be quite narrow: "the settings where the conditions for successful counterinsurgency by foreign powers are met—the existence of allies able to gather high-quality intelligence from local people and to help build local institutions to deliver services—are the very settings where counterinsurgency is least 'needed'" (Branch and Wood 2010: 4). Economic assistance by the counterinsurgent coalition in Afghanistan has had little effect on civilian attitudes in particularly violent Pashtun villages, the critical setting for counterinsurgency efforts (Lyall et al. 2013). Moreover, the effects of violence against civilians on civilian support for the group carrying out the violence appears to be conditional on who carried out the violence: civilian support for the Taliban increased after coalition violence against civilians, but support for the coalition did not increase after Taliban violence (Lyall et al. 2013).

Despite the supposed benefits of the hearts-and-minds approach to counterinsurgency, states nonetheless often employ indiscriminate violence. Although many scholars argue that it is counterproductive, in part because it may render joining the insurgents less risky than not doing so (Kalyvas 2006; Kalyvas and Kocher 2007), it is sometimes effective, as in Chechnya (Lyall 2009). In her exploration of the conditions under which it results in sustained collective action by civilians in support of the state, Livia Schubiger (2013, 2014) argues that direct and collective violence by the state against civilians weakens insurgents both because local communities seek to signal to the state their renewed loyalty by forming local militias, and because insurgents cannot in the face of such violence successfully integrate the flood of new recruits it generates and is therefore likely to fragment. Yet in the long run, she suggests, such violence prolongs the conflict as it destroys the insurgent coherence needed for negotiated resolution and fuels conditions for the later resurgence of conflict.

THE SOCIAL LEGACIES OF CIVIL WAR

Civil wars leave death, devastation and destruction in their wake, legacies that pose challenges for post-war development and reconciliation. Civil wars result—to sharply varying degree across countries—in lower incomes, investment rates, and social service provision (Chen et al. 2008). Legacies for civil society may be latent for decades and then re-emerge when conditions allow, as in the debate in newly democratic Spain about appropriate memorialization of those killed in the civil war in 1936–39. Indeed, Laia Balcells (2012) found that patterns of extreme violence were associated with political identities a generation later. In Guatemala, Regina Bateson (2013) found that post-war violence against suspected criminals took the collective form of public lynching in areas where pro-state militias had patrolled communities during the war, whereas elsewhere it took the form of individual killing.

Yet legacies are not uniformly negative: the wartime destruction of some forms of political and social domination and the emergence of new actors may facilitate new forms of political order and participation in its wake. In oligarchic societies, sustained insurgency—either violent as in El Salvador or primarily nonviolent as in South Africa—may lead to democratic rule (Wood 2000). This path to democracy is likely uncommon, however: it is nonviolent forms of mass mobilization that play an essential role in many transitions to democratic rule (Collier 1999, 2004). Moreover, Chenoweth and Stephan (2011) show that nonviolent campaigns more frequently succeed than violent ones: in their analysis of the more than 300 campaigns for major political change between 1900 and 2006, more than half of the nonviolent campaigns succeeded while only about a quarter of the violent ones did so. They argue against the suggestion that nonviolent campaigns succeed more often because they emerge in "easier" settings, but more work needs to be done on the conditions under which distinct types of campaigns emerge as well as when they succeed.

Turning from regimes to local legacies, in Wood (2008) I pointed to some surprisingly positive social legacies of some civil wars including more egalitarian gender roles, a more equitable distribution of property rights, an empowered civil society, and unprecedented political participation. Recent works confirm the existence of "pro-social" legacies of war. Survey evidence gathered during and after civil war demonstrates that exposure to civil war violence sometimes increases pro-social behavior by both individuals and communities. John Bellows and Edward Miguel (2009) found that the individuals more exposed to violence during Sierra Leone's civil war were more likely to vote, join community groups, and attend community meetings in its aftermath. Christopher Blattman (2009) similarly found that former child soldiers in Uganda were more likely to participate politically than their civilian peers; his qualitative evidence suggests that it is child soldiers who witnessed violence who were particularly likely to participate after the war.

Scholars increasingly use behavioral game experiments to measure the extent to which war and violence generate these pro-social outcomes and to identify the underlying mechanisms. In Tel Aviv, senior citizens were more likely to cooperate with one another (and to punish those who did not cooperate) during Israel's war with Hezbollah in 2006 than either before or after (Gneezy and Fessler 2011). Greater exposure to violence led to more altruistic behavior in the post-war period in Burundi (Voors et al. 2012). Michael Bauer and his collaborators (2013) found increased egalitarian motivations towards in-group but not out-group members among children and youth between 7 and 20 years of age at the time of war in both Georgia (six months after the war with Russia) and in Sierra Leone (a decade after the civil war), suggesting that exposure to violence at those ages is particularly consequential. Communities affected by violence during Nepal's civil war exhibited more pro-social motivation, an outcome possibly driven by the flight of individuals not inclined to cooperate and the coalescing of those remaining to cope with wartime challenges (Gilligan et al. 2014).

In my earlier analysis, I traced the social legacies of civil war to six local social processes—political mobilization, military socialization, the polarization of social identities, the militarization of local authority, the transformation of gender roles, and the fragmentation of local political economies (Wood 2008). I showed that their incidence varied sharply across the civil wars in Sierra Leone, Peru, El Salvador, and Sri Lanka, which suggests that variation in those processes may contribute to variation in the pro-social outcomes just discussed. In contrast to the pro-social legacies discussed earlier, Alessandra Cassar and her co-authors (2013) found that violence undermined trust within localities after civil war in Tajikistan. The authors suggest that the discrepancy with other studies reflects differences in how war is fought locally: in Tajikistan war was fought between different Tajik factions within local communities. Variation in wartime processes may also explain variation in post-war political mobilization. For example, the erosion of rural secret societies during the civil war in Liberia was followed by massive mobilization by women that pushed elites to negotiate an end to the conflict; in contrast, in neighboring Sierra Leone the secret societies emerged relatively unscathed and women's political participation remained limited in the post-war period (Nielsen 2015).

Conclusion

Recent literature on social mobilization and violence in civil war analyzes their variation across not only conflicts but also across armed actors within each conflict. Scholars continue to develop and test theories to account for that observed variation, with increasing success in the case of patterns of violence, including repertoires. Variation in social mobilization during civil war is less well understood, perhaps in part because of challenges in analyzing political opportunity, framing processes, and mobilizing structures during war. And scholars are only beginning to document and analyze the varied social legacies of civil war. Among the topics likely to benefit from increased exchange between scholars of civil wars and social movements as forms of contentious politics are the determinants of repertoires of violence and contention; the origins of group institutions and ideology, including diffusion across groups; the dynamics of escalation and de-escalation; the emergence of dual political opportunity structures—one defined by the state, the other by the insurgents—as insurgent organizations build territorial control; the evolution of framing processes and mobilizing structures as mobilization becomes violent or the state more repressive; the conditions for movement success; and the unintended as well as intended social legacies of mobilization and violence.

REFERENCES

Alimi, Eitan Y., Bosi, Lorenzo, and Demetriou, Chares (2012). "Relational Dynamics and Processes of Radicalization: A Comparative Framework," *Mobilization.* 17(1): 85–98.

Arjona, Ana (2010). "Social Order in Civil War." PhD diss., Yale University.

Balcells, Laia (2010). "Rivalry and Revenge: Violence Against Civilians in Conventional Civil Wars," *International Studies Quarterly.* 54(2): 291–313.

Balcells, Laia (2012). "The Consequences of Victimization on Political Identities: Evidence from Spain," *Politics & Society.* 40(3): 311–347.

Balcells, Laia and Kalyvas, Stathis N. (2014). "Does Warfare Matter? Severity, Duration and Outcomes of Civil Wars," *Journal of Conflict Resolution.* 58(8): 1390–1418.

Bateson, Regina Anne (2013). "Order and Violence in Postwar Guatemala." PhD diss., Yale University.

Bauer, Michal, Cassar, Alessandra, Chytilová, Julie, and Henrich, Joseph (2013). "War's Enduring Effects on the Development of Egalitarian Motivations and In-Group Biases," *Psychological Science.* 25(1): 47–57.

Bellows, John and Miguel, Edward (2009). "War and Local Collective Action in Sierra Leone," *Journal of Public Economics.* 93: 1144–1157.

Berman, Eli, Shapiro, Jacob N., and Felter, Joseph H. (2011). "Can Hearts and Minds Be Bought? The Economics of Counterinsurgency in Iraq," *Journal of Political Economy.* 119(4): 766–819.

Blattman, Christopher (2009). "From Violence to Voting: War and Political Participation in Uganda," *American Political Science Review.* 103(2): 231–247.

Bosi, Lorenzo and Giugni, Marco (2012). "The Study of the Consequences of Armed Groups: Lessons from the Social Movement Literature," *Mobilization: An International Journal.* 17(1): 85–98.

Branch, Daniel (2010). "Footprints in the Sand: British Colonial Counterinsurgency and the War in Iraq," *Politics & Society.* 38: 15–34.

Branch, Daniel and Wood, Elisabeth Jean (2010). "Revisiting Counterinsurgency," *Politics & Society.* 38(1): 3–14.

Brockett, Charles D. (2005). *Political Movements and Violence in Central America.* New York: Cambridge University Press.

Cassar, Alessandra, Grosjean, Pauline, and Whitt, Sam (2013). "Legacies of Violence: Trust and Market Development," *Journal of Economic Growth.* 18: 285–318.

Cederman, Lars-Erik, Skrede Gleditsch, Kristian, Salehyan, Idean, and Wucherpfennig, Julian (2013). "Transborder Ethnic Kin and Civil War," *International Organization.* 67(2): 389–410.

Chen, Siyan, Loayza, Norman V., and Reynal-Querol, Marta (2008). "The Aftermath of Civil War," *The World Bank Economic Review.* 22(1): 63–85.

Chenoweth, Erica and Lewis, Orion A. (2013). "Unpacking Nonviolent Campaigns: Introducing the NAVCO 2.0 Dataset," *Journal of Peace Research.* 50(3): 415–423.

Chenoweth, Erica and Stephan, Maria J. (2011). *Why Civil Resistance Works: The Strategic Logic of Nonviolent Conflict*. New York: Columbia University Press.

Cohen, Dara Kay (2013). "Explaining Rape During Civil War: Cross-National Evidence (1980–2009)," *American Political Science Review*. 107(3): 461–477.

Cohen, Dara Kay, Hoover Green, Amelia, and Wood, Elisabeth Jean (2013). *Wartime Sexual Violence: Misconceptions, Implications, and Ways Forward*. United States Institute of Peace Special Report 323, February 2013.

Collier, Paul (2004). "Greed and Grievance in Civil War," *Oxford Economic Papers*. 56(4): 563–595.

Collier, Paul and Hoeffler, Anke (2001). *Greed and Grievance in Civil War*. Washington, DC: World Bank Working Papers.

Collier, Paul and Hoeffler, Anke (2004) "Greed and Grievance in Civil War," *Oxford Economic Papers* 56(4): 563–595.

Collier, Ruth Berins (1999). *Paths Toward Democracy: The Working Class and Elites in Western Europe and South America*. Cambridge: Cambridge University Press.

Cunningham, Kathleen Gallagher (2013). "Understanding Strategic Choice: The Determinants of Civil War and Nonviolent Campaign in Self-Determination Disputes," *Journal of Peace Research*. 50: 291–304.

Fearon, James and Laitin, David (2003). "Ethnicity, Insurgency, and Civil War," *American Political Science Review*. 97(1): 75–90.

Freeden, Michael (2004). "Ideology, Political Theory and Political Philosophy." In *Handbook of Political Theory*, edited by Gerald F. Gaus and Chandran Kukathas, 3–17. London and New Delhi: Sage.

Fujii, Lee Ann (2011). *Killing Neighbors: Webs of Violence in Rwanda*. Ithaca: Cornell University Press.

Gates, Scott (2002). "Recruitment and Allegiance: the Microfoundations of Rebellion," *Journal of Conflict Resolution*. 46(1): 111–130.

Gilligan, Michael J., Pasquale, Benjamin J., and Samii, Cyrua (2014). "Civil War and Social Cohesion: Lab-in-the-Field Evidence from Nepal," *American Journal of Political Science*. 58: 604–619.

Gneezy, Ayelet and Fessler, David M. T. (2011). "Conflict, Sticks and Carrots: War Increases Prosocial Punishments and Rewards," *Proceedings of the Royal Society*. B. 279: 219–223.

Goodwin, Jeff (2001). *No Other Way Out: States and Revolutionary Movements, 1945–1991*. Cambridge: Cambridge University Press.

Goodwin, Jeff (2012). "Introduction to a Special Issue on Political Violence and Terrorism: Political Violence as Contentious Politics," *Mobilization: An International Journal*. 17(1): 1–5.

Guevara, Che ([1961] 1998). *Guerrilla Warfare*. Lincoln, NE: University of Nebraska Press.

Gutiérrez Sanín, Francisco and Wood, Elisabeth Jean (2014a). "Ideology in Civil War: Instrumental Adoption and Beyond," *Journal of Peace Research*. 51(2): 213–226.

Gutiérrez Sanín, Francisco and Wood, Elisabeth Jean (2014b). "What Should We Mean By 'Pattern of Political Violence'? Repertoire, Targeting, Frequency and Technique." Paper presented at the annual meeting of the American Political Science Association, Washington D.C., August 29.

Hegre, Håvard and Sambanis, Nicholas (2006). "Sensitivity Analysis of Empirical Results on Civil War Onset," *Journal of Conflict Resolution*. 50(4): 508–535.

Hoddie, Matthew and Hartzell, Caroline A. (2007). *Crafting Peace: Power-Sharing Institutions and the Negotiated Settlement of Civil Wars*. University Park: Pennsylvania State University.

Hoover Green, Amelia (2011). "Repertoires of Violence Against Non-combatants: The Role of Armed Group Institutions and Ideologies." PhD diss., Yale University.

Hoover Green, Amelia (2014). "Armed Group Institutions and Conflict-Related Sexual Violence in Cross-National Perspective." Paper presented at the Workshop on Sexual Violence and Armed Conflict: New Research Frontiers held at the Harvard Kennedy School, Harvard University, September 2–3.

Hultman, Lisa (2007). "Battle Losses and Rebel Violence: Raising the Costs for Fighting," *Terrorism and Political Violence*. 19(2): 205–222.

Hunt, David (2010). "Dirty Wars: Counterinsurgency in Vietnam and Today," *Politics & Society*. 38: 35–66.

Jentzsch, Corinna (2014). "Militias and the Dynamics of Civil Wars." PhD diss., Yale University.

Kalyvas, Stathis N. (2006). *The Logic of Violence in Civil War*. Cambridge: Cambridge University Press.

Kalyvas, Stathis N. (2008). "Ethnic Defection in Civil War," *Comparative Political Studies*. 41(8): 1043–1068.

Kalyvas, Stathis N. (2012). "Micro-Level Studies of Violence in Civil War: Refining and Extending the Control-Collaboration Model," *Terrorism and Political Violence*. 24(4): 658–668.

Kalyvas, Stathis N. and Balcells, Laia (2010). "International System and Technologies of Rebellion: How the End of the Cold War Shaped Internal Conflict," *American Political Science Review*. 104(3): 415–429.

Kalyvas, Stathis N. and Kocher, Adam (2007). "How 'Free' is Free Riding in Civil Wars? Violence, Insurgency, and the Collective Action Problem," *World Politics*. 59(2): 177–216.

Kalyvas, Stathis N. and Kocher, Matthew Adam System (2009). "The Dynamics of Violence in Vietnam: An Analysis of the Hamlet Evaluation," *Journal of Peace Research*. 46(3): 335–355.

Kocher, Matthew Adam, Pepinsky, Thomas B., and Kalyvas, Stathis N. (2011). "Aerial Bombing and Counterinsurgency in the Vietnam War," *American Journal of Political Science*. 55(2): 201–218.

Leiby, Michele (2009). "Wartime Sexual Violence in Guatemala and Peru," *International Studies Quarterly*. 53: 445–468.

Leiby, Michele (2011). "State-Perpetrated Wartime Sexual Violence in Latin America." PhD diss., University of New Mexico.

Lyall, Jason (2009). "Does Indiscriminate Violence Incite Insurgent Attacks? Evidence from Chechnya," *Journal of Conflict Resolution*. 53(2): 331–362.

Lyall, Jason, Blair, Graeme, and Imai, Kosuke (2013). "Explaining Support for Combatants during Wartime: A Survey Experiment in Afghanistan," *American Political Science Review*. 107(4): 679–705.

Mampilly, Zachariah Cherian (2011). *Rebel Rulers: Insurgent Governance and Civilian Life during War*. Ithaca: Cornell University Press.

Manekin, Devorah (2012). "Waging War among Civilians: The Production and Restraint of Counterinsurgent Violence in the Second Intifada." PhD diss., University of California Los Angeles.

McAdam, Doug, Tarrow, Sidney, and Tilly, Charles (2001). *Dynamics of Contention*. New York: Cambridge University Press.

Metelits, Claire (2010). *Inside Insurgencies. Violence, Civilians, and Revolutionary Group Behavior*. New York: New York University Press.

Mitchell, Neil (2004). *Agents of Atrocity: Leaders, Followers, and the Violation of Human Rights in Civil War*. New York: Palgrave MacMillian.

Nielsen, Rebecca (2015). "War, Networks, and Women in Politics: Female Secret Societies in Liberia and Sierra Leone." PhD diss., Yale University.

Nordås, Ragnhild (2011). *Sexual Violence in African Conflicts*, PRIO Policy Brief 01.

Parkinson, Sarah Elizabeth (2013). "Organizing Rebellion: Rethinking High-Risk Mobilization and Social Networks in War," *American Political Science Review*. 107(3): 418–432.

Peceny, Mark and Stanley, William D. (2010). "Counterinsurgency in El Salvador," *Politics & Society*. 38: 67–94.

Perspectives on Politics Review Symposium (2008). Review of *The New U.S. Army/Marine Corps Counterinsurgency Field Manual*. Articles by Stephen Biddle, Jeffrey C. Issac, Stathis N. Kalyvas, Wendy Brown, and Douglas A. Ollivant. *Perspectives on Politics*. 6: 347–360.

Romero, Mauricio (2003). *Paramilitares y autodefensas, 1982–2003*. Bogotá: Instituto de Estudios Políticos y Relaciones Internacionales, Universidad Nacional de Colombia.

Schubiger, Livia Isabella (2013). "Repression and Mobilization in Civil War: The Consequences of State Violence for Wartime Collective Action." PhD diss., University of Zurich.

Schubiger, Livia Isabella (2014). "State Violence and Counterinsurgent Collective Action: Evidence from Peru." Paper presented at the 2014 annual meeting of the American Political Science Association, Washington D.C., August 29.

Sharp, Gene (2005). *Waging Nonviolent Struggle: 20th Century Practice and 21st Century Potential*. Boston: Extending Horizons Books.

Staniland, Paul (2012). "States, Insurgents, and Wartime Political Orders," *Perspectives on Politics*. 10(2): 243–264.

Staniland, Paul (2014). *Networks of Rebellion: Explaining Insurgent Cohesion and Collapse*. Ithaca: Cornell University Press.

Stanton, Jessica (2009). "Strategies of Violence and Restraint in Civil War." PhD diss., Columbia University.

Stanton, Jessica (2013). "Strategies of Restraint in Civil War." Unpublished paper.

Stearns, Jason (2015). "The Social Rebel: Interest, Social Locus, and the Longevity of Armed Groups." PhD diss., Yale University.

Steele, Abbey (2009). "Seeking Safety: Avoiding Displacement and Choosing Destinations in Civil Wars," *Journal of Peace Research*. 46(3): 419–430.

Straus, Scott (2012). "Retreating from the Brink: Theorizing Mass Violence and the Dynamics of Restraint," *Perspectives on Politics*. 10(2): 343–362.

Tarrow, Sidney (2007). "Inside Insurgencies: Politics and Violence in an Age of Civil War," *Perspectives on Politics*. 5(3): 587–600.

Tarrow, Sidney (2014). "Contentious Politics." In *Oxford Handbook of Social Movements*, edited by Donatella della Porta and Mario Diani. Oxford: Oxford University Press.

Tilly, Charles (2003). *The Politics of Collective Violence*. Cambridge: Cambridge University Press.

Tilly, Charles (2008). *Contentious Performances*. New York and Cambridge: Cambridge University Press.

Tilly, Charles and Tarrow, Sidney, (2006). *Contentious Politics*. Oxford: Oxford University Press.

Toft, Monica Duffy (2009). *Securing the Peace: The Durable Settlement of Civil War*. Princeton: Princeton University Press.

United States Army and Marine Corps (2007). *Counterinsurgency Field Manual.* Chicago: University of Chicago Press.

Voors, Maarten J., Nillesen, Eleonora E. M., Verwimp, Philip, Bulte, Erwin H., Lensink, Robert, and Van Soest, Daan P. (2012). "Violent Conflict and Behavior: A Field Experiment in Burundi," *American Economic Review.* 102(2): 941–964.

Walter, Barbara F. (2002). *Committing to Peace: The Successful Settlement of Civil Wars.* Princeton: Princeton University Press.

Walter, Barbara F. (2009). "Bargaining Failures and Civil War," *Annual Review of Political Science.* 12: 243–261.

Wasser, Louis (2014). "Ballot Boxes, Bushwhackers, and Bebsi-Soaked Bandanas: Calculating Contention from Appalachia to the Arab World." Unpublished paper, Yale University.

Weber, Eugen (1976). *Peasants into Frenchmen: The Modernization of France, 1870–1914.* Stanford: Stanford University Press.

Weinstein, Jeremy (2007). *Inside Rebellion: The Politics of Insurgent Violence.* Cambridge: Cambridge University Press.

Wood, Elisabeth Jean (2000). *Forging Democracy from Below: Insurgent Transitions in South Africa and El Salvador.* Cambridge: Cambridge University Press.

Wood, Elisabeth Jean (2003). *Insurgent Collective Action and Civil War in El Salvador.* Cambridge: Cambridge University Press.

Wood, Elisabeth Jean (2006). "Variation in Sexual Violence During War," *Politics and Society.* 34(3): 307–342.

Wood, Elisabeth Jean (2008). "The Social Processes of Civil War: The Wartime Transformation of Social Networks," *Annual Review of Political Science.* 11: 539–561.

Wood, Elisabeth Jean (2009). "Armed Groups and Sexual Violence: When is Wartime Rape Rare?" *Politics and Society.* 37(1): 131–161.

Wood, Elisabeth Jean (2012). "Rape During War is Not Inevitable: Variation in Wartime Sexual Violence." In *Understanding and Proving International Sex Crimes*, edited by Morten Bergsmo, Alf B. Skre, and Elisabeth Jean Wood, 389–419. Oslo: Torkel Opsahl Academic Epublisher.

Wood, Elisabeth Jean (2013). "Transnational Dynamics of Civil War: Where Do We Go From Here?" In *Transnational Dynamics of Civil War*, edited by Jeffrey T Checkel, 231–258. Cambridge: Cambridge University Press.

Wood, Elisabeth Jean (2015). "Conflict-Related Sexual Violence and the Policy Implications of Recent Research," *The International Review of the Red Cross.* 894: 1–22.

CHAPTER 30

CIVIL RESISTANCE

DANIEL P. RITTER

DESPITE having been employed for millennia, civil resistance, or nonviolent action, has only relatively recently begun to attract systematic attention from social scientists. Defined as the sustained use of "non-routine political acts that do not involve violence or the threat of violence" (Schock 2013: 277), civil resistance is a social phenomenon closely related to social movements. But despite obvious theoretical overlaps, the civil resistance literature has developed in virtual isolation of social movement studies. One of the objectives of this chapter is therefore to encourage social movement scholars and students of civil resistance to consider more deliberately the potential for cross-fertilization.

Nonviolent forms of activism can be been traced back as far as 449 BCE, when Roman workers abandoned the city—in effect inventing the general strike—and refused to return until their demands for political rights had been met (Schock 2013: 278). Prior to the twentieth century, civil resistance was mostly employed by individuals and groups harboring religious convictions that prohibited the use of violence (Solomonow 1981; Paige, Satha-Anand, and Gilliatt 1993; Arapura 1997; Long 2011; Schock 2013), and the religious roots of nonviolent action can still be discerned today. Contemporary civil resistance was shaped by Mohandas K. Gandhi's South African experience. As a lawyer hired to represent an Indian company in the then-British colony, the Mahatma-to-be encountered severe racial discrimination that drove him onto the path of nonviolent resistance (Gandhi 1928). Inspired by Christian and Hindu thought, including Jesus' Sermon on the Mount, Leo Tolstoy's (1984) *The Kingdom of God is Within You*, and Henry David Thoreau's (2002) "Civil Disobedience," Gandhi eventually concluded that oppression is most effectively countered with nonviolent means of struggle.

Convinced that violent responses were morally wrong, but that submission was unsatisfactory as well, Gandhi developed an alternative that aimed to avoid both ills. *Satyagraha* ("clinging to the truth") was his conceptualization of a spiritually inspired form of resistance. The method, which was eventually applied by the masses in both South Africa and India, resulted in considerable successes in both countries. Still, Gandhi's legacy has since reached far beyond those two countries with activists on every continent adopting Gandhian tactics to press for democracy, human rights, independence, and a host of other political goods, ranging from the local level to the international one. Over the years, however, Gandhi's emphasis on the moral aspect of nonviolent resistance has been progressively marginalized (Chabot and Sharifi 2013). What remains, however, is a powerful method of social and political change.

This chapter aims to introduce the reader to the phenomenon of civil resistance and the academic research that accompanies it. To that end, I begin by exploring what civil resistance is. Next, I survey some of the existing research on the subject. Third, I identify the outcomes generated by movements employing civil resistance. Finally, I speculate on how greater interaction between civil resistance studies and social movement research should be able to advance our understanding of both subjects.

What is Civil Resistance?

Civil resistance is a form of contentious politics that eschews violent repertoires in favor of nonviolent ones. Unarmed mobilization can be employed against virtually any type of adversary, although the state usually features as the principal antagonist in most episodes of civil resistance. While few, if any, major nonviolent social movements have managed to completely avoid the use of violence, it is the clear preference for nonviolent tactics, not an absolute devotion to them, that characterizes nonviolent mass mobilization. Since states are sometimes inclined to resort to violence in the face of a sustained challenge against them, there is always the risk that the civil resisters fail to maintain their nonviolent discipline and reciprocate state violence. Remarkably often, however, movements have managed to remain predominantly nonviolent.

Gene Sharp, the most influential scholar on the topic, has defined civil resistance as "a technique of action by which the population can restrict and sever the sources of power of their rulers or other oppressors and mobilize their own power potential into effective power" (2005: 39). Sharp's understanding of civil resistance is based on a particular, Gandhi-inspired "pluralistic" conception of power that deems rulers dependent on the consent of the governed. Sharp's contention is that no leader, regardless how powerful he or she may seem, can retain power unless granted the cooperation of key social groups, the ruler's "pillars of support" (Sharp 2005: 35). For instance, no leader personally represses protesters, with that task instead befalling the security forces under the ruler's control. Consequently, if the police and other coercive forces decide to withdraw their support for the regime by refraining from repressing large gatherings, then the leader has in one stroke lost his or her coercive powers. Civil resisters, the thinking goes, should therefore seek to unravel the relationships on which the regime depends by compelling the pillars of support to withdraw their cooperation from the government (Sharp 1973, 2005). This can be done either through acts of *omission*, that is, the refusal to perform acts that one usually performs, such as go to work, or through *commission*, the performance of acts one usually does not perform or is forbidden to perform, such as demonstrations and marches (Sharp 2005: 41). Sharp identified 198 nonviolent methods that can weaken a regime through omission, commission, or a combination of the two (Sharp 1973). The list has become famous in its own right and suggests the nearly limitless variations of civil resistance–only the activists' imagination sets the boundaries for what nonviolent tactics can be devised.

Civil resistance has had a tremendous impact on the world, causing repressive regimes to fall and allowing people to successfully claim their rights. Despite this the phenomenon remains misunderstood in a variety of ways (Schock 2003, 2005). First, nonviolent action is often equated with pacifism or passive resistance. While both of these concepts are related to civil resistance, they differ in important ways. Most importantly, civil resistance is neither passive nor conflict evading: civil resisters eschew violence, but they do not eschew conflict. Indeed, nonviolent resistance is intended precisely to be used in, or even to instigate, conflict situations. Second, a tactic's absence of violence does not necessarily make it an act of civil resistance. Conversing with an adversary is not a nonviolent action, since it is neither a non-routine nor sustained activity. Also, institutionalized, routine political actions, such as vote casting, do not qualify as civil resistance despite their nonviolent character. Third, civil resistance does not require a moral commitment to nonviolent ideals. On the contrary, many formerly violent activists have turned to civil resistance for purely pragmatic reasons. There is thus no requirement for nonviolent activists to be "good people" with just intentions. Finally, nonviolent resistance does not mean that no violence will occur and that nobody will be hurt or die. On the contrary, many nonviolent struggles have resulted in relatively large casualty figures for the simple reason that a movement's adherence to nonviolent tactics does not guarantee that the state, or any adversary for that matter, responds in kind (Sharp 1973: 70–71, 2005, 21–22; Schock 2005: 6–12).

CIVIL RESISTANCE RESEARCH

Although the twentieth century was the bloodiest in human history, it arguably also witnessed more civil resistance than any preceding it. The diffusion of unarmed struggle has generated substantial interest in the topic and given birth to an academic subfield. While researchers have examined a plethora of issues pertaining to civil resistance, they have been particularly inclined to understand why and how nonviolent movements succeed.

The scholarship on civil resistance has progressed through several phases (Carter 2009; Schock 2013). Early scholarship on nonviolent resistance often embraced the "principled" Gandhian view of the method by accepting the religious/ideological foundations of both the Indian independence movement and the American Civil Rights Movement. Furthermore, it was not unusual for writers to focus on Gandhi specifically and, importantly, on Gandhi's belief that nonviolence should be used to make the world a better place, not simply to emerge victorious from conflicts (Gregg 1935; Bondurant

1958; Brown 1972, 1977). The principled approach was however soon overtaken by a distinct interest in the political and strategic dimensions of civil resistance that has since become a dominant feature of the subfield, even though researchers embracing "principled nonviolence" continue to thrive and criticize the strategic turn (Dalton 1993; Cortwright 2006; Chabot and Vinthagen 2007; Chabot and Sharifi 2013).

Sharp (1973) revolutionized the field with the publication of his three-volume *The Politics of Nonviolent Action* in which he emphasized the strategic and pragmatic dimensions of civil resistance. The power of nonviolent action, Sharp argued, stems not from its moral superiority over violence, but rather from the fact that it is a powerful technique of conflict behavior. Many scholars have since embraced Sharp's focus on nonviolent strategy and contributed to its growing prominence. Since the early 1990s, a number of books and many articles have been published that take civil resistance "campaigns"—"sequence[s] of strategic interactions in which the participants try to pursue more or less known objectives" (Ackerman and Kruegler 1994: 10)—as their units of analysis in order to dissect nonviolent activists' strategic choices and their consequences (Ackerman and DuVall 2000; Helvey 2004; Stephan and Chenoweth 2008; Stephan 2009; Chenoweth and Stephan 2011). The conclusions generated by this strand of research has largely been that nonviolent struggle can succeed in any political context as long as the movement employs sounds strategy and manages to mobilize large numbers of participants. The Sharpian school of civil resistance studies has exercised great influence not only in academia, but also within the activist camp. Movement organizers from all over the world, including Burma (Beer 1999), Serbia (Ackerman and Duvall 2000), and Egypt (Chabot and Sharifi 2013), have read Sharp's writings and employed them as civil resistance manuals, often to great effect.

But although nonviolent campaigns are frequently successful, many have also failed to accomplish their objectives (Chenoweth and Stephan 2011). This outcome divergence has led social movement and revolution scholars with an interest in nonviolent resistance to apply insights from these related subfields to the study of civil resistance (Schock 2005; Nepstad 2011; Ritter 2015). In particular, they have sought to add a structural dimension to the actor-driven frameworks that dominate civil resistance scholarship. In one of the earliest attempts to apply social movement theory to nonviolent resistance studies, Kurt Schock (2005) analyzed six nonviolent campaigns that challenged the national governments in South Africa, the Philippines, Burma, China, Nepal, and Thailand. Drawing on political process models, Schock found that although activists' strategic choices and tactical execution represent the single most important factor in determining whether a movement turns out to be successful or a failure, structural factors such as political opportunities and international contexts matter as well.

Sharon Erickson Nepstad's (2011) examination of "nonviolent revolutions" in China, East Germany, Panama, Chile, Kenya, and the Philippines showed that the responses of armed forces to civil resistance campaigns help explain the fate of unarmed movements. Nepstad found that when security forces remain coherent and repress activists, nonviolent movements tend to fall apart. However, if soldiers and police officers refused to use overwhelming force against the protesters that often signaled that the regime was in grave danger of collapse. Consequently, Nepstad argues that the use of civil resistance is a potential explanation for security force behavior, since soldiers tend to be disinclined to respond with violence unless attacked. Nepstad also shows that international sanctions, often assumed to be harmful to authoritarian states, may in actuality be beneficial to dictators as they can undermine the opposition movement's narrative and generate domestic support for the regime.

In an important contribution that breaks new ground in the study of civil resistance, not least methodologically, Erica Chenoweth and Maria Stephan (2011) undertook the immense task of analyzing over 300 violent and nonviolent campaigns for regime change, the end of foreign occupation, or secession. Whereas research on civil resistance had previously been almost exclusively qualitative in nature with a heavy emphasis on case studies, Chenoweth and Stephan employed quantitative methods of analysis. As a result, they were able to empirically show that nonviolent campaigns are on average more likely to succeed than their violent counterparts. In fact, their "most striking finding is that between 1900 and 2006, nonviolent resistance campaigns were nearly twice as likely to achieve full or partial success as their violent counterparts" (Chenoweth and Stephan 2011: 7). The authors explain the greater success rate of nonviolent campaigns by pointing to their "participation advantage" over violent movements, concluding that civil resistance "facilitates the active participation of many more people than violent campaigns, thereby broadening the base of resistance and raising the costs to opponents of maintaining the status quo" (Chenoweth and Stephan 2011: 10–11).

Recently, Daniel Ritter (2015) has attempted to explain unarmed revolutionary success in a more structural manner. Focusing on unarmed revolutions in the Middle East and North Africa, Ritter draws on revolution theory to argue that both the activists' use of nonviolent tactics and certain regimes' unwillingness to repress can be linked to long-term historical processes. Authoritarian regimes that are well integrated into the Western political system of trade, aid, and military collaboration may eventually find themselves constrained by their rhetorical embrace of Western values, such as democracy and human rights when challenged nonviolently by domestic opposition coalitions. Trapped by its discursive, albeit hypocritical, espousal of democratic values, Western-aligned regimes cannot resort to repression without risking the external, and indirectly internal, support on which it depends. As a result they vacillate, which allows the revolutionary movement to grow until it becomes nearly impossible to control.

THE OUTCOMES OF CIVIL RESISTANCE

Civil resistance has been used throughout the world in many different types of struggles. The most famous Western nonviolent campaign is probably the US Civil Rights Movement, in which sit-ins, marches, and boycotts eventually put so much pressure on the American government that it introduced the Civil Rights Act of 1964 (McAdam 2009). Other Western social movements that have relied primarily on nonviolent methods of struggle include the women's movement, the peace movement, and the global justice movement (Clark 2009; Smith and Wiest 2012; Schock 2013).

While social movements in democratic countries often employ nonviolent methods in their struggles, much of the academic study on nonviolent resistance has focussed on struggles for maximalist objectives in non-democratic settings. For instance, Chenoweth and Stephan's (2008, 2011) large quantitative study examined movements that strove for regime change, the end of foreign occupation, or secession. Similarly, Schock (2005), Nepstad (2011), and Ritter (2015) studied nonviolent movements that either sought to overthrow authoritarian regimes, or, at the very least, tried to challenge the state's monopoly on power.

One of the subjects most frequently addressed by civil resistance scholars is regime change in non-democratic countries (Zunes 1994). Although unarmed tactics played important parts in a few such occurrences prior to the late 1970s, for instance in Guatemala and El Salvador in 1944 (Sharp 2005) as well as in Portugal in 1974–75 (Maxwell 2009), the practice of ousting authoritarian leaders through nonviolent resistance has proliferated since the late 1970s. Following the example set by the pre-dominantly unarmed overthrow of Mohammad Reza Pahlavi, the last "shah" of Iran, in January 1979 (Goodwin 2001: 294–295; Foran 2005: 259), dictators and authoritarian regimes on virtually every continent have met the same fate. In countries like the Philippines (Zunes 1999; Mendoza 2009), Chile (Huneeus 2009; Nepstad 2011), Thailand (Satha-Anand 1999; Schock 2005), East Germany (Garton Ash 1990; Maier 2009), Czechoslovakia (Garton Ash 1990; Ritter 2012), South Africa (Schock 2005; Lodge 2009), Serbia (Ackerman and DuVall 2000), Ukraine (Bunce and Wolchik 2010), Tunisia, and Egypt (Nepstad 2013; Ritter 2015), to mention a few of the most spectacular cases, autocrats have fallen at the hands of unarmed revolutionaries. While these democratizing movements assumed somewhat different forms due to a variety of contextual factors, they still looked strikingly similar: Initially small groups of demonstrators helped others cross the barrier of fear that had kept terrorized populations in check for years or even decades. Once the crowds in the streets began to grow, so did the pressure on the state, which eventually caused it to collapse. While the final outcome of these movements were often disappointing to their protagonists (Chabot and Sharifi 2013)—for instance, Islamic Iran is arguably more authoritarian than the state the revolution overthrew—the accomplishment of the movements' most pressing objectives can hardly be questioned, and unarmed revolutionary movements have, as noted, more often than not been successful in accomplishing political change on the national level (Chenoweth and Stephan 2011).

In addition to their immediate achievements, civil resistance has also changed the face of contentious politics. Whereas young and violent males have historically been the drivers of revolutionary movements, nonviolent action has increased the potential for mass-based, non-institutionalized political participation. Due to the immediate risks associated with violently attacking the state, participants in such struggles need to be physically strong and "biographically available," that is, free of the responsibilities of family life. Besides any normative concerns one might have with this arrangement, violent movements have also tended to generate new repressive regimes (Karatnycky and Ackerman 2005). Since virtually anyone can participate in a nonviolent movement, regardless of age, gender, or physical ability, such forms of contention permit a greater number of people to claim ownership of movements for change (Chenoweth and Stephan 2011: 10–11). Often, but not always, this participation advantage has lead to better long-term outcomes as far as democratization and the spread of political and civil rights are concerned (Karatnycky and Ackerman 2005).

Contribution to Social Movement Studies

For decades, civil resistance researchers examined their subject in isolation from the closely related fields of social movement and revolutions studies. Even though students of nonviolent action in effect examined social movements, the emphasis on a particular form of resistance seemingly distracted analysts from drawing on the wealth of knowledge available in the social movement literature. Despite investigating similar phenomena, the development of unarmed resistance studies and social movement research have in some ways progressed in opposite directions of one another. Nonviolent action scholars have only recently begun to broaden their investigations to permit structural factors to complement the subfield's heavy emphasis on agency and strategy (Schock 2013). Social movement studies, on the other hand, have long been criticized for being overly structural (Mahoney and Snyder 1999; Goodwin and Jasper 2004a, 2004b; Morris 2004). The political process model that dominates the field emphasizes political opportunities that make structural conditions primordial in their relationship with human agency. Even though resource mobilization and framing approaches have mitigated this development, social movement theory remains dominated by structural perspectives (Schock 2013). Consequently, both social movement scholars and nonviolent resistance researchers can learn a great deal from each other's work. In fact, cross-fertilization seems necessary if either field is to progress beyond their current states. Social movement studies can benefit greatly from taking into greater account actors' choices and tactics, which civil resistance research has shown impacts a movement's chances of success (Chenoweth and Stephan 2011) and its long-term outcomes (Karatnycky and Ackerman 2005).

While these empirical correlations should be enough to entice students of social movement to take seriously the importance of movement choices and, by extension, agency in movements, more research is necessary in order to establish how and why nonviolent tactics pose such a difficult challenge to repressive regimes. Here, it is civil resistance scholarship that can benefit from insights from the fields of social movement and revolution theory. Tactical choices certainly do matter, but as social movement theorists have pointed out, those choices must be analyzed within their broader political and social contexts (Meyer 2004: 54). It is no more misguided to assume that humans play no role in social change than to argue that agents of change restructure society as they please, when they please. A full understanding of civil resistance—or any form of contentious politics—therefore requires researchers to place the strategic dimensions of a movement in relation to the structural conditions that encapsulate it.

In addition to addressing the "agency deficit" in social movement studies, civil resistance research can help counter another common criticism of the former, namely the tendency to focus on social movement in the Western world. While social movement researchers have dedicated most of their time to "new social movements" in the United States and Europe, students of civil resistance have often examined popular mobilization against repressive regimes in non-Western settings (Zunes, Kurtz, and Asher 1999; Roberts and Garton Ash 2009; Schock 2005; Sharp 2005; Nepstad 2011; Ritter 2015). A plausible explanation for the non-Western focus of civil resistance research is that only in non-democratic setting does nonviolent action constitute deviant, non-institutionalized behavior. Since peaceful protest is an accepted and routinized response to social grievances in democratic countries, a radical conceptualization of civil resistance might suggest that it cannot, by definition, occur in a democratic context. By virtue of being an acceptable and normalized component of politics, authorized demonstrations are no more "resistance" or "protest" than voting is. From this perspective, civil resistance can only occur in countries where such protests behavior is—either explicitly or implicitly—forbidden.

CONCLUSION

This brief chapter has described the nature of civil resistance, surveyed the academic study of the subject, explored its outcomes, and reflected on the subfield's relationship to social movement research. Due to its substantial impact on political and social developments in many parts of the world, civil resistance warrants further research. Students of social movements may find the literature on civil resistance a fruitful source of inspiration, and combining the strategy-focus of civil resistance research with the more structural approach of social movement studies should be of significant benefit to both sub-disciplines.

REFERENCES

Ackerman, Peter and DuVall, Jack (2000). *A Force More Powerful: A Century of Nonviolent Conflict*. New York: St. Martin's.
Ackerman, Peter and Kruegler, Christopher (1994). *Strategic Nonviolent Conflict: The Dynamics of People Power in the Twentieth Century*. Westport, CT: Praeger.
Arapura, John G. (1997). "The Spirituality of Ahimsa (Nonviolence): Traditional and Gandhian. In *Hindu Spirituality: Postclassical and Modern*, edited by KR Sundaraja and Bhitika Mukeri, 392–420. New York: Crossroad.

Beer, Michael A. (1999). "Violent and Nonviolent Struggle in Burma: Is a Unified Strategy Workable?" In *Nonviolent Social Movements: A Geographical Perspective*, edited by Stephen Zunes, Lester R. Kurtz, and Sarah Beth Asher, 174–184. Malden, MA: Blackwell.

Bondurant, Joan (1958). *Conquest of Violence: The Gandhian Philosophy of Conflict*. Princeton, NJ: Princeton University Press.

Brown, Judith M. (1972). *Gandhi's Rise to Power*. Cambridge: Cambridge University Press.

Brown, Judith M. (1977). *Gandhi and Civil Disobedience*. Cambridge: Cambridge University Press.

Bunce, Valerie J. and Wolchik, Sharon L. (2011). *Defeating Authoritarian Leaders in Postcommunist Countries*. New York: Cambridge University Press.

Carter, April (2009). "People Power and Protest: The Literature on Civil Resistance in Historical Context." In *Civil Resistance and Power Politics: The Experience of Non-violent Action from Gandhi to the Present*, edited by Adam Roberts and Timothy Garton Ash, 25–42. New York: Oxford University Press.

Chabot, Sean and Sharifi, Majid (2013). "The Violence of Nonviolence: Problematizing Nonviolent Resistance in Iran and Egypt," *Societies Without Borders*. 8(2): 205–232.

Chabot, Sean and Vinthagen, Stellan (2007). "Rethinking Nonviolent Action and Contentious Politics: Political Cultures of Nonviolent Opposition in the Indian Independence Movement and Brazil's Landless Workers' Movement," *Research in Social Movements, Conflicts and Change*. 27: 91–121.

Chenoweth, Erica and Stephan, Maria J. (2011). *Why Civil Resistance Works: The Strategic Logic of Nonviolent Conflict*. New York: Columbia University Press.

Clark, Howard, ed. (2009). *Unarmed Resistance and Global Solidarity*. London: Pluto.

Cortwright, David (2006). *Gandhi and Beyond: Nonviolence for an Age of Terrorism*. Boulder, CO: Paradigm.

Dalton, Dennis (1993). *Nonviolent Power in Action*. New York: Columbia University Press.

Foran, John (2005). *Taking Power: On the Origin of Third World Revolutions*. New York: Cambridge University Press.

Gandhi, Mohandas K. (1950 [1928]). *Satyagraha in South Africa* (2nd ed.). Ahmedabad: Navajivan.

Garton Ash, Timothy (1990). *The Magic Lantern: The Revolution of '89 Witnessed in Warsaw, Budapest, Berlin, and Prague*. New York: Random House.

Gregg, Richard B. (1935). *The Power of Non-Violence*. London: George Routledge.

Goodwin, Jeff (2001). *No Other Way Out: States and Revolutionary Movements, 1945–1991*. New York: Cambridge University Press.

Goodwin, Jeff and Jasper, James M. (2004a). "Caught in a Winding, Snarling Vine: The Structural Bias of Political Process Theory." In *Rethinking Social Movement: Structure, Meaning, and Emotion*, edited by Jeff Goodwin and James M. Jasper, 3–30. Lanham, MD: Rowman & Littlefield.

Goodwin, Jeff and Jasper, James M., eds. (2004b). *Rethinking Social Movement: Structure, Meaning, and Emotion*. Lanham, MD: Rowman & Littlefield.

Helvey, Robert L. (2004). *On Strategic Nonviolent Conflict: Thinking About the Fundamentals*. Boston, MA: The Albert Einstein Institution.

Huneeus, Carlos (2009). "Political Mass Mobilization against Authoritarian Rule: Pinochet's Chile 1983–88." In *Civil Resistance and Power Politics: The Experience of Non-violent Action from Gandhi to the Present*, edited by Adam Roberts and Timothy Garton Ash, 197–212. New York: Oxford University Press.

Karatnycky, Adrian and Ackerman, Peter (2005). *How Freedom is Won: From Civic Resistance to Durable Democracy*. Washington, DC: Freedom House.

Lodge, Tom (2009). "The Interplay of Non-violent and Violent Action in the Movement against Apartheid in South Africa." In *Civil Resistance and Power Politics: The Experience of Non-violent Action from Gandhi to the Present*, edited by Adam Roberts and Timothy Garton Ash, 213–230. New York: Oxford University Press.

Long, Michael G., ed. (2011). *Christian Peace and Nonviolence: A Documentary History*. Maryknoll, NY: Orbis.

Mahoney, James and Snyder, Richard (1999). "Rethinking Agency and Structure in the Study of Regime Change," *Studies in Comparative International Development*. 34(2): 3–32.

Maier, Charles S. (2009). "Civil Resistance and Civil Society: Lessons from the Collapse of the German Democratic Republic in 1989." In *Civil Resistance and Power Politics: The Experience of Non-violent Action from Gandhi to the Present*, edited by Adam Roberts and Timothy Garton Ash, 260–276. New York: Oxford University Press.

Maxwell, Kenneth (2009). "Portugal: 'The Revolution of the Carnations,' 1974–75." In *Civil Resistance and Power Politics: The Experience of Non-violent Action from Gandhi to the Present*, edited by Adam Roberts and Timothy Garton Ash, 144–161. New York: Oxford University Press.

McAdam, Doug (2009). "The US Civil Rights Movement: Power from Below and Above, 1945–70." In *Civil Resistance and Power Politics: The Experience of Non-violent Action from Gandhi to the Present*, edited by Adam Roberts and Timothy Garton Ash, 58–74. New York: Oxford University Press.

Mendoza, Amado Jr. (2009). "'People Power' in the Philippines, 1983–6." In *Civil Resistance and Power Politics: The Experience of Non-violent Action from Gandhi to the Present*, edited by Adam Roberts and Timothy Garton Ash, 179–196. New York: Oxford University Press.

Meyer, David S. (2004). "Tending the Vineyard: Cultivating Political Process Research." In *Rethinking Social Movement: Structure, Meaning, and Emotion*, edited by Jeff Goodwin and James M. Jasper, 47–60. Lanham, MD: Rowman & Littlefield.

Morris, Aldon (2004). "Reflections on Social Movement Theory: Criticisms and Proposals." In *Rethinking Social Movement: Structure, Meaning, and Emotion*, edited by Jeff Goodwin and James M. Jasper, 233–246. Lanham, MD: Rowman & Littlefield.

Nepstad, Sharon Erickson (2011). *Nonviolent Revolutions: Civil Resistance in the Late 20th Century*. New York: Oxford University Press.

Nepstad, Sharon Erickson (2013). "Mutiny and Nonviolence in the Arab Spring: Exploring Military Defections and Loyalty in Egypt, Bahrain, and Syria," *Journal of Peace Research*. 50(3): 337–349.

Paige, Glenn D., Satha-Anand, Chaiwat, and Gilliatt, Sara, eds. (1993). *Islam and Nonviolence*. Honolulu, HI: Center for Global Nonviolence Planning Project.

Ritter, Daniel P. (2012). "Civil Society and the Velvet Revolution: Mobilizing for Democracy in Czechoslovakia." *COSMOS Working Paper 2012/4*. Department of Political and Social Sciences, European University Institute. http://cadmus.eui.eu/bitstream/handle/1814/26177/2012WP04COSMOS.pdf?sequence=1

Ritter, Daniel P. (2015). *The Iron Cage of Liberalism: International Politics and Unarmed Revolutions in the Middle East and North Africa*. Oxford: Oxford University Press.

Roberts, Adam and Garton Ash, Timothy, eds. (2009). *Civil Resistance and Power Politics: The Experience of Non-violent Action from Gandhi to the Present*. New York: Oxford University Press.

Satha-Anand, Chaiwat (1999). "Imagery in the 1992 Nonviolent Uprising in Thailand." In *Nonviolent Social Movements: A Geographical Perspective*, edited by Stephen Zunes, Lester R. Kurtz, and Sarah Beth Asher, 158–173. Malden: MA: Blackwell.

Solomonow, Allan, ed. (1981). *Roots of Jewish Nonviolence*. Nyack, NY: Jewish Peace Fellowship.

Schock, Kurt (2003). "Nonviolent action and its Misconceptions: Insights for Social Scientists," *PS: Political Science and Politics*. 36(4): 705–712.

Schock, Kurt (2005). *Unarmed Insurrections: People Power Movements in Nondemocracies*. Minneapolis, MN: University of Minnesota Press.

Schock, Kurt (2013). "The Practice and Study of Civil Resistance," *Journal of Peace Research*. 50(3): 277–290.

Sharp, Gene (1973). *The Politics of Nonviolent Action*. Boston, MA: Porter Sargent.

Sharp, Gene (2005). *Waging Nonviolent Struggle: 20th Century Practice and 21st Century Potential*. Boston, MA: Porter Sargent.

Sharp, Gene (2010 [1993]). *From Dictatorship to Democracy* (4th ed.). Boston: The Albert Einstein Institution.

Smith, Jackie and Wiest, Dawn (2012). *Social Movements in the World-System: The Politics of Crisis and Transformation*. New York: Russell Sage Foundation.

Stephan, Maria J., ed. (2009). *Civilian Jihad: Nonviolent Struggle, Democratization, and Governance in the Middle East*. New York: Palgrave Macmillan.

Stephan, Maria J, and Chenoweth, Erica (2008). "Why Civil Resistance Works: The Strategic Logic of Nonviolent Conflict," *International Security*. 33(1): 7–44.

Thoreau, Henry D. (2002 [1849]). "Civil Disobedience." In *An Anthology of Nonviolence: Historical and Contemporary Voices*, edited by Krishna Mallick and Doris Hunter, 51–66. Westport, CT: Greenwood.

Tolstoy, Leo (1984 [1894]). *The Kingdom of God is Within You: Christianity Not as a Mystic Religion but as a New Theory of Life*. Translated by Constance Garnett. Lincoln, NE: Bison Books.

Zunes, Stephen (1994). "Unarmed Insurrections against Authoritarian Governments in the Third World: A New Kind of Revolution," *Third World Quarterly*. 15: 403–426.

Zunes, Stephen (1999a). "The Origins of People Power in the Philippines." In *Nonviolent Social Movements: A Geographical Perspective*, edited by Stephen Zunes, Lester R. Kurtz, and Sarah Beth Asher, 129–157. Malden, MA: Blackwell.

Zunes, Stephen, Kurtz, Lester R., and Asher, Sarah B., eds. (1999). *Nonviolent Social Movements: A Geographical Perspective*. Malden, MA: Blackwell.

CHAPTER 31

....

CONSUMER STRATEGIES IN SOCIAL MOVEMENTS

....

MICHELE MICHELETTI AND DIETLIND STOLLE

Introduction

....

WHERE do people learn about organic eggs, fairtrade coffee, and other forms of alter-consumerism or even more radical practices of anti-consumerism? What kinds of collectivities help them decide which products are better for political, ethical, and environmental reasons and how they should relate to consumer society? More generally, who makes growing numbers of people aware of the politics of products, and how are they mobilized into more politically oriented consumer practices? Research shows that such ideas in one way or another come from political consumer market campaigns (cf. O'Rourke 2005; Stolle and Micheletti 2013) run by groups engaged in multi-leveled and multi-issued fields of contestation within production and consumption (cf. Melucci 1996). This chapter discusses the informal networks, civic groups, and institutions involved in this field of contention and why and how they adopt political consumer strategies and campaigns into their cause advocacy and toolkits of collective action (Taylor and van Dyke 2004). It illustrates how social movements have extended action repertoires to use the market as their arena for politics. It focusses on how they create public awareness about the relationship between their goals and consumer practices, mobilize for greater public concern about the politics of products, change lifestyles and, therefore, even conceptions of politics and consumer culture. The chapter discusses the four different forms of consumer-oriented political activism: boycotts, buycotts, discursive consumer strategies, and lifestyle politics, and illustrates how social movements have historically and recently used consumer practices.

WHAT ARE POLITICAL CONSUMER
PRACTICES?

Consumer choice has been a tool for activism throughout the centuries. It was part of the historical grand anti-slavery movement in the 1700s, instrumental in Gandhi's nonviolent struggle for independence from Britain, and part of the Nazi campaign against Jewish business. Over the years campaigns about consumer choice have become increasingly important for activism around the world. Social movements recognize that not only can people be mobilized to take a stand on important political issues, for instance GMOs, animal treatment, or worker welfare, when demonstrating and protesting but also when they go shopping. Social movements believe that these and other identified multi-leveled and complex problems (e.g., overfishing, deforestation, and climate change) might be dealt with and perhaps even solved if consumers globally are mobilized to put economic pressure on corporations and other institutions. Using the market as an arena for social movement activism can also, however, support nationalism, intolerance, exclusiveness, and discrimination for example, the Klu Klux Klan's market-based "racial terrorism" (Safianow 2004).[1]

The concept "political consumerism" identifies these different kinds of efforts as a form of collective action, formally defined as consumers' use of the market as an arena for politics in order to change institutional or market practices found to be ethically, environmentally, or politically objectionable (see Stolle and Micheletti 2013: ch. 2). When people mobilize politically in the market and use their economic means to attempt to influence political matters they function as "citizen-consumers" who believe that citizen responsibility also applies to private market transactions. This term indicates both how public and private life becomes intermeshed within the activities of social movements and other civic efforts (Soper and Trentmann 2008) as well as how contemporary collective action can shift its focus from the state to become more variable, individualized, and dispersed (cf. Melucci 1996; Micheletti 2010).

Consumer *boycott* is the rejection of a product with the purpose of limiting a corporation's profit margin, influencing its stockmarket value, damaging its reputation, or more broadly mobilizing public awareness about a matter concerning the politics of products. Social movements mobilize boycott actions. Such market-oriented campaigns have included or still include boycotting Nike, Nestlé, Coca-Cola, Shell, McDonalds, and other corporate multinational corporations. These long-running boycotts, in similar fashion to the South African anti-Apartheid boycott and divestment campaign (Sikkink 1986; Bar-Yam 1995), teach collective action and communicate arguments for market-based political action. However, more recently social movements have begun to view boycotts as problematic because it is increasingly difficult to decide which corporations to boycott and boycotts may do more harm than good to the cause. Boycotts have, for instance, been found to be threatening the livelihood of workers in targeted firms: many global social justice networks have, therefore, been cautious about mobilizing support for them or supporting them officially. Thus important groups in the anti-sweatshop movement have only actively supported boycotts if asked to do so by the garment workers themselves.[2] Sometimes corporations even listen to boycott demands but social movements have difficulty in calling them off, thus complicating problem solving between civil society and business.

Therefore the use of *buycotts* or deliberately choosing certain products over others from, for instance, organic and green labeling schemes or fairtrade shopping guides, has been promoted more since the 1990s. These are social movements that have called or call for product labeling, which seeks to guarantee that goods are produced under certain conditions, such as least damaging to the environment, without child labor, locally grown, better for farm animals, or with a fairer wage to producers. However as history shows, without mobilization of awareness and support it may be difficult to convince corporations to seek certification from such labeling schemes. Moreover, certain product categories—for instance clothing and shoes—are not covered by labeling schemes, or if they are, they require a price premium and are more costly than non-labeled ones (see also Hamm, Gronefeld, and Halpin 2002). From a social movement perspective, some activist groups also feel that buycotts lack the mobilizing potential of more protest-oriented and lifestyle changing forms of political consumerism.

This explains why buycotts are often accompanied by discursive political consumerism, or the expression of opinions about corporate policy and practice in communicative efforts directed at business, the public at large, and various political institutions. Here an important example used frequently by consumer-oriented social movements to mobilize support and communicate their causes is culture jamming or adbusting. This entails changing the meaning of corporate advertising through artistic techniques that alter corporate logos visually and assign marketing slogans new meaning. This action tool also encourages individuals to use corporate platforms (automated customer service functions, chat sites, e-mail systems, logotypes) as arenas (locus) for political action. Other forms of movement-oriented discursive actions include street performances that target particular consumer goods and even holiday gift-giving messages. Notable examples of such culture jamming have been included in market campaigns against Nike, McDonalds, Coca-Cola, and the Walt Disney Company.

Lifestyle commitments are also advocated by some social movements that believe that citizens must take greater responsibility for the effects of consumption on the planet and, therefore, play a role in broader and deeper social change. Good examples of this form of political consumerism that implies committing one's lifestyle to political principles ("lifestyle politics") are veganism, freeganism, voluntary simplicity, and some forms of vegetarianism. These efforts can be said to form movements that not only promote new consumer lifestyles but also, implicitly if not explicitly, newer worldviews that challenge present-day political, social, economic, and cultural thinking and structures. They thereby affect diverse arenas of social life and, in so doing, create new solidarity networks (for more discussion on the significance of this kind of collective action (see Melucci 1996). They mobilize people to commit themselves to reject what they believe is reckless freedom of choice and overconsumption, thus challenging contemporary capitalism and advocating deep alter-consumerism and also anti-consumerism. Lifestyle politics, therefore, goes well beyond the other three forms of political consumerism, and requires the adamant practice of them all. Vegans are, for example, asked to reject all animal products (boycott), buy products (buycott) that are labeled "cruelty free," advocate alternative food choices and animal rights with others (discursive political consumerism), and even to implement a lifestyle at odds with dominant society to suit their convictions. For freegans the important act is to challenge eating conventions by using discarded but edible food; for the followers of voluntary simplicity (or voluntary poverty) it implies directly confronting prevalent notions about the need for more economic growth and consumer possessions by untangling oneself from the lures of shopping and advocating an "outwardly simply [but] inwardly rich" life (Elgin 1993: 2). This type of activity appears to be on the rise particularly in countries experiencing austerity because it implies less consumption and even ownership sharing (Olaison et al. 2013).

In sum, the diverse and multiple social movements that promote these questioning consumer activities all attempt to cultivate awareness and a sense of active responsibility in people about the significance of production and consumption for planetary politics in multiple and diverse fields. They seek to convince individuals to think solidaristically, collectively, and strategically when they shop and that they use their vast resources (money, time, lifestyles) to help shape consumer culture. The ultimate goal is influence over political development and social change.

Why do Social Movements Increasingly Use Consumer Practices in Cause Activism?

By the mid-1900s and early 2000s, using the market as an arena for politics became an increasingly important activity for social movements and civil society generally (Stolle and Micheletti 2013). Why? Aside from its attractiveness in mobilizing support and public awareness for movement causes, targeting consumer choice has on several occasions emerged as the most viable or even only option for working with solving complex problems. This is particularly true for movements whose engagements are transnational (cross-border) or involve a multitude of actors, or levels of action. Focussing on consumer choice has been judged as a good way of affecting positive change in today's more globalized and free-trade-oriented world. However even national politics has been targeted and at times re-oriented through the power of politically mobilized consumer choice.

Social movements put consumer-oriented strategies in their action repertoire for different reasons: their grievances or causes are ignored in the public discourse; governments do not or cannot address them, and corporations refuse to listen, respond, or cooperate with them. They protest this neglect by using the market as their arena for collective action to address for instance civil, children's, and human rights, and environmental issues, as illustrated in the cases that follow.

First, African–Americans have used the market successfully in their struggle for recognition, respect, and equality. Boycotts became a central part of their nonviolent action repertoire along with political fasts and civil disobedience, two other typical protest tools. Although they boycotted public transportation in the early 1900s, the Montgomery Bus Boycott in 1955 is most famous. It started when Rosa Parks, a woman schooled in Mahatma Gandhi's nonviolent protest tools, refused to accept that the money she paid for a bus ticket did not entitle her to sit anywhere on the city bus. Her subsequent arrest for violating segregation laws was viewed as a good test of the effectiveness of a boycott as a means of resistance. The civil rights movement viewed the city's bus system as a good boycott target because many African–Americans rode them but could walk the distance instead. African–American church leaders, supporting the boycott, opened their churches as mobilizing meeting spots. The year-long boycott both tested the commitment of the black community to fight for equality and gave them the courage to organize collectively for their democratic rights. As Martin Luther King stated, black Americans were more willing to walk in dignity than ride in humiliation. The boycott ended when the US Supreme Court declared local laws requiring segregation on buses unconstitutional. This example demonstrates how consumer-oriented actions draw attention to a public issue and also create feelings of empowerment for politics of recognition struggles. Many social movements in later years have referred to this successful way of mobilizing and protesting as a reason for using boycotts in their own causes (Frank, Dana et al. 2003).

A well-known international boycott of an iconic food brand is the decades-long, still ongoing and now multi-issued and multi-leveled Nestlé boycott. The boycott shows how movement campaigning can mobilize and sustain consumer choice over time, lead to certain changes in corporate practice, but it also reveals the limitations of boycotting in solving even relatively simple problems, such as regulations to prohibit certain infant formula marketing. Nevertheless, it is often evoked within social movement circles and scholarship. Since the 1930s experts had publicly and forcefully warned about the connection between infant formula and high infant mortality in developing countries. They even used shareholder activism in attempts to change corporate policy (Miller 2005). Anti-formula movement activists were, however, disappointed by corporate responses. Therefore, they chose Nestlé as their boycott target because it was the largest global infant formula manufacturing company and manufactured many popular products. Health, international solidarity, church, and other groups mobilized for the boycott that was kicked off in the United States in 1977 and then spread to other countries. This brought the issue to the US Congress and then to the United Nations; in 1981 the International Code of Marketing of Breastmilk Substitutes (or infant formula) was adopted. Boycott campaigners called off the boycott. However, because infant formula producers, including Nestlé, found loopholes in the Code, few countries incorporated it into their legislation, and no provision had been made for implementation monitoring (Sikkink 1986; Bar-Yam 1995;

Keck and Sikkink 1998), the boycott was reinstated. International governmental regulation proved to be too weak. Today activists target additional large global infant formula producers and use other consumer movement strategies (e.g., calling on parliaments to regulate how infant formula is marketed). The boycott leader Baby Milk Action still targets Nestlé and lists more political, ethical, and environmental reasons for this.[3] This example shows how a carefully framed boycott with considerable support can focus international public attention on an issue not directly concerning one's own country or well-being, thereby creating a sense of solidarity with less fortunate people globally and mobilizing diverse parts of civil society. It also indicates how cross-border issues cannot easily be solved through national legislation but require additional movement and international governmental action.

More recently, the gay rights movement has mobilized consumer choice for its struggle for recognition (Friedman 1999; Chasin 2000). Here gay activists have focussed on legislation allowing gay marriage, corporate benefits for gay couples, and general civil rights for gay people (Friedman 1996; Ayres and Brown 2005). The movement's strategy includes a varied action repertoire involving protests, legal challenges, petitions, labor union collaborations (Swank and Breanne 2013), many of which have been only moderately successful (Santora 2001). Mobilizing consumer power is an additional tool and implies a strategy that expands the field of identity political protest by boycotting anti-gay companies, events, and societal groups (see e.g. Mathews, 1995). This has contributed greatly and symbolically to raising general public awareness and changing policy (Goldberg 1993–94). Recently, attempts were even made to boycott cultural events featuring top Russian artists and, importantly, the Winter Olympics in Sochi, Russia, as well as Stolychnaya vodka, because of Russia's stance on gay rights. Even major sponsors, such as Coca-Cola, the Coors Brewing Company, and Disney, were targeted for not taking a forceful stance against Russia's anti-gay legislation and attitude. Boycotts have also been called on states in the United States that do not support gay rights (e.g., in Colorado) (Goodstein 1992; Lee 1992; Anonymous 1993; Goldberg 1993–94). Exactly what role market-oriented actions are playing in gaining recognition for gay rights is not clear. However, if comparisons are made to the South African boycott, it appears that consumer-oriented strategies, including the targeting of the tourist industry through the so-called "pink dollar," have expanded awareness and in scope over the last decades.

Other important struggles are also influenced by consumer strategies. The International Boycott, Divestment and Sanctions Campaign against Israel (BDS campaign) uses an action repertoire similar to the movement against anti-Apartheid in South Africa (McMahon 2014). Initiated by civil groups in Palestine in the mid-2000s, it calls for boycotts of settlement goods (i.e., Israeli goods produced in the occupied territories) and even academic, tourist, sports, and cultural boycotts, all of which directly or indirectly target relationships with businesses and government, and asks individuals and institutions to divest in businesses involved in transactions in the occupied territories (also known as negative social responsible investing, see Stolle and Micheletti 2013 for discussion of this form of activism). It also wants government sanctions.[4] Many academic, moral, and pop culture celebrities support the campaign, including Archbishop Desmond Tutu and Naomi Klein, author of *No Logo*, a strong mobilizing manifesto for the anti-sweatshop movement. The European Union has been working on legislation in this regard, including guidelines for a non-binding labeling system of settlement products. Some countries have already done so.[5] Noteworthy is the campaign's highly sensitive nature: Jewish merchants were targeted in anti-Semitic boycotts in what has been called the "cold pogrom" of the inter-war years (*Encyclopædia Judaica Jerusalem* 1971: 1279) and Arab boycotts of Israel since 1948 have created fear that the BDS movement will be identified with causes other than condemnation of Israel's policies in the occupied territories. This example illustrates how individual and institutional consumers (e.g., universities) globally can be drawn into complex international issues (in this case the status of Palestine in the international community), how movements use consumer actions as ways to communicate their cause, how consumers can feel that they have played a role through boycotting goods, and how consumer actions can become entangled with other and perhaps contradictory causes and forces.

Lastly, political consumer strategies are on the rise because they represent "feel-good activism" or what has been labeled as easy activism or clicktivism (Gladwell 2010). This implies a form of engagement that mobilizes people on an individual basis to feel that they have acted positively and contributed to solving a political problem. Some of the more emotional frames we are now going to discuss fit this category because they communicate guilt relief from purchasing certain goods over others.

In sum, there are multiple and at times complex reasons for why consumer strategies have become more important and integral for social movements. First and foremost, successful boycotts, as some discussed earlier, have established that this form of collective action is a useful strategy. Second, many societal problems such as cross-border issues or identity politics have either failed to be solved or cannot be solved by conventional social movement action or through the parliamentary sphere alone. Thus movements not only develop new strategies to raise public awareness and seek cause resolution, they also, as discussed in the following section, re-orient or transform themselves.

How do Social Movements Put Political Consumer Strategies into Practice?

Special political consumer-oriented groups and networks have emerged in several more traditional social movements focussing, for example, on international solidarity, labor rights, nature conservation, and animal protection. Older civil society associations, in particular labor unions in various countries (e.g., the United States), once again focus more on market campaigns in light of recent political developments. On certain issues, the new groups and old ones coordinate large national and transnational campaigns (e.g., for better conditions in outsourced manufacturing, global human rights, and against GMOs) to help form a multifaceted critical mass of market demand for alternatively produced consumer goods. Additionally, in the 1990s and early 2000s more national and global labeling schemes (e.g., for organic food, fairtrade, and forest certification), now important governance institutions, were established. These schemes also create a stable infrastructure for movement cause advocacy and activism. What additional mobilizing strategies do movements use to elicit consumer actions for their causes? We discuss two aspects: commercialization and the triangle of change.

Both aspects bring market strategies and actors more directly into social movement fields. As will be discussed, the first aspect implies at times that cause framing is now marketing for satisfying emotions, for example when movements evoke the emotional attachments involved in holiday spirit to market alternatively labeled goods. Here they employ pop culture, anti-branding, peer pressure, and personal desire (e.g., sex appeal and good health) to draw individuals into giving their gifts that also aim at relieving guilt about responsibility for complex political problems. This development, similar to commercial marketing is not approved by all involved movement network groups, which fear that mainstream marketing threatens the original cause, draining it of its true social movement character (for a discussion, see Stolle and Micheletti 2013: ch. 5).

Another development is that movements collaborate with several partners in order to push for alternative consumer choice. For example, governments come into the picture as large consumers of certain products (public procurers of paper, energy, food, clothing, furniture, etc.) and because of their general legitimacy as public representatives. Corporations are involved as targets of activism and increasingly as key partners for the building of problem-solving initiatives. This collaboration between movements, the state, and business has been called the "triangle of change" (if more institutionalized "multi-stakeholder initiatives") and reflect ongoing global societal transformation based on the enhanced role of individual choice, looser governmental regulation, and general globalization processes. Thus, contemporary social movements work in the globalized market as an arena for globalized politics together with corporations, governments, and consumers in apparently crafting a social contract for global society, perhaps even a "market-based" transnational societal corporatism. This situation differs greatly from how most movements worked in the 1900s. If this analysis is correct, it reflects a development following a similar role to yesteryear's societal corporatism: from aggressive movement campaigning to mobilize support and raise public awareness, to a period of internal discussion about movement visions and goals, and resulting in the ability to sit down and discuss common matters with corporations, governments, and other stakeholders. Key illustrations of this development are provided in the following section.

Examples of Social Movement Consumer Practices

Traditional consumer movements, such as those concerned with consumer protection and rights, have characteristically promoted mechanisms that provide transparent and simple information about consumer products so that consumers can make more informed choice. The assumption is that this will help consumers make safer choices, protect their health, safeguard against false advertisement and business fraud, and ultimately improve the position of consumers in the marketplace (Mayer 1989; Brobeck 1990, 1997). For instance, Consumer International, founded in 1960 with over 240 member organizations in 120 countries, advocates governmental regulation to enhance consumer protection and rights in various business sectors and branches. Other social movements use consumer strategies to protect producers and others affected by the production process. This section focuses on two prominent examples.

Organic Food Movement

Different goals, values, and opinions form what is often identified as the organic food movement. The movement includes groups supporting the principles of small-scale organic farming, community-supported agriculture, slow food, animal welfare, certain religious communities, lifestyle and health consumers, public procurement of organic food, as well as activist networks demanding that transnational agri-businesses take more responsibility for how they produce food. This movement can be traced back at least to the mid-1800s. However, the "new" organic movement emerged in the late 1960s and 1970s when the issues of pesticide use, farm animal treatment, and transnational agri-business were emerging on the political agenda. As with other new movements from the 1970s, it became more confrontational; this was triggered by the so-called food scares in the 1980s and 1990s. Organic food advocates also started emphasizing more the personal health angle to mobilize support along with other-oriented interests (climate change, the environment, world poverty, and farm animal treatment), thus using concerns of the traditional consumer movement (protection and rights of consumers against business) along with other-regarding frames. For example, they framed their message as the need for "pure" and "natural" food and played off popular culture when they called GE food "Frankenstein food" from "terminator seeds" as a way to profile the broader environmental issues involved in GMOs (cf. Conford 2001; West and Larue 2005).

Involved groups from different movement fields employed different means to advocate their cause and reach their goals. They targeted national governments, litigated, mobilized people globally to sign petitions and engage in protest demonstrations, boycotts, and letter-writing campaigns directed at both industry and government. The environmental movement was important here. Greenpeace used spectacular and theatrical political performances, blockaded ports of destination for the first delivery of Monsanto GMO seed for the European market and even, as typical of this green activist group, had activists chaining themselves to gates in Spain as part of the broad 1999 European campaign "Take the GM out of Animal Feed." Most of these activities are reminiscent of those used by social movements generally.

The strategy was to target the well-known food brands and to mobilize food consumers cross-nationally to boycott certain popular ones (e.g., Gerber, Kraft, Kellogg) and several globalized fast-food chains, among them McDonald's (Schurman and Munro 2009). The Monsanto Company was targeted particularly. It was sued and culture jammed into "Monsatan" and "Global Leader Cereal Killer." In 2006 the Organic Consumers Association, an online grass-roots mobilizing group campaigning for health, justice, and sustainability, started its now annual "Millions against Monsanto" campaign. Founded in 1998, it also campaigned against certain governmental agricultural and food policy efforts. Some companies, for example, Tesco, Sainsbury's, and Marks & Spencer, decided to follow this multiple network mobilized consumer pressure and ban certain GMO food products (e.g., poultry fed with GM feed) from their lines; others created their own private GM labels.[6] Over time European food activism became less confrontational due to governmental and corporate action. But US groups continued to target Monsanto, demand a government mandatory GM label, and campaign, in a way similar to earlier consumer movements, for the right of consumers to know and choose what is in their food. The GMO campaign also led to multiple mobilization efforts for organic food more globally but particularly in the Northern world. Activist groups even run responsibility-taking information and mobilization campaigns close to major gift-giving and food-eating holidays (e.g., Valentine's Day, Thanksgiving, Christmas, Mother's Day, etc.) in order to create additional market venues for the practice of consumer choice that draws on both solidarity emotions and personal guilt when claiming that "by purchasing organic and fairtrade chocolate and flowers…. your consumer dollars will no longer be going towards toxic pesticides, child slavery, and farm worker exploitation" (Organic Consumers Association 2011). In Europe, mainstream supermarkets stock a growing assortment of organically labeled goods, feature them in advertisements, and discuss their benefits on their websites. Some governments even have target goals for the percentage of organic food to be served in public institutions, for example, schools, thus illustrating how a triangle of change can develop with the help of public procurement policy and consumer sensitive retailers.

While mobilization has created consumer awareness about the politics of food and increased the demand for organically labeled goods, it has also affected the movement. IFOAM, the most established institution in the new organic food movement,[7] continually, for example, mediates between the ideological small-scale farming faction and the large-scale labeling mainstream "market" segments; this division can be compared to the "realos" and "fundis" factions found in other broad social movements. Certain activist mobilizing groups critical to how these two almost contradictory interests are balanced now advocate "beyond organic," that is, eating fresh and locally produced organic food and slow food over agri-business food certified with the organic label (Thompson and Coskuner-Balli 2007; Nijhius 2007). Thus, successes in mobilizing more consumer choice can also create problems within complex movements with different factions and conflicting values. Nevertheless, interest in purchasing organic food is growing among consumers. The sale of organically grown labeled products has risen, and consumers spend increasingly more money on them. In 1997, global sales of organic food totaled $11 billion USD; and they more than tripled to reach $39 billion by 2006 (Willer and Yussefi 2006). Today (2014) the figure stands at $63 billion USD and is rising steadily.[8]

Anti-Sweatshop Movement

Anti-sweatshop activism also has a long history, involves multiple movements, and is particularly attractive to young people (Sklar 1998; Boris 2003). In North America it developed more confrontational strategies to name and shame garment corporations. It has called boycotts, publicly criticized how popular brands manufacture their apparel and shoes, and sued corporations (e.g., Nike) for false advertising. A lack of trust between activists and corporations, explains this strategy. The movement's aggressive stance as well as corporate reactions to movement demands has made it more difficult to generate "triangle of change" mechanisms in North America; even the collaboration between anti-sweatshop activists and trade unions have played a role here. The European development is different: European-based corporations have been more favorable to labor unions; activist groups have considered European business as more trustworthy, cooperative, forward-looking, and willing to help generate "triangle of change" mechanisms. All this reflects the lack or the presence of a legacy of societal corporatism. Most likely the less confrontational atmosphere in Europe also helps to explain why the anti-sweatshop cause has received less public visibility in Europe than North America.

The global contemporary anti-sweatshop movement started to mobilize more systematically in the late 1980s. It used traditional social movement tactics, for example, picketing, protests, etc. but also anti-sweatshop fashion shows, a kind of street performance, to call attention to labor practices primarily in outsourced manufacturing. In Europe and particularly the United States there was confrontation with the police. New groups specifically focussing on the sweatshop issue emerged, and older labor and international humanitarian groups found new ways to campaign for their causes.

The term "year of the sweatshop" identifies the period August 1995 to August 1996 as one of heightened mobilization, public campaigning, and media coverage of the hidden politics of apparel (Ross 1997; Greenberg and Knight 2004; De Winter-Schmitt 2007: 201). Also characteristic of the "year of the sweatshop" is focussed media reporting, and some governmental efforts particularly in the United States, for instance, the executive branch's decision to initiate a problem-solving strategy involving consumer education, more labor enforcement, and the establishment of a voluntary task force (the Apparel

Industry Partnership) to improve the situation in outsourced garment manufacturing). The European Union gave economic support to the Clean Clothes Campaign's (CCC, founded in 1989 and with branches in fifteen European countries) efforts to improve its mobilization skills and for better collaboration with Southern partners. These efforts illustrate how triangles of change can emerge. Other parts of the world also mobilized against sweatshop practices.

As has been the case in the history of activism and protest (e.g., the anti-war movements), universities became an increasingly central venue for mobilization. US student involvement grew "sudden and sharp" (Elliot and Freeman 2000: 12) in the late 1990s to mid-2000s. Students targeted brand corporations (particularly Nike because it supplied many college teams with apparel and equipment) and university administrations for not sufficiently taking responsibility to protect workers in their procurement policies for sports and their own logo apparel (sweatshirts, etc.). Campus activism had effects. College administrators changed their procurement policies, student and public consciousness was raised, and important "triangle of change" institutions were created to help solve the sweatshop problem, in particular the university-based multi-stakeholder Workers Rights Consortium (WRC). The CCC noted these successes and decided to target public procurement in Europe. Anti-sweatshop activism shows how big consuming institutions (universities and governments particularly in Europe) can be drawn into complex consumer-oriented solidarity causes. Importantly for later developments on other sensitive societal issues, the movement began to target big international sporting events, playing off the promotional visibility and vulnerability of sportswear brands and even the spirit of sportsmanship itself. While these activities mobilize new groups (e.g., team supporter organizations and youth groups), they are reported as only having marginal effects on problem-solving (see Sluiter 2009; Merk 2008).

Unlike the organic food movement discussed earlier, anti-sweatshop activism has not produced a global labeling scheme and has generally not striven to do so. For various reasons, it considers its problem too complex, resource-intensive, and risky for this kind of problem-solving (for a discussion, see Stolle and Micheletti 2013). Instead it has preferred proactive, forerunning "no sweat" ethical businesses, mobilization of support into clean clothes or "sweatfree" communities, multi-stakeholder initiatives, and, due to problems in developing legislation on different levels of government, adoption of ethical procurement policies by public bodies. The movement became an innovative player in various "triangle of change" problem-solving efforts. One recent achievement is the Accord on Fire and Building Safety in Bangladesh, signed in 2013 by over 100 international brands, global and local unions, NGOs and the International Labour Organisation (ILO). This governmental, NGO, and corporate collaboration is considered an unprecedented coordinated approach.

Over time many anti-sweatshop groups decided to focus more on lesser-known brands and even other industries where they consider workers to be denied sufficient labor rights (e.g., fast-food services, the beverage industry and particularly Coca-Cola, farm labor, electronics, toys, mining of diamonds and other minerals). They also started to pressure large heterogeneous discount retailers (e.g., Wal-Mart, Aldi, Tesco, Carrefour), and movement groups advocate that a sustainable living wage is a human right for workers and continue to strive to develop "triangle of change" ways to solve the problem of underpaid labor.[9]

CONCLUSION

Many social movements today draw increasingly on consumer strategies to advocate and aid their causes. An important reason for the spread of consumer-oriented strategies outside the conventional consumer rights and protection movement is the ramification of globalization and privatization on the balance of power between government and business. These two mega-processes have weakened the regulatory force of nation-state governments and given corporations greater freedom domestically and abroad. Social movements are, therefore, re-orienting their action repertoires and strategies and finding new arenas, targets, and partners to further their causes. They differ significantly from past movements, which also could employ consumer strategies but focussed primarily on governmental regulation as their preferred goal for societal change. Contemporary social movements are even transforming themselves organizationally into transnational platforms for complex and varied forms of collective action, thus again illustrating the changing opportunity structure for movement collective action. Not surprisingly, then, the enhanced role of consumer choice, more individualized and public–private forms of looser collective action (particularly individual lifestyle change) and general responsibility-taking for the planet through, for instance, simple shopping choices have become central features in contemporary social movement activism. Unlike the past, contemporary movements are also innovating political problem-solving through triangle of change institutions and initiatives that tie together activists, consumers, corporations, and government as equal partners in the solving of problems both domestically and globally. They represent, therefore, a new kind of movement with a different understanding of the workings of politics and different view of who can be mobilized into collective action.

NOTES

1. See also here for an overview: www.wkkk.wikidot.com/organized-boycotts
2. For a movement stance on this, see www.cleanclothes.org/issues/faq/boycotts
3. See www.nestlecritics.org/ and www.babymilkaction.org/nestlefree
4. See more www.bdsmovement.net/bdsintro
5. See www.euobserver.com/economic/116272 and www.spiegel.de/international/europe/eu-to-crack-down-on-products-from-israeli-settlements-a-882623.html
6. Some large food suppliers now state that they are dropping this ban because of the complexities in the food supply chain. The organic food movement has criticized this and asks

why other chains have successes in continuing the ban. See further www.thegrocer.co.uk/
fmcg/fresh/sainsburys-ms-and-the-co-op-follow-tescos-lead-on-gmfeed/238400 and
www.soilassociation.org/news/newsstory/articleid/5191/china-moves-to-source-gm-
free-soya-supplies-why-will-tesco-not-do-the-same-in-britain

7. IFOAM is a member or accredited participant in eight UN bodies, see more information
at www.ifoam.org/
8. www.agprofessional.com/news/212753341.html
9. See more at www.cleanclothes.org/livingwage

REFERENCES

Anonymous (1993). "Colorado Gay Rights Ban Ruled Unconstitutional," *The Washington Post
(1974–Current file)*. December 15: 1.
Ayres, Ian and Brown, Jennifer Gerarda (2005). *Straightforward: How to Mobilize Heterosexual
Support for Gay Rights*. Princeton, NJ: Princeton University Press, 64.
Bar-Yam, Naomi Bromberg (1995). "The Nestlé Boycott: The Story of the WHO/UNICE Code
for Marketing Breastmilk Substitutes," *Mothering* (winter). 56–63.
Boris, Eileen (2003). "Consumers of the World Unite!," *Sweatshop USA: The American
Sweatshop in Historical and Global Perspective*. 203–224.
Brobeck, Stephen (1990). *The Modern Consumer Movement: References and Resources*. Boston,
MA: G.K. Hall.
Brobeck, Stephen (1997). *Encyclopedia of the Consumer Movement*. Santa Barbara,
CA: ABC-CLIO.
Chasin, Alexandra (2000). *Selling Out: The Gay and Lesbian Movement Goes to Market*.
New York: St. Martin's Press.
Conford, Philip (2001). *The Origins of the Organic Movement*. Edinburgh: Floris Books.
DeWinter-Schmitt, Rececca (2007). "Business as Usual? The Mobilization of the Anti-
Sweatshop Movement and the Social Construction of Corporate Identity," Ph.D disserta-
tion. American University (AU), School of International Service (SIS), Washington, DC.
Elgin, Duane (1993). *Voluntary Simplicity: Toward a Way of Life That Is Outwardly Simple,
Inwardly Rich*, Revised edn. New York: William Morrow and Company.
Elliot, Kimberly Ann and Richard B. Freeman. 2000. "White Hats or Don Quixotes? Human
Rights Vigilantes in the Global Economy," Paper for the National Bureau of Economic
Research Conference on Emerging Labor Market Institutions http://www.asiafloorwage.
org/documents/Resources-onwages/Backgroundreading/ONActivism/White%20Hats%20
or%20Don%20Quixotes.pdf
Encyclopædia Judaica Jerusalem. (1971). *Boycott, Anti-Jewish*, Band 4, 1278–1280.
Jerusalem: Keter Publishing House.
Frank, Dana et al. (2003). "Beyond the Boycott: The Future of Worker–Consumer Alliances,"
Politics and Society. 31(3): 359.
Friedman, Monroe (1996). "A Positive Approach to Organized Consumer Action: The
"Buycott" as an Alternative to the Boycott," *Journal of Consumer Policy*. 19(4): 439.
Friedman, Monroe (1999). *Consumer Boycotts: Effecting Change Through the Marketplace and
the Media*. New York: Routledge.
Gladwell, Malcolm (2010). "Small Change: Why the Revolution will not be Tweeted,"
New Yorker, October 4.

Greenberg, Josh and Knight, Graham (2004). "Framing Sweatshops: Nike, Global Production, and the American News," *Media Communication and Critical/Cultural Studies.* 1(2): 151–175.

Goldberg, Suzanne B. (1993–94). "Gay Right through the Looking Glass: Politics, Morality and the Trial of Colorado's Amendment," *Fordham Urban Law Journal.* 2, 21.

Goodstein, Laurie (1992). "New York Joins Boycott On Colorado Gay Law," *The Washington Post (1974–Current file).* December 9, 1.

Hamm, Ulrich, Gronefeld, Friederike, and Halpin, Darren (2002). *Analysis of the European Market for Organic Food.* Aberystwyth, Wales: University of Wales Aberystwyth School of Management and Business.

Keck, Margaret E. and Sikkink, Kathryn (1998). *Activists Beyond Borders: Advocacy Networks in International Politics.* Ithaca, NY: Cornell University Press.

Lee, Gary (1992). "More Groups Join Boycott Of Colorado," *The Washington Post (1974–Current file).* December 23, 1.

Mathews, Jay. 1995. "At Coors, a Brewing Dilemma Over Gay Rights." *The Washington Post (1974-Current file),* September 16.

Mayer, Robert N. (1989). *The Consumer Movement: Guardians of the Marketplace.* Boston: Twayne Publishers.

McMahon, Sean F. (2014). "The Boycott, Divestment, Sanctions Campaign: Contradictions and Challenges," *Race & Class.* 55: 65–81.

Melucci, Alberto. 1996. *Challenging Codes: Collective Action in the Information Age.* Cambridge: Cambridge University Press.

Merk, Jeroen (2008). *The Structural Crisis of Labour Flexibility: Strategies and Prospects for Transnational Labour Organising in the Garment and Sportswear Industries.* Amsterdam: International Secretariat Clean Clothes Campaign.

Micheletti, Michele (2010 [2003]). *Political Virtue and Shopping: Individuals, Consumerism, and Collective Action,* 2nd edn. New York: Palgrave.

Miller, Fred Dycus (2005). *Out of the Mouths of Babes: The Infant Formula Controversy.* Piscataway, NJ: Transaction Publishers.

Nijhius, Michelle (2007). "Beyond the Pale Green: Activists and Small-Scale Farmers are going 'Beyond Organic' to push Local Foods," *Grist.* November 12.

O'Rourke, Dara (2005). "Market Movements: Nongovernmental Organization Strategies to Influence Global Production and Consumption," *Journal of Industrial Ecology.* 9(1–2): 115–128.

Olaison, Lena, Birke, Otto, and Vollmer, Hans (2013). " 'Saving the City': Collective Low-budget Organizing and Urban Practice," *Ephemera: Theory & Politics in Organization.* http://www.ephemerajournal.org/sites/default/files/pdfs/papers/CfPSavingTheCity_.pdf

Organic Consumers Association (2011). "Unchain Your Heart." Available at www.organicconsumers.org/valentines/alert.htm.

Ross, Andrew (1997). *No Sweat: Fashion, Free Trade, and the Rights of Garment Workers.* London: Verso.

Safianow, Allen (2004). " 'You Can't Burn History': Getting Right with the Klan in Noblesville, Indiana," *indimagahist: Indiana Magazine of History.* 100(2): 109–154.

Santora, T. (2001). "What's Good for the Goose: A Critical Review of Unions as Employers and the Continuing Struggle Toward Equal Benefits in the Workplace," *Working USA.* 4(4): 98.

Schurman, Rachel and Munro, William (2009). "Targeting Capital: A Cultural Economy Approach to Understanding the Efficacy of two Anti-Genetic Engineering Movements," *American Journal of Sociology.* 115(1): 155–202.

Sikkink, Kathryn (1986). "Codes of Conduct for Transnational Corporations: The Case of the WHO/UNICEF Code," *International Organization.* 40: 815–840.

Sklar, Kathryn Kish (1998). *The Consumers' White Label Campaign of the National Consumers' League 1898–1919, Getting and Spending: European and American Consumer Societies in the 20th Century.* Cambridge: Cambridge University Press, 17–36.

Sluiter, Liesbeth (2009). *Clean Clothes: A Global Movement to end Sweatshops.* New York: Pluto Press.

Soper, Kate and Trentmann, Frank (2008). *Citizenship and Consumption.* New York: Palgrave MacMillan.

Stolle, Dietlind and Micheletti, Michele (2013). *Political Consumerism: Global Responsibility in Action.* Cambridge: Cambridge University Press.

Swank, Eric and Fahs, Breanne (2013). "An Intersectional Analysis of Gender and Race for Sexual Minorities Who Engage in Gay and Lesbian Rights Activism," *Sex Roles.* 68(11–12): 660–674.

Taylor, V. and Van Dyke, N. (2004). *Get up, Stand up: Tactical Repertoires of Social Movements.* Malden, MA: Blackwell Publishing, 262–293.

Thompson, C.J. and Coskuner-Bali, G. (2007). "Enchanting Ethical Consumerism: The Case of Community Supported Agriculture," *Journal of Consumer Culture.* 7(3): 275–303.

West, Gale E. and Larue, Bruno (2005). "Determinants of anti-GM Food Activism," *Journal of Public Affairs.* 5(3–4): 236–250.

Willer, Helga and Yussefi, Minou (2006). *The World of Organic Agriculture 2006: Statistics and Emerging Trends,* 8th Revised edn. Bonn: IFOAM.

Websites cited

www.agprofessional.com/news/Global-organic-sales-reach-63-billion-US-is-largest-market—212753341.html

www.babymilkaction.org/nestle-boycott-successes

www.consumersinternational.org/who-we-are/about-us/we-are-50/history-of-the-consumer-movement/

www.ec.europa.eu/consumers/strategy-programme/financial-programme/index_en.htm

www.oecd.org/internet/consumer/promotingconsumerinterest.htm

www.nytimes.com/2013/12/23/world/asia/bangladeshi-factory-owners-charged-in-fatal-fire.html

www.nytimes.com/2013/04/25/world/asia/bangladesh-buildingcollapse.html?pagewanted=all

CHAPTER 32

....

VOLUNTARY ACTIONS AND SOCIAL MOVEMENTS

....

HELMUT K. ANHEIER AND NIKOLAS SCHERER

INTRODUCTION

....

For a long time, the research agendas for civil society, volunteering, and social movements have developed in parallel, and remained largely unconnected. Typically, seminal
work on social movements rarely references seminal work on volunteering and civic
engagement, and vice versa (McAdam, McCarthy and Zald 1996; Anheier and Salomon
1999; Putnam 2000; della Porta and Diani 2006; Musick and Wilson 2008). This is at
first surprising given the overlap in subject matter; but it is also understandable since all
three fields have made great efforts to develop an interdisciplinary approach to highlight
different aspects of social reality. Only more recently has a growing body of academic
work emerged and begun to integrate these distinct literatures (Andrews and Edwards
2004; Hasenfeld and Gidron 2005; Eliasoph 2013). What explains this recent engagement with each other's perspective?

First, social movement theorists have increasingly approached key theoretical problems
within the literature such as the determinants behind participation or alliance-building
under the heading of "collective action," whereby "collective action" is defined in broader
terms than mere rational choice[1] (see, e.g., Baldassarri 2009). Approaching these problems as "collective action" phenomena invited scholars to look more at the interplay
between individual attitudes and social networks to capture the formation of common
identities and interests. By doing so, social movement theorists have also been motivated
to look beyond their field and to import key theoretical insights from other fields.

Second, non-profit, voluntary or non-governmental organizations have become more
important in many countries socially as well as economically (Anheier 2014: ch. 4);
and taken together as a sector, they have become the target of policy initiatives on local,
national, and international levels (Handy and Hustinx 2009: 552; Anheier 2014: ch. 18).
Activities such as volunteering—that is, the voluntary contributions of money, in-kind,
and of time—and political activism increasingly take place in such formal settings. These

organizations pursue political goals and uphold social or political values (Eliasoph 2013). The recognition of the increasing importance of these organizations adds to our understanding of why this dialogue has come about.

Third, it has been learned that social movements require the participation of both civic activists and volunteers to give voice to their demands and build up successful advocacy coalitions; and, as social movements develop, their activities become more formalized in organizational settings; they often transform into non-governmental or voluntary organizations. Non-governmental or voluntary organizations are thus often both vehicle and outcome of social movements.

Following the recent engagement of different bodies of academic work this chapter outlines the contribution approaches to volunteering and civic engagement could make to the study of social movements. First, we clarify the notions of volunteering and social movements, then present various approaches to explain why people become active. Finally, we look at the relationship between volunteering and social movements by drawing on different country experiences, but with a focus on the United States and Germany as illustrative cases.

Understanding Volunteering and Social Movements

Volunteering

Volunteering is a complex social phenomenon. Definitions vary according to the disciplinary perspectives taken as well as by geographical, cultural, and political context (Anheier and Salamon 1999). In their seminal *Volunteers: A Social Profile*, Musick and Wilson conclude that "words such as 'volunteering' are folk concepts as well as scientific concepts" (Musick and Wilson 2008: 25).

"Volunteering" is as a particular form of civic engagement that involves some meaningful degree of *voluntary participation in some form of collectivity for some purpose or cause*: Individuals or groups thereof come together, give their time or other resources (monetary and non-monetary resources, including in-kind contributions, social ties, knowledge, etc.), and engage in the operation, management, and support of an organization, associations, or any other form of organized collectivity. In the following discussion, voluntary work is defined as work without monetary pay or legal obligation provided for persons living outside the volunteer's own household (Badelt 1999). The definition refers to a four-fold distinction:

- First, it draws a demarcation line between paid and volunteer work. In fact, in some cases volunteers receive some kind of remuneration, which may be monetary. The borderline between paid work and voluntary work may therefore overlap. For example, an activist for a political advocacy groups may receive a stipend or honorarium.

- Second, the definition provides a distinction between household work and volunteering. Household and family work is a form of unpaid work that relates to issues distinctive from those concerning volunteers and should therefore be treated separately. However, there remain borderline cases such as services provided for relatives living close to the volunteer's own household.
- Third, according to the definition, other people have to benefit from the result of voluntary work. Hence it excludes sole consumptive activities such as certain forms of hobbies like wine-tasting or walking. Since activities may contain consumptive aspects as well as productive ones the decisive factor is usually the "third person." If another person could carry out the respective activity, it is considered productive. For instance practicing a musical instrument is not a voluntary service in terms of the definition, whereas playing in an orchestra can be regarded as such.
- Fourth, persons who are legally obliged to provide "voluntary" services—like civil servants as part of their job description—are not considered volunteers, even if they do not receive adequate compensation.

Not surprisingly, the notion of what is volunteering and what is a volunteer varies across countries and is closely related to aspects of culture and history. Before turning to more economic aspects, it is useful to take a brief look at some of the sociological factors that shape the meaning, form, and pattern of volunteering. Certainly, the British and American concept of volunteering, the French *voluntariat*, the Italian *volontariato*, the Swedish *frivillig verksamhet* or the German *Ehrenamt* have different histories, and carry different cultural and political connotations (see Anheier and Salamon 1999).

In Australia or the United Kingdom, volunteering is closely related to the concept of a voluntary sector, a part of society that is seen as separate from both the business sector and the statutory sector of government and public administration. This notion of voluntarism has its roots in Lockeian concepts of a self-organizing society outside the confines of the state. Civil society and voluntary action also resonate in the thinking of Scottish enlightenment philosophy, yet find their most eloquent expression in the work of Alexis de Tocqueville's "Democracy in America." For Tocqueville, voluntary action and voluntary association become cornerstones of a functioning democratic polity, in which a voluntary sector shields society from the tyranny of the majority. The link between voluntarism and democracy became deeply imprinted in American culture and the country's political self-understanding.

In other countries, however, the notion of volunteering is different in that it puts emphasis on communal service to the public good rather than social inclusion and democracy. The German term *Ehrenamt* (or honorary office) comes closest to this tradition. In the nineteenth century, the modernization of public administration and the development of an efficient, professional civil service within an autocratic state under the reformer Lorenz von Stein, allocated a specific role to voluntarism. Voluntary office in the sense of trusteeship of associations and foundations became the domain of the growing urban middle class (Pankoke 1994; Anheier and Seibel 2001).

A vast network of associations and foundations emerged in the middle and late nineteenth century, frequently involving paid staff, but run and managed by volunteers. But unlike in the United States, the German notion of voluntarism as a system of "honorary officers" took place in a still basically autocratic society where local and national democratic institutions remained underdeveloped. This trusteeship aspect of voluntarism began to be seen separately from other voluntary service activities such as caring for the poor, visiting the sick or assisting at school. These latter volunteer activities remained the domain of the Church and, increasingly, also became part of the emerging workers' movement during the industrialization period.

It is, however, important to emphasize that at least in their cultural and historical development, notions of volunteering are seen in relation to the public good, social participation, political mobilization, and service to the community—and hence with different implications for social movements.

In addition to different national traditions, voluntarism is also closely linked to the self-understanding of larger non-profit organizations like the Red Cross. Voluntary service is regarded next to the notions of humanity, impartiality, neutrality, independence, unity, and universality—the seven fundamental principles of the International Federation of the Red Cross and Red Crescent Movement (IFRC 1993 and 1999). It defines volunteers as "individuals who reach out beyond the confines of paid employment and normal responsibilities to contribute in different ways without expectation of profit or reward in the belief that their activities are beneficial to the community as well as satisfying to themselves" (IFRC 1993).

The UN offers a broader definition of volunteering as "contributions that individuals make as non-profit, non-wage, and non-career action for the well-being of their neighbours, and society at large" (UN 1999)—a definition that is rather broad and includes mutual self-help and many forms of collective action. The UN sees volunteering primarily in its service function: "voluntary service is called for more than ever before to tackle areas of priority concern in the social, economic, cultural, humanitarian and peacekeeping fields" (UN 1999: 2).

How do the social sciences approach volunteering? In economics, volunteer work is a somewhat problematic concept because no market price exists to establish its value relative to changes in supply and demand. The United Nations System of National Accounts (SNA) is a case in point. The system treats volunteer work as a non-market activity just like housework or leisure activities such as gardening. Chadeau and Roy (1986) suggest breaking down economic activities into five categories:

- activities that are remunerated, reported, and typically included in official statistics, for example, full-time and part-time work covered by a formal contract;
- remunerated activities that are either legal or illegal but remain unreported, for example, activities in the underground or shadow economy;
- activities that are unpaid and intended for parties outside households, for example, volunteering;

- unpaid activities within households, for example, household chores such as cooking and ironing; and
- other activities.

The third category mentioned by Chadeau and Roy (1986) is of special interest and includes all unpaid activities carried out for the benefit of an economic unit other than the household itself. These non-market activities are set apart from both mutual aid and forms of barter. Volunteering work is work in the sense that it is different from leisure; and it is voluntary and therefore distinct from paid work. The objective distinction between volunteer work and leisure is based on the third-party criterion, that is, the fact that some activities are non-marketable (Hawrylyshyn 1977), since "it is impossible for one person to obtain another person to perform instead" (UN 1993: 6–16). For example, a sports club can either hire a paid coach or opt for asking someone to volunteer. Yet if members choose to play some sport like tennis or soccer, they cannot pay a third party to play for them without losing the benefits of playing (pleasure, fitness). Thus, membership participation is leisure, coaching is work. Likewise, attending an environmentalist rally involves participation and is therefore leisure, while organizing the rally without pay is voluntary work.

From the subjective point of view, however, this distinction is not always clear (Archambault et al. 1998). One source of confusion is tied to personal motivations and dispositions, especially when volunteering is mixed with advocacy functions: can I pay somebody to visit the sick or the handicapped instead of me? Another is the mix of membership and volunteering. For example, some national Red Cross societies traditionally make little distinction between members and volunteers, as do many political parties, unions, and social movement organizations.

The distinction between voluntary and paid work is easier to make, and there is a clear difference in the status of volunteers as opposed to employees, even though the differences in atypical forms of work are increasingly becoming blurred. As a result, intermediate positions exist between totally unpaid work and work paid at labor market price. For example, volunteers, in particular when serving on boards, are frequently reimbursed for related expenses, and some receive in-kind compensation. Similarly, larger non-profit organizations in Germany provide benefits like health and accident insurance to volunteers, and some charities cover the pension payments for those working as volunteers overseas.

By contrast, some paid employees work for wages that are below market value. There are a variety of reasons for this. For one, employees may be sympathetic to the aim of the non-profit organization (e.g., humanitarian assistance, environmental protection, peace movement) and not demand wages at the prevailing market rate. What is more, they may see volunteering as an investment for gaining skills and experience, which is typically the case for apprentices in many European countries, or trainees generally. Or they may be required to take on lower wages because of labor market imperfections. Such is the case in countries with structural unemployment problems such as Spain or France, but also in virtually all developing countries where large portions of the population work in a "gray zone" of paid and unpaid labor. Certainly, these examples go beyond the narrower meaning of volunteering.

In sociology, there has been a tendency to understand volunteering as an enactment of civil culture *outside* the realm of politics. Volunteering has been primarily associated with voluntary engagements in *non-political* forms of voluntary associations such as charities, soup kitchens, neighborhood groups, fraternal organizations, choral groups, and other pleasure and leisure groups (Walker 2013). Such a perspective is, however, incomplete. On the one hand, it neglects that some voluntary associations seek social change and greater social justice (Rochester 2013: 16): Voluntary associations have "politicized" many issues that were once considered to be private and pressured governments alongside associated social movements. Taylor and Kendall (1996), for example, stressed the role of British voluntary associations by campaigning for social change (Taylor and Kendall 1996).

On the other hand, the focus on the service provision aspects of voluntary work overlooks the broader political implications and dimensions of *any* form of volunteering. Civil society scholars have interpreted voluntary associations as schools of democratic practice—as sites that allow citizens the acquisition of social and democratic skills they subsequently utilize in social as well as political contexts (Putnam 1993; Verba, Schlozman, and Brady 1995). Other scholars, in turn, have pointed to the political economic dimensions that underpin the very development and practice of voluntary associations with a philanthropic or charity mission (Anheier and Salamon 2006; Hall 2006; Anheier 2014). They stressed how non-profits developed out of prevailing socio-economic and political order by delivering and complementing services of the emerging welfare state.

Hence, following Eliasoph (2013), it could be argued that volunteering in any form of voluntary association, professional or not, is an inherently political act. Volunteering and associated non-political forms of voluntary organizations are also political if they do *not* advocate for social or political change since they contribute to maintain the prevailing social and political order with attended problems.

Social Movements

Tilly (2004) and Tarrow (1994) locate the historical origin of social movements in the late eighteenth century, following the great economic, technological, social, and political changes that accompanied these times (Rochester 2013: 28). "Social movements" can and usually have been understood as "a loosely organized, sustained effort to promote or resist change in society that relies at least in part on noninstitutionalized forms of collective action" (McAdam and Boudet 2012: 56). They are themselves not formally organized, but rather "networks of interaction" held together by shared goals, beliefs, and concerns (Diani 1992: 13).

In this sense, social movements constitute a *form of voluntary association* (see later); although they are much broader than the notion of a formal association, political or not (Walker 2013: 1): they involve multiple actors including individuals, coalitions, and other groups as well as movements, at local, national or even international levels. The environmental movements of the 1980s and Occupy and Indignados movements of the 2010s are cases in point (Anheier, Kaldor, and Glasius 2012).

"Advocacy" *outside* existing institutional channels of a political system is a feature distinguishing social movements from other interest groups. Social movements use a broad range of strategies and methods to challenge the status quo, and to persuade others about their concerns, including actions that deliberately break the law (Taylor and van Dyke 2004). Collective actions include occupations, sit-ins, strikes, riots, boycotts, flashmobs, and more recently online activism such as hacking and leaking. The repertoires also include moreover civic forms of advocacy such as protests, campaigning or litigation; in other words, activities that are typically associated with NGOs promoting political or social goals (Meyersen and Scully 1995; Alexander 2006).

While the activities of social movement have historically targeted the state authorities, they have also concentrated on "other forms of authority, including firms, industry and cultural systems" (de Bakker, den Hond, King, and Weber 2013: 576). It is important to underline that, while voluntary associations have, generally speaking, a rather *implicit* political dimension, social movements have an *explicit* political dimension: they have specific political concerns and, in case, draw on "contentious politics," that is, on other political means than those provided by the existing institutional structure to express these concerns and attain related goals.

Social movement theorists tend to pay only little attention to the activists and followers that make up social movements, and who are typically the volunteers described earlier. What is more, the boundaries between (non-)political forms of voluntary associations and social movements are, *in practice*, not clear-cut. Overall, both represent forms of civic engagement that encompass a political dimension; both are vehicles for their members' shared enthusiasm, beliefs, and concerns and provide them with opportunities to interact voluntarily, to develop common goals, values, norms, and ideologies; both contribute to the social and political order—in particular as a great deal of political advocacy by social movements happens in and through voluntary associations and NGOs. Moreover, volunteering—the voluntary contributions of money, in-kind, and of time by individuals, etc.—is the fundamental basis upon which social movements are able to put forward their political cause. We argue that this common ground also justifies treating social movements as a form of voluntary association. This suggests a look at theories of civic engagement and volunteering to see, as proposed at the outset, how they could contribute to our understanding of social movements.

What Social Movement Studies Can Learn from Theories of Civic Engagement and Volunteering

Who Volunteers and Why Do People Volunteer?

Although the systematic empirical study of volunteering is relatively new, the literature on civic engagement suggests several main factors facilitating or inhibiting civic engagement, in particular:

- Social capital
- Socio-economic factors
- Subjective dispositions

First, in terms of social capital, people's social networks and thus group membership helps to explain why people volunteer. Friends, family members, and colleagues, for example, report about their experiences of volunteering thereby mobilizing others to do so (Janoski 2010). Frequent interactions with peer groups enable the development of a sense of solidary, which, in turn, "makes it more likely we will respond to calls to volunteer on behalf of that group" (Musick and Wilson 2008: 218). Thus, social micro-mobilization processes serve as one explanation: the broader a person's social network and the greater the number of different groups a person belongs to, the higher the likelihood of volunteering. Putnam's social capital thesis argues that participation in voluntary activity provides individuals with social skills and by engendering trust in others on an interpersonal basis increases the likelihood of a future civic engagement (Putnam 1993). The thesis that previous civic engagement contributes to future engagement has been substantiated by researchers in the UK (Pattie, Seyd, and Whiteley 2003).

Second, various studies have found that socio-economic factors have a significant positive correlation with an individual's disposition to volunteer. Both middle class membership and higher formal levels of education make civic engagement more likely. The 2010 *Civic Life in America Report* provides an illustration of the effect of the level of education on volunteering (NCoC and CNCS 2011). A similar effect can be observed with regard to higher incomes.

However, the effects of such variables are mitigated by structural factors. A meta-analysis of fifteen studies by Costa and Khan (2003: 104) found that "in more diverse communities people participate less as measured by how they allocate their time, their money, their voting, and their willingness to take risks to help others." This finding underscores Almond and Verba's (1963) key insight: the "context of participation" explains volunteering. In a "participant culture," characterized by a close relationship between citizens and governments, volunteering is higher, they argue. Similarly,

Anheier (2014) suggests that specific non-profit regimes are related to higher volunteering rates. Volunteering is thus an institutional outcome of a regime type.

Third, subjective dispositions such as motives, values, norms, attitudes, and personality traits play a key role. Barker (1993) has provided a range of motives why people volunteer. He distinguishes between altruistic motives (such as a compassion for those in need), instrumental motives (such as to gain new experiences and new skills or personal satisfaction), and obligation motives (moral, religious duty). Of course, these motivations rarely occur in isolation.

In several studies, the degree of religiosity, for example, has been identified as being one of the most important factors in explaining variations in volunteering both within and across countries (see, e.g., Wuthnow and Hodgkinson 1990). Einolf (2011) found a positive and robust link between religiosity, pro-social orientation, and volunteering. Son and Wilson (2011) interpreted the link as a function of socialization. Churches, as well as schools, promote certain attitudes, among them the desire to help and do something good for future generations.

Penner (2004) argues that personality traits such as "other-orientated" empathy or "helpfulness" help to differentiate volunteers from non-volunteers. He stresses that these traits have to be seen in a broader social context. They interact with socio-demographic characteristics (e.g., social status, gender, age, ethnic background) and social pressure to volunteer. What turns these motivations and dispositions into the act of volunteering? Research found that among the most important factor is being asked to do so (Musick and Wilson 2008). A survey among more than 3,200 adults in the United States in 2002 found out that six out of ten of the "DotNet" generation (those born after 1976) responded to external impetus to engage in volunteering (Keeter, Andolina, and Jenkins 2002: 36).

Analogous to Max Weber's charismatic leader, the social entrepreneur is an individual who "with his entrepreneurial spirit and personality" will act as a change agent and leader "to tackle social problems by recognizing new opportunities and finding innovative solutions" (Brouard and Larivet 2010: 45). The social entrepreneur is "more concerned with creating social value than financial value" (Brouard and Larivet 2010: 45). It internalizes "positive externalities" in the economic system and seeks to empower disadvantaged actors by incorporating them into new, innovative solutions.

According to Mair and Martí (2006: 37) social entrepreneurship involves:

- a process of creating value by combining resources in a new way;
- resource combinations that are intended primarily to explore and exploit opportunities to create social value by stimulating social change or meeting social needs; and
- the offering of services and products, as well as the creation of new organizations.

Social entrepreneurs have complex motivations, yet they basically center around a mission to create social change (Swedberg 2009: 102). Referring to "social origins theory"

Mair (2010) argues that liberal regimes produce the most social entrepreneurs, largely due to greater institutional flexibility and hence more opportunities to become active.

Volunteering and Social Movements in the United States and Germany

This section illustrates the relationships between volunteering and social movements in the context of the non-profit sector or civil society generally by looking as two different cases: the United States and Germany. In each case, we will look at one specific social movement and the role voluntary organizations have played as vehicle (United States) and outcome (Germany) of social movements. By doing so, we want to suggest that discussing the historical involvement of non-governmental organizations, non-profit, and voluntary organizations provides a fuller picture of the variety of ways through which people come together and interact to fuel and secure social and political change.

United States—The Civil Rights Movement

Historically, US civil society is rooted in a reaction against eighteenth-century European absolutism and the rigidities of its social and political order, the so-called "old world." From the very beginning, voluntary associations and philanthropy became linked to the constitution of US society and its political order (McCarthy 2003; Hall 2006; Zunz 2011). McCarthy (2003), for example, traced the impact of philanthropy and volunteerism on America from 1700 to 1865. She examines how charities and reform associations forged partnerships with government, provided important safety nets for popular discontent, and sparked much-needed economic development. She demonstrates that during the nineteenth century philanthropy became a crucial factor in the abolitionist movement and in the struggle for social justice in the broadest sense, in particular against the exclusion of women and minorities from effective political voice.

Hall (2006) provides an historical account of the role of non-profit organizations in American religious, educational, social and political life. Hall stresses how non-profit organizations have facilitated the success of social movements (such as the 1960s civil rights movement) but also how they have worked to stabilize elite hegemony (such as the "conservative revolution" of the 1990s). He finds that a great deal of the characteristics, size, and scope of today's US non-profit sector—along with its very name—is the result of the 1950s institutional changes, namely the federal tax reform, which exempted non-profit organizations from taxation, and subsequent changes of the post-Second

World War welfare regime settlement. Non-profit organizations became increasingly favored as recipients of direct and indirect subsidies from the state and became, if not an extension of the government, an essential part in its governance. Following the re-invention of US government in terms of a shift from "big government" to governing through and with private actors, non-profit organizations took over increasingly active roles in advocating and formulating public policies.

The civil rights movement emerged in the mid-1950s and was sustained through the mid-1960s. It challenged the racial inequality between blacks and whites and "relied on diverse tactics including litigation, community organizing and direct action to pursue political empowerment, expanding economic opportunities, desegregating major institutions, altering social relations, and transforming the broader culture" (Andrews 2013: 1). One key event in the movement's struggle for equality was the 1954 litigation over school segregation, the *Brown v. Board of Education* case. In the *Brown* decision the federal court finally decided that school segregation in Kansas violated the US constitution which guaranteed all citizens equal protection of the laws.

The decision was the successful highpoint of a series of legal actions by the National Association for the Advancement of Colored People (NAACP), one of the nation's oldest and largest NGOs to promote the end of ethnic racism. NAACP was founded in 1909 and grew out of the Niagara Movement which fought for racial desegregation. While the immediate impact of the *Brown* decision led to "massive resistance by white Southerners to challenge civil rights initiatives" (Andrews 2013, quoting Klarman 1994), a variety of non-profit organizations including churches, foundations, and other advocacy groups such as the Student Non-violent Coordinating Committee (SNCC), the Congress of Racial Equality (CORE), and the Southern Christian Leadership Conference (SCLC) worked together and used their social infrastructure, ties, and networks "to mobilize demonstrators and voters to fight segregation" (Hall 2006: 53). In other words, they formed a broader alliance to promote social change and justice.

The SNCC, for example, founded in 1960 by black students at Shaw University, played a major role with its voluntary activities such as the coordination of sit-ins across the South, voter registrations drives in the Southern US states of Georgia, Alabama, and Mississippi, the organization of the March to Washington in 1963, the "freedom rides"—bus trips by racially mixed groups across the Southern US states—to test out the new laws. These voluntary actions and the violent local response in the Southern states brought not only national attention but also substantial sympathy to the civil rights movement's political causes.

As we know by now, the civil rights movement was ultimately successful in changing public opinion and policy. Moreover, following the *Brown* case the practice of litigation used by the NAACP was soon used by other advocacy groups and movements such as physically and mentally disabled persons, women, and gays and lesbians that sought an end to discrimination and gender inequality (Hall 2006: 53). This rights-orientated approach—and thus the use of existing institutional channels to advocate a political concern—helped these groups and movements to realize their political goals over time.

But again, it could be questioned if advocacy groups such as the NAACP would have been that successful if they were not joined and supported by volunteers.

GERMANY—THE ENVIRONMENTAL MOVEMENT

In contrast to other European countries, Germany became a nation-state only in 1871 after the Franco–Prussian War. Moreover, it did not see successful anti-feudal revolutions as, for example, France or the United States. Germany's history during the eighteenth and nineteenth centuries can be described one of "compromises between a 'self-modernizing' feudal order on the one and the emergent civil society on the other" (Anheier 2014: 43). Moreover, major conflicts that emerged in the context of the industrial revolution, and led to the rise of the labor and other mass movements, ended in compromises.

A vast network of private cooperatives, mutual associations, local institutions, and professional associations developed while the still autocratic state started building up a welfare system to pre-empt political challenges. To a large extent the German non-profit sector developed not in antithesis to the state but in interaction with it. The development sparked in the subsidiarity principle, the idea that the state is the *primary* financier of social welfare services while the voluntary or non-profit sector is the primary provider. The pattern of incorporating societal and corporate actors, in particular of trade unions and business associations, into public policy making has been reinforced and expanded throughout (West) Germany's social welfare history.

Germany provides therefore a textbook example of corporatist arrangement, particular in the field of health care and social services (Zimmer 1999). The corporatist model does, however, not mean that (West) Germany's political system has not been challenged from below, as the emergence of the environmental movement, which then led into the Green Party (Alliance 90/The Greens) illustrates.

The green environmental movement arose out of several loosely coordinated social movements at the local and national level of which the anti-nuclear movement and the peace movement were most central (Müller-Rommel 1985). The green movement began with loosely organized citizens' initiatives at the local level in the mid-1970s. The term "citizens' initiative" is important here as it points to the fact that citizens independently—that is, *voluntarily* and thus without being promoted by others—came together to develop political proposals. These grass-roots were supported and developed as many volunteers gave their time. By means of self-help and out of the established political settings they developed fresh, alternative proposals to public urban planning. As such, they were also largely reactive to the state and promoted a grass-roots democracy. They organized protests which were against urban renewal, new highways, and the construction of nuclear energy plants. The initiatives also used the established institutional means, that is, local and federal law, and liaison and consultations with local authorities to change policy decisions (Müller-Rommel 1985: 55). Their success led to the establishment of the Federal Association of Environment Citizens Initiative (BBU), an umbrella association "to promote the professionalization and politicization of the environmental movement all over Germany" (Müller-Rommel 1985: 55).

The BBU, although a conventional organization setting, used the unconventional and voluntary practices of the 1960s' student movements to mobilize public opinion: protests, sit-ins, illegal occupations, information campaigns, etc. The BBU quickly gained more than 300,000 members and united more than 1,000 local action groups. The BBU concentrated more and more on nuclear energy, since this was a policy field where local groups could achieve very little if they did not act together. Over time, the practices attracted more left-leaning supporters. As attempts to influence the ruling Social Democratic/Liberal coalition to create an advocacy coalition with the trade unions and other interest groups did not work, some of the factions that were turned away founded Die Gruenen in 1980. The party began as an "anti-party party," as a political institution that was against the system, and was founded on four pillars: sound ecology, social responsibility, grass-roots democracy, and pacifisim (Trump 2009).

These principles were attractive to conservative and alternative forces alike. The stationing of NATO missiles in Germany in 1983 drove many protestors of the peace movement (which had been growing constantly since 1979) to join the Greens and helped them to succeed in the 1983 federal elections, with the Greens gaining more than 5 per cent of the votes. Most importantly for our discussion is that the electoral success of the Greens can be ascribed in particular to the support of local grass-roots and the activists of the ecological anti-nuclear and peace movement (Müller-Rommel 1985: 56).

The result was another institutional compromise, where a social movement was successfully integrated into the country's political system as both party and an infrastructure of organizations and associations supporting it, and serving its wider constituencies—just as the labor movement developed an infrastructure of associations linked loosely to the social democrats, and just as the Catholic and Protestant welfare associations maintain some affinity to the Christian Democratic Party.

Conclusion

This chapter's assertion has been that the study of the emergence, mobilization, and success of social movements could be enriched from existing research on volunteering, civic engagement, and the non-profit sector. The fields do complement each other in a meaningful way as they cover overlapping terrain.

To that end, we first discussed some common associations underlying the theoretical concepts of volunteering and social movements, suggesting that social movements could also be understood as a form of voluntary association. We then turned our attention to two theoretical insights by voluntary research: who volunteers and what motivates people to volunteer. Finally, we sought to demonstrate the relevance of voluntary research with two illustrative case studies: The success of the civil rights movement in the United States and the emergence of the Green party in Germany. The first case outlined the empowering effect of civic engagement in NGOs and local grass-roots on the civil rights movement. The second case epitomized the opposite effect, the role of social movements on the constitution of NGOs. Against the background of these brief analyses we sought to point out that the historical and dynamic interplay in the civil society–market–state relation, has affected the way the volunteering–social movement relationship played out in various ways.

In concluding, we want to stress that a common research agenda lies in finding out how and why people voluntarily come together and organize themselves. Having outlined different factors: social, socio-economic, and personal ones, that facilitate or inhibit civic engagement, we believe that it would be a worthwhile endeavour to further intensify the dialogue between students of civil society, non-profit organizations, and social movements around theories of civic action and self-organization. Such a dialogue should allow for more comprehensive theoretical perspectives on the emergence, mobilization, and success of social movements, and how they impact social and political change.

Suggested Readings

Anheier, H. K. (2014). *Nonprofit Organisations—Theory, Management, Policy*. Abingdon, New York: Routledge.

Eliasoph, N. (2013). *The Politics of Volunteering*. Malden, MA: Polity Press.

Hall, P. D. (2006). "A historical overview of philanthropy, voluntary associations, and non-profit organizations in the United States, 1600–2000. In *The Non-profit Sector: A Research Handbook*, edited by W. Powell and R. Steinberg, 32–65. New Haven and London: Yale University Press.

Musick, M. A., and Wilson, J. (2008). *Volunteers: A Social Profile*. Bloomington, IN: Indiana University Press.

Rochester, C. (2013). *Rediscovering Voluntary Action*. Basingstoke: Palgrave Macmillan.

  1. We thank Mario Diani for this very useful comment.

References

Alexander, J. (2006). *The Civil Sphere*. New York: Oxford University Press.

Almond, G. A., and Verba, S. (1963). *The Civic Culture: Political Attitudes and Democracy in Five Nations*. New Jersey: Princeton University Press.

Andrews, K. T. (2013). "Civil Rights Movement (United States)." In *The Wiley-Blackwell Encyclopedia of Social and Political Movements*, edited by D. A. Snow, D. della Porta, B. Klandermans, and D. McAdam, 1–6.

Andrews, K. T. and Edwards, B. (2004). "Advocacy Organizations in the US Political Process," *Annual Review of Sociology*. 30: 479–508.

Anheier, H. K. (2014). *Nonprofit Organisations—Theory, Management, Policy*. Abingdon: New York: Routledge.

Anheier, H. K. and Salamon, L. M. (1999). "Volunteering in Cross-National Perspective: Initial Comparisons," *Law and Contemporary Problems*. 62(4): 43–66.

Anheier, H. K. and Salamon, L. M. (2006). The Nonprofit Sector in Comparative Perspective. In *The Non-profit Sector: A Research Handbook*, edited by W. Powell and R. Steinberg, 89–116. New Haven and London: Yale University Press.

Anheier. H. A. and Seibel, W. 2001. *The Non-profit Sector in Germany*. Manchester: Manchester University Press.

Anheier. H. K., Kaldor, M., and Glasius, M. (2012). "The Global Civil Society Yearbook: Lessons and Insights 2001–2011." In *Global Civil Society 2012. Ten Years of Critical Reflection*, edited by M. Kaldor, H. L. Moore and S. Selchow, 2–26. Houndmills: Palgrave Macmillan.

Archambault, E. et al. (1998). *The Monetary Value of Volunteer Time: A Comparative Analysis of France, Germany and the United States*, Paper presented at the Annual Conference of the Review of Income and Wealth, Lillehammer, Norway.

Badelt, C. (1999). "Ehrenamtliche Arbeit im Non-profit Sektor." In *Handbuch der Non-profit Organisationen. Strukturen und Management*, edited by C. Badelt, 433–462. Stuttgart: Schäffer-Poeschl.

Barker, D. G. (1993). "Values and Volunteering." In *Volunteering in Europe*, edited by J. D. Smith, 10–31. London: Voluntary Action Research.

Baldassarri, D. (2009). "Collective Action." In *Oxford Handbook of Analytic Sociology*, edited by P. Hedström and P. Bearman, 391–418. Oxford: Oxford University Press.

Brouard, F., and Larivet, S. (2010). "Essay of Clarifications and Definitions of the Related Concepts of Social Enterprise, Social Entrepreneur and Social Entrepreneurship." In *Handbook of Research on Social Entrepreneurship*, edited by A. Fayolle and H. Matlay, 29–56. Northampton, MA: Edward Elgar Publishing.

Chadeau, A and Roy, C. (1986). "Relating Households Final Consumption to Household Activities: Subsidiarity or Complementary Between Market and Non-Market Production," *The Review on Income and Wealth*. 32(4).

Costa, D. L., and Khan, M. E. (2003). "Civic Engagement and Community Heterogenity: An Economist's Perspective," *Perspectives on Politics*. 1(1): 103–111.

De Bakker, F. G. a., den Hond, F., King, B., and Weber, K. (2013). "Social Movements, Civil Society and Corporations: Taking Stock and Looking Ahead," *Organization Studies*. 34(5–6): 573–593.

della Porta, D. and Diani, Mario (2006). *Social Movements: An Introduction*. Malden, MA: Blackwell Publishing.

Diani, Mario (1992). "The Concept of Social Movement," *Sociological Review*. 40(1): 1–25.

Einolf, C. J. (2011). "The Link Between Religion and Helping Others: The Role of Values, Ideas, Language," *Sociology of Religion*. 72(40): 435–455.

Eliasoph, N. (2013). *The Politics of Volunteering*. Malden, MA: Polity Press.

Hall, P. D. (2006). "A Historical Overview of Philanthropy, Voluntary Associations, and Non-profit Organizations in the United States, 1600–2000." In *The Non-profit Sector: A Research Handbook*, edited by W. W. Powell and R. Steinberg, 32–65. New Haven and London: Yale University Press.

Handy, F., and Hustinx, L. (2009). "The Why and How of," *Nonprofit Management and Leadership*. 19(4): 549–558.

Hasenfeld Y. and Gidron, B. (2005). "Understanding Multi-Purpose Hybrid Organizations: The Contributions of Theories of Civil Society, Social Movements and Non-Profit Organizations," *Journal of Civil Society*. 1(2): 97–112.

Hawrylyshyn, O. (1977). "Towards a Definition of Non-Market Activities." *The Review on Income and Wealth*. Series 23(1).

International Federation of Red Cross and Red Crescent Societies (IFRC) (1993). *Code of Ethics*. Geneva: IFRC.

International Federation of Red Cross and Red Crescent Societies (IFRC) (1999). *Strategy 2010: Learning from the Nineties and Other Supporting Documents*. Geneva: IFRC.

Janoski, T. (2010). "The Dynamic Processes of Volunteering in Civil Society: A Group and Multi-Level Approach," *Journal of Civil Society*. 6(2): 99–118.

Keeter, Z. S., Andolina, M., and Jenkins, K. (2002). *The Civic and Political Health of the Nation: A Generational Portrait*. College Park, MD: University of Maryland Center for Information and Research on Civic Learning and Engagement.

Klarman, M. J. (1994). "How Brown Changed Race Relations: The Backlash Thesis," *Journal of American History*. 81: 81–118.

Mair, J. (2010). "Social Entrepreneurship: Taking Stock and Looking Ahead." In *Handbook of Research on Social Entrepreneurship*, edited by A. Fayolle and H. Matlay, 15–28. Northampton, MA: Edward Elgar Publishing.

Mair, J., and Martí, I. (2006). "Social Entrepreneurship Research: A Source of Explanation, Prediction and Delight," *Journal of World Business*. 41(1): 36–44.

McAdam, D., McCarthy, J. and Zald, M. N. (1996). *Comparative Perspectives on Social Movements: Political Opportunities, Mobilizing Structures, and Cultural Framings*. New York, NY: Cambridge University Press

McAdam, D. and Boudet, H. (2012). *Putting Social Movements in their Place: Explaining Opposition to Energy Projects in the United States, 2000–2005*, New York, NY: Cambridge University Press.

McCarthy, K. (2003). *American Creed: Philanthropy and the Rise of Civil Society, 1700–1865*. Chicago: Chicago University Press.

Meyersen, D. and Scully, M. (1995). "Tempered Radicalism and the Politics of Ambivalence and Change," *Organization Science*. 6(5): 585–600.

Müller-Rommel, F. (1985). "Social Movements and the Greens: New Internal Politics in Germany," *European Journal of Political Research*. 13(1): 53–67.

Musick, M. A. and Wilson, J. (2008). *Volunteers: A Social Profile*. Bloomington, IN: Indiana University Press.

NCoC and CNCS. (2011). *Civic Life in America: Key Findings on the Civic Health of the Nation.*: Washington, D.C: Diane Publishing.

Pankoke, E. (1994). "Zwischen Enthusiasmus und Dilletantismus. Gesellschaftlicher Wandel freien Engagements." In *Ehre*, edited by L. Vogt and A. Zwingerle, 151–171. Frankfurt: Suhrkamp.

Pattie, C., Seyd, P., and Whiteley, P. (2003). "Citizenship and Civic Engagement: Attitudes and Behaviour in Britain," *Political Studies*. 51(3): 443–468.

Penner, L. (2004). "Volunteerism and Social Problems," *Journal of Social Issues*. 645–666.

Putnam, R. (1993). *Making Democracy Work*. Princeton, NJ: Princeton University Press.

Putnam, R. (2000). *Bowling Alone: The Collapse and Revival of American Community*. New York, NY: Simon & Schuster Paperbacks.

Rochester, C. (2013). *Rediscovering Voluntary Action*. Basingstoke: Palgrave Macmillan.

Son, J., and Wilson, J. (2011). "Generativity and Volunteering," *Sociological Forum.* 26(3): 644–667.

Swedberg, R. (2009). "Schumpeter's Full Model of Entrepreneurship: Economic, Non-Economic and Institutions." In *An Introduction to Social Entrepreneurship: Voices, Preconditions, Contexts*, edited by R. Ziegler, 77–106. Cheltenham and Northhampton, MA: Edward Elgar.

Tarrow, S. (1994). *Power in Movement*. Cambridge: Cambridge University Press.

Taylor, M. and Kendall, J. (1996). "History of the Voluntary Sector." In *The Voluntary Sector in the UK*, edited by J. Kendall and M. Knapp, 28–60, Manchester: Manchester University Press.

Taylor, V., and van Dyke, N. (2004). "'Get Up, Stand Up': Tactical Repertoires of Social Movements." In *The Blackwell Companion to Social Movements*, edited by D. Snow, S. Soule, and H. Kriesi, 262–293. Oxford: Blackwell.

Tilly, C. (2004). *Social Movements 1768-2004*. Boulder, CO: Paradigm Publishers.

Trump, E. (2009). Germany, Green Movement, In *The International Encyclopedia of Revolution and Protest*, edited by I. Ness. Oxford: Blackwell, Blackwell Reference Online, http://www.revolutionprotestencyclopedia.com/subscriber/tocnode.html?id=g9781405184649_chunk_g9781405184649624 (last accessed 27 March 2015).

United Nations (UN) (1993). *System of National Accounts*. New York: United Nations.

Verba, S., Schlozman, K., and Brady, H. (1995). *Voice and Equality*. Cambridge, MA: Harvard University Press.

Walker, E. (2013). "Voluntary Associations and Social Movements." In *The Wiley-Blackwell Encyclopedia of Social and Political Movements*, edited by D. Snow, D. della Porta, B. Klandermans, and D. McAdam, 1385–1388. New York: Blackwell.

Wuthnow, R., and Hodgkinson, V. A. (1990). *Faith and Philanthropy in America: Exploring the Role of Religion in America's Voluntary Sector*. San Francisco, CA: Jossey-Bass.

Zimmer, A. (1999). "Corporatism Revisited—The Legacy of History and the German Nonprofit Sector," *International Journal of Voluntary and Nonprofit Organizations.* 10(1): 37–49.

Zunz, O. (2011). *Philanthropy in America—A History*. Princeton, NJ: Princeton University Press.

PART VI

CULTURES
OF CONTENTION

....

CHAPTER 33

CULTURAL CONFLICTS AND SOCIAL MOVEMENTS

....

ANNA E. TAN AND DAVID A. SNOW

In this chapter we examine the relationship between culture and social movements, but with a particular focus on two critical aspects of that relationship: culture as a seedbed for many of the conflicts generative of social movements, and the utilization of culture as an instrument of challenge and social change. In exploring these two central aspects of the relationship between culture and social movements, we go beyond the work of Johnston and Klandermans (1995), Earl (2004), and Williams (2004), among others, to establish further, indeed cement, the centrality of that linkage to a more thorough understanding of the emergence and operation of social movements.

To that end, we begin with the elaboration of complementary conceptualizations of culture and social movements—that is, conceptualizations that allow for a clear apprehension and articulation of the relationship between culture and social movements. With these conceptualizations in hand, we turn to an exploration of the relationship between cultural conflicts and social movements, arguing and illustrating how many, if not most, of the animating grievances associated with the emergence of social movements are rooted, at least in part, in cultural conflicts. Next, we examine how culture is used as an instrument of challenge by identifying and illuminating a number of mechanisms through which social movements make their challenges and claims.

COMMENSURATE CONCEPTUALIZATIONS OF CULTURE AND SOCIAL MOVEMENTS

....

As with most key social science concepts, there is no consensual definition of culture. While there is general agreement that culture manifests itself in the products of social action, in the practices and tools keyed to producing or using those products, and in the ideas, values, recipes/norms, and various forms of symbolization associated with both practices and products, such as identities, the actual conceptualization of culture remains ambiguous. This ambiguity is evident in the various metaphors used for conceptualizing culture, including "ideological system" (Geertz 1973), "tool kit" (Swidler 1986), "repertoire" and "habitus" (Bourdieu 1993), cultural "codes" (Melucci 1996; Alexander 2003), and, most recently "library" (Snow et al. 2014). Each of these analogical metaphors is useful analytically depending on one's focal interests. Given our interest in cultural conflict in relation to movement emergence and the utilization of culture as an instrument of challenge and change, we find more commensurate with these interests the metaphoric conceptions that accent the plasticity and fungibility of cultural items or resources—that is, the products, practices, and symbols constitutive of culture—as well as the creative potential of human agency. Accordingly, we opt for a conceptualization of culture that is skewed clearly in the direction of the "tool kit" and "library" metaphors, a conception which views culture as a system of rules and resources that, while constraining, may be creatively used in novel contexts and circumstances (Sewell 1992, 1996).

To accompany this understanding of culture and its relationship to movements, we conceptualize social movements commensurately not merely as challenges to the state or existing polities but more broadly and elastically as collective challenges to, or defense of, extant systems of authority, be they institutional, organizational, or cultural (Snow 2004a; Van Dyke, Soule, and Taylor 2004; Snow and Soule 2010). Additionally, we contend that social movements challenge authorities not only directly, but also indirectly, as with many communal and religious movements that seek to exit the system (Snow 2004a: 16–19; Tierney 2013). In conceptualizing social movements primarily as challenges to structures or systems of authority, including but not limited to the state or polity, we observe a much larger range and number of cases better understood as cultural challenges that are embedded in cultural conflict.

CULTURAL CONFLICTS AND SOCIAL MOVEMENTS

Our orienting proposition is that cultural conflict, though not limited to social movement challenges, remains at the core of many of the most impactful collective actions throughout modern history. To grasp the locus and range of cultural conflicts, we propose a heuristic typology that cross-classifies the core aspects of culture about which there is often conflict and the posture or stance of movements in relation to these core cultural elements. The core cultural elements, arrayed horizontally across the top in Table 33.1, include, as noted earlier, cultural products, cultural practices, and the regulative and sense-making, cognitively encoded stuff of culture—the norms and recipes, values, and ideologies. Arrayed vertically on the left are three movement stances or positions in relation to the core cultural elements. They include embracement, modification or reform, and rejection, which we will elaborate and illustrate shortly. We propose that it is at the intersections of the three movement stances and the core cultural elements that the locus of movement-related cultural challenges and conflicts can be readily identified.

Since cultural products, practices, and the ideational complex of values, beliefs, and rules are all intertwined, it follows that they are all implicated in some fashion in all movements rooted in cultural conflict The cells of the typology are thus permeable. However, the degree of implication of the cultural elements is variable. Thus, we contend that for most movements there is a primary, defining intersectional nexus. Thus, for the movement against smoking in public places, the focus has been on banning the practice of smoking in such places rather than prohibiting the production of cigarettes per se. Similarly, in the case of the movement against drunk driving, the focus has been on monitoring and reducing the conjoint practices of drinking and driving, not on the prohibition of alcohol in general, even though some members or wings of the movement might favor that as well. Just as the key cultural elements are not mutually exclusive but often overlap in different configurations, such is also the case with the movement stances or postures. Embracement of certain values and beliefs, for example, is often predicated on the rejection of another set of values and beliefs, but it is typically either the embracement or the rejection that is accented and can thus be considered the primary or defining stance.

The utility of such a flexible categorization is two-fold: first, in its permeability, the table allows for the categorization of a range of cases in terms of their objectives and cultural framework; and secondly, it readily allows for the inclusion of movements within non-Western and non-democratic contexts as easily as the array of well-known cases in the United States and modern Western world. In considering our following discussion of the three orientations of cultural challenges by social movements (embracement, reform, and rejection), we reiterate the importance of this permeability in categorizing movements according to our typology. These and other core intersectional nexuses are illustrated in Table 33.1, which cross-classifies the core aspects of culture about which there is often conflict and the stance of movements in relation to these core cultural elements.

Using this table as a point of departure, we turn to an illustrative elaboration of the way in which culture functions as a seedbed for movement grievances and claims by focussing on movement embracement, modification, and rejection of key cultural elements.

Forms of Cultural Conflict

In considering this classification of the various movement orientations, Wallis's (1984) functionally analogous typology, with his distinction between *world-rejecting* and *world-affirming* movements, merits discussion (see also Wilson's [1973] more elaborated

Table 33.1 Dimensions and Nexuses of Culture Conflict

Movement Stance or Position	Key Cultural Elements		
	Products	Practices	Values/Beliefs/Identities
Embrace	Drug legalization (Marijuana legalization - NORMAL US); Guns (National Rifle Association, US)	Most rights movements; Pro-choice; Christian Evangelical movements (Promise Keepers, US; South Korean Fatherhood Movement)	Many religious movements & cults (Melenesian cargo cults; Falun Gong, China); Identity movements (Fat acceptance movement) Peace movements (Plowshares movement, US and Europe)
Modify/Reform	Gun control advocacy; Obesity awareness movement (Public health campaigns)	Modern and Early Reforms in Catholic Church; Anti-smoking; Environmental sustainability movements	Consciousness raising movements (Black is Beautiful; Women's liberation); some identity movements
Reject	Anti-technology movements (Luddites UK); Alcohol Prohibition (US Temperance Movement)	Abolitionist movements (England and US); Radical left anarchists (Autonomen, Germany and Netherlands); Anti-sweat shop (US and Latin America); Anti-abortion; Anti-nuclear	Anti-imperialist movements (May 4th Movement & Boxer Rebellion, China); Millenarian religious movements (Peoples' Temple, Guyana/US)

typology of "responses to the world"). The world-rejecting movement condemns the dominant social order, including both its values and institutional arrangements. The world-affirming movement is used here as an analogous form to cultural embracement, referring to a movement that not only accepts but rather champions some or all of the extant social order. Finally, Wallis advances the concept of a middle-ground orientation in the form of the world-accommodating movement. Such movements are often functionally analogous to our concept of modification or reform-oriented movements, though we dispute Wallis' contention that such movements have little to no consequence on the lives of their adherents. In considering the spectrum of movements featured in our discussion, one would be hard pressed to identify any movements that were or are inconsequential to the lives of adherents.

Embracement

Although movements are often understood in terms of their objections to structural relationships and associated cultural elements, there is, in fact, a wealth of movements centered on the embracement of cultural products and/or practices, as well their underlying beliefs and values. Embracement, in the way we are conceptualizing it, goes beyond the approval or acceptance of a past or current cultural element to celebrating, valorizing, and championing that product, practice or meaning and its underlying values. The concept of "embracement" lays at the most culturally conciliatory pole of the cultural engagement continuum, ranging from affirmation and thus embracement at one end to rejection at the other, with varying degrees of reform in between. Movements embracing elements of culture can be found on both the right and the left of the political spectrum, and employ a range of tactics, from the unobtrusive embracement of non-binary gender identities through drag queen performance (Rupp and Taylor 2003) to the often vitriolic defense of the idealized, traditional Christian family, as seen in the US religious right.

In the United States, few cultural doctrines have aroused more zealous and vocal embracement than that of "traditional Christian family values." One such movement anchored in these values and which gained prominence in the United States is the Promise Keepers movement. Beginning as a modest-sized grass-roots men's ministry, the Promise Keepers soon grew into a fully fledged men's evangelical movement, holding massive rallies in football stadiums at the height of their popularity in the 1990s (Hardisty 2000; Bartkowski 2004). The movement's popularity peaked with the "Stand in the Gap: A Sacred Assembly of Men" demonstration, as roughly 800,000 supporters congregated at the National Mall in Washington, DC. Despite the movement's apparent subsequent decline, its values base has been adopted and embraced by similar movements outside of the United States, such as the South Korean transnational fatherhood movement with an estimated 200,000 male graduates of its "Father Schools" in some 230 cities in forty-five countries (Kim 2013). Other movements associated with the embracement of traditional patriarchal familial structure and the values of the Christian Right continue to proliferate in the United States, as evidenced by the strength of organizations such as the Family Research Council (FRC). Operating on its mandate of "Advancing Faith, Family and Freedom," the FRC's opposition to same-sex equality and reproductive rights has resulted in its labeling as a "hate group" by the Southern Poverty Law Center (Schlatter 2010). This controversial designation highlights the organization's strategy, including challenging marriage equality measures and engaging in anti-gay lobbying. However, the movement's leadership and supporters object to this negative labeling or counter-framing, identifying themselves as advocates of traditional Christian values rather than opponents of social equality. Thus, it is this fervent embracement that lies at the heart of the movement's relationship to culture. Such organizations often present themselves as the last line of the defense against the erosion of traditional values and thus assume the role of cultural guardians in their activism.

In line with these examples of cultural embracement, many of the movements discussed herein will occupy one or more of these domains in their advocacy, but remain focussed on the embracement of one or more cultural elements. For example, the Fat Acceptance movement targets both the individual and institutions. While highly visible anti-obesity frames and public health outreach have gained prominence in recent decades, the discourse around obesity remains crowded with competing obesity-acceptance frames and its organizational carriers, such as the National Association to Advance Fat Acceptance (Snow and Lessor 2010; Saguy 2013). The obesity-acceptance frames of the fat acceptance movement advance not only the embracement of positive meanings surrounding obesity, but also the individual level practices surrounding the so-called "fat-body" (Kwan 2009). With the embracement of fatness and "fat" as an acceptable identity, the movement not only affirms but champions fatness much in the same way as the earlier "black is beautiful" component of the civil rights movement embraced Afrocentric beauty. Although these movements may propose some modifications of their affirmed identities or cultural elements, they are mobilized around their advocacy rather than critique of selected products, practices, and meanings.

Reform

Reform entails calls for modification, but not wholesale rejection, of some cultural product and/or practices associated with it. Thus, reform-oriented movements in relation to culture can be characterized by their more moderate objectives; though the moderate, reform-centered nature of their goals hardly dictates the tactics they may use in the process of securing these sought changes. This diversity is reflected in the cases noted in this chapter, ranging from the diverse and largely institutionalized advocates of gun control to the highly theatrical and often controversial tactics of the People for the Ethical Treatment of Animals (PETA). Similarly, the movement for smoking cessation can be characterized by its efforts to fundamentally alter the cultural practices associated with smoking through large-scale media campaigns and lobbying, while not seeking bans on tobacco products entirely. The common thread of these disparate movements is their effort to modify rather than do away with specific cultural elements. Their proposed reforms range from the minor and incremental, to the drastic, thus spanning the continuum between the embracement and rejection orientations and their associated movements.

Although opposition to certain cultural elements characterizes these movements, they generally advocate not for their abolition but rather the deployment of alternatives to the cultural connotations attached to their use. While some more extreme opponents of gun ownership advocate for a full ban on firearms, the gun control movement is predominately concerned with the framing of acceptable forms of gun ownership, while problematizing those forms of firearms associated with gun violence (Spitzer 1995). Similarly, although the animal rights movement is comprised of both reformists and abolitionists of animal products, high-profile organizations such as PETA have adopted reform-oriented strategies advocating reduced meat consumption, selective endorsement of fast food restaurants, and amicable animal-product industry relationships. In spite of these conciliatory goals, the organization itself has established a reputation for theatrical protest tactics, and controversial and often disturbing information campaigns (Jasper and Nelkin 1992). These examples serve to illustrate the critical point that a reformist orientation towards cultural elements does not dictate a conciliatory strategy.

To illustrate further, we may look to another prominent form of reformist move-ment: those oriented towards consciousness-raising. Such movements gained vis-ibility with the 1960s and 1970s incarnations of the women's liberation movement (Shreve 1989; Hanisch 2000; Snow and Lessor 2013), as well as the rise of the Black Consciousness anti-apartheid movement of South Africa in the 1960s (Hirschmann 1990). In the case of the women's liberation movement, the Miss America picket of 1968 marked a critical point in the movement's mythology. The enduring associa-tion of second wave feminism with the media-fabricated bra burnings that allegedly took place at this protest continues to perpetuate the notion that feminism is an out-right rejection of femininity (Dow 2003). Protest organizer and prominent feminist author of *The Personal is Political* reflected on the protest's intention not as a rejec-tion of womanhood but an effort to challenge normative notions of femininity, as constructed by pageants such as the Miss America competition (Hanisch 2000). Women's liberation, as partly a consciousness-raising movement, does not seek to fundamentally dismantle a cultural institution, but rather problematize, critique, and reshape it.

Rejection

We now turn to those movements overtly centered on the abolition, rejection or destruc-tion of certain cultural elements. Rejection, in this context, entails not only the disap-proval of a cultural product, practice, and/or associated underlying values and beliefs but, even more strongly, the condemnation and desired elimination of the product or practice in question. Such movements are characterized by antagonistic and often dichotomous framing of the present culture with their proposed alternatives, with the unambiguous rejection of the targeted cultural elements. Arguably less common than their embracement or reform-centered peers, movements based on the rejection of cul-tural elements task themselves with the challenge of unseating specific cultural products, practices, and meanings from the cultural canon.

The anti-industrial Luddite movement of the nineteenth century provides such an iconic example of cultural rejection that the term "Luddite" has entered the cultural lexi-con as a general label for any individual who vehemently rejects technology. Luddism emerged at the turn of the nineteenth century as a working-class movement comprised of increasingly discontent textile laborers, in the wake of new labor saving technological developments during the English industrial revolution (Hobsbawm 1952). To charac-terize the movement thinly as merely anti-technological, as the contemporary usage of "Luddite" would suggest, obscures the importance of industrial technology as not only the grievance itself but as a cultural symbol. Hobsbawm emphasizes this nuance, recall-ing that Luddites destroyed both old and new industrial machinery as a form of coercive and often symbolic collective bargaining. The cultural meanings and symbolic value of targets are often of immense significance when considering movement activities seem-ingly focussed upon the destruction of material targets, whether it be the sabotage of farming or fur operations by animal and earth liberationists or nineteenth-century machine-breaking.

More recently, Theodore Kaczynski gained notoriety as the Unabomber, penning an incendiary manifesto to accompany his widespread campaign of bombings from the late 1970s to 1995. Just as Kaczynski framed his efforts not only as the rejection of cultural products, but also the normative meanings and definitions of progress attached with them, numerous historical and contemporaneous movements have advocated for the rejection of entire value systems. Despite widespread condemnation of his actions, Kaczynski's manifesto and beliefs did find favorable audience among existing critics of technology, ranging from those in the speculative science fiction community (Kurzweil 2000) to primitivist factions of the anarchist and environmentalist movements (Taylor 1998). These movements have experienced varying levels of success throughout history, but rarely attain the widespread and sustained cultural change they seek. More often, these movements serve as linchpins of opposition that heightens visibility of criticisms of their targeted cultural elements, and thus pave the way for more moderate reform-oriented movements to effect change.

It can be observed that world-rejecting movements are often religious in character, from the ascetic pronouncement of "Death to the World" by the canonized hermit Isaac of Nineveh (Alfeyev 2000) to the counter culture-inspired Children of God new religious movement emerging in the 1960s and such contemporaneous, kindred movements as Jim Jones' Peoples Temple and the Heaven's Gate cult, both of which culminated in mass suicide, the former in Jonestown, Guyana, and the later in San Diego. For such movements, the rejection of the contemporary social order is often accompanied with apocalyptic religious prophecy (Hall 1987, 2000; Kaplan 1997; Tierney 2013). Conversely, non-religious world-rejecting movements have dogmatic characteristics in their belief systems, as observed in counter-cultural utopian communities (Kanter 1972; Gardner 1978; Berger 1981). These two distinct variants of world-rejecting movements share a prefigurative character, coinciding with their rejection of the present cultural milieu; these movements view their various intentional communities and communal spaces as ideological praxis.

Non-religious world-rejecting movements have emerged intermittently throughout history. Anti-Western and isolationist sentiments in China have historically fomented into periodically violent movements, as observed in the Boxer Rebellion of 1898–1900 (Wallace 1956) and the May 4th Movement of 1919 associated with the New Culture Movement (Cadot-Wood 2013). These movements framed themselves antagonistically in relation to all aspects of culture, such that all cultural products, practices, aesthetics, and values associated with the so-called Imperial influences were vilified. These movements were organized around symbolic linkages and diagnostic frames that identified a diverse range of both concrete and largely symbolic foreign activities as emblematic of China's eroding national sovereignty. Although these movements advanced their own claims and cultural alternatives, it is their mobilization *against* elements of their respective political and cultural milieus that defines them.

CONTEXTS OF CULTURAL CONFLICT

When we consider the varieties of cultural challenges advanced by social movements, whether it is via embracement, reform, rejection, or a configuration thereof, it is evident that any discussion of cultural contention would be incomplete without considering the relational or interactional context of the conflict. The contexts of cultural conflicts can be divided into at least three main clusters: conflicts with institutional and cultural authorities or gatekeepers, conflicts within movements, and conflicts between movements. The distinct dynamics of each of these settings for cultural conflict provide yet another set of intersecting conditions consequential to social movements. In further distinguishing movements by the settings in which their cultural challenges occur, we extend understanding of the contextual conditions that both facilitate and constrain the types of cultural contention in which social movements engage.

Conflicts with Institutional and Cultural Authorities

Cases of contention over culture between movement challengers and institutional authorities have probably constituted the most extensively studied cases of cultural conflict. These conflicts take place at the most micro-level in the form of disputes over specific practices or symbols in a single setting, as in the case of protests against school uniform policies in individual institutions (Malone 2002) and recent attempts to ban the *niqab* (veil) in both France and Quebec (Scott 2009), or across a whole socio-cultural context, as with Mao Zedong's attempts to overthrow the entire cultural framework of institutional authority in the case of the Cultural Revolution in the Peoples' Republic of China and its ensuing purge of political figures associated with the previous "revisionist" regime (Walder and Su 2003; Wu 2013). Although the role of institutions of power as authorizing agents of culture remains insufficiently examined in extant social movements literature, Bourdieu (1984) provides a parsimonious theory of power rooted in cultural and symbolic processes. Social movements, no doubt, are critical agents in these social change processes, whether these engagements are sweeping rejections of the dominant cultural order or isolated challenges within institutions.

Despite the relatively recent so-called cultural turn in the study of collective action, some of the earliest examples of cultural challenges mounted by social movements can be found in the insurgencies of early Jewish zealots and Christians in response to Roman cultural imperialism (see Montefiore 2011). History is populated with rejectionist responses to cultural imperialism, rather actual or constructed and thus perceived, as evidenced in recent modern times by the rise of "militant" Islam as manifested and the Taliban and al-Qaeda movements, among others (Jansen 1979; Snow and Marshall 1984; Rashid 2000, 2002; Wiktorowicz 2004).

Although, religious movements—new and old—may focus attention on particular facets of culture, they oftentimes engage with a vigorous rejection of multiple dimensions of culture. Such challenges tend to draw the ire of established institutions. For example, the internationally condemned repression of the Falun Gong spiritual movement in the People's Republic of China is perhaps more widely known in the West than the teachings of the movement itself. The withdrawal of the movement and practitioners of Falun Gong from state supervision signaled a shift in the relationship between the spiritual movement and Chinese authority, reorienting the perception of the practice of Falun Gong from benign to outright subversive (Chang 2004; Sun 2013). Though contemporary social movements may see far fewer constituents go to their own martyrdom, cultural grievances and claims against institutions and figures of authority continue to lay the foundation for violent repression.

Agents of violence in the cultural conflicts of movements are not confined to state actors. In the case of the Chinese Cultural Revolution, much of the most egregious acts of mass killing perpetrated ostensibly on behalf of the Revolution were not committed by the Red Guard, but rather by private citizens empowered by the wave of anti-bourgeois sentiment and heightened conflict within their communities (Su 2011). Thus, the boundaries between conceptualizations of cultural conflicts with authorities, and cultural conflicts between movements, are necessarily permeable.

Conflicts between Movements

Similarly, we may look to conflicts between movements as both generative and reflective of cultural conflicts. These conflicts may be both emergent challenges arising in the contemporary cultural sphere or longstanding conflicts revived. The movements referenced here are not easily relegated to the status of petty squabbles or insubstantial grievances. The reality is far from it; those challenges deployed from one movement to another have their bases in deeply rooted beliefs, often compounded by resultant disparities in social status and capital, and cultural or institutional legitimacy. For example, though the schism between the Shia and Sunni denominations of Islam dates back to the death of the prophet Muhammad, the longstanding rifts surrounding matters of doctrine and tradition (*hadith*) have since become entangled in more recent elaborations on the part of religious leaders, thus generating conflict that is as much cultural as it is territorial and geopolitical (Nasr 2006). The Shia minority itself has experienced a cultural revitalization of sorts, transforming from a scattered, outnumbered denomination to deeply embattled social movement.

More recently, the conflict between the radical environmental movement, represented in part by organizations such as the Earth Liberation Front and Animal Liberation Front, and the organized labor movement has demonstrated the fragility of solidarity on the far-left. Despite alignments on a range of social issues, the starkest of boundaries between these militant environmentalists and even the most progressive of labor activists is rooted in culture as much as class (Obach 2002). Characterized as privileged hippies and callous anthropocentrists respectively by the opposing sides, it is divergent cultural conceptions of the appropriate relationships for humans and their environment that have been most consistently generative of conflict between these movements.

Conflict between movements need not be a hindrance to the progress of both, however. Fetner (2008) finds that the religious right, comprised of a number of movements in its own right, shaped gay and lesbian activism. More concretely, Fetner argues that the emergence of a vocal anti-gay movement on the Christian right led to the crystallization of the frames and discourses in the Lesbian Gay Bisexual and Transgender (LGBT) movement. These shifts occurred in response to the specific claims and mobilizing issues addressed by the anti-gay countermovement. These findings highlight the importance of inter-movement dynamics in understanding resultant social and cultural changes. However, although the specific iteration of anti-gay mobilization in Fetner's study emerged largely in response to LGBT mobilization in the 1970s, care must be taken not to broadly classify all conservative and right-wing movements as countermovements.

Ultimately, to characterize the dynamics between movements to be comprised entirely of movements and subsequent countermovements is both reductive and imprecise. In those movements emerging from the aforementioned cultural gulfs of America, the terms "countermovement" and "reactionary" often obscure their distinct grievances and the autonomy of their emergence. Such is the case of the anti-abortion movement, or rather movements, and its equally complicated counterpart in the form of the pro-choice movement (Munson 2010). Although Meyer and Staggenborg (1996) have demonstrated the utility of the terminology of the countermovement in illuminating the complex interactions between movement challengers, the state, and reactive movements, temporal sequencing of a movement's emergence in relation to an opposing movement alone should not be used as a classification heuristic in labeling countermovements.

Conflicts within Movements

Less understood are conflicts emerging within movements. Much of the extant literature on social movements supports the notion that intra-movement conflict can be strategically disadvantageous (Polletta 2012), diminishing the capacity for tactical adaptation and often collapsing mobilization potential under the weight of movement in-fighting (Ryan 1989). Such internal conflict can diminish the effectiveness of the movement's claims-making strategies as seen in the New Christian Right (Bates 2000), and is particularly evident in studies of labor movements (Hiltermann 1993; Balser 1997). However, some scholars have challenged this notion, demonstrating the capacity for within-movement conflict to potentially foment new discourses and identities (Ghaziani 2008; Moon 2012) and bring sharper focus to issues within a movement (Haines 1984). In this section, we accent the role of within-movement conflict in a range of cases, from the various "great" schisms within Christianity (including the East–West bisection of the Catholic Church in 1054 A.D., the Western or Papal schism in the Catholic Church from 1378–1418, and the Protestant Reformation beginning around 1512 with the publication of Luther's *Ninety-Five Theses* and concluding around 1548 with the Peace of Westphalia) to the contemporary LGBT movement. Such examples serve to illustrate that within-movement cultural conflicts need not be limited to the kinds of cleavages that lead to factionalism, and may manifest themselves far more ambiguously. The fluidity of such conflicts to boil over into crisis or simmer in the form of near-constant low-level bickering, is particularly relevant to understanding the role of cultural conflict within movements.

While some scholars may characterize inquiry into internal movement conflicts as the study of in-fighting and squabbling, such conflicts have constituted perhaps some of the most influential cultural shifts in Western history. Consider the example given earlier of the East–West Schism at the turn of the millennium fracturing Catholicism into the Roman Catholic and Eastern Orthodox churches. While powerful geopolitical interests were certainly salient in the conflicts leading up to the Great Schism in 1054 A.D., underlying theological and ecclesiastical disagreements between the East and West remain the most enduring consequence of this historic divide (Barrett et al. 1982).

More recently, scholars have examined the consequences of within-movement conflict in a host of contemporary movements in both Western and non-Western settings. The LGBT community is a particularly notable example, as evident in its terminology alone: the evolution of this acronym is the result of ongoing debate as to who ought to be included within the collective banner of "LGBT" and what it is to be gender or sexually non-conforming (Stone 2009). Both Ghaziani (2008) and Moon (2012), in their respective studies of conflict within the LGBT movement, found that these internal conflicts have not detracted from the movement's aims but rather contributed to the claims-making outcomes of the movement.

Similarly, such debates over inclusion of certain constituencies and acceptability of various movement identities continue in a host of movements, spanning the entire social and political spectrum (Blee and Creasap 2010; Laraña et al. 1994; Polletta 2012; Shupe and Bromley 1980). Although the white power movement is frequently labeled by external watchdogs, such as the Southern Poverty Law Center (SPLC), as a monolithic movement rooted entirely in hatred, within-movement distinctions are constantly being debated and constructed. A recent study of white power discourse by Snow, Tan, and Owens (2013) in an online discussion community reveals not only divergent movement frames and identities within a highly fragmented movement, but a constant process of low-level conflict (described as "contentious chatter"). Moreover, movements themselves may evolve as amalgamations of various sub-cultures, whose boundaries do not simply dissolve upon coalescence into a social movement. Using the typology of accommodative versus oppositional sub-cultures developed by Johnston and Snow (1998) in their study of mobilization in former Soviet Estonia, we may observe that many movements, including the white power movement, are comprised not of a single sub-culture but rather a loosely assembled amalgamation of various sub-cultures with shared interests and grievances (Simi and Futrell 2010).

However, as suggested earlier, internal contentious chatter and cultural conflict need not lead to fractionalization or diminished capacity of a movement. Recent work on the role of emotion in social movements by Summers-Effler (2010) demonstrates that internal conflict may, in fact, be informally institutionalized and built into the so-called emotional rhythm of the organization. This steady state of conflict therefore contributes to the long-term evolution of the organization. This finding, although novel in its expounding upon the sparse literature on emotion in movements, builds upon an established body of literature on the capacity for internal movement cultures to sustain a movement, even in unfavorable conditions (Taylor 1989; Staggenborg 1989).

Movement cultures themselves can, and often are, consequential outside of the confines of their organizations and constituencies. Meyer and Whittier (1994) conceptualize this process of diffusion as social movement *spillover*. Regardless of the terminology, it is understood that movements contribute to broader cultural change, even through internal conflict.

Mechanisms

We have argued and illustrated that cultural conflict germinates in the intersections of various cultural elements and movement stances or orientations to those elements, and in different relational contexts. But we have said little about how movements give cultural substance to their claims and challenges other than through the embracement, modification, or rejection of one or more cultural elements. Here we address this gloss in part by elaborating two mechanisms through which social movements may both use and affect cultural change. Consistent with our introductory conceptualization of culture, we see culture not as a single malleable monolith but rather as an ever changing field, acting as the context in which actors engage with culture and negotiate their respective relations of power, drawing from synthetic perspectives on culture (see Sewell 1992; Snow et al. 2014). We argue that the cultural field is then subject to a range of mechanisms through which various agents attempt to affect sociocultural change. Drawing from this recent work by Snow and his colleagues (2013), we suggest two related mechanisms—cultural revitalization and cultural fabrication—that illustrate conceptually both how culture may be used and altered by social movements.

Revitalization

Revitalization involves the resuscitation of a forgotten, jettisoned, or unused cultural item—be it a cultural practice, product, or sign or symbol—and aligning it with movement claims and goals and/or imbuing it with new meanings and associations that are resonant with present issues and concerns. Revitalization need not be a wholesale recovery from antiquity; in reviving some cultural artifact, the product, practice or symbol is made contemporaneous and situated within the present cultural context. A notable historical example can be readily seen in the 1933s to WWII period, with the National Socialist Party of Germany's revival of symbolism and terminologies of the Holy Roman Empire—the so-called First Reich. The *Aquila*, or eagle, of the Roman legion battle standard joined the colors of the Nazi party to become the ubiquitous Iron Eagle. More recently, the Guy Fawkes mask has been revived, far removed from its origins in the failed Gunpowder Plot of 1605, to become a highly visible symbol of post-modern anarchism and leftist libertarian, as in popularized fiction such as Alan Moore's 1981 graphic novel *V for Vendetta* (Call 2008). And an even more recent example is provided by the former FOX news showman, Glenn Beck's rescue and revitalization of obscure conservative thinkers, such as W. Cleon Skousen and his writings, namely *The 5,000 Year Leap*, which Beck said was "essential to understanding why our Founders built this Republic the way they did" (Wilentz 2010: 36). Beck, among other others, rescued and revitalized such dust-collecting items and their arguments to help frame various contemporary issues and events of particular relevance to the Tea Party movement. As one Tea Party observer noted, it "is a thoroughly modern movement, organizing on Twitter and Facebook ... [b]ut when it comes to ideology, it has reached back to dusty bookshelves for long-dormant ideas" (Zernike 2010). As evidenced in these examples, cultural revitalizations need not be carried out wholesale or without some fusion of additional elements to suit the cultural artifacts' new contemporary context.

Fabrication

Fabrication involves the construction or creation of something relatively new out of existing cultural resources, drawing from the cultural cache of these resources but fusing them together in a *bricolage* fashion. The fabrication may be a straightforward construction devoid of any deception or misrepresentation, or it may intentionally misrepresent and deceive.

In reconsidering the concept of fabrication, freed of the baggage of negative connotation, there are a plethora of illustrative cases. One prominent case of the modern age involved Heinrich Himmler, the head of the Nazi SS and arguably the second most influential leader in the Nazi movement and regime, and his use of the Roman Senator, historian, and author Cornelius Tacitus's book titled, *Germania* (AD 98), as the basis for elaborating and legitimating the highly mobilizing master frame of Aryan Supremacy (see Krebs 2011; Snow et al. 2013). We may also look to a variety of liberation movements influenced by the *satyagraha* principle of forceful, non-violent resistance developed by Mahatma Gandhi, including Nelson Mandela's campaigns against South African Apartheid (Mandela 1999) and Martin Luther King Jr.'s role in the civil rights movement, characterized by his self-avowed "pilgrimage to non-violence" (King 2008). The Rastafarian socio-religious movement may also be understood as a particularly enduring cultural fabrication, fusing Jamaican and Ethiopian lineages of Christianity, with more recent anti-colonial interpretations of Babylon (aligned closely with Western colonialism and cultural hegemony) and youth counterculture symbols from across the Caribbean and African sphere (Chevannes 1994).

At the foundation of such religious movements formed on elaborate cultural fabrications is the character of syncretism that can also be observed in the profusion of new religious movements emerging in the twentieth century. Constructed from once disparate cultural elements, fused from old and new, and imbued with often drastically new meanings and beliefs, syncretic movements can range from the benevolent to the violent, as in the case of the Aum Shinrikyo movement responsible for the sarin gas attack on the Tokyo subway in 1995 (Hall 2000; Juergensmeyer 2000).

Configurational Processes

Cultural change processes may also result from any configuration of these two mechanisms. One notable example of such hybrid revitalization and fabrication can be found in the once-vital American militia movement of the 1990s and 2000s. Drawing from both the letter, but perhaps not spirit, of the Second Amendment of the Constitution, these militia organizations often revived long-since discarded state militia insignia and organization names while simultaneously aligning them with contemporary far-right libertarian politics (Crothers 2004). In these highly recognizable symbols and historical meanings attached with the American Revolution and the emergent American identity, the militia movement found a powerful metaphor for their contemporary anti-government and anti-regulatory frames. However, they did not simply revive these historical resonant symbols and meanings but rather reconfigured them alongside more recent racialist and libertarian frames to novel effect. The resultant cultural forms provided the framework for the late twentieth-century wave of survivalist, separatist, anti-government, anti-tax, and often racialist movements, loosely organized under the militia banner. However, these movements bore little resemblance to the Patriot militias of the American Revolutionary War that they so readily invoked. Militia movement leaders then composited the cultural resonance of such struggles for US independence with contemporary libertarian and sometimes millenarian discourses, thus fabricating the basis for an entirely new movement while retaining the namesake of its historical forebears.

The deployment of cultural and historically resonant symbols, such as the iconography of the American Patriot, is a well-established practice among social movement actors. The resurgence of the Islamic Fundamentalist Taliban in Afghanistan has been accompanied with a great deal of popular misapprehension about the movement's roots, or lack thereof, in traditional Islamic beliefs. Rashid (2000) suggests that the often barbaric practices and ideologies of the Taliban are rooted not in the Qur'an but rather the contemporary socio-political climate of its founders. He argues that these refugees, emerging from the Soviet invasion of Afghanistan, invoked antiquated interpretations of sharia law and its provisions for the treatment of women, as well as the principles of fundamentalist Takfiri organizations, as a means of sanctioning violence against their political opponents. The configuration of these militant, fundamentalist Islamic beliefs with often-drastic departures from the Qur'an, alongside tribal codes previously unincorporated into sharia law, thus provided the leaders of the Taliban with the veneer of legitimacy, all the while forging a radically new movement amidst the devastation and corruption of Afghanistan's sociopolitical climate at the time of its emergence.

Conclusion

In this chapter, we have examined culture as a seedbed for many of the conflicts generative of social movements, and the utilization of culture as an instrument of challenge and social change. To get a handle on the locus and range of cultural conflicts, we conceptualized the diverse assortment of cultural elements and artifacts in a given cultural field into three main categories: products, practices, and meanings. We then identified three primary forms of social movement orientations in relation to these cultural elements as a way of systematically classifying the broad range of cultural claims and challenges advanced by movement actors: embracement, reform, and rejection. In doing so and in light of the array of movements that populate, or might populate Table 33.1's cells, we think scholars of social movements would be hard pressed to identify a profusion of movements, past or present, in which cultural conflicts and challenges were not significant factors in their emergence and character. With the rise of such rapidly spreading movements as those contained within the Occupy and Arab Spring waves, emerging in 2011 and 2013 respectively, it is evident that even material grievances are rarely deployed without accompanying cultural challenges. Moreover, the strategies employed in these twenty-first century movements appear to be informed, in part, by cultural concerns: Arab Spring's non-violence rooted in anti-authoritarian and anti-military cultural values (Nepstad 2011) and the decentralized practices of the Occupy movement, heavily informed by the social media networks that fueled the movement (Costanza-Chock 2012). These recent movements are not entirely novel but rather extensions and syntheses of the many culturally rooted movements that have preceded them, a handful of which we have referenced here.

Throughout our discussion, we have emphasized and now reiterate the permeability of these classifications, recognizing that few movements fit neatly in any one intersectional configuration throughout its life course. It is this possible immensity in dynamic variation that characterizes the empirical reality of the nexus of social movements and cultural conflict and change processes. We also noted that these conflicts and challenges do not emerge and play out randomly across the socio-cultural landscape but are, instead, nested in three core contexts—in relation to intuitional and/or cultural authorities, between movements, and within movements. We observed, however, that the role of social movements in influencing cultural change processes often extends far beyond the immediate contexts and cultural fields in which movements operate.

Finally, we identified and illustrated two mechanisms through which movements use and affect culture: cultural revitalization and cultural fabrication. These mechanisms of cultural engagement, associated with and activated in part by the framing processes of alignment, articulation, and elaboration (Snow et al. 1986; Benford and Snow 2000; Snow 2004b), highlight the role of social movements as important socio-cultural actors irrespective of their targets of change. "By reaching back, dusting off, and bringing forth into the present various cultural relics or traditions, movements are important agents of cultural reclamation, revitalization, and/or fabrication. And, in the process, they are important cultural actors" (Snow et al. 2013: 239), particularly in contexts of cultural conflict.

REFERENCES

Alfeyev, Hilarion (2000). *The Spiritual World of Isaac the Syrian*. Collegeville, MN: Cistercian Publications/Liturgical Press.

Alexander, Jeffrey C. (2003). *The Meanings of Social Life: A Cultural Sociology*. Oxford: Oxford University Press.

Balser, Deborah B. (1997). "The Impact of Environmental Factors on Factionalism and Schism in Social Movement Organizations," *Social Forces*. 76: 199–228.

Barrett, David B., Kurian, George Thomas, and Johnson, Todd M. (1982) *World Christian Encyclopedia*. Nairobi: Oxford University Press.

Bartkowski, John P. (2004). *The Promise Keepers: Servants, Soldiers, and Godly Men*. New Brunswick, NJ: Rutgers University Press.

Bates, Vernon L. (2000). "The Decline of a New Christian Right Social Movement Organization: Opportunities and Constraints," *Review of Religious Research*. 42: 19–40.

Benford, Robert D. and Snow, David A. (2000). "Framing Processes and Social Movements: An Overview and Assessment," *Annual Review of Sociology*. 26: 611–639.

Blee, Kathleen M. and Creasap, Kimberly A. (2010). "Conservative and Right-wing Movements," *Annual Review of Sociology*. 36: 269–286.

Berger, Bennett M. (1981). *The Survival of a Counterculture: Ideological Work and Everyday Life among Rural Communards*. Berkeley: University of California Press.

Bourdieu, Pierre (1984). *Distinction: A Social Critique of the Judgment of Taste*. Cambridge, MA: Harvard University Press.

Bourdieu, Pierre (1993). *The Field of Cultural Production: Essays on Art and Literature*. New York: Columbia University Press.

Cadot-Wood, A. (2013). "May Fourth Movement (China)." In *The Wiley-Blackwell Encyclopedia of Social and Political Movements*, Vol. II, edited by D. A. Snow, D. della Porta, B. Klandermans, and D. McAdam, 726–728. Oxford: Wiley/Blackwell.

Call, Lewis (2008). "A is for Anarchy, V is for Vendetta: Images of Guy Fawkes and the Creation of Postmodern Anarchism," *Anarchist Studies*. 16: 154–172.

Chang, Maria Hsia (2004). *Falun Gong: The End of Days*. New Haven, CT: Yale University Press.

Chevannes, Barry (1994). *Rastafari: Roots and Ideology*. Syracuse, NY: Syracuse University Press.

Costanza-Chock, Sasha (2012). "Mic Check! Media Cultures and the Occupy Movement," *Social Movement Studies*. 11: 375–385.

Crothers, Lane (2004). *Rage on the Right: The American Militia Movement from Ruby Ridge to Homeland Security*. Lanham, MY: Rowman & Littlefield Publishers.

Dow, Bonnie J. (2003). "Feminism, Miss America, and Media Mythology," *Rhetoric & Public Affairs*. 6: 127–149.

Earl, Jennifer (2004). "The Cultural Consequences of Social Movements." In *The Blackwell Companion to Social Movements*, edited by David A. Snow, Sarah A. Soule, and Hanspeter Kriesi, 508–530. Malden, MA: Blackwell Publishing.

Fetner, Tina (2008). *How the Religious Right Shaped Lesbian and Gay Activism*. Minneapolis: University of Minnesota Press.

Gardner, Hugh (1978). *The Children of Prosperity: Thirteen Modern American Communes*. New York: St. Martin's Press.

Geertz, Clifford (1973). *The Interpretation of Cultures: Selected Essays*. New York: Basic Books

Ghaziani, Amin (2008). *The Dividends of Dissent: How Conflict and Culture Work in Lesbian and Gay Marches on Washington*. Chicago: University of Chicago Press.

Haines, Herbert H. (1984). "Black Radicalization and the Funding of Civil Rights: 1957–1970," *Social Problems*. 32: 31–43.

Hall, John R. (1987). *Gone from the Promised Land: Jonestown in American Cultural History*. Brunswick. NJ: Transaction.

Hall, John R. (2000). *Apocalypse Observed: Religious Movements and Violence in North America, Europe, and Japan*. London: Routledge.

Hanisch, Carol (2000). "A Critique of the Miss America Protest." In *Radical Feminism: A Documentary Reader*, edited by Barbara A. Crow, 378–381. New York: New York University Press.

Hardisty, Jean (2000). *Mobilizing Resentment: Conservative Resurgence from the John Birch Society to the Promise Keepers*. Boston: Beacon Press.

Hiltermann, Joost R. (1993). *Behind the Intifada: Labor and Women's Movements in the Occupied Territories*. Princeton, NJ: Princeton University Press.

Hirschmann, David (1990). "The Black Consciousness Movement in South Africa," *The Journal of Modern African Studies*. 28: 1–22.

Hobsbawm, Eric J. (1952). "The Machine Breakers," *Past & Present*. 1: 57–70.

Jansen, G. H. (1979). *Militant Islam*. New York: Harper & Row.

Jasper, James M. and Nelkin, Dorothy (1992). *The Animal Rights Crusade: The Growth of a Moral Protest*. New York: The Free Press.

Johnston, Hank and Klandermans, Bert, eds. 1995. *Social Movements and Culture*. Minneapolis, MN: University of Minnesota Press.

Johnston, Hank and Snow, David A. (1998). "Subcultures and the Emergence of the Estonian Nationalist Opposition 1945–1990," *Sociological Perspectives*. 41: 473–497.

Juergensmeyer, Mark (2000). *Terror in the Mind of God: The Global Rise of Religious Violence*. Berkeley, CA: University of California Press.

Kanter, Rosabeth Moss (1972). *Commitment and Community: Communes and Utopias in Sociological Perspective*. Cambridge, MA: Harvard University Press.

Kaplan, Jeffrey (1997). *Radical Religion in America: Millenarian Movements from the Far Right to the Children of Noah*. Syracuse, NY: Syracuse University Press.

Kim, Allen (2013). "South Korean Transnational Fatherhood Movement." In *The Wiley-Blackwell Encyclopedia of Social and Political Movements*, Vol. III, edited by D. A. Snow, D. della Porta, B. Klandermans, and D. McAdam, 1232–1234. Oxford: Wiley/Blackwell.

King, Coretta Scott, ed. (2008). *The Words of Martin Luther King, Jr.* New York: Newmarket Press.

Krebs, Christopher B. (2011). *A Most Dangerous Book: Tacitus's "Germania": From the Roman Empire to the Third Reich.* New York: W.W. Norton & Company.

Kurzweil, Ray (2000) *The Age of Spiritual Machines: When Computers Exceed Human Intelligence.* London: Penguin.

Kwan, Samantha (2009). "Framing the Fat Body: Contested Meanings between Government, Activists, and Industry," *Sociological Inquiry.* 79: 25–50.

Laraña, Enrique, Johnson, Hank, and Gusfield, R., eds. (1994). *New Social Movements: From Ideology to Identity.* Philadelphia: Temple University Press.

Malone, Karen. (2002). "Street Life: Youth, Culture and Competing Uses of Public Space." *Environment and Urbanization,* 14: 157–168.

Mandela, Nelson (1999). "The Sacred Warrior," *Time.* 154: 124–126.

Melucci, Alberto (1996). *Challenging Codes: Collective Action in the Information Age.* New York: Cambridge University Press.

Meyer, David S. and Staggenborg, Suzanne (1996). "Movements, Countermovements, and the Structure of Political Opportunity," *American Journal of Sociology.* 101: 1628–1660.

Meyer, David S. and Whittier, Nancy (1994). "Social Movement Spillover," *Social Problems.* 41: 277–298.

Moon, Dawne (2012). "Who Am I and Who Are We? Conflicting Narratives of Collective Selfhood in Stigmatized Groups," *American Journal of Sociology.* 117: 1336–1379.

Munson, Ziad (2010). *The Making of Pro-Life Activists: How Social Movement Mobilization Works.* Chicago: University of Chicago Press.

Nasr, Vali (2006). *The Shia Revival: How Conflicts within Islam will Shape the Future.* New York: W.W. Norton & Company.

Nepstad, Sharon Erikson (2011). "Nonviolent Resistance in the Arab Spring: The Critical Role of Military Opposition Alliances," *Swiss Political Science Review.* 17: 485–491.

Obach, Brian K. (2002). "Labor-Environmental Relations: An Analysis of the Relationship between Labor Unions and Environmentalists," *Social Science Quarterly.* 83: 82–100.

Polletta, Francesca (2012). *Freedom is an Endless Meeting: Democracy in American Social Movements.* Chicago: University of Chicago Press.

Rashid, Ahmed (2000). *Taliban: Militant Islam, Oil & Fundamentalism in Central Asia.* New Haven, CN: Yale University Press.

Rashid, Ahmed (2002). *Jihad: The Rise of Militant Islam in Central Asia.* New Haven, CN: Yale University

Rupp, Leila J. and Taylor, Verta A. (2003). *Drag Queens at the 801 Cabaret.* Chicago: University of Chicago Press.

Ryan, Barbara (1989). "Ideological Purity and Feminism: The US Women's Movement from 1966 to 1975," *Gender & Society.* 3: 239–257.

Saguy, Abigail C. (2013). *What's Wrong with Fat?* New York: Oxford University Press.

Schlatter, Evelyn (2010). "18 Anti-Gay Groups and Their Propaganda." *Intelligence Report.* Southern Poverty Law Center. Issue 140.

Scott, Joan Wallach (2009). *The Politics of the Veil.* Princeton: Princeton University Press.

Sewell, William H. (1992). "A Theory of Structure: Duality, Agency, and Transformation," *American Journal of Sociology.* 98: 1–29.

Sewell, William H. (1996). "Historical Events as Transformations of Structures: Inventing Revolution at the Bastille," *Theory and Society.* 25: 841–881.

Shreve, Anita (1989). *Women Together, Women Alone: The Legacy of the Consciousness-raising Movement*. New York: Viking.

Shupe, Anson and Bromley, David G. (1980). *The New Vigilantes: Deprogrammers, Anti-Cultists, and the New Religious*. Beverly Hills, CA: Sage.

Simi, Pete and Futrell, Robert (2010). *American Swastika: Inside the White Power Movement's Hidden Spaces of Hate*. Lenham, MD: Rowman & Littlefield Publishers.

Snow, David A. (2004a). "Social Movements as Challenges to Authority: Resistance to an Emerging Conceptual Hegemony," *Research in Social Movements, Conflicts and Change*. 25: 3–25.

Snow, David A. (2004b). "Framing Processes, Ideology, and Discursive Fields." In *The Blackwell Companion to Social Movements*, edited by David A. Snow, Sarah Soule, Hanspeter Kriesi, 380–412. Oxford: Blackwell Publishing.

Snow, David A. and Lessor, Roberta G. (2010). "Framing Hazards in the Health Arena: The Cases of Obesity, Work-Related Illnesses, and Human Egg Donation." In *Social Movements and the Transformation of American Health Care*, edited by Jane C. Banaszak-Holl, Sandra R. Levitsky, and Mayer N. Zald, 284–299. New York: Oxford University Press.

Snow, David A. and Lessor, Roberta G. (2013). "Consciousness, Conscience, and Social Movements." In *The Wiley-Blackwell Encyclopedia of Social and Political Movements*, Vol. I, edited by D.A. Snow, D. della Porta, B. Klandermans, and D. McAdam, 244–249. Oxford: Wiley/Blackwell.

Snow, David. A. and Marshall, Susan E. (1984). "Cultural Imperialism, Social Movements, and the Islamic Revival," *Research in Social Movements, Conflict and Change*. 7: 131–152.

Snow, David A., Rochford, R. Burke, Jr., Worden, Steven K., and Benford, Robert D. (1986). "Frame Alignment Processes, Micromobilization, and Movement Participation," *American Sociological Review*. 51: 464–481.

Snow, David A., Tan, Anna E. Tan, and Owens, Peter B. (2013). "Social Movements, Framing Processes, and Cultural Revitalization and Fabrication," *Mobilization*. 18: 225–242.

Snow, David A., Owens, Peter B., and Tan, Anna E. (2014). "Libraries, Social Movements, and Cultural Change: Toward and Alternative Conceptualization of Culture," *Social Currents*. 1: 35–43.

Spitzer, Robert J. (1995). *The Politics of Gun Control*. Chatham, NJ: Chatham House.

Staggenborg, Suzanne (1989). "Stability and Innovation in the Women's Movement: A Comparison of Two Movement Organizations," *Social Problems*. 36: 75–92.

Stone, Amy L. (2009). "More than Adding a T: American Lesbian and Gay Activists' Attitudes towards Transgender Inclusion" *Sexualities*. 12: 334–354.

Su, Yang (2011). *Collective Killings in Rural China during the Cultural Revolution*. New York: Cambridge University Press.

Summers-Effler, Erika (2010). *Laughing Saints and Righteous Heroes: Emotional Rhythms in Social Movement Groups*. Chicago: University of Chicago Press.

Sun, Yanfei (2013). "Falun Gong (China)." In *The Wiley-Blackwell Encyclopedia of Social and Political Movements*, Vol. II, edited by D. A. Snow, D. della Porta, B. Klandermans, and D. McAdam, 446–447. Oxford: Wiley/Blackwell

Swidler, Ann (1986). "Culture in Action: Symbols and Strategies," *American Sociological Review*. 51: 273–286.

Taylor, Bron (1998). "Religion, Violence and Radical Environmentalism: From Earth First! To the Unabomber to the Earth Liberation Front," *Terrorism and Political Violence*. 10: 1–42.

Taylor, Verta (1989). "Social Movement Continuity: The Women's Movement in Abeyance," *American Sociological Review*. 54: 761–775.

Tierney, Amber C. (2013). "System Exiting and Social Movements." In *The Wiley-Blackwell Encyclopedia of Social and Political Movements*, Vol. III, edited by D. A. Snow, D. della Porta, B. Klandermans, and D. McAdam, 1310–1312. Oxford: Wiley/Blackwell.

Van Dyke, Nella, Soule, Sarah A., and Taylor, Verta A. (2004). "The Targets of Social Movements: Beyond a Focus on the State," *Research in Social Movements, Conflict and Change*. 25: 27–51.

Walder, Andrew G., and Su, Yang (2003). "The Cultural Revolution in the Countryside: Scope, Timing and Human Impact," *The China Quarterly*. 173: 74–99.

Wallace, Anthony F. C. (1956). "Revitalization Movements," *American Anthropologist*. 58: 264–281.

Wallis, Roy. (1984). *The Elementary Forms of the New Religious Life*. London: Routledge and Kegan Paul.

Wiktorowicz, Quintan, ed. (2004). *Islamic Activism: A Social Movement Theory Approach*. Bloomington, IN: Indiana University Press.

Wilentz, Jean (2010). "Confounding Fathers: The Tea Party's Cold War Roots," *The New Yorker*. October 18: 32–39.

Williams, Rhys H. (2004). "The Cultural Contexts of Collective Action: Constraints, Opportunities, and the Symbolic Life of Social Movements." In *The Blackwell Companion to Social Movements*, edited by David A. Snow, Sarah A. Soule, and Hanspeter Kriesi, 90–115, London: Blackwell.

Wilson, Brian R. (1973). *Magic and the Millennium*. London: Heinemann.

Wu, Lili (2013). "Cultural Revolution (China)." In *The Wiley-Blackwell Encyclopedia of Social and Political Movements*, Vol. I, edited by D. A. Snow, D. della Porta, B. Klandermans, and D. McAdam, 305–311. Oxford: Wiley/Blackwell.

Xu, Jin. and Dingxin Zhao (2013). "Chinese Communist Revolution." In *The Wiley-Blackwell Encyclopedia of Social and Political Movements*, Vol. I, edited by D. A. Snow, D. della Porta, B. Klandermans, and D. McAdam, 180–183. Oxford: Wiley/Blackwell.

Zernike, Kate (2010). "Movement of the Moment Looks to Long-Ago Texts." Available at www.nytimes.com/2010/10/02/us/politics/02teaparty.html?_1=...

CHAPTER 34

....

NARRATIVE AND SOCIAL
MOVEMENTS

....

FRANCESCA POLLETTA AND
BETH GHARRITY GARDNER

A woman pulled up to a drive-through McDonald's and ordered a cup of coffee. She spilled the coffee and burned her leg. Then she sued McDonald's successfully for three million dollars.

In the late 1990s, this story was told and retold by activists who were seeking to reform the American laws around civil litigation. The story captured the points that tort reform activists were making: that people were blaming their own carelessness on companies and that they were seeking and winning outrageous sums of money from pushover juries. The real story, however, was different from the one that was told. The woman did not just burn her leg: she suffered third-degree burns that left permanent scarring over sixteen per cent of her body and rendered her disabled for the next two years. McDonald's, it was revealed, had received over seven hundred complaints about its scalding coffee over the previous decade. And the punitive damages the woman was awarded were later reduced to one-fifth of the original amount. But the true story did not strike the chords that the fictive one did. Told alongside other stories of litigation-happy Americans—the woman who claimed a hospital-administered test had caused her to lose her psychic powers, the burglar who sued his victim when he fell through the skylight, the man who sued the manufacturer of his power mower when he strained his back pushing the machine—the McDonald's story helped the tort reform movement to win legislation limiting litigation in almost every American state (Haltom and McCann 2004).

Stories can serve as a crucial resource to activists. Poignant or outrageous stories can gain support for the movements' claims. In addition, however, sometimes gaining acceptance for the story *is* winning. In this case, tort reform activists used the McDonald's story and others like it to gain acceptance for a more general story about torts. In this story, Americans' propensity for litigation was driving up the cost of medical malpractice insurance. This was not, in fact, true. The reason that malpractice insurance was getting more expensive had nothing to do with litigation and everything to do with fluctuations in insurance companies investments. That this conflicting account was so rarely heard attests to the power of the story that tort reform activists told.

Activists use stories to mobilize participants, enlist supporters, and influence decision makers. Stories, in this sense, are strategic. But stories also figure as a cultural backdrop against which activists' stories (as well as the claims they advance by way of stories) are heard. These background stories help determine whether activists' claims are treated as plausible or exaggerated, as morally compelling or as trivial, as coherent or nonsensical. These stories are important also because, insofar as they undergird policy making, they generate advantages for some groups rather than others. Changing those deeper stories is thus a target and measure of protest's success.

In this essay, we take up both kinds of stories, and try to demonstrate their importance to movements' emergence, trajectories, and outcomes.[1] We begin by defining narrative and distinguishing it from other terms that sociologists have used to capture the cultural dimensions of social movements. Then we show how scholars have used concepts of story and storytelling to answer questions that are typically asked about social movements. Why do movements emerge when they do? Under what conditions are movements able to mobilize participation and support? When are movements successful and what counts as success? In discussing the first question, we show how scholars have used narrative to account for the constitution of collective actors, that is, to explain why people come to see themselves as a group with stakes in protest. In discussing the second question, about the dynamics of and conditions for mobilization, we show why stories are so persuasive. But we also draw attention to the institutional norms of storytelling that make it difficult for activists to tell the stories they want to tell. In discussing movement outcomes, we sketch several ways in which gaining acceptance for a story may constitute success. Finally, we devote a brief section to the use of narrative as data and method for social movement analysis. Throughout, we draw insights from outside the sociology of social movements as well as from within it. We also highlight issues that would benefit from an even fuller engagement with narrative scholarship.

WHAT IS NARRATIVE?

A narrative is an account of a sequence of events in the order in which they occurred to make a point.[2] Beyond that minimal definition, most scholars see narratives as having characters (who are human or human-like in their characteristics or perceptions). Audiences should feel an emotional connection with at least one character. Only relevant events are included in the story and later events are assumed to explain earlier ones. Following Labov (Labov and Waletsky 1967), scholars typically look in a text for an orientation, which sets the stage for the events to be recounted, a series of "and then" clauses, and an evaluation, which communicates why the story is important to tell. The causal links between events, however, are based not on formal logic or probability but on plot. Plot is the structure of the story. It is the means by which what would otherwise be mere occurrences are made into moments in the unfolding of the story. Plots are familiar to audiences from stories they have heard before, although the relationship between the underlying plot structure and a particular story is complex. Finally, events in a story project a desirable or undesirable future. They make a normative point. Storytellers rarely say explicitly to their audiences, "and the moral of the story is…." Rather, the story's larger meaning seems to be given by the events themselves (Polletta 2006, and see Bal 1985 and Polkinghorne 1988 for good discussions of narrative's elements).

Unlike an explanation, then, a narrative represents cause and effect relations through its sequencing of events rather than by appeal to standards of logic and proof. Reports also explain through their representation of events, but they do not organize events as carefully and, in particular, do not rely on suspense to make a normative point. An argument makes a normative point, but the point is not integrated into the account of events and revealed by the story's dénouement. More than arguments, analyses, reports, or descriptions, audiences expect stories to be open to multiple interpretations. Audiences are less likely to hear ambiguity in stories as imprecision or error.

Narratives are forms of discourse, vehicles of ideology, and elements of collective action frames, but unlike all three, they can often be identified in a chunk of text or speech by their formal features (Polletta 2012). That said, some of the most effective stories are those that are not fully recounted (Gerteis 2002). They are instead simply alluded to, or presented in capsule form (Kalcik 1975). Narrative does have another analytical virtue, however. Unlike frames, ideologies, or discourses, narrative is a folk concept as well as a scholarly one. Most people know how to construct a story, and when and why they should tell stories, and how to respond to a story. Some conventions of storytelling are formalized, such as those in courtroom testimony. Others are less formal, but their breach may come with penalties: for example, losing credibility for violating storytelling norms in a television news interview or congressional testimony. As we will show, activists are often in a difficult position with respect to these conventions. Sometimes they are unable to conform to narrative conventions and sometimes they are unwilling to suffer the political costs of doing so. Paying attention to the institutional norms of storytelling thus offers insight into movement dynamics obscured by these other cultural concepts.

WHY DO MOVEMENTS EMERGE WHEN THEY DO?

Social movement scholars in recent years have sought to move beyond an account of movement emergence centered on so-called political opportunities. Certainly, changes in alignments in the institutional political sphere sometimes signal to movement actors that mobilizing the broader group may secure concessions that were previously unavailable. But in many cases, the relevant question is why a movement actor came into being in the first place. In other cases, the task is to explain the emergence of movements outside the institutional political sphere, such as movements targeting the Catholic Church, schools, or academic science. A conceptual idiom of political opportunities is not especially useful in cases like these (Snow 2005; Armstrong and Bernstein 2008).

Paying attention to the stories that people tell may be more useful. In one vein of scholarship, scholars have accounted for the emergence of mobilizing collective identities by way of changes in the stories that people commonly tell. Stories' configurational and emotional dimensions are important here. Stories turn discrete events into an evolving whole. They link past, present, and future, and invest events with moral significance and an emotional charge. For example, Somers (1992) challenges standard accounts of English working class formation in the early nineteenth century by arguing that English laborers were motivated to act collectively not by economic grievances but rather by a powerful and longstanding narrative of legal rights in a political community. Kane (2000) traces the "narrative competition" between conciliatory and retributive accounts of British domination that preceded the establishment of an Irish national identity. Plummer (1995) argues that the mutual constitution of an audience for new stories and the new stories themselves explains why a homosexual identity emerged but an identity around the enjoyment of pornography did not. Behind American class identity in the nineteenth-century Knights of Labor, Gerteis (2002) shows, was not one story but several stories that together defined working white Americans both against and in solidarity with racial others. In each case, people developed stakes in collective action that followed from the stories they told rather than from pre-existing interests.

In another vein of research and theorizing, scholars have shown that protest is likely when the stories that govern action and interaction in a particular institutional arena lose their force or when new stories gain purchase. For example, Luker (1984) argues that American physicians who routinely performed abortions sought abortion reform when medical advances rendered implausible the moral story that they were acting to save the life of the mother. Since stories integrate description, explanation, and evaluation, institutional stories, in this view, both describe institutional practices and legitimate them. When the description is no longer accurate, the moral warrant suffers too. Newly vulnerable to challenge, physicians mobilized to gain legal protection for abortion.

People may also gain reasons to protest when new stories come to animate an institutional arena. Illustrating this dynamic, Davis (2005) attributes the rise of a movement against child sexual abuse to the institutionalization of a new story, one that was derived from the anti-rape movement. Before the 1970s, child sexual abuse was seen through the lens of family systems and psychoanalytic therapies. Harm to the victim was not considered inevitable and was rarely thought to be long-lasting. Family members, including the victim, were often seen as collusive with the abuser in tolerating the abuse. That account changed when anti-rape and child protection movements converged on the issue of child sexual abuse. The rape experience was transposed to the experience of sexually abused children. In the new story, abuse was widespread but unrecognized, even by victims themselves, victimization was clear-cut, and harm was profound and permanent. The appropriate response to such abuse was for victims to mobilize to speak out and gain rights.

In Luker's case, it was the lack of a justificatory story that led physicians to mobilize, while in Davis's case, it was the production of one that led adult survivors of child abuse to mobilize. In both cases, though, institutional dynamics were critical to stories' importance. Physicians would not have lacked for a justificatory story if medical technological advances had not made abortion increasingly unnecessary to save the life of the mother. The story of child sexual abuse that spurred mobilization would not have been available had it not been for the institutional power of the feminist anti-rape movement in promoting it. Accounts such as Luker's and Davis's thus converge with organizational scholarship that has probed the role of *institutional schemas* both in sustaining institutions and in spurring challenges to them (Polletta and Gardner, 2015; Schneiberg and Clemens 2006). Institutional schemas are enacted in rules, rituals, and routines, as well as stories, but stories' integration of the particular with the universal and the descriptive with the normative makes them especially illuminating of the logics or models that govern institutional action (Polletta 2006). We should see in people's stories, then, the shifts and conflicts in institutional schemas that may precede overt contention.

STORYTELLING IN BIDS FOR PARTICIPATION AND SUPPORT

Once movements are underway, activists use stories strategically to recruit participants (Armstrong and Crage 2006; Viterna 2013) and sustain their commitment (Owens 2009; Steinberg and Ewick 2013), to enlist support (Mische 2003), justify violence (Fine 1999), and make claims in diverse political contexts (Khalili 2008; Braunstein 2012). Activists use other rhetorical forms, of course, such as arguments and logical explanations. But stories seem uniquely equipped to simultaneously appeal to and transform people's identities in a way that motivates action (Viterna 2013). Again, stories' configurational dimension, and specifically its capacity to link past, present, and future into a coherent whole, may explain its use in movement decision making. Indeed, della Porta and Rucht (2012) found that global justice activists often told stories of the movement as a way to defuse conflict in meetings.

Recent research shows that stories are also better able than other kinds of messages to change people's opinions (Slater and Rouner 2002; Jones 2013). This is especially true when audiences are not already invested in the issue in question, a situation that movement activists confront routinely. The reason seems to be that when people are absorbed in a story, they stop treating new information critically. They truly suspend disbelief (Green and Brock 2000). And they do so in a way that has lasting effects. The attitudinal change brought about by stories tends to persist or even increase over time (Appel and Richter 2007).

Not all stories are equally persuasive, of course. Effective stories are relevant and believable. Activists with access to widely known and oft-told stories of collective resistance presumably have an advantage in enlisting support over those who do not have such access. Polish Solidarity activists, for example, were able to draw on "fortifying myths" from Catholicism to interpret setbacks as tests of character on the way to victory (Voss 1998; see also Nepstad 2001). Yet the very familiarity of stories also poses obstacles. As a case in point, Nicaraguan Sandinistas could claim the historical figure of Augusto Sandino as inspiration and guide because Sandino had largely dropped out of official memory; he was thus available for the taking. By contrast, since Emile Zapata remained prominent in Mexican national memory, Zapatistas had to struggle with the state to claim his legacy (Jansen 2007).

It makes sense that successful stories would be those that meshed with deeply held ideological values. Pro-business tort reformers' story of litigation-happy Americans, however much it conflicted with the empirical evidence, tapped a deep-rooted American belief in individual responsibility along with a nostalgic longing for an era of self-restraint (Haltom and McCann 2004). But in contrast to that case, activists who campaigned against sex education in American schools were able to capitalize on brand new stories about child-victims and the abusive power of words (Irvine 2002). American reformers who called for drastically cutting welfare benefits in the 1990s argued that people's dependency on welfare inhibited their ability to become autonomous people. The idea that economic dependency was a psychological problem rather than a structural relationship only made sense in the wake of the wide circulation of stories about (chiefly women's) dependency on drugs, alcohol, and destructive relationships (Fraser and Gordon 1994). Further support for the idea that persuasive stories may produce ideological beliefs rather than reflecting them comes from Somers and Block (2005), who argue that American welfare reformers' power lie in their ability to tell a conversion story in which right-thinking people would wake up to the stunning perversity of the fact that the government was fostering people's weakness.

Additional features of stories may be important to their influence. Polletta argues that stories' reliance on ambiguity serves to engage listeners—and to mobilize them (2006; see also Auyero 2002). Stewart (2012) found that stories about immigration that were told in "low mimetic" mode, with a focus on logic and evidence, were less effective in gaining American policy makers' support than stories told in an "apocalyptic" mode, with immigration connected to crime and terrorism. Mische (2003) argues that Brazilian activists who told fairly short-term stories of reform were better able to forge alliances than those who insisted on longer-term revolutionary narratives. Taken together, these studies suggest that while successful stories seem familiar, simple, urgently important, and commonsensical, each of those perceptions may actually represent strategic accomplishments.

Unsurprisingly, political entrepreneurs with deep financial resources and wide political connections are better able to secure a favorable hearing for their preferred story (Fine 1995; Irvine 2002; Meyer 2006; Esacove 2010). In addition, some people may be better able than others to exploit influential features of stories. Take genre. Jones (2013) found that stories about climate change that cast environmental organizations as heroes led respondents to express preferences for renewable energy rather than market or expert-driven policy solutions. But Higgins and Brush (2006) argue that when poor people represent themselves as heroic in the stories they tell, they are disbelieved. Polletta et al.'s (2013) experimental data suggest that something else stands in the way of poor people effectively telling heroic stories: the fact that people read along the lines of genre (i.e., read a heroic protagonist as heroic) only when the protagonists match stereotypes of people in that role. Armstrong and Crage (2006) identify a narrative resource that some groups have and some do not: *mnemonic capacity*. Gay rights activists in New York City were able to secure a perception of the 1969 Stonewall riots as having originated the gay rights movement, even though this was not the case, because they joined the story of the riots to a commemorative ritual, namely a gay pride parade.

Along with features of stories' form and the resources and status of their tellers, the contexts of stories' telling matters for how effective stories are. Scholars of social movements can draw here from a literature on storytelling in institutional contexts such as courts, medical interviews, and self-help groups (see Polletta et al. 2011 for a review). People in settings like these are required to tell their personal stories, but they are also expected to conform to institutional norms of storytelling. To be successful (to win the case, get treatment, stay in the group, etc.), people often have to tell stories that are not their own. In Belgian political asylum cases, for example, African applicants were asked to tell briefly a complex story about political developments in a foreign country, and then the story was translated, reproduced, and evaluated in numerous materials. Yet the applicant was held responsible for any inconsistencies in the story anywhere along the line (Blommaert 2001). Those who testified about their experiences of brutal state repression in South Africa's Truth and Reconciliation Commission hearings were supplied with a twenty-page protocol that, among other things, discouraged them for talking about the larger context of their experiences (Andrews 2007).

Studies like these trace the consequences of storytelling norms for individuals. But insofar as movements involve affected participants telling their stories in court, in legislative hearings, to the media, and to funders, one can see how such norms have consequences beyond individuals. For example, plaintiffs making claims of gender discrimination in employment have been pressed by American judges to provide stories of individual episodes of discrimination, even when their claims have rested rather on patterns of disparate treatment (Schultz 1990). Adult survivors of child abuse who appeared in court seeking monetary damages were advised to emphasize the debilitating consequences of their past abuse. They were discouraged from presenting themselves as survivors who were in control of their lives (Whittier 2009). In each case, conforming to the institutional norms of narration came with strategic costs.

The media is another venue in which activists struggle to tell stories appropriately but still effectively. Gaining media coverage is critical to movements' ability to get their issues on the public agenda, as well as to gain support from elected officials, many of whom rely on mainstream news sources (Ferree, Gamson, Gerhards, and Rucht 2002).

But the norms of journalistic storytelling may make it difficult for activists to get their causes covered favorably. Reporters' tendency to tell stories about people and events may make it difficult for activists to communicate the structural causes of the injustices they fight (Smith et al. 2001). On the other hand, the fact that the American media, at least in contrast to the German media, relies much more on personal profiles of movement leaders affords activists the opportunity to get their message out in a relatively unfettered way (Ferree et al. 2002; Gamson 2002). However, there may be another problem. As Sarah Sobieraj's (2010) study of movement coverage suggests, reporters may be eager to hear activists' stories, but only if they fit with reporters' notions of authenticity. While the activists Sobieraj observed strove to come across as professional and focused on the movement's message, reporters wanted them to be spontaneous, emotional, and talk only about their own experiences.

Like other cultural constraints, those imposed by the conventions of narrative's use and evaluation are not insuperable. For example, savvy activists have produced the people directly affected by an issue that reporters want to interview, but coached them on how to link their experience to the movement's goals (Salzman 2003). Doing so is difficult, however. Like other kinds of structures such as the distribution of financial resources or the structure of mainstream politics, the conventions of narrative's performance operate for the most part to support the status quo.

Stories as Collective Good

In accounting for movement impacts, scholars have tended to locate cultural changes only in the realm of everyday life, treating political changes, such as new laws or policies, as noncultural (Polletta 2004). But significant changes in the political sphere are often cultural: for example, the recognition of new political actors or a new understanding of a cluster of problems that cuts across policies. The study of narrative offers a way to capture the role of movements in effecting such changes.

Do policy makers' acceptance of a movement's preferred story lead to favorable policies? While some policy scholars have argued that the stories told about particular issues directly shapes the policies that are adopted (Stone 1989), others have argued that, in the United States at least, the framing of political issues does not change much after issues reach Congress (Baumgartner et al. 2009). Jones and McBeth (2010) argue, accordingly, that the stories groups tell may affect policy indirectly, through the policy coalitions they produce. This is an interesting idea for scholars of social movements since it points to a way in which movements may have impact: by telling stories that are capable of enlisting effective political allies. In this vein, Bail (2012) shows that although organizations communicating anti-Muslim messages after 9/11 were in the minority, they captured disproportionate media attention by way of emotional displays of anger and fear. They were then able to convert media attention into political standing, moving from the fringe of expert opinion about Islam to the mainstream.

Clearly, we need to know much more about the points in the policy process at which movements have the best chances of getting their stories accepted as the authoritative ones. However, there are other routes to impact. One is by way of the redistribution of storytelling authority. Most of the time, the stories of the relatively powerless are "just" stories, that is, seen as idiosyncratic, subjective, implausible, and/ or unimportant (Polletta 2006). But movements are sometimes able to gain authority for a new class of storytellers. This was the case for American AIDS activists, who in the 1980s gained recognition for AIDS patients' personal accounts of their illnesses as authoritative knowledge in drug research (Epstein 1996). Latin American movements against military dictatorships secured recognition for the literary form of *testimonio*, in which an individual's story of political trauma stands in for the experience of the group (Nance 2006). The 1980s American movement against child abuse successfully reformed laws around the admissibility of children's stories of abuse (McGough 1994). The strategy of publicly telling personal stories that became prominent in the women's and gay and lesbian movements in the 1970s is now a familiar feature of movements organized around different identities: for example, economic marginality in the case of the Spanish *Indignados* and Occupy Wall Street, and immigration status in the case of the American "DREAMers" (Plummer 1995; Gaby and Caren 2012; Nicholls 2013).

The stories that activists tell *about* the movement may also have political impacts. Certainly, we know that efforts to gain acceptance for particular versions of history are often hard-fought (Conway 2008). This applies to movement history, too. Getting Martin Luther King, Jr. Day made an official American holiday undoubtedly has had cultural effects. But has it changed who gets what from American political institutions? We do not know. Savelsberg and King (2005) argue that differences in the way the United States and Germany commemorate the past is in part responsible for differences in how each country deals legislatively with acts of hate against vulnerable groups. Analogous studies might probe the connections between the commemoration of movements and legislative or policy outcomes. Focusing instead on individual attitudes, Griffin and Bollen (2009) found that survey respondents who spontaneously evoked the American struggle for civil rights as an important historical moment evinced more liberal racial beliefs. Together, these studies point to strong connections between culture and policy, and suggest that winning the battle over how the past is storied may have tangible effects.

Stories as Data and Method

Much social movement research involves interviewing activists, who recount, usually in narrative form, their experiences in a movement or movements. Whether or not they rely primarily on interviews, scholars often analyze movements and movement organizations in terms of their rise and fall. But scholarship on narrative points to problems with both strategies. The notion that one can use activists' stories as a transparent window onto movement developments and processes is questionable. One of the things that movements do, we know, is to help participants to recount new stories about themselves. Indeed, sometimes participants are strategically coached on how to tell their stories in a way that will win them public support (Plummer 1995; Whittier 2009; Braunstein 2012). Winners and losers in contentious episodes tell different stories after the fact (Auyero 2002). These are fascinating processes. But they make clear the limitations of interviews for explaining what happened in past movements.

Scholars of narrative have taken two positions with respect to the stories told in interviews. One holds that the life stories people tell offer enough in the way of factual data that such stories can be verified (Bertaux 2003). Collect enough stories and the result should be a fairly accurate account of events. The other position on narrative is that empirical accuracy is not the point. People perform selves in the stories they tell. Narrative analysis can provide insight into key conflicts and turning points in a life, shedding light on how people experienced historical developments in patterned ways (see Riessman 2001 for a good example). Either way, supplementing individual stories with documentary sources and/or ethnographic observation undoubtedly yields a fuller picture both of events and experience (Auyero 2002).

Representing movements' trajectories in narrative form poses different problems. Narratives have a beginning, middle, and end. Since we take the beginning of the story as the beginning of when things start to matter ("once upon a time"), we may not question the chronological starting point of an analysis even though a different starting point would yield a different analysis. Or take narrative's dependence on characters whose actions drive events and whose fates tender normative conclusions. The protagonists of stories stand in for larger groups or identities yet stories often do not specify the criteria for their representativeness. Difference within groups or in experiences may be obscured as a result. In analyses of past contention, we may talk about "challengers," that is, the story's protagonists, without fully exploring their internally differentiated, tenuously unified, and emergent character.

Another danger stems from the fact that narratives smuggle explanation into description, thus obscuring the fact that what came before a particular development may not be responsible for it. Narratives relax the demands of causal explanation. "Following, not verifying, the story is essential to successful narrative," Griffin (1993: 1099) observes. Griffin recommends that analysts pose counterfactuals at critical causal junctures to determine whether a particular event would have occurred had certain antecedent conditions not been present. In another analytic strategy, Bearman, Faris, and Moody (1999) use network methods to model connections among events as a way to specify the relevant beginnings and endings of historical episodes. Franzosi (2004) uses the storied form of newspaper data to analyze patterns of Italian strikes and the rise of Italian fascism. Wada (2004) does the same to account for why Mexicans shifted from making social claims to political ones in a context of neoliberalism.

Conclusion

People in movements, like people outside them, tell stories all the time. The task for social movement scholars is to figure out why the stories activists tell sometimes lead people to enlist in the cause, provide favorable coverage of it, support it financially, and enact policies in line with it—and sometimes to do none of those things. We have argued that, as much as stories' form and content, the context in which stories are heard matters for their effectiveness. We have drawn special attention to the institutional contexts in which activists are compelled to tell their stories, and to the tensions activists face between telling institutionally appropriate stories and telling what in fact might be more effective political stories.

We have also probed the cultural contexts in which activists' stories are heard, or better, the cultural backdrop of beliefs, assumptions, and feeling norms against which activists' stories are heard. While the stories that gain traction often seem to be the ones that are simple, coherent, and aligned with deep cultural values, research suggests that none of those may be the case. Instead, we have just begun to scratch the surface of what makes stories seem to hang together and seem to reflect reality straightforwardly—even as they constitute it.

Future work should probe these issues. The political consequences of popular stories also warrant more attention. We need to know more about the points in the policy-making process at which movement stories are most influential. We also need to know much more about how contention over popular memories affects institutional practices. In other words, are the rewards of winning only symbolic? Finally, we urge more systematic comparison of cultural forms such as stories, arguments, frames, and identities as they figure in processes of contention. For example, when are stories more effective than statistics in persuading policy makers to support the movement's cause? Are some groups more receptive to arguments than stories (see e.g., Ghoshal 2009)? The study of culture in movements has advanced far enough that we should be able to tease out culture's constitutive elements in accounting for culture's role in contention.

Notes

1. We use the term "narrative" and "story" interchangeably. Many scholars have distinguished between the two, but they have done so in so many ways that we have opted instead to use more specific terms such as background narrative where appropriate.
2. Scholars typically describe narratives as accounts of past events. However, Gibson (2012) makes a plausible case for treating anticipated events as narratives.

References

Andrews, Molly. (2007). *Shaping History: Narratives of Political Change*. Cambridge: Cambridge University Press.
Appel, Markus, and Richter, Tobias. (2007). "Persuasive Effects of Fictional Narratives Increase Over Time," *Media Psychology*. 10: 113–134.

Armstrong, Elizabeth A. and Bernstein, Mary. (2008). "Culture, Power, and Institutions: A Multi-institutional Politics Approach to Social Movements," *Sociological Theory*. 26(1): 74–99.

Armstrong, Elizabeth A. and Crage, Suzanna. M. (2006). "Movements and Memory: The Making of the Stonewall Myth," *American Sociological Review*. 71(5): 724–751.

Auyero, Javier. (2002). "The Judge, the Cop, and the Queen of Carnival: Ethnography, Storytelling, and the (Contested) Meanings of Protest," *Theory and Society*. 31(2): 15–187.

Bal, Mieke. (1985). *Narratology: Introduction to the Theory of Narrative*, trans. C. van Boheemen. Toronto: University of Toronto Press.

Baumgartner, Frank R., Berry, Jeffrey M., Hojnacki, Marie, Leech, Beth L. and Kimball, David C. (2009). *Lobbying and Policy Change: Who Wins, Who Loses, and Why*. Chicago: University of Chicago Press.

Bearman, Peter, Faris, Robert, and Moody, James (1999). "Blocking the Future: New Solutions for Old Problems in Historical Social Science," *Social Science History*. 23: 501–533.

Bertaux, Daniel. (2003). "The Usefulness of Life Stories for a Realist and Meaningful Sociology." In *Biographical Research in Eastern Europe: Altered Lives and Broken Biographies*, edited by R. Humphrey, R. Miller, and E. Zdravomyslova, 39–52. Burlington: Ashgate Publishing Company.

Blommaert, Jan. (2001). "Investigating Narrative Inequality: African Asylum Seekers' Stories in Belgium," *Discourse & Society*. 12(4): 413–449.

Braunstein, Ruth. (2012). "Storytelling in Liberal Religious Advocacy," *Journal for the Scientific Study of Religion*. 51(1): 110–127.

Conway, Brian. (2008). Local Conditions, Global Environment and Transnational Discourses in Memory Work: The Case of Bloody Sunday (1972)," *Memory Studies*. 1: 187–209.

Davis, Joseph E. (2005). *Accounts of Innocence: Sexual Abuse, Trauma, and the Self.* Chicago: University of Chicago Press.

della Porta, Donatella, and Rucht, Dierter, eds. (2012). *Meeting Democracy: Power and Deliberation in Global Justice Movements*. New York: Cambridge University Press.

Epstein, Steven. (1996). *Impure Science: AIDS, Activism, and the Politics of Knowledge*. Berkeley: University of California Press.

Esacove, Anne W. (2010). "Love Matches Heteronormativity, Modernity, and AIDS Prevention in Malawi," *Gender & Society*. 24(1): 83–109.

Ferree, Myra Marx, Gamson, William A., Gerhards, Jurgen, and Rucht, Dieter. (2002). *Shaping Abortion Discourse: Democracy and the Public Sphere in Germany and the United States*. New York: Cambridge University Press.

Fine, G. A. (1995). "Public Narration and Group Culture: Discerning Discourse in Social Movements." In *Social Movements and Culture*, edited by H. Johnston and B. Klandermans, 127–143. Minneapolis: University of Minnesota Press.

Fine, Gary Alan. (1999). "John Brown's Body: Elites, Heroic Embodiment, and the Legitimation Of Political Violence," *Social Problems*. 46: 225–249.

Franzosi, Roberto. (2004). *From Words to Numbers: Narrative, Data, and Social Science*. Vol. 22. Cambridge: Cambridge University Press.

Fraser, Nancy, and Gordon, Linda. (1994). A Genealogy of Dependency: Tracing a Keyword of the U.S. Welfare State," *Signs*. 19: 309–336.

Gaby, Sarah, and Caren, Neal. (2012). "Occupy Online: How Cute Old Men and Malcolm X Recruited 400,000 US Users to OWS on Facebook," *Social Movement Studies*. 11(3–4): 367–374.

Gamson, William A. (2002). "How Storytelling Can be Empowering." In *Culture in Mind: Toward a Sociology of Culture and Cognition*, edited by K. A. Cerulo, 187–198. New York: Routledge.

Gerteis, Joseph. (2002). "The Possession of Civic Virtue: Movement Narratives of Race and Class in the Knights of Labor," *American Journal of Sociology*. 108(3): 580–615.

Gibson, David R. (2012). *Talk at the Brink: Deliberation and Decision Making during the Cuban Missile Crisis*. Princeton, NJ: Princeton Univ. Press.

Ghoshal, Raj. (2009). "Argument Forms, Frames, and Value Conflict: Persuasion in the Case of Same-sex Marriage," *Cultural Sociology*. 3(1): 76–101.

Green, Melanie C. and Brock, Timothy C. (2000). "The Role of Transportation in the Persuasiveness of Public Narratives," *Journal of Personality and Social Psychology*. 79: 701–721.

Griffin, Larry J. (1993). "Narrative, Event-Structure Analysis, and Causal Interpretation in Historical Sociology," *American Journal of Sociology*. 98: 1094–1133.

Griffin, Larry J., and Bollen, Kenneth A. (2009). "What Do These Memories Do? Civil Rights Remembrance and Racial Attitudes," *American Sociological Review*. 74(4): 594–614.

Haltom William, and McCann, Michael. (2004). *Distorting the Law: Politics, Media, and the Litigation Crisis*. Chicago: University of Chicago Press.

Higgins, Lorraine, and Brush, Lisa. (2006). "Personal Experience Narrative and Public Debate: Writing the Wrongs of Welfare," *College Composition and Communication*. 57: 694–729.

Irvine Janice. (2002). *Talk About Sex: The Battles over Sex Education in the United States*. Berkeley: University of California Press.

Jansen, Robert S. (2007). "Resurrection and Appropriation: Reputational Trajectories, Memory Work, and the Political Use of Historical Figures," *American Journal of Sociology*. 112: 953–1007.

Jones, Michael D. (2013). "Cultural Characters and Climate Change: How Heroes Shape our Perception of Climate Science," *Social Science Quarterly*. 95: 1–39.

Jones, Michael D. and McBeth, Mark K. (2010). "A Narrative Policy Framework: Clear Enough to be Wrong?" *Policy Studies Journal*. 38(2): 329–353.

Kalcik, Susan. (1975). "… like Ann's gynecologist or the time I was almost raped." In *Women and Folklore*, edited by C. R. Farrer, 3–11. Austin: University of Texas Press.

Kane, Anne. (2000). "Narratives Of Nationalism: Constructing Irish National Identity During the Land War, 1879–1882," *National Identities*. 2(3): 245–264.

Khalili, Laleh. (2008). "Commemorating Battles and Massacres in the Palestinian Refugee Camps of Lebanon," *American Behavioral Scientist*. 51(11): 1562–1574.

Labov, William, and Waletsky, Joshua. (1967). "Narrative Analysis: Oral Versions of Personal Experience." In *Essays on the Verbal and Visual Arts*, edited by J. Helm, 12–44. Seattle: University of Washington Press.

Luker, Kristen. (1984). *Abortion and the Politics of Motherhood*. Berkeley: University of California Press.

McGough, Lucy S. (1994). *Child Witnesses: Fragile Voices in the American Legal System*. New Haven: Yale University Press.

Meyer, David S. (2006). "Claiming Credit: Stories of Movement Influence as Outcomes," *Mobilization*. 11: 281–298.

Mische, Ann. (2003). "Cross-talk in Movements: Reconceiving the Culture-Network Link." In *Social Movements and Networks: Relational Approaches to Collective Action*, edited by M. Diani and D. McAdam, 258–280. London: Oxford University Press.

Nance, Kimberly A. (2006). *Can Literature Promote Justice? Trauma Narrative and Social Action in Latin American Testimonio*. Nashville: Vanderbilt University Press.

Nepstad, Sharon Erickson. (2001). "Creating Transnational Solidarity: The Use of Narrative in the U.S.-Central America Peace Movement," *Mobilization*. 6: 21–36.

Nicholls, Walter. (2013). *The DREAMers: How the Undocumented Youth Movement Transformed the Immigrant Rights Debate*. Stanford: Stanford University Press.

Owens, Lynn. (2009). *Cracking Under Pressure: Narrating the Decline of the Amsterdam Squatters Movements*. Amsterdam: University of Amsterdam Press.

Plummer, Kenneth. (1995). *Telling Sexual Stories: Power, Change, and Social Worlds*. New York: Routledge.

Polkinghorne, Donald E. (1988). *Narrative Knowing and the Human Sciences*. Albany: SUNY Press.

Polletta, Francesca. (2004). "Culture In and Outside Institutions." In *Authority in Contention (Research in Social Movements, Conflicts and Change, Volume 25)*, edited by D. J. Myers and D. M. Cress, 161–183. New York: Emerald Group Publishing Limited.

Polletta, Francesca. (2006). *It Was Like a Fever: Storytelling in Protest and Politics*. Chicago: University Chicago Press.

Polletta, Francesca. (2012). "Popular Beliefs About Storytelling." In *Varieties of Narrative Analysis*, edited by J. A. Holstein and J. F. Gubrium, 229–250. Thousand Oaks: Sage Publications.

Polletta, Francesca, and Gardner, Beth Gharrity. (2015). "Emerging Trends in the Study of Culture and Social Movements." In *Emerging Trends in the Social and Behavioral Sciences*, edited by R. A. Scott and S. M. Kosslyn. Hoboken, NJ: Wiley.

Polletta, Francesca, Chen, Pang Ching Bobby, Gardner, Beth Gharrity, and Motes, Alice. (2011). The Sociology of Storytelling," *Annual Review of Sociology*. 37: 109–130.

Polletta, Francesca, Trigoso, Monica, Adams, Britni, and Ebner, Amanda. (2013). "The Limits of Plot: Accounting for How Women Interpret Stories of Sexual Assault.," *American Journal of Cultural Sociology*. 1(3): 289–320.

Riessman, Catherine K. (2001). "Analysis of Personal Narratives." In *Handbook of Interview Research: Context and Method*, edited by J. F. Gubrium and J. A. Holstein, 695–710. Thousand Oaks: Sage Publications.

Salzman, Jason. (2003). *Making the News: A Guide for Activists and Nonprofits*, revised edition Boulder: Westview.

Savelsberg, Joachim J., and King, Ryan D. (2005). "Institutionalizing Collective Memories of Hate: Law and Law Enforcement in Germany and the United States," *American Journal of Sociology*. 111(2): 579–616.

Schneiberg, Marc, and Clemens, Elisabeth S. (2006). "The Typical Tools for the Job: Research Strategies in Institutional Analysis," *Sociological Theory*. 24: 195–227.

Schultz, Vicki. (1990). "Telling Stories About Women and Work: Judicial Interpretations of Sex Segregation in the Workplace in Title VII Cases Raising the Lack of Interest Argument," *Harvard Law Review*. 103: 1749–1843.

Slater, Michael D., and Rouner, Donna. (2002). "Entertainment-education and Elaboration Likelihood: Understanding the Processing of Narrative Persuasion," *Communication Theory*. 12: 173–191.

Smith, Jackie, McCarthy, John D., McPhail, Clark, and Augustyn, Boguslaw. (2001). "From Protest to Agenda Building: Description Bias in Media Coverage of Protest Events in Washington, D.C.," *Social Forces*. 79(4) 1397–1423.

Snow, David A. (2005). "Social Movements as Challenges to Authority: Resistance to an Emerging Conceptual Hegemony." In *Authority in Contention (Research in Social*

Movements, Conflicts and Change, Volume 25), edited by D. J. Meyers and D. M. Cress, 3–25. New York: Emerald Group Publishing Limited.

Sobieraj, Sarah. (2010). "Reporting Conventions: Journalists, Activists, and the Thorny Struggle for Political Visibility," *Social Problems*. 57(4): 505–528.

Somers, Margaret R. (1992). "Narrativity, Narrative Identity, and Social Action: Rethinking English Working-class Formation," *Social Science History*. 16(4): 591–629.

Somers, Margaret R. and Block, Fred. (2005). "From Poverty to Perversity: Ideas, Markets, and Institutions Over 200 Years of Welfare Debate," *American Sociological Review*. 70(2): 260–287.

Steinberg, Marc W. and Ewick, Patricia. (2013). "The Work Stories Do: Charles Tilly's Legacy on the Provision of Reasons, Storytelling, and Trust in Contentious Performances," In *Advances in the Visual Analysis of Social Movements (Research in Social Movements, Conflicts and Change, Volume 35)*, edited by N. Doerr, A. Mattoni, and S. Teune, 147–173. New York: Emerald Group Publishing Limited.

Stewart, Julie. (2012). "Fiction Over Facts: How Competing Narrative Forms Explain Policy in a New Immigration Destination," *Sociological Forum*. 27(3): 591–616.

Stone, Deborah. A. (1989). "Causal Stories and the Formation of Policy Agendas," *Political Science Quarterly*. 104(2): 281–300.

Viterna, Jocelyn. (2013). *Women in War: The Micro-processes of Mobilization in El Salvador*. New York: Oxford University Press.

Voss, Kim. (1998). "Claim Making and the Framing of Defeats: The Interpretation of Losses by American and British Labor Activists, 1886–1895." In *Challenging Authority: The Historical Study of Contentious Politics*, edited by M. P. Hanagan, L. P. Moch, and W.T. Brake, 136–148. Minneapolis: University of Minnesota Press.

Wada, Takeshi. (2004). "Event Analysis of Claim Making in Mexico: How are Social Protests Transformed into Political Protests?" *Mobilization: An International Quarterly*. 9(3): 241–257.

Whittier, Nancy. (2009). *The Politics of Child Sexual Abuse: Emotion, Social Movements, and the State*. New York: Oxford University Press.

CHAPTER 35

THE ART OF SOCIAL MOVEMENT

RON EYERMAN

THE arts, most particularly music, are an established part of social movement reper-toire (Eyerman and Jamison 1998; Roscigno and Danaher 2004; Reed 2005; Roy 2010; Rosenthal and Flacks 2012). Artistic representations are important to internal move-ment dynamics such as recruitment, mobilizing solidarity, and forming collective iden-tity. They are also important in communicating movement ideas to the wider world and creating a reservoir of cultural resources for future reference. Social movements can be considered expressive public performances that are meaningful and which provoke meaningful response. Charles Tilly (1999) calls social movements "repeated public dis-plays." One can identify at least three audiences for such displays, the internal dynamics of the movement itself, those it opposes and, finally, the general public of bystanders and potential supporters (Eyerman 2006).

A social movement emerges when groups of disparate and ever-changing individu-als sense they are united and moving in the same direction. People and organizations move in and out of social movements, but this sense of collective engagement, continu-ous over time and place, is what makes a movement. To achieve this, collective identity and solidarity must be forged, a process which necessarily involves marking off those inside from those outside. The arts play a significant role in such boundary drawing, as well as in the construction and maintenance of internal cohesiveness. In addition, the arts can be a tool in opening public debate around the issues that movements consider important. Music, as activist-performers from Pete Seeger and Woody Guthrie to Billy Bragg knew so well, draws and fuses a crowd. In skillful hands, music is also a tool in popular education. One can covey a political message in a very amenable way and, at the same time, draw the bonds and boundaries of community. Films, most particularly documentaries, and theater can be used in a similar way (Adams 2002; Andits 2013). Through artistic representation movements identify and communicate who they, what they are for, and what they are against. Needless to say, the content of this message will vary across the political spectrum, but the forms remain quite similar.

INTERNAL MOVEMENT DYNAMICS

Artistic expression and representation are important recruitment tools, helping to draw sympathizers into a movement. Music and collective singing are obvious examples. With the simple transformation of popular hymns, the Swedish-American labor organizer Joe Hill (Joel Hagglund), helped to recruit many into the International Workers of the World (IWW) in the early part of the twentieth century. More than 100 years later, singer-activists Joan Baez and Billy Bragg "dreamed" of Joe Hill at rallies and concerts, as they engaged their audiences with memories of past protest: "I dreamed I saw Joe Hill last night, alive as you and me." Making use of popular melodies for political purpose is a common tactic. While Hill parodied religious musical traditions, others in the American civil rights movement transformed the tunes of a commercial popular culture into mobilizing manifestos. Broadening our notion of "art" to include advertisements and graphic design, more contemporary movements such as ACT UP and Occupy Wall Street, use the visual forms common in the commercial world in a subversive way. Artfully conceived posters and stickers have been a staple of movement expression, communication, and recruitment at least since the 1960s. The evolving digital media will make this even more accessible and instantaneous.

Another aspect of internal movement dynamics where the arts make a significant contribution are in collective bonding, forging group solidarity and strength. Movements bind individuals together in common projects through collective identification and forms of social interaction, such as public demonstration and other collective rituals. There is no better mechanism for this than collective singing and visual displays of solidarity through dress and other symbolic forms (Doerr et al., this volume). Think of the Orange Revolution in the Ukraine, where the wearing of brightly colored clothing signified solidarity within a movement and projected this outward. The American Civil Rights Movement is perhaps best known for its transformation of traditional practices for political purpose, but similar processes were at work in South Africa as opposition forces built their struggle against the apartheid regime. Building on traditions rooted in religious celebration and the slave experience, African Americans created a powerful force for civil rights and inclusion in the dominant society. Similarly, South African oppositional movements transformed long-standing cultural traditions, including voice and dance, into expressions of protest which eventually led to fundamental political change. Within these movements and many others, forms of cultural expression became sources of solidarity and empowerment.

Collective singing and music more generally can provide courage and resilience in trying situations, such as being confronted by violent opposition or imprisonment. This was the case in both the American and South African struggles against racism. College students reacted similarly during various building occupations in the United States and elsewhere, reviving musical practices inherited from earlier protest traditions. Labor struggles around the world involved similar practices, where music and other forms of cultural expression provided solace and solidarity in the face of great opposition.

Hearing a piece of music or viewing an image can invoke a sense of identification even in the absence of others. The strains of a national anthem or of a recognized protest song can stir emotional response and memory. This latter example points to another aspect of artistic representation in the internal dynamics of social movements, namely the forming of collective identity. Artistic representations carry the potential of collective representation, becoming the means through which individuals come to recognize themselves as part of a group. This is perhaps most apparent in music and especially in collective singing, where form and content meld easily together. Singing together binds individual and group. At the same time, a common message, the text of a song, can convey a common vision and purpose. Such practices create group solidarity. When done in public, collective singing becomes a demonstration of collective identity where participants exemplify who they are and what they stand for.

Movement Art as Communication

The last observation points to the second role of the arts in social movement: communicating ideas and emotions to those outside the movement, including potential supporters and the public at large. Social movements demonstrate who they are and what they stand for through public display. Tilly's (2003) well-known WUNC, the necessity of displaying worthiness, unity, numbers, and commitment, applies to movements generally, as they publically perform their collectivity. Clothing as Tarlo (1996) has shown, and other symbols, such as flags and banners, along with distinctive music and dance, are an important part of this. Tarlo reveals how Gandhi's independence movement developed material objects, bits of clothing, and the traditional tools of their manufacture to convey opposition. Gandhi's famous spinning wheel now appears on the Indian national flag, while the cloth cap he donned still carries its symbolic weight. Movements make use of visual, textual, and sonic sources in order to be seen and heard. Social movement scholars have long recognized this but have only recently begun to develop analytic tools and research methodologies to take them more seriously into account (Doerr 2014).

Beyond symbols and invented traditions, more formal art works play a part in displaying and evoking collective feeling. Artists and art works of all sorts were a central part of the global movement against America's war in Vietnam. In 1965, as the antiwar movement slowly escalated at pace with direct military engagement, the American artist Carolee Schneemann filmed newspaper photographs to create powerful images of the pain and suffering of war in a work entitled "Viet Flakes": (Israel 2013). She was one of hundreds of artists who actively participated in the social movements of the time. Even as such works were displayed in formal gallery or museum settings, the political meaning could be ascertained, at least during the highpoints of protest. This can also be true of seemingly abstract or non-representational artworks, such as Wally Hedrick's "black works," which were layers of black paint on canvas. One such painting bore the title "Vietnam." When it was viewed in 1968, its meaning must have been very suggestive to those who viewed it, perhaps even more so than the representational protest art of the period.

Artists helped to give a visual coherence to the protest. During periods of intense protest, established art institutions can become movement spaces, whether intended or not. Perhaps the most well known piece of political art, Picasso's "Guernica," became an important symbol not only for anti-fascist movements even when displayed at New York's Museum of Modern Art (MoMA). The painting was a major source inspiration for American artists seeking points of reference for political art. The hegemony of modernism and abstract art in the United States in the 1950s helped to turn the art world and artists against political art. When searching for reference in constructing such art during the Vietnam War, American artists turned to Guernica, if not Picasso himself, for a model (Israel 2013).

In addition to creating art works with a political content, artists have often lent their names, performances, and even money to support and help identify movement causes. Artists have been important in lending credence to political protest through signing petitions, publicizing manifestos, and donating their work. This has been true even of works with no obvious political content. Popular musicians were important public figures in the American civil rights movement, the Chinese protests in 1989, and in the Arab Spring revolts. The documentary "The Square" (2013) about the wave of protests in Cairo's Tahrir Square reveals the power of music as well as the danger facing musician-activists. Movements often turn to popular artists, as well as art, to legitimate their cause. On the other side, the global waves of feminism and of women's movements generated empowering art works and stimulated artistic as well as political movements. Viewing these works today recalls the visions and evokes some of the power of those movements. In this way, art works can become transmitters of protest traditions, even when the movements that inspired them may have ended in terms of public protest. An example is the wave of protests in the Ukraine in early 2014 which eventually led to the fall of the seated government and then dissipated. Calling this an "unfinished revolution," the *New York Times* (30 April 2014: C1) reporting on an exhibition at the National Art Museum of Ukraine, stated "the demonstrations have ended, for now, but Ukrainians continue to turn to culture to assert and define themselves in a time of upheaval, just as their counterparts have in recent years after uprisings from Cairo to Rio de Janeiro." If the notion of cycles of protest has any validity, one can argue that artworks of all sorts provide lasting retainers of the ideas and values that past or passing social movements expressed.

In addition to visual images and music (both recorded and performed), literature, theater and film are also important carriers of protest traditions. Part of the collective memory of protest, these aesthetic forms embed and disperse movement ideas and practices. Poets and playwrights inspired rebellious national liberation movements around the globe over the past centuries. This was clearly the case in Ireland, Poland, Hungary, and the Czech Republic where the poet and playwright Vaclav Havel became its first president in 1993. This was equally true in Africa, Asia, and South America. While perhaps not as directly inspirational, commercial films and documentaries, intended or not, serve as carriers of protest traditions. The documentary "Berkeley in the Sixties," which chronicles the rise and transformation of the Free Speech Movement at the University of California at Berkeley in the early 1960s, provides a rousing introduction to social movements to younger generations of students. Street murals and other forms of outsider art can have a similar function. The murals painted on the side of university buildings in Mexico City recall social struggles of previous eras, and while they may have become part of the taken-for-granted urban landscape, they still serve as reminders of protest traditions. Social movements carve themselves out of past traditions, reinventing repertoires in new contexts. Here again the arts continue to play an important role.

Representing the Other

In their performances, social movements articulate what they stand for by representing who and what they are against. The arts are important here. A well-known song that emerged out of the organizing struggles of American coal miners in the 1930s asked "Which side are you on?" The lyrics made clear that there were only two sides from which to chose, one was for or against the union. On the other side stood "the thug" and behind him, the mine owner. The song, written by the wife of an organizer, became a staple in the American protest music tradition and was sung at rallies and demonstrations although the 1960s, where the named other was altered to fit the new situation. Activists have employed street theater to identify and name the other they opposed. During the Vietnam War protests in the United States, the San Francisco Mime Troupe acted out their skits in parks and on streets across the country, portraying villains, from the chemical companies that produced napalm to political and military leaders. Using techniques developed by Brecht they created a "guerrilla theater" that was mobile and effective. One of the most powerful uses of Brecht's theater of pedagogical protest techniques was "The Laramie Project" (2000), a traveling theater production about the murder of a gay man in Laramie, Wyoming. While not street theater, the actors speak directly to the audience, making clear the distinction between "we" and "they" at the same time and the social distance between actor and audience is disrupted. The project remains a powerful force in articulating some of the concerns of the LGBT movements. Novels, such as *Uncle Tom's Cabin* (1852) which helped fuel the Abolitionist movement, have also been important in naming those a movement opposes. In its popular melodramatic way, Stowe's novel not only created heroes and villains for its contemporary audience, its title character (Uncle Tom) provided the civil rights movement with a rallying counter-figure. No black activist in the 1960s wanted to be an "Uncle Tom."

More directly connected to public protests in the naming of the "other," movement artists create highly visible and clearly identifiable "others" to mobilize against. While the commonplace use of placards and chanted slogans might not qualify as art, the guerilla notion associated with the San Fransisco Mime Troupe has been adopted by artist/activists around the world. The Guerilla Girls, self-named "feminist masked avengers" working in the agitprop tradition, create interactive street art, such as a pink painted wall declaring: "I'm not a feminist, but if I were, this is what I would complain about….," with a large blank space for viewers to fill in. Here the audience names those it opposes. Graffiti and other forms of street art were very prominent in the Arab Spring protests that shook the Middle East and North Africa in 2013, where caricatures of dictators were sprayed onto walls along with mobilizing slogans. The concept and practice of "guerilla art" has now passed into the social movement lexicon and one might even call it a movement in itself.

MOVEMENT AGAINST THE ARTS

It seems fitting to discuss movements against the arts in the context of the art of movements. Authoritarian regimes and their related movements have very often viewed artists and the arts with suspicion. Nazism is a well-known example, where claims to artistic freedom and autonomy were met with the severest forms of repression. The infamous "degenerate" art exhibition in Munich in 1937 ordered by Adolf Hitler to display all that was wrong with artistic modernism was only part of a wider attempt to purge German culture of what were considered to be polluting tendencies. Certain forms of music, literature, film, and theater were deemed equally threatening to "purity" and national health. To such regimes, control of the arts is considered essential to control of the population. This has been equally true of dictatorial regimes in Greece, Spain, and Latin America. It is also true in Moslem countries, where religious based regimes and movements have made art and artists targets of sanction and repression. The *fatwa* issued by Ayatollah Khomeini of Iran against the author Salman Rushdie was both a life-threatening sanction and a mobilizing tool. Visual representations of the author were important in mobilizing those who had most likely read or even heard of the book. The same can be said of the more recent Muhammad cartoons, where the enemy was more collective than individual, though threats to individuals were also made. Any claims to free expression, from artists to intellectuals and journalists, are threatening to authoritarian regimes, especially as they are newly forming or unstable. There is an underside to such repression however, as it often unites as it forces underground such individuals. Authoritarian attempts at social control help to create subcultures which may actually spur artistic unity as well as development. Franco's regime in Spain can be credited with catalyzing the emergence of a socially reflective film industry after his death, similar developments have occurred in Iran, both amongst exiles living abroad and within the country itself.

THE ART OF SOCIAL MOVEMENT

When connected to social movements, art practices form the core of the symbolic and expressive aspects of social movements. Eyerman and Jamison (1991, 1998) use the term "cognitive praxis" to call attention to such knowledge bearing and knowledge producing practices. For them, movement art is truth-bearing; revealing something about the world as it is and as it might be. When created within movement contexts, art reveals truth as the movement sees it. The music of social movements, for example, tells the story of the movement as much as it is meant to mobilize activists and recruit new participants. At the same time and through the same process, artistic representations and expressions make the movement visible to itself. Movement art in other words, is part of the coming-to-be of a social movement. The art created within a social movement objectifies the ideas and emotions which motivate and guide that movement, providing a mirror for the movement to know itself. The same processes of objectification and representation make it possible to transmit protest traditions over time and space. Objectified and materialized, the art of social movements re-creates protest traditions which become ready-made resources for other movements. Such traditions are more than mere resources to be mobilized, for they embody a way of knowing and being-in-the world. As such, they are more than tools in a protest tool kit; to adopt them is to become them. At the same time, movement art provides a glimpse of how the world ought to be or might have been. Even at its most angry and critical, the protest art of social movements contains a utopian moment, articulating and exemplifying how the world might be, should the aims of the movement be achieved.

As a form of communication, movement art addresses its audience on an equal plane, as an audience capable of understanding, of being reasoned with, and moved. In this sense movement art exemplifies a central ideal of movements, to recruit as many to their cause as possible. This is not to imply that all social movements are democratic, but merely that they are necessarily open to new participants in ways different from other forms of collective behavior. Unlike formal organizations, social movements do not have members, they have participants and supporters who must be constantly recruited and incorporated, fused with knowledge and power. Movement art is central to that purpose.

References

Adams, Jacqueline (2002). "Art in Social Movements: Shantytown Women's Protests in Pinochet's Chile." *Sociological Forum.* 17(1): 21–56.

Andits, Petra (2013). "Movies and Movements." In *Wiley-Blackwell Encyclopedia of Social Movements,* edited by David Snow et al. Malden, MA: Blackwell Publishing.

Doerr, Nicole (2014). "Working with Images." In *Methodological Practices in Social Movement Research,* edited by Donatella della Porta. Oxford: Oxford University Press.

Doerr, Nicole et al. (this volume). "Visuals in Social Movements." In *Oxford Handbook of Social Movements.* New York: Oxford University Press.

Eyerman, Ron (2006). "Performing Opposition or, How Movements Move." In *Social Performance,* edited by Alexander et al. Cambridge: Cambridge University Press.

Eyerman, Ron and Jamison, Andrew (1991). *Social Movements: A Cognitive Approach.* Cambridge: Polity Press.

Eyerman, Ron, and Jamison, Andrew (1998). *Music and Social Movements*. Cambridge: Cambridge University Press.

Israel, Matthew (2013). *Kill for Peace American Artists Against the Vietnam War*. Austin: University of Texas Press.

Reed, T. V. (2005). *The Art of Protest*. Minneapolis: University of Minnesota Press.

Roscigno, Vincent, and Danaher, William (2004). *The Voice of Southern Labor*. Minneapolis: University of Minnesota Press.

Rosenthal, Rob, and Flacks, Richard (2012). *Playing for Change*. Boulder, CO: Paradigm Publishers.

Roy, William (2010). *Reds, Whites and Blues: Social Movement, Folk Music, and Race in America*. Princeton, NJ: Princeton University Press.

Tarlo, Emma (1996). *Clothing Matters*. London: Hurst & Company.

Tilly, Charles (1999). "From Interactions to Outcomes in Social Movements." In *How Social Movements Matter*, edited by Mario Giugni, Doug McAdam, and Charles Tilly, 253–270. Minneapolis: University of Minnesota Press.

Tilly, Charles (2003). *Collective Violence*. New York: Cambridge University Press.

CHAPTER 36

VISUALS IN SOCIAL MOVEMENTS

NICOLE DOERR, ALICE MATTONI,
AND SIMON TEUNE

INTRODUCTION

APPROACHING social movements as visual phenomena has not been at the core of scholarly interest. There is no doubt among researchers that the visual forms in which movements express themselves matter. Moreover, it is hardly controversial to assume that movements are pivotally perceived through vision. Thus, clothing and bodily gestures, images and symbols, posters and videos are not only crucial forms of movements' representation but also potentially rich materials to answer central research questions in social movement studies. However, like other domains of the social sciences, work on social movements has kept its focus on textual sources in the form of manifestos, leaflets, websites, newspaper articles or interviews, while visual information, if used, has remained an illustrative appendage.

Despite the dominant focus on written texts, the past decades have seen a lively debate on visuals in many disciplines in the field of humanities and, also, in the social sciences. In the context of what was emphatically referred to as the "pictorial turn" (Mitchell 1994), scholars emphasized the centrality of vision in contemporary societies. In disciplines such as art history and media studies, anthropology and sociology "visual culture" was identified as a crucial field of knowledge. In this perspective, the production, circulation, and interpretation of images is part of the collective elaboration of meaning and thus an intrinsically political process (Rogoff 1998). Even though the concept of symbolic politics has played an important role in the understanding of political processes and political culture (Edelman 1964), political scientists were hesitant to transfer the debate on images to their field of study. However, some scholars argued for the recognition of visual analysis in political science (Mueller and Oezcan 2007) and proposed appropriate methods (Mueller 2007; Doerr and Milman 2014). Triggered by the terrorist attacks of September

11, philosophers and cultural theorists discussed the artistic and political relevance of image events such as 9/11 that take place in real time on a global scale (Baudrillard 2001). In the wake of this debate, a few political scientists started to analyze empirically what exactly constitutes the alleged power of images (see, e.g., Bleiker 2001). Others criticized the focus on a somewhat mysterious "power" of images urging scholars to systematically explore which *actors* actually create, distribute, and interpret contested images (see, for instance, Falk 2010). Finally, technological developments added to the attention to visual aspects of political processes. Digital photography has enlarged the number of poten-tial producers of images and it allowed for low-cost and immediate ways of distribution. Images of torture that spread during the war in Iraq (Sontag 2004) brought the attention to ordinary people, protesters, and their opponents as actors in the diffusion of social and visual media in contentious global publics.

The rising interest in visual studies has also started to echo in the field of social move-ments. In her analysis of popular art in Pinochet's Chile, Jacqueline Adams under-lines the potential use of visual studies for established concepts of social movement research: "movements can use art to carry out framing work, mobilize resources, communicate information about themselves, and, finally, as a symbol of the move-ment" (Adams 2002: 22). Even though visual studies could be combined with different approaches to social movements, most of the relevant literature developed separately from what has been termed the "classical agenda" of social movement research (McAdam et al. 2001: 14–19), namely political opportunities, mobilizing structures, collective action frames, and repertoires of action. Framing approaches have already been used to under-stand both the ways in which movements are depicted and their attempts to visualize what they see at stake. However, the bulk of the contributions to the field leave classical concepts of social movement studies aside and build on more generic concepts such as visual culture, visibility, or visual discourse.

We develop our argument in this chapter along two crucial aspects, which are by no means mutually exclusive, but highlight different foci in the visual analysis of social movements. In the next section, we summarize research about the performative dimen-sion of social movements becoming visible, by focusing on collective practices that are developed to express and represent a movement's cause. We then present literature that discusses visual aspects in the mediatization of social movements to underline the fact that visualization is largely dependent on different kinds of media technologies. In the concluding section we consider some relevant lines of investigation that might deepen our understanding of both social movements and the images they are associated with.

BECOMING VISIBLE
THROUGH PERFORMANCE

A first field of interest in the visual analysis of social movements is the immediate expression of dissent in performative acts of movement constituencies. By using the concept of performance we highlight the (mainly) embodied practices of protest and the visual codes routinely used to display dissent—from wearing badges to marching in street demonstrations to sharing and commenting on activist videos on social network sites (Alexander 2011; Tilly 2008; see also Eyerman 2006). This aspect of social movements connects to two established strands of social movement research: on the one hand, the interactionist perspective building on Goffman's concepts of framing and dramaturgy; on the other hand, the socio-historical perspective that takes interest in the forms of contentious claim-making. The first strand of research subsumed under the label "framing" highlights collective attempts to make sense of social problems, their origins and the role that movements can play to bring about change. The classical framing literature touches upon visual aspects, but it does not systematically address the issue. Yet, scholars have used the concept of framing to understand the ways in which movements present themselves (Morrison and Isaac 2012; Luhtakallio 2013). The second strand of research under the rubric of "repertoires of contention" also neglected visual information. Even though Tilly, who coined the concept of repertoires, acknowledges that activists "make publicly visible collective claims" (Tilly 2008: 8), the central role of vision for the practice and understanding of protest is not very prominent in his work nor in research that builds upon Tilly's ideas (for an exception, see Leslie Wood's 2012 work on puppets).

Apart from the literature on framing and repertoires, the performative aspect of social movements has also been highlighted by authors with particular interest in the cultural embedding of contention. Scholars such as James Jasper have highlighted the creative expression of dissent that taps into the available imagery and adds to this cultural environment (Jasper 1997). Jasper is among the few canonical authors who pays explicit tribute to the role of images in the cultural dynamics of social movements (Jasper 2014). In earlier research, together with his colleague Jane Poulsen, he also describes the capacity of drastic images to invoke a "moral shock" (Jasper and Poulsen 1995) that recruits even formerly uninvolved citizens into social movement activism.

Generally, visual analysis provides potent tools to study the performance of emotions in movements. Images play a vital role in social movements' shaping of emotions from shame and anger (Halfmann and Young 2010) to irony and pride (Mattoni and Doerr 2007; Mattoni 2008). Images are used to ridicule opponents (Howell 2012) and to picture them as vicious and cruel (Streeby 2013). As Flam and Doerr (2015) demonstrate, right-wing activists in different European countries use visual tools to mobilize hatred and fear against immigrants, while global justice protesters and immigrants' right coalitions aim at breaking such visualized stereotypes. They find that right-wing groups who display and perform images of hatred needed little organizing effort to make their message visible. Activists who organized performances of solidarity with immigrants, by contrast, invested much energy in deliberative processes to make sure their challenge of visualized stereotypes reached out to different groups (Doerr 2010).

Looking at visual aspects of activist performances, the very act of taking to the streets and forming a collective body can be seen as a practice that makes a conflict visible. As Jesus Casquete (2006) shows for nationalist demonstrations in the Basque Country, demonstrations are a means both to represent and to experience a community of challengers.

This is particularly relevant in a repressive environment that seeks to blind out protest (see also Guano 2002). As with Basque nationalists, any social movement seeks to gain visibility through collective action. However, the attempts of some collective actors have been investigated in more detail. The American gay movement is a prominent example. Activists developed visual strategies such as drag performances (Taylor et al. 2004) and reappropriating the pink triangle, a symbol for gay prisoners in Nazi concentration camps (Gamson 1989). These strategies served to confront mainstream audiences with the existence and stigmatization of the gay community. The use of symbols and colors, in particular, has been the subject of several studies. Worn and displayed to mark affiliation to a common cause, such visual markers are a constituent of social movements (Linke 1988; Lahusen 1996; Goodnow 2006). The sanguine of the labor movement as well as the green, white, and purple of the Women's Social and Political Union are only two examples for colors representing movements (Sawer 2007). Colors and symbols that emerge as signifiers of political struggles lead to a more general perspective on visual aspects of social movements. Visual elements are indeed part of a larger context that might be better understood through two paramount concepts: discourse and visual culture.

Social movement theorists have discussed the role of narratives and symbols which help activists perform the perspective and experiences of disadvantaged groups in mainstream arenas of political talk (Polletta 2006) in global protest summits (Wood 2012), and in transnational movement publics (Doerr and Mattoni 2014). In this vein, empirical studies combining visual and textual discourse analysis explore the role of images and texts as a source or constraint for social movements' organizing, outreach, and fostering the diffusion of new ideas (Doerr 2010). The notion of discourse is also present in a Foucaultian perspective on vision and activism that highlights the formative gaze of normalization (Gamson 1989). Looking at the organization of lesbian, gay, bisexual, and transgender (LGBT) activists in South Africa and Namibia, two countries with an intertwined history, but contrasting legal frameworks, Ashley Currier (2012) shows that national contexts and cultural environments matter. She emphasizes the ambivalence of visibility. For people of color, those who are gender diverse, or live with obvious disabilities visibility is also connected to stigmatization and threat, whereas the invisibility of people in a normalized position has to be considered a privilege.

The second concept used to understand the context in which social movements are set is the rather loosely defined notion of visual culture. It is predominantly understood as an umbrella term that highlights the embedding of visual artifacts such as images or films in a cultural environment. The contributions that take interest in social movements from this perspective emphasize an interactionist understanding of culture and thus a focus on agency (Streeby 2013). Visual culture is a context for activism that is by no means set. It is reproduced and changed in the practices of both social movement activists and relevant counterparts. In his analysis of the Iranian Green Movement, Mazyar Lotfalian (2013) emphasizes the intertwining of street protests and an innovative use of new technologies to visualize and interpret both the protests and state repression. In a similar vein, Lina Khatib (2012) explores the country-specific conditions under which protesters across the Maghreb and Iran used images to call for protest. She underlines the contentious struggles over meaning between regimes and challengers that are fought out with images.

BECOMING VISIBLE THROUGH MEDIA

A second field of inquiry into visual aspects of social movements includes the mediatized aspect of mobilization. As it happened with other social, cultural, and political phenomena, changes at the level of the media environment brought with them deep transformations in activism as well. Mediatization processes (Krotz 2009; Couldry and Hepp 2013; Hepp 2013) indeed also affected social movements that increasingly take into consideration the diverse range of media technologies and organizations with which they interact, often developing a pragmatic attitude towards the combination of diverse media logics that co-exist in contemporary societies. More generally, mediatization processes are at work also in the case of images that social movement actors produce and diffuse (Ibrahim 2009). Across history, the visual side of social movements was shaped by different constellations of media technologies and organizations (Mattoni and Teune 2014).

Scholars of communication and cultural studies interested in political activism have addressed framing processes and the dynamics of political conflict in media discourse, hence considering the mediatized dimension of visuals in the context of social movements. Images are, like texts, a key medium used by protesters to communicate a message. Visual theorists in media studies and art history agree that images are associated with a complex stock of cultural knowledge and experiences, frames and identifications, while they are also interpreted, framed and re-framed by political actors (Mitchell 1994; Fahlenbrach 2014). The main focus, in this regard, has been the construction, also through visuals, of activist discourses able to counterbalance, or openly challenge, mainstream dominant discourses on contentious issues. Indeed, images produced by social movements are part of the general struggle over meaning within societies. Oldfield (1995), for instance, shows that the circulation of images is part and parcel of a movement's attempts to raise public attention and to garner support. In particular, he focusses on the British abolitionist movement and its use of Josiah Wedgwood's kneeling slave that was reproduced hundreds of thousands times to serve as a marker of support for the abolitionist cause.

As such, these images become a reference point for those who seek to understand or interpret a social movement as well as for those who seek to support, co-opt, de-legitimize or demobilize it. As images can serve as a medium for the representation of complex messages, visual codes play a significant role in the framing work of social movements. In her analysis of Chilean *arpilleras*, Jacqueline Adams (2002) underlines three framing functions of these works of art: depicting the terrible conditions of life in Chile, portraying the Pinochet regime as evil, and conveying an alternative way of thinking. Christian

Lahusen (1996) reaches similar conclusions in his analysis of public campaigns, devoting a significant part of his study to the use of visual media in general and to campaign and organization logos in particular. However, due to the characteristic openness of visual forms, that follow a logic of association usually absent from written texts (Mueller and Oezcan 2007), images require a particularly careful and hence challenging reading by social movement scholars. Moreover, given the complex and contentious reception of culturally coded images in fragmented audiences across the world, these attempts are likely to have varied and potentially ambiguous effects.

Another strand of research pays attention to the mediatized dimension of visuals with reference to the mainstream and commercial press. Media scholars, more than others, have shown the impact of images on the reception of contentious actors (Arpan et al. 2006), their role in attracting media attention (Routledge 1997), and mainstreaming social movement claims (Delicath and DeLuca 2003). Because the resonance of social movements is essentially tied to their image in public and commercial mass media, visual representations of protest constitute a key concern of social movement organizing (Ryan 1991). Indeed, although movements may try to use images as a sort of Trojan horse to convey their messages, especially before the advent of information and communication technologies, they remain dependent on mass media for the formation and dissemination of their visual codes (Gamson et al. 1992). Several authors have pointed to the condensation of movement messages in media images. As "news icons," images can be used to refer to social problems as they are seen by social movements (Szasz 1994; Bennett and Lawrence 1995; Juris 2008). They may also replace proper arguments with "argumentative fragments" (Delicath and DeLuca 2003).

However, the mediatized dimension of visuals in social movements goes well beyond the representation of contentious performances and issues within the mainstream and commercial press. Especially with regard to recent protests in Middle Eastern and North African countries, literature is flourishing on the work of signification by political activists and sympathetic audiences in social media platforms and other media outlets. The issue at stake, in these studies, is the very process of mediatization that occurs with regard to visuals across, and due to a combination of, different media platforms. Relevant examples are Neda Agha-Soltan, killed in Iran during the 2009 protests against the government after the contested presidential elections (Olesen 2014; Assmann and Assmann 2010); the 28-year-old blogger Khaled Said, killed by the Egyptian police in Alexandria on June, 6, 2010 (Olesen 2013); and the suicide of Mohamed Bouazizi who set himself on fire and died shortly after his extreme act, quickly becoming a symbol of the injustices that triggered the Tunisian uprising (Lim 2013). These violent deaths were first captured through visual materials, then spread through social media platforms and cultural artifacts, and finally transformed into global injustice symbols (Olesen 2014; Olesen 2013) and global icons (Assmann and Assman 2010). Media practices that manipulated and transformed the original images, often through collaborative image making (Loftalian 2013), were crucial in the creation of such global injustice symbols. Equally relevant were the resonances that these images were able to have at the global level (Olesen 2014; Lim 2013) and the processes of meaning adaptation that they underwent while travelling across the globe (Olesen 2014). In fact, it seems that the number of such global images diffused via digital media platforms changed familiar visual representations in the media coverage of political conflict (Halfmann and Young 2010).

Conclusions

If visual appearance is crucial in the performance and mediatization of social move-ments, what are the opportunities and challenges for future research? As means of symbolic production (Goffman 1959), images have external effects, like mobilizing attention for a problem, and internal effects, like creating and sustaining collective iden-tity (Melucci 1996). A complement to textual sources, images allow for the refining and expanding of our understanding of such social processes.

The work on injustice symbols shows that images may become a focus around which experiences and injustice frames are organized. Building on this strand of research as well as on Jasper and Poulsen's (1995) work on moral shocks, images should be seen as an organizational resource that helps to connect formerly unlinked people, even more so in the contemporary media environment that facilitates such connections through computer-mediated social networks (Bennett and Segerberg 2013). Images are particu-larly rewarding when it comes to understanding emotions in this context. Social move-ment activists diffuse still and moving images to arouse emotions that raise attention and ultimately help to mobilize people into action.

Visual analysis also adds to the available knowledge on other aspects of the context in which social movements act. Studying the ways in which images are re-contextualized and re-interpreted by external actors will help us to understand the discursive oppor-tunities for a social movement. Third wave feminists, for instance, are confronted with the normalizing use of images of their protests in the commercial context of mainstream media. By selecting "sexy" images for their coverage media producers reinforce the formative gaze on the female body and counter the activists' message of self-determination.

In a time of transnational flows of communication, visual practices are likely to be effective in diffusing new ideas, thus empowering movements for social change across borders. This leads to the increased need for research on the visual conditions of diffu-sion of social movement organizing strategies in global (social) media spheres and yet across culturally diverse and fragmented audiences. By combining framing approaches with visual analysis we should be in a better position to understand pathways of dif-fusion of slogans, images, and visual objects that spread ideas and movements across countries. Future research should focus particularly on transcultural aspects of diffu-sion. Images are key to grasping different understandings of the protesting body and the ways in which it is re-interpreted across the globe.

References

Adams, Jacqueline (2002). "Art in Social Movements: Shantytown Women's Protest in Pinochet's Chile," *Sociological Forum.* 17(1): 21–56.

Alexander, Jeffrey (2011). *Performance and Power.* London: Polity.

Arpan, Laura M., Baker, Kaysee, Lee, Youngwon, Jung, Taejin, Lorusso, Lori, and Smith, Jason (2006). News Coverage of Social Protests and the Effects of Photographs and Prior Attitudes." *Mass Communication and Society.* 9(1): 1–20.

Assmann, Aleida and Assmann, Corinna (2010). "Neda—the Career of a Global Icon" In *Memory in a Global Age: Discourses, Practices and Trajectories,* edited by Aleida Assmann and Sebastian Conrad, 225–242. Basingstoke: Palgrave Macmillan.

Baudrillard, Jean (2001). *The Spirit of Terrorism.* Translated by Rachel Bloul. *Le Monde* 2 November.

Bennett, W. Lance and Lawrence, Regina G. (1995). "News Icons and the Mainstreaming of Social Change," *Journal of Communication.* 45(3): 20–39.

Bennett, W. Lance and Segerberg, Alexandra (2013). *The Logic of Connective Action: Digital Media and the Personalization of Contentious Politics.* Cambridge: Cambridge University Press.

Bleiker, Roland (2001). "The Aesthetic Turn in International Political Theory," *Millennium.* 30/2.

Casquete, Jesus (2006). "The Power of Demonstrations," *Social Movement Studies.* 5(1): 45–60.

Currier, Ashley (2012). *Out in Africa: LGBT Organizing in Namibia and South Africa.* Minneapolis: University of Minnesota Press.

Delicath, John W. and DeLuca, Kevin Michael (2003). "Image Events, the Public Sphere, and Argumentative Practice: The Case of Radical Environmental Groups," *Argumentation.* 17 (3) (September 1): 315–333.

Doerr, Nicole (2010). "Politicizing Precarity, Producing Visual Dialogues on Migration: Transnational Public Spaces in Social Movements." *Forum Qualitative Social Research* 11(2). No page numbers, available at www.qualitative-research.net/index.php/fqs/article/view/1485.

Doerr, Nicole and Mattoni, Alice (2014). "Public Spaces and Alternative Media Practices in Europe. The Case of the EuroMayDay Parade Against Precarity." In *Media And Revolt: Strategies and Performances from the 1960s to the Present,* edited by K. Fahlenbrach, E. Sivertsen, and R. Werenskjold, 386–405. New York, NY: Berghahn Books.

Doerr, Nicole and Milman, Noa (2014). "Working with Images." In *Methods of Social Movement Analysis,* edited by Donatella della Porta, 418–445. Oxford: Oxford University Press.

Edelman, Murray (1964). *The Symbolic Uses of Politics.* Urbana: University of Illinois Press.

Fahlenbrach, Kathrin (2014). "Protest in Television. Visual Protest on Screen." In *Media and Revolt. Strategies and Performances from the 1960s to the Present,* edited by Kathrin Fahlenbrach, Rolf Werenskjold, and Erling Sivertsen, 234–250. New York/Oxford: Berghahn Books.

Falk, Francesca (2010). "Invasion, Infection, Invisibility: An Iconology of Illegalized Immigration." In *Images of Illegalized Immigration. Towards a Critical Iconology of Politics,* edited by C. Bischoff, F. Falk, and S. Kafehsy, 83–100. Bielefeld: transcript.

Flam, Helena and Doerr, Nicole (2015). "Visuals and Emotions in Social Movements." In *Methods in Pursuit of Emotion,* edited by Flam and Jochen Kleres, 229–239. London: Routledge.

Gamson, Joshua (1989). "Silence, Death, and the Invisible Enemy: AIDS Activism and Social Movement 'Newness'," *Social Problems*. 36: 351–367.

Gamson, William A., Croteau, David, Hoynes, William, and Sasson, Theodore (1992). "Media Images and the Social Construction of Reality," *Annual Review of Sociology*. 18 (January 1): 373–393.

Goodnow, Trischa (2006). "On Black Panthers, Blue Ribbons, & Peace Signs: The Function of Symbols in Social Campaigns. Visual Communication Quarterly," *Visual Communication Quarterly*. 13: 166–179.

Goffman, Erving (1959). *The Presentation of Self in Everyday Life*. Garden City, NY: Doubleday.

Guano, Emanuela (2002). "Ruining the President's Spectacle: Theatricality and Telepolitics in the Buenos Aires Public Sphere," *Journal of Visual Culture*. 1: 303–323.

Halfmann, Drew, and Young, Michael P. (2010). "War Pictures: The Grotesque as Mobilizing Tactic," *Mobilization*. 15(1): 1–24.

Howell, Jayne (2012). "Beauty, Beasts, and Burlas: Imagery of Resistance in Southern Mexico," *Latin American Perspectives*. 39(3): 27–50.

Ibrahim, Yasmin (2009). "The Art of Shoe-Throwing: Shoes as a Symbol of Protest and Popular Imagination," *Media, War & Conflict*. 2: 213–226.

Jasper, James M. (2014). *Protest: A Cultural Introduction to Social Movements* Hoboken, NJ: Wiley.

Jasper, James D. and Poulsen, Jane D. (1995). "Recruiting Strangers and Friends. Moral Shocks and Social Networks in Animal Rights and Anti-nuclear Protests," *Social Problems*. 42: 493–512.

Juris, Jeffrey S. (2008). "Performing Politics: Image, Embodiment, and Affective Solidarity During Anti-corporate Globalization Protests," *Ethnography*. 9(1): 61–97.

Khatib, Lina (2012). *Image Politics in the Middle East: The Role of the Visual in Political Struggle*. London: I.B.Tauris.

Lahusen, Christian (1996). *The Rhetoric of Moral Protest: Public Campaigns, Celebrity Endorsement, and Political Mobilization*. Berlin, New York: Walter de Gruyter.

Lim, Merlyna (2013). "Framing Bouazizi: 'White Lies', Hybrid Network, and Collective/connective Action in the 2010–11 Tunisian Uprising," *Journalism* 14(7). (March 1), 921–941.

Linke, Uli (1988). "The Language of Resistance: Rhetorical Tactics and Symbols of Popular Protest in Germany," *City & Society*. 2(2): 127–133.

Lotfalian, Mazyar (2013). "Green Movement, Aestheticized Politics, Visual Culture, and Emergent Forms of Digital Practice," *International Journal of Communication*. 7(1) (June 30): 1371–1390.

Luhtakallio, Eeva (2013). "Bodies Keying Politics. A Visual Frame Analysis of Gendered Local Activism in France and Finland." In *Advances in the Visual Analysis of Social Movements*, edited by Nicole Doerr, Alice Mattoni, and Simon Teune, 27–54. *Research in Social Movements, Conflict and Change*, vol. 35. Bingley: Emerald.

Mattoni, Alice (2008). *Serpica Naro and the Others. The Social Media Experience in the Italian Precarious Workers Struggles*. Portal, 5(2). Available at: www.epress.lib.uts.edu.au/ojs/index.php/portal/issue/view/35/showToc.

Mattoni, Alice and Doerr, Nicole (2007). "Images within the Precarity Movement in Italy." *Feminist Review*. 87(1):130–135.

Mattoni, Alice and Teune, Simon (2014). "Visions of Protest. A Media-Historic Perspective on Images in Social Movements," *Sociology Compass*. 8(6):876–887.

McAdam, Doug, Tarrow, Sidney, and Tilly, Charles (2001). *Dynamics of Contention*. Cambridge, New York: Cambridge University Press.

Melucci, Alberto (1996). *Challenging Codes: Collective Action in the Information Age.* Cambridge Cultural Social Studies. Cambridge (England); New York: Cambridge University Press.

Mitchell, William John Thomas (1994). *Picture Theory: Essays on Verbal and Visual Representation.* Chicago: University of Chicago Press.

Morrison, Daniel R. and Isaac, Larry W. (2012). "Insurgent Images: Genre Selection and Visual Frame Amplification in IWW Cartoon Art," *Social Movement Studies.* 11(1): 61–78.

Mueller, Marion G. (2007). "What is Visual Communication? Past and Future of an Emerging Field of Communication Research," *Studies in Communication Sciences.* 7(2): 7–34.

Mueller, Marion G., and Oezcan, Esra (2007). "The Political Iconography of Muhammad Cartoons: Understanding Cultural Conflict and Political Action," PS: *Political Science and Politics.* 40(2): 287–291.

Oldfield, John R. (1995). *Popular Politics and British Anti-Slavery: The Mobilization of Public Opinion against the Slave Trade, 1784–1807.* Manchester: Manchester University Press.

Olesen, Thomas (2013). "'We Are All Khaled Said': Visual Injustice Symbols in the Egyptian Revolution, 2010–2011," *Research in Social Movements, Conflicts and Change.* 35 (March 1): 3–25.

Olesen, T. (2014). "Dramatic Diffusion and Meaning Adaptation: The Case of Neda." In *Spreading Protest. Social Movements in Times of Crisis,* edited by D. della Porta and A. Mattoni. Wivenhoe Park: ecpr press.

Rogoff, Iris (1998). "Studying Visual Culture." In *Visual Culture Reader,* edited by Mirzoeff, Nicholas, 14–27. New York: Routledge.

Ryan, Charlotte (1991). *Prime Time Activism. Media Strategies for Grassroots Organizing.* Boston, MA: South End Press.

Sawer, Marian (2007). "Wearing your Politics on your Sleeve: The Role of Political Colours in Social Movements," *Social Movement Studies.* 6: 39–56.

Sontag, Susan (2004). "Regarding the Torture of Others." *New York Times,* May 23.

Streeby, Shelley (2013). *Radical Sensations: World Movements, Violence, and Visual Culture.* Durham: Duke University Press.

Szasz, Andrew (1994). *Ecopopulism: Toxic Waste and the Movement for Environmental Justice.* Minneapolis: University of Minnesota Press.

Taylor, Verta, Rupp, Leila J., and Gamson, Joshua (2004). "Performing Protest: Drag Shows as Tactical Repertoire of the Gay and Lesbian Movement." In *Authority in Contention,* edited by Daniel J. Myers and Daniel M. Cress, 25: 105–137. Research in Social Movements, Conflicts and Change. Greenwich and CT: JAI Press.

Tilly, Charles (2008). *Contentious Performances.* Cambridge: Cambridge University Press.

Wood, Leslie (2012). *Direct Action, Deliberation, and Diffusion: Collective Action after the WTO Protests in Seattle.* Cambridge: Cambridge University Press.

....

CHAPTER 37

PRACTICE MOVEMENTS

The Politics of Non-Sovereign Power

....

JULIA ECKERT

WHO "does" politics and how do they do it? When does "politics" happen, and what makes for political change? Considering the ever growing expressions of varied dissatisfactions with representative forms of politics, which are not restricted to formal democratic representation but also include representations by conventional social movements, a reconsideration of what has been called "insurgent citizenship" (Holston 2007), "non-movements" (Bayat 2010), "the politics of the governed" (Chatterjee 2004), and, of course, "the weapons of the weak" in the formulation of James Scott (1985) might be fruitful for generating a conceptualization of "politics" and "political change," which does justice to the fact that unorganized and unrepresented but nonetheless collective action is and always has been a central site of politics in most political systems.

In the following I will first outline the defining characteristics of practice movements, that is: forms of unorganized collective action, which are distinct from conventional social movements in various ways, first and foremost by the direct expression of their goals in their practices. Secondly, I will consider why the attention to practice movements is necessary for our conceptualization of politics not only in situations in which conventional social movements are circumscribed by governmental restrictions, but more generally as moves for a livable life, in which "the subaltern speak." This raises, thirdly, the question of how their unrepresented expressions of visions of a good life relate to hegemonial understandings of the social order, and how we can understand the relation of resistance and projective-ness in the inherent transgression of the normative grounds of the social order in which they arise. Stressing their projective character rather than restricting them to their resisting dimensions, I conclude this examination of practice movements with a discussion of the effects practice movements might have, both on the level of either oppressive or responsive regulative reactions, and on normative standards.

PRACTICE MOVEMENTS

Unorganized collective action is distinct from social movements "proper" in several ways. James Scott once described it as "a social movement with no formal organization, no formal leaders, no manifestoes, no dues, no name and no banner" (Scott 1985: 35; cf. Bayat 2010: 14). Rather, such movements are defined by forms of practice that are oriented towards goals that reside above all in some improvement of everyday possibilities of living. These goals are shared by many, even if they might not strive to achieve them collectively. We can know of these goals and the numbers who adhere to them only and only insofar as they are expressed through what people do and how many do it that way. Goals and claims are articulated not in manifestos or declarations but rather in "acts of citizenship" (Isin/Nielsen 2008), and in everyday practice. Thus, practice is at the centre of these movements, and I will therefore refer to them as "practice movements."

The defining practices of such unorganized collective action are more often than not part of everyday living (Bayat 2010: 111; Das 2011) rather than being performed in the extraordinary (as is implied by Isin 2008). They are in many respects practices of going about one's life: working, housing, moving, dressing, and acquiring food. However, in other respects these practices stand out from other quotidian practices in that they explicitly transgress restrictions inherent in the nexus of the material organization of space, property relations, status orders, and almost always normative regulations, be they laws, morals, or customs. As such, these practices are pragmatically striving to overcome restrictions or aiming at the redistribution of goods, whether material or symbolic. They are "concerned largely with immediate, de facto gains" (Scott 1985: 33) and as such, they are "pre-ideological" (Bayat 2010: 19). Whether they strive to improve access to material goods, symbolic representation or participation in societal institutions, or all of the above at the same time, these practices can be defined as expanding the space of action of those who pursue them. They produce—often in incremental ways—temporary or lasting changes in the material grounds or in the normative regulation of the everyday life of those who pursue them.

In their transgressive character, the practices of such practice movements are distinct from other transgressive practices, be they individual criminal acts or organized crime, in that they implicitly or explicitly challenge the normative grounds of the rules that they transgress. Those who engage in practice movements often develop alternative normative legitimations for their practices.

Such practice movements are thus collective in a specific sense: while not collectively organized, they are more than the aggregate of individual action in that within them, different individual acts and ways of doing inform and inspire each other and can, if need be, refer to each other by way of comparison, justification, and explanation. Although not necessarily articulated collectively, they are thus nonetheless fundamentally social: visions of possibilities, ways of realizing them, ideas of oneself as rights bearing subjects, and delineations of the addressees of demands emerge in social relations, collectively or by comparison, and by recognizing the similarities in forms of subjection and in the needs of life (Das 2011: 320–322). Sometimes it is by way of witnessing, often by way of rumors (Harney 2006; Das 2011; Eckert 2012) that people know of each other's practices of transgression, and that they are propelled towards a common practice. Such forms of knowledge rely on the identification of similarity, of comparability (Eckert 2012): what happened there could happen here; their situation is in some way comparable to ours; what they have done we could do, etc. This identification of comparability is often as far as any collective identity goes for such movements. They thus challenge us to conceptualize the aggregation of such practices, and to examine the generation of collective goals, norms, and identities, and to reflect on their ways of effecting change.

Today we see such movements in the multitudinous squatting of urban land (e.g., Bayat 2000), the unregulated construction of homes thereupon (e.g., Holston 2007), the occupation of public space in which to work (e.g., Anjaria 2011), the assertion of access to public space (e.g., Göle 2006; Bayat 2010: 96–114), and the practical insistence on one's own freedom of movement (e.g., Mezzadra 2006; De Genova 2009) to seek work and a better living: next to urban squatters, I would count as the currently possibly largest of such moves that of the millions of illegalized migrants who cross borders despite their ever increasing fortifications.[1]

However, there are also less visible practices such as pilfering, or sharing (e.g., Gold 2004), and even forms of recycling. The latter two examples are less clearly infringing on dominant norms or legal rules; however, one could say that they are circumventions of established forms of exchange which affect both the possibilities of those who circumvent these conventional forms, as well as the conventional (market) forms in themselves, redistributing resources from one chain of exchange into another. There are of course also the classical examples of draft-dodging or deserting. These could be said to be what Alfred Hirschman (1970) once described as "exit," while all other examples seem to make it necessary to add a third dimension to his distinction of exit and voice as the two forms of protest: Squatting, pilfering, and also migrating are not, or not only, exits from an unwanted situation; neither are they simply voice or protest, demanding change from a competent authority. Rather, in their pragmatic and practical approach to their goals, they strive to produce such change themselves. They might be better described as forms of appropriation or, as Asef Bayat called it, encroachments (Bayat 2000). They attempt to access or realize what they claim.[2]

The current relevance of movements of appropriation might relate to the fact that today exclusion (e.g., Castells 1997: III, 70–161) is a predominant form of social relations. Both voice and exits necessitate other forms of relation to be possible: "voice" is highly contingent on someone being interested to hear; exits need something to turn to, something to enter into from where one leaves. When nobody listens, and there is nothing to turn to due to various forms of exclusion, appropriation appears as the only option to reclaim access. Thus, I would venture the thesis that practice movements are above all about access, participation, and having a share rather than about autonomy or other forms of exits from a relation.

THE SUBALTERN SPEAK

The possibly particular historical significance of practice movements points us to the question of why it is important to incorporate such practice movements when we consider social movements. Bayat has looked at what he has called non-movements in contexts in which, as he holds, they are politically so relevant because "real" social movements are oppressed or outlawed by authoritarian governments, and have no space for action. Since oppositional collective action in such contexts cannot take the forms that Western academia is used to classify as such, we are in danger of overlooking relevant political forces at work. Such considerations should not be restricted to authoritarian political systems, but need to be examined in contexts in which many forms of civil protest are criminalized or their legal protections curtailed by expansive security legislation or the extension of discretionary powers of the executive.

However, we do not encounter practice movements only in contexts in which social movements "proper" are oppressed. Practice movements operate also in contexts in which conventional social movements exist, and may indeed be thriving. There, too, they have a political significance independent of social movements proper that we cannot ignore. First, on a more particular level, paying attention to such non-organized practice movements is important because they are one form in which "the subaltern can speak"; ignoring them would be to silence the subaltern once more (cf. Spivak 1988). Practice movements express goals and desires "unrepresented" and before their articulation within the framework of a particular vision of social and political change. Sometimes they are expressions of hopes, intentions, and visions in explicit or implicit opposition to those formulations developed within social movements. "I do not want any movements anymore. I have had enough movements. Movements only exploit the poor for their own political ends" shouted the president of a slum dweller association in Mumbai at me once. Thus, those who are engaged in practice movements for their everyday futures sometimes deliberately refrain from participating in conventional social movements because that would be to align themselves with particular ideological positions. Others are engaged in such conventional social movements for one cause, but in their everyday lives engage in the multitudinous uncoordinated struggles beyond organized social movements.

The relation of such "pre-ideological" (Bayat 2010: 19) practice movements to conventional social movements of whatever ideological hue concern the questions of the relations of power between and within them. Practice movements can turn into social movements when they start to organize more formally, often triggered by an adverse event such as the demolition of a slum, or other dissipations of the practices of practice movements.

Social movements "proper" can at times also support or strengthen practice movements, one example possibly being the role of women's movements for the globalization of a discourse of women's rights which entered into local women's practice movements in various ways (Bayat 2010: 96–114; Eckert 2012). Practice movements can be absorbed into populist programmatics, these constructing the political (cf. Laclau 2005) by addressing precisely the everyday woes of the "common man" in a way that takes up the everyday understandings of such woes, and forges political identities around them. But social movements can also side-line practice movements, or demand of them an ideological positioning, which is exactly what the president of the slum association quoted earlier resented. These questions of agenda setting, of which representations of goals and needs and the proper ways to achieve them become dominant, seem to be of particular relevance today when various transnational movement networks, be it the Global Justice Movement and its venue, the World Social Forum, or various chapters of Occupy or the "Real Democracy Movement" attempt to include disparate practice movement. It is a question of what issues can be raised within these forums and what is relegated to silence (Lukes 1974), what goals are legitimate, which moral or ethical frames are deemed emancipatory, and which are attributed to the realm of reaction, defence, or protection. These questions are pertinent not only to the relations between social movements and practice movement, but also to our academic perspective on them: the academic sorting of movements into emancipatory or defensive (protective, reactionary) movements (Castells 1997: II; Fraser 2013) participates in this pre-determination of what emancipation can consist of, and whether it is or needs to be the predominant goal at all (cf. Mahmoud 2001). These questions are given greater urgency by the pre-ideological normative positioning of practice movements.

The second reason why we need to take account of such practice movements is located on a more general level. Practice movements are a ubiquitous transformative force that shapes social institutions; in their aggregation they can transform the distribution of resources, social practice, legal interpretation, and the legitimacy of modes of governing—in a different but no lesser way than social movements. The attention to social movements once overcame the narrow focus on formal political institutions to come to an understanding of political processes. For an adequate understanding of the realm of politics, however, we need to expand our perspective even further and look beyond organized collective action to include the transformative effects of the practices of practice movements on normative and institutional structures. In as much as they are unrepresented or rather, self-representative, and strive not to rule but to live a "liveable life" (Butler 2004), they could be considered examples of non-sovereign forms of political power (Jennings 2011: 39f) which necessitate a rethinking of sovereignty-centered political theory.

EVERYDAY RESISTANCE

The overall orientation towards inclusion of practice movements that I propose points us to the question of their normativity, and their relation to the structures within which they operate.

As mentioned earlier, the practices of everyday living defining practice movements are different from other such everyday practices in as much they directly transgress particular hindrances and denials inherent in regulations and property relations.[3] Although not all practice movements breach law, their circumventing of different kinds of normative regulations could be said to be a defining characteristic, distinguishing them from other forms of everyday practice that might likewise transform aspects of social order despite being in accordance with societal norms.

Because of their transgressive character, such practices have sometimes been considered under the term "resistance." Most prominently, it was James Scott who examined in "the Weapons of the Weak" the "social avalanche of petty acts of insubordination" (Scott 1985: 31) by which peasants sought to resist those who dominated and exploited them. Michel de Certeau, too, developed a terminology of a well-nigh warlike opposition between strategies of regulation by governments and corporations and the subversive tactics of "consumers" to point us to the transformative potential of routine practices such as walking, reading, or eating (De Certeau 1984). Such attention to the subversive potentials of "use" mirrors the regard that British cultural studies authors inspired by Gramsci, such as Raymond Williams (1981), Stuart Hall (1980), or Dick Hebdige (1979), have given to the transformations of meaning effected by use and consumption.

Such assumptions of "resistance" have, however, been criticized for several weaknesses. For one: discovering resistance in every act ever so trivial might lead to a one-dimensional analysis of human behavior, obliterating the possibility and force of cooperative and reciprocal orientations (Ortner 1984: 157; Brown 1996: 733). Moreover, it is not even that clear whether we can easily distinguish between resisting and compliant practices, and whether all expressions of an awareness of domination are already resistance. If we thus restrict our attention to those practices that explicitly express the aim to resist the status quo, we are faced with the problem of how exactly intentions matter: We see manifold examples of where intentions to change actually reproduce the structures they set about to change, as Marshall Sahlins once demonstrated (Sahlins 1981), and others where change obtained without being intended. Thus, we are not better off if we focus on the effects of "resistance," since we then encounter the question what precisely the effects of resistance are, or what the relation between change and resistance is precisely. What degree or type of transformation should we count as indicative of resistance?

More importantly, resistors do more than resist. Not only do they have their own politics, as Sherry Ortner has highlighted (1995: 177), dealing with the frictions and tensions amongst their own ranks, between old and young, women and men, reformers and revolutionaries, etc. which point us to the complexity of their normative perspectives; they have, moreover, projects that cannot fully be appreciated when restricting one's perspective to their resisting dimensions. These projects are projective, pointing towards goals that are perceived as worthwhile in themselves rather than simply as an aversion or avoidance of the status quo.

Again, the term "appropriation" seems to offer conceptual possibilities that overcome the lacunae of "resistance."[4] Appropriation connotes taking something, which was not in your purview before, had been withheld or unreachable or simply alien. It means making something your own. "Appropriation" has, however, a double connotation: taking over something, and taking something up as a practice of your own. "Taking over something" resonates with the notion of the "encroachment" of Bayat (2000).[5] Its affinity with a slow "occupation" of something points towards the expansion of spatial possibilities, of room to maneuver. "Taking up something as your own practice" entails the notion of a transformation through use that de Certeau had in mind, and like him, many of the cultural studies authors.

Using the term "appropriation" rather than resistance thus makes it possible to abstain from presupposing any "critical" intentionality associated with "resistance" or the subversive connotation of de Certeau's "tactics." Appropriation also makes it possible not to think of such practices as necessarily zero-sum games, but rather as an issue of transformation and innovation in which practices (incrementally and often only partially) produce what they aim at. Any further ideas for the future thereby need not be reduced to an oppositional reaction to the status quo but can more fully be appreciated in their potentially polyvalent normative and projective dimensions, taking into view creativity, "complicity" (Brown 1996: 733), and affirmative practices, that might transform the status quo by using rather than rejecting it (Eckert 2006).

Normativity and Hegemony

I have suggested in this chapter that more often than not practice movements actually demand better access to the goods of the status quo, more participation, and recognition in the body politic.[6] Their opposition is against their exclusion from the status quo, rather than necessarily towards its institutions in general. Furthermore, their opposition, on the face of it, might directly target only those specific norms deemed responsible for the specific exclusions that people struggle against, such as dress codes by women in Iran (Bayat 2010: 96–114), zoning laws by hawkers in India (Anjaria 2011), building regulations by squatters all over the world, or property laws. Other norms might be considered legitimate or valid, and practice movements might actually distinguish between their legitimate and their illegitimate infringements of law (Eckert 2006), even though "legitimate" rules might be equally part of a larger systemic regulatory apparatus in which their exclusion is grounded. The general striving for inclusion indicates a valuation of the goods that the status quo could offer if one were included in it in a more privileged position.[7] In short, their practical oppositions do not explicitly formulate an alternative systemic model; revolution is rarely on the agenda of practice movements, and whether their orientation leads towards more inclusive or more exclusive societal relations is contingent on many factors within such movements and also within the reactions they trigger in the institutional context within which they operate.

When this ambivalent relation to the status quo has been perceived and not been "neutralized" by assumptions about hidden spheres of oppositional authenticity, the refusal—explicit or implicit—of many practice movements to align their vision of the good life with a coherent formulation of an alternative, has led to analyses that consider practices aiming for inclusion as effects of hegemony: the striving of the marginalized to be part of the system of marginalization seemed to prove the hegemonic force of this system.

Lacking or even renouncing any explicit ideological stance has never meant that these movements have no normative positions, or that these positions are merely reproducing the dominant norms. In their aiming for specific changes in the material or symbolic order they live in, practices of practice movements express clear moral and ethical norms, and sometimes, when asked, also make them explicit.

Central here are the legitimations that undergird these struggles. In all the negotiations, practices, and struggles, different grounds of legitimation are at play, different ways of reasoning as to why one is owed something from someone else and from the body politic. People refer to their labor (Eckert 2011, 2012), to their contributions to a body politic (Holston 2007), to their shared humanity (Das 2011).

These legitimations express certain normative ideas. Often they might stem from the very legitimatory grounds that the status quo purports to, but does not, fulfil. Unfulfilled normative promises are certainly one driving force of claims and demands for inclusion; they are ubiquitous as the universalist claims of most modern orders have nowhere fulfilled their promises to all they deemed to include. Struggles are shaped by the aspirations grounded in these promises and their contrast to the experiences people have had. Promises are interpreted in ways that mesh moral or ethical and future imaginations possibly stemming from realms other than the dominant normative orders. Moreover, comparisons to others deemed comparable in ethic, moral, legal, economic, or other respects can "import" norms of how things should be from other situations in time or space: The golden past is as much a point of reference as the government of a neighboring state might be one.

Practice movements thus might provide insights into the room to maneuver between hegemonies and counter-hegemonies in a space that is certainly socially formed in its normativity, but in which different normative realms encounter each other, and are thereby each transformed.

EFFECTS

Practice movements set in motion different processes at the same time. They often effectively alter access to material goods and public space at least temporarily. At the same time, they might trigger adverse sanctions against their violation of law, such as the further fortification of border controls, or the demolition or confiscation of houses, machines, or other goods. Furthermore, state administrations and government authorities might forge particular relations with such movements, that are not based on contracts or rights but rather on bio-political forms of "assistance" to life, thereby continuing their exclusion from "civil society" (Chatterjee 2004). Sometimes, however, such movements might actually initiate a process of re-regulation or law reform, that is, the adaptation of law to their social practice: titles to land might be transferred; slums might be regularized and "improved"; legal migration schemes might be elaborated or illegalized migrants might be amnestied; minorities (whether this be racial, sexual, ethnic, religious, or other) might formally be granted participatory rights that had previously been withheld, thus institutionalizing the changes wrought by practice.

That such legal and institutional change, within which rights might be "waxing and waning " (Das 2011: 327) is related to practice movements, that is, to "the struggles of the multitudes of mass illegalities which enact forms of citizen understandings" (Baxi 2004: 362) is precisely the reason why we cannot come to an adequate understanding of political change without taking them into view. Upendra Baxi has argued that "the rule of law is always and everywhere a terrain of people's struggle to make power accountable, governance just, and state ethical" (Baxi 2004: 372). His intention is to overcome the Eurocentric understanding of the shaping of norms of the rule of law (Baxi 2004: 340; cf. Rajagopal 2003) by pointing to the ways in which these norms were reformulated and creatively constituted in the interpretations of different historical struggles. This could be taken further, to look at the shaping of norms and institutions not only in respect to their interpretation, but to their fundamental constitution through what Seyla Benhabib has called "democratic iterations" (Benhabib 2004: 179–181). Again, however, it needs to be stressed that the effects of democratic iterations can veer into various directions ideologically and in terms of structures of inclusion and exclusion.

The corrosion of the normative status quo that often goes along with its partial affirmation in the practices of practice movements lies in the incremental transformations of the legitimacy of claims (Holston 2007: 13; Das 2011: 327). It consists first and foremost in slow and sometimes contradictory changes of the norms of what is "normal." The slow and small transformations in the ideas about the acceptable and the right way of governing can add up to rather substantive changes in the relations of domination— without necessarily ending many forms of exploitation, injustice, oppression, or cruelty and sometimes producing new ones. These practices and forms of action constitute social change: They "succeed" when they affect what is considered "normal," "standard," and legitimate practice, or even when they shift the line between legal and illegal.

NOTES

1. Economic strategies of illegalized migrants in the places they have migrated to can also be counted among such practice movements.
2. As Albert Hirschman (1993) showed for the combination of exit and voice in his study of the dissolution of the GDR, we might consider the various combinations of exit, voice, and appropriation: exit from the system and appropriating its resources in sharing and recycling, e.g., or of all three together.
3. Attention to these forms of aggregate transformative practices in the everyday struggles for a better life might provide insights also into the relation between practices of living and

transformative politics, which have always been part of some, and play an increasingly important role in "conventional" social movements.

4. Both resistance and appropriation are not confined to subordinate segments of society, of course. Dominant groups and classes also resist: they can resist any move to re-distribution or to the regulation of their privilege. They appropriate space or the means of production. They often appropriate these also against the formal rules that support their privileges anyhow, further expanding their reach and encroaching on the livelihood chances of the already marginalized. Thus, these terms do not necessarily denote a movement against the dominant, or towards greater equality.

5. I prefer "appropriation" to Bayat's "encroachment" as encroachment seems to imply a restriction to the aspect of "taking over" something, while appropriation serves better to allude also to the transformative aspects of using what one has taken over or taken up.

6. It is to some degree an empirical question whether they strive for greater inclusion, or rather for greater autonomy (Bayat 2000: 548). Such directions might also transform over the course of certain struggles.

7. This might also imply that achieving greater inclusion in the system will be to the detriment of others who remain excluded by the very norms that have not been transformed due to the limited opposition to, or the affirmation of, the status quo. Solidarity is possibly not necessarily an element of practice movements.

References

Anjaria, Jonathan Shapiro (2011). "Ordinary States: Everyday Corruption and the Politics of Space in Mumbai," *American Ethnologist.* 38(1): 58–72.

Baxi, Upendra (2004). "Rule of Law in India, Theory and Practice." In *Asian Discourses of Rule of Law: Theories and Implementation of Rule of Law in twelve Asian Countries, France and the U. S.*, edited by R. Peerenboom, 324–345. London: Routledge Curzon.

Bayat, Asef (2000). "From Dangerous Classes to Quiet Rebels: Politics of the Urban Subaltern in the Global South," *International Sociology.* 15: 533–557.

Bayat, Asef (2010). *Life as Politics; How Ordinary People Change the Middle East.* Stanford: Stanford University Press.

Benhabib, Seyla (2004). *The Rights of Others; Aliens, Residents and Citizens.* Cambridge: Cambride University Press.

Brown, Michael (1996). "On Resisting Resistance," *American Anthropologist.* 98(4): 729–749.

Butler, Judith (2004). *Precarious Life: The Powers of Mourning and Violence.* London, New York: Verso.

Castells, Manuel (1997). *The Information Age: Economy, Society and Culture; The Power of Identity.* Oxford: Blackwell.

Chatterjee, Partha (2004). *The Politics of the Governed: Reflections on Popular Politics in Most of the World.* New York: Columbia University Press.

Das, Veena (2011). "State, Citizenship and the Urban Poor," *Citizenship Studies.* 15(3–4): 319–333.

De Certeau, Michel (1984). *The Practice of Everyday Life.* Berkeley: University of California Press.

De Genova, Nicholas (2009). "Conflicts of Mobility and the Mobility of Conflict: Rightlessness, Presence, Subjectivity, Freedom," *Subjectivity.* 29(1): 445–466.

Eckert, Julia (2006). "From Subjects to Citizens: Legalisation from Below and the Homogenisation of the Legal Sphere," *Journal of Legal Pluralism*. 38: 45–75.

Eckert, Julia (2011). "Subjects of Citizenship." *Citizenship Studies*. 3–4: 309–317.

Eckert, Julia (2012). "Rumours of Rights." In *Law against the State: Ethnographic Foray's into Law's Transformations*, edited by J. Eckert, B. Donahoe, Ch. Struempell, Z.Ö. Biner, 147–170. Cambridge: Cambridge University Press.

Fraser, Nancy (2013). "A Triple Movement?" *New Left Review*. 81: 119–132.

Gold, Lorna (2004). *The Sharing Economy: Solidarity Networks transforming Globalisation*. Aldershot: Routledge.

Göle, Nilüfer (2006). "Islamic Visibilities." In *Islam in Public: Turkey, Iran and Europe*, edited by N. Göle, L. Ammann. 3–43. Istanbul, Bilgi University Press.

Hall, Stuart (1980). "Encoding / Decoding," In *Culture, Media, Language: Working Papers in Cultural Studies*, edited by S. Hall, D. Hobson, A. Lowe, and P. Willis, 128–138. London: Hutchinson.

Harney, Nicholas (2006). "Rumour, Migrants, and the Informal Economies of Naples, Italy," *International Journal of Sociology and Social Policy*. 26(9/10): 374–384.

Hebdige, Dick (1979). *Subculture, the Meaning of Style*. London: Routledge.

Hirschman, Albert O. (1970). *Exit, Voice and Loyalty: Responses to Decline in Firms, Organisations and States*. Cambridge, MA: Harvard University Press.

Hirschman, Albert O. (1993). "Exit, Voice, and the Fate of the German Democratic Republic: An Essay in Conceptual History," *World Politics*. 45(2): 173–202.

Holston, James (2007). *Insurgent Citizenship: Disjunctions of Democracy and Modernity in Brazil*. Princeton: Princeton University Press.

Isin, Engin (2008). "Theorizing Acts of Citizenship." In *Acts of Citizenship*, edited by E. F. Isin and G. Nielsen, 15–43. London: Macmillan.

Isin, Engin and Nielsen, Greg, eds. (2008). *Acts of Citizenship*. London: Macmillan.

Jennings, Ronald (2011). "Sovereignty and Political Modernity: A Genealogy of Agamben's Critique of Sovereignty," *Anthropological Theory*. 11: 23–61.

Laclau, Ernesto (2005). *On Populist Reason*. London: Verso.

Lukes, Stephen (1974). *Power, a Radical View*. London: Palgrave Macmillan.

Mahmoud, Saba (2001). "Feminist Theory, Embodiment, and the Docile Agent: Some Reflections on the Egyptian Islamic Revival," *Cultural Anthropology*. 6(2): 202–236.

Mezzadra, Sandro (2006). *Diritto di fuga. Migrazioni, cittadinanza, globalizzazione*. Verona: ombre corte.

Ortner, Sherry (1984). Theory in Anthropology since the Sixties." *Comparative Studies in Society and History*. 1: 126–166.

Ortner, Sherry (1995). "Resistance and the Problem of Ethnographic Refusal," *Comparative Studies in Society and History*. 1: 173–193.

Rajagopal, Balakrishnan (2003). *International Law from Below: Development, Social Movements, and Third World Resistance*. Cambridge: Cambridge University Press.

Sahlins, Marshall (1981). *Historical Metaphors and Mythical Realities: Structure in the Early History of the Sandwich Islands Kingdom*. Ann Arbor: University of Michigan Press.

Scott, James (1985). *Weapons of the Weak: Everyday Forms of Peasant Resistance*. New Haven: Yale University Press.

Spivak, Gayatri (1988). "Can the Subaltern Speak?" In *Marxism and the Interpretation of Culture*, edited by C. Nelson and L. Grossberg, 271–313. Chicago: University of Illinois Press.

Williams, Raymond (1981). *Culture*. Glasgow: Collins.

CHAPTER 38

....

IMMANENT ACCOUNTS

Ethnography, Engagement, and
Social Movement Practices

....

JEFFREY S. JURIS AND ALEX KHASNABISH

SOCIAL movements can be passionate and inspiring affairs, sustained efforts on the part of highly motivated collective actors to change the world and their place within it. Whether through mass protest or everyday grass-roots struggle, activists organize to confront the sources of their grievances, challenge existing relations of power, and build alternatives to the status quo. At the same time, social movements are also products of collective imagination and labor. Even during their most mundane and intimate moments, social movements are forums for experimenting with new ideas, relationships, and identities. Ethnography, including participant observation *together with* a group in struggle, would seem to be a logical and effective way of capturing the emotions, lived experiences, and everyday struggles of activists. Yet as Paul Lichterman (2013) points out, ethnographic methods are underused in the mainstream social movements literature. In contrast, much recent writing and theorizing about and with social movements in disciplines such as anthropology and critical geography have made extensive use of ethnographic methods (see Juris and Khasnabish 2013), but such work remains disconnected from dominant trends in the study of social movements in sociology and political science.[1] Part of this is epistemological: sociologists and political scientists tend to view empirical data, including ethnographic observations, as grist for the mill of theory building, while interpretivist anthropologists and geographers approach theory as a framework for analyzing particular cases (Hess 2013), generating new concepts through the ethnographic encounter itself.

Despite such differences ethnographic approaches to the study of social movements hold great potential for bridging disciplinary divides, particularly in relation to our understanding of movement practices. That is to say, if we want to understand what activists and movements actually do—from the day-to-day work of their own reproduction to the diverse and often unexpected ways they struggle for social change—we need to make greater use of a range of ethnographic practices and sensibilities from a variety of fields. While mainstream social movements research has largely focused on struggles located in the cosmopolitan centers of the Global North, in anthropology and geography ethnographies of social movements have explored a wider range of locales, both inside and outside of core western states, as well as transnational movements that seek to transcend north-south divisions.

Social movements are complex assemblages that overflow with contradiction and possibility and produce cultural-political meaning. Resistance, rebellion, and revolution are reproduced across space and through time, in part, via the circulation of stories of struggle (Polletta 2006: Selbin 2010). Ethnographic approaches are well-positioned to explore such movement meaning-making and the complex lived realities it portrays, encounters, and generates. Ethnographies of social movements also allow for a complex interrogation of the dynamic encounters between activists, organizers, allies, opponents, and the broader public. Moreover, given its attention to daily life, ethnography can help us see past static accounts of movement "success" and "failure" that rest upon political categories many radical movements seek to resist and displace, emphasizing less obvious and predictable but often more significant and durable effects (see Haiven and Khasnabish 2013).

This chapter explores a range of ethnographic examples from diverse geographic settings and disciplinary perspectives. We argue that ethnography is particularly useful for understanding the logic of activist practice. We begin by considering the importance of ethnography for the study of movement practices, and then explore four modes of activist practice that ethnography can shed light on—everyday cultural production, local-global networking, new media activism, and performative protest—before concluding with reflections about the need for collaboration among social movement ethnographers from multiple disciplinary traditions and perspectives.

Ethnography and Practice in the Study of Social Movements

As critical anthropologists and politically engaged ethnographers of social movements, we view ethnography as more than a set of research methods, including participant observation and open-ended, narrative-oriented interviews; we also see ethnography as a mode of analysis and writing that allows us to capture the subjective mood, tone, and feeling of social movement events, activities, and encounters. This has long been viewed as an important role for ethnography, even among positivist social movement scholars. However, ethnography is not restricted to thick description. Ethnographic analyses are able to uncover important empirical issues and generate critical theoretical insights that are not accessible through traditional objectivist methods. In particular, it is ethnography's attention to everyday lived experience, the production of meaning and subjectivity, as well as internal power differences and political-cultural struggles that allows us to grasp the complexity, contingency, promise, and limitations of contemporary activism.

Just as importantly, we view ethnography as an attitude and perspective involving an ethic of openness and flexibility and a willingness to allow oneself to be transformed in the research process. In this sense, ethnography fundamentally challenges, even if it does not overcome, the (researching) subject-(researched) object divide. We suggest that the best social movement ethnographies are carried out from within grass-roots social movements, generating experiential and practical knowledge. Partially inspired by engaged feminist methods (see Naples 2003), such "militant" ethnographic approaches (Juris 2008a)—although not without obstacles and contradictions (see Juris and Khasnabish 2013)—are not only important for gaining access to activist groups and networks, they also provide critical purchase on key tensions and issues that speak directly to activist concerns. When we are situated within a particular network or struggle, and are thus a constitutive part of that struggle, our contributions as researchers are potentially less instrumental and more strategic (Méndez 2008).

Because they are concerned with the practices and underlying logics of action, engaged ethnographic accounts speak to a dual audience: activists and movement scholars in the academy (Hale 2006). Regardless of an ethnographer's degree of identification with a movement—there is room for a wide range of positionalities, ranging from casual support to full-scale "observant-participation" (Costa Vargas 2006)—engaged ethnography thus has to engage intellectual and political concerns. Politically engaged ethnography, rather than analyzing movements from the outside as objects to decode, is particularly well-suited to the analysis of everyday movement practices. In order to grasp the logic of activist practice, ethnographers enter into the everyday flow and rhythm of movement activity, which means not only taking part in but also—to varying degrees—helping to organize political protests, meetings, and activities (Juris 2008a). At the same time, during moments when movements are nascent, demobilized, or reconsolidating, ethnography can also examine and facilitate the work of radical imagination—the prefigurative capacity to envision and work toward more just social worlds (Khasnabish and Haiven 2012).

However, ethnographic engagement raises unavoidable empirical and ethical questions. What happens when our own views and analyses differ from those of our collaborators? And is there not a risk of providing intelligence to agents of surveillance and repression? Moreover, if movement-based ethnographies are grounded in solidarity, what kinds of movements never get studied? The politics of such knowledge production refuses easy answers, but we believe there is considerable value in conducting engaged ethnographic work with movements for social justice (see Khasnabish and Haiven 2012; Juris and Khasnabish 2013). In what follows, we draw on multiple fields and examples from diverse social movements to examine the utility of engaged ethnography for understanding various domains of social movement practice.

EVERYDAY CULTURAL PRODUCTION

Beginning with the focus on culture and identity among new social movement (NSM) theorists, and particularly since the "cultural turn" in the study of social movements, the mainstream social movements literature has paid increasing attention to the symbolic and experiential domains of social movement activity, yet full-scale ethnographic analyses remain few and far between. This is surprising given that ethnography, with its focus on meaning and experience, is "well-suited" to the study of such symbolic processes (Lichterman 2013). Although a handful of sociological ethnographers have examined interactive cultural dynamics within social movement groups and networks (see below), it has been largely in the field of anthropology where cultural production and contestation have come to the fore.

The anthropology of social movements has followed the lead of NSM theorists with respect to the importance of culture to contemporary social movements yet anthropologists have also veered from NSM theory in at least two important ways: first, perhaps reflecting the Latin American origin of much of the early anthropology of social movements, anthropologists have recognized that social movement struggles are at once cultural *and* material, both symbolic and political-economic (see Escobar and Alvarez 1992). Second, reflecting the influence of cultural studies approaches to culture and power, anthropologists have viewed culture and identity as not only produced by social movements but also challenged and contested within movements. As Kay Warren (1998) argues in her ethnographic study of identity in Guatemala's Pan-Maya movement, "It is not uncommon for scholars of new social movements to treat their goals and organizations as self-evident ... Much less attention is directed to the internal dynamics of these movements: to the particular ways participants contest, create, and consume culture" (209).

In his ethnographic work on Afro-Brazilian movements, John Burdick (1995) similarly suggests, "anthropology can deepen our understanding of social movements by viewing them in light of one of the key (postwar) insights of our discipline: that culture, rather than a seamless whole, is best understood as an arena in which multiple, differently empowered actors and groups generate and employ discourses that compete with each other for dominance" (362). This allows us to understand social movements as complex fields defined by social and ideological heterogeneity, not only as vehicles *for* struggle but sites *of* struggle. Given the importance of consciousness, framing, and struggles over meaning, internally and externally, ethnographic knowledge can help illuminate the "processes of growth, shrinkage, rupture, and disintegration of social movements" (362), providing strategic tools for movement organizers themselves.

Social movement ethnographies have explored the politics of cultural production in relation to internal movement cultures, practices, identities, and struggles, as well as efforts to generate novel cultural-political meanings. With respect the latter, social movements wage struggles to produce alternative conceptions of categories such as woman, nature, race, economy, democracy, or citizenship that overturn dominant cultural-political understandings while transforming the terrain of institutional-political and material struggle (Alvarez, Dagnino, and Escobar 1998). Whereas mainstream accounts of social movements tend to focus on the formal properties of movement "frames," ethnographic approaches understand culture as more complex, deeper, and contested (see also Polletta 1997). Anthropologists have thus been interested in the everyday practices whereby activists create new meanings, subjectivities, and imaginaries in the context of transnational struggles, including the Zapatista, global justice, occupy, and global indigenous movements (see Juris 2008a; Khasnabish 2008; Escárcega 2013).

Ethnographic approaches have been particularly fruitful for studying internal movement cultures, practices, and struggles, including contests over visions, identities, strategies, decision making, and organizational forms. It is in the realm of internal cultural dynamics within and between movement groups where sociological ethnographers have had the greatest impact. For example, Rick Fantasia (1988) employs a deeply embedded ethnographic approach among labor activists to explore how "cultures of solidarity" are produced in the context of struggle. For her part, Sharon Kurtz (2002) makes use of an engaged ethnographic approach to examine "identity practices" within grass-roots labor mobilizations, emphasizing the importance of intersectional identities to campaign success. Paul Lichterman and Nina Eliasoph have been particularly influential in their use of an interactivist approach to culture to ethnographically explore how diverse cultural forms, values, and practices are produced and operate in a variety of activist, religious, and secular volunteer organizations (see Lichterman 1996, 2005; Eliasoph 1998). They also show how alternative movement cultures differentially engage multiple constituencies, leading to contrasting forms of political commitment, such as the "personalized" politics practiced within many green party groups and the "communitarian" politics associated with grass-roots community-based environmental organizations (Lichterman 1996).

Similarly, the sociologist Geoffrey Pleyers (2011) has used ethnography among various sectors of the global justice movement in Europe and Latin America to explore contrasting "logics of action": the pathway of "experience" rooted in personalized modes of commitment, directly democratic participation, and novel direct action practices; and the pathway of "reason" shaped by traditional bureaucratic organizational forms and logics, institutional practices, and an orientation toward state-oriented political reforms. A number of ethnographers in sociology, anthropology, and geography have also used politically engaged ethnography to explore the everyday meanings, practices, and values associated with experiential modes of anarchist, autonomous, and/or direct action organizing within a variety of grass-roots counter-institutions, such as autonomous social centers, neighborhood assemblies, and pirate radios in Europe and Latin America (see, e.g., Chatterton 2010; Juris 2012a; Razsa and Kurnik 2012; Sitrin 2012). Ethnography is particularly good at teasing out the alternative logics of such activist practices in order to grasp and represent alternative models of social and political organization arising within social movements and to communicate those back to scholars and activists (see Graeber 2009).

A distinctively anthropological approach to contrasting movement cultures sees them as characterized by differences not only *between* but also *within* movements. For example, Juris (2008a) uses ethnography among alternative global justice movement networks in Catalonia and the Spanish State, as well as internationally, to explore complex internal struggles over ideology, organization, decision making, strategy, and tactics. Elsewhere he explores a tension between "openness" and "intentionality" in the US Social Forum process as organizers focused on recruiting grass-roots communities of color, sometimes to the exclusion of other groups (Juris 2008b). In her ethnographic study of Brazilian youth activism, the sociologist Anne Mische (2008) similarly explores the divergent cultural and political dynamics—and the contrasting communicational styles—that characterize different networks, while also examining bridging practices whereby activists generate discursive and organizational links between networks.

Perhaps nowhere are internal cultural struggles within movements fiercer than in the context of organizational form and decision making. Ethnographic and historical accounts of global justice and other movements since the 1960s have noted the rise of "prefigurative" forms of organization and decision making that reflect activists' directly democratic values and political visions. Not only have scholars noted struggles between supporters of different organizational forms and practices, they have explored tensions related to unequal distributions of power and authority, as well as informal hierarchies, within purportedly horizontal and directly democratic processes (see Polletta 2002; Doerr 2008; Juris 2008a; Maeckelbergh 2009; Wood 2012). In these cases, ethnography is well-suited to observing particular decision-making practices and organizational forms, while grasping the subtleties of complex internal struggles.

A final domain of everyday cultural production social movement ethnographers have explored involves what the sociologists Ron Eyerman and Andrew Jamison (1991) refer to as "cognitive praxis," the knowledge-making activity of social movements. The anthropologists Casas-Cortés, Osterweil, and Powell (2013) have argued that social movements should be seen as knowledge producers engaged in multiple kinds of "knowledge practices" that exist alongside the knowledge production activities of scholars. The political scientist and ethnographer Janet Conway (2006) similarly explores the subaltern knowledges of local activists in Toronto as they confront entrenched systems of power, while Arturo Escobar (2008) examines the production of knowledge about biodiversity, nature, and territory on the part of Afro-Colombian movements.

The recognition that social movements and activists create their own knowledge forces us to re-evaluate the status of our own ethnographic knowledge production. As the anthropologist Julia Paley (2001) illustrates in her research on health care organizing during the transition to democracy in Chile, ethnographers can contribute to the knowledge practices of the movements they study even as they generate ethnographic knowledge with and about those movements. Juris (2008a) suggests that ethnographers of the global justice movements can use their writing to contribute to existing activist circuits of research, strategizing, and theorizing. Haiven and Khasnabish (2013, 2012) further contend that ethnographers can work with activists during moments of fragmentation or demobilization to help summon the radical imagination—the collective, prefigurative force that animates radical social movements—into being as well as to assist in identifying and addressing internalized barriers and oppressions that inhibit movement reproduction. In all of these senses, there is a confluence between practical movement knowledge required for effective mobilization and the kinds of embedded knowledge generated by militant ethnography. In this sense, as Casas-Cortés, Osterweil, and Powell (2013) point out, ethnographers of social movements have to confront the fact that they are increasingly just one voice in a "crowded field" of knowledge producers.

LOCAL-GLOBAL NETWORKING

Ethnography can also shed critical light on the intersection of space, place, and practice within social movements. In this section, we emphasize macro-level spatial practices, including the defense of local territories and their transnational extension. There has been much high quality inter-disciplinary ethnographic work in recent years—within anthropology, geography, and sociology—that has examined the transnational dimensions of contemporary activism, including a focus on local-global networking practices (see Juris and Khasnabish 2013). Ethnography enables us to capture the underlying logics and strategies of such practices, and the complex micro-political struggles that give shape to shifting networks formations (Juris 2008a).

The study of globalization poses a challenge to ethnographic practice, as the method was developed to encompass long-term participant observation in resolutely local settings. How can ethnography be used to study processes at a global scale or to examine mobile phenomena that cross borders? One strategy has been to focus on local sites, but extend the analysis outward to consider how global forces, connections, and imaginations impact and articulate with local contexts (Burawoy 2000). "Multi-sited" ethnography is a contrasting strategy: following people, ideas, objects, conflicts, and other phenomena across networks of geographically dispersed sites (Marcus 1995). Many ethnographic studies of transnational processes combine elements of emplacement and mobility. In this sense, there is no necessary contradiction between local and global scales, and, in fact, ethnographic attention to the lived experience and everyday practices of activists often reveals a dual focus on locally rooted, place-based politics and transnational networking, suggesting a need for practice-based "networked ethnographies" (see Escobar 2008).

Many ethnographies of transnational networking, even if they recognize the articulation of local-global forces, tend to emphasize one or the other. In most cases, however, attention is given to the complex power relations and micro-political struggles through which transnational movements and networks are constituted. Ethnographies that primarily focus on local, place-based politics, albeit in the context of wider transnational activist connections include Escobar's (2008) innovative ethnography of

Afro-Colombian movements focusing on the relationship between local conceptions of nature, territory, and identity and global forces related to capital, development, and transnational activist networking practices as well as the geographer Wendy Wolford's (2010) study of the contrasting fates of two settlements of the Brazilian Landless Workers' Movement—a quintessential locally rooted, yet transnationally linked struggle—one in the southern state of Santa Catarina and the other in the northeastern state of Pernambuco.

Other ethnographic accounts have focused on the transnational dimension of local-global networking, while providing similarly nuanced analyses of internal differentiation and struggle. Transnational feminism has provided a source of inspiration for much early ethnographic work on transnational activism. Through an analysis of NGO-sponsored forums held in conjunction with UN conferences, the political scientist Sonia Alvarez (1998) explores the rift between the "ethical-cultural" and "structural-institutional" dimensions of second-wave feminism in Latin America. Her focus on plural feminist practices and the cultural-political struggles between them emphasizes power imbalances and unequal access to cultural, material, and political resources.

Building on these issues, the sociologist Millie Thayer (2010) explores how transnational feminism based in northeastern Brazil articulates local, regional, and transnational women's organizing in complex, often contradictory ways. In her ethnographic account of the strategies and practices of an autonomous women's labor collective in Nicaragua, the sociologist Jennifer Bickham Méndez (2005) similarly examines power dynamics in the context of local, national, and transnational processes. Such tensions and power struggles among transnational activists point to the inevitable "friction" that shapes local-global activist networks, an important insight emerging from Anna Tsing's (2005) fine-tuned ethnography of transnational forest activists in Indonesia. Alpa Shah's (2010) analysis of the contrasting perspectives on indigenous people, rights, and development between global indigenous rights activists and local adivasis in rural Jharkhand, India and Shannon Speed's (2008) study of the articulations and divergences between local-global human rights discourses in Chiapas, Mexico provide further ethnographic accounts of "friction" within local-global activist contexts.

Transnational Zapatismo and global justice movements have perhaps provided the most fertile terrain for the ethnographic analysis of transnational activism. Carving out a practice-based approach to networks, for example, Juris (2008a) argues that global justice movements involve an increasing confluence among network technologies, network-based organizational forms, and network-based political norms, mediated by activist practice. The network, beyond technology and organizational infrastructure, has thus become a widespread cultural ideal, a model of and for emerging forms of radical, directly democratic practice.

Similarly stressing the links between imagination and political practice, Alex Khasnabish (2008) explores how Zapatismo resonates among US and Canadian activists who, rather than "importing" Zapatismo, "encounter" it through politico-cultural and technological processes of transmission and translation, practices of imagination through which activists seek to ground Zapatismo in their everyday fabrics of struggle. Transnational Zapatista and global justice networks are also marked by cultural, political, and organizational tensions, power imbalances, and struggles, for example, between direct action-oriented activists (see, e.g., Graeber 2009) and other global justice movement sectors. Ethnographies of regional and world social forums have paid particular attention to the differential experiences and exclusions of, and internal struggles between, multiple constituencies and groups within particular social forum processes (Juris 2008b; Conway 2013).

Actor-network theory (ANT) and complexity theory have also inspired practice-oriented studies of global justice activism. Complexity theory, which emphasizes the recursive self-generation of complex, adaptive systems through myriad micro-level interactions, has become increasingly influential among activists and ethnographers alike (see Escobar 2008). For his part, based on fieldwork among grass-roots activists in Bangladesh, the geographer Paul Routledge (2008) draws on ANT to analyze shifting patterns of connection, association, and translation within transnational global justice networks, paying particular attention to issues of culture, power, and human agency.

New Media Activism

New media practices, including activist usage of websites, listservs, and social media, have been central to the dynamics of local-global networking. The general literature on this topic is too vast to cover here, but for our purposes it is sufficient to point out that ethnographers are particularly well-situated to examine not only the everyday practices of media activists, but also how new and other media have shaped the organizational logic and cultural dynamics of contemporary social movements. For example, ethnographers such as Arturo Escobar (2008) and Jeffrey Juris (2008a) have examined the resonance between the reticulate, self-organizing properties of the internet and the rhizomatic structure and dynamics of the global justice movements. In this sense, online and offline practices do not simply mirror one another, they are also mutually constitutive, while particular media practices and organizing logics are always contested.

New media and communication technologies are also sites of struggle, as revealed in the conflicts over participatory democracy that Anastasia Kavada (2010), a communications scholar, has explored in her online/offline ethnographic research on a European Social Forum organizing listserv. Juris and his colleagues (2013) similarly found that free and open source software emerged as a terrain of struggle between tech workers, other forum organizers, and grass-roots activists within various regional and world social forums. Ethnographic research thus helps to illuminate not only emerging logics and practices facilitated by new media and technology, but also the contests over their meaning and legitimate usages.

The rise of social media platforms such as Facebook and Twitter has continued to shape the dynamics of contemporary protest. John Postill's (2014) ethnographic account of the use of Twitter in Spain's indignados movement reveals the emergence of a new "viral reality" shaped by the incessant sharing of information by activists and media professionals via new social media platforms. Juris (2012b) further identifies an emerging "logic of aggregation" within the occupy movements fueled by the capacity of social media to convene large numbers of dispersed individuals within concrete physical spaces, a subtle shift from the networking logics of the global justice movements.

Beyond the internet, activists increasingly use multiple media platforms to organize and communicate protest. In her ethnographic research on an Indymedia collective, Tish Stringer (2013) examines not only the circulation of written texts via Indymedia websites, but also the production of activist videos. Social movements have also made extensive use of public, low-power, and pirate radio, as anthropological ethnographers have explored in relation to urban youth activism in the Basque Country (Urla 1997) and Mexico City (Juris 2012a) as well as popular and indigenous struggles in Oaxaca (Stephen 2013). Multimedia tools and formats have not only provided forums for cultural production and meaning-making, they have also facilitated grass-roots networking and movement building.

PERFORMATIVE PROTEST

Ethnography is also an important method for grasping the more visible moments of activism, including mass marches, direct actions, rallies, and other modes of performative protest. An embodied and politically engaged ethnography is particularly important for understanding the highly emotional dynamics of public protests, as well as the complex forms of interaction and negotiation that go into their organization. Activists employ various "techniques of the body" and diverse protest styles to occupy space and resist domination, while conveying political messages and expressing alternative values and identities. When studying political protests and actions, the ethnographer's body thus becomes an important research tool (Juris 2008a).

Mass marches and actions bring together the visual, embodied, and spatial dimensions of activist practice. Engaged ethnographic research carried out from within the heat of struggle is particularly attuned to the complex micro-level spatial practices and dynamics of street protest. In his ethnographies of street protest in India and Nepal, Routledge (1994) employs the concept of "terrain of resistance" to denote culturally and spatially contextualized sites of contestation between forces of domination and resistance, as well as between different values, beliefs, and goals (560–561). Terrains of resistance are both physical and symbolic, conflict spaces within which protest action is set, represented, and interpreted (1997). In this sense, diverse protest tactics inscribe differential cultural and political meanings on the surrounding landscape.

Ethnographers have also examined how political meanings are represented and conveyed through embodied protest performance. Interpretivist ethnographers are particularly adept at examining the symbolic and theatrical aspects of activist performance. The anthropologist Angelique Haugerud (2013), for example, explores the performance practices of Billionaires for Bush, a satirical activist performance troupe that uses humor and satire to challenge corporate globalization and economic inequality. The sociologist Ben Shepard (2010) uses politically engaged ethnography with ActUp and other queer protest groups to analyze similarly colorful performances in the struggle against HIV/AIDS and in support of queer liberation. Finally, Juris (2008a, 2012b) uses militant ethnography to explore the intersections between embodied action, cultural performance, and diverse spatial practices during mass anti-corporate globalization and occupy protests. In all of these examples, an engaged and embodied ethnography captures the diverse and intersecting modes of spatial, bodily, and performative practice that constitute mass actions, marches, and other forms of public protest.

As the sociologist Javier Auyero's (2003) study of two young Argentine women's remembrances of their participation in anti-IMF and anti-corruption protests attests, quasi-ethnographic methods such as life histories can also reveal how individual actors experience collective action, illuminating the intersections between personal biographies, public protest, and historical events. Similarly, the anthropologist Lynn Stephen (2013) uses oral testimonies collected from indigenous women in Oaxaca to shed important ethnographic and experiential light on the dynamics of street protest, communal life at the barricades, and mass media take-overs during the 2006 Oaxaca uprising.

Conclusion

Ethnographic methods, and particularly politically engaged ethnography, can help illuminate movement dynamics that are less accessible to traditional objectivist social movement research. Ethnographers are in a better position to observe and to directly experience the everyday lived realities of movement activists, providing a strategic vantage point from which to examine the ongoing practices, forms of interaction, and emotional dynamics of social movement activity. As we have argued, rather than approaching social movements as an object for testing universal laws or a hermeneutic representation to decode, engaged ethnography allows us to grasp the logic of activist practice, including diverse forms of cultural production, local-global networking, new media activism, and performative protest. In particular, an anthropological approach to culture as always produced and contested within complex fields of power allows us to examine the ongoing cultural-political practices and struggles enacted by and within grass-roots social movements. Such engaged ethnography comes with its own politics of knowledge production, of course, and issues related to the power relations and divergences between ethnographers and the movements they work with and study, as well as the kinds of movements ethnographers engage, continue to demand further consideration.

We have also noted that ethnographic approaches have been much more prevalent among anthropologists and critical geographers engaged in the study of social movements. Ethnography has been far less common within mainstream social movement studies, although a number of cultural sociologists have produced high quality ethnographic accounts of movement cultures in the context of mobilization and/or ongoing social interaction. Nonetheless, there has been little cross-fertilization between ethnographic approaches to movements in sociology and interpretivist approaches in fields such as anthropology and critical geography.

Despite important epistemological differences, greater interaction between mainstream social movement theorists, participant observers in sociology, and interpretivist ethnographers can be mutually beneficial. Ethnographers in anthropology and critical geography often produce sophisticated, richly descriptive, and theoretically innovative accounts of social movement activity, yet they have a tendency to remain *sui generis*, failing to contribute to larger discussions and frameworks. Meanwhile, the mainstream scholarship on social movements, including ethnographic work by sociologists, could benefit from the alternative perspectives and theoretical innovation provided by more critical-interpretivist ethnographic accounts, particularly in relation to culture, power, and more radical, non-modernist forms of movement activity, as well as the greater geographic diversity represented by ethnographies of social movements in anthropology and geography. Some of this cross-fertilization is already starting to happen, particularly in relation to global justice movements and the social forum process, yet there is still a need for further exchanges across disciplinary, epistemological, and geographic divides.

NOTE

1. This is actually a long-standing trend, already noted by the anthropologist Arturo Escobar in his early work on social movements (see, e.g., Escobar 1992).

REFERENCES

Alvarez, Sonia E. (1998). "Latin American Feminisms 'Go Global.'" In *Cultures of Politics, Politics of Cultures*, edited by Sonia E. Alvarez, Evelina Dagnino, and Arturo Escobar, 293–324. Boulder, CO: Westview Press.

Alvarez, Sonia E., Dagnino, Evelina, and Escobar, Arturo (1998). "Introduction." In *Cultures of Politics, Politics of Cultures*, edited by Sonia E. Alvarez, Evelina Dagnino, and Arturo Escobar, 1–29. Boulder, CO: Westview Press.

Auyero, Javier (2003). *Contentious Lives*. Durham, NC: Duke University Press.

Burdick, John (1995). "Uniting Theory and Practice in the Ethnography of Social Movements," *Dialectical Anthropology*. 20: 361–385.

Burawoy, Michael (2000). "Grounding Globalization." In *Global Ethnography*, edited by Michael Burawoy, et al., 337–350. Berkeley: University of California Press.

Casas-Cortés, Maria Isabel, Osterweil, Michal, and Powell, Dana E. (2013). "Transformation in Engaged Ethnography." In *Insurgent Encounters*, edited by Jeffrey S. Juris and Alex Khasnabish, 199–228. Durham, NC: Duke University Press.

Chatterton, Paul (2010). "Autonomy," *Antipode*. 42(4): 897–908.

Conway, Janet (2006). *Praxis and Politics*. London: Routledge.

Conway, Janet (2013). *Edges of Global Justice*. London: Routledge.

Costa Vargas, João H. (2006). *Catching Hell in the City of Angels*. Minneapolis: University of Minnesota Press.

Doerr, Nicole (2008). "Deliberative Discussion, Language, and Efficiency in The World Social Forum Process," *Mobilization*. 13(4): 395–410.

Eliasoph, Nina (1998). *Avoiding Politics*. Cambridge: Cambridge University Press.

Escárcega, Sylvia (2013). "The Global Indigenous Movement and Paradigm Wars." In *Insurgent Encounters*, edited by Jeffrey S. Juris and Alex Khasnabish, 129–150. Durham, NC: Duke University Press.

Escobar, Arturo (1992). "Culture, Practice and Politics," *Critique of Anthropology*. 12(4): 395–432.

Escobar, Arturo (2008). *Territories of Difference*. Durham, NC: Duke University Press.

Escobar, Arturo and Alvarez, Sonia E., eds. (1992). *The Making of Social Movements in Latin America*. Boulder: Westview Press.

Eyerman, Ron and Jamison, Andrew (1991). *Social Movements: A Cognitive Approach*. University Park, PA: The Penn State University Press.

Fantasia, Rick (1988). *Cultures of Solidarity*. Berkeley: University of California Press.

Graeber, David (2009). *Direct Action*. Oakland, CA: AK Press.

Haiven, Max, and Khasnabish, Alex (2013). "Between Success and Failure." *Interface*. 5(2): 472–498.

Hale, Charles R. (2006). "Activist Research v. Cultural Critique," *Cultural Anthropology*. 21(1): 96–120.

Haugerud, Angelique (2013). *No Billionaire Left Behind*. Stanford, CA: Stanford University Press.

Hess, David J. (2013). "Local and Not-So-Local Exchanges: Alternative Economies, Ethnography, and Social Science." In *Insurgent Encounters*, edited by Jeffrey S. Juris and Alex Khasnabish, 151–170. Durham, NC: Duke University Press.

Juris, Jeffrey S. (2008a). *Networking Futures: The Movements against Corporate Globalization*. Durham, NC: Duke University Press.

Juris, Jeffrey S. (2008b). "Spaces of Intentionality," *Mobilization*. 13(4): 353–371.

Juris, Jeffrey S. (2012a). "Frequencies of Transgression." In *Radio Fields*, edited by Lucas Bessire and Daniel Fisher, 160–178. New York: New York University Press.

Juris, Jeffrey S. (2012b). "Reflections on #Occupy Everywhere," *American Ethnologist*. 39(2): 259–279.

Juris, Jeffrey S. and Alex Khasnabish, eds. (2013). *Insurgent Encounters: Transnational Activism, Ethnography, and the Political*. Durham, NC: Duke University Press.

Juris, Jeffrey S., Caruso, Guiseppe, Couture, Stéphane, and Mosca, Lorenzo (2013). "The Cultural Politics of Free Software and Technology within the Social Forum Process." In *Insurgent Encounters*, edited by Jeffrey S. Juris and Alex Khasnabish, 342–366. Durham, NC: Duke University Press.

Kavada, Anastasia (2010). "Email Lists and Participatory Democracy in the European Social Forum," *Media, Culture, & Society*. 32(3): 355–372.

Khasnabish, Alex (2008). *Zapatismo beyond Borders*. Toronto: University of Toronto Press.

Khasnabish, Alex, and Haiven, Max (2012). "Convoking the Radical Imagination," *Cultural Studies/Critical Methodologies*. 12(5): 408–421.

Kurtz, Sharon (2002). *Workplace Justice*. Minneapolis: University of Minnesota Press.

Lichterman, Paul (1996). *The Search for Political Community*. Cambridge: Cambridge University Press.

Lichterman, Paul (2005). *Elusive Togetherness*. Princeton: Princeton University Press.

Lichterman, Paul (2013). "Ethnography and Social Movements." In *The Wiley-Blackwell Encyclopedia of Social and Political Movements*, edited by David A. Snow, Donatella della Porta, Bert Klandermans, and Doug McAdam, 428–431. Malden, MA: Wiley-Blackwell.

Maeckelbergh, Marianne (2009). *The Will of the Many*. London: Pluto Press.

Marcus, George E. (1995). "Ethnography in/of the World System," *Annual Review of Anthropology*. 24: 95–117.

Méndez, Jennifer Bickham (2005). *From the Revolution to the Maquiladoras*. Durham: Duke University Press.

Méndez, Jennifer Bickham (2008). "Globalizing Scholar Activism." In *Engaging Contradictions*, edited by Charles R. Hale, 136–163. Berkeley: University of California Press.

Mische, Anne (2008). *Partisan Publics*. Princeton: Princeton University Press.

Naples, Nancy A. (2003). *Feminism and Method*. London: Routledge.

Paley, Julia (2001). *Marketing Democracy*. Berkeley: University of California Press.

Pleyers, Geoffrey (2011). *Alter-Globalization*. London: Polity.

Polletta, Francesca (1997). "Culture and its Discontents," *Sociological Inquiry*. 67(4): 431–450.

Polletta, Francesca (2002). *Freedom is an Endless Meeting*. Chicago: University of Chicago Press.

Polletta, Francesca (2006). *It Was Like a Fever*. Chicago: University of Chicago Press.

Postill, John (2014). "Democracy in an Age of Viral Reality," *Ethnography*. 15(1): 51–69.

Razsa, Maple and Kurnik, Andrej (2012). "The Occupy Movement in Žižek's Hometown," *American Ethnologist*. 39(2): 238–258.

Routledge, Paul (1994). "Backstreets, Barricades, and Blackouts," *Environment and Planning D*. 12: 559–578.

Routledge, Paul (2008). "Acting in the Network," *Environment and Planning D*. 26: 199–217.

Selbin, Eric (2010). *Revolution, Rebellion, Resistance*. London: Zed Books.

Shah, Alpa (2010). *In the Shadows of the State*. Durham, NC: Duke University Press.

Shepard, Benjamin (2010). *Queer Political Performance and Protest*. New York: Routledge.

Sitrin, Marina (2012). *Everyday Revolutions*. London: Zed.

Speed, Shannon (2008). *Rights in Rebellion*. Stanford, CA: Stanford University Press.

Stephen, Lynn (2013). *We are the Face of Oaxaca*. Durham, NC: Duke University Press.

Stringer, Tish (2013). "This is What Democracy Looked Like." In *Insurgent Encounters*, edited by Jeffrey S. Juris and Alex Khasnabish, 318–341. Durham, NC: Duke University Press.

Thayer, Millie (2010). *Making Transnational Feminism*. London: Routledge.

Tsing, Anna (2005). *Friction*. Princeton: Princeton University Press.

Urla, Jacqueline (1997). "Outlaw Language." In *The Politics of Culture in the Shadow of Capital*, edited by Lisa Lowe and David Lloyd, 280–300. Durham, NC: Duke University Press.

Wood, Lesley J. (2012). *Direct Action, Deliberation, and Diffusion*. Cambridge: Cambridge University Press.

Warren, Kay (1998). *Indigenous Movements and their Critics*. Princeton: Princeton University Press.

Wolford, Wendy (2010). *This Land is Ours Now*. Durham, NC: Duke University Press.

PART VII

POLITICAL AND NON-POLITICAL OPPORTUNITIES AND CONSTRAINTS

CHAPTER 39

··

CONTENTIOUS COLLECTIVE ACTION AND THE EVOLVING NATION-STATE

··

MARK R. BEISSINGER

OF the variety of large-scale structural influences on contentious collective action, the state is often considered among the most consequential. The reasons are multiple and fundamental. Given their defining claim to supremacy in binding rule making within the territories under their authority,[1] states naturally become arenas within which collective action flows. No other authority is made to bear such direct responsibility for the conditions under which we live, nor is thought to possess such means for altering those conditions. Some social movements aim primarily to bring about alterations in lifestyles and social norms rather than in the political sphere; yet, more often than not, even these movements seem inexorably drawn to the state as a source of grievance or a vehicle for achieving social change.

States attract resistance not only due to their claims of ultimate authority, but also because of their penetration and presence in everyday life, the ambitions of those who control them, and the ways in which state power has been readily subject to abuse (at times, on a massive scale). In contrast to earlier periods in human history, in the modern era how state power is exercised has come to be associated with vast stakes, exerting enormous influence on the life chances of most individuals and their offspring. As a result of their ability to award licenses and contracts, distribute and redistribute resources, regulate trade and the supply of money, and enforce laws and regulations, livelihoods and fortunes hang on even the most rudimentary of state decisions. States also attract collective action because of how state power has become thoroughly entangled in the politics of identity and cultural difference, raising difficult issues not only about the cultural rules underpinning the state (and the enormous distributional stakes these can involve), but also about the proper boundaries of political communities and the affective ties associated with them.

But modern states are much more than just a source of grievance and a central object of and arena for collective action. As much of the social movement literature emphasizes, states are also key players within contentious politics in their own right. Most states have amassed significant coercive capabilities to back up their claimed supremacy in rule making, and many have substantial material capabilities as well. As a result, states usually possess considerable capacity to shape society, reward those who support them, and punish those who challenge them. The repressive, material, and regulatory capacities of states and how these are wielded are widely considered among the most important factors shaping mobilization. But states also have more subtle means for influencing collective action through their control over public imaginations. Through their enormous powers to socialize, normalize, and mobilize affect, states can define and constrain how individuals understand themselves and pursue their interests, shaping collective action in constitutive ways.

Conversations about "the state" are readily susceptible to reification, and it is easy to forget that states represent a range of possibilities and configurations. Some exercise enormous power within and beyond their borders. Others exist nominally and persist largely due to their recognition by the international community of states, possessing little more than juridical sovereignty (Jackson and Rosberg 1982). Still others assume a more predatory posture, blurring the line between states and organized crime (Levi 1981; Tilly 1985; Olson 1993). Most states, however, combine elements of all three of these potentialities to varying degrees. Whole-cloth descriptors such as weak or strong, though deeply embedded in discourse about states, cannot capture the complexity within and across cases. Moreover, despite the prevalence of the notion of state "failure" in writings about states, few states ever completely fail in the sense of a total collapse of state institutions (Somalia is a rare example). Even in the midst of civil war, state institutions usually continue to function (though with limited reach and effectiveness), and revolutionary movements claiming sovereignty vis-à-vis states often attempt to construct alternative state institutions.

It is also wrong to imagine states as bounded organizations crisply distinct from the societies over which they rule. Throughout history, states have tended to be closely aligned with dominant economic interests. However, as even the Marxist literature on the state came to recognize (Poulantzas 1975; Skocpol 1979), states have as often shaped these interests as they have been shaped by them. States and societies are thus closely intertwined, with social relationships penetrating state institutions and political relationships infiltrating society (Evans 1995; Migdal 2001). Indeed, these network ties between states and societies are often critical to the ways in which social movements exert influence over states.

Much of what states become depends on the political regimes that control them. By "political regime," scholars have in mind "the choice of procedures that regulate access to state power" (Munck 2001: 123). But particularly in states that have been built by specific regimes and are closely associated with them, it has often been difficult to distinguish analytically between the two. Some states are so closely intertwined with specific regimes that the collapse of the regime has essentially meant the unravelling of the state. (This was the case, for instance, in the demise of Soviet communism.) Other states endure a succession of regimes of various sorts with little effect on state power (though frequent regime turnover can exercise a cumulative effect on state legitimacy and capacity). Irrespective of regime-type, it has never been easy to transform entrenched state–society relationships, in large part because of the expectations of behavior that they generate, the interests associated with them, and the enormous collective action problems involved. Moments of heightened contention have provided rare opportunities to move these relationships in new directions. Still, many of the deep-seated ways in which populations relate to states have been known to survive even the most violent and disruptive of revolutionary upheavals.

Temporally, states are subject to the variable rhythms of their institutions and the regimes that control them—the openings and closings posited by political opportunity theories. But viewed within a longer time frame, states have themselves been subject to a series of long-term transformations that have influenced the form, content, and process of mobilization. In the remainder of this chapter, I examine three such transformations and the effects that they have had (and continue to have) on contentious politics: the growth and complexity of state institutions; national self-determination and states; and the effects of globalization on states.

CONTENTION AND THE GROWTH OF THE INSTITUTIONAL STATE

While there is no generally accepted scholarly definition of a state, as Michael Mann (1986) noted, states have generally been defined either functionally (in terms of their monopoly of violence or dominance in rule making) or institutionally (as a set of organizations from which political relations radiate). In the contemporary world modern states are widely associated with a set of institutions that most states possess to one degree or another: permanent bureaucracies that carry out fiscal, regulatory, and administrative tasks; standing armies; legislatures and political parties; courts and police; central banks; foreign ministries and embassies. Today only 13 per cent of states do not have standing armies (almost all of these, islands); only 12 per cent have tax burdens less than 10 per cent of GDP (mainly oil states that collect significant rents from energy production); only 1 per cent have no legislative institutions; only 18 per cent have chief executives not associated with a political party (mostly monarchies and military dictatorships); and only 17 per cent have no legislative opposition parties.[2] Moreover, only four countries have no central bank. Significantly, almost all of these institutions emerged over the last four hundred years. Whether due to institutional isomorphism, to extensive borrowing, or to a global culture positing what states should look like (Meyer et al. 1997), there has been a formal institutional convergence among states on a global scale, as states today look much more similar to one another than did political units in earlier periods of history.

With some important exceptions, what Mann called the "infrastructural" power of states (their ability to penetrate the daily lives of those they govern) remained relatively underdeveloped in the ancient and medieval worlds. But beginning in the sixteenth century, a revolution in state power unfolded on the European continent. As European absolutist rulers grew in strength, wealth, and ambition and projected their power outward, they began to develop a set of increasingly permanent institutions (standing armies, bureaucracies, and universal taxation) that are today widely associated with the modern state. The ways in which the rise of the modern state altered contentious politics was a central theme of the work of Charles Tilly (1998), embodied in particular in his notion of the collective action repertoire. As Tilly (2004) documented, the growth of the institutional state and its increasing encroachment on the lives of its subjects in the form of levies, taxation, regulation, and conscription evoked into being the earliest social movements and gave rise to revolution as a modern form of politics. The growth of central state power transformed the locus and character of claims away from local authority and toward the central state and fostered more direct and sustained forms of organized collective action.

Indeed, there has long been an endogenous relationship between the growth of states and the evolution of political contention. While the growth of state institutions became a source of new forms of contention, mobilization in turn exercised a significant influence on the development of state institutions. Modern legislatures were originally conceived as a way of providing a veneer of consent for state extraction of resources. But legislatures soon gained a will of their own, and parliamentary campaigns aimed at legitimating legislative representation unwittingly opened up new spaces for public influence on politics. Thus, as contention over the growing demands of states increased, the rule-making institutions of states grew more complex, divided, and subject to mass influence. Early political parties developed as legislative factions, but under the influence of electoral incentives quickly evolved into vehicles for linking public sentiment to state institutions. In addition to institutionalizing division within government, parties in turn transformed mobilizational politics by creating organized standing oppositions permanently interested in mobilizing populations. Tilly (2004) has suggested that the demonstration as a form of collective action prospered with the rise of elected assemblies. Demonstrations resembled a type of public counter-assembly, and through their visible display of support for or against particular policies, took advantage of politicians' increasing dependence on public consent. In this respect, the vulnerabilities of state institutions exercise an important influence on choices of mobilizational forms and tactics. The growth and diversification of the legitimating institutions of states also opened up many of the channels commonly associated with political opportunity—elections, divided government, splits within ruling coalitions, and realignments within government (Tarrow 2011).

The industrial revolution brought about an enormous expansion in the size and responsibilities of states (Polyani 1944; Gerschenkron 1962; North 1990) and infused states with a rationalist perspective that has shaped global repertoires of rule (Scott 1998). Industrialization led to the rise of the labor movement and the growth of significant urban unrest, which in turn led to a significant increase in the state's role in regulating the dysfunctions of capitalism and the further growth of state institutions. Prior to the nineteenth century, European states maintained order through ad hoc institutions like constables or night watchmen, dealing with major unrest by calling in military force or volunteer militias. But as urban crime, industrial strife, and revolutionary challenges multiplied, states embraced the need for a professional police force to manage and regulate dissent (della Porta and Reiter 1998). In their further efforts to stave off revolutionary challenges (and sometimes as a result of successful revolutionary challenges), states assumed additional responsibilities for alleviating poverty and inequality. By the second half of the twentieth century, with the mushrooming of the state's welfare functions, the size and weight of states proportionately within societies had grown tremendously. In 2010 total government expenses (cash payments for the operating activities of government in providing goods and services) for 113 non-socialist countries ranged from 11 per cent of GDP for Bangladesh to 62 per cent of GDP for Ireland, with the average across countries being 28 per cent of GDP.[3] Thus, in interaction with contentious politics, by the early twenty-first century states had truly grown into Leviathans in ways that Hobbes could hardly have imagined.

The institutional growth of states raises a number of questions about the relationship between states and contentious politics that have yet to receive adequate answers. Scott (1998) suggests certain common ways in which states view reality through the prism of high modernism and points to shared repertoires of rule typical of modern states. To what extent do these incite common repertoires of contentious challenges? Even in authoritarian states, the formal presence of elections and legislatures may impart consistent rhythms to contentious politics. Beneath the veneer of formal institutional convergence around the world lies enormous variety in the quality and functioning of state institutions. For some states, coercive capacities have far outstripped institutional development in other spheres, orienting them toward violent responses to the mobilizational challenges that they face. Indeed, states remain the greatest source of violence in the world today, responsible for the most heinous instances of mass murder over the last two centuries. In a large number of states formal institutions remain rife with corruption and permeated by organized criminal groups, familial ties, and patronage relationships. Despite its prevalence, we know little about the circumstances under which informality mobilizes or de-mobilizes. State corruption and fraud, for instance, have been manifest grievances within urban civic revolutions; but in peasant revolutions involvement in patronage relationships is known to prevent individual participation in revolutionary challenges. Moreover, as James Scott (2009) has shown, there are still large geographic swathes that have never come under the real control of states and into which state power has failed to penetrate, even though these areas fall within the formal territories of states. These regions—usually mountainous terrain—sometimes serve as bases for militarized revolutionary challenges (Goodwin 2001; Fearon and Laitin 2003). Still, many states have found ways of surviving even when large portions of their territory remain beyond their sway. In much of the world, the cost of state institutions has become increasingly difficult to sustain economically, particularly as globalization has forced states to lower taxes to compete for private investment. Heavy debt has compelled many states to engage in significant contraction—a development that has become a significant grievance and occasion for substantial mobilization. Thus, today it may not be the growth of the institutional state that lies at the basis of contention, but rather its contraction, as the world has come to rely upon the supply of public goods that only states have been able to provide on a large scale, but which states are increasingly less capable of supplying.

Contention, Culture, and the National State

A second vector of structural change in the character of states that has been closely intertwined with contention is the rise of national self-determination as a principle for constituting states and the state's entanglement in issues of mass culture and identity. Most people throughout history have thought of themselves primarily in local, religious, urban, class, tribal, or clan terms—not as belonging to state or national communities. But beginning in the sixteenth century, the growing power of the state evoked a series of changes in the ways in which individuals related to state power—and in particular, in the relationship of cultural identities to the state.

As Ernest Gellner (1983) observed, nationalism emerges only where politically centralized units are already taken for granted. In the pre-modern world, power was functionally rather than geographically differentiated, with multiple authorities often piled up over the same territory and population. The key feature of sovereignty, by contrast, was the closure of political power—that is, the unlimited authority of the state within a geographically bounded territory rather than its limitation to particular functional spheres (Wendt 1992). The emergence of sovereignty within Europe secularized political power and undermined its longstanding connection with religion and the universal claims of the Church. But it also created a focal point of shared fate among all subject to the common rule of the sovereign (Anderson 1983). Sovereignty and the closure it entailed were closely tied with the development of the modern notion of the citizen—a person who legally belongs to a state, is subject to its laws and entitled to its protections, and therefore owes the state loyalty and obligations (such as the duty to pay taxes, support it in time of war, and obey its laws). But if the state did not live up to its contractual obligations to protect, loyalty to the state could just as easily be withdrawn.

Many scholars date the first large-scale nationalist mobilizations to the revolutions of the late eighteenth century and the contention that emerged over the burdens imposed on populations due to the growth of the institutional state. These early nationalist mobilizations asserted the rights of citizens vis-à-vis monarchs and posited that the source of sovereignty lay with the nation—a mass membership community from which the state and its rulers drew their right to rule. In the form of citizen armies, civic nationalism of this sort proved its superiority in motivating participation and commitment over the mercenary forces of monarchs. But by the early nineteenth century nationalism underwent tremendous evolution, as culture began to be asserted as the proper basis for constituting nations. In this ethnicized version of national community, nationalism became a theory of political legitimacy positing that "ethnic boundaries should not cut across political ones," and that "ethnic boundaries within a given state.... should not separate the power-holders from the rest" (Gellner 1983: 1). The principle of national self-determination has been a profoundly destabilizing force for states, coming to justify anti-colonial, separatist, and irredentist mobilizations around the world, as well as revolt against domination by privileged racial or ethnic minorities within states. As a result, over time the number of independent states in the world has multiplied from fifty-one countries in 1945 to approximately 196 by 2013—a process of fragmentation that continues within developing and advanced industrial countries alike.

As many movements have discovered, the shared cultural symbols associated with civic and ethnic nationalisms constitute some of the most efficient means for mobilizing affect and for overcoming collective action problems. However, as experience has also shown, these symbols can be used as easily to justify liberation from a culturally alien state as to motivate ethnic cleansing and genocide in the name of creating a culturally homogenous society. Moreover, culture has been as much a force underpinning mobilizational challenges to states as it has been used by states to undermine mobilizational challenges. As Eric Hobsbawm (1990) observed, in response to separatist challenges and the threat of revolution and separatist nationalism, nineteenth-century European monarchs devised official nationalist projects aimed at fashioning national communities around states through the invention of tradition, the establishment of large-scale public education, and language standardization and assimilation. By most estimates, the power of states to foster language rationalization and construct identities has led overall to a reduction of the number of independent cultures around the world.[4] And through their everyday manipulation of culture, states aim to reinforce loyalty to the state within their populations, preparing them to assume willingly the sacrifices asked of them—including the ultimate sacrifice of life itself (Billig 1995).

While today all states (even monarchies) claim to represent nations (variously defined), conflict over the proper boundaries of the nation and over who deserves membership status remains ubiquitous. There is no such thing as a culturally neutral state; all states, to varying degrees, represent repositories of cultural interest—even more so in a world beset by massive movements of populations across state borders. Despite the power of states to foster assimilation and homogenization, all states remain culturally diverse in key respects and experience conflict over access to the state by the cultural groups within their borders. Given widespread expectations that states should represent particular ethnic interests, those who run states often find that building legitimacy involves ethnic favoritism in the distribution of public goods and jobs—a practice that constitutes a frequent grievance within contentious politics. Empirical studies have shown that violent ethnic rebellion is inversely related to the degree to which an ethnic group enjoys access to and representation within the state (Cederman, Wimmer, and Min 2010). But there is also considerable variation across cultural groups in their abilities to contest situations of ethnic domination that relate to group size, the degree of assimilation, the resources available, and the density of network structures (Beissinger 2002). The ways in which states classify citizens and code cultural difference—in censuses, identity cards, and in categories of public policy—also exercise profound effects on how individuals understand and mobilize around cultural identities. And the spatial organization of states and ways in which internal boundaries intersect with cultural difference can serve as an obstacle or facilitation to nationalist mobilization. Thus, as constructivist theories have emphasized, which cultural categories among the many competing for our attention become the basis for mobilization is usually the product of the policies, behaviors, and institutional configurations of states.

GLOBALIZATION AND THE STATE

States are Janus-like entities, with one face positioned toward those they govern, and another toward what lies beyond their boundaries. Indeed, the consolidation of the modern state system involved the emergence of an international community of states that mutually recognized one another's sovereignty and status (Spruyt 1994). As Tilly (1992) noted, the establishment of the modern state system was also a violent process, as states assimilated territories, eliminated competitors, and amassed resources through war and conquest. In some cases it also involved a marriage between incipient capitalism and states, with trade, transnational borrowing, and mercantilist commerce enriching state coffers and strengthening the capabilities of rulers. While European rulers were recognizing one another's sovereignty, they were also expanding globally, establishing the first truly global international system. When European colonialism collapsed in the mid-twentieth century, the nation-state was left behind as universal political form, with a global system of states blanketing the planet.

Much as states have straddled domestic and international spheres, there has always been an international component to contentious politics as well. Defeat in wars and international financial crises have served as moments of state weakness that have precipitated contentious challenges, and early social movements (such as the abolitionist, labor, or temperance movements) sought connections with kindred movements across state borders and often organized transnationally. Nevertheless, in the last several decades the relationship between states and civil society has changed dramatically as a result of radical changes in the international context of mobilization, due specifically to the impacts of globalization, the internet and social media, and the consolidation of an international legal and normative order above the nation-state.

Globalization, in the sense of the intensification of social relationships across state boundaries in ways that link distant locations around the world (Giddens 1991: 64), is not a new phenomenon. But globalization in the late twentieth and early twenty-first centuries is quantitatively and qualitatively different from the past, as the scale and speed of interactions across state borders have intensified at an exponential rate, and trade, capital, people, and information move across state borders as never before in human history. Globalization has influenced contentious politics in multiple ways. But some of its most important effects have had subversive effects on the power and control of states. The growth and rapidity of cross-border movement of capital has not only undermined the ability of states to tax and regulate business; it has also been associated with periodic financial bubbles whose disruptive effects ripple across states, creating punctuated crises of state legitimacy and setting in motion contentious challenges simultaneously across multiple contexts. Flows of communication now move across state borders with enormous speed, evading censorship and injecting greater volatility into the political sphere. Oppositions themselves have increasingly organized transnationally, using websites and social media to coordinate action across state borders and to disseminate information outside the reach of states. In this saturated information environment, contention can spread rapidly across states merely from challengers emulating the prior successes of others. Such connections are facilitated by a sense of interconnectedness produced by common institutional characteristics, histories, cultural affinities, or modes of domination across states (Beissinger 2007).

At the same time, the emergence of an international human rights normative regime has added an additional layer of constraints that have given some leaders pause before engaging in violent crackdowns against opponents. As Margaret Keck and Kathryn Sikkink (1998) have shown, movements and transnational NGOs have learned to utilize these norms to shame states engaging in gross human rights violation and to generate pressures on them from the international community of states. Transnational NGOs also play important roles in supporting civil society association and aiding domestic opposition. And the presence of an increasingly robust layer of international institutions above the nation-state offers an additional source of political opportunities for movements, at times providing a supplementary venue from which challengers can communicate messages and exert influence (Tarrow 2005). Indeed, under the influence of globalization and the global communications revolution, a transformation in collective action repertoires may be taking place, as transnational actors and social media grow increasingly important to the organization of protest action, traversing the boundaries of nation-states with great frequency, providing safe haven for information beyond the reach of censorship, and impugning state capacities for control.

CONCLUSION

Looked at from a global vantage point, until recently the power of states had been on the rise over the past four hundred years, as states became the hegemonic form of political organization around the world and constituted, by most accounts, the most significant factor structuring contentious collective action. But states today are under significant stress on a number of different fronts: the incoherence and growing cost of state institutions, raising questions over the ability of states to supply public goods; endemic conflict over the proper boundaries of the membership communities of states and the cultural rules underpinning them; and the erosion of state capacities to control burgeoning transnational processes and the constraints imposed by global norms and institutions on state actions. As a result, the capacities of states to structure collective action may be eroding across much of the world (Rosenau 1990). Still, while the power of states to shape collective action may be under stress due to institutional corrosion, national fragmentation, and globalization, states will remain the central objects, arenas, and actors within contentious politics for the foreseeable future, as the world has yet to imagine a viable model for constituting authority that might take their place.

NOTES

1. Like Mann (1986), I de-emphasize the monopoly of legitimate violence as the defining feature of states and focus instead on the state's claim to supremacy in binding rule making within a particular territory—a feature akin to sovereignty (the exclusive right to rule within a particular territory). Contrary to the Weberian conception of states, many states perennially lack a monopoly of legitimate violence within their territories, and the legitimacy of state violence is subject to considerable contention.
2. Data computed from Bennett and Scott (2000); Beck et al. (2001); Fish and Kroenig (2009); Miller, Holmes, and Feulner (2013).
3. Data from The World Bank, World Development Indicators, available at: http://data.worldbank.org/indicator/GC.XPN.TOTL.GD.ZS?display=default Data are missing for all state socialist countries, where government expenses as a proportion of GDP are vastly higher.
4. The number of languages in the world has been decreasing significantly over time. According to *Ethnologue*, which has tracked language use around the world since 1951, of approximately 7,000 known languages, 10 per cent are "institutional languages" in the sense of being used by institutions outside the family or local community, while 34 per cent of languages are endangered or dying. See http://www.ethnologue.com/statistics/status.

REFERENCES

Anderson, Benedict (1983). *Imagined Communities: Reflections on the Origin and Spread of Nationalism*. London: Verso.

Beck, Thorsten, et al. (2001). "New Tools in Comparative Political Economy: The Database of Political Institutions." *World Bank Economic Review*. 15(1): 165–176 (data available at http://go.worldbank.org/2EAGGLRZ40).

Beissinger, Mark R. (2002). *Nationalist Mobilization and the Collapse of the Soviet State*. Cambridge: Cambridge University Press.

Beissinger, Mark R. (2007). "Structure and Example in Modular Political Phenomena: The Diffusion of Bulldozer/Rose/Orange/Tulip Revolutions," *Perspectives on Politics*. 5(2): 259–276.

Billig, Michael (1995). *Banal Nationalism*. London: Sage.

Bennett, D. Scott and Stam, Allan (2000). "EUGene: A Conceptual Manual." International Interactions 26: 179–204 (data available at: http://eugenesoftware.org).

Cederman, Lars-Erik, Wimmer, Andreas, and Min, Brian (2010). "Why Do Ethnic Groups Rebel?: New Data and Analysis," *World Politics*. 62(1): 87–119.

della Porta, Donatella and Reiter, Herbert, eds. (1998). *Policing Protest: The Control of Mass Demonstrations in Western Democracies*. Minneapolis, MN: University of Minnesota Press.

Evans, Peter B. (1995). *Embedded Autonomy: States and Industrial Transformation*. Princeton, NJ: Princeton University Press.

Fearon, James D. and Laitin, David D. (2003). "Ethnicity, Insurgency, and Civil War," *American Political Science Review*. 97(1): 75–90.

Fish, M. Steven and Kroenig, Matthew (2009). *The Handbook of National Legislatures: A Global Survey*. New York, NY: Cambridge University Press.

Gellner, Ernest (1983). *Nations and Nationalism*. Ithaca, NY: Cornell University Press.

Gerschenkron, Alexander (1962). *Economic Backwardness in Historical Perspective*. Cambridge, MA: Harvard University Press.

Giddens, Anthony (1991). *The Consequences of Modernity*. Cambridge: Polity Press.

Goodwin, Jeff (2001). *No Other Way Out: States and Revolutionary Movements, 1945–1991*. Cambridge: Cambridge University Press.

Hobsbawm, Eric J. (1990). *Nations and Nationalism Since 1780: Programme, Myth, Reality*. Cambridge: Cambridge University Press.

Jackson, Robert and Rosberg, Carl (1982). "Why Africa's Weak States Persist." *World Politics* 35: 1–24.

Keck, Margaret E. and Sikkink, Kathryn (1998). *Activists Beyond Borders: Advocacy Networks in International Politics*. Ithaca, NY: Cornell University Press.

Levi, Margaret (1981). "The Predatory Theory of Rule," *Politics & Society*. 10(4): 431–465.

Mann, Michael (1986). *The Sources of Social Power, vol. 1: A History of Power from the Beginning to AD 1760*. Cambridge: Cambridge University Press.

Meyer, John W. et al. (1997). "World Society and the Nation-State," *American Journal of Sociology*. 103(1): 144–181.

Migdal, Joel S. (2001). *State in Society*. Cambridge: Cambridge University Press.

Miller, Terry, Holmes, Kim R., Feulner, Edwin J. (2013). *Index of Economic Freedom* Washington, DC: The Heritage Foundation (data available at http://www.heritage.org/index/download)

Munck, Gerardo L. (2001). "The Regime Question," *World Politics*. 54(1): 119–145.

North, Douglass C. (1990). *Institutions, Institutional Change and Economic Performance*. Cambridge: Cambridge University Press.

Olson, Mancur (1993). "Dictatorship, Democracy, and Development," *American Political Science Review*. 87(3): 567–576.

Polyani, Karl (1944). *The Great Transformation*. New York, NY: Rinehart.

Poulantzas, Nicos (1975). *Political Power and Social Classes*. London: NLB.

Rosenau, James N. (1990). *Turbulence in World Politics: A Theory of Change and Continuity*. Princeton, NJ: Princeton University Press.

Scott, James C. (1998). *Seeing Like a State: How Certain Schemes to Improve the Human Condition Have Failed*. New Haven, CT: Yale University Press.

Scott, James C. (2009). *The Art of Not Being Governed: An Anarchist History of Upland Southeast Asia*. New Haven, CT: Yale University Press.

Skocpol, Theda (1979). *States and Social Revolutions*. Cambridge: Cambridge University Press.

Spruyt, Hendryk (1994). *The Sovereign State and its Competitors*. Princeton, NJ: Princeton University Press.

Tilly, Charles (1985). "War Making and State Making as Organized Crime." In *Bringing the State Back In*, edited by Peter B. Evans, Dietrich Rueschemeyer, and Theda Skocpol, 169–191. Cambridge: Cambridge University Press.

Tilly, Charles (1992). *Coercion, Capital, and European States, AD 990–1992*. Oxford: Blackwell.

Tilly, Charles (1998). *Popular Contention in Great Britain, 1758–1834*. Cambridge, MA: Harvard University Press.

Tilly, Charles (2004). *Social Movements, 1768–2004*. Boulder, CO: Paradigm.

Tarrow, Sidney (2011). *Power in Movement: Social Movements and Contentious Politics*, 3rd edn. Cambridge: Cambridge University Press.

Tarrow, Sidney (2005). *The New Transnational Activism*. Cambridge: Cambridge University Press.

Wendt, Alexander (1992). "Anarchy is What States Make of It: The Social Construction of Power Politics," *International Organization*. 46(2): 391–425.

CHAPTER 40

SOCIAL MOVEMENTS AND THE MULTILATERAL ARENA

JACKIE SMITH

GLOBALIZATION, the process of expanding and intensification of transnational exchanges and relationships, affects social movements. As states have become more inter-connected, ideas, goods, people, money, and communications flow more quickly and easily across national borders. This has shaped both the grievances around which people organize as well as the resources with which challengers can wage their struggles. Nevertheless, much social movement research continues to privilege the state as the main, if not the sole arena where social movement contestation takes place. By drawing from work in political sociology, international relations, and political economy of the world system, scholars can improve understandings of the ways political conflicts are embedded in extra-local contexts. This essay clarifies some assumptions embedded in state-centric approaches and explores ideas at the borders of social movement scholarship and related fields about how the world beyond states impacts conflicts on local, national, and global scales.

Research on transnational dimensions of social movements, like earlier social movement research, shows that ongoing processes of contention between social movements and political authorities shape the basic institutions of societies, namely states (cf. Tilly 1978; Tarrow 2011). What we've learned from this latest work is that social movements have shaped transnational institutions—including inter-governmental organizations and law—in ways similar to their influences on national institutions (Rajagopal 2003; Khagram 2004; Smith 2008). In short, by engaging in transnational claims making, social movement actors helped generate more democratic and inclusive international norms and create institutional practices and procedures that expand participation in politics and otherwise reflect and reinforce these norms. They have helped define states' legitimacy to reflect popular demands for participation and elite accountability, rather than merely military and economic priorities. In the course of their varied struggles for human rights, environmental protection, peace, and other claims, movements have secured a place for civil society actors in the world of states. Yet, although they have become recognized actors in world politics, the contradictions between the democratic impulses of movements and the requirements of the global capitalist system are becoming more apparent, and there is evidence that many are looking outside the system of states to address the world's most pressing conflicts. Having engaged the interstate arena in unprecedented ways during the 1990s, many activist groups saw more clearly this system's limited capacities for responding to growing problems. The early twenty-first century thus saw a growth in transnational social movement activity *outside* the boundaries of interstate politics. This development encourages us to re-think relationships between social movements and not just the state, but also the interstate system itself. It also raises the question about what roles and actions social movements may play in efforts to fundamentally transform states and the capitalist world system.

TRANSNATIONAL SOCIAL MOVEMENTS AND INTERNATIONAL INSTITUTIONS

Early work on how movements transcend national boundaries demonstrated that social movement engagement in transnational political arenas helped define global institutions and norms, engage transnational actors in domestic or national conflicts, and challenge or resist global institutions. The global arena, in short, was a source of political opportunities for social movement at the same time as it helped define the conflicts around which popular groups mobilized and the constraints on popular contention. Considerable evidence shows how movements help lay the foundations for international human rights laws and institutions and defined limits on the legitimate uses of military power. They have played similar roles in enhancing attention to international environmental issues (Willetts 1996; Risse et al. 1999; Khagram 2004; Smith 2008). Social movements have also helped institutionalize international norms by aiding the "domestication" of international law (see Tarrow 2005). Engaging what Keck and Sikkink (1998) famously referred to as the "boomerang effect," transnational advocacy groups draw attention to states' violations of international norms, drawing various forms of international pressure on violators aimed at changing their practices. They may also use legal mechanisms to transform domestic practices and laws in less overtly contentious ways. More recent years especially have seen rising levels of contention against international institutions (Sikkink 2005). While the bulk of this confrontation has been against the global financial institutions—the World Bank, International Monetary Fund, and World Trade Organization—the United Nations and its various conferences have become more frequent targets of movement critics.

Studies of changes in transnational activism over time show that movements' engagement with global institutions and the related work of building transnational organizations and alliances has transformed their analyses and organizing capacities. For instance, UN conferences provided spaces in which activists from many countries could converge to exchange experiences, discuss strategies for advancing global change, and defining shared visions, identities, and priorities (Friedman et al. 2005). As activists developed relationships with their counterparts from around the world, they learned about the complex impacts of global economic policies in different settings. They also learned how to use international mechanisms to press their own, and other states to conform to global norms, and in many cases discovered how ineffective these mechanisms are at changing state practices (Smith and Wiest 2012). Women's movement activists in particular helped articulate critiques of the interstate system and its capacity for addressing the claims movements raised (Alvarez 1999; Meyer and Prügl 1999; Conway 2012). But a key outcome of some of the earlier transnational activism was its success at expanding the possibilities for individual activists to encounter the global political sphere. By inviting activism around UN conferences, transnational social movements helped expand activists' political analyses and their self-understanding beyond the confines of a single state. This latter point is essential, since the ability to imagine one's self as a citizen of not just a single country but of the world, and to understand a local struggle as connected to global structures is what helps to sustain and grow transnational activism. Moreover, by extending the political beyond the bounds of the state, it helps lead activists to more systemic critiques that target the international system or even global capitalism. For instance, through repeated transnational encounters, feminist activists have deepened their analyses of patriarchy and the intersectionality of various oppressions, leading to more radical critiques of globalization and the state (Vargas 2005; Dufour and Giraud 2007; Moghadam 2012).

Understanding States and the Global System: Multi-Disciplinary Perspectives

Studies of global social change in particular have engaged multiple disciplines in attempts to gain understandings of the multiple, complex processes at work in this sphere. Conflicts in international arenas reflect interests arising from multiple national contexts and play out within institutional frameworks that have their own languages, laws, and logic. At times, international institutional arenas overlap and contradict one another, as when trade agreements impinge on human rights or environmental claims. And the machinations of interstate politics reflect complex histories—often involving colonial and post-colonial relations—and rules of diplomacy. Thus, an appreciation for the mechanics of institutions and international law in addition to an understanding of geopolitics and the global economy are required to fully comprehend the struggles taking place on the global stage. I have found several traditions helpful in developing my own understanding of this global space.

A logical starting point is the field of international relations which, at least in the United States, is populated mainly by political scientists. Beginning in the 1970s, but especially in the 1990s the field saw a growing recognition of non-state actors, which forced a re-thinking of international relations' conventional emphasis on states as the main if not the only agents of international affairs. This shift has contributed to new developments in this field, and most noteworthy for scholars of social movements is the perspective known as *constructivism*. This sub-field is informed by work in the sociology of institutions (see, e.g., Powell and DiMaggio 1991), and it stresses the ways that states' interests and priorities are shaped through their engagement in international organizations. In contrast to earlier approaches in the field, constructivists stress the importance of ideas and organizational roles and relationships over power and geopolitics for explaining states' behaviors. International institutions help legitimize states by providing a context within which states' primacy in governance is recognized and reinforced. At the same time, they define state agendas and priorities, insofar as a state's connections with an international organization may impact its interests vis-à-vis other states (e.g., Finnemore 1997; Keck and Sikkink 1998; Friedman et al. 2005). We see interesting parallels with thinking in the sociology of social movements in ideas such as "norm entrepreneurs," and notions that institutions provide resources and opportunities for change advocates. Sikkink's discussion of "norms cascades" and their reliance on institutional dynamics is a particularly helpful illustration of constructivist logics (2011). While much constructivist literature remains centered around questions of how institutional dynamics affect interstate politics, some recent work emerging from the constructivist international relations field has placed more focus on the organizational dynamics of non-state actors. For instance, von Bülow (2010) examines long-term changes in transnational networks among South American groups working on trade issues, and Wong (2012) explores the organizational choices of transnational human rights groups make their campaigns more or less effective at influencing politics.

Constructivists' analyses of global political change complement and indeed draw heavily from research in the sociological tradition of world culture or world polity. This tradition is grounded in institutional analysis and stresses the ways organizations help define actors and their interests. Thus, they view global change as an outcome of organizational logics such as isomorphism—the tendency for actors to mimic dominant organizational practices and forms. Thus, the diffusion of ideas such as human rights, practices such as the national regulation and operation of public schools, and values such as progress and economic growth result from underlying organizational logics (Meyer et al. 1997; Boli and Thomas 1999).

Where world cultural approaches are weak, however, are in helping us account for the inequities of power in the interstate arena and for how these inequities shape the negotiation of conflicts and contradictions in world cultural values. Here is where research in the tradition of the political economy of the world system is especially helpful. This tradition emphasizes a world-historical perspective for understanding conflict and social change, and a key point scholars in this area make is that all states are necessarily embedded in a broader set of structural relations that are global in nature. Thus, conflicts within those states should be understood in this larger context, since the interests and vulnerabilities of states and social movements are shaped by these world-systemic relations. While institutions are important, central to world-systemic analyses are considerations of a state's position in the world economy—that is, is it part of the core that helps define the terms of the world economy, or is it on the periphery and therefore more subject to the influences of core states. In addition, the world-historical context can be important for understanding conflicts at the national or transnational level, and this is particularly so at times of hegemonic decline and systemic crisis, like we are seeing in the current political moment (see, e.g., Arrighi et al. 1989; Arrighi and Silver 1999; Wallerstein 1974 (2011)).[1]

ELITE RESPONSES TO TRANSNATIONAL ACTIVISM

As scholars began to pay more attention to the place of non-state actors in global politics, their growing participation and influence began to generate responses from more powerful actors. By the mid-1990s, the United Nations began re-assessing the place of civil society groups, and many governments were pushing for more restrictions on civil society access. Reform proposals tended to stress functionalist and corporatist approaches to UN–civil society relations and did not provide for effective participation of civil society or for greater access to influential UN bodies such as the General Assembly or Security Council (Charnovitz 1997; Willetts 2006). At the same time, corporations began paying more attention to international arenas, and formed their own civil society groups—known as "business NGOs" or "BINGOs" to lobby UN officials and government delegates to international meetings (Bruno and Karliner 2002). Right wing and fundamentalist religious organizations also mobilized across borders, in reaction to the progressive gains made by feminists and environmentalists (Buss and Herman 2003; Bob 2012).

This time also saw growth in corporate efforts to "greenwash" their images by, for instance, giving grants to human rights or environmental groups to build schools or clinics or to support social services activities and even environmentally oriented projects that do not threaten corporate interests. Under pressure from the United States, the UN initiated a "Global Compact" in 1999 to provide a mechanism to allow corporations to deflect criticisms from a growing anti-corporate globalization movement. Under the guise of promoting "corporate social responsibility," the Global Compact asks corporate "partners" to adhere to a set of principles, but it has no mechanisms for monitoring or enforcing these. Thus, it allows corporations to restore their tarnished image without changing their practices (Smith 2010).

In addition to more direct attempts to constrain the participation and impacts of civil society activists, elite actors also found ways to channel and co-opt the energies of activist groups. This process of professionalization, institutionalization, and bureaucratization—known as "NGOization"—refers to the institutionalization and deradicalization of social movement demands. Faced with movement challenges, elites seek to diffuse threats to the status quo by incorporating popular actors into the political process and "demobilizing" discourses that threaten dominant interests and agendas (Lynch 2013). The process is not unlike that used in the administration of colonial territories, and indeed has many parallels with colonialism. As Rajagopal observed, "international institutions have played a crucial role in mediating and often deradicalizing the contentious relationship between development interventions and many non-European societies, ... [acting as] shock absorbers against mass resistance" (2003: 48).

Groups that become more deeply involved in the day-to-day work of organizations like the UN and dependent upon what Aksartova (2009) calls the "Western grant economy" tend to stray from their more radical commitments as they attend to elite agendas, discourses, and operating practices. Lang's work uncovers how the institutional logics of states and interstate politics encourage "advocacy without publics" (2013: 93). They do so by structuring incentives in ways that reinforce elite agendas and preferences rather than to encourage public engagement. Ironically, elite interest in engaging with NGOs rests on the notion that these groups represent a public; yet NGOs in this system have little time or capacity for cultivating or activating popular constituencies. This phenomenon has been described as "global governmentality," as civil society organizations are mobilized to advance global neoliberal projects and to reproduce elite-defined policy agendas and models (Goldman 2005; Ferguson 2006; Hammack and Haydemann 2009).

In addition to efforts to limit civil society participation through formal rules of political access and through the provision of resources, governments have increasingly engaged in direct efforts to repress popular participation in multilateral politics. The most dramatic instances of such repression have occurred at the sites of global trade negotiations, including meetings of the Group of 7/8 in the late 1990s and of the World Trade Organization in 1999 and early 2000s. Protesters similarly had escalated tactics to move beyond rallies and demonstrations to employ direct action aimed at blocking delegates' access to these meetings. The growing contention around the rules of the global economy has spread to the environmental arena as well, and since 2007 the global climate negotiations have seen increasingly confrontational protests (Hadden 2015; Bond 2012). The global justice movement's impact at building transnational networks around more radical analyses of the global capitalist economy that link economic policies with environmental concerns, human rights, and other outcomes is likely to shape a more contentious future trajectory of interactions between movements and the multilateral political arena.

CONCEPTUAL AND EPISTEMOLOGICAL
BORDERLANDS

Scholarship on globalization and on transnational social movements challenges basic assumptions and concepts in predominant social science traditions.[2] This research has sensitized scholars to the ways our thinking is both shaped by and reinforces existing power relations. Academic specialization has served to obscure the impacts of world-historical factors in social relations. Moreover, the organization of academic work and the structuring of professional incentives privileges methodologies and perspectives of scholars in the global North, effectively "erasing" the experiences and perspectives of those outside the core of the world-economy (see, e.g., Connell 2007; Santos 2007).

A world-historical perspective on social movements is essential to any effort to understand the political significance of struggles in a given time and place. This overview demonstrates how social movements have always been transgressing the boundaries of politics which elites have sought to enforce. In the process they have helped define the modern state and the interstate system. Even as national states were first becoming consolidated, popular groups were actively mobilizing to define limits of state authority and legitimate uses of state power. Struggles over these definitions of the modern democratic state have always been transnational, even though much of the theorizing of social movements is cast in state-centered terms (Markoff 1996).

Attention to the world-historical context of social movements also helps situate a given conflict within the larger set of social relations, which often include histories of imperialism, colonialism, or other forms of exploitation. This attention to history serves as an important reminder that the state is a fairly recent social innovation and a constantly changing one at that. By the 1990s growing numbers of activists were recognizing that human rights or environmental protection could not be advanced with traditional appeals to the state, since by then neoliberal policies had severely weakened even core states' capacities to address these concerns (see, e.g., Tilly 1995; Seidman 2004). Activists in the South are especially aware of the limitations of nationalist projects for achieving emancipatory goals. Rajagopal reflects discussions in many activist circles claiming that "emphasizing the predominant role of the state in the realization of human rights simply reproduces the same structures that have prevented the realization of those rights in the first place.... [Is] it possible to think of public action that does not depend entirely on traditional state structures to be carried out?" (2003: 193). Indeed, global justice activists have been discussing ideas like that expressed in John Holloway's *Changing the World Without Taking Power* (2002, 2010), rethinking the place of the state in social movement strategies. Social movement research, however, has been slow to escape its methodological nationalism. For instance, many early discussions of transnational social movements centered on the question of whether or not globalization made the state irrelevant. This state-centric framing of the debate obscured the ways global changes were transforming social relations and the state itself (cf. Smith and Kutz-Flamenbaum 2010).

Along with deconstructing conventional notions of the state, transnational social movements help bring into focus the problematic distinction in much scholarship between "the local" and "the global" and between institutional and cultural or pre-figurative politics. Many analyses tend to compartmentalize these ideas in ways that masks how movement discourse and practice defy such categorization. For instance, Subramaniam, Gupte, and Misra (2003) demonstrate the complex sub-national networks that connect rural activist networks to national and global anti-neoliberal struggles. Examples such as the World Social Forum process and the World March of Women reveal the innovative ways movements help bridge the local and global, and expand the possibilities for local participation in global networks of resistance. More recently, a transnational initiative of activists in the Arab Spring, Occupy Wall Street, and other anti-austerity protests called the "Global Square"—organized for the 2013 World Social Forum in Tunis—performed a similar role. Indeed, their major threat to existing power relations is movements' ability to engage people locally in projects of global social change.

In addition to questioning conventional distinctions between local and global, activists and critical scholars—especially those from the global South—have articulated an increasingly sharp critique of the modernist development project that highlights the centrality of cultural resistance to movements' efforts to change policies (see, e.g., Escobar 2004; Quan 2012). Although integrating this critique into the actual practices of social movements has proved challenging, the emergence of movement spaces like the World Social Forum and the networks it supports has allowed activists to confront and examine the tensions between transformative visions such as those expressed in feminist circles and the actual practices of movements, which tend to reproduce inequities of the dominant order (see, e.g., Hewitt and Karides 2011; Conway 2012). This tension between what social movement scholars have referred to as instrumental and prefigurative politics is being actively engaged in contemporary transnational activist networks, inspired and supported by many years of transnational feminist organizing (see, e.g., Vargas 2005; Alvarez 2009; Moghadam 2012).

POLITICAL IMAGINATION AND THE SOCIOLOGY OF EMERGENCES

Now that we've established social movements as active participants in the construction of political institutions, we can better appreciate what role they might play in the ongoing transformation of the modern state and the interstate system itself. There is a growing consciousness among activists that they play such a role (Pleyers 2011). This has been possible in large part because social movements have expanded the spaces where they can engage in transnational activity outside of formal institutional spaces, expand popular political imaginations, and advance new models of social organization.

Given that states have developed in tandem with and have played an essential role in the development of the capitalist world system, it follows that any movements envisioning a non-capitalist order must transcend the institutional logics of states. This includes a transcendence of conventional discourses and conceptualizations of revolutions, as these are also firmly grounded in the historical context of the modern state. The ability to engage with one another outside of the United Nations conferences and to discuss agendas that do not emanate from national or interstate politics is imperative for such movements. With the establishment of the World Social Forum in 2001 and the proliferation of other sites of autonomous transnational civil society engagement in the early twenty-first century,[3] I believe we are witnessing the foundations for a crucial transformation of what we now understand as "international politics." These autonomous spaces for transnational movement engagement expand their capacities for what Zapatista activists call "political imagination" (see Khasnabish 2008), fostering creative responses to the institutional dilemmas imposed by the internal contradictions of states and the interstate order. No longer forced to work within these contradictory logics, activists can imagine new orienting principles for social relations that are not based in violence, exploitation, and exclusion.

Thus, research on social movements requires attention to what Boaventura de Sousa Santos (2007) calls the "sociology of emergences." In other words, we need to redefine how we select instances of social movement struggle to investigate and theorize. Rather than privileging movements deemed "significant" somehow within the existing political and institutional logics, we must open up our field of vision to include those movements rendered invisible (or largely invisible) by prevailing scholarly conventions and public and media agenda-setting processes. Rather than privileging projects that seem viable within existing institutional arrangements, scholars need to be sensitive to the ways new arrangements may be forming through the practices of actors who are now relegated to the margins of "politics." The transnational relations among social movement actors have altered the place of the state in social movement politics. As they seek ways to address persistent and increasingly urgent problems of securing access to people's basic needs (i.e., for clean water, food, jobs, etc.) and mitigating climate change, movements are finding that they must transgress the boundaries of the interstate system. In doing so they are helping to reinvent the notion of revolution as they constitute organizations and projects that enable transnational dialogue and collaboration.

NOTES

1. For a more extensive review of these literatures, see Smith and Wiest (2012).
2. I am grateful to Saskia Sassen for suggesting the terminology used in the heading of this section.
3. On the World Social Forum and its impacts, see, e.g., Sen (2007); Smith et al. (2011); Sen et al. (2012).

References

Aksartova, Sada (2009). "Promoting Civil Society or Diffusing NGOs? U.S. Donors in the Former Soviet Union." In *Globalization, Philanthropy, and Civil Society*, edited by D. C. Hammack and S. Heydemann, 160–191. Bloomington: Indiana University Press.

Alvarez, Sonia E. (1999). "The Latin American Feminist NGO 'Boom,'" *International Feminist Journal of Politics*. 1: 181–209.

Alvarez, Sonia E. (2009). "Beyond NGO-ization? Reflections from Latin America," *Development*. 52: 175–184.

Arrighi, Giovanni and Silver, Beverly J. (1999). *Chaos and Governance in the Modern World System*. Minneapolis, MN: University of Minnesota Press.

Arrighi, Giovanni, Hopkins, Terence K., and Wallerstein, Immanuel (1989). *Antisystemic Movements*. New York: Verso.

Bob, Clifford (2012). *The Global Right Wing and the Clash of World Politics*. New York: Cambridge University Press.

Boli, John and Thomas, George M. (1999). *Constructing World Culture: International Nongovernmental Organizations Since 1875*. Stanford: Stanford University Press.

Bond, Patrick (2012). *Politics of Climate Justice: Paralysis Above, Movement Below*. Scottsville: South Africa University of Kwazulu-Natal Press.

Bruno, Kenny and Karliner, Joshua (2002). *Earthsummit.biz: The Corporate Takeover of Sustainable Development*. Oakland: Food First Books.

Buss, Doris and Herman, Didi (2003). *Globalizing Family Values: The Christian Right in International Politics*. Minneapolis, MN: University of Minnesota Press.

Charnovitz, Steve (1997). "Two Centuries of Participation: NGOs and International Governance," *Michigan Journal of International Law*. 18: 183–286.

Conway, Janet (2012). *Edges of Global Justice*. New York: Routledge.

Connell, Raewyn (2007). "The Northern Theory of Globalization," *Sociological Theory*. 25: 368–385.

Dufour, Pascale and Giraud, Isabelle (2007). "Globalization and Political Change in the Women's Movement: The Politics of Scale and Political Empowerment in the World March of Women," *Social Science Quarterly*. 88: 1152–1173.

Escobar, Arturo (2004). "Development, Violence and the New Imperial Order," *Development*. 47: 15–21.

Finnemore, Martha (1997). "Norms, Culture, and World Politics: Insights from Sociology's Institutionalism," *International Organization*. 50: 325–347.

Friedman, Elisabeth Jay, Clark, Ann Marie, and Hochstetler, Kathryn (2005). *Sovereignty, Democracy, and Global Civil Society: State-Society Relations at the UN World Conferences*. New York: State University of New York Press.

Ferguson, James (2006). *Global Shadows: Africa in the Neoliberal World Order*. Durham, NC: Duke University Press.

Goldman, Michael (2005). *Imperial Nature: The World Bank and Struggles for Social Justice in the Age of Globalization*. New Haven: Yale University Press.

Hadden, Jennifer. (2015). *Networks in Contention: Global Civil Society and the Divisive Politics of Climate Change*. New York: Cambridge University Press.

Hammack, David C. and Heydemann, Steven (2009). *Globalization, Philanthropy, and Civil Society*. Bloomington: Indiana University Press.

Hewitt, Lyndi and Karides, Marina (2011). "More than a Shadow of a Difference? Feminists at the World Social Forums." In *Handbook of World Social Forum Activism*, edited by J. Smith, S. Byrd, E. Reese, and E. Smythe, 85–104. Boulder, CO: Paradigm Publishers.

Holloway, John (2002, 2010). *Changing the World Without Taking Power*. New York: Pluto Publishers.

Keck, Margaret and Sikkink, Kathryn (1998). *Activists Beyond Borders*. Ithaca: Cornell University Press.

Khagram, Sanjeev (2004). *Dams and Development: Transnational Struggles for Water and Power*. Ithaca: Cornell University Press.

Khasnabish, Alex (2008). *Zapatismo Beyond Borders: New Imaginations of Political Possibility*. Toronto: University of Toronto Press.

Lang, Sabine (2013). *NGOs, Civil Society, and the Public Sphere*. New York: Cambridge University Press.

Lynch, Cecelia (2013). "Neoliberal Ethics, the Humanitarian International, and Practices of Peacebuilding." In *Globalization, Social Movements, and Peacebuilding*, edited by J. Smith and E. Verdeja, 47–68. Syracuse, NY: Syracuse University Press.

Markoff, John (1996). *Waves of Democracy: Social Movements and Political Change*. Thousand Oaks: Pine Forge Press.

Meyer, John W., Boli, John, Thomas, George M., and Ramirez, Francisco O. (1997). "World Society and the Nation-State," *American Journal of Sociology*. 103: 144–181.

Meyer, Mary K. and Prügl, Elisabeth, eds. (1999). *Gender Politics in Global Governance*. Boulder, CO: Rowman & Littlefield Publishers, Inc.

Moghadam, Valentine (2012). *Globalization and Social Movements: Islamism, Feminism and the Global Justice Movement*, 2nd edn. Boulder, CO: Rowman & Littlefield.

Pleyers, Geoffrey (2011). *Alter-Globalization: Becoming Actors in the Global Age*. Malden, MA: Polity Press.

Powell, Walter W. and DiMaggio, Paul J. (1991). *The New Institutionalism in Organizational Analysis*. Chicago: University of Chicago Press.

Quan, H.L.T. (2012). *Growth Against Democracy: Savage Developmentalism in the Modern World*. Lanham, MD: Lexington Books.

Rajagopal, Balakrishnan (2003). *International Law from Below: Development, Social Movements, and Third World Resistance*. New York: Cambridge University Press.

Risse, Thomas, Ropp, Stephen C., and Sikkink, Kathryn (1999). *The Power of Human Rights: International Norms and Domestic Change*. New York: Cambridge University Press.

Santos, Boaventura de Sousa (2007). "Beyond Abyssal Thinking: From Global Lines to Ecologies of Knowledges," *Eurozine*, 35. http://www.eurozine.com/pdf/2007-06-29-santos-en.pdf

Seidman, Gay (2004). "Deflated Citizenship: Labor Rights in a Global Era." In *People Out of Place: Globalization, Human Rights, and the Citizenship Gap*, edited by A. Brysk and G. Shafir, 109–129. New York: Routledge.

Sen, Jai (2007). "The World Social Forum as an Emergent Learning Process," *Futures*. 39: 507–522.

Sen, Jai and Waterman, Peter, eds. (2012). *The World Social Forum: Critical Explorations, Volume 3, Challenging Empires*. New Delhi: OpenWord.

Sikkink, Kathryn (2005). "Patterns of Dynamic Multilevel Governance and the Insider-Outsider Coalition." In *Transnational Protest and Global Activism*, edited by D. della Porta and S. Tarrow, 151–173. Lanham, Md.: Rowman & Littlefield.

Sikkink, Kathryn (2011). *The Justice Cascade: How Human Rights Prosecutions Are Changing World Politics*. New York: W.W. Norton & Company.

Smith, Jackie (2008). *Social Movements for Global Democracy*. Baltimore, Md.: Johns Hopkins University Press.

Smith, Jackie (2010). "Power, Interests, and the United Nations Global Compact." In *Globalization, Private-Sector Authority, and New Modes of Democratic Policy-Making*, edited by T. Porter and K. Ronit, 89–113. New York: State University of New York Press.

Smith, Jackie and Kutz-Flamenbaum, Rachel (2010). "Prisoners of our Concepts: Liberating Social Movement Theory." In *The Transnational Condition: Protest Dynamics in an Entangled Europe*, edited by S. Teune, 211–227. Oxford: Berghahn Books.

Smith, Jackie and Wiest, Dawn (2012). *Social Movements in the World-System: The Politics of Crisis and Transformation*. New York: Russell Sage Foundation.

Tarrow, Sidney (2005). *The New Transnational Activism*. New York: Cambridge University Press.

Tarrow, Sidney (2011). *Power in Movement: Social Movements, Collective Action and Politics*, 3rd edn. New York: Cambridge University Press.

Tilly, Charles (1978). *From Mobilization to Revolution*. Reading, MA: Addison Wesley.

Tilly, Charles (1995). "Globalization Threatens Labor Rights," *International Labor and Working Class History*. 47: 1–23.

Vargas, Virginia (2005). "Feminisms and the World Social Forum: Space for Dialogue and Confrontation," *Development*. 48: 107–110.

von Bülow, Marisa (2010). *Building Transnational Networks: Civil Society and the Politics of Trade in the Americas*. New York: Cambridge University Press.

Wallerstein, Immanuel (1974, 2011). *The Modern World-System I: Capitalist Agriculture and the Origins of the European World-Economy in the Sixteenth Century*. New York: Academic Press.

Willetts, Peter (1996). *The Conscience of the World: The Influence of NGOs in the United Nations System*. London: C. Hurst.

Willetts, Peter (2006). "The Cardoso Report on the UN and Civil Society: Functionalism, Global Corporatism, or Global Democracy?" *Global Governance*. 12: 305–324.

Wong, Wendy H. (2012). *Internal Affairs: How the Structure of NGOs Transforms Human Rights*. Ithaca: Cornell University Press.

CHAPTER 41

"THE GAME'S AFOOT"

Social Movements in Authoritarian States

HANK JOHNSTON

DESPITE waves of democratization in the late twentieth century, repressive, authoritarian states are still common in the twenty-first. All state regimes, including democratic ones, differ on their degree of openness, legal protections, social control, and responsiveness to citizens, but authoritarian states are characterized by their severe restrictions of democratic freedoms and reliance on violence and preemptive surveillance to repress political dissent and collective action. Although these are not conditions conducive to social movement development, it is incorrect to say that movements do not occur in authoritarian states. Rather, when movements do mobilize, their organization, trajectories, and targets of collective action often are different from those of movements in democratic contexts.

This chapter paints a broad landscape of social movements in authoritarian regimes. It considers the institutional and organizational differences among these states, and how these variably shape social movement processes. It discusses how a broadened conception of what constitutes a social movement helps capture unique strategic and organizational considerations of authoritarian settings. Finally, this chapter draws on recent theoretical trends and applies them to the dynamics of state-movement interaction in repressive contexts. It suggests a fine-grained approach to *the strategic field of play* (Fligstein and McAdam 2012) in which various state actors—ranging from political and economic elites to various levels of state security to local thugs and shakedown artists—interact with the diverse activist groups that constitute the movement at different stages in its development. It is an approach that recognizes elite alignments, class relations, and the determining force of social control, but also stresses the on-the-ground creative agency of relevant actors and the "eventfulness" of protest mobilizations (della Porta 2014)—locales where "the game's afoot" among challengers and state agencies.

In authoritarian states, the familiar forms of social movement action—demonstrations, marches, rallies, and so on—are less widely practised compared to open democracies. Nevertheless, the pace of "mass incidents" in the modular repertoire has increased significantly in China: from less than 10,000 per year in the mid-1990s to about 180,000 in 2011. This indicates a degree of tolerance of protest performances, but within parameters established by the state and local officials and widely recognized by participants. An overall theme of this chapter is that social movements in authoritarian states adapt to their constrained and less open environments. Networked relations among groups, shared identities, continuity over time, and extrainstitutional collective action—the constituent elements of social movements everywhere (Diani 1997; della Porta and Diani 2006; Johnston 2014)—define social movements in authoritarian contexts as well, but public manifestations of these elements are often limited and less overt, and in some phases of movement development, assume novel configurations in what I call the *repressive repertoire*. I use this term to describe the unique early patterns of challenge and claim-making characteristic of repressive contexts, and as a contrast to protest forms typical of open and democratic political regimes. The *modern social movement repertoire*—marches, rallies, demonstrations, and petitions—is a familiar and modular template for collective action (Tilly 1995, 2008), but one that, in authoritarian contexts, emerges under specific conditions of tentative liberalization by the state, and strategic agency on the part of movement actors. Prior to that, the analyst needs to be sensitive to different forms of contention.

THE AUTHORITARIAN CONTEXT

Fifty years ago, Juan Linz (1964) was instrumental in refining the concept of authoritarianism based in part on his analysis of Francoist Spain. He characterized authoritarian states as less developed state systems compared to Western democracies. This meant that they had weaker direct-rule capacities, underdeveloped legitimizing ideologies (but guiding "mentalities" such as economic development, nationalism, anticorruption, or anticommunism), limited rule-of-law protections, and attenuated responsiveness to citizen demands. However, key to our focus in this chapter, Linz and Stepan (1996) noted that the constrained capacity of authoritarian states permits space for limited pluralism and civil society to exist, and for oppositional networks to percolate below the surface of civic life, which are potential locales where oppositional movements may develop.

Linz and Stepan (1996) further elaborated two additional types of repressive nondemocracies, which again vary on the dimension of state capacity. First, *totalitarian states* evince highly developed capacities to penetrate and control the lives of their citizens. An extensive security apparatus, strong ideological socialization, ongoing propagandizing, internal monitoring of state and party organizations, and the absence of autonomous civic organization are characteristics of totalitarian systems. It is best to think of these characteristics as variables. For example, North Korea offers very little social space outside official and party organizations for collective action, and relies on high levels of official populist mobilization to legitimate its juche regime. Belarus is less developed on these dimensions, offering more space, but relies heavily on its security apparatus to limit collective action. But, an often overlooked fact is that collective protest occurs in these regimes too.

Another part of the Linz-Stepan typology draws on Max Weber's concept of the *sultanistic regime*. These states are autocracies whose guidance rests on the whims of a supreme leader. They are personalistic dictatorships, characteristic of less economically developed states and less elaborated civil society. Power, corruption, and plunder are concentrated in a small circle dependent on the leader's beneficence. For our purposes, the key variables are (1) lower state capacity compared to totalitarian and authoritarian regimes, (2) a reliance on patrimonial-clientalistic relations that benefit political elites, and (3) a tendency for brutal repression because legitimacy concerns are less relevant to the regime. These combine to increase the likelihood of armed insurgencies, which Boudreau (2004: 154) points out changes "how participants and authorities calculate victory and defeat, expense and opportunity."

The concept of state capacity has been identified as a key variable by research in political and social revolutions (Tilly 1992; Goodwin 2001). It refers to a state's ability to control activities within its borders and to regulate the actions of its citizens, and is measured by the development of a state's administrative bureaucracy and its police and military functions. Nicaragua under Somoza presented sultanistic qualities, and was faced with a guerrilla insurgency in some rural regions, and, later, mass popular mobilization in the cities. Burma too, although a military regime, brutally repressed its opposition and forced it into the forests where it waged armed resistance. However, Iran under Pahlavi, and Romania under Ceausescu were regimes with sultanistic characteristics that fell to popular movements without sustained armed uprisings. Insurgent armies are not social movements in themselves, but their tendency to concentrate in sultanistic states emphasizes the importance of state capacity as variable that can shape the composition of the opposition movement broadly defined. This was the case in the Philippines where armed rebels waged battle against the Marcos regime, and in South Africa, where ANC guerrillas played an important role in the antiapartheid movement's trajectory (Seidman 2001).

A typological approach, while useful in identifying key variables, offers only a static view of state systems, which are, in fact, increasingly recognized as dynamic and fluid over the long term. Elite interests shift (Slater 2010), and popular sentiments, pushed by movement activity, global pressures, and (today) digital media, move, congeal, and move again, putting new pressures on regime officials. Also, conspicuous by its absence, the Linz-Stepan typology underestimates the effect of state corruption. While present in all state systems, including democracies (della Porta and Vannucci 2012), the absence of checks and balances, of independent branches of government, and of rule of law allows official kleptocracy to permeate state and party from top to the bottom in authoritarian systems. On the one hand, norms of corruption may ease fissures among state actors for whom self-enrichment is the common goal, but on the other—and this is important for our social movement approach—it imparts a persistent grass-roots-level illegitimacy to the state. Ubiquitous corruption and elite conspicuous consumption are widely apparent and frequently discussed among citizens in authoritarian states where there are few official channels of recourse. Recall that a minor bribe, the shakedown of a fruit vendor in Tunisia, was the spark that ignited the Arab Spring. Recall the pervasiveness of anti-corruption protests in China and India.

Another drawback of this typology is that emphasizing the centrality of repressive control glosses over the fact that no regime, regardless of its high-capacity apparatus, is a hermetically sealed system of mind-control where all collective action is precluded and/or immediately stamped out. When Soviet archives were opened, it became clear that even the Stalinist terror was not monolithic (Priestland 2007). Even in North Korea, probably the highest-capacity repressive state today, protests erupted in late 2009 when the currency was devalued by 100 to 1, wiping out the savings of millions of citizens and skyrocketing food prices. Protests in Pyongyang were hostile outbursts, not sustained social movements, but if greater space for autonomous groups were available—as in authoritarian states as opposed to a totalitarian one—they could have evolved into a networked web of oppositional activist groups.

DYNAMICS OF THE STATE

Analytical approaches to social movements in authoritarian states cut many ways. The comparative study of social and political revolutions is relevant because all revolutions begin as social movements, that is, broad and diverse networks of groups and organizations united by their shared opposition to the *anciens régimes*—Iran, Nicaragua, Philippines, China, South Africa, to name a few. Recent perspectives on revolution emphasize the social movement angle by their focus on agency, culture, and middle-level dynamics (as antidotes to the structuralist approaches of forty years ago).

There is also a large literature on democratic transitions that follows the same structuralist-agentic fault line. Transition studies gained purchase during the 1980s and 1990s in response to the Spanish democratization (Maravall 1982) and to several democratic transitions in Latin America (O'Donnell and Schmitter 1986; Linz and Stepan 1992). In contrast to earlier structuralist approaches, these too tend to focus on the agency of social movement mobilization, especially working-class strike waves, urban activist groups, and elite adjustments. Several recent studies approach democratic change from different mesolevel perspectives: tactical considerations (Schock 2005), elite opportunism (Slater 2010), generalizable mechanisms and processes (McAdam, Tarrow, and Tilly 2001), a dynamic, multiplayer focus (Parsa 2000), and the on-the-ground role of disruptive action and how it shapes movement trajectories (della Porta 2014). From these different threads of social science research several general patterns can be discerned.

Comparative studies of democratic oppositions have increasingly recognized the state's response dynamics in ways that go beyond simple measures of repression such as deaths or arrests. Boudreau's analysis (2004) of democratic movements in Philippines, Burma, and Indonesia focusses on how elite response strategies shape mobilization trajectories. He emphasizes the dynamic unfolding of state actions by examining the antecedents of contemporary oppositions, such as the independence struggles in these countries, and how templates of state response influence subsequent actions as well as expectations of activists. Broadly drawing on a dynamics of contention approach (McAdam, Tarrow, and Tilly 2001; McAdam and Tarrow 2011), he focusses on how cycles of "state attack and movement response" unfold. In the Philippines, Marcos tolerated moderate activists, which allowed for a network of civic groups to develop and push for policy reforms without directly challenging his rule. It is important to note that, in this authoritarianism, movements that pursued discreet claims and policy reforms existed, and the persistence of an armed insurgency cast civic groups as people the regime could work with. However, the regime's tendency to brand all activists as communists alienated many moderates and helped solidify a broad opposition. In contrast, draconian repression in Burma drove most opposition groups to join the armed insurgency there.

Boudreau's study offers a first step toward more fine-grained approach to the state, its dynamics, and the relationship to movement development. Slater's (2010) analysis of repressive states—also a comparison of Southeast Asian cases—mirrors this strategy by focussing specifically on elite actors, but with the goal of analyzing the formation of repressive regimes in the context of popular challenges. Like Boudreau, he identifies key historical junctures, which Slater labels "critical antecedents," in the dynamic unfolding of state strategies. Based on antecedent experiences, Slater explores elite defections and breaks from the political leadership, which foster the cross-class coalitions of broad democratic movements (the Philippines). He also probes the making of "protection pacts," whereby elites unify behind durable authoritarianisms and provide resources for state maintenance (Malaysia).

Slater's comparisons echo the theorizing of McAdam, Tarrow, and Tilly (2001), whose analysis of democratic movements and state building identifies elite division and brokerage as key causal mechanisms in contentious politics, writ large. But in terms of social movements in authoritarian regimes, Slater's approach is an important step in deconstructing the authoritarian state as a Leviathan of repressive control. It may seem like that at times, but in reality its repressive apparatus and strategies reflect complex collective actions of various elite actors rather than a unified self-interest or ideological agenda. Future research can take this deconstruction several steps further to more accurately portray the dynamics of the mobilization-repression relationship. I have in mind the way that policy divisions and divergent interests not only occur in the capital among political and economic elites, but also in provinces, cities and towns in the periphery, among local elites—and, a step further, among security agencies, military, and police.

Elite-level decisions and national-level strategies of repression are important factors in shaping the space available for social movements in authoritarian regimes, but the complexity of state administration opens the door for broader conceptions of the agency. There are numerous levels of enforcement—national-level security apparatus, secret police, military intelligence units, networks of spies for the state and ruling party, special militias, and party enforcers—all of which hold the potential for conflicting interests at the mesolevel. An important player here too is the military, which has its distinct interests. The role of armed forces can be further deconstructed by recognizing that special units, elite divisions, and republican guards chosen for loyalty to the president can play key roles in regime transition. Finally—and often overlooked—are informally organized bands of thugs, ruffians, vigilantes, local militias, and even foreign mercenaries, which are commonly employed as enforcers and who look out for their spheres of influence and graft. These groups include gangsters and/or party members known for their brutality, physical intimidation, and violent efficiency. They are used as agents of enforcement and fear, especially during periods of increased dissident activity, or to terrorize individual citizens whose actions pose threats to political elites. An example of the complexity is that in al-Assad's Syria, prior to the civil war, there were eighteen different branches of police and security in the major cities. Regarding social movements in authoritarian regimes, the key point is that complexity and diversity in interests, levels of authority, and modes of enforcement create cracks and lapses in repressive surveillance that create free spaces where dissent can be voiced, rudimentary mobilization structures take shape, and protest actions occur.

MOVEMENT DYNAMICS

Slater's (2010) comparisons of Southeast Asian states emphasize that elite perceptions are major determinants of repressive strategies and imply ways that movements can strategize to create spaces that mitigate elite responses. Both he and Boudreau concentrate their analysis on the state's side of engagement, but several other comparative studies incorporate an expanded social-movement focus to the field play (see Fligstein and McAdam 2012). Parsa's (2000) comparisons are anchored in the comparative-revolutions tradition, looking at social revolutions in Iran and Nicaragua, and contrasting them with the Philippines' "people power" revolution—a *political revolution* that only changed the regime and not class structures and political institutions. Importantly, his study shifts analytical focus to the dynamic and multiplex nature of the opposition by tracing the role of four key actors in the movement phase of the revolutions. Students were a perennial thorn in the side of the authoritarian regimes because universities were free spaces of discussion and ideological debate and regime elites were often hesitant to kick the hornet's nest. The clergy were also key actors who were able to act with "relative impunity" because they occupied sacred ground on which regime elites generally did not tread for fear of popular reaction. This created another free space from which the early opposition could organize, and, in its later stages, mobilize. The working class and its unions were "rebels with dual targets." Demands about wages and working conditions had obvious economic dimensions, but they also assumed a political color because the authoritarian state typically had heavy intervention in the economy and was repressive of worker mobilization. Finally, echoing our last section, economic elites were reluctant partisans of social change, joining when they saw opportunities to challenge the state's role in the economy and demurring when they feared the radicalism of students and workers.

Parsa's approach stresses the complex dynamics of the oppositional movement prior mobilization phases and especially the agency of its diverse leadership. He shows how radical groups in Philippines and Iran strategically moderated their positions to foster the antiregime coalitions to attract economic elites. A related aspect of movement dynamics is the ideological diversity of the opposition and the way its radical-moderate balance shapes elite perceptions. Diversity in ideology and frames of the groups that make up an opposition movement are often glossed over during mass popular mobilizations and the dramas of central-square occupations, but Parsa points out that how these differences are managed can be important determinants of the revolution's course. Parsa's consideration of ideology distinguishes his study from structural approaches to revolutions and locates him among the new generation of comparative-revolution scholars, but from the perspective of a social movements approach to regime change, the strategic framing of ideological agendas and coalition formation among the main actors direct attention to agency and creativity in the mobilization process.

Creativity and strategic agency are the central themes of Schock's (2005) comparisons of successful people-power movements in South Africa, Philippines, Thailand, and Nepal. He too argues for the importance of coalition building, and stresses agency in organizational strategy to foster durability and resiliency in the face of state repression. Schock's study focusses on movement strategies of nonviolence based on the modern modular repertoire—marches, strikes, demonstrations, meetings, and petitions—as opposed to the cadre-led armed insurgencies characteristic of the post-war period. Organizational strategies that contribute to long-term survival of the opposition include creating a decentralized network of activist groups and organizations, and uniting them under a broad democratic front or umbrella organization that facilitates communication. This was the accomplishment of the UDF in South Africa and the UNIDO in Philippines. His comparisons reveal that under repressive conditions strategic flexibility and tactical variety are key elements of movement success.

Importantly, Schock's approach looks at maco shifts in regime type in terms of micro strategies and tactics of the movement. He complements Slater's emphasis on mesolevel elite actions by showing how movement strategies at a more microlevel identify certain elite sectors for recruitment and target the state's international dependency ties (e.g., Philippines regarding the United States) to foster elite division. Rather than focussing on how elite divisions merely reflect shifting interests, Schock shows how the strategic agency of movement groups can foster these divisions. This is an important step towards a more fine-grained analysis of the "field of play" in authoritarian contexts, one that recognizes the interaction of elite agency, state agency, and movement agency.

Schock's analysis points towards analyzing social movements in authoritarian states as a three-way collision of moving targets by which assessments of what may be possible and prudent courses of action cascade over the course of movement development. In this three-way play, movements can convert the repressive tactics of the state to opportunities by what Schock terms the "political jujitsu dynamic" (2005: 42), whereby nonviolent movements confront the violence of the state. Strategic adjustments by activists convert instances of repression to *increases* in mobilization. The shift to strategic agency among players offers a more nuanced, contingent, and—in terms of understanding the mobilization-repression relationship—promising approach compared to the linear model of increased repression → increased fear/costs → decreased mobilization, which may make sense logically, but empirically has been undermined several times since 2011, a recent example being the 2014 Ukrainian protests against the Yanukovych regime. The key difference in Schock's approach is the adaptation of organizational strategy and movement tactics to the application of state repression. Schock shows that the importance of movement resilience to take advantage of the state's increasing illegitimacy rests on this dynamic.

THE REPRESSIVE REPERTOIRE

Schock's fine-grained approach to movements' organizations and strategies introduces a temporal dimension to the analysis—a reflection of ongoing strategic assessment of opportunities and threats by key actors. His focus on agency and temporality mirror Beissinger's (2002) and della Porta's (2014) analyses of democratization processes, but for our purposes, it brings in another body of literature on everyday resistance and covert protests (Bayat 1997, 2003; Johnston 2006, 2011), and their links with more recognizable, public collective actions within the modular social movement repertoire. The bridge is that these covert protests are accomplished by activist groups that are, in fact, often seeds of collective actions that develop later in the movement's trajectory, and that continuity in actors is not uncommon. Pushing the analytical focus further back reveals how the dispersed network organization, which Schock sees as central to movement resilience and success, is incubated in earlier periods of movement development that Schock's comparative data do not access.

The term *repressive repertoire* captures the various forms of collective action that reside between the abeyance phase of a movement, when heavy repression and/or its recent historical memory drive oppositional sentiments into private spaces, and their dramatic expression via mobilization in the module repertoire. Thus, the repressive repertoire represents a middle phase of collective action where crucial first steps are taken—creatively and intentionally—to socially organize dissatisfaction and slowly move oppositional sentiments into more public forms. The key characteristics of the repressive repertoire are duplicity, creativity, and triggering.

Duplicity

Research in the former Soviet Union and Eastern Europe (Johnston and Mueller 2001; Johnston 2006), has shown how duplicity permeates public discourse in repressive settings. Citizens reflecting back upon daily life often mention the "double-minded" quality of public discourse. In authoritarian states, one learns not to speak one's mind publicly, but rather to guard one's words and monitor reactions. However, among trusted friends and in circles of acquaintances considered safe, with careful vigilance to who is participating, one can "speak the truth."

Because civil society is highly constrained in authoritarian contexts, this principle is sometimes translated to select official organizations such that their legal status serves as a protective shield behind which members can cautiously engage in oppositional speech—hence their duplicity. Members gather, talk, and sometimes take part in activities that push the limits of what the regime may define as acceptable. Calhoun's (1994) analysis of the democracy movement in China notes how the official infrastructure of university groups and informal student networks provided the basis of mobilization. It is common that duplicitous groups use public buildings and file official budgets and political reports, but their activities frequently have an implicit oppositional character. People who are private opponents of the regime concentrate in these activities as locales where the duplicity of public discourse and general oppositional quiescence can be transcended. The key point is that, although not numerous, such groups and organizations occur throughout repressive states as free spaces of guarded oppositional discourse. Their occurrence rests on the gaps in social control that was discussed earlier.

Johnston's field research in several former authoritarian regimes (2005, 2006) reports that respondents had no trouble identifying groups and organizations known for their veiled oppositional milieu. Social and recreational groups sometimes perform this role (folk-dancing groups, ethnographic study groups, folk music groups, local historical societies, and drama clubs). In line with Parsa's (2000) observations about Iran, Nicaragua, and Philippines, religious organizations are often covert centers of veiled political activity, accorded free-space status by repressive regimes that, nevertheless, dare not repress the sacred. In Poland, the central role of the Roman Catholic Church is prototypical, but this pattern is also evident in Buddhist temples in Tibet and Myanmar, Sufi orders in Chechnya, the Muslim Brotherhood in Egypt's political conflict and in the outbreaks of Syrian violence in 2000. Finally, networks of dissidents often overlap with intellectual and artistic groups (jazz circles, literary salons, book clubs, theater groups, cinema societies, and language study groups). They cluster as centers of oppositional speech because members' creativity and/or inquisitiveness are stifled by the authoritarian state.

Creativity

Numerous small collective actions in the resistance repertoire stand out by virtue of their creativity to mitigate the fear of participants. In 2011 the authoritarian regime of Belarus had difficulty breaking up protest actions by students who gathered publicly to set their mobile phones to go off simultaneously. The cacophony of ring tones said nothing overtly about political protest, but that it was collectively organized and accomplished despite police presence creatively communicates a vague symbolic protest. Tactical creativity in the use of mobile phones and microblogs for protest coordination is another way activists can stay one step ahead of the security forces.

Symbolic actions are another form of creative protest, often accomplished stealthily to mitigate risks. Flowers appeared at the gates of the Gdansk shipyard to commemorate the anniversary of the deaths of striking workers, and in Tallinn, Estonia, flowers appeared on the anniversary of the republic at the site of a statue of a national hero, which was demolished by the Soviets in 1940. The planting of flags, crosses, and painting of political graffiti are usually collective actions rather than individual ones, and displays of opposition. Political graffiti were common sights in Latin American authoritarian regimes, in Egypt during the Arab Spring, in the Iranian democracy movement in 2009, and in Syria before the civil war. Taking advantage of public locations, many of which carry heavy symbolism for the democratic opposition, these kinds of actions remind the broader population that there is an opposition out there that is willing to take risks; and that with guile and creativity, oppositional statements can be made public.

Triggering

The term refers to events or actions that precipitate a change in the prevailing discourse. It was a central concept in Gamson, Fireman, and Rytina's (1982) seminal analysis of how quiescence is transformed into collective action by breaking the by surface tension of group conformity. Gamson, Fireman, and Rytina's (1982) focus-group exercises demonstrated that just one or two outspoken group members can be critical to fomenting rebellion in small group settings. As an element of the repressive repertoire, the activities described earlier, first, in duplicitous groups, and, second, the small collective acts of creative protest, also function to break public quiescence about dissatisfaction with authoritarian rule, its lack of responsiveness, and its rampant corruption.

Kuran (1995) accorded public conformity a critical role in authoritarian stability in his analysis of East European communism. His concept of preference falsification describes a mass "group think," which operates during periods of protest quiescence to stifle communication about regime dissatisfaction (see also Ermakoff 2008). Kuran reasoned that fear of reprisals imparts a veil of silence that keeps most citizens from voicing their true attitudes, and fosters the incorrect belief that they are alone in their dissatisfaction. He went on to suggest that developments in other countries, such as the rise of Solidarity in Poland or the fall of the Berlin Wall, served as the triggers to break quiescence. Although international trends can play a role—as evident in how protest diffused in the Arab Spring—Kuran's hypothesis of preference falsification misses role of actions within the repressive repertoire. As discussed earlier, the social control apparatus of any authoritarian regime is never monolithic such that it hermetically seals off all dissent. The fundamental point of the repressive repertoire is that its small acts of protest and opposition are creatively carved out of situations where social control breaks down and islands of freedom are creatively and agentically claimed by dissident actors.

The repressive repertoire confirms the analytical centrality of the strategic field of play whereby each actor—the several levels of state security and the dissidents they pursue—monitors the other to seek an advantage. Moreover, from the ground view, the stronger hand in this game would seem to be not with the security forces but with the creative and adaptable opposition, at least in the long run. According to a former intelligence analyst of the Cuban government, "Pushing for change in Cuba is likened to the punishment of Sisyphus, rolling a stone up a hill only to watch it roll to the bottom. But sometimes, the stone comes to rest in a different position" (quoted in Burnett 2013: 6). The free spaces created by actions within the repressive repertoire are fundamental to subsequent activist organization, and serve as base camps of yet more activism. Moreover, they have a resonance much broader than the regime could ever imagine because their public performance proclaims to the majority of nonengaged citizens that there is indeed an opposition out there.

Recognition of the repressive repertoire broadens the definition of social movements in repressive states to include less public actions of dissident activists and more risk-adverse ordinary citizens. It also includes the ephemeral forms of network organization and oppositional identity that anchor those actors. Further support for this broadened definition is the finding that there is continuity of participation of early activists in later collective actions that are more public and recognizable.

Repertoire Transition to the Modular Forms

Actions within the repressive repertoire bridge the crucial period of movement development when the social-psychological processes of conformist quiescence and preference falsification increasingly break down for wider segments of the population. It is a common pattern that, prior to mass oppositional mobilizations such as the Tahrir Square protests in Egypt, 2011, there are usually sequences of smaller public actions that represent the first tentative ventures by submerged movement groups into the public arena. These are actions of *repertoire transition* that point to more recognizable and modular forms characteristic of open societies. In Tunisia and Egypt prior to the mass mobilizations of the Arab Spring, despite repressive conditions, there had been a rising tide of bounded and focussed labor and policy-focussed protest over the last five years (Clarke 2011; Kurzman 2012).

These protest mobilizations are typically focussed on issues such as the environment, labor concerns, corruption, neighborhood NIMBY grievances, household and family claims, and women's demands (Cai 2010)—rather than mass antiregime protests. It is typical that these transitional collective actions are characterized by a tension with the repressive state. This occurs in part at the policy level because, by permitting public protests to occur, the regime acknowledges—at least to a minimal degree—popular sovereignty. This tension is also manifested in the streets, because security apparatuses are not accustomed to moderation and restraint, even though there is often a strong self-limiting quality to the public demonstrations so that they remain overwhelmingly peaceful. At the policy level, the party and/or state may choose not to unleash the police and security apparatus for ideological reasons, for reasons of international politics, or to provide a safety value to reduce more direct antiregime protests.

Since Tiananmen Square, a transition to modular tactics has been occurring rapidly in China over the past quarter century. In the city of Xiamen, there were large protests in 2007 against the construction of a petrochemical plant that lasted several days. Organizers called for participation in several NIMBY mobilizations of "concerned citizens" looking out for the well-being of the city and the nation. Protest participation was characterized as "going for a stroll," a common tactic in China that was later seen in the aborted, post-Arab Spring, jasmine revolution there. The idea of taking a stroll (rather than a march of coordinated protesters) duplicitously cloaks the risks collective action during the period of repertoire transition. Under the guise of a simple afternoon walk, the mid-stage ambiguity of the transitional repertoire is vividly captured (Johnston and Carnesecca 2014).

In China, situating protester claims within regime-defined legality has emerged as an important tactic to voice claims against various levels of state administration (O'Brien and Li 2006; Ho 2008). Moreover, as in the Xiamen protests, strategic-field factors frequently come into play as local officials, concerned how their handling of the movement might jeopardize their position vis-à-vis the central government, on the one hand, and protesters, on the other, equivocate in their responses to movement calls for action. In Xiamen, the movement's tactical boldness increased as officials demonstrated a reduced capacity to respond. Increasing numbers of participants (which reached 10,000 during the height of protests) mitigated risks and made policing the protests less certain, less efficient, and more haphazard. However, movements in China whose claims more openly challenge political elites, even though they too seek the cloak of legality and citizen reform, are not tolerated. We see this in the repression directed at the New Citizens Movement, an anticorruption campaign calling on Communist Party officials to reveal their hidden wealth. It had been attracting increasing middle-class support, to which the state has responded with the arrests of its leader, Xu Zhihong, and several other movement activists.

Early in the repertoire transition, public events ostensibly convened for one purpose often serve as opportunities to briefly and quickly assert broad oppositional claims. One frequent tactic is to exploit the funerals of activists and martyrs for the cause as opportunities for protest. Another common tactic is that activists intone prohibited songs or initiate oppositional chants at mass public events such as concerts and football matches. The presumption is that more risk-adverse bystanders will see the safety accorded by the number of people present and join in. These examples represent gradual and irregular shifts in the repressive repertoire toward more familiar public forms of collective of action closer to the modular repertoire. They change even more the perception of political opportunity in repressive states by suggesting openings for hundreds—sometimes thousands—of citizens who witness them or spontaneously participate. As such actions mount, the quiescence characteristic of authoritarian polities is broken, bridging the gap between "private truths and public lies"—to use Kuran's phrase.

For all these reasons, the more the authoritarian state tolerates these forms of protests, the more it runs the risk of more public and broadly supported protest actions in the future—a proverbial slippery slope from the regime's point of view that poses significant strategic challenges. Moreover, in the field of play between the various agencies of social control and the creativity of the repressive repertoire, the long-term advantage would seem to reside with the activists. This is a suggestive hypothesis for further research.

Social science has analyzed the more recognizable collective action forms of protest mobilization as repressive states crumble. The trend over the years has been a shift from macrolevel factors characteristic of modernization theory (fifty years ago) and structural approaches to revolution (forty years ago) to increasingly meso- and microlevel analyses of strategic interactions among different players. The concepts of the repressive repertoire and repertoire transition shift focus to the less apparent foundations that activists lay before the modern repertoire publicly appears. Their creative and duplicitous collective actions represent microlevel assertions of agency and strategic adjustment. They are the first public utterances that, indeed, the Emperor has no clothes, thereby planting the seeds from which broad-based social movements grow in repressive contexts.

References

Bayat, Asef. (1997). *Street Politics: Poor People's Movements in Iran*. New York: Columbia University Press.

Bayat, Asef. (2003). "The Street and Politics of Dissent in the Arab World," *Middle East Report*. 226: 10–17.

Beissinger, Mark. (2002). *Nationalist Mobilization and the Collapse of the Soviet State*. New York: Cambridge University Press.

Boudreau, Vincent. (2004). *Resisting Dictatorship: Repression and Protest in Southeast Asia*. New York: Cambridge University Press.

Burnett, Victoria. (2013). "Glimmers of Tolerance Emerge within Cuba's Revolution for Voices of Dissent," *New York Times*. December 8: A6.

Cai, Yongshun. 2010. *Collective Resistance in China*. Stanford, CA: Stanford University Press.

Calhoun, Craig. (1994). *Neither Gods nor Emperors: Students and the Struggle for Democracy in China*. Berkeley: University of California Press.

Clarke, Killian. (2011). "Saying 'Enough': Authoritarianism in Egypt's Kefaya Movement," *Mobilization: An International Quarterly*. 16: 397–416.

della Porta, Donatella. (2014). *Mobilizing for Democracy*. New York: Oxford University Press.

della Porta, Donatella, and Diani, Mario. (2006). *Social Movements. An Introduction*. Second edition. Malden, MA: Blackwell Publishing.

della Porta, Donatella, and Vannucci, Alberto. (2012). *The Hidden Order of Corruption*. Farnham: Ashgate.

Diani, Mario. (1997). "Social Movements and Social Capital: A Network Perspective on Social Movements," *Mobilization*. 2: 129–147.

Ermakoff, Ivan. (2008). *Ruling Oneself Out: A Theory of Collective Abdications.* Durham, NC: Duke University Press.

Fligstein, Neil, and McAdam, Doug. (2012). *A Theory of Fields.* New York: Oxford University Press.

Gamson, William A., Fireman, Bruce, and Rytina, Steven. (1982). *Encounters with Unjust Authority.* Homewood, IL: Dorsey Press.

Goodwin, Jeff. (2001). *No Other Way Out: States and Revolutionary Movements, 1945–1991.* New York: Cambridge University Press.

Ho, Peter. (2008). "Introduction: Embedded Activism and Political Change in a Semi-Authoritarian Context." In *China's Embedded Activism*, edited by P. Ho and R. L. Edmonds, 1–32. New York: Routledge Press.

Johnston, Hank. (2006). "The Dynamics of (Small) Contention in Repressive States," *Mobilization: An International Quarterly.* 11: 195–212.

Johnston, Hank. (2011). *States and Social Movements.* Cambridge: Polity Press.

Johnston, Hank. (2014). *What is a Social Movement?* Cambridge: Polity Press.

Johnston, Hank, and Carnesecca, Cole. (2014). "Fear Management in Contemporary Antiauthoritarian Oppositions." In *From Silence to Protest,* edited by Frédéric Royall and Didier Chabanet, 27–50. Farnham: Ashgate.

Johnston, Hank, and Mueller, Carol. (2001). "Unobtrusive Practices of Contention in Leninist Regimes," *Sociological Perspectives.* 44: 351–376.

Kuran, Timur. (1995). *Private Lives, Public Truths.* Cambridge, MA: Harvard University Press.

Kurzman, Charles. (2012). "The Arab Spring Uncoiled," *Mobilization: An International Quarterly.* 17: 377–390.

Linz, Juan J. (1964). "An Authoritarian Regime: Spain." In *Cleavages, Ideologies, and Party Systems: Contributions to Comparative Political Sociology*, edited by Eirk Allart and Yrjö Kittunen, 291–341. Helsinki: Academic Bookstore.

Linz, Juan J., and Stepan, Alfred. (1996). *Problems of Democratic Transition and Consolidation.* Baltimore, MD: Johns Hopkins Press.

McAdam, Doug, and Tarrow, Sidney. (2011). "Dynamics of Contention Ten Years On: A Special of Mobilization," *Mobilization: An International Quarterly.* 16: 1–116.

McAdam, Doug, Tarrow, Sidney G., and Tilly, Charles. (2001). *Dynamics of Contention.* New York: Cambridge University Press.

Maravall, José M. (1982). *Transition to Democracy in Spain.* London: Croom Helm Ltd.

O'Brien, Kevin J., and Li, Lianjiang. (2006). *Rightful Resistance in Rural China.* New York: Cambridge University Press.

O'Donnell, Guillermo, and Schmitter, Philippe C. (1986). *Transitions from Authoritarian Rule: Tentative Conclusions about Uncertain Democracies.* Baltimore, MD: Johns Hopkins University Press.

Parsa, Misagh. (2000). *States, Ideologies, and Social Revolutions: A Comparative Analysis of Iran, Nicaragua, and the Philippines.* New York: Cambridge University Press.

Priestland, David. (2007). *Stalinism and the Politics of Mobilization.* New York: Oxford University Press.

Schock, Kurt. (2005). *Unarmed Insurrections.* Minneapolis: University of Minnesota Press.

Seidman, Gay, (2001). "Guerrillas in their Midst: Armed Struggle in the South African Anti-Apartheid Movement," *Mobilization.* 6: 111–127.

Slater, Daniel. (2010). *Ordering Power: Contentious Politics and Authoritarian Leviathans in Southeast Asia.* New York: Cambridge University Press.

Tilly, Charles, (1992). *Coercion, Capital, and European States.* Malden, MA: Blackwell.

Tilly, Charles (1995). *Popular Contention in Great Britain 1758–1834.* Cambridge, MA: Harvard University Press.

Tilly, Charles. (2008). *Contentious Performances.* New York: Cambridge University Press.

CHAPTER 42

REPRESSION

The Governance of Domestic Dissent

ABBY PETERSON AND MATTIAS WAHLSTRÖM

SOCIAL movement research has a long tradition of studying repression. For all its short-comings, the concept of repression is paradigmatic for the multi-disciplinary research field, and any broader review of the field must depart from it, even though there are good reasons to favor alternative conceptualizations that avoid the concept's normative connotations (see Earl 2006). In this chapter we will make a case for conceptualizing repression as *the governance of domestic dissent*. Institutional actors meet the perceived threats of oppositional forces with actions designed to "steer the conduct of civil society" (Loader 2000: 344) so as not to threaten or disrupt the dominant political and economic order (cf. Thörn 2012). Repression or policing contention[1] is a dispersed mechanism *for* the governance of the dominant political and economic order. The multidimensional model of repression that we will be using to organize this chapter builds upon previous theoretical definitions but is modified to grasp a wider disciplinary field of research and geographical context (e.g., Tilly 1978; Davenport 1995 and 2007a; and in particular, Earl 2003).

Our ambition is to provide a multi-disciplinary overview, which can shed light on possible loci for new multi-disciplinary collaboration as well as lacunae in the research field. In order to survey the vast literature on repression our model for understanding the forms of governing dissent departs from three conceptual dimensions: a scale dimension along the axis of the supra-national level to the local level; an institutional dimension capturing the institutional relationships of the "governors of dissent" and the nation-state, and a functional dimension which distinguishes the activities of governing (see Figure 42.1). The scale dimension denotes the geographic and operational scale of the governance of dissent—implying positions both in organizational hierarchies and geographic scope. The institutional dimension tackles the identity of the actors governing dissent—from actors more or less tightly linked to the national government to private and civil society actors that act more or less independently of any state. Finally, the functional dimension

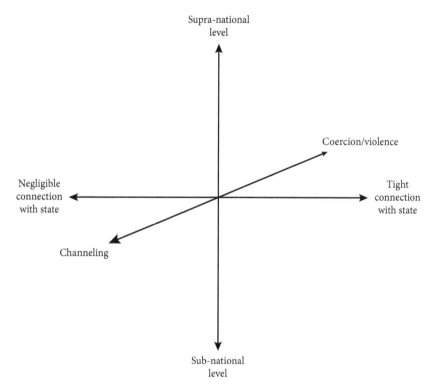

Supra-national
level

Coercion/violence

Negligible
connection
with state

Tight
connection
with state

Channeling

Sub-national
level

FIGURE 42.1 Core dimensions of repression: scale (vertical axis); institutional (horizontal axis); and functional (depth axis).

addresses the ways that dissent is governed—ranging from subtle forms of chan-neling, through intimidation and symbolic violence, to violent coercion at the other end of the spectrum.

THE SCALE DIMENSION

The plural forms of policing, *sic* governing contention, are exercised in local and national, and increasingly, in international contexts. This latter aspect is encapsulated in the scale dimension, which is inherited from discussions in geography (cf. Marston 2000). We regard scale in this context as the geographic scope of an agent's aspiration of governance, which in some cases (as in supra- and sub-national governmental insti-tutions) also implies a hierarchical relation between institutions. However, there is no mechanical relation between the scale of an agent's governing capacity and the scale of any specific repressive action. A national institution may well enact repression on the local level, and several local institutions can, at least in principle, co-organize repression of a larger scale.

Repression is typically thought of as being exercised at the national scale, and in many cases this is correct in terms of the steering, that is, law making and coordination of repressive capacities. However, in order to capture the whole range of activities associated with the governance of dissent one needs to study activities on both larger and smaller scales. On an international level, there is not only coordination of protest policing strategies (Reiter and Fillieule 2006), but also more importantly, an increasing exchange of intelligence and concomitant regulation of national borders in order to restrict the international movement of protesters. When public protest events are governed on scales beyond the immediate event, this typically makes coercive governing less publicly visible (D'Arcus 2003).

Since 9/11 2001 the US-defined "war on terror" has dramatically extended the geopolitical scope of the governance of dissent to the global scale (Croft 2006; Oliver 2006; Donohue 2008; Awan and Blakemore 2013) and with this extension clouded the traditional distinction between domestic threat and foreign threats. In response to terrorist actions or the threat of terrorist actions numerous democracies across the globe enacted anti-terrorist acts, such as the Patriot Act in the United States and the Prevention of Terrorism Act in India, which have radically expanded the repressive powers of the federal government thereby infringing on civil rights of assembly and protest (Cole 2003; Abdolian and Takooshian 2002; Kristnan 2004). Post-9/11 has witnessed an unparalleled international cooperation and intelligence sharing between police authorities and security services and private corporate intelligence agencies in this new situation for the governance of dissent.

The smallest scale of repression is arguably the interpersonal level. Ferree (2005) calls attention to the ridicule directed at feminist activists, as an example of what she designates as "soft repression." Albeit not centrally coordinated, it can be classified as repression to the extent that the aggregate effect is repressive. Small-scale repression can also involve attacks on activists by local thugs and vigilantes supporting a regime. According to Johnston (2012: 72), in high-capacity authoritarian regimes "this is violence of the state at the microlevel, and is where the majority of citizens encounter an unjust and arbitrary state."

THE INSTITUTIONAL DIMENSION

The institutional dimension recognizes that repression is *both* governmental and non-governmental regulatory action exercised against collective actors challenging the existing relations of power. While our overview highlights state repression, which has been the most researched, our point of departure is sensitive to the plurality of the policing forms unfolding *within, above, beyond, and below the state* (Bayley and Shearing 1996; Jones and Newburn 1998 and 2006; Crawford and Lister 2004). So while policing domestic dissent *by the state* is still significant and the linchpin for the governance of domestic dissent, state authorities, for example, military, police authorities at both the national and local levels, together with state security police, are increasingly joined by policing actors within the private security industry, in international fora between states, for example, Interpol and Europol, and lastly, by countermovements operating below the state. The institutional dimension includes the following categories: *public*, for example, the state's coercive arm, state bureaucracies such as the tax authorities, etc.; *private*, for example, the private security industry, business corporations, private foundations, etc.; and *civil*, for example, powerful countermovements.

As Pierskalla (2010: 136) points out, effective repression crucially depends on the willingness of the policing enforcers to carry out the orders of the governors. As the case in Egypt after the 2013 overthrow of democratically elected President Mursi the military grasped governmental power by incarcerating the President, confronting the ensuing protests with violence, carrying out mass arrests amongst his supporters, and declaring his power base the "Muslim Brotherhood" illegal. In a comparative study of Latin American and African countries Carey (2006) found that differences in the exercise of overt coercion could be best explained by the position of the military to the government. Also in Western democratic states, the police organizations are not clear-cut extensions of state power, but act semi-autonomously according to their institutional logics (P. A. J. Waddington 1994). Police responses to dissent in Western democracies are typically less expressions of government interests, and rather have the character of organizational coping in order to maintain "order" and control over situations (see Earl and Soule 2006).

Research on repression has little interrogated the role of private actors for the governance of domestic dissent. However, as Earl (2004: 68ff.) points out, US labor history abounds with cases of private business enterprises employing private security forces to control protest through both overt and covert coercion (Griffen et al. 1986). While this avenue of governance had declined in importance in liberal democracies it has gained renewed vitality since the early 1990s with the extraordinary rise of the global corporate security sector (Singer 2004). Private global actors are localizing repression within nation-states for the governance of (their) economic order. Particularly in conjunction with extraction industries operating in weak states, private security corporations have been contracted to quell protest among, for example, striking oil workers in Nigeria 2003 (Bebbington et al. 2008). Holmqvist (2005: 14) maintains that global corporations involved in natural resource extraction are, with the involvement of private security corporations, creating "unnatural enclaves of security in otherwise unstable environments." The private security industry is governing dissent over grievances generated by the extraction industries themselves by creating "secure" areas independently of the state, which she argues risks throwing the process of democratic state building off track thereby generating further sources of popular grievances. In these cases, extraction industries in collusion with the corporate security industry are effectively circumventing the state as major actors in the governance of domestic dissent (cf. Campbell 2003; Ferguson 2006).

Not only global corporations contract private security, weak national governments have contracted these services to suppress political and social unrest as was the case in

Angola and Sierra Leone in 1995–98 when Executive Outcomes, and later in the conflict, Sandline, were hired to wage civil war (Musah and Fayemi 2000). While Holmqvist (2005: 3) maintains that there were few instances of genuine "contract wars," a wider industry of private security provision has proliferated that offers weak states a variety of security activities to beef up their own coercive capacity. Not only weak states engage the private security sector, even so-called "strong states" use private security actors to supplement state institutions. For example, Mitchell and Staeheli (2005) claim that restrictions on police spying on oppositional groups in the United States have led to the privatization of spying rather than its elimination. "More and more police began working with private security and detective firms to gain intelligence on political organisations" (Mitchell and Staeheli 2005: 802).

Lastly along our institutional dimension we have the case of civil actors governing dissent. The social movement discussion regarding the repression exercised by countermovements classically invokes the case of the state of Mississippi and the powerful anti-civil rights countermovement during the latter 1950s and early 1960s (Zald and Useem 1987; Luders 2003), as reflecting perhaps the singular role of powerful countermovements for the governance of dissent in the United States. Mississippi state, county, and city authorities were seen as being aligned with countermovement suppression of social change in a struggle with federal authorities. States are characteristically interpreted as supporting, mediating, or constraining countermovements (e.g., Meyer and Staggenborg 1996; Irons 2006 and 2010).

The Functional Dimension

The functional dimension in our model builds upon Osborne and Gaebler's (1992) distinction between aspects of governance that involve policy formation, agenda setting, and catalyzing change ("steering"), and those concerned with implementation and the on-the-ground enforcement of control ("rowing"). Our governance emphasis calls attention to the role of the various branches of government that steer the forms of policing contention through executive orders, legislative measures, laws and courts, etc., as well as steering the deployment of the policing enforcers (cf. Loader 2000). First, when police authorities and/or military are deployed to control dissent we find coercive action taken by the government that directly, and in some cases dramatically, raises the costs of collective oppositional social action (cf. Tilly 1978). Other more subtle forms of policing contention reside in the channeling of dissent into less threatening avenues. Contention can be governed by legislative and legal means that selectively lower the costs of dissent for some oppositional actors and indirectly raise the costs for others. Earl (2006: 130) argues that protest control "may be occurring long before insurgency is evident. In fact, protest control may play an important role as a switchman, effectively preventing protest mobilization around some grievances and ineffectively allowing some troubles to boil into protest." Nevertheless, it is the coercive actions of protest control, overt and covert, which has garnered the lion's share of the attention of researchers. Violent and even deadly confrontations with oppositional actors have been in focus. A brutal massacre of dissidents unswervingly communicates a state's (or a private security force's) resolve to directly repress public protest. At the same time, as observed by Arendt (1970), the use of physical violence to achieve one's ends can be interpreted as a sign of a relative lack of power, an inability to govern protest through means closer to the channeling end of the spectrum.

Using ethnographic and case studies, the brutality of protest policing in authoritarian regimes has been analyzed (e.g., De Nardo 1985; Francisco 2005; Sheptycky 2002 and 2005; Boudreau 2004/2009; Bedford 2009), but it has been the difficult balance police authorities must tread between the protection of order and the protection of civil and political liberties in liberal democratic contexts that has been most widely researched (e.g., Waddington, Jones, and Critcher 1989; P.A.J. Waddington 1991, 1994, and 1999; D. Waddington 1992; Critcher and Waddington 1996; della Porta 1995; Fillieule and Jobard 1998; della Porta and Fillieule 2004; Peterson 2006). della Porta and Reiter (1998) introduced the notion of protest policing, calling attention to the importance of under- standing the strategies of controlling protest. This work has led to rich case studies that reveal the complicated interactions between protesters and police authorities. King and Brearley (1996), McPhail, Schweingruber, and McCarthy (1998), and della Porta and Fillieule (2004), equally argue that police forces have gradually moved from the 1970s onwards from the traditional "escalated force" strategy with harsh repression to a more tolerant strategy of "negotiated management" of protest involving the search for dialogue. In the wake of increasing transnational protest the new challenges and chal- lengers have awakened new response strategies from police authorities (della Porta, Peterson, and Reiter 2006; Ferndandez 2008). Noakes and Gillham (2006) maintain that the recent transnational protest waves, in combination with the growing impact of a "new penology" (Feeley and Simon 1992), have led to a move from negotiated man- agement to a strategy that selectively incapacitates "risk demonstrators" while retain- ing dialogue and negotiation with compliant demonstrators (cf. Vitale 2005; Wahlström 2010; Gorringe et al. 2012). Whereas this is indeed a pattern that has been a consistent aspect of the negotiated management approach, the underlying logic of selective proac- tive incapacitation has become more prominent. However, the policing of transnational summit protests is not necessarily representative of domestic protest policing more gen- erally, and some studies direct attention to the trend of "dialogue policing" in several European police forces, which represents a less coercive—albeit not unproblematic— form of governing dissent (Wahlström and Oskarsson 2006; Stott et al. 2013; Baker 2013).

Related to the enduring importance of public space for popular dissent (Mitchell 2003a), the spatial dimensions of protest policing have attracted growing scholarly interest (e.g., Mitchell and Staeheli 2005; Noakes et al. 2005; Peterson 2006; Zajko and Béland 2008). In democratic countries the police have the dual goal of securing the pos- sibility of free speech in public space, and at the same time maintaining law and order. Therefore, authorities prefer to direct protesters to easily controlled spaces, which are not always those preferred by the challengers, in terms of political impact and/or symbolic significance (Mitchell 2003b). Several observers have noted an increasing sophistication on the part of the police in the use of zoning techniques and other forms of spatial separation to more effectively govern public space (Gillham et al. 2013). This governance is essentially about police territoriality (Herbert 2007), typically focussed on either maintaining the dominant order within an area or through protecting a border that dissenters wish to cross (Wahlström 2010).

While overt coercion has undeniably captured the most attention, covert surveillance, intelligence gathering, harassment, and disinformation campaigns have not been neglected (on the more invisible forms of harassment, see Forminaya and Wood 2011: 1). Marx (1979), and Churchill and Wall (1988), Cunningham (2004) all found that the Federal Bureau of Investigation (FBI) and its COINTELPRO operation targeted groups and organizations during the 1960s and 1970s that were not necessarily posing a significant level of threat to the surrounding community. In short, these researchers found that covert coercion was draconian in its scope thereby violating civil liberties (see also Lyon 1994; Carley 1997; Boykoff 2006 and 2007; Starr et al. 2008).

Abdolian and Takooshian (2002: 1446) point out "historically, during times of crisis, it has been natural for democratic nations, including the United States, to temporarily abridge individual liberties in ways that would never be considered in more halcyon times." The US Patriot Act of October 2001 dramatically reduced restrictions on law enforcement agencies' capability to search telephone and e-mail communications, and medical, financial, and other records. The act also allows for unprecedented sharing of intelligence between law enforcement agencies. The act expanded the definition of terrorism to include what it defined as domestic terrorism, thus enlarging the number of activities to which the Patriot Act's extended law enforcement powers could be applied. For example, animal rights organizations and ecological organizations could fall within its reach making it potentially a "felony to, among other things, 'deter' the business activities of industries engaged in the exploitation of animals and natural resources by protesting the actions of a … corporation or influencing a unit of government to take a specific action" (Eddy 2005: 262). These changes in the statutes have, according to Eddy, boosted the governance capacities in some states to protect economic interests and threaten to significantly raise the costs of involvement in nonviolent environmental protest.

Policing theorists have warned that democratic societies have progressively shifted towards becoming "surveillance societies" where "surveillance displaces crime control for the efficient production of knowledge useful in the administration of suspect populations" (Ericson 1994: 139; see also Dandeker 1990). Since 9/11 security services are increasingly targeting Muslim communities as suspect populations. By casting a wide net in their counterterrorism measures, security services have introduced a "religious profiling," which in effect risks criminalizing Muslims per se. Counterterrorism policing in many Western European countries now gives priority to what are called preventive strategies in which cooperation with Muslim communities is sought by the security service. Security services seek to initiate a dialogue with Muslim communities in order to enhance their information gathering capacity as well as encouraging

Muslim communities' self-policing to prevent radicalization processes among Muslim youth (e.g., Akram and Johnson 2002; Bigo and Tsoukala 2008; Birt 2009; Kundnani 2009; Spalek 2009; Thomas 2010; Lindkilde 2012). According to Peterson (2012), the "soft coercion" of the security service is an attempt to create new spaces of governance, where Muslim communities (and individuals) are ostensibly "invited" to participate in the state's counterterrorism program. These invited spaces reflect what Raco (2003: 78) describes as the state's "increased concern with defining and shaping 'appropriate' individual and community conduct, regulation and control," which in effect extends the scope of repression from political dissidents to targeted communities. While many liberal democracies are selectively targeting Muslim communities, Earl (2011: 275) points out that in authoritarian or totalitarian regimes a large share of the population is subjected to insidious forms of repression.

Robertson (2009 and 2011) has analyzed Russia under Putin as a paradigmatic case for the new authoritarianism evolving with innovative channeling techniques to govern dissent with a range of indirect means for controlling and limiting protest, while retaining the range of coercive measures to directly police protest. The use of preventive detention and harassment to pre-empt protest is widespread. But the real innovation has occurred in the restructuring of state-civil society relations in Russia with the development of a system of licensing and governmental support for non-governmental organizations (NGOs), which favors NGOs willing to work with the regime and inhibiting more critical and thereby threatening NGOs. Secondly, the Putin regime has created what Robertson calls "ersatz social movements," particularly youth "movements" which, while they look like social movements and can provide mass mobilization, do so to counter potential challenges to the regime on the streets. As Robertson (2009: 545) points out, a broad approach to repression is not new. "Rulers in both authoritarian and democratic states alike have long understood the importance of channelling protest actions and political energy in non-threatening directions."

VARIATIONS IN THE LEVEL AND CHARACTER OF THE GOVERNANCE OF DOMESTIC DISSENT

The case study approach has led to the development of an explanatory model that emphasizes the processual, relational nature of protest policing in liberal democracies calling attention to a number of factors that impact upon how the police authorities respond to protesters. Within a specific political, media, and juridical context (e.g., Wisler and Tackenberg 2000) external factors influence police behavior such as who is challenging and how they are challenging. Significant differences can be found not only on the state level but also on the city level (MacSheoin and Yeates 2009; Rafail 2010). Since local and national institutions are nested within an international institutional context (Meyer 2003), political opportunities on several levels may contribute to the character and level of repression of a social movement. della Porta and Reiter (2006) maintain that the main explanation for the brutality of Italian policing at the 2001 G8 summit in Genoa was the relative closure of domestic as well as transnational political opportunities for the claims of the new global justice challengers. Researchers have found that police meet more radical protesters employing more radical confrontational tactics with harsher measures (e.g., McAdam 1982; Bromley and Shupe 1983; Koopmans 1993; Davenport 1995; Earl 2003; della Porta and Fillieule 2004; Lee 2013) as they will when meeting protesters poorer in material and political resources (Piven and Cloward 1977; Waddington 1992; della Porta 1998; Wisler and Guigni 1999; Earl, Soule, and McCarthy 2003). Earl and Soule (2006: 159) found "overwhelming support for a blue, or police-centered approach to protest policing in the US" arguing that the institutional features of policing with its emphasis on control together with organizational variations between police agencies structure protest policing. Police authorities meet with more coercive force what they perceive as a threat that they could lose control over the protest situation, for example in protest situations with counterdemonstrators, missile throwing by protesters and other confrontational protest tactics. However, it is not always clear to what extent police coercion is merely a reaction to activist violence or actually constitutes the flashpoint that sparks violent reactions from the protesters (Wahlström 2011). The protest situation, for example, the presence of political dignitaries and heads of state, will amplify the level of repression (Ericson and Doyle 1999; P. A. J. Waddington 2003; King and D. Waddington 2006). The range of external factors—institutional, situational, and contextual—are filtered through what della Porta (1998) called "police knowledge," that is, how the police interpret their role and the surrounding environment, and consequently police knowledge shapes how police authorities perceive threats posed by challengers and subsequently the measures taken to govern challenges. Police knowledge is neither static nor uniform within police organizations, and may change both through experiences as well as through training in the context of tactical reform (Wahlström 2007).

While case studies have often focussed protest events that resulted in notorious instances of police repression, even "police riots" (Stark 1972; Peterson 2006), Earl, Soule, and McCarthy (2003), using a quantitative approach instead, found that heavy-handed police repression in the period associated with the escalated force style of protest policing was the exception rather than the rule. On the basis of their analysis they argue that in the cases that the police were present and acted it was concrete situational threats such as the use of confrontational tactics and protest size that triggered an escalated response by the police. Their analysis found little support for the theoretical approach launched by Gamson (1990 [1975]) and developed by Stockdill (2003) that suggests that protester weakness produces repression, rather that a threat based model of repression, according to these researchers, offers the most robust explanation for police presence and action at protest events. Their study is in line with Davenport (2000), who argues that the threat model is the most empirically supported model. However, it is worth pointing out that Earl, Soule, and McCarthy's study is empirically limited to the United States and does not consider other regimes or government contexts. Carey (2010) and MacSheoin and

Yeates (2009) remind us that governments respond differently to protest. While situational and institutional factors may offer robust explanations in established democracies, how the government and elites perceive the threat of domestic dissent can have more significant causal power in other regime types.

Davenport (1995), among others, emphasizes that perceived threats to the political and economic order are defined and responded to differently across contexts. Empirical research has found that the likelihood of threats being perceived by the government and repression exercised is significantly reduced in stable liberal democratic regimes where overt coercive action is often not an attractive option and which are committed to tolerate at least certain aspects of dissident behavior—the "domestic democratic peace" hypothesis (Davenport 2007b; see even Regan and Henderson 2002). Conversely, in stable consolidated autocracies the governments have the capacity to deter any public protest, hence, repression is rarely necessary. This leads to the prominent "murder in the middle" hypothesis (cf. Fein 1995), which posits that regimes between these two poles are those that will most often resort to overt coercive actions to govern domestic dissent. The problem with the murder in the middle hypothesis is that the "middle" is not specified. It includes what researchers intermittently have called semi-democracies, semi-autocracies, hybrid regimes, so-called transitional regimes in various degrees of evolution, and interim regimes (Fearon and Laitin 2003). Research is lacking that addresses and untangles the range of regimes in the leftover category of the middle—the varieties of capacity and resolve to govern domestic dissent with coercive actions and/or channeling actions.

Transitions from authoritarian regimes to post-authoritarian regimes follow uneven paths. The transition to democracy in Eastern European countries in the post-1989 era differed from the transition made by the former Soviet republics. The former Soviet states had to different degrees burgeoning civil societies and regimes struggling for recognition by Western Europe. Robertson (2011) calls post-authoritarian regimes in the former Soviet Republics that hold elections with at least some form of opposition for "hybrid regimes," which he claims are now the most common form of the "new" authoritarian regime. These regimes are faced with the challenge that control of the streets is both more difficult and more important for regime stability than before in order to maintain elite unity and at least the appearance of invincibility—the hallmark of a stable authoritarian regime. Titarenko et al. (2001) in an analysis of repression in Minsk, Belarus, demonstrate how the state after transition on the one hand governed dissent by developing a very restrictive permit system, but shifted tactics towards more frequent coercive actions under President Lukashenko.

Other transitional regimes seeking to establish democracy are more unstable and less consolidated and we can expect that they do not have the capacity, in the same way as hybrid regimes, to utilize channeling measures. Schatzman (2005) found evidence that in the transition to democracy in eighteen South American countries rebellion and collective protest did not diminish; violent rebellions continued. Furthermore in the transition from authoritarian regimes to democratic, the coercive arms of the state—the police and military—are not readily "civilized" due to inertia and their self-perpetuating behavior (Poe and Tate 1994; Davenport 1995; Carey 2010). The intensity of the level of protest directly influences the level of state response to its repression. Carey (2010) points out that what she calls semi-democracies are more likely than full democracies or autocracies to endure severe forms of dissent. She argues that guerrilla warfare significantly increases the risk of state terror—understood as widespread killing and torture of civilians—by 50 per cent.

THE OUTCOMES OF REPRESSION

The research on how repression affects subsequent protest has been studied by a number of researchers (e.g., McAdam 1982; Lichbach 1987; Fantasia 1988; Khawaja 1993; Koopmans 1993; Kriesi et al. 1995; Bosi et al. 2014). Research can substantiate that repression both sparks more protest *and* inhibits further protest. How can we understand this ostensible anomaly? Moore (1998) used statistical sequential tests of events data and found support for Lichbach's substitution model that suggests that repression can steer the behavior of dissidents from violent protest to nonviolent forms of protest, and vice versa, but it cannot eliminate protest. Departing from a choice-theoretical approach Moore (2000) further argues that governments mix accommodation of protesters' demands and repression of protest to achieve a (for the state) tolerable policy level at minimal costs.

Pierskalla (2010) argues that repression and protest are interrelated strategic decisions, a game played by rational actors in which outcomes observed in reality emerge as equilibrium strategies on the part of governments—trade-offs between governments and opposition. The state seeks to govern dissent so as to best maintain the status quo. The considerable literature on the relationship between repression and protest has found mixed evidence with regard to the effectiveness of government repression in defusing domestic dissent (e.g., Hibbs 1973; Muller and Opp 1986; Muller and Weede 1990; Rasler 1996; Dickson 2007; Chang 2008; Davenport and Loyle 2012). Johnston (2012) argues that the contradictory results are partly due to unwarranted aggregation of different regime types in the same models, partly because of complexities and tensions within the state apparatus that may give rise to possibilities for resistance. In short, government repression can be successful *or* lead to violent escalation and public outrage—"backfire"—even ending in regime collapse (e.g., Koopmans 1998; Francisco 2004; Hess and Martin 2006), a phenomenon Schock (2005) called the "paradox of repression."

CONCLUSIONS

We conclude with three lessons from our review. First, the field of repression research is truly inter-disciplinary. We have culled valuable insights from the disciplines of sociology, political science, international relations, law, criminology, geography, and development studies. While the inter-disciplinary nature of the field brings with it a muddle of terminologies, theoretical frameworks, methodologies, and geographical foci, dialogues across disciplinary boundaries appear far from unachievable and should bring the rewards of valuable cross-fertilizations that can better address the lacunae in our understanding of repression. Our conceptual definition of repression as the govern-ance of domestic dissent is one suggestion that might provide a common ground for dialogue.

Secondly, our three-dimensional model of the governance of dissent has proved a use-ful heuristic device for our overview and will hopefully stimulate new inquiries into the relationship between mobilization and scale, type of institutional governor, and func-tional character of repression. The model allows for mapping various "configurations of repression," which are composed of the scope of different scales or levels of repression, the multiplicity of the institutions of repression, together with the repressive strategies that confront a social movement.

Thirdly, we have learned that domestic dissent unequivocally provokes repression. Governments appear compelled to govern dissent so as to protect the political and economic order from threats and disruption. Governments may be joined by private security actors and to a far lesser degree civil actors in their efforts to steer dissent in less challenging directions. But dissent *is* governed, by sheer coercive force or by less strong-arm and subtle means, in order to maintain the status quo. Social movement protest and repression are inextricably joined.

NOTE

1. Repression and policing are used interchangeably to avoid redundancy, as are dissent, pro-test, and contention.

REFERENCES

Abdolian, Lisa Finnegan and Takooshian, Harold (2002). "The USA Patriot Act: Civil Liberties, the Media, and Public Opinion," *Fordham Urban Law Journal.* 30(4): 1429–1453.

Akram, Susan M. and Kevin R. Johnson (2002). "Race, Civil Rights, and Immigration Law After September 11, 2001: The Targeting of Arabs and Muslims," *New York University Annual Survey of American Law.* 58: 295–355.

Arendt, Hannah (1970). *On Violence.* New York: Harcourt, Brace & Company.

Awan, Imran and Blakemore, Brian (2013). *Extremism, Counter-Terrorism and Policing.* Aldershot: Ashgate.

Bayley, David and Shearing, Clifford (1996). "The Future of Policing," *Law and Society Review.* 30(3): 585–606.

Bebbington, Anthony, Hinojosa, Leonith, Bebbington, Denise Humphreys, Burneo, Maria Luisa and Warnaars, Ximena (2008). "Contention and Ambiguity: Mining and the Possibilities of Development," *Development and Change.* 39(6): 965–992.

Bedford, Sophie (2009). "Islamic Activism in Azerbaijan: Repression and Mobilization in a Post-Soviet Context," *Stockholm Studies in Politics 129*. Stockholm: Södertörn Doctoral Dissertations 33.

Bigo, Didier and Tsoukala, Anastassia (2008). *Terror, Insecurity and Liberty*. New York: Routledge.

Birt, Yahya (2009). "Promoting Virulent Envy? Reconsidering the UK's Terrorist Prevention Strategy," *Royal United Services Institute Journal*. 154(4): 52–58.

Bosi, Lorenzo, Demetriou, Charles, and Malthaner, Stefan (2014). *Dynamics of Political Violence: A Process-Oriented Perspective on Radicalization and the Escalation of Political Conflict*. Aldershot: Ashgate.

Boudreau, Vincent (2004/2009). *Resisting Dictatorship: Repression and Protest in Southeast Asia*. Cambridge: Cambridge University Press.

Boykoff, Jules (2006). *The Suppression of Dissent: How the State and Mass Media Squelch USAmerican Social Movements*. New York: Routledge.

Boykoff, Jules (2007). *Beyond Bullets: The Suppression of Dissent in the United States*. Oakland, CA: AK Press.

Campbell, Bonnie (2003). "Good Governance, Security and Mining in Africa," *Minerals and Energy*. 21(1): 31–44.

Carey, Sabine C. (2006). "The Dynamic Relationship Between Protest and Repression," *Political Research Quarterly*. 59(1): 1–11.

Carey, Sabine C. (2010). "The Use of Repression as a Response to Domestic Dissent," *Political Studies*. 58: 167–186.

Carley, Michael (1997) "Defining Forms of Successful State Repression of Social Movement Organizations: A Case Study of the FBI's COINTELPRO and the American Indian Movement," *Research in Social Movements, Conflicts and Change*. 20: 151–176.

Chang, Paul Y. (2008). "Unintended Consequences of Repression: Alliance Formation in South Korea's Democracy Movement (1970–1979)," *Social Forces*. 87(2): 1–28.

Churchill, Ward and Wall, Vander Jim (1988). *Agents of Repression: The FBI's Secret Wars Against the Black Panther Party and the American Indian Movement*. Boston, MA: South End Press.

Cole, David (2003). *Enemy Aliens: Double Standards and Constitutional Freedoms in the War on Terror*. New York: The New Press.

Crawford, Adam and Lister, Stephen (2004). *The Extended Policing Family*. New York: Joseph Roundtree Foundation.

Critcher, Chas and Waddington, David, eds. (1996). *Policing Public Order: Theoretical and Practical Issues*. Aldershot: Avebury.

Croft, Stuart (2006). *Culture, Crisis and America's War on Terror*. New York: Cambridge University Press.

Cunningham, David (2004). *There's Something Happening Here: The New Left, the Klan and FBI Counterintelligence*. Berkeley: University of California Press.

Dandeker, Christopher (1990). *Surveillance, Power and Modernity*. Cambridge: Polity Press.

D'Arcus, Bruce (2003). "Protest, Scale, and Publicity: The FBI and the H Rap Brown Act," *Antipode*. 35(4): 718–741.

Davenport, Christian (1995). "Multi-Dimensional Threat Perception and State Repression: An Inquiry Into Why States Apply Negative Sanctions," *American Journal of Political Science*. 39(3): 683–713.

Davenport, Christian (2000). "Introduction." In *Paths to State Repression*, edited by Christian Davenport, 1–24. Lanham, MD: Rowman and Littlefield.

Davenport, Christian (2007a). "State Repression and Political Order," *Annual Review of Political Science*. 10: 1–23.

Davenport, Christian (2007b). *State Repression and the Domestic Democratic Peace*. New York: Cambridge University Press.

Davenport, Christian and Loyle, Cyanne (2012). "The States Must Be Crazy: Dissent and the Puzzle of Repressive Persistence," *International Journal of Conflict and Violence*. 6(1): 75–96.

De Nardo, James (1985). *Power in Numbers: The Political Strategy of Protest and Rebellion*. Princeton, NJ: Princeton University Press.

della Porta, Donatella (1995). *Social Movements, Political Violence, and the State: A Comparative Analysis of Italy and Germany*. Cambridge: Cambridge University Press.

della Porta, Donatella (1998). "Police Knowledge and Protest Policing: Some Reflections on the Italian Case." In *Policing Protest: The Control of Mass Demonstrations in Western Democracies*, edited by Donatella della Porta and Herbert Reiter, 175–202. Minneapolis, MN: University of Minnesota Press.

della Porta, Donatella and Reiter, Herbert, eds. (1998) *Policing Protest: The Control of Mass Demonstrations in Western Democracies*. Minneapolis, MN: University of Minnesota Press.

della Porta, Donatella and Fillieule, Olivier (2004). "Policing Social Movements." In *The Blackwell Companion to Social Movements*, edited by David Snow, Sarah Soule, and Hans Kriesi, 217–241. Oxford: Blackwell.

della Porta, Donatella and Reiter, Herbert (2006). "The Policing of Global Protest: The G8 at Genoa and its Aftermath." In *The Policing of Transnational Protest*, edited by Donatella della Porta, Abby Peterson, and Herbert Reiter, 13–42. Aldershot: Ashgate.

della Porta, Donatella, Peterson, Abby, and Reiter, Herbert, eds. (2006). *The Policing of Transnational Protest*. Aldershot: Ashgate.

Dickson, Eric (2007). "On the (In)effectiveness of Collective Punishment: An Experimental Investigation." Working Paper no. 2451/26056, New York University.

Donohue, Laura (2008). *The Cost of Counterterrorism: Politics, Politics, and Liberty*. Cambridge: Cambridge University Press.

Earl, Jennifer (2003). "Tanks, Tear Gas, and Taxes: Toward a Theory of Movement Repression," *Sociological Theory*. 21(1): 44–68.

Earl, Jennifer (2004). "Controlling Protest: New Directions for Research on the Social Control of Protest," *Authority in Contention. Research in Social Movements, Conflicts and Change*. 25: 55–83.

Earl, Jennifer (2006). "Introduction: Repression and the Social Control of Protest," *Mobilization*. 11(2): 129–143.

Earl, Jennifer (2011). "Political Repression: Iron Fists, Velvet Gloves, and Diffuse Control," *Annual Review of Sociology*. 37: 261–284.

Earl, Jennifer and Soule, Sarah (2006). "Seeing Blue: A Police-Centered Explanation of Protest Policing," *Mobilization*. 11(2): 145–164.

Earl, Jennifer, Soule, Sarah, and McCarthy, John (2003). "Protest Under Fire? Explaining Protest Policing," *American Sociological Review*. 69: 581–606.

Eddy, Ethan Carson (2005). "Privatizing the Patriot Act: The Criminalization of Environmental and Animal Protectionists as Terrorists," *Pace Environmental Law Review*. 22(2): 261–327.

Ericson, Richard V. (1994). "The Royal Commission on Criminal Justice System Surveillance." In *Criminal Justice in Crisis*, edited by Michael McConville and Lee Bridges, 113–149. Aldershot: Edward Elgar.

Ericson, Richard and Doyle, Aaron (1999). "Globalization and the Policing of Protest: The Case of APEC 1997," *British Journal of Sociology*. 50(4): 589–608.

Fantasia, Rick (1988). *Cultures of Solidarity: Consciousness, Action, and Contemporary American Workers*. Berkeley, CA: University of California Press.

Fearon, James D. and Laitin, David D. (2003). "Ethnicity, Insurgency, and Civil War," *American Political Science Review*. 97(1): 75–90.

Fein, Helen (1995). "More Murder in the Middle: Life-integrity Violations and Democracy in the World, 1987," *Human Rights Quarterly*. 17(1): 170–191.

Ferree, Myra Marx (2005). "Soft Repression: Ridicule, Stigma, and Silencing in Gender-based Movements," *Research in Social Movements, Conflicts and Change* 25: 85–101.

Ferguson, James (2006). *Global Shadows: Africa in the Neo-Liberal World Order*. Durham, NC: Duke University Press.

Fernandez, Luis A. (2008). *Policing Dissent: Social Control and the Anti-Globalization Movement*. New Brunswick, NJ: Rutgers University Press.

Fillieule, Olivier and Jobard, Fabien (1998). "The Policing of Protest in France: Towards a Model of Protest Policing." In *Policing Protest: The Control of Mass Demonstrations in Western Democracies*, edited by Donatella della Porta and Herbert Reiter, 70–90. Minneapolis, MN: University of Minnesota Press.

Fominaya, Cristina Flesher and Wood, Lesley (2011). "Repression and Social Movements," *Interface*. 3(1): 1–11.

Francisco, Ronald A. (2004). "After the Massacre: Mobilization in the Wake of Harsh Repression." *Mobilization*. 9(2): 107–126.

Gamson, William A. (1990 [1975]). *The Strategy of Social Protest*. Homewood, IL: Dorsey.

Gillham, Patrick F., Edwards, Bob, and Noakes, John A. (2013). "Strategic Incapacitation and the Policing of Occupy Wall Street Protests in New York City, 2011," *Policing and Society*. 23(1): 81–102.

Gorringe, Hugo, Rosie, Michael, Waddington, David, and Kominou, Margarita (2012). "Facilitating Ineffective Protest? The Policing of the 2009 Edinburgh NATO Protests," *Policing & Society*. 22(2): 115–132.

Griffen, Larry J., Wallace, Michael E., and Rubin, Beth A. (1986). "Capitalist resistance to the organization of labor before the new deal: Why? How? Success?" *American Sociological Review*. 51(2): 147–167.

Hess, David and Martin, Brian (2006). "Repression, Backfire, and the Theory of Transformative Events," *Mobilization*. 11(2): 249–267.

Hibbs, Douglas A. (1973). *Mass Political Violence: A Cross-National Causal Analysis*. New York: John Wiley.

Holmqvist, Caroline (2005). *Private Security Companies: The Case for Regulation*. SIPRI Policy Paper no. 9. Stockholm: SIPRI.

Johnston, Hank (2012). "State Violence and Oppositional Protest in High-capacity Authoritarian Regimes," *International Journal of Conflict and Violence*. 6(1): 55–74.

Jones, Trevor and Newburn, Tim (1998). *Private Security and Public Policing*. Oxford: Clarendon Press.

Jones, Trevor and Newburn, Tim, eds. (2006). *Plural Policing: A Comparative Perspective*. New York: Routledge.

Khawaja, Marwan (1993). "Repression and Popular Collective Action: Evidence from the West Bank," *Sociological Forum*. 8: 47–71.

King, Mike and Brearley, Nigel (1996). *Public Order Policing: Contemporary Perspectives on Strategy and Tactics*. Leicester: Perpetuity Press.

King, Mike and Waddington, David (2006). "The Policing of Transnational Protest in Canada." In *The Policing of Transnational Protest*, edited by Donatella della Porta, Abby Peterson, and Herbert Reiter, 75–96. Aldershot: Ashgate.

Koopmans, Ruud (1993). "The Dynamics of Protest Waves: West Germany, 1965 to 1989," *American Sociological Review*. 58: 637–658.

Koopmans, Ruud (1998). "Dynamics of Repression and Mobilization: The German Extreme Right in the 1990s," *Mobilization*. 2(2): 637–658.

Kriesi, Hanspeter, Koopmans, Ruud, Dyvendak, Jan Wilem, and Giugni, Marco (1995). *New Social Movements in Western Europe*. Minneapolis, MN: University of Minnesota Press.

Kundnani, Arun (2009). *Spooked! How Not to Prevent Violent Extremism*. London: Institute of Race Relations.

Lee, Jung-eun (2013). "Categorical Threat and Protest Policing: Patterns of Repression Before and After Democratic Transition in South Korea," *Journal of Contemporary Asia*. 43(3): 475–496.

Lichbach, Mark (1987). "Deterrence of Escalation? The Puzzle of Aggregate Studies of Repression and Dissent," *Journal of Conflict Resolution*. 31: 266–297.

Lindekilde, Lasse (2012). "Neo-liberal Governing of "Radicals": Danish Radicalization Prevention Policies and Potential Iatrogenic Effects," *International Journal of Conflict and Violence*. 6(1): 109–125.

Loader, Ian (2000). "Plural Policing and Democratic Governance," *Social and Legal Studies*. 9(3): 323–345.

Luders, Joseph (2003). "Countermovements, the State, and the Intensity of Racial Contention in the American South." In *States, Parties, and Social Movements*, edited by Jack A. Goldstone, 27–44. New York: Cambridge University Press.

Lyon, David (1994). *The Electronic Eye: The Rise of Surveillance Society*. Cambridge: Polity.

MacSheoin, Tomás and Yeates, Nicola (2009). "Policing Anti-globalisation Protests: Patterns and Variations in State Responses." In *The Politics of Globalization*, edited by Samir Dasgupta and Jan Nederveen Pieterse, 197–241. New Delhi: Sage.

Marx, Gary (1979). "External Efforts to Damage or Facilitate Social Movements: Some Patterns, Explanations, Outcomes, and Complications." In *The Dynamics of Social Movements*, edited by Mayer Zald and John D. McCarthy, 94–125. Cambridge, MA: Winthrop.

McAdam, Douglas (1999 [1982]). *Political Process and the Development of Black Insurgency*. Chicago: Chicago University Press.

McPhail, Clark, Schweingruber, David, and McCarthy, Clark (1998). "Policing Protest in the United States: 1960–1995." In *Policing Protest: The Control of Mass Demonstrations in Western Democracies*, edited by Donatella della Porta and Herbert Reiter, 49–69. Minneapolis, MN: University of Minnesota Press.

Meyer, David S. (2003). "Political Opportunity and Nested Institutions," *Social Movement Studies*. 2(1): 17–35.

Meyer, David S. and Staggenborg, Suzanne (1996). "Movements, Countermovements, and the Structure of Political Opportunity," *American Journal of Sociology*. 101(6): 1628–1660.

Mitchell, Don (2003a). *The Right to the City: Social Justice and the Fight for Public Space*. New York: Guilford Press.

Mitchell, Don (2003b). "The Liberalization of Free Speech: Or How Protest in Public Space Is Silenced," *Stanford Agora* 4.

Mitchell, Don and Staeheli, Lynn A. (2005). "Permitting Protest: Parsing the Fine Geography of Dissent in America," *International Journal of Urban and Regional Research.* 29(4): 796–813.

Moore, Will H. (1998). "Repression and Dissent: Substitution, Context, and Timing," *American Journal of Political Science.* 42(3): 851–873.

Moore, Will H. (2000) "Repression and Dissent: A Substitution Model of Government Coercion," *Journal of Conflict Resolution.* 44: 107–127.

Muller, Edward N. and Opp, Karl-Dieter (1986). "Rational Choice and Rebellious Collective Action," *American Political Science Review.* 80(2): 471–488.

Muller, Edward D. and Weede, Erich (1990). "Cross-National Variation in Political Violence," *Journal of Conflict Resolution.* 34: 624–651.

Musah, Abdel-Fatau and Fayemi, J. 'Kayode, eds. (2000). *Mercenaries: An African Security Dilemma.* London: Pluto Press.

Noakes, John and Gillham, Patrick F. (2006). "Aspects of the 'New Penology' in the Police Response to Major Political Protest in the United States, 1999–2000." In *The Policing of Transnational Protest*, edited by Donatella della Porta, Abby Peterson, and Herbert Reiter, 97–118. Aldershot: Ashgate.

Oliver, William M. (2006). *Homeland Security for Policing.* New Jersey: Pearson Prentice Hall.

Peterson, Abby (2006). "Policing Contentious Politics at Transnational Summits: Darth Vader or the Keystone Cops." In *The Policing of Transnational Protest*, edited by Donatella della Porta, Abby Peterson, and Herbert Reiter, 43–74. Aldershot: Ashgate.

Peterson, Abby (2012). "Legitimacy and the Swedish Security Service's Attempts to Mobilize Muslim Communities," *International Journal of Criminology and Sociology.* 1(1): 1–12.

Pierskalla, Jan Henryk (2010). "Protest, Deterrence, and Escalation: The Strategic Calculus of Government Repression," *Journal of Conflict Resolution.* 54(1): 117–145.

Piven, Frances Fox and Cloward, Richard A. (1977). *Poor Peoples Movements: Why They Succeed, How They Fail.* New York: Vintage.

Poe, Steven C. and Tate, C. Neal (1994). "Repression of Human Rights and Personal Integrity Revisited: A Global Analysis," *American Political Science Review.* 43(2): 291–313.

Raco, Mike (2003). "Governmentality, Subject-building, and the Discourses and Practices of Devolution in the UK," *Transactions of the Institute of British Geographers.* 28: 75–95.

Rasler, Karen (1996). "Concession, Repression, and Political Protest in the Iranian Revolution," *American Political Science Review.* 61(1): 132–152.

Regan, Patrick M. and Henderson, Errol A. (2002). "Democracy, Threats and Political Repression in Developing Countries: Are Democracies Internally Less Violent?" *Third World Quarterly: Journal of Emerging Areas.* 23(1): 119–136.

Reiter, Herbert and Fillieule, Olivier (2006). "Formalizing the Informal: The EU Approach to Transnational Protest Policing." In *The Policing of Transnational Protest*, edited by Donatella della Porta, Abby Peterson, and Herbert Reiter, 145–173. Aldershot: Ashgate.

Robertson, Graeme B. (2009). "Managing Society: Protest, Civil Society, and Regime in Putin's Russia," *Slavic Review.* 68(3): 528–547.

Robertson, Graeme B. (2011). *The Politics of Protest in Hybrid Regimes: Managing Dissent in Post-Communist Russia.* New York: Cambridge University Press.

Schatzman, Christina (2005). "Political Challenge in Latin America: Rebellion and Collective Protest in an Era of Democratization," *Journal of Peace Research.* 42(3): 291–310.

Schock, Kurt (2005). *Unarmed Insurrections: People Power Movements in Nondemocracies.* Minneapolis, MN: University of Minnesota Press.

Sheptycki, James W. E. (2002). *In Search of Transnational Policing. Towards a Sociology of Global Policing*. Aldershot: Ashgate.

Sheptycki, James W. E. (2005). "Policing Protest When Politics Go Global. Comparing Public Order Policing in Canada and Bolivia," *Policing and Society*. 15(3): 327–352.

Singer, Peter W. (2004). *Corporate Warriors: The Rise of the Privatized Military Industry*. Ithaca, NY: Cornell University Press.

Spalek, Basia, S., El-Awa, McDonald, Laura Zahra, and Lampert, Robert (2009). *Policy— Muslim Engagement and Partnerships for the Purposes of Counter-Terrorism: An Examination*. Birmingham: University of Birmingham.

Stark, Rodney (1972). *Police Riots: Collective Violence and Law Enforcement*. Belmont, CA: Wadsworth.

Starr, Amory, Fernandez, Luis A., Amster, Randall, Wood, Lesley J., and Caro, Manuel J. (2008). "The Impacts of State Surveillance on Political Assembly and Association: A Socio-Legal Analysis," *Qualitative Sociology*. 31(3): 251–270.

Stockdill, Brett C. (2003). *Activism Against AIDS: At the Intersections of Sexuality, Race, Gender, and Class*. Boulder, CO and London: Lynne Rienner Publishers.

Thomas, Paul (2010). "Failed and Friendless: The UK's 'Preventing Violent Extremism' Programme," *British Journal of Politics and International Relations*. 12(3): 442–458.

Thörn, Håkan (2012). "Governing movements in urban space." In *Transformations of the Swedish Welfare State: From Social Engineering to Governance?*, edited by Bengt Larsson, Martin Letell, and Håkan Thörn, 199–214. Basingstoke: Palgrave.

Tilly, Charles (1978). *From Mobilization to Revolution*. Reading, MA: Addison-Wesley Publishing Company.

Titarenko, Larisso, McCarthy, John D., McPhail, Clark, and Augustyn, Boguslaw (2001). "The Interaction of State Repression, Protest Form and Protest Sponsor Strength During the Transition From Communism in Minsk, Belarus, 1990–1995," *Mobilization*. 6(2): 129–150.

Vitale, Alex (2005). "From Negotiated Management to Command and Control: How the New York Police Department Polices Protests," *Policing and Society*. 15: 283–304.

Waddington, David (1992). *Contemporary Issues in Public Disorder: A Comparative and Historical Approach*. London: Routledge.

Waddington, P. A. J. (1991). *The Strong Arm of the Law: Armed and Public Order Policing*. Oxford: Oxford University Press.

Waddington, P. A. J. (1994). *Liberty and Order: Public Order Policing in a Capital City*. London: UCL Press.

Waddington, P. A. J. (1999). *Policing Citizens: Authority and Rights*. London: UCL Press.

Waddington, P. A. J. (2003). "Policing Public Order and Political Contention." In *Handbook of Policing*, edited by Tim Newburn, 394–421. Cullompton: Willan.

Wahlström, Mattias (2007). "Forestalling Violence: Police Knowledge of Interaction with Political Activists," *Mobilization*. 12(4): 389–402.

Wahlström, Mattias (2010). "Producing Spaces for Representation: Racist Marches, Counterdemonstrations, and Public-order Policing," *Environment and Planning D: Society and Space*. 28(5): 811–827.

Wahlström, Mattias (2011). "Taking Control or Losing Control? Activist Narratives of Provocation and Collective Violence," *Social Movement Studies*. 10(4): 367–385.

Wahlström, Mattias and Oskarsson, Mikael (2006). "Negotiating Political Protest in Gothenburg and Copenhagen." In *The Policing of Transnational Protest*, edited by Donatella della Porta, Abby Peterson, and Herbert Reiter, 117–143. Aldershot: Ashgate.

Wisler, Dominique and Giugni, Marco (1999). "Under the Spotlight: The Impact of Media Attention on Protest Policing," *Mobilization*. 4(2): 171–187.

Zald, Mayer N. and Useem, Bert (1987). "Movement and Countermovement Interaction: Mobilization, Tactics and State Involvement." In *Social Movements in an Organizational Society*, edited by Mayer Zald and John D. McCarthy, 247–272. New Brunswick, NJ: Transaction Books.

CHAPTER 43

MANAGING PROTEST

The Political Action Repertoires of Corporations

PHILIP BALSIGER

> Another fascinating and almost completely unstudied source of external mobilization and constraint is the corporation. In the age of the multinational corporation, increased overt and covert intervention efforts may be expected.
>
> (Marx 1979)

SCHOLARS of interest groups, comparative political economy, and—in management studies—of "corporate political activity" have provided insights into the political power of corporations and the various strategies they use to shape legislation in their favor (Culpepper 2010; Werner 2012; Lawton, McGuire et al. 2013; Walker and Rea 2014). Yet besides the role of corporations in the policy-making process of the state, another form of politics exists, which has been termed "private politics" (Soule 2009; Baron 2010). Corporations and industries are often the targets of social movement activism, and increasingly so (Walker, Martin et al. 2008; Soule 2009). Social movement groups build coalitions and conduct campaigns to challenge corporations with tactical repertoires adapted to the marketplace (Balsiger 2010, 2014a). Targeted firms, in turn, have developed a wide repertoire of tactics to respond to social movement demands. Large transnational corporations have equipped themselves with specialized units dealing with risk management, corporate social responsibility (CSR), or public affairs, with the purpose of observing a company's "contentious" environment and developing strategies to respond to demands from civil society. These "overt and covert intervention efforts"—that is, corporate political actions and reactions to movement challenges—are still poorly understood.

Many studies have analyzed the outcomes of movement–corporate interactions. In private politics, markets and corporations themselves are "policy-making venues" (Baumgartner and Jones 1991). Regulation scholars have studied forms of private regulation (Bartley 2007; Fransen 2012; Locke 2013), and management scholars have been interested in the rise of corporate–NGO partnerships (Yaziji and Doh 2009) and different forms of CSR (Vogel 2005; Crouch 2006; Egels-Zandén and Wahlqvist 2007; de Bakker and den Hond 2008; Gond, Kang et al. 2011). But often, firms use CSR policies and forms of self-regulation strategically, as a way to respond to challenges, deflect attention or prevent more encompassing and binding regulations and policy changes (Fooks, Gilmore et al. 2013; Scherer, Palazzo et al. 2014). And firms' repertoires to respond to and "manage" protest do not stop there: other, more explicitly political and sometimes contentious strategies exist. Examples include communication strategies of "reputation management" (McDonnell and King 2013), or counter-campaigns to defy and decry particular opponents.

The first goal of this chapter is to map and classify this repertoire of corporate protest management. Second, the chapter discusses some principles of variation of corporate tactics and develops hypotheses that could be empirically tested and that have not yet been fully addressed. Beyond variations of corporate and industry opportunity structures, which have been covered prominently in the existing literature (Schurman 2004; King and Soule 2007; King 2008, Werner 2012; Waldron, Navis et al. 2013; see Soule and King, this volume), the chapter focusses on institutional and cultural features that are likely to affect corporate political actions: the development of specialized firm-internal units to deal with protest management, and the possible role of state capacity and national "varieties of capitalism" for corporate political strategies.

STATE POLITICS AND PRIVATE POLITICS

In state politics, firms use their resources to influence governments, legislations, administrations, and public opinion through their institutional integration into policy making as well as through lobbying efforts and opinion campaigns, either as part of business associations or as individual corporations (Hall and Soskice 2001; Maloney, Jordan et al. 2007; Wilks 2013). Many times, firms use their resources to keep certain issues from the public agenda, through public persuasion efforts to "suppress public discussion of the grand issues of politico-economic organization" (Werner 2012). Business power is often the greatest when politics is "quiet" (Culpepper 2010). Sometimes, however, regulative threat or outside challengers force firms to take public stances and defend their interests publicly.

Next to traditional forms of state politics, scholars have pointed at the rising prominence of "private politics," where corporations directly oppose civil society challengers. Baron (2010) defines private politics as "politics (which) pertains to individual and collective action to influence the conduct of private agents, including oneself, as in the case of NGOs that apply social pressure to change the conduct of firms" (Baron 2010: 1299). In private politics, the state plays only a minimal role, if any. NGOs target corporations directly; forms of private voluntary regulation (Locke 2013) can emerge without the contribution of any national or transnational governmental institutions, solely between NGOs and firms or driven by businesses alone.

Management scholars have repeatedly pointed out that firms have started to engage in activities that have traditionally been regarded as core government activities: public health, education, social security, or the protection of human rights (Scherer and Palazzo 2011). This "new political role" of corporations (Scherer and Palazzo 2011) is interpreted as the result of regulatory gaps that emerge due to increased globalization of markets and the limited reach of states and international regulation. Matten and Crane (2005) speak of the need to "reframe corporate citizenship away from the notion that the corporation is a citizen in itself (as individuals are) and toward the acknowledgement that the corporation administers certain aspects of citizenship for other constituencies" (Matten and Crane 2005: 173). In sum, firms do not just *do* political activities (as when trying to influence legislation in their favor), they *are* political (Scherer, Palazzo et al. 2014). But what business scholars often fail to acknowledge is that this increasingly political role of corporations is not just a response to regulatory gaps, but is inserted into contentious dynamics of the "private politics" kind that oppose civil society actors and firms. National and transnational markets have increasingly become arenas of contentious interactions. Regulatory gaps are often only addressed once social movement actors formulate grievances and publicly oppose corporate policies.

Private politics seems to have become more important in recent decades, but it is not historically new. In the history of the modern welfare state, for instance, direct negotiations between firms and labor unions have a long tradition, and in some cases, certain welfare and health programs are still employer-run. Governance scholars have suggested that such modes of self-governance—which occur also in other fields such as environmental protection or quality control—emerge in the "shadow of hierarchy." When facing threats for binding and encompassing legislation, companies and business associations prefer to self-regulate rather than submit to public regulation (Héritier and Lehmkuhl 2008; Werner 2012). There is thus a close relationship between private and state politics: private politics can be used by firms to prevent state regulation. But private politics is also an arena strategically chosen by activist when there is no progress in state politics (Balsiger 2014b), and it becomes more important because state politics lacks legislative authority on many prominent contemporary issues in a globalized world. Finally, firms can also use their access to state politics to fight back against their direct challengers. In sum, the political repertoire of corporations in private politics needs to be seen in close association with state politics, as firms' strategic repertoires in private and state politics can overlap and may be intimately linked.

MAPPING CORPORATE STRATEGIES AND TACTICS TO MANAGE PROTEST

What is the action repertoire of firms in private politics? Building on and complementing existing typologies of corporate political action (Oliver 1991; Kneip 2012, 2013; Walker and Rea 2014), we can distinguish between six strategic orientations of corporate action to respond to and manage protest: avoidance, acquiescence, compromise, side-stepping, confrontation, and prevention (see Table 43.1).

The strategies go from no resistance to new demands to an increasingly active role by firms in opposing demands and shaping the terms of the public debate themselves. Each of these strategies can be pursued through different tactics, and firms can either act as single firms, or they can cooperate with other firms in business associations (Walker and Rea 2014). In general, the firms in question are large, most of the time transnationally active multinational corporations: those are the ones that are most often targeted by social movement actors and have the resources to actively respond to movement challengers.

Before illustrating the tactics used within the different strategic orientations, two general features of tactical responses should be kept in mind. First, as many authors have pointed out (Vogel 2005; Kneip 2012), tactics can be either substantive or symbolic, that is, they may consist of concrete actions or merely of communication. The two often go together, but not necessarily. Firms publish press releases to communicate on a charity program they are launching, and at the same time initiate steps to launch the program. But firms may also just pay lip service to certain demands without following up with concrete actions. In this case, they make discursive concessions without substantive ones. Second, some tactics can be used to pursue several strategic orientations, while others are more closely associated with one particular strategy. For example, suing protesters for libel belongs to the strategic orientation of confrontation. But a tactic such as

Table 43.1 Strategic orientations of corporate reactions to activist challenges

Strategic orientation	Possible tactics
Avoidance	Non-reaction Denying responsibility
Acquiescence	Collaboration with activist organization
Compromise	Self-regulation Negotiations Compensations Labels
Sidestepping	Reputation/Impression management Collaboration with competing activist organization Labels
Confrontation	Public relations campaign Grass-roots lobbying Coalition formation Collaboration with competing activist organization Legal action
Prevention	Media monitoring Research Infiltration

putting in place a specific corporate policy can be both a case of sidestepping, of compromise, or even acquiescence, depending on the exact nature of the policy and of the demands. Only a contextual analysis can tell us which case applies.

The different tactics used within these strategic orientations are illustrated by drawing on examples from the literature of contentious markets. The examples thereby focus on corporate strategies to respond to *outside* challengers. Important challenges can also be voiced from *within* firms, by unions and employee groups in particular. Although the range of strategic orientations of responses may be similar in these cases of inside challenges, the actual tactics are likely to differ substantively and are left aside in this contribution.

Avoidance

Avoidance is a form of reaction that is actually a non-reaction, but a deliberate one: Firms simply ignore demands. It is thus not the same as when firms are not even aware of a particular demand: avoidance means that firms choose not to react to a demand. They just wait it out, hoping that "the storm will pass." In the anti-sweatshop struggle, for instance, many of the targeted retailers did not respond to campaign demands and did not take any measures regarding social standards in supply chains (Balsiger 2014b). When they did react, they often first denied their responsibility—a more active form of avoidance—pointing at subcontractors instead. Actually, avoidance is often a paying strategy. Activist groups usually focus on big firms and firms that show some willingness to respond to demands. Once a firm makes some commitments, activists can hold managers accountable to their own declarations. Ensuring a good reputation has thus mixed impact for corporations—it also attracts further protest (Vogel 2005).

Acquiescence

Acquiescence means that companies accept activist demands and change their policies accordingly. For example, one of the chief strategies of the European anti-GMO movement was to target supermarket chains demanding them to go GMO free. The first store which agreed to do this was a small frozen food company called Iceland Foods; but over the next few years, many other European retailers followed this lead (Schurman and Munro 2010). The determinants of compliance are the object of many studies (see Soule and King, this volume) and have to do with management capacities and commitment (Zald, Morrill et al. 2005). At least two different mechanisms are at play: public pressure and reputational damage may provoke companies to accept demands—but more often, this probably leads to some kind of compromise. Secondly, acquiescence can also be a paying "social strategy" for firms, who can thereby distinguish themselves from their competitors. Activist campaigns can provide firms with what Husted and Allen (2011: 92) call "social issue opportunities" and thus create a potential competitive advantage This does not necessarily mean that such behavior is purely opportunistic and driven solely by economic interests. It can also resonate with managers' or owners' ideology and political convictions. In this case, firms can become allies to activist struggles: they are a source of external mobilization rather than a source of constraint.

Compromise

Compromise involves some kind of implicit or explicit negotiation of demands. Another term would be concessions. When compromising, firms may focus on one site or object of the contention but disregard others. In their reaction against NGO campaigns for socially accountable finance, big banks cooperated to create the Equator Principles, a set of environmental and social risk management guidelines for project finance (O'Sullivan and O'Dwyer 2014). The principles took up a number of social movement demands, but left out others: in particular, it focussed only on project finance instead of all financial operations and lacked accountability mechanisms that were demanded by activists. In this case, banks thus put in place forms of self-regulation that took up movement demands, but kept the regulation firmly under their own control. Similar to self-regulation "in the shadow of hierarchy" (Héritier and Lehmkuhl 2008), firms and industries develop their own modes of regulation in the "shadow of public campaigning."

Another example of compromise and concession is when companies enter into negotiations and offer compensations for the consequences of their practices. In mining conflicts with local communities, for instance, transnational mining companies build hospitals or schools and pay for healthcare and education for local populations. They collaborate and fund moderate groups to push for such agreements and thus hope to marginalize more radicalized groups (Gustaffson 2014).

Sidestepping

Depending on the point of view, the last example contains actions that also qualify as a form of confronting opponents or as sidestepping tactics by giving concessions on aspects that are unrelated to core movement demands. Sidestepping means that companies use tactics to respond to movement demands that do not address the actual demands, but concern other issues. Reputation or impression management tactics (McDonnell and King 2013) most of the time belong in this category. As a reaction to activist challenges, firms put forward particular social or environmental commitments that are however unrelated to the concrete demands and are commonly denounced as greenwashing or window-dressing by critical observers. They can be mere communication strategies or actually consist of undertakings like reporting, auditing, or donations. Often, firms make donations to nonprofits: for instance, Wal Mart increased donations to conservation programs in response to criticism by environmental groups (Vogel

2005). The nonprofits that benefit from such generosity are usually moderate, noncritical NGOs with whom firms like to associate (Vogel 2005). Firms also sometimes cherry pick benevolent SMOs to start partnerships with them.

Sidestepping strategies also concern the market arena. A widespread market tactic is the development of product labels that take up specific social movement issues—green, organic, fair trade, pesticide-free, etc. Sometimes, social movement organizations are behind such labels and they are thus not necessarily sidestepping tactics. But in certain contexts, even such movement-approved labels can be used as sidestepping tactics.

Confrontation

Confrontation strategies are designed to actively counter activist groups and their demands. Firms can for instance counter-frame the issue at stake through public campaigns. In the case of the French anti-sweatshop campaign, retailers cooperated with each other and created their own monitoring initiative. But they went further than that: they publicly attacked their opponents through a carefully orchestrated media campaign, featuring an open letter that questioned the legitimacy of the campaigners (Balsiger 2014b). Counter-framing can consist in delegitimizing opponents, but it can also mean that a company reframes its own practices and policies in a way that appeals to a broader coalition. For instance, when the Canadian log industry was attacked by Greenpeace for the environmental damage it caused, industry officials argued that bans and increased regulation would lead to job losses. They managed to gain workers and their unions as allies in opposing environmentalists (Zietsma and Winn 2008). Informing and mobilizing different social groups on their behalf is a common strategy that corporations and industries use. For the US case in particular, E. Walker (2009, 2014) has shown how companies use agencies specialized in grass-roots mobilization not just to seek out allies among civil society, but to actively mobilize them, by funding groups, developing tools of mobilization like flyers, leaflets, etc. "Grass-roots mobilization" by corporations thus goes even further: it means actively creating support and mobilizing it, while hiding behind specialized agencies. Of course, this kind of tactic can be used not just against threats by social movements, but also proactively to shape public policy making.

The tactics firms use to counter their social movement opponents also play out in other arenas. In issues where science plays a prominent role, industries challenge scientific findings and propose their own studies. The biotech industry funded and conducted studies on the benefits and on the lack of risks of biotechnology (Schurman and Munro 2010). Often, it is sufficient for industries to create doubt about the consequences of practices like smoking or pesticide use to prevent regulation (Michaels 2008) and counter activist demands.

Firms also go to court to fight their challengers and try to silence them. Reacting against "culture jammers," that is, activists subverting brand logos and advertisement, firms like Nike or Coca-Cola have taken activists to court for tampering with their brand imagery (Micheletti and Stolle 2013: 177). Often, the mere threat of legal action is enough to cause activists to back away. Sometimes corporations also pressure legislators or governments into taking action against activists and their tactics. In many US states, for instance, legislators voted for bills criminalizing the secret filming of animal abuse in agricultural facilities under pressure from the agricultural industry. Finally, firms can also use direct forms of repression. They can call upon the police when it comes to protecting private property from attacks. In other cases, they may have their own private security forces to move protestors away, repress or arrest them, such as in private settings like malls or in contexts with relatively weak states. As these examples show, state and private politics are not always clearly separated.

Prevention

Firms do not only react to movement demands, they also try to prevent them from arising in the first place and put in place measures to be better prepared when they do arise. A lot of this is information gathering on the social movement sector. A fine knowledge of social movement actors is very useful when it comes to finding allies or negotiating and striking deals with big NGOs. Public affairs or risk management units within big firms employ specialists who deal with this, or mandate agencies specialized in public relations or public affairs. Large firms also monitor the media and, increasingly, social media to follow the public debate mentioning them in order to be ready to intervene quickly if an issue arises. In parallel, they try to shape this public debate by intervening in social media and by providing content to traditional media organizations. This form of surveillance can go much further, as illustrated by a case that was uncovered a few years ago in Switzerland: Nestlé had managed to infiltrate a local group that was researching a book on the company, by placing a person working for a private security company in the group.

Some Principles of Variation

Scholars have used the concepts of corporate and industry opportunity structure to analyze how corporations and markets influence social movement dynamics and outcomes. Many studies convincingly show that corporate and industry characteristics shape the strategic responses by firms to movement challengers. Beyond such factors reviewed by Soule and King (this volume), this discussion focusses on two, so far mostly overlooked, aspects that are likely to shape corporate strategic responses: the political–institutional context within which movement–corporate interactions take place, and the rise of specialized "public affairs" units within firms.

Political–Institutional Contexts

The "varieties of capitalism" literature reveals the organization of capitalism into a number of national institutional configurations. It distinguishes between coordinated, state-led, and liberal market economies (Hall and Soskice 2001). Within such different contextual settings, firms are organized differently and differ in their relationship to the state. It is possible that such differences are also reflected in the reactions of firms to activist campaigns. For instance, in Germany, workers are represented on company boards, giving unions an institutionalized role in corporate decision making that is not found in many other countries. This rule of corporate governance, together with other corporate arrangements, means that companies are used to cooperating and negotiating with unions, which could predispose them also to reach compromises with activist challengers (Kang and Moon 2012). In a country like France, in contrast, state regulation is the norm and not bipartite arrangements at the firm or industry level; corporate governance does not include employee representation. Here, firms could be less inclined to cooperation and instead more likely to ignore demands, reject voluntary regulation, and expect the state to intervene.

Walker (2015) claims that the use of grass-roots lobbying differs greatly depending on the national organization of capitalism. Similarly, Gond, Kang, and Moon (2011) discuss the national shaping of CSR policies. But this last study also points out a trend that cuts across national traditions: the move towards deregulation and open markets has made CSR an instrument of public policy in many European countries. This indicates a countervailing force that might suppress distinct national characteristics. In addition, many of the firms that are targeted by activists are multinational companies that operate globally and perhaps no longer belong to any distinct national tradition. One can thus have different expectations around the role of political contexts for corporate strategies. On the one hand, following the varieties of capitalism approach, one could expect strong national differences clustering into national corporate repertoires. But another hypothesis, taking up theories of capitalist globalization, would make us think that those differences are declining because both firms and their challengers operate transnationally. At least for big multinational companies, we might also witness the rise of a transnational repertoire of protest management.

If we move beyond the Western world, state capacity is an additional political–institutional dimension that is likely to affect corporate strategies. When states have less resources and coercive capacities or even lack control of parts of their national territory, firms have much greater leverage in developing strategies. Scholars of corporate citizenship often use examples from such contexts to show how corporations come to assume tasks that in other circumstances constitute the prerogative of the state, such as education or even policing. The complex relationship between weak local states depending on foreign investment, multinational companies pursuing profit-seeking activities, and local and transnational activists, has not been sufficiently addressed. On the other hand, in authoritarian states, the corporate repertoire to manage protest may also be different from democratic contexts. More generally, this points at the question of the relative autonomy between the corporate sector and governments.

Public Affairs Departments and Protest Management Styles

Examining the characteristics of those who are in charge of the management of protest within firms is a further promising aspect for study. The range of repertoires used is also likely to depend on the amount of expertise and specialization one finds within companies. Large transnational firms, in particular, consist of different units and factions and often have complex governance structures. The rise of specialized units within firms to deal with public affairs or CSR has been a trend in recent years, and is an unintended effect of increasing activist campaigns (McDonnell, King, and Soule 2014). Such units lead firms to develop more conscious strategic responses and may also bring about routinized relationships between corporate officials and activist organizations. Here, an analogy with the study of protest policing proves useful: the police force is an important actor in dealing with street protest and its organizational culture and institutional environment shape different policing styles (della Porta and Fillieule 2004). Public relations and public affairs personnel similarly constitute a professional group specialized in managing protest within big firms, albeit very different from police forces.

Drawing on findings from policing studies, one could assume that personal knowledge between firm officials and activists is important not only from the perspective of social movements (as "internal allies" (Raeburn 2004)), but also from the perspective of firms, for whom such relationships can provide valuable information and, therefore, predictability. Policing studies have also revealed the selectiveness of policing strategies, depending on police perception of opponent groups. A similar sociology of public affairs personnel could inquire whether such routines also exist within corporations, and how perception of different groups and causes affects the strategies companies use to respond to challenges. Management literature routinely distinguishes between moderate and radical groups, for example (den Hond and de Bakker 2007; Yaziji and Doh 2009). This kind of categorization, built on previous experiences, activist tactics, and diffuse perception categories, might lead to selective corporate reactions depending on groups. Similarly, different causes may be treated differently by public affairs managers; causes that are seen as radical or marginal, for instance animal rights or executive compensation, could be treated with less benevolence than more mainstream causes such as environmental issues.

Conclusion

Although "the politics of business are nuanced, multifaceted, and focused on winning hearts and minds as much as on votes and pocketbooks" (Walker and Rea 2014), there are still very few studies, especially with a political sociological perspective, that consider how corporations act politically by trying to shape public opinion, foster their legitimacy, and respond to challenges from activists. In parallel with increased movement pressures, corporations have developed their arsenal of tactics and the sophistication of their counter-strategies. This chapter has offered a typology of those strategies and discussed some as yet rarely addressed aspects of contextual and firm-internal institutional variation that are likely to shape corporate reactions to challenges. The existing literature indicates that corporations are very active "sources of constraint" for social movement mobilization. Within the different types of strategic orientations, the more contentious tactics of sidestepping, confronting, and preventing particularly reveal corporations' ability to shape movement demands according to their interests and indicate the political nature of corporate actions. But at the same time, scholars must also acknowledge that corporations can be "sources of external mobilization," too: social entrepreneurs, green start-ups, or LGBT-friendly companies can be allies of movements and advocate stricter regulations or the acceptance of rights along with movements.

Acknowledgment

I would like to thank the participants of the "Bringing capitalism back" workshop at the European University Institute (EUI) in May 2014 for their very insightful comments on a previous draft of this chapter.

References

Balsiger, Philip. (2010). "Making Political Consumers: The Tactical Action Repertoire of a Campaign for Clean Clothes," *Social Movement Studies*. 9(3): 311–329.

Balsiger, Philip. (2014a). "Between Shaming Corporations and Proposing Alternatives: The Politics of an 'Ethical Shopping Map'," *Journal of Consumer Culture*. 14(2): 218–235.

Balsiger, Philip. (2014b). *The Fight for Ethical Fashion. The Origins and Interactions of the Clean Clothes Campaign*. Farnham, Burlington VT: Ashgate.

Baron, David P. (2010). "Morally-Motivated Self-Regulation," *American Economic Review*. 100(4): 1299–1329.

Bartley, Tim. (2007). "Institutional Emergence in an Era of Globalization: The Rise of Transnational Private Regulation of Labor and Environmental Conditions," *American Journal of Sociology*. 113(2): 297–351.

Baumgartner, Frank. R. and Jones, Bryan D. (1991). "Agenda Dynamics and Policy Subsystems," *The Journal of Politics*. 53(4): 1044–1074.

Crouch, Colin. (2006). "Modelling the Firm in its Market and Organizational Environment: Methodologies for Studying Corporate Social Responsibility," *Organization Studies*. 27(10): 1533–1551.

Culpepper, Pepper. (2010). *Quiet Politics and Business Power. Corporate Control in Europe and Japan*. Cambridge: Cambridge University Press.

de Bakker, Frank G. A. and den Hond, Frank. (2008). "Introducing the Politics of Stakeholder Influence. A Review Essay," *Business & Society*. 47(1): 8–20.

della Porta, Donatella and Fillieule, Olivier. (2004). "Policing Social Protest." In *The Blackwell Companion to Social Movements*, edited by David A. Snow, Sarah A. Soule and Hanspeter Kriesi, 232–241. Malden, MA, Oxford, Victoria: Blackwell..

den Hond, Frank and de Bakker, Frank G. A. (2007). "Ideologically Motivated Activism: How Activist Groups Influence Corporate Social Change Activities," *Academy of Management Review*. 32(3): 901–924.

Egels-Zandén, Niklas and Wahlqvist, Evelina. (2007). "Post-Partnership Strategies for Defining Corporate Responsibility: The Business Social Compliance Initiative," *Journal of Business Ethics*. 70(2): 175–189.

Fooks, Gary, et al. (2013). "The Limits of Corporate Social Responsibility: Techniques of Neutralization, Stakeholder Management and Political CSR," *Journal of Business Ethics*. 112(2): 283–299.

Fransen, Luc. (2012). *Corporate Social Responsibility and Global Labor Standards*. New York: Routledge.

Gond, Jean-Pierre, Kang, Nahee and Moon, Jeremy. (2011). "The Government of Self-regulation: On the Comparative Dynamics of Corporate Social Responsibility," *Economy and Society*. 40(4): 640–671.

Gustaffson, Maria Therese. (2016). "Private Conflict Regulation and the Influence of Indigenous Peasants Over Natural Resources," *Latin American Research Review*, 5: 86–106.

Hall, Peter A. and Soskice, David. (2001). *Varieties of Capitalism: The Institutional Foundations of Comparative Advantage*. Oxford, New York: Oxford University Press.

Héritier, Adrienne and Lehmkuhl, Dirk. (2008). "The Shadow of Hierarchy and New Modes of Governance," *Journal of Public Policy*. 28(1): 1–17.

Husted, Bryan and Allen, David B. (2011) *Corporate Social Strategy. Stakeholder Engagement and Competitive Advantage*. Cambridge, Cambridge University Press.

Kang, Nahee and Moon, Jeremy. (2012). "Institutional Complementarity between Corporate Governance and Corporate Social Responsibility: A Comparative Institutional Analysis of Three Capitalisms," *Socio-Economic Review*. 10(1): 85–108.

King, Brayden G. (2008). "A Political Mediation Model of Corporate Response to Social Movement Activism," *Administrative Science Quarterly*. 53: 395–421.

King, Brayden G. and Soule, Sarah A. (2007). "Social Movements as Extra-institutional Entrepreneurs: The Effect of Protest on Stock Price Returns," *Administrative Science Quarterly*. 52(3): 413–442.

Kneip, Veronika. (2012). "Corporate Reaction to Anticorporate Protest: Multinational Corporations and Anticorporate Campaigns." In *The Establishment Responds. Power, Politics, and Protest since 1945*, edited by K. Fahlenbach, M. Klimke, J. Scharloth and L. Wong, 211–228. Houndsmills, New York: Palgrave Macmillan..

Kneip, Veronika. (2013). "Protest Campaigns and Corporations: Cooperative Conflicts?" *Journal of Business Ethics*. 118(1): 189–202.

Lawton, Thomas, McGuire, Steven and Rajwani, Tazeeb. (2013). "Corporate Political Activity: A Literature Review and Research Agenda," *International Journal of Management Reviews*. 15: 86–105.

Locke, Richard. (2013). *The Promise and Limits of Private Power: Promoting Labor Standards in a Global Economy*. Cambridge: Cambridge University Press.

Maloney, William Jordan, Grant and Clarence, Emma. (2007). *Democracy and Interest Groups*. Houndsmills, Basingstoke: Palgrave Macmillan.

Matten, Dirk and Crane, Andrew. (2005) "Corporate Citizenship: Toward an Extended Theoretical Conceptualization," *Academy of Management Review*. 30(1): 166–179.

Marx, Gary. (1979) "External Efforts to Damage or Facilitate Social Movements: Some Patterns, Explanations, Outcomes, and Complications." In *The Dynamics of Social Movements*, edited by M. Zald, J. McCarthy. Cambridge, MA: Winthrop Publishers.

McDonnell, Mary-Hunter and King, Brayden G. (2013). "Keeping up Appearances: Reputational Threat and Impression Management after Social Movement Boycotts," *Administrative Science Quarterly*. 58(3): 387–419.

McDonnell, Mary-Hunter, King, Brayden G., and Soule, Sarah A. (2014). "A Dynamic Process Model of Contentious Politics: Activist Targeting and Corporate Receptivity to Social Challenges" Paper presented at the EGOS Colloquium, July 4–7, Rotterdam.

Michaels, David. (2008). *Doubt is their Product: How Industry's Assault on Science Threatens your Health*. Oxford, New York: Oxford University Press.

Micheletti, Michele and Stolle, Dietlind. (2013). *Political Consumerism. Global Responsibility in Action*. Cambridge: Cambridge University Press.

Oliver, Christine (1991). "Strategic Responses to Institutional Processes," *The Academy of Management Review*. 16(1): 145–179.

O'Sullivan, Niamh and O'Dwyer, Brendan. (2014). "The Structuration of Issue-Based Fields: Social Accountability, Social Movements and the Equator Principles Issue-based Field," paper presented at the EGOS Colloquium, July 4–7, Rotterdam.

Raeburn, Nicole C. (2004). *Changing Corporate America from Inside Out. Lesbian and Gay Workplace Rights*. Minneapolis, London: University of Minnesota Press.

Scherer, Andreas G. Palazzo, Guido and Matten, Dirk. (2014). "The Business Firm as a Political Actor: A New Theory of the Firm for a Globalized World," *Business & Society*. 53(2): 143–156.

Schurman, Rachel. (2004). "Fighting "Frankenfoods": Industrial Opportunity Structures and the Efficacy of the Anti-Biotech Movement in Western Europe," *Social Problems*. 51(2): 243–268.

Schurman, Rachel and Munro, William. (2010). *Fighting for the Future of Food: Activists versus Agribusiness in the Struggle over Biotechnology*. Minneapolis: Minnesota University Press.

Soule, Sarah A. (2009). *Contention and Corporate Social Responsibility*. Cambridge: Cambridge University Press.

Vogel, David. (2005). *The Market for Virtue*. Washington DC: The Brookings Institution.

Waldron, Theodore L., Navis, Chad and Fisher Greg. (2013). "Explaining Differences in Firms' Responses to Activism," *Academy of Management Review*. 38(3): 397–417.

Walker, Edward T. (2014). *Grassroots for Hire: Public Affairs Consultants in American Democracy*. Cambridge: Cambridge University Press.

Walker, Edward T. (2015). "Global Corporate Resistance to Public Pressures: Corporate Stakeholder Mobilizations in the U.S., Norway, Germany, and France." In *Corporate Social Responsibility in a Globalizing World*, edited by Kiyoteru Tsutsui and Alwyn Lim, 321–361. Cambridge: Cambridge University Press.

Walker, Edward T. and Rea, Christopher M. (2014). "The Political Mobilization of Firms and Industries," *Annual Review of Sociology*. 40: 281–304.

Walker, Edward, T., Martin, Andrew W. and McCarthy John. (2008). "Confronting the State, the Corporation, and the Academy: The Influence of Institutional Targets on Social Movement Repertoires," *American Journal of Sociology*. 114(1): 35–76.

Werner, Timothy. (2012). *Public Forces and Private Politics in American Big Business*. Cambridge: Cambridge University Press.

Wilks, Stephen. (2013). *The Political Power of the Business Corporation*. Cheltenham, Northampton, MA: Edward Elgar.

Yaziji, Michael and Doh, Jonathan. (2009). *NGOs and Corporations. Conflict and Collaboration*. Cambridge: Cambridge University Press.

Zald, Mayer N., Morrill, Calvin and Rao Hayagreeva. (2005). "The Impact of Social Movements on Organizations." In *Social Movements and Organization Theory*, edited by Gerald F. Davis, Doug McAdam, W. Richard Scott, and Mayer N. Zald, 253–279. Cambridge: Cambridge University Press.

Zietsma, Charlene and Winn, Monika I. (2008). "Building Chains and Directing Flows. Strategies and Tactics of Mutual Influence in Stakeholder Conflicts," *Business & Society*. 47(1): 68–101.

CHAPTER 44

PARTY SYSTEMS, ELECTORAL SYSTEMS, AND SOCIAL MOVEMENTS

HANSPETER KRIESI

> Instead of attempting to exterminate all political forms, organizations, and alignments that do not qualify as pressure groups, would it not be better to attempt to make a synthesis, covering the whole political system and finding a place for all kind of political life.
>
> (E. E. Schattschneider (1960 [1988]).
> *The Semi-sovereign People*. London: Wadsworth, 38)

THE Schattschneider quote I use as an introduction here was directed against the American group theorists who saw pressure groups everywhere, but did not have the parties on their conceptual screen. When reading this quote, I was reminded of social movement scholars who tend to see movements everywhere, but do not connect them to political parties. In the political process approach, of course, political parties enter the fray as part of the political environment of social movements. That is, political parties are part of the alliance and conflict structure in which social movements are embedded. The party system, in turn, is seen as shaped by the institutional structure, most importantly, by the electoral system, which determines to a large extent the number and orientation of the parties available as possible allies of the social movements. Barring a few exceptions (e.g., Diani 1992, 1995), the social movement literature has tended to overlook that political parties are linked to social movements not only as possible allies, but in more fundamental ways as well. This does not necessarily mean that we should put aside Tilly's enormously influential polity model, which has introduced a separation of movement politics from institutionalized politics by distinguishing between social movements as "challengers" seeking access to the institutionalized realm of politics and "polity members" who already have such routinized access. It means, however, that the two worlds of inside (institutionalized, conventional) and outside (protest, unconventional) politics are not as neatly separated as this model suggests to the non-attentive reader. Following Goldstone's (2003: 2) lead, we should start from the assumption that "social movements constitute an essential element of normal politics in modern societies, and that there is only a fuzzy and permeable boundary between institutionalized and non-institutionalized politics."

On the one hand, in a "movement society" (Meyer and Tarrow 1998), some forms of moderate protest have become part of the conventional repertoire that is, from time to time, they are also adopted by polity insiders. With respect to political parties, this means that certain established parties tend to expand the scope of contest beyond the narrow boundaries of the polity in order to strengthen their hand inside of the polity. On the other hand, some types of outsiders prefer to articulate their protest inside of the polity and tend to refrain from mobilizing protest in the streets. With respect to political parties, this means that some social movements prefer to organize in the form of political parties, or their cause is co-opted and integrated into the program of established political parties. My discussion of the relationship between political parties and social movements starts out with the conventional view of the political process approach by conceptualizing the parties as part of the political context the configuration of which is determined by the institutional structure. It then moves on to consider parties as social movement organizations. Finally, it goes one step further by also taking into account the effect of social movements on party systems. As I shall argue, some social movements have the capacity to fundamentally transform individual parties and entire party systems.

INSTITUTIONAL CONTEXTS

There are different types of democracies, even if we are only considering established democracies as I am going to do here, and different typologies to distinguish between these types. Among comparative political scientists, Lijphart's (1999) distinction between majoritarian and consensus democracies has become prevalent, and it is useful to put the present discussion in the context of this distinction. Lijphart's criterion for classifying democracies is the concentration of political power. Majoritarian democracies concentrate political power, while consensus democracies divide it. Lijphart's scheme uses two dimensions for summarizing how power is divided—the "executive–parties" dimension and the "federalism–centralism" dimension. For our purposes, his "executive–parties" dimension is more important. It is characterized by five aspects: the number of parties (two-party systems vs multiparty systems), the electoral system (majority and plurality methods vs proportional representation), the concentration of power in the cabinet (single party vs coalition governments), the executive–legislative relations (dominance by the executive vs balance between the two), and interest group arrangements (pluralism vs corporatism). The dimension mixes formal, institutional, and informal power arrangements, but the resulting pattern in a given country is ultimately driven by the electoral system. This means that majoritarian electoral systems tend to produce two-party systems with single party governments, executive dominance, and interest group pluralism, while proportional systems tend to lead to multiparty systems with coalition governments, more balanced executive–legislative relations, and interest group coordination (corporatism). The paradigmatic cases are the United Kingdom for majoritarian systems, and Belgium or the Netherlands for consensus systems. Lijphart's typology is well suited for parliamentary systems, while presidential systems are more difficult to accommodate within this framework. On the one hand, presidentialism is an extreme form of majoritarianism. The classic presidential system of the United States is also characterized by a majoritarian electoral system for the election of Congress, a two-party system, and single party governments (under the leadership of the President). On the other hand, the American presidential system divides power between the President and Congress (and a powerful judiciary). Moreover, Congress is divided into two equally powerful chambers, and the federalist division of power between the federal government and the state governments divides power even more. In other words, the system of checks and balances brings this system closer to the consensus system, which is taken into account by Lijphart's second dimension.

For our purposes, two aspects of Lijphart's distinction are crucial: a) in majoritarian systems, it is much more difficult to successfully create new parties, that is, access to the political system via the creation of new parties is rather more closed than in consensual systems. This means that b), in majoritarian systems, instead of creating his own party, a challenger has a strong incentive to introduce his demands into the program of one of the existing parties. That is the capture of existing parties by new challengers is much more likely in majoritarian systems than in consensus systems, as is the co-optation of such challengers by existing parties.

There is one important exception to this generalization: regional concentration of challenging minorities and of the corresponding ethnic and nationalist movements. If a challenging group is regionally concentrated, it can gain political representation by creating its own party even in a majoritarian system. The reason is that electoral constituencies are territorially defined, which means that in a given region, a regionally concentrated minority may constitute the majority and get its representatives elected to the national parliament. In the case of federalist systems, the party of a national minority may even become the governing party at the regional level. An example that illustrates this point is the Scottish National Party (SNP), which won a plurality of seats in the Scottish Parliament for the first time in the 2007 elections, and formed a minority government with party leader Alex Salmond elected First Minister of Scotland. In the 2011 general election, the SNP won a landslide victory and was able to form a majority government in Scotland. Other illustrations include the Catalonian or Basque minorities in Spain (whose proportional system is rather restrictive due to the small size of the electoral districts), as well as the many ethnic minorities in India, which are able to rule in their own state within the Indian federalist system.

Parties as Allies

Within this general context, parties can become important allies of social movements, and, as already pointed out in the introduction, it is this aspect that has above all been on the mind of scholars adopting the political process approach. According to their line of argument, social movements expand a given issue-specific conflict in the general public, that is, they create public controversy where there was none before, they draw the public's attention to the issue in question and frame it in line with their own demands, and, by doing so, they strengthen the hand of allies of their cause—political parties within the parliamentary arena, interest groups, and public officials within the administrative arena. Protesters on their own, Tarrow (1994: 98) explains, seldom have the power to affect policy priorities of elites. The goal of challengers is, as Wolfsfeld (1997: 29) points out, "to generate dissensus among the powerful. Challengers attempt to make inroads among elites, who represent more legitimate sources for providing alternative frames." The expansion of conflict in the public sphere is the general "weapon of the weak" that allows social movements to create political opportunities for elites—as Tarrow (1994: 98) has observed, not only in the negative sense of repression, but also in the positive sense when politicians seize the opportunity created by the challengers and defend their cause within the political system. Parties and their representatives may pick up the cause of the challengers for opportunistic reasons, as is the case when political entrepreneurs seize the opportunity created by the challengers to proclaim themselves tribunes of the people. They may also do so for more substantive or ideological reasons. Viewed from the party's perspective, the challenger's outside mobilization may be a welcome support for the party's long-term agenda in a given policy sub-system, which may help the party to undermine the established policy monopoly in the sub-system in question.

To discuss the possible alliances between parties and social movements more systematically, I propose two distinctions: we should distinguish between mainstream parties and peripheral parties, as well as between government and opposition. Mainstream parties are parties that habitually govern, and that, even if they are in the opposition, are part of the "cartel" in the sense of Katz and Mair (1995). These parties are, as Mair (2009) has observed, exposed to an increasing tension between their role as representatives of the national citizen public, and their role as responsible governments. As representatives of the national citizen public, they are expected to be responsive and accountable to their voters; as responsible governments, they are expected to take into account the increasing number of principals constituted by the many veto players who now surround the government in its multilevel institutional setting. This extension of the scope of accountability not only implies that the governing parties' maneuvering space is reduced, but also and most importantly that their accountability to the national constituency of voters, that is, their representative function, is diminished. Peripheral parties, whose chances to participate in government are slim, are less exposed to such pressures. This is why, Mair (2011) suggested, that we might observe a division of labor between the two types of parties: on the one side, we have the mainstream parties or the core of the party system who fulfil the task of responsible government, on the other side, the peripheral parties which give voice to the people, that is, which fulfil the representation function and which often adopt a rather populist style. In other words, Mair (2011: 14) thought that "it is possible to speak of a growing divide in the European party system between parties which claim to represent, but don't deliver, and those which deliver, but are no longer seen to represent." In other words, Mair suggested that, while mainstream parties may generally be non-accessible for social movements, the peripheral parties constitute a conduit for popular challenges within the party system.

Mair's point applies, of course, only to multiparty systems, and even for these systems, it may be somewhat overdrawn. On the one hand, even some of the peripheral parties have taken up government responsibilities and influenced government policy accordingly. This is illustrated by the fact that some of the challengers from the new populist right have, indeed, participated in government (e.g., the Swiss People's Party (SVP) in Switzerland, the FPÖ in Austria, the Lega and the PdL in Italy) or supported minority governments without becoming formal members of governing coalitions (e.g., the Danish People's Party, and the Dutch PVV). On the other hand, mainstream opposition parties are more accessible to outside challengers than members of government. This has been one of my arguments for explaining the differential accessibility of the mainstream left (social democrats) for new social movements in the seventies and eighties of the last century (Kriesi 1995). More recently, this is also shown by Green-Pedersen and Mortensen's (2010) study of agenda-setting by parties in the Danish parliament. As this study indicates, opposition parties exert greater influence on the party-system agenda than governing parties, while governing parties are more responsive to the party-system agenda than opposition parties. Governing parties also directly pick up some of the issues (although not issues related to the economy) raised by the opposition. That is, indirectly, via the opposition parties' influence on the party-system agenda and on the governing parties' agenda, challengers may have an influence on the government's agenda. At least, this applies to a multiparty system in a consensus democracy like Denmark.

PARTIES AS SOCIAL MOVEMENT
ORGANIZATIONS: THE DIFFERENCE
BETWEEN THE NEW LEFT AND
THE NEW RIGHT

As suggested in the introduction, parties may not only serve as allies of social movements, social movements may choose to organize themselves in the form of parties in the first place. That is, social movements may create their own parties (in consensus systems), or they may try to capture mainstream parties (in majoritarian systems). When it comes to parties as social movement organizations (SMOs), it is crucial to distinguish between movements from the (new) left and movements from the (new) right. To be sure, some social movements of both sides have created their own parties, but the left is more likely to rely on public protest outside of the party system than the right, and the mobilization of protest outside of the established channels is considered much more legitimate on the new left than on the new right in particular (of course with the exception of extreme right parties that often promote their own aggressive version of radical street politics).

The classic movement of the left, the labor movement has, of course, not only created its own interest organizations (trade unions), but also its own social-democratic and communist parties. At the same time, the established organizations of the old left have not given up mobilizing protest outside of the political system. Moreover, the more recent left-libertarian new social movements which were responsible for the wave of protest that swept across Western Europe and North America from the late sixties to the eighties of the last century were highly critical of representative democracy and of parliamentary procedures in particular. They sought more participatory modes of mobilization, and engaged heavily in protest activities to push their claims onto the agenda (Nedelmann 1984; Kitschelt 1993).

By contrast, the new populist right, which arguably has been the driving force behind a second wave of protest that has been following upon the new left's wave during the nineties and two-thousands, has mainly mobilized in the channels of electoral politics and (if available) more institutionalized direct democratic channels, even if it has also been highly critical of the mainstream parties and of representative democracy. Moreover, it has mainly relied on *populist mobilization strategies*. Contrary to the "bottom up" strategy of the new left, the new right's populist strategy is a "top down" strategy that establishes a direct link between the monolithically conceived people and those who govern by a personalistic leader who "seeks or exercises government power based on direct, unmediated, non-institutionalized support from large numbers of mostly unorganized followers" (Weyland 2001: 14). In contrast to Weyland's definition that draws on the Latin American experience, several populist parties in Western Europe (e.g., the Lega or the SVP) are probably better organized at the grass-roots level than

most of their competitors. But the element of the personalistic leadership is not necessarily incompatible with the existence of more formal organizations. In some cases, the
personalistic mobilization strategy may be the only one available for a political leader, in
other cases (such as the Lega or the SVP) it may co-exist with more organized forms of
mobilization. Thus, even if we allow for less than pure cases of populist strategies, we can
still define them in terms of personalistic leadership. Typically, the personalistic leader
does not belong to the established political elites, but is an outsider (a new challenger),
who incarnates the demands of 'the people.' This leader has direct, unmediated access to
the people's grievances, and acts as *the* spokesperson of the *vox populi* (Abts 2011: 930).

This key strategic difference between the new left and the new right is linked to the
basic *value-orientations* characterizing the left and the right, respectively. Rebels on
the right tend to have authoritarian and materialist values, and prefer (orderly) conventional political action over (disorderly) protest politics, while rebels on the left tend
to share libertarian and post-materialist values, which predispose them for unconventional protest politics. For both the challengers on the left and on the right, the "medium
is the message," that is, the choice of the channel in which they express themselves is
at the same time an expression of their underlying message. Thus, Flanagan and Lee
(2003, 260ff), in their comparative analysis of authoritarian–libertarian value change
in the twelve largest and most affluent Western nations, find differing orientations
toward political involvement between authoritarians (who tend to be closer to the right)
and libertarians (who tend to be closer to the left). Authoritarians are joiners of conventional groups in essentially equal proportions with libertarians. However, they are
not as likely to join political action-oriented groups. Authoritarians have a more parochial and less cosmopolitan outlook on politics, and, above all, they have a much lower
protest potential than libertarians. Finally, libertarians seem to prefer less continuous,
more task-specific, more individualistic forms of political involvement—such as those
provided by public protesting, while the more traditional forms of political involvement provided by party politics seem to correspond more to the world views of the
authoritarians.

Similarly, Gundelach (1998) explains the individuals' involvement in four types of
protest activities (signing a petition, attending lawful demonstrations, boycotts, and
occupying buildings), what he calls "grass-roots activity," mainly with value orientations characteristic of the left. In the twelve West European countries he analyzed, he
found that social or political libertarianism and post-materialism were all associated
with grass-roots activity, and post-materialism turned out to be most important in
stimulating such activity. More recently, Inglehart (2008) has confirmed the positive
relation between post-materialist values and protest activities, and van der Meer et al.
(2009: 15) have shown that left-wing citizens are more likely to turn to protest activities than their counterparts on the right in all twenty Western democracies that they
studied during the early 2000s. Finally, Dalton et al. (2010) confirm the significant
effect of post-materialism and left ideology on protest behavior in their eighty-seven
nations study based on World Value Survey (WVS) (wave 1999–2002). Moreover, using
multilevel models, they show that both the effects of left–right self-placement and

post-materialist attitudes are magnified in democratic and economically developed countries—that is in the countries which I am focussing on here.

It is, of course, true that, in multiparty systems, the new left has also created its own parties, above all the Green parties. However, these parties have some characteristics which correspond to the values of their partisans and which distinguish them from the personalistic strategies of the parties of the new right: they are parties of "individual participation" which attribute great importance to their grass-roots, and which have continued to mobilize outside of the party system to a much greater extent than the new populist right (Poguntke 1993). For the new left, mobilization outside of the party system is part of its standard repertoire, while for the new populist right, such mobilization is a second best solution when it turns out to be unsuccessful within the partisan channel of mobilization. This is confirmed by Hutter and Kriesi's (2013) analyses, which show that the success of the radical right in electoral terms leads it to abstain from protest activities, while electoral success incites the radical left to engage more intensively in protest politics. More specifically, their analysis of six West European countries—Austria, France, Germany, the Netherlands, Switzerland, and the United Kingdom—documents the dominance in terms of public protest of both left over right, and of radical parties over moderate ones. In the protest arena, the left is more present than the right and the radical left dominates over the moderate left in five out of the six countries; only the United Kingdom deviates in this respect because of the protest activities of the National Front in the seventies and of the BNP later on. The two most successful right-populist challengers—the Austrian and the Swiss parties from the populist right—have been particularly protest averse.

The Transformation of the Party System by Social Movements

Some social movements not only organize as parties, but the parties of these movements transform the party system. That is, the party system is not only a crucial context condition shaping the emergence, mobilization, and eventual success or failure of social movements, some powerful movements may, in turn, also be capable of transforming the entire party system. This has, of course, been the case of the labor movement: all the West European party systems have been similarly transformed by the rise of its parties, and they have been differentially shaped by whether or not the parties of this movement subsequently split into a social-democratic and a communist branch (Bartolini 2000).

More recently, the rise of the Green parties and of the parties of the new populist right has similarly been driving the transformation of the party systems in Western democracies. The two types of parties that have emerged out of the last two great waves of protest in these countries have both contributed to the reinterpretation and reinforcement of the competition on the cultural dimension of the party space. The Green parties have become the most clear-cut defenders of a universalistic–multicultural, libertarian position that is opposed by the particularistic–nationalistic, authoritarian position of the new populist right. As a study of the impact of cultural (universalistic vs particularistic) and economic (state vs market) preferences on the electoral choices of European citizens reveals, the cultural preferences are crucial with respect to the vote for these two types of parties, while the economic preferences are more discriminating between mainstream parties (Häusermann and Kriesi 2015). Moreover, the impact of the preferences on the cultural dimension on the vote choice has generally become greater than the impact of the economic preferences. For the case of France in particular, this overall finding based on a cross-sectional study is confirmed by a longitudinal analysis (Tiberj 2013). According to the argument I have advanced together with my colleagues (Kriesi et al. 2006, 2008, 2012), the new populist right, rather than simply articulating a populist challenge to the mainstream parties which habitually govern, has instead given voice to a new structural conflict that opposes globalization "losers" to globalization "winners." At this point, I might add that the Green parties constitute their most clear-cut opponents on this new structural conflict.

In consensus democracies, the Green and right-wing populist challengers have partly given rise to new parties, partly they have been co-opted by mainstream parties that have been transformed in due course. Thus, some social-democratic parties—the French socialists being an example—have been co-opting the multicultural program of the Greens, thereby almost entirely closing off their electoral niche. On the other hand, some conservative or liberal-conservative parties, such as the SVP and the Austrian Liberal Party (FPÖ), have transformed themselves under the impact of the new structural conflict to become the key parties of the new populist right in their respective countries.

As already pointed out, in majoritarian democracies, the rise of new parties coming out of social movements is much more difficult, which means that the transformation of existing parties by social movements is more likely. This is illustrated by the US case, where third parties have a very difficult time and where cooperation with major parties or capture of major parties is a promising alternative for social movements. Thus, after having built its own People's Party and having experienced the only limited success of this party, the American populist movement of the late nineteenth century made a compromise with the Democrats and, in the presidential elections of 1896, supported William Jennings Bryan, the Democratic candidate who was close to its own cause—with fatal consequences for both the Democratic party and the populists. Bryan lost the race and went down to the first of three national defeats, and "the People's Party rapidly shrank from the spearhead of a social movement into an insignificant sect (before expiring in 1908)" (Kazan 1995: 45). More recent attempts of presidential candidates close to social movements met with similar fates—either as third party candidates (Ralph Nader, Ross Perrot or George Wallace) or as candidates of one of the major parties (George McGovern for the Democrats in 1972; and Barry Goldwater for the Republicans in 1964).

The most recent transformative force in the US party system has been the Tea Party—a variant of long-standing forms of conservative populism in America and, arguably, the equivalent of the new populist right in West European party systems. It is worth having a closer look at the fate of this movement for an appreciation of the effect social movements may have in a two-party system. As is explained by Skocpol and Williamson (2012), Tea Party efforts moved forward within and across the edges of the GOP, but not under party control. The Tea Party had its greatest effect on the party system in the mid-term elections 2010, when it contributed (in addition to the economic crisis conditions) to the victory of many very conservative Republican candidates, and allowed the Republicans to take control of the House, and of both the governorships and the legislatures in twelve states (Drew 2013). The Republican Party had been moving toward the right for some time, and the movement only quickened after the advent of the Tea Party. The Tea Party activists fulfilled "watchdog functions," barking at the GOP heels. According to Skocpol and Williamson (2012: 183), the bottom line for the Tea Party's impact on Congress—and on state legislatures—lies in its capacity to coordinate national pressures from wealthy funders and ideological advocates with contacts from grass-roots Tea Partyers who have a reputation for clout in local districts. When coordinated pressure can be mounted—as it did in budget battles—the Tea Party delivers a loud and clear absolutist message to legislators, a message that comes both from advocates in Washington, DC, and from local districts. In spite of the fading popularity of the symbolism of the "Tea Party," the power of hard-right ideologues consolidated during the first years of the Obama Administration has continued to drive Republican politics, crowding Republicans into an ultra-right corner and contributing to the paralysis of the American political system (Drew 2013).

The transformation processes I have discussed so far are part of long-term trends that are enhanced by social movement actors. Party systems may, however, also be transformed as a result of short-term exogenous shocks. Such shocks may give rise to mobilization processes which result in a *political crisis* with profound consequences for the national party system. In the context of the Great Recession, we have witnessed such transformation processes in several countries. More specifically, against the background of the crisis, we have seen the rise of an entirely new phenomenon—the "anti-party," which is a contradiction in terms, but nevertheless an empirical reality: it is a political organization that mobilizes against the established party system as a whole by competing with the established parties in the electoral channel. In other words, this is a protest movement that participates in elections in order to defeat the established parties with their own weapons. The most successful case in point so far has been the Italian "Five star movement" (M5S) of the comic Beppe Grillo, but the "Grillini" have by no means been the only movement of this kind. For example, in the 2010 local elections in Iceland, a country that was immediately and very heavily struck by the Great Recession in late 2008, the voters of the country's capital Reykjavik turned to the "best party" of the comic Jon Gunnar Kristinsson, which became the largest party with 35 per cent of the vote. "Jon Gnarr" had founded the "best party" at the end of 2009—as a parody of established party politics—asking, among other things, for a "transparent" handling of corruption.

Similarly, the Italian Five-star movement has set out to fight against "la casta," the political establishment of the country, its privileges and immoral behavior: although it also has some environmental goals in its program, the Five-star movement above all seeks to change the political process, to introduce more direct forms of participation, to reduce the costs of politics, and to limit the power of individual politicians by forbidding the cumulation of roles, introducing term limits, and cutting their expenditures and personal allowances (Biorcio and Natale 2013: 49). In the 2013 Italian national elections, the movement obtained 25.6 per cent of the vote and became the largest party of the country. Given that it subsequently refused to enter into any coalition and to participate constructively in the legislative process, its success led to a stalemate in Italian politics (De Sio et al. 2013: 12). The impasse created by the movement's policy of non-cooperation could only be overcome by forcing the two major adversaries in the party system into an oversized coalition government, which, predictably, has not been able to solve any of Italy's pressing economic and institutional problems so far. Although the outcome of the political crisis in which the rise of the new movement has precipitated Italian politics is still open, it may very well result in a profound transformation of the Italian party system.

Such a transformation has already taken place in Greece, arguably the country that was hardest hit by the Great Recession. For more than three years, Greece saw an enormous, sustained mobilization against the government's austerity policies, which were imposed by the international "Troika" (composed of the European Central Bank ECB, the European Commission, and the International Monetary Fund (IMF)), with far-reaching consequences for electoral politics. The party system reconfigured under the impact of a new political conflict opposing the partisans and foes of the bailout agreement that imposed this very harsh policy (Dinar and Rori 2013: 274–6). The new political conflict dimension of the bailout issue, which could be regarded as the Greek version of the "integration–demarcation" cleavage that we have identified in North-West European countries (Kriesi et al. 2006, 2008), confronted the two pro-European mainstream parties with the peripheral parties from the left (the Communist KKE and the more left-libertarian Syriza) and the right (LAOS). The specifically Greek aspect is that this conflict has predominantly been articulated by the old and new left (KKE and Syriza) and not by the new populist right. Eventually, Greece experienced a deep political crisis that culminated in the collapse of its party system during the consecutive parliamentary elections of May and June 2012. In these elections, the punishment meted out to the two major parties was exemplary: together they lost no less than 45 per cent of total vote, jointly obtaining no more than 32 per cent. The socialist PASOK was literally destroyed losing more than 30 per cent, but its traditional conservative opponent, the ND, was not able to benefit from this collapse and also lost 15 per cent. The May election resulted in a deadlock, which led to the organization of a second election in June and a limited comeback of ND to become the largest party with 29.7 per cent. The big winner of the elections was Syriza, which saw its vote share sky-rocket, placing it in second place, only three percentage points below the leading party (Dinar and Rori 2013: 279). Joining forces, the two traditional major parties only barely succeeded in excluding the new forces from government.

Conclusion

In my discussion of the relationship between political parties and social movements, I have argued that the borderline between insiders (political parties) and outsiders (social movements) in politics is not as clear-cut as is often assumed by social movement scholars. More specifically, I have tried to show that, in addition to the conventional political process view of this relationship that conceives of political parties mainly in terms of allies of social movements, social movements may, in turn, also create or reshape individual parties and transform entire party systems. Let me conclude by stating the obvious: this kind of impact is, of course, not given to any kind of movement, but only to important movements capable of expanding the scope of conflict society-wide. The impact of such movements on the party system is likely to be particularly profound, when they operate in times of crisis, where they may serve as the catalyst of a political crisis leading to a realignment of political forces and to profound institutional reforms.

References

Abts, Koen (2011). Maatschappelijk onbehagen en ethnopopulisme. Burgers, ressentiment, vreemdelingen, politiek en extreem rechts. *Proefschrift*, Katholieke Universiteit Leuven.

Bartolini, Stefano (2000). *The Political Mobilization of the European Left, 1860–1980: The Class Cleavage*. Cambridge University Press.

Biorcio, Roberto and Natale, Paolo (2013). *Politica a 5 stelle. Idee, storia e strategie del movimento di Grillo*. Milano: Feltrinelli.

Dalton, Russell, Van Sickle, Alix, and Weldon, Steven (2010). "The Individual–Institutional Nexus of Protest Behaviour," *British Journal of Political Science*. 40: 51–73.

De Sio, Lorenzo, Emanuele, Vincenzo, Maggini, Nicola, and Paparo, Aldo (2013). "Introduction: A Perfect Storm?" In *The Italian General Election of 2013. A Dangerous stalement?*, edited by Lorenzo De Sio, Vincenzo Emanuele, Nicola Maggini, and Aldo Paparo, 11–13. Roma: CISE.

Diani, Mario (1992). "The Concept of Social Movement," *Sociological Review*. 40: 1–25.

Diani, Mario (1995). *Green Networks. A Structural Analysis of the Italian Environmental Movement*. Edinburgh: Edinburgh University Press.

Dinar, Elias and Rori, Lamprini (2013). "The 2012 Greek Parliamentary Elections: Fear and Loathing in the Polls," *West European Politics*. 36(1): 270–282.

Drew, Elizabeth (2013). "The Stranglehold on Our Politics," *New York Review of Books*, September 26.

Flanagan, Scott C. and Lee, Aie-Rie (2003). "The New Politics, Cultural Wars, and the Authoritarian-Libertarian Value Change in Advanced Industrial Democracies," *Comparative Political Studies*. 36: 235–270.

Goldstone, Jack A. (2003). "Introduction: Bridging Institutionalized and Noninstitutionalized Politics." In *States, Parties, and Social Movements*, edited by Jack A. Goldstone, 1–24. Cambridge: Cambridge University Press.

Green-Pedersen, Christoffer and Mortensen, Peter B. (2010). "Who Sets the Agenda and Who Responds to it in the Danish Parliament? A New Model of Issue Competition and Agenda-setting," *European Journal of Political Research.* 49: 257–281.

Gundelach, Peter (1998). "Grass-Roots Activity." In *The Impact of Values*, edited by Jan W. Van Deth and Elinor Scarbrough, 412–440. Oxford: Oxford University Press.

Häusermann, Silja and Kriesi, Hanspeter (2015). "What Do Voters Want? Dimensions and Configurations in Individual-level Preferences and Party Choice." In *The Politics of Advanced Capitalism*, edited by Pablo Beramendi, Silja Häusermann, Herbert Kitschelt and Hanspeter Kriesi, 202–230. Cambridge: Cambridge University Press.

Hutter, Swen and Kriesi, Hanspeter (2013). "Movements of the Left, Movements of the Right Reconsidered." In *The Future of Social Movement Research. Dynamics, Mechanisms, and Processes*, edited by Jacquelien van Stekelenburg, Conny Roggeband, and Bert Klandermans, 281–298. Minneapolis: University of Minnesota Press.

Inglehart, Ronald (2008). "Changing Values among Western Publics form 1970 to 2006," *West European Politics.* 31: 130–146.

Katz, Richard S. and Mair, Peter (1995). "Changing Models of Party Organization and Party Democracy: The Emergence of the Cartel Party," *Party Politics.* 1(1): 5–28.

Kazan, Michael (1995). *The Populist Persuasion. An American History.* New York: Harper-Collins: Basic Books.

Kitschelt, Herbert (1993). "Social Movements, Political Parties, and Democratic Theory," *The Annals of the American Academy of Political and Social Science.* 528: 13–29.

Kriesi, Hanspeter (1995). "Alliance Structures." In *New Social Movements in Western Europe. A Comparative Analysis*, edited by Hanspeter Kriesi, Ruud Koopmans, Jan Willem Duyvendak, and Marco Giugni, 53–81. Minneapolis: University of Minnesota Press.

Kriesi, Hanspeter, Grande, Edgar, Dolezal, Martin, Helbling, Marc, Hutter, Swen, Höglinger, Dominic, and Wüest, Bruno (2012). *Political conflict in Western Europe.* Cambridge: Cambridge University Press.

Kriesi, Hanspeter, Grande, Edgar, Lachat, Romain, Dolezal, Martin, Bornschier, Simon, and Frey, Tim (2006). "Globalization and the Transformation of the National Political Space: Six European Countries Compared," *European Journal of Political Research.* 45(6): 921–957.

Kriesi, Hanspeter, Grande, Edgar, Lachat, Romain, Dolezal, Martin, Bornschier, Simon, and Frey, Timotheos (2008). *West European Politics in the Age of Globalization.* Cambridge: Cambridge University Press.

Lijphart, Arend (1999). *Patterns of Democracy. Government Forms and Performance in Thirty-Six Democracies.* New Haven: Yale University Press.

Mair, Peter (2009). "Representative versus Responsible Government," *MplfG Working Paper* 09/8.

Mair, Peter (2011). "Bini Smaghi vs. the Parties: Representative Government and Institutional Constraints," *EUI Working Paper, RSCAS 2011/22.*

Meyer, David S. and Tarrow, Sidney, eds. (1998). *The Social Movement Society: Contentious Politics for a New Century.* Lanham: Rowman & Littlefield.

Nedelmann, Brigitta (1984). "New Political Movements and Changes in Processes of Intermediation," *Social Science Information.* 23: 1029–1048.

Poguntke, Thomas (1993). *Alternative Politics. The German Green Party.* Edinburgh: Edinburgh University Press.

Skocpol, Theda and Williamson, Vanessa (2012). *The Tea Party and the Remaking of Republican Conservatism*. Oxford: Oxford University Press.

Tarrow, Sidney (1994). *Power in Movement: Social Movements, Collective Action and Politics*. Cambridge: Cambridge University Press.

Tiberj, Vincent (2013). "Values and the Votes from Mitterand to Hollande: The Rise of the Two-axis Politics," *Parliamentary Affairs*. 66: 69–86.

Van der Meer, Tom W. G., van Deth, Jan, and Scheepers, Peer L. H. (2009). "The Politicized Participant. Ideology and Political Action in 20 Democracies," *Comparative Political Studies*. 42: 1426–1457.

Weyland, Kurt (2001). "Clarifying a Contested Concept—Populism in the Study of Latin American Politics," *Comparative Politics*. 34(1): 1–22.

Wolfsfeld, Gadi (1997). *Media and Political Conflict: News from the Middle East*. Cambridge: Cambridge University Press.

CHAPTER 45

···

POPULISM, SOCIAL MOVEMENTS, AND POPULAR SUBJECTIVITY

···

KENNETH M. ROBERTS

THE relationship between populism and social movements has long been opaque, and rarely has it been a focal point of scholarly attention. Indeed, research on populism and social movements has tended to follow separate paths, with neither paying much heed to intellectual developments on the other path. Neither scholarly tradition has devoted much energy to a search for common spawning grounds or points of intersection between the two phenomena. Even less have they engaged in a systematic analysis of potential tensions or contradictions between populism and social movements. Although both concepts are widely used to refer to the political mobilization of common citizens in opposition to established elites, there is no consensus regarding their similarities and differences, the boundaries that demarcate them, the areas where they might overlap, or their status as distinct sub-types of a shared political genus.

Drawing primarily from the recent Latin American experience, this chapter suggests that this mutual intellectual disengagement is both unfortunate and unnecessary. The study of both phenomena—populism and social movements—would be enriched by more systematic attention to the origins, dynamics, and characteristics of the other. Both, after all, can be characterized as non-institutionalized forms of contentious politics, and as I will argue, they share a common political opportunity structure. Indeed, they tend to appear sequentially, with mass social protest often preceding and setting the stage for populism. The two do not often coincide, however, and they are not synonymous with each other; to the contrary, there is an inherent tension between populism and social movements, as they generally entail quite different forms of collective action and popular subjectivity. Whereas social movements emerge from autonomous forms of collective action undertaken by self-constituted civic groups or networks, populism typically involves an appropriation of popular subjectivity by dominant personalities who control the channels, rhythms, and organizational forms of social mobilization. Indeed, populism does not require that mass constituencies engage in collective action at all, beyond the individual act of casting a ballot in national elections or popular referendums. Although both forms of popular subjectivity contest established elites, social movements mobilize such contestation from the bottom-up, whereas populism typically mobilizes mass constituencies from the top-down behind the leadership of a counter-elite.

These distinctions are not universally recognized or acknowledged, in part because populism is a notoriously elastic and contested concept that is subject to different meanings (Weyland 2001). When conceptualized in minimalist discursive or ideological terms, populism is easily conflated with social movements that discursively construct the political order as a binary realm of contestation between an authentic popular will and an unaccountable and unrepresentative power elite. When conceptualized as a distinct mode of popular subjectivity, however, populism can be analytically separated from social movements, making it possible to explore the interrelationships between them and potential areas of convergence or conflict.

Following this latter course, it quickly becomes apparent that mass social protest has often been a prelude to populist eruptions in contemporary Latin America, in part because such protests both trigger and reflect a crisis of institutionalized, party-mediated democratic representation. Such representational crises create a political opportunity structure that is conducive to the rise of anti-establishment movements or populist outsiders. Regimes formed by such anti-establishment actors, however, vary dramatically in their relationships to the social movements that presaged their rise. Likewise, they vary in their compatibility with autonomous forms of social mobilization under their watch.

To understand these varying relationships, it is essential not only to break down the artificial boundaries that separate the study of populism from that of social movements, but also the boundaries that separate both of these fields from the study of party politics (see McAdam and Tarrow 2011). Populism, social movements, and political parties are alternative but inter-related modes of articulating and representing mass constituencies in the political domain, and one mode can hardly be understood in isolation from the others. These inter-relationships are mapped out in this chapter through a comparative analysis of recent populist experiences in Latin America and the patterns of social mobilization that preceded and followed their ascendance.

Populist Discourse and Political Subjectivity

The relationship between populism and social movements is inevitably muddled by the conceptual inconsistencies that surround the use of the populist concept in the social sciences (Roxborough 1984). As Tarrow (2013: 15) presciently states, "words for contentious politics are polysemic, and that makes their meaning both ambiguous and available." Economists, for example, have long equated populism with profligate social spending, polarizing redistributive measures, and other patterns of unsustainable state intervention that prioritize mass consumption over capital accumulation and market efficiency (Dornbusch and Edwards 1991; Edwards 2010). Political scientists, however, have increasingly decoupled the populist concept from any particular set of economic policies or historical stage of economic development; in so doing, they allow for the identification of populist political appeals by anti-establishment leaders or movements who adopt a wide range of economic policies, from neoliberal orthodoxy to statist heterodoxy (Roberts 1995; Weyland 1996). Such approaches locate populism squarely in the political domain and insist on its essential political characteristics.

These essential political characteristics, however, remain a source of considerable debate. As Canovan (1981: 294) argues, all forms of populism "involve some kind of exaltation of and appeal to 'the people', and all are in one sense or another anti-elitist." The "people," however, can enter the political arena in a variety of different ways, through multiple forms of political subjectivity (Roberts 2006; Ostiguy 2009). The contested meanings of populism largely center on this question of popular subjectivity and the range of mobilizational patterns encompassed by the populist label. Clarifying these contested meanings is especially critical at a time when democratization is creating new opportunities for populist mobilization in countries and regions that have rarely experienced it in the past, such as Thailand (Hewison 2010; McCargo 2001) and a number of countries in Africa (Resnick 2012). Indeed, economic crises and political disenchantment have recently spawned diverse forms of socio-political mobilization that exalt "the people" and contest established elites in Europe, Latin America, and even the United States (Castells 2012; Hutter and Kriesi 2013; Skocpol and Williamson 2013; della Porta 2014; de la Torre 2014). Which of these can—or should—be characterized as "populist," however, remains unclear.

For advocates of a discursive or ideological approach, populism is not defined by any particular pattern of popular subjectivity or socio-political mobilization, and no such pattern is intrinsic to populism. Populism, therefore, is polymorphic in its mobilizational expressions; the elite-popular cleavage can generate multiple and diverse forms of popular subjectivity or collective action. Mudde (2007: 23), for example, conceptualizes populism as a "thin-centered ideology that considers society to be ultimately separated into two homogeneous and antagonistic groups, 'the pure people' and 'the corrupt elite,' and which argues that politics should be an expression of the *volonté générale* (general will) of the people" (see also Mudde and Rovira Kaltwasser 2012: 8). Such a minimalist conceptualization travels easily across temporal and spatial boundaries and allows the populist label to be applied to a diverse array of anti-elite or anti-establishment political phenomena, from right-wing nationalism in Europe (Berezin 2009) and the United States to socialist-inspired mass mobilizations in Latin America. It also allows populism to assume a variety of organizational forms and mobilizational patterns, including political parties (such as new national-ist parties in Europe), charismatic movements (such as those formed behind iconic figures such as Juan Domingo Perón in Argentina, Hugo Chávez in Venezuela, and Thaksin Shinawatra in Thailand), and grass-roots social movements (such as agrar-ian movements in nineteenth-century US politics, recent indigenous and popular movements in Bolivia, or the anti-austerity protest movement of the *indignados* in Spain).

So conceived, populism is defined by its redemptive discourse and an anti-elite or anti-establishment ideology, rather than any particular mode of popular subjectiv-ity. Indeed, the latter is almost infinitely malleable, allowing for top-down as well as bottom-up (or plebiscitary and participatory) patterns of mobilization, and both insti-tutionalized and non-institutionalized organizational forms. In short, in the discursive tradition, populism has no systematic relationship to social movements and collective action; the rhythms and forms of popular mobilization are epiphenomenal or context specific, and they are not constitutive of populism.

As della Porta (2014) suggests, following Laclau (2005), the Spanish *indignados* and other contemporary grass-roots protest movements in Europe manifest a populist logic in their efforts to reconstruct "the people" as a democratic subject in contexts where traditional representative institutions are increasingly detached or unrespon-sive. As she recognizes, however, such grass-roots movements are more participatory, deliberative, and culturally inclusive than the party-based forms of right-wing nation-alism that are routinely characterized as populist in Europe (Mudde 2007; Berezin 2009). The distinctions between different mobilizational patterns identified by della Porta and other scholars like Hutter and Kriesi (2013) resonate with an alternative scholarly tradition that places popular subjectivity—or, more properly, the appropria-tion of it—at the very center of its conceptualization of populism. In this tradition, autonomous forms of collective action that generate grass-roots social movements are not considered to be populist, whatever their discourse; to the contrary, they are understood to be in tension with populist leadership, even in contexts where the two might co-exist. The populist label, therefore, is restricted to cases where socio-political mobilization is controlled from above and dependent on a dominant authority figure to weld together diverse popular interests and articulate a shared political project for "the people."

This tradition is especially prevalent in Latin American scholarship, where the study of populism developed in the middle of the twentieth century as an attempt to differ-entiate regional patterns of mass political incorporation from the class-based forms of socialist mobilization that historically characterized the West European experience. This differentiation rested in part on the ideological diffuseness of Latin American populism and its heterogeneous, multi-class base of appeal. More fundamentally, however, it also rested on distinctive patterns of popular subjectivity and socio-political mobilization in contexts of delayed industrialization, where the limited size and organizational strength of the proletariat impeded the autonomous construction of a class-based political subject from below. Instead, popular subjects were routinely constructed around the figure of a charismatic leader who articulated the claims of socially diverse and often poorly organized mass constituencies that otherwise lacked a capacity for autonomous political expression (see, e.g., di Tella 1965; Laclau 1977; Germani 1978; Collier and Collier 1991; Laclau 2005; Oxhorn 2011).

In this tradition, a basic distinction is made between what Barr (2009) calls plebiscitary and participatory linkages between mass constituencies and the leaders or movements who claim to represent "the people." These linkages ultimately embody very different forms of popular subjectivity and collective action. Participatory linkages or patterns of subjectivity provide citizens with a direct role in contesting established elites or in deliberative and policy making processes. As such, they tend to rely on autonomous and self-constituted forms of collective action at the grass-roots, inside or out of (and sometimes against) formal institutional channels. By contrast, under plebiscitary linkages or patterns of subjectivity, mass constituencies—often unorganized—are mobilized from above to acclaim an authority figure or ratify their leader's political initiatives. Such plebiscitary acclamation often resides in the voting booth or popular referendums, and is not predicated on autonomous forms of collective action at the grass-roots. Indeed, plebiscitary appeals often rest on a direct, unmediated relationship between a populist figure and highly fragmented mass constituencies. Although both patterns of subjectivity routinely invoke "the people" and employ an anti-elite or anti-establishment discourse, Barr restricts the populist label to plebiscitary forms of mobilization. Weyland (2001), likewise, conceptualizes populism in terms of plebiscitary authority, and claims that populism "does not empower 'the people,' but invokes the people to empower a leader."[1]

Clearly, then, any hypothesized empirical relationship between populism and social movements hinges on the conceptualization of populism being employed. Whereas a discursive conceptualization allows a wide range of social movements to be characterized as populist, a plebiscitary conceptualization consigns populism and social movements to separate and distinct categories of popular subjectivity, with social movements referring to more participatory and bottom-up forms of political mobilization. Both approaches, it should be noted, are inherently minimalist or essentialist, rather than multi-dimensional; they merely differ on what they consider to be the essential attribute or meaning of populist mobilization.

It is not the purpose of this essay to adjudicate among these alternative scholarly conventions and meanings. Instead, it seeks to demonstrate that considerable analytical traction can be gained by decoupling populism from social movements and exploring how different patterns of popular subjectivity—both top-down and bottom-up, or plebiscitary and participatory—interact in contemporary anti-establishment movements in Latin America. Doing so requires that both populism and social movements be analytically linked to the study of institutionalized forms of partisan representation (McAdam and Tarrow 2011)—or, more precisely, to the representational failures that trigger anti-establishment patterns of political contestation.

PARTIES, POPULISM, AND SOCIAL PROTEST
IN LATIN AMERICA'S POST-ADJUSTMENT ERA

Populism and social movements have both flourished on the contemporary Latin American political landscape, leading many observers to assume that they are a natural response to the market-based structural adjustment policies that were adopted in the region following the debt crisis of the 1980s. Market liberalization, however—which occurred throughout the region—cannot readily explain the considerable cross-national variation that emerged in the strength of populism and social movements in the post-adjustment era. Such variation, I argue, was not a function of market liberalization per se, but rather a response to the representational failures produced by particular types of partisan alignments around the process of market reform. Whereas some partisan alignments channeled societal resistance to market orthodoxy towards institutionalized parties of the left, other alignments channeled such resistance into extra-systemic forms of social and/or electoral protest, including populism. These different political responses to market liberalization—in essence, alternative political expressions of Polanyi's (1944) celebrated "double movement"—are an essential starting point for understanding the complex interrelationships between populism and social movements in contemporary Latin America.

In most of Latin America, the period of economic crisis and structural adjustment in the 1980s and early 1990s was associated with the disarticulation and demobilization of historic labor and popular movements (Roberts 2002; Kurtz 2004; Rice 2012). Populism, where it existed during this period, was highly detached from social movements or any other form of grass-roots collective action; indeed, it could thrive in contexts of economic crisis and social fragmentation that enabled populist outsiders like Alberto Fujimori in Peru to appeal to unorganized mass constituencies by attacking a discredited political establishment. Such forms of populism—clearly plebiscitary in form—could even be embedded in neoliberal projects that allowed populist leaders to challenge organized interests in a broad range of settings (Roberts 1995; Weyland 1996).

Following stabilization and structural adjustment, however—in particular, the defeat of hyperinflation across the region by the mid-1990s—the political winds began to shift. Social and political resistance to market liberalization intensified in the post-adjustment era, helping to revive leftist parties, strengthen social movements, and push populism back toward more statist and redistributive policy orientations. The specific form of this Polanyian backlash, however, depended heavily on the politics of market liberalization in each country, and in particular on partisan alignments around the process of market reform. In short, the political opportunity structure was more conducive to mass social protest in some countries than others. Where conservative actors led the process of market reform and a major party of the left was consistently present as an opposition force, the Polanyian backlash in the post-adjustment era was largely contained within institutional channels. Indeed, societal resistance to market orthodoxy strengthened established parties of the left and eventually enabled them to win the presidency in countries like Chile, Brazil, Uruguay, and El Salvador. In each case, levels of social protest were relatively moderate in the post-adjustment era, established parties remained electorally dominant, and anti-establishment populist figures made little headway in the electoral arena (Roberts 2014).

The political legacies of market liberalization, however, and the political opportunity structure for mass social or electoral protest, were strikingly different where center-left or labor-based populist parties played a major role in the process of structural adjustment. In the short-term, "bait-and-switch" market reforms imposed by parties that campaigned against them and historically championed more statist and redistributive policies contributed to the broad technocratic consensus around the neoliberal model in the late 1980s and early 1990s—what aptly came to be known as the "Washington Consensus" (see Williamson 1990). Such bait-and-switch patterns of reform, however, proved to be highly destabilizing in the post-adjustment era, as they de-aligned party systems programmatically and left them without institutionalized outlets for dissent from market orthodoxy. Such dissent, therefore, was often channeled into social protest movements and varied forms of electoral protest, including support for populist outsiders or new "movement parties" on the left (Kitschelt 2006). In countries like Argentina, Bolivia, Ecuador, and Venezuela,[2] bait-and-switch market reforms left a sequel of explosive social protest that directly or indirectly toppled presidents, led to partial or complete party system breakdowns, and (in the latter three cases) ushered in the election of an anti-system populist figure or a new movement party of the left (Silva 2009). The political character of Latin America's "left turn," therefore, varied dramatically across countries depending on political alignments during the critical juncture of structural adjustment (Madrid 2009; Levitsky and Roberts 2011; Roberts 2014).

In short, although every country in the region experienced at least scattered and isolated forms of social protest against market liberalization, the types of sustained, mass-based protest movements that produced systemic political change were limited to a relatively small number of countries. Levels of social protest were heavily conditioned by party politics; destabilizing protest cycles did not occur where party systems provided institutionalized outlets for dissent from market orthodoxy. Conversely, where all the major parties participated in the reform process and converged on the neoliberal model, dissent was far more likely to be channeled into widespread and destabilizing forms of social protest. The iconic cases included the mass urban riots known as the *caracazo* that followed a bait-and-switch process of structural adjustment in Venezuela in 1989; the cycles of indigenous and urban popular protests in Ecuador in the 1990s and early 2000s; the *piquetero* (picketers) movement of unemployed workers and the urban riots that rocked Argentina during the 2001–02 financial crisis; and the so-called "water wars" and "gas wars" that erupted in Bolivia in 2000 and 2003, respectively (Silva 2009; Rice 2012).

These protest cycles were veritable political earthquakes in their respective countries. All produced systemic political change, and all opened the door for new populist tendencies to emerge, if not full-blown experiments with populist authority. Mass social protest led to the resignation or removal of three consecutive elected presidents in Ecuador and two presidents in Argentina and Bolivia, and it contributed to the impeachment of Carlos Andrés Pérez in Venezuela. Likewise, in all four countries mass social protest was followed by major electoral change, with the demise or collapse of traditional parties. Indeed, entire party systems essentially collapsed in Venezuela, Bolivia, and Ecuador, while the anti-Peronist side of the party system suffered a steep decline in Argentina. Among the major traditional parties in the four countries, only the Peronist PJ in Argentina weathered the storm; alone in the region, the PJ successfully veered back to the left after leading the process of market reform in order to channel much of the social backlash that erupted when a financial crisis occurred under the watch of its partisan rivals in 2001. In the other three cases, entire party systems were outflanked on the left by the rise of new populist leaders (Hugo Chávez in Venezuela and Rafael Correa in Ecuador) or a new movement party empowered by the protest cycles (the *Movimiento al Socialismo* (MAS) in Bolivia).

These latter three cases are routinely lumped together as examples of populism in contemporary Latin America (see, e.g., de la Torre 2013; Levitsky and Loxton 2013; Weyland 2013). In narrow discursive terms, the appellation surely fits (Hawkins 2009). Nevertheless, these countries experienced quite different patterns of socio-political mobilization, collective action, and popular subjectivity following their initial cycles of mass social protest. As such, they help to crystallize the debate over different conceptualizations of populism and its relationship to social movements, both before and after taking state power. It is to these relationships that I now turn.

POPULISM AND POPULAR SUBJECTIVITY IN LATIN AMERICA'S "LEFT TURN"

Although mass social protest played a central role in the demise of the old order and the rise of new populist or leftist alternatives in Venezuela, Bolivia, and Ecuador, the relationship between social movements and these new alternatives varied dramatically (de la Torre 2013). The Bolivian case is *sui generis*, as new partisan and electoral alternatives emerged organically from social movements themselves. As Santiago Anria states (2013: 19), Bolivia "is the only case in the region where social movements, originally in the rural areas, created a political leadership of their own, formed a political organization—the MAS—as their electoral vehicle, and captured state power through their participation in democratic elections after leading a series of mass protests." President Evo Morales began his political career as an activist in Bolivia's largely indigenous coca growers union, which joined with other highlands peasant organizations to found a series of electoral vehicles that culminated in the MAS in the late 1990s. According to Van Cott (2008: 103), when the MAS originally formed, "there was little difference between the coca growers'/campesino movement and the party—the latter was merely the political instrument of the former." The MAS subsequently capitalized on the explosion of anti-neoliberal social protests in the "water wars" and "gas wars" of the early 2000s, extending its organizational networks to urban areas and broadening its base of electoral support. Although Morales undoubtedly played an important role in forging a common political project out of the diverse rural and urban movements that ultimately converged in the MAS, his leadership was deeply rooted in an autonomous and bottom-up dynamic of socio-political mobilization—in short, a highly participatory form of popular subjectivity.

By contrast, the rise of Chávez in Venezuela and Correa in Ecuador relied overwhelmingly on plebiscitary forms of popular subjectivity. The electoral victories of both leaders had been preceded by cycles of mass protest, but neither rose to prominence through their involvement with social movements or movement organizations. Both leaders founded parties from the top-down that were electoral vehicles for their personal leadership, rather than extensions of movement organizations like the MAS in Bolivia. Chávez' party, the *Movimiento Quinta República* (MVR), had origins in the clandestine military network organized by the charismatic young leader when he was an army officer. After leading a failed military coup in 1992 and serving time in prison, Chávez became a symbol of rebellion against an increasingly discredited political establishment, and founded the MVR as a vehicle for his outsider presidential campaign in 1998 (López Maya 2011). Correa, likewise, did not emerge from the protest movements that toppled successive Ecuadorean presidents in 1997, 2000, and 2005. A US-trained economist who had served a short-lived stint as an anti-neoliberal economy minister, Correa cobbled together a media-savvy campaign team from academic and technocratic circles in order to make an outsider bid for the presidency in 2006. To accentuate Correa's political independence and anti-establishment credentials, his hastily organized party vehicle declined to sponsor a list of congressional candidates to accompany his presidential campaign (de la Torre 2009; Conaghan 2011). In neither Venezuela nor Ecuador, then, did social movements generate the political leadership of populist figures or the partisan vehicles that carried them to power; popular subjects undermined the *ancien regime* through social protest, but they did not play a constitutive role in the creation of populist alternatives. Their role, in short, was one of plebiscitary acclamation in the voting booth rather than active participation.

Although these genetic traits continued to influence patterns of governance after new populist and leftist alternatives took public office, the ideal-typical distinctions between plebiscitary and participatory forms of popular subjectivity began to fade. This was especially true in Bolivia and Venezuela, where hybrid forms of subjectivity developed under Morales and Chávez, pushing the former in a more populist and plebiscitary direction and the latter toward higher levels of grass-roots participation. In Bolivia, social protest was quickly channeled into electoral protest; in the process, the MAS "personalized its campaigns, relying heavily on the charismatic appeal of Evo Morales to win support" (Madrid 2012: 62). In office, Morales and the MAS convoked elections for a constituent assembly and relied on the plebiscitary instrument of a popular referendum to approve a new constitution, thoroughly refounding regime institutions. Furthermore, as Anria

(2013: 33–35) notes, the rapid expansion of the MAS into urban areas in response to electoral imperatives in 2005 did not rest on the same types of organic, participatory social networks that had spawned the formation of the party in rural coca-growing regions a decade before. Instead, the party achieved territorial penetration by negotiating informal alliances with pre-existing community organizations and co-opting their leaders into government positions, in the process threatening the autonomy of many civic groups. The gradual bureaucratization of the MAS produced "detachment … from the social organizations that brought it to power" and made the party "reminiscent of a populist machine" in urban areas (Anria 2013: 35).

The tensions between charismatic authority, party bureaucratization, and popular participation, however, did not mean that social movements and civic networks ceased to be important political actors in Bolivia, or that they relinquished their capacity for autonomous political mobilization. Even before the MAS took power at the national level, new institutional channels had been opened for social actors to participate in municipal governance (Van Cott 2008), and popular assemblies continued to be active in debates over constitutional reforms and the selection of party candidates for public office (Crabtree 2013: 285). As stated by Madrid (2011: 254), the Morales government "consulted regularly with its social movement bases through assemblies and congresses," and it created "new channels for such consultation to take place," including a national coordinating body that brought together "the heads of the social movement organizations with the president, his ministers, and congressional leaders in order to discuss government policies." Although MAS-affiliated social movements routinely mobilized to defend the government against regional and elite-based political opposition (de la Torre 2013: 35), neither the government nor the MAS was able to fully control popular mobilization. Indeed, social mobilization often escaped the confines of formal institutional channels and challenged government policies. Independent mining cooperatives and lowlands indigenous communities mobilized against policy initiatives of the MAS government, with the latter forcing Morales to put on hold plans to build a highway through the TIPNIS indigenous territory and national preserve. Even many MAS-affiliated groups participated in widespread protests in 2010 against a government decree to cancel fuel price subsidies, inducing Morales to annul the decree (Anria 2013: 35–36; Crabtree 2013: 286). The ongoing capacity for autonomous collective action thus helped to hold the government accountable to its social bases and at least partially counteract the tendencies toward top-down control associated with party bureaucratization and concentrated, charismatic executive authority.

Similarly, a hybrid articulation of plebiscitary and participatory forms of subjectivity emerged in Venezuela under Chávez, despite the highly plebiscitary character of Chávez's authority and of the regime he founded. Following his election in 1998, Chávez relied heavily on plebiscitary measures to bypass and dismantle existing regime institutions and refound the constitutional order, using a series of popular referendums to convoke a constituent assembly, ratify a new constitution that empowered the executive branch, and defeat a recall campaign by the political opposition. The new constitution, however, also called for the establishment of a "protagonistic democracy" that created spaces for grass-roots participation in multiple governing arenas. Community-based "Bolivarian circles" began to emerge in the early 2000s and played a central role in the popular mobilization that helped to restore Chávez to power after a short-lived military coup in April 2002. After defeating a management strike in the state-owned oil industry in 2003 and centralizing control over windfall oil rents, Chávez deepened redistributive social and economic reforms, launching a series of social "missions" that encouraged community planning and popular participation in education, health care, land use, and food programs. He also established highly participatory "communal councils" that operated parallel to municipal governments and played a central role in the design of social programs and development projects (Hawkins 2010a; Hawkins 2010b; Handlin and Collier 2011; López Maya 2011). Although the plethora of organizational spaces for popular participation were structured from above, mobilization at the grass-roots was often loosely connected or even independent of Chávez's party machine, attesting to the hybrid character of popular subjectivity in Venezuela's Bolivarian revolution.

Such hybridity was much less prevalent in Ecuador, where the plebiscitary character of Rafael Correa's populist authority clashed more directly with autonomous social movements and civic networks. Ecuador's indigenous movement was the strongest in Latin America in the 1990s, with lowland and highland organizations converging in a national confederation that founded its own party vehicle, *Pachakutik*, and played a central role in mass protests that drove presidents from office in 1997 and 2000 (see Yashar 2005; Van Cott 2005; Madrid 2012). *Pachakutik*, however, was far less successful in the electoral arena than the more heterogeneous MAS in Bolivia, which wove together ethnic, class, and nationalist identities in an over-arching anti-establishment and anti-neoliberal discourse (Madrid 2008). Given its limited electoral appeal, *Pachakutik* supported independent populist figures in presidential campaigns in 1996, 1998, and 2002, helping to elect Lucio Gutiérrez to the presidency in the latter race and briefly placing a number of party members in his initial cabinet. Gutiérrez, however, quickly abandoned his campaign platform by adopting orthodox market reforms, leading *Pachakutik* to withdraw from the government, although the president's efforts to co-opt other indigenous leaders divided and weakened the national confederation (Wolff 2007).

After yet another cycle of more urban-based mass protests forced Gutiérrez from office in 2005, the stage was set for the election of the left-leaning populist figure Rafael Correa in 2006. Correa had no significant ties to the indigenous movement, which for the first time had run a presidential candidate from its own ranks, with little success. Indeed, in contrast to Bolivia, "Correa was elected when the indigenous movement entered into a crisis, temporarily losing its capacity to engage in sustained collective action" (de la Torre 2013: 28). Although Correa proclaimed a "Citizens' Revolution" and adopted a wide range of redistributive social measures, he did so in a technocratic manner, with relatively few of the grass-roots organizations and participatory channels that flourished in Venezuela under Chávez, or the consultative mechanisms and popular assemblies that helped hold the MAS accountable in Bolivia. Popular referendums were held to convoke a constituent assembly and ratify a new constitution, but popular mobilization was restricted to the electoral arena, and the government clashed with virtually all forms of autonomous social organization. As Conaghan states (2011: 274), "Correa regarded Ecuador's turbulent and intrusive civil society as an obstacle, not a building block, for his revolution," and he dismissed organized interests as "privileged interlocutors representing special interests, while his elected government was deemed the only legitimate guardian of the 'national' interest." Organizations of students, teachers, public sector employees, environmentalists, and indigenous peoples all entered into conflict with Correa's plebiscitary and technocratic brand of populism, and they contested a wide range of issues, from control over high school and university curricula to union prerogatives, community autonomy, and a development model based largely on natural resource extraction (de la Torre 2013: 37–39).

In short, legacies of market reform, social protest, and party system collapse paved the way for the emergence of new leftist alternatives in Bolivia, Ecuador, and Venezuela, but these alternatives varied in their relationships to social movements, and they encompassed radically different forms of popular subjectivity and collective action. Whether or not all of these experiments are characterized as populist, it is essential to understand how both plebiscitary and participatory patterns of popular subjectivity have reshaped the political arena in Latin America's post-adjustment era.

Conclusion

The study of populism and social movements has for too long been segregated into separate camps. Although populism's contested meanings make it difficult to pin down a precise relationship to social movements, the recent Latin American experience leaves little doubt that the two phenomena can hardly be understood in isolation from each other. Populism and social movements both tend to be rooted in representational failures that trigger non-institutionalized patterns of popular subjectivity. This subjectivity can take alternative plebiscitary or participatory forms that are inevitably in tension with one another, even when they coincide in hybrid political expressions, as in Bolivia and Venezuela in the early 2000s. This tension lies at the very heart of the debate over the meaning of populism and its essential characteristics.

Notes

1. Personal communication with the author, January 15, 2012.
2. Structural adjustment policies were imposed by the major historic labor-affiliated populist party in Argentina (the Peronist *Partido Justicialista,* or PJ), Bolivia (the *Movimiento Nacinalista Revolucionario,* or MNR), and Venezuela (*Acción Democrática,* or AD). In Ecuador, the leading center-left and populist parties both adopted market liberalization policies when they held executive office in the late 1980s and mid-1990s, respectively.

References

Anria, Santiago (2013). "Social Movements, Party Organization, and Populism: Insights from the Bolivian MAS," *Latin American Politics and Society*. 55(3) (Fall): 19–46.

Barr, Robert R. (2009). "Populists, Outsiders and Anti-Establishment Politics," *Party Politics*. 15(1): 29–48.

Berezin, Mabel (2009). *Illiberal Politics in Neoliberal Times: Culture, Security and Populism in a New Europe*. New York: Cambridge University Press.

Canovan, Margaret (1981). *Populism*. London: Junction Books.

Castañeda, Ernesto (2012). "The Indignados of Spain: A Precedent to Occupy Wall Street," *Social Movement Studies*. 11(3–4): 309–319.

Castells, Manuel (2012). *Networks of Outrage and Hope: Social Movements in the Internet Age*. Cambridge: Polity Press.

Collier, Ruth Berins and Collier, David (1991). *Shaping the Political Arena: Critical Junctures, the Labor Movement, and Regime Dynamics in Latin America*. Princeton: Princeton University Press.

Conaghan, Catherine (2011). "Ecuador: Rafael Correa and the Citizens' Revolution." In *The Resurgence of the Latin American Left*, edited by Steven Levitsky and Kenneth M. Roberts, 260–282. Baltimore: Johns Hopkins University Press.

Conniff, Michael L., ed. (2012). *Populism in Latin America*, 2nd ed. Tuscaloosa, AL: University of Alabama Press.

Crabtree, John (2013). "From the MNR to the MAS: Populism, Parties, the State, and Social Movements in Bolivia since 1952." In *Latin American Populism in the 21st Century*, edited by Carlos de la Torre and Cynthia J. Arnson, 269–293. Washington, DC: Woodrow Wilson Center Press.

de la Torre, Carlos (2009). *Populist Seduction in Latin America*. Athens, OH: Ohio University Press.

de la Torre, Carlos (2013). "In the Name of the People: Democratization, Popular Organizations, and Populism in Venezuela, Bolivia, and Ecuador," *European Review of Latin American and Caribbean Studies*. 95 (October): 27–48.

de la Torre, Carlos (2014). *The Promise and Perils of Populism: Global Perspectives*. Lexington: University of Kentucky Press.

de la Torre, Carlos and Arnson, Cynthia J., eds. (2013). *Latin American Populism in the Twenty-First Century*. Washington, DC: Woodrow Wilson Center Press.

della Porta, Donatella (2014). *Social Movements in Times of Austerity: Bringing Capitalism Back In*. Cambridge: Polity Press.

di Tella, Torcuato S. (1965). "Populism and Reform in Latin America." In *Obstacles to Change in Latin America*, edited by Claudio Véliz, 47–74. Cambridge: Cambridge University Press.

Dornbusch, Rudiger and Edwards, Sebastian (1991). "The Macroeconomics of Populism." In *The Macroeconomics of Populism in Latin America*, edited by Rudiger Dornbusch and Sebastian Edwards, 7–13. Chicago: University of Chicago Press.

Edwards, Sebastian (2010). *Left Behind: Latin America and the False Promise of Populism*. Chicago: University of Chicago Press.

Germani, Gino (1978). *Authoritarianism, Fascism, and National Populism*. New Brunswick, NJ: Transaction Books.

Handlin, Samuel and Collier, Ruth Berins (2011). "The Diversity of Left Party Linkages and Competitive Advantages." In *The Resurgence of the Latin American Left*, Steven Levitsky and Kenneth M. Roberts, 139–161. Baltimore: Johns Hopkins University Press.

Hawkins, Kirk (2009). "Is Chávez Populist? Measuring Populist Discourse in Comparative Perspective," *Comparative Political Studies*. 42(8): 1040–1067.

Hawkins, Kirk (2010a). *Venezuela's Chavismo and Populism in Comparative Perspective.* New York: Cambridge University Press.

Hawkins, Kirk (2010b). "Who Mobilizes? Participatory Democracy in Chávez's Bolivarian Revolution," *Latin American Politics and Society*. 52(3): 31–66.

Hewison, Kevin (2010). "Thaksin Shinawatra and the Reshaping of Thai Politics," *Contemporary Politics*. 16(2) (June): 119–133.

Hutter, Swen and Kriesi, Hanspeter (2013). "Movements of the Left, Movements of the Right Reconsidered." In *The Future of Social Movement Research*, edited by Jacquelien von Stekelenburg, Conny Roggeband, and Bert Klandermans, 281–298. Minneapolis: University of Minnesota Press.

Kitschelt, Herbert (2006). "Movement Parties." In *Handbook of Party Politics*, edited by Richard S. Katz and William Crotty, 278–290. London: Sage Publications.

Kurtz, Marcus (2004). "The Dilemmas of Democracy in the Open Economy: Lessons from Latin America," *World Politics*. 56(2) (January): 262–302.

Laclau, Ernesto (1977). *Politics and Ideology in Marxist Theory*. London: Verso.

Laclau, Ernesto (2005). *On Populist Reason*. London: Verso.

Levitsky, Steven and Loxton, James (2013). "Populism and Competitive Authoritarianism in the Andes," *Democratization*. 20(1): 107–136.

Levitsky, Steven and Roberts, Kenneth M., eds. (2011). *The Resurgence of the Latin American Left*. Baltimore: Johns Hopkins University Press.

López Maya, Margarita (2011). "Venezuela: Hugo Chávez and the Populist Left." In *The Resurgence of the Latin American Left*, edited by Steven Levitsky and Kenneth M. Roberts, 213–238. Baltimore: Johns Hopkins University Press.

Madrid, Raúl L. (2008). "The Rise of Ethnopopulism in Bolivia," *World Politics*. 60(3) (April): 475–508.

Madrid, Raúl L. (2009). "The Origins of the Two Lefts in Latin America," *Political Science Quarterly*. 125(4) (Winter): 1–23.

Madrid, Raúl L. (2011). "Bolivia: Origins and Policies of the Movimiento al Socialismo." In *The Resurgence of the Latin American Left*, edited by Steven Levitsky and Kenneth M. Roberts, 239–259. Baltimore: Johns Hopkins University Press.

Madrid, Raúl L. (2012). *The Rise of Ethnic Politics in Latin America*. New York: Cambridge University Press.

McAdam, Doug and Tarrow, Sidney (2011). "Ballots and Barricades: On the Reciprocal Relationship between Elections and Social Movements," *Perspectives on Politics*. 8(2) (June): 529–542.

McCargo, Duncan (2001). "Populism and Reformism in Contemporary Thailand," *South East Asia Research*. 9(1) (March): 89–107.

Mudde, Cas. (2007). *Populist Radical Right Parties in Europe*. Cambridge: Cambridge University Press.

Mudde, Cas and Rovira Kaltwasser, Cristóbal (2012). "Populism and (Liberal) Democracy: A Framework for Analysis." In *Populism in Europe and the Americas: Threat or Corrective to Democracy?*, edited by Cas Mudde and Cristóbal Rovira Kaltwasser, 1–26. Cambridge: Cambridge University Press.

Ostiguy, Pierre (2009). *The High and the Low in Politics: A Two-Dimensional Political Space for Comparative Analysis and Electoral Studies*. Helen Kellogg Institute for International Studies, Working Paper #360. South Bend, IN: University of Notre Dame.

Oxhorn, Philip (2011). *Sustaining Civil Society: Economic Change, Democracy, and the Social Construction of Citizenship in Latin America*. University Park, PA: Pennsylvania State University Press.

Panizza, Francisco (2005). "Populism and the Mirror of Democracy." In *Populism and the Mirror of Democracy*, edited by Francisco Panizza, 1–31. London: Verso.

Polanyi, Karl (1944). *The Great Transformation*. New York: Farrar and Rinehart.

Resnick, Danielle (2012). "Opposition Parties and the Urban Poor in African Democracies," *Comparative Political Studies*. 45(11) (November).

Rice, Roberta (2012). *The New Politics of Protest: Indigenous Mobilization in Latin America's Neoliberal Era*. Tucson: University of Arizona Press.

Roberts, Kenneth M. (1995). "Neoliberalism and the Transformation of Populism in Latin America: The Peruvian Case," *World Politics*. 48(1): 82–116.

Roberts, Kenneth M. (2002). "Social Inequalities Without Class Cleavages in Latin America's Neoliberal Era," *Studies in Comparative International Development*. 36(4): 3–34.

Roberts, Kenneth M. (2006). "Populism, Political Conflict, and Grass-Roots Organization in Latin America," *Comparative Politics*. 38(2).

Roberts, Kenneth M. (2014). *Changing Course in Latin America: Party Systems in the Neoliberal Era*. New York: Cambridge University Press.

Roxborough, Ian (1984). "Unity and Diversity in Latin American History," *Journal of Latin American Studies*. 16: 1–26.

Silva, Eduardo (2009). *Challenging Neoliberalism in Latin America*. New York: Cambridge University Press.

Skocpol, Theda and Williamson, Vanessa (2013). *The Tea Party and the Remaking of Republican Conservatism*. New York: Oxford University Press.

Van Cott, Donna Lee (2005). *From Movements to Parties in Latin America: The Evolution of Ethnic Politics*. Cambridge: Cambridge University Press.

Van Cott, Donna Lee (2008). *Radical Democracy in the Andes*. New York: Cambridge University Press.

Tarrow, Sidney (2013). *The Language of Contention: Revolutions in Words, 1688-2012*. New York: Cambridge University Press.

Weyland, Kurt. 1996. "Neopopulism and Neoliberalism in Latin America: Unexpected Affinities," *Studies in Comparative International Development*. 31(3): 3–31.

Weyland, K. (2001). "Clarifying a Contested Concept: Populism in the Study of Latin American Politics," *Comparative Politics*. 34(1): 1–22.

Weyland, K. (2013). "The Threat from the Populist Left," *Journal of Democracy*. 24(3) (July): 13–32.

Williamson, John (1990). "What Washington Means by Policy Reform." In *Latin American Adjustment: How Much Has Happened?*, edited by John Williamson, 7–20. Washington, DC: Institute for International Economics.

Wolff, Jonas (2007). "(De-)Mobilising the Marginalised: A Comparison of the Argentine *Piqueteros* and Ecuador's Indigenous Movement," *Journal of Latin American Studies*. 39(1) (February): 1–29.

Yashar, Deborah (2005). *Contesting Citizenship in Latin America: The Rise of Indigenous Movements and the Postliberal Challenge*. Cambridge: Cambridge University Press.

....

CHAPTER 46

MARKETS, BUSINESS, AND SOCIAL MOVEMENTS

....

SARAH A. SOULE AND BRAYDEN G. KING

INTRODUCTION

....

OVER the past several years, scholars of social movements have turned their attention to a number of questions related to the interaction of firms, markets, and social movements (see recent reviews, such as King and Pearce 2010 or Soule 2012a). Some study how the activities of social movements impact some firm-level outcome (e.g., Lounsbury, Ventresca, and Hirsch 2003; King and Soule 2007; King 2008b; Bartley and Child 2011; Soule et al. 2013), while others focus on the way in which businesses can sometimes act as social movements (e.g., Davis and Thompson 1994; Vogel 2005; Vogus and Davis 2005; Walker and Rea 2014). This literature has drawn extensively, and appropriately, on both organizational and social movement theories.

One area of work that has received comparatively less attention is that which takes as central the idea that markets and firms impact social movements, just as movements impact firms and markets. That is, rather than focussing on the way in which movements matter to firms and markets, this work has switched the causal arrow, and seeks to uncover the variety of ways in which firms and markets influence basic movement processes.

The purpose of this essay is twofold. First, we review existing research on how the facets and characteristics of organizations and industries impact social movement organizations. In general, this work has drawn inspiration from the political opportunity structure model, and has taken the perspective of the *corporate* or *industry opportunity structure*. Second, we describe a set of recent changes to businesses and industries, and how these may be expected to impact social movements via changing the nature of the corporate and industry opportunity structures within which movements operate. As we describe, some of these may facilitate movements and movement processes, while others may constrain them.

Corporate and Industry Opportunity Structures

To understand the way in which markets and firms influence movements, it is important to understand the concepts of the *corporate* (King 2008a) and *industry opportunity structures* (Schurman 2004). These concepts are derived from the older political opportunity structure concept, which is best understood as the "consistent ... dimensions of the political environment that provide incentives for people to undertake collective action by affecting their expectations for success or failure" (Tarrow 1998: 76). The basic idea is that the activities of social movements directed at state institutions are dramatically structured by changes in the level of elite receptivity to protesters, changes in elite ability and willingness to repress movements, and the presence of elite allies (Tarrow 1998).

This idea was adopted by Schurman (2004) who argues that, in the case of movements directed at markets and firms, the *industry opportunity structure* provides the opportunities and constraints that influence the activities of movements in the relevant industry. Schurman (2004) defines the industry opportunity structure as the set of "economic, organizational, cultural, and commodity-related" factors that facilitate and constrain movements and their effects on corporate targets (Schurman 2004: 251). Key dimensions of the industry opportunity structure include the relationships among actors in the industry's organizational field and the nature of the goods or services produced by the industry, which, to the extent that these can be harmful, may offer more opportunities for activism than do others (Schurman 2004). One example of the industry opportunity structure is the level of competition in the industry, which can encourage companies to acquiesce more quickly to the demands of activists. This appears to have been the case with respect to the adoption of domestic partnership benefits amongst the top-US airlines (Raeburn 2004).

King (2008a, 2008b) also builds on the idea of the political opportunity structure, by suggesting that *corporate opportunity structures* and *corporate mediation* can impact the activities and processes of social movements (see also Dauvergne and LeBaron 2014). Corporations are similar to states in that they are political entities with structural characteristics that shape their openness to movement influence (Zald 1970). Key dimensions of the corporate opportunity structure are various realignments within the corporate elite, signals from the elite within the corporation, and a general openness to movement claims. For example, Raeburn (2004) showed the employee-led lesbian, gay, bisexual, and transgender (LGBT) movement experienced greater receptiveness in companies in which there were elite allies in the upper echelon of corporate leadership.

This early work did an excellent job of analogizing from the political opportunity structure to the industry and corporate opportunity structures. Inspired by this idea, many scholars have set out to measure these concepts in various empirical settings.

Operationalizing Industry Opportunity Structures

Research examining the industry opportunity structures of mobilization has tended to focus on the aggregate characteristics of firms within an industry or on the institutional dynamics of specific markets. These studies suggest a number of fruitful ways to operationalize opportunity structures at a macro-comparative level of analysis (i.e., between industry differences).

First, some scholars have suggested that the *competitive dynamics* of an industry ought to shape the opportunities for activists to influence the industry. For instance, Kapstein and Busby (2013) argue that the small number of competitors in the AIDS antiretroviral drug market made it easier for activists to encourage all suppliers of the drugs to lower their prices and to engage in differential pricing whereby patients in wealthier countries could subsidize patients in poorer countries. A single defector from this pricing scheme would have suffered greater reputational penalties than would have been true in an industry with many competitors.

Resource partitioning theory has demonstrated that industry concentration (a specific form of competition) creates opportunities for movement-like conditions to emerge at the periphery inasmuch as it creates a common enemy for identity movements who mobilize in opposition to mass producers (Carroll and Swaminathan 2000; Greve et al. 2006; Sikavica and Pozner 2013). For example, a highly concentrated brewing industry in the United States set the stage for the emergence of a craft beer "movement" (Carroll and Swaminathan 2000). Concentrated competition ought to be associated, in particular, with the emergence of specialist movements (see Soule and King 2008 for an application of these ideas to three social movement industries).

Second, in addition to the competitive dynamics of an industry, other research demonstrates that *regulatory differences* between industries are important determinants of movement dynamics. For example, Rao et al. (2011) find that variation in regulatory labor laws make protestors more or less effective when trying to impede the location of new large retail stores like Walmart. Their analysis suggests that regulatory differences change the competitive dynamics in industries and subsequently make activists' attempts to shape corporate behavior more or less viable.

Third, several scholars point to the existence of *private regulatory associations* as an important dimension of the industry opportunity structure. In addition to state regulatory differences, the emergence of private regulation, such as associations and certification systems, which firms voluntarily join to signal their compliance with socially responsible norms, create opportunities for movements to gain access to firms within an industry (Bartley 2007). The emergence of such standards signals activist influence and may draw new movements to an industry as they see opportunities for exerting leverage over previously resistant firms (Dubuisson-Quellier 2013).

Operationalizing Corporate Opportunity Structures

Research examining the corporate opportunity structures for mobilization has tended to focus on the characteristics of firms and how these impact movement dynamics. These studies suggest a number of fruitful ways to operationalize opportunity structures at a corporate level.

First, some scholars have argued that the *characteristics of the chief executive officer (CEO)* are an important dimension of the corporate opportunity structure. A company's CEO has more power and sway over a company's policies than any other individual; therefore, their personal dispositions and values are likely to shape how receptive a company would be to movement mobilization. Briscoe et al. (2014), for example, demonstrate that companies with liberal CEOs who donate to the Democratic Party are more likely to foster mobilization by LGBT activists. CEOs' past experiences ought to influence their values, their receptivity to employees' demands, and their general disposition to engage in "social responsibility" (Chin et al. 2013). For example, CEOs who had recently experienced the birth of a daughter were more receptive to women's pay equality in the future (Dahl et al. 2012).

Scholars have also pointed to characteristics of the *corporate board and board governance* as factors that ought to matter to activists and movements. Surprisingly, there is little past research directly related to corporate governance and social movements (although see McAteer and Pulver 2009); however, research on social responsibility suggests that corporate board and shareholder dynamics ought to influence the firm's receptiveness to social issues (Aguilera et al. 2006). In particular, the presence of outsider board members (i.e., board members not employed by the organization) makes firms more responsive to social concerns and outsider constituents (Ibrahim et al. 2003; Barnea and Rubin 2010) and more sensitive to negative media attention, more generally (Bednar et al. 2013). As well, firms with more women on their boards tend to have higher responsibility ratings than firms dominated by men (Bear et al. 2010). Finally, companies whose boards give more voice to outsider constituents are more favorable to movements. Vasi and King (2012) demonstrate that corporations with strong shareholder rights are more likely to respond positively to the demands of activists. To evaluate governance rights, they used the Governance Index developed by Gompers, Ishii, and Metrick (2003) that ranges from a democracy portfolio (low managerial power, high shareholder rights) to a dictatorship portfolio (high managerial power, low shareholder rights).

Third, scholars have looked at *firms' reputation, status, and visibility* as dimensions of the corporate opportunity structure. A common finding in much of the research examining movements and corporations is that activists mobilize against highly visible, prestigious firms. Organizational size, dominant competitive position, and having high status or a positive reputation make firms attractive targets (Florida 1996; Etzion 2007; King 2008b; Lenox and Eesley 2009; McAteer and Pulver 2009). Activists seek highly visible targets because public demonstrations against these firms generate more media attention (King 2011), which in turn makes their targets more susceptible to reputation threat and enhances the movement's influence (King 2008b; McDonnell and King 2013). Thus, activists will often ignore low status firms altogether (King 2011; Model et al., working paper). King and McDonnell (2015) show that firms that have reputations for engaging in socially responsible activities (e.g., corporate philanthropy) are especially likely to foster movement mobilization, in part because these firms could be accused of organizational hypocrisy, which creates more outrage in the media and broader public. Similarly, Micheletti and Stolle (2008) show that Nike made itself more vulnerable to activists' challenges because it tried to brand itself as a good corporate citizen.

Finally, some have noted that the overall *corporate culture and receptiveness* to activism is an important dimension of the corporate opportunity structure, arguing that certain firms engender cultures that make them more receptive to movement influence. Vasi and King (2012) note that companies with a green corporate culture will respond more favorably to environmental demands of activists and find that a progressive culture lowers the amount of environmental risk to which firms are exposed. McDonnell et al. (working paper) argue that companies often adopt certain policies like corporate social responsibility (CSR) reports and committees initially to protect their reputation and public image but that these "social management devices" change the internal culture of firms and make them more receptive to activists in the future. Rojas et al. (2012) find that a company's culture shapes how they respond to shareholder resolutions.

Suggestions for Future Research: Altering the Opportunities for Movements

The interactions between movements and corporations have transformed the corporate field, which in turn has sometimes created new opportunities for movement influence, yet at other times has presented constraints on movement influence. We will go on to outline some trends and transformations that ought to impact industry and corporate opportunities for movements in the future.

Benefit Corporations

A benefit corporation (or "B Corporation") is a relatively new form of corporate entity in the United States, which is designed for for-profit organizations that wish to consider social and environmental issues alongside profit. The general purpose of a B corporation is to have a positive impact on society. B Corporations' directors have the same authority and function similarly to a traditional corporation, but a B Corporation's shareholders agree that social motives have equal weight over company's decisions as financial rewards, and they seek feedback from society on whether or not the corporation is, in fact, having a positive impact. At the time of this writing, fourteen states allow those so inclined to incorporate as B Corporations.

In terms of corporate opportunity structure, these are pretty interesting. We might expect that they are far less likely to be targeted, since activists (at least those on the left) will implicitly trust them to be good corporate citizens. However, if one of these fails to deliver positive societal impact, citizens will have direct channels to influence them; in other words, they are extremely open to citizen input. This is different from a normal corporate structure, which has fewer channels for seeking the input of outside constituents. The relative openness of B Corporations and their implicit recognition of social issues as a priority in their charter suggest that social movements ought to have ongoing influence within these companies. Moreover, it is possible that B Corporations that appear to have adopted the form for superficial reasons might attract more criticism from activists who are angered by perceived organizational hypocrisy.

The challenge for executives of B Corporations will be to figure out how to allocate their attention among the various demands made on them by external stakeholders; whereas, the challenge for activists will be to develop tactics, akin to those used by movements primarily aimed at influence legislative change, that make their issues more salient and more likely to be considered on the corporate agenda.

Professional Grass-roots Lobbying Firms

Professional grass-roots lobbying firms (PGLF), popularly known as "astroturf" organizations, specialize in mobilizing stakeholders who then act on behalf of the political goals of the firm (Walker 2014). This particular organizational form is not especially new. For example, the Public Cup Vendor Company (now the Dixie Cup Company) was behind a mass public health campaign in the United States designed to encourage the use of disposable drinking cups in an effort to prevent the spread of disease by using the common shared, metal cups available in the early 1900s (Lee 2010). But, the form proliferated dramatically in the late twentieth century, much to the dismay of critics, who argue that unsuspecting activists are tricked into grass-roots mobilization by clever organizers, who really have only the interest of corporations in mind. For example, the National Smokers Alliance, an organization that opposed restrictions on smoking in public places, was created and funded by Burson-Marsteller, a PR firm hired by Phillip Morris.

Lee and Romano (2013) demonstrate that a new cadre of professional organizers have emerged that seemingly promote civil society and democracy by organizing public deliberation events in which community members are given opportunities to express their opinion and mobilize support for local issues. However, despite their appearances as community organizers, these professionals are guns-for-hire who often work for private companies and organize grass-roots activities around issues that align with those companies' interests.

The proliferation of privately sponsored community organizing has the potential to create new forms of social movement organizations. Fetner and King (2014) described these as "three layer movements" or movement organizations that acquire resources both from below, drawing on grass-roots support, and in a top-down fashion, as they are injected with financial support, expertise, and infrastructure from private funders. Only time will tell how such movement organizations alter the landscape of the social movement sector.

Security and Exchange Commission Rules

A recent article in *The Economist* noted that over time, the Security and Exchange Commission (SEC) rules have been more or less favorable to activist investors submitting resolutions to firms (*Economist* 2014). A shareholder resolution is a shareholder's (or group of shareholders') recommendation (which is intended to be presented at the annual meeting of shareholders) that a company take some action (SEC 2004). The barriers to filing a resolution are quite low. Shareholders must own at least $2,000 worth of shares and commit to holding these shares until after the annual meeting when the proposal would be presented (SEC 2004). They must also file the resolution more than 120 days prior to the company's annual meeting.

While these particular SEC rules have not changed over time, the SEC frequently changes the rules stipulating the grounds on which a company can challenge a resolution. A firm's challenge to a resolution must argue that the resolution does not meet one of the thirteen rules documented in SEC Rule 14a-8.[1] The most common objections raised by firms are that the shareholder resolution: 1) relates to operations accounting for less than 5 per cent of the firm's assets, sales and revenue, or 2) directly "deals with a matter relating to the company's ordinary business operations" (Tkac 2006). Observers have commented that these rules are vague, and that the SEC has historically vacillated on their interpretation of the rules, providing firms significant latitude for attempting a challenge (Ackerly 1998). Thus one area for future research should examine the changes to SEC rules, and the enforcement thereof, and how this alters the industry opportunity structure by making shareholder activism more or less likely to succeed.

Corporate Social Responsibility

The expansion of corporate social responsibility as a reaction to social movement activism is another example of how movement-corporate interactions can change corporations and markets (Soule 2009). Firms targeted by activists often respond by adopting corporate social responsibility policies, practices, and positions (Soule 2009; McDonnell and King 2013). One view of the rationale behind adopting such "social management devices" is that firms do this in an effort to buffer themselves from future criticism (McDonnell and King 2013). But rather than protect them from future social movement targeting, these activities ironically create new opportunities for engagement and dialogue with activists (McDonnell and King 2013; McDonnell et al. working paper).

This implies the need for research that looks at how activism impacts a fundamental characteristic of the corporate opportunity structure (e.g., the presence of a CSR officer, CSR policies, and so on), which in turn impacts fundamental movement processes (see Soule et al. 1999 for a similar argument regarding the political opportunity structure). And indeed, recent evidence suggests that exposure to movements may make firms more inclined to develop future social responsibility measures. In a study of the "urgent appeals" tactic used by the Clean Clothes Campaign, den Hond et al (2014) show that the level of experience with prior activism was an important predictor of how the firm responded to this tactic, since prior activism often led to an integration of corporate social responsibility initiatives into a firm's basic operations.

Crowdfunding and Co-production

A final interesting trend in movement mobilization that is likely to shape how industry and corporate opportunity structures evolve in the future is the use of online technology to aid in crowdfunding and other forms of co-production. Websites such as Kickstarter, Indiegogo, and Rockethub offer forums where people can evaluate projects of different types, some of which are purely market-based and others that have a clearer social mission intent, and potentially fund those projects with voluntary donations. Crowdfunding sites combine an ethic of entrepreneurialism with a collective action model for generating enthusiasm and support for new causes.

Practically speaking, crowdfunding enables far-flung activists to attract resources from likeminded individuals who are otherwise disconnected from their causes. Consider, for example, the success of the Indiegogo project, "Full Page Ad for Turkish Democracy in Action," which raised over $100,000 to put a full page advertisement in support of Turkish activists in the New York Times.[2] Another effective use of crowdfunding by social movements was Scottish independence activists' use of Bloomvc to raise money to fund "volunteers to reach undecided voters in their local communities and ensure a Yes vote at the independence referendum."[3]

Crowdfunding has a similar logic to other types of co-production, which refers to "situations in which consumers collaborate with companies or with other consumers to produce things of value" (Humphreys and Grayson 2008: 963). In co-production forms of organizing, consumers are activists in their own right, taking a proactive role alongside companies in producing markets and goods. Companies, for example, might decide which styles of clothing they will make next season based on consumer polls.[4]

But in other instances, co-production might allow consumers to have a more direct say over a company's social practices, leading to a greater expression of values and ethics (Arvidsson 2011).

Both crowdfunding and co-production represent a new logic for mobilizing consumers and activists around the production of economic and social goods. In both forms, corporations are being bypassed altogether or they are allowing for more democratic participation. Both forms of expression involve significant decentralization. The question remains, what kinds of new opportunities do crowdfunding and co-production create for activists seeking to have a more direct and immediate impact? One interpretation is that these forms might facilitate a more open opportunity structure and create spaces of democratic association outside the norms of traditional capitalism. Whereas most corporate producers are averse to direct participation by consumers, communities, and other stakeholders, these new forms of organizing hold the promise of breaking down hierarchies and facilitating more direct communication, which perhaps may give expression to a greater diversity of voices and grievances. Another possibility is that these new forms may simply open up the possibility for "personalized politics," similar to that which observers of online activism have seen, as movements begin using social media (Bennett and Segerberg 2013). Rather than breaking down the walls of traditional corporations, crowdfunding and co-production might merely create a new outlet for personal expression and displace more engaged forms of activism (Kristofferson et al. 2014).

Conclusion

This essay sought to contribute to the exciting and growing literature at the intersection of social movement and organizational studies by reviewing a slice of this literature that examines how the characteristics of firms, markets, and industries impacts social movement activities and processes. We did this with an eye toward understanding how it is that scholars working on this general question have operationalized the corporate and industry opportunity structures. While there are a number of excellent reviews of research on how movements impact firms, to the best of our knowledge, this is the first attempt to review work that reverses this causal arrow, asking instead how it is that changes in firms, markets, and industries impact how social movements operate.

Beyond this review, we also discuss a number of changes in the nature of firms, markets, and industries, and suggest some possibilities for how these changes may impact social movements going forward. Although most research has focused on the industry and firm dynamics that shape movement-corporation interactions, we should not forget that industry and corporate opportunities are also situated within a political context. The political environment of a firm's home country alters how movement activists view the potential receptivity of corporate targets (McAteer and Pulver 2009) or may change the strategic calculations of firms responding to movement pressures (Vogel 1986; Soule et al. 2013).

Opportunity structures—political, industry, and corporate—are nested within one another, making the lower-level effects of corporate characteristics conditional on variation in the political environment (Soule 2009, 2012b; Soule et al. 2013). Moreover, it is likely that individual activists' behaviors, as well as those of employees and consumers, are likely shaped by the political conditions of their home country as well. Koos (2012), for example, shows that in countries with historically "statist institutions" and weak civil society, consumers are less politically-minded and less willing to mobilize against firms. Thus, we suggest that future research ought to focus more on the interplay between political, industry, and corporate opportunity structures.

NOTES

1. For a list of these, see www.sec.gov/interps/legal/cfslb14.htm accessed January 28, 2014.
2. www.indiegogo.com/projects/full-page-ad-for-turkish-democracy-in-action accessed March 18, 2014.
3. www.bloomvc.com/project/Support-a-Yes-vote-for-Scottish-independence accessed March 18, 2014.
4. Threadless.com, an online retailer of t-shirts and other products, uses this strategy for producing clothing products.

REFERENCES

Ackerly, Dana T. (1998). "SEC Makes Changes in Shareholder Proposal System," *Public Company Advocate.* 4–5.

Aguilera, Ruth V., Williams, Cynthia A., Conley, John M., and Rupp, Deborah E. (2006). "Corporate Governance and Social Responsibility: A Comparative Analysis of the UK and the US," *Corporate Governance: An International Review.* 14(3): 147–158.

Arvidsson, Adam (2011). "Ethics and Value in Customer Co-production," *Marketing Theory.* 11: 261–278.

Barnea, Amir and Rubin, Amir (2010). "Corporate Social Responsibility as a Conflict between Shareholders," *Journal of Business Ethics.* 97: 71–86.

Bartley, Tim (2007). "Institutional Emergence in an Era of Globalization: The Rise of Transnational Private Regulation of Labor and Environmental Conditions," *American Journal of Sociology.* 113(2): 297–351.

Bartley, Tim and Child, Curtis (2011). "Movements, Markets and Fields: the Effects of Anti-sweatshop Campaigns on US Firms, 1993–2000," *Social Forces.* 90: 425–451.

Bear, Stephen, Rahman, Noushi and Post, Corinne (2010). "The Impact of Board Diversity and Gender Composition on Corporate Social Responsibility and Firm Reputation," *Journal of Business Ethics.* 97(2): 207–221.

Bednar, Michael K., Boivie, Steven, and Prince, Nicholas R. (2013). "Burr under the Saddle: How Media Coverage Influences Strategic Change," *Organization Science.* 24(3): 910–925.

Bennett, W Lance and Segerberg, Alexandra (2013). *The Logic of Connective Action: Digital Media and the Personalization of Contentious Politics.* Cambridge: Cambridge University Press.

Briscoe, Forrest, Chin, MK, and Hambrick, Donald C. (2014). "CEO Ideology as an Element of the Corporate Opportunity Structure for Social Activists," *Academy of Management Journal,* 57: 1786–1809.

Carroll, Glenn R. and Swaminathan, Anand (2000). "Why the Microbrewery Movement? Organizational Dynamics of Resource Partitioning in the U.S. Brewing Industry," *American Journal of Sociology.* 106(3): 715–762.

Chin, MK, Hambrick, Donald C., and Treviño, Linda K. (2013). "Political Ideologies of CEOs the Influence of Executives' Values on Corporate Social Responsibility," *Administrative Science Quarterly.* 58(2): 197–232.

Dahl, Michael S., Dezső, Cristian L., and Gaddis Ross, David (2012). "Fatherhood and Managerial Style How a Male CEO's Children Affect the Wages of His Employees," *Administrative Science Quarterly.* 57(4): 669–693.

Dauvergne, Peter and LeBaron, Genevieve (2014). *Protest, Inc.* Cambridge, England: Polity Press.

Davis, Gerald F. and Thompson, Tracy A. (1994). "A Social-Movement Perspective on Corporate-Control," *Administrative Science Quarterly.* 39: 141–173.

den Hond, Frank, Stolwijk, Sjoerd, and Merk, Jeroen (2014). "A Strategic-Interaction Analysis of an Urgent Appeal System and its Outcomes for Garment Workers," *Mobilization.* 19(1): 83–111.

Dubuisson-Quellier, Sophie (2013). "A Market Mediation Strategy: How Social Movements Seek to Change Firms' Practices by Promoting New Principles of Product Valuation," *Organization Studies.* 34(5–6): 683–703.

Economist (2014). "Corporate Upgraders: America Should Make Life Easier, Not Harder, for Activist Investors." www.economist.com/news/leaders/21596518-america-should-make-l ife-easier-not-harder-activist-investors-corporate-upgraders, accessed February 15, 2014.

Etzion, Dror (2007). "Research on Organizations and the Natural Environment, 1992–Present: A Review," *Journal of Management.* 33: 637–664.

Fetner, Tina and King, Brayden G. (2014). "Three Layer Movements, Resources, and the Tea Party." Pp. 35-54 in *Understanding the Tea Party Movement,* edited by N. Van Dyke and D. S. Meyer. Surrey: Ashgate.

Florida, Richard (1996). "Lean and Green: The Move to Environmentally Conscious Manufacturing," *California Management Review.* 39.

Gompers, Paul, Ishii, Joy, and Metrick, Andrew (2003). "Corporate Governance and Equity Prices," *The Quarterly Journal of Economics.* 118(1): 107–156.

Greve, Henrich R., Pozner, Jo-Ellen, and Rao, Hayagreeva (2006). "Vox Populi: Resource Partitioning, Organizational Proliferation, and the Cultural Impact of the Insurgent Microradio Movement." *American Journal of Sociology.* 112(3): 802–837.

Humphreys, Ashlee and Grayson, Kent (2008). "The Intersecting Roles of Consumer and Producer: A Critical Perspective on Co-production, Co-creation and Prosumption," *Sociology Compass.* 2: 963–980.

Ibrahim, Nabil A., Howard, Donald P., and Angelidis, John P. (2003). "Board Members in the Service Industry: An Empirical Examination of the Relationship between Corporate Social Responsibility Orientation and Directorial Type," *Journal of Business Ethics.* 47(4): 393–401.

Kapstein, Ethan B. and Busby, Joshua W. (2013). *AIDS Drugs for All.* Cambridge: Cambridge University Press.

King, Brayden G. (2008a). "A Social Movement Perspective of the Stakeholder Collective Action and Influence," *Business and Society.* 47: 21–49.

King, Brayden G. (2008b). "A Political Mediation Model of Corporate Response to Social Movement Activism," *Administrative Science Quarterly*. 53: 395–421.

King, Brayden G. (2011). "The Tactical Disruptiveness of Social Movements: Sources of Market and Mediated Disruption in Corporate Boycotts," *Social Problems*. 58(4): 491–517.

King, Brayden G. and McDonnell, Mary-Hunter (2015). "Good Firms, Good Targets: The Relationship between Corporate Social Responsibility, Reputation, and Activist Targeting." In *Corporate Social Responsibility in a Globalizing World: Toward Effective Global CSR Frameworks*, edited by K. Tsutsui and A. Lim, 393–429. Cambridge: Cambridge University Press.

King, Brayden G. and Pearce, Nicholas A. (2010). "The Contentiousness of Markets: Politics, Social Movements, and Institutional Change in Markets," *Annual Review of Sociology*. 36: 249–267.

King, Brayden G. and Soule, Sarah A. (2007). "Social Movements as Extra-institutional Entrepreneurs: The Effect of Protests on Stock Price Returns," *Administrative Science Quarterly*. 52: 413–442.

Koos, Sebastian (2012). "What Drives Political Consumption in Europe? A Multi-level Analysis on Individual Characteristics, Opportunity Structures and Globalization," *Acta Sociologica*. 55: 37–57.

Kristofferson, Kirk, White, Katherine, and Peloza, John (2014). "The Nature of Slacktivism: How the Social Observability of an Initial Act of Token Support Affects Subsequent Prosocial Action," *Journal of Consumer Research*. 40(6): 1149–1165.

Lee, Caroline W. (2010). "The Roots of Astroturfing," *Contexts*. 9: 73–75.

Lee, Caroline W. and Romano, Zachary (2013). "Democracy's New Discipline: Public Deliberation as Organizational Strategy," *Organization Studies*. 34(5–6): 733–753.

Lenox, Michael J. and Eesley, Charles E. (2009). "Private Environmental Activism and the Selection and Response of Firm Targets," *Journal of Economics & Management Strategy*. 18: 45–73.

Lounsbury, Michael, Ventresca, Marc, and Hirsch, Paul M. (2003). "Social Movements, Field Frames and Industry Emergence: A Cultural–Political Perspective on US Recycling," *Socioeconomic Review*. 1(1): 71–104.

McAteer, Emily and Pulver, Simone (2009). "The Corporate Boomerang: Shareholder Transnational Advocacy Networks Targeting Oil Companies in the Ecuadorian Amazon," *Global Environmental Politics*. 9(1): 1–30.

McDonnell, Mary-Hunter and King, Brayden (2013). "Keeping up Appearances Reputational Threat and Impression Management after Social Movement Boycotts," *Administrative Science Quarterly*. 58(3): 387–419.

Micheletti, Michele and Stolle, Dietlind (2008). "Fashioning Social Justice Through Political Consumerism, Capitalism, and the Internet," *Cultural Studies*. 22(5): 749–769.

Model, Jacob, Soule, Sarah A., and King, Brayden G. (2014). "Shareholder Activism in the US: A Processual Approach." Unpublished Paper.

Raeburn, Nicole (2004). *Lesbian and Gay Workplace Rights: Changing Corporate America from inside Out*. Minneapolis, MN: University of Minnesota Press.

Rao, Hayagreeva, Yue, Lori Q., and Ingram, Paul. (2011). "Laws of Attraction: Regulatory Arbitrage in the Face of Activism in Right-to-Work States," *American Sociological Review*. 76(3): 365–385.

Rojas, Miguel, M'Zali, Bouchra, Turcotte, Marie-France, and Merrigan, Philip (2012). "Characteristics of Companies Targeted by Social Proxies: An Empirical Analysis in the Context of the United States," *Business and Society Review*. 117(4): 515–534.

Schurman, Rachel (2004). "Fighting "Frankenfoods": Industry Opportunity Structures and the Efficacy of the Anti-biotech Movement in Western Europe," *Social Problems*. 51: 243–268. au

Sikavica, Katarina and Pozner, Jo-Ellen (2013). "Paradise Sold: Resource Partitioning and the Organic Movement in the US Farming Industry," *Organization Studies*. 34: 623–651.

SEC (2004). "Staff Legal Bulletin No. 14B." Retrieved from www.sec.gov/interps/legal/cfslb14b. htm, accessed March 18, 2014.

Soule, Sarah A. (2009). *Contentious and Private Politics and Corporate Social Responsibility*. Cambridge: Cambridge University Press.

Soule, Sarah A. (2012a). "Social Movements and Markets, Industries, and Firms," *Organization Studies*. 33: 1715–1733.

Soule, Sarah A. (2012b). "Targeting Organizations: Private and Contentious Politics," *Research in the Sociology of Organizations*. 34: 261–285.

Soule, Sarah A. and King, Brayden G. (2008). "Competition and Resource Partitioning in three Social Movement Industries," *American Journal of Sociology*. 113: 1568–1610.

Tarrow, Sidney G. (1998). *Power In Movement*. Cambridge: Cambridge University Press.

Tkac, Paula. (2006). "One Proxy at a Time: Pursuing Social Change Through Shareholder Proposals," *Economic Review-Federal Reserve Bank of Atlanta*. 91: 1.

Vasi, Ion Bogdan and King, Brayden G. (2012). "Social Movements, Risk Perceptions, and Economic Outcomes," *American Sociological Review*. 77: 573–596.

Vogel, David (1986). *National Styles of Regulation: Environmental Policy in Great Britain and the United States*. Ithaca, NY: Cornell University Press.

Vogel, David (2005). *The Market for Virtue*. Washington, DC: The Brookings Institution.

Vogus, Timothy J. and Davis, Gerald F. (2005). "Elite Mobilizations for Antitakeover Legislation, 1982–1990." In *Social movements and organization theory*, edited by G. F. Davis, D. McAdam, W. R. Scott, and M. N. Zald, 96–121. Cambridge: Cambridge University Press.

Walker, Edward T. (2014). *Grassroots for Hire: Public Affairs Consultants in American Democracy*. Cambridge: Cambridge University Press.

Walker, Edward T. and Rea, Christopher M. (2014). "The Political Mobilization of Firms and Industries," *Annual Review of Sociology*, 40: 281–304.

Zald, Mayer N. (1970). *Power in Organizations*. Nashville, TN: Vanderbilt University Press.

PART VIII

MOVEMENTS' CONTRIBUTIONS TO SOCIAL AND POLITICAL CHANGE

....

CHAPTER 47

WELFARE CHANGES AND SOCIAL MOVEMENTS

....

COLIN BARKER AND MICHAEL LAVALETTE

WHAT is the relationship between social movements and welfare systems and forms of welfare delivery? The question is deceptively simple. There is a history of movement struggles over provision of housing, monetary or "welfare" benefits, education and health and all manner of social and public policies and services. Yet the relationship between movement activity and welfare change is not straightforward. This is partly due to the vastly different ways of conceptualizing "welfare" under capitalism and the range of interests that shape "welfare settlements" (including movements, political parties, individual and collective units of capital, pressure groups, state bureaucracies, and governments). Here, we attempt to pick our way through this maze and offer an analysis of welfare, welfare changes, and social movement activity.

CAPITALISM AND WELFARE REGIMES

Within capitalism, most people meet their material needs through the wages system. By itself, however, this system has serious deficiencies. Sections of the potential labor force suffer unemployment and under-employment. Children, old people, the sick and disabled, for example, are often excluded from wage-work. The wages system does not automatically provide the educated and relatively healthy workforce capital needs. Urbanization and market-dependence generate additional problems of housing, public health, food safety, etc.

In short, capitalism not only entails continuous "commodification," and especially the commodification of labor power, but also requires measures of "de-commodification," that is, of regulation and socio-economic provision on "non-market" principles. The resolution of that contradiction—deciding what measures, how extensive and how organized—remains an open question, determined by *politics*. Here different interests clash, define alternative projects, make claims and counter-claims, assert opposed "rights." Many agencies combine to contest the nature of extra-market regulation and material provision: parties, states, different capitalist interests, and of course *social movements*. All attempt to elaborate all manner of arguments, to mobilize support and to exert pressure. The underlying class struggle that marks the capitalist system finds expression in the clash of movements and other forces (Barker 2013).

The idea of "welfare regimes" was developed by Esping-Andersen (1990). Among OECD countries, he discerned three "ideal-type" regimes: "social-democratic," "corporatist," and "liberal." Around these three ideal-types are "clusters" of countries: the Scandinavian countries broadly represented the first type, Germany, Italy, and France, for example, the second, and the United States, Canada, and Australia the third. The three types were classified in terms of the "de-commodification" of welfare services. The central principle of the social-democratic type is "universalism," where benefits and services are based simply on citizenship, with limited means-testing of applicants. The corporatist type rests on the social insurance principle, with benefits tied to contributions. In the liberal type, where the market is predominant, most citizens rely on private and corporate provision while a residual minority receives state provision on a means-tested basis.

None of Esping-Andersen's types involve *complete* de-commodification. He focusses on monetary provisions—pensions, sickness, and unemployment benefits—but says little about education and health services, factory legislation, housing, minimum wage laws or environmental safety. Any of these might in principle be explored as sources of variation, not least in "de-commodification." Further, his typology is limited to OECD countries, or "rich democracies." In many regimes in the global South, post-war authoritarian regimes sought hegemony by welfare measures like subsidized food and fuel prices, some measures of land reform, etc.

The way states meet popular needs shapes their relationship with beneficiaries. "Universalism" requires less bureaucratic investigation in and interference with the lives of the needy than do systems where welfare assistance is limited to those "most in need" (Rothstein 1998). "Liberalism" in welfare regimes has an authoritarian aspect. In Britain, where "universalism" applies in some settings (e.g., the National Health Service) but not others (e.g., unemployment benefits), people's transactions with state institutions are markedly different in each sphere.

In practice, welfare systems involve different combinations of provision.

First, states are uniquely placed to offer solutions to welfare problems, given their particular non-market power of taxation and fiscal redistribution. One characteristic of modern states is the growth of what has been termed their "infrastructural" power (Mann 1984), that is their capacity to "penetrate civil society" and to implement political decisions throughout their realms. The growth of states' capacities to "intervene" in the organization of civil society depends on their ability to gather and process knowledge about their own subjects, and to develop bureaucratic machineries able to follow centrally determined distinctions and procedures. This growth of infrastructural capacity underlies the unstable amalgam of "coercion" and "hegemony" that, for Gramsci (1971), characterizes modern states.

Second, modern states develop in an overall capitalist setting. As Esping-Andersen notes, "we cannot grasp the welfare state without locating its activities in relation to the private sector" (1990: 4, 103). The private capitalist sector itself often plays a significant direct part in welfare systems, whether through private insurance, pensions, health facilities, housing, and the like, or through the wage supplements which provide various "benefits" to employees, sometimes through collective bargaining with trade unions. "Liberal" regimes involve a greater predominance of private and corporate capitalist provision, as for example with the "for-profit" hospital systems in the United States.

Third, at different junctures "charities" and NGOs have supplied significant inputs into welfare provision. These range from individual charitable donations to food banks and social housing schemes.

Fourth, families account for much direct provision of care of children, the sick, the disabled, and the aged, with many of the burdens falling on the shoulders of women.

Finally, in different periods, movements have themselves attempted a variety of forms of collective self-provision, aiming to provide democratic and self-organized forms of welfare free from both state or charitable "interference" and market principles.

The character of a welfare regime has consequences for class stratification. For example, different welfare regimes are linked to different levels of inequality and poverty (Wilkinson and Pickett 2010). After the application of state welfare measures, for instance, the relative poverty rates in Sweden and Norway were 4.8 per cent and 4.0 per cent respectively; but in the United Kingdom and the United States they were 8.2 per cent and 15.1 per cent (Moller et al. 2003).

This is especially so if we do not limit "welfare" to aid only to the poor. Some states spend enormous sums on fiscal welfare in the form of tax privileges to private insurance plans, private education, and the like that mainly benefit the middle classes. As these tax "reliefs" do not show up on expenditure accounts, they are often ignored (Titmuss 1958). Taking "tax breaks" and other kinds of "fiscal welfare" into account sharpens the effects on class stratification. In any case, a key function of states within the capitalist order is precisely to assist capitalist concerns with all manner of both fiscal and direct aid. Forgetting these matters permits a very lop-sided account of "welfare regimes."

Given the actual complexity of "welfare" provision within capitalist states, questions about the relationship of social movements to welfare changes become quite difficult. "The principal difficulty is how to establish a causal relationship between a series of events that we can reasonably classify as social movement actions and an observed change in society, be it minor or fundamental, durable or temporary" (Guigni 1998).

Saville (1983: 11) suggested that three kinds of factors interact to produce different welfare systems: (1) the economic and social requirements of an increasingly complex globalized capitalism; (2) the political calculations of national ruling groups; and (3) the pressures arising from the mass of the population as their own perceptions of economic and social needs have widened. As the role of social movements in the post-colonial states of the global South has become more prominent, a broader analysis might suggest add a further factor to this list: (4) the place of each state in the international division of labor and power.

There seems to be no necessary direct association between the establishment of parliamentary democracy and the formation of "welfare states": modern "welfare state" measures were first introduced in nations without parliamentary democracy, while they were passed rather late in states where democracy arrived early. In essence, authoritarian states were freer to pass laws enforcing the necessary revenues than were states where the vote was the property of a mass of small farmers and artisans and business people who resisted state taxation (Esping-Andersen 1990: 15–16).

Sometimes, the *threat* of popular movements induced elites to introduce welfare regime changes. In Britain, the "Captain Swing" movement of 1830, when farm laborers across the south of England set fire to hayricks and attacked poor law overseers, provided a key motive in the state's determination to "reform" the administration of poverty (Hobsbawm and Rude 1973). Later in the century, in Bismarck's Germany social insurance policies were explicitly intended to counter the growth of popular movements, notably the expanding social democratic parties.

Some important differences in welfare settlements, as between different countries, are due to the different ways in which popular movements evolved. Until late in the nineteenth century, it seemed that workers' movements in Western Europe and the United States were moving in broadly parallel directions (Katznelson and Zolberg 1986). From the 1880s, however, these movements took divergent paths. European union organization began broadening out from skilled artisans to less skilled workers, serious beginnings were made toward forming national social democratic parties, and reforming governments introduced national social insurance schemes and other "welfare state" measures. In the United States, by contrast, the defeat of the Knights of Labor set any such projects backwards (Voss 1994). Thereafter, the predominant stress in militant labor struggles in the United States was "syndicalism, pure and simple" (Kimeldorf 1999); no independent workers' party succeeded in claiming the mass allegiance of American workers, and it was not until the 1930s that serious beginnings were made in the construction of any kind of federal "welfare state."

Katznelson reflects on the heritage. Deploying Gramsci's metaphor of First World War battlefields, he argues that national patterns of the "trenches" of workplaces, streets, and "normal" political channels provide bases for different kinds of anti-systemic resistance. The configuration of these trenches "defines the terrain of battle and thus imparts a logic to the war itself" (Katznelson 1982: 19). Each country possesses a unique configuration of sites of struggle, and this shapes its special history of class and politics—and of social movements. Distinguishing between work and community-based conflicts, he concludes that what characterizes the United States has been that the links between them "have been unusually tenuous.... Each kind of conflict has had its own separate vocabulary and set of institutions.... Class, in short, has been lived and fought as a series of partial relationships, and it has therefore been experienced and talked about as only one of a number of competing bases of social life."

This experience helps to account for the relative weakness of radical politics in America (Katznelson 1982: 19).

This experience also helps to explain the dominance of America's "liberal" welfare regime: workers in strong unions can bargain with their employers for quite generous corporate welfare schemes that provide pensions and health insurance, but weaker sections of the workforce and the unemployed have, at best, to rely on means-tested benefits.

CHANGES IN WELFARE SYSTEMS AND THE ROLE OF SOCIAL MOVEMENTS

Welfare changes occur discontinuously. While any regime is subject to small accretions of change in detail, there are also periods of more or less large "transformation" when whole welfare systems are re-configured. New "welfare settlements" are established, or—in Gramscian terms—new "truce lines" are drawn (Lavalette and Penketh 2003; Cox and Nilsen 2014).

Institutional reform occurs in bursts. Every so often, Lockwood (1992) argues, society must adjust its "status order" to the shifting realities of its "class system." Movements from below compel elites to re-negotiate the meaning of rights and citizenship (Scott 1990). However, this leaves unresolved just how "permanent" changes in welfare regimes are. Writers in the optimistic climate of the "long boom" saw welfare reforms as long-lasting (Heclo 1971; Marshall 1992); later critics suggested that popular advances made in periods of struggle were later subjected to "clawback" by elites (Piven and Cloward 1977).

The circumstances of periods of regime transformation are quite various. They include the aftermath of wars, economic crises, popular insurgency, state building in the aftermath of de-colonization, state-led development in Latin America. Out of the turmoil of economic crises can emerge both "regressive" and more "progressive" transformations: the 1930s produced Nazi Germany, but also the United States. Most recently, neoliberalism's advance has generated further reconstructions of state–society relations.

We can't, it seems, discuss movement impacts on welfare outside their active relationships with political forces like states, parties, lobbies, countermovements, along with the world contexts in which they occur. Movements struggle within and with welfare systems, variously rising to challenge existing arrangements, contributing to changing them, defending existing provisions against attack, or seeking to implant their own direct means of solving welfare problems. But they do so discontinuously. Much of the time, actual and potential recipients of state and corporate welfare do not engage in collective protest (Piven and Cloward 1977). Their relative "passivity" is due less to any positive belief in existing arrangements than to "informed fatalism" (Bagguley 1996).

Those who *might* protest may be "confused" by contradictory interventions into their existence, or be so subjected to repressive humiliation by the everyday functioning of welfare systems that the risks and difficulties of collective organization and action seem overwhelming (Auyero and Swistun 2009; Auyero 2012). Yet popular passivity is always conditional and potentially open to unexpected reversals, if new threats or opportunities arise.

"Welfare systems" certainly offer many grounds for recipients' dissatisfaction, and engender irregular popular mobilization. Protestors may resist a specific injustice: refusal of a benefit, bullying administrators, or a family's eviction from rented housing. Like the Unemployed Workers Movements of the 1930s, they may demand higher benefits. Or they may seek greater control over the activities of welfare personnel, like the multiple campaigns over health provision launched by women's organizations, and disability and anti-racist campaigners from the 1970s.

In authoritarian states, battles for democratization are not disconnected from struggles over welfare. Nineteenth-century Chartism was after all not only a political but a "knife and fork question." Demands for female suffrage were rarely about abstract "rights" alone. Underlying the wave of democratization across the global South from the 1980s was growing resistance to the impact of neoliberalism on popular living standards.

Movements vary in their solutions to the "social problems" they confront. Tilly suggests that, in general, social movements come close to being mass lobbies, centered on *indirect* forms of action. They deploy

> ... actions that display will and capacity, but that would not in themselves accomplish the objectives on behalf of which they make claims. Social movements call instead for powerholders to take the crucial actions.... (T)hey organize around the demand that powerholders recognize, protect, endorse, forward, or even impose a given program. (Tilly 1994: 7)

This discounts the possibility that movements may attempt to develop means to enforce their own conceptions of welfare. Or, more precisely, *sections* of movements may. For, since movements are not coherent organizations with defined memberships, but rather take the form of "networks" drawn from multiple groupings, they mostly lack unified views about such matters. What they should seek to achieve, and how, is regularly *disputed* within movements.

Challenges to the everyday functioning of existing welfare regimes can draw on a quite wide-ranging repertoire of contention, ranging from conventional "lobbying" of influential persons and institutions, through public meetings and street demonstrations to occupations of facilities, blockading of ports, roads and railways, and other forms of "civil disobedience."

Mostly, such movement activities are quite small-scale in their scope of mobilization. Movements that contribute to significant changes in welfare *systems*, on the other hand, are commonly wider in the scope of their mobilization, more differentiated in their aims and participants, and sometimes approach the phenomena that Tarrow (1994) and others have identified as "protest waves" or "cycles of protest," historical periods when the *possibility* of large-scale historical transformation appears to enlarge.

The phenomenon of the "protest wave" has been revealed in studies of trade union strikes, demonstrations, and the like (Shorter and Tilly 1974; Haynes 1985). The fundamental pattern is of "an increasing then declining magnitude in the use of disruptive direct action" (Tarrow 1983: 27), and an expansion in the numbers of people involved via "diffusion" and "escalation" processes that draw different social layers into overt collective activity (Tarrow 1994). General protest waves tend to "spill over" from one social sector to others, with "reciprocal action" (Luxemburg 1986) between them. Those already prone to collective action become more active and organized, while the normally less active begin to participate.

Some accounts of "waves" assume a too-simple curve of development, passing from an initiating stage to a peak, followed by an inevitable winding down toward final dissipation. But their progress is probably better conceptualized as a complex series of "climaxes," each representing a potential fork in the path of movement development. At a particular climax, events may occur and decisions be taken whose effect is, indeed, to begin to wind a movement down. Various mechanisms of containment may come into effective play to limit further expansion and development (Sewell 1996). However, each climax, as a moment of significant conflict and decision, is inherently open-ended, with more than one possible outcome. "Containment"—whether by repression or co-optation—doesn't always work.

Protest waves involve quite dynamic re-orderings of popular experience, all relevant to questions concerning "welfare." Insofar as they mobilize formerly "passive" layers of the population, they start to alter the social relations, ideas, identities, and aspirations of those newly involved. They are significant too as periods when innovation in "contentious repertoires" occurs: they are "the crucibles within which the repertoire of collective action expands" (Tarrow 1989: 20). Protest waves often involve the development of new organizational forms, as well as challenges to existing organizations, from parties and unions to movement bodies. Some innovations arise from the direct experience of collective action, like soup kitchens in strikes or self-organized "security" during occupations of workplaces or public squares. People's sense of who they are and *might* be begins to be challenged, along with conceptions of "welfare." The sense of relative powerlessness which infects the politics of everyday life can be transmuted, quite quickly, into a more active and cheerful apprehension of new horizons of possibility. Protest waves adjust angles of vision, shifts patterns of deference, alter the balance of fear and confidence.

If any movement pattern is likely to alter a whole welfare system, it is this kind of protest wave. However, not every protest wave does achieve this, or achieve it for long. The simple scale of a protest wave does not determine its material effectiveness. The "May events," though they won a rise in the minimum wage, left no lasting mark on France's welfare system. Nor did Solidarity in Poland, despite compelling the regime, briefly, to promise improvements in the food supply, pensions, the health service, nursery care, and housing (Barker 1986).

Questions of *timing* may determine which welfare settlements possess lasting power. Both Sweden's and America's 1930s welfare settlements displayed considerable longevity, along with Britain's NHS. President Johnson's "Great Society" programs, however, were rapidly pulled back. "What came next" in the larger economic and institutional context seems to matter. Sweden recovered rapidly from a slump, avoided direct entanglement in the World War, then joined the United States and United Kingdom in the long post-war boom—a period when, globally, states' involvement in economic management expanded. However, the 1960s reforms in the United States were rapidly succeeded by urban fiscal crises and the onset of neoliberalism.

Most welfare studies focus attention on *state* provision, and less on movements' efforts to provide popular welfare through their own activities. "Welfare from below" has been attempted especially in two conditions: first, where states simply fail to provide, or their provision was too demeaning; second, at the peak of protest waves.

Movement bodies like Friendly Societies, burial clubs, and self-funded schools developed in nineteenth-century Britain, when state provision was almost non-existent or highly punitive in form. In practice, they often excluded less well-organized and less skilled workers and their families. These bodies commonly failed to survive sudden runs on their funds occasioned by widespread unemployment, or major strikes. In contemporary Palestine, with no state aid available, activists struggle to establish "home-made" social services to help deal with traumatized individuals and families (Jones and Lavalette 2011, 2013).

Examples of collective self-help can be found in the welfare activities carried out by the German SPD prior to the First World War, and behind republican lines during the Spanish Civil War. In the post-war world, efforts at welfare from below have recurred, notably during protest waves. Practical experiments in collective self-help emerged as an alternative to bureaucratic state forms of welfare delivery. In the late 1960s in Italy,

> [i]t was in civil society... that radical alternatives spread most rapidly: "red" markets, kindergartens, restaurants, surgeries, social clubs, etc. opened (and often shut) one after another. Their aim was to organise social life along quite different lines. (Ginsborg 1990: 323)

In the same period the Black Panther Party set out to provide programs of "survival pending revolution" to America's urban ghettoes. These included "free breakfast programs for school children and food aid for families; schools, adult education, and childcare; medical care, medical research, and clothing; free plumbing, home maintenance, and pest control; and protective escort for the elderly and ambulance services; cooperative housing; employment assistance; free shoes" (Pope and Flanigan 2013). In the aftermath of the *Argentinazo* of 2001, workers attempted to run numbers of abandoned factories under their own control. In South Africa's townships, activists illegally reconnect electricity to cut-off homes. In 2012, former "Occupy" activists in New York provided relief to neighborhoods smashed up by Hurricane Sandy, when state responses proved inadequate.

Such experiments in democratic welfare organization involve efforts to re-make welfare systems under principles different from bureaucratic state or market-based schemes. It is, as Zolberg (1972) notes, especially during protest waves that such ideas, previously the property of small minorities, have the possibility to become more widespread. The fate of most is to be repressed, or—like Britain's Friendly Societies (Yeo 1980)—colonized by states and markets. They nonetheless constitute part of the history of welfare change, always liable to re-emerge during popular insurgency.

The Post-war World

There were two periods in the post-war decades when the relationship between welfare and social movements was rather differently posed. The first was the "long boom" after 1945, and the second the period of "neoliberalism" initiated by the crisis of the early 1970s. The transition between them was marked by a broad protest wave in which movements opened up new questions about welfare. Neoliberalism has witnessed an extensive re-making of welfare systems, confronting movements with new problems.

State involvement was central to the different governing doctrines in most states following the Second World War, whether as "Keynesian," "communism" or "state-developmentalism." Crouch's judgment on the post-1945 British state could be generalized: there was "a belief in the capacity of the state to do public good, but also of its almost Jacobin lack of a need to consult with or embed itself within the wider population" (Crouch 2001: 114).

Corporate and state capital alike flourished in the longest boom in capitalist history. Living standards rose across much of the globe. Social movement challenges to welfare regimes were at best weak. Across the West, "The welfare state... served as the major peace formula of advanced capitalist democracies" (Offe 1984: 147). Across Western capitalism, there was some small redistribution of income toward the working class, but the degree of "de-commodification" achieved was small. Across the global South "state-led development" policies were predominant, largely under authoritarian regimes which encompassed a variety of state-organized "welfare" measures, including price controls on food, housing, and public transport, expanded health and education services, social security, and public health programs.

Leading figures in West European social democratic parties (Crosland 1956) concluded that Keynesian welfare state policies had solved capitalism's economic problems, leading their parties to abandonment of even rhetorical commitment to socialist transformation. After all, the major conservative parties shared the same broad commitments. If the German SPD led the way, others followed.

The boom also changed the composition of the workforce. State-promoted higher education expanded student numbers enormously. Millions of women were drawn into richer countries' labor markets, along with migrants from less industrialized regions and countries. The new workers met with various forms of gender and racial discrimination.

The post-war welfare settlements had developed on the explicit assumption that married women would be dependent on male wage earners, and that women were the appropriate providers of care and welfare services (Wilson 1977). Immigrant workers faced discrimination in access to better-paid jobs, housing, and access to social services (Jacobs 1985); "Keynesian welfare states" were shaped by strong gender and racist biases (Bakshi et al. 1995). In the ghettoes of US cities, unemployment among Blacks "reached depression levels" (Piven and Cloward 1977: 12), fuelling insurgency in the 1960s.

Out of the political militancy of the protest wave of the 1960s came new kinds of demands on welfare systems. Some were strong economic demands. In US cities, "poor people's movements" targeted the welfare system, with some impressive results: between 1960 and 1972 the numbers of families winning Aid to Families with Dependent Children quadrupled, and payments grew six times. Applicants' chances of success also increased as they became more demanding, putting pressure on relief officers to employ "their discretion more permissively" (Piven and Cloward 1977: 264–275).

Others targeted the bureaucratic, masculinist, and top-down organizational assumptions of state organizations, from universities to the health services. Campaigners fought for abortion rights, disability rights, nursery provision, domestic violence refuges, and gay and lesbian rights. They opposed racism in welfare institutions, and demanded that medical institutions allow women more control over their bodies and their treatments. Feminism, anti-racism, revolutionary socialism, and anarchism all contributed impulses (Ferguson et al. 2006). There was a cross-fertilization between movements: thus mental health campaigners drew on the rhetoric and practices of both liberation and rank-and-file workers' movements (Crossley 1999; Slorach 2014). Workforce changes facilitated these movements. Public sector white-collar workers unionized in large numbers in response to a "proletarianization" of their condition, providing sympathetic encouragement. Many were women, radicalized by second-wave feminism.

These "post-sixties" movements won some significant gains. Anti-racist movements backed by unions successfully opened up recruitment in welfare institutions and local governments (where they had more potential purchase) to Black and Asian workers (Virdee 2010), as well as challenging broader societal racism (Farrar 2004). The hierarchical and masculinist ethos of medical practice was widely undermined. In America, gay and lesbian activists moved from protesting against official indifference to the HIV–AIDS plague to directly demanding involvement with drug companies' research into treatments, forcing open the secretive world of the Federal Drug Administration (Shephard and Hayduk 2002).

Neoliberalism and Crisis

From the 1970s, world capitalism entered a new phase, "neoliberalism." The 1973 crisis found states no longer able to apply "Keynesian" remedies. Inflation, unemployment, fiscal crises, and slower growth demanded new policies, in an environment where capital demanded freer mobility and cuts in taxation, compelling states to compete in new ways for investment (Gerstenberger 2013). The inherited framework of welfare systems was challenged.

Neoliberalism was not introduced at one fell swoop across the globe. Among the leading capitalist democracies, politicians in the United States and United Kingdom played the part of "vanguards" (Davidson 2013), leading where other states followed more slowly. In both America and Britain, governments set out to break major strikes. As well as attacking union power head-on, the Reagan administration nearly halved corporate taxes between 1980 and 1983 (Esping-Andersen 181). America led the world in establishing a "Great U-turn" in inequality, which widened sharply as neoliberalism took hold (Moller et al. 2003: 25): industrial productivity continued to rise, but real wages stagnated and, for many workers, fell in real terms, while executive remuneration soared.

From the beginning, neoliberal measures meant attacks on welfare provision and the workforces that provide it. In New York, an acute fiscal crisis in 1975 saw financiers take charge of the city budget: benefit levels were cut, and "two-fifths of the blacks on the city's work force (and half of the Hispanics) were fired at the same time as recession-induced unemployment reached near-depression levels" (Piven and Cloward 1977: 357). In 1976, the IMF instructed the British Labour government to slash its welfare program as a condition for loans—a forerunner of the "Structural Adjustment Policies" (SAPs) it imposed on numerous regimes in the global South as sovereign debt levels sky-rocketed.

If at first neoliberal policies seemed to be the property of the Right, liberal and social democratic parties eventually fell in behind. Even in "social democratic" Sweden, large parts of the welfare state were privatized (Bott 2014). In Britain, Labour governments promoted "private finance initiatives" that burdened the education and health sectors with long-term repayments to finance capital, often with extraordinarily high profit returns. In the name of "market reform" the much-cherished National Health Service became a "brand" umbrella under which a web of public and private agencies compete (Pollock 2005). Neoliberalization of "left" parties was not limited to Europe. In South Africa, within two years of the fall of Apartheid, the ANC government adopted neoliberal economic policies. So later did Brazil's Workers' Party, and the MAS government in Bolivia (Amann and Baer 2002; Webber 2011; Bond et al. 2013).

Initially, some of the strongest popular resistance to the introduction of neoliberal policies came in the global South, where SAPs were imposed. The IMF demanded heavy cuts in welfare spending, food and fuel subsidies, and the opening of economies to private and especially foreign investment. Resistance's first shape was "food riots": Walton and Seddon (1994: 39–40) counted 146 of these between 1976 and 1992. This period was also one marked by a wave of "democratic transitions" that reshaped political regimes across much of Latin America, sub-Saharan Africa, and Asia, as the earlier state-developmentalist systems in less developed countries broke down. By the late 1990s and early 2000s, "nearly two-thirds of the world could be considered nominally democratic… including West Africa and Latin America" (Almeida 2010: 313; Barker 2012).

At first, the advent of democracy in the global South produced some short-term decline in movement activity. However, the new neoliberal regimes generated a second wave of popular contention—now focussed on predominantly economic questions, including "welfare" issues. In what Almeida (2007, 2014) terms "defensive mobilization," public sector workers, students, indigenous communities, and others combined in new ways to oppose cutbacks in welfare provision, privatizations of public facilities, and the subordination of everyday need to the "dictatorship of the debt." The advent of democracy increased the potential for protest, for it permitted the legalization of unions, space for civic organizations like South Africa's Anti-Privatisation Forum, for NGO activity and for oppositional parties (Almeida 2010).

Capital's increasingly rapid "globalization" began to translate itself into a globalization of movement impulses, many flowing from the less- to the more-developed world. From the later 1990s, *general* questions about welfare within neoliberalism began to re-emerge in movements within developed countries, both before and after the protests at the WTO meetings in Seattle in November 1999. New slogans generalized: "Another world is possible," "Our world is not for sale." The "Global Justice Movement" ("GJM") began to counterpose alternative conceptions of popular welfare *against* the priorities of the IMF, WTO, etc. However, the generalization of resistance was made more difficult by two inter-related processes.

First, in a whole series of major states, trade union strength was seriously weakened. In some cases, as in the United States, Italy, and Britain, major industrial battles had been fought and lost in the 1980s. There were major workforce reductions in formerly core industries, and while new forms of employment developed to take up much of the slack, unions were largely unsuccessful in organizing these. Outside Austria and Scandinavia, the proportion of the workforce in unions dropped markedly. At the same time, indices of unemployment and part-time and casual employment rose, especially among younger workers. The movement scene as a whole has thus altered quite dramatically.

Second, across much of Europe, previously "social democratic" parties had themselves become proponents of neoliberal assumptions. The first development weakened the biggest source of resistance to practical neoliberalism, with the unions retreating to "new realist" policies. The second deprived welfare movements of previously important allies within both national and local governments. Not only "social democratic" welfare regimes were undermined by neoliberalism. In the United States, the trade union strategy of winning "fringe benefits" in bargaining with large companies lost headway, as employers ceased to accommodate unions, whose membership bases shrank remarkably (Moody 2014).

If the first post-war world economic crisis in 1973 signaled the beginnings of neoliberalism, the second, from 2008, was both a crisis in neoliberalism itself and a further revelation of its nature. Governments responded to the financial system's threatened collapse with history's largest ever welfare handout, spending at least $20 trillion shoring up banks and corporations that were "too big to fail" (McNally 2013: 2). This generated a massive rise in sovereign debt—reaching toward levels previously associated with world wars (Konzelmann 2014: 704)—which was then off-loaded onto the backs of workers, as the core of the capitalist world entered "the age of austerity." Wage levels and pension entitlements have been cut, privatization of core parts of former welfare states has speeded up. Inequalities continued to grow. SAPs, formerly the fate of "Third World" states, were now imposed on European countries like Greece, Spain, and Ireland. States not subject to these strictures nonetheless acted similarly to *prevent* such outturns, generating the "competitive austerity" policies that now dominate governments across Europe. What official responses to the crisis revealed, more sharply than ever, is that neoliberalism is not, first and foremost, an economic doctrine about market freedom, but an ongoing class assault to reduce labor rewards (whether by wages or by "state welfare") in the interests of restoring profitability (Harvey 2005; Harman 2009).

Although there are elements of continuity with the earlier "GJM," movement responses to the crisis have, to date, been more nationally focussed. The imposition of unprecedently large cuts in state welfare provision, in conjunction with other "neoliberal" policy responses, has set off a wave of sometimes spectacular movement responses, including large general strikes, occupations of public squares, demonstrations against all manner of cuts, movements defending people from house evictions, etc. These have often involved a high level of political generalization. All the significant movements of the past few years have, in one manner or another, focussed on "welfare" issues.

In some cases, public anger at social democratic parties' backing for neoliberal policies has produced major upsets in existing party attachments, with voters shifting both to right and left. There is widespread evidence of disaffection from "official politics." To date, movements have claimed only a few government scalps: Iceland's 2010 "saucepan revolution" brought down the government, as did the Quebec student movement of 2012.

The crisis poses new problems for social movements. One whole wing of the "social movement as a whole" has been weakened seriously by forty years of neoliberalism. It is not just that union membership, especially in the private sector, has shrunk, or that unions have not penetrated many new areas of employment, leaving many young workers outside their ranks. Day-to-day resistance to increasingly assertive managements in workplaces—a powerful root of everyday "union consciousness"—has declined. On the other hand, new kinds of social movement bodies and activities have arisen and developed, drawing on relatively new sources of energy. In Europe and North America, they include the precarious workers and the "graduates with no future" that Mason (2013) identified as playing new roles in current movements. Across Latin America and the global South, indigenous communities and informal urban workers have participated in new ways in revolts.

Taken separately, none of these social forces possesses the capacity to mount a sufficient challenge to neoliberalism's global assault on general welfare. Analyzing South Africa, in some ways "the protest capital of the world," Alexander and Pfaffe (2014) point to two parallel movements of resistance, each the product of a distinct layer of the black working class: a high level of strikes by employed and unionized workers, and an equally widespread level of township revolts, involving most unemployed and semi-employed youth. In the struggle against Apartheid, there was a reciprocal division of labor between unions and townships, but today a "hinge" has opened, with little cross-fertilization and sometimes open tension between them. They point to small signs that these divisions might be overcome, and thus the "possibility, though only a possibility, that the hinge will close."

Across the global South, public sector unions have been central in many protests over privatization, pay and welfare cuts, etc. As in the North, their power has been reduced by a whole series of defeats, but there are, nonetheless, suggestions that movement success may be possible against neoliberal policies to the degree that wider coalitions by multiple social sectors develop, using innovative tactics (McNally 2013). Developments of this kind, though imply major reorientations of unions, challenges to the conservatism of many of their leaderships, and the loosening of union attachments to neoliberalized parties—whether South Africa's ANC, Brazil's Workers Party or Bolivia's MAS.

Are there also such "open hinges" in the North? The movements that created "M-15" in Spain or "Occupy" across America in 2011 had tangential, often tense, relationships with unions. Drawing on repertoires that emerged within the post-1960s movements and the "GJM," they relied on more "horizontalist" forms of organizing. The Spanish "Indignados," rejecting the main union federations' acceptance of a cut in pensions, initially refused to allow union banners and stalls during their occupations of city squares in 2011. Subsequently, however, their activists collaborated with more radical parts of the trade unions in a series of movements—the *mareas* (tides)—that took up and generalized M-15's slogans and some of their organizing practices (Martinez and Domingo 2014).

Without a strengthening and renewal of union organization and workplace resistance, the "movements of the squares" can only make limited progress. Without some of their energies and imagination, union decline will continue. If the hinge can be closed, then the kinds of movements that brought down Apartheid and ended many dictatorships in the global South may yet succeed in pushing back neoliberalism's assaults on welfare, perhaps even opening the way to new kinds of welfare systems.

References

Alexander, Peter and Pfaffe, Peter (2014). "Social Relationships to the Means and Ends of Protest in South Africa's Ongoing Rebellion of the Poor: The Balfour Insurrections," *Social Movement Studies*. 13(2): 204–221.

Almeida, Paul D. (2007). "Defensive Mobilization. Popular Movements against Economic Adjustment Policies in Latin America," *Latin American Perspectives*. 34(3): 127–139.

Almeida, Paul D. (2010). "Social Movement Partyism: Collective Action and Oppositional Political Parties." In *Strategic Alliances: Coalition Building and Social Movements*, edited by Nella Van Dyke and Holly J. McCammon, 170–196. Minneapolis: University of Minnesota Press.

Almeida, Paul D. (2014). *Mobilizing Democracy. Globalization and Citizen Protest*. Baltimore: Johns Hopkins University Press.

Amann, Edmund and Baer, Werner (2002). "Neoliberalism and its Consequences in Brazil," *Journal of Latin American Studies*. 34(2): 945–959.

Auyero, Javier (2012). *Patients of the State: The Politics of Waiting in Argentina*. Durham: Duke University Press, 2012.

Auyero Javier and Swistun, Débora Alejandra (2009). *Flammable: Environmental Suffering in an Argentine Shantytown*. New York: Oxford University Press.

Bagguley, Paul (1996). "The Moral Economy of Anti-poll Tax Protest." In *To Make Another World: Studies in Protest and Collective Action*, edited by Colin Barker and Paul Kennedy, 7–24. Aldershot: Avebury.

Bakshi, P., Goodwin, M., Painter, J., and Southern, A. (1995), "Gender, Race, and Class in the Local Welfare State: Moving Beyond Regulation Theory in Analysing the Transition from Fordism," *Environment and Planning A*. 27: 1539–1554.

Barker, Colin (1986). *Festival of the Oppressed: Solidarity, Reform and Revolution in Poland, 1980–1981*. London: Bookmarks.

Barker, Colin (2012). "Twenty Five Years of Revolution," *International Socialism*. 135, 147–156.

Barker, Colin (2013). "Class Struggle and Social Movements." In *Marxism and Social Movements*, edited by Colin Barker, Laurence Cox, John Krinsky, and Alf Gunwald Nilsen, 41–62. Boston: Brill.

Bond, Patrick, Desai, Ashwin, and Ngwane, Trevor (2013). "Uneven and Combined Marxisms within South Africa's Urban Social Movements." In *Marxism and Social Movements*, edited by Colin Barker, Laurence Cox, John Krinsky, and Alf Gunvald Nilsen, 233–255. Boston: Brill.

Bott, Adam. "Sweden's Great Welfare Heist" *Red Pepper*, April http://europe.redpepper.org.uk/swedens-great-welfare-heist/ (accessed 30 April 2014).

Cox, Laurence and Nilsen, Alf Gunvald (2014). *We Make Our Own History. Marxism and Social Movements in the Twilight of Neoliberalism*. London: Pluto.

Crosland, Anthony (1956). *The Future of Socialism*. London: Cape.

Crossley, Nick (1999). "Fish, Field, Habitus and Madness: the First Wave Mental Health Users Movement in Great Britain," *British Journal of Sociology*. 50(4): 647–670.

Crouch, Colin (2001). "Welfare State Regimes and Industrial Relations Systems: The Questionable Role of Path Dependency Theory." In *Comparing Welfare Capitalism: Social Policy and Political Economy in Europe, Japan and the USA*, edited by Bernhard Ebbinghaus and Philip Manow, 105–124. London: Routledge.

Davidson, Neil (2013). "The Neoliberal Era in Britain: Historical Developments and Current Perspectives," *International Socialism*. 139, 171–223.

Esping-Andersen, Gøsta (1990). *The Three Worlds of Welfare Capitalism*. New York: Princeton University Press.

Farrar, Max (2004). "Social Movements and the Struggle Over 'Race.'" In *Democracy and Participation—Popular Protest and New Social Movements*, edited by Malcolm J Todd and Gary Taylor, 218–247. London: Merlin Press.

Ferguson, Iain, Lavalette, Michael, and Mooney, Gerry (2006). *Rethinking Welfare*. London: Sage.

Gerstenberger, Heide (2013). "State, Capital, Crisis," *ACME: An International E-Journal for Critical Geographies*. 12(2): 349–365.

Ginsborg, Paul (1990). *A History of Contemporary Italy*. Harmondsworth: Penguin.

Gramsci, Antonio (1971). *Selections from the Prison Notebooks*. London: Lawrence & Wishart.

Guigni, Marco (1998). "Was It Worth the Effort? The Outcomes and Consequences of Social Movements," *Annual Review of Sociology*. 371–393.

Harman, Chris (2009). *Zombie Capitalism: Global Crisis and the Relevance of Marx*. London: Bookmarks.

Harvey, David (2005). *A Brief History of Neoliberalism*. Oxford: Oxford University Press.

Haynes, M. J. (1985). "Strikes." In *The Working Class in England 1875–1914*, edited by John Benson, 89–132. London: Croom Helm.

Heclo, Hugh (1971). *Modern Social Politics in Britain and Sweden*. New Haven: Yale University Press.

Hobsbawm, Eric and Rude, George (1973). *Captain Swing*. Harmondsworth: Penguin.

Jacobs, Sidney (1985). "Race, Empire and the Welfare State: Racism and Council Housing," *Critical Social Policy*. 5(13): 6–28.

Jones, Chris and Lavalette, Michael (2011). "'Popular Social Work' in the Palestinian West Bank: Dispatches from the Front Line." In *Social Work In Extremis*, edited by Michael Lavalette and Vasilios Ioakimidis, 8–31. Bristol: Policy Press.

Jones, Chris and Lavalette, Michael (2013). "The Two Souls of Social Work: Exploring the Roots of Popular Social Work," *Critical and Radical Social Work*. 1(2): 147–166.

Katznelson, Ira (1982). *City Trenches: Urban Politics and the Patterning of Class in the United States*. Chicago: University of Chicago Press.

Katznelson, Ira and Zolberg, Aristide R., eds. (1986). *Working-Class Formation: Nineteenth-Century Patterns in Western Europe and the United States*. New York: Princeton University Press.

Kimeldorf, Howard (1999). *Battling for American Labor. Wobblies, Craft Workers and the Making of the Union Movement*. Oakland: University of California Press.

Konzelmann, Suzanne J. (2014). "The Political Economics of Austerity," *Cambridge Journal of Economics*. 38: 701–741.

Lavalette, Michael and Penketh, Laura (2003). "The Welfare State in the UK. "In *Welfare Capitalism Around the World*, edited by Christian Aspalter, 61–86. Taipei: Casa Verde.

Lockwood, David (1992). *Solidarity and Schism: "The Problem of Disorder" in Durkheimian and Marxist Sociology*. Oxford: Clarendon Press.

Luxemburg, Rosa (1986). *The Mass Strike, The Political Party and the Trade Unions*. London: Bookmarks.

McNally, David (2013). "'Unity of the Diverse': Working-class Formations and Popular Uprisings from Cochabamba to Cairo." In *Marxism and Social Movements*, edited by Colin Barker, Laurence Cox, John Krinsky, and Alf Gunvald Nilsen, 401–423. Boston: Brill.

Mann, Michael (1984). "The Autonomous Power of the State: Its Origins, Mechanisms and Results," *European Journal of Sociology*. 25(2): 185–213.

Marshall, T.H. (1992) "Citizenship and Social Class" in *Citizenship and Social Class*, edited by TH Marshall and T Bottomore, 3–49 London: Pluto Press.

Martinez, Miguel and Domingo, Elena (2014). Social and Political Impacts of the 15M Movement in Spain. Paper presented at the Nineteenth International Conference on Alternative Futures and Popular Protest Conference, Manchester. http://www.miguel-angelmartinez.net/?Social-and-political-impacts-of

Mason, Paul (2013). *Why It's Still Kicking Off Everywhere: The New Global Revolutions.* London: Verso.

Moller, Stephanie, Bradley, David, Huber, Evelyne, Nielson, Francois, and Stephens, John D. (2003). "Determinants of Relative Poverty in Advanced Capitalist Democracies," *American Sociological Review.* 68(1): 22–51.

Moody, Kim (2014). *In Solidarity: Essays on Working-Class Organization and Strategy in the United States.* Chicago: Haymarket.

Offe, Claus (1984). *Contradictions of the Welfare State.* London: Hutchinson.

Pollock, Allyson M. (2005). *NHS Plc: The Privatisation of Our Health Care.* London: Verso.

Piven, Frances Fox and Cloward, Richard A. (1977). *Poor People's Movements: Why They Succeed, How They Fail.* New York: Vintage Books.

Pope, Ricky J. and Flanigan, Shawn T. (2013). "Revolution for Breakfast: Intersections of Activism, Service, and Violence in the Black Panther Party's Community Service Programs," *Social Justice Research.* 28(3): 445–470.

Rothstein, Bo (1998). *Just Institutions Matter: The Moral and Political Logic of the Universal Welfare State.* Cambridge: Cambridge University Press.

Saville, John (1954/1983). "The Welfare State: An Historical Approach." In *The New Reasoner* (reprinted as the "Origins of the Welfare State" in *Social Policy and Social Welfare*, edited by Martin Loney, David Boswell, and John Clarke, 8–17. Milton Keynes: Open University Press).

Scott, Alan (1990). *Ideology and the New Social Movements.* London: Unwin Hyman.

Sewell, William (1996). "Historical Events as Transformations of Structures: Inventing Revolution at the Bastille," *Theory and Society.* 25: 841–881.

Shepard, Benjamin and Hayduk, Ronald (2002). *From ACT UP to the WTO: Urban Protest and Community Building in the Era of Globalisation.* London: Verso.

Shorter, Edward and Tilly, Charles (1974). *Strikes in France, 1830 to 1968.* Cambridge: Cambridge University Press.

Slorach, Roddy (2014). "Out of the Shadows; Disability Movements," *Critical and Radical Social Work.* 2(2): 159–174.

Tarrow, Sidney (1983). *Struggling to Reform: Social Movements and Policy Change During Cycles of Protest.* Ithaca: Western Societies Program, New York, Cornell University.

Tarrow, Sidney (1989). *Democracy and Disorder: Protest and Politics in Italy 1965–1975.* New York: Oxford University Press.

Tarrow, Sidney (1994). *Power in Movement: Social Movements, Collective Action and Politics.* New York: Cambridge University Press.

Tilly, Charles (1993–94). "Social Movements as Historically Specific Clusters of Political Performances," *Berkeley Journal of Sociology.* 38: 1–30.

Titmuss, Richard (1958). *Essays on "The Welfare State."* London: Allen & Unwin.

Virdee, Satnam (2010). "The Continuing Significance of 'Race': Racism, Antiracist Politics and Labour Markets." In *Race and Ethnicity in the 21st Century*, edited by A. Bloch and J. Solomos, 66–92. London: Palgrave Macmillan.

Voss, Kim (1994). *The Making of American Exceptionalism: Knights of Labor and Class Formation in the Nineteenth Century.* New York: Cornell University Press.

Walton, John K. and Seddon, David (1994). *Free Markets and Food Riots: The Politics of Global Adjustment.* Basingstoke: Wiley-Blackwell.

Webber, Jeffery R. (2011). *From Rebellion to Reform in Bolivia: Class Struggle, Indigenous Liberation, and the Politics of Evo Morales.* Chicago: Haymarket.

Wilkinson, Richard and Pickett, Kate (2010). *The Spirit Level: Why Equality is Better for Everyone*. Harmondsworth: Penguin.

Wilson, Elizabeth (1977). *Women and the Welfare State*. London: Tavistock.

Yeo, Stephen (1980). "State and Anti-state: Reflections on Social Forms and Struggles from 1850." In *Capitalism, State Formation and Marxist Theory*, edited by Philip Corrigan, 111–142. London: Quartet.

Zolberg, Aristide R. (1972). "Moments of Madness," *Politics and Society*. 2: 183–207.

....

CHAPTER 48

THE IMPACTS OF ENVIRONMENTAL MOVEMENTS

....

CHRISTOPHER ROOTES AND EUGENE NULMAN

IN the academic and—especially—in the activist literature, claims or assumptions about the impacts of environmental movements upon policy, practice, and outcomes are legion. Indeed, grand, often inflated claims have been made for the influence of environmental movements by their activists and opponents alike. Yet, because the impacts of social movements are notoriously difficult to assess, the impacts of environmental movements have been relatively under-investigated, and because such competing claims are so difficult to assess, the impact of environmental movements remains highly contested.

From the 1970s onwards, the history of environmental movements in North America, western Europe, and Australia has generally been told as one of a series of inspiring victories as one relatively unspoiled fragment of the natural environment after another has been spared from developers, and as some of the most egregious instances of pollution of air, land, and water have been mitigated. Yet, even since the 1960s, the great strides that have been made toward effective environmental protection have not been solely the products of environmental movements. The US Clean Air Acts, for example, resulted from initiatives of Congress even before anything recognizable as an environmental movement emerged. In many cases, despite the undoubted value of the efforts of environmental movements, there is a pervasive chicken and egg problem: did the movement discover the problem or did it, rather, amplify existing public or elite opinion and, by mobilizing some of the public, channel it into the policy arena?

Environmental Movements

Since the 1960s, we have become accustomed to speaking of "the environmental movement." Although many of its constituents do not take action as demonstrative or conflictual, even confrontational, as that we commonly associate with other social movements, some do. Indeed, "environmental movement" is a problematic denotation of a phenomenon that is highly diverse in its forms of organization and action, from the radical, but sometimes covert, direct action of the "green" movement (Doherty 2002), through demonstrative public protest, to the often publicly invisible actions of bureaucratized formal organizations that lobby governments or work in concert with governments and/or corporations to achieve desired environmental outcomes.

The latter end of the continuum presents particular difficulties, and some have suggested that it is better referred to as a "public interest lobby" or an "advocacy coalition" rather than a movement (Bosso 2005). Some environmental NGOs, however, rarely lobby, let alone protest, but are preoccupied with practical action to remedy environmental degradation or to protect remnants of relatively pristine natural environments.

To define "environmental movements" restrictively would be at odds with the discourse of environmentalists themselves, which is generally inclusive and recognizes commonalities among environmental groups and organizations that are rooted in the shared concern to protect the natural environment that exists among the members and supporters of environmental organizations of various kinds. Thus, we define an environmental movement as a loose, non-institutionalized network of informal interactions that includes, as well as individuals and groups who have no organizational affiliation, organizations of varying degrees of formality, and is engaged in collective action motivated by shared identity or concern about environmental issues (Rootes 2004).

Much grass-roots environmental activism is only loosely linked to mainstream environmental movement organizations (EMOs) or, indeed, to other instances of grass-roots action. Yet though the links and networks may be precarious, such local action is informed by the climate of opinion to which EMOs have contributed, and has often played a discovery role for national EMOs (Carmin 1999) and served to train activists who have gone on to rejuvenate wider environmental movements.

The Bases of Impact

The impact of environmental movements, and the pressure they exert on governments, corporations, and other actors, is not simply proportional to the frequency or intensity of their mobilization of public protests or, indeed, of the numbers of participants therein. Indeed, recourse to street demonstrations may mark not the strength but the weakness of a movement, and its embrace of confrontational tactics may reflect the desperation of the politically excluded. For the most part, in highly economically developed Northern states, especially in Europe, the environment has generally been a valence issue that attracts a relatively high measure of endorsement across the political spectrum and does not sharply divide mainstream political parties. Under such conditions, environmentalists may enjoy relatively easy access to policy makers and decision makers.

Environmental NGOs, especially in the North, generally ground their influence and legitimacy upon their insistence that their claims are based on the best available scientific evidence. Sometimes they commission original research; more generally, they deploy published research. As a result of long engagement with particular issues, such NGOs earn respect for their expertise and are, as a result, sometimes drawn into advising or acting as contractors to governments and corporations that lack either scientific expertise or the capacity effectively to communicate to the public the environmental issues that they confront.

Nevertheless, if their reliance upon scientific evidence gives such environmental NGOs credibility with the powerful, it inhibits NGOs' ability to campaign on issues where scientific evidence is weak. This is especially problematic where public concern about an issue, such as incinerator emissions, cannot be warranted by scientific evidence of harm. Even in the absence of such evidence, and without overt support from established NGOs, local environmental campaigns may nevertheless be successful in mobilizing against proposed developments, not only in Northern countries with nominally democratically accountable governments and officials, but even in authoritarian states such as China (Lang and Xu 2013) where governments' desire to avoid sustained civil unrest may outweigh concern to implement development policies. Although it is by no means inevitable, the frequency of local environmental campaigns may lead governments and corporations to avoid particular strategies and technologies altogether, and so local campaigners may achieve impacts where environmental NGOs cannot.

The impacts of environmental movements may be direct or indirect, negative or positive. Thus environmental movements may embrace action designed to head-off, derail or obstruct the formation or development of draft or mooted policies, or they may promote the formation or development of policies designed to achieve desired environmental ends. Equally, once policy is formulated and promulgated, environmental movements may oppose or obstruct its implementation, or contrive to make the implementation of environmentally desirable policy more effective.

Impacts on Policy Formation

Examples of the negative impacts of environmental movements on policy formation or development are legion. In the United States, anti-nuclear and anti-incineration campaigners have been credited with preventing the commissioning of any new nuclear power stations or waste incinerators for three decades from 1980. In the UK, the Blair/Brown Labour government (1997–2010) essayed a series of policies concerning genetically modified organisms (GMOs) and new housing on greenfield sites, and repeatedly backed down when faced by environmental movement protests. Similarly, that government's coalition successor watered down proposed changes to land-use planning in the face of concerted opposition.

Of the many cases in which EMOs have positively influenced the shaping of environmental policy, perhaps none is more iconic than the role EMOs played in securing passage of the UK Climate Change Act 2008, then the most ambitious and potentially consequential environmental legislation in the world. Beginning in 2005, Friends of the Earth (FoE) and other EMOs began to mobilize public support for decisive action to combat climate change. FoE proposed a draft Climate Change Bill requiring annual 3 per cent reductions in greenhouse gas emissions leading to an 80 per cent reduction by 2050, and worked with representatives of each major political party to steer the issue into parliamentary debate. FoE encouraged its supporters to lobby their Members of Parliament to sign declarations of support for the Bill, which 412 of the 646 MPs eventually did. This led the government to adopt the Bill, whilst watering down its more ambitious provisions. However, as the Bill proceeded through the parliamentary process, FoE urged its members to continue to lobby MPs to strengthen the Bill. Public and private lobbying persuaded many MPs to press the government to accept the 80 per cent reduction target and to include annual indicative targets while maintaining five-year binding targets (Nulman 2015).

Not the least interesting aspect of this case is the extent to which an EMO successfully engaged with the formal political and legislative process to secure passage of legislation that realized most of its objectives; even when it sought to mobilize its supporters it did so by conventional means: a petition, albeit online, and a campaign of writing letters and sending emails and postcards to MPs. In securing passage of unprecedentedly ambitious legislation, FoE undoubtedly made an impact, but it did so by means not generally central to the repertoires of social movements. Yet FoE's methods were appropriate to the circumstances. Whilst it is unlikely that any such ambitious legislation would have made its way to the statute books without FoE's initiative and persistence, it was widely perceived to be timely, as the ease with which so many MPs were persuaded to support it attests.

The experience of the US environmental movement with respect to climate change is in stark contrast. With federal government action on climate change blocked by hostile Republican majorities in Congress, the US climate movement has more often taken the form of protest, and its impacts have been greatest in states and cities where legislators have been sympathetic.

Although the influence of environmental movements is mediated by the variety of other actors and interests, and identifying specifically movement impacts is accordingly difficult, it appears that the influence of environmental movements upon policy is greatest in the early, agenda-setting stages of policy formation, when policy preferences are malleable rather than entrenched (Olzak and Soule 2009). Thus, at this liminal stage, movement organizations may strategically frame policy issues so as to shape the preferences of elite actors. Some, however, may seek to raise awareness even of issues on which attitudes are culturally embedded or politically entrenched in order to problematize them and to mobilize public opinion to demand policy change.

IMPACTS ON POLICY IMPLEMENTATION

The impacts of environmental movements upon policy implementation may be positive as well as negative. Thus environmental campaigns and mobilizations may ensure local implementation of national policies and international treaties. In many countries, wildlife conservation organizations campaign principally to ensure the implementation of protective legislation.

Often, however, environmental campaigners have resisted, and sometimes successfully obstructed the implementation of government policy. In some cases the impact of the environmental movement appears clear, as, for example, in the case of the protests in Germany that disrupted the transport of nuclear waste. In both Germany and the United States, protests have prevented the construction of permanent nuclear waste repositories. Yet although it was sustained pressure from environmentalists that maintained the high profile of the nuclear issue in Germany from the 1970s onward, it was an external event—the nuclear disaster at Fukushima, Japan—that triggered the decision to close Germany's nuclear reactors.

The 1990s campaign against the UK road-building program stimulated a series of protracted and innovative protests that delayed and escalated the costs of road-building, but it is less clear that it was their impact, rather than a recession-induced state fiscal crisis, that brought the program to a premature end.

In general, the impact of environmental movements upon policy implementation is often indirect and difficult to distinguish from the impacts of other actors, processes, and events.

IMPACTS ON PUBLIC OPINION

Social movements are usually conceived of as phenomena of civil society. However large the initial mobilization, most movements, in the attempt to build a constituency for social and/or political change, appeal to wider sections of the public, either directly to change social practice or in order to enlist public opinion in the struggle to persuade governments or corporations to change policy and/or practice. Indeed, Burstein (1999) concludes that movements influence policy outcomes only when their actions are mediated by public opinion.

Many of the achievements of environmental movements have resulted from lobbying and persuasion that is not usually publicly visible. Precisely because it is not visible, the extent of its impact is disputable and cannot easily be assessed (Giugni 2004). But even where the actions of environmental movements are highly visible, determining the extent and significance of their impact is more art than science. Studies that purport to demonstrate the impact of movements on public opinion are generally correlational, observing the correlation between a movement's articulation of a discourse and the appearance of its traces in public opinion, ideally after a plausible elapse of time. In a notably sophisticated study of the impact of protest upon public policy, Agnone (2007) found that, controlling for media attention, legislative context, and election cycles, more federal environmental protection legislation was passed in the United States when environmental movement protest amplified, or raised the salience of, pro-environmental public opinion. Such impacts may be amplified by the relatively high levels of public approval of the environmental movement and trust in environmental NGOs (Dunlap and Scarce 1991; Inglehart 1995).

In general, in democratic states, the impact of environmental movements upon public policy is greatest where it runs with the grain of public opinion, and especially where the movement's diagnostic and prognostic frames resonate with (significant parts of) the public. In an apparently infinite iterative process, environmental activists seek to shape public opinion and thereby influence the formation of environmental policy. In this the mass media have been an indispensable tool, for it is through the mass media that most people gain information about the environment as about other issues. Of environmental NGOs, Greenpeace has been the most consistently adroit and assiduous in its exploitation of the opportunities provided by mass media to reach the public and thence to bring pressure to bear upon governments and corporations. Whether campaigning against nuclear weapons testing, whaling or sealing, or latterly against transnational oil companies, Greenpeace has highlighted environmental degradation and parlayed public opinion into persuading governments and corporations to change policy and practice (Zelko 2013).

By engaging the public, environmental movements have often been credited with setting the agenda for public policy on environmental matters, but in general their impact is perhaps better conceived not as agenda-setting so much as highlighting neglected issues, maintaining their salience, keeping public concern alive even at times when the attentions of policy makers are diverted elsewhere by other pressing issues such as those of economic crisis management, and pressing their advantage when windows of political opportunity are opened.

Thus Rucht (1999) concluded that, although environmental movement pressure was correlated with improvements in the quality of the environment, that pressure appeared to be mediated by public opinion, and it was by no means sufficient to guarantee favorable outcomes; likewise in some countries, the United States included, strong movement pressure was associated with only moderately favorable public opinion and environmental outcomes. Nor should government resistance be simply assumed; ministers in the 1997–2010 UK Labour government actively encouraged the environmental movement to mobilize in favor of policies that ministers desired but which they feared lacked sufficient public support.

Variations in the relationships between movement pressure, public opinion, and environmental outcomes may be explained by variations in political opportunity, both structural and conjunctural. But another element Rucht did not attempt to measure was the strength of corporate and political opposition to environmental protection measures that conflict with libertarian political ideology and/or corporate interests entrenched in and protected by informal networks of power and influence.

The widely celebrated successes of environmental movements often exert a constraining effect on corporations which are obliged, when devising policies and strategy, to consider the possible impacts of antagonizing Greenpeace or other campaigning NGOs, but they have also stimulated the development of vigorous countermovements both in the industrialized North and in the developing South. It may be a tribute to the effectiveness of environmental movements that coal-mining, oil, and other resource extracting corporations have funded pre-emptive campaigns to counter the claims of environmental NGOs, but the corporate fightback has made the struggle for environmental justice more hazardous, especially for activists in developing countries in the global South, where modernizing elites often see their interests as aligned with those of resource-extracting corporations.

It might be supposed that the dramatic increase in the numbers of environmental organizations and the numbers of their members and supporters is testimony to the impact of the mobilizing efforts of those organizations upon a wider public. But there is an equally plausible case to be made that EMOs were often largely passive beneficiaries of wider secular changes in societies. The case of FoE in England is instructive. FoE set out in 1971 to be a lobbying organization and did not seek or expect a mass membership, but its first public action—a "bottle drop" outside a drinks manufacturer in London—attracted so many calls from people asking "how can I join" that FoE responded by licensing the formation of more than 100 local FoE groups. FoE had not so much mobilized the public as it had taken an action that chimed with the public mood at the time and, by its existence, provided a vehicle for the organizational reflection of that mood.

It is clear that public opinion alone does not provide sufficient opportunities for the environmental movement to influence policy, but others conditions have been identified that bolster the impacts of EMOs.

How Movements Make an Impact

Political opportunities are important factors in the ability of environmental movements to influence policy. The opening of an environmental policy window during periods of electoral competition is particularly important as it gives EMOs greater access to policy makers. In these contexts, EMOs often work to generate solutions to policy problems or influence the designs of existing or government-proposed policies, working as expert stakeholders. EMOs are at a particular advantage here as they are regarded as a "scientific social movement" (Yearley 1989).

Yet movements do not make an impact only through the direct efforts of NGOs that engage with policy makers. Radical activists also make an impact, often by creating a "radical flank" effect that enables more institutionalized NGOs to gain an audience. Thus environmental movement impacts are often better considered as the outcomes of a variety of strategies and tactics all directed to broadly shared ends, than simply to the efforts of a single NGO.

As well as attempting to address specific issues or policies, EMOs participate in electoral campaigning around the environment more generally. Green parties do this in many countries, but in the United States the League of Conservation Voters (LCV) works to promote environmentally friendly policy makers and shame others. In 1971, the LVC began compiling a record of Congressional environmental votes and giving each Congressman a score between 0 and 100. Analysis of these scores revealed some correspondence with the strength of the movement in the Congressman's state. Thus, in 1971, Pennsylvania, New York, and New Jersey received scores of 50, 68, and 70, respectively; of the three states, Pennsylvania had a weaker environmental movement (Hays 1993: 41).

This strategy was favored particularly in contexts where the environmental movement had little access to policy makers. Such was the case in the United States following George W. Bush's first presidency, when the environmental movement's distaste for Bush after his administration attempted to undermine the Clean Air Act, the Endangered Species Act, and forest protection and pollutant regulations led the Sierra Club, LCV, and other environmental organizations to spend over $15 million during the 2004 campaign (Bosso and Guber 2005: 79). However, environmental organizations spent significantly less on campaign contributions than other advocacy groups, and the movement's attempt to determine the outcome of the election failed. Bush's rival in the 2004 race, John Kerry, was unable to generate media coverage through support for environmental initiatives despite high levels of public support for environmental legislation, probably due to its relatively low salience following the terrorist attacks of 2001 and the subsequent war in Iraq (Bosso and Guber 2005).

INFLUENCE OF ENVIRONMENTAL MOVEMENTS ON INTERNATIONAL AGREEMENTS

The increasing number and scope of international agreements concerning the environment has presented a new pattern of opportunities to environmental NGOs. The limited capacities of new supranational institutions of environmental governance have some-times led them to deliberately foster the development of networks of environmental groups, as, for example the European Commission did when, in seeking to expand its competence in the hitherto neglected environmental sphere, it funded the establish-ment of the European Environmental Bureau. Environmental NGOs were presented with a platform and opportunities to participate in the shaping of agreements at the 1992 Rio Earth Summit, and they have made influential contributions to international Conventions on a wide range of topics, including biosafety, desertification, endangered species, forestry and whaling (see, e.g., contributors to Betsill and Corell 2008).

Environmental activists have also demonstrated and made representations at sev-eral global climate summits, none more spectacularly than the 2000 Conference of the Parties to the UN Framework Convention on Climate Change (COP-9) when concerted action by environmental NGOs persuaded the US delegation to drop its proposal to include nuclear energy in the Clean Development Mechanism associated with the Kyoto Protocol. That victory proved short-lived when, unable to secure EU agreement that the United States might offset its greenhouse gas emissions by treat-ing its forests as "carbon sinks," the United States withdrew from the Kyoto process. The 2009 (COP-15) meeting in Copenhagen, billed as the summit at which a successor climate agreement to Kyoto would be developed, was an even more devastating failure for environmental campaigners; present in unprecedented numbers and with different groups employing a variety of insider and outsider strategies, the meeting ended with all non-official delegates excluded from the conference center and with no new agree-ment (Hadden 2015).

Access in itself is only as useful as is the level of seriousness of policy makers in advancing environmental protection in relation to other interests. EMOs were given significant levels of access both formally in the climate change negotiations process and as advisors to (or even members of) national delegations but, despite their formal inclusion in the governance process, EMOs failed to influence many important decisions as they were unable to affect the incentive structures of national delegations.

In other international negotiations, NGOs were able to affect debates on carbon sinks and emissions trading in addition to having some influence on positions taken by the US and EU delegations (Betsill 2008; also see Burgiel 2008 on the Cartagena Protocol on Biosafety; Corell 2008 on the Desertification Convention; Andersen and Skodvin 2008 on the International Whaling Commission; and Humphreys 2008 on Forest Conversation and the Trade in Forest Products).

In general, the impacts of EMOs in international negotiations, and upon the even-tual agreements, have been limited both by movement actors' relative outsider status compared to industry groups (Lund 2013), and, most critically, by their frequent need to be perceived to act transparently, in public, when most of the real work of such nego-tiations takes place behind closed doors. It is noteworthy that environmental NGOs have had most influence when they have engaged practically in areas in which they had accumulated expertise and where they were able to act as brokers between North and South. On climate change, by contrast, where environmental NGOs have no special expertise commensurate with the magnitude and complexity of the problem, and where the issues have become polarized and politicized, they have, despite their intermittently highly public interventions, been much less influential.

The two major international EMOs—FoE and Greenpeace—present different patterns of response to the dilemmas of attempting to make an impact on global environment politics.

Greenpeace International has privileged efficiency and campaign effectiveness over internal democracy, and has retained the capacity to restructure and sometimes amalgamate national Greenpeace organizations, which are concentrated in the global North. The result is that it is sometimes viewed with suspicion not only by national governments but also by the citizens of states whose cultures and interests it offends, most notably in the case of Norway (Strømsnes et al. 2009). Yet its organizational structure has given Greenpeace the flexibility and capacity to respond to issues as they arise, and has contributed to its becoming the most formidable environmental campaigning NGO in the world, particularly on marine issues.

FoE International, by contrast, has over seventy national affiliates, and is well represented in the global South. It has insisted upon preserving internal democracy even at the expense of operational efficiency and, very likely, the effectiveness of some of its short-term campaigns (Doherty and Doyle 2013). In the longer term, however, its respect for the autonomy of its national affiliates, deliberate inclusiveness in the determination of policy priorities, and determination to keep together a disparate grouping may increase its impact and make it a more important player in global environmental politics.

Often in the global South, environmental movements have utilized a "boomerang effect" in order to bring international resources to bear upon local and national concerns. An early example occurred during a campaign to clean up the "valley of death" in Cubatao, Brazil in the 1980s when campaigners sought to reduce international funding for development that increased pollution and deforestation (Hochstetler 2002). Environmental movements in the global South often called upon allies in the North for support, particularly regarding the halting of environmentally destructive practices associated with large projects funded or commissioned by actors from the North, but as transnational environmental networks developed, the boomerang effect was put into play more frequently even without the clear presence of Northern interests (as in the case of the campaign against the Narmada Dams in India, which persuaded the World Bank to withdraw funding).

It should not be imagined, however, that all the effective initiatives of environmental movements at international level originate in the global North. GAIA, the global alliance against waste incinerators, began in the Philippines and thence spread through the South and to the North. More generally, assisted by improving communications networks, South–South environmental movement networks are becoming increasingly common.

WIDER IMPACTS OF ENVIRONMENTAL MOVEMENTS

Environmental movements have been credited with enlarging the space for civil society and democratic participation in authoritarian states in central and eastern Europe and in the newly industrializing states of east Asia (Lee and So 1999).

Because environmental movements address universal issues and the health and well-being of whole populations, issues that can be construed as questions of national patrimony rather than sectional or subversive interests, environmental movements have been more easily tolerated by authoritarian regimes than have groups and movements that directly challenge the character of the state itself.

In China, for example, whereas human rights activists suffer restrictions and worse, environmental activists, treading carefully to sidestep official restrictions on fund-raising, have succeeded in steadily enlarging their scope of activity. This they have done by exploiting the legal gray area in which environmental NGOs are positioned—neither officially recognized nor expressly proscribed. Rather than seeking to influence policy directly, Chinese environmental NGOs have pragmatically adapted their aims and approaches based on the needs of the public, focussing upon the health and livelihood impacts of environmental degradation. Moreover, seeking to demonstrate to the public that they are there to help rather than to make trouble, many Chinese environmental NGOs have sought to work on what the government has identified as areas for improvement, in order to accelerate and influence environmental improvements rather than campaigning for radical restructuring (Zhang and Barr 2013).

Whilst the ultimate outcomes of environmental activism in China remain obscure, elsewhere in east Asia and in central and eastern Europe under state socialism, environmental movements permitted a certain space in which to organize, and attracted activists who might otherwise have campaigned more directly for regime change. But if environmental movements thus became schools for civil society organization and cover for activists with other aspirations, when regime change occurred, environmental movements were often marginalized and effectively demobilized as activists exploited the space to address other neglected issues. This was most evident in central and eastern Europe where the collapse of state socialist regimes entailed a precipitate decline in economic activity. As a result, not only were citizens distracted from environmental concerns by the need to augment their sharply reduced real incomes, but the evident need for environmental improvement was reduced by the dramatic contraction of polluting industries, which was less the product of environmental campaigning than of the collapse of protectionist economic policies and the introduction of market economics.

In a much more modest way, environmental movements appear to have contributed to the vitality of civil society and, tentatively, to the rejuvenation of the political processes of liberal democratic states. If conventional politics holds little attraction for young people in most such states, it is among the youngest age cohorts than support for environmental movements and, especially, Green parties is greatest. Similarly, women tend to be more prominent in local environmental campaigns than they are in mainstream politics, probably because the barriers to entry are lower in the former than in the latter. Thus the existence of environmental movements may provide a path into politics for people who would otherwise remain outside the political realm.

Conclusion

The striking thing about environmental movements is that despite their many successes, and justified celebration of their increasing influence in many policy arenas, the assault on the global environment proceeds at an unprecedented pace. Scarcely a week goes by without new evidence of continuing degradation of the global environment: the concentrations of greenhouse gases in the atmosphere are at unprecedentedly high levels and rising; tropical rainforests continue to be logged and burned so that the "lungs of the planet" are an ever smaller proportion of the surface area of the Earth; biodiversity continues to decline at an alarming rate; overfishing and acidification of the oceans increasingly endanger tropical reefs and marine ecology.

This increasing global environmental degradation is only partly offset by significant local gains, of which examples include the improving condition of Europe's rivers, better air quality in many cities in the global North, and even the re-naturalization of some previously degraded landscapes and rivers. Even in the North, it is difficult to be sanguine about the prospects of environmental improvement because the business-as-usual operations of (government and) corporations and other economic actors, including, not least, consumers, continue to contribute to environmental degradation. It is this that justifies the focus of many environmental activists upon practical action at the local level because at least here the impacts of action may be demonstrable. Nevertheless, the dilemma of local action remains that its impacts are largely determined by institutional arrangements that it is beyond the power of local actors to change, or upon the actions or reactions of more powerful non-local actors (Rootes 2013).

The general paradox of environmental improvements in the domestic environments of the de-industrializing/ecologically modernized countries of the global North is that much of it has been achieved at the expense of increasing impacts abroad, especially in the global South, not simply by direct exploitation of the natural environmental resources of less affluent/less industrialized countries, but also via the normal operation of the terms of trade by which the industrial production that fulfils the aspirations of the consumers of the North has been increasingly located in the South.

However, the spread of environmental awareness is now global, transnational EMOs now exist, and the campaigns of national environmental EMOs address not merely national but, increasingly, global issues. In their interventions in international negotiations, EMOs have begun to make an impact and, although various national and corporate interests are powerfully arrayed against them, it is likely that, through their continued advocacy and deployment of scientific evidence, environmental movements will make significant impacts upon global environmental policies and their implementation.

REFERENCES

Agnone, Jon (2007). "Amplifying Public Opinion: The Policy Impact of the U.S. Environmental Movement." *Social Forces*. 85(4): 1593–1620.

Andresen, Steinar and Skodvin, Tora (2008). "Non-state Influence in the International Whaling Commission, 1970–2006." In *NGO Diplomacy: The Influence of Nongovernmental Organizations in International Environmental Negotiations*, edited by Michele M. Betsill and Elisabeth Corell, 119–148. Cambridge, MA: MIT Press.

Betsill, Michele M. (2008). "Environmental NGOs and the Kyoto Protocol Negotiations: 1995 to 1997." In *NGO Diplomacy: The Influence of Nongovernmental Organizations in International Environmental Negotiations*, edited by Michele M. Betsill and Elisabeth Corell, 43–66. Cambridge, MA: MIT Press.

Betsill, Michele M. and Corell, Elisabeth, eds. (2008). *NGO Diplomacy: The Influence of Nongovernmental Organizations in International Environmental Negotiations*. Cambridge, MA: MIT Press.

Bosso, Christopher J. (2005). *Environment, Inc.: From Grassroots to Beltway*. Lawrence: University Press of Kansas.

Bosso, Christopher J. and Guber, Deborah Lynn (2005). "Maintaining Presence: Environmental Advocacy and the Permanent Campaign." In *Environmental Policy: New Directions for the 21st Century*, edited by Norman Vig and Michael Kraft, 78–99. Washington, DC: CQ Press.

Burgiel, Stanley W. (2008). "Non-state Actors and the Cartagena Protocol on Biosafety." In *NGO Diplomacy: The Influence of Nongovernmental Organizations in International Environmental Negotiations*, edited by Michele M. Betsill and Elisabeth Corell, 67–100. Cambridge, MA: MIT Press.

Burstein, P. (1999). "Social Movements and Public Policy." In *How Social Movements Matter*, edited by M. Giugni, D. McAdam, and C. Tilly, 3–21. Minneapolis, London: University of Minnesota Press.

Carmin, JoAnn (1999). "Voluntary Associations, Professional Organizations and the Environmental Movement in the United States," *Environmental Politics*. 8(3): 101–121.

Corell, Elisabeth (2008). "NGO Influence in the Negotiations on the Desertification Convention." In *NGO Diplomacy: The Influence of Nongovernmental Organizations in International Environmental Negotiations*, edited by Michele M. Betsill and Elisabeth Corell, 101–118. Cambridge, MA: MIT Press.

Doherty, Brian (2002). *Ideas and Actions in the Green Movement*. London: Routledge.

Doherty, Brian and Doyle, Timothy (2013). *Environmentalism, Resistance and Solidarity: The Politics of Friends of the Earth*. Basingstoke: Palgrave Macmillan.

Dunlap, Riley E. and Scarce, Rik (1991). "Poll Trends: Environmental Problems and Protection," *The Public Opinion Quarterly*. 55(4): 651–672.

Giugni, Marco (2004). *Social Protest and Policy Change: Ecology, Antinuclear, and Peace Movements in Comparative Perspective*. Lanham: Rowman & Littlefield Publishers.

Hadden, Jennifer (2015). *Networks in Contention: The Divisive Politics of Global Climate Change*. New York: Cambridge University Press.

Hays, Samuel P. (1993). *Beauty, Health, and Permanence: Environmental Politics in the United States, 1955–1985.* Cambridge: Cambridge University Press.

Hochstetler, Kathryn (2002). "After the Boomerang: Environmental Movements and Politics in the La Plata River Basin," *Global Environmental Politics.* 2(4): 35–57.

Humphreys, David (2008). "NGO Influence on International Policy on Forest Conservation and the Trade in Forest Products." In *NGO Diplomacy: The Influence of Nongovernmental Organizations in International Environmental Negotiations,* edited by Michele M. Betsill and Elisabeth Corell, 149–176. Cambridge, MA: MIT Press.

Inglehart, Ronald (1995). "Public Support for Environmental Protection: Objective Problems and Subjective Values in 43 Societies," *PS: Political Science and Politics.* 28(1): 57–72.

Lang, Graeme and Xu, Ying (2013). "Anti-incinerator Campaigns and the Evolution of Protest Politics in China," *Environmental Politics.* 22(5): 832–848.

Lee, Y. F. and So, Alvin, eds. (1999). *Asia's Environmental Movements.* Armonk NY and London: M. E. Sharpe.

Lund, Emma (2013). "Environmental Diplomacy: Comparing the Influence of Business and Environmental NGOs in Negotiations on Reform of the Clean Development Mechanism," *Environmental Politics.* 22(5): 739–759.

Nulman, Eugene (2015). *Climate Change and Social Movements: Civil Society and the Development of National Climate Change Policy.* Basingstoke: Palgrave Macmillan.

Olzak, Susan and Soule, Sarah A. (2009). "Cross-Cutting Influences of Environmental Protest and Legislation," *Social Forces.* 88(1): 201–225.

Rootes, Christopher (2004). "Environmental Movements." In *The Blackwell Companion to Social Movements,* edited by David A. Snow, Sarah A. Soule, and Hanspeter Kriesi, 608–640. Malden, MA: Blackwell.

Rootes, Christopher (2013). "From Local Conflict to National Issue: When and How Environmental Campaigns Succeed in Transcending the Local," *Environmental Politics.* 22(1): 95–114.

Rucht, Dieter (1999). "The Impact of Environmental Movements in Western Societies." In *How Social Movements Matter,* edited by M. Giugni, D. McAdam, and C. Tilly, 204–224. Minneapolis: University of Minnesota.

Strømsnes, Kristin et al. (2009). "Environmentalism between State and Local Community: Why Greenpeace has Failed in Norway," *Environmental Politics.* 18(3): 391–417.

Yearley, Steven (1989). "Environmentalism: Science and a Social Movement," *Social Studies of Science.* 2(19): 343–355.

Zelko, Frank (2013). *Make It a Green Peace! The Rise of a Countercultural Environmentalism.* New York and Oxford: Oxford University Press.

Zhang, Joy Y. and Barr, Michael (2013). *Green Politics in China: Environmental Governance and State-Society Relations.* London: Pluto Press.

....

CHAPTER 49

IS IT SOCIAL MOVEMENTS THAT CONSTRUCT HUMAN RIGHTS?

....

KATE NASH

WHAT is the link between human rights and social movements? Today human rights are very often considered in the terms of international law. There is no doubt that this is due in part to the work of non-governmental organizations (NGOs), pushing for accountability and norm change at international and national levels since the 1970s (Keck and Sikkink 1998). But if human rights are really to make a difference, if they are to become a language that can address injustices, it is clear that far more than law has to be changed. People must be able to define human rights in ways that are appropriate to help them overcome the obstacles they face, and they must know how, and where, to address their grievances if the language of human rights is really to improve their lives. The study of social movements is precisely concerned with questions about how people frame "wrongs" in ways that make a difference, how they build solidarity and create organizations to further their aims, and how and where they direct their actions to make a difference. It would seem quite obvious, then, that how human rights are constructed by social movements *should* be a focus of scholarly attention (see Stammers 1999, 2009).

In fact, however, the term "movement" is used very loosely in the human rights literature, and social movements have not been systematically studied in relation to human rights. In the first section of this chapter I will discuss how "movement" has been used in inter-disciplinary studies of human rights in a way that is primarily *normative*, to legitimate ideals of global justice. In the second section I will discuss "transnational advocacy networks." This is the main way NGO constructions of human rights have been studied. Transnational advocacy networks are similar to social movements in some respects, but they are not the same. I discuss how the focus on elite transformation in studies of transnational advocacy networks needs to be supplemented to study the construction of human rights by social movements. In the third section I consider what such studies might look like on the basis of existing work on human rights advocacy, before concluding with some comments on the value of studying social movements and human rights. Studying how human rights are constructed, how they circulate between elites *and* in grassroots forms of organization opens up a rich field of investigation for anyone interested in collective action in our globalizing times.

THEORIZING HUMAN RIGHTS MOVEMENT(S)

In the inter-disciplinary literature on human rights, it is quite common to refer in passing to the "human rights movement." In the fourth edition of their authoritative textbook on international human rights, Alston and Goodman assert that: "In today's world, human rights is characteristically imagined as a movement involving international law and institutions, as well as a movement involving the spread of liberal constitutions among states" (Alston and Goodman 2012: 59). Similarly, Aryeh Neier, former executive director of Human Rights Watch, states that: "The international human rights movement is made up of men and women ... who are united by their commitment to promote human rights for all, everywhere ... " He goes on to list civil liberties as "the fundamental rights to which they are committed ... " (Neier 2012: 2).

Passing references to "the human rights movement" amongst what we might call "global constitutionalists" (focussed as these analysts are on advancing international human rights law) are intended to legitimate human rights advocacy. "Human rights movement" suggests that international non-governmental organizations (INGOs) are channelling popular demands for human rights "from below." This is especially important given that INGOs are based in the Northwest while the injustices they address very often take place elsewhere.[1] In contrast, *critics* of globalizing human rights see a singular and unified global human rights movement as *problematic*—though again without specifying what they mean by "movement." From a critical legal perspective, David Kennedy argues that what he calls "the human rights movement" is caught in a series of traps that limit political imagination and action through an overestimation of the value and power of international law. According to this view, the human rights movement consolidates global elites, putting too much faith in lawyers and procedures rather than challenging grossly unequal relations of power and voice through struggles to articulate more utopian visions (Kennedy 2002).

From the point of view of "global constitutionalists," grievances are brought to the United Nations (UN), where they are mostly dealt with by setting standards and monitoring, occasionally through "peacekeeping operations." For Neier, the wealth and military power of the United States has been a help, not a hindrance to the cause of human rights (Neier 2012). In contrast, for those who focus on human rights activism outside the Northwest, rather than a single, unified, and elite-oriented human rights movement (singular), there is a plurality of grassroots human rights movements (plural). Santos's theory of "subaltern cosmopolitanism" is the most interesting version of this argument, but he too conceives of social movements and human rights in highly normative terms (Santos 2002a, 2002b). He aims to show how social movements can be united in a counter-hegemonic project of anti-capitalist, anti-imperialist globalization. For Santos, human rights are only of value when they are defined in ways that remain close to every-day life and communities mobilized against capitalism and imperialism.

If "global constitutionalists" neglect how people make use of human rights where they live, Santos's theory of human rights movements neglects the *range* of human rights advocacy. In fact, the empirical case studies that have been linked to "subaltern cosmopolitanism" are more interesting and diverse than the analytic framework itself would suggest. Studies of social movements that have been engaged in human rights advocacy in the volume edited by Santos and Rodríguez-Garavito include, for example, studies of resistance to the Narmada Dam project that (amongst other tactics, including direct action) involved an application to the Indian Supreme Court to put a stop to it; of the Treatment Action Campaign that involved (amongst other tactics, again includ-ing direct action) appealing to South African courts; and the Movement of Landless Rural Workers that (amongst other tactics, once again including direct action) has also engaged (albeit somewhat reactively and indirectly) with the Brazilian courts to try and bring about land reform (Santos and Rodríguez-Garavito 2005).

Privileging the local, "subaltern cosmopolitanism" cannot help us to understand how institutions at the national and international scales may be *intrinsically* (not acci-dentally) important to progressive constructions of human rights (see Nash 2012). The international human rights regime remains state-centric to the extent that it is state actors that sign and ratify international human rights agreements, that commit to respecting and enforcing human rights within their territories (against their own violations), and that submit to (or evade) being monitored and judged by UN agen-cies and regional intergovernmental organizations (IGOs) (especially European and Inter-American) in terms of their compliance with those agreements. Ultimately too, it is states that donate the resources to set up international courts and commis-sions, and—exceptionally, in very extreme cases—invite or allow external agencies to monitor, administer, and enforce law within their territories (Donnelly 2003: 33–7). Increasingly states are "internationalizing," becoming enmeshed in regulation and law across borders—including that related to human rights. It is vital, therefore, to theorize and to study how the politics of human rights is organized at *multiple* scales, how advo-cacy engages local, national, and international norms and law whilst remaining virtu-ally always oriented towards states.

TRANSNATIONAL ADVOCACY NETWORKS

"Transnational advocacy networks" is the dominant analytic framework through which the construction of human rights has been studied. The theory is normative in similar ways to "global constitutionalism" in that it is quite uncritical of international human rights norms, and of the geopolitical dimensions of their development. But it does explicitly make analytic room for social movements as a distinct form of organization, rather than collapsing everything into a "human rights movement."

Transnational advocacy networks resemble social movements. According to the international relations (IR) theorists Margaret Keck and Katherine Sikkink who developed the perspective, a transnational advocacy network "includes those relevant actors working internationally on an issue, who are bound together by shared values, a common discourse, and dense exchanges of information and services" (Keck and Sikkink 1998: 3). Keck and Sikkink argue that transnational advocacy networks try to shame political elites into changing how they construct their state's interests as belonging to an international community of states, and—eventually—the policies and practices that led to human rights abuses. Transnational advocacy networks are like social movements in that they are made up of informal networks that link individuals, groups, and organizations. And like social movements, transnational advocacy networks are involved in political and cultural conflict over radically opposed values and visions of society (Diani 2000).

But transnational advocacy networks are not the same as social movements. Above all, the main difference as I see it is that social movements involve the formation of collective identity amongst ordinary people, as well as (sometimes) of elites. Social movements are different from interest groups and parties in that they do not assume common goals, and nor do they just try to realize goals set by professionals employed in NGOs. Social movements are concerned with fundamental questions about who "we" are and who "we" oppose. They challenge and change "commonsense" amongst ordinary people, and empower individuals and groups as a crucial aspect of transforming structures and practices. The formation of collective identity is discursive: it involves debate, the forging of new symbols, struggles over values and visions of how life in common should be lived. We can think of social movements as spaces for challenging what is "known" and for constructing new definitions of injustice, equality, and rights. It is on this basis that Nancy Fraser suggests that we think of social movements as "counter-public spheres" (Fraser 1997; see also Melucci 1989; della Porta and Diani 2005).

Studies of transnational advocacy networks have focussed on the transformation of elites, not on the formation of collective identity amongst activists and ordinary people. As social constructivists in IR, Keck's and Sikkink's argument is with realists: they want to show that ideas and norms can make a difference in international politics, that outcomes are not determined solely by calculations of state interest, wealth, and force. In particular, they want to show the importance of non-state actors, NGOs, to institutionalizing norms. Under the right conditions, they argue, persuasion by NGOs can shame elites into working to end the torture and murder in which state agents have been involved—with their knowledge or their active participation. Once valuing human rights becomes part of the *identity* of elites, they will work actively to *prevent* human rights abuses (Keck and Sikkink 1998; see also Risse et al. 1999; Clark 2001). Although they do not put it in these terms themselves, Keck and Sikkink are concerned with reforming the collective identity of international elites. They have practically no interest in how meanings are negotiated outside those elites. In this respect, in fact, they seem to *assume* that all the actors involved in transnational advocacy networks share the same "values" and a "common discourse." They must effectively assume *either* that grassroots organizations (GROs) construct human rights in exactly the same way as the NGOs that represent their campaigns at the international level, *or* (against their social constructivist premises) that it is in the (real, and therefore unquestionable) interests of ordinary people to be represented as the victims of human rights violations in precisely the terms that are used by INGOs.

Although (as Keck and Sikkink do) it is quite usual to refer to "NGOs" in general terms when they are being distinguished as the "third sector" independent of states and privately owned businesses there are huge variation within this category. As a matter of definition *international* NGOs have branches in several countries (each with voting rights on the organization's board), whereas NGOs are nationally based (Keck and Smith 2002: 26). This means that, in general, INGOs are far larger than NGOs, and have far more influence on intergovernmental organizations and states. Some NGOs are large and influential too, but others are tiny. Both these types of organization can be formally distinguished from grassroots organizations (though in practice it can be more difficult to distinguish NGOs and GROs). In general GROs involve volunteers rather than paid staff, they are smaller and "flatter" in terms of their bureaucracy and decision-making, and—above all—they involve people in their localities who make human rights claims on their own behalf (Batliwala 2002).

Since the 1970s, the international human rights field has been dominated by Amnesty (AI) and, more recently, Human Rights Watch (HRW). AI and HRW have been joined in the last decade by even larger INGOs including Oxfam, Save the Children, and CARE. Previously exclusively concerned with humanitarianism, they have become involved, to a greater or lesser extent, in advocacy for human rights in relation to development. Human rights INGOs receive funding from members (Amnesty), donors (Human Rights Watch), or governments (Oxfam and CARE take money from donors and governments). Money flows from members, donors, and governments who are overwhelmingly based in the Northwest to INGOs, also based in the Northwest, while those they represent mostly live elsewhere. All these organizations have influence with governments, with the UN, and in some cases (Oxfam, for example), with the World Bank. Each of them has budgets of millions of dollars, a highly professional workforce, and a hierarchical and bureaucratic structure (Gready and Ensor 2005; Nelson and Dorsey 2008; Stroup 2012).

In my view the important question for social movement studies, and for those interested in how human rights are constructed, is: can INGOs be part of social movements? This question raises others, quite different from those we are likely to ask if we see INGOs as actors in transnational advocacy networks. Rather than focussing only on elite transformation, we will ask what *kind* of relationships INGOs have with ordinary people who are not just *victims* of human rights violations, but who are also organizing in NGOs and GROs to construct and claim human rights *on their own behalf*. Thinking of INGOs in terms of social movements raises the question of how INGOs are connected to smaller NGOs and to GROs. What difference do these connections make to how human rights are constructed? What kinds of collective identity are formed through constructions of human rights? And what kinds of collective action do these constructions enable?

Distorting and Adding Weight

Clearly a good deal of conceptual, methodological, and empirical work is needed if we are to begin to address these questions. By way of making a beginning, from existing studies I have identified two diametrically opposed models of the relationships between INGOs, NGOs, and GROs.

The first model focusses on how INGOs *distort* the aims and the means of social movements for audiences elsewhere. In *Marketing Rebellion* Clifford Bob argues that human rights INGOs are not just concerned with justice: they also aim to enhance the brand name and the success of the INGO itself. INGOs manage the competition between "causes" they could, in principle, support, selecting aspects of human suffering and delivering them to Northwestern audiences in forms that make sense to us. Bob argues that how "causes" are chosen and packaged may distort or leave out aspects of people's experience that are simply too complex or too controversial for mainstream audiences in Northwestern states. In fact, in some cases, he suggests, the way INGO support is offered may even make people's situation worse. Bob found that the violent repression of the Movement for the Survival of the Ogoni People (MOSOP) by the Nigerian state increased *at the same time* as support in Northwest states for their environmental and human rights. Bob is clear that NGOs in the South are not passive in relation to INGOs: they are not just victims. They act strategically to try to make their causes attractive to gain support for their aims and interests. In part, Bob argues, the damaging consequences of an international human rights campaign for the Ogoni people was due to the decision of Ken Saro-Wiwa, the movement's leader, to risk escalating non-violent confrontation with the state in order to attract external attention and to put pressure on the government. It was a strategy for which he ultimately paid with his life when he was summarily hanged along with nine other members of the movement after a hasty military tribunal in 1995. Saro-Wiwa's strategy was very successful in attracting attention from the international media, INGOs, Northwestern states and activists, and it has changed how people think about links between environmental and human rights issues. Bob argues, however, that it is doubtful that it led to any long-term gains for the Ogoni people. MOSOP initially mobilized to demand regional autonomy within Nigeria. But these demands were too complex and too Nigeria-specific to find adequate representation in campaigns at the international level (Bob 2005).

The "distortion" model of the relationship between INGOs and grassroots movements confirms criticisms (such as those of David Kennedy) that human rights are inherently problematic because they are elitist. Bob's research on the relationship between INGOs and MOSOP models the problems that arise when INGOs are more responsive to funders and supporters in the Northwest than they are to the people on whose behalf they campaign. In this case it seems that there was a mismatch between collective identity formation in MOSOP, which was focussed on regional autonomy, and the translation of values and aims into the language of human rights that Ken Saro-Wiwa used strategically to attract international support.

In contrast, perhaps a more surprising model is that in which INGOs *add weight* to existing campaigns by NGOs and GROs. The celebrated Treatment Action Campaign in South Africa is an example of INGOs "adding weight." The Treatment Action Campaign was largely made up of young, urban South Africans allied with the Congress of South African Trade Unions and the South African Council of Churches, and used tactics typically associated with social movements, including demonstrations and illegal sit-ins, to put pressure on the state at local, national, and international levels to deliver drugs to treat HIV/AIDs. Oxfam joined the campaigners to put pressure on transnational pharmaceutical corporations to allow drugs to be distributed more cheaply. And later, when the South African government was still reluctant to organize a national programme of treatment, Oxfam was also involved in demonstrations in Europe, the United States, and Asia to make the politicians think again (Friedman and Mottiar 2005; Forbath et al. 2011). In this case, Oxfam seems to have taken its lead from campaigners at the grassroots rather than setting the agenda, including associating its "brand name" with radical forms of political protest and civil disobedience.

The example of the Treatment Action Campaign is an interesting one for the study of how human rights are constructed by social movements. William Forbath and his colleagues (some of whom led the campaign) suggest that the formation of collective identity was vital to its success. They conclude that the people involved not only gained knowledge about how to pursue social rights through the national state, they also developed a sense of themselves as having a "right to rights." In both these respects, the campaign was not *just* focussed narrowly on achieving particular goals: it was empowering to some of the poorest and most marginalized people in South African society. Forbath et al. suggest that human rights education in the South African townships involved:

> untidy, uneven, many-layered process of new rights-bearing identities in the making. Religious structures of thought and feeling and customary local knowledge, witchcraft, and spirit worlds merge and jostle with medico-scientific "enlightenment" and liberal and social rights consciousness. (Forbath et al. 2011: 81)

Unfortunately, however, Forbath et al. tell us very little about *how* these identities were negotiated. How was "folk medicine" negotiated in relation to Western medicine, for example (Decoteau 2013)? What is the effect on peoples' identities, their understanding of who they are in relation to others, of grafting an understanding of oneself as a claimant of human rights onto local understandings? And precisely what role did constructions of human rights play in the formation of collective identity in this case?

What we *do* learn very clearly from accounts of the Treatment Action Campaign is that INGOs do not *necessarily* distort the values and aims of grassroots mobilizations. Friedman and Mottiar, who have made an in-depth study of the Treatment Action

Campaign's organization and strategies, argue that the leadership of the Treatment Action Campaign took care that INGOs it made links to did *not* influence their campaign (Friedman and Mottiar 2005). There was a range of organizations eager to fund and promote the campaign, including INGOs, foundations, governments, the European Union (EU) and the UN, as well as individuals. In this respect the leaders of the Treatment Action Campaign were in a very different situation from Ken Saro-Wiwa.

Conclusion

Although there are very good reasons to study how human rights are constructed by social movements, remarkably little empirical work has actually been done in this area. As Khagram, Riker, and Sikkink note, this is in part for disciplinary reasons: there has been little discussion between IR theorists who work on transnational advocacy networks and sociologists and political scientists who work on social movements (Khagram, Riker, and Sikkink 2002; see also Tarrow 2001; Eschle and Stammers 2004).

Social movements have a crucial role to play in constructing human rights if they are to be realized in practice. Rights are never effective simply because they are legal rights. Enjoying human rights in practice depends on how people use them—on what they claim, and how they make rights claims. This, in turn, depends on collective identity, on the pressure that people bring to bear because they have a "right to rights"—even where they do not have rights in law, or law is administered unjustly. The administration of human rights creates its own status hierarchies and cruelties, even at the local level (Englund 2006). Collective action is needed at every level if human rights are to make a real difference. Grassroots organizing is necessary if people are to be able to define human rights in ways that are appropriate to dealing with the injustices they face. And more often than not the wrongs people suffer benefit national and global elites. Then it is not enough to remain "local," and links to INGOs that can influence state actors, intergovernmental organizations, and even, sometimes, the CEOs of transnational corporations, are invaluable. INGOs *can* add weight to local campaigns and it is often impossible for social movements to achieve their aims without that help.

What is needed to understand social movements and human rights is systematic study of how defining and claiming human rights contribute to collective identity at different scales, and in different forms of organization. How do the relationships between organizations affect which definitions of human rights are taken up, where, by whom, and to what effect? Although my interest is in human rights, it seems to me that this research agenda also represents an opportunity for those involved in social movement studies. The problem with organizing human rights claims so that they are really effective is the very problem that has concerned social movements themselves since 1968: how to address elites whilst at the same time avoiding oligarchic manipulation (della Porta and Diani 2005: 160). We know something about the difficulties of forming transnational social movements (Tarrow 2001; della Porta and Tarrow 2005). What we know less about are emerging forms of transnational activism that involve the grass-roots mobilizations outside institutions that are typically associated with social movements and that at the same time address global elites through INGOs. Studying human rights claims offers social scientists a focus for understanding contemporary forms of transnational activism that extends the classic agenda of social movement studies.

NOTE

1. "Northwestern" is an attempt to generalize in a way that gets beyond West/East, North/South dichotomies that oversimplify complex and overlapping historical, cultural, and economic interconnections and diversity. I use "Northwestern" to denote Western European and European settler states, the United States, Canada, Australia, and New Zealand. Though imperfect, this categorization lumps together states that share broad commonalities in terms of the history of their formation in terms of citizens' rights and capitalist industrialization, as well as in terms of their centrality to twentieth century geopolitics—all of which are important to the study of human rights.

REFERENCES

Alston, Philip, and Goodman, Ryan (2012). *International Human Rights in Context: Law, Politics, Morals.* Oxford: Oxford University Press.

Batliwala, Srilatha (2002). "Grassroots Movements as Transnational Actors: Implications for Global Civil Society," *Voluntas: International Journal of Voluntary and Nonprofit Organizations.* 13(4): 393–409.

Bob, Clifford (2005). *The Marketing of Rebellion: Insurgents, Media and International Activism.* Cambridge: Cambridge University Press.

Clark, Ann Marie (2001). *Diplomacy of Conscience: Amnesty International and Changing Human Rights Norms.* Princeton: Princeton University Press.

Decoteau, Claire Laurier (2013). "Hybrid Habitus: Toward a Post-Colonial Theory of Practice." In *Postcolonial Sociology,* edited by Julian Go, *Political Power and Social Theory.* 24: 263–294.

della Porta, Donatella and Diani, Mario (2005). *Social Movements.* Chichester: Wiley-Blackwell.

della Porta, Donatella and Tarrow, Sidney, eds. (2005). *Transnational Protest and Global Activism.* Lanham: Rowman & Littlefield.

Diani, Mario (2000). "The Concept of Social Movement." In *Readings in Contemporary Political Sociology,* edited by Kate Nash, 155–176. Oxford: Blackwell.

Donnelly. Jack (2003). *Universal Human Rights in Theory and Practice.* Ithaca, NY: Cornell University Press.

Englund, Harri (2006). *Prisoners of Freedom: Human Rights and the African Poor.* Berkeley: University of California Press.

Eschle, Catherine and Stammers, Neil (2004). "Taking Part: Social Movements, INGOs and Global Change," *Alternatives.* 29: 333–372.

Forbath, William, with Achmat, Zackie, Budlender, Geoff, and Heywood, Mark (2001). "Cultural Transformation, Deep Institutional Reform and ESR Practice: South Africa's Treatment Action Campaign." In *Stones of Hope: How African Activists Reclaim Human*

Rights to Challenge Global Poverty, edited by Lucie White and Jeremy Perelman, 51–90. Stanford: Stanford University Press.

Fraser, Nancy (1997). "Rethinking the Public Sphere: A Contribution to the Critique of Actually Existing Democracy." In *Justice Interruptus: Critical Reflections on the "Postsocialist" Condition*, 69–98. New York: Routledge.

Friedman, Steven, and Mottiar, Shauna (2005). "A Rewarding Engagement? The Treatment Action Campaign and the Politics of HIV/AIDS," *Politics and Society*. 33(4): 511–565.

Gready, Paul, and Ensor, Jonathan, eds. (2005). *Reinventing Development? Translating Rights-Based Approaches from Theory into Practice*. London: Zed Books.

Keck, Margaret, and Sikkink, Katherine (1998). *Activists beyond Borders: Advocacy Networks in International Politics*. Ithaca, New York: Cornell University Press.

Keck, Margaret, and Smith, Jackie (2002). "Transnational Organisations, 1953–93." In *Restructuring World Politics: Transnational Social Movements, Networks, and Norms*, edited by Sanjeev Khagram, James Riker, and Katherine Sikkink, 24–46. Minneapolis: University of Minnesota Press.

Kennedy, David (2002). "The International Human Rights Movement: Part of the Problem?" *Harvard Human Rights Journal*. 15: 101–125.

Khagram, Sanjeev, Riker, James, and Sikkink, Katherine (2002). "From Santiago to Seattle: Transnational Advocacy Groups Restructuring World Politics." In *Restructuring World Politics: Transnational Social Movements, Networks, and Norms*, edited by Sanjeev Khagram, James Riker, and Katherine Sikkink, 3–23. Minneapolis: University of Minnesota Press.

Melucci, Alberto (1989). *Nomads of the Present: Social Movements and Individual Needs in Contemporary Society*. Philadelphia: Temple University Press.

Nash, Kate (2012). "Human Rights, Movements and Law: On Not Researching Legitimacy," *Sociology*. 46(5): 1–16.

Neier, Aryeh (2012). *The International Human Rights Movement: A History*. Princeton: Princeton University Press.

Nelson, Paul J. and Dorsey, Ellen (2008). *New Rights Advocacy: Changing Strategies of Development and Human Rights NGOs*. Washington: Georgetown University Press.

Risse, Thomas, Ropp, Stephen, and Sikkink, Katherine, eds. (1999). *The Power of Human Rights: International Norms and Domestic Change*. Cambridge: Cambridge University Press.

Santos, Boaventura De Sousa (2002a). *Towards a New Legal Common Sense*. London: Butterworths LexisNexis.

Santos, Boaventura De Sousa (2002b). "Toward a Multicultural Conception of Human Rights." In *Moral Imperialism: a Critical Anthology*, edited by Berta Hernandez-Truyol, 39–60. New York: New York University.

Santos, Boaventura De Sousa and Rodríguez-Garavito, Cesar, eds. (2005). *Law and Globalization from Below: Towards a Cosmopolitan Legality*. Cambridge: Cambridge University Press.

Stammers, Neil (1999). "Social Movements and the Social Construction of Human Rights," *Human Rights Quarterly*. 21: 980–1008.

Stammers, Neil (2009). *Human Rights and Social Movements*. London: Pluto.

Stroup, Sarah (2012). *Borders Among Activists: International NGOs in the United States, Britain, and France*. Ithaca, New York: Cornell University Press.

Tarrow, Sidney (2001). "Transnational Politics: Contention and Institutions in International Politics," *Annual Review of Political Science*. 4: 1–20.

CHAPTER 50

THE CONDITIONS FOR CIVIL SOCIETY PARTICIPATION IN INTERNATIONAL DECISION MAKING

RAFFAELE MARCHETTI

THIS chapter examines the international conditions that have been relevant in determining the strengthening of transnational activism during the last three decades. Specific attention is paid to those conditions that allowed for a limited but continuing inclusion of civil society organizations (CSOs) within the international decision-making process. In order to understand this gradual shift, the chapter examines the ideational contribution of CSOs in relation to the contemporary debate on globalization. The chapter is structured in the following way: it first examines the socio-economic and normative-institutional conditions that favored transnational activism. It then sketches an interpretative model for understanding the contextual impact of CSOs and their politics of norm change at the transnational level. Next, the chapter goes on to survey the debate on globalization and scrutinizes the main global master frames developed thereby. From this exercise, a common denomination is identified in the pro-civil society participatory norm, which is then analyzed in the context of a number of concrete institutionalizations. These institutional instances contribute to trace the spreading of this new norm within the current global governance arrangements, while at the same time showing that its implementation is inevitably subject to partisan interpretation and consequently political controversy.

CONTEXTUAL CONDITIONS
FOR TRANSNATIONAL ACTIVISM

It is now widely recognized that civil society, from traditional international non-governmental organizations (INGOs) to transnational social movements, plays a significant role in global governance (Risse-Kappen 1995; Keck and Sikkink 1998; Tarrow 2005; Smith and Wiest 2012). What is perhaps less debated are the contextual conditions that created an environment conducive to such transnational activism. The transnational mobilizations of the last thirty years have taken place within particular political circumstances. The conditions that constituted a favorable environment for the strengthening of transnational activism and its progressive inclusion in international decision making can be categorized into two main types: socio-economic and institutional-normative conditions. I will begin by listing these factors, then I will analyze them individually in more detail. Among the socio-economic conditions, there are four main factors—first, the transformation of the state's functions; second, the process of globalization; third, the information technology (IT) revolution; and, finally, a number of socio-economic processes related to education and travelling. Among the institutional-normative conditions, there are three main elements—first, the new rules for participation; second, the transformation of authority and modes of compliance; and, finally, the specific set of liberal principles as embedded in the system of global governance.

Within the four socio-economic conditions, undoubtedly the privatization of the functions previously performed by the state opened new political spaces for CSOs. The state's financial resources declined in the 1980s and 1990s and its overall role in international affairs was consequently reduced. At the same time, a number of differing ideological perspectives (including neoliberalism and the third way, but also the principle of subsidiarity) suggested a similar acknowledgment of the value of non-state actors. As a consequence of this new context, CSOs were able to mobilize resources both from the state itself (which opted for the cheaper and most effective way of subcontracting its tasks, mainly to NGOs) and from other private and public sources (Hulme and Edwards 1997).

The globalization process generated a sense of common purpose among civil society actors, and triggered both internal unification, increasing the sense of solidarity among civil society organizations, and the contestation of the socio-economic consequences of globalization (Van Rooy 2004). For the first time, a number of ad hoc coalitions and campaigns were organized on a trans-ideological basis, going beyond the traditional political barriers of previous forms of national mobilization, and targeting a number of controversial aspects of globalization.

Also, the technological innovations in the IT field revolutionized the organizational patterns within civil society (Hill and Hughes 1998; Warkentin 2001). Through the internet, groups from different parts of the world have been able to increase their political know-how and their ability to join forces transnationally, addressing common targets.

Moreover, changes in social behavior, such as the proliferation of higher education and the expansion of international travel, have empowered CSOs, allowing an enlarged group of activists to get in contact with each other. The spread of knowledge and the building of new transnational trustworthy relations increased the awareness of social inequality and the political mechanisms underpinning such a situation, providing the bases for mobilization (Smith and Wiest 2012: 168).

Three further institutional-normative conditions related to the system of global governance are relevant. The current global governance arrangements allow for the participation of a number of different political actors considered to be relevant stakeholders. This has created a significant opportunity for the inclusion of civil society organizations in what were previously closed government rooms (Higgott, Underhill, and Bieler 2000; Hale and Held 2011).

The transformation of authority from its traditional understanding in terms of institutional delegation, to one according to which authority is granted on the bases of expertise, principles, or simply capacity to deliver has made extra room for the claims from CSOs (Avant, Finnemore, and Sell 2010). In the same vein, compliance today is more and more a matter of improving actors' ability and willingness to comply with international standards rather than coercing them into obedience. This context, centered on soft modes such as capacity building, dissemination of best practices, and normative persuasion, is very favorable for CSOs as norm-creators and agent-persuaders.

In addition, the wider international system, based as it is primarily on liberal Western principles, has created an environment conducive to the development of these kinds of activities (Boli and Thomas 1999; Smith and Wiest 2012: 163). The widespread recognition of the transnational value of: human rights, civic participation, accountability, good governance and democracy, social empowerment, and gender equality, have enhanced the possibilities for CSOs to gain space and legitimacy in the international system beyond the traditional framework of state-based representation.

The specific political constellation that has facilitated the growth and consolidation of civil activism at the international level may help not only in understanding the origins of this phenomenon, but also in deciphering the contours of any future development of global civil society's role. If the support of international institutions diminishes; if the states regain their exclusive role in international affairs; if the globalization process becomes constrained by nationalistic policies; if technological innovations remain compartmentalized and obstructed by censorship; and finally, if the international system turns towards authoritarian forms of state-centrism and evolves into a realpolitik-dominated multipolar system (thereby including forms of macro-regionalization) hostile to non-governmental actors, then the aforementioned conditions for the transnational flourishing of civil society may fade away, and activists may find themselves under pressure to find alternative forms of political action (and indeed of political agency) that are more suitable to the new scenario.

The Contextual Impact of Social Movements' Action

The conditions examined in the previous section have proven essential for the transnational mobilizations of the last decades. It would be mistaken, however, to take them as given, solely as a sort of external constraint on the action of CSOs. While they decisively shape the realm of possibilities for mobilization, they are in turn shaped by the action of CSOs themselves. Any mobilization in fact can have a material impact and/or a contextual impact (or indeed a null impact). Actions having a contextual impact are those that are able to shape the socio-economic and institutional context for the future mobilizations. In this sense, their immediate value might be low, but their long-term significance is high. More specifically, this chapter understands the political agency of CSOs active at the transnational level as in-between the overall contextual preconditions that shape their existence and the political opportunity structure that provides them with favorable/unfavorable specific circumstances for action. Political agency is here seen as the combination of a specific identity (rooted in the frame of reference of the organization), with the goals and strategies that are set by the CSOs. The combination of these factors then generates the different impact of the CSOs (see Figure 50.1).

The contextual impact is often seen in normative-institutional terms. It is precisely by changing the norms and the institutions within which all political actors have to play at the international level that CSOs may increase their relative weight. Based as it is on the state-centered Westphalian model, the baseline at the international level is particularly hostile to non-governmental actors. Given this context, any reform in terms of

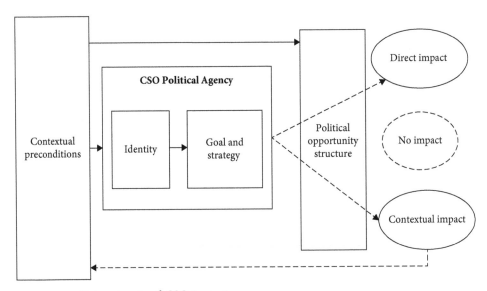

FIGURE 50.1 Determinants of CSO impact.

increased inclusion of non-state actors is going to be beneficial to future transnational mobilizations. The analytical model most used to interpret the mobilizations leading to normative-institutional reform is the model of the politics of norm change. It is to this model that we now turn.

THE POLITICS OF NORMS CHANGE

At the base of one of the core dynamics leading to the emergence and operation of transnational activism resides the perception of the possibility of normative change (or conversely the possibility to resist a threatening change) in one specific global issue area. This possibility might be due either to the "discovery" of a new issue as significant, or to the re-interpretation of a long-standing issue in a different way. Ultimately a key component of transnational activism in global governance lies exactly in its stubborn attempt to influence the normative battle on the right and legitimate interpretation of key global issues. In this perspective, CSOs should be seen not only as traditionally "problem solvers" (providing solutions which governments are less suited to deliver), but also as "problem generators" (imposing new problematic issues on the international agenda). While the perception of an unjust situation necessarily constitutes a precondition for action, it is only when the actor recognizes the possibility of having a positive impact on such a situation that mobilization may start. Transnational mobilizations on global issues should be interpreted as the development of the politics of change through several political steps (Keck and Sikkink 1998; Price 2003).

A first, crucial challenge for any transnational network is the ability to present the issue at stake in such a way that it is perceived as problematic, urgent, and yet soluble. Each issue of contention should be clearly and singly identified: protest on broad or fuzzy issues tend to be less effective. Any issue at stake should be presented to the public as problematic and therefore in need of action. It should be also seen as urgent, that is, no postponement should be accepted. And finally, it should be assessed as feasible, as a problem that can be solved, for otherwise no action would be initiated. The issue of political feasibility is particularly controversial, and it is exactly within this controversy that CSOs may have a first impact by suggesting that something that was previously considered as unproblematic, not urgent, and especially unsolvable, can indeed now be judged as worthy of public attention. The first step in cross-border mobilizations is therefore the production of knowledge and the creation of frames through which the correct interpretation of the issue at stake is proposed.

A second step consists of the external dissemination and strategic use of such knowledge: Here information acquires a fully public dimension, thus a political significance (Kolb 2005). Global public opinion needs to be attracted and its imagination captured for the framing of the terms of the conflict in such a way that the issue at stake becomes associated with a general interest which requires a public engagement. Information politics is at work here. Often, when networks become active players in the epistemic communities of experts of global issues, they tend to be perceived by public opinion as credible sources of information and increase their influence on policy making. It is in this phase that CSOs need to play well within the windows of opportunities that the system provides in order to be as effective as possible in reaching the right target audience, be it politicians, opinion leaders, or citizens.

A third step is, however, necessary in order to promote change. This consists in enacting the process of acquisition of legitimate representation of the general interests at stake (Jordan and van Tuijl 2000; Tilly 2004; Van Rooy 2004; Collingwood 2006; Brown 2008). Contrasting the situation of international affairs in which states monopolize power and social actors are structurally excluded, the task consists here in the appropriation of a recognized role in the public sphere, as rightful advocates of general interests. To the question "in whose name do you speak?" transnational networks need to offer a response in terms of reclaiming for themselves the representation of a more general interest than that relevant for economic and political decision makers (Florini 2000; Rajagopal 2003).

Once transnational networks succeed, through the process just outlined, in shaping a challenge associated to a particular global issue, the political opportunity for mobilizing and network building arises. Once a norm has emerged, it may be embedded into institutions and travel among them in a dynamic that is well studied in the field of international relations (IR) (Johnston 2001; Acharya 2004; Checkel 2005). What is important to note in this respect is that according to the perspective of many civil society activists, institutions tend to be seen as norm receivers and norm institutionalizers rather than norm-generators, or at least as partners in political synergies. The role of wider civil society remains indispensable for generating new normative narratives.

The competitive nature of the politics of norm change is at times underestimated or simply overlooked by many studies. However, the dynamics generating new norms is inherently contentious. Any time a new reading is advanced by CSOs, a different, most often opposite interpretation is vigorously promoted by antagonist socio-economic actors (Santos 2006; Bob 2012). The case of the normative debate on the nature of the political control of the globalization process is a clear case in point.

The Normative Debate about Globalization

One of the most heated debates on the political agenda concerns the social consequences and the political control of what is usually referred to as globalization. There can be no doubt that world ethical consciousness has been altered by the global transformations of the last decades. In this process, characterized by the intensification of interaction and by the deepening enmeshment of local and global, economic concerns have undoubtedly taken the lead, but politics, law, and culture are also experiencing radical mutations that increasingly throw into doubt the legitimacy of traditional codes of conduct. From the assemblies of international institutions to national parliaments, from private sector meetings to civil society fora, the theme of the effects of the increased global intercon-nectedness on the life of citizens occupies the center of public discussion.

The focus of this debate on globalization is the inadequacy of the current institutional framework and its normative bases for a full development of the political sphere at the global level. Traditional political canons anchored in the nation-state and its domes-tic jurisdiction are increasingly perceived as insufficient, or indeed, self-defeating in a world in which socio-economical interaction is, to a significant degree, interdepend-ent. Unstable financial markets, environmental crises, and unregulated migratory flows offer just a few examples of phenomena that all too clearly remind us of the heavy inter-dependence of the contemporary international system and of its political deprivation. These intense processes of global transformation functionally require increased trans-national cooperation, and yet pose a continuous challenge to the effectiveness and legit-imacy of "traditional" political life.

Acknowledging the limits of this political tension, alternative projects of global politics have been developed and mooted publicly in recent decades. Their common denominator consists of the attempt to go beyond the centrality of the sovereign state towards forms of political participation that allow for new subjects to "get into transna-tional politics." These new would-be or quasi-global political actors are part of the broad category of non-state actors, which includes: international non-governmental organiza-tions, transnational corporations, networks and campaigns of civil society organizations and faith-based groups, transnational social movements, transnational political parties, international private bodies, and individuals. Despite minor institutional experiments, most of these actors share the characteristics of effectively being excluded from interna-tional decision-making mechanisms, and yet being more and more active on the global stage. International exclusion constitutes the critical target of most of the alternative projects of global politics that occupy the center of the public debate on globalization.

Underpinning this debate on the political deficits of the global system are a number of ideological readings of globalization and global political phenomena that can be consid-ered to be species of archetypes or master frames of global politics. These master frames can be considered as "meta-tanks," or cultural resources from which political actors draw their ideas and principles in order to formulate their political reference for action (Snow and Benford 2000: 58). Political actors actively deploy global master frames to construct their contentious political references in their politics of norm change (Goffman 1974; McAdam, McCarthy, and Zald 1996; Benford and Snow 2000). What distinguishes mas-ter frames from political projects is precisely their detachment from any specific politi-cal actor or action (content-orientation rather than action-orientation) (Oliver and Johnston 2000; Snow and Benford 2000). In opposition to the hybrid characteristics of political projects, a master frame remains "uncontaminated," more static, and clearly distinguishable from other master frames.

Historically speaking, the first master frame with a global scope tended to have a rather negative outlook. In the 1970, among the very widespread negative master frames was the anti-Americanism master frame, but also that of anti-colonialism. Earlier on, the master frame of anti-Nazism was dominant. In more positive terms, the master frame of human rights also played a crucial role for many decades. We can call these first generation global master frames. They were the first and the less articulated master frames. With time, some of them lost their political centrality (the anti-Nazism frame) whilst some flowed into other more sophisticated global master frames. Anti-Americanism often turned into localism or civilizationism; anti-colonialism partly disappeared and partly flowed into civilizationism; the master frame of human rights was further developed within the global master frames of cosmopolitanism, but also to some extent within that of localism. In order to understand better the different between first and second generation global master frames we now need to move to the current debate on the master frames of global politics.

GLOBAL POLITICS AND ITS MASTER FRAMES

A typical phenomenon of any transition process occurring at the international level is precisely the sense of instability generated by the emergence of un-institutionalized actors and new legitimacy claims (previously unheard) in the public domain. Within this context of new political agency, an unprecedented global public domain consolidates in which old, state-centered visions of international affairs mix with new non-state-centered visions of global politics, producing a complex map of ideological positions. The global public domain remains thus a central place where new dimensions and new applications of global legitimacy are developed and advanced in contrast to current interpretations. This does not necessarily entail reformist or indeed revolutionary transformations, but the mere possibility of starting a dynamic of norms change in international politics makes this global public arena and its ideal content extremely important for current global politics (Finnemore and Sikkink 1998; Clark 2007). It is to this global public discourse and to its components that we need to look in order to understand the future, long-term transformation of global politics.[1]

In this under-explored arena of discussion and contestation over the legitimate global social purposes, a number of distinct political positions can be identified. Few scholars have attempted such classification. Bond identifies five principal positions: specifically, global justice movements, third world nationalism, post-Washington consensus, Washington consensus, and resurgent rightwing populism (Bond 2004: 20–1). Held and McGrew acknowledge six positions: radicalism, statism/protectionism, global transformation, institutional reformer, liberal internationalism, and neoliberalism (Held and McGrew 2002: 99). Pianta distinguishes three projects that go by the names of neoliberal globalization, globalization of rights and responsibilities, and globalization from below (Pianta 2001). Aguiton discerns three groups, called radical internationalist (beyond state and capitalism), nationalist (south), and neoreformist (global governance) (Aguiton 2001). These categorizations provide a useful first orientation in the debate, nonetheless they are not completely satisfactory for at least three reasons: a) they provide only a limited range of alternatives (Held and McGrew; Pianta; Aguiton); b) they fail to clearly distinguish between conventional (state-based) and the new non-conventional models (Bond; Held and McGrew; Aguiton); and more importantly, c) they fail to provide a valid method of politically interpreting these categories in the context of globalization.

Building on the previous discussion and expanding the perspective to include other marginalized master frames of non-state actors, four key interpretations of the notion of world polity can be identified as delimiting the range of non-conventional ideal alternatives available to the global political debate (see Table 50.1 below): 1) the vision of world capitalism as associated with a global free market and private economic actors; 2) the project for the democratization of international institutions as formulated in the cosmopolitan model with reference to individuals and supra-national institutions; 3) the radical vision held by the vast majority of the social movements in terms of alter-globalism and that of ethnic localism; and finally, 4) the discourse on the dialogue or clash of civilizations which refers to macro-regional actors often defined in religious terms (Marchetti 2009).

Table 50.1 Main characteristics of global master frames

	Cosmopolitanism	Localism	Civilizationism	Neoliberalism
Political power	Bottom up by individuals	Bottom up by civic groups	Top down by cultural élites	Top down (and bottom up) by economic actors
Reading of globalization	Reformist	Radical antagonism	Conservative antagonism	Supportive
Human bond	Political	Social	Cultural-Religious	Economic
Agency	Individual (citizens)	Collective (grassroots groups)	Collective (civilisations and cultural élites)	Individual/ Collective (firms and consumers)
Ontology	Universalism; Homogeneity	Pluralism; Heterogeneity	Pluralism; Heterogeneity	Universalism; Homogeneity
Political principles	Globalism; Delegated participation; Sameness; Hierarchy; Institutional fairness	Place-basedness; Direct participation; Diversity; Autonomy; Solidarity	Culture-basedness; Elites guidance; Diversity; Respect; Goodwill and non violence	Globalism; Technocracy; Sameness; Freedom; Competition
Responsibility for public goods	Institutions (formal)	Society (substantive)	Elites (substantive)	None (formal)
Institutional project	Supra-national integration of individuals	Local groups, Transnational networks	Macro-regionalism	Global self-regulation

The Institutionalization of the New Pro-civil Society Participatory Norm and its Controversies

A pro-civil society participatory norm constitutes the underpinning element of the global master frames just presented. The norm paves the way for a positive welcoming of NGOs and to a lesser extent social movements, not least for their alleged potential in terms of legitimacy and (cost-)effectiveness (the so-called "new policy agenda"). While each frame draws the norm in a slightly different form, the central pivot remains the same: non-governmental actors should have a voice in the decision-making mechanisms at the international and transnational level. This new understanding of the political agency of non-governmental actors at the international level is revolutionary. Until a few years ago, it was unthinkable to consider non-state actors as relevant subjects in the international realm. However, as argued by Reinman, in the 1980s this new norm began to emerge in international development circles and later became institutionalized within the United Nations (UN) system in the 1990s. As a consequence, civil society has since been seen, together with the private sector, as the right (at time even indispensable) functional partner to the delegitimized states and intergovernmental organizations (Reiman 2006: 59–60). Today this seems more and more accepted, if not absolutely encouraged. A number of examples prove that this new norm, differently interpreted and differently implemented, has been endorsed by a growing number of international institutions.

The UN is showing signs of opening towards civil society, the so-called stakeholders, though in different forms (United Nations 2004). At least four mechanisms can be singled out. The first by now well-developed formula for the inclusion of stakeholders adopted by the UN for many years is the classical consultation with CSOs. A second mechanism for engagement with civil society is the subcontracting of specific functions. A third mechanism more recently observed concerns the founding, financing, aggregating, or simply sponsoring of newly created CSOs. Finally, a fourth mechanism that has been envisaged and implemented in the last few years is the formal inclusion of non-governmental organizations (NGOs) into the decision-making process of the UN. This is a particularly innovative transformation in that it significantly erodes the pure intergovernmental nature of the UN. With this fourth mechanism, non-governmental actors move inside intergovernmental organizations. Two instances of such formalized inclusion of CSOs have occurred in the last seven years. In 2007 CSOs were included in the workings of UNAIDS, the Joint United Nations Program on HIV/AIDS, and perhaps more importantly in 2009, in the working of the Committee on Food Security (CFS) of the Food and Agriculture Organization (FAO).

The European Commission also has a long history of interaction with civil society experts that has changed and expanded over time. In the 1960s and 1970s the

Commission focussed on "consultation" within European economic integration and dialogue with primarily economic experts within industrial and agrarian interest groups. Later on, in the 1980s and 1990s, it focussed on developing a "partnership" with non-governmental actors within the social dialogue on specific policy areas such as security, social, and educational policy. However, only in the late 1990s and 2000s, did attention move to the idea of "participation" itself and the concept of participatory democracy. The White Paper on Governance drew up the framework for such cooperation (European Commission 2001) and the Leaken Conference of 2001 established a qualitative milestone for the recognition of the participation of CSOs in European governance by including for the first time the representation of civil society in the Convention working on the Constitutional Treaty. As a result, the process of policy formation widened beyond the classical intergovernmental method and included voluntary, informal, inclusive, and participatory forms of coordination, the so-called new era of EU multilevel governance.

Finally, the World Commission on Dams (WCD), established in 1998 to review the effectiveness of large dams and develop new standards, represents a third, different case of inclusion of non-state actors in international institutions. The novelty of such an organization consisted in its hybrid nature in that it relied on extensive public consultations with a different range of CSOs, and pioneered a new funding model with both private and CSO funding contributing to the financing of the process. Especially important were its recommendations affirming, among other things, that all stakeholders, including indigenous peoples, should have the opportunity for informed participation in decision-making processes related to large dams through stakeholder fora. The WCD successfully contributed to change, with a soft governance-multistakeholder approach, the paradigm of large infrastructures management.

These examples suggest a rather rosy scenario in terms of the increased participation of CSOs in the wider international decision-making process, compared with the past. However, these and other examples do not necessarily entail either any broad consensus on, or support for, the role played by CSOs for a number of reasons: first, the examples constitute different implementations of the pro-civil society norm rather than a single instance; second, the norm itself is subject to different, competing interpretations; third, alternative norms are advanced in the global public debates concerning the role CSOs should play in the international system. As already mentioned, the normative competition at the global level is very intense. Any norm generates benefits and costs, it has beneficiaries and victims. As a matter of fact, in its implementation, the pro-CSOs norm has tended so far to favor by and large a specific set of organizations (big INGOs, strong transnational networks), marginalizing less organized grassroots movements and small local groups. As a consequence, while still leaving windows of opportunities for mobilizations on different levels, overall, the current global governance scheme has been de facto selective in its interaction with civil society. Institutionalized, professional CSOs are part and parcel of the functional mode of governance insofar as they act as governance partners in the implementation of sector-comprehensive strategies on different policy levels or in the promotion of a pro-global integration agenda thereby providing alternative, deliberative paths for the re-legitimization of many international organizations.

At the level of principles, however, a difference remains between participatory governance (with stakeholders) and participatory democracy from below. Participatory governance is centered on an instrumental input legitimacy and an output legitimacy anchored on private-public partnerships, whereas participatory democracy is based on a mode of intrinsic input legitimacy in which discursive involvement in policy formation is promoted by transnational civil society. The contrast between these divergent readings also highlights a serious political dilemma for civil society in global governance. The more international organizations seek professionalized NGOs, the less they will have bottom up civil society actors, which entails a diminution of the very legitimizing and communicative role of civil society (Heidbreder 2012: 19). It is a sort of catch 22 situation in which CSOs need to be simultaneously highly professionalized in order to have a voice in governance circles, and remain deeply rooted in order to provide genuine legitimacy from below. This political dilemma is one of the reasons for the increasing skepticism of many social movements about the real availability of opportunities at EU, UN, or other international institutions' level.

Conclusions

This chapter has analyzed the contextual conditions that have favored the ascendancy of transnational activism in global politics in the last thirty years. Among these conditions, particularly important is the normative background that has allowed for the recognition of CSOs as relevant stakeholders in global governance. The pro-civil society participatory norm that is now embedded in a number of international organizations has been shown not only to be a contextual condition, but also in line with the politics of norm change forcefully enacted by CSOs themselves. It is in fact in the debate on globalization and world orders that a number of competing master frames have been constructed by CSOs which, despite their ideological differences, share the acknowledgment of the political significance of non-state actors. By suggesting this double vision of international norms (as a constraining factor, but also as a product of contentious politics), this chapter has pointed to the inherently competitive nature of global politics: a domain in which CSOs' contribution in terms of norm contestation and norm creation is more and more incisive.

Note

1. Such interpretative endeavor is only possible by combining inputs from different disciplinary agendas, including the research on: transnational activism (della Porta and Tarrow 2005); the politics of norm change (Finnemore and Sikkink 1998); and on globalization and global governance (Held and McGrew 2002), which include contributions from international relations, political sociology, and international political theory.

References

Acharya, A. (2004). "How Ideas Spread: Whose Norms Matter? Norm Localization and Institutional Change in Asian Regionalism," *International Organization*. 58(2): 239–275.

Aguiton, C. (2001). *Le monde nous appartient*. Paris: Plon.

Avant, D.D., Finnemore, M. and Sell, S.K., eds. (2010). *Who Governs the Globe?* Cambridge: Cambridge University Press.

Benford, R.D. and Snow, D.A. (2000). "Framing Processes and Social Movements: An Overview and Assessment," *Annual Review of Sociology*. 26(August): 611–639.

Bob, C. (2012). *The Right Wing and the Clash of World Politics*. Cambridge: Cambridge University Press.

Boli, J. and Thomas, G.M., eds. (1999). *Constructing World Culture: International Non-Governmental Organizations Since 1875*. Stanford, CA: Stanford University Press.

Bond, P. (2004). *Talk Left, Walk Right: South Africa's Frustrated Global Reforms*. Scottsville: University of KwaZulu-Natal Press.

Brown, L.D. (2008). *Creating Credibility. Legitimacy and Accountability for Transnational Civil Society*. Sterling VA: Kumarian Press.

Checkel, J.T. (2005). "International Institutions and Socialization in Europe: Introduction and Framework," *International Organization*. 59(4): 801–826.

Clark, I. (2007). *International Legitimacy and World Society*. Oxford: Oxford University Press.

Collingwood, V. (2006). "Non-Governmental Organisations, Power and Legitimacy in International Society," *Review of International Studies*. 32(3): 439–454.

De Sousa Santos, B. (2006). *The Rise of the Global Left: The World Social Forum and Beyond*. London: Zed Books.

della Porta, D. and Tarrow, S., eds. (2005). *Transnational Protest and Global Activism*. Lanham, MD: Rowan and Littlefield.

European Commission. (2001). *European Governance: A White Paper*. Brussels: COM (2001) 428 final.

Finnemore, M. and Sikkink, K. (1998). "International Norms Dynamics and Political Change," *International Organization*. 52(4): 887–917.

Florini, A., ed. (2000). *The Third Force: The Rise of Transnational Civil Society*. Tokyo and Washington: JCIE and CEIP.

Goffman, E. (1974). *Frame Analysis: An Essay on the Organisation of the Experience*. New York: Harper Colophon.

Hale, T. and Held, D., eds. (2011). *Handbook of Transnational Governance. New Institutions and Innovations*. Cambridge: Polity.

Heidbreder, E.G. (2012). "Civil Society Participation in EU Governance," *Living Reviews in European Governance*. 7(2). Cited on March 2014 http://europeangovernance.livingreviews. org/Articles/lreg-2012-2/.

Held, D. and McGrew, A. (2002). *Globalization/Anti-Globalization*. Cambridge: Polity.

Higgott, R.A., Underhill, G.R.D. and Bieler, A., eds. (2000). *Non-State Actors and Authority in the Global System*. New York: Routledge.

Hill, K.A. and Hughes, J.E. (1998). *Cyberpolitics: Citizen Activism in the Age of the Internet*. Lanham, MD: Rowan and Littlefield.

Hulme, D. and Edwards, M., eds. (1997). *NGOs, States and Donors: Too Close for Comfort?* London: Macmillan.

Johnston, A.I. (2001). "Treating International Institutions as Social Environments," *International Studies Quarterly*. 45: 487–515.

Jordan, L. and van Tuijl, P. (2000). "Political Responsibility in Transnational NGO Advocacy," *World Development*. 28(12): 2051–2065.

Keck, M. and Sikkink, K. (1998). *Activists Beyond Borders: Advocacy Networks in International Politics*. Ithaca, NY: Cornell University Press.

Kolb, F. (2005). "The Impact of Transnational Protest on Social Movement Organizations: Mass Media and the Making of ATTAC Germany." In *Transnational Protest and Global Activism* edited by D. della Porta and S. Tarrow, 95–120. Lanham: Rowan and Littlefield.

Marchetti, R. (2009). "Mapping Alternative Models of Global Politics," *International Studies Review*. 11(1): 133–156.

McAdam, D., McCarthy, J.D. and Zald, M.N. (1996). *Comparative Perspectives on Social Movements: Political Opportunities, Mobilizing Structures, and Cultural Framings*. Cambridge: Cambridge University Press.

Oliver, P. and Johnston, H. (2000). "What A Good Idea! Ideology and Frames in Social Movement Research," *Mobilization*. 5(1): 37–54.

Pianta, M. (2001). *Globalizzazione dal basso. Economia mondiale e movimenti sociali*. Roma: ManifestoLibri.

Price, R. (2003). "Transnational Civil Society and Advocacy," *World Politics*. 55(4): 579–607.

Rajagopal, B. (2003). *International Law from Below. Development, Social Movements and Third World Resistance*. Cambridge: Cambridge University Press.

Reiman, K. (2006). "A View from the Top: International Politics, Norms, and the Worldwide Growth of NGOs," *International Studies Quarterly*. 50: 45–67.

Risse-Kappen, T., ed. (1995). *Bringing Transnational Relations Back In: Non-State Actors, Domestic Structure and International Institutions*. Ithaca, NY: Cornell University Press.

Smith, J. and Wiest, D. (2012). *Social Movements in the World-System: The Politics of Crisis and Transformation*. New York: Russell Sage Foundation.

Snow, D.A. and Benford, R.D. (2000). "Clarifying the Relationship between Framing and Ideology," *Mobilization*. 5(1): 55–60.

Tarrow, S. (2005). *The New Transnational Activism*. Cambridge: Cambridge University Press.

Tilly, C. (2004). *Social Movements, 1768–2004*. Bouder, CO: Paradigm.

United Nations. (2004). *We the Peoples: Civil Society, the United Nations and Global Governance* (No. A/58/817/2004). New York: Report of the Panel of Eminent Persons on United Nations-Civil Society Relations. Commission Cardoso (UN A/58/817).

Van Rooy, A. (2004). *The Global Legitimacy Game: Civil Society, Globalization, and Protest*. Houndmills, Basingstoke: Palgrave.

Warkentin, C. (2001). *Reshaping World Politics. NGOs, the Internet and Global Civil Society*. Lanham, MD: Rowan and Littlefield.

CHAPTER 51

··

DEMOCRACY IN SOCIAL MOVEMENTS

··

DONATELLA DELLA PORTA

SOCIAL MOVEMENTS AND DEMOCRACY: AN INTRODUCTION

··

SOCIAL movements do not only transform democratic states through struggles for policy changes, but they also express a fundamental critique of conventional politics, thus addressing meta-political issues (Offe 1985). Since the nineteenth century, the labor movement has been a pivotal actor in the broadening of citizens' rights, bridging claims for freedom with those for social justice (della Porta 2013). Since the 1970s, the so-called "new social movements" (including environmental and women's movements) have challenged existing conceptions of democracy, calling for decentralized and participatory organizational structures as well as the defence of interpersonal solidarity against state and corporate bureaucracies. They have claimed free spaces, liberated from the dominion of the states and the market (Offe 1985). At the turn of the millennium, the global justice movement has bridged the traditional emphasis on participatory democracy with a new one on deliberative democracy (della Porta 2009a). Since 2011, importing some forms of protest from the Arab Spring, anti-austerity protestors called for new forms of direct democracy (della Porta 2014).

While never a central concern for social movement studies, in recent times there has in fact been some increased attention to democracy within movements, that is visible in these movements' attempts to make their internal organizational structures more open and egalitarian, without losing (too much) in efficiency. If the resource mobilization approach had focussed on strategic choices, the "cultural turn" in social movement studies has prompted a recognition of the symbolic and emotional dimension of social movements, opening the way to considering the "passionate" dimension of social movement politics also as far as the internal life of movement organizations is concerned.

Second, in normative theory, the debate on participative and deliberative forms of democracy oriented attention towards the visions of democracy inside and outside social movements. Third, as neoliberalism developed as a political and economic ideology, opportunities for social movements shirked, following the shift from politics to the market. The increasing influence of some international institutions, primarily financial (the World Bank (WB), International Monetary Fund (IMF), and the World Trade Organisation (WTO)) and some macro-regional (mainly the EU) ones, brought about the challenges to develop global conceptions of democracy. In 2011, with and after the Arab Spring, calls for "real democracy" were voiced at the core and at the periphery of the capitalist system. In these circumstances, social movements appear to play a potentially crucial role.

Protest and social movements are in fact considered as more and more relevant for conceptions of democracy in which society has a voice, collective sentiments can be articulated, judgments on the governments and its actions are formed, counter-knowledge (or counter-expertise) is formulated, and demands are issued (Rosanvallon 2008, 20). In particular, attempts have come from the Global South to develop democratic decision making based on the principle of autonomy from the state (Starr, Martinez-Torres and Rosset 2011).

As social movements seem to respond to these transformations, additional stimuli to analyze the conceptions of democracy in social movements came from observed internal changes. Studies focussing on conceptions and visions of democracy in social movements (della Porta 2009a and 2009b) confirm their growing concern with the development of proposals for reform of state institutions, which go in directions which are resonant with the growing legitimacy to different forms of political participation, so transforming challenges into opportunities. What is more, they point at the experimentation, within social movements, of democratic conceptions that openly challenge the liberal vision of democracy as a representative system based on majoritarian decision making.

In what follows, I will look at the ways in which social movement organizations have, over time, developed their structures and functions. While by far not all social movements have aimed at achieving internal democracy (Tilly 2007), progressive movements have often attempted to develop inclusive and transparent decision making. If these attempts often failed, and power structures did indeed survived within the social movement organizations, social movements have, however, been very self-reflective, trying to learn from previous mistakes and devise (partial) solutions to specific problems.

PARTICIPATORY DEMOCRACY IN MOVEMENTS

If liberal democracy—and therefore the democratic state—is mainly based on principles of delegation and majority votes, social movements have long been considered to be the carriers of *participatory* visions and practices of democracy, with their criticism of delegation and positive emphasis on the importance of directly involving citizens in decision making.

In European history, a participatory vision of democracy developed with the mobilization of the labor movement, also bringing about relevant institutional changes. The initial steps of the democratic state have been characterized by widespread activism in the public sphere (cf. Eder 2010), which remained autonomous from political parties. It is in this phase—which in the history of England and France stretches from the end of the eighteenth century to the beginning of the next one—that a public sphere is formed, and not only for the bourgeoisie. Studies on the "making" of the labor movement describe this period as being characterized by identities still oriented to trades, fragmented organizational structures and local, sporadic protests, but also by a certain participatory ferment. Notwithstanding the low levels of electoral participation, participation in the public sphere was intense, with the multiplication of autonomous and influential opinion movements. Summarizing various historical studies, Alessandro Pizzorno observes that halfway through the eighteenth century, in England, public opinion "manifested itself in ever more numerous petitions, in discussions in public places, or in semi-private places (taverns, cafés, clubs), where the new middle class of tradesmen and professionals, readers of periodicals.... Numerous societies and associations were formed.... the political press spread in a manner previously unimaginable" (Pizzorno 1996: 972). During what E.P. Thompson (1991) influentially defined as "the making of the English working class," street marches for reform mobilized hundreds of thousands of citizens, while some of the radical magazines achieved a circulation of tens of thousands of copies. In many European countries, extra-parliamentary political associations gathered hundreds of thousands of signatures for petitions on themes such as the freedom of the press, the emancipation of slaves, freedom of religion, electoral reform, and public education (Pizzorno 1996: 488–489). Petitions, processions, and barricades mobilized many thousands of people (Sewell 1980).

At the origins of democracy lies in fact "the entrance of the masses into history." Indeed, "the 18th century represents a rupture on a grand scale in the history of western Europe. Before that moment, the masses were barred from exercising their public rights. From that moment, they became citizens and in this sense members of the political community" (Bendix 1964: 72). The struggle for universal suffrage is thus also and principally a struggle for recognition of emerging groups: "it is to oppose a conception of foreignness and social invisibility that impacted the majority of society. Overcoming existing discrimination in the name of equality meant being recognised as full members of society" (Costa 2010: 13).

The social and political claims of the budding workers' movement intertwined with claims that may be defined as meta-democratic, addressing the very conceptions and practices of democracy. The battle for the freedom of the press was a founding experience of the English working class (Thompson 1991: 805). A central claim for the worker movement, the right "to combine" began with the right to associate, but differentiated itself from this (Bendix 1964). While the freedom to associate with others formed a part of the freedom of conscience, of speech, of industry, of religious belief, and of the press, it had not, like these others, been promoted by the revolution, which had rather aimed to abolish the bodies between the state and nation of the old order. It emerged instead as an invention of the workers' organizations that, exploiting the ambiguities of the revolutionary discourse, defined the demands for collective negotiations in terms of brotherhood. In the burgeoning workers' movement, associations were thought of as workers' corporations, cooperatives, but also as confraternities of proletarians, initially with a mutual aid function, and then as instruments for opposing a vision of freedom as isolation, promoting associations as a reciprocal link and common intelligence (Sewell 1980: 216).

In the protest campaigns for the widening of citizenship rights, other models of democracy were also conceptualized and practiced: direct, horizontal, and self-managed. In the public sphere, old and new intertwined: traditional forms of associationism (corporations, etc.) combined with emerging forms. Under pressure from social movements of various types, the system of representation that had been constituted, with continuities and discontinuities with respect to the old order, soon began to build institutions and practices for recognizing collective identities. Notwithstanding the individualizing rhetoric, the democratic state in formation shows traits of organized or associative democracy, developing channels of access for interests organized in parties or associations.

Conceptions and practices of different models of democracy (and different democratic qualities) with respect to those foreseen in the definition of the liberal state, were developed and prefigured especially during waves of protest. Pushed by the workers' movement, the debate on democracy spread to include not only an emphasis on participation, but also themes of social equality. In the first period of the development of capitalism, equality in civil and political rights sanctioned by the concept of citizenship was not normally considered as being in conflict with the social inequalities produced by the market, notwithstanding the fact that this weakened the enjoyment of civil and political rights. According to Marshall's (1992: 27) influential reconstruction, in the twentieth century, the growth of economic wellbeing, the diffusion of education, and the use of those same civil and political rights affected this balance: "Social integration spread from the sphere of sentiments and patriotism to that of material satisfaction. The components of a civilized and cultivated life, at first the monopoly of the few, were progressively placed within reach of the many, who were encouraged to reach out their hand to those who still eluded their claims. The diminution of inequality reinforced the pressures for its abolition, at least with regard to the essential elements of social wellbeing. These aspirations were in part heeded by incorporating social rights in the *status* of citizenship and thus creating a universal right to a real income that is not proportional to the market value of the claimer" (Marshall 1992: 28). Social rights then began to be discussed as indefeasible conditions for a true enjoyment of political rights, and therefore democracy.

As with the labor movement in the past, other movements also became arenas for debating and experimenting with different conceptions of democracy. The protest movements of the late 1960s were already interpreted as an indication of the widening gap between parties and citizens—and indeed of the parties' inability to represent new lines of conflict (Offe 1985). This could be seen in the growing separation between movements and parties, that had together contributed to the development of some of the main cleavages.

Faced with more and more bureaucratized parties, the democratic quality of participation has become central in the visions and practices of so-called new social movements. The 1968 movement called for a widening of civil rights and forms of political participation. The Berkeley Free Speech Movement influenced European student movements, which also organized debates on freedom of opinion as well as the "state of emergence of democracy." The anti-authoritarian frame, central for these movements, was in fact articulated in claims for "democracy from below." Democracies of councils and self-management were also practiced in the workers' movements of those years. Beyond the widening of forms of political participation, the '68 movement and those that followed it (the first being the women's movement) experimented internally with new democratic practices, considered as early indications for the realization of non-authoritarian (libertarian) relations.

The social movements of the 1970s and the 1980s also insisted on the legitimacy— if not the prevalence—of alternative forms of democracy. As Herbert Kitschelt noted, "The struggle of the left libertarian movements thus recalls an ancient element of democratic theory, which promotes the organisation of the collective decision-making process variously defined as classical, populist, communitarian, strong, grassroots or direct democracy, against a democratic practice defined in contemporary democracies as realist, liberal, elitist, republican or representative democracy" (Kitschelt 1993: 15). Against a liberal democracy based on delegation to representatives who may be controlled only at elections, but legitimated to take decisions between one election and another, movements affirmed that citizens, naturally interested in politics, must directly assume the task of intervening in political decisions. As carriers of a participatory conception of democracy, movements also criticized the monopoly of mediation through mass parties and a "strong" structuring of interests, aiming to shift policy making toward more visible and controllable places. Democracy as self-management was much discussed among social movements in this period.

Research on democracy in social movements increased greatly in the last two decades, together with the expansion of movements that put democracy at the center of their thinking and practices. Investigating recent movements, Francesca Polletta stressed that activists "expected each other to provide legitimate reasons for preferring one option to another. They strove to recognize the merits of each other's reasons for favouring a particular option.... the goal was not unanimity, so much as discourse. But it was a particular kind of discourse, governed by norms of openness and mutual respect" (Polletta 2002: 7). In her in-depth analysis of civic engagement in grass-roots groups on environmental and gender issues, Kathleen Blee (2012) noted the different values promoted by the activists and their evolution in time.

In part, these conceptions did penetrate the democratic state through reforms that widened participation, in schools, in factories, and in local areas but also through the political recognition of movement organizations and the "right to dissent."

DELIBERATIVE DEMOCRACY IN THE GLOBAL JUSTICE MOVEMENT

Recent research on the global justice movement has pointed at the widening of a participatory and deliberative framing of democracy (della Porta 2009a and 2009b; della Porta and Rucht 2013).

Participation has not been the only innovation pushed forward by social movements on conceptions and practices of democracy. Especially in some recent social movements, such as those active on issues of global justice, the development of arenas—such as the social forums—of reflections and exchange of ideas among a plurality of different social and political actors testifies to the growing democratic importance assigned to the construction of multiple and critical public spheres. Their visions and practices in fact resonate with what normative theory has defined as *deliberative* democracy, referring to decisional processes in which under conditions of equality, inclusiveness, and transparency, a communicative process based on reason (the strength of a good argument) is able to transform individual preferences, leading to decisions oriented to the public good (della Porta 2005). Linked to the (more traditional) participatory values, have been emerging values, such as attention to communication, practices of consensus building, emphasis on the inclusion of diverse groups, and especially, respect for such diversity (della Porta 2005). Nowadays, progressive social movement organizations experiment with consensual methods of decision making, and values such as plurality, diversity, and inclusivity are mentioned in their fundamental documents (della Porta 2009a and 2009b).

Over the last decades, transnational protest campaigns have multiplied, in particular on issues such as environmental protection, gender discrimination, and human rights, targeting the international financial organizations as well as other IGOs. During these campaigns, common frames developed around global justice and global democracy, and transnational networks were consolidated (Marchetti 2008).

In terms of conceptions of democracy, a stress on participation (re)emerged. As mentioned earlier, social movements have, at least since the 1960s, criticized delegation as well as oligarchic and centralized power, instead legitimating forms of direct participation and grass-roots, horizontal, egalitarian organizational models. In the global justice movement, however, participation acquires different meanings in different movement areas (Reiter 2009). In organizations coming from the Old Left, participation and delegation are seen as highly compatible, and the stress on participation appears as a recovery of the original values of democratic centralism. For the New Left, the emphasis is on direct democracy and self-organization, while the solidarity groups and new social movement organizations stress the prefigurative role of participation as "school of democracy" (della Porta 2009a and 2009b).

If participation is also valued in conceptions of deliberative democracy that acquired support in the global justice movement, particular attention is given to the discursive quality of democracy with an emphasis on four elements: the transformation of preferences, the orientation to the public good, the use of arguments, and the development of consensus. Sometimes explicitly, more often not, organizations and activists within the global justice movement have in fact adopted deliberative norms (della Porta 2009a and 2009b). First of all, they have stressed that, given a complex reality, no easy solution is at hand nor can it be derived from the ideologies of the movements of the past; potential conflicts must therefore be approached by reliance on the potential for mutual understanding that might develop in an open, high-quality debate. The notion of a common good is often recalled (including democracy as a common good), as well as the need to achieve it through communication, exchanges of ideas, and knowledge sharing. The value of discussion among "free and equal" citizens is reflected in a positive stress on diversity and inclusion as well as in the attention paid to the development of structured arenas for the exchange of ideas, with the experimentation with some rules that should allow for horizontal flows of communication and reciprocal listening. Even though social movement actors have often presented conflict as a dynamic element in society, they tend increasingly to balance it with a commitment to different values such as dialogue and mutual understanding. Consensus is supported as an alternative to majoritarian decision making, which is accused of repressing and/or alienating the minorities, also within social movements. Through consensual decision making, instead, not only is legitimacy supposed to increase with the awareness of a collective contribution to decisions, but the acknowledgment of different points of views helps to develop that which unites, constructing a shared vision while respecting diversity. In fact, in the global justice movement, consensual methods spread transnationally, thanks in particular to the symbolic impact and concrete networks built around the Zapatistas experience (Starr, Martinez-Torres, and Rosset 2011), and the successive adoption of consensual principles and practices in the social forum process. Dedicated publications, workshops, and training courses helped in the diffusion of consensual practices and the principle of consensus in the movement.

However, consensus acquired a different meaning for different organizations and activists. In particular, when coupled with an assembleary, horizontal tradition, consensual decision making is perceived as a way to reach a collective agreement that reflects a strong communitarian identity. This prefigurative vision, particularly widespread among small and often local groups within the autonomous tradition, resonates with an anti-authoritarian emphasis and an egalitarian view (Leach 2009). An alternative, more pragmatic view is spread in the new (even transnational) networks, with consensual decision making being accompanied especially by an emphasis on diversity and the need to respect it, but also to improve mutual understanding through good communication (della Porta 2009b).

While some aspects of this participatory and deliberative vision spread with institutional experiments inspired by the Porto Alegre participatory budget (Font, della Porta and Sintomer 2014), the tensions within the social forum process increased between "horizontal" and "vertical" visions (della Porta 2009a; Smith et al. 2014).

Prefiguring "Real Democracy": Deliberation and Participation in the Anti-austerity Protests

Conceptions and practices of democracy developed within the global justice movement remained central also to the activities and identities of the movements which followed it, inheriting in part its emphasis on participation and deliberation. Attention to direct participation and deliberation in fact became all the more central in the movements against austerity which emerged especially since 2011. The protestors in Tahrir Square in Egypt were calling for freedom, but also practicing other conceptions of democracy that, if not opposed to, are certainly different from liberal representative democracy, resonating instead with ideas of participatory and deliberative democracy. Those who camped in Puerta del Sol in Madrid, Syntagma Square in Athens, or Zuccotti Park in New York, did indeed go back to conceptions of participation from below, cherished by the progressive social movements of the past. However, they combined them with a special attention to the creation of egalitarian and inclusive public spheres, in what they called "real" or "direct" democracy.

In anti-austerity protests, the activists' discourse on democracy is articulate and complex, taking up some of the principal criticisms of the ever-decreasing quality of liberal democracies, but also of the poor quality of internal democracy in previous movements. They do develop proposals which resonate with (more traditional) participatory visions, but also with new deliberative conceptions that underline the importance of creating multiple public spaces, egalitarian but plural. A participatory and deliberative conception of democracy is prefigured in the occupied squares, transformed into public spheres inhabited by "normal citizens." It is an attempt to create high-quality discursive democracy, recognizing the equal rights of all (not only delegates and experts) to speak (and be listened to) in a public and plural space, open to discussion and deliberation on themes that range from situations suffered to concrete solutions to specific problems, from the elaboration of proposals on common goods to the formation of collective solidarity and emerging identities.

The occupations in fact represented not only occasions to protest but also experimentations with participatory and deliberative forms of democracy. A consensual, horizontal decision-making process developed based on the continuous formation of small groups, that then reconvened in the larger assembly. Describing Occupying Boston, and citing an activist that talked about the "small slice of utopia we are creating," Juris (2012: 268) singled out some tactical, incubating, and infrastructural roles of the occupied free spaces: among the first are attracting media attention and inspiring participation; among the second, "providing a space for grassroots participatory democracy; ritual and community building, strategizing and action planning, public education and prefiguring alternative worlds that embody movement visions"; among the third, networking and coordination. Beyond the prefiguration of a different society that the activists already imagine, these spaces are also important in the invention of alternative, but not yet imagined, futures, through what has been called the politics of becoming. In the occupying movement Razsa and Kurnik (2012) studied in Slovenia, the encounters of diverse minorities transform the movements and their visions. The occupations of open public spaces facilitate the creation of intense ties (Graeber 2012; Postill 2012).

In a different way to the movements of the previous decades, which had used a varied and plural repertoire, the *acampadas* (protest camps) became much entrenched with the very identity of the movement, not just, as for other social movements, one form of action among others. Occupied spaces were in fact "vibrant sites of human interaction that modeled alternative communities and generated intense feeling of solidarity" (Juris 2012: 268). Police evictions took away these vital spaces, exposing the risk of transforming the camps into a sort of fetish, difficult to keep, but also difficult to substitute for.

In sum, calls for and prefiguration of deliberative democracy follow a vision of democracy profoundly different from the one which legitimates representative democracy based on the principle of majority decisions. Democratic quality here is in fact measured by the possibility to elaborate ideas within discursive, open, and public arenas, where citizens play an active role in identifying problems, but also in elaborating possible solutions. In protests against the crisis (and ineffective and unjust responses to it) protestors started to prefigure, in occupied public spaces, different conceptions of democracy, based on participation and deliberative values.

Explaining Changes in Conceptions of Democracy

Transformations in conceptions of democracy in social movements are affected by various elements. First, like any organizational population, social movement organizations are subject to environmental selection. This means that in each wave of protest, various models are tried and tested; but only a few survive, usually transformed in order to adapt to the quick evolution (ups and downs) of the mobilization. The context with which they interact strongly influences the range of choices available, especially the successful ones. In social movement studies, some reflections have indeed developed on the effects of political institutions, with inclusive systems said to allow for the development of large, unitary, and moderate movement organizational structures, and exclusive systems instead favoring weak, fragmented, and radical ones.

As for the new social movements, a networked, loosely coordinated structure emerged as a better fit to address the various and variable needs of mobilization as well as those of survival in the doldrums (Diani 1995). The network structure allows movements to maintain a plural repertoire, testing various potential options and combining their effects. The capacity to form and sustain these networks is therefore a very central task in resource mobilization: categorical traits (such as class) are not sufficient for collective action; they need to be supported by dense network ties. Observing that social movements have a greater opportunity to spread in groups endowed with material resources and dense ties, new social movement theorists have linked the decline of a hierarchical organizational model to the weakening of the reference basis of industrial workers, who had supported that model. Organizational adaptation then required a shift from hierarchy to networks. New social movements have been said in fact to represent new social groups, which have more heterogeneous categorical tracts and are spatially less concentrated (Offe 1985).

Within each movement and protest wave, different democratic models are present in different organizations. Looking at the global justice movement, the DEMOS project singled out some internal explanations. So, even though participation as an internal principle is more likely to be mentioned where delegation in decision making is low, participation is considered as a positive general value by organizations at all levels in the scale of delegation (Reiter 2009). While mentioned by large and small groups, participation in actual decision making of organizations of the Global Justice Movement decreases with their size. Similarly, critiques of delegation and the appeal to consensual values resonate more with smaller, poorer, and more participatory groups (della Porta 2009c). Significantly, mention of democratic values is associated with references to alter-globalist issues; in particular, consensual values are more often mentioned by groups that were founded in the most recent wave of protest on global issues, that experiment with new organizational forms (such as the modern networks) or stress horizontal structures, and that maintain a more multi-issue focus (della Porta 2009c).

The global justice movement adopted and adapted principles of rotation, consensus, use of mediators, and autonomy which had been promoted by social movements such as the Zapatistas or the Sem Tierra (Starr, Martinez-Torres and Rosset 2011). In the *acampadas*, the principle of deliberative and participatory democracy—inherited from the previous movements—was adapted to the characteristics of a movement of "common people" rather than activists, that privileged persons over associations (della Porta 2015). Equality in public spaces was indeed more radical in the anti-austerity movement's appeals to "the 99%." To a certain extent, the emphasis on plurality as a positive value and the related need to be inclusive increased with the diversity of the citizens affected by the austerity measures. Radical inclusivity and equality are reflected in the choice of public spaces—such as parks and squares—as the pulsating heart of the movement, where there were no walls or fences to reduce the transparency and publicity of the process. The orientation to public goods to be obtained through the participation of all citizens in a high-quality discourse is embedded in the generalization of the use of consensual methods, even to large assemblies. The alternative management of the commons is indeed prefigured in the camps.

Beyond social structures, *normative preferences* also affect the choice of an organizational formula. As Elisabeth Clemens observed, an organizational model is more likely to be adopted to the extent that it "is believed to work, involves practices and organizational relations that are already familiar, and is consonant with the organization of the rest of those individuals' social world" (1996: 154). As symbolic incentives are particularly important for activists, in order to be rewarding, participation requires social movement organizations that embody the activists' norms and values—in what Blee (2012: 92) defines as "moral sensitivity." Research on social movements has linked new organizational forms to cultural changes as well. Recent cultural transformations have been said to bring about the need to adapt mobilizing strategies to multiple identities, with organizational structures that allow for multiple choices and give individuals a voice. Some attention was paid to the emergence of "light communities"—with soft identities, loose ties, short-term engagement, and low identification—as people are less and less willing to create strong collective bonds (Roggeband and Duyvendak 2013: 95). That is to say, identities tend to be less and less pervasive (as broadly applied) and salient (Snow 2013), in a society that is more fragmented, differentiated, plural, but also characterized by multiple identities. Organizational formats must adapt to these cultural characteristics. The assumption is that, "[i]n late modern societies, people become increasingly connected as individuals rather than as members of a community or group; they operate their own personal community networks. Traditional greedy institutions, such as trade unions and churches, which made significant demands on members' time, loyalty and energy, are replaced by light groups and associations that are loose, easy to join, and easy to leave" (van Skelenburg and Boekkooi 2013: 218).

New *technologies* have been considered not only as an enhancing instrument of protest, but also as capable of shaping the organizational format through their influence on the culture of participation. Social media (and new digital technologies in general) are expected to change participation in protest, as they make protesting less risky and help in forming and joining groups; but they are also less capable of producing strong bonds of solidarity (Polletta et al. 2013: 19). While even virtual collective identity seems able to mobilize, digital technologies facilitate especially some limited forms of democracy commitment such as consumption-based forms of sociability rather than more political forms of commitment (Polletta et al. 2013: 30). In fact, personalization of politics has been linked to different organizational models, in particular through the use of digital media. As Lance Bennett and Alexandra Segerberg (2013) observed, personalized politics is not necessarily ineffective or disorganized, but can be organized in different ways. In particular, connective action can be activated when "interpersonal networks are enabled by technological platforms of various designs that coordinate and scale the networks" (Bennett and Segerberg 2013: 35).

Conceptions of democracy tend moreover to *spread* from one movement to the next, through processes of adaptation. If we look at the recent anti-austerity protests, the complex rules and norms of their horizontal conceptions of participation and deliberation were adopted from various groups, more or less embedded in national traditions. Spanish activists thus cited anarchism and US activists pointed to the Quakers as progenitors of horizontalism, but also important were the ways in which the original ideas had been transformed through and by other movements, from the feminist to the anti-nuclear and the autonomous squatted youth centers. In fact, the strength of these streams of national movement cultures influenced and limited the capacity of the *acampadas*, as specific democratic forms, to travel from one country to the next (Roos and Oikonomakis 2014). Moreover, it affected the adaptation of a long lasting form of protest, the camp, as it travels from Iceland to Egypt, and then to Europe and the United States, becoming along the way more and more conceptualized by activists as a prefiguration of a different society.

Learning from previous movements does not, however, mean just adopting their forms by imitation, but also (and even more) reflecting upon their mistakes. So, even the experiences of the global justice movement, the immediate progenitor, were not taken for granted, but criticized because of an allegedly increasingly associational, or even hierarchical, vision of participation and deliberation, that the new generations of activists in particular did not find resonant with their taste and experiences. While representative democracy became increasingly affected by a deep legitimacy crisis, conceptions of direct democracy (re)emerged as more apt to organize highly critical citizens.

Conclusion

In sum, social movements are, among other things, important actors in the experimentations with different models of democracy. This does not mean they are successful in their search. Rather, the continuous self-reflexivity and adaptation of their internal structure testifies to a never achieved goal, while power reproduces inequalities (Dorr 2007). While democracy in movement has never been central in social movement studies, attention is growing, together with movements' open call for "another democracy." While we are starting to learn about determinants, dynamics, and consequences of internal practices of democracy, more systematic comparison is needed on the different democratic models and movements' differential success in their implementation, on democratic tradeoffs and evolution.

Author Note

The author gratefully acknowledges the support of an ERC Advanced Grant on the project "Mobilizing for Democracy."

REFERENCES

Bendix, Reinhard (1964). *Nation Building and Citizenship*. New York: Wiley & Sons.

Bennet, Lance and Segerberg, Alexandra (2013). *The Logic of Connective Action. Digital Media and the Personalization of Contentious Politics*. Cambridge: Cambridge University Press.

Blee, Kathleen M. (2012). *Democracy in the Making. How Activists Groups Form*. Oxford: Oxford University Press.

Clemens, Elisabeth S. (1996). "Organizational Forms as Frames." In *Comparative Perspectives on Social Movements*, edited by Doug McAdam, John McCarthy and Meyer Zald, 205–225. New York: Cambridge University Press.

Costa, Pietro (2010) "Democrazia e diritti." In *La democrazia di fronte allo stato*, edited by Alessandro Pizzorno. 1-48. Milano: Feltrinelli.

della Porta, Donatella. 2005, "Multiple Belongings, Tolerant Identities, and the Construction of 'Another Politics': Between the European Social Forum and the Local Social Fora." In *Transnational Protest and Global Activism*, edited by Donatella della Porta and Sidney Tarrow, 175–202. New York: Rowman and Littlefield.

della Porta, Donatella, ed. (2009a). *Another Europe*. London: Routledge.

della Porta, Donatella, ed. (2009b). *Democracy in Social Movements*. London: Palgrave.

della Porta, Donatella (2009c). "Consensus in Movements." In *Democracy in Social Movements*, edited by Donatella della Porta, 73–99. London: Palgrave.

della Porta, Donatella (2013). *Can Democracy Be Saved?* Oxford: Polity Press.

della Porta, Donatella (2014). *Mobilizing for Democracy*. Oxford: Oxford University Press.

della Porta, Donatella (2015). *Social Movements in Times of Austerity*. Oxford: Polity Press.

della Porta, Donatella and Rucht, Dieter, eds. (2013). *Meeting Democracy*. Cambridge: Cambridge University Press.

Diani, Mario (1995). *Green Networks. A Structural Analysis of the Italian Environmental Movement*. Edinburgh: Edinburgh University Press.

Dorr, Nicole (2007). "Is 'Another' Public Sphere Actually Possible? The Case of the Women Without' in the European Social Forum Process as a Critical Test for Deliberative Democracy," *Journal of International Women's Studies*. 8: 71–88.

Eder, Klau (2010). "The Transformations of the Public Sphere and their Impact on Democratization." In *La democrazia di fronte allo stato democratico*, edited by Alessandro Pizzorno, 247–283. Milano: Feltrinelli.

Font, Joan, della Porta, Donatella, and Sintomer, Yves, eds. (2014). *Participatory Democracy in Southern Europe*. New York: Rowman and Littlefield.

Graeber, David (2012). *The Democracy Project. A History. A Crisis. A Movements*: London: All en Lane.

Juris, Jeffrey F. (2012). "Reflections on #Occupy Everywhere: Social Media, Public Spaces, and Emerging Logics of Aggregation," *American Ethnologist*. 39(2): 259–279.

Kitschelt, Herbert (1993). "Social Movements, Political Parties, and Democratic Theory," *The Annals of The AAPSS*, 528: 13–29.

Leach, Darcy (2009). "An Elusive 'We': Anti-Dogmatiam, Democratic Practice, and the Contradictory Identity of the German Autonomen," *American Behavioral Scientist*. 52: 1042–1068.

Marchetti, Raffaele (2008). *Global Democracy: For and Against. Ethical Theory, Institutional Design and Social Struggles*. London: Routledge.

Marshall, T.H. (1992). "Citizenship and Social Class." In *Citizenship and Social Class*, edited by T.H. Marshall, and H.D. Bottomore, 3–51. London: Pluto Press.

Offe, Claus (1985). "New Social Movements: Changing Boundaries of the Political," *Social Research*. 52: 817–868.

Pizzorno, Alessandro (1996). "Mutamenti nelle istituzioni rappresentative e sviluppo dei partiti politici." In Paul Bairoch and Eric Hobsbaum (eds), *La storia dell'Europa contemporanea*. Torino: Einaudi, 961–1031.

Polletta, Francesca (2002). *Freedom is an Endless Meeting. Democracy in American Social Movements*. Chicago: University of Chicago Press.

Polletta, Francesca (2013). "Participatory Democracy in Social Movements." In *Blackwell Encyclopedia on Social and Political Movements*, edited by David Snow, Donatella della Porta, Bert Klandermans, and Doug McAdam, 907–910. London: Blackwell.

Postill, John (2012). "New Protest Movements and Viral Media," *Media/anthropology*. March 26. http://johnpostill.com/2012/03/

Razsa, Mapel and Kurnik, Andrej (2012). "The Occupy Movement in Žižek's Hometown: Direct Democracy and a Politics of Becoming," *American Ethnologist*. 39(2): 238–258.

Reiter, Herbert (2009). "Participatory Democracy." In *Democracy in Social Movements*, edited by Donatella della Porta, 44–73. Houndsmill: Palgrave.

Roggeband, Conny and Duyvendak, Jan Willem (2013). "The Changing Supply Side of Mobilization: Questions for Discussion." In *The Future of Social Movement Research. Dynamics, Mechanisms, and Processes*, edited by Jacquelien van Skelenburg, Conny Roggeband, and Bert Klandermans, 95–106. Minneapolis: University of Minnesota Press.

Roos, Jerome and Oikonomakis, Leonidas (2014). "They Don't Represent Us! The Global Resonance of the Real Democracy Movement from Indignados to Occupy." In *Looking for the Transnational Dimension of Protest from the Arab Spring to Occupy Wall Street*, edited by Donatella della Porta and Alice Mattoni, 117-136. Essex: ECPR Press.

Rosanvallon, Pierre (2008). *Counter-Democracy. Politics in an Age of Distrust*. Cambridge: Cambridge University Press.

Sewell, William H. Jr. (1980). *Work and Revolution in France, The Language of Labour from the Old Regime to 1848*. Cambridge: Cambridge University Press.

Smith, Jackie et al. (2014). *Global Democracy and the World Social Forums*. Boulder Co.: Paradigm. Second edition.

Snow, David A. (2013). "Identity Dilemmas, Discoursive Fields, Identity Work and Mobilization: Clarifying the Identity–Movement Nexus." In *The Future of Social Movement Research. Dynamics, Mechanisms, and Processes*, edited by Jacquelien van Skelenburg, Conny Roggeband, and Bert Klandermans, 263–280. Minneapolis: University of Minnesota Press.

Starr, Amory, Martinez-Torres, Maria Elena, and Rosset, Peter (2011). "Participatory Democracy in Action. Practices of the Zapatistas and the Movimento Sem Terra," *Latin American Perspectives*. 30(1): 102–119.

Tilly, Charles (2007). *Democracy*. Cambridge: Cambridge University Press.

Thompson, E.P. 1991 (or 1963). *The Making of the English Working Class*. London: Penguin Books.

van Skelenburg, Jacquelien and Boekkooi, Marije (2013). "Mobilizing for Change in Changing Societies." In *The Future of Social Movement Research. Dynamics, Mechanisms, and Processes*, edited by Jacquelien van Skelenburg, Conny Roggeband, and Bert Klandermans, 217–234. Minneapolis: University of Minnesota Press.

CHAPTER 52

....

DEMOCRATIC INNOVATIONS

....

JULIEN TALPIN

DELIBERATIVE democracy and collective action have often been opposed as offering conflicting ways of constructing the common good, based on cooperative discussion on the one hand, and adversarial protest and negotiation on the other (Mouffe 1999; Young 2001). Social movements have however shaped the inception and organization of democratic innovations to a large extent. Historically, the first wave of deliberative and participatory institutions appeared in the 1970s as a response to social movements' claims for a greater inclusiveness of the political process. Social movements also influence the way democratic innovations work, by participating, or on the contrary boycotting, new forms of democratic engagement. Finally, social movements' internal democratic practices and reflections about the limits of informal decision making have inspired the field of deliberative democracy, which has, in turn, influenced collective action research. Social movement scholarship can learn from research on deliberative democracy to pay particular attention to micro processes and especially to the central role of discursive interactions in the making of groups and in shaping of the social order. In contrast, deliberative democrats can get insights from collective action research on the role of power and the broader political processes and opportunity structures shaping democratic interactions.

DEMOCRATIC INNOVATIONS AS ANSWERS TO SOCIAL MOVEMENTS' CLAIMS

....

Collective mobilizations have shaped political institutions across history. The emergence of liberal democracies is, at least in part, the product of mass protest, leading to revolutions and regime changes (Tilly 1978; Skocpol 1979). The nineteenth-century labor movement also spurred democratization, from enfranchisement to claims about how representation should work (Thompson 1963). The emergence of direct-democratic procedures at the end of the nineteenth century in both Switzerland and the United States was the product of the mobilization of populist movements in times of crisis surrounding representative governments' legitimacy (Kriesi and Wieser 1999). More recently, democratic innovations, understood as institutional arrangements allowing for participation, deliberation, and sometimes decisions of lay citizens and non-professionalized political actors beyond the ballot (Smith 2009), have appeared as answers to claims for greater inclusiveness made by activists. Democratic innovations embody the opening of the policy process to claims coming from civil society, and institutionalized through original mechanisms. While forms of discursive participation (Delli Carpini et al. 2004) have existed at different points in time, from town meetings (Mansbridge 1980; Frank 2004) to the US forum movement (Mattson 1998), such innovations have mushroomed since the 1960s. They have emerged as an answer to the declining legitimacy of representative government and electoral democracy. They take the form of neighborhood councils, planning cells, consensus conferences, citizen juries, public debates, participatory budgets, or e-town meetings among others.

The term "participatory democracy" was coined in 1962 in the Students for a Democratic Society (SDS) Port Huron Statement (Polletta 2002). While vague in its content, this claim for a deepening of democracy first targeted greater participation from below in workplaces and universities (Pateman 1970), but not necessarily the transformation of the policy process or the institutional system. In the wake of unrest in 1968 however, many social movements emerged at the local level asking for better environmental conditions in the urban context. While some doubt of the efficacy of such claims persisted, facing the resistance of both political elites and capitalist structures (Castells 1983), they nevertheless resulted in the creation of new democratic spaces at the local level. Neighborhood councils and committees in France, Italy, or the United States (Berry, Portney, Thompson 1993) are direct offspring of urban social movements' claims for a greater voice in local decisions. These new participatory bodies can be seen as "procedural concessions" of the state (Kitschelt 1986) facing growing criticisms at the local level. In France for instance, the paradigmatic example is that of Roubaix's Alma-Gare neighborhood opposition to brutal renovation. The creation of a "popular urban planning workshop," self-organized by the residents, pushed elected officials to create neighborhood councils in the rest of the city, mostly to avoid the diffusion of an adversarial style of participation (Cossart and Talpin 2015). Democratic innovations stemming from protest have often been, however, empty shells, creations from above lacking the necessary participatory dynamics. Demands for participation resulted in an opening of the political opportunity structure, which does not necessarily mean a democratization of the political process. Another striking example is the "war on poverty" program launched at the end of the 1960s by the US government as a response to the riots that affected many American inner-cities at the time, from Watts in Los Angeles to Newark (Gillette 2010). The program sought "maximum feasible participation," mostly through "community action programs" financed by the state. Here, as has happened since the 1980s in the UK and France, urban planning and renovation progressively included residents in the definition of programs. In this case, democratic innovations stemmed from riots and political violence, rather than from peaceful forms of organizing. However, in the United States and elsewhere, it often resulted in the patronizing of community groups.

The impact of social movements' claims for democratization is clearer in Latin America. Not only did protest foster the transition to democracy (O'Donnell and Schmitter 1986), it also pushed for deeper participatory mechanisms. The creation of the participatory budget (PB) in the city of Porto Alegre, Brazil, offers a paradigmatic illustration, which has subsequently been transferred to the rest of the country, before traveling to other continents (Sintomer, Herberg, Röcke 2008; Ganuza and Allegretti 2012). The creation of a PB in Porto Alegre is largely the product of pressure from below on the local government. At the beginning of the 1980s, residents' associations formed a coalition of most of the city's community groups, the Union of Neighborhood Associations, which backed a center-left candidate in the first post-dictatorship municipal elections. The latter became mayor and had to address the claims of those who considered themselves responsible for his election victory. The coalition, tired of the endless fights with previous local administrations to get their needs heard (access to water, public transport, and specific investments), expected the election of a progressive mayor would allow a broad discussion on city-wide investment priorities. Asking for an opening of the budget and policy processes black box, the Union of Neighborhood Associations started formulating the idea of a participatory budget. Whilst the previous mayor, who was not re-elected mainly because of a corruption scandal, had remained deaf to such claims, his successor, from the Workers' Party, known for its grass-roots and participatory style, cooperated with associations to design the city's first PB in 1989 (Abers 2000; Baiocchi 2005). While the creation of such democratic innovations can be seen as a way for a rising political party to get a hold on local civil society, it is also undeniably the product of intense mobilization from local social movements. Emphasizing the central role of the budget in local decision-making power, residents' associations creatively initiated, even though the process was progressively refined, an innovation that was to meet with tremendous success. The PB was then reproduced in other cities of the country, before being exported to the rest of the continent and then Europe. The location of the World Social Forum, the annual gathering of the Global Justice Movement, in Porto Alegre since 2002 (before moving to other cities across the globe) embodies the convergence between social movements and democratic innovations, the Brazilian city appearing to some as a paradigmatic illustration of the idea that "another world is possible" (della Porta and Tarrow 2005). More than a procedural concession in this case, participatory democracy appears as the product of direct cooperation between social movements and a leftist political party (Wampler and Avrtizer, 2004). Democratic innovations have spread all across Latin America (particularly in Bolivia, Ecuador, Peru, Uruguay, Argentina, and Mexico), more than anywhere else, due to pressure from social movements and cooperation with left-wing political coalitions, significantly transforming the political system (Goldfrank 2011), sometimes resulting in novel constitutional arrangements.

Democratic innovations often fail to fulfill social movements' ambitions however, unless the latter play an active, critical role in the newly created mechanisms. Playing the game of the institution, however, is a risk for organizations, who risk losing their critical stance by being co-opted.

SOCIAL MOVEMENTS AS COUNTERVAILING POWERS IN DEMOCRATIC INNOVATIONS

Social movements' engagement in democratic innovations should not be taken for granted. As Fung and Wright (2003) suggest, the involvement of social movements' organizations (SMOs) in participatory institutions has to face specific obstacles. First, their adversarial cognitive frames, seeing protest and bargaining as the means of promoting their cause, might not fit the more collaborative attitude required in democratic innovations. Also, activists might not acquire the skills required by participatory engagement: protest implies capacities other than the facilitation and organization of democratic processes. Finally, the most powerful SMOs might not be ready for engagement in institutions taking place mostly at the local level. Despite these hurdles, social movements' engagement in democratic innovations is considered a crucial condition for the success of participatory experiments.

Fung and Wright (2003) define their role as one of "countervailing power" within democratic innovations. Social movements should be able to counter-balance the domination of the most powerful in deliberative processes, and especially of business and industry interest groups, as well as the silencing of minority or working class participants by the wealthy and the educated. Formal institutions of participatory collaboration are usually characterized by large asymmetries in prior knowledge, skills, and intensity of interest. While institutional design might counter-balance some of these trends, the involvement of organized critical actors appears crucial too.

Social movements can play two key roles in democratic innovations: involving the public and making public authorities accountable for the outputs of participation. Community group, NGO and association members generally represent a large portion of the public making up democratic innovations (Ryfe 2005; Jacobs et al. 2009). Their absence or boycotting of the process automatically translates into a smaller turnout, jeopardizing the legitimacy of the institution. Beyond their own membership, SMOs have unique mobilization capacities. While the large turnout observed in Porto Alegre can be attributed to the "demonstration effect" of the PB, it also largely stemmed from the active organizing work done by neighborhood associations (Avritzer 2002). One of the most striking examples of the role organized groups can play in democratic innovations comes from the Kerala region in India. The decentralized planning process in Kerala created highly empowered institutions that included an impressive number of working-class citizens. When the Communist Party of India-Marxist (CPM) returned to power in 1996, the state government rapidly launched the "People's Campaign for Decentralized Planning." First of all, fiscal devolution took place, 40 per cent of all developmental expenditure being allocated to the local self-governing institutions. Political power was then devolved to local governments, elected representatives now having the possibility to define, finance, and implement development plans and projects (Heller 2001). These plans take shape through a multi-stage participatory process of iterated deliberation, between elected representatives, government officials, activists, and lay citizens. At once a top-down decentralizing movement initiated by elected representatives, the Kerala People's Campaign is also the product of twenty-five years of local experimentation by NGOs. The inception of the Campaign was made possible by the engagement of members of the CPM in a social movement, the Kerala People's Science Movement (KSSP), which offered room for experimentation, unthinkable in the traditional Leninist framework of the party. As Heller (2001: 154) emphasizes: "most of the techniques and favored projects of the Campaign—rapid rural appraisal, local resource mapping, community water management, rotating credit-schemes, self-help associations—come from a repertoire of practices that NGOs have been developing for years." The KSSP also provided a tremendous platform for participation, the Campaign being attended by more than 100,000 people during its early years. The collaboration between civil society actors and leftist political parties emerged as the key to success.

In contrast, the absence or withdrawal of social movements from democratic innovations shows how they can shape participatory dynamics. Limited turnout rates and low popular control over participatory budgeting in European cases appear directly linked to the minimal involvement of civil society in the process (Sintomer, Herzberg, Röcke. 2008). In the case of the city of Cordoba, Spain, the will of the municipal government to reform the PB process to make more room for individuals and non-organized participants in an institution otherwise largely dominated by existing neighborhood associations, resulted in a lockout, and then the decline of the experiment. In this case, neighborhood associations' pressure to keep a hold on the process entailed lengthy negotiations—the participation process was delayed for two years—which ended with the ruling Communist party losing the town hall. Similarly, in Chicago, the municipal government reformed the process to exclude community organizations from the innovative community policing program in which they had invested massively (Fung 2004). Police administration and politicians indeed became increasingly uncomfortable with the countervailing power acquired by community groups that they used to challenge dominant institutional and professional routines. The exclusion of SMOs resulted in a decline in the quality of deliberative processes, as community groups were no longer present to provide facilitation and training to residents. As a consequence, Chicago police became increasingly dominant in the discussions, and were able to reframe what community policing meant in more traditional terms, less challenging for their professional habits and identities. The absence of social movements in democratic innovations might therefore transform them into participatory window-dressing institutions.

In contrast, in Porto Alegre, the strength of residents' associations and the emergence of coalitions of organizations avoided such control of the government over the PB process, pushing it to remain accountable to the electoral base that brings it to power. The political context appears crucial: the Workers' Party facing powerful opposition from interest groups and other parties could not "betray" its electoral base, largely composed of community activists and PB participants. It appeared more important to the party to strengthen its base than to influence concrete policy decisions by controlling the PB (Abers 2000). As a result, the Workers' Party remained in power for four consecutive terms totaling sixteen years. The way the participatory forum impacted local civil society also made patronizing and politicians' control more difficult. Indeed, the PB fostered the creation of many new associations, the intensification of civil society cooperation networks, and the renewal of civic organization leadership (Baiocchi 2005). By strengthening civil society, the PB created the conditions to remain empowered and autonomous from public authorities. As a result however, the level of protest activities in this city has declined due to activists' involvement in the PB, sometimes increasing the bureaucratization of once-radical social movements.

Critical to the dynamics of democratic innovations, social movements' participation is nevertheless the exception more than the rule in deliberative institutions. This absence can be the product of SMOs' strategies, but it can also stem from institutions' procedural design. As a way of counter-balancing the numerical domination of activists and politicized participants over processes aimed at including lay citizens in policy discussions, random selection has undergone a tremendous revival in the last thirty years. Many democratic innovations, from citizen juries and consensus conferences to deliberative polls, are indeed based on the random selection of its participants, in order to offer a fair representation of genders, generations, and educational levels in the discussion. While academic justifications of random selection range from democratic inclusion (Sintomer 2007; Smith 2009), to enlarging the diversity of opinions heard in the deliberation (Goodin 2003), and to the representativeness of the participants (Fishkin 2009), its political use appears more instrumental. In many cases, mini-publics are set up by public authorities to avoid conflict with organized civil society actors; random selection legitimizing the absence of community leaders from the deliberation. While not systematic, such strategies delegitimize democratic innovations in the eyes of many SMOs, being seen as merely manipulative. While SMOs and interest groups might influence mini-publics' deliberation by framing the discussion when they are invited to present their views as experts, this remains a marginal position in the institution. Hendricks (2006), comparing four mini-publics, shows that while some agree to engage in deliberative forums (to distribute what they consider to be the right information to the people, improve their public image, and sometimes facilitate reform), they often fear co-option and prefer to opt out. Those who do engage are the weakest or minority interests groups, who have little to lose by playing the game of the public authorities.

While few deliberativists disagree on the need to include countervailing power in democratic innovations, the emphasis put on mini-publics in the literature often fails to acknowledge their atomistic nature—participation cannot be other than individualized—and depoliticizing consequences. As top-down institutions, they are used by public authorities or academics to serve their agendas, rather than as creative solutions to civil society claims. The deliberative supply might therefore fail to reach a real demand for participation. Some, in the Habermasian tradition, have argued for turning back to deliberation in the public sphere rather than at the micro level, as this is where politics takes place (Chambers 2009). In this case, social movements would contribute to deliberation by the formulation of opinions and discourses, even by means of protest and collective action, rather than through direct inclusion in democratic innovations (Habermas 1997; Dryzek 2000). Some have tried to build a multi-layered synthesis by advocating deliberation at all levels of society, from the local level to the wider national and global public spheres, within a fragmented, pluralistic, and heterogeneous deliberative system (Parkinson and Mansbridge 2012). So far, however, democratic innovations have been isolated innovations at the local level, rather than forming a unified system. This fragmented picture may also stem from research strategies that have mostly adopted case-study or monographic designs, which fail to account more systematically for the meso or macro consequences of institutional change.

DELIBERATION AND DEMOCRATIC PRACTICES: FROM MOVEMENTS TO INSTITUTIONS AND BACK

Social movements' scholarship has also influenced democratic innovations through its emphasis on domination in discursive interactions and the need to organize deliberation to deliver their democratic ambitions. Beyond the influence of the New Left, the most direct inspiration comes from the feminist movement of the 1970s, which developed thorough reflections on internal democratic practices (Mansbridge 1993; Polletta 2002). Jo Freeman's (1973) seminal article on the "power of structurelessness" emphasizes how informal decision-making processes, friendships, and the use of consensus resulted in the domination of males in the movement's discussions and general assemblies. These reflections on men's symbolic domination and gender inequities led the feminist movement to innovate, first by developing non-mixed groups and then by using more formal and proceduralized ways of organizing discussion and decision making. Rotating leadership, turn-taking, and lot systems to allocate tasks appeared in the feminist movement before being transferred in other sectors of the new social movements.

While such reflections on domination processes in linguistic interactions have led some to refuse the deliberative paradigm altogether (Bourdieu 1990; Fraser 1992; Sanders 1997; Mouffe 1999), it has urged others to refine their democratic theories. Some of the most influential deliberative theorists have indeed either been active in the feminist movement or been formed in gender studies (Young 1990; Mansbridge 1993; Benhabib 1996). Beyond the influence of feminism, social movements' reflections on how to overcome the iron law of oligarchy (Michels 1915) and develop proper internal democratic procedures then spread to democratic innovation literature. This has resulted, from a theoretical perspective, in strong emphasis being placed by the deliberativists on adequate participatory procedures. Joshua Cohen (1989) and Jürgen Habermas (1993) have established a list of criteria that deliberation has to meet to be inclusive, fair, and democratic and therefore fulfill its empowering potential. Considering the academic success of the deliberative paradigm, it has had practical consequences too.

Democratic innovations, at first little reflective about how to organize discussion, became increasingly proceduralized (Gastil and Levine 2005), as the rise of mini-publics illustrates. A similar trend can also be observed within social movements. The Global Justice Movement (GJM) has, for instance, been a formidable democratic laboratory since its emergence. Not only does it clamor for participatory democracy both externally and internally, but it has also developed innovative deliberative practices. The need for communication and mutual understanding across heterogeneous organizations and linguistic boundaries led to original translation practices in counter-summits and Social Forums (Doerr 2012). To avoid the flaws of past "assemblyism," Social Forums tried to limit the delegation of powers and the emergence of permanent leaders by rotating the chairs at meetings or replacing leaders by "facilitators" or "spokepersons," embodying a different conception of what representation means in the movement (della Porta 2005). This also entailed an increased proceduralization of decision-making processes, organizations participating in GJM displaying a unique taste for deliberation and consensus, as Polletta sums up (2002: 190–1): "a 60s activist would be surprised by the procedural machinery that today accompanies the democratic deciding process. There are formal roles—timekeepers, facilitators, observers of feelings—and a sophisticated range of gestures. Raising moving fingers as if playing a piano indicates support for a point; making a triangle in the air with forefinger and thumb of both hands indicates concern with respect for rules of the deliberative process; a raised fist indicates an intention to veto the decision." Similar forms of deliberative procedures have recently been observed in the Indignados/Occupy movement that comprises many former GJM activists.

The increased formalization of decision-making processes in social movements led scholars to use methodological devices first conceived in the field of deliberative democracy. Operationalizing Habermas' deliberative criteria, in the line of others empirical deliberativists (Steiner et al. 2005), della Porta and her colleagues in the "Democracy in Europe and Mobilization of Society" (DEMOS) project coded the GJM meeting discussions. The results confirm the centrality of deliberation within most of the organization: 40 per cent of the 244 organizations studied relied on low-delegation decision-making processes and consensus in 60 per cent of cases (Haug and Teune 2008; della Porta 2009; Rucht 2012). The research also highlights the fact that smaller and more recent groups are more deliberative and participatory than larger and older ones. Organizations' internal structures also influence their strategies and repertoires of action. The more participatory the internal democratic processes, the less ready organizations are to cooperate with the state, including democratic innovations. In contrast, the larger and more professionalized groups, having more classical, representative internal decision-making procedures, interact more easily with participatory institutions.

This indicates a tension between internal and external forms of participatory democracy that need to be investigated further. While the small groups of the GJM practicing consensual democracy may be clearly oppositional, are less politicized groups also practicing horizontal decision making more ready for cooperation with deliberative bodies?

While democratic innovations and social movements have undergone a quasi-simultaneous turn to increasingly proceduralized deliberative practices, little research has been conducted so far on whether these practical changes are interrelated. The influence of democratic theory on actors' practices can be noted in some cases, but more systematic research is needed on how former activists moved from one arena to the other, and how their previous organizational practices have shaped their activities within democratic innovations. Many politicians and professionals who set up the first participatory innovations were active in the new social movements of the 1970s. In some regards, the emergence of a sphere of participation professionals and experts (see Jacobs et al. 2009) is the product of the reinvestment of the skills and knowledge acquired in movements by former activists getting older and seeking establishment status. From this perspective, the World Social Forum in Porto Alegre has constituted an arena of exchange and cross-fertilization between activists and democratic innovators.

The influence of social movements on democratic innovations can also be observed in scientific scholarship. Francesca Polletta for instance, having studied American social movements' democratic practices over the twentieth century, also studied a twenty-first-century town meeting held in New York City in 2004 (Polletta and Wood 2005), the research reflecting a distinctive sensibility towards informal and narrative interactions within democratic innovations. In the reverse direction, deliberative theory and the fine-grained analysis of discursive practices have already significantly impacted research on social movements' internal practices and democratic structures. Another important field of study deals with the impact of deliberation on the formation of individual preferences. Most research agrees (Goodin and Niemeyer 2003; Fishkin 2009; Rosenberg 2009) that properly designed deliberation makes preferences more enlightened and robust. Such research could usefully inform social movements' scholarship on how organizations' deliberative practices shape participants' opinions and values over time. It could usefully be matched with the existing literature on the biographical consequences of activism (McAdam 1989).

References

Abers, Rebecca (2000). *Inventing Local Democracy: Grassroots Politics in Brazil*. Boulder, CO: Lynne Riener.

Avritzer, Leonardo (2002). *Democracy and the Public Sphere in Latin America*. Princeton, NJ: Princeton University Press.

Baiocchi, Giovanni (2005). *Militants and Citizens: The Politics of Participatory Democracy in Porto Alegre*. Princeton, NJ: Princeton University Press.

Benhabib, Seyla, ed. (1996). *Democracy and Difference, Contesting the Boundaries of the Political*. Princeton, NJ: Princeton University Press.

Berry, Jeffrey, Portney, Ken, and Thomson, Ken (1993). *The Rebirth of Urban Democracy.* Washington, DC: The Brookings Institution.

Bourdieu, Pierre (1990). *Language and Symbolic Power.* Harvard, MA: Harvard University Press.

Bryan, Frank (2004). *Real Democracy: The New England Town Meeting and How It Works.* Chicago, IL: Chicago University Press.

Castells, Manuel (1983). *The City and the Grassroots: A Cross-cultural Theory of Urban Social Movements.* Berkeley: University of California Press.

Chambers, Simone (2009). "Rhetoric and the Public Sphere. Has Deliberative Democracy Abandoned Mass Democracy?" *Political Theory.* 37(3): 323–350.

Cohen, Joshua (1989). "Deliberation and Democratic Legitimacy." In *The Good Polity*, edited by Alan P. Hamlin and Philip Pettit, 17–34. Oxford: Basil Blackwell.

Cossart, Paula, and Talpin, Julien (2015). *Participation piège à cons? Quand l'Alma-Gare prouve le contraire (Roubaix, 1968–1989).* Paris, France: Le Croquant.

della Porta, Donatella (2005). "Deliberation in Movement: Why and How to Stud Deliberative Democracy and Social Movements." *Acta Politica.* 40(3): 336–350.

della Porta, Donatella, eds. (2009). *Democracy in Social Movements.* Basingstoke: Palgrave MacMillan.

della Porta, Donatella, and Tarrow, Sidney, eds. (2005). *Transnational Protest and Global Activism.* New York: Rowman and Littlefield.

Delli Carpini, Michael, Cook, Francis, and Jacobs, Laurence (2004). "Public Deliberation, Discursive Participation, and Citizen Engagement." *Annual Review of Political Science.* 7(1): 315–344.

Doerr, Nicole (2012). "Translating Democracy: How Activists in the European Social Forum Practice Multilingual Deliberation." *European Political Science Review.* 4(3): 361–384.

Dryzek, John (2000). *Deliberative Democracy and Beyond.* Oxford: Oxford University Press.

Fishkin, James (2009). *When the People Speak. Deliberative Democracy and Public Consultation.* Oxford: Oxford University Press.

Fraser, Nancy (1992). "Rethinking the Public Sphere: A Contribution to the Critique of Actually Existing Democracy." In *Habermas and the Public Sphere*, edited by Craig Calhoun, 109–142. Cambridge, MA: The MIT Press.

Freeman, Jo (1973). "The Tyranny of Structurelessness." *The Berkeley Journal of Sociology.* 17: 151–165.

Fung, Archon (2004). *Empowered Participation.* Princeton, NJ: Princeton University Press.

Fung, Archon, and Wright, Erik Olin (2003). "Countervailing Power in Empowered Participatory Governance." In *Deepening Democracy, Institutional Innovations in Empowered Participatory Governance*, edited by Archon Fung and Erik Olin Wright, 259–289. London: Verso.

Ganuza, Ernesto, and Allegretti, Giovanni (2012). "The Power of Ambiguity: How Participatory Budgeting Travels the Globe." *Journal of public deliberation* 8(2).

Gastil, John, and Levine, Peter, eds. (2005). *The Deliberative Democracy Handbook: Strategies for Effective Civic Engagement in the Twenty-First Century.* San Francisco, CA: Joey-Bass.

Gillette, Michale (2010). *Launching the War on Poverty: An Oral History.* Oxford: Oxford University Press.

Goldfrank, Benjamin (2011). *Deepening Democracy in Latin America. Participation, Decentralization and the Left.* Philadelphia, PA: Penn State University Press.

Goodin, Robert (2003). *Reflective Democracy.* Oxford: Oxford University Press.

Goodin, Robert, and Niemeyer, Simon (2003). "When Does Deliberation Begin? Internal Reflection versus Public Discussion in Deliberative Democracy." *Political Studies*. 51(4): 627–649.

Habermas, Jürgen (1997). *Between Facts and Norms: Contributions to a Discourse Theory of Law and Democracy*. Cambridge: Polity Press.

Haug, Christoph, and Teun, Simon (2008). "Identifying Deliberation in Social Movement Assemblies: Challenges of Comparative Participant Observation." *Journal of Public Deliberation*. 4(1).

Heller, Patrick (2001). "Moving the State: The Politics of Decentralization in Kerala, South Africa, and Porto Alegre." *Politics & Society*. 29(1): 131–163.

Hendricks, Caroline (2006). "When the Forum Meets Interest Politics: Strategic Uses of Public Deliberation." *Politics and Society*. 34(4): 571–602.

Jacobs, Laurence, Cook, Frances Lomax, and Delli Carpini, Michael (2009). *Talking Together. Public Deliberation and Political Participation in America*. Chicago, IL: The University of Chicago Press.

Kitschelt, Herbert (1986). "Political Opportunity Structures and Political Protest: Anti-Nuclear Movements in Four Democracies." *British Journal of Political Science*. 16(1): 57–85.

Kriesi, Hanspeter, and Wisler, Dominique (1999). "The Impact of Social Movements on Political Institutions: A Comparison of the Introduction of Direct Legislation in Switzerland and the United State." In *How Social Movements Matter*, edited by Marco Giugni, Doug McAdam, and Charles Tilly, 42–65. Minneapolis: Minnesota University Press.

Mansbridge, Jane (1980). *Beyond Adversary Democracy*. New York: Basic Books.

Mansbridge, Jane (1993). "Feminism and Democratic Community." In *Democratic Community: NOMOS XXXV*, edited by John Chapman and Ian Shapiro, 342–377. New York: New York University Press.

Mattson, Kevin (1998). *Creating a Democratic Public: The Struggle for Urban Participatory Democracy during the Progressive Era*. University Park, PA: Penn State Press.

McAdam, Doug (1989). "The Biographical Consequences of Activism." *American Sociological Review*. 54(5): 744–760.

Michels, Roberto (1915). *Political Parties: A Sociological Study of the Oligarchical Tendencies of Modern Democracies*. New York: Free Press.

Mouffe, Chantal (1999). "Deliberative Democracy or Agonistic Pluralism." *Social Research*. 66(3): 745–758.

O'Donnell, Guillermo, and Schmitter, Philip (1986). *Transitions from Authoritarian Rule: Prospects for Democracy*. Baltimore, MD: The John Hopkins University Press.

Parkinson, John, and Mansbridge, Jane (2012). *Deliberative Systems: Deliberative Democracy at the Large Scale*. Cambridge: Cambridge University Press.

Pateman, Carol (1970). *Participation and Democratic Theory*. Cambridge: Cambridge University Press.

Polletta, Francesca (2002). *Freedom Is an Endless Meeting. Democracy in American Social Movements*. Chicago, IL: The University Press of Chicago.

Polletta, Francesca, and Wood, Lesley (2005). "Public Deliberation after 9/11." In *Wounded City: The Social Effects of the World Trade Center Attack on New York City*, edited by Nancy Foner. New York: Russell Sage Foundation.

Rosenberg, Shawn, eds. (2009). *Deliberation, Participation and Democracy. Can the People Govern?* London: Palgrave McMillan.

Rucht, Dieter (2012). "Deliberation as an Ideal and Practice in Progressive Social Movements." In *Evaluating Democratic Innovations, Curing the Democratic Malaise?* edited by Brigitte Geisel and Ken Newton, 112–133. London: Routledge.

Ryfe, David (2005). "Does Deliberative Democracy Work?" *Annual Review of Political Science.* 8(1): 49–71.

Sanders, Lynn (1997). "Against Deliberation." *Political Theory.* 25(3): 347–376.

Sintomer, Yves (2007). *Le pouvoir au peuple. Jurys citoyens, tirage au sort et démocratie participative.* Paris, France: La Découverte.

Sintomer, Yves, Herzberg, Carsten, and Röcke, Anja (2008). "Participatory Budgeting in Europe: Potentials and Challenges." *International Journal of Urban and Regional Research.* 32(1): 164–178.

Skopol, Theda (1979). *States and Social Revolutions: A Comparative Analysis of France, Russia and China.* Cambridge: Cambridge University Press.

Smith, Graham (2009). *Democratic Innovations: Designing Institutions for Citizen Participation.* Cambridge: Cambridge University Press.

Steiner Jürg, Bachtiger, André, Spörnli, Marcus, and Steenbergen, Marco (2005). *Deliberative Politics in Action: Analysing Parliamentary Discourse.* Cambridge: Cambridge University Press.

Thompson, Edward (1963). *The Making of the English Working Class.* London: Penguin.

Tilly, Charles (1978). *From Mobilization to Revolution.* Reading, MA: Addison-Wesley Publishing.

Wampler, Brian, and Avritzer, Leonardo (2004). "Participatory Publics: Civil Society and New Institutions in Democratic Brazil." *Comparative Politics.* 36(3): 291–312.

Young, Iris Marion (1990). *Justice and the Politics of Difference.* Princeton, NJ: Princeton University Press.

Young, Iris Marion (2001). "Activist Challenges to Deliberative Democracy." *Political Theory.* 29(5): 670–690.

CHAPTER 53

REVOLUTIONS AND REGIME CHANGE

JEFF GOODWIN AND RENE ROJAS

SOCIAL movements usually attempt to reform societies by changing laws, public policies, or cultural norms. However, some movements—revolutionary movements—try
to bring about more fundamental changes, including, minimally, a change of political
regime. This is the very definition of a "revolutionary movement." Such movements
may also seek to transform radically social and economic institutions. Revolutionary
movements usually fail, but when they succeed, they bring about revolutions or regime
change of one type or another.

REVOLUTIONS AND REVOLUTIONARY
SITUATIONS

In everyday language, "revolution" has come to mean virtually any substantial change.
Changes in forms of thinking, technology, and even consumer goods or fashions are often
described as "revolutionary." However, social scientists usually define revolution in two
ways. First, a revolution may refer, very broadly, to the overthrow or fundamental transformation of a political regime or state by a social movement or rebellion, whether by violent or nonviolent means (Tilly 1978). Although government officials sometimes support
revolutionaries, a revolution differs from a *coup d'etat*, which refers to the overthrow of a
government by elites, including military officers, who have little if any popular support.

Alternatively, a revolution may refer, more narrowly, to one of those rare historical
episodes in which the overthrow of a regime or state is accompanied by fundamental changes in a society's economic institutions and class structure (e.g., the French,
Russian, and Chinese revolutions). This latter type of revolution is often called a "social
revolution" (or "great revolution") to distinguish it from those revolutions (or "political

revolutions") that entail new political regimes, but little, if any, change in economic institutions or class structures (e.g., the English and American revolutions) (Skocpol 1979). What begins as a political revolution, however, may end up becoming a social revolution.

For Marxist analysts, revolutions necessarily involve a substantial redistribution of property or the creation of a new type of economy or "mode of production." Other scholars argue that revolutions may fundamentally change the everyday lives of millions of people without entailing radical economic change—by changing politics and culture, for example. The Iranian Revolution of 1979 may be an example of this (McDaniel 1991; Parsa 2000). But however conceptualized, social scientists agree that "social" or "great" revolutions have been relatively rare occurrences. By most counts, fewer than two dozen social revolutions have taken place during the past two centuries (see Table 53.1).

While political revolutions have occurred as long as states have existed, the French Revolution of 1789 is generally recognized as the first social revolution. Prior to it, the word "revolution" was often used in its literal sense as a return to some prior state of affairs. "Revolution," in other words, was synonymous with "restoration." However, the French Revolution revolutionized the word itself. The word no longer suggested a

Table 53.1 Social revolutions

Country	Year
France	1789
Saint-Dominigue (Haiti)	1791
Mexico	1910
Russia	1917
Yugoslavia	1945
Vietnam	1945
China	1949
Bolivia	1952
Cuba	1959
Algeria	1962
Ethiopia	1974
Angola	1975
Mozambique	1975
Cambodia	1975
Laos	1975
Iran	1979
Nicaragua	1979
Eastern Europe	1989

Note: The listed dates are conventional markers that refer to the year in which revolutionaries initially overthrew the extant political regime. But revolutions are best conceptualized not as single events but as conflicts that typically span many years.

cyclical return to the *status quo ante*, but instead a linear progression to a fundamentally different (and implicitly superior or more advanced) type of society. "Revolution" became not just a popular idea and a social science concept after the French Revolution, but also a moral ideal and even imperative for millions of people who hoped to create a better world. A great many social movements have arisen over the past two centuries which have had the explicit objective of overthrowing oppressive political regimes and, often, fundamentally remaking the social and economic order. When such movements have mobilized substantial popular support, one may speak of the existence of a "revolutionary situation"—a situation in which political loyalties are divided between the government and the revolutionaries, a situation also known as "dual power" (Trotsky 1961 [1932]).

There have been hundreds of revolutionary situations around the globe during the past three or four centuries. Charles Tilly (1993) found that there were a dozen to two dozen revolutionary situations in each of the major European countries alone between 1492 and 1992. Most revolutionary movements, however, do not succeed in overthrowing political regimes. If the state's armed forces remain cohesive and strong, rebellions are usually defeated or at least contained in peripheral regions within the territory governed by that state. Revolutionary situations, in other words, do not automatically result in actual political, let alone social, revolutions. Revolutions usually require the prior collapse or at least weakening of the state's "infrastructural power"—that is, the state's capacity to enforce its laws and policies upon the people whom it claims to govern. And although it is true that revolutionary movements themselves sometimes accumulate the power to incapacitate states—for example, by winning over soldiers, military officers, and government officials as well as ordinary people—revolutionary movements just as frequently topple states that have already been fatally weakened by economic and fiscal crises, interstate wars, and/or elite divisions and conflicts (Goldstone 1991; Goodwin 2001).

Social scientists often consider violence to be a defining characteristic of revolutions, and many, if not most, revolutions have in fact involved considerable violence among the movements and states contending for power. Moreover, foreign states have often intervened militarily in revolutionary situations or have attacked recently empowered revolutionary regimes. Many revolutionary governments, furthermore, have employed considerable violence in order to reorganize society along new lines, including extensive state terrorism (e.g., in France and Russia) and even genocide (e.g., in Cambodia). Nonetheless, the extent of violence in revolutions is extremely variable, and some revolutions—especially political revolutions that have not challenged dominant classes—have occurred with relatively little bloodshed. Some social scientists, furthermore, have detected a trend in recent decades toward nonviolent revolutions (Chenoweth and Stephan 2011). Violence is best understood, accordingly, as a potential and variable component of revolution, not as one of its defining characteristics. In other words, "nonviolent revolution" is not an oxymoron (Nepstad 2011).

While a certain type of social movement—the revolutionary movement—may bring about a revolution, the two concepts are clearly distinct. The idea of revolution—whether one uses the broader or narrower definition—stands apart analytically from such kindred forms of contentious politics as social movements, popular rebellions, riots, wars (civil or interstate), and *coups d'etat*. These latter forms of contention, however, have often been closely connected with revolutionary situations or with actual revolutions (McAdam, Tarrow, and Tilly 2001). Revolutionary movements and popular rebellions, for example, may create revolutionary situations, and these often result in civil wars, and of course revolutionary movements bring about actual revolutions if they successfully seize state power. Also, social movements that initially seek reforms within the existing political system may become revolutionary movements should they ultimately attempt to overthrow the state, which often happens when the political order breaks down or when the state persistently refuses to implement the reforms desired by such movements (e.g., in Mexico in 1910–11). More or less spontaneous riots, for their part, may help to precipitate revolutions, and they have occurred frequently as a result of the breakdown of state power that characterizes revolutionary situations. Interstate wars, moreover, sometimes help to cause revolutions by weakening states, as well as by inflaming popular grievances, including perceived threats to "the nation" or "the people" (e.g., in Russia and Vietnam). Revolutions, in turn, often bring about interstate wars, typically because foreign states try to destroy those revolutionary movements or regimes they consider threats. And coups, finally, may become "revolutions from above" if their leaders subsequently implement radical political or socio-economic changes, as arguably occurred in Japan after the Meiji Restoration and in Turkey after Ataturk's consolidation of power (Trimberger 1978). In short, while revolutions (especially social revolutions) are a distinct and relatively rare form of contentious politics, they are often connected, whether as cause or consequence, with other and more frequently recurring types of contention.

CLASS CONFLICT AND REVOLUTION

Classical Marxists have understood revolutions as systemic change resulting from conflicts between polarized classes with clashing economic and political interests and aims. The goals and struggles of opposing classes have in fact stood behind the modern era's major revolutions. Although the concept of class conflict has virtually disappeared from social movement theory (Hetland and Goodwin 2013), class conflict is surely the principal factor driving most revolutionary situations and outcomes. Yet classes or class coalitions do not confront each other directly as discrete and monolithic adversaries in revolutionary situations. Rather, revolutions are shaped by state institutions and non-state political organizations, as well as by the ideas and resources that each of these deploys. Moreover, revolutionary conflict is never uniform or linear. Revolutionary conflicts intensify during critical junctures that generate opportunities for collective action by disrupting existing political arrangements and thus altering the balance of forces among opposing groups. Finally, particular political expressions of class con-flict are shaped by international developments, chiefly geostrategic competition among states—contests aggravated by capitalism's uneven global development—but also by transnational ideologies and flows of resources.

Most significantly, class conflict is substantially shaped and organized by the institu-tional make-up of political regimes. Class structures do not directly determine political rules and behaviors. Just as a particular level of economic development is character-ized by a specific social structure and delineates the interests and capacities of social classes, a society's economic organization conditions the formal and informal rules of governing institutions and rule-making processes of its political regime. Political regimes thus constrain the action of social groups, promoting the power of some while at times reducing if not altogether suppressing the political influence of others.

In short, political regimes articulate and mediate class interests by arbitrating between rival dominant groups and by demarcating prospects for cooperation among usually antagonistic forces. The rules governing the participation and influence of class actors may be more or less democratic. Regimes vary in their incorporation of non-elite sec-tors by according them more or less institutionalized access to political influence and material welfare. In addition, the level of economic development also offers regimes varying degrees of organizational and ideological resources. These are employed by the state but also by political and civil associations that promote the interests of the social groups they represent. Lastly, and quite importantly, whereas political elites—heads of state institutions and partisan rulers—generally attend to the needs and demands of economic elites, they seldom present a uniform response to non-elite claims. The effi-cacy and adeptness of state actors and bureaucracies in addressing demands from below, the forms and intensity of the fights around these grievances, and the cohesion and flex-ibility with which elites accommodate intensifying protest all influence the emergence (or absence) of revolutionary situations. Throughout history, revolutionary conflicts have typically unfolded under authoritarian conditions when non-elites are repressed and excluded from power—yet have some capacity for collective action—while elites are simultaneously badly divided.

Revolutionary situations—or situations of "dual power"—can be understood as moments when mobilized non-elite forces collide with a regimes' institutions, that is, when the competing claims of groups that states attempt to govern and control escape established rules and channels of political participation and incorporation. A dual-power situation arises when extra-institutional conflict is acute enough and has sufficient popular support to open the possibility of deep political and social change. According to Lenin, revolutionary situations display "three major symptoms":

> (1) ... when there is a crisis, in one form or another, among the "upper classes", a crisis in the policy of the ruling class, leading to a fissure through which the discon-tent and indignation of the oppressed classes burst forth...; (2) when the suffering and want of the oppressed classes have grown more acute than usual; (3) when, as a consequence of the above causes, there is a considerable increase in the activity of

the masses, who.... are drawn both by all the circumstances of the crisis *and by the*
"upper classes" themselves into independent historical action.

(Lenin 1915: 213; emphasis in original)

Scholars of revolutions have since elaborated on these core insights. Acute "suffering
and want"—maybe the most crucial of Lenin's "symptoms"—usually entail a dramatic
and generalized deterioration in living standards, leading some scholars to view revolutions as a result of intense "relative deprivation." Lenin was more plausibly alluding to
the disruptions of people's daily routines which encourage their defiance of economic
and political authority. Understood in this way, the weakening or breakdown of what
Piven and Cloward (1977: 11) describe as "the regulatory controls inherent in the structures of institutional life" are preconditions for dual power. Economic crises, wars, and
even natural disasters often provoke such dislocations. In these scenarios, ordinary people suffer the impact of the loss of work or income and of being sent into bloody and
often unpopular wars. Significantly, the breakdown or even collapse of institutions upon
which daily survival depends—work, commerce, transportation, and other services
such as health and education—has the potential to thrust normally quiescent people
into militant protest. In sum, one precondition for dual power consists of deep dislocations that break down routinized systems of social stability and control.

Though necessary for the emergence of destabilizing mass protest, such dislocations
alone do not produce revolutionary situations. Lenin identifies a second indispensable
condition for dual power: The shock must open up "fissures" among elites that eventually destabilize the very foundations of the regime and thereby provide a necessary
opening for protest from below. Crises of elite cohesion generally occur when growing fiscal pressures resulting from wars and state-led modernization efforts cause established consensus over arrangements for settling competing elite claims to collapse (as
in prerevolutionary France and China). As disagreement over how the costs of fiscal
and institutional reform should be distributed grows, some elites may come to oppose
the regime, whose institutional coherence consequently erodes. The state's capacity to
control and enforce its will and rules upon the population within the territory that it
governs—that is, its infrastructural power—may begin to contract and even collapse.
State breakdown driven by elite division magnifies, in turn, the efficacy of non-elite
mobilization.

Scholars have identified two related paths from elite conflict and state breakdown
to situations of dual power. In the first, the shock unleashes mounting and threatening pressure by non-elite political forces as discussed above. No longer checked by
the institutions of social control, uncontainable unrest from below generates the crisis among elites who are pulled into opposing directions by the developing insurgency
itself. One elite faction might be compelled to clamp down on non-elites, extracting
more resources to cover fiscal gaps, restricting democratic rights, and even unleashing
repression; other elites, by contrast, might advocate for reformist incorporation, aiming
to accommodate non-elite demands for the restoration of stability and the preservation
of their overall rule. In this view, the mounting stress from non-elite demands impedes

convergence around a unified and stabilizing elite response that would prevent regime collapse.

A second and more robustly theorized scenario involves an elite crisis driving non-elites into revolutionary action. Typically, a fiscal emergency provoked by international conflict, in the form of war or geopolitical competition, may generate instability as elites resist additional burdens imposed by more autonomous state officials. The ensuing institutional breakdown, involving the disintegration of state power and legitimacy, in turn facilitates or exacerbates rebellion by powerless groups who enjoy the capacity for effective mobilization. This is the influential model offered by Theda Skocpol in *States and Social Revolutions* (1979), which analyzes the revolutions in France, Russia, and China. In either scenario, the cohesion of the police and armed forces is crucial for preventing the fall of the regime. If the costs of war, repression, and/or reform divide or weaken the military and undermine its ability to act in a unified and decisive manner against popular protest, then the likelihood of revolution greatly increases (Chorley 1943).

The second condition listed by Lenin has been emphasized by so-called "political opportunity" and "state-centered" theorists. Whether elite division and institutional collapse result either from or in revolutionary movements, ruling elites find it impossible to satisfy their claims under the existing regime. The revolutionary crisis intensifies as the actions of disaffected elite groups impair state capacity.

Combined, Lenin's first two conditions might appear sufficient to generate a dual-power situation. Yet even when non-elite actors escape the regulatory capacity of key institutions, and elite divisions undermine the state's infrastructural power, a revolutionary crisis is not assured. Adding a third and final condition, Lenin stipulates that non-elites, "drawn both by all the circumstances of the crisis *and by the 'upper classes' themselves*," must display "independent historical action." By "historical" Lenin seems to mean a qualitatively superior capacity for collective action on the part of groups who seek a new social order. In other words, revolutionary movements must exhibit the ability to take advantage of the institutional shock and collapse in order to place radical transformation on the national agenda. Otherwise, if non-elite groups are incapable of organizing into a political force that can topple it, the regime will likely weather the unrest resulting from dislocations, even amid a weakening of state institutions.

The development of such "historical" capacity depends at a minimum on two factors. First, revolutionary movements must have leverage over central areas of the regime. This occurs when their supporters play necessary and valued roles in key institutions, increasing the disruptive potential of withdrawing their contributions to such institutions. That is, when non-elites enjoy "structural power" rooted in indispensable institutional roles, their *collective capacity for imposing costs on elites* who depend on their contribution is enhanced. Michael Schwartz (1976), in his important study of radical protest movements, explicates this mechanism at a micro-level. Significantly, elite vulnerability to such structural leverage grows in times of crisis and collapse. Moreover, this form of non-elite power is reinforced at the level of the state when ruling factions, in a bid to restore stability, formalize non-elite leverage by sharing governing responsibilities with them. Understandably, if revolutionary movements cannot utilize such institutional leverage, elite domination will remain robust.

On a macro-historical level, some have posited that patterns of economic development generate non-elite capacity in broader structural terms. In Marx's classical formulation, increased capitalist competition and industrial concentration brings together larger and larger swaths of working-class populations with similar experiences, cooperative predispositions, uniform interests, and shared antagonists. He held that workers would deploy their increasingly coherent and concentrated influence over production to overturn the existing order as capitalist crises became more pronounced. Though his predictions of inevitable radical aspirations and polarized class conflict are questionable, his framework for understanding variations in non-elite leverage over the entire social edifice remains relevant. In a variation of the standard Marxian account, Trotsky (1961 [1932]) argued that uneven economic development in Russia gave industrial workers unprecedented influence and allowed them to turn a struggle against autocracy into a fight for radical social and economic transformation—an example of a political revolution growing into a social revolution. The central point is that insurgents' capacity to undertake "historical" action against elite rule is a function of the leverage rooted in their structural position in society.

Secondly, non-elites must mobilize associational and ideological resources if their increased activity and leverage is to translate into an "independent" and "historical" revolutionary movement. Elaborating on this requirement, many scholars have underscored the importance of organization, tactics, and ideas. These factors involve the practical tools needed for gathering, processing, producing, and deploying information among insurgents and their followers. These practical dimensions of revolutionary conflict are by no means epiphenomena of class structure and institutional configurations. Organizational cultures and ideology play an undeniable role in the origins and outcomes of revolutions. However, they are not independent of the larger political arena in which revolutionary situations unfold. Radical ideologies have existed and enjoyed significant appeal in most modern regimes. Yet they have never by themselves fostered movements, much less brought about dual-power situations.

The contributing effects of culture are evident when ideologies and tactics correspond to and take advantage of the shifting balance of forces that weakens regime elites and extant insurgent capacities. That is, the effective deployment of ideologies and the agency of their "carriers" are circumscribed by prevailing material and political conditions. When dislocations and state crises open opportunities for movements to challenge dominant classes, the decisions of revolutionaries and the impacts of their particular "framings" of the conflict matter and may end up being decisive. When the strategies and ideologies promoted by revolutionaries give meaning to and serve to guide popular movements, and when they also serve to intensify popular mobilization, thereby maximizing its disruptive impact, they can be the crucial factor that gives ordinary people the momentous capacity to "make" revolution. Accordingly, Lenin concluded his statement on revolutionary situations with the following qualification: "Not every revolutionary situation," he explained, "gives rise to a revolution; revolution arises only out of a situation in which the above-mentioned objective changes are accompanied by a sub-jective change, namely, the ability of the revolutionary *class* to take revolutionary mass action *strong* enough to break (or dislocate) the old government, which never, not even in a period of crisis, 'falls', if it is not toppled over" (Lenin 1915: 213; emphasis in original).

REGIMES AND REVOLUTION

Revolutionary situations are much more likely to develop in authoritarian and repressive political contexts than in democratic and liberal ones. No revolutionary movement, in fact, has ever overthrown a long-consolidated democratic regime. For example, the social revolutions of the Cold War era overthrew extremely repressive colonial regimes (as in Vietnam and Algeria), personalist dictatorships (as in Cuba, Iran, and Nicaragua), and the Soviet-imposed and backed single-party regimes of Eastern Europe (Wickham-Crowley 1992; Goodwin 2001). None overthrew a government that even remotely resembled a democracy.

Revolutionary movements tend to win popular support when the regimes they oppose sponsor or defend—typically with violence—social and economic arrangements that are widely viewed as unfair or discriminatory. Economic and social arrangements may be widely regarded as unjust (i.e., as not simply unfortunate or inevitable), but unless government officials sponsor or protect those arrangements—through laws, taxes, conscription, and, ultimately, coercion—collective efforts to overthrowing the government are unlikely to become widely supported. For example, people may attribute their plight to their social "superiors," but the state itself may not be frontally challenged unless there is a broadly shared view that it stands behind and defends elites.

Revolutionary movements may also attract support when the state excludes non-elite groups from state power or resources. Even if such groups direct their claims at the state, they are usually unlikely to seek its overthrow if they can win some significant share of political power or influence—for example, through elections. Even when such groups view their political influence as unfairly limited, their inclusion in political decision making may preclude them from becoming radicalized. The political incorporation of mobilized groups into parliamentary and other political institutions—including the putatively revolutionary working class of Marxist theory—has usually prevented or reversed the radicalization of such groups. These groups may understand such inclusion as the first step in the potential accumulation of greater influence and resources; they are thus unlikely to jeopardize relatively low-cost access to state institutions by supporting "disloyal" and illegal revolutionary movements. By contrast, authoritarian regimes tend to foster or "incubate" revolutionary forms of political contention. Movements that call for revolution tend to win support under such regimes, because they come to be regarded as more realistic and potentially more effective than political moderates and reformists—who come to be seen, paradoxically, as idealistic and utopian, given the repressiveness of the regime.

Indiscriminate yet inconsistent violence by weak states against mobilized groups also tends to help revolutionary movements. People who are targeted by the state may take up arms or join clandestine groups simply in order to defend themselves. People whose families or friends have been killed or arrested by the state may also back revolutionary movements in order to avenge them. Thus, unless state violence is targeted at unpopular groups or is simply overwhelming, indiscriminate coercion often backfires, leading to growing popular support for revolutionary movements. Such movements may win sympathy not so much because of their ideologies alone (although these are undoubtedly important), but because they can offer people some form of protection from, and the means for striking back at, violent authoritarian regimes. Mobilized groups have usually only turned to disruptive strategies, including armed struggle, after their previous efforts to secure change through legal means were violently repressed. Under repressive conditions, ordinary people often view militant, disruptive protest—including but not limited to armed struggle—as a legitimate and reasonable means of political contestation. Revolution is simply politics by other means.

Indiscriminate state violence, finally, also reinforces the plausibility of revolutionary ideologies and "frames," that is, ideologies and frames that (1) depict the existing political and perhaps social order as fundamentally unjust and (2) call for a radically new political system and perhaps social order as well. Violent and exclusionary regimes, in other words, often unintentionally foster the popularity of their most radical critics—be they religious activists, socialist militants, or radical nationalists—who regard extant institutions as corrupt, incapable of reform, and thus requiring a complete and perhaps violent reconstruction. Which radical leaders or group will come to lead or dominate a revolutionary movement, however, is contingent upon a great many factors, including how much coercive force they can muster and how well or poorly their ideologies or frames resonate with political activists and ordinary people.

In conclusion, repressive authoritarian regimes may unintentionally foster the growth of revolutionary movements by generating or reinforcing widespread popular grievances, by contributing to widespread feelings of anger and outrage, by focussing these emotions on the state and political authorities, by closing off possibilities for peaceful reform, by enhancing the plausibility of revolutionary ideologies and frames, and by inducing people to use disruptive and even violent strategies in order to defend themselves and to pursue effectively their collective interests and ideals. By contrast, more liberal and democratic regimes tend to pacify and institutionalize, but hardly eliminate, class struggle and other types of social conflict. Elections have been aptly described as a "democratic expression of the class struggle" (Lipset 1981). Democracy, that is, channels a variety of social conflicts—including, but not limited to, class conflicts—into a competition for votes during elections and into the lobbying of representatives by "interest groups" between elections. The temptation to rebel against the state, which is rarely followed without trepidation under any circumstances, is generally suppressed under democratic regimes by the knowledge that new elections are but a few years off, and with them the chance to "throw out" unpopular leaders and elect new ones. Democratic regimes have of course also provided a context in which social movements of various types can win concessions from economic, political, and cultural elites, although this often requires a good deal of disruption (Piven and Cloward 1977). However, movements that call for the overthrow of elected governments rarely win much popular backing, unless such governments push people into such movements by indiscriminately repressing government opponents—by abandoning, in other words, democratic principles.

One should not conclude from this that political radicalism and militancy go unrewarded in democratic societies. Democracy, as noted, by no means eliminates social conflict; in fact, democracy encourages a veritable explosion of social conflict, however pacific, by providing the "political space" within which those groups outside elite circles can make claims on political, economic, and cultural authorities. Political parties as well as a range of interest groups, trade unions, professional associations, and of course social movements generally become the organizational vehicles of political struggle in democratic societies. But these pillars of "civil society" are generally just that—civil. Their tactical repertoires include electoral campaigns, strikes, demonstrations, lobbying, boycotts, and civil disobedience—forms of collective action that may be quite disruptive and undertaken for quite radical ends, but which are not intended to overthrow the state or remake society as a whole.

Democracy, in sum, dramatically reduces the likelihood of revolutionary change, but not because it brings about social justice. Democracy, as Marx emphasized more than 150 years ago, is fully compatible with widespread poverty, inequality, exploitation, and social problems of many kinds. Movements for social justice arise so often in democratic contexts for just this reason. And yet these movements, to repeat, almost always view the state as an instrument to be pressured or influenced—not as an institution to be smashed and rebuilt. Revolutionary movements, however, develop not simply because people are angry or aggrieved, but because the state under which they live provides no other mechanisms for social change, violently repressing those who seek incremental reforms.

References

Chenoweth, Erica and Stephan, Maria J. (2011). *Why Civil Resistance Works: The Strategic Logic of Nonviolent Conflict*. New York: Columbia University Press.

Chorley, Katharine (1943). *Armies and the Art of Revolution*. Boston: Beacon Press.

Goldstone, Jack A. (1991). *Revolution and Rebellion in the Early Modern World*. Berkeley and Los Angeles: University of California Press.

Goodwin, Jeff (2001). *No Other Way Out: States and Revolutionary Movements, 1945–1991*. Cambridge: Cambridge University Press.

Hetland, Gabriel and Goodwin, Jeff (2013). "The Strange Disappearance of Capitalism from Social Movement Studies." In *Marxism and Social Movements*, edited by Colin Barker, Laurence Cox, John Krinsky, and Alf Gunvald Nilsen, 83–102. Chicago: Haymarket Books.

Lenin, V. I. (1915). "The Collapse of the Second International." In Lenin: Collected Works, Vol. 21. Moscow: Progress Publishers.

Lipset, Seymour Martin (1981). *Political Man: The Social Bases of Politics.* Expanded edition. Baltimore: Johns Hopkins University Press.

McAdam, Doug, Tarrow, Sidney, and Tilly, Charles (2001). *Dynamics of Contention.* Cambridge: Cambridge University Press.

McDaniel, Timothy (1991). *Autocracy, Modernization, and Revolution in Russia and Iran.* Princeton, NJ: Princeton University Press.

Nepstad, Sharon Erickson (2011). *Nonviolent Revolutions: Civil Resistance in the Late 20th Century.* Oxford: Oxford University Press.

Parsa, Misagh (2000). *States, Ideologies, and Social Revolutions: A Comparative Analysis of Iran, Nicaragua, and the Philippines.* Cambridge: Cambridge University Press.

Piven, Frances Fox and Cloward, Richard A. (1977). *Poor People's Movements: Why They Succeed, How They Fail.* New York: Vintage.

Schwartz, Michael (1976). *Radical Protest and Social Structure: The Southern Farmers' Alliance and Cotton Tenancy, 1880–1890.* Chicago: University of Chicago Press.

Skocpol, Theda (1979). *States and Social Revolutions: A Comparative Analysis of France, Russia, and China.* Cambridge: Cambridge University Press.

Tilly, Charles (1978). *From Mobilization to Revolution.* Reading, MA: Addison-Wesley.

Tilly, Charles (1993). *European Revolutions, 1492–1992.* Oxford: Blackwell.

Trimberger, Ellen Kay (1978). *Revolution from Above: Military Bureaucrats and Development in Japan, Turkey, Egypt, and Peru.* New Brunswick, NJ: Transaction Books.

Trotsky, Leon (1961 [1932]). *The History of the Russian Revolution.* New York: Pathfinder.

Wickham-Crowley, Timothy P. (1992). *Guerrillas and Revolution in Latin America: A Comparative Study of Insurgents and Regimes since 1956.* Princeton, NJ: Princeton University Press.

Author Index

Numbers in **bold** refer to tables and figures.

General Index

Numbers in **bold** refer to tables and figures.

political violence, 10, 15, 55, 71, 78, 80, 88, 414–416
  al-Qaeda movement, 96, 173, 179, 521
  armed rebellion and resistance, 414, 621
  assassination, 414, 416, 439
  Black Panther Party, 152, 718
  Black Power movements, 152, 279
  communication goals, 444
  culture-dependence, 439
  effect of "youth bulge", 150
  EOKA movement (Cyprus), 96
  escalation dynamics, 15–16, 96, 441–442
  ethnic cleansing/genocide, 191, 601
  hijacking, 439
  Japanese Red Army, 150
  kidnapping, 414, 416, 439
  mechanisms and dynamics, 97, 441
  mobilization pathways, 443–445
  moral disengagement and legitimation of violence, 180
  movement rivalries, 442
  Northern Ireland, 93–94, 99–100
  radicalization, 96, 180, 442, 444
  Red Army Faction (Baader-Meinhoff; Germany), 150
  Red Brigades (Italy), 96, 150
  role of police and security forces, 416–417, 425–436, 442
  social movement perspective, 439–448
  state reactions, 442
  use of torture, 268, 270, 439, 558, 644, 746
  violent/non-violent repertoire continuum, 440–441, 447
  Weather Underground (USA), 150
  see also civil wars; revolution; riots; terrorism; suicide bombing; wars/warfare
poor people's movements, 720
populism, 20–21, 63, 161, 671–676, 681–692
  Latin American, 686–692
  top-down leadership and mobilization, 20, 681–682, 684–685, 689–690
  see also color revolutions; Egyptian revolution; Tea Party movement
power relations/structures, 1, 5, 8, 307, 388, 391–392
  asymmetry, 50, 194, 264, 269–270, 273, 441, 610–611

emergence of counter-power, 44, 614–615
hegemons, 141
institutional, 114–116
Marxist conception, 114
multidimensional, 114
pluralistic, 468
power-sharing vs. power concentration, 55–56
reproduction of, 38
practice movements, 18, 348, 567–576
  acts of citizenship, 568
  appropriation, 569, 572–573, 576n4, 576n5
  effects, 574–575
  everyday practice, 568
  everyday resistance, 346–349, 571–573, 626
  goals, 568, 572
  land occupation, 75, 79, 385, 569
  migrants, 569, 575
  norms and legitimation, 573–575
  squatting, 75, 201–202, 207–209, 414, 569, 573
  transgressive challenge, 568, 571
  use of public space, 569
private politics
  corporate actors, 20–21
  governance of protest, 20
protest cycles, 5, 69, 71, 75–77, 80, 258, 282, 318–320, 687–688, 716
protest patterns, 8, 55, 70, 73–76, 80, 312–315
protest repertoires
  bodily gestures, 78, 587
  civil disobedience, 151–152, 369–370, 429, 482, 716, 749, 803
  conscientious objection, 414
  demand and supply of protest, 221–222
  electoral protest, 98
  flash mobs, 60, 500
  hybrid and multi-issue activism, 373
  land occupation, 75, 79, 385, 569
  military mutiny, 81
  rent strikes, 93
  road blockades, 78
  self-immolation and suicide, 91, 268, 272, 439, 520
  sit-ins, 151–152, 414, 431, 471, 500, 504, 506, 749
  squatting, 75, 201–202, 207–209, 414, 569, 573

opportunity structures, 203–209
  politics of place, 200–201
  social housing, 210, 713
  social mobilization, 10, 200–211
  space and contentious politics, 10, 200
  subaltern mobilization, 204, 210
  urban planning, 10, 201–202,
    204–205, 505, 782
  urban sociology, 201
  urban transformation, 10, 202–211
  urbanization, 386

voluntary and non-profit organizations, 3,
    16–17, 150, 267, 494–507
  citizens' initiatives, 505–506
  civic voluntarism, 61
  collaborative activity, 504
  cultural contexts, 496–497
  implicit politics, 500
  participation and motivation, 500–503
  politicized aims, 499
  social capital, 501
  social entrepreneurship, 502–503
  social movements as forms of voluntary
    association, 499–500
  vehicles and outcomes of social movements,
    495, 503–507
  volunteering, 494–499
  see also charities; non-governmental
    organizations

wars/warfare
  American Civil War, 92, 94
  asymmetric, 192
  automation of, 141

child soldiers, 460
Cold War, 185, 191, 456, 801
  effects on social movements and collective
    action, 80–82, 141
  ethno-national, 191–192
  First World War, 81, 90, 141, 148, 714, 718
  Iraq War, 224, 334, 350, 368, 558, 736
  private actors and mercenaries, 141, 637–638
  pro-social outcomes, 460–461
  Second World War, 58, 71, 118, 140, 148–149,
    151, 160, 264, 314, 503–504, 719
  South African (Boer) War, 141
  Spanish–American War, 141
  Vietnam War, 61, 280, 282, 284, 453, 551–553
  see also civil war
welfare provision, 3, 21, 137, 140–141, 176, 208,
    210, 387, 499, 504–505, 539, 599, 655,
    711–724
  charities and NGOs, 713
  de-commodification, 711–712, 719
  effects of neoliberalism, 721–724
  fiscal welfare, 713
  inequality and poverty, 713
  Keynesian, 719–720
  private/corporate provision, 713
  social insurance, 712, 714
  social movement activism, 714–724
  universalism, 712
  welfare from below and self-help,
    208, 348, 718
  welfare regimes, 712
world systems theory, 4, 610–611

Zapatismo movement (Mexico), 371, 384, 539,
    582, 585–586, 615, 773, 776

Lightning Source UK Ltd.
Milton Keynes UK
UKHW030623220520
363693UK00003B/4